RUGBY VICTORIANA

RUGBY VICTORIANA

THE HIGHS AND LOWS OF VICTORIAN RUGBY IN NORTHERN ENGLAND

GRAHAM MORRIS

Scratching Shed Publishing Ltd

Copyright © Graham Morris 2024
All rights reserved
The moral right of the author has been asserted.
First published by Scratching Shed Publishing Ltd in 2024
Registered in England & Wales No. 6588772.
Registered office:
47 Street Lane, Leeds, West Yorkshire. LS8 1AP
www.scratchingshedpublishing.co.uk
ISBN 978-1068618987

Photographs provided by Graham Morris
unless otherwise stated
Page design: Tony Hannan
Cover design: Louise Woodward-Styles

No part of this book may be reproduced or transmitted in any form or by any other means without the written permission of the publisher, except by a reviewer who wishes to quote brief passages in connection with a review written for insertion in a magazine, newspaper or broadcast.

A catalogue record for this book is available
from the British Library.

Typeset in Warnock Pro Semi Bold and Palatino
Printed and bound in the United Kingdom by
Short Run Press Ltd
Bittern Road, Sowton Industrial Estate, Exeter. EX2 7LW
Tel: 01392 211909   Fax: 01392 444134

Contents

Football and the Victorian Era vii

Preface ix

The Great Contest xiii

Introduction xv

Acknowledgements xix

Milestones & Stats

1837-1868 1	1885-1886 117
1869-1870 3	1886-1887 129
1870-1871 5	1887-1888 143
1871-1872 7	1888-1889 165
1872-1873 9	1889-1890 185
1873-1874 11	1890-1891 201
1874-1875 17	1891-1892 221
1875-1876 21	1892-1893 239
1876-1877 25	1893-1894 263
1877-1878 31	1894-1895 287
1878-1879 39	1895-1896 313
1879-1880 47	1896-1897 341
1880-1881 55	1897-1898 365
1881-1882 67	1898-1899 395
1882-1883 77	1899-1900 425
1883-1884 91	1900-1901 453
1884-1885 105	

Notes 475

Appendices 481

Statistics Notes 553

Representative Team Abbreviations 559

Bibliography 567

Football and the Victorian Era

When the historian comes to deal with the reign of Queen Victoria, and reaches that magic word 'football', he will be struck by the fact that the Victorian era was the golden age of football – the era in which football, with an almost startling suddenness, became the national game of the United Kingdom.

When the last century dawned there were no clubs, or regular or codified rules, and between 1800 and 1850 football itself lost much of its popularity. The game during those 50 years seemed fated to die and might have died, had it not been for our great public schools. They saved football's life, at least in England, for up North (Scotland) there was plenty of vitality of a kind left in the game.

Possibly the schools to which the greatest credit belong are Rugby, Eton and Charterhouse. The former had a fine open park, and hence played what we now call the Rugby game. Rugby was played at Rugby School during the whole half-century, while the character of the game played at Eton and Charterhouse is often ascribed, and perhaps rightly, to the nature of the field of play.

What strides the game has made during the past thirty years we all know. From some points of view the growth of football is not the least marvellous feature of the Victorian era. That the social changes for the better, and the wise legislation of that era, have helped the growth of the game that has done so much to make soldiers out of shop-keepers, no one can doubt, although it is an aspect of the question too wide for treatment here.

By Hamish Stuart (*Athletic News*, 4th February 1901, following the death of Queen Victoria).

Rugby Football by B. Fletcher Robinson, 1896

Preface

The headline title of this volume is *Rugby Victoriana* which, admittedly, may appear to be a strange choice. For myself, though, it gives a nod to the rapidly changing times embraced by the Victorian era when so many advancements took place within sport, particularly the various codes of 'football' that became firmly established in society's consciousness. Queen Victoria came to the throne in 1837, just eight years before the first Rugby School football rules were drawn up, and died in January 1901, a few months before the scope of this book concludes. During her reign the first football annuals appeared and football – round and oval ball – grew from a few sparse newspaper sentences in its earliest years to full page reports by the turn of the century.

I have held the ambition for quite some time to fill the gap that exists in rugby record keeping prior to the creation of the breakaway Northern Union in 1895. It was a period that embraced the early history of many of today's leading northern rugby union and rugby league organisations. In particular it is notable that in the case of today's rugby league outfits – those founded during Victorian times – that most club history books tend to focus only on the facts and figures from the time they defected from the Rugby Football Union (RFU). The achievements of club and players during the formative, embryonic years in rugby union are often absent.

To some extent this is due to the authors basing their information on the ground-breaking work of the original Rugby League Record Keepers'

Club (RLRKC) of which I was proud to be a contributing member. This of course is how it should be because the whole point behind the RLRKC publishing their data was to provide comprehensive, reliable information that could be referenced and used by others, hopefully done with due acknowledgement to its original source although this is not always the case! It was thanks to the work of RLRKC members that it was possible to determine, for instance, how many matches each player had taken part in or who had scored the most tries, goals and points for club, county or country.

The RLRKC was the brainchild of Irvin Saxton who, as editor supported by a small army of likewise enthusiasts, set forth on the mammoth task of compiling a complete statistical record of British rugby league since it began life as the Northern Union. Hitherto there had been little in the way of record keeping and what did exist was generally unreliable. The compilation and publication of all the team line-ups, results, scorers, etc., began in 1972 and continued until 1999 when, mission apparently accomplished, the RLRKC was discontinued. Its disappearance, however, left a void, one that has now happily been filled by its reformation in 2020 under the leadership of Neil Ormston.

By its very definition the RLRKC did not, and does not, cover the period prior to that split from the RFU in August 1895, consequently many individual and club achievements prior to that time are overlooked, forgotten even. I set myself the task of attempting to rectify that situation by researching the statistical history of those early years of rugby in the northern counties, covering each club competition and representative match. In setting out the results of my research in this volume I have modelled my output on the season-by-season format as used by Saxton in producing those much-prized booklets issued by the original RLRKC.

This publication – my fifteenth book on rugby – has been the biggest, most challenging task I have undertaken, the research alone occupying most of my spare time over the past ten years or so. Whilst it would seem natural that I covered the counties of Cheshire, Cumberland, Lancashire and Yorkshire – who all had clubs that joined the Northern Union – I have also included Durham, Northumberland and Westmorland because during the late-1800s the fortunes of all seven aforementioned counties was intertwined. Together they made up the northern section of the county championship and jointly provided players to represent the North (of England) in the annual and prestigious contest versus the South.

My decision to take this project up to 1900-01 – a further six seasons beyond the 1895 breakaway – was due, in part, to the fact that several of today's well known rugby league clubs remained with the RFU after the initial defections. In this category are Salford and Swinton (who both resigned from the RFU in 1896), Barrow and Hull Kingston Rovers (1897), York (1898), and Keighley (1900). Bramley also defected in 1896 continuing as Rugby Football League members until 1999, whilst Dewsbury entered with a new club in 1898, replacing the town's disbanded rugby union outfit. There was also a vast number of other – more 'junior' – clubs that joined the Northern Union in those latter years including virtually all those based in Cumberland.

The following pages, therefore, embrace matches under the auspices of the Rugby Football Union and Northern Football Union up to and including season 1900-01. This covers details of 622 representative matches (involving county and international teams), 90 league tables and 99 cup competitions (including details of the finals) plus notes on contemporary issues to help provide the reader with a flavour of how rugby matters were reported during that period. Hopefully, I have fulfilled my self-imposed task of placing once more the names of those long forgotten Victorian northern rugby heroes onto the printed page.

Graham Morris
Worsley
October 2024

Inter-county rivalry as Bradford – who won by two goals, two tries to one goal – host Manchester at Park Avenue on 1st November 1884 *Toby, The Yorkshire Tyke, 1884*

The Great Contest

'Tis Cup-tie-tide, and the excitement attending the various encounters is at its height. All round 'touch' there is a seething mass of people – an enormous concourse of human beings ever on the qui vive. On the stands we listen to the silver stream of valuable opinion expressed by the knowing ones, in order, if possible, to find the winner of the great contest. At the time at which the game is to be started approaches the excitement becomes fiercer and more burning in its intensity. At last the contestants appear on the scene, and a mighty shout proclaims that the ball has been kicked off, and the clamour of voices round the ground ceases. The struggle is desperate, and with the cheers of the onlookers and their own impetuosity the players strive with might and main to win the day. Bruises and hurts are not noticed in the heat of the last few moments. The ball is skilfully shot over the bar or taken over the line after a marvellous run, and the call of time afterwards proclaims the game at an end. If the play is crowned with festivities in the evening, in no other circumstances could festivity be so innocuous. In any case a week's pent-up energy has had its outlet, and a departure made whereby the spirits and muscles of the hardy Tykes have been thoroughly recreated.

    Football 'Notes' (*Yorkshire Post*, 1st March 1886, anticipating the opening round of the 1886 Yorkshire Challenge Cup).

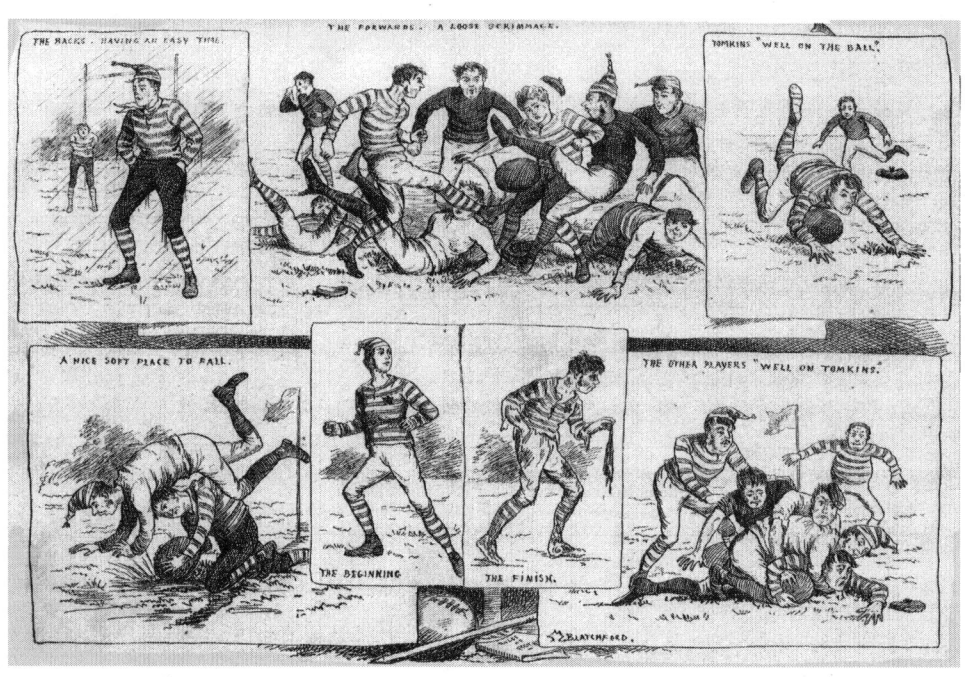

An artist's impression of 'A Football Match'. *Illustrated Sporting and Dramatic News, 1880*

Introduction

During the Victorian era rugby union in the north of England grew to unprecedented heights, reaching its zenith during the 1880s. Its rise was based around the communal rivalries that built up in the working class northern towns as the game, which had its roots in the public schools and universities, gained wider appeal. Support for rugby, particularly in the mill towns and mining communities of Lancashire and Yorkshire, created a phenomenon that appeared to have no bounds. But its success was also its downfall.

In a period where the ethos of amateurism ruled in sport, rugby in northern England was riddled with politics and intrigue, especially when it came to alleged payments and inducements to players – particularly the better performers – to switch allegiance. Rumour and counter rumour, accusation and denial dominated the newspapers of the day. No one was safe from a ban or suspension, although many cases remained unproved. During that period the waters appeared to be muddied but, looking back at events today with a clearer head and armed with further evidence, there is no doubt that the rewarding of the essentially working class players was a prolific practice. The fear of professionalism in rugby meant that its rulers were reluctant to allow competitive club matches because of their belief that it would lead to remuneration as clubs attempted to procure better players in order to achieve success.

Prior to the rise of intense club rivalries, the earliest matches that could be considered to have had a competitive element were representative fixtures. The very first was a county game, arranged between Lancashire and Yorkshire in 1870. From that tentative start, more county teams slowly emerged across the nation, and inter-county contests such as the annual meetings of Durham and Northumberland, captured the public imagination. Such encounters led to calls for a county championship but the idea fell on deaf ears. Almost two decades after that initial Lancashire-Yorkshire 'Roses' clash an apprehensive Rugby Football Union gave its hesitant stamp of approval, Yorkshire being declared the first official champion county in 1888-89.

Similarly the inaugural international fixture, arranged in 1871 between England and Scotland, had a semi-official quality about it but, as the first of what became an annual contest, its significance quickly grew. Ireland (in 1875) and Wales (1881) also picked up the baton and the first Home Nations tournament (which evolved into today's Six Nations) began in 1882-83, although not officially recognised as such at the time.

It was at club level, particularly in the north of England, that competitive rugby was inevitable, Yorkshire leading the way through the introduction of its Yorkshire Challenge Cup knock-out tournament in 1877-78. As its popularity grew, clubs in other northern counties were not slow to introduce similar cup contests. A further giant step was taken in 1889-90 when the West Lancashire Rugby League appeared, the first league competition instituted by 'senior' clubs. It was a pathway soon followed by other Unions in the north.

But whereas rugby had been the dominant code of football in the north of England prior to the 1880s, the Association game would gain the upper hand in terms of appealing to the masses. The Football Association Cup began in 1872 developing into a nation-wide contest with Blackburn Rovers becoming the first northern finalist in 1882. Professionalism in that sport was subsequently sanctioned in 1885 and the Football League commenced operations in 1888-89 with six Lancashire and six Midland clubs.

Whilst the attraction to soccer grew stronger due to its endorsement of payments and competitive fixtures, rugby struggled on with the nagging belief that competition would unavoidably lead to the dreaded word 'professionalism'. In fact that was exactly how it panned out but its denial had helped give Association the lead and it ultimately led to the formation of the Northern Football Union (now known as the Rugby Football League) in 1895 as the leading Lancashire and Yorkshire clubs, plus two from Cheshire, sought to control their own destiny. Rugby Union in the north was on a downward path.

Professionalism would not be officially recognised by the Rugby Union authorities until 1995, a full century later. It has since led to that code gaining far greater prominence, its increased competitiveness resulting in higher attendance figures at club level and a stronger media profile. However, Rugby League still retains its grip on the counties of Lancashire, Yorkshire and Cumbria.

So it appears that Rugby Union has gone full circle by finally taking the steps that many, particularly in the north of England, thought it should have during the Victorian era. Had it done so, perhaps the Northern Union would not have seen the light of day. Possibly the timing was wrong all those years ago? Maybe semi-professional rugby union was not then the appropriate route to take? Whatever the rights and wrongs of 1895's so-called 'Great Schism', the achievements of those pioneering clubs and players of the north should not be forgotten, something that has, hopefully, been addressed in this publication.

Tempers appear frayed at Richmond on 22nd November 1884 when Bradford comfortably defeated Marlborough Nomads by seven goals, four tries to nil.
Toby, The Yorkshire Tyke, 1884

Acknowledgements

It is impossible to compile a volume such as this without the help and goodwill of others. Mike Latham, Robert Gate and Graham Williams have been particularly supportive with their knowledge and expertise and there are so many others who I am indebted to including Tony Collins, Paul Cotham, Bill Dalton, John Dewhirst, Craig Evans, Stephen Fox, Mick Harrop, Dave Huitson, John Jenkins, Tom Little, Tom Mather, Martin O'Keefe, Iain Robson, Mike Rylance, Alex Service, Gary Slater, Philip Tarleton, and Michael Turner.

Also staff at the National Football Museum Archive (Preston), the Preston Harris Library (Preston), Birkenhead Park (Rugby) Football Club, Cheshire Rugby Football Union, Sale (Rugby) Football Club, King's School (Parramatta, New South Wales, particularly its archivist Jenny Pierce), Wirral Archives (Birkenhead) and local history libraries at Bury, Castleford, Durham, Huddersfield, Kendal, Leeds, Leigh, Macclesfield, Manchester, Newcastle, Oldham, Radcliffe, Rochdale, St Helens, Sale, Salford, Tameside (Ashton-under-Lyne), Warrington, Wigan, and Workington.

I would especially like to thank Louise Woodward-Styles for producing the book cover and enhancing many of the photographs therein, and Tony Hannan, who painstakingly designed the pages that follow.

So-called 'big side' games, often involving 100 or more participants, were the regular football fare at Rugby School during the mid-1800s. *The Graphic, 1870*

1837-1868

1837
DAWN OF AN ERA
The Victorian era begins on 20th June 1837 when Queen Victoria succeeds to the throne, the Coronation subsequently taking place during June 1838.

1845
THE FIRST RUGBY RULES
The first Rugby School football rules are drawn up, including the H-shaped posts.

1857
TOM BROWN
Tom Brown's Schooldays first published. Written by Thomas Hughes, it depicted life at Rugby School in Warwickshire and helped to popularise the code of football as played at that school.

SHEFFIELD FOUNDED
Sheffield Football Club was founded on 24th October, initially playing under 'Sheffield' rules, although five of its players represented Yorkshire under 'Rugby' rules in the first rugby union county match against Lancashire in 1870. Sheffield adopted Association rules during 1878, and is believed to be the oldest existing football club in the world still playing under Association rules. Notts County Football Club, founded in 1862, is claimed to be oldest club in the world to have continually played under Association rules only.

THE NORTH'S FIRST RUGBY MATCH
Teams labelled 'Rugby' and 'The World' met on 19th December at Liverpool Cricket Club, Edge Hill. It is believed to be the north's first organised football match based on Rugby School rules.

LIVERPOOL FOUNDED
Liverpool (Rugby) Football Club founded and believed the oldest rugby club in England, amalgamating with St Helens RU (founded 1919) as Liverpool St Helens in 1986. Guy's Hospital (London) claims to date from 1843 but no contemporary evidence supports this. Some historians believe it began in the 1860s. Other early claims are Dublin University (1854 as Trinity College) and Edinburgh Academicals (1857).[1]

1860
MANCHESTER FOUNDED
The Manchester (Rugby) Football Club was founded.

1861
SALE FOUNDED
The Sale (Rugby) Football Club was founded.

1862
RUGBY RULES REVISED
The Rugby School rules were revised due to football's growing popularity. Previously, games were based on those learned at different public schools and played to an agreed set of hybrid rules.

1864
HUDDERSFIELD FOUNDED
Huddersfield founded as the Huddersfield Athletic Club, subsequently amalgamating with the Huddersfield Cricket Club in 1875 to form the Huddersfield Cricket, Athletic and Football Club, the forerunner of today's Huddersfield rugby league club.

1865
HULL FOUNDED
Hull (Rugby) Football Club founded.

1868
YORK FOUNDED
The York club was founded as the York Amateurs.

1869-1870

FIRST REPRESENTATIVE MATCH

The first representative rugby match took place on 26th March at the Leeds (Rugby) Football Club ground when Yorkshire met Lancashire. The Yorkshire team was selected solely from Bradford, Huddersfield, Hull, Leeds and Sheffield players, Lancashire choosing from the Manchester and Rochdale clubs, Liverpool deciding not to participate.

1869-1870 STATISTICS

COUNTY MATCH

Saturday 26 March 1870 at Whitehall Road, Leeds
YORKSHIRE 0 *Backs*: HW Chambers (Shef), CE Freeman (Hud). *Half-backs*: A Firth (Brad), T Plint (Lee). *Forwards*: H Beardsell (Hud), A Bradley (Hud), Brown (Brad), B Cariss (Lee), JR Eyre (Shef), A Holmes (Brad), WHH Hutchinson (Hull), Johnson (Shef), CB Lambert (Hull), W Lockwood (Shef), WC Lupton (Brad), A Macauley (Lee), Thomson (Shef), RJ Wade (Hull), R Waltham (Hull), H Wright (capt, Lee).
LANCASHIRE 1 goal *Backs*: FD Broughton (Man), R Osborne (Roch). *Half-backs*: W Grave (Man, c), W MacLaren (capt, Man). *Forwards*: A Arnott (Man), JJ Bolton (Man), F Brierley (Roch), JC Brierley (Roch), WF Colley (Roch), JS Genth (Man), CG Hulton (Roch), J Hulton (Man), J MacLaren (Man), H Radcliffe (Roch), EEM Royds (Roch), W Sharpe (Man), CE Sidebotham (Man), CM Taylor (Roch), HJC Turner (Man, t), W Welsh (Man).
Attendance: 'fair'
Note: Some reports imply Lancashire scored three other tries, in addition to the converted try.

Rugby football as depicted in the early 1870s. *Illustrated London News, 1871*

1870-1871

THE F.A. CUP BEGINS
The Football Association Challenge Cup began in November with 15 entries. It remains as the oldest 'football' cup competition in the world.

RUGBY FOOTBALL UNION FOUNDED
The Rugby Football Union was founded on 26th January, subsequently publishing the Laws of the Game in June 1871, based on the Rugby School rules.

FIRST INTERNATIONAL MATCH
The first international rugby match, Scotland versus England, was played in Edinburgh on Monday 27th March. It took place just two days after the Lancashire versus Yorkshire county match, four of Manchester's players appearing in both games. The *London Daily News*, looking ahead to the international, commented: 'The challenge issued by the leading Scottish [Rugby] Football Clubs has not fallen upon stony ground, and we are glad to be in a position to state that all the preliminaries of an international match worthy of the title have been satisfactorily arranged. The challenge [was] signed by the captains of the Edinburgh Academy, Academical, Merchistonian, St Andrews, and West of Scotland clubs, professing their readiness to meet a picked Twenty of the members of English clubs and play them in Scotland, according to the rules of the game as played at Rugby School. The undertaking [by English clubs] was, indeed, no small one; cricket secretaries often enough find it far from an easy matter to collect an Eleven for a distant match. But in this case it would be necessary

to find Twenty players, a worthy representative body of innumerable clubs, willing to undertake a journey of some hundreds of miles to join a match which, at the most, could not last longer than a couple of hours.'[2]

ROCHDALE HORNETS FOUNDED
Rochdale Hornets was founded on 20th April when Rochdale (formed 1867) merged with Rochdale Wasps and Rochdale United.

1870-1871 STATISTICS

COUNTY MATCH

Saturday 25 March 1871 at Whalley Range, Manchester
LANCASHIRE 3 tries *Backs*: F Lemonius (Liv), RR Osborne (Man). *Half-backs*: W Grave (Man), SA Hermon (PresG), W MacLaren (capt, Man), J Penny (Liv). *Forwards*: CE Armytage (Man), WF Colley (Roch), AS Gibson (Man), PM Gibson (Liv), JR Hay-Gordon (Liv), CG Hulton (Roch), E Kewley (Liv), JR Kewley (Liv), EA McIntosh (Liv), D MacLaren (Man), C Moore (Liv), R Taylor (Roch), HJC Turner (Man), W Welsh (Man).
YORKSHIRE 1 goal *Backs*: C Gibson (Lee), AJ Griesbach (Lee), W Hodgson (Hull). *Half-backs*: A Bradley (Hud), T Naylor (Lee), H Wright (Lee). *Forwards*: CW Beardsell (Hud), H Beardsell (Hud, fg), GS Brook (Hud), HS Brook (Hud), R Butler (Lee), A Champion (Brad), A Firth (Brad), CE Freeman (Hud), T Heron (Hud), B Hirst (Lee), A Holmes (Brad), AW Lassen (Brad), A McLaurin (Brad), RJ Wade (Hull).
Attendance: 'large'
Note 1: Yorkshire won as only goals are counted.
Note 2: Scorers of Lancashire's three tries not reported.
Note 3: H. Beardsell's field goal for Yorkshire reported as 'from a flying kick'.

INTERNATIONAL MATCH

Monday 27 March 1871 at Raeburn Place, Edinburgh
SCOTLAND 1 goal, 1 try *Backs*: WD Brown (GlasA), T Chalmers (GlasA), A Clunies-Ross (StAndU). *Half-backs*: JW Arthur (GlasA), TR Marshall (EdinA), W Cross (Mer, t, c). *Forwards*: A Buchanan (EdinU, t), AG Colville (Mer), D Drew (GlasA), JF Finlay (EdinA), J Forsyth (EdinU), RW Irvine (EdinA), WJC Lyall (EdinA), JLH Macfarlane (EdinU), JAW Mein (EdinA), FJ Moncreiff (capt, EdinA), R Munro (StAndU), G Ritchie (Mer), AH Robertson (WoS), JS Thomson (StAndU).
ENGLAND 1 try *Backs*: A Lyon (Liv), AG Guillemard (WKent), RR Osborne (Man). *Three-quarter*: W MacLaren (Man). *Half-backs*: F Tobin (Liv), JE Bentley (Gip), JF Green (WKent). *Forwards*: RH Birkett (ClapR, t), BH Burns (Black), JH Clayton (Liv), CA Crompton (Black), A Davenport (RavPk), JM Dugdale (RavPk), AS Gibson (Man), A St G Hamersley (MarlN), JH Luscombe (Gip), CW Sherrard (Black), F Stokes (capt, Black), DP Turner (Rich), HJC Turner (Man).
Attendance: 2,000

1871-1872

SWINTON FOUNDED
Swinton was founded on 16th October as Swinton and Pendlebury Football Club, although its roots can be traced back to the 1866-67 season.

TEAMS TOO LARGE?
The third annual county fixture between Lancashire and Yorkshire took place at the Huddersfield club ground, Fieldhouse, on 20th January. As with its predecessors, it was played 20-a-side, a number that some observers felt was too high, one reporter commenting: 'It was evident that both teams were too large, it being almost impossible for one man to run the gauntlet of 20, however good his chances at the onset.'[3]

ENGLAND: NO NORTHERN PRESENCE
When England met Scotland at Kennington Oval on 5th February, they did not select anyone from a northern club. This contrasted with the previous year's inaugural international in Edinburgh when seven northern-based players were included. The third England-Scotland encounter, which took place in Glasgow during March 1873, again lacked a northern presence. This led to lobbying for an annual North versus South 'trial' match, the first being in January 1874. It turned the tide of opinion amongst selectors and, when England met Ireland in February 1885, it was the first time the majority chosen were from northern clubs.

1871-1872 STATISTICS

COUNTY MATCH

Saturday 20 January 1872 at Fieldhouse, Huddersfield
YORKSHIRE 0 H Beardsell (Hud), A Bradley (capt, Hud), GS Brook (Hud), R Butler (Lee), WA Dawson (Brad), A Firth (Brad), CE Freeman (Hud), AJ Griesbach (Lee), EW Harrison (Hull), T Heron (Hud), W Hodgson (Hull), WHH Hutchinson (Hull), CB Lambert (Hull), AW Lassen (Brad), FB Moss (Hull), FS Ramsbotham (Lee), J Riley (Lud), EJ Tennant (Lee), J Tennant (Lee), RJ Wade (Hull).
LANCASHIRE 1 goal *Backs*: JG Gibson (Liv), JR Hay-Gordon (Liv), A Lyon (capt, Liv). *Three-quarters*: RW Colquhoun (Liv), C Grey (Man), GJ Warren (Liv). *Half-back*: C Moore (Liv). *Forwards*: J Blythe (Liv), WF Colley (Man), J Drew (Man), JS Genth (Man), W Grave (Man), W Greg (Man), CG Hulton (PresG), D MacLaren (Man), J MacLaren (Man), C Pilkington (Man), CE Sidebotham (Man), HJC Turner (Man), R Walker (Man).
Attendance: 2,500/3,000
Note 1: Playing positions for Yorkshire not reported.
Note 2: Scorers for Lancashire not reported.

INTERNATIONAL MATCH

Monday 5 February 1872 at Kennington Oval, London
ENGLAND 2 goals, 2 tries *Backs:* AG Guillemard (WKent), FW Mills (MarlN), WO Moberley (RavPk). *Three-quarter*: H Freeman (MarlN, dg). *Half-backs*: JE Bentley (Gip), S Finney (RIEC, t), P Wilkinson (Law Club). *Forwards*: T Batson (Black), JA Body (Gip), JA Bush (Clif), FI Currey (MarlN), FBG D'Aguilar (RE, t), A St G Hamersley (MarlN, t), FW Isherwood (RavPk, c), F Luscombe (Gip), JEH Mackinlay (StGHosp), WW Pinching (GuyHosp), CW Sherrard (Black), F Stokes (capt, Black), DP Turner (Rich).
SCOTLAND 1 goal *Backs*: LM Balfour (EdinA), WD Brown (GlasA), T Chalmers (GlasA). *Half-backs*: RP Maitland (RA), TR Marshall (EdinA). *Quarter-backs*: JW Arthur (GlasA), W Cross (Mer), FJ Moncreiff (capt, EdinA). *Forwards*: J Anderson (WoS), EM Bannerman (EdinA), CW Cathcart (Lor, dg), AG Colville (Mer), JF Finlay (EdinA), RW Irvine (EdinA), JH McClure (WoS), JLH Macfarlane (EdinU), W Marshall (EdinA), FT Maxwell (RE), JAW Mein (EdinA), HW Renny-Tailyour (RE).
Attendance: 4,000
Note: No northern-based players in England team.

1872-1873

WAKEFIELD TRINITY FOUNDED
Wakefield Trinity was founded as the 'Football' (rugby) section of the existing Holy Trinity Church Young Men's Society, the name evolving into Wakefield Trinity during 1873-74. A separate Wakefield Football Club also took up the rugby code in 1872-73 but disbanded in 1879, its most well known player being Charles Fernandes of England and Yorkshire.

OXFORD UNIVERSITY GO NORTH
The first meeting between a northern county and a team representing a university took place in Leeds during January when Yorkshire met Oxford University. It was not subsequently recognised by the University as an official fixture, the Yorkshire Rugby Union's *Commemoration Book 1914-19 and Official Handbook 1919-20* stating the University claimed it to be 'a vacation game got up by individuals'. That view is supported by the fact that only their captain, C. W. Hamilton, played in the Oxford versus Cambridge 'Varsity' match the following month and none had appeared in their inaugural meeting the previous season. However, it was advertised in the press by Yorkshire's Honorary Secretary J. W. Beattie as 'Yorkshire v. Oxford University', hence the reason for including it in this publication.[4]

1872-1873 STATISTICS

COUNTY MATCHES

Saturday 11 January 1873 at Wortley Cricket Ground, Leeds
YORKSHIRE 3 goals, 3 tries *Backs*: WA Dawson (Brad), JB Vickerman (Hud).
Half-backs: A Bradley (Hud, c), CE Freeman (capt, Hud, c), EA Hollingbury (Hull, t),
EJ Tennant (Lee, 2t). *Forwards*: LE Ashby (Brad, t), H Beardsell (Hud, 2t, c), GS Brook
(Hud), G Brooke (Hud), M Dawson (Brad), N Ellershaw (Hull), H Freeman (Brad),
WHH Hutchinson (Hull), CB Lambert (Hull), R Margerison (Appleby Bridge), FB Moss
(Hull), WS Sykes (Lee), C Ullathorne (Hull)
OXFORD UNIVERSITY 0 *Back*: AJ Griesbach. *Three-quarters*: H Wright, JG Wylie.
Half-backs: T Gant, WS Shirley. *Forwards*: JE Ashworth, R Butler, Eden, JB Ellis,
CW Hamilton (capt), Macmichael, W Millhouse, RE Norris, FS Ramsbotham, LW Shirley,
FW Slingsby, AJ Tuckwell, JC Wheatley, E Williamson, T Williamson
Attendance: 3,000. *Note*: Yorkshire had 19 players.

Saturday 1 February 1873 at Whalley Range, Manchester
LANCASHIRE 2 goals, 6 tries *Backs*: CG Hulton (PresG), A Lyon (Liv, c), F Radcliffe
(Man). *Half-backs*: W Grave (Man, dg), JR Hay-Gordon (Liv, t). *Forwards*: J Blythe (Liv),
CW Carver (Liv), RW Colquhoun (Liv), G Dunlop (Liv), M Edwards (Liv), JS Genth
(Man), W Greg (Man), E Kewley (Liv, t), D MacLaren (Man), F Patteson (Man), R Peel
(Man), A Pilkington (Man), CE Sidebotham (Man), R Walker (Man)
YORKSHIRE 1 goal, 1 try *Backs*: WA Dawson (Brad, t), W Hodgson (Hull, c), B Osborne.
Three-quarter: A Bradley (Hud). *Half-back*: EA Hollingbury (Hull). *Forwards*: LE Ashby
(Brad), H Beardsell (Hud), Bennett, GS Brook (Hud), HS Brook (Hud), CE Freeman (Hud),
JJ Freeman (Brad), R Hodgson (Hull), C Hustwick (Hull), WHH Hutchinson (capt, Hull),
CB Lambert (Hull), FB Moss (Hull), F Schutt (Brad), WS Sykes (Lee), Thompson
Attendance: 3,000.
Note 1: Name of one Lancashire player missing from match reports.
Note 2: Scorers for five Lancashire tries and one Yorkshire try not reported.
Note 3: Clubs not identified for Osborne, Bennett and Thompson (Yorkshire).

INTERNATIONAL MATCH

Monday 3 March 1873 at Hamilton Crescent, Glasgow
SCOTLAND 0 *Backs*: WD Brown (GlasA), T Chalmers (GlasA), JLP Sanderson (EdinA).
Half-backs: W St C Grant (Craig), TR Marshall (EdinA.). *Quarter-backs*: GB McClure
(WoS), JLH Macfarlane (EdinU). *Forwards*: HW Allen (GlasA), P Anton (StAndU),
EM Bannerman (EdinA), CC Bryce (GlasA), CW Cathcart (EdinU), JP Davidson (RIEC),
RW Irvine (EdinA), JAW Mein (EdinA), FJ Moncrieff (capt, EdinA), AG Petrie (RHSFP),
TP Whittington (Mer), RW Wilson (WoS), AT Wood (RHSFP)
ENGLAND 0 *Backs*: FW Mills (MarlN), S Morse (MarlN), CHR Vanderspar (Rich).
Three-quarter: H Freeman (MarlN). *Half-backs*: CW Boyle (OxfU), S Finney (RIEC).
Forwards: JA Body (Gip), JA Bush (Clif), EC Cheston (Rich), WRB Fletcher (MarlN),
A St G Hamersley (MarlN), HA Lawrence (Rich), F Luscombe (Gip), JEH Mackinlay
(StGHosp), H Marsh (RIEC), MW Marshall (Black), CH Rickards (Gip), ER Still (RavPk),
F Stokes (capt, Black), DP Turner (Rich)
Attendance: 4,000   *Note*: No northern-based players in England team.

1873-1874

HALIFAX FOUNDED
The Halifax club was founded.

ST HELENS FOUNDED
The St Helens club was founded, being subsequently renamed Eccleston Rangers, then St Helens Rangers before reverting to St Helens in 1885.

SALFORD FOUNDED
The Salford club was founded as Cavendish, changing its name to Salford in 1879.

WIDNES FOUNDED
The Widnes club was founded as the Farnworth and Appleton Cricket and Football Club, changing its name to Widnes in 1875.

VARYING MATCH DURATIONS
Durham played its first county match, opposing Yorkshire at the Darlington cricket ground on 6th December. It took place over four quarters of 20 minutes each in an era when matches often varied in duration, usually determined by the captains, based on criteria like inclement weather or the late arrival of the away team (a regular event usually blamed on the railway system). Match reports often quoted halves lasting 25, 30, 35 or 40 minutes and the first England versus Scotland game in 1871 was played over two 50-minute periods. Another arrangement

sometimes used was to change ends after a goal had been scored, playing a maximum of two hours. In the Laws of the Game published by the Rugby Football Union in 1871, none of its 59 laws referred to the duration of a match, and did not do so until 1926.

REDUCED TEAM SIZES
The aforementioned Durham versus Yorkshire match at Darlington was the first county fixture in the north of England to be played with 15 players each instead of 20, beginning a trend that saw all county games evolve into 15-a-side contests over the next three seasons. The 1871 Laws of the Game did not stipulate the number of players per team and, like the duration of matches, appear to have evolved through tradition. It was not until 1892 that the number of players was incorporated into the laws.

CALL IT A DRAW
The result of the Yorkshire versus Lancashire match, played at the Bradford cricket ground in Great Horton on 17th January, was declared as 'drawn in favour of Lancashire,' a common description for the outcome during a period when only goals counted towards the result. As neither side had registered a goal the match was declared a draw with Lancashire's two tries earning them the plaudit. The practice of only counting goals continued until November 1875 after which tries were also taken into account. This match was arranged as 20-a-side but only 19 arrived for each team, Lancashire starting with 17, two arriving later.

NORTH VERSUS SOUTH
The first North (of England) versus South match took place at the Market Field in Rugby on 31st January. The fixture came about after complaints by northern clubs that their players were being overlooked for England selection. It was reported that 'the only way out of the difficulty was thought to be that a match should take place between two picked twenties of the North and South to partake, in its nature, more of a trial match than a struggle between the two,' and 'it was arranged that the weathercock on Rugby Church should be the line of demarcation'.[5] Despite the implied non-combative nature of the trial, it quickly established itself as a prestigious, competitive annual fixture in its own right, providing a bridge between international and county selection. With few exceptions, the North selected its players from Cheshire, Cumberland, Durham, Lancashire, Northumberland, Westmorland and Yorkshire.

SHEFFIELD TURNS ITS BACK ON RUGBY

For the return Yorkshire versus Durham match, at Holbeck Recreation Ground, Leeds, on 11th April, it was reported: 'Invitations sent by the Yorkshire committee to the Sheffield men were unfortunately not accepted. Sheffield notoriously possesses the best footballers in the county, and either at their own game, which is almost peculiar to themselves, or any other of the prevailing games, are fully capable of tackling the remainder of the county. It is, therefore, all the more to be deplored that they are always conspicuous by their absence at every county match.'[6] In fact Sheffield players, having contributed to the first county match in 1870, made no further appearances. Their 'own game' was commonly referred to as the 'Sheffield Rules' which, during this embryonic period for 'football', was devised in 1857, continuing until 1878 when Association rules were adopted. This was an era when athletes with prowess at one sport often demonstrated capability in other disciplines, hence the invitation to play the 'Rugby' code at county level.

YORKSHIRE COUNTY FOOTBALL CLUB FOUNDED

The Yorkshire County Football Club was founded this season by five clubs (Bradford, Huddersfield, Hull, Leeds and York). The exact date is not recorded but believed to be during April.

1873-1874 STATISTICS

COUNTY MATCHES

Saturday 6 December 1873 at Feethams Cricket Ground, Darlington
DURHAM 1 goal, 2 tries *Backs*: CE Bell (capt, Darl, t, c), WC Best (Darl). *Half-backs*: JL Bell (Darl, t), T Watson (Darl). *Forwards*: CE Barnes (DurC), CJ Coleby (Darl), EH Dykes (Gate), WS Elliot (Sund), OA Leatham (Darl, t), JC Shewell (Darl), J Taylor (Gate). *Also in team (positions not reported)*: GA Fisher, WJ Gibson (Darl), RE Hall (Darl), CHS James (Otterburn).
YORKSHIRE 0 J Baldwin (Ilkley), F Fawcett (Harr), T Fawcett (Harr), JJ Freeman (Lee), HWT Garnett (Brad), W Hodgson (Hull), C Hustwick (Hull), WHH Hutchinson (capt, Hull), CB Lambert (Hull), A Sidgwick (Brad), J Sharpe (Hull), WSykes (Lee), TS Tetley (Brad, AJ Tuckwell (Lee), J Young (Harr).
Attendance: 'good'
Note 1: Club not identified for G. A. Fisher (Durham).
Note 2: Playing positions for Yorkshire not reported.

Saturday 17 January 1874 at Bradford Cricket Ground, Great Horton Road
YORKSHIRE 0 *Backs*: W Hodgson (Hull), JB Vickerman (Hud). *Two-thirds*: H Harris (York), R Mills (Brad). *Half-backs*: R Hodgson (Hull), H Huth (Hud). *Forwards*: C Bethell (Hull), GS Brook (Hud), HS Brook (Hud), G Brooke (Hud), JJ Freeman (Lee), HWT Garnett (capt, Brad), WH Griffiths (Brad), WHH Hutchinson (Hull), CC Lapage (Lee), R Margerison (Brad), HC Shann (Lee), A Sidgwick (Brad), TS Tetley (Brad).
LANCASHIRE 2 tries *Backs*: RW Colquhoun (Liv), D MacLaren (Man). *Three-quarter*: A Irving (RochH). *Half-backs*: J Hulton (PresG), A Lyon (Liv). *Forwards*: AJ Bulteel (Man), CW Carver (Liv), JS Genth (Man, t), W Greg (Man), E Kewley (capt, Liv, t), MacLaren (Man), EE Marriott (Man), A Pilkington (Man), C Pilkington (Man), G Shawe (Liv), CJC Touzel (Liv), R Walker (Man), W Welch (Man), H Woolley (Man).
Attendance: 'small'
Note: Both teams had 19 players.

Saturday 11 April 1874 at Holbeck Recreation Ground, Leeds
YORKSHIRE 1 try *Backs*: R Hodgson (Hull), W Hodgson (Hull). *Three-quarter*: JG Wylie (Don). *Half-backs*: B Cariss (capt, Lee), R Mills (Brad). *Forwards*: JD Brown (Lee), E Dunsford (Brad), F Fawcett (Harr), HWT Garnett (Brad), WHH Hutchinson (Hull), CB Lambert (Hull), CC Lapage (Lee), HC Shann (Lee, t), A Sidgwick (Brad), TS Tetley (Brad).
DURHAM 1 goal *Back*: WS Elliot (Sund). *Half-backs*: E Penny (Gate), T Watson (capt, Darl). *Quarter-backs*: PB Junor (Sund, t, c), C Kidson (Sund). *Forwards*: WC Best (Darl), FW Brooks (Darl), JH Brooks (Darl), HW Fawcus (SSh), HP Kayll (Sund), OA Leatham (Darl), W Ogden (Sund), J Radford (Gate), G Sowerby (Darl), J Taylor (Gate).
Attendance: 2,000

ENGLAND TRIAL MATCH

Saturday 31 January 1874 at Market Field, Rugby
NORTH 1 try *Backs*: R Hodgson (Hull), F Lemonius (Liv), D MacLaren (Man). *Half-backs*: S Finney (Crewe, t), JR Hay-Gordon (Liv), A Lyon (capt, Liv). *Forwards*: CW Carver (Liv), E Cliff (Liv), SG Colquhoun (Liv), JS Genth (Man), W Greg (Man), WHH Hutchinson (Hull), E Kewley (Liv), J MacLaren (Man), S Parker (Liv), A Pilkington (Man), C Pilkington (Man), R Walker (Man), H Woolley (Man), TR Wynne (Liv).
SOUTH 3 tries *Backs*: JM Batten (CamU), GF Congreve (RavPk), FW Mills (MarlN). *Three-quarter*: H Freeman (MarlN). *Half-backs*: J St G Ord (RA, t), GA Pearson (Black, t). *Forwards*: T Batson (Black), EC Cheston (Rich), FL Cunliffe (RMA), WR Fletcher (MarlN), P Gooding (OxfU), A St G Hamersley (capt, MarlN), C Hewitt (QH), HA Lawrence (Rich), MW Marshall (Black), R Peile (Rich), WW Pinching (GuyHosp), HJ Rawson (Black, t), CP Sclater (Gip), WH Stafford (RE).
Attendance: n/a
Note: Match drawn as only goals are counted.

INTERNATIONAL MATCH

Monday 23 February 1874 at Kennington Oval, London
ENGLAND 1 goal *Backs*: JM Batten (CamU), MJ Brooks (OxfU). *Three-quarter*: H Freeman (MarlN, dg). *Half-backs*: WE Collins (OChelt), WH Milton (MarlN), S Morse (MarlN). *Forwards*: T Batson (Black), HA Bryden (ClapR), EC Cheston (Rich), CW Crosse (OxfU), FL Cunliffe (RMA), JS Genth (Man), A St G Hamersley (capt, MarlN), E Kewley (Liv), HA Lawrence (Rich), MW Marshall (Black), S Parker (Liv), WFH Stafford (RE), DP Turner (Rich), R Walker (Man).
SCOTLAND 1 try *Backs*: WD Brown (capt, GlasA), T Chalmers (GlasA.). *Half-backs*: HM Hamilton (WoS), TR Marshall (EdinA), WH Kidston (WoS). *Quarter-backs*: W St C Grant (Craig), AK Stewart (EdinU). *Forwards*: CC Bryce (GlasA), JP Davidson (RIEC), JF Finlay (EdinA, t), G Heron (GlasA), RW Irvine (EdinA), JAW Mein (EdinA), T Neilson (WoS), AG Petrie (RHSFP), J Reid (EdinW), JK Todd (GlasA), RW Wilson (WoS), AT Wood (RHSFP), AH Young (EdinA).
Attendance: 4,000

FOOTBALL.
LANCASHIRE v. YORKSHIRE.

A football match between representative players of of these counties took place on Saturday afternoon on the ground of the Manchester Football Club, at Whalley Range. The teams were composed as follows:—Lancashire: Jellicorse (Wanderers, Didsbury), back; Leech (Liverpool), back; Dunsmure (Sale), three quarters back; J. R. Hay-Gordon (Liverpool), half back; A. Lyon (Liverpool), half back; R. Walker (Manchester), E. Kewley (Liverpool), J. S. Genth (Manchester), J. Maclaren (Manchester), C. W. Carver (Liverpool), C. Pilkington (Manchester), E. Marriott (Manchester), Darbyshire (Manchester), R. W. Dean (Liverpool), R. Greg (Manchester), F. Pattison (Manchester), R. Colquhoun (Liverpool), C. Gray (Liverpool), W. Higgin (Liverpool), A. Bulteel (Manchester), forwards. Yorkshire: D. F. Burton (Hull), back; Richardson (Bradford), back; Hodgson (Hull), three quarters back; Mills (Bradford), half back; Huth (Huddersfield) back; Tetley (Bradford), back; Hutchinson (Hull), captain; Garnett (Bradford), Schutt (Bradford), Wither (Bradford), Champney, Manning (Leeds), Welsh (Huddersfield), Macaulay (Huddersfield), B. Schofield (Huddersfield), C. Hastwick (Hull), F. H. Calvert (Huddersfield), B. Wrigley (Huddersfield), F. Watkinson (Huddersfield), J. H. Connacher (Huddersfield), forwards. The umpires were Mr. W. Maclaren for Lancashire and Mr. J. Bradley for Yorkshire. Despite the adverse state of the weather, a large number of spectators, including many ladies, were present, and the progress of the match, which at times was very exciting, was watched with much interest. The kick off took place shortly before three o'clock, and when, at half-past four, time was called, no goal had been obtained by either party, and the game stood as follows:—Lancashire, four tries and two touchdowns; Yorkshire, nothing. Hay-Gordon obtained two tries, Kewley one try, and one try was obtained from a free catch. On the part of Lancashire the players who especially distinguished themselves were Hay-Gordon, Kewley, Walker, Dunsmure, Carver, Bulteel, Darbyshire, and Marriott; and on the part of Yorkshire, Burton, Hodgson, Mills, Hutchinson, Garnett, and Macaulay.

A contemporary report of the sixth annual Lancashire-Yorkshire clash.
Manchester Guardian, January 1875

1874-1875

14 VERSUS 14
The Durham versus Yorkshire match at Darlington cricket ground on 12th December was played with 14 players on each side. Yorkshire arrived one short so Durham generously stood down one of their own players to even the numbers.

AT YOUR CONVENIENCE
The Lancashire versus Yorkshire match in January was scheduled for Liverpool, but, as the *Leeds Mercury* reported, 'it was thought desirable to change the locality to Manchester, that city being more central and convenient for all the Yorkshire players, several of whom came as far as from Hull'.[7]

THE WORLD'S OLDEST RUGBY CUP COMPETITION BEGINS
The United (London) Hospitals Challenge Cup was instituted, seven hospitals taking part in this knock-out contest during February and March. It remains today as the world's oldest rugby cup competition.

1874-1875 STATISTICS

COUNTY MATCHES

Saturday 12 December 1874 at Feethams Cricket Ground, Darlington
DURHAM 1 goal, 1 try *Back*: T Thompson (Darl). *Half-backs*: W Hill (Sto), HP Kayll (Sund). *Quarter-backs*: JL Bell (capt, Darl), WA Kidson (Sund, t). *Forwards*: WC Best (Darl, c), JH Brooks (Darl), JJ Kayll (Sund), H Peters (Sund), Powell (Sto), Russell (Darl), SC Shewell (Darl), GMD Trotter (Sto), JG Wilkes (Darl).
YORKSHIRE 0 *Backs*: W Hodgson (Hull), A Milner (Harr). *Three-quarter*: B Cariss (capt, Lee). *Half-backs*: H Huth (Hud), R Mills (Brad). *Forwards*: TP Crosland (Hud), E Dunsford (Brad), HWT Garnett (Brad), R Hodgson (Hull), CC Lapage (Lee), HJ Manning (Lee), F Schutt (Brad), HC Shann (Lee), TS Tetley (Brad).
Attendance: 'not large'
Note 1: Yorkshire had one player missing so Durham decided to also have 14.
Note 2: One Durham try scorer not reported

Saturday 16 January 1875 at Whalley Range, Manchester
LANCASHIRE 4 tries *Backs*: EH Jellicorse (Man), WE Leach (Liv). *Three-quarter*: G Dunsmuir (Man). *Half-backs*: JR Hay-Gordon (Liv, 2t), A Lyon (Liv). *Forwards*: AJ Bulteel (Man), CW Carver (Liv), RW Colquhoun (Liv), G Darbishire (Man), RW Dean (Liv), JS Genth (Man), A Gray (Liv), W Greg (Man), WF Higgins (Liv), E Kewley (Liv, t), J MacLaren (Man), EE Marriott Man), F Patteson (Man), C Pilkington (Man), R Walker (Man).
YORKSHIRE 0 *Backs*: DF Burton (Hull), J Richardson (Brad). *Three-quarter*: R Hodgson (Hull). *Half-back*: R Mills (Brad). *Quarter-backs*: H Huth (Hud), TS Tetley (Brad). *Forwards*: TH Calvert (Hud), C Champney (Hal), JHS Conacher (Hud), HWT Garnett (Brad), RF Gwyther (Brad), C Hustwick (Hull), WHH Hutchinson (capt, Hull), A Macauley (Hud), HJ Manning (Lee), B Schofield (Hud), F Schutt (Brad), F Watkinson (Hud), R Welsh (Hud), PT Wrigley Hud).
Attendance: 'large'
Note 1: Match drawn as only goals are counted.
Note 2: One Lancashire 'try' scored from a 'free catch'.

Saturday 20 March 1875 at Holbeck Recreation Groubd, Leeds
YORKSHIRE 2 goals *Backs*: FW Mills (Esholt), A Milner (Harr). *Three-quarter*: B Cariss (capt, Lee, dg). *Half-backs*: H Huth (Hud), R Mills (Brad), TS Tetley (Brad, dg). *Forwards*: GS Brook (Hud), HS Brook (Hud), A Christison (York), E Dunsford (Brad), HWT Garnett (Brad), E Glaisby (York), RF Gwyther (Brad), WHH Hutchinson (Hull), HJ Manning (Lee), TJ Ogden (LeeStJ), F Schutt (Brad), HC Shann (Lee), RJ Wade (Hull), R Welsh (Hud).
DURHAM 1 goal *Backs*: HP Kayll (Sund), T Thompson (Darl). *Half-backs*: W Hill (Sto, c), C Kidson (Sund). *Quarter-backs*: WC Best (Darl), WA Kidson (capt, Sund, t). *Forwards*: JH Brooks (Darl), CL Bell (Durham), RH Bicknell (Sto), RH Christison (Gate), CO Fawcus (Sto), HW Fawcus (SSh), HE Kayll (Sund), W Ogden (Sund), TR Read (Darl), SC Shewell (Darl), G Sowerby (Darl), J Taylor (Gate), R Welford (Darl), JG Wilkes (Darl).
Attendance: 'good'

ENGLAND TRIAL MATCH

Saturday 19 December 1874 at Kennington Oval, London
SOUTH 1 try *Backs*: AW Pearson (GuyHosp), L Stokes (Black). *Three-quarter*: WH Milton (MarlN). *Half-backs*: WE Collins, (StGHosp, t), S Morse (MarlN), R Sedgwick (Rich). *Forwards*: F Adams (Rich), T Batson (Black), J Bush (Clif), EC Cheston (Rich), KR Fletcher (Black), WRB Fletcher (OxfU), EC Fraser (OxfU), HA Lawrence (capt, Rich), F Luscombe (Gip), MW Marshall (Black), AE Pinching (Black), H Stafford (RE), R Stokes (Black), H Wace (CamU).
NORTH 0 *Backs*: GF Congreve (RavPk), WE Leach (Liv). *Three-quarter*: GF Griffin (RavPk). *Half-backs*: JR Hay-Gordon (Liv), A Lyon (Liv). *Forwards*: FH Bucknill (Crewe), AJ Bulteel (Man), CW Carver (Liv), HWT Garnett (Brad), JS Genth (Man), W Greg (Man), WHH Hutchinson (Hull), E Kewley (capt, Liv), CW Moss (Sou), TAR Littledale (Liv), J MacLaren (Man), W Marriott (Man), S Parker (Liv), C Pilkington (Man), R Walker (Man).
Attendance: 500
Note: Match drawn as only goals are counted.

INTERNATIONAL MATCHES

Monday 15 February 1875 at Kennington Oval, London
ENGLAND 2 goals, 1 try *Backs*: AW Pearson (Black, c), L Stokes (Black). *Three-quarter*: WH Milton (MarlN). *Half-backs*: WE Collins (OChelt), AT Mitchell (OxfU, t), EH Nash (Rich, dg). *Forwards*: FR Adams (Rich), T Batson (Black), EC Cheston (Rich, t), CW Crosse (OxfU), EC Fraser (Black), HJ Graham (Wim), WHH Hutchinson (Hull), HA Lawrence (capt, Rich), F Luscombe (Gip), JEH Mackinlay (StGHosp), MW Marshall (Black), ES Perrott (OChelt), DP Turner (Rich), R Walker (Man).
IRELAND 0 *Backs*: HL Cox (DubU), RB Walkington (NIFC). *Three-quarters*: RJ Bell (NIFC), AP Cronyn (DubU). *Half-backs*: R Galbraith (DubU), EN McIlwaine (NIFC), J Myles (DubU). *Forwards*: WS Allen (Wand), G Andrews (NIFC), WH Ash (NIFC), M Barlow (Wand), BN Casement (DubU), A Combe (NIFC), W Gaffikin (Wind), E Galbraith (DubU), FT Hewson (Wand), JA Macdonald (MethC), RM Maginiss (DubU), GH Stack (capt, DubU), HD Walsh (DubU).
Attendance: 2,000

Monday 8 March 1875 at Raeburn Place, Edinburgh
SCOTLAND 0 *Backs*: WD Brown (capt, GlasA), T Chalmers (GlasA). *Half-backs*: NJ Finlay (EdinA), M Cross (Mer), HM Hamilton (WoS). *Quarter-backs*: JR Hay-Gordon (EdinA), JK Tod (GlasA). *Forwards*: A Arthur (GlasA), JW Dunlop (WoS), AB Finlay (EdinA), JF Finlay (EdinA), GR Fleming (GlasA), G Heron (GlasA), RW Irvine (EdinA), A Marshall (EdinA), JAW Mein (EdinA), AG Petrie (RHSFP), J Reid (EdinW), D Robertson (EdinA), A Wood (RHSFP).
ENGLAND 0 *Backs*: LH Birkett (ClapR), AW Pearson (Black). *Three-quarter*: S Morse (MarlN). *Half-backs*: WE Collins (OChelt), WAD Evanson (Rich), AT Mitchell (OxfU). *Forwards*: FR Adams (Rich), RH Birkett (ClapR), JA Bush (Clif), EC Cheston (Rich), WRB Fletcher (MarlN), JS Genth (Man), HJ Graham (Wim), E Kewley (Liv), HA Lawrence (capt, Rich), F Luscombe (Gip), MW Marshall (Black), S Parker (Liv), JE Paul (RIEC), DP Turner (Rich).
Attendance: 7,000

NORTH v. SOUTH.

On Saturday afternoon, a grand match took place at Manchester between representatives of North and South of England Football Clubs. The ground was in excellent condition, and the delightfully fine and bright weather brought between 3000 and 4000 spectators. There were twenty players on each side. For the North: W. Grave, Manchester; J. Huth, Huddersfield (backs); A. N. Hornby, Manchester, and H. Tetley, Bradford (three-quarter backs); J. R. Hay-Gordon, Liverpool, and C. W. H. Clarke, Liverpool (half backs); R. Walker, W. Greg, J. S. Genth, A. Bulteel, E. Todd, E. E. Marriott, and C. Gray, Manchester; H. M. Brooke, Huddersfield; — Markendale, Manchester; G. Garnett, Bradford; W. H. Hunt, Preston; E. Kewley, C. S. Verelst, and E. Cliffe, Liverpool. For the South, the following played:—A. Miller and E. J. Taylor, Clifton (backs); W. Gray, Guy's Hospital, and C. R. Gunner, Marlborough Nomads (three-quarter backs); A. R. Butterworth, Marlborough Nomads, and W. E. Collins, St. George's Hospital (half backs); F. Luscombe, J. A. Body, and J. A. Brewer, Gipsies; H. J. Graham and J. D. Graham, Wimbledon; E. B. Turner and T. R. Turner, St. George's Hospital; E. H. Birkett, Clapham Rovers; H. R. Armstrong, Marlborough Nomads; M. Curtis, Clifton; W. R. B. Fletcher, Oxford University; F. J. Newton, Ravenscourt Park; H. W. Whyatt, Guy's Hospital; W. Slade, West Kent. Mr. Walker was captain of the northern team, and Mr. Luscombe of the southern. Mr. J. Maclaren acted as referee. The match was very even throughout. The southerners worked well together, and had the advantage of superior weight; but the north played well on the ball, and finally won with one try and a touch down, their opponents only gaining two touch downs. No goal was scored.

Newspaper report of 'a grand match' between the North and South.
Sheffield Independent, January 1876

1875-1876

BARROW FOUNDED
The Barrow club was founded this season.

INTELLIGIBLE TERMS
In an era when terminology in rugby football was changing rapidly as the game evolved, the Honorary Secretary of the Manchester (Rugby) Football Club, Ernest E. Marriott, wrote the following letter to the Manchester-based *Athletic News* with reference to comments in the latest edition of Charles Alcock's *Football Annual*, published in London: 'May I call the attention of local secretaries of football clubs and others to the following extract from page 13 of the *Football Annual* for 1875:- "It is to be regretted that *rouge* and other inexplicable terms still crop up in the accounts of Rugby football published in the sporting pages. The term *rouge* has no existence either at Rugby [School] or in the [Rugby Football] Union Code; why will clubs belonging to the Union persist in using it! A *touchdown* occurs when the defending side are compelled to touch the ball down in their own goal [in-goal area]. When the attacking side touch the ball down in their opponents' goal [in-goal area], they gain a *try* or a *punt out*, according to whatever means they adopt with a view to obtaining a goal. These definitions are simple enough, and if secretaries of clubs following the Union rules would remember them, their accounts of matches would be intelligible to others besides themselves." I have noticed these errors particular in the Manchester papers, and hope this letter, if you can kindly publish it, will help to make football accounts more intelligible in future.'[8]

THE FIRST INTERNATIONAL REFEREE

Abram Combe was the first to referee an international match when Ireland entertained England in Dublin on 13th December. When rugby football became more organised in the 1860s it was the team captains who attempted to settle disagreements. By the early 1870s this evolved into each club appointing its own umpire, the pair effectively taking over the decision making from the team captains. This inevitably led to disputes and referees were introduced in 1875-76 to act as arbitrators although lacking any real decision making power.

A LARGE AND OPEN FIELD

When Yorkshire met Lancashire at Fieldhouse, Huddersfield, on 15th January it was noted that 'the field in which the match was played is a large and open one, abutting on the Leeds and Liverpool Canal on the north-west side, and near the Leeds and Huddersfield road on the other. The distance between the goals was 150 yards and the breadth between the boundaries 80 yards'.[9] Apart from that, its huge size warranted no further comment in the report. In fact, pitch dimensions was another item not covered by the *Laws of the Game* published in 1871, eventually being regulated in 1879. Perhaps the enormous field of play could be justified by the presence of 20 players on each side which, in this case, was the last time an inter-county fixture took place between two 20s.

BEST IN THE RUGBY UNION

The *Athletic News* heralded Huddersfield as the best club in the country, stating 'Yorkshiremen have reason to be proud of the Huddersfield club, which is undoubtedly, by a long way, the foremost in the country of those playing the Rugby Union game'.[10]

1875-1876 STATISTICS

COUNTY MATCHES

Saturday 15 January 1876 at Fieldhouse, Huddersfield
YORKSHIRE 0 *Backs*: DF Burton (Hull), R Hodgson (Hull). *Three-quarter*: H Huth (Hud). *Half-backs*: R Mills (Brad), CM Sharpe (Hud), TS Tetley (Brad). *Forwards*: GS Brook (Hud), HS Brook (capt, Hud), A Christison (York), JHS Conacher (Hud), HWT Garnett (Brad), G Harrison (Hull), W Hodgson (Hull), WHH Hutchinson (Hull), B Schofield (Hud), F Schutt (Brad), C Tennant (Lee), F Thursby (York), R Welsh (Hud), PT Wrigley (Hud).
LANCASHIRE 0 *Backs*: W Grave (Man), A Knowles (Man). *Three-quarters*: JR Hay-Gordon (Liv), AN Hornby (Blackburn), L Knowles (Man). *Half-back*: CWH Clarke (Liv). *Forwards*: H Burder (Man), E Cliff (Liv), JS Genth (Man), A Gray (Liv), W Greg (Man), WF Higgins (Liv), WH Hunt (PresG), E Mann (Man), ET Markendale (ManR), EE Marriott (Man), R Mellor (ManFW), R Todd (Man), CL Verelst (Liv), R Walker (capt, Man).
Attendance: 1,500   *Referee*: n/a

Friday 25 February 1876 at Edge Hill, Liverpool
LIVERPOOL 0 – Liverpool team not reported.
CHESHIRE 2 tries *Backs*: J Healing (BirkPk), WH Wallace (BirkPk). *Three-quarters*: HM Blythe (BirkPk), C Spence (Birkenhead School). *Half-backs*: JB Parry (RockF), H Watson (BirkPk). *Forwards*: F Baker (Sale), WH Bleakley (Sale), Burton (RockF), Crawford (Parkgate), W Ewer (NewB), J Goodwin (BirkPk), W Healing (BirkPk), Houlder (BirkPk), EC Kendall (RockF), Leece (BirkPk), Moysey (BirkPk), W Rickman (BirkPk), GH Smythe (BirkPk), RL Stewart (BirkPk).
Attendance: n/a   *Referee*: n/a
Note: Scorers for Cheshire not reported.

Saturday 26 February 1876 at Carlisle
CUMBERLAND 0 *Backs*: Essex, Norrie. *Half-back*: Stewart. *Quarter-backs*: EL Hough (capt, Carl), CW Murray. *Forwards*: Abbot, Busch, Fidler, Graham, Holder, Johnstone, Maxwell (Carl), Pike, Scott, Thompson.
NORTHUMBERLAND 2 tries *Backs*: H Hughes (NorFC), A Hutchinson (NorFC). *Half-back*: G Sowerby (Bensham). *Quarter-backs*: B Hodge (NorFC, t), F Logan (NorFC). *Forwards*: J Adamson, R Atkinson (NorFC), R Braithwaite (NorFC), FCT Challoner (NorFC), Cobbold (t), JE de Jersey (NorFC), F Dunford (NorFC), JT Harding (NorFC), FG Radford (NorFC).
Attendance: n/a   *Referee*: n/a
Note 1: Northumberland had 14 players.
Note 2: Clubs not identified for majority of Cumberland team.
Note 3: Clubs not identified for J. Adamson and Cobbold (Northumberland).

ENGLAND TRIAL MATCH

Saturday 29 January 1876 at Whalley Range, Manchester
NORTH 1 try *Backs*: W Grave (Man), J Huth (Hud). *Three-quarters*: AN Hornby (Man), TS Tetley (Brad). *Half-backs*: CWH Clarke (Liv), JR Hay-Gordon (Liv, t). *Forwards*: HS Brook (Hud), AJ Bulteel (Man), E Cliff (Liv), HWT Garnett (Brad), JS Genth (Man), W Greg (Man), C Grey (Man), WH Hunt (PresG), E Kewley (Liv), J Markendale (Man), EE Marriott (Man), R Todd (Man), CL Verelst (Liv), R Walker (capt, Man).
SOUTH 0 *Backs*: A Miller (Clif), EJ Taylor (Clif). *Three-quarters*: W Gray (GuyHosp), CR Gunner (MarlN). *Half-backs*: AR Butterworth (MarlN), WE Collins (StGHosp). *Forwards*: HR Armstrong (MarlN), RH Birkett (ClapR), JA Body (Gip), JV Brewer (Gip), MM Curtis (Clif), WHB Fletcher (OxfU), HJ Graham (Wim), JD Graham (Wim), F Luscombe (capt, Gip), FJ Newton (RavPk), AW Pinching (GuyHosp), W Slade (WKent), EB Turner (StGHosp), TR Turner (StGHosp).
Attendance: 3,000/4,000
Referees: J MacLaren (Manchester), CE Sidebotham (Manchester)

INTERNATIONAL MATCHES

Monday 13 December 1875 at Rathmines, Dublin
IRELAND 0 *Backs*: H Moore (Wind), RB Walkington (NIFC). *Three-quarters*: BN Casement (DubU), EW Hobson (DubU). *Half-backs*: RJ Bell (capt, NIFC), AP Cronyn (DubU). *Forwards*: G Andrews (NIFC), DT Arnott (Lans), WH Ash (NIFC), HL Cox (DubU) WA Cuscaden (Bray), W Finlay (NIFC), R Galbraith (DubU), R Greer (King), J Ireland (Wind), JA Macdonald (MethC), EN McIlwaine (NIFC), RM Maginiss (DubU), HD Walsh (DubU), AJ Westby (DubU).
ENGLAND 1 goal, 1 try *Backs*: SHM Login (RNC), AW Pearson (Black, c). *Three-quarters*: CR Gunner (MarlN), AT Mitchell (OxfU). *Half-backs*: CWH Clarke (Liv, t), WE Collins (OChelt). *Forwards*: JV Brewer (Gip), CC Bryden (ClapR), AJ Bulteel (Man), JA Bush (Clif), HJ Graham (Wim), JD Graham (Wim), W Greg (Man), WHH Hutchinson (Hull), E Kewley (Liv, t), F Luscombe (capt, Gip), EE Marriott (Man), MW Marshall (Black), EB Turner (StGHosp), CL Verelst (Liv).
Attendance: 'large'   *Referee*: A Combe (Ireland)

Monday 6 March 1876 at Kennington Oval, London
ENGLAND 1 goal, 1 try *Backs*: AH Heath (OxfU), AW Pearson (Black). *Three-quarters*: RH Birkett (ClapR), JS Tetley (Brad), L Stokes (Black, c). *Half-backs*: WE Collins (OChelt, t), WC Hutchinson (RIEC). *Forwards*: FR Adams (Rich), JA Bush (Clif), EC Cheston (Rich), HJ Graham (Wim), W Greg (Man), WH Hunt (Man), E Kewley (Liv), FH Lee (MarlN, t), F Luscombe (capt, Gip), MW Marshall (Black), WCW Rawlinson (Black), GR Turner (StGHosp), R Walker (Man).
SCOTLAND 0 *Backs*: JS Carrick (WoS), T Chalmers (GlasA). *Half-backs*: M Cross (GlasA), NJ Finlay (EdinA). *Quarter-backs*: GQ Paterson (EdinA), AK Stewart (EdinU). *Forwards*: A Arthur (Mer), WH Bolton (WoS), NT Brewis (EdinIFP), CW Cathcart (EdinU), D Drew (GlasA), GR Fleming (GlasA), JHS Graham (EdinA), RW Irvine (capt, EdinA), JE Junor (GlasA), D Lang (Paisley), AG Petrie (RHSFP), J Reid (EdinW), C Villar (EdinW), DH Watson (GlasA).
Attendance: 2,000   *Referee*: A Rutter (England)

1876-1877

WARRINGTON FOUNDED
Warrington founded as Warrington Zingari in August, renamed Warrington in 1879. A different Warrington rugby club had existed prior to that.

OLDHAM FOUNDED
Oldham founded during September.

KEIGHLEY FOUNDED
Keighley founded on 17th October, originally as a Rugby and Association Football Club.

DURHAM COUNTY UNION FOUNDED
Durham County Rugby Union founded by seven clubs on 31st October.

CHESHIRE COUNTY UNION FOUNDED
Cheshire County Rugby Union believed founded during 1876-77, although the exact date is unknown. There are no surviving minutes for that period.

THUMBS UP FOR 15-A-SIDE
This was the first season when virtually all matches were played with 15-a-side, including international matches, the North versus South fixture, and inter-county games. The Yorkshire versus Durham match, played at Holbeck Recreation Ground, Leeds, on 11th November, drew the following comment: 'The game was very fast owing no doubt to the fact that only 15 a side played instead of 20 as usual in big matches.'[11]

THE LAST COUNTY 20
When Cheshire met Liverpool at Edge Hill on 25th November, it was the last occasion that a northern county used 20 players. Liverpool, however, was short-handed and fielded 16. Due to a late start, only one hour was played.

DUAL-SPORTSMAN
As the Durham and Northumberland teams emerged for their county match at Sunderland on 27th January 'Mr. Fawcus, on entering the field, was loudly cheered for his victory on the Tyne just an hour or two previous to his arrival'.[12] The explanation was that Northumberland and Tynemouth forward William Fawcus had just beaten J. G. Sowerby of Gateshead in a one mile amateur skiff race on the River Tyne, winning a silver cup in the process!

SMALL GROUND
Cheshire hosted its first inter-county match on 24th February, opposing Lancashire on Sale's ground at Brooklands. It attracted a fairly modest '400 to 500 spectators', the *Manchester Guardian* claiming 'this ground is much too small for a match of this importance'.[13] Nonetheless, a reported 1,500 were packed into the same ground the following season when Yorkshire visited.

1876-1877 STATISTICS

COUNTY MATCHES

Saturday 11 November 1876 at Holbeck Recreation Ground, Leeds
YORKSHIRE 0 *Backs*: RH Christison (York), R Hodgson (Hull). *Three-quarters*: EW Harrison (Hull), W Hodgson (Hull). *Half-backs*: R Mills (Brad), TS Tetley (Brad). *Forwards*: A Christison (York), RH Fowler (Leeds), HWT Garnett (Brad), E Glaisby (York), G Harrison (Hull), WHH Hutchinson (capt, Hull), O Leatham (Lee), HJ Manning (Lee), F Schutt (Brad).
DURHAM 1 try *Back*: HE Kayll (Sund). *Half-backs*: JL Bell (Darl, t), PB Junor (capt, DurC). *Quarter-backs*: RF Boyd (Sund), JH Twining (DurU). *Forwards*: CE Barnes (DurC), RH Bicknell (Sto), R Brierley (Hou), JH Brooks (Darl), EH Dykes (DurC), J Fowles (Sund), AGM Hudson (Sund), HP Kayll (Sund), SF Prest (Bensham), SC Shewell (Darl).
Attendance: 'large'   *Referee*: n/a

Saturday 25 November 1876 at Edge Hill, Liverpool
LIVERPOOL 0 *Backs*: J Garnett, P Hunter. *Half-backs*: Dixon, G Warren. *Quarter-backs*: HD Bateson, JR Hay-Gordon. *Forwards*: E Cliff, SG Colquhoun, Dempsey, Gardener, M Hull, TAR Littledale, Steele.

CHESHIRE 1 goal, 3 tries *Backs*: S Marsland (Sale), JC Wilson (Sale, c).
Three-quarter: HM Blythe (capt, BirkPk). *Half-backs*: WH Green (West Derby, t),
GP Pagden (Sale, t). *Quarter-backs*: JB Parry (RockF, t), HC Rowley (Bow).
Forwards: G Andrews (Ald), WH Bleakley (Sale), CE Dearden (Ald), TH Harrison
(RockF), EC Kendall (RockF, t), Leece (BirkPk), BB Middleton (RockF), H Potter, Rowley,
GH Smythe (BirkPk), FS Swainwick (Ald), JWH Thorp (Macc), WH Wallace (BirkPk).
Attendance: n/a   *Referee*: n/a
Note 1: Liverpool had 16 players instead of 20 (13 as listed plus three forwards reported as 'three others').
Note 2: Clubs not identified for forwards H. Potter and Rowley (Cheshire).
Note 3: Played for one hour only, due to late start.

Saturday 16 December 1876 at Holmside, Sunderland
DURHAM 1 goal, 1 try *Back*: HE Kayll (Sund, fg). *Half-backs*: H Brooks (Darl), C Kidson
(capt, Sund, t). *Quarter-backs*: RF Boyd (Sund), J Laing (Sund). *Forwards:* R Brierley (Hou),
JH Brooks (Darl), OC Carr (DurU), HW Edlin (Darl), T Elstob (Hou), J Fowles (Sund),
HP Kayll (Sund), A Laing (Sund), SC Shewell (Darl), JG Wilkes (Darl).
NORTHUMBERLAND 1 goal *Backs*: W Carr (NorFC), B Hodge (NorFC). *Half-backs*:
CNM Dale (NorFC), T Wilson (Tynm). *Quarter-backs*: JL Bell (capt, NorFC), JT Harding
(NorFC). *Forwards*: C Adamson, CE Barnes (DurC), C Bramwell (Tynm), A Cadle
(NorFC), FCT Challoner (NorFC), B Dale (NorFC), W Fawcus (Tynm), HL Pattinson
(NorFC), JS Pattinson (NorFC).
Attendance: 'large'   *Referee*: n/a
Note 1: Club not identified for C. Adamson (Northumberland).
Note 2: Scorer(s) for Northumberland not reported.

Saturday 20 January 1877 at Whalley Range, Manchester
LANCASHIRE 0 *Backs*: A Knowles (Man), ET Smith (ManR). *Three-quarters*: AN Hornby
(PresG), L Knowles (Man). *Half-backs*: WS Butterworth (RochH), JR Hay-Gordon (Liv).
Forwards: E Cliff (Liv), D Drew (Man), W Greg (Man), WH Hunt (PresG), E Kewley
(capt, Liv), GF Schofield (Sou), R Todd (Man), CJC Touzel (Liv), H Wyles (Bro).
YORKSHIRE 0 *Backs*: A Christison (York), R Hodgson (Hull). *Three-quarters*: TS Tetley
(Brad), PT Wrigley (Hud). *Half-backs*: R Mills (Brad), E Seaton (Lee). *Forwards*: TH Calvert
(Hud), JHS Conacher (Hud), RH Fowler (Leeds), HWT Garnett (capt, Brad), G Harrison
(Hull), O Leatham (Lee), F Schutt (Brad), C Tennant (Lee), GT Thomson (Hal).
Attendance: 3,000/4,000   *Referee*: W MacLaren (Manchester)

Saturday 27 January 1877 at Chester Road, Sunderland
DURHAM 2 tries *Back*: HE Kayll (Sund). *Half-backs*: WC Best (Darl), E Scott (Sund).
Quarter-backs: WA Kidson (Sund), J Laing (Sund). *Forwards*: HW Edlin (Darl),
AGM Hudson (Sund), HP Kayll (capt, Sund), A Laing (Sund), AC Mann (Sund),
Pinchin (Sund), SF Prest (Bensham), JC Shewell (Darl).
NORTHUMBERLAND 1 try *Back*: B Hodge (NorFC). *Half-backs*: B Dale (capt, NorFC),
T Wilson (Tynm). *Quarter-backs*: JT Harding (NorFC), F Logan (NorFC). *Forwards*:
WR Bagley (Darl), CE Barnes (DurC), A Cadle (NorFC), J Edwards (NorFC), GD Fawcus
(Tynm), W Fawcus (Tynm), Hendlands, HL Pattinson (NorFC), JS Pattinson (NorFC),
F Redford (NorFC), F Richards.

Attendance: n/a   *Referee*: n/a
Note 1: Names for two Durham forwards not reported.
Note 2: Reports list 16 Northumberland players which is probably incorrect.
Note 3: Clubs not identified for Hendlands and F. Richards (Northumberland).
Note 4: Scorers for both teams not reported.

Saturday 10 February 1877 at Feethams Cricket Ground, Darlington
DURHAM 0 *Back*: HE Kayll (Sund). *Half-backs*: W Hill (Sto), WA Kidson (Sund), SC Shewell (capt, Darl). *Quarter-backs*: H Brooks (Darl), J Laing (Sund). *Forwards*: CE Barnes (DurC), JH Brooks (Darl), OC Carr (DurU), HW Edlin (Darl), AGM Hudson (Sund), HP Kayll (Sund), A Laing (Sund), Pinchin (Sund), GMD Trotter (Sto).
YORKSHIRE 0 *Backs*: B Cariss (Lee), R Hodgson (Hull). *Three-quarter*: F Steinthal (Brad). *Half-backs*: R Mills (Brad), E Seaton (Lee). *Forwards*: JC Atkinson (Lee), JHS Conacher (Hud), RH Fowler (Leeds), HWT Garnett (capt, Brad), E Glaisby (York), JH Jolly (York), F Schutt (Brad), F Thursby (York), P Wilkinson (Lee).
Attendance: 'not large'   *Referee*: n/a
Note: Yorkshire had 14 players.

Saturday 24 February 1877 at Brooklands, Sale
CHESHIRE 1 try *Backs*: H Marsland (Sale), JC Wilson (Sale). *Three-quarter*: GP Pagden (Sale), WH Wallace (capt, BirkPk). *Half-backs*: JB Parry (RockF), HC Rowley (Bow, t). *Forwards*: G Andrews (Ald), WH Bleakley (Sale), W Ewer (NewB), TH Harrison (RockF), EC Kendall (RockF), BB Middleton (RockF), FS Swainwick (Ald), JWH Thorp (Macc), JN Wilson (Sale).
LANCASHIRE 1 goal, 2 tries *Backs*: CM Sawyer (Bro, c), ET Smith (ManR). *Three-quarters*: JH Hulton (PresG), A Irving (RochH). *Half-backs*: WS Butterworth (RochH), A Knowles (Man, t). *Forwards*: E Cliff (Liv), D Drew (Man), W Greg (Man), WH Hunt (PresG), E Kewley (capt, Liv, t), ET Markendale (ManR), GF Schofield (Sou), R Todd (Man, t), A Whalley (Bro).
Attendance: 400/500   *Referee*: HM Blythe (Birkenhead Park)

Saturday 10 March 1877 at Bath Lane, Newcastle
NORTHUMBERLAND 0 *Back*: B Hodge (NorFC). *Half-backs*: B Dale (capt, NorFC), JB Richards (NorFC). *Quarter-backs*: JT Harding (NorFC), F Logan (NorFC). *Forwards*: FCT Challoner (NorFC), GD Fawcus (Tynm), W Fawcus (Tynm), WH Gabbatt (NorFC), R Graves (NorFC), HA Hughes, HL Pattinson (NorFC), JS Pattinson (NorFC), SF Prest (NorFC).
CUMBERLAND 0 *Back*: Lishman (Carl). *Half-backs*: R Braithwaite (Carl), Crow (Carl). *Quarter-backs*: Bell (Carl), Hadley (Carl). *Forwards*: Beagle (Carl), J Buck (capt, Carl), J Corbitt (Carl), R Fothergill (Carl), Henderson (Carl), H McCallum (Carl), Richardson (Carl), J Walker (Carl), Whitehead (Carl).
Attendance: 'large'   *Referee:* n/a
Note 1: Name of one Cumberland forward and one Northumberland forward not reported.
Note 2: Club not identified for H. A. Hughes (Northumberland).

ENGLAND TRIAL MATCH

Saturday 9 December 1876 at Kennington Oval, London
SOUTH 0 *Backs*: LH Birkett (ClapR), AW Pearson (GuyHosp). *Three-quarter*: L Stokes (Black). *Half-backs*: WE Collins (capt, StGHosp), WC Hutchinson (RIEC). *Forwards*: FR Adams (Rich), RH Birkett (ClapR), EC Cheston (Rich), TA Fison (Rich), FD Fowler (RIEC), HJ Graham (Wim), HP Henderson (Wim), MW Marhall (Black), CW Rawlinson (Black), CAS Trevor (RIEC).
NORTH 1 goal, 1 try *Backs*: DH Brownfield (RavPk, c), DF Burton (Hull). *Three-quarters*: AN Hornby (PresG, t), H Huth (Hud, t). *Half-backs*: JL Bell (Darl), JR Hay-Gordon (Liv). *Forwards*: E Cliff (Liv), A Fenton (RochH), HWT Garnett (Brad), W Greg (Man), G Harrison (Hull), WH Hunt (PresG), E Kewley (capt, Liv), O Leatham (Lee), R Todd (Man).
Attendance: 'good'   *Referee*: AG Guillemard (RFU Vice-President)

INTERNATIONAL MATCHES

Monday 5 February 1877 at Kennington Oval London
ENGLAND 2 goals, 2 tries *Backs*: LH Birkett (ClapR), L Stokes (Black, 2c). *Three-quarters*: RH Birkett (ClapR), AN Hornby (Man, t). *Half-backs*: WC Hutchinson (RIEC, 2t), PLA Price (RIEC). *Forwards*: FR Adams (Rich, t), RH Fowler (Lee), G Harrison (Hull), WH Hunt (Man), E Kewley (capt, Liv), FH Lee (MarlN), MW Marshall (Black), CJC Touzel (Liv), EB Turner (StGHosp).
IRELAND 0 *Backs*: R Galbraith (capt, DubU), RB Walkington (NIFC). *Half-backs*: H Brown (Wind), FW Kidd (Lans). *Quarter-backs*: TG Gurdon (NIFC), AM Whitestone (DubU). *Forwards*: T Brown (Wind), HL Cox (DubU), HG Edwards (DubU), W Finlay (NIFC), WJ Hamilton (DubU), J Ireland (Wind), HW Jackson (DubU), HC Kelly (NIFC), WH Wilson (DubU).
Attendance: 1,500   *Referee*: AG Guillemard (England)

Monday 5 Mar 1877 at Raeburn Place, Edinburgh
SCOTLAND 1 goal *Backs*: JS Carrick (GlasA), HH Johnston (Edinburgh Collegians). *Half-backs*: M Cross (GlasA, dg), RC Mackenzie (GlasA). *Quarter-backs*: JR Hay-Gordon (EdinA), EJ Pocock (EdinW). *Forwards*: JHS Graham (EdinA), RW Irvine (capt, EdinA), JE Junor (GlasA), HM Napier (WoS), AG Petrie (RHSFP), J Reid (EdinW), TJ Torrie (EdinA), C Villar (EdinW), DH Watson (GlasA).
ENGLAND 0 *Backs*: LH Birkett (ClapR), AW Pearson (Black). *Three-quarters*: AN Hornby (Man), L Stokes (Black). *Half-backs*: WAD Evanson (Rich), PLA Price (RIEC). *Forwards*: CC Bryden (ClapR), HWT Garnett (Brad), G Harrison (Hull), WH Hunt (Man), E Kewley (capt, Liv), AF Law (Rich), MW Marshall (Black), R Todd (Man), CJC Touzel (Liv).
Attendance: 3,000   *Referee*: W Cross (Scotland)

COUNTY FOOTBALL MATCH.

YORKSHIRE versus DURHAM,
HOLBECK RECREATION GROUNDS,
SATURDAY, NOV. 11, 1876.

TEAMS.

YORKSHIRE.	DURHAM.
BACKS.	**BACKS.**
R. H. Christison - *York.*	H. E. Kayll - *Sunderland.*
R. Hodgson - - - *Hull.*	
THREE-QUARTER BACKS	**THREE-QUARTER BACKS**
E. W. Harrison - *Hull.*	R. F. Boyd - *Sunderland.*
W. Hodgson - - - ,,	J. H. Twining { *University* Durham. }
HALF-BACKS.	**HALF-BACKS.**
T. S. Tetley - *Bradford.*	P. B. Junor (Captain) *Darlington.*
Reg. Mills - - ,,	J. L. Bell ,,
FORWARDS.	**FORWARDS.**
W. H. Hutchinson (Captain) *Hull.*	S. C. Shewell *Darlington.*
G. Harrison - - - ,, ,,	J. H. Brooks - - ,,
R. H. Fowler - - *Leeds.*	H. P. Kayll - *Sunderland.*
Oct. Leatham - - ,,	Fowles - - ,,
H. J. Manning - - ,,	Hudson - - ,,
F. Schutt - - - ,,	H. Dykes - - - *Durham.*
H. W. T. Garnett *Bradford.*	Barnes - - - ,,
A. Christison - - *York.*	Bickwell - - - *Stockton.*
E. Glaisby - - - ,,	Prest - - - *Bensham.*
	Byerley *Houghton-le-Spring.*
UMPIRE.	**UMPIRE.**
A. M. Bulteel *Manchester F.C.*	

Team sheet for Yorkshire versus Durham in Leeds, November 1876.

1877-1878

CARLISLE AND THE CUMBERLAND TEAM

After Cumberland had met Northumberland at Edenside, Carlisle, on 24th November, the *Carlisle Patriot* commented that 'several players from Whitehaven and other places declined at the last moment to attend, and a team had to be picked the night previous, so that it was consequently weak and could hardly be reckoned as representing the county'. It was the second consecutive year that Cumberland had taken on Northumberland with an all-Carlisle line-up, the other clubs taking the stance that their players had not been invited.[14] Disputes over player selection for the various county teams was a common occurrence during this period, whereby some 'senior' clubs were perceived by their rivals as controlling the process in favour of their own players. For example the situation in Cumberland – with Carlisle viewed by some as taking up a parental stance – was similar to accusations aimed at the Manchester club, leading to the creation of a more democratic Lancashire County Union in 1881.

THE YORKSHIRE CUP BEGINS

The Yorkshire County Challenge Cup, famously known as 'T'owd Tin Pot', was launched this season with 16 clubs, evolving into England's premier county cup contest. With the opening round about to take place, the *Yorkshire Post* wrote: 'This cup, valued at 50 guineas, is offered by the County Football Club to be competed for annually by the various clubs in Yorkshire. That the supporters of the game in this county have shown that they take the liveliest interest in the contests for the possession of the prize may be at once understood from the fact that the best clubs have entered the lists with an eagerness altogether beyond expectation. Nowhere has this most exhilarating and manly of winter games made such rapid and gigantic strides as it has done, and still continues to do, in Yorkshire.'[15]

THE FIRST YORKSHIRE CUP FINAL

The first Yorkshire Cup finalists were Halifax and York, the decisive match taking place on 29th December. The venue was to have been the Fieldhouse Ground at Huddersfield but heavy snow necessitated a late switch to the Holbeck Recreation Ground, home of the Leeds club. The *Yorkshire Post* commented that 'it must be very gratifying to the committee that, despite the short notice given of their intention to play the final tie at Leeds, such a large number of onlookers [estimated at 3,000] should be present. The play in the various rounds has been of the closest character, results proving how evenly the teams engaged have been matched. Although the clubs engaged on Saturday [in the final] are well known, they had never previously met, and there was consequently a certain amount of uncertainty as to the result. That the object the Yorkshire Football Committee had in view when they offered this cup – the further development of the game in this county – has been fully realised there can be no doubt, and now the contests have been brought to a most successful close they certainly deserve the best thanks not only of football players but the public in general, for the admirable manner in which the matches have been conducted throughout'.[16] Despite the optimism evoked by those closing words, the misconduct of clubs, players, and spectators was often the subject of debate in the years that followed.

YORKSHIRE GO SOUTH

Yorkshire was the first northern county to play outside the north of England when they met Middlesex at Kennington Oval, on Monday 25th February. Originally scheduled for the Richmond club's ground in Old Deer Park, a decision was taken on the preceding Thursday to transfer to the more expansive Surrey Cricket Club headquarters.

WEST CUMBERLAND TAKES TO THE FIELD

Following on from their dispute with Carlisle over the legitimacy of the Cumberland county team, Whitehaven and Workington combined to produce a West Cumberland side that took on Northumberland in Hexham on 16th March. As with the earlier Carlisle-based selection the previous November, the Cumbrians were heavily defeated, increasing the argument for a properly constituted county side.

THE CHESHIRE CUP BEGINS

The Cheshire County Challenge Cup commenced this season with clubs split into East, West and Mid-divisions for the opening rounds. The Bowdon and Lymm team won the latter section and met Stalybridge (East winners) to decide who opposed Birkenhead Park (West) in the final. It was reported that the decider would take place 'at Whalley Range, the ground having been kindly granted by the Manchester Football Club. The contest will commence after the match between the Manchester and Broughton Wasps 2nd teams has been concluded, which is arranged for an earlier hour than usual, viz., 2.15 pm'.[17]

1877-1878 STATISTICS

CHESHIRE COUNTY CHALLENGE CUP (7 entries)
Most goals wins. If equal, most tries. If still equal, most minor points.

East Division
Macclesfield 0, Stalybridge 1t

Mid-Division
First Round
Northwich 0, Sale 1t
Bye: Bowdon and Lymm

Second Round
Sale 0, Bowdon and Lymm 0

Second Round Replay
Bowdon and Lymm 2g, Sale 0

West Division
Birkenhead Park 1t, New Brighton 0

Semi-final
Bowdon and Lymm 2g, 4t, Stalybridge 0
Bye: Birkenhead Park

FINAL
Saturday 23 March 1878 at Whalley Range, Manchester
BIRKENHEAD PARK 1 goal, 1 try *Backs*: GM Christian, R Wood. *Three-quarters*: AH Boucher, JJ Ravenscroft. *Half-backs*: JB Parry, JW Sinclair. *Forwards*: E Goodwin, J Healing (t), W Healing, R Hulton (c), EC Kendall (capt), BB Middleton (t), WS Smythe, G Stewart, WH Wallace
BOWDON AND LYMM 0 *Backs*: R Hind, Walkinshaw. *Three-quarters*: Hoggridge, HC Rowley. *Half-Backs*: E Crossfield (capt), Mathison. *Forwards*: Alexander, Draper, Hutchings, Maw, Moss, Owen, W Rycroft, Saville, Whittall.
Attendance: 1,200   *Referee*: J MacLaren (Manchester)

YORKSHIRE COUNTY FOOTBALL CHALLENGE CUP (16 entries)
Most goals wins. If equal, most tries. If still equal, most minor points.

First Round
Bradford 0, Huddersfield 0 (mp: 1-0)
Dewsbury 2g, Bradford Zingari 0
Halifax 3g, 4t, Wakefield FC 0
Heckmondwike 0, Bradford Junior 0 (mp: 1-0)
Hull 1g, 1t, Mirfield 1t
Leeds 1t, Kirkstall 2g
Wakefield Trinity 0, Leeds St John's 0 (mp: 4-0)
York 0, Bradford Caledonians 0 (mp: 1-0)

Second Round
Dewsbury 0, Bradford 1t
Heckmondwike 0, Hull 0 (mp: 0-0)
Kirkstall 0, York 1g
Wakefield Trinity 0, Halifax 1t

Second Round Replay
Hull 1g, 1t, Heckmondwike 0 (at York)

Third Round (semi-finals)
Bradford 0, Halifax 0 (mp: 0-1)
York 1g, 1t, Hull 0

FINAL
Saturday 29 December 1877 at Holbeck Recreation Ground, Leeds
HALIFAX 1 goal, 1 try *Back*: J Wood. *Three-quarters*: J Dodd, R Ward (t). *Half-backs*: J Robinson (t), A Walsh (capt, c). *Forwards*: H Aspinall, SM Cockin, C Cooper, S Duckett, A Firth, JH Hartley, J Helliwell, GT Thomson, W Whiteley, F Wood
YORK 0 *Backs*: H Harris, H Maughan. *Three-quarters*: WE Christison, G Milner. *Half-backs*: C Christison, C Wood. *Forwards*: RH Christison, RD Eves, E Glaisby (capt), JH Jolley, WJ Mackenzie, W Milner, WE Nicholson, E Smith, M Williamson.
Attendance: 3,000   *Referee*: HWT Garnett (Bradford)

COUNTY MATCHES

Saturday 17 November 1877 at Holbeck Recreation Ground, Leeds
YORKSHIRE 2 tries *Backs*: R Hodgson (Hull), Fred Huth (Hud). *Three-quarters*: H Harris (York), H Huth (Hud). *Half-backs*: W Hodgson (Hull), R Mills (Brad, t). *Forwards*: JC Atkinson (Lee), JHS Conacher (Hud), G Darbyshire (Hull), FR Dawson (LeeStJ), JE Fairburn (Mir), HWT Garnett (capt, Brad), E Glaisby (York), G Harrison (Hull, t), HF Henderson (Lee).
DURHAM 0 *Back*: WC Best (Darl). *Half-backs*: SJ Elstob (DurU), PB Junor (capt, DurC). *Quarter-backs*: JL Bell (Darl), EC Wilson (DurC). *Forwards*: WB Bagley (Darl), JH Brooks (Darl), OC Carr (DurU), EH Dykes (DurC), J Eden (Darl), HW Edlin (Darl), T Elstob (Hou), JE Fletcher (DurC), D Parry (DurU), T Todd (Hou).
Attendance: 2,000   *Referee*: n/a

Saturday 24 November 1877 at Edenside Cricket Ground, Carlisle
CUMBERLAND 0 *Back*: Holmes (Carl). *Half-backs*: Baker (Carl), Milburn Carl). *Quarter-backs*: Capon (Carl), Scott (Carl). *Forwards*: Brockbank (Carl), J Buck (capt, Carl), Fish (Carl), Main (Carl), Maxwell (Carl), Murray (Carl), Ormerston (Carl), Ramsay (Carl), Thompson (Carl), Webster (Carl).
NORTHUMBERLAND 8 goals, 2 tries *Backs*: E Scott (NorFC), T Wilson (Tynm). *Half-backs*: B Hodge (NorFC), E Milvain (NorFC). *Quarter-backs*: JL Bell (capt, NorFC),

F Logan (NorFC). *Forwards*: DC Beadon (NorFC), R Braithwaite (NDur), S Burridge (NorFC), A Cadle (NorFC), A Eichholtz (NorFC), GD Fawcus (Tynm), JE Fletcher (NorFC), R Graves (NorFC), G Sowerby (NDur).
Attendance: n/a   *Referee*: n/a
Note: Scorers for Northumberland not reported.

Saturday 19 January 1878 at Hanson Lane, Halifax
YORKSHIRE 1 try *Backs*: R Hodgson (Hull), J Wood (Hal). *Three-quarters*: ET Hirst (Lee), H Huth (capt, Hud). *Half-back*: W Hodgson (Hull). *Forwards*: HE Briggs (Brad), EH Dykes (LeePC), CWL Fernandes (Wakefield FC, t), HWT Garnett (Brad), G Harrison (Hull), WG Mackenzie (York), GT Thomson (Hal), JH Walker (Mir), RA Ward (Hal), PT Wrigley (Hud).
LANCASHIRE 2 goals, 1 try *Backs*: AN Hornby (capt, PresG/Man), WS Sawyer (Bro). *Three-quarters*: H Farr (Swi, t), R Hunt (PresG/Man, c, dg). *Half-backs*: JH Hulton (PresG/Man), WE Openshaw (Man, t). *Forwards*: T Blatherwick (Man), W Emery (Birch), WH Hunt (PresG), GC Lindsay (ManR), W Longshaw (Swi), GF Schofield (Sou), R Shutt (Bro), HL Storey (PresG), JWH Thorp (Man).
Attendance: 10,000   *Referee*: HP Henderson (Leeds)

Saturday 16 February 1878 at Whalley Range, Manchester
LANCASHIRE 3 goals, 1 try *Backs*: AN Hornby (capt, PresG/Man), ET Smith (ManR). *Three-quarters*: H Farr (Swi, t), R Hunt (PresG/Man, t, 3c). *Half-backs*: JH Hulton (PresG/Man, 2t), WE Openshaw (Man). *Forwards*: T Blatherwick (Man), G Bromilow (Sou), O Heggs (Birch), WH Hunt (PresG), ET Markendale (ManR), CL Verelst (Liv), EF Woodforder (Man), H Wyles (Bro), H Yates (Swi).
CHESHIRE 0 *Backs*: McIlwaine (BirkPk), WH Wallace (BirkPk). *Three-quarters*: W Boucher (BirkPk), PF Shaw (NewB). *Half-backs*: JB Parry (BirkPk), R Percival (Nord). *Forwards*: WH Bleakley (Sale), J Crawford (BirkPk), CE Dearden (Ald), EC Kendall (capt, BirkPk), W Middleton (BirkPk), W Rycroft (Bow), GH Smythe (BirkPk), JWH Thorp (Macc), JN Wilson (Sale).
Attendance: 2,000   *Referee*: W Grave (Manchester)

Monday 25 February 1878 at Kennington Oval, London
MIDDLESEX 2 goals, 2 tries *Backs*: WJ Penny (KCHosp), N Thursby (OChelt). *Three-quarters*: LH Birkett (capt, ClapR, t), WAD Evanson (Rich, 2t). *Half-backs*: J Litle (StBHosp), TH Rawson (Ken, c, dg). *Forwards*: JM Biggs (UCHosp), JV Brewer (Gip), HP Gardner (Rich), ET Gurdon (Rich), EA Hunt (StGHosp), E Langdon (StTHosp), P Oswald (Rich), EB Turner (StGHosp), GF Vernon (Black).
YORKSHIRE 2 goals, 1 try *Backs*: H Harris (York), R Hodgson (Hull). *Three-quarters*: H Hayley (Wak), H Huth (Hud). *Half-backs*: R Mills (Brad), C Wood (York). *Forwards*: JC Atkinson (Lee, t), DS Denehey (LeeStJ), CWL Fernandes (Wakefield FC), HWT Garnett (capt, Brad, gm), JH Greenhalgh (Brad), G Harrison (Hull), HP Henderson (Lee, dg), Fred Huth (Hud), GT Thomson (Hal).
Attendance: 'small'   *Referee*: MW Marshall (Blackheath)

Saturday 2 March 1878 at Brooklands, Sale
CHESHIRE 3 tries *Backs*: WE Coubrough (NewB), W Nicholson (NewB). *Three-quarters*: W Boucher (BirkPk), PF Shaw (NewB). *Half-backs*: R Percival (Nord), TW Shaw (NewB, t).

Forwards: A Coubrough (NewB, t), CE Dearden (Ald), T Hardy (Sale, t), EC Kendall (capt, BirkPk), WJ Kerr (NewB), W Middleton (BirkPk), W Stewart (BirkPk), JWH Thorp (Macc), JN Wilson (Sale).
YORKSHIRE 1 try *Backs*: Frank Huth (Hud), Fred Huth (Hud). *Three-quarter*: H Huth (Hud, t). *Half-backs*: FT Gordon (LeeStJ), E Mann (Brad). *Forwards*: JC Atkinson (Lee), G Darbyshire (Hull), DS Denehey (LeeStJ), JE Fairburn (Mir), CWL Fernandes (Wakefield FC), HWT Garnett (capt, Brad), JH Hartley (Hal), G Hastings (Brad), HP Henderson (Lee), A Schutt (Brad).
Attendance: 1,500 *Referee*: W Grave (Manchester)

Saturday 16 March 1878 at Tynedale FC, Hexham
NORTHUMBERLAND 6 goals, 7 tries *Back*: E Scott (NorFC). *Half-backs*: HE Kayll (Sund, t), E Milvain (NorFC, t). *Quarter-backs*: JL Bell (capt, NorFC, 5t), F Logan (NorFC, t). *Forwards*: DC Beadon (NorFC), R Braithwaite (NDur), S Burridge (NorFC), FCT Challoner (NorFC, t), A Eichholtz (NorFC, t), GD Fawcus (Tynm, 2t), J Fowles (Sund), R Hargreaves (t), SF Prest (NorFC), G Sowerby (NDur).
WEST CUMBERLAND 0 *Back*: WT Wilson (Whi). *Half-backs*: JD Bain (Work), RY Sutton (Whi). *Quarter-backs*: JC Hellon (Whi), E Ridgway (Whi). *Forwards*: G Atkinson, C Blair (Work), R Blair (Work), FE Eddis (Whi), JD Fidler (Whi), E Henley (Whi), J Hodgson (Work), R Hodgson (Work), FE Wood (Work).
Attendance: n/a *Referee*: n/a
Note 1: Scorers of Northumberland's six conversions not reported.
Note 2: Clubs not identified for R. Hargreaves (Northumberland), and G. Atkinson (West Cumberland).

ENGLAND TRIAL MATCH

Saturday 15 December 1877 at Whalley Range, Manchester
NORTH 0 *Backs*: DH Brownfield (RavPk), HE Kayll (Sund). *Three-quarters*: AN Hornby (Man/PresG), H Huth (Hud). *Half-backs*: JR Hay-Gordon (Liv), JL Bell (Darl). *Forwards*: JC Atkinson (Lee), HWT Garnett (Brad), W Greg (Man), WH Hunt (Man/PresG), E Kewley (capt, Liv), ET Markendale (ManR), GF Schofield (Sou), R Todd (Man), R Walker (Man).
SOUTH 1 goal, 2 tries *Backs*: AW Pearson (Black), WJ Penny (KCHosp). *Three-quarters*: WAD Evanson (Rich), L Stokes (Black, dg). *Half-backs*: AH Jackson (GuyHosp), PL Price (RIEC). *Forwards*: JM Biggs (UCHosp), A Budd (Black), GW Burton (Black), FD Fowler (RIEC), H Fowler (OxfU), MW Marshall (Black), FR Ormond (capt, Rich), EB Turner (StGHosp), GF Vernon (Black, 2t).
Attendance: 4,000 *Referee*: AT Stuart (Scotland)

INTERNATIONAL MATCHES

Monday 4 March 1878 at Kennington Oval, London
ENGLAND 0 *Backs*: HE Kayll (Sun), AW Pearson (Black). *Three-quarters*: AN Hornby (Man), L Stokes (Black). *Half-backs*: WAD Evanson (Rich), PLA Price (RIEC). *Forwards*: FR Adams (Rich), JM Biggs (UCHosp), FD Fowler (Man), H Fowler (OxfU), ET Gurdon (Rich), E Kewley (capt, Liv), MW Marshall (Black), GT Thomson (Hal), GF Vernon (Black)

SCOTLAND 0 *Back*: WE Maclagan (EdinA). *Half-backs*: M Cross (GlasA), NJ Finlay (EdinA). *Quarter-backs*: JA Campbell (MerCS), JA Neilson (GlasA). *Forwards*: LJ Auldjo (Abertay), NT Brewis (EdinIFP), JHS Graham (EdinA), DR Irvine (EdinA), RW Irvine (capt, EdinA), JE Junor (GlasA), G MacLeod (EdinA), HM Napier (WoS), AG Petrie (RHSFP), SH Smith (GlasA).
Attendance: 8,000   *Referee*: AG Guillemard (England)

Monday 11 March 1878 at Lansdowne Road, Dublin
IRELAND 0 *Back*: RB Walkington (capt, NIFC). *Half-backs*: FW Kidd (DubU), RN Matier (NIFC). *Quarter-backs*: GL Fagan (Kingstown School), TG Gordon (NIFC). *Forwards*: EWD Croker (Lim), HG Edwards (DubU), W Finley (NIFC), W Griffiths (Lim), RW Hughes (QCB), HC Kelly (NIFC), JA Macdonald (MethC), WD Moore (QCB), HW Murray (DubU), F Schutt (Wand).
ENGLAND 2 goals, 1 try *Backs*: AW Pearson (Black, 2c), WJ Penny (KCHosp, t). *Three-quarters*: HJ Enthoven (Rich), AN Hornby (Man). *Half-backs*: JL Bell (Darl), AH Jackson (Black). *Forwards*: T Blatherwick (Man), A Budd (Black), EF Dawson (RIEC), HP Gardner (Rich, t), WH Hunt (Man), MW Marshall (capt, Black), EB Turner (StGHosp, t), CL Verelst (Liv), GF Vernon (Black).
Attendance: 3,000   *Referee*: E Swainston (England)

A depiction of rugby in Calcutta, India, in 1875. When the Calcutta club ceased in 1878, its remaining silver rupees were melted down to create what is now known as the Calcutta Cup. *Illustrated Sporting and Dramatic News, 1875*

1878-1879

LEIGH FOUNDED
The Leigh club was founded during August.

THE COMBINED COUNTIES
For the only time during the Victorian era the north-east England counties of Northumberland and Durham combined, opposing Lancashire at Whalley Range on 30th November. The two teams emerged at 2.50 pm, 'the Lancashire players wearing the county jersey of red and white stripes, whilst the combined counties sported the colours of their respective clubs'.[18]

THE KAYLL BROTHERS
The appearance of Alfred Kayll and John Kayll in the combined Northumberland and Durham team against Lancashire on 30th November completed a unique family foursome, Henry Kayll and Hartley Kayll having represented Durham against Yorkshire at Sunderland, 14 days earlier. It meant that all four brothers, who each played for Sunderland, had taken part in county rugby during November.

THE YORKSHIRE CHALLENGE CUP
Problems began to surface in the Yorkshire Challenge Cup competition, as explained by the *Yorkshire Post*: 'The County Football Committee have heard that certain clubs, entered to compete for the County Challenge Cup, are engaging the services of players from other clubs to assist them in their cup ties, and they have been asked to decide upon the validity of such

action. They reserve the right to disqualify any club on such objection being made, and proved to their satisfaction. The committee also wish special attention to be directed to the rule which fixes one hour and twenty minutes as the duration of play, but which in special circumstances be reduced to a minimum of one hour's play. They would strongly urge that matches should be commenced as soon after half-past two as possible, and that three p.m. should be the latest hour for starting play. Instructions have been issued to the appointed referees that touch-downs are to be held to include dead-balls and touches-in-goal. In consequence of this, clubs having a tie played on their own ground, are expected either by erecting barriers or by other means to obviate any difficulty that might be occasioned by spectators encroaching on the space behind goal.'[19]

A FROSTY OUTCOME

For the first time since it began in 1870, the annual Lancashire versus Yorkshire fixture did not take place. It was originally due to be played on Saturday 18th January at Whalley Range, Manchester, but postponed due to frost. It was rescheduled for the following Wednesday, 22nd January, but frost again intervened and it was not subsequently played.

THE CALCUTTA CUP

The Scotland versus England match, played at Raeburn Place, Edinburgh, on Monday 10th March, was the first time that the Calcutta Cup was at stake although, on this occasion, the result was a draw. The trophy was originally provided by the dissolved Calcutta Football Club (in India) who converted their assets to silver rupees which were then melted down to produce the cup. The intention behind their gesture was to initiate a national rugby union knock-out competition to rival the Football Association Cup (inaugurated in 1871-72) but the Rugby Football Union, already less than enthusiastic about the launch of the Yorkshire and Cheshire Cups, rejected the idea as too competitive and against the amateur ethos.

THE FIRST YORKSHIRE CUP DISQUALIFICATION

It seemed it was just a matter of time before a team competing in the Yorkshire Cup contravened the competitions soon to be infamous 'Rule 4' that stated players must be *bona fide* members of the club they represented. The first transgressor was Badsworth Hunt, who had apparently beaten Leeds St John's in the second round at Cardigan Fields on 15th March. The draw for the following round, including Badsworth Hunt, had already appeared in the press before it was decided at a Competition Committee meeting, in the Queen's Hotel, Leeds, on Monday evening (17th March), that they had used an ineligible player. Leeds St John's offered to replay the match the following weekend, again at home (minus the ineligible player) but Badsworth refused and were consequently disqualified.[20]

THE YORKSHIRE CUP FINAL: THE GOOD
The second Yorkshire Cup Final took place at Hanson Lane, Halifax, on 12th April, Wakefield Trinity defeating Kirkstall by two goals and one try to nil. The contest was already proving a hit; a reported 12,000 quadrupling the previous year's attendance at the final, despite snowy conditions. The *Yorkshire Post* reported that 'special trains ran to Halifax from Wakefield, Dewsbury, York, Leeds, Bradford, and other Yorkshire towns, and the gate [receipts] was announced to be devoted to the Mansion House Fund for the relief of the widows and orphans of soldiers who fell [in the Anglo-Zulu War] at Isandlwana [22nd January 1879] and Rorke's Drift [22nd-23rd January 1879]'. The same report went on to state that 'shortly after the receipt of the intelligence that Wakefield was victorious, the [Wakefield] Parish Church bells began to ring in honour of the event. On the arrival at Wakefield of the special train [carrying the team] the victors were met by the Parish Church Association band and an immense concourse of people. They were received with great cheering by the crowd, and marched from the station to the Woolpack Inn, the cheering in the streets being again and again renewed. The cup was carried at the head of the team, and on the party arriving at the Woolpack it was inspected by a large number of people'.[21]

THE YORKSHIRE CUP FINAL: THE BAD AND THE UGLY
Unfortunately there were some ugly scenes in Halifax at the conclusion of the Yorkshire Cup Final. The *Huddersfield Chronicle* reported that 'as the teams were being conveyed from the field, the windows of the [Wakefield Trinity] omnibus in, and on, which they were seated was smashed, stones being thrown at the players by ill-disposed roughs, and some of the players were hurt. The [Wakefield] football players [later] complained very much of the treatment they had received at Halifax from their opponents [Kirkstall] and also from some of the Halifax football players, and Mr. Barron Kilner [a prominent Trinity player] returned to Wakefield with one of his eyes covered by a bandage'.[22] The involvement of Halifax players reportedly had its roots in ill-feeling arising from the Wakefield Trinity-Halifax semi-final tie.

1878-1879 STATISTICS

CHESHIRE COUNTY CHALLENGE CUP (7 entries)
Most goals wins. If equal, most tries. If still equal, most minor points.

Preliminary Round
Birkenhead Park 2g, 2t, Bowdon and Lymm 0
Sale 2g, 5t, Northwich 0
Northenden 3g, 4t, Alderley and Macclesfield 0
Bye: New Brighton

Semi-finals
Northenden 0, New Brighton 2t
Birkenhead Park w/o Sale
(result not found)

FINAL
At Waterloo Park, Liverpool (date unknown)
BIRKENHEAD PARK w/o NEW BRIGHTON
Result not found
Note: Refer to Appendix 9 for further information.

YORKSHIRE COUNTY FOOTBALL CHALLENGE CUP (24 entries)
Most goals wins. If equal, most tries. If still equal, most minor points.

First Round
Badsworth Hunt 4g, 1t, Leeds Athletic 0
Bradford Albion 0, Ravensthorpe 1t
Bradford Zingari w/o Hull (withdrew)
Cleckheaton w/o Hull White Star (withdrew)
Dewsbury 5g, 4t, Huddersfield Junior 0
Halifax 1g, 4t, Mirfield 0
Heckmondwike Cricket and FC 1t, Leeds 2g
Huddersfield 1g, 1t, Heckmondwike 0
Leeds St John's 0, Bradford Junior 0 (mp: 3-0)
Wakefield FC 1g, Bradford United 3g, 1t
Wakefield Trinity 2g, 1t, Bradford 0
York 0, Kirkstall 1t

Second Round
Cleckheaton 0, Kirkstall 1t
Halifax 1g, 1t, Huddersfield 0
Leeds 1t, Bradford United 0
Leeds St John's 1g, 1t, Badsworth Hunt 2g (awarded to Leeds St John's after protest)
Ravensthorpe 0, Dewsbury 2g, 3t
Wakefield Trinity 2g, 2t, Bradford Zingari 0

Third Round
Halifax 1g, 2t, Dewsbury 0
Kirkstall 1g, 1t, Leeds St John's 0
Wakefield Trinity 2t, Leeds 0

Fourth Round (semi-final)
Wakefield Trinity 0, Halifax 0 (mp: 10-2)
Bye: Kirkstall

Milestones & Stats 1869-1901

FINAL

Saturday 12 April 1879 at Hanson Lane, Halifax
WAKEFIELD TRINITY 2 goals, 1 try *Backs*: A. Hayley (capt, dg), B Longbottom (t).
Three-quarters: CE Bartram, H Hayley. *Half-backs*: CT Baldwin, JW Whitehead (c).
Forwards: TO Bennett, W Ellis, A Hirst, W Jackson, B Kilner (t), JW Kilner, J Longbottom, TB Parry, G Steele.
KIRKSTALL 0 *Back*: WR Harrison. *Three-quarters*: JW Helliwell, H Sewell. *Half-backs*: H Broadbent, F Cookson, A Denton. *Forwards*: S Binks, R Clapham, JW Clarke H Cooper, F Greenwood, J Pitt, S Speight, H Walker, J Wrightson.
Attendance: 12,000   *Referee*: H Huth (Huddersfield)

COUNTY MATCHES

Saturday 16 November 1878 at Chester Road, Sunderland
DURHAM 0 *Backs*: HE Kayll (Sund), RH Mallett (Darl). *Half-backs*: GH Green (Hou), WA Kidson (Sund). *Quarter-backs*: C Kidson (capt, Sund), JW Sowerby (NDur). *Forwards*: JH Brooks (Darl), J Eden (Darl), SJ Elstob (Darl/DurU), J Fowles (Sund), GW Grey (NDur), WT Hallimond (BishA), HP Kayll (Sund), A Laing (Sund), T Potts (Hou).
YORKSHIRE 3 goals, 3 tries *Backs*: WR Harrison (Kirk), JA Wylde (Lee). *Three-quarters*: Fred Huth (Hud), H Huth (Hud, dg). *Half-backs*: C Scharff (Brad, 2t), C Wood (York, 2t). *Forwards*: JC Atkinson (Lee), GW Bottomley (Hud), CWL Fernandes (Lee), HWT Garnett (capt, Brad, c), G Harrison (Hull, t), EM Jones (Lee, c), JR Ormerod (LeeStJ), WR Pierce (Badsworth Hunt), G Steele (Wak).
Attendance: 'large'   *Referee*: n/a

Saturday 30 November 1878 at Whalley Range, Manchester
LANCASHIRE 4 tries *Backs*: J Marsh (Bolton, t), W Morgan (Bro). *Three-quarters*: R Hunt (Man, t), W Massey (ManFW). *Half-backs*: W Grave (Man), G Nicholson (Sou). *Forwards*: L Aitken (Man), WJ Andrew (ManR), HD Bateson (Liv), T Blatherwick (Man), J Brickill (Che, t), J D'Aguilar (ManFW), FD Fowler (Man, t), HH Springmann (Liv), R Walker (capt, Man)
NORTHUMBERLAND AND DURHAM 0 *Back*: JL Bell (capt, Darl). *Half-backs*: PB Junor (DurC), J Laing (Sund). *Quarter-backs*: JT Harding (NorFC), WA Kidson (Sund), LG Morgan (Sund). *Forwards*: JE Fletcher (DurC), AC Kayll (Sund), JJ Kayll (Sund), A Laing (Sund), J Laing (Sund), AE Lees (NorFC), H Mason (NorFC), JRC Nicholls (NorFC), E Scott (NorFC).
Attendance: 3,000/4,000   *Referee*: H Greg (Manchester)

Monday 2 December 1878 at Kennington Oval, London
KENT 1 goal *Backs*: A Poland (Black), C Hewitt (QH). *Three-quarters*: J Readman (Laus), L Stokes (capt, Black, dg). *Half-backs*: S Fry (QH), HH Taylor (StGHosp). *Forwards*: GW Burton (Black), S Ellis (QH), JA Fraser (Black), W Hewitt (QH), AR Layman (Cleve), AP Marsden (Cleve), S Neame (OChelt), GS Robertson (Black), A Spurling (Black).
YORKSHIRE 0 *Backs*: H Harris (York), Fred Huth (Hud). *Three-quarters*: ET Hirst (Lee), H Huth (Hud). *Half-backs*: C Scharff (Brad), E Seaton (Lee). *Forwards*: JC Atkinson (Lee), GW Bottomley (Hud), EH Dykes (Lee), CWL Fernandes (Lee), A Firth (Hal), HWT Garnett (capt, Brad), G Harrison (Hull), EM Jones (Lee), GT Thomas (Hal).
Attendance: 300   *Referee*: AK Stewart (Scotland)

Saturday 1 March 1879 at Fartown, Huddersfield
YORKSHIRE 2 goals *Backs*: M Newsome (Dew), JA Wylde (Lee). *Three-quarters*: H Hayley (Wak), Fred Huth (Hud, 2c). *Half-backs*: JC Broadhead (Kirk, t), C Scharff (Brad, t). *Forwards*: JC Atkinson (Lee), CWL Fernandes (Lee), HWT Garnett (capt, Brad), G Harrison (Hull), A Macauley (Mir), WR Pierce (Badsworth Hunt), G Steele (Wak), GT Thomas (Hal), E Woodhead (Hud).
CHESHIRE 0 *Backs*: WE Coubrough (NewB), R Wood (BirkPk). *Three-quarters*: GP Pagden (Sale), PF Shaw (NewB). *Half-backs*: CWH Clark (BirkPk), J Ravenscroft (BirkPk). *Forwards*: CE Dearden (Ald), R Forrest (Sale), EC Kendall (capt, Birk Pk), WJ Kerr (NewB), AW McIlwaine (BirkPk), BB Middleton (BirkPk), WS Smythe (BirkPk), JWH Thorp (Macc), JN Wilson (Sale).
Attendance: 5,000 *Referee*: H Huth (Huddersfield)

Saturday 29 March 1879 at Devisdale, Bowdon
CHESHIRE 0 *Backs*: WE Coubrough (NewB), F Marsland (Northenden). *Three-quarters*: PF Shaw (NewB), AB Wilson (BirkPk). *Half-backs*: CWH Clark (BirkPk), A Coubrough (NewB). *Forwards*: BS Atkinson (NewB), BD Beevor (Bow), AW McIlwaine (BirkPk), W Middleton (BirkPk), GP Pagden (Sale), W Rycroft (Bow), GH Smythe (BirkPk), JWH Thorp (capt, Macc), B Wallace (BirkPk).
LANCASHIRE 2 goals, 5 tries *Backs*: WA Gordon (Sou), ET Smith (ManR). *Three-quarters*: CM Sawyer (Bro, t), CW Smith (ManR, 2t). *Half-backs*: G Nicholson (Sou), JH Payne (Bro). *Forwards*: T Blatherwick (Man), WS Butterworth (RochH), JW Fletcher (ManR), FD Fowler (capt, Man, t), W Henderson (ManFW, t), HC Rowley (Man, c), JB Rye (Old), HH Springmann (Liv, 2t, c), H Yates (Swi).
Attendance: 2,000 *Referee*: CJ Hughes (Northwich)

Saturday 29 March 1879 at Elm Tree Street, Wakefield
YORKSHIRE 4 goals *Backs*: M Newsome (Dew), JA Wylde (Lee). *Three-quarters*: H Hayley (Wak), H Huth (Hud). *Half-backs*: J Dodd (Hal), C Scharff (Brad, 2t). *Forwards*: JC Atkinson (Lee), GW Bottomley (hud), CWL Fernandes (Lee, t), HWT Garnett (capt, Brad), G Harrison (Hull), B Kilner (Wak), A Macauley (Mir), WR Pierce (Badsworth Hunt, 4c), GT Thomas (Hal, t).
MIDDLESEX 4 tries *Backs*: G Perham (Wim), GA Rimmington (Gip). *Three-quarter*: GF Cooper (Flam). *Half-backs*: HL Ashmore (Walth, t), JR Davies (Black). *Forwards*: FR Adams (capt, Rich, t), R Barlow (Rich, t), AS Bremner (Rich), A Curle (Laus, t), HP Gardner (Rich), AF Law (Richmond), CE Macrae (Harl), A Tillyer (Harl), GF Vernon (Black), FS Watts (Harl).
Attendance: 3,000 *Referee*: n/a

ENGLAND TRIAL MATCH

Monday 17 February 1879 at Kennington Oval, London
SOUTH 2 goals, 1 try *Backs*: WJ Penny (KCHosp), T Fry (QH). *Three-quarters*: WAD Evanson (Rich), L Stokes (Black, t, 2c). *Half-backs*: HH Taylor (Black), LT Williams (Rich). *Forwards*: FR Adams (capt, Rich, t), A Budd (Black), GW Burton (Black), AH Evans (OxfU), ET Gurdon (Rich), WH McConnell (RIEC), NF McLeod (RIEC), S Neame (OChelt, t), GF Vernon (Black).
NORTH 1 goal *Backs*: HE Kayll (Sund), ET Smith (ManR). *Three-quarters*: R Hunt (Man, c), H Huth (Hud). *Half-backs*: T Blatherwick (Man, t), JT Harding (NorFC). *Forwards*: HD Bateson (Liv), EH Dykes (Lee), CWL Fernandes (Lee), FD Fowler (Man), G Harrison (Hull), W Middleton (BirkPk), HC Rowley (Man), HH Springmann (Liv), R Walker (capt, Man)
Attendance: 'fair'   *Referee*: n/a

INTERNATIONAL MATCHES

Monday 10 March 1879 at Raeburn Place, Edinburgh
SCOTLAND 1 goal *Back*: WE Maclagan (EdinA). *Half-backs*: M Cross (GlasA), NJ Finlay (EdinA, dg). *Quarter-backs*: JA Campbell (GlasA), JA Neilson (GlasA). *Forwards*: R Ainslie (EdinIFP), NT Brewis (EdinIFP), JB Brown (GlasA.), EN Ewart (GlasA), JHS Graham (EdinA), DR Irvine (EdinA), RW Irvine (capt, EdinA), JE Junor (GlasA), HM Napier (WoS), AG Petrie (RHSFP).
ENGLAND 1 goal *Backs*: H Huth (Hud), WJ Penny (KCHosp). *Three-quarter*: L Stokes (Black, c). *Half-backs*: WAD Evanson (Rich), HH Taylor (Black). *Forwards*: FR Adams (capt, Rich), A Budd (Black), GW Burton (Black, t), FD Fowler (Man), G Harrison (Hull), NF McLeod (RIEC), S Neame (OChelt), HC Rowley (Man), HH Springmann (Liv), R Walker (Man).
Attendance: 10,000   *Referee*: GR Fleming (Scotland)

Monday 24 March 1879 at Kennington Oval, London
ENGLAND 3 goals, 2 tries *Back*: WJ Penny (KCHosp). *Three-quarters*: WAD Evanson (Rich, t), L Stokes (Black, 2c, dg). *Half-backs*: WE Openshaw (Man), HT Twynam (Rich, t). *Forwards*: FR Adams (capt, Rich, t), HD Bateson (Liv), JM Biggs (UCHosp), A Budd (Black), GW Burton (Black), ET Gurdon (Rich), G Harrison (Hull), NF McLeod (RIEC), S Neame (OChelt), HC Rowley (Man, t).
IRELAND 0 *Back*: WW Pike (King), *Half-backs*: JC Bagot (DubU), WJ Willis (Lans). *Quarter-backs*: J Heron (NIFC), AM Whitestone (DubU). *Forwards*: JR Bristow (NIFC), BN Casement (DubU), JL Cuppaidge (DubU), W Finlay (NIFC), JJ Keon (Lim), HW Murray (DubU), WC Neville (capt, DubU), H Purdon (NIFC), F Schutt (Wand), G Scriven (DubU).
Attendance: 500   *Referee*: AG Guillemard (England)

Oxford versus Cambridge at Kennington Oval on 25th February 1880. The annual varsity match often featured Northern players and Cambridge – winners by two goal to one – included Charles Coates, John Payne, Edgar Storey and P. T. Wrigley, Oxford fielding E. T. Hirst and Charles Phillips. *Illustrated Sporting and Dramatic News, 1880*

1879-1880

BRAMLEY FOUNDED
The Bramley club was founded.

WIGAN FOUNDED
Wigan founded as Wigan Wasps during September and renamed Wigan in 1881. A previous Wigan rugby club had existed from 1872 until 1878.

INCLUSIVITY IN YORKSHIRE
The question of fair selection for county teams was a theme picked up by the *Yorkshire Post* when it appealed for the composition of the Yorkshire side to be more inclusive: 'As the dates for the trial matches to select the Yorkshire team … are close at hand, we trust that the Yorkshire County Committee will see their way clear this season to allow other clubs than those already on the board [Leeds, Hull, York, Bradford and Huddersfield] to have a voice in the matter of selecting the players. We fail to see any reason why such organisations as Halifax, Kirkstall, Wakefield Trinity, Leeds St John's, and Dewsbury should not participate in the doings of the committee; the more so as they are all members of the Union and possess, as is well known, some of the best players in the county.'[23]

SCORED FROM THE KICK-OFF
When Lancashire entertained Cheshire at Whalley Range, Manchester, on 29th November, Liverpool forward Herman Springmann (often reported as 'Harry Springman') scored directly from the kick-off for Lancashire. The

Manchester Courier described the moment: '[Thomas] Blatherwick [Manchester] kicked off for Lancashire and Springmann, following up with such smartness as to take the ball before the Cestrians could get near, and after a clever run, gained a try in less than a minute amidst loud cheers.'[24]

A LANCASHIRE AND YORKSHIRE STALEMATE

Lancashire, having cancelled last season's match with Yorkshire due to the weather, felt it was still their right to host the 1879-80 fixture in Manchester. Yorkshire, however, believed it was their turn and a stalemate ensued. The matter was finally referred to the Rugby Football Union, the decision being that Yorkshire play host at either Huddersfield or Dewsbury. It was scheduled for the St John's Cricket Ground, Huddersfield, on 13th December but, for the second consecutive season, was postponed due to frost. However, on this occasion it was successfully restaged, taking place at that venue on 17th January.

FIRST INTERNATIONAL MATCH IN THE NORTH

England met Scotland at Whalley Range, Manchester, on 28th February. It was the first of 12 international matches that took place in the north during the Victorian era; eight in Manchester, three in Leeds, one in Dewsbury.

EXTRA TIME IN THE YORKSHIRE CUP

When Horbury Athletic Club led visitors Ossett by three tries to nil in the latter stages of their Yorkshire Cup second round tie on 13th March, the result seemed certain. Ossett, however, only required a goal to sneak a victory. The finish, as described by the *Yorkshire Post*, was dramatic: 'Time was nearly up now, but the referee [William Peake of Kirkstall] decided to extend it by five minutes to make up for time lost in disputing points, and the Ossett men made good use of it, and took the ball across the field and obtained a try. The kick [at goal, which would have won the match] failed.' Spectators, however, were unclear as to whether the goal had been scored and 'the referee was completely hemmed in by the now excited crowd, all eager to hear the decision, but for some reason or other the Ossett umpire left the field and Mr. Peake decided not to give his decision until he arrived at the King's Arms [the Horbury club head-quarters] where the point was contested by the two umpires, Mr. Peate deciding in favour of Horbury by three tries to Ossett one try'. Ossett subsequently lodged an appeal but the referee's verdict was upheld.[25]

NORTHUMBERLAND COUNTY UNION FOUNDED

The Northumberland County RU was founded by six clubs on 14th April.

1879-1880 STATISTICS

CHESHIRE COUNTY CHALLENGE CUP (6 entries)
Most goals wins. If equal, most tries. If still equal, most minor points.

First Round
New Brighton 1g, Marple 1t
Northenden 0, Birkenhead Park 1g, 2t
Byes: Bowdon, Sale

Semi-Finals
New Brighton w/o Bowdon (result not found)
Birkenhead Park w/o Sale (Sale withdrew)

FINAL
Saturday 13 March 1880 at Rock Ferry La Crosse Ground, Birkenhead
NEW BRIGHTON 1 try *Back*: JB Keyworth. *Three-quarters*: AK Bulley, WE Coubrough, PF Shaw (capt). *Half-backs*: AS Coubrough, E Holt. *Forwards*: A Eskrigge, JR Herron, WJ Kerr, O Leatham, RP Leitch, D McDonald, WC Milburn, J Muir, HJ Ryalls (t).
BIRKENHEAD PARK 0 *Backs*: AW McIlwaine, AB Wilson. *Three-quarters*: JJ Ravenscroft, R Wood. *Half-backs*: G Cowie, JB Parry (capt). *Forwards*: E Crawley, England, P Martin, BB Middleton, GH Smythe, G Stewart, WH Wallace, A Williamson, WG Wride.
Attendance: 500   *Referee*: n/a

YORKSHIRE COUNTY FOOTBALL CHALLENGE CUP (23 entries)
Most goals wins. If equal, most tries. If still equal, most minor points.

First Round
Bradford 1g, Halifax 1g (mp: 1-4)
Bradford Junior 1g, 1t, York 0
Cleckheaton 3g, 3t, Hull 0
Dewsbury 3g, 2t, Potternewton 0
Horbury Athletic 1g, 1t, Bradford Zingari 0
Kirkstall 3g, 1t, Barnsley 0
Leeds Blenheim 0, West Town Shamrock (Dewsbury) 1t
Leeds Parish Church 0, Ossett 1g
Leeds St John's 0, Huddersfield 1g
Mirfield 0, Heckmondwike 2g, 1t
Salterhebble 0, Wakefield Trinity 2g
Bye: Leeds

Second Round
Cleckheaton 0, Wakefield Trinity 2g, 1t
Dewsbury 2g, 3t, Bradford Junior 1t
Halifax 3t, Kirkstall 0
Heckmondwike 1g, 1t, Huddersfield 3t
Horbury Athletic 3t, Ossett 1t
West Town Shamrock 0, Leeds 1g

Third Round
Dewsbury 2t, Leeds 0
Horbury Athletic 0, Heckmondwike 1t
Wakefield Trinity 2t, Halifax 0

Fourth Round (semi-final)
Dewsbury 0, Wakefield Trinity 1g
Bye: Heckmondwike

FINAL
Saturday 3 April 1880 at Cardigan Fields, Leeds
WAKEFIELD TRINITY 3 goals, 6 tries *Back*: A Hayley. *Three-quarters*: CE Bartram (c, dg), H Hayley (t, dg). *Half-backs*: H Hutchinson (3t), CT Baldwin (capt, t). *Forwards*: TO Bennett, W Ellis, W Jackson, B Kilner, JW Kilner, B Longbottom, HB Pickersgill (t), A Shires, EJ Spink (t), G Steele.
HECKMONDWIKE 1 try *Back*: M Riley. *Three-quarters*: J Garbutt, JT Gill. *Half-backs*: H Bentley, R Sykes. *Forwards*: GH Banks, J Bardon, B Firth, A Fitton, J France, H Harpin, H Heaton (capt), J Holmes (t), JP Humble, H Wilson.
Attendance: 6,000   *Referee*: HWT Garnett (Bradford)

COUNTY MATCHES

Saturday 15 November 1879 at The Parks, Oxford
OXFORD UNIVERSITY 2 goals, 1 try *Backs*: N Maclachlan, PA Newton. *Three-quarters*: AH Heath, HA Tudor (t). *Half-backs*: RL Knight (t), L Watkins. *Forwards*: E Astley, RN Blandy, AH Evans (capt, 2c), H Fowler, GO Jacob, C Phillips, M Shearman, HK Tunstall, H Vassall (t).
CHESHIRE 0 *Backs*: WE Coubrough (NewB), R Sleigh (BirkPk). *Three-quarters*: PF Shaw (NewB), AW Wilson (Sale). *Half-backs*: HA Dixon (NewB), JB Parry (BirkPk). *Forwards*: B Atkinson (BirkPk), H Brandon (BirkPk), HD Hulme (Bow), WJ Kerr (NewB), BB Middleton (BirkPk), R Percival (Nord), G Stewart (BirkPk), JWH Thorp (capt, Macc), JN Wilson (Sale).
Attendance: 'large'   *Referee*: n/a

Saturday 15 November 1879 at Elland Road, Leeds
YORKSHIRE 2 goals, 4 tries *Back*: JA Wylde (Lee). *Three-quarters*: A Hayley (Wak, c), A Newsome (Dew). *Half-backs*: J Dodd (Hal, t, c), C Scharff (Lee, t). *Forwards*: JC Atkinson (Lee), GW Bottomley (Hud, t), G Darbyshire (Hull), HWT Garnett (capt, Brad), G Harrison (Lee), B Kilner (Wak, t), J Pitt (Kirk), G Steele (Wak), GT Thomson (Hal, t), E Woodhead (Hud, t).
DURHAM 1 goal *Backs*: HE Kayll (Sund), RH Mallett (Darl, c). *Half-backs*: PB Junor (capt, DurC), JL Watson (Darl). *Quarter-backs*: WA Kidson (Sund), G Morgan (DurU). *Forwards*: JH Brooks (Darl), J Eden (Darl, t), J Fowler (Darl), WT Hallimond (BishA), A Hill (Hart), JJ Kayll (Sund), D Parry (DurU), JT Todd (Hou), T Todd (Hou).
Attendance: 4,000   *Referee*: AJ Bulteel (Manchester)

Saturday 29 November 1879 at Whalley Range, Manchester
LANCASHIRE 1 goal, 2 tries *Backs*: F Bagshaw (Che), W Hopper (Bolton). *Three-quarters*: E Beswick (Swi), CM Sawyer (Bro, 2t, c). *Half-backs*: T Deane (Bro), CW Trevor-Smith (ManR). *Forwards*: HH Andrew (ManR), HD Bateson (Liv), T Blatherwick (capt, Man), WS Butterworth (RochH), AM Fletcher (Old), T Hunter (Birch), ET Markendale (ManR), HH Springmann (Liv, t), JD Wormald (Bolton).
CHESHIRE 1 try *Backs*: WE Coubrough (NewB), AW Wilson (Sale). *Three-quarters*: PF Shaw (NewB), R Wood (BirkPk). *Half-backs*: HA Dixon (NewB), JB Parry (BirkPk). *Forwards*: B Atkinson (BirkPk), H Brandon (BirkPk, t), E Crawley

Milestones & Stats 1869-1901

(BirkPk), HD Hulme (Bow), AW McIlwaine (BirkPk), W Rycroft (Bow), GH Smythe (BirkPk), JWH Thorp (Macc), A Williamson (BirkPk).
Attendance: 2,300   *Referee*: n/a

Monday 5 January 1880 at Old Deer Park, Richmond
MIDDLESEX 0 *Backs*: AS Bremner (Rich), N Thursby (OChelt). *Three-quarters*: WH Stiles (ClapR), CM Wilkins (MarlN). *Half-backs*: E Ashmore (Walth), HL Ashmore (Walth). *Forwards*: R Barlow (Rich), FWF Collier (ClapR), H Fowler (capt, OxfU), C Gurdon (Rich), ET Gurdon (Rich), WW Northcott (Rich), A Tillyer (Harl),
GF Vernon (Black), JJ Ward (Gip).
YORKSHIRE 2 tries *Backs*: H Harris (York), A Hayley (Wak). *Three-quarters*: Fred Huth (Hud), M Newsome (Dew). *Half-backs*: J Dodd (Hal), C Scharff (Lee, t). *Forwards*:
G Harrison (Lee), EB Holwell (Lee), B Kilner (Wak), A Macauley (Hud, t), JB Ogden (LeeStJ), J Pitt (Kirk), GT Thomson (capt, Hal), JE Wood (Hal), E Woodhead (Hud).
Attendance: 200   *Referee*: J MacLaren (RFU Vice-President)

Saturday 17 January 1880 at Fartown, Huddersfield
YORKSHIRE 2 tries *Backs*: A Hayley (Wak), H Huth (Hud, t). *Three-quarters*: J Dodd (Hal), A Newsome (Dew). *Half-backs*: C Scharff (Lee), C Wood (York, t). *Forwards*:
GW Bottomley (Hud), HE Briggs (Brad), HWT Garnett (capt, Brad), G Harrison (Lee), B Kilner (Wak), A Macauley (Hud), J Pitt (Kirk), JE Wood (Hal), E Woodhead (Hud).
LANCASHIRE 2 goals, 2 tries *Back*: AN Hornby (Man). *Three-quarters*: R Hunt (Man, 2c), CM Sawyer (Bro, 2t). *Half-backs*: JH Payne (Bro), WR Richardson (Man, t). *Forwards*:
HH Andrew (ManR), T Blatherwick (Man), WS Butterworth (RochH), RJ Clegg (Man), JM Reid (Liv), HC Rowley (Man), JS Sawyer (Bro, t), JW Schofield (Man), H Sherriff (Che), R Walker (Man).
Attendance: 3,000/4,000   *Referee*: n/a*
*No referee appointed, two umpires only (*Leeds Mercury*, 19 January 1880).

Saturday 14 February 1880 at Meadow Cricket Ground, Burton-on-Trent
MIDLAND COUNTIES 1 goal, 2 tries *Backs*: AG Piper (Burt), G Ratliff (Cov).
Three-quarters: HC King (Leam, dg), HE Ratliff (Cov, t). *Half-backs*: SH Evershed (Burt), A Mason (Rugby). *Forwards*: CD Curry (Leam, t), GM Day (Burt), PH Evans (Derby), E Field (Leam), EE Hopewell (Rugby), JF Hunt (capt, Burt), H Rotherham (Cov),
HE Sugden (Burt), J Whittaker (Rugby).
YORKSHIRE 1 try *Back*: WR Harrison (Kirk). *Three-quarters*: JC Broadhead (Kirk),
H Broughton (Bradford Junior). *Half-backs*: F Bedford (Hal), TP Peacock (LeeStJ).
Forwards: JO Beutler (Brad), JE French (Hal, t), EB Holwell (Lee), WB Lindley (LeeStJ), B Longbottom (Wak), A Macauley (capt, Hud), JA Miller (LeeStJ), B Schofield (Hud),
FJ Smith (Brad), S Speight (Kirk).
Attendance: 2,000   *Referee*: n/a

Saturday 21 February 1880 at Smithdown Road, Liverpool
CHESHIRE 0 *Backs*: WE Coubrough (NewB), R Wood (BirkPk). *Three-quarters*:
J Ravenscroft (BirkPk), PF Shaw (NewB). *Half-backs*: JB Parry (capt, BirkPk), R Percival (Nord). *Forwards*: H Brandon (BirkPk), A Coubrough (NewB), HD Hulme (Bow),
WJ Kerr (NewB), BB Middleton (BirkPk), W Rycroft (Bow), G Stewart (BirkPk),
JWH Thorp (Macc), A Williamson (BirkPk).

YORKSHIRE 1 try *Back*: CE Bartram (Wak). *Three-quarters*: A Newsome (Dew, t), M Newsome (Dew). *Half-backs*: J Dodd (Hal), C Scharff (Lee). *Forwards*: GW Bottomley (Hud), JE French (Hal), HWT Garrett (capt, Brad), EB Holwell (Lee), WH Hudson (Lee), JW Ibbotson (Dew), B Kilner (Wak), A Macauley (Hud), JB Ogden (LeeStJ), G Steele (Wak).
Attendance: 2,000   *Referee*: n/a

Saturday 21 February 1880 at Whalley Range, Manchester
LANCASHIRE 3 goals, 7 tries *Back*: AN Hornby (Man, t). *Three-quarters*: R Hunt (Man, t, dg), CM Sawyer (Bro, 2t). *Half-backs*: A Knowles (Man, t), JH Payne (Bro, t, c). *Forwards*: HH Andrew (ManR), T Blatherwick (Man), WS Butterworth (RochH), ET Markendale (ManR), AB Rowley (Man), HC Rowley (Man, 2t, c), JS Sawyer (Bro), WS Sawyer (Bro), JW Schofield (Man), R Walker (Man, t).
MIDDLESEX 0 *Back*: ET Turner (Black). *Three-quarters*: J Duffie (KCHosp), J Styles (ClapR). *Half-backs*: HT Twynam (Rich), A Tillyer (Harl). *Forwards*: E Bunn (Laus), HR Clayton (Rich), WE Clifton (Rich), W Edwards (ClapR), HP Gardner (Rich), C Gurdon (Rich), ET Gurdon (capt, Rich), B Leonard (Ken), W Mothershill (Rich), GF Vernon (Black).
Attendance: 3,000/4,000   *Referee*: n/a

Monday 1 March 1880 at Belle Vue, Wakefield
YORKSHIRE 1 goal, 4 tries *Back*: CE Bartram (Wak, c). *Three-quarters*: A Newsome (Dew), M Newsome (Dew). *Half-backs*: HE Briggs (Brad, t), H Huth (Hud, t). *Forwards*: TO Bennett (Wak), GW Bottomley (Hud), HWT Garrett (capt, Brad), G Harrison (Lee), JW Ibbotson (Dew), B Kilner (Wak), JB Ogden (LeeStJ), G Steele (Wak, t), JE Wood (Hal, t), E Woodhead (Hud, t).
SURREY 0 *Backs*: GL Lyons (Gip), CO Master (Gip). *Three-quarters*: FS Clarke (OChelt), PH Clifford (ClapR). *Half-backs*: RRH Ross (ESh), J Shearman (Rich). *Forwards*: A Back (ESh), CH Coates (capt, CamU), HS Holloway (Flam), WA Jellicoe (Laus), RB Kennard (OChelt), EJ Lamb (OChelt), HS Ross (ESh), AC Slee (Wim), JN Turney (Laus).
Attendance: 3,000   *Referee*: n/a

ENGLAND TRIAL MATCH

Saturday 14 February 1880 at Hanson Lane, Halifax
NORTH 2 goals, 1 try *Backs*: AN Hornby (capt, Man), H Huth (Hud).
Three-quarters: R Hunt (Man), CM Sawyer (Bro). *Half-backs*: J Dodd (Hal), JB Parry (BirkPk). *Forwards*: GW Bottomley (Hud), WS Butterworth (RochH), G Harrison (Lee, t), B Kilner (Wak), ET Markendale (ManR), W Middleton (BirkPk), HC Rowley (Man), JS Sawyer (Bro), E Woodhead (Hud).
SOUTH 3 goals, 2 tries *Backs*: WJ Penny (KCHosp), RH White (StTHosp, 2t).
Three-quarters: L Stokes (capt, Black, 3c). *Half-backs*: HH Taylor (StGHosp), HT Twynam (Rich). *Forwards*: GW Burton (Black, 2t), CH Coates (CamU), SS Ellis (QH), C Gurdon (Rich, t), ET Gurdon (Rich), S Neame (OChelt), FL Pattison (Black), C Phillips (BirkPk/OxfU), A Spurling (Black), GF Vernon (Black).
Attendance: 10,000   *Referee*: J MacLaren (RFU Vice-President)

INTERNATIONAL MATCHES

Monday 2 February 1880 at Lansdowne Road, Dublin
IRELAND 1 try *Back*: RB Walkington (NIFC). *Half-backs*: JC Bagot (DubU),
AM Whitestone (DubU). *Quarter-backs*: WT Heron (NIFC), M Johnston (DubU).
Forwards: JL Cuppaidge (DubU, t), AJ Forrest (Wand), RW Hughes (QCB), HC Kelly
(capt, NIFC), F Kennedy (Wand), JA Macdonald (Wind), A Millar (King), H Purdon
(NIFC), G Scriven (DubU), JW Taylor (NIFC).
ENGLAND 1 goal, 1 try *Backs*: TW Fry (QH), AN Hornby (Man). *Three-quarters*: R Hunt
(Man), L Stokes (capt, Black, c). *Half-backs*: AH Jackson (Black), HT Twynam (Rich).
Forwards: SS Ellis (QH, t), C Gurdon (Rich), B Kilner (Wak), ET Markendale (ManR, t),
S Neame (OChelt), HC Rowley (Man), JW Schofield (Man), GF Vernon (Black),
E Woodhead (Hud).
Attendance: 2,000   *Referee*: GP Nugent (Ireland)

Saturday 28 February 1880 at Whalley Range, Manchester
ENGLAND 2 goals, 3 tries *Backs*: TW Fry (QH, t), L Stokes (capt, Black, 2c).
Three-quarters: HC Rowley (Man), CM Sawyer (Bro). *Half-backs*: RT Finch (CamU),
HH Taylor (Black, 2t). *Forwards*: GW Burton (Black, t), CH Coates (CamU), C Gurdon
(Rich), ET Gurdon (Rich, t), G Harrison (Hull), S Neame (OChelt), C Phillips
(BirkPk/OxfU), GF Vernon (Black), R Walker (Man).
SCOTLAND 1 goal *Back*: WE Maclagan (EdinA). *Half-backs*: M Cross (GlasA, c),
NJ Finlay (EdinA). *Quarter-backs*: WS Brown (EdinIFP, t), WH Masters (EdinIFP).
Forwards: R Ainslie (EdinIFP), NT Brewis (EdinIFP), JB Brown (GlasA), DY Cassels
(WoS), EN Ewart (GlasA), JHS Graham (EdinA), RW Irvine (capt, EdinA), D McCowan
(WoS), AG Petrie (RHSFP), CR Stewart (WoS).
Attendance: 9,000   *Referee*: AG Guillemard (England)

John Payne of Broughton made 31 Lancashire appearances, also representing the North and England. *Athletic News, 1888*

1880-1881

BATLEY FOUNDED
The Batley club was founded during October 1880 as the Batley Cricket, Athletic and Football Club through the amalgamation of Batley Athletic Football Club and the Batley Cricket Club.

THE NORTHUMBERLAND CUP BEGINS
The Northumberland County Challenge Cup was introduced this season, commencing in November with six clubs competing for a cup described as 'a massive and chaste piece of workmanship' that cost £70.

THE FLYING MAN
When Durham met Northumberland on 4th December, they included William Kidson in the rarely defined position of 'flying-man', sometimes referred to as 'flyman'. A decade ahead of the introduction of 'fly-half' into rugby union terminology, the role provided a link between half-backs and three-quarters and in common use in north-east England during the early 1880s.[26]

CHESHIRE'S APPRECIATION
Cheshire's home fixture against Lancashire took place at the Broughton Football Club ground, based in Salford, Lancashire, on 11th December, following a postponement at Birkenhead on 20th November due to frost. It was reported as 'a concession made by the Broughton club which was greatly appreciated by the Cheshire executive'.[27]

APPEAL FOR A NATIONAL RUGBY COMPETITION

With the latest Yorkshire Cup contest about to start again and the level of interest continuing to grow, the *Yorkshire Post* argued for the introduction of a national competition: 'During the past few years a mania has sprung up for challenge cups, the result of enterprise on the part of the Football Association and the Rugby Union. The first [national] trophy [F.A. Cup] was instituted by the former in 1870-71. Since that time [it has grown] to such an extent that the entries are now so great that it has been found necessary to divide the clubs into districts. It is to be regretted that the Rugby Union have not yet shown any disposition to follow the excellent example [of creating a national trophy]. Such a step would give our first rate northern fifteens a fine opportunity of measuring strength with the best southern teams.'[28]

THE DURHAM CUP BEGINS

The Durham County Challenge Cup was introduced this season with ten clubs entering, the first final being contested by Sunderland and Houghton-le-Spring at Feetham's Ground, Darlington, on 26th March. It was reported: 'There was a good attendance, but the gathering would have been much greater to witness the final had more notice been given to it. It was, however, only decided on the previous night that the game should be played at Darlington, as some neutral ground had to be selected. The game excited the greatest interest, and there was a good number in attendance from Sunderland and different parts of the county, including Darlington.'[29]

CHESHIRE CUP TO BE DISCONTINUED

After four consecutive Cheshire Cup competitions, the county committee decided, on 21st April, 'that the cup ties be discontinued as detrimental to the best interests of the game in Cheshire and tending to promote bad feeling between clubs'.[30] The competition was not resurrected until 1969-70.

LANCASHIRE COUNTY UNION FOUNDED

The creation of a Lancashire Football Union was finalised at the Mitre Hotel, Manchester, on Tuesday evening, 31st May, when its proposed rules were adopted. It was stated that 'there was a good attendance of representatives. About eleven of the sixteen Rugby Union organisations have signified their intention of joining the Lancashire Union. There was no communication from the Manchester Football Club, which club embraces some of the best players in the county'.[31] The stance taken by Manchester was significant because it was due to its perceived dominance of county affairs that the decision to create a county union was instigated by five clubs; Birch, Broughton, Free Wanderers (Manchester), Manchester Rangers and Swinton. The gathering followed two previous meetings, also held at the Mitre Hotel, on the 3rd and 17th of May. After the latter, it was reported: 'For a considerable time past, the management of county affairs has been a self-imposed task of the Manchester F. C., but the leading clubs decided to have a voice in the matter. At the first meeting held a fortnight ago it was resolved that a deputation should wait upon the Manchester F. C. to endeavour to secure their co-operation along with the 16 clubs which have approved of the formation of a county union. Twelve clubs sent representatives on Tuesday night [17th May], and it was decided that a union for the management of the county affairs should be formed.'[32]

LEEDS FOOTBALL CLUB RENAMED
Having completed five seasons since its formation, the Leeds (Rugby) Football Club was renamed. At its annual general meeting in May 1881 at the Griffin Hotel in Leeds it was unanimously decided that the club would be known as the Yorkshire Wanderers in the belief that 'by losing its local designation the club expects to gain considerably by an increase of new members'. The club would continue to be based in Leeds with the team 'uniform' unchanged except that the Leeds coat of arms would no longer appear on the jersey.[33]

1880-1881 STATISTICS

CHESHIRE COUNTY CHALLENGE CUP (9 entries)
Most goals wins. If equal, most tries. If still equal, most minor points.

First Round
Bowdon 1g, 3t, Egremont (Wallasey) 0
Marple 4t, Hyde 1t
New Brighton w/o Sale (result not found)
Northenden 0 Birkenhead Park 1g, 2t
Bye: Dukinfield

Second Round
Marple 0, Birkenhead Park 1t
New Brighton 3g, 3t, Dukinfield 1t
Bye: Bowdon

Third Round (Semi-final)
Birkenhead Park 11g, 6t, Bowdon 0
Bye: New Brighton

FINAL
Saturday 26 March 1881 at Smithdown Lane, Wavertree, Liverpool
BIRKENHEAD PARK 0 *Back*: JA Black. *Three-quarters*: R Wood, AC Blain, JJ Ravenscroft (capt). *Half-backs*: G Cowie, JB Parry. *Forwards*: EA Beazley, DA Bingham, H Brandon, WP Evans, FW Jones, BB Middleton, C Phillips, GH Smythe, G Stewart.
NEW BRIGHTON 0 *Back*: JB Keyworth. *Three-quarters*: PF Shaw (capt), C Cameron, WE Coubrough. *Half-backs*: HS Patterson, H Wrigley. *Forwards*: AS Coubrough, ER Harpin, E Holt, WJ Kerr, O Leatham, RP Leitch, D McDonald, WC Milburn, H Sinclair.
Attendance: 'large'   *Referee*: CWH Clark (Liverpool)

FINAL REPLAY
Monday 4 April 1881 at Smithdown Lane, Wavertree, Liverpool
BIRKENHEAD PARK 1 goal, 1 try *Back*: JA Black. *Three-quarters*: R Wood (dg), AC Blain, JJ Ravenscroft (capt). *Half-backs*: G Cowie, JB Parry. *Forwards*: EA Beazley, DA Bingham, H Brandon, WP Evans, BB Middleton, C Phillips, GH Smythe, G Stewart, JR Wilson (t).
NEW BRIGHTON 0 *Back*: JB Keyworth. *Three-quarters*: PF Shaw (capt), C Cameron, WE Coubrough. *Half-backs*: HS Patterson, H Wrigley. *Forwards*: A Coubrough, CE Geddes, A Herron, JR Herron, E Holt, WJ Kerr, O Leatham, RP Leitch, H Sinclair.
Attendance: 'large'   *Referee*: JM Reid (Liverpool)

DURHAM COUNTY CHALLENGE CUP (10 entries)
Most goals wins. If equal, most tries.

First Round
Darlington 3t, Durham City 0
Houghton-le-Spring 1t, North Durham 0
Sunderland w/o Durham University
Sunderland Rovers 1g, 1t, Hartlepools 0
Westoe w/o Bishop Auckland

Second Round
Darlington 0, Sunderland 1g, 1t
Houghton-le-Spring 1g, 1t Westoe 0
Bye: Sunderland Rovers

Third Round (semi-final)
Sunderland Rovers 0, Houghton-le-Spring 2t
Bye: Sunderland

Milestones & Stats 1869-1901

FINAL
Saturday 26 March 1881 at Feethams Ground, Darlington
SUNDERLAND 3 tries *Back*: HE Kayll. *Three-quarters*: RGR Eden, O Thompson (t).
Half-backs: AGM Hudson (2t), C Kidson, WA Kidson. *Forwards*: W Dickinson, J Fowles,
WA Gales, R Hitchcock, DS Inman, JJ Kayll, A Laing (capt), J Laing, H Thompson.
HOUGHTON-LE-SPRING 0 *Back*: RD Proud. *Three-quarters*: G Moore, FT Richie.
Half-backs: AT Crow, TM Jamieson. *Forwards*: WC Blackett, T Elstob, F Forrest, W Forster,
GH Green (capt), R Leary, JR Rowntree, JT Todd, T Todd, WC Wetherell.
Attendance: 'good'   *Referee*: JH Brooks (Darlington)

NORTHUMBERLAND COUNTY FOOTBALL CHALLENGE CUP (6 entries)
Most goals wins. If equal, most tries. If still equal, majority of 3 minor points.

First Round
Gosforth 2t, Tynedale 1t
Northern 1g, 1t, Percy Park 0
Tynemouth 0, Northumberland FC 0 (mp: 0-6)

Second Round (semi-final)
Northumberland FC 1g, 2t, Gosforth 0
Bye: Northern

FINAL
Saturday 19 February 1881 at Burdon Terrace, Newcastle
NORTHERN 1 goal, 2 tries *Back*: JW Swinburne. *Three-quarters*: E Liddell (dg),
JVW Rutherford (capt, t). *Half-backs*: AC Challoner (t), C Gibson.
Forwards: WR Dickinson, K Guthrie, R Henzell, G Maitland, GA Mason, GW Ridley,
W Ridley, D Ross, CE Winship, WA Winship.
NORTHUMBERLAND FC 0 *Back*: FS Strickland. *Three-quarters*: JL Bell (capt), B Reed.
Half-backs: GA Bell, SF Prest. *Forwards*: DC Beadon, A Cadle, F Corbett, Fox, F Marshall,
J Morrison, CR Pattinson, JS Pattinson, Rogers, WS Williams.
Attendance: 1,500   *Referee*: PB Junor (Durham RU)

YORKSHIRE COUNTY FOOTBALL CHALLENGE CUP (32 entries)
Most goals wins. If equal, most tries. If still equal, most minor points.

First Round
Barnsley 2t, Leeds Parish Church 0
Dewsbury 1t, Huddersfield 0
Dewsbury Shamrocks 1g, Leeds St John's 0
Gildersome and Morley 1t, Leeds 2g, 1t
Halifax w/o Bradford Zingari (withdrew)
Halifax Free Wanderers 2g, 4t, Leeds Rovers 0
Harrogate 0, Batley 1t
Horbury 1g, 2t, Bradford Rangers 1g, 1t
Hull 0, Bingley 2t
Kirkstall 1t, Cleckheaton 1g, 1t
Mytholmroyd 1t, Bradford 1g, 5t
Ossett 4g, 1t, Tadcaster 0
Salterhebble 1t, Heckmondwike 0
Thornes 1g, Sowerby Bridge 0
Wakefield Trinity 3g, 1t, Mirfield 0
York w/o Potternewton (disbanded)

Second Round
Barnsley 0, Horbury 1g
Batley 0, Halifax Free Wanderers 1g
Bingley 0, Leeds 3t
Bradford 0, Dewsbury 1t
Cleckheaton 1g, 1t, Ossett 1g
Halifax 1g, 1t, Thornes 1g
Salterhebble 1t, Dewsbury Shamrocks 3t
York 0, Wakefield Trinity 4g

Third Round
Cleckheaton 1t, Horbury 1g
Dewsbury 3g, Halifax Free Wanderers 0
Halifax 1g, 2t, Leeds 1g, 1t
Wakefield Trin 1g, 2t, Dewsbury Shamrocks 0

Fourth Round (semi-finals)
Halifax 0, Dewsbury 1g
Horbury 1t, Wakefield Trinity 1g, 1t

FINAL
Saturday 9 April 1881 at Cardigan Fields, Leeds
DEWSBURY 1 goal *Back*: GE Pyrah. *Three-quarters*: A Newsome (capt, dg), M Newsome. *Half-backs*: C Marsden, S Mortimer. *Forwards*: H Broadbent, EL Fisher, WK Fisher, J Fligg, WE Hanson, JW Ibbotson, H Purdy, J Scholes, D Varley, S Wolstenholme.
WAKEFIELD TRINITY 0 *Back*: A Hayley. *Three-quarters*: CE Bartram, H Hayley. *Half-backs*: JH Cuthbert, H Hutchinson. *Forwards*: W Ellis, W Jackson, J Jubb, B Kilner (capt), JW Kilner, G Logan, B Longbottom, A Shires, EJ Spink, G Steele.
Attendance: 10,000   *Referee*: PB Junor (Durham RU)

COUNTY MATCHES

Saturday 16 October 1880 at Whitehaven Cricket Ground
CUMBERLAND 1 goal *Backs*: J Harker (Asp), J Scott (Work, c). *Three-quarters*: F Nicholson (Cock), RY Sutton (Whi). *Half-backs*: J Lister (Cock), JC Nicholson (Cock). *Forwards*: J Blair (Work), T Dobie (Asp, t), FE Eddis (Whi), JC Hellon (Whi), Lees (Whi), C Milligan (Whi), R Strathern (Whi), W Thompson (Asp), EH Williams (capt, Whi).
BARROW 2 goals, 1 try *Back*: J Atkinson (capt, t, 2c). *Three-quarters*: T Carlton (t), S Troughton (t). Half-backs: GB Ashburner, R Tyson. *Forwards*: GT Ashburner, E Brown, J Carlton, R Cross, T Gerrard, E Gradwell, BU Hearn, P Robinson, A Smyth, E Stables.
Attendance: n/a   *Referee*: n/a

Saturday 23 October 1880 at Whitehaven Cricket Ground
CUMBERLAND 2 tries *Backs*: J Scott (Work), S Troughton (Bar). *Three-quarters*: GB Ashburner (Bar/Whi), RY Sutton (Whi, t). *Half-backs*: J Lister (Cock), JC Nicholson (Cock). *Forwards*: J Blair (capt, Work), JC Brockbank (Whi), T Dobie (Asp), JC Hellon (Whi), Lees (Whi), F Nicholson (Cock), R Strathern (Whi), W Thompson (Asp, t), R Tyson (Bar).
NORTHUMBERLAND 1 try *Backs*: S Oliver (Tynm), RH Robb (Tynd). *Three-quarters*: J Cowper (Tynd), W Farr (Gos). *Half-backs*: J McConnell (PerPk), SF Prest (capt, NorFC, t). *Forwards*: JG Burdon (NorFC), WR Dickinson (Nor), C Gibson (Nor), JT Maling (Nor), J Morrison (NorFC), TH Morrison (PerPk), WH Pattinson (NorFC), GW Ridley (Nor), W Ridley (Nor).
Attendance: n/a   *Referee*: JR Bain (Cumberland)

Saturday 13 November 1880 at Feethams Cricket Ground, Darlington
DURHAM 0 *Backs*: RH Mallett (Darl), TF Wilson (Wes). *Three-quarters*: F Robson (SundR), J White (NDur). *Half-backs*: PB Junor (DurC), JL Watson (Darl). *Forwards*: WB Bagley (Darl), W Crozier (DurC), JK Dearden (DurU), J Eden (Darl), WT Hallimond (BishA), A Laing (capt, Sund), R Leary (Hou), JR Rowntree (Hou), O Stephenson (Hart).
YORKSHIRE 1 goal, 4 tries *Back*: H Broughton (BradR), JA Wylde (Lee). *Three-quarters*: H Huth (Hud, t), A Newsome (Dew). *Half-backs*: TP Peacock (LeeStJ), C Wood (York, 3t). *Forwards*: GW Bottomley (Hud), H Broadbent (Dew), CH Coates (Lee), EH Dykes (Lee, t), CWL Fernandes (Lee), G Harrison (capt, Lee), JA Miller (LeeStJ), J Pitt (Kirk), WH Smith (Brad, c).
Attendance: 'not great'   *Referee*: JH Brooks (Durham)

Monday 15 November 1880 at The Parks, Oxford
OXFORD UNIVERSITY 2 tries *Back*: A Brooker. *Three-quarters*: WE Collins, B Evanson. *Half-backs*: AP Irwin, RL Knight (t). *Forwards*: WF Barwick, CF Leslie, GA Mackenzie, (capt), WL Patterson, CF Sanctuary, HF Tatham, V Varral, J Walker, T Walker (t).
CHESHIRE 1 goal, 2 tries *Back*: AW McIlwaine (BirkPk, dg). *Three-quarters*: R Wood (BirkPk), PF Shaw (NewB, t), WE Coubrough (NewB). *Half-backs*: G Cowie (BirkPk), Royds. *Forwards*: WJ Kerr (NewB), W Lucas (Hyde), D McDonald (NewB, t), W Middleton (BirkPk), C Phillips (BirkPk), J Ravenscroft (capt, BirkPk), HJ Ryalls (NewB), GH Smythe (BirkPk), G Stewart (BirkPk).
Attendance: n/a   *Referee*: n/a
Note: Club not identified for Royds (Cheshire)

Saturday 20 November 1880 at Belle Vue, Wakefield
YORKSHIRE 2 goals, 1 try *Back*: A Hayley (capt, Wak, 2c), H Wade (LeeStJ). *Three-quarters*: AR Atkinson (Lee), TL Scarborough (Hal). *Half-backs*: MS Dawson (Lee), H Hutchinson (Wak, 2t). *Forwards*: F Booth (BradR), T Chambers (Hal), W Ellis (Wak), WK Fisher (Dew), JF Griffith (York), EB Holwell (Lee), JW Kilner (Wak, t), J Watson (LeeStJ), JE Wood (Hal).
MIDLAND COUNTIES 1 try *Backs*: DH Brownfield (Stoke), EW Piper (Burt). *Three-quarters*: H Brook (Bedford), HE Ratliff (capt, Cov). *Half-backs*: SH Evershed (Burt, t), EH Richards (Derby). *Forwards*: PH Evans (Derby), FS Hunt (Burt), JH Paget (Leic), CF Skilton (Burt), HE Sugden (Burt), A Tapp (Nott), W Turral (Cov), R Twyford (North Stafford), E Worthington (Leic).
Attendance: 3,000   *Referee*: HWT Garnett (Yorkshire)

Saturday 27 November 1880 at Edenside Cricket Ground, Carlisle
NORTHUMBERLAND 4 goals *Back*: DJ Pigg (Gos). *Three-quarters*: GA Bell (NorFC), S Oliver (Tynm, t). *Half-backs*: SF Prest (NorFC), JVW Rutherford (capt, Nor, 3c). *Forwards*: S Burridge (NorFC), P Campbell (NEls), S Crawford (Tynm), W Cummins (Tynm, t), GD Fawcus (Tynm, 2t, c), TH Morrison (PerPk), GR Palmer (Tynm), CR Pattinson (NorFC), JS Pattinson (NorFC), GW Ridley (Nor).
DUMFRIESSHIRE 0 *Back*: CH Whitelaw (Canonbie). *Half-backs*: J Nicholson (Annan), J Fletcher (Langholm), J Maxwell (Canonbie). *Quarter-backs*: JN Saunders (Annan), WJ Johnston (Annan). *Forwards*: Blithe (Dumfries), Brown (Dumfries), Elliot,

G Goodfellow (Canonbie), T Graham (Canonbie), G Little (Langholm), Tennant (capt, Dumfries), Turnbull, Walker (Dumfries).
Attendance: n/a   *Referee*: J Nanson (Cumberland)
Note: Clubs not identified for Elliott and Turnbull (Dumfriesshire).

Saturday 4 December 1880 at Chester Road, Sunderland
DURHAM 0 *Back*: HE Kayll (Sund). *Three-quarters*: A Hill (Hart), F Robson (SundR). *Flying-man*: WA Kidson (Sund). *Half-backs*: JW Sowerby (NDur), JL Watson (Darl). *Forwards*: WB Bagley (Darl), FC Dearden (DurU), HW Edlin (Darl), J Fowles (Sund), A Laing (capt, Sund), J Laing (Sund), A Paget (Sund), ET Pease-Watkin (Darl), O Stephenson (Hart).
NORTHUMBERLAND 1 goal *Backs*: GA Bell (NorFC), B Reed (NorFC). *Three-quarters*: JL Bell (capt, NorFC, c), SF Prest (NorFC). *Half-backs*: J McConnell (PerPk), JVW Rutherford (Nor). *Forwards*: SF Bates (Gos), S Crawford (Tynm), GD Fawcus (Tynm, t), F Marshall (NorFC), S Oliver (Tynm), JS Pattinson (NorFC), GW Ridley (Nor), RH Robb (Tynd), WA Winship (Nor).
Attendance: 'large'   *Referee*: G Sowerby (Durham)

Saturday 4 December 1880 at Whalley Range, Manchester
LANCASHIRE 4 goals, 2 tries *Back*: AN Hornby (Man). *Three-quarters*: R Hunt (Man, t, 3c, dg), HC Rowley (Man), CM Sawyer (Bro). *Half-backs*: JH Payne (Bro, t), WR Richardson (Man, 2t). *Forwards*: HH Andrew (ManR), T Blatherwick (capt, Man), WS Butterworth (RochH), J Fletcher (Man), JT Hunt (Man, t), ET Markendale (ManR), AB Rowley (Man), JS Sawyer (Bro), JW Schofield (Man)
YORKSHIRE 0 *Back*: J Dodd (Hal). *Three-quarters*: CE Bartram (Wak), TL Scarborough (Hal), A Newsome (Dew). *Half-backs*: H Hutchinson (Wak), C Wood (York). *Forwards*: GW Bottomley (Hud), CWL Fernandes (Lee), G Harrison (Lee), JW Kilner (Wak), JA Miller (LeeStJ), WH Smith (Brad), G Steele (Wak), GT Thomson (capt, Hal), JE Wood (Hal).
Attendance: 5,000   *Referee*: HM Blythe (Cheshire)

Saturday 11 December 1880 at Broughton FC, Lower Broughton Road, Salford
CHESHIRE 0 *Back*: AW McIlwaine (BirkPk). *Three-quarters*: PF Shaw (NewB), WE Coubrough (NewB), AC Blain (BirkPk). *Half-backs*: G Cowie (BirkPk), JB Parry (BirkPk). *Forwards*: H Brandon (BirkPk), HD Hulme (Bow), O Leatham (NewB), C Phillips (BirkPk), J Ravenscroft (capt, BirkPk), W Rycroft (Bow), GH Smythe (BirkPk), G Stewart (BirkPk), JWH Thorp (Macc).
LANCASHIRE 2 goals, 1 try *Back*: AN Hornby (capt, Man). *Three-quarters*: R Hunt (Man, 2c), CM Sawyer (Bro, 2t), HC Rowley (Man). *Half-backs*: JH Payne (Bro), WR Richardson (Man). *Forwards*: HH Andrew (ManR), T Blatherwick (Man, t), WS Butterworth (RochH), J Fletcher (Man), JT Hunt (Man), AB Rowley (Man), JS Sawyer (Bro), JW Schofield (Man), W Woodcock (Bro).
Attendance: 2,000   *Referee*: AE Ward (Cheshire)

Monday 20 December 1880 at Richardson's Field, Blackheath
MIDDLESEX 0 *Back*: GB Mills (Walth). *Three-quarters*: HR Ladell (Rich), CB Ashmore (Walth), HT Twynam (Rich). *Half-backs*: HL Ashmore (Walth), AH Jackson (Black). *Forwards*: G Fowler (Walth), H Fowler OxfU), H Freeborn (StGHosp), HP Gardner (Rich),

C Gurdon (Rich), ET Gurdon (capt, Rich), JE Howe (StBHosp), GF Vernon (Black), JJ Ward (Rich).
LANCASHIRE 0 *Back*: AN Hornby (capt, Man). *Three-quarters*: R Hunt (Man), JH Payne (Bro). *Half-backs*: WS Butterworth (RochH), WR Richardson (Man). *Forwards*: HH Andrew (ManR), T Blatherwick (Man), RJ Clegg (Man), J Fletcher (Man), TH Higgins (Liv), JT Hunt (Man), AT Roberts (Birch), JS Sawyer (Bro), WS Sawyer (Bro), JW Schofield (Man).
Attendance: 'few'   *Referee*: L Stokes (Kent)

Monday 20 December 1880 at Old Deer Park, Richmond
SURREY 0 *Backs*: PH Clifford (ClapR), FH Pym (RIEC). *Three-quarters*: LR Colledge (StTHosp), EF White (StTHosp). *Half-backs*: ES Chapman (CamU), FS Clarke (OChelt). *Forwards*: A Back (ESh), AS Bryden (ClapR), HT Creswell (Walth), RH Hedderwick (LonS), HS Holloway (Flam), J Payne (Ken), M Shearman (capt, Rich), JN Turney (Laus), H Urwick (ClapR).
YORKSHIRE 1 try *Back*: H Broughton (BradR). *Three-quarters*: TL Scarborough (Hal), H Wade (LeeStJ). *Half-backs*: J Dodd (Hal), WL Wise (Lee, t). *Forwards*: J Bardon (Heck), H Broadbent (Dew), T Chambers (Hal), CH Coates (Lee), CWL Fernandes (Lee), WK Fisher (Dew), G Harrison (Lee), JA Miller (LeeStJ), WH Smith (Brad), GT Thomson (capt, Hal).
Attendance: 30*   *Referee*: n/a
*'scarcely more than thirty' (Bradford Observer, 21 December 1880).

Saturday 12 February 1881 at Burdon Terrace, Newcastle
NORTHUMBERLAND 1 goal *Back*: JW Swinburne (Nor). *Three-quarters*: SF Prest (NorFC), W Farr (Gos), GA Bell (NorFC). *Half-backs*: J McConnell (PerPk), JVW Rutherford (Nor). *Forwards*: JH Bennett (NEls), S Crawford (Tynm), WR Dickinson (Nor), R Henzell (Nor), JS Pattinson (NorFC, fg), GW Ridley (Nor), RH Robb (Tynd), WS Williams (NorFC), CE Winship (Nor).
EDINBURGH UNIVERSITY 1 goal, 3 tries *Back*: J Clegg. *Half-backs*: F Brooks (2t), F Hunter. *Quarter-backs*: WK Morton, A Playfair (dg). *Forwards*: F Abraham, F Bateman, GB Batten, J Blanchard, W Ferguson, LC Haslip, RSF Henderson (capt), JG Houseman, AS Paterson, WA Peterkin (t).
Attendance: n/a   *Referee*: JF Ogilvie (Northumberland)

Saturday 26 February 1881 at Burdon Terrace, Newcastle
DURHAM 0 *Back*: HW Sample (Wes). *Three-quarters*: F Robson (SundR), O Thompson (Sund). *Half-backs*: WA Kidson (Sund), JW Sowerby (NDur), JL Watson (Darl). *Forwards*: WB Bagley (Darl), RF Crosthwaite ((Wes), W Crozier (DurC), J Fowles (Sund), A Laing (capt, Sund), J Laing (Sund), H Mason (DurC), ET Pease-Watkin (Darl), O Stephenson (Hart).
NORTHUMBERLAND 1 try *Back*: JW Swinburne (Nor). *Three-quarters*: JVW Rutherford (capt, Nor), E Liddell (Nor), W Farr (Gos). *Half-backs*: GA Bell (NorFC), J McConnell (PerPk, t). *Forwards*: SF Bates (Gos), JW Coward (PerPk), R Dale (Tynm), WR Dickinson (Nor), S Oliver (Tynm), JS Pattinson (NorFC), GW Ridley (Nor), J Smith (Gos), WS Williams (NorFC).
Attendance: 'good'   *Referee*: JL Bell (Northumberland)

Saturday 26 February 1881 at Crown Flatts, Dewsbury
YORKSHIRE 0 *Back*: H Broughton (BradR), M Newsome (Dew). *Three-quarters*:
A Newsome (Dew), TL Scarborough (Hal). *Half-backs*: WL Wise (Lee), C Wood (York).
Forwards: T Chambers (Hal), CWL Fernandes (Lee), WK Fisher (Dew), G Harrison (Lee),
B Kilner (Wak), JA Miller (LeeStJ), G Steele (Wak), GT Thomson (capt, Hal), W Watson (LeeStJ).
CHESHIRE 1 goal *Back*: H Maxwell (NewB). *Three-quarters*: J Ravenscroft (capt, BirkPk),
PF Shaw (NewB), WE Coubrough (NewB, c). *Half-backs*: AC Blain (BirkPk), G Cowie
(BirkPk). *Forwards*: W Andrew (Mar), HD Hulme (Bow, t), O Leatham (NewB),
D McDonald (NewB), BB Middleton (BirkPk), C Phillips (BirkPk), GH Smythe (BirkPk),
G Stewart (BirkPk), JWH Thorp (Macc).
Attendance: 3,000   *Referee*: HWT Garnett (Yorkshire)

Saturday 19 March 1881 at Burdon Terrace, Newcastle
NORTHUMBERLAND 2 tries *Back*: R Robb (Tynd). *Three-quarters*: GA Bell (NorFC),
B Reed (NorFC), W Farr (Gos). *Half-backs*: GD Fawcus (capt, Tynm, 2t), J McConnell
(PerPk). *Forwards*: A Cadle (NorFC), R Dale (Tynm), T Hedley (Tynd), F Marshall
(NorFC), TH Morrison (PerPk), S Oliver (Tynm), CR Pattinson (NorFC), T Robson
(Tynd), J Smith (Gos).
CUMBERLAND 0 *Back*: J Scott (Work). *Three-quarters*: RY Sutton (Whi), T Carlton
(Bar/Whi), J Atkinson (Bar/Egr). *Half-backs*: GB Ashburner (Bar/Whi), JC Nicholson
(Cock). *Forwards*: C Blair (Work), R Blair (Work), T Dobie (Asp), Hayton (Cock),
G Highton (Kes), Hilton (Whi), Lees (Whi), J Lister (Cock), W Thompson (Asp).
Attendance: 'large'   *Referee*: JL Bell (Northumberland)

ENGLAND TRIAL MATCH

Saturday 18 December 1880 at Kennington Oval, London
SOUTH 2 goals, 1 try *Back*: TW Fry (QH). *Three-quarters*: M Shearman (Rich), L Stokes
(capt, Black, t, 2c). *Half-backs*: AH Jackson (Black), HH Taylor (Black). *Forwards*: A Budd
(Black, t), G W Burton (Black, t), H Fowler (OxfU), C Gurdon (Rich), ET Gurdon (Rich),
WW Hewitt (QH), S Neame (OChelt), GF Vernon (Black), JI Ward (Rich), CP Wilson
(CamU).
NORTH 0 *Back*: AN Hornby (capt, Man). *Three-quarters*: R Hunt (Man), HC Rowley
(Man), CM Sawyer (Bro). *Half-backs*: JH Payne (Bro), WR Richardson (Man). *Forwards*:
HH Andrews (ManR), T Blatherwick (Man), WS Butterworth (RochH), CWL Fernandes
(Lee), JT Hunt (Man), C Phillips (BirkPk), J Ravenscroft (BirkPk), W Rycroft (Bow),
JS Sawyer (Bro).
Attendance: 2,000   *Referee*: AG Guillemard (RFU President)

Milestones & Stats 1869-1901 65

INTERNATIONAL MATCHES

Saturday 5 February 1881 at Whalley Range, Manchester
ENGLAND 2 goals, 2 tries *Back*: AN Hornby (Man). *Three-quarters*: CM Sawyer (Bro, t), L Stokes (capt, Black, 2c). *Half-backs*: WR Richardson (Man), HH Taylor (Black, 3t). *Forwards*: GW Burton (Black), CWL Fernandes (Lee), C Gurdon (Rich), ET Gurdon (Rich), WW Hewitt (QH), C Phillips (BirkPk), JJ Ravenscroft (BirkPk), HC Rowley (Man), GF Vernon (Black), JI Ward (Rich).
IRELAND 0 *Back*: T Harrison (Cork). *Half-backs*: W Peirce (Cork), WW Pike (King). *Quarter-backs*: M Johnston (DubU), HF Spunner (Wand). *Forwards*: DR Browning (Wand), JCS Burkitt (Cork), WEA Cummins (Cork), AJ Forrest (capt, Wand), F Kennedy (Wand), AR McMullen (Cork), HB Morell (DubU), H Purdon (NIFC), G Scriven (DubU), WA Wallis (Wand).
Attendance: 2,000   *Referee*: AG Guillemard (England)

Saturday 19 February 1881 at Richardson's Field, Blackheath
ENGLAND 8 goals, 6 tries *Back*: TW Fry (QH). *Three-quarters*: R Hunt (Man, t, c, dg), L Stokes (capt, Black, 6c). *Half-backs*: HH Taylor (Black, t), HT Twynam (Rich, t). *Forwards*: A Budd (Black, t), GW Burton (Black, 4t), CWL Fernandes (Lee, t), H Fowler (OxfU), C Gurdon (Rich), ET Gurdon (Rich), WW Hewitt (QH), HC Rowley (Man, t), H Vassall (MarlN/OxfU, 3t), CP Wilson (CamU).
WALES 0 *Backs*: CH Newman (New), RHB Summers (Haverfordwest). *Three-quarters*: JA Bevan (capt, CamU), E Peake (Chepstow). *Half-backs*: EJ Lewis (LlanC), L Watkins (Llandaff). *Forwards*: G Darbishire (Bangor), BE Girling (Car), GF Harding (New), BB Mann (Car), WD Phillips (Car), FT Purdon (New), TA Rees (LlanC), E Treharne (Pon), RDG Williams (New).
Attendance: 'large'   *Referee*: AG Guillemard (England)

Saturday 19 March 1881 at Raeburn Place, Edinburgh
SCOTLAND 1 goal, 1 try *Back*: TA Begbie (EdinW, c). *Half-backs*: WE Maclagan (EdinA), NJ Finlay (EdinA), RC Mackenzie (GlasA). *Quarter-backs*: JA Campbell (GlasA), AR Don-Wauchope (CamU). *Forwards*: R Ainslie (EdinIFP), T Ainslie (EdinIFP), JB Brown (GlasA, t), JW Fraser (EdinIFP), JHS Graham (capt, EdinA), D McCowan (WoS), R Maitland (EdinIFP), WA Peterkin (EdinU), C Reid (EdinAy).
ENGLAND 1 goal, 1 try *Back*: AN Hornby (Man). *Three-quarters*: R Hunt (Man), L Stokes (capt, Black, dg). *Half-backs*: HC Rowley (Man, t), FT Wright (Man). *Forwards*: A Budd (Black), GW Burton (Black), CH Coates (Lee), CWL Fernandes (Lee), H Fowler (OxfU), C Gurdon (Rich), ET Gurdon (Rich), WW Hewitt (QH), C Phillips (BirkPk), H Vassall (MarlN/OxfU).
Attendance: 12,000   *Referee*: DH Watson (Scotland)

Jimmy Dodd of Halifax made 31 Yorkshire appearances and represented the North. *Athletic News, 1888*

1881-1882

ASSOCIATION GAINS GROUND IN THE NORTH-EAST
Rugby, hitherto the dominant football code in the north-east of England was, in the words of the *Northern Echo* correspondent, under threat: 'Not so many years ago the game, as played under Association rules, was almost unknown in the North of England, but lately a great amount of success has attended it, and there are now at least twenty-five clubs in Durham and Northumberland. Not only has the number of players, now estimated at nearly 1,500, rapidly increased, but the interest taken by spectators may be said to have risen in a like proportion, and at the good matches spectators may be counted by hundreds.'[34]

CUMBERLAND NOT REPRESENTATIVE
Four years on from complaints that the Cumberland county team was based around the Carlisle club came renewed accusations, only this time aimed at Whitehaven. Following Cumberland's heavy defeat to Northumberland by five goals and five tries to nil at Burdon Terrace, Newcastle, on 3rd December, several irate letters were published in the Carlisle press including one from 'Half-back of Cockermouth F. C.', who wrote: 'This match was not played between Northumberland and Cumberland, but between Northumberland and Whitehaven. The [Cumberland] team consisted of eleven of the Whitehaven team, two from Maryport, and two from Aspatria [and] representatives from the following towns were not asked to assist: Carlisle, Cockermouth, Keswick and Workington. In fact the secretaries of those clubs did not know anything about the match till it was over. This is a disgraceful state of things. If the

Whitehaven secretary had politely sent a note to the secretaries of those clubs, there is no doubt Cumberland would have been represented by a different set of men to that which went to Newcastle.'[35]

LANCASHIRE COUNTY CLUB FOUNDED

The Lancashire County Club was founded by 16 clubs at the Albion Hotel, Manchester, on 22nd December. This came about after the Manchester Football Club had sent out a circular inviting clubs to attend a meeting at the same hotel on 16th December 'for the purpose of considering a scheme on the basis of which the Manchester Football Club is prepared to hand over the management of county affairs to a society to be called the Lancashire County Football Club'.[36] That was clearly an attempt to heal the rift that had existed between the Manchester club and the Lancashire County Union since the latter's formation the previous May. Following that initial meeting (16th December) the creation of the new Lancashire County Club was confirmed (22nd December) when the county's two premier clubs – Manchester and Liverpool – united with Birch, Bolton, Broughton, Broughton Rangers, Cheetham, Cheetham Hill, Free Wanderers (Manchester), Manchester Athletic, Manchester Rangers, Oldham, Rochdale Hornets, Salford, Swinton, and Walton.

THE NORTH COUNTRY CANTABS

Cheshire entertained the curiously named North Country Cantabs at the St Ann's Ground, Birkenhead, on Wednesday 11th January, winning by a comfortable one goal and four tries to nil. The Cantabs were a touring side made up of leading Cambridge University players, referred to in match reports as the 'Light Blues'.[37]

THE NORTH TAKES ON WALES

The North (of England), having met the South on eight occasions, took on Wales at Newport on 14th January, winning by one goal to one try. Wales had played its inaugural international the previous season, losing heavily to England at Blackheath.

YORKSHIRE CUP OBJECTIONS

Following the opening round of the Yorkshire Cup, three objections were raised as to the eligibility of opposition players. Farsley complained that Bramley had been assisted by Flynn of Leeds Rangers, and Woodhead of Pudsey. Barnsley cited opponents Hope Foundry for the use of Watson and Dawson, two retired members of Leeds St John's, who they claimed were ineligible. Dewsbury Shamrocks disputed the legality of the Hipperholme and Lightcliffe club in selecting Tyas Wood, Albert Wood and Jimmy Lockhead, three well-known Halifax players. Bramley and Hope Foundry were found not guilty but Hipperholme and Lightcliffe was disqualified, Dewsbury Shamrocks progressing to the next round.[38]

1881-1882 STATISTICS

DURHAM COUNTY CHALLENGE CUP (10 entries)
Most goals wins. If equal, most tries. If still equal, majority of 3 minor points.

First Round
Durham City 0, Houghton-le-Spring 2t
Hartlepool Rovers 2t, Westoe 2g, 2t
North Durham 1g, Sunderland Rovers 2t
Ryton 2t, Hartlepools 0
Sunderland 2t, Darlington 0

Second Round
North Durham 1t, Westoe 5g, 2t
Sunderland 1t, Houghton-le-Spring 0
(replay ordered after protest)
Bye: Ryton

Second Round Replay
Sunderland 1t, Houghton-le-Spring 2t

Third Round (semi-final)
Houghton-le-Spring 0, Ryton 0 (mp: 6-1)
Bye: Westoe

FINAL
Saturday 1 April 1882 at Chester Road, Sunderland
HOUGHTON-LE-SPRING 1 try *Back*: N Meiklejohn. *Three-quarters*: GF Moore, GH Brown, EA Crow. *Half-backs*: AT Crow (capt), TM Jamieson. *Forwards*: T Burton, W Coxon, T Elstob, W Forster (t), R Leary, W Nicholson, T Potts, JT Todd, T Todd.
WESTOE 0 *Back*: HW Sample. *Three-quarters*: TF Wilson (capt), WH Wilson, HG Crosthwaite. *Half-backs*: CR Green, JJ Ker. *Forwards*: TT Anderson, HB Buckland, RF Crosthwaite, WW Crosthwaite, HL Green, DU Law, C Ward, CE White, WS Young.
After extra time   *Attendance*: 'large'   *Referee*: W Crozier (Durham City)

NORTHUMBERLAND COUNTY FOOTBALL CHALLENGE CUP (7 entries)
Most goals wins. If equal, most tries. If still equal, majority of 3 minor points.

First Round
Gosforth 0, Tynemouth 2g
Northern 1t, Tynedale 0
Northumberland FC 1g, 5t, North Elswick 0
Bye: Percy Park

Second Round (semi-finals)
Northern 1t, Tynemouth 0
Northumberland FC 1t, Percy Park 0

FINAL
Saturday 18 February 1882 at Burdon Terrace, Newcastle
NORTHERN 1 goal, 3 tries *Backs*: JVW Rutherford, JW Swinburne. *Three-quarters*:
E Liddell, J May (capt, t). *Half-backs*: H Saunders, H Symington (t). *Forwards*: G Maitland,
GA Mason, A Mursell, S Reid, W Ridley, D Ross (t), J Warwick, CE Winship (t),
WA Winship.
NORTHUMBERLAND FC 0 *Back*: FS Strickland. *Three-quarters*: JG Burdon, SF Prest (capt).
Half-backs: A Cadle, W Farr. *Forwards*: R Blunt, A Eichholtz, F Marshall, CR Pattinson,
HL Pattinson, JS Pattinson, RM Richardson, B Shaw, SB Tritton, WS Williams.
Attendance: 3,000   *Referee*: PB Junor (Durham)
Note: Scorer of Northern conversion not reported.

YORKSHIRE COUNTY FOOTBALL CHALLENGE CUP (32 entries)
Most goals wins. If equal, most tries. If still equal, majority of 3 minor points.

First Round
Batley 4t, Hull 0
Bierley 1t, Headingley 0
Dewsbury Shamrocks 2t, Hipperholme and Lightcliffe 1g, 1t (awarded to Dewsbury
Shamrocks after protest)
Farsley 0, Bramley 0 (mp: 1-3, aet)
Halifax Free Wanderers 1g, Mirfield 1g, 2t
Heckmondwike 2t, Castleford 0
Hope Foundry (Leeds) 1t, Barnsley 1t (mp: 6-0)
Horbury 1g, 1t, Bradford 1t
Keighley 0, Wakefield Trinity 1g, 3t
Leeds Parish Church 0, Harrogate 0 (mp: 1-0, aet)
Leeds St John's 0, Ossett 1t
Manningham 1g, 3t, Gildersome and Morley 0
Otley 0, Kirkstall 1t
Salterhebble 4t, Mytholmroyd 0
Selby 0, Cleckheaton 1t
Thornes 3g, 3t, Shipley 0

First Round Replays
Bramley 1g, 2t, Farsley 0
Harrogate 1g, 1t, Leeds Parish Church 0
Second Round
Batley 0, Kirkstall 1g, 1t
Bramley 0, Thornes 3g, 1t
Cleckheaton 2t, Mirfield 1t
Harrogate 0, Manningham 0 (mp: 4-3, aet)
Hope Foundry 0, Wakefield Trinity 7g, 3t
Horbury 1g, 1t, Bierley 1t
Ossett 1g, Heckmondwike 0
Salterhebble 0, Dewsbury Shamrocks 0 (mp: 2-3, aet)

Second Round Replays
Dewsbury Shamrocks 0, Salterhebble 1g, 1t
Manningham 1g, 1t, Harrogate 1g

Third Round
Horbury 2t, Cleckheaton 1g
Kirkstall 1g, 6t, Manningham 0
Thornes 2g, 2t, Ossett 0
Wakefield Trinity 1g, 6t, Salterhebble 1t

Semi-finals
Thornes 2t, Kirkstall 0
Wakefield Trinity 1g, 2t, Cleckheaton 1g

FINAL
Saturday 1 April 1882 at Cardigan Fields, Leeds
THORNES 1 goal *Back*: E Varley. *Three-quarters*: J Fothergill (capt), H Wigglesworth (pg).
Half-backs: H Dawson, TH Sampson. *Forwards*: JW Dawson, G Dobson, F Evans,
G Fawcett, T Harrison, A Horner, TW Kitson, JA Liddington, J Simpson, A Whiteley.
WAKEFIELD TRINITY 1 try *Back*: A Hayley. *Three-quarters*: CE Brartram, H Hayley,
G Jubb. *Half-backs*: JH Cuthbert, H Hutchinson. *Forwards*: W Ellis, W Jackson, J Jubb,
B Kilner (capt), JW Kilner, F Mawer, EJ Spink, G Steele, WG Thompson (t).
Attendance: 5,000   *Referee*: HWT Garnett (Bradford)

COUNTY MATCHES

Saturday 12 November 1881 at Cardigan Fields, Leeds
YORKSHIRE 2 goals, 3 tries *Backs*: J Dodd (Hal). *Three-quarters*: TL Scarborough (Hal,
dg), CE Bartram (Wak), A Newsome (Dew). *Half-backs*: E Buckley (Hal, dg), S Mortimer
(Dew, t). *Forwards*: GW Bottomley (Hud), WK Fisher (Dew), G Harrison (YorksW),
Fred Huth (Hud, t), B Kilner (Wak, t), J Lockhead (Hal), JW Marshall (Brad), B Schofield
(Hud), GT Thomson (capt, Hal).
DURHAM 0 *Back*: TF Wilson (Wes). *Three-quarters*: O Thompson (Sund), W Taylor (Hart),
F Oliver (Ryton). *Half-backs*: JJ Ker (Wes), F Robson (SundR). *Forwards*: HB Buckland
(Wes), RF Crosthwaite (Wes), W Crozier (DurC), W Dickinson (Sund), A Hill (Hart),
J Laing (Sund), RE Reed (Sund), JW Sowerby (capt, NDur), JT Todd (Hou).
Attendance: 4,000   *Referee*: HWT Garnett (Yorkshire)

Saturday 19 November 1881 at Whalley Range, Manchester
LANCASHIRE 2 goals, 6 tries *Back*: AN Hornby (capt, Man, t, 2c). *Three-quarters*:
E Beswick (Swi, 3t), CM Sawyer (Bro, t). *Half-backs*: T Deane (Bro), JH Payne (Bro).
Forwards: T Blatherwick (Man), WS Butterworth (RochH), CH Horley (Swi), WS Hulse
(ManFW, t), JT Hunt (Man), AB Rowley (Man), HC Rowley (Man, t), JW Schofield (Man),
RL Seddon (Bro), E Wood (Che, t).
CHESHIRE 0 *Back*: H Maxwell (NewB). *Three-quarters*: PF Shaw (NewB), R Wood
(BirkPk), WE Coubrough (NewB). *Half-backs*: AC Blain (BirkPk), WN Fletcher (Mar).
Forwards: W Andrew (Mar), BS Atkinson (NewB), F Barlow (Mar), EA Beazley (BirkPk),
DA Bingham (BirkPk), HD Hulme (Mar), JWH Thorp (Macc), W Turner (Mar),
R Twyford (Con).
Attendance: 3,500   *Referee*: WH Hutchinson (Yorkshire)

Saturday, 19 November 1881 at Aston Lower Grounds, Birmingham
MIDLAND COUNTIES 0 *Back*: EW Piper (Leam). *Three-quarters*: G Ratliff (Cov), JR Deykin (Edg), J Wilson (Edg). *Half-backs*: WW Cassells (Burt), SH Evershed (Burt). *Forwards*: CA Crane (Wolv), CD Currie (Strat), JJ Gover (Edg), JF Hunt (Burt), HF Keep (Rush), CR Radclyffe (Edg), WH Rawlinson (Leam), A Stewart-Brown (Leam), E Worthington (Leic).
YORKSHIRE 3 goals, 3 tries *Backs*: HB Wilson (Hud, dg). *Three-quarters*: A Newsome (Dew, t, c), CE Bartram (Wak, 2t, dg), G Jubb (Wak). *Half-backs*: F Bonsor (Brad), PF Holmes (Hud). *Forwards*: GW Bottomley (Hud), WK Fisher (Dew), Fred Huth (Hud), B Kilner (Wak), B Schofield (Hud), AC Sharpe (Hud), T Stericker (Brad), GT Thomson (capt, Hal, t), W Watson (LeeStJ).
Attendance: 1,000   *Referee*: EB Holmes (Midland Counties)

Saturday 26 November 1881 at Hanson Lane, Halifax
YORKSHIRE 0 *Backs*: J Dodd (Hal). *Three-quarters*: TL Scarborough (Hal), CE Bartram (Wak), A Newsome (Dew). *Half-backs*: E Buckley (Hal), PF Holmes (Hud). *Forwards*: GW Bottomley (Hud), CH Coates (YorksW), EH Dykes (LeePC), G Harrison (YorksW), B Kilner (Wak), J Lockhead (Hal), JW Marshall (Brad), T Stericker (Brad), GT Thomson (capt, Hal).
LANCASHIRE 0 *Back*: AN Hornby (capt, Man). *Three-quarters*: E Beswick (Swi), R Hunt (Man), CM Sawyer (Bro). *Half-backs*: JH Payne (Bro), HC Rowley (Man). *Forwards*: JA Brodie (Walton), WS Butterworth (RochH), JB Cooke (ManFW), CH Horley (Swi), WS Hulse (ManFW), JT Hunt (Man), AB Rowley (Man), JH Wilson (Man), E Wood (Che).
Attendance: 10,000   *Referee*: PB Junor (Durham)

Saturday 3 December 1881 at Burdon Terrace, Newcastle
NORTHUMBERLAND 5 goals, 5 tries *Back*: FS Strickland (NorFC). *Three-quarters*: SF Prest (NorFC, t), GD Fawcus (Tynm), JW Rutherford (Nor, 5c). *Half-backs*: J McConnell (PerPk, t), H Symington (Nor, 3t). *Forwards*: JG Burdon (NorFC), A Cadle (NorFC, t), T Hadley (Tynd), G Maitland (Nor, t), F Marshall (NorFC), JS Pattinson (NorFC), RH Robb (Tynd, 3t), D Ross (Nor), CE Winship (Nor).
CUMBERLAND 0 *Back*: Sharpe (Mary). *Three-quarters*: AC Challoner (Nor), S Palmer (Whi), Nicholson (Mary). *Half-backs*: WH Alderson (Whi), RY Sutton (Whi). *Forwards*: Carruthers (Mary), Collins (Whi), T Dobie (Asp), J Doran (Whi), JE Eddis (Whi), JC Hellon (Whi), W Hursthwaite (Whi), W Thompson (Asp), J Tyson (Whi).
Attendance: 500   *Referee*: n/a
Note: A. C. Challoner (Northern) replaced a Cumberland player who did not arrive.

Wednesday 11 January 1882 at St Annes Ground, Birkenhead
CHESHIRE 1 goal, 4 tries *Back*: W Rome (NewB). *Three-quarters*: PF Shaw (capt, NewB, c), WE Coubrough (NewB), AC Blain (BirkPk). *Half-backs*: G Cowie (BirkPk), HS Patterson (NewB). *Forwards*: W Andrew (Mar), DA Bingham (BirkPk), H Court (BirkPk), LF Potts (NewB, t), HJ Ryalls (NewB, t), W Turner (Mar), R Twyford (Con, 2t), JR Wilson (BirkPk, t).
NORTH COUNTRY CANTABS 0 *Backs*: PH Clifford, H Lewis. *Three-quarters*: A Durandu, A Wilson. *Half-backs*: BS Biram, A St H Gibbons (capt). *Forwards*: J Bushby, HS Cliff, J Gilmore, WER Littledale, R Threlfall, HS Timmis, GA Webster, A Whitehead, CM Wilson.
Attendance: n/a   *Referee*: n/a
Note: One unnamed Cheshire forward reported as 'A N Other'.

Milestones & Stats 1869-1901 73

Saturday 21 January 1882 at Burdon Terrace, Newcastle
NORTHUMBERLAND 0 *Back*: EB Brutton (Tynm). *Three-quarters*: JW Rutherford (Nor), SF Prest (capt, NorFC), T Robson (Tynd). *Half-backs*: J McConnell (PerPk), H Symington (Nor). *Forwards*: JW Coward (PerPk), G Maitland (Nor), F Marshall (NorFC), G Mason (Nor), S Oliver (Tynm), JS Pattinson (NorFC), RH Robb (Tynd), D Ross (Nor), J Walton (Tynm).
YORKSHIRE 1 goal *Back*: H Wade (LeeStJ, c). *Three-quarters*: G Jubb (Wak), FT Ritchie (Brad), C Chadwick (Dew). *Half-backs*: F Bonsor (Brad), JH Potter (LeeStJ). *Forwards*: F Cookson (Kirk), JH Crossland (Hal), G Harrison (capt, YorksW), J Lockhead (Hal), JW Marshall (Brad), JB Ogden (LeeStJ), R Petty (York), EJ Spink (Wak, t), T Stericker (Brad).
Attendance: 2,000/3,000   *Referee*: Dr JG Robertson (Durham)

Saturday 4 February 1882 at Corstorphine, Edinburgh
EDINBURGH UNIVERSITY 1 goal, 3 tries *Back*: J Clegg (t, c). *Half-backs*: H Brooks, F Hunter (t). *Quarter-backs*: GF Chadwick, WK Morton. *Forwards*: F Abraham (t), WTC Barrett, GB Batten, W Davidson, JF Griffin, CG Guthrie, LC Haslip, RSF Henderson (capt), LC Keep (t), J Tod.
NORTHUMBERLAND 0 *Back*: FS Strickland (NorFC). *Three-quarters*: SF Prest (NorFC), E Liddell (Nor), T Robson (Tynd). *Half-backs*: JT Dodd (Tynd), H Symington (Nor). *Forwards*: A Cadle (NorFC), HF Calder, JW Coward (PerPk), HE Jones (NorFC), D Mansell (NorFC), F Marshall (NorFC), G Mason (Nor), S Oliver (Tynm), JS Pattinson (NorFC).
Attendance: n/a   *Referee*: n/a.
Note: HF Calder (club not identified) replaced Northumberland player who missed train.

Saturday 25 February 1882 at St Annes Ground, Birkenhead
CHESHIRE 1 try *Back*: WE Coubrough (NewB). *Three-quarters*: PF Shaw (NewB), W Rome (NewB), H Williamson (Sal/Sale). *Half-backs*: HS Patterson (NewB), SE Pullen (NewB). *Forwards*: G Cowie (BirkPk), E Crawley (BirkPk), HD Hulme (Mar), FW Huntington (NewB), BB Middleton (BirkPk, t), HJ Ryalls (NewB), H Sinclair (Mar), JWH Thorp (Macc), JR Wilson (BirkPk).
YORKSHIRE 1 goal *Backs*: H Wade (LeeStJ). *Three-quarters*: CE Bartram (Wak), A Newsome (Dew, dg), FT Ritchie (Brad). *Half-backs*: E Buckley (Hal), PF Holmes (Hud). *Forwards*: GW Bottomley (Hud), T Chambers (Hal), WK Fisher (Dew), WE Hanson (Dew), W Jackson (Wak), TP Peacock (LeeStJ), R Petty (York), GT Thomson (capt, Hal), W Watson (LeeStJ).
Attendance: 3,000   *Referee*: J MacLaren (RFU Vice-President)

Saturday 25 February 1882 at Chester Road, Sunderland
DURHAM 0 *Back*: WC Wetherell (DurC). *Three-quarters*: WA Kidson (Sund), O Thompson (Sund), TM Jamieson (Hou). *Half-backs*: JJ Ker (Wes), F Robson (SundR). *Forwards*: HB Buckland (Wes), RF Crosthwaite (Wes), G Dickinson, W Dickinson (Sund), J Fowles (Sund), A Hill (Hart), RE Reed (Sund), JW Sowerby (capt, NDur), JT Todd (Hou).
NORTHUMBERLAND 0 *Back*: JW Swinburne (Nor). *Three-quarters*: T Robson (capt, Tynd), JT Dodd (Tynd), EB Brutton (Tynm). *Half-backs*: J McConnell (PerPk), H Symington (Nor). *Forwards*: Dunn, S Oliver (Tynm), CR Pattinson (NorFC), GW Ridley (Nor), RH Robb (Tynd), D Ross (Nor), G Steward, J Warwick (Nor), CE Winship (Nor).
Attendance: 2,500   *Referee*: A Laing (Durham)
Note: Clubs not identified G. Dickinson (Durham); Dunn, G. Steward (Northumberland).

Saturday 25 March 1882 at The Butts, Coventry
MIDLAND COUNTIES 1 try *Back*: H Phillips (Wolv, t). *Three-quarters*: G Fowler (Mose), A Smith (Mose), HV Hasluck (Mose), W Hasluck (Mose). *Half-backs*: R Child (Cov), F Reeve (Mose). *Forwards*: CE Cobb (Edg), CA Crane (Wolv), CD Currie (Strat), GM Day (Burt), P Evershed (Burt), JJ Gover (capt, Edg), AJ Otter (Mose), E Worthington (Leic).
LANCASHIRE 1 goal, 3 tries *Back*: WW Higgins (Che). *Three-quarters*: E Beswick (Swi, t), JW Hulse (ManFW, t), F Bagshaw (ManR). *Half-backs*: J Mills (Swi, c), AH Wrigley (Liv). *Forwards*: JB Cooke (ManFW), W Dickenson (Swi), CH Horley (Swi), WS Hulse (ManFW), JT Hunt (capt, Man), J Kneen (Che, t), JP Pattinson (Man), AS Roberts (Che), R Seddon (Swi, t).
Attendance: 3,500   *Referee*: EB Holmes (Midland Counties)

ENGLAND TRIAL MATCH

Saturday 3 December 1881 at Fartown, Huddersfield
NORTH 1 goal, 1 try *Back*: J Dodd (Hal). *Three-quarters*: CE Bartram (Wak, t, c), E Beswick (Swi), CM Sawyer (Bro). *Half-backs*: JH Payne (Bro), HC Rowley (Man). *Forwards*: JA Brodie (Walton), CH Coates (YorksW), JT Hunt (Man, t), JW Marshall (Brad), BB Middleton (BirkPk), JJ Ravenscroft (BirkPk), T Stericker (Brad), GT Thomson (capt, Hal), E Wood (Che).
SOUTH 0 *Backs*: GB Mills (Walth), AS Taylor (CamU). *Three-quarters*: AM Evanson (OxfU), CM Wilkins (MarlN). *Half-backs*: HH Taylor (Black), HT Twynam (Rich). *Forwards*: HG Fuller (CamU), C Gurdon (Rich), ET Gurdon (capt, Rich), WW Hewitt (QH), PA Newton (Black), A Spurling (Black), WM Tatham (MarlN/OxfU), H Vassall (MarlN/OxfU), JI Ward (Rich).
Attendance: 7,000/8,000   *Referee*: J MacLaren (RFU Vice-President)

REPRESENTATIVE MATCH

Saturday 14 January 1882 at Rodney Parade, Newport
WALES 1 try *Backs*: SS Clark (Nea), WD Phillips (Car). *Three-quarters*: CH Newman (capt, New), GF Harding (New). *Half-backs*: WB Norton (Car), J Bridie (New), WF Evans (Rhymney). *Forwards*: TGS Clapp (Nan), BE Girling (Car), R Gould (New), CP Lewis (LlanC), FT Purdon (New), E Treharne (Pon, t), TB Jones (New), T Williams (Car).
NORTH 1 goal *Back*: R Wood (BirkPk). *Three-quarters*: CE Bartram (Wak, c), E Beswick (Swi), A Newsome (Dew). *Half-backs*: JH Payne (capt, Bro), WR Richardson (Man). *Forwards*: GW Bottomley (Hud), WS Hulse (ManFW), JT Hunt (Man, t), F Huth (Hud), JW Marshall (Brad), BB Middleton (BirkPk), HC Rowley (Man), JWH Thorp (Macc), E Wood (Che).
Attendance: 5,000   *Referee*: JD Miller (Gloucestershire)

INTERNATIONAL MATCHES

Monday 6 February 1882 at Lansdowne Road, Dublin
IRELAND 2 tries *Back*: RB Walkington (NIFC). *Half-backs*: RE McLean (DubU), EJ Wolfe (Arm), WW Pike (King). *Quarter-backs*: GC Bent (DubU), M Johnston (DubU, t). *Forwards*: WEA Cummins (Cork), AJ Forrest (Wand), RW Hughes (NIFC), TR Johnson-Smyth (Lans), JA Macdonald (MethC), HB Morell (DubU), R Nelson (QCB), OS Stokes (Cork Bankers, t), JW Taylor (capt, NIFC).
ENGLAND 2 tries *Back*: AH Hornby (Man). *Three-quarters*: E Beswick (Swi), WN Bolton (Black, t), R Hunt (Man, t). *Half-backs*: HC Rowley (Man), HT Twynam (Rich). *Forwards*: HG Fuller (Bath), C Gurdon (capt, Rich), WW Hewitt (QH), JT Hunt (Man), BB Middleton (BirkPk), A Spurling (Black), GT Thomson (Hal), H Vassall (MarlN/OxfU), JI Ward (Rich).
Attendance: 5,000   *Referee*: WC Neville (Ireland)

Saturday 4 March 1882 at Whalley Range, Manchester
ENGLAND 0 *Back*: AH Hornby (capt, Man). *Three-quarters*: E Beswick (Swi), WN Bolton (Black). *Half-backs*: JH Payne (Bro), HH Taylor (Black). *Forwards*: CH Coates (YorksW), HG Fuller (Bath), C Gurdon (Rich), ET Gurdon (Rich), JT Hunt (Man), PA Newton (Black), HC Rowley (Man), WM Tatham (MarlN/OxfU), GT Thomson (Hal), H Vassall (MarlN/OxfU).
SCOTLAND 2 tries *Back*: JP Veitch (RHSFP). *Half-backs*: WE Maclagan (EdinA), A Philp (EdinIFP). *Quarter-backs*: WS Brown (EdinIFP), AR Don-Wauchope (CamU). *Forwards*: R Ainslie (EdinIFP, 2t), T Ainslie (EdinIFP), JB Brown (GlasA), DY Cassels (capt, WoS), D McCowan (WoS), R Maitland (EdinIFP), C Reid (EdinA), A Walker (WoS), JG Walker (WoS), WA Walls (GlasA).
Attendance: 16,000   *Referee*: HL Robinson (Ireland)

Fred Bonsor of Bradford made 32 Yorkshire appearances, also representing the North and England. *Athletic News, 1888*

1882-1883

HULL KINGSTON ROVERS
Kingston Amateurs founded this season and renamed Kingston Rovers in 1885, evolving into the more familiar Hull Kingston Rovers around 1890.

FOOTBALL: THE NATIONAL WINTER PASTIME
As the 1882-83 season began, the *Manchester Guardian* provided an interesting summation of the state of affairs in the world of football: 'The popularity of the game of football is more pronounced year by year, the season which has just commenced bidding fair to be the busiest on record.

In the North of England, Lancashire, Yorkshire, Cheshire, Northumberland, Cumberland, Durham, Staffordshire and the Midland Counties, and in the South, Middlesex, Surrey, Kent, Norfolk, Suffolk, Gloucestershire, Somersetshire, and Devonshire have arranged inter-county matches, and so universally is the game played from one end of the kingdom to the other that it may fairly be called the national winter pastime.

Footballers are divided into two distinct organisations, Rugby Union and Association, a player seldom being found expert at both games. The Universities of Oxford and Cambridge and most of the public schools practice both styles of play, but, as a rule, the two organisations do not flourish in the same locality, and it will be found that where Rugby Union clubs are strong those who play the Association game are weak, and vice versa. In Manchester and district, for instance, the former [Rugby] is almost exclusively played, whilst in East Lancashire the dribbling game [Association] only is cared for. In Yorkshire also it will be found that in

Sheffield the Association holds entire sway, the opposite being the case in Huddersfield, Halifax, Wakefield, etc.'[39]

THE ROLE OF THE UMPIRE
A continuing theme, especially in club matches – and cup-ties in particular – was the number of disputes over decisions that often resulted in appeals being referred to a committee who had the power to overturn a result or order a replay. The *Manchester Guardian* commented that 'among the most unsatisfactory features of football are the frequency of disputes and the reluctance and disfavour with which at times the decisions of umpires and referees are received. The question of umpires is one that has been freely discussed during the past season in connection with the kindred game of cricket, and pretty much the same objection applies to both games; the inadvisability of choosing persons interested in the success of the teams engaged. The remedy appears to consist in appointing – either from those present or by pre-arrangement – well known and competent past or present players, entirely disinterested [in the clubs involved], who from pure love of the game are in most localities generally to be found willing to undertake the responsible posts of umpires and referees'.

The introduction of referees in 1875-76 had not resolved the problem and some matches went ahead with just two umpires, such as the Lancashire versus Yorkshire fixture on 17th January 1880, a fiercely disputed encounter that prompted the *Leeds Mercury* to state 'there was no referee but there ought to have been one'.[40]

WENDING THEIR WAY TO THE GROUNDS
At a time when pedestrianism was often the best means of local transport, one scribe made an interesting observation about the coming and going of footballers on match day, stating 'Saturday last found footballers busy in all directions, the suburbs of Manchester literally swarming with groups of young men, easily recognised by their Gladstone bags or attire, wending their way to the various football grounds'.[41] On the day referred to, 14th October, several prominent matches took place in the area including Manchester's final club trial at Whalley Range, (Manchester) Free Wanderers versus Huddersfield at Fallowfield, and Manchester Athletic hosting Wavertree in Alexandra Park.

GIVE IT A TRY
The imbalance in scoring that gave tries a secondary role to goals was starting to be challenged. The *Manchester Guardian* noted: 'In the early days

of the Rugby Union game, goals only were counted, and any number of tries had no effect on the result. It will, however, be evident to anyone who takes an interest in the game that in the getting of tries lies the real strength, and that kicking a goal from a favourable "place" is a comparatively easy matter, whilst to drop a goal from the field partakes of the nature of chance as often as not. It is, therefore, manifestly unjust that a goal, particularly if dropped, should outweigh any number of tries. Attempts have been made to induce the Rugby Union to adopt a system of counting by points, but a strong conservative feeling exists in that body, and beyond agreeing, in 1876, to allow tries to decide a game in the event of goals being equal, the efforts made to induce them to adopt a reasonable and logical system of scoring has been unsuccessful.'[42]

SELECTING THE LANCASHIRE TEAM

The *Manchester Guardian* gave guarded approval to the new Lancashire County Club stating 'until last year the Manchester club had full and entire control of all appertaining to Lancashire county football, but as the game developed and advanced in popularity protests were loudly raised by other strong and powerful clubs in the county against that state of affairs continuing, and the result has been the formation of a Lancashire County Club. On Monday last [30th October] the Committee selected the Lancashire team to meet the Midland Counties, and little objection can be taken to their choice. It would have been the wiser course, perhaps, to follow the example of Yorkshire and Cheshire, and to have organised a series of trial matches, thereby attaining the twofold object of accustoming the players to each other's peculiarities, and enabling the Committee to make their selection after testing the ability of the aspirants to county honours in a practical manner'.[43]

FIVE TRIES TO NONE NOT ENOUGH

After Yorkshire defeated Lancashire by five tries to nil at Whalley Range on 25th November, the *Manchester Guardian* renewed its criticism of the scoring system: '[Teddy] Bartram [Yorkshire] was somewhat disappointing, his attempts at goal especially not coming up to expectations. One of his place kicks was in a very good position, and that five tries should be obtained without a goal being registered is surprising. A lucky goal by the losers would have turned a crushing defeat into a victory, and shows forcibly the necessity for accurate kicking at goal, and the ridiculousness of the present value put on the winning points.'[44] Bartram redeemed himself in Yorkshire's next match, his try and two drop goals – one from the centre of the field – helping defeat Northumberland at Cardigan Fields, Leeds, during February.

CUMBERLAND COUNTY UNION FOUNDED

The Cumberland County (Rugby) Football Club was founded on 2nd December during a meeting at the Golden Hotel in Maryport, its committee to consist of one representative from each club. It was agreed they would arrange county games and administer the new (Cumberland) Challenge Cup.[45] An earlier meeting had taken place on 25th October at the Station Hotel, Workington, when six clubs had been represented; Aspatria, Keswick, Maryport, Whitehaven, Workington and Eden Wanderers (the latter sending a letter of intent). It appears to have been organised in an effort to improve co-operation amongst the clubs, although Carlisle did not attend. None of the press reports that referred to the 25th October meeting mentioned the possible founding of a county club, although it was reported that they arranged a match with Northumberland – which took place on 11th November – 'the proceeds of which are to be appropriated for the purchase of a silver challenge cup worthy of the county and district'.[46]

THE UNOFFICIAL CHAMPIONSHIP

What is now looked upon as the first international rugby championship began during this season when Wales met England in Swansea on 16th December. Initially embracing the four home nations, the concept of it being a championship was not officially endorsed and, as such, there was no table published until *The Times* produced what is thought to be the first on 16th March 1896. Nonetheless, the so-called International Rugby Championship remained unofficial throughout the Victorian era and beyond, although several publications have, retrospectively, produced tables and lists of 'winners'.

THE NORTHUMBERLAND CUP GAINS POPULARITY

The third Northumberland Cup final was contested by Tynemouth and Tynedale at the Burdon Terrace Ground, Newcastle, on 17th March, and interest in the competition was evidently growing. It was decided to play the match in four quarters of 20 minutes each and, during the second period, as the *Shields Daily News* reported: 'The excitement among the spectators was intense, and the pressure from the crowd having broken the wire roping, it was with the utmost difficulty that the police and committee could keep the spectators off the field of play. A few minutes before time someone in the crowd called "time," and in an instant the ground was covered with spectators, and a considerable delay took place before it could again be cleared. During the whole of the last period it was with the very greatest difficulty that the ground could be kept clear, and from the number of spectators present and the intense interest taken in the game, it is remarkably evident that since the [Northumberland] Cup was first played for, the Rugby game has become very popular indeed.'[47]

YORKSHIRE CUP SEMI-FINAL DISPUTE

At the Yorkshire County meeting on Monday 2nd April, Dewsbury was disqualified for playing a non *bona fide* member in their semi-final 'win' over Halifax on Saturday 31st March. The player concerned was J. Hampton Jones of the Walton (Liverpool) club. The news caused disruptions in Dewsbury, the *Dewsbury Reporter* stating that 'on Tuesday night [3rd April] over 4,000 persons assembled in front of the Man and Saddle Hotel [the club headquarters] when the appearance of Mr. Mark Newsome [team captain] and his brother [Alf] on the balcony was a signal for an outburst of cheering'. Although he had 'little to tell them' he did say 'they had lodged an objection against Barratt of the Halifax club', adding the county committee would meet next evening [Wednesday] to consider the claim. A reported 8,000 appeared outside the same hotel on Wednesday night when 'the cheering of the crowd was something tremendous' as they was told the match would be replayed. Halifax, although found not guilty in the case of Barratt, had offered to replay the match, the accusation against Jones and Dewsbury being upheld. Halifax won the rematch in which, in addition to the ban on Jones, Alf and Mark Newsome declined to play for Dewsbury in protest. Due to the replay, the final was delayed one week.[48]

THE MISSING PLAYER

When Lancashire travelled to Newcastle to play Northumberland on 14th April, it led to a tiresome journey and a missing player. The *Athletic News* related the tale: 'The announcement made a week or two ago that a county match had been arranged for last Saturday came as a great surprise, as the Rugby season for matches of such importance was supposed to be over. The team selected by the Lancashire Committee was considered a remarkably good one, but several of the players chosen found it inconvenient to take part in the match, and struck out their names accordingly. A special saloon was attached to the 6.30 pm train from Manchester on Friday evening for the convenience of the Lancashire players, and the only incident on the outward journey to the banks of the Tyne was the sudden strange disappearance of one of the Lancashire team at Leeds. The Walton representative [R. Wilcock] was spirited away in a mysterious manner; but to the great relief of the [Lancashire] captain [John Payne], the lost player turned up safe and sound at Thirsk, his reappearance being hailed with tremendous cheering. Newcastle was reached after a somewhat tiresome journey of nearly seven hours, and the Lancastrians were glad to retire to rest at the Douglas Hotel.' One of the Lancashire players who had withdrawn was J. Hampton Jones of Walton who 'evidently acting under instructions from Yorkshire, refused to play'. Just over a week previous, he had been the central figure in Dewsbury's Yorkshire Cup disqualification.[49]

HUNSLET FOUNDED

Hunslet was founded on 21st May as the football section of the Hunslet Cricket and Football Club through the amalgamation of Hunslet Albion and Leeds Excelsior.

1882-1883 STATISTICS

CUMBERLAND COUNTY CHALLENGE CUP (7 entries)
Most goals wins. If equal, most tries. If still equal, majority of 3 minor points.

First Round
Aspatria w/o Keswick
Ellensiders (Maryport) 0, Cockermouth 1g, 1t
Whitehaven w/o Eden Wanderers (Carlisle)
Bye: Workington

Semi-finals
Aspatria 2g, Cockermouth 0 (at Workington)
Whitehaven 2g, 2t, Workington 0 (at Cockermouth)

FINAL
Saturday 7 April 1883 at Cockermouth
ASPATRIA 0 (3 minor points) *Back*: G Gordon. *Three-quarters*: G Bell, W Lauriston, H Monkhouse. *Half-backs*: T Holliday, WT Ridley. *Forwards*: W Blaylock, T Dobie (capt), C Graham, J Graham, J Kendal, W McGee, J McKenzie, G Rayson, J Sandwith.
WHITEHAVEN 0 (4 minor points) *Back*: J Shippen. *Three-quarters*: S Palmer, RY Sutton (capt). *Half-backs*: WH Alderson, D Atkinson. *Forwards*: JT Anderson, C Davidson, J Doran, FE Eddis, J Glaister, T Herd, C Harrison, T Shippen, T Smith, J Spittal.
After extra time   *Attendance*: 'large'   *Referee*: JE Birkett (Workington)

FINAL REPLAY
Saturday 14 April 1883 at Workington
ASPATRIA 1 goal *Back*: G Gordon. *Three-quarters*: G Bell (gm), W Lauriston, H Monkhouse. *Half-backs*: T Holliday, WT Ridley. *Forwards*: W Blaylock, T Dobie (capt), C Graham, J Graham, J Kendal, W McGee, J McKenzie, G Rayson, J Sandwith.
WHITEHAVEN 0 *Back*: J Shippen. *Three-quarters*: S Palmer, RY Sutton (capt). *Half-backs*: D Atkinson, W Hursthwaite. *Forwards*: JT Anderson, W Brockbank, J Doran, FE Eddis, J Glaister, T Herd, C Harrison, T Shippen, T Smith, J Spittal.
Attendance: n/a   *Referee*: JM Mawson (Barrow)

DURHAM COUNTY CHALLENGE CUP (11 entries)
Most goals wins. If equal, most tries. If still equal, majority of 3 minor points.

First Round
Darlington 0, Durham City 3t
Ryton 2t, Houghton-le-Spring 1t
Sunderland 1t, North Durham 1g
Sunderland Rovers 0, Boldon 0 (mp: 4-0)
Westoe 1t, Hartlepool Rovers 0
Bye: Hartlepools

Second Round
Durham City 0, Sunderland Rovers 2t
Hartlepools 1t, Ryton 2t
Westoe 0, North Durham 4t

Third Round (semi-final)
Sunderland Rovers 0, Ryton 3t
Bye: North Durham

FINAL
Saturday 14 April 1883 at Feethams Ground, Darlington
NORTH DURHAM 1 goal, 1 try *Back*: H Ferguson. *Three-quarters*: WW Forster (dg), T Davidson, WT Dance. *Half-backs*: H Furness, W Pentney (t). *Forwards*: RR Chapman (capt), AC Frith, GW Gray, E Heston, W Kimpster, JL Scope, JW Sowerby, F Taylor, JE White.
RYTON 1 try *Back*: R Lishman. *Three-quarters*: JT Taylor, R Bennett, C Prest. *Half-backs*: J Stobart (t), J Stowell (capt). *Forwards*: J Bennett, Alf Benson, Ambrose Benson, J Douglas, JB Richardson, E Sample, J Wallace, T Wallace, J Whitfield.
Attendance: 'good'   *Referee*: Rev CH Coates (Stockton-on-Tees)

NORTHUMBERLAND COUNTY FOOTBALL CHALLENGE CUP (9 entries)
Most goals wins. If equal, most tries. If still equal, majority of 3 minor points.

First Round
Tynemouth 2g, 2t, Tankerville (Newcastle) 0
Northern 1g, 1t, North Elswick 0
Northumberland FC w/o Rockcliff (disbanded)
Tynedale 1t, Percy Park 0
Bye: Gosforth

Second Round
Tynemouth 1g, 1t, Northumberland FC 0
Northern 3g, 4t, Gosforth 0
Bye: Tynedale

Semi-final
Northern 1t, Tynedale 2g, 1t
Bye: Tynemouth

FINAL
Saturday 17 March 1883 at Burdon Terrace, Newcastle
TYNEMOUTH 2 tries *Back*: MF Elsdon. *Three-quarters*: EB Brutton, A Hunter.
Half-backs: J Foreman, J McConnell (t). *Forwards*: C Bramwell, J Brown, N Clark, R Dale,
J Dall (t), WH Farrow, S Oliver, JR Palmer, J Walton, JT Watkin (capt).
TYNEDALE 0 *Back*: RH Robb. *Three-quarters*: T Robson (capt), J Elliott, W Pattinson.
Half-backs: J Gregg, T Elliott. *Forwards*: C Callender, CW Harrison, E Harrison, T Hedley,
T McDonald, T Oliver, JT Robb, G Robson, T White.
Attendance: 2,000   *Referee*: PB Junor (Durham)

YORKSHIRE COUNTY FOOTBALL CHALLENGE CUP (32 entries)
Most goals wins. If equal, most tries. If still equal, majority of 3 minor points.

First Round
Batley 1g, 6t, Shipley 1t
Bramley 0, Dewsbury Shamrocks 0 (mp: 1-4, aet)
Castleford 0, Kirkstall 2t
Farsley 0, Cleckheaton 2g, 8t
Halifax 1g, 5t, Mytholmroyd 0
Halifax Free Wanderers 1g, 2t, Mirfield 1g
Harrogate 1t, Dewsbury 2g, 5t
Heckmondwike 1t, Bradford 2g, 4t
Leeds Parish Church 2t, Selby 0
Manningham 2t, Ossett 1g, 2t
Morley 1t, Thornes 1t (mp: 0-8)
Otley 1t, Bierley 2t
Salterhebble 1g, 1t, Horbury 0
Wakefield Trinity 2g, 8t, Keighley 0
York Melbourne 1t, Hull 2t
Yorkshire Wanderers (Leeds) 1t, Leeds St John's 1g

Second Round
Batley 1g, 1t, Kirkstall 0
Cleckheaton 1g, 5t, Bierley 0
Halifax Free Wanderers 1t, Bradford 4g, 4t (at Bradford)
Hull 1g, Thornes 1g (mp: 1-9)
Leeds Parish Church 1t, Dewsbury Shamrocks 2g, 1t
Leeds St John's 0, Dewsbury 1g, 4t
Ossett 0, Wakefield Trinity 1g
Salterhebble 0, Halifax 2g, 2t

Milestones & Stats 1869-1901

Third Round
Cleckheaton 0, Halifax 3g, 1t
Dewsbury 1t, Bradford 0
Thornes 2g, 1t, Dewsbury Shamrocks 0
Wakefield Trinity 1g, 2t, Batley 0

Semi-finals
Dewsbury 1g, 1t, Halifax 2t (at Belle Vue, Wakefield – replay ordered after protest)
Wakefield Trinity 1g, 1t, Thornes 2t (at Hanson Lane, Halifax)

Semi-final Replay
Halifax 2g, Dewsbury 1g, 1t (at Cardigan Fields, Leeds)

FINAL
Saturday 21 April 1883 at Cardigan Fields, Leeds
WAKEFIELD TRINITY 1 goal, 2 tries *Back*: HO Hamshaw (c). *Three-quarters*: H Fallas (t), WE Hartley, CE Bartram. *Half-backs*: A Fisher (t), H Hutchinson. *Forwards*: H Dawson, W Ellis, JH Fallas, W Jackson (t), G Jubb, J Lathom, MB Oldroyd, T Shires, G Steele (capt).
HALIFAX 0 *Back*: W Barrett. *Three-quarters*: TL Scarborough, J Dodd (capt), A Wood. *Half-backs*: E Buckley, J Parker. *Forwards*: T Allbutt, T Chambers, JH Crossland, WH Marshall, J Smithson, GT Thomson, J Wood, JH Wood, W Wood.
Attendance: 7,000   *Referee*: GR Hill (RFU Honorary Secretary)

COUNTY MATCHES

Saturday 4 November 1882 at Whalley Range, Manchester
LANCASHIRE 4 goals, 5 tries *Back*: WW Higgins (Che). *Three-quarters*: T Farr (Swi, 2t), JW Hulse (Man, t, 4c), E Storey (Man, t). *Half-backs*: J Mills (Swi), JH Payne (Bro, t). *Forwards*: A Hope (Swi), WS Hulse (Man), E Lings (ManFW), FS Moss (Bro), A Murray (Walk), JP Pattinson (Man), JW Schofield (Man), JT Seddon (Swi, 2t), JD Wormald (Man, 2t).
MIDLAND COUNTIES 1 goal *Back*: G Jones (Mose). *Three-quarters*: H Phillips (Wolv), A Smith (Mose, t, c), R Bullock (Leam). *Half-backs*: SH Evershed (capt, Burt), P Lea (Mose). *Forwards*: C Cobb (Edg), CA Crane (Wolv), GM Day (Burt), F Fowler (Burt), JJ Gover (Edg), A Miller (Leam), CN Milner (Mose), AG Otter (Mose), HE Sugden (Burt).
Attendance: 2,000   *Referee*: HM Blythe (Cheshire)

Saturday 11 November 1882 at Liscard, Wallasey
CHESHIRE 2 goals, 1 try *Back*: H Maxwell (NewB). *Three-quarters*: PF Shaw (NewB), F Marsland (Sale, 2t, dg), AC Blain (BirkPk). *Half-backs*: SE Pullen (NewB), W Rome (NewB, c). *Forwards*: H Bell (NewB), DA Bingham (BirkPk), WH Broady (Run), W Carroll (Sale), G Cowie (BirkPk), G Crossland (BirkPk), HD Hulme (Mar), BB Middleton (BirkPk), HJ Ryalls (NewB).
LANCASHIRE 2 tries *Back*: T Farr (Swi). *Three-quarters*: JW Hulse (Man), E Storey (Man, t), J Robertson (BroR). *Half-backs*: JH Payne (capt, Bro), FT Wright (Man). *Forwards*: SB Beard (RochH), H Brandon (Liv), JB Cooke (ManFW), A Hope (Swi), CH Horley (Swi), WS Hulse (Man, t), JW Schofield (Man), JT Seddon (Swi), JD Wormald (Man).
Attendance: 2,000   *Referee*: W Walton (Cheshire)

Saturday 11 November 1882 at Whitehaven Cricket Ground
CUMBERLAND 1 goal, 1 try *Back*: G Bell (Asp). *Three-quarters*: H Pooley (Kes), H Hutchinson (Work), S Palmer (Whi, c). *Half-backs*: J Steel (EdW), RY Sutton (capt, Whi). *Forwards*: JT Anderson (Whi), D Atkinson (Whi, t), T Dobie (Asp, t), G Highton (Kes), W McGee (Asp), R Sharpe (Mary), CE Smith (Work), J Turnbull (Work), HC Wynne-Edwardes (EdW).
NORTHUMBERLAND 1 goal, 1 try *Back*: HB Lockhart (Nor). *Three-quarters*: T Robson (Tynd), G Robson (Tynd), FS Ogilvie (Tynm, c). *Half-backs*: GA Bell (capt, NorFC), JT Todd (Tynd). *Forwards*: WH Farrow (Tynm), W Heywood (Rock, t), O Morgan (Wallsend Wanderers), GR Palmer (Tynm), ET Ridley (Nor), GW Ridley (Nor, t), RH Robb (Tynd), H Shotton (NEls), JW Swinburne (Nor).
Attendance: 'large'   *Referee*: WH Atkinson (Cumberland)

Saturday 11 November 1882 at Friarage Field, Hartlepool
DURHAM 0 *Back*: TF Wilson (Wes). *Three-quarters*: R Eden (Darl), EA Crow (SundR), N Meiklejohn (Hou). *Half-backs*: TM Jamieson (Hou), FG Reed (Sund). *Forwards*: L Briggs (Sund), RF Crosthwaite (Wes), CH Elliot (Sund), F Forrest (SundR), A Hill (capt, Hart), H Prior (Darl), RE Reed (Sund), HJ Robinson (Darl), JW Sowerby (NDur).
YORKSHIRE 5 goals, 6 tries *Back*: H Wade (LeeStJ). *Three-quarters*: CE Bartram (Wak, t, 2dg), H Fallas (Wak), FT Ritchie (Brad, t). *Half-backs*: F Bonsor (Brad), JH Potter (LeeStJ, t, 2dg). *Forwards*: T Allbut (Hal), GW Bottomley (Hud), AJ Forrest (YorksW), J Garforth (Dew, t), JW Marshall (Brad), P Redfern (Dew), G Steele (Wak), GT Thomson (capt, Hal, 2t), A Wood (Hal).
Attendance: 1,000   *Referee*: PB Junor (Durham)

Saturday 18 November 1882 at Belle Vue, Wakefield
YORKSHIRE 5 goals, 7 tries *Back*: JA Wylde (YorksW). *Three-quarters*: CE Bartram (Wak, t, c, 2dg), H Fallas (Wak, t, c), WFB Calvert (Hull, t). *Half-backs*: PF Holmes (Hud, dg), JH Potter (LeeStJ, t). *Forwards:* GW Bottomley (Hud), AJ Forrest (YorksW, t), J Garforth (Dew), G Harrison (YorksW, t), JW Marshall (Brad, t), P Redfern (Dew, 2t), G Steele (Wak), GT Thomson (capt, Hal), JH Wood (Hal).
MIDLAND COUNTIES 0 *Back*: R Moore (Burt). *Three-quarters*: HV Bailey (Wolv), J Eadie (Burt), SH Evershed (capt, Burt). *Half-backs*: G Gill (Leam), H Green (Wolv). *Forwards*: CA Crane (Wolv), J Cressy (Leic), JJ Gover (Edg), A Jackson (Leam), J Linnet (Rush), WJ Rawlinson (Leam), CR Wagstaffe (Rush), E Worthington (Leic).
Attendance: 2,500   *Referee*: HWT Garnett (Yorkshire)
Note: Midland Counties had 14 players.

Saturday 25 November 1882 at Whalley Range, Manchester
LANCASHIRE 0 *Back*: W Cooke (Swi). *Three-quarters*: E Beswick (Swi), T Farr (Swi), JW Hulse (Man). *Half-backs*: JH Payne (Bro), FT Wright (Man). *Forwards*: JB Cooke (ManFW), W Dickenson (Swi), A Hope (Swi), CH Horley (Swi), WS Hulse (Man), JP Pattinson (Man), JW Schofield (Man), JT Seddon (Swi), R Seddon (Swi).
YORKSHIRE 5 tries *Back*: J Dodd (Hal). *Three-quarters*: CE Bartram (Wak), TL Scarborough (Hal), H Fallas (Wak). *Half-backs*: PF Holmes (Hud), JH Potter (LeeStJ). *Forwards*: GW Bottomley (Hud), AJ Forrest (YorksW, 2t), J Garforth (Dew, 2t), G Harrison

(YorksW), JW Marshall (Brad), P Redfern (Dew), G Steele (Wak), GT Thomson (capt, Hal, t), A Wood (Hal).
Attendance: 5,000   *Referee*: L Stokes (Kent)

Saturday 3 February 1883 at Cardigan Fields, Leeds
YORKSHIRE 2 goals, 2 tries *Back*: J Dodd (Hal). *Three-quarters*: CE Bartram (Wak, t, 2dg), A Newsome (Dew), H Wigglesworth (Tho). *Half-backs*: JW Bottomley (Brad, t), JH Potter (LeeStJ). *Forwards*: S Asquith (Hal), JH Crossland (Hal), J Garforth (Dew), A Greenwood (Cleck), WE Hanson (Dew), G Harrison (YorksW), GT Thomson (capt, Hal), W Watson (LeeStJ), A Wood (Hal).
NORTHUMBERLAND 1 try *Back*: HB Lockhart (Nor). *Three-quarters*: CH Sample (NorFC/CamU), EB Brutton (Tynm), T Robson (Tynd). *Half-backs*: JT Todd (Tynd), H Symington (Nor). *Forwards*: C Bramwell (Tynm), JW Coward (PerPk), J Gee (PerPk), A Mursell (Nor), GR Palmer (Tynm, t), GW Ridley (Nor), RH Robb (Tynd), WC Sample (NorFC), CE Winship (Nor).
Attendance: 4,000   *Referee*: J MacLaren (RFU President)

Saturday 24 February 1883 at Burdon Terrace, Newcastle
NORTHUMBERLAND 1 goal *Back*: HB Lockhart (Nor). *Three-quarters*: JVW Rutherford (Nor, c), T Robson (Tynd), GA Bell (NorFC). *Half-backs*: JT Todd (Tynd), H Symington (Nor). *Forwards*: C Bramwell (Tynm), JW Coward (PerPk), R Dale (Tynm), J Gee (PerPk), GR Palmer (Tynm), GW Ridley (Nor), RH Robb (Tynd, t), WC Sample (NorFC), CE Winship (Nor).
DURHAM 0 *Back*: TF Wilson (Wes). *Three-quarters*: N Meiklejohn (Hou), EA Crow (Hou), HE Ferens (DurU). *Half-backs*: JJ Ker (Wes), FG Reed (Sund). *Forwards*: HB Buckland (Wes), J Crozier (DurC), F Forrest (SundR), A Hill (Hart), W Kimpster (NDur), WL Oakes (HartR), H Prior (Darl), HJ Robinson (Darl), JW Sowerby (NDur).
Attendance: n/a   *Referee*: n/a

Saturday 24 February 1883 at Crown Flatts, Dewsbury
YORKSHIRE 1 goal, 1 try *Back*: J Dodd (Hal). *Three-quarters*: H Fallas (Wak, t), H Wigglesworth (Tho, c), A Newsome (Dew). *Half-backs*: F Bonsor (Brad), JH Potter (LeeStJ). *Forwards*: S Asquith (Hal), T Chambers (Hal), J Garforth (Dew), WE Hanson (Dew), G Harrison (capt, YorksW), AB Perkins (Dew), G Steele (Wak), H Whiteley (Tho), A Wood (Hal, t).
CHESHIRE 2 tries *Back*: H Maxwell (NewB). *Three-quarters*: G Carrington (Sale), F Marsland (Sale), PF Shaw (NewB). *Half-backs*: WN Fletcher (Mar, t), W Rome (NewB). *Forwards*: H Bell (NewB), W Carroll (Sale), G Cowie (BirkPk), G Crossland (BirkPk), SO Hart-Davies (BirkPk), HD Hulme (Mar), FW Huntington (NewB, t), BB Middleton (capt, BirkPk), HJ Ryalls (NewB).
Attendance: 6,000   *Referee*: W Cail (Northumberland)

Saturday 24 March 1883 at Burdon Terrace, Newcastle
NORTHUMBERLAND 1 try *Back*: HB Lockhart (Nor). *Three-quarters*: CH Sample (NorFC/CamU), EB Brutton (Tynm), FS Ogilvie (Tynm). *Half-backs*: JT Todd (Tynd), H Symington (Nor, t). *Forwards*: JW Coward (PerPk), R Dale (Tynm), A Mursell (Nor), GR Palmer (Tynm), GW Ridley (capt, Nor), RH Robb (Tynd), WC Sample (NorFC), JT Watkin (Tynm), CE Winship (Nor).

EDINBURGH COLLEGIATE FORMER PUPILS 1 try *Back*: D Underwood. *Half-backs*: R Hartley, H Brooks. *Quarter-backs*: J Maclaren, A Park. *Forwards*: G Beattie, H Craigie, T Croil, W Douglas, R Gordon, R Laird, J McGregor, W Shand (capt), J Walton (t), A Whyte.
Attendance: 'large'   *Referee:* n/a

Saturday 14 April 1883 at Burdon Terrace, Newcastle
NORTHUMBERLAND 1 goal *Back*: HB Lockhart (Nor). *Three-quarters*: CH Sample (NorFC/CamU, dg), GA Bell (NorFC), J Elliott (Tynd). *Half-backs*: JT Todd (Tynd), H Symington (Nor). *Forwards*: C Bramwell (Tynm), JW Coward (PerPk), T Elliott (Tynd), A Mursell (Nor), GW Ridley (Nor), RH Robb (Tynd), T Robson (Tynd), WC Sample (NorFC), CE Winship (Nor).
LANCASHIRE 3 goals, 5 tries *Back*: TM Holt (RochH). *Three-quarters*: T Farr (Swi, 2t), EJ Jordan (Bro, c), J Robertson (BroR, dg). *Half-backs*: J Mills (Swi, t, c), JH Payne (capt, Bro, t). *Forwards*: H Court (Old), CH Horley (Swi, 2t), FS Moss (Bro), JT Seddon (Swi), R Seddon (Swi, t), RL Seddon (Bro), A Smith (Bro), A Teggin (BroR), R Wilcock (Walk).
Attendance: 3,500   *Referee*: WA Kidson (Durham)

ENGLAND TRIAL MATCH

Saturday 2 December 1882 at Richardson's Field, Blackheath
SOUTH 4 goals, 4 tries *Back*: AS Taylor (Black, dg). *Three-quarters*: WN Bolton (Black, 2t, c), CG Wade (OxfU), AM Evason (OxfU, 2t, c, dg). *Half-backs*: Alan Rotherham (OxfU, t), HT Twynam (Rich). *Forwards*: HG Fuller (CamU), ET Gurdon (capt, Rich), RFS Henderson (Black), RS Kindersley (OxfU), G Standing (Black, t), EL Strong (OxfU), WM Tatham (MarlN/OxfU), H Vassall (MarlN/OxfU), CS Wooldridge (OxfU).
NORTH 0 *Back*: J Dodd (Hal). *Three-quarters*: CE Bartram (Wak), PF Shaw (NewB), SH Evershed (Burt). *Half-backs*: JH Payne (Bro), JH Potter (LeeStJ). *Forwards*: GW Bottomley (Hud), G Cowie (BirkPk), J Garforth (Dew), G Harrison (YorksW), WS Hulse (Man), BB Middleton (BirkPk), HJ Ryalls (NewB), GT Thomas (Hal), JD Wormald (Man).
Attendance: 1,800   *Referee*: GR Hill (RFU Honorary Secretary)

INTERNATIONAL CHAMPIONSHIP

Saturday 16 December 1882 at St Helen's, Swansea
WALES 0 *Backs*: DH Bowen (Llan), CP Lewis (capt, LlanC). *Three-quarters*: WB Norton (Car), J Clare (Car), D Gwynn (Swa). *Half-backs*: CH Newman (New), E Treharne (Pon). *Forwards*: T Baker Jones (New), A Cattell (Llan), TKS Clapp (Nan), R Gould (New), GF Harding (New), JH Judson (Llan), GL Morris (Swa), FJ Purdon (Swa).
ENGLAND 2 goals, 4 tries *Back*: AS Taylor (Black). *Three-quarters*: WN Bolton (Black, t), AM Evason (OxfU, 2c), CG Wade (OxfU, 3t). *Half-backs*: JH Payne (Bro), Alan Rotherham (OxfU). *Forwards*: HG Fuller (CamU), ET Gurdon (capt, Rich), RSF Henderson (Black, t), RS Kindersley (OxfU), G Standing (Black), GT Thomas (Hal, t), WM Tatham (MarlN/OxfU), H Vassall (MarlN/OxfU), CS Wooldridge (OxfU).
Attendance: 3,000   *Referee*: A Herbert (Wales)

Milestones & Stats 1869-1901

Monday 5 February 1883 at Whalley Range, Manchester
ENGLAND 1 goal, 3 tries *Back*: AS Taylor (Black). *Three-quarters*: WN Bolton (Black, t), AM Evanson (OxfU, c), CG Wade (OxfU, t). *Half-backs*: JH Payne (Bro), HT Twyman (Rich, t). *Forwards*: HG Fuller (CamU), ET Gurdon (capt, Rich), BB Middleton (BirkPk), EJ Moore (OxfU), PM Pattisson (CamU), GT Thomas (Hal), G Standing (Black), WM Tatham (MarlN/OxfU, t), CS Wooldridge (OxfU).
IRELAND 1 try *Back*: JWR Morrow (QCB). *Half-backs*: RE McLean (NIFC), RH Scovell (King). *Quarter-backs*: WW Fletcher (King), JP Warren (King). *Forwards*: SAM Bruce (NIFC), AJ Forrest (Wand, t), FS Heuston (King), RW Hughes (NIFC), H King (DubU), JA Macdonald (MethC), A Millar (King), DF Moore (Wand), G Scriven (capt, DubU), JW Taylor (NIFC).
Attendance: 5,000   *Referee*: AS Pattison (Scotland)

Saturday 3 March 1883 at Raeburn Place, Edinburgh
SCOTLAND 1 try *Back*: DW Kidston (GlasA). *Half-backs*: WE MacLagan (LonS), MF Reid (Lor, t). *Quarter-backs*: WS Brown (EdinIFP), PW Smeaton (EdinA). *Forwards*: T Ainslie (EdinIFP), JB Brown (GlasA), DY Cassels (capt, WoS), D McCowan (WoS), JG Mowat (GlasA), C Reid (EdinA), D Somerville (EdinIFP), J Jamieson (WoS), A Walker (WoS), WA Walls (GlasA).
ENGLAND 2 tries *Back*: HB Tristram (OxfU). *Three-quarters*: WN Bolton (Black, t), AM Evanson (OxfU), CG Wade (OxfU). *Half-backs*: JH Payne (Bro), Alan Rotherham (OxfU, t). *Forwards*: HG Fuller (CamU), C Gurdon (Rich), ET Gurdon (capt, Rich), RSF Henderson (Black), EJ Moore (OxfU), RM Pattisson (CamU), WM Tatham (MarlN/OxfU), GT Thomson (Hal), CS Wooldridge (OxfU).
Attendance: 10,000   *Referee*: HC Kelly (Ireland)

Other results
Scotland 3g, Wales 1g
Ireland 0, Scotland 1g, 1t
(Ireland and Wales did not arrange a fixture)

Final table

	P	W	D	L	G-T	G-T
England	3	3	0	0	3-9	0-2
Scotland	3	2	0	1	4-2	1-2
Ireland	2	0	0	2	0-1	2-4
Wales	2	0	0	2	1-0	5-4

Herbert Robertshaw is depicted scoring Bradford's final try in the Yorkshire Cup final victory over Hull at Cardigan Fields, Leeds, April 1884. *Toby, The Yorkshire Tyke, 1884*

1883-1884

GOOD FOR THE MIND AND BODY

With the 1883-84 season about to unfold, the *Hull Packet* praised the virtues of rugby football: 'It is but a very few years ago since football was in its infancy, especially in this county [Yorkshire], whilst, at the present time, it is estimated that considerably over 100,000 men and youths are engaged in it every week. It is a healthy, invigorating exercise, good for the mind and body, and it has this advantage over any other game, that members can play at it altogether; and not only is it exciting to the players, but it is also interesting, and in some instances exciting to the spectator. The "Rugby" is now generally preferred to the "Association," and the use of the hands in the former, varies the monotony of the latter. The game of "Rugby" under the revised rules is made exciting from beginning to end, and as it is, is by far the best of all winter games. To be a footballer a man should have a quick eye and be fleet of foot as well as be possessed of those grand qualities, self-possession and courage. He also needs a broad chest, a good pair of legs, a great amount of wind, as well as a considerable amount of strength and pluck.'[50]

COUNTY QUALIFICATION AMBIGUITY

The *Manchester Guardian* echoed concerns being raised on the ambiguity of county qualification, a subject due to be debated by the Rugby Football Union: 'The importance that county football has assumed has forced attention to the nature of the qualification of many of the players taking part in them. The necessity for a definite rule is so important [and] obvious that it seems strange that the Rugby Union, the authority in all that relates to football when played under Union rules, has not before now followed the example of the dribbling [Association] organisation. Several cases occurred last season in which one player was chosen to represent two different counties, and the absence of any recognised credentials for county players under Rugby rules caused some confusion.'[51]

COUNTY QUALIFICATION DEFINED
During the Rugby Football Union's annual meeting at the Westminster Palace Hotel, London, on Wednesday 24th October, rules defining county qualification were adopted with immediate operation. The following was agreed:

1. A man may play for the county in which he was born; for the county in which he has resided for the six months previous to the time of playing; or for the county in which he is residing at school or college at the time of playing.
2. A man shall still be qualified to play for a county, having previously played for that county for three years and not having played for any other county.
3. No man shall play for more than one county during the same season.
4. Should any question arise as to qualification the same shall be left to the decision of the Rugby Union.[52]

OXFORD UNIVERSITY: A TEAM WITHOUT EQUAL
The Oxford University team was building a strong reputation, their exploits even being extolled by the northern press. A report in the *Liverpool Mercury*, which followed the University's victory over Cheshire on 27th October, exclaimed 'the Oxford University fifteen are undoubtedly without their equal in the country and last year they went through a brilliant array of fixtures without a single defeat, and they bid fair to repeat the feat this year'. The praise was echoed in the *Manchester Guardian*, which described them as the 'premier team in England' following their win against Yorkshire on 20th February.[53]

THE VALUE OF TRIAL MATCHES
Yorkshire's county selection policy was praised by the *Manchester Guardian* whilst deriding that of Lancashire: 'The determination of Yorkshire to maintain the position they last year obtained of champion county of football

The England team that met Scotland in the first ever international rugby match, played at Raeburn Place, Edinburgh on 27th March 1871. For ease of identification a number has been imposed on each player's jersey: JE Bentley (1), HJC Turner (2), F Tobin (3), DP Turner (4), F Stokes (5), JH Clayton (6), RR Osborne (7), AS Gibson (8), JH Luscombe (9), RH Birkett (10), JF Green (11), A St G Hamersley (12), W MacLaren (13), CW Sherrard (14), A Lyon (15), CA Crompton (16), A Davenport (17), AG Guillemard (18), JM Dugdale (19), BH Burns (20). The northern-based players are Clayton, Lyon, and Tobin (all Liverpool), Gibson, MacLaren, Osborne, and HJC Turner (all Manchester).

Manchester 1875-76, taken on the occasion of a match arranged between Manchester and 'The Veterans' at Whalley Range. Despite five of them wearing England jerseys the lack of a surviving caption makes it impossible to correctly identify all the players. Those known to have taken part are: J Armitage, T Blatherwick, W Bleakley, AJ Bulteel, H Burder, HE Carter, D Drew, JS Genth, L Genth, W Greg, G Gunton, RC Longridge, JC Lowe, J MacLaren, W MacLaren, E Mann, D Marriage, EE Marriott, J Rowley, WW Rowley, CE Sidebotham, TN Speakman, WHA Thorpe, R Todd, HJC Turner, R Walker.

Roger Walker captained the Manchester club in its earliest days. A reliable, hard-working forward, he played for Lancashire (8 times), the North (5), and England (5), later enhancing his reputation as an administrator when elected President of the Rugby Football Union in 1894.

George Thomson was a member of the Halifax pack that won the inaugural Yorkshire County Cup in 1877-78. A strong, mobile forward, he made 29 appearances for Yorkshire, many as captain, and represented the North four times and England nine.

Preston Grasshoppers provided Lancashire with five players for the match against Yorkshire on 19th January 1878, some of whom also played for Manchester. Back: JH Hulton, R Hunt, HL Storey. Front: WH Hunt, AN Hornby.

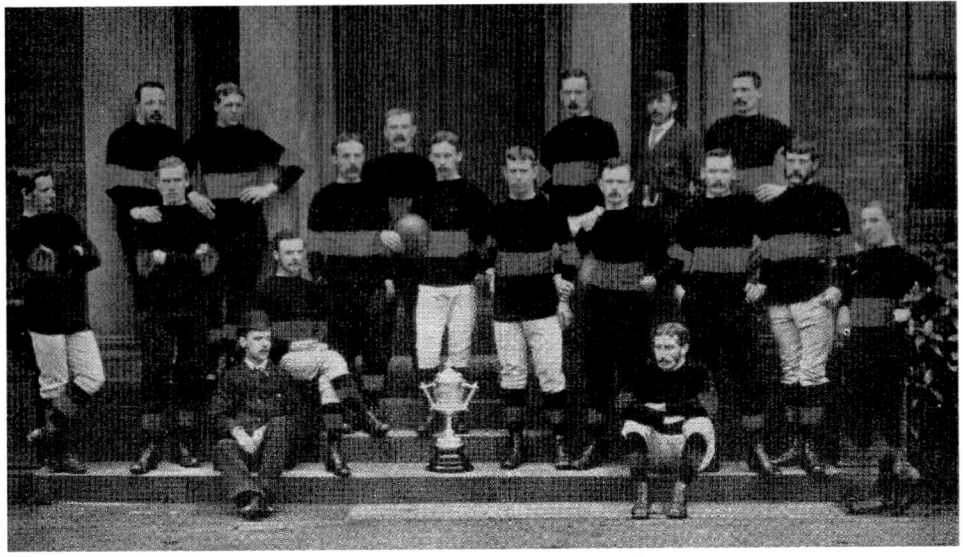

Wakefield Trinity 1878-79, winners of the Yorkshire County Cup. Back: A Hirst, W Jackson, B Longbottom, TO Bennett, J Bell (umpire), J Longbottom. Middle: B Kilner, W Ellis, JW Whitehead (seated), H Pickersgill, A Hayley, G Steele, H Haley, JW Kilner, TB Parry. Front: J Leach (secretary), CT Baldwin.

Kendal Town 1879-80. Back (standing): A Harrison, TR Barrow, M Thompson, JR Illingworth, JC Garnett, J Holmes, W Head, L Winder, J Farrer. Middle (kneeling): J Kemp, A Peake, C Hoggarth, W Craghill, R Archer. Front (lay on ground): EM Braithwaite. Along with Kendal Hornets, Town provided the backbone of Westmorland rugby during the Victorian era.

George Ashburner was an outstanding three-quarter and one of the early pioneers of the Barrow club, taking on the role of captain in 1881. Although born in Ulverston, Lancashire, he played twice for Cumberland during 1880-81. In the first of those, versus Northumberland at Whitehaven on 23rd October, he shared the distinction with Stephen Troughton and Rowell Tyson as the first Barrow players selected for a county match.

John Atkinson was another of Barrow's players to effectively 'guest' for Cumberland during the 1880-81 season, making just one appearance in the return match against Northumberland in Newcastle on 19th March. A three-quarter, he was another Lancastrian, born in Lancaster.

Birkenhead Park 1880-81, winners of the Cheshire County Cup. Back: WP Evans (against railings), G Cowie, C Phillips, G Stewart, BB Middleton, R Wood, H Brandon, JA Black, JR Wilson (against railings). Middle: A Williamson, JJ Ravenscroft, HM Blythe, DA Bingham. Front: AC Blain, GH Smythe, JB Parry, EA Beazley.

Sunderland 1880-81, winners of the Durham County Cup. Back: O Thompson, H Thompson, J Fowles, WA Gales, DS Inman, W Dickinson. Middle: J Laing, AGM Hudson, A Laing, C Kidson, JJ Kayll. Front: RGR Eden, WA Kidson, HE Kayll, R Hitchcock.

Hull 1881-82. Back: L Whitehead, HL Smith, GW Braithwaite, DR Lovell, F Winter, J Wilson, F Jones, AH Tyacke, E Robinson. Middle: W Close, GA Hoskins, WFB Calvert. Front: LA Smith, A Smithson, JFB Calvert, EM Braithwaite.

Robert Lionel 'Bob' Seddon made 18 appearances for Lancashire, four for the North and three for England. The Swinton and former Broughton Rangers forward had the honour of captaining the first British touring team in 1888 but sadly drowned in a boating accident in Australia midway through the tour. A memorial was subsequently erected near the scene in Maitland, New South Wales.

Jim Valentine is considered by many to be Swinton's most legendary player. An outstanding three-quarter, he first played for Lancashire in 1884 (his 56 appearances the most for a northern county in the Victorian era), and represented the North (7 times) and England (4). After Swinton joined the Northern Union in 1896, he led them to Challenge Cup success in 1900 and played five more times for Lancashire.

Bradford 1883-84, winners of the Yorkshire County Cup. Back: H Robertshaw, S Asquith. Middle: WP Carter, AB Perkins, JW Bottomley, FT Ritchie, T Atkinson, FD Richmond, F Booth, J Barker, JF Wright, E Critchley, S Haigh. Front: R Bonsor, JW Marshall, JL Hickson, F Bonsor, E Wilkinson, AR Robertshaw, J Potter.

Richard Evison 'Dicky' Lockwood was an exceptionally talented three-quarter who represented Yorkshire (46 times), the North (7), and England (14). He debuted for the original Dewsbury club in 1884, transferring to Heckmondwike in 1889. In 1895 he switched to Wakefield Trinity after they had joined the Northern Union, adding a further Yorkshire appearance under that code. He moved on in 1900 to the reformed Dewsbury team, continuing to play for them until 1903.

William 'Buller' Stadden was a brilliant Wales international half-back who moved from the Cardiff club to Dewsbury in 1886, qualifying him for Yorkshire with whom he appeared 21 times. In 1895 he joined Huddersfield in the breakaway Northern Union, retiring in 1896 and taking a coaching role at the club. During March 1899 he made a comeback with the resurrected Dewsbury club but played just once.

Percy Park 1885-86, winners of the Northumberland County Cup. Back: JA Williamson, A McConnell (secretary). Third row (standing): RE Herbertson, G Brewis, F Kirk, JW Coward, G Leighton, A Gee, T Glover. Second row (seated): T Gee, L Rhode, RH Spence. Front (on ground): H Douglas, E Biggs, W Ryder, W Dodds.

Harry Eagles was the most celebrated Salford player in its early history, a forward regarded for his energetic play and leadership. His 1886 Lancashire debut was the first of 18 appearances, followed by three for the North. Selected for the 1888 tour to Australia and New Zealand, he played in all 52 matches, plus an additional 19 arranged under Australian Rules.

Will Walker of Kendal Hornets appeared 8 times for Westmorland from 1886 to 1888. Rated as one of the county's finest three-quarters he took over as the Hornets' captain in 1879, a position he retained until 1890.

The Durham team that played against Middlesex at Sunderland on 21st February 1887. Back: CJ Sadler, TM Swinburne (vice-president), HO Hoy, W Hodgson, W Yiend, CH Newman, HH Carrick, R Barwick. Middle: G Pimbury, FE Pease, JW Sowerby, WL Oakes, JC Wilford, CH Elliot, GH Eyre, WF Greenwell (honorary secretary). Front: TM Jamieson, VT Thompson.

in the North is evidenced by the steps which have been taken to secure the best available team to represent the county. The Yorkshire Executive invited the Rugby clubs to send in the names of players willing to take part in a series of trial matches from which the Committee selected sides, and a first trial match was played at Wakefield. The result of this contest was the selection of two teams, "Probables" and "Possibles", who met at Dewsbury on Wednesday [7th November], and played a second trial game. The Committee have thus obtained by personal observation more reliable evidence of the players' ability to represent the county than is afforded by club recommendations, which, though given in good faith, are more or less partial and unreliable. The value attached to trial matches by Yorkshire is in striking contrast to the cavalier treatment from Lancashire at its annual meeting, when it was curtly dismissed with the remark that trial games "served no practical purpose," and that they had in the past been "miserable failures." Times have changed, and no single club now boasts a monopoly of the best players; while no county which aspires to the highest position can afford to neglect taking what appears the first and most reliable step to secure the strongest team to represent it.'[54]

FOUR THREE-QUARTERS INTRODUCED
The idea of increasing the number of three-quarters from three to four is credited to the Cardiff club who successfully introduced the concept in a home match with Gloucester on 23rd February. It happened more by accident than design as the club sought a solution to accommodating all four of its outstanding three-quarters. The format was unsuccessfully replicated by Wales against Scotland at Cardiff Arms Park on 9th January 1886 and shelved until resurrected in December 1888 against the touring New Zealand Native side. It was not until early 1894 that England, Ireland and Scotland adopted a four-man line.

THE RAPIDITY OF LANCASHIRE
After Lancashire had convincingly defeated the Midland Counties by six goals and three tries to nil at Moseley, Birmingham, on 23rd February, one journalist praised the speed of the visitors stating 'the rapidity of the Lancashire scoring in the second half was marvellously quick, for three goals and two tries were chalked up in two and a half minutes'.[55]

CUP FOOTBALL: UNHEALTHY EXCITEMENT?
As the Yorkshire Cup competition kicked off once more, the *Yorkshire Post* captured the mood, both good and bad: 'The Rugby game was at the

zenith of its glory in Yorkshire on Saturday last [1st March], the occasion being the playing off of the now famous games in connection with the Challenge Cup. Altogether the initial round was a marked success in every way, the sport itself being of surprising excellence, and the attendance everywhere very large. A great deal has recently been said and written respecting the evil influences of Challenge Cups; how they encourage rough play, create betting, and in other ways cause an unhealthy excitement to prevail. Mr Rowland Hill, the Honorary Secretary of the Rugby Union, has gone so far as to say "that a great service would be rendered to football by the abandonment of these competitions".'[56]

NORTH-EAST DECIDER

An innovation this season was the meeting of the Durham and Northumberland county cup winners, Northern (Northumberland) defeating Hartlepool Rovers (Durham) at the Chester Road Cricket Ground, Sunderland, on 29th March.

CUMBERLAND CUP FINAL CHAOS

The Cumberland Cup competition ended in chaos after two scoreless finals on the Aspatria ground, Carlisle City refusing to meet Whitehaven for a third time. The *Athletic News* related the sorry story: 'The Cumberland Cup has been settled at last, but in a most unsatisfactory manner. In the first match Carlisle gained what most people thought was a try, and in the second tussle they crossed the Whitehaven line five times. Four of these tries were disallowed, the umpires disagreed about the other, and the referee, not being in a position to see, refused to give a decision. Carlisle kicked a goal under dispute. At a county committee meeting held to consider whether the goal should be allowed, it was decided by the casting vote of the chairman that it should not. The committee ordered the match to be played over again. Carlisle, however, refused [and] the cup was presented to the Whitehaven captain, Mr. [Richard] Sutton, last Thursday [1st May], and on arrival home with the trophy, he was immediately chaired, and a procession formed, the members of the club being seated on a large bus preceded by the Volunteer Band, which paraded several of the principle streets.'[57]

1883-1884 STATISTICS

CUMBERLAND COUNTY CHALLENGE CUP (7 entries)
Most goals wins. If equal, most tries. If still equal, majority of 3 minor points.

First Round
Aspatria 1g, Whitehaven 2g
Cockermouth 3t, Workington 0
Ellensiders 0, Carlisle City 0 (mp: 0-3)
Bye: Eden Wanderers

Semi-finals
Carlisle City w/o Eden Wanderers (withdrew)
Whitehaven 2t, Cockermouth 0 (at Noble Croft, Aspatria)

FINAL
Saturday 29 March 1884 at Noble Croft, Aspatria
WHITEHAVEN 0 (2 minor points) *Back*: R Simpson. *Three-quarters*: J Shippen, D Atkinson, SB Ridgway. *Half-backs*: WH Alderson, RY Sutton (capt). *Forwards*: E Ackroyd, JT Anderson, C Davidson, J Doran, C Douglas, C Harris, C Harrison, T Shippen, T Smith.
CARLISLE CITY 0 (2 minor points) *Back*: A Lee. *Three-quarters*: F Telford, G Bell, J Dodgshon. *Half-backs*: T Hilton, RH Tinkler. *Forwards*: L Chambers, EH Dawson, JS Dodgshon, W Dodgshon (capt), H Etchells, W Harding, T Kirkbride, B Rickerby, J Sutton.
Attendance: 'large'   *Referee*: JR Bain (Harrington)
Note: Whitehaven refused to play extra time.

FINAL REPLAY
Saturday 5 April 1884 at Noble Croft, Aspatria
WHITEHAVEN 0 (2 minor points) *Back*: J Shippen. *Three-quarters*: D Atkinson, T Shippen, SB Ridgway. *Half-backs*: WH Alderson, RY Sutton (capt). *Forwards*: E Ackroyd, JT Anderson, C Davidson, J Doran, C Douglas, C Harris, C Harrison, T Smith, J Stamper.
CARLISLE CITY 0 (3 minor points) *Back*: A Lee. *Three-quarters*: F Telford, G Bell, J Dodgshon. *Half-backs*: W Dodgshon (capt), T Hilton, RH Tinkler. *Forwards*: J Black, L Chambers, EH Dawson, JS Dodgshon, H Etchells, T Kirkbride, B Rickerby, J Sutton.
After extra time   *Attendance*: 'large'   *Referee*: H Stancliffe (Manchester)

FINAL SECOND REPLAY
WHITEHAVEN w/o CARLISLE CITY
Cup awarded to Whitehaven after Carlisle City refused to play due to a dispute.

DURHAM COUNTY CHALLENGE CUP (10 entries)
Most goals wins. If equal, most tries. If still equal, majority of 3 minor points.

First Round
Hartlepool Rovers 1g, 1try, Darlington 0
Ryton 0, North Durham 1t
Sunderland 0, Durham City 1g, 1t
Sunderland Rovers 1g, Houghton-le-Spring 1g (mp: 5-5, aet)
Westoe 0, Boldon 1t

First Round Replay
Sunderland Rovers 1g, Houghton-le-Spring 0 (aet)

Second Round
Hartlepool Rovers 2g, Sunderland Rovers 1t
North Durham 1g, 2t, Durham City 0
Bye: Boldon

Semi-final
Hartlepool Rovers 4t, Boldon 0
Bye: North Durham

FINAL
Saturday 22 March 1884 at Chester Road, Sunderland
HARTLEPOOL ROVERS 2 tries *Back*: HO Hoy. *Three-quarters*: R Williams, FW Purves, A Hill. *Half-backs*: J Armstrong, G Smith. *Forwards*: J Brewster, H Geipel, F Harrold, R Marshall, WL Oakes (capt), R Ogden, AE Towers (2t), WH Towers, T Watson.
NORTH DURHAM 1 try *Back*: WT Dance. *Three-quarters*: T Davidson, F Hutchinson, WW Forster. *Half-backs*: CH Newman, W Pentney. *Forwards*: HH Carrick, RS Ferguson, W Furness, GW Gray, E Histon, JL Scope, JW Sowerby (capt, t), W Swinburne, F Taylor.
After extra time   *Attendance*: 1,500   *Referee*: Rev CH Coates (Stockton-on-Tees)

NORTHUMBERLAND COUNTY FOOTBALL CHALLENGE CUP (6 entries)
Most goals wins. If equal, most tries. If still equal, majority of 3 minor points.

First Round
Northumberland FC 0, Percy Park 0
Northern 2g, Tynemouth 0
Tynedale 2g, 2t, North Elswick 0

First Round Replay
Northumberland FC 2g, Percy Park 0

Semi-final
Northern 1t, Northumberland FC 0
Bye: Tynedale

FINAL
Saturday 15 March 1884 at Burdon Terrace, Newcastle
NORTHERN 1 try *Back*: CE Morgan. *Three-quarters*: CS Gill, V Rutherford, H Macarthy. *Half-backs*: JVW Rutherford (capt, t), H Symington. *Forwards*: CH Coates, HB Lockhart, A Mursell, ET Ridley, GW Ridley, D Ross, FJ Scott, H Spence, JW Swinburne.
TYNEDALE 0 *Back*: RH Robb. *Three-quarters*: T Robson (capt), J Robinson, W Pattinson. *Half-backs*: JT Dodd, J Gregg. *Forwards*: J Bailey, GH Bell, T Elliott, CW Harrison, E Harrison, T Hedley, W Robson, T Rogers, T White.
Attendance: 4,000   *Referee*: JT Todd (Durham RU President)

Milestones & Stats 1869-1901

DURHAM v NORTHUMBERLAND CHALLENGE MATCH
Saturday 29 March 1884 at Chester Road, Sunderland
NORTHERN (Northumberland Cup winners) **1 try** *Back*: CE Morgan. *Three-quarters*: CS Gill, HB Lockhart, H Macarthy. *Half-backs*: JVW Rutherford (capt), H Symington. *Forwards*: CH Coates, Haswell, A Mursell, ET Ridley, GW Ridley, D Ross, FJ Scott, H Spence, JW Swinburne (t).
HARTLEPOOL ROVERS (Durham Cup winners) **0** *Back*: HO Hoy. *Three-quarters*: R Williams, FW Purves, A Hill. *Half-backs*: J Armstrong, G Smith. *Forwards*: J Brewster, H Geipel, F Harrold, R Marshall, WL Oakes (capt), R Ogden, AE Towers, WH Towers, T Watson.
Attendance: 1,500 *Referee*: JT Todd (Durham RU President)

YORKSHIRE COUNTY FOOTBALL CHALLENGE CUP (57 entries)
Most goals wins. If equal, most tries. If still equal, majority of 3 minor points.

First Round
Barnsley 0, Manningham 6g, 4t
Batley 1g, 2t, Dewsbury Shamrocks 0
Batley Mountaineers 3g, 6t, Newmillerdam 0
Bingley 4t, Brighouse Rangers 1t
Birstall 0, Castleford 2g, 1t
Bramley 0, Ossett 0 (mp: 3-3, aet)
Buttershaw Mills (Bradford) 0, Heckmondwike 1g, 3t
Denfield 1t, Wakefield St Austin's 1g, 1t
Dewsbury 0, Wakefield Trinity 1g
Dodworth 1g, 1t, Bowling 0
Dudley Hill 2t, Shipley 0
Eastmoor 0, Thornes 7g, 2t
Gildersome 0, Hull 4g, 6t
Goole 1t, Bradford Trinity 1t (mp: 3-0)
Halifax 1g, 2t, Halifax Free Wanderers 0
Hipperholme and Lightcliffe 0, Keighley 1t
Holbeck 1t, Elland 0
Hull Southcoates 3g, 3t, Skipton 1t
Leeds Parish Church 4t, Otley 0
Leeds St John's 1g, 4t, Bradford Rangers 0
Mirfield 1t, Liversedge 0
Morley 0, Horbury 1t
Mytholmroyd 1t, Halifax St Joseph's 0
Pudsey 1g, 3t, Luddendenfoot 2t
Salterhebble 1g, 1t, Wortley 0
Selby 1t, Cleckheaton 0
Stanley 0, Bradford 6g, 5t
York 0, Kirkstall 1t
Bye: Middlesbrough Rovers

First Round Replay Ossett 2g, 1t, Bramley 0

Second Round
Batley 1g, 2t, Goole 1g
Bradford 4g, 3t, Wakefield St Austin's 2t
Dodworth 0, Castleford 2t
Heckmondwike 1g, Wakefield Trinity 2t
Horbury 2t, Selby 0
Hull 1t, Leeds St John's 1t (mp: 3-4, aet)
Keighley 2t, Dudley Hill 0
Kirkstall 0, Mirfield 1t
Leeds Parish Church 0, Halifax 1t
Manningham 1g, 3t, Batley Mountaineers 0
Middlesbrough Rovers 1t, Pudsey 1g, 1t
Mytholmroyd 1t, Hull Southcoates 1g, 1t
Ossett 1t, Bingley 0
Salterhebble 1t, Thornes 0
Bye: Holbeck

Second Round Replay
Leeds St John's 1g, Hull 1g, 2t

Third Round
Batley 2g, 3t, Keighley 1t
Bradford 5g, 1t, Manningham 0
Horbury 2g, 1t, Salterhebble 0
Hull 1t, Heckmondwike 0
Hull Southcoates 0, Halifax 5g
Mirfield 0, Castleford 1g, 2t
Ossett 2t, Pudsey 0
Bye: Holbeck

Fourth Round
Castleford 2g, Halifax 2t
Holbeck 2t, Hull 3g, 1t
Horbury 0, Batley 4t
Ossett 0, Bradford 2g

Semi-finals
Bradford 2t, Batley 0 (at Hanson Lane, Halifax)
Hull 1g, 1t, Castleford 1g (at Belle Vue, Wakefield)

FINAL
Saturday 5 April 1884 at Cardigan Fields, Leeds
BRADFORD 1 goal, 4 tries *Back*: FD Richmond. *Three-quarters*: AR Robertshaw, E Critchley, FT Ritchie. *Half-backs*: F Bonsor (capt, 2t), JF Wright. *Forwards*: S Asquith (t), T Atkinson, WP Carter (t), S Haigh, JL Hickson (c), JW Marshall, J Potter, H Robertshaw (t), E Wilkinson
HULL 1 try *Back*: W Tomlinson. *Three-quarters*: GE Calvert, JR James, BR Wilson. *Half-backs*: H Bell, GE Belt. *Forwards*: JFB Calvert, WFB Calvert (capt), G Harrison (t), G Jacketts, F Mawer, C Simpson, W Teal, L Whitehead, J Wilson.
Attendance: 15,000   *Referee*: GT Thomson (Halifax)

COUNTY MATCHES

Saturday 27 October 1883 at The Parks, Oxford
OXFORD UNIVERSITY 5 goals, 3 tries *Back*: HJ King. *Three-quarters*: AM Evanson (t), GC Lindsay (t), HW Cave (t, 3c, dg). *Half-backs*: AGG Asher (dg), Alan Rotherham (2t). *Forwards*: CW Berry, GF Bradby, ED Court (t), FJC Mackenzie, EJ Moore, AR Patterson, WH Squire, EL Strong, WM Tatham (capt).
CHESHIRE 1 goal *Back*: E Whitehead (Duk). *Three-quarters*: W Rome (capt, NewB, t, c), WS Leitch (NewB), JA Black (BirkPk). *Half-backs*: RH Jackson (BirkPk), JH Pierce (NewB). *Forwards*: J Barber (NewB), H Bell (NewB), H Blocksage (Duk), H Cookson (Sale), SD Crawford (NewB), JE Davies (Run), J Dunlop (BirkPk), E Lings (Sale), HJ Ryalls (NewB).
Attendance: 4,000   *Referee*: n/a

Saturday 3 November 1883 at Whalley Range, Manchester
LANCASHIRE 2 goals *Back*: WW Higgins (Man). *Three-quarters*: E Storey (Man, t),
T Farr (Swi), CE Barlow (Old). *Half-backs*: J Mills (Swi, 2c), AH Wrigley (Liv, t). *Forwards*:
C Anderton (ManFW), H Court (Old), WS Hulse (Man), JT Hunt (capt, Man/PresG),
JH Jones (Walk), HFB Moore (Man), RL Seddon (Bro), A Teggin (BroR), J Welsh (Liv).
NORTHUMBERLAND 0 *Back*: REE Spencer (NorFC). *Three-quarters*: W Pattinson
(Tynd), GA Bell (NorFC), JW Swinburne (Nor). *Half-backs*: JVW Rutherford (capt, Nor),
H Symington (Nor). *Forwards*: GH Armstrong (NorFC), R Dale (Tynm), A Mursell (Nor),
S Oliver (Tynm), GR Palmer (Tynm), FW Ramsay (NorFC), GW Ridley (Nor),
WC Sample (NorFC), CE Winship (Nor).
Attendance: 4,000   *Referee*: WH Wallace (Cheshire)

Saturday 10 November 1883 at Burdon Terrace, Newcastle
NORTHUMBERLAND 1 goal, 1 try *Back*: REE Spencer (NorFC). *Three-quarters*:
JW Swinburne (Nor), MF Elsdon (Tynm), GA Bell (NorFC). *Half-backs*: Dr Hogg (Tynd),
JVW Rutherford (capt, Nor, gm). *Forwards*: R Dale (Tynm), A Mursell (Nor), S Oliver
(Tynm), GR Palmer (Tynm), FW Ramsay (NorFC), GW Ridley (Nor, t), HS Rowell (Nor),
WC Sample (NorFC), CE Winship (Nor).
CUMBERLAND 1 try *Back*: J Shippen (Whi). *Three-quarters*: RY Sutton (Whi), G Bell
(Asp), S Palmer (Whi, t). *Half-backs*: WH Alderson (Whi), D Atkinson (Whi). *Forwards*:
JT Anderson (Whi), J Beattie (Work), J Brown (Mary), T Dobie (Asp), G Fielden (Work),
G Gibson (Cock), W Holmes (Cock), H Monkhouse (Asp), HC Wynne-Edwardes (EdW).
Attendance: 'fair'   *Referee*: W Cail (Northumberland)

Saturday 10 November 1883 at Park Avenue, Bradford
YORKSHIRE 2 goals, 3 tries *Back*: J Dodd (Hal). *Three-quarters*: CE Bartram (Wak, 3t),
H Fallas (Wak), H Wigglesworth (Tho, 2c). *Half-backs*: F Bonsor (Brad), H Hutchinson
(Wak). *Forwards*: T Chambers (Hal), J Garforth (Dew), G Harrison (Hull), J Lathom (Wak),
JW Marshall (Brad), AC Sharpe (Hud), GT Thomson (capt, Hal, t), W Wolstenholme
(Dew, t), A Wood (Hal).
DURHAM 1 goal *Back*: WC Wetherell (DurC). *Three-quarters*: FR Simpson (Sund),
EA Crow (Hou), N Meiklejohn (Hou). *Half-backs*: JJ Ker (Wes), FG Reed (Sund). *Forwards*:
W Coxon (Hou), WF Cross (SundR), J Crozier (DurC), W Forster (Hou), A Hill (capt,
HartR), WL Oakes (HartR), RE Reed (Sund), JW Sowerby (NDur), WH Towers (HartR,
dg).
Attendance: 5,000   *Referee*: HWT Garnett (Yorkshire)

Saturday 17 November 1883 at Whalley Range, Manchester
LANCASHIRE 2 tries *Back*: WW Higgins (Man). *Three-quarters*: E Storey (capt, Man, t),
J Robertson (BroR, t), A Durandu (Liv). *Half-backs*: J Mills (Swi), AH Wrigley (Liv).
Forwards: J Bagshaw (Swi), WS Hulse (Man), JH Jones (Walk), AT Kemble (Liv), FS Moss
(Bro), RL Seddon (Bro), A Teggin (BroR), E Trevor-Smith (Man), JD Wormald (Man).
CHESHIRE 0 *Back*: PF Shaw (capt, NewB). *Three-quarters*: JA Black (BirkPk), AC Blain
(BirkPk), G Carrington (Sale). *Half-backs*: WN Fletcher (Man/BirkPk), WS Leitch (NewB).
Forwards: H Bell (NewB), H Blocksage (Duk), H Cookson (Sale), G Cowie (BirkPk), HD
Hulme (BirkPk), E Lings (Sale), HJ Ryalls (NewB), A Williamson (BirkPk), W Wright (Run).
Attendance: 2,000   *Referee*: H Huth (Yorkshire)

Saturday 17 November 1883 at Burton Cricket Ground, Burton-on-Trent
MIDLAND COUNTIES 1 try *Back*: R Byrne (Mose). *Three-quarters*: SH Evershed (capt, Burt), WS Eadie (Burt), G Fowler (Mose). *Half-backs*: W Allen (Burt), H Player (Edg). *Forwards*: C Cobb (Edg), CA Crane (Wolv), JR Deykin (Edg), P Evershed (Burt), F Fowler (Mose), J Morrison (Wolv), E Napier (Burt), E Radcliffe (Mose), K Wilson (Mose, t).
YORKSHIRE 3 goals, 3 tries *Back*: J Dodd (Hal). *Three-quarters*: CE Bartram (Wak, 2t), H Fallas (Wak, t), H Wigglesworth (Tho, 3c). *Half-backs*: F Bonsor (Brad), H Hutchinson (Wak). *Forwards*: T Chambers (Hal), J Garforth (Dew), G Jubb (Wak), J Lathom (Wak), JW Marshall (Brad), AC Sharpe (Hud, t), GT Thomson (capt, Hal), W Wolstenholme (Dew, t), A Wood (Hal, t).
Attendance: 500   *Referee*: GR Hill (RFU Honorary Secretary)

Saturday 24 November 1883 at Hanson Lane, Halifax
YORKSHIRE 2 goals *Back*: J Dodd (Hal). *Three-quarters*: CE Bartram (Wak, t, 2c), H Fallas (Wak), H Wigglesworth (Tho). *Half-backs*: F Bonsor (Brad), H Hutchinson (Wak). *Forwards*: J Garforth (Dew), JL Hickson (Brad, t), J Lathom (Wak), JW Marshall (Brad), AC Sharpe (Hud), G Steele (Wak), GT Thomson (capt, Hal), W Wolstenholme (Dew), A Wood (Hal).
LANCASHIRE 0 *Back*: WW Higgins (Man). *Three-quarters*: E Storey (Man), J Robertson (BroR), AH Wrigley (Liv). *Half-backs*: J Mills (Swi), JH Payne (capt, Bro). *Forwards*: J Bagshaw (Swi), WS Hulse (Man), JT Hunt (Man/PresG), JH Jones (Walk), AT Kemble (Liv), FS Moss (Bro), A Teggin (BroR), E Trevor-Smith (Man), JD Wormald (Man).
Attendance: 8,000   *Referee*: GR Hill (RFU Honorary Secretary)

Saturday 24 November 1883 at Burdon Terrace, Newcastle
NORTHUMBERLAND 0 *Back*: REE Spencer (NorFC). *Three-quarters*: JT Todd (Tynd), JW Swinburne (Nor), HB Lockhart (Nor). *Half-backs*: MF Elsdon (Tynm), JVW Rutherford (capt, Nor). *Forwards*: R Dale (Tynm), A Mursell (Nor), S Oliver (Tynm), GR Palmer (Tynm), FW Ramsay (NorFC), GW Ridley (Nor), HS Rowell (Nor), WC Sample (NorFC), CE Winship (Nor).
EDINBURGH UNIVERSITY 2 goals, 1 try *Back*: H Chambers. *Half-backs*: G Macdonald, H Brooks. *Quarter-backs*: LH Evans (t0, LG Fischer (2t). *Forwards*: GB Batten, WH Campbell, G Hardyman (2c), LC Haslip, RSF Henderson, G Knowles, EL McClure, WA Peterkin (capt), FS Westenra, JW Williams.
Attendance: 2,000   *Referee*: PB Junor (Durham)

Saturday 8 December 1883 at Whitehaven Cricket Ground
CUMBERLAND 2 tries *Back*: J Shippen (Whi). *Three-quarters*: S Palmer (Whi, t), G Bell (Asp), RY Sutton (capt, Whi). *Half-backs*: WH Alderson (Whi), D Atkinson (Whi). *Forwards*: JT Anderson (Whi), J Brown (Mary), T Dobie (Asp), G Gibson (Cock), J Graham (Asp), J Harrison (Cock), W Holmes (Cock, t), R Simpson (Whi), J Steel (EdW).
DURHAM 1 try *Back*: T Davidson (NDur). *Three-quarters*: TF Wilson (Wes), JT Taylor (Ryton), A Hill (capt, HartR). *Half-backs*: FG Reed (Sund), FR Simpson (Sund). *Forwards*: W Coxon (Hou), WF Cross (SundR), CH Elliot (Sund), W Forster (Hou), WL Oakes (HartR, t), RE Reed (Sund), JW Sowerby (NDur), W Swinburne (NDur), WH Towers (HartR).
Attendance: n/a   *Referee*: JM Mawson (Barrow)

Monday 31 December 1883 at Whitehaven Cricket Ground
CUMBERLAND 0 *Back*: J Shippen (Whi). *Three-quarters*: RY Sutton (capt, Whi), J Hunter (Work), JW McQuhae (Cock). *Half-backs*: D Atkinson (Whi), SB Ridgway (Whi). *Forwards*: JT Anderson (Whi), J Brown (Mary), G Gibson (Cock), C Harrison (Whi), W Holmes (Cock), J Murchie (Work), HP Senhouse (Cock), W Sewell (Work), J Skelton (Cock).
DEWSBURY 1 goal, 5 tries *Back*: B Haigh. *Three-quarters*: WJ Fawcett (c), TP Bate (t), A Collins (t). *Half-backs*: WE Hanson (capt), J Taylor (2t). *Forwards*: WK Fisher, J Fligg, J Garforth, A Hirst, JH Jones, J Neville (t), P Redfearn, E Wolstenholme (t), W Wolstenholme.
Attendance: 2,000   *Referee*: n/a

Wednesday 2 January 1884 at Burdon Terrace, Newcastle
NORTHUMBERLAND 1 goal, 1 try *Back*: GA Bell (NorFC). *Three-quarters*: CH Sample (NorFC/CamU, c), EB Brutton (Tynm), T Robson (Tynd). *Half-backs*: WR Gray (PerPk), H Symington (Nor). *Forwards*: GH Armstrong (NorFC), R Dale (Tynm), A Eichholtz (NorFC, t), S Oliver (Tynm, t), GW Ridley (Nor), HS Rowell (Nor), FJ Scott (Nor), H Shotton (NEls), JW Swinburne (Nor).
DURHAM 1 try *Back*: T Davidson (NDur). *Three-quarters*: TF Wilson (Wes), JT Taylor (Ryton), FR Simpson (Sund). *Half-backs*: FG Reed (Sund), VT Thompson (Sund). *Forwards*: W Coxon (Hou), WF Cross (SundR), W Forster (Hou), A Hill (capt, HartR), RE Reed (Sund), JW Sowerby (NDur, t), W Swinburne (NDur), WH Towers (HartR), Willis (Boldon).
Attendance: n/a   *Referee*: n/a

Saturday 26 January 1884 at Cardigan Fields, Leeds
CHESHIRE 0 *Back*: E Whitehead (Duk). *Three-quarters*: H Murdoch (NewB), W Rome (NewB), J Cockerell (Cheadle). *Half-backs*: WN Fletcher (Man/BirkPk), H Hughes (Run). *Forwards*: J Barber (NewB), DA Bingham (BirkPk), H Blocksage (Duk), G Cowie (BirkPk), SD Crawford (NewB), HD Hulme (BirkPk), HJ Ryalls (NewB), A Williamson (BirkPk), W Wright (Run).
NORTHUMBERLAND 3 goals, 2 tries *Back*: RH Robb (Tynd). *Three-quarters*: CH Sample (NorFC/CamU, 2t, 2c, dg), MF Elsdon (Tynm), T Robson (Tynd). *Half-backs*: WR Gray (PerPk, t), H Symington (Nor). *Forwards*: R Dale (Tynm), A Eichholtz (NorFC), A Mursell (Nor), S Oliver (Tynm), FW Ramsay (NorFC), GW Ridley (capt, Nor), WC Sample (NorFC, t), JW Swinburne (Nor), CE Winship (Nor).
Attendance: n/a   *Referee*: T Glover (Yorkshire)

Saturday 9 February 1884 at Burdon Terrace, Newcastle
NORTHUMBERLAND 0 *Back*: RH Robb (Tynd). *Three-quarters*: T Robson (Tynd), WM Scott (NorFC), MF Elsdon (Tynm). *Half-backs*: JVW Rutherford (capt, Nor), H Symington (Nor). *Forwards*: JW Coward (PerPk), R Dale (Tynm), A Eichholtz (NorFC), A Mursell (Nor), S Oliver (Tynm), FW Ramsay (NorFC), GW Ridley (Nor), WC Sample (NorFC), JW Swinburne (Nor).
YORKSHIRE 1 goal, 2 tries *Back*: J Dodd (Hal). *Three-quarters*: JJ Hawcridge (Mann), A Wood (Hal), H Fallas (Wak, dg). *Half-backs*: F Bonsor (Brad), H Hutchinson (Wak, t). *Forwards*: GW Bottomley (Hud), J Garforth (Dew), G Harrison (Hull), J Lathom (Wak), H Robertshaw (Brad), GT Thomson (capt, Hal), H Ward (Wak), E Wilkinson (Brad, t), E Wolstenholme (Dew).
Attendance: 2,000   *Referee*: JT Todd (Durham)

Saturday 16 February 1884 at Liscard, Wallasey
CHESHIRE 0 *Back:* W McFarlane (Sale). *Three-quarters*: PF Shaw (capt, NewB), F Warburton (Sale), AC Blain (BirkPk). *Half-backs*: WN Fletcher (Man/BirkPk), E Reynolds (NewB). *Forwards*: H Bell (NewB), DA Bingham (BirkPk), H Blocksage (Duk), R Bolton (Sale), G Cowie (BirkPk), HD Hulme (BirkPk), E Lings (Sale), HJ Ryalls (NewB), A Williamson (BirkPk).
YORKSHIRE 1 goal *Back*: HO Hamshaw (Wak). *Three-quarters*: H Fallas (Wak), JJ Hawcridge (Mann), J Dodd (Hal, c). *Half-backs*: H Dawson (Wak), H Hutchinson (Wak). *Forwards*: GW Bottomley (Hud), WFB Calvert (Hull, t), JH Crossland (Hal), J Garforth (Dew), J Lathom (Wak), GT Thomson (capt, Hal), E Wilkinson (Brad), W Wolstenholme (Dew), A Wood (Hal).
Attendance: 2,000/3,000   *Referee*: n/a

Wednesday 20 February 1884 at University Running Ground, Iffley Road, Oxford
OXFORD UNIVERSITY 1 goal *Back*: HB Tristram. *Three-quarters*: CP Allen, HW Cave, CG Wade. *Half-backs*: AGG Asher, Alan Rotherham (t). *Forwards*: CW Berry (c), ED Court, RS Kindersley, FJC Mackenzie, EJ Moore, WH Squire, EL Strong, WM Tatham (capt), CS Wooldridge.
YORKSHIRE 0 *Back*: J Dodd (Hal). *Three-quarters*: H Fallas (Wak), H Wigglesworth (Tho), JJ Hawcridge (Mann). *Half-backs*: F Bonsor (Brad), H Hutchinson (Wak). *Forwards*: GW Bottomley (Hud), WFB Calvert (Hull), JH Crossland (Hal), J Garforth (Dew), J Lathom (Wak), GT Thomson (capt, Hal), E Wilkinson (Brad), W Wolstenholme (Dew), A Wood (Hal).
Attendance: 5,000   *Referee*: GR Hill (RFU Honorary Secretary)

Saturday 23 February 1884 at Chester Road, Sunderland
DURHAM 1 goal, 1 try *Back*: T Davidson (NDur). *Three-quarters*: FW Purves (HartR), H Brooks (Darl/EdinU, dg), FR Simpson (Sund). *Half-backs*: CH Newman (NDur), FG Reed (Sund). *Forwards*: W Coxon (Hou), WF Cross (SundR), CH Elliot (Sund), W Forster (Hou), WL Oakes (HartR), RE Reed (Sund), JW Sowerby (capt, NDur), W Swinburne (NDur), WH Towers (HartR, t).
NORTHUMBERLAND 0 *Back*: RH Robb (Tynd). *Three-quarters*: MF Elsdon (Tynm), GA Bell (NorFC), WM Scott (NorFC). *Half-backs*: JVW Rutherford (capt, Nor), H Symington (Nor). *Forwards*: GH Armstrong (NorFC), JW Coward (PerPk), R Dale (Tynm), A Darling (NorFC), A Eichholtz (NorFC), HB Lockhart (Nor), A Mursell (Nor), WC Sample (NorFC), JW Swinburne (Nor).
Attendance: 'large'   *Referee*: Rev CH Coates (Yorkshire)

Saturday 23 February 1884 at The Reddings, Moseley, Birmingham
MIDLAND COUNTIES 0 *Back*: R Byrne (Mose). *Three-quarters*: SH Evershed (capt, Burt), A Smith (Mose), JR Reid (Edg). *Half-backs*: P Lea (Mose), H Player (Edg). *Forwards*: C Cobb (Stour), CA Crane (Wolv), JR Deykin (Stour), P Evershed (Burt), G Fowler (Mose), AJ Otter (Stour), A Thompson (Stafford), G Ward (Mose), K Wilson (Mose).
LANCASHIRE 6 goals, 3 tries *Back*: WW Higgins (Man). *Three-quarters*: JW Hulse (Man, t), TH Hunt (Man/PresG), FT Wright (Man, 2t, 4c, 2dg). *Half-backs*: T Deane (Bro), JH Payne (capt, Bro). *Forwards*: J Bagshaw (Swi), WS Hulse (Man, t), JT Hunt (Man/PresG), JH Jones (Walk, t), FS Moss (Bro), JB Rye (Old, t), A Teggin (BroR), E Trevor-Smith (Man, t), J Welsh (Liv).
Attendance: 1,000   *Referee*: EB Holmes (Midland Counties)

ENGLAND TRIAL MATCH

Saturday 15 December 1883 at Whalley Range, Manchester
NORTH 0 *Back*: HB Tristram (OxfU). *Three-quarters*: SH Evershed (Burt), H Wigglesworth (Tho), CE Bartram (Wak). *Half-backs*: F Bonsor (Brad), H Hutchinson (Wak). *Forwards*: H Bell (NewB), J Garforth (Dew), JL Hickson (Brad), JT Hunt (Man/PresG), FS Moss (Bro), HJ Ryalls (NewB), A Teggin (BroR), GT Thomson (capt, Hal), A Wood (Hal).
SOUTH 2 goals, 3 tries *Back*: CH Sample (CamU, 2c). *Three-quarters*: AM Evanson (Rich, t), GC Wade (OxfU, 2t), WN Bolton (Black). *Half-backs*: Alan Rotherham (OxfU, t), HT Twynam (Rich). *Forwards*: HG Fuller (CamU), C Gurdon (Rich), ET Gurdon (capt, Rich), RSF Henderson (Black), CJB Marriott (CamU), HF Ransome (Man/CamU, t), EL Strong (OxfU), WM Tatham (MarlN/OxfU), CS Wooldridge (Black).
Attendance: 4,000   *Referee*: J MacLaren (RFU President)

INTERNATIONAL CHAMPIONSHIP

Saturday 5 January 1884 at Cardigan Fields, Leeds
ENGLAND 1 goal, 2 tries *Back*: HB Tristram (OxfU). *Three-quarters*: CG Wade (OxfU, t), CE Chapman (CamU), WN Bolton (Black, c). *Half-backs*: Alan Rotherham (OxfU, t), HT Twynam (Rich, t). *Forwards*: HG Fuller (CamU), G Gurdon (Rich), ET Gurdon (capt, Rich), RSF Henderson (Black), JT Hunt (Man), CJB Marriott (CamU), EL Strong (OxfU), WM Tatham (MarlN/OxfU), CS Wooldridge (Black).
WALES 1 goal *Back*: CP Lewis (LlanC, c). *Three-quarters*: CP Allen (OxfU, t), WB Norton (Car), CG Taylor (Rua). *Half-backs*: WH Gwynn (Swa), CH Newman (capt, New). *Forwards*: FG Andrews (Swa), TJS Clapp (New), R Gould (New), HS Lyne (New), FL Margrave (Llan), GL Morris (Swa), WD Phillips (Car), HJ Simpson (Car), JS Smith (Car).
Attendance: 2,000   *Referee*: JA Gardner (Scotland)

Monday 4 February 1884 at Lansdowne Road, Dublin
IRELAND 0 *Back*: JWR Morrow (QCB). *Half-backs*: RE McLean (NIFC), RH Scovell (DubU), DJ Ross (BelA). *Quarter-backs*: WW Higgins (NIFC), M Johnston (DubU). *Forwards*: HM Brabazon (DubU), JBW Buchanan (DubU), SAM Bruce (NIFC), RW Hughes (NIFC), FH Levis (Wand), JA Macdonald (capt, MethC), DF Moore (Wand), WG Rutherford (Tip), OS Stokes (Cork Bankers).
ENGLAND 1 goal *Back*: CH Sample (CamU, c). *Three-quarters*: WN Bolton (Black, t), HJ Wigglesworth (Tho), H Fallas (Wak). *Half-backs*: JH Payne (Bro), HT Twynam (Rich). *Forwards*: H Bell (NewB), ET Gurdon (capt, Rich), CJB Marriott (CamU), EL Strong (OxfU), WM Tatham (MarlN/OxfU), A Teggin (BroR), GT Thomson (Hal), A Wood (Hal), CS Wooldridge (Black).
Attendance: 6,000   *Referee*: JS Laing (Scotland)

Saturday 1 March 1884 at Rectory Field, Blackheath
ENGLAND 1 goal *Back*: HB Tristram (OxfU). *Three-quarters*: WN Bolton (Black, c), AM Evanson (Rich), CG Wade (OxfU). *Half-backs*: Alan Rotherham (OxfU), HT Twynam (Rich). *Forwards*: C Gurdon (Rich), ET Gurdon (capt, Rich), RSF Henderson (Black), RS Kindersley (OxfU, t), CJB Marriott (CamU), EL Strong (OxfU), WM Tatham (MarlN/OxfU), GT Thomson (Hal), CS Wooldridge (Black).

SCOTLAND 1 try *Back*: JP Veitch (RHSFP). *Half-backs*: WE Maclagan (capt, LonS), ET Roland (EdinW), DJ McFarlan (LonS). *Quarter-backs*: AGG Asher (FetLor), AR Don-Wauchope (FetLor). *Forwards*: T Ainslie (EdinIFP), CW Berry (FetLor), JB Brown (GlasA), J Jamieson (WoS, t), D McCowan (WoS), WA Peterkin (EdinU), C Reid (EdinA), J Tod (Wat), WA Walls (GlasA).
Attendance: 8,000   *Referee*: G Scriven (Ireland)

Other results
Wales 0, Scotland 1g, 1t
Scotland 2g, 2t, Ireland 1t
Wales 1g, 2t, Ireland 0

Final table

	P	W	D	L	G-T	G-T
England	3	3	0	0	3-2	1-1
Scotland	3	2	0	1	3-4	1-1
Wales	3	1	0	2	2-2	2-3
Ireland	3	0	0	3	0-1	4-4

1884-1885

THE YORKSHIRE CUP: MINOR POINTS
In an effort to avoid replays in the Yorkshire Cup it was decided to take so-called 'minor points' into account. When the Yorkshire Committee met at the Queen's Hotel, Leeds, on 14th July 1884, they decided that when a match would otherwise be considered drawn, the team scoring not less than a majority of three minor points shall be declared the winners, anything less still being considered a draw.[58]

THE WEST LANCASHIRE AND BORDER TOWNS UNION
The West Lancashire and Border Towns Union was founded at a crowded meeting in Liverpool Gymnasium on the 10th November with the creation of a challenge cup competition its prime motive. It was seen as 'the only means to which Rugby Union could be maintained as an institution and hold its own against the increased popularity of the Association game'.[59] The West Lancashire and Border Towns Challenge Cup subsequently began in 1885-86.

UNABLE TO RAISE A TEAM
Yorkshire's home fixture with Midland Counties, scheduled for Dewsbury on 15th November, was cancelled as the visitors were unable to raise a team.

THE YORKSHIRE CUP: A DISGRACEFUL SCENE
When Leeds Parish Church defeated visitors Bradford Trinity in the Yorkshire Cup first round on 28th February, the *Yorkshire Post* reported that

'the one great blot of the week was the disgraceful scene enacted at Crown Point, Leeds. From a reliable source we learn that the game was a series of squabbles, which ultimately ended in the spectators breaking into the field and Bradford Trinity retiring some five or six minutes before the call of "no side". In this instance the referee seemed to have lost his head, his decisions being neither prompt nor decisive'.[60]

THE YORKSHIRE CUP: A FEAT NEVER EQUALLED
After Manningham entertained Brighouse (not to be confused with Brighouse Rangers) in the Yorkshire Cup first round on 28th February, it was reported that Manningham's Billy Fawcett 'carried off the palm' (indicating he was the outstanding player) scoring four tries and ten goals from eleven attempts, claimed as 'a feat which has never been equalled in one match'.[61]

THE CUMBERLAND CUP: A BIASED UMPIRE
The *Athletic News* made a good case for neutral umpires with the following comment: 'It has often been said that the umpire is the sixteenth player in a team; but this was never better shown than in the cup-tie on Saturday [7th March] between Whitehaven and Cockermouth for the Cumberland Challenge Cup, when the Cockermouth umpire repeatedly clapped his hands on the referee deciding in favour of Cockermouth.'[62]

THE DURHAM CUP: A FRIVOLOUS OBJECTION
After Sunderland Rovers defeated Hartlepool Rovers by one try to nil in a Durham Cup semi-final on 7th March, the latter lodged an appeal on the grounds that the Sunderland Rovers umpire had bet on the game. The County Committee decided it was a 'frivolous objection' and dismissed the claim.[63]

THE DURHAM CUP COMPETITION SUSPENDED
The Durham County Union, at a meeting held at Walton's Hotel, Sunderland, on 20th March, decided to withdraw the Durham Cup for the following 1885-86 season. The *Northern Echo* did not pull any punches: 'A great deal of indignation has been aroused by the announcement. It is said the County Committee think bringing clubs together in such a competition begets an unfriendly spirit amongst players. If this is the only excuse for what is looked upon as their outrageous action, the spirit of gentleness must indeed be powerful in the bosoms of those committeemen. If it is the outcome of the dispute as to the Sunderland [Rovers] and Hartlepool

[Rovers] match, [it] does not give us a favourable idea of their wisdom. It is part of the committee's duty to settle any unfortunate dispute, and it seems a petty schoolboy course for them to put a check on the progress of football in the county at the first appeal that is made to them. Their action does not prove the existence in our clubs of any reprehensible spirit, but simply tells of the weakness of the county committee.'[64]

THE YORKSHIRE CUP FINAL: A MINOR VICTORY

The Yorkshire Cup final was unusual in that it was won without a goal or try being scored, being decided on the new secondary criteria of minors, Batley defeating Manningham by eight minor points to two. Held at the Leeds St John's ground at Cardigan Fields on 4th April in front of a reported 15,000 crowd, the *Leeds Mercury* relayed an imaginative description of the scene: 'An extra grandstand, capable of holding over 2,000 spectators, had been erected. This structure, however, must have been improperly put together, as it gave way in the middle, unable to bear the weight of the crowd. Fortunately no one was injured, but many who would otherwise have had a good view of the game, were prevented from seeing so well. Behind the barriers a number of wherries [long rowing boats used for canal passenger transport] had been placed, but even these were insufficient to accommodate all the spectators, and hundreds can have had glimpses only of the game. Special stands, too, had been erected for the press and for the members of the County Committee, and every arrangement made for the comfort of those present that the careful thought of St. John's executive could suggest. Hundreds witnessed the match from the hill on the Armley side of the river, and other points of vantage in the neighbourhood were well patronised.'[65]

1884-1885 STATISTICS

CUMBERLAND COUNTY CHALLENGE CUP (11 entries)
Most goals. If equal, most tries. If still equal, majority of 3 minor points.

First Round
Aspatria 1t, Carlisle City 0
Maryport 1t, Penrith 0
Parton 0, Cockermouth 0 (mp: 2-5)
Whitehaven 1g, 2t, Workington 1g, 1t
Wigton 0, Millom 2g, 2t
Bye: Millom St James's

Second Round
Cockermouth 1t, Whitehaven 1g, 1t
Maryport 2t, Millom St James's 1t
Millom 0, Aspatria 1t

Semi-final
Whitehaven 2t, Maryport 0
(at Noble Croft, Aspatria). *Bye*: Aspatria

FINAL
Saturday 28 March 1885 at Waterworks Lane, Carlisle
ASPATRIA 1 goal, 1 try *Back*: W Lauriston. *Three-quarters*: CJ Irving, G Bell (capt, c), J Tremble. *Half-backs*: H Monkhouse, WT Ridley (t). *Forwards*: W Blaylock, J Harker, T Holliday, T McKenzie, J Mumberson. G Rayson, W Sanderson, J Sandwith (t), J Todd.
WHITEHAVEN 0 *Back*: J Shippen. *Three-quarters*: R Simpson, SR Palmer, D Atkinson. *Half-backs*: I Stamper, RY Sutton (capt). *Forwards*: W Brockbank, J Doran, R Douglas, C Harrison, W Hayton, C Milligan, T Shippen, T Smith, J Wright.
Attendance: 2,000/3,000   *Referee*: W Dodgshon (Carlisle)

DURHAM COUNTY CHALLENGE CUP (11 entries)
Most goals wins. If equal, most tries. If still equal, majority of 3 minor points.

First Round
Durham City 3g, Boldon 0
Hartlepool Rovers 2g, 1t, Sunderland 0
Humbledon (Sunderland) 2g, 1t, Houghton-le-Spring 1g, 1t
North Durham 1t, Ryton 0
Westoe 0, Sunderland Rovers 0 (mp: 3-6)
Bye: Darlington

Second Round
Humbledon 1g, Durham City 2g, 1t
North Durham 0, Hartlepool Rovers 1g, 1t
Sunderland Rovers 1g, 1t, Darlington 0

Semi-finals
Hartlepool Rovers 0, Sunderland Rovers 1t
Bye: Durham City

FINAL
Saturday 21 March 1885 at Friarage Field, Hartlepool
DURHAM CITY 1 goal, 4 tries *Back*: HB Tristram. *Three-quarters*: HE Ferens, FA Ker, JT Robinson. *Half-backs*: J Turnbull (2t), AR Wilson (t). *Forwards*: J Crozier (c), W Crozier (t), FJ Hall, R Harrison, F Lumsden (t), FW Morgan, TE Rickerby (capt), WP Root, QH Warden.
SUNDERLAND ROVERS 0 *Back*: WH Bell. *Three-quarters*: WE Thompson, EH Toft, W Crisp. *Half-backs*: T Lee, JC Wilford. *Forwards*: T Annison, R Barwick, E Bell (capt), WF Cross, F Forrest, R Noton, T Robson, A Toft, W Waddell.
Attendance: 3,000/4,000   *Referee*: JT Todd (Durham RU President)

NORTHUMBERLAND COUNTY FOOTBALL CHALLENGE CUP (6 entries)
Most goals wins. If equal, most tries. If still equal, majority of 3 minor points.

First Round
Northern 5g, 2t, North Elswick 0
Northumberland FC 1t, Percy Park 2t
Tynedale 0, Tynemouth 1g

Semi-finals
Northern 2g, 2t, Percy Park 0
Bye: Tynemouth

FINAL
Saturday 21 March 1885 at Burdon Terrace, Newcastle
TYNEMOUTH 2 goals *Back*: G Oliver. *Three-quarters*: MF Elsdon (dg), J Sisterton, J Dall.
Half-backs: H Bramwell, J Foreman (t). *Forwards*: R Dale (capt), TR Dixon, WH Farrow,
W Frazier, JH Greenwell, R Grieves, S Oliver (c), GR Palmer, J Walton.
NORTHERN 1 goal *Back*: CE Morgan. *Three-quarters*: CS Gill, HB Lockhart, H Symington.
Half-backs: RE Herbertson, B Sutherland. *Forwards*: SJ Allden, J Brown, H Coates, P Jones,
J Livingstone, A Mursell, JA Robertson, FJ Scott, JW Swinburne (capt).
Attendance: 4,000/5,000   *Referee*: n/a
Note: Scorer of Northern drop-goal reported as CE Winship, although not listed in team.

DURHAM v NORTHUMBERLAND CHALLENGE MATCH
Saturday 28 March 1885 at Chester Road, Sunderland
DURHAM CITY (Durham Cup winners) **3 goals, 1 try** *Back*: HB Tristram (dg). *Three-quarters*: HE Ferens, FA Ker, JT Robinson. *Half-backs*: J Turnbull, AR Wilson. *Forwards*:
J Crozier (2c), W Crozier (t), FJ Hall (t), R Harrison, F Lumsden (t), FW Morgan,
TE Rickerby (capt), WP Root, QH Warden.
TYNEMOUTH (Northumberland Cup winners) **1 try** *Back*: G Oliver. *Three-quarters*:
AE Hunter, J Sisterson, MF Elsdon. *Half-backs*: H Bramwell, J Foreman. *Forwards*:
W Cummins, R Dale (capt), WH Farrow, W Frazier, JH Greenwell (t), R Grieves, S Oliver,
GR Palmer, J Walton.
Attendance: 2,500   *Referee*: Rev CH Newman (North Durham)

YORKSHIRE COUNTY FOOTBALL CHALLENGE CUP (64 entries)
Most goals wins. If equal, most tries. If still equal, majority of 3 minor points.

First Round
Barnsley 1g, Bramley 1g (mp: 0-8)
Batley 1g, 2t, Heckmondwike 0
Batley Carr Trinity 0, Keighley 2t
Bingley 1g, 2t, Buttershaw 1t
Bowling 2g, 1t, Bradford Rangers 2t
Bradford 3g, 3t, Hull 0
Bradford Trinity 2g, Leeds Parish Church 2g, 3t (replay ordered after protest)
Brighouse 0, Manningham 10g, 5t
Brighouse Rangers 4g, 3t, Gildersome 0
Castleford 4g, 3t, Denfield 0
Dewsbury 1g, 1t, Hull Southcoates 1t
Doncaster Town 1t, Leeds St John's 2g, 4t
Dudley Hill 1g, Morley 1t
Eastmoor 1t, Dodworth 0
Halifax 4g, 7t, Hebden Bridge 0
Halifax Free Wanderers 1g, 2t, Hipperholme and Lightcliffe 1t
Harrogate White Star 1g, 1t, Mytholmroyd 1g
Huddersfield St Paul's 0, Cleckheaton 2g, 2t

First Round *continued*
Hunslet 2g, Elland 1g
Luddendenfoot 0, Pudsey 2g, 1t
Mirfield 1g, 2t, Halifax St Joseph's 0
Normanton 0, Goole 0 (mp: 4-1)
Ossett 1t, Wakefield St Austin's 1t (mp: 4-2, aet)
Otley 0, Horbury 1t
Pontefract 0, Liversedge 2t
Ravensthorpe 0, Selby 1t
Salterhebble 5g, 4t, Beverley 0
Shipley 2g, 2t, Middlesbrough Rovers 1t
Stanley 3t, Thornhill 1g
Thornes 0, Wakefield Trinity 1g
Wortley 0, Kirkstall 1g
York 2t, Birstall 0

First Round Replays
Leeds Parish Church 2t, Bradford Trinity 0 (at Dewbury)
Wakefield St Austin's 0, Ossett 1t

Second Round
Bowling 0, Bramley 1g
Brighouse Rangers 4t, Keighley 0
Castleford 0, Bradford 1g, 2t (aet)
Cleckheaton 0, Wakefield Trinity 0 (mp: 3-8)
Dewsbury 1g, 3t, York 0
Dudley Hill 0, Manningham 2t
Halifax 0, Horbury 0 (mp: 4-0)
Halifax Free Wanderers 1g, 3t, Normanton 0
Hunslet 1g, 1t, Bingley 0
Leeds Parish Church 2g, Shipley 0
Leeds St John's 5g, 2t, Harrogate White Star 0
Liversedge 2g, 6t, Thornhill 0
Mirfield 1g, 1t, Eastmoor 0
Pudsey 1t, Batley 4g, 2t
Salterhebble 1g, 2t, Ossett 0
Selby 1g, Kirkstall 0

Third Round
Bramley 0, Bradford 1g, 2t
Dewsbury 3t, Halifax Free Wanderers 1g (replay ordered after protest)
Halifax 0, Batley 1g
Hunslet 1t, Leeds St John's 0
Liversedge 1g, 1t, Mirfield 0
Salterhebble 1t, Brighouse Rangers 0
Selby 1g, Manningham 1g, 2t
Wakefield Trinity 3g, 2t, Leeds Parish Church 1t

Third Round Replay
Halifax Free Wanderers 0, Dewsbury 1g

Fourth Round
Bradford 7g, 3t, Hunslet 0
Dewsbury 1t, Wakefield Trinity 1t (mp: 4-0)
Manningham 2t, Liversedge 0
Salterhebble 0, Batley 1t

Semi-finals
Batley 1g, Bradford 1t
(at Hanson Lane, Halifax)
Manningham 3g, 2t, Dewsbury 1g
(at Fartown, Huddersfield)

Milestones & Stats 1869-1901

FINAL

Saturday 4 April 1885 at Cardigan Fields, Leeds
BATLEY 0 (8 minor points) *Back*: H Ratcliffe. *Three-quarters*: JT Haslam, A Ineson, H Simms. *Half-backs*: A Hirst, J Naylor. *Forwards*: CE Carter, T Nicholson, A Parker, J Parker (capt), A Scholes, J Stoner, JW Sykes, H Terry, W Wolstenholme.
MANNINGHAM 0 (2 minor points) *Back*: W Robinson. *Three-quarters*: WJ Fawcett, Fred W Richmond, H Archer (capt). *Half-backs*: D Halfyard, RS Snowden. *Forwards*: E Holmes, H Jowett, M Kitchen, W Knowles, J Lorimer, Frank D Richmond, T Robinson, J West, F Wigglesworth.
Attendance: 15,000   *Referee*: GT Thomson (Halifax)

COUNTY MATCHES

Saturday 8 November 1884 at Friarage Field, Hartlepool
DURHAM 1 try *Back*: HO Hoy (HartR). *Three-quarters*: FW Purves (HartR), H Brooks (Darl/EdinU), JT Taylor (Ryton). *Half-backs*: CH Newman (NDur), AR Wilson (DurU, t). *Forwards*: HH Carrick (NDur), B Cox (Sund), WF Cross (SundR), CH Elliot (Sund), A Hill (capt, HartR), WL Oakes (HartR), RE Reed (Sund), JW Sowerby (NDur), WH Towers (HartR).
YORKSHIRE 1 goal, 1 try *Back*: HO Hamshaw (Wak). *Three-quarters*: CE Bartram (Wak), H Fallas (Wak, dg), JT Haslam (Bat). *Half-backs*: GE Belt (Hull), F Bonsor (Brad, t). *Forwards*: AJ Forrest (LeeStJ), J Garforth (Dew), G Harrison (Hull), G Jubb (Wak), G Millar (Hal), TP Peacock (LeeStJ), H Robertshaw (Brad), GT Thomson (capt, Hal), E Wilkinson (Brad).
Attendance: 6,000   *Referee*: Dr GW Ridley (Northumberland)

Saturday 15 November 1884 at Liscard, Wallasey
CHESHIRE 1 goal, 1 try *Back*: F Wainwright (Bow, c). *Three-quarters*: R Barber (NewB, t), WN Fletcher (capt, Man/BirkPk), JA Black (BirkPk). *Half-backs*: LM Holden (NewB), RH Jackson (BirkPk). *Forwards*: J Barber (NewB), DA Bingham (BirkPk), WH Broady (Run), JE Davies (NewB), C Hardy (Bow), JH Jones (NewB), E Lings (Sale), HJ Ryalls (NewB, t), A Williamson (BirkPk).
LANCASHIRE 1 goal, 3 tries *Back*: AN Hornby (capt, Man). *Three-quarters*: FT Wright (Man, t, c), J Robertson (BroR, t), WS Sawyer (Bro, t). *Half-backs*: T Deane (Bro), JH Payne (Bro). *Forwards*: C Anderton (ManFW), J Bagshaw (Swi), CH Horley (Swi), WS Hulse (Man), AT Kemble (Liv, t), FS Moss (Bro), JB Rye (Old), A Teggin (BroR), J Welsh (Liv).
Attendance: 6,000   *Referee*: GT Thomson (Yorkshire)

Saturday 15 November 1884 at Waterworks Lane, Carlisle
CUMBERLAND 1 try *Back*: J Shippen (Whi). *Three-quarters*: D Atkinson (Whi), CE Chapman (EdW/CamU), JW McQuhae (Cock). *Half-backs*: W Dodgshon (CarlC), RY Sutton (capt, Whi, t). *Forwards*: J Bayman (Par), GB Blake (EdW), J Brown (Mary), G Gibson (Cock), C Harris (Whi), W Holmes (Cock), SR McPhail (EdW/EdinU), JL Smith (Work), J Steel (EdW).
NORTHUMBERLAND 2 tries *Back*: RH Robb (Tynd). *Three-quarters*: MF Elsdon (Tynm), HB Lockhart (Nor), WM Scott (NorFC). *Half-backs*: GA Bell (capt, NorFC), WR Gray (PerPk, t). *Forwards*: GH Armstrong (NorFC), J Bailey (Tynd), GH Bell (Tynd), CH Coates

(Nor), S Oliver (Tynm), FW Ramsay (NorFC, t), JA Robertson (Nor), M Thompson (NorFC), J Walton (Tynm).
Attendance: 'fair'   *Referee*: AR Don-Wauchope (Scotland)

Saturday 22 November 1884 at Whalley Range, Manchester
LANCASHIRE 1 goal, 2 tries *Back*: WW Higgins (Man). *Three-quarters*: J Valentine (Swi), JW Hulse (Man, c), FT Wright (Man, 2t). *Half-backs*: J Mills (Swi), JH Payne (capt, Bro). *Forwards*: T Banks (Swi), H Bell (LivOB), HC Chapman (LivOB), CH Horley (Swi), WS Hulse (Man), AT Kemble (Liv, t), FS Moss (Bro), RL Seddon (BroR), A Teggin (BroR).
YORKSHIRE 0 *Back*: J Dodd (Hal). *Three-quarters*: CE Bartram (Wak), H Fallas (Wak), TL Scarborough (Hal). *Half-backs*: H Hutchinson (Wak), JH Potter (LeeStJ). *Forwards*: WFB Calvert (Hull), J Garforth (Dew), S Haigh (Brad), G Harrison (Hull), G Jacketts (Hull), A Parker (Bat), TP Peacock (LeeStJ), G Steele (Wak), GT Thomson (capt, Hal).
Attendance: 8,000/10,000   *Referee*: GR Hill (RFU Honorary Secretary)

Saturday 6 December 1884 at Chester Road, Sunderland
DURHAM 2 goals *Back*: HO Hoy (HartR). *Three-quarters*: FW Purves (HartR), H Brooks (Darl/EdinU, 2c), JT Taylor (Ryton). *Half-backs*: CH Newman (capt, NDur), AR Wilson (DurU). *Forwards*: HH Carrick (NDur, t), B Cox (Sund), WF Cross (SundR, t), J Crozier (DurC), CH Elliot (Sund), FJ Hall (DurC), RE Reed (Sund), JW Sowerby (NDur), WW Wilkin (Wes).
CUMBERLAND 1 goal *Back*: RS Bailey (CarlC). *Three-quarters*: W Lewthwaite (Mary), CE Chapman (EdW/CamU, dg), J Hunter (Work). *Half-backs*: J Robley (Mary), Joe Wilson (Work). *Forwards*: J Bayman (Par), J Brown (Mary), EH Dawson (CarlC), G Gibson (Cock), MJ Huthart (EdW), SR McPhail (EdW/EdinU), J Skelton (Mary), JL Smith (Work), W Wood (Par).
Attendance: n/a   *Referee*: Dr GW Ridley (Northumberland)

Saturday 6 December 1884 at Burdon Terrace, Newcastle
NORTHUMBERLAND 0 *Back*: CE Morgan (Nor). *Three-quarters*: CH Sample (capt, NorFC/CamU), HB Lockhart (Nor), W Pattinson (Tynd). *Half-backs*: WR Gray (PerPk), H Symington (Nor). *Forwards*: GH Armstrong (NorFC), JW Coward (PerPk), CW Harrison (Tynd), A Mursell (Nor), GR Palmer (Tynm), FW Ramsay (NorFC), JA Robertson (Nor), M Thompson (NorFC), CE Winship (Nor).
LANCASHIRE 1 goal, 3 tries *Back*: WW Higgins (Man). *Three-quarters*: JB Lonsdale (Walk), J Robertson (BroR, t), EH Flower (Bro, t, c). *Half-backs*: T Deane (Bro), JH Payne (capt, Bro, t). *Forwards*: C Anderton (ManFW), JA Brodie (Walton), HC Chapman (LivOB), WS Hulse (Man), AT Kemble (Liv, t), FS Moss (Bro), WA Scholes (RochH), RL Seddon (BroR), A Teggin (BroR).
Attendance: 3,000   *Referee*: AN Hornby (Lancashire)

Friday 2 January 1885 at Chester Road, Sunderland
DURHAM 0 *Back*: HO Hoy (HartR). *Three-quarters*: H Brooks (Darl/EdinU), A Hill (capt, HartR), FR Simpson (Sund). *Half-backs*: EA Douglas (Crook/CamU), J Stobart (Ryton). *Forwards*: R Barwick (SundR), HH Carrick (NDur), B Cox (Sund), W Forster (Hou), W Kimpster (NDur), WL Oakes (HartR), TE Rickerby (DurC), JW Sowerby (NDur), WH Towers (HartR).

NORTHUMBERLAND 0 *Back*: HB Lockhart (Nor). *Three-quarters*: C Charles (Nor), V Rutherford (Nor), AE Bainbridge (NorFC). *Half-backs*: WM Scott (NorFC), H Symington (Nor). *Forwards*: GH Armstrong (NorFC), JW Coward (PerPk), A Eichholtz (NorFC), A Mursell (Nor), GR Palmer (Tynm), JA Robertson (Nor), M Thompson (NorFC), G Walters (capt, Nor), CE Winship (Nor).
Attendance: 'large'   *Referee*: CWL Fendandes (Yorkshire)

Saturday 17 January 1885 at Cardigan Fields, Leeds
CHESHIRE 1 goal, 1 try *Back*: LJW Clegg (Bow). *Three-quarters*: R Barber (NewB), CFS Lathom (Bow), W Rome (NewB). *Half-backs*: WN Fletcher (capt, Man/BirkPk), RH Jackson (BirkPk). *Forwards*: J Barber (NewB, t), DA Bingham (BirkPk), G Cowie (BirkPk), J Herron (NewB, c), JH Jones (NewB, t), E Lings (Sale), HF Ransome (Bow), ET Trevor-Smith (Sale), A Williamson (BirkPk).
NORTHUMBERLAND 0 *Back*: RH Robb (Tynd). *Three-quarters*: H Shotton (NEls), CH Sample (NorFC/CamU), AE Bainbridge (NorFC). *Half-backs*: V Rutherford (Nor), WM Scott (NorFC). *Forwards*: GH Armstrong (NorFC), JW Coward (PerPk), CW Harrison (Tynd), J Honeyman (NEls), GW Mole (NEls), FW Ramsay (NorFC), JA Robertson (Nor), HW Sample (NorFC/CamU), M Thompson (NorFC).
Attendance: 'moderate'   *Referee*: JA Miller (Yorkshire)

Saturday 17 January 1885 at Whitehaven Cricket Ground
CUMBERLAND 1 try *Back*: J Shippen (Whi). *Three-quarters*: WH Musgrave (Whi), W Lewthwaite (Mary), D Atkinson (Whi). *Half-backs*: J Hunter (Work), RY Sutton (capt, Whi). *Forwards*: J Brown (Mary), G Gibson (Cock), C Harris (Whi), B Hodgson (Whi), W Holmes (Cock, t), T Shippen (Whi), J Thomson (Pen), John Wilson (Work), W Wood (Par).
FURNESS 1 goal, 1 try *Back*: JR Harley (Barrow). *Three-quarters*: S Troughton (capt, Askam, c), GB Ashburner (Barrow), WH Nurton (Askam, 2t). *Half-backs*: JH Walton (Barrow), J Trenwith (Askam). *Forwards*: FS Ainslie (Barrow), J Anderson (Askam), A Dixon (Askam), RK Grey (Askam), H Leak (Barrow), T MacDonald (Askam), J Todd (Dalton), R Wilson (Ulverston), JJ Woodburn (Askam).
Attendance: 'large'   *Referee*: n/a

Saturday 31 January 1885 at Whalley Range, Manchester
LANCASHIRE 4 tries *Back*: WW Higgins (Man). *Three-quarters*: FT Wright (Man), EH Flower (Bro), J Robertson (BroR). *Half-backs*: T Deane (Bro), JH Payne (capt, Bro). *Forwards*: C Anderton (ManFW), H Bell (LivOB), CH Horley (Swi), AT Kemble (Liv, t), FS Moss (Bro, t), JB Rye (Old), WA Scholes (RochH), RL Seddon (BroR, t), A Teggin (BroR, t).
DURHAM 1 try *Back*: HO Hoy (HartR). *Three-quarters*: H Brooks (Darl/EdinU), FW Purves (HartR), FR Simpson (Sund). *Half-backs*: CH Newman (capt, NDur), AR Wilson (DurU). *Forwards*: R Barwick (SundR), HH Carrick (NDur), B Cox (Sund), CH Elliot (Sund), A Hill (HartR), WL Oakes (HartR), TE Rickerby (DurC, t), JW Sowerby (NDur), WH Towers (HartR).
Attendance: 2,000   *Referee*: GR Hill (RFU Honorary Secretary)

Saturday 7 February 1885 at Park Avenue, Bradford
YORKSHIRE 2 goals *Back*: HB Wilson (Hud). *Three-quarters*: H Simms (Bat), AR Robertshaw (Brad, dg), TL Scarborough (Hal). *Half-backs*: F Bonsor (capt, Brad), JH Potter (LeeStJ, c). *Forwards*: WFB Calvert (Hull), WP Carter (Brad), FL Mawer (Hull), J Oddy (LeePC), TP Peacock (LeeStJ), H Robertshaw (Brad), H Ward (Wak), E Wilkinson (Brad), E Wolstenholme (Dew, t).
NORTHUMBERLAND 1 try *Back*: CE Morgan (Nor). *Three-quarters*: W Pattinson (Tynd), V Rutherford (Nor), MF Elsdon (Tynm). *Half-backs*: WR Gray (PerPk), H Symington (capt, Nor). *Forwards*: GH Armstrong (NorFC), JW Coward (PerPk), TR Dixon (Tynm), T Gee (PerPk), J Honeyman (NEls), GR Palmer (Tynm), RH Robb (Tynd), T Rogan (NorFC), JW Swinburne (Nor, t).
Attendance: 6,000   *Referee*: PB Junor (Durham)

Monday 9 February 1885 at Crown Flatts, Dewsbury
YORKSHIRE 0 *Back*: J Dodd (Hal). *Three-quarters*: H Fallas (Wak), JJ Hawcridge (Brad), H Simms (Bat). *Half-backs*: J Parker (Hal), JH Potter (LeeStJ). *Forwards*: WP Carter (Brad), J Garforth (Dew), G Harrison (Hull), TP Peacock (LeeStJ), GD Scarborough (Hal), GT Thomson (capt, Hal), H Ward (Wak), E Wilkinson (Brad), E Wolstenholme (Dew).
MIDDLESEX 0 *Back*: PB Harrower (LonS). *Three-quarters*: WE Maclagan (LonS), AE Stoddart (Black), CM Wilkins (MarlN). *Half-backs*: WK Arber (Rich), JH Roberts (Rich). *Forwards*: WG Clibborn (Rich), WE Clifton (Rich), C Gurdon (Rich), ET Gurdon (Rich), J Hammond (Black), EH Lawrie (MarlN), CJB Marriott (Black), WJ Payne (ClapR), JD Vans Agnew (capt, MarlN).
Attendance: 4,000/5,000   *Referee*: W Cail (Northumberland)

Saturday 14 February 1885 at Belle Vue, Wakefield
YORKSHIRE 1 goal, 3 tries *Back*: HB Wilson (Hud). *Three-quarters*: H Fallas (Wak, c), JT Haslam (Bat), JJ Hawcridge (Brad, t). *Half-backs*: J Parker (Hal), JH Potter (LeeStJ). *Forwards*: J Garforth (Dew, t), G Harrison (Hull), C Mathers (Bram), TP Peacock (LeeStJ, t), GD Scarborough (Hal), GT Thomson (capt, Hal, t), H Ward (Wak), E Wilkinson (Brad), E Wolstenholme (Dew).
CHESHIRE 2 tries *Back*: C Holden (BirkPk). *Three-quarters*: JA Black (BirkPk, 2t), LJW Clegg (Bow), AC Blain (BirkPk). *Half-backs*: WN Fletcher (capt, Man/BirkPk), RH Jackson (BirkPk). *Forwards*: DA Bingham (BirkPk), F Dun (BirkPk), JH Jones (NewB), E Lings (Sale), H Marsland (Sale), HF Ransome (Bow), HJ Ryalls (NewB), ET Trevor-Smith (Sale), A Williamson (BirkPk).
Attendance: 5,000   *Referee*: GR Hill (RFU Honorary Secretary)

Saturday 21 February 1885 at Burdon Terrace, Newcastle
NORTHUMBERLAND 1 goal *Back*: CE Morgan (Nor). *Three-quarters*: CH Sample (NorFC/CamU, dg), H Symington (Nor), MF Elsdon (Tynm). *Half-backs*: GA Bell (capt, NorFC), WM Scott (NorFC). *Forwards*: GH Armstrong (NorFC), JW Coward (PerPk), TR Dixon (Tynm), T Gee (PerPk), J Honeyman (NEls), A Mursell (Nor), FW Ramsay (NorFC), JW Swinburne (Nor), T Wallace (NorFC).
DURHAM 1 goal *Back*: HO Hoy (HartR). *Three-quarters*: H Brooks (Darl/EdinU), AE Emmerson (HartR, dg), H Hodgson (Darl). *Half-backs*: CH Newman (capt, NDur), AR Wilson (DurU). *Forwards*: R Barwick (SundR), HH Carrick (NDur), B Cox (Sund),

A Hill (HartR), WL Oakes (HartR), RE Reed (Sund), TE Rickerby (DurC), JW Sowerby (NDur), WH Towers (HartR).
Attendance: 'large'   *Referee*: JA Miller (Yorkshire)

ENGLAND TRIAL MATCH

Saturday 20 December 1884 at Rectory Field, Blackheath
SOUTH 1 try *Back*: D Dryden (Tiv). *Three-quarters*: CG Wade (OxfU), AE Stoddart (Black), WN Bolton (Black). *Half-backs*: Alan Rotherham (OxfU), HT Twynam (Rich). *Forwards*: ED Court (Black, t), C Gurdon (Rich), ET Gurdon (capt, Rich), J Hammond (Black), RSF Henderson (Black), RS Kindersley (OxfU), VC le Fanu (CamU), EJ Moore (Black/OxfU), WM Tatham (MarlN).
NORTH 0 *Back*: WW Higgins (Man). *Three-quarters*: JJ Hawcridge (Brad), H Brooks (Darl/EdinU), CH Sample (NorFC/CamU). *Half-backs*: JH Payne (capt, Bro), JH Potter (LeeStJ). *Forwards*: DA Bingham (BirkPk), G Harrison (Hull), CH Horley (Swi), AT Kemble (Liv), FS Moss (Bro), A Teggin (BroR). HF Ransome (Man/CamU), JW Sowerby (NDur), GT Thomson (Hal).
Attendance: 3,000   *Referee*: FI Currey (RFU President)

INTERNATIONAL CHAMPIONSHIP

Saturday 3 January 1885 at St Helen's, Swansea
WALES 1 goal, 1 try *Back*: JA Gould (New). *Three-quarters*: HM Jordan (New, 2t), FE Hancock (Car), CG Taylor (Rua, c). *Half-backs*: WH Gwynn (Swa), CH Newman (capt, New). *Forwards*: TJS Clapp (New), S Goldsworthy (Swa), R Gould (New), T B Jones (New), HS Lyne (New), ES Richards (Swa), J Rowlands (Lampeter), JS Smith (Car), LC Thomas (Car).
ENGLAND 1 goal, 4 tries *Back*: HB Tristram (OxfU). *Three-quarters*: CG Wade (OxfU, t), AE Stoddart (Black), JJ Hawcridge (Brad, t). *Half-backs*: JH Payne (Bro, c), Alan Rotherham (OxfU). *Forwards*: ED Court (Black), ET Gurdon (capt, Rich), G Harrison (Hull), RSF Henderson (Black), AT Kemble (Liv), RS Kindersley (OxfU, t), FS Moss (Bro), HJ Ryalls (NewB, t), A Teggin (BroR, t).
Attendance: 5,000   *Referee*: CP Lewis (Wales)

Saturday 7 February 1885 at Whalley Range, Manchester
ENGLAND 2 tries *Back*: CH Sample (CamU). *Three-quarters*: JJ Hawcridge (Brad, t), AE Stoddart (Black), WN Bolton (Black, t). *Half-backs*: JH Payne (Bro), Alan Rotherham (OxfU). *Forwards*: C Gurdon (Rich), ET Gurdon (capt, Rich), G Harrison (Hull), CH Horley (Swi), AT Kemble (Liv), FS Moss (Bro), HJ Ryalls (NewB), GT Thomson (Hal), CS Wooldridge (Black).
IRELAND 1 try *Back*: GH Wheeler (QCB). *Half-backs*: RE McLean (NIFC), JP Ross (Lans), EH Greene (DubU, t). *Quarter-backs*: EC Crawford (DubU), RG Warren (Lans). *Forwards*: TC Allen (NIFC), RM Bradshaw (Wand), THM Hobbs (DubU), RW Hughes (NIFC), TR Lyle (DubU), FW Moore (Wand), HJ Neill (NIFC), WG Rutherford (capt, Tip), T Shanahan (Lans).
Attendance: 6,000   *Referee*: HS Lyne (Wales)
Note: First time majority of England team selected from northern clubs (eight players).

Other results
Scotland 0, Wales 0
Scotland 1g, 2t, Ireland 0

Final table

	P	W	D	L	G-T	G-T
England	2	2	0	0	1-6	1-2
Scotland	2	1	1	0	1-2	0-0
Wales	2	0	1	1	1-1	1-4
Ireland	2	0	0	2	0-1	1-4

(Championship incomplete. England and Scotland did not meet due to a scoring dispute in previous season's match. Wales and Ireland did not meet due to dispute after latter arrived two players short for previous season's match.)

1885-1886

NORTH VERSUS NORTH

The growing status of the North versus South fixture – introduced in 1874 as an England trial – was demonstrated when it was decided to organise a North East against North West match to help determine who should represent the North. The North East included players from Durham (4), Northumberland (3) and Yorkshire (8) whilst the North West selected from Cheshire (3), Cumberland (1) and Lancashire (11). Scheduled for Dewsbury's Crown Flatts on 12th December, the match was subsequently called off due to severe frost. With the meeting against the South just one week away there was insufficient time to reschedule.

SIXTEEN PUDSEY MEN

When Manningham met Pudsey in the Yorkshire Cup first round on 27th February, the tie was brought to a halt after 20 minutes play when the referee discovered that Pudsey had 16 men on the field. The game, which was scoreless at that point, was then restarted from the beginning. Afterwards Pudsey, who had lost, alleged that to two of the Manningham players – Pulleyn and Birmingham – were professionals 'having been paid for their services over and above their expenses'. In what was probably the most serious allegation related to the competition to date, the Yorkshire Committee, during their meeting at the Queen's Hotel, Leeds, on 2nd March, decided that the allegation was not proved 'on the evidence before them'.[66]

THE YORKSHIRE CUP: FROM STRENGTH TO STRENGTH
The Yorkshire Cup continued to gain popularity, going from strength to strength. The *Yorkshire Post* commented: 'From an unpretentious competition how its entries have doubled! And how the [Rugby] football-loving community have taken to and upheld it! Tens of thousands now witness the various struggles [compared to] the hundreds who graced the proceedings a few seasons ago. The history and status of the teams engaged are perfectly well known, while the sporting prophets have each sung the praises of the same. And here we must protest against the manner in which southerners, as a rule, write respecting the evil influence of such contests. Why, the Yorkshire trophy, and that trophy alone, has made that county what it is.'[67]

WESTMORLAND COUNTY CLUB FOUNDED
The Westmorland County Football Club was founded on 2nd March at the Mechanics' Institute, Windermere, by four clubs; Ambleside, Kendal Hornets, Kendal Town, and Windermere.

THE WEST LANCASHIRE CUP: LANCASHIRE'S FIRST CUP CONTEST
The West Lancashire and Border Towns Challenge Cup commenced during March with 24 clubs taking part. The *Athletic News* enthused: 'There can be no doubt that the [West Lancashire and Border Towns] Union, although yet in its infancy, has done much to resuscitate the drooping interests of the Rugby code in West Lancashire, and it may truthfully be stated that from Runcorn to Wigan, and thence to Southport, there never was greater interest shown in the pastime than is now apparent under the fostering care of the West Lancashire and Border Towns Union. The interest in and around Liverpool has not yet been subjected to such an awakening influence as that which has aroused the enthusiasm of Widnes, Warrington, Runcorn and Wigan.'[68]

ROUGH PLAY IN THE YORKSHIRE CUP
Several letters were published in the *Yorkshire Post* referring to unsavoury play in the Yorkshire Cup ties. One of them, from 'J. H. M.', was typical: 'Having seen for myself the rough and brutal play that takes place in a large proportion of Cup matches, by which many of our ablest players are placed hors de combat every week, I think that it is time some measures were taken to put a stop to it. There is a rule by which a referee may stop altogether a game where rough play is persisted in; but where is the

referee, who, when the home team is transgressing, will dare anger the spectators, which, he well knows, would fall on his luckless head in a shower of stones or sods were he to adopt such a course.'[69]

THE YORKSHIRE CUP SEMI-FINAL: SUSPENSE AND ANXIETY
A bizarre situation occurred after Batley believed they had beaten Halifax by one try to nil in the Yorkshire Cup semi-final at Crown Flatts, Dewsbury, on 3rd April. Halifax protested against Batley's try, claiming the referee had stopped play by blowing his whistle. During the Yorkshire Committee meeting at the Queen's Hotel, Leeds, on 5th April, the referee, Mr. Glover, stated he blew his whistle after umpire Mr. Shaw raised his stick for off-side play, but then saw both umpires conferring together, claiming they had agreed to the try. Mr. Shaw denied raising his stick and said he was surprised to hear the whistle. The committee decided Mr. Glover had blown under the impression an appeal had been made and ordered a replay the following Wednesday (7th April) at Huddersfield. Batley said it was impossible to raise a team for Wednesday but stated a willingness to play on Saturday (10th April), the date set for the final. Their request was turned down and, as they did not turn up at Huddersfield, Halifax were awarded the match. Despite further protests, Batley, the previous year's winners, were out of the cup.[70]

THE WEST LANCASHIRE CUP: A BEAUTIFUL TROPHY
The first West Lancashire and Border Towns Challenge Cup Competition was concluded on 10th April when Warrington beat Aspull by eight points to one at Fairfield, Liverpool, one scribe stating the cup 'is as beautiful and valuable as its name is long'.[71] The competition was hailed a success, Warrington attracting 10,000 for the their second round tie with Widnes, and a reported 12,000 attending their semi-final with Runcorn at Widnes.

NORTH-EAST CHALLENGE MATCH SUSPENDED
A consequence of the Durham Challenge Cup cancellation was that the annual challenge match between its winning club and the Northumberland Cup victors could not, for obvious reasons, take place. The inter-county contest was eventually revived in 1891-92.

1885-1886 STATISTICS

CUMBERLAND COUNTY CHALLENGE CUP (8 entries)
Most goals wins. If equal, most tries. If still equal, majority of 3 minor points.

First Round
Brookland Rovers (Maryport) 2t, Workington 2t
(mp: 3-3, no extra time due to ground conditions)
Carlisle City 1g, 3t, Millom 0
Maryport 1g, Maryport St James's 0
Byes: Aspatria, Cockermouth

First Round Replay
Workington 1t, Brookland Rovers 0

Second Round
Aspatria 1t, Cockermouth 0 (replay ordered after protest)
Carlisle City 0, Workington 0 (mp: 4-0)
Bye: Maryport

Second Round Replay
Aspatria 0, Cockermouth 0 (mp: 9-0, at Maryport)

Semi-finals
Carlisle City 1t, Maryport 0 (at Noble Croft, Aspatria)
Bye: Aspatria

FINAL
Saturday 27 March 1886 at Maryport Cricket Ground
CARLISLE CITY 1 goal *Back*: A Lee. *Three-quarters*: JH Fetherby, J Dodgshon, J Bowman.
Half-backs: W Dodgshon (capt), F Telford. *Forwards*: G Bell (fg), J Black, RN Burgess,
L Chambers, EH Dawson, H Etchells, T Hetherington, T Metcalfe, B Rickerby.
ASPATRIA 0 *Back*: L Beattie. *Three-quarters*: J Temble (capt), W Lauriston, H Sandwith.
Half-backs: H Monkhouse, WT Ridley. *Forwards*: T Allison, J Armstrong, J Harker,
J Kendal, J Mumberson, G Rayson, W Sanderson, J Sandwith, J Todd.
Attendance: 1,500   *Referee*: JM Mawson (Barrow)

NORTHUMBERLAND COUNTY FOOTBALL CHALLENGE CUP (8 entries)
Most goals wins. If equal, most tries. If still equal, majority of 3 minor points.

First Round
North Elswick 1g, Benwell (Newcastle) 0
Northumberland FC 1g, Tynemouth 1t
Percy Park 1g, 1t, Bellingham 0
Tynedale 0, Northern 0 (mp: 2-2, aet)

First Round Replay
Northern 1g, Tynedale 0

Semi-finals
Percy Park 1g, 2t, Northumberland FC 1g
North Elswick 1t, Northern 0
(Both semi-finals same day at Jesmond Ground, Newcastle)

Milestones & Stats 1869-1901

FINAL
Saturday 10 April 1886 at Jesmond Ground, Newcastle
PERCY PARK 1 goal, 1 try *Back*: JA Williamson (c). *Three-quarters*: F Finney, G Leighton (2t), RE Herbertson. *Half-backs*: H Douglas, W Ryder. *Forwards*: E Biggs, G Brewis, JW Coward (capt), W Dodds, A Gee, T Gee, T Glover, L Rhode, RH Spence.
NORTH ELSWICK 1 goal *Back*: S Atkinson. *Three-quarters*: H Shotton (c), E Dixon, JT Taylor. *Half-backs*: G Stewart (t), H Welford. *Forwards*: E Allison, C Atkinson, W Douglas, T Downs, G Gillespie, W Morrell, J Ross, P Spicer, Williams (capt).
Attendance: 2,000   *Referee*: n/a

WEST LANCASHIRE AND BORDER TOWNS CHALLENGE CUP (24 entries)
Try – 4 points; conversion – 4; drop-goal, field goal – 6; minor – 1. Majority of 3 points required to win.

First Round
Blackrod 7, Wigan 22
Blundellsands 4, St Helens Recreation 35
Bootle 9, Walton 19
Edge Hill 21. Lowton 6
Leigh 58, Kirkdale 0
Litherland 18, New Brighton Olympic 0
Pagefield (Wigan) 20, Newton-le-Willows 9
Runcorn 70, Sutton (St Helens) 1

Southport Olympic 2, Aspull 11
Warrington 70, Lymm and Oughtrington 0
Wavertree 3, St Helens 5 (aet)
Widnes Recreation 0, Widnes 52

First Round Replay
Wavertree 9, St Helens 12 (aet)

Second Round
Aspull 51, Pagefield 0
Leigh 17, Runcorn 19 (aet)
Litherland 2, St Helens Recreation 6
Walton 2, St Helens 12
Warrington 14, Widnes 0
Wigan 29, Edge Hill 0

Second Round Replay
Runcorn w/o Leigh (refused to play due to disagreement over venue)

Third Round
Runcorn 46, Wigan 0
Warrington 52, St Helens 0
Byes: Aspull, St Helens Recreation

Semi-finals
Aspull 4, St Helens Recreation 6 (no extra time)
(at Dentons Green Lane, St Helens)
Warrington 2, Runcorn 2 (abandoned due to altercation – replay ordered)
(at Lowerhouse Lane, Widnes)

Semi-final Replays
Aspull 13, St Helens Recreation 5 (at Upper Dicconson Street, Wigan)
Warrington 30, Runcorn 13 (at Southport)

FINAL

Saturday 10 April 1886 at Liverpool College Ground, Fairfield
WARRINGTON 9 *Back*: J Buxton. *Three-quarters*: J Jolley, T Barnes (dg), H Boardman.
Half-backs: E Gilbert, W Speakman. *Forwards*: H Ashton (capt), A Davies, E Dillon,
W Dillon, W Hayes, W Povey, J Rigby, Fairfield Turner, Frank Turner.
ASPULL 1 *Back*: Dawber. *Three-quarters*: J Roberts (capt), R Seddon, JC Samuels.
Half-backs: J Cartwright, D Hulme. *Forwards*: H Bramwell, Brooks, Hampson,
W Haydock, T Hesketh, L Hickson, R Lawson, T Monks, J Pilkington.
Attendance: 5,000/6,000   *Referee*: AT Kemble (Liverpool)
Note: Warrington's score includes 3 minor points, Aspull's score is from one minor point.

YORKSHIRE COUNTY FOOTBALL CHALLENGE CUP (64 entries)
Most goals wins. If equal, most tries. If still equal, majority of 3 minor points.

First Round
Alverthorpe Rangers 1t, Sheffield 0
Batley 3g, 1t, Heckmondwike 0
Batley Carr Trinity 1t, Barnsley 0
Birstall 0, Leeds Parish Church 1g
Brighouse Rangers 1g, 1t, Bowling 0
Castleford 3t, Bingley 0
Cleckheaton 3g, 1t, Selby 1t
Dewsbury 1g, 2t, Normanton 0
Dudley Hill 3t, Ossett 0
Eastmoor 2g, 2t, Hull Athletic 1t
Elland 0, Hull Southcoates 1g
Goole 1t, Mytholmroyd 0 (aet)
Halifax 1g, Wakefield Trinity 0
Halifax St Joseph's 0, Bradford Trinity 3g, 2t
Holbeck 3g, 2t, Middlesbrough Rovers 0
Hunslet 0, Bramley 1g, 1t
Keighley 3g, York 0
Leeds Rovers 0, Leeds St John's 2g, 4t
Liversedge 1g, Halifax Free Wanderers 0
Luddendenfoot 0, Batley Mountaineers 2t
Manningham 1g, 2t, Pudsey 1t
Mirfield 1t, Thornes 0
Morley 1g, Bradford 1g, 3t
Otley 1t, Buttershaw 1t (mp: 2-4, aet)
Ovenden 1g, 2t, Doncaster Town 0
Pontefract 0, Horbury 0 (mp: 5-6, aet)
Ravensthorpe 1g, Dodworth 0
Salterhebble 1g, 1t, Hull 1g, 1t (mp: 0-6)
Settle 3t, Harrogate 1t (replay ordered after protest)
Shipley 0, Kirkstall 2t
Wakefield St Austin's 5g, 8t, Beverley 0
Wortley 2t, Huddersfield 1t

First Round Replays
Buttershaw 1t, Otley 0
Harrogate 1t, Settle 0 (at Keighley)
Horbury 1g, Pontefract 1t

Second Round
Bradford 5g, 7t, Bradford Trinity 0
Buttershaw 2g, Batley 2g, 2t
Cleckheaton 4g, 7t, Batley Mountaineers 0
Dewsbury 6g, 4t, Batley Carr Trinity 0
Dudley Hill 0, Brighouse Rangers 4t
Eastmoor 1t, Leeds St John's 1g
Goole 0, Hull Southcoates 0 (mp: 2-5)
Halifax 3t, Castleford 0
Harrogate 0, Wortley 1g, 2t
Holbeck 3g, 1t, Keighley 2t
Horbury 1t, Leeds Parish Church 0
Hull 3g, 6t, Ovenden 0
Kirkstall 1t, Mirfield 1g, 1t
Manningham 2g, 3t, Liversedge 0
Ravensthorpe 0, Alverthorpe Rangers 1g
Wakefield St Austin's 2t, Bramley 1t

Third Round
Alverthorpe Rangers 0, Mirfield 1t
Bradford w/o Horbury (disqualified)
Brighouse Rangers 1g, Wakefield St Austin's 0
Halifax 2t, Dewsbury 0
Holbeck 1g, Cleckheaton 1g, 1t
Leeds St John's 0, Batley 2g
Manningham 2g, Hull 1t
Wortley 1g, Hull Southcoates 0

Fourth Round
Bradford 1g, 1t, Manningham 1g
Cleckheaton 0, Halifax 3t
Mirfield 0, Batley 1t
Wortley 0, Brighouse Rangers 1g

Semi-finals
Batley 1t, Halifax 0 (at Crown Flatts, Dewsbury – replay ordered after protest)
Bradford 2t, Brighouse Rangers 0 (at Belle Vue, Wakefield)

Semi-final replay
Halifax w/o Batley (disqualified)

FINAL
Saturday 10 April 1886 at Cardigan Fields, Leeds
HALIFAX 1 goal *Back*: F Murgatroyd. *Three-quarters*: TL Scarborough (capt), J Dodd (c), D Welsh. *Half-backs*: E Buckley (t), J Parker. *Forwards*: T Albutt, JP Clowes, JH Crossland, A Dennis, G Millar, JH Pollard, TW Watson, I Webster, W Wood.
BRADFORD 0 *Back*: P Robertshaw. *Three-quarters*: AR Robertshaw (capt), FT Ritchie, E Critchley. *Half-backs*: F Bonsor, JF Wright. *Forwards*: T Atkinson, M Bonsor, S Haigh, JL Hickson, H Inman, E Nelson, J Potter, H Robertshaw, E Wilkinson.
Attendance: 14,000   *Referee*: G Harrison (Hull)

COUNTY MATCHES

Saturday 7 November 1885 at Tynedale FC, Hexham
NORTHUMBERLAND 1 goal, 1 try *Back*: RH Robb (Tynd). *Three-quarters*: CS Gill (Nor), CH Sample (capt, NorFC), T Robson (Tynd). *Half-backs*: GA Bell (NorFC, 2t), AC Challoner (Nor). *Forwards*: J Baty (Tynd), CH Coates (Nor), JH Greenwell (Tynm), CW Harrison (Tynd), J Livingstone (Nor), GW Mole (NEls), S Oliver (Tynm, c), GW Ridley (Nor), HW Sample (NorFC).
CUMBERLAND 0 *Back*: W Bleasdale (Cock). *Three-quarters*: G Bell (Asp), G Bell (CarlC), J Tremble (Asp). *Half-backs*: WT Ridley (Asp), RH Tinkler (CarlC). *Forwards*: GB Blake (EdW), J Higmore (Work), W Holmes (Cock), HP Senhouse (Cock), J Skelton (Mary), J Steel (capt, EdW), J Thompson (Mary), J Todd (Asp). TJ White* (Tynd).
Attendance: 'large'   *Referee*: CR Green (Durham)
*Guest from Northumberland to replace unavailable player.

Saturday 14 November 1885 at Aigburth, Liverpool
LANCASHIRE 2 goals *Back*: WW Higgins (Man). *Three-quarters*: EH Flower (Bro, t), J Robertson (BroR), J Valentine (Swi). *Half-backs*: W Bumby (Swi), JH Payne (capt, Bro). *Forwards*: HC Chapman (LivOB), CH Horley (Swi), WS Hulse (Man), AT Kemble (Liv), W Kinnish (Bar), FS Moss (Bro), RL Seddon (BroR, t), A Strang (Liv, 2c), A Teggin (BroR).

CHESHIRE 0 *Back*: F Wainwright (NewB). *Three-quarters*: JA Black (BirkPk), AB Wilson (BirkPk), R Barber (NewB). *Half-backs*: RH Jackson (BirkPk), FW Spence (BirkPk). *Forwards*: G Cowie (BirkPk), F Dun (BirkPk), W Hughes (Run), JH Jones (NewB), J Lewis (Run), E Lings (Sale), T Lings (Sale), HF Ransome (Bow), HJ Ryalls (capt, NewB).
Attendance: 5,000   *Referee*: GR Hill (RFU Honorary Secretary)

Saturday 14 November 1885 at Holderness Road, Hull
YORKSHIRE 1 goal *Back*: CE Fox (Salt, c). *Three-quarters*: JT Haslam (Bat), AR Robertshaw (Brad), FT Ritchie (Brad). *Half-backs*: F Bonsor (Brad), J Parker (Hal). *Forwards*: G Harrison (capt, Hull), J Heron (Selby), JL Hickson (Brad), AP Iveson (Hull), C Mathers (Bram, t), TP Peacock (LeeStJ), H Robertshaw (Brad), TW Watson (Salt), E Wilkinson (Brad).
DURHAM 1 goal *Back*: HO Hoy (HartR). *Three-quarters*: AE Emmerson (HartR), MH Horsley (HartR), GH Eyre (Sund). *Half-backs*: CH Newman (NDur), AR Wilson (DurU, t). *Forwards*: R Barwick (SundR), B Cox (Sund), CH Elliot (Sund), RS Ferguson (DurU), A Hill (HartR, c), F Lumsden (DurC), FE Pease (Darl), JW Sowerby (NDur), WH Towers (HartR).
Attendance: 8,000   *Referee*: R Henzell (Northumberland)

Saturday 21 November 1885 at Jesmond Ground, Newcastle
NORTHUMBERLAND 1 try *Back*: CE Morgan (Nor). *Three-quarters*: CS Gill (Nor, t), CH Sample (capt, NorFC), W Pattinson (Tynd). *Half-backs*: GA Bell (NorFC), V Rutherford (Nor). *Forwards*: CH Coates (Nor), JW Coward (PerPk), A Eichholtz (NorFC), JH Greenwell (Tynm), CW Harrison (Tynd), J Livingstone (Nor), RH Robb (Tynd), HW Sample (NorFC), G Walters (Nor).
YORKSHIRE 2 goals, 2 tries *Back*: HB Wilson (Hud). *Three-quarters*: JT Haslam (Bat, t, dg), AR Robertshaw (Brad, t, dg), CE Fox (Salt). *Half-backs*: F Bonsor (Brad), JH Potter (LeeStJ). *Forwards*: M Bonsor (Brad), J Garforth (Dew), G Harrison (capt, Hull), JL Hickson (Brad), C Mathers (Bram), TP Peacock (LeeStJ), H Robertshaw (Brad), TW Watson (Hal), E Wilkinson (Brad).
Attendance: 3,000   *Referee*: JT Todd (Durham)

Saturday 28 November 1885 at Fartown, Huddersfield
YORKSHIRE 1 goal, 1 try *Back*: HB Wilson (Hud). *Three-quarters*: JT Haslam (Bat, dg), AR Robertshaw (Brad), CE Fox (Salt). *Half-backs*: F Bonsor (Brad), JH Potter (LeeStJ). *Forwards*: G Harrison (capt, Hull), JL Hickson (Brad), E Jackson (Bat, t), C Mathers (Bram), TP Peacock (LeeStJ), H Robertshaw (Brad), TW Watson (Hal), E Wilkinson (Brad), E Wolstenholme (Dew).
LANCASHIRE 1 try *Back*: WW Higgins (Man). *Three-quarters*: EH Flower (Bro), J Robertson (BroR), J Valentine (Swi). *Half-backs*: T Deane (Bro), JH Payne (capt, Bro). *Forwards*: HC Chapman (LivOB), CH Horley (Swi), WS Hulse (Man), AT Kemble (Liv), HFB Moore (Man), FS Moss (Bro, t), RL Seddon (BroR), A Strang (Liv), A Teggin (BroR).
Attendance: 5,000   *Referee*: W Cail (Northumberland)

Saturday 5 December 1885 at Waterworks Lane, Carlisle
CUMBERLAND 0 *Back*: W Bleasdale (Cock). *Three-quarters*: G Bell (CarlC), G Bell (Asp), JH Fotherby (CarlC). *Half-backs*: J Murchie (Work), RH Tinkler (CarlC). *Forwards*: J Brown

(Mary), J Flynn (Millom St James's), G Gibson (Cock), J Hewitson (Mil), J Pender (CarlC), J Steel (capt, EdW), J Todd (Asp). J Tremble (Asp), HC Wynne-Edwardes (EdW).
DURHAM 2 goals, 2 tries *Back*: HB Tristram (DurC). *Three-quarters*: A Hill (HartR, c), AE Emmerson (HartR, t), GH Eyre (Sund). *Half-backs*: CH Newman (capt, NDur, dg), AR Wilson (DurU). *Forwards*: R Barwick (SundR, t), B Cox (Sund), CH Elliot (Sund), W Forster (Hou), F Lumsden (DurC), FE Pease (Darl), RJ Simey (Sund), JW Sowerby (NDur), WH Towers (HartR, t).
Attendance: 'fair'   *Referee*: AB Perkins (Yorkshire)

Saturday 5 December 1885 at Whalley Range, Manchester
LANCASHIRE 1 goal, 4 tries *Back*: WW Higgins (Man). *Three-quarters*: HJ McNiven (Man, 2t), J Robertson (BroR), J Valentine (Swi, t). *Half-backs*: T Deane (Bro), JH Payne (capt, Bro). *Forwards*: C Anderton (ManFW, t), HC Chapman (LivOB), CH Horley (Swi), WS Hulse (Man), AT Kemble (Liv), FS Moss (Bro), RL Seddon (BroR), A Strang (Liv, c), A Teggin (BroR, t).
NORTHUMBERLAND 1 try *Back*: CH Sample (capt, NorFC). *Three-quarters*: W Pattinson (Tynd), GA Bell (NorFC), AE Watts (Nor). *Half-backs*: JT Dodd (Tynd), V Rutherford (Nor). *Forwards*: CH Coates (Nor), JW Coward (PerPk), A Eichholtz (NorFC), A Gee (PerPk), CW Harrison (Tynd), J Livingstone (Nor), FW Ramsay (NorFC), HW Sample (NorFC, t), JW Swinburne (Nor).
Attendance: 3,000/4,000   *Referee*: JWH Thorp (Cheshire)

Saturday 2 January 1886 at Liscard, Wallasey
CHESHIRE 1 try *Back*: F Wainwright (NewB). *Three-quarters*: JA Black (BirkPk), EDW Davies (BirkPk), HC Speakman (Run), W Rome (NewB). *Half-backs*: RH Jackson (BirkPk), FW Spence (BirkPk). *Forwards*: DA Bingham (BirkPk), WH Broady (Run), F Dun (BirkPk), J Hampson (BirkPk), W Hughes (Run, t), J Lewis (Run), T Lings (Sale), HJ Ryalls (capt, NewB).
FETTESIAN-LORETTONIAN 3 goals *Back*: HB Tristram. *Half-backs*: MF Reid, AAD Sewell, DJ McFarlane. *Quarter-backs*: AGG Asher, AR Don-Wauchope (capt, t). *Forwards*: PH Blyth, JD Boswell, HF Caldwell, DA McLeod (2c, dg), WM McLeod, HF Menzies, CJB Milne, J Steel, JG Walker (t).
Attendance: 3,000   *Referee*: AT Kemble (Lancashire)

Saturday 30 January 1886 at Friarage Field, Hartlepool
DURHAM 1 try *Back*: GA Kerrich-Walker (DurC). *Three-quarters*: GH Eyre (Sund), MH Horsley (HartR), JH Walker (HartR). *Half-backs*: CH Newman (NDur), AR Wilson (DurU). *Forwards*: R Barwick (SundR, t), B Cox (Sund), CH Elliot (Sund), RS Ferguson (DurU), F Lumsden (DurC), FE Pease (Darl), RJ Simey (Sund), JW Sowerby (NDur), WH Towers (HartR).
LANCASHIRE 3 tries *Back*: JT Walkden (Old). *Three-quarters*: EJ Jordan (Bro, t), EH Flower (Bro), HJ McNiven (Man). *Half-backs*: JH Payne (capt, Bro), S Simpson (BroR, t). *Forwards*: C Anderton (ManFW), CH Horley (Swi), N Hotchkiss (Swi), WS Hulse (Man), J Jackson (Sal), AT Kemble (Liv), W Kinnish (Bar), A Teggin (BroR, t), JH Tune (BroR).
Attendance: 6,000   *Referee*: GR Hill (RFU Honorary Secretary)

Saturday 13 February 1886 at Liscard, Wallasey
CHESHIRE 0 *Back*: C Holden (BirkPk). *Three-quarters*: JA Black (BirkPk), HC Speakman (Run), R Barber (NewB). *Half-backs*: RH Jackson (BirkPk), FW Spence (BirkPk). *Forwards*: DA Bingham (BirkPk), G Cowie (BirkPk), F Dun (BirkPk), J Herron (NewB), W Hughes (Run), J Lewis (Run), HF Ransome (Bow), HJ Ryalls (capt, NewB), W Wright (Run).
YORKSHIRE 3 goals, 1 try *Back*: CE Fox (Salt, 2c). *Three-quarters*: JW Graham (Dew), AR Robertshaw (Brad, dg), E Coulman (Hull). *Half-backs*: F Bonsor (Brad), E Buckley (Hal). *Forwards*: G Harrison (capt, Hull, t), JL Hickson (Brad), C Mathers (Bram), TP Peacock (LeeStJ), H Robertshaw (Brad), H Ward (Wak), TW Watson (Hal), E Wilkinson (Brad, 2t), E Wolstenholme (Dew).
Attendance: 4,000   *Referee*: J MacLaren (Lancashire)

Saturday 13 February 1886 at Chester Road, Sunderland
DURHAM 1 goal, 1 try *Back*: MH Horsley (HartR). *Three-quarters*: GH Eyre (Sund, c), CH Newman (capt, NDur), JH Walker (HartR). *Half-backs*: EA Douglas (Sund, t), AR Wilson (DurU). *Forwards*: R Barwick (SundR), RS Ferguson (DurU), W Kimpster (NDur), F Lumsden (DurC), FE Pease (Darl), RE Reed (Sund), RJ Simey (Sund), JW Sowerby (NDur, t), WH Towers (HartR).
NORTHUMBERLAND 1 goal *Back*: CH Sample (NorFC). *Three-quarters*: F Finney (PerPk), CS Gill (Nor), GA Bell (NorFC). *Half-backs*: MT Scott (Nor/CamU, dg), B Sutherland (Nor). *Forwards*: JW Coward (PerPk), JH Greenwell (Tynm), FW Ramsay (NorFC), RH Robb (Tynd), T Rogan (Tynd), HW Sample (NorFC), D Spencer (Nor), JW Swinburne (Nor), CE Winship (Nor).
Attendance: 2,000/3,000   *Referee*: JB Junor (Durham)

Monday 22 February 1886 at Grove Park, Chiswick, London
MIDDLESEX 1 goal *Back*: PB Harrower (LonS). *Three-quarters*: JE Edwards (Black, dg), JD Vans Agnew (MarlN), GC Lindsay (LonS). *Half-backs*: WK Arber (Rich), D Montgomery (LonS). *Forwards*: JG Anderson (LonS), WG Clibborn (Rich), C Gurdon (Rich), ET Gurdon (capt, Rich), J Hammond (Black), GL Jeffery (Black), EH Lawrie (MarlN), CJB Marriott (Black), JG Tait (LonS).
YORKSHIRE 3 tries *Back*: J Dodd (Hal). *Three-quarters*: A Ineson (Bat), AR Robertshaw (Brad), E Coulman (Hull). *Half-backs*: F Bonsor (Brad), JH Potter (LeeStJ, 2t). *Forwards*: J Garforth (Dew), G Harrison (capt, Hull), JL Hickson (Brad), E Jackson (Bat, t), C Mathers (Bram), TP Peacock (LeeStJ), H Ward (Wak), TW Watson (Hal), E Wilkinson (Brad).
Attendance: 2,000   *Referee*: GR Hill (RFU Honorary Secretary)
Note: Middlesex won due to scoring most goals.

ENGLAND TRIAL MATCH

Saturday 19 December 1885 at Park Avenue, Bradford
NORTH 1 try *Back*: CH Sample (NorFC). *Three-quarters*: EB Brutton* (CamU), AR Robertshaw (Brad), HJ McNiven (Man). *Half-backs*: F Bonsor (Brad), JH Payne (Bro). *Forwards*: CH Elliot (Sund), G Harrison (capt, Hull), CH Horley (Swi, t), FS Moss (Bro), TP Peacock (LStJ), H Robertshaw (Brad), RL Seddon (BroR), J Steel (EdW), E Wilkinson (Brad).

Milestones & Stats 1869-1901

SOUTH 2 goals, 3 tries *Back*: AS Taylor (Black). *Three-quarters*: CG Wade (Rich, t), AE Stoddart (Black, 2t, 2c), AR St L Fagan (LonHosp). *Half-backs*: JH Roberts (Rich), Alan Rotherham (Rich, 2t). *Forwards*: WG Clibborn (Rich), C Gurdon (Rich), ET Gurdon (capt, Rich), PF Hancock (Wivel/Black), RE Inglis (Black), GL Jeffery (Black), CJB Marriott (Black), N Spurling (Black), WH Squire (Rich).
Attendance: 10,000/12,000   *Referee*: GT Thomson (Yorkshire)
*Born in Durham and selected by both North and South decided to represent the former.

INTERNATIONAL CHAMPIONSHIP

Saturday 2 January 1886 at Rectory Field, Blackheath
ENGLAND 1 goal, 2 tries *Back*: AS Taylor (Black). *Three-quarters*: CG Wade (Rich, t), AR Robertshaw (Brad), AE Stoddart (Black, gm). *Half-backs*: F Bonsor (Brad), Alan Rotherham (Rich). *Forwards*: WG Clibborn (Rich), CH Elliot (Sund), C Gurdon (Rich), PF Hancock (Wivel/Black), RE Inglis (Black), GL Jeffery (Black), CJB Marriott (capt, Black), FS Moss (Bro), E Wilkinson (Brad, t).
WALES 1 goal *Back*: DH Bowen (Llan). *Three-quarters*: CG Taylor (Rua, c), JA Gould (New), WM Douglas (Car). *Half-backs*: CH Newman (capt, New), WJ Stadden (Car, t). *Forwards*: EP Alexander (CamU), W Bowen (Swa), R Gould (New), AF Hill (Car), DH Lewis (Car), D Morgan (Swa), E Roberts (Llan), WH Thomas (LlanC), GA Young (Car).
Attendance: 6,000   *Referee*: DF Moore (Ireland)

Saturday 6 February 1886 at Lansdowne Road, Dublin
IRELAND 0 *Back*: JWR Morrow (Lis). *Half-backs*: DJ Ross (Belfast Academy), JP Ross (NIFC), EH Greene (Wand). *Quarter-backs*: M Johnston (capt, Wand), RG Warren (Lans). *Forwards*: HM Brabazon (DubU), J Chambers (DubU), RW Hughes (NIFC), J Johnston (BelA), VC le Fanu (CamU), TR Lyle (DubU), RH Massey-Westropp (Lim), WG Rutherford (Tip), T Shanahan (Lans).
ENGLAND 1 try *Back*: AS Taylor (Black). *Three-quarters*: CG Wade (Rich), AR Robertshaw (Brad), AE Stoddart (Black). *Half-backs*: F Bonsor (Brad), Alan Rotherham (Rich). *Forwards*: WG Clibborn (Rich), C Gurdon (Rich), PF Hancock (Wivel/Black), RE Inglis (Black), GL Jeffery (Black), CJB Marriott (capt, Black), N Spurling (Black), A Teggin (BroR), E Wilkinson (Brad, t).
Attendance: 7,000   *Referee*: R Mullock (Wales)

Saturday 13 March 1886 at Raeburn Place, Edinburgh
SCOTLAND 0 *Back*: JP Veitch (RHSFP). *Half-backs*: WF Holms (RIEC), GR Wilson (RHSFP), RH Morrison (EdinU). *Quarter-backs*: AR Don-Wauchope (FetLor), AGG Asher (FetLor). *Forwards*: JB Brown (capt, GlasA), AT Clay (EdinA), TW Irvine (EdinA), MC McEwan (EdinA), DA MacLeod (GlasU), CJB Milne (WoS), C Reid (EdinA), J Tod (Wat), WA Walls (GlasA).
ENGLAND 0 *Back*: CH Sample (NorFC). *Three-quarters*: AE Stoddart (Black), AR Robertshaw (Brad), EB Brutton (CamU). *Half-backs*: F Bonsor (Brad), Alan Rotherham (Rich). *Forwards*: WG Clibborn (Rich), C Gurdon (Rich), ET Gurdon (capt, Rich), RE Inglis (Black), GL Jeffery (Black), CJB Marriott (Black), N Spurling (Black), A Teggin (BroR), E Wilkinson (Brad).
Attendance: 8,000   *Referee*: HG Cook (Ireland)

Other results
Wales 0, Scotland 2g, 1t
Scotland 4g, 2t, Ireland 0
Ireland v Wales not played

Final table

	P	W	D	L	G-T	G-T
Scotland	3	2	1	0	6-3	0-0
England	3	2	1	0	1-3	1-0
Wales	2	0	0	2	1-0	3-3
Ireland	2	0	0	2	0-0	4-3

(Scotland and England share Championship. Ireland and Wales again did not meet due to their continuing dispute.)

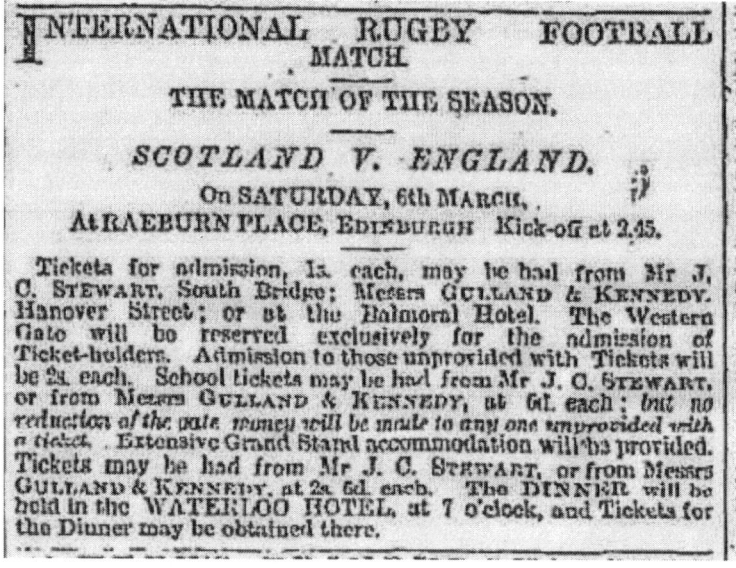

Unfortunately 'the match of the season' had to be postponed due to poor conditions following a snowfall and rearranged for 13th March. *The Scotsman, 1886*

1886-1887

THE DURHAM CUP RESURRECTED

The Durham County Rugby Football Union, at its annual meeting held at the Walton's Hotel, Sunderland, on 23rd September, decided that the Durham Cup would again be competed for. It was also reported that there were 20 clubs in the Durham Union during the previous season.[72]

AN IMPORTANT MEETING

The *London Evening Standard* reported on what it referred to as 'probably the most important meeting held by the Rugby [Football] Union' which took place at the Westminster Palace Hotel, London, on 4th October. On the agenda was a proposed alteration to the scoring system and a sub-committee report on professionalism. Point systems had already been introduced in the various county competitions but this was the first endorsement of points by the Union. The following rules, to be introduced immediately, were agreed:

1. A match shall be decided by a majority of points
2. A goal shall equal three points and a try one point.
3. If the number of points be equal, or no goal be kicked or try obtained, the match shall be drawn.
4. When a goal is kicked from a try, the goal only is scored.

The verdict on whether to allow professionalism was, however, disappointing for many of the northern clubs and players in their bid to be on the right side of the law. It was reported that 'the proposed rules as to professionals [which declared it illegal] caused considerable discussion, especially that referring to the player who receives remuneration for loss of [work] time. Several of those present thought that this law would prove great hardship among the working classes, but eventually the rules recommended by the Sub-Committee were passed en bloc'.[73]

MORE CUMBERLAND SELECTION ISSUES

Following the Cumberland versus Northumberland match at Carlisle on 30th October, the *Carlisle Patriot* reported 'the match was robbed of any interest it might otherwise have possessed by the absurdly non-representative character of the Cumberland team which, for reason well known to the reader, did not include any players from Carlisle or Whitehaven'. In the case of Carlisle, this was, reportedly, because no Carlisle or Eden Wanderers [also based in Carlisle] players had taken part in the county trial at Maryport on 16th October, and 'it was decided to choose the team from players who took part in the trial match'. Meanwhile, five Whitehaven players withdrew because 'they do not regard the Cumberland team as representative of the strength of the county'.[74]

LARGE CROWD AT THE ROSES MATCH

The Lancashire versus Yorkshire match on 20th November was played in front of 'perhaps the largest number of spectators ever present at a football match at Whalley Range', estimates generally being reported as 20,000. The match, which was drawn with one converted try each, had an exciting finish due to a last minute try by Dewsbury's Dicky Lockwood who 'grounded the ball among the spectators at the back'.[75]

WESTMORLAND DEBUT

Westmorland played its first match on 27th November when it entertained a team representing the West Lancashire and Border Towns Union in Kendal. Curiously the *Ambleside Herald* referred to the referee as 'Mr. E. Walmsley, of Football Times, Blackburn'. In fact Edmund Walmsley, who was not a rugby official, was the proprietor of the Blackburn-based publication *Cricketers' Herald, Athletic and Football Times*.[76]

NORTH EAST VERSUS NORTH WEST

The first North East versus North West match took place at Whalley Range, Manchester, on 13th December, following the cancellation of the inaugural fixture 12 months earlier. Intended as a trial for the North team to oppose the South, it proved to be its only staging during the Victorian era.

ROYALTY AT THE RUGBY

H. R. H. The Prince of Wales attended the 'Football Jubilee Festival' at Kennington Oval, London, on 12th March. The afternoon commenced with a rugby match, Lancashire defeating Middlesex by one try to nil, followed by an Association game between the Corinthians and Preston North End. The occasion drew a reported 12,000, the proceeds going to the Imperial Institute Fund, a London Charity. The Prince stayed for one hour and a quarter, arriving at half-time during the rugby clash and leaving whilst the Association fixture was in progress. This followed up the previous year's 'Charity Festival', also at Kennington Oval, when a combined London Scottish and London Welsh side played against (the rest of) London at rugby, and The Gentlemen opposed The Players at Association, again attended by the Prince of Wales.

BRADFORD FAIL TO CLEAR THE SNOW

Bradford had a central role in the latest Yorkshire Cup drama after their home third round tie with Manningham was postponed on 12th March. Manningham successfully protested that Bradford failed to clear their Park Avenue ground of snow and the tie was rescheduled for Cardigan Fields, Leeds, on 16th March. Bradford consequently held a meeting on 15th March, over 1,500 members attending, and decided to refuse to replay in Leeds. In a bizarre act of determination, Manningham turned out at Leeds, kicked off, scored, and claimed the 'win' whilst, at the same time, Bradford went through a similar routine at Park Avenue 'to assert their rights'.

The County Committee decided to disqualify Bradford who subsequently took their grievance to the High Court of Justice in London on 17th March. Mr. Waddy QC, 'on behalf of Bradford Football Club', tried to obtain an interim injunction against the Yorkshire Committee, preventing the playing of the Ossett versus Manningham match in the next round of the Yorkshire Cup. The request was refused, an outcome that was generally well received by the press, one report concluding that 'in the interests of manly sport their lordships said that the matter was such as ought to be left to the proper tribunal – the County Committee. On this ground, and this ground alone, the injunction asked for was properly refused'.[77]

A BIG DAY FOR ASPULL

The second West Lancashire and Border Towns Challenge Cup final took place on 26th March, Aspull beating Wigan by 20 points to one. The *Athletic News* commented: 'According to the rules the final tie is bound to be played in Liverpool. Last year Warrington won the trophy on the Liverpool College Grounds at Fairfield, and this time the meeting was on the new enclosure of the Liverpool Athletic Company. The first batch of arrivals at the ground was a nice little party from Aspull, each bearing the inevitable ticket, "Play up, Aspull". Then came a lot of Wiganers, each adorned with a more elaborate favour than that adopted by the opposition. I may say, for the benefit of those of readers whose geography may have been somewhat neglected, that Aspull is a colliery village, some three miles out of Wigan, and the members of the Aspull Club are mostly composed of men who toil underground for their daily bread. Between them and Wigan there is naturally a great amount of rivalry.'[78]

1886-1887 STATISTICS

CUMBERLAND COUNTY CHALLENGE CUP (12 entries)
Try – 4 points; conversion – 4; drop-goal, field goal – 6; minor – 1. Majority of 3 points required to win.

First Round
Cockermouth w/o Whitehaven
Greysouthen v Aspatria (draw – score not given)
Maryport 3, Brookland Rovers 11
Millom w/o Penrith (withdrew)
Seaton 25, Dearham 7
Workington 8, Broughton 10 (aet)

First Round Replays
Broughton 8, Workington 4
Greysouthen 0, Aspatria 7

Second Round
Aspatria 4, Broughton 1
Cockermouth 2, Brookland Rovers 1 (aet)
Seaton 4, Millom 10

Second Round Replay
Brookland Rovers 14, Cockermouth 0

Semi-final
Millom 18, Brookland Rovers 10 (at Workington Cricket Ground)
Bye: Aspatria

FINAL
Saturday 2 April 1887 at the Maryport Cricket Ground
MILLOM 6 *Back*: J Moore. *Three-quarters*: I Moore, CW Dove, J Davy. *Half-backs*: J Denwood, J McGuire. *Forwards*: H Barlow-Massicks (capt), A Flynn, T Harris, J Hewitson, J Hudson, B Kendall, T Pascoe, G Thompson, T Whalen (t),

ASPATRIA 4 *Back*: Jerry Saul. *Three-quarters*: H Sandwith, L Beattie, W Lauriston (capt).
Half-backs: Joseph Saul, WT Ridley. *Forwards*: JW Cowen, J Dixon, Green, T Grieve, J
Harker, Harrison, J Mumberson, G Rayson, J Rumney.
After extra time   *Attendance*: 'large'   *Referee*: Rev M Dykes (Barrow)
Note: Millom's score includes 2 minor points, Aspatria's score was from 4 minor points.

FINAL REPLAY
Saturday 16 April 1887 at the Maryport Cricket Ground
MILLOM 4 *Back*: J Moore. *Three-quarters*: I Moore, CW Dove (t), J Davy. *Half-backs*:
J Denwood, J McGuire. *Forwards*: H Barlow-Massicks (capt), A Flynn, T Harris, J Hudson,
A Jordan, B Kendall, T Pascoe, G Thompson, T Whalen.
ASPATRIA 1 *Back*: Jerry Saul. *Three-quarters*: G Bell (capt), L Beattie, H Sandwith.
Half-backs: Joseph Saul, WT Ridley. *Forwards*: T Allison, J Dixon, T Grieve, J Kendal,
H Monkhouse, J Mumberson, G Rayson, W Sanderson, J Sandwith.
Attendance: 'large'   *Referee*: J Paisley (Greysouthen)
Note: Aspatria's score is from one minor point.

DURHAM COUNTY CHALLENGE CUP (15 entries)
Most goals wins. If equal, most tries. If still equal, majority of 3 minor points.

First Round
Durham City 1g, 1t, Sunderland 0
Hartlepool Rangers 1g, Houghton-le-Spring 0
Hartlepool Rovers 2g, Ryton 0
North Durham w/o Darlington (disbanded)
Tudhoe 1g, 1t, Gateshead Institute 2t
West Hartlepool 1g, Consett 1t
Westoe w/o Sunderland Rovers (disbanded)
Bye: Humbledon

Second Round
Durham City 1t, Westoe 1t (mp: 4-0)
Hartlepool Rangers 1g, 1t,
North Durham 1t
Hartlepool Rovers 2g, 1t, Tudhoe 0
Humbledon 2t, West Hartlepool 0

Semi-finals
Hartlepool Rovers 1t, Durham City 0 (aet)
Humbledon 1g, Hartlepool Rangers 0

FINAL
Saturday 2 April 1887 at Friarage Field, Hartlepool
HARTLEPOOL ROVERS 2 goals, 3 tries *Back*: HO Hoy. *Three-quarters*: JH Walker,
AE Emmerson (2t), MH Horsley (t), *Half-backs*: WG Lohden (t), G Smith. *Forwards*:
G Bell, A Hill (t), CM Huntley, W L Oakes (capt), R Ogden, FE Prease, W Thwaites,
T Watson (2c), W Yiend.
HUMBLEDON 0 *Back*: W Chrisp. *Three-quarters*: J Branfoot, H Burkett, M Barron.
Half-backs: JW Featherstone, G Morgan. *Forwards*: C Alderson, W Bartram (capt),
J Carmichael, D Ranken, FW Ranken, J Ranken, CH Raper, J Sugden, G Vaux.
Attendance: 6,000   *Referee*: TM Swinburne (Durham RU Vice-President).

NORTHUMBERLAND COUNTY FOOTBALL CHALLENGE CUP (9 entries)
Most goals wins. If equal, most tries.

First Round
North Elswick 1g, 2t, Tynemouth 0
Northern 1g, 1t, Benwell 0
Percy Park 1g, 2t, Newcastle Rangers 0
Tynedale w/o Bellingham (withdrew)
Bye: Northumberland FC

Second Round
Northumberland FC 1g, 1t, North Elswick 0
Tynedale 1t, Percy Park 0
Bye: Northern

Semi-final
Northern 1t, Northumberland FC 0
Bye: Tynedale

FINAL
Saturday 2 April 1887 at Jesmond Ground, Newcastle
TYNEDALE 1 goal, 1 try *Back*: RH Robb. *Three-quarters*: T Robson (capt), W Pattinson, JT Dodd (dg). *Half-backs*: FHR Alderson, W Farthing. *Forwards*: J Bailey, I Baty, T Elliott (t), CW Harrison, JJ McIntyre, Dr Mackie, JC Robertson, T Rogan, J Scott.
NORTHERN 1 try *Back*: A Park. *Three-quarters*: CS Gill, V Rutherford, E Edwards. *Half-backs*: AC Challoner, HB Lockhart (capt). *Forwards*: SJ Allden, H Angus, T Latham, J Livingstone, F Manford, HWE Spencer, P Stanton, JW Swinburne (t), A Watson.
Attendance: 5,000   *Referee*: n/a

WEST LANCASHIRE AND BORDER TOWNS CHALLENGE CUP (16 entries)
Try – 4 points; conversion – 4; drop-goal, field goal – 6; minor – 1. Majority of 3 points required to win.

First Round
Aspull 30, Southport Olympic 10
Litherland 8, Wigan 26
Liverpool Wanderers 2, Walton 12
St Helens 3, Warrington 6

St Helens Recreation 53, Bootle 1
Tuebrook 2, Tyldesley 10
Walkden 7, Leigh 2
Widnes 25, Blackrod 2

Second Round
Aspull 15, St Helens Recreation 4
Walkden 11, Wigan 26
Walton 1, Tyldesley 27
Warrington 9, Widnes 2

Semi-finals
Aspull 6, Tyldesley 3
(at Prescott Street, Wigan)
Wigan 12, Warrington 6
(at Boundary Road, St Helens)

FINAL
Saturday 26 March 1887 at Liverpool College Ground, Fairfield
ASPULL 20 *Back*: J Pilkington. *Three-quarters*: E Bullough, R Seddon (capt), J Roberts (t). *Half-backs*: J Cartwright, D Hulme. *Forwards*: E Baxendale, H Bramwell, G Croston, W Haydock (t), T Hesketh, R Lawson, James Lindsay, John Lindsay, T Monks.
WIGAN 1 *Back*: J Slevin (capt). *Three-quarters*: J Anderton, JC Samuels, J Hunter. *Half-backs*: J Mitchinson, T Morris. *Forwards*: W Atkinson, J Booth, T Brayshay, E Dempsey, J Ellison, S Kay, JE Lowe, EF Wardle, L Whittle.
Attendance: 5,000   *Referee*: E Beswick (Swinton)
Note: Aspull's score includes 12 minor points, Wigan's score was from one minor point.

YORKSHIRE COUNTY FOOTBALL CHALLENGE CUP (64 entries)
Most goals wins (3 tries count as one 'goal'). If equal, most tries (excluding any already counted as equalling a 'goal'). If still equal, majority of 3 minor points.

First Round
Alverthorpe 2g, 2t, Bradford Trinity 0
Bingley 0, Shipley 1g (aet)
Bowling 1g, Manningham 1g, 1t
Bradford 5g, 6t, Keighley 0
Bramley 1g, 2t, Ravensthorpe 1t
Brighouse Rangers 1g, 4t, Barnsley 0
Buttershaw 0, Mytholmroyd 0
(mp: 3-4, aet)
Eastmoor 0, Holbeck 1g, 2t
Goole 0, Wakefield St Austin's 1g
Guiseley 1g, Cleckheaton 3t (mp: 4-4, aet)
Halifax 1g, 1t, Otley 1t
Hipperholme and Lightcliffe 1t,
Dudley Hill 1g, 1t
Harrogate 1g, Dewsbury 2g, 1t
Horsforth 0, Leeds Rovers 0 (mp: 1-10)
Huddersfield 1t, Castleford 2t
Hull 3g, 3t, Thornes 0
Hull Athletic 2g, 1t, Shepley 1t
Hunslet 1g, 2t, Salterhebble 0
Kirkstall 1t, Elland 0
Leeds Parish Church 1g, 1t, Saltaire 0
Leeds Rifles 1t, Horbury 1g, 2t
Lockwood 1g, Dewsbury Clarence 1g, 1t
Morley 4t, Heckmondwike 0
Normanton 3g, 1t, Hebden Bridge 0
Ossett 1g, 4t, Halifax Free Wanderers 0
Pontefract 2t, Skipton 0
Pudsey 1g, York St George's 0
Ripon 1g, Mirfield 2g, 3t
Selby 0, Leeds St John's 1t (aet)
Wakefield Trinity 5g, 7t, Doncaster Town 0
Wortley 1t, Batley 1g, 1t
York 0, Liversedge 2g

First Round Replays
Cleckheaton 1g, Guiseley 0
Mytholmroyd 0, Buttershaw 1t

Second Round
Alverthorpe 1g, Hull 1t
Batley 1g, 3t, Hunslet 1t
Bramley 0, Liversedge 1g
Brighouse Rangers 1g, 3t, Pontefract 1t
Buttershaw 1t, Ossett 2g, 3t
Castleford 1t, Hull Athletic 0
Cleckheaton 0, Kirkstall 2t
Dewsbury Clarence 0, Bradford 5g, 3t
Holbeck 0, Morley 1g
Leeds Parish Church 1g, 2t, Horbury 0
Leeds Rovers 2t, Normanton 1g
Leeds St John's 1g, Dewsbury 0
Manningham 1g, Halifax 0
Mirfield 3t, Wakefield St Austin's 1t
Shipley 2t, Dudley Hill 1g
Wakefield Trinity 2g, 3t, Pudsey 0

Third Round
Brighouse Rangers 0, Batley 1g, 1t
Castleford 1t, Leeds St John's 2g
Kirkstall 1g, 1t, Dudley Hill 0
Leeds Parish Church 1t, Morley 0
Liversedge 1g, 1t, Mirfield 1g, 1t (mp: 10-1)
Manningham w/o Bradford (disqualified)
Normanton 0, Wakefield Trinity 1g, 2t
Ossett 2g, 1t, Alverthorpe 0

Fourth Round
Batley 0, Wakefield Trinity 0 (mp: 1-3, aet)
Leeds Parish Church 1t, Leeds St John's 1g
Liversedge 2g, 1t, Kirkstall 1t
Ossett 0, Manningham 0 (mp: 5-2)

Fourth Round Replay
Wakefield Trinity 1g, 2t, Batley 0

Semi-finals
Leeds St John's 0, Liversedge 0
(mp: 7-3, at Crown Point, Leeds)
Wakefield Trinity 1g, 1t, Ossett 0
(at Crown Flatts, Dewsbury)

FINAL

Saturday 2 April 1887 at Thrum Hall, Halifax
WAKEFIELD TRINITY 2 goals *Back*: HO Hamshaw. *Three-quarters*: CE Bartram, H Fallas, A Ash. *Half-backs*: H Dawson (capt, t), H Hutchinson (2c). *Forwards*: P Booth, T Harrison, G Jubb, J Lathom, FW Lowrie, F Ross (t), J Thompson, H Ward, H Whiteley.
LEEDS ST JOHN'S 0 *Back*: JW Hutton. *Three-quarters*: W Gray, R Walton, JH Potter. *Half-backs*: B Burrell (capt), W Place. *Forwards*: J Illingworth, EG Load, C McMillan, J Milnes, JW Moore, GB Naylor, JA Shirer, J Watmough, B West.
Attendance: 14,000   *Referee*: A Cattell (Sheffield)

COUNTY MATCHES

Saturday 30 October 1886 at Lismore Place, Carlisle
CUMBERLAND 1 try *Back*: L Beattie (Asp). *Three-quarters*: H Sandwith (Asp), W Lewthwaite (Mary), T Armstrong (Pen). *Half-backs:* G Tandy (Pen), W Thompson (Dear). *Forwards*: F Crump (Pen), J Harrison (Mil), T Lister (Dear), J Mumberson (Asp), E Murray (Mary, t), H Paisley (Grey), J Sandwith (Asp), H Temperley (Asp), J Thomson (capt, Pen).
NORTHUMBERLAND 2 tries *Back*: JA Williamson (PerPk). *Three-quarters*: AC Challoner (Nor), RE Herbertson (PerPk), S Atkinson (NEls). *Half-backs*: B Sutherland (Nor), H Welford (NEls). *Forwards*: JW Coward (capt, PerPk), A Gee (PerPk), T Gee (PerPk, t), AS Haslam (NEls, t), J Livingstone (Nor), HB Lockhart (Nor), GW Mole (NEls), FW Ramsay (Nor), HWE Spencer (Nor).
Attendance: n/a   *Referee*: JM Mawson (Barrow)

Saturday 6 November 1886 at Friarage Field, Hartlepool
DURHAM 1 goal *Back*: MH Horsley (HartR). *Three-quarters*: GH Eyre (Sund, c), AE Emmerson (HartR), JH Walker (HartR). *Half-backs*: CH Newman (NDur), JC Wilford (Sund). *Forwards*: R Barwick (Sund), HH Carrick (NDur), B Cox (Sund), CH Elliot (Sund), A Hill (HartR, t), W Hodgson (Tud), F Lumsden (DurC), FE Pease (Darl), W Yiend (HartR).
YORKSHIRE 1 goal *Back*: CE Fox (Salt, c). *Three-quarters*: RE Lockwood (Dew), AR Robertshaw (Brad), JT Haslam (Bat). *Half-backs*: F Bonsor (Brad), Jim Naylor (Bat). *Forwards*: P Dickenson (Cas), G Harrison (capt, Hull), JL Hickson (Brad, t), E Jackson (Bat), C Mathers (Bram), JW Sykes (Bat), H Ward (Wak), TW Watson (Hal), E Wilkinson (Brad).
Attendance: 2,000   *Referee*: GR Hill (RFU Honorary Secretary)

Saturday 13 November 1886 at Upper Park, Birkenhead
CHESHIRE 0 *Back*: TH Woods (Run). *Three-quarters*: JA Black (BirkPk), C Holden (BirkPk), WA Riley (Run). *Half-backs*: H Hughes (Run), FW Spence (BirkPk). *Forwards*: WH Broady (Run), J Cowan (BirkPk), G Cowie (capt, BirkPk), J Lewis (Run), E Lings (Sale), H Ransome (Bow), J Scurfield (BirkPk), A Williams (NewB), W Wright (Run).
LANCASHIRE 3 goals, 3 tries *Back*: S Roberts (Swi, 3c). *Three-quarters*: A Durandu (Liv, t), V Slater (Sal, t), J Valentine (Swi, t). *Half-backs*: J Mills (Swi), LB Stoddart (Liv). *Forwards*: C Anderton (ManFW), HC Chapman (LivOB), H Eagles (Sal, t), N Hotchkiss (Swi), AT Kemble (capt, Liv), RL Seddon (BroR), HH Springmann (Liv), A Teggin (BroR), S Williams (Sal, 2t).
Attendance: 3,000   *Referee*: GR Hill (RFU Honorary Secretary)

Saturday 13 November 1886 at Crown Flatts, Dewsbury
YORKSHIRE 3 goals, 4 tries *Back*: CE Fox (Salt, c). *Three-quarters*: RE Lockwood (Dew, dg), AR Robertshaw (Brad), JT Haslam (Bat). *Half-backs*: F Bonsor (Brad, t), JH Potter (LeeStJ, 2t, c). *Forwards*: T Allbutt (Hal), H Bedford (Bat), P Dickenson (Cas), G Harrison (capt, Hull, t), E Jackson (Bat), W Jowett (Brad), C Thompson (Dew), H Ward (Wak, t), E Wilkinson (Brad, t).
NORTHUMBERLAND 1 goal *Back*: JA Williamson (PerPk, c). *Three-quarters*: CS Gill (Nor), V Rutherford (Nor), AC Challoner (Nor). *Half-backs*: H Scott (Nor), B Sutherland (Nor, t). *Forwards*: JW Coward (capt, PerPk), T Gee (PerPk), JH Greenwell (Tynm), AS Haslam (NEls), J Livingstone (Nor), GW Mole (NEls), FW Ramsay (Nor), T Rogan (Tynd), HWE Spencer (Nor).
Attendance: 4,000   *Referee*: JT Todd (Durham)

Saturday 20 November 1886 at Whalley Range, Manchester
LANCASHIRE 1 goal *Back*: S Roberts (Swi, c). *Three-quarters*: V Slater (Sal), J Valentine (Swi), A Durandu (Liv). *Half-backs*: J Mills (Swi), LB Stoddart (Liv). *Forwards*: C Anderton (ManFW), HC Chapman (LivOB), H Eagles (Sal), N Hotchkiss (Swi), AT Kemble (capt, Liv), RL Seddon (BroR, t), HH Springmann (Liv), A Teggin (BroR), S Williams (Sal).
YORKSHIRE 1 goal *Back*: CE Fox (Salt). *Three-quarters*: RE Lockwood (Dew, t), AR Robertshaw (Brad), JT Haslam (Bat). *Half-backs*: F Bonsor (Brad), JH Potter (LeeStJ, c). *Forwards*: H Bedford (Bat), P Dickenson (Cas), G Harrison (capt, Hull), JL Hickson (Brad), E Holmes (Mann), E Jackson (Bat), W Jowett (Brad), C Thompson (Dew), E Wilkinson (Brad).
Attendance: 20,000   *Referee*: GR Hill (RFU Honorary Secretary)

Saturday 27 November 1886 at Jesmond Ground, Newcastle
NORTHUMBERLAND 1 try *Back*: MF Elsdon (Tynm). *Three-quarters*: H Scott (Nor), T Thomas (PerPk), CS Gill (Nor). *Half-backs*: S Brutton (Tynm), H Welford (NEls). *Forwards*: JW Coward (PerPk), A Gee (PerPk), T Gee (PerPk), AS Haslam (NEls), J Livingstone (Nor), GW Mole (NEls), RH Spence (PerPk, t), HWE Spencer (Nor), JW Swinburne (capt, Nor).
LANCASHIRE 3 goals, 1 try *Back*: S Roberts (Swi, 2c). *Three-quarters*: A Durandu (Liv, dg), J Valentine (Swi), V Slater (Sal). *Half-backs*: J Mills (Swi), LB Stoddart (Liv). *Forwards*: C Anderton (ManFW), T Banks (Swi, t), HC Chapman (LivOB), H Eagles (Sal, t), J Groves (RochH), AT Kemble (capt, Liv), A Little (Bar), FS Moss (Bro), S Williams (Sal, t).
Attendance: 2,000   *Referee*: JT Todd (Durham)

Saturday 27 November 1886 at Mint's Feet, Kendal
WESTMORLAND 1 try *Back*: CH Knight (KenH). *Three-quarters*: WJ Walker (capt, KenH), J Armstrong (KenH), E Hoggarth (KenT). *Half-backs*: R Chorley (KenT), R Saul (Amb). *Forwards*: J Alexander (KenT, t), JJ Armer (KenT), RC Beard (KenT), L Beetham (Amb), J Berry (KenH), W Cross (KenH), R Fisher (Amb), W Martin (Wind), A Tucker (Wind).
WEST LANCASHIRE 1 try *Back*: TH Woods (Run). *Three-quarters*: HC Speakman (Run), J Slevin (Wig, t), E Foreman (StH). *Half-backs*: JE Farrell (Wid), D Hulme (Asp). *Forwards*: T Brayshay (Wig), J Clarke (Run), W Faulkner (Run), WL Goodman (LivW), R Lawson (Asp), J Pyke (StHR), JH Smith (Wid), L Whittle (Wig), R Wilcock (capt, LivW).
Attendance: 3,000   *Referee*: E Walmsley (Blackburn)

Saturday 11 December 1886 at Houghton-le-Spring
DURHAM 1 goal, 1 try *Back*: WH Bell (Sund, c). *Three-quarters*: MH Horsley (HartR), JH Walker (HartR), JC Wilford (Sund). *Half-backs*: EA Douglas (Hendon Church Institute), CH Newman (NDur, t). *Forwards*: R Barwick (Sund), HH Carrick (NDur), B Cox (Sund), CH Elliot (Sund), A Hill (HartR), W Hodgson (Tud), F Lumsden (DurC), FE Pease (Darl, t), W Yiend (HartR).
CUMBERLAND 0 *Back*: L Beattie (Asp). *Three-quarters*: H Paisley (Grey), W Lewthwaite (Mary), H Sandwith (Asp). *Half-backs*: WT Ridley (Asp), J Robley (Mary). *Forwards*: J Dixon (Asp), WH Farrow* (Tynm), J Lewthwaite (Mary), T Lister (Dear), J Mumberson (Asp), J Paisley (Grey), G Rayson (Asp), J Sandwith (Asp), J Skelton (Mary).
Attendance: 1,000   *Referee*: W Cail (Northumberland)
*Guest from Northumberland to replace unavailable player.

Saturday 29 January 1887 at Whalley Range, Manchester
LANCASHIRE 1 goal, 1 try *Back*: S Roberts (Swi, c). *Three-quarters*: FC Withers (Liv, 2t), A Durandu (Liv), V Slater (Sal). *Half-backs*: J Mills (Swi), JH Payne (Bro). *Forwards*: T Banks (Swi), H Eagles (Sal), AT Kemble (capt, Liv), A Little (Bar), RL Seddon (BroR), HH Springmann (Liv), A Teggin (BroR), F Turner (War), S Williams (Sal).
DURHAM 1 try *Back*: HO Hoy (HartR). *Three-quarters*: JH Walker (HartR), AE Emmerson (HartR), JC Wilford (Sund). *Half-backs*: EA Douglas (Hendon Church Institute), CH Newman (capt, NDur). *Forwards*: R Barwick (Sund), B Cox (Sund), CH Elliot (Sund), A Hill (HartR), W Hodgson (Tud), WL Oakes (HartR), FE Pease (Darl), JW Sowerby (NDur), W Yiend (HartR, t).
Attendance: 6,000   *Referee*: WH Wallace (Cheshire)

Saturday 29 January 1887 at Cavendish Park, Barrow
NORTH LANCASHIRE 0 *Back*: JJ Woodburn (Bar). *Three-quarters*: JR Harley (capt, Bar), T Forshaw (Bar), J Tyson (Ask). *Half-backs*: R Crawley (Ask), JH Walton (Bar). *Forwards*: A Barton (Carn), J Johnson (More), J Kidd (Ask), H Leak (Bar), N Leigh (Lanc), A Little (Bar), T MacDonald (Ask), J Todd (Ask), S Vickers (Ask).
WESTMORLAND 3 tries *Back*: CH Knight (KenH). *Three-quarters*: WJ Walker (capt, KenH, t), J Armstrong (KenH, t), E Hoggarth (KenT). *Half-backs*: WE Banks (KenT), J Berry (KenH). *Forwards*: J Alexander (KenT), JJ Armer (KenT), TG Baines (KenH), RC Beard (KenT, t), L Beetham (Amb), W Cross (KenH), R Fisher (Amb), W Hill (KenH), W Martin (Wind).
Attendance: 2,500/3,000   *Referee*: n/a

Saturday 5 February 1887 at Fitz Mill Lane, Cockermouth
CUMBERLAND 0 *Back*: L Beattie (Asp). *Three-quarters*: H Sandwith (Asp), W Lewthwaite (Mary), G Dobson (Cock). *Half-backs:* WT Ridley (Asp), J Robley (Mary). *Forwards*: J Grave (Cock), J Lewthwaite (Mary), J Mumberson (Asp), T Nettleton (Cock), Newton (Brou), NJ Paisley (Grey), G Rayson (Asp), HP Senhouse (capt, Cock), J Thomson (Pen).
WESTMORLAND 1 goal, 1 try *Back*: WG Hoggarth (KenT). *Three-quarters*: WJ Walker (capt, KenH), E Hoggarth (KenT), J Armstrong (KenH, t). *Half-backs*: WE Banks (KenT), J Berry (KenH). *Forwards*: TG Baines (KenH), RC Beard (KenT, t), L Beetham (Amb), W Cross (KenH, c), R Fisher (Amb), W Hill (KenH), W Hodgson (Amb), W Martin (Wind), JW Wilkinson (KenH).
Attendance: 2,000   *Referee*: S Troughton (Lancashire)

Saturday 12 February 1887 at Jesmond Ground, Newcastle
NORTHUMBERLAND 1 goal, 1 try *Back*: MF Elsdon (Tynm). *Three-quarters*: CS Gill (Nor, dg), T Thomas (PerPk), F Finney (PerPk). *Half-backs*: FHR Alderson (Tynd, t), AC Challoner (Nor). *Forwards*: A Gee (PerPk), T Gee (PerPk), JH Greenwell (Tynm), AS Haslam (NEls), GW Mole (NEls), W Morrell (NEls), RH Spence (PerPk), HWE Spencer (Nor), JW Swinburne (capt, Nor).
DURHAM 0 *Back*: HO Hoy (HartR). *Three-quarters*: JH Walker (HartR), VT Thompson (Sund), JC Wilford (Sund). *Half-backs*: TM Jamieson (Con), G Smith (HartR). *Forwards*: R Barwick (Sund), B Cox (Sund), CH Elliot (Sund), W Hodgson (Tud), WL Oakes (HartR), R Pattinson (HartR), FE Pease (Darl), JW Sowerby (NDur), W Yiend (HartR).
Attendance: 2,000/4,000   *Referee*: T Swinburne (Durham)

Saturday 12 February 1887 at Thrum Hall, Halifax
YORKSHIRE 2 goals, 3 tries *Back*: CE Fox (Salt, c). *Three-quarters*: WJ Fawcett (Mann, c), J Dodd (Hal), JW Graham (Dew). *Half-backs*: H Archer (Hud, 2t), H Hutchinson (Wak). *Forwards*: T Allbutt (Hal), H Bedford (Bat, 2t), E Birch (York), P Dickenson (Cas, t), G Harrison (capt, Hull), E Holmes (Mann), E Jackson (Bat), W Teal (Hull), H Ward (Wak).
CHESHIRE 1 goal *Back*: H Murdoch (NewB). *Three-quarters*: JA Black (BirkPk), HC Speakman (Run), F Davies (Run). *Half-backs*: LM Holden (BirkPk), FW Spence (BirkPk). *Forwards*: DA Bingham (capt, BirkPk), WH Broady (Run, c), J Cowan (BirkPk, t), W Faulkner (Run), JG Gifford (NewB), H Hughes (Run), A Williams (NewB), AG Wood (BirkPk), W Wright (Run).
Attendance: 5,000   *Referee*: H Vassall (RFU Honorary Treasurer)

Monday 14 February 1887 at Mount Pleasant, Batley
YORKSHIRE 4 goals, 2 tries *Back*: HO Hamshaw (Wak). *Three-quarters*: RE Lockwood (Dew, 2t), WJ Fawcett (Mann, 3c), J Dodd (Hal). *Half-backs*: H Archer (Hud), T Elliker (Bat). *Forwards*: H Bedford (Bat), E Birch (York, t), P Dickenson (Cas), G Harrison (capt, Hull), E Holmes (Mann, t, dg), E Jackson (Bat), W Teal (Hull), H Ward (Wak), E Wilkinson (Brad, t).
SURREY 0 *Back*: FA Coles (ClapR). *Three-quarters*: AB Whitehead (OLey), G Dale (ClapR), FW Weeks (ClapR). *Half-backs*: A Bishop (Harl), HC Carpmael (ClapR). *Forwards*: A Allport (ClapR), WP Carpmael (ClapR), CT Codrington (MarlN), HJ Cooper (StTHosp), LF Elliott (Ken), TAM Forde (StTHosp), JH Gould (OLey), McHutchen (Harl), CC Moxon (StTHosp).
Attendance: 4,000   *Referee*: Rev F Marshall (Yorkshire)

Saturday 19 February 1887 at Whalley Range, Manchester
LANCASHIRE 3 tries *Back*: S Roberts (Swi). *Three-quarters*: V Slater (Sal), D Worthington (Tottington, t), FC Withers (Liv, t). *Half-backs*: J Mills (Swi), JH Payne (capt, Bro). *Forwards*: C Anderton (ManFW), FA Andrew (Man), HC Chapman (LivOB), H Eagles (Sal), AT Kemble (capt, Liv, t), A Little (Bar), RL Seddon (BroR), A Teggin (BroR), F Turner (War).
SOMERSETSHIRE 1 goal, 2 tries *Back*: SMJ Woods (Bridg, dg). *Three-quarters*: BWL Ashford (Exe, 2t), H Merry (Well), SC Smith (Wes). *Half-backs*: FC Duckworth (Wes), FH Fox (Well/MarlN). *Forwards*: AA Glass (Wivel/OChelt), HT Gilmore (Wes), AA Hammill (Bridg), EL Hancock (Wivel), PF Hancock (Wivel/Black), HG Manfield (Yeo), RMP Parsons (Yeo), H Paterson (Wes), JR Walter (Well).
Attendance: 5,000   *Referee*: WH Wallace (Cheshire)
Note: Somersetshire won due to scoring most goals.

Saturday 19 February 1887 at Park Avenue, Bradford
YORKSHIRE 2 tries *Back*: CE Fox (Salt). *Three-quarters*: RE Lockwood (Dew), J Dodd (Hal), WJ Fawcett (Mann). *Half-backs*: H Archer (Hud, t), J Wright (Brad). *Forwards*: H Bedford (Bat), P Dickenson (Cas), G Harrison (capt, Hull), JL Hickson (Brad), E Holmes (Mann, t), E Jackson (Bat), W Jowett (Brad), H Ward (Wak), E Wilkinson (Brad).
MIDDLESEX 3 tries *Back*: AS Johnson (Black). *Three-quarters*: JA Gould (Rich, t), AE Stoddart (Black, t), SH Baker (Ken). *Half-backs*: JH Roberts (Rich), Alan Rotherham (capt, Rich). *Forwards*: CJ Arkle (Rich), WG Clibborn (Rich), WE Clifton (Rich), C Collier (Rich), HM Elder (MarlN), J Hammond (Black), GB James (Harl), GL Jeffery (Black), ES McEwan (OChelt, t).
Attendance: 12,000   *Referee*: W Cail (Northumberland)

Monday 21 February 1887 at Chester Road, Sunderland
DURHAM 1 goal *Back*: HO Hoy (HartR). *Three-quarters*: GH Eyre (Sund), VT Thompson (Sund), JC Wilford (Sund). *Half-backs*: TM Jamieson (Con, c), CJ Sadler (Durham School). *Forwards*: R Barwick (Sund), HH Carrick (NDur), CH Elliot (Sund), W Hodgson (Tud), WL Oakes (HartR), FE Pease (HartR), G Pimbury (DurC), JW Sowerby (NDur), W Yiend (HartR, t).
MIDDLESEX 1 goal, 2 tries *Back*: AS Johnson (Black). *Three-quarters*: JA Gould (Rich, t, dg), AE Stoddart (Black), SH Baker (Ken). *Half-backs*: J Anderson (Rich, t), JH Roberts (Rich). *Forwards*: CJ Arkle (Rich), WE Clifton (Rich), C Collier (Rich), HM Elder (MarlN), J Hammond (Black), GB James (Harl), GL Jeffery (Black), ES McEwan (OChelt), CE Ward (Rich).
Attendance: 2,500   *Referee*: W Cail (Northumberland)

Monday 21 February 1887 at Belle Vue, Wakefield
YORKSHIRE 3 tries *Back*: HO Hamshaw (Wak). *Three-quarters*: RE Lockwood (Dew, 3t), J Dodd (Hal), JW Graham (Dew). *Half-backs*: F Bonsor (capt, Brad), T Elliker (Bat). *Forwards*: H Bedford (Bat), P Dickenson (Cas), J Garforth (Dew), JL Hickson (Brad), E Holmes (Mann), E Jackson (Bat), A Parker (Bat), W Teal (Hull), E Wilkinson (Brad).
SOMERSETSHIRE 1 try *Back*: H Merry (Well). *Three-quarters*: R Escott (Wivel), SMJ Woods (Bridg), BWL Ashford (Exe). *Half-backs*: FC Duckworth (Wes), FH Fox (Well/MarlN, t). *Forwards*: HT Gilmore (Wes), AA Glass (Wivel/OChelt), EL Hancock (Wivel), WH Manfield (Yeo), RMP Parsons (Yeo), H Paterson (Wes), JR Walter (Wivel).
Attendance: 4,000   *Referee*: GR Hill (RFU Honorary Secretary)

Saturday 12 March 1887 at Kennington Oval, London
MIDDLESEX 0 *Back*: AS Johnstone (Black). *Three-quarters*: WE Maclagan (LonS), GC Lindsay (LonS), AE Stoddart (Black). *Half-backs*: Alan Rotherham (Rich), JH Roberts (Rich). *Forwards*: CJ Arkle (Rich), C Collier (Rich), ET Gurdon (capt, Rich), WG Clibborn (Rich), J Hammond (Black), GL Jeffery (Black), ES McEwan (OChelt), CJB Marriott (Black), T Riddell (LonS).
LANCASHIRE 1 try *Back*: S Roberts (Swi). *Three-quarters*: J Valentine (Swi), J Robertson (BroR), V Slater (Sal, t). *Half-backs*: J Mills (Swi), JH Payne (capt, Bro). *Forwards*: C Anderton (ManFW), HC Chapman (LivOB), H Eagles (Sal), AT Kemble (capt, Liv), FS Moss (Bro), JW Roberts (Sal), RL Seddon (BroR), AH Stockley (Liv), A Teggin (BroR).
Attendance: 12,000   *Referee*: L Stokes (RFU President)

Thursday 21 April 1887 at Lowerhouse Lane, Widnes
WEST LANCASHIRE 1 goal *Back*: J Pilkington (Asp). *Three-quarters*: TH Davies (Run), T Barnes (War), J Jolley (War). *Half-backs*: D Hulme (Asp), J Pilkington (StHR). *Forwards*: WH Broady (Run, c), J Holmes (Litherland, t), W Kiddie (Wid), T Monks (Asp), W Parr (StHR), JH Smith (Wid), F Turner (War), L Whittle (Wig), W Wilcock (LivW).
WESTMORLAND 1 goal, 3 tries *Back*: WG Hoggarth (KenT). *Three-quarters*: WJ Walker (capt, KenH), J Armstrong (KenH, t), E Hoggarth (KenT). *Half-backs*: J Berry (KenH, t), W Cross (KenH, c). *Forwards*: J Banks (Amb), RC Beard (KenT), L Beetham (Amb, t), T Henderson (KenH), W Hodgson (Amb), RH Moore (Amb), R Nicholson (KenT), WJ Parsons (KenH), JW Wilkinson (KenH, t).
Attendance: 2,000   *Referee*: GR Hill (RFU Honorary Secretary)

ENGLAND TRIAL MATCH

Saturday 18 December 1886 at Rectory Field, Blackheath
SOUTH 1 goal, 1 try *Back*: HB Tristram (Rich). *Three-quarters*: AE Stoddart (Black), J le Fleming (Black), AR St L Fagan (LonHosp). *Half-backs*: Alan Rotherham (Rich), MT Scott (CamU). *Forwards*: CJ Arkle (Rich), HC Baker (Clif), CR Cleveland (OxfU), WG Clibborn (Rich, 2t), JH Dewhurst (CamU), GL Jeffery (Black), CJB Marriott (capt, Black), N Spurling (Black), FG Swayne (CamU, c).
NORTH 2 tries *Back*: S Roberts (Swi). *Three-quarters*: A Durandu (Liv), JA Black (BirkPk, t), RE Lockwood (Dew, t). *Half-backs*: F Bonsor (Brad, J Mills (Swi). *Forwards*: G Harrison (capt, Hull), JL Hickson (Brad), AT Kemble (Liv), FE Pease (Darl), RL Seddon (BroR), HH Springmann (Liv), A Teggin (BroR), E Wilkinson (Brad), S Williams (Sal).
Attendance: 5,000   *Referee*: WAD McClachan (London Scottish)

INTERNATIONAL CHAMPIONSHIP

Saturday 8 January 1887 at Stradey Park, Llanelli*
WALES 0 *Back*: DH Bowen (Llan). *Three-quarters*: CG Taylor (Black), JA Gould (New), WM Douglas (Car). *Half-backs*: OJ Evans (Car), CH Newman (capt, New). *Forwards*: EP Alexander (CamU), AF Bland (Car), W Bowen (Swa), TJS Clapp (New), R Gould (New), AJ Hybart (Car), TW Lockwood (New), D Morgan (Swa), WH Thomas (CamU).
ENGLAND 0 *Back*: S Roberts (Swi). *Three-quarters*: J le Fleming (Black), AR Robertshaw (Brad), RE Lockwood (Dew). *Half-backs*: F Bonsor (Brad), Alan Rotherham (capt, Rich). *Forwards*: HC Baker (Clif), CR Cleveland (OxfU), WG Clibborn (Rich), JH Dewhurst (CamU), JL Hickson (Brad), GL Jeffery (Black), RL Seddon (BroR), N Spurling (Black), E Wilkinson (Brad).
Attendance: 8,000   *Referee*: GR Hill (England)
*Transferred from rugby ground to adjoining cricket ground due to frost.

Saturday 5 February 1887 at Lansdowne Road, Dublin
IRELAND 2 goals *Back*: DB Walkington (NIFC). *Half-backs*: CR Tillie (DubU, t), DF Rambaut (DubU, 2c), R Montgomery (CamU, t). *Quarter-backs*: JH McLaughlin (Der), RG Warren (capt, Lans). *Forwards*: J Chambers (DubU), JS Dick (QCC), J Johnston (BelA), VC le Fanu (CamU), J Macaulay (Lim), HJ Neill (NIFC), TR Lyle (DubU.), R Stevenson (Lis), EJ Walsh (Lans).

ENGLAND 0 *Back*: S Roberts (Swi). *Three-quarters*: WN Bolton (Black), AR St L Fagan (LonHosp), RE Lockwood (Dew). *Half-backs*: Alan Rotherham (capt, Rich), MT Scott (CamU). *Forwards*: WG Clibborn (Rich), JH Dewhurst (CamU), JL Hickson (Brad), GL Jeffery (Black), AT Kemble (Liv), CJB Marriott (Black), FE Pease (Darl), RL Seddon (BroR), A Teggin (BroR).
Attendance: 7,000   *Referee*: WD Phillips (Wales)

Saturday 5 March 1887 at Whalley Range, Manchester
ENGLAND 1 try *Back*: HB Tristram (Rich). *Three-quarters*: WN Bolton (Black), AR Robertshaw (Brad), RE Lockwood (Dew). *Half-backs*: F Bonsor (Brad), Alan Rotherham (capt, Rich). *Forwards*: CR Cleveland (OxfU), WG Clibborn (Rich), JH Dewhurst (CamU), JL Hickson (Brad), GL Jeffery (Black, t), RL Seddon (BroR), HH Springmann (Liv), A Teggin (BroR), E Wilkinson (Brad).
SCOTLAND 1 try *Back*: WF Holms (LonS). *Half-backs*: WE Maclagan (LonS), GC Lindsay (LonS), AN Woodrow (GlasA). *Quarter-backs*: PH Don-Wauchope (EdinW), CE Orr (WoS). *Forwards*: CW Berry (EdinW), AT Clay (EdinA), J French (GlasA), TW Irvine (EdinA), HT Ker (GlasA), MC McEwan (EdinA), RG Macmillan (LonS), DS Morton (WoS, t), C Reid (capt, EdinA).
Attendance: 12,000   *Referee*: TR Lyle (Ireland)

Other results
Ireland 0, Scotland 2g, 2t
Scotland 4g, 8t, Wales 0
Wales 1g, 1t, Ireland 3t

Final table

	P	W	D	L	G-T	G-T
Scotland	3	2	1	0	6-11	0-1
Wales	3	1	1	1	1-1	4-11
Ireland	3	1	0	2	2-3	3-3
England	3	0	2	1	0-1	2-1

1887-1888

WEST LANCASHIRE UNION ANNUAL MEETING
The West Lancashire and Border Towns Union held their annual meeting at the Goat Hotel, Liverpool, on 30th September. Amongst the decisions made it was agreed that semi-final receipts from the Cup competition be divided between the contending clubs instead of going to the West Lancashire and Border Towns Union. Also, it was resolved not to adopt the new point scoring values created the previous season by the Rugby Football Union, but to continue with the system they already used; converted tries counted as eight points, dropped goals six points, unconverted tries four points, with a majority of three minors required to win a match that would otherwise be drawn.[79]

NORTHAMPTONSHIRE TRAVEL NORTH
Northamptonshire made their only appearance in the north during the Victorian era when they visited Cheshire at Runcorn on 2nd November. A further fixture against Northumberland at Newcastle was arranged for 31st December but cancelled at the last moment as Northamptonshire was unable to raise a team.

YORKSHIRE MEET IRISH OPPOSITION
Yorkshire entertained overseas opposition for the first time when Ulster visited Belle Vue, Wakefield, on Monday 5th December. Unfortunately the home county did not have 15 players available at the start and had to call

on three from hosts Wakefield Trinity; Paul Booth, Jack Fotherby and Jack Gomersall. The time taken for Yorkshire to obtain a full complement caused 'considerable delay' in starting the match.[80]

THE TOUR TO AUSTRALIA AND NEW ZEALAND: A WARNING

During November 1887, reports began to surface of a proposed (Rugby) football tour to Australia and New Zealand. The men behind it were the entrepreneurial cricketing trio of Alfred Shaw, Arthur Shrewsbury and James Lillywhite. Throughout December and January, speculation was rife as to who would be in the touring party, resulting in the following notice appearing in the press: 'The Rugby Football Union Committee wish it to be known that in response to a request from the promoters to give their support and approval to the proposed tour to Australia, they decline to do so. They do not consider it within their province to forbid their players joining the undertaking, but they feel it their duty to let gentlemen who may be thinking of going know that they must be careful in any arrangements made that they do not transgress their laws for the prevention of professionalism. The Committee will look with a jealous eye upon any infringements of such laws, and they desire specially to call attention to the fact that players must not be compensated for loss of time.'[81]

YORKSHIRE RUGBY FOOTBALL UNION

At a meeting held at the Queen's Hotel, Leeds, on 13th December, it was agreed to form the Yorkshire Rugby Football Union, effectively replacing the Yorkshire County Football Club which was perceived as biased towards its senior clubs.

WESTMORLAND WOES

Westmorland hosted North Lancashire at the Mint's Feet ground in Kendal on Thursday 19th January. Although Westmorland won comfortably it had been pre-determined that the match would be considered a 'draw' due to 'the Barrow contingent failing to put in an appearance'. Their absence left North Lancashire four short so they borrowed three from Westmorland, both teams fielding fourteen players.[82]

DURHAM PROTEST AT COUNTY RESULT

Durham met Lancashire at Friarage Field, Hartlepool, on 28th January, in a match played in driving wind and snowstorms. Lancashire claimed a half-time lead of one goal to nil after a Harry Eagles try was converted by Arthur Durandu shortly before the interval. Durham, however, protested that the ball did not pass through the goal correctly. With an unconverted Durham try being the only second half score, Lancashire left the field as winners by one 'disputed' goal to one try. It was agreed to refer the matter to the next Rugby Football Union meeting at The Westminster Palace Hotel, London, on 3rd February. The evidence was duly considered and the goal overruled, the result being declared a draw with one try each.

THE INTERNATIONAL BOARD: ENGLAND IN DISPUTE

England did not fulfil their annual fixtures against Scotland, Ireland and Wales during 1887-88 due to their opposition to the International Rugby Football Board, founded by the latter three countries at a meeting held on 4th February at the King's Head Hotel, Newport. Although England was invited to join the Board, they declined and the dispute continued on through 1888-89. Following conciliatory discussions, England again played their three rivals during February and March 1890, the issues finally being settled by arbitration in April 1890.

NORTH VERSUS SOUTH RIVALRY EXTENDED

Due to England's matches against the three other home nations being cancelled after the first North versus South 'trial' match had taken place in Manchester on 17th December, it was decided to arrange a second meeting that was subsequently played at Blackheath on 4th February.

THE YORKSHIRE CUP: OSSETT DISQUALIFIED

Following the first round of the Yorkshire Cup on 25th February, there was the usual batch of disputes for the County Committee to deal with at the Queen's Hotel in Leeds two days later. Leeds St John's appealed against the 'unfair' tactics pursued by Ossett, who had won their tie at Cardigan Fields. Evidence was presented concerning the foul tackling 'indulged in' by Ossett, the referee and both umpires speaking about the 'rough' play. The committee decided to disqualify Ossett, awarding the match to Leeds St John's.[83]

THE YORKSHIRE CUP: JACK CLOWES PROFESSIONALISED

The second round of the Yorkshire Cup on 3rd March produced accusations of professionalism against Angus Stuart (Dewsbury), Tom Haslam (Batley) and Jack Clowes (Halifax), each of them having, reportedly, received £15 expenses towards the upcoming tour to Australia and New Zealand. Their respective clubs elected not to select Haslam and Stuart for the cup ties but Halifax played Clowes, who scored a late winning try in their win at Dewsbury. The Yorkshire Committee, in its meeting at the Queen's Hotel, Leeds, on 5th March, adopted the following resolution: 'That J. P. Clowes of the Halifax club, having received £15 from Mr. Turner, of Nottingham, for an outfit in connection with a football tour in Australia, has thereby received money consideration for playing football, and, in the opinion of the committee, is a professional football player, according to the Rugby Union Rules as to professionalism adopted October, 1886.' Halifax – deemed to be unaware of the payment – was ordered to meet Dewsbury again on Wednesday 7th March at Park Avenue, Bradford, when they won again.[84]

THE TOUR TO AUSTRALIA AND NEW ZEALAND: PROFESSIONALISM

On Thursday 8th March, the tour party departed from Tilbury on the steamship *Kaikoura* heading, via Plymouth, for Wellington, New Zealand. Meanwhile, on the previous evening a special meeting was convened by the Yorkshire Committee at the Queen's Hotel, Leeds, attended by a Commission of the English Union. This was arranged in consequence of the conviction of Halifax's Jack Clowes as a professional. The following resolution was agreed: 'The Rugby Football Union have decided on the evidence before them that J. P. Clowes is a professional within the meaning of their laws. On the same evidence they have formed a very strong opinion that others composing the team have also infringed these laws, and they require from them such explanations as they may think fit on their return to England.'[85] Clowes did not play on tour to avoid 'professionalising' his colleagues.

LEIGH WITHDRAW FROM THE WEST LANCASHIRE UNION

Leigh was so incensed after losing their first round West Lancashire cup-tie with St Helens Recreation on 3th March that they resigned. The *Leigh Chronicle* reported that the Leigh secretary 'sent a strongly worded letter to the West Lancashire and Border Towns Rugby Football Union, stating that owing to the decisions of the referee the Leigh club withdraws from the Union. It is almost impossible, the letter states, for the Leigh players to get over the line at least seven times and be wrong every time'. A week earlier, the *Manchester Times* had painted an optimistic picture as the competition was about to start: 'The names of one or two clubs are certainly conspicuous by their absence this season, but on the whole there seems to be little falling off in the amount of enthusiasm which has hitherto characterised the contests in the West Lancashire Cup.'[86]

THE YORKSHIRE CUP: HUDDERSFIELD'S ATTENDANCE RECORD?

There was great interest in Huddersfield's fifth round Yorkshire Cup tie against Brighouse Rangers at Fartown on 24th March. With Huddersfield recapturing their form of a few seasons earlier the tie drew a reported 10,000, claimed to be 'the largest that has ever been seen on that ground, and even with the low prices of 6 [old] pence, and 3 [old] pence, realised £177, 10 shillings'.[87] Despite a subsequent protest by Brighouse, Huddersfield progressed with a comfortable win.

A DAY TRIP TO TUDHOE

When Hartlepool Rovers and its supporters travelled to Tudhoe on 24th March for the third round of the Durham Cup, postponed seven days earlier due to snow, it was a day to remember. The *Northern Daily Mail* provided an illuminating description: 'On Saturday afternoon, a very heavily laden trip, which included a number of ladies, left the Hartlepools for Spennymoor. A saloon carriage was on for the exclusive use of the Rovers' team, and as the train steamed on for the village the general talk was about the encounter. The train arrived at Spennymoor at quarter past three, and all flocked for the Tudhoe Brewery Field. No one seemed to know the way, but going up the main street we soon noticed a red flag flying, showing us that we were within reasonable distance of the field. Arriving there, it was seen that the Tudhoe club were not used to large "gates", for the arrangements were nothing short of disgraceful, a box was fixed up against the railings, where money was taken and tickets given in return admitting the bearer into the field. Here soon gathered a crowd of immense magnitude, being jolted and jostled about in all directions endeavouring to get within arm's length of the box and thus get the much coveted ticket. Seeing that this arrangement was not sufficient after about half-an-hour's trial it was announced that people could pay at the gate, and then a tremendous rush followed. Ultimately all anxious to witness the match gained admission, and naturally made for the grandstand as the ground was covered in water [from the thaw]. But the stand being very small, only accommodating three or four hundred, it was soon crowded, and those unable to enter the much coveted enclosure had to content themselves by finding pieces of wood on which to stand. An omnibus which had been running people up to the field from the station entered the field, with a few spectators on the top. Others soon found their way on to this place of vantage and most were very much taken aback when they were met by the conductor who asked for a shilling a head. There was no place for the players to put their coats and hats, and consequently they lay them at the side of the field. This reminded one of the olden days of football, when coats were laid at the side of the field to mark the touchline.'[88]

CUMBERLAND IN THE MONEY

The Cumberland County Union was enjoying its most financially successful season to date, the *Lancashire Evening Post* reporting: '£63 was taken at the final match for the Cumberland County Cup [Millom v Broughton] at Egremont last Saturday [7th April], by far the largest taken at any football match in the county. At the semi-final between Millom and Carlisle at Maryport the sum was £43, [in the other semi-final] at Egremont between Maryport and Broughton £26, and at Carlisle when Broughton and Maryport replayed the sum was £24. Although but small compared with football in Lancashire, in Cumberland they are regarded as very large gates insomuch as in former years the money taken has been exceedingly scanty, indeed, it is not too much to say that the County Committee has never before been free of debt.'[89]

THE FIRST SOUTH-EAST LANCASHIRE CUP FINAL

The inaugural South East Lancashire Cup final saw Blackley beat Cheetham Hill 18-15 at New Barnes, Salford, on 5th May. The *Athletic News*, who supplied the trophy, noted: 'The Blackley people were very sanguine about winning, and drove over from their village retreat to the scene of action in Salford in four four-in-hand conveyances [horse-drawn omnibus]. They also had some slips printed as "Won the Cup," and these they carefully affixed to the windows of the omnibuses at the conclusion of the match.'[90]

THE TOUR TO AUSTRALIA AND NEW ZEALAND:
A GRUELLING SCHEDULE

The tour of Australia and New Zealand began in April 1888 and continued until early October. The gruelling schedule covered 35 matches, plus a further 19 under Australian Rules (winning six and drawing one). Incredibly, Harry Eagles (Salford) appeared in all 54 matches. Tour captain Bob Seddon (Swinton) was drowned in a boating accident in West Maitland, Australia, on 15th August, the captaincy passing to Andrew Stoddart (Blackheath). The Rugby Football Union now acknowledge this to be the first British Lions tour although, at the time, they did not endorse it, considering it to be a privately arranged unofficial tour. It was often labelled as the '[Alfred] Shaw and [Arthur] Shrewsbury Team', after the names of two of its three promoters (the other was James Lillywhite). In Australia and New Zealand the press mostly referred to the tourists as England or 'the English', although they included players born in Scotland (Bob Burnett, Willie Burnett, Alex Laing, John Smith and Angus Stuart), Ireland (Arthur Paul), Wales (Willie Thomas) and the Isle of Man (Alf Penketh), whilst Jack Clowes was born in the United States to English parents. To reflect contemporary reports the tourists are referred to as England in the statistics section.

1887-1888 STATISTICS

CUMBERLAND COUNTY CHALLENGE CUP (16 entries)
Try – 4 points; conversion – 4; drop-goal, field goal – 6; minor – 1. Majority of 3 points required to win.

First Round
Broughton 25, Moresby 0
Ellenborough 0, Carlisle City 5
Flimby 30, Penrith 0
Egremont 1, Maryport 2 (aet)
Millom 14, Aspatria 2
Seaton 27, Greysouthen 1
Whitehaven 60, Cockermouth 3
Workington 27, Dearham 7

First Round Replay
Maryport 16, Egremont 0

Second Round
Flimby 6, Broughton 16
Carlisle City 11, Workington 6
Maryport 10, Seaton 2
Millom 26, Whitehaven 0

Semi-finals
Broughton 5, Maryport 5
(aet, at Egremont Athletic Club Grounds)
Millom 12, Carlisle City 6
(at Maryport Cricket Ground)

Semi-final Replay
Broughton 15, Maryport 5
(at Lismore Place, Carlisle)

FINAL
Saturday 7 April 1888 at Egremont Athletic Club Grounds
MILLOM 21 *Back*: J Moore (c). *Three-quarters*: J Davy, CW Dove, I Moore.
Half-backs: J Denwood, J McGuire. *Forwards*: H Barlow-Massicks (capt), JH Buckett (2t), J Burns (t), A Flynn, J Flynn, T Harris, B Kendall, G Thomas, T Whalen.
BROUGHTON 6 *Back*: T Lister. *Three-quarters*: J Tremble (capt), W Harrison, R Burns.
Half-backs: W Black, J Neen. *Forwards*: G Clark, W Clark, T Kirkpatrick, J Lawson, G Lister, J Lister, J Newman, J Rennie, T Rennie.
Attendance: 3,000   *Referee*: GR Hill (RFU Honorary Secretary)
Note: Millom's score includes 5 minor points, Broughton's score was from six minor points.

DURHAM COUNTY CHALLENGE CUP (18 entries)
Most goals wins. If equal, most tries. If still equal, majority of 3 minor points.

First Round
Consett w/o Bishopwearmouth (withdrew)
Durham City 2g, 2t, West Hartlepool 0
Hartlepool Rangers 1t, Boldon 2g
Hartlepool Rovers 3g, 2t, Westoe 0
Henderson's Wanderers (Durham) w/o Durham University (withdrew)
Houghton-le-Spring 0, North Durham 0 (mp: 1-0, aet)
Ryton 0, Tudhoe 1g
Stockton 0, Humbledon 2t
Sunderland 0, Gateshead Institute 0 (mp: 4-0)

First Round Replay
Houghton-le-Spring 0, North Durham 0 (mp: 4-0)

Second Round
Durham City 3g, 2t, Henderson's Wanderers 0
Hartlepool Rovers 3g, 5t, Consett 0
Sunderland 1g, 2t, Boldon 0
Tudhoe 2t, Humbledon 0
Bye: Houghton-le-Spring

Third Round
Sunderland 1g, 2t, Houghton-le-Spring 0 (replay ordered after protest)
Tudhoe 0, Hartlepool Rovers 0 (mp: 1-3, no extra time)
Bye: Durham City

Third Round Replays
Sunderland 2g, 1t, Houghton-le-Spring 1g, 1t
Tudhoe 0, Hartlepool Rovers 2t

Semi-final
Sunderland 0, Durham City 3g
Bye: Hartlepool Rovers

FINAL
Saturday 14 April 1888 at Ashbrooke Ground, Sunderland
DURHAM CITY 1 goal *Back*: GA Kerrich-Walker (c). *Three-quarters*: HB Tristram, FA Bulman, JH Smeddle (t). *Half-backs*: N Cochrane, J Turnbull (capt). *Forwards*: JW Fogg-Elliot, FJ Hall, JB Johnson, F Lumsden, P McPherson, T Raine, R Shields, RJ Simey, JT Wetherell
HARTLEPOOL ROVERS 0 *Back*: AE Morrison. *Three-quarters*: A Hill (capt), AE Emmerson, MH Horsley. *Half-backs*: AC Scott, G Smith. *Forwards*: T Danby, CM Huntley, W Mould, WL Oakes, R Ogden, FE Pease, A Robinson, W Thwaites, W Yiend.
Attendance: 5,000   *Referee*: W Cail (Northumberland RU President)

NORTHUMBERLAND COUNTY FOOTBALL CHALLENGE CUP (8 entries)
Most goals wins. If equal, most tries.

First Round
North Elwick 1t, Percy Park 4t
Northern 2g, 2t, Benwell 0
Northumberland FC 1g, 2t, Newcastle Rangers 0
Tynedale 0, Tynemouth 1t

Semi-finals
Northern 1g, 5t, Northumberland FC 0
Percy Park 1g, 1t, Tynemouth 1g

FINAL
Tuesday 3 April 1888 at Jesmond Ground, Newcastle
NORTHERN 1 goal, 3 tries *Back*: E Emley. *Three-quarters*: CS Gill (2t), HB Lockhart (capt), AC Challoner. *Half-backs*: MT Scott, WM Scott (dg). *Forwards*: H Angus, J Livingstone, F Manford, JA Robertson, P Stanton (t), G Walters, A Watson, W Watson, CE Winship.
PERCY PARK 0 *Back*: P Horsley. *Three-quarters*: F Finney, RE Herbertson, W Bentham. *Half-backs*: H Douglas, T Stewart. *Forwards*: G Brewis, J Burn, JW Coward (capt), W Dodds, A Gee, T Gee, G Leighton, A Phillips, RH Spence.
Attendance: 'large'   *Referee*: CH Sample (Northumberland RU)

WEST LANCASHIRE AND BORDER TOWNS CHALLENGE CUP (14 entries)
Try – 4 points; conversion – 4; drop-goal, field goal – 6; minor – 1. Majority of 3 points required to win.

First Round
Boothstown 0, Tyldesley 8
Leigh 2, St Helens Recreation 5
Pemberton 15, Tuebrook 1
St Helens 12, Blackrod 2
Widnes 6, Aspull 0
Wigan 47, Southport Olympic 0
Byes: Litherland, Walkden

Second Round
Litherland 6, Walkden 1
Pemberton 1, Widnes 10
St Helens Recreation 2, Wigan 6
Tyldesley 23, St Helens 0

Semi-finals
Tyldesley 13, Wigan 5
(at Wilderspool, Warrington)
Widnes 28, Litherland 1
(at Dentons Green Lane, St Helens)

FINAL
Saturday 24 March 1888 at Wilderspool, Warrington
TYLDESLEY 9 *Back*: H Pearson. *Three-quarters*: F Shaw (capt, c), WH Ramsden, J Fearnley. *Half-backs*: J Berry, C Hardman. *Forwards*: P Eckersley, J Hampson, W Hesley, T Hilton, J Hodgkinson (t), W Ramsden, A Smith, W Sutcliffe, G Woodward.
WIDNES 1 *Back*: S Bingham. *Three-quarters*: F Plumpton, J Parkinson, R Barker. *Half-backs*: JE Farrell, T Wilkinson. *Forwards*: W Barber, J Bingham, J Gandy, J Hardman, T Hughes, W Kiddie, T Pennington, JH Smith (capt), G Woods.
Attendance: 14,000   *Referee*: E Beswick (Swinton)
Note: Tyldesley's score includes one minor point, Widnes' score was from one minor point.

YORKSHIRE COUNTY FOOTBALL CHALLENGE CUP (97 entries)
Most goals wins (3 tries count as one 'goal'). If equal, most tries (excluding any already counted as equalling a 'goal'). If still equal, majority of 3 minor points.

First Round
Barnsley 0, Buttershaw 1t
Batley 1g, 3t, Ovenden 0
Bingley 2t, Gomersal Albion 0
Bowling 0, Keighley 1g, 1t
Castleford 2t, Kirkburton 0
Cleckheaton 2g, 7t, Dodworth 0
Doncaster Town 0, Heckmondwike 2g, 6t
Dudley Hill w/o Nortonthorpe (withdrew)
Elland 0, Churwell 0 (mp: 2-6)
Greengates 1g, Keighley Shamrocks 0
Greetland 3g, 5t, Stanningley and Farsley 0
Guiseley 0, Thornes 1t
Halifax Free Wanderers 1t, Wakefield St Austin's 0 (aet)
Horbury 3g, 2t, Lockwood 0
Horsforth 0, Calverley 0 (mp: 6-4, aet)
Huddersfield 4t, Bowling Old Lane 0
Hunslet 2t, Brighouse Rangers 1g
Laisterdyke 0, Birstall 1g
Leeds St John's 1g, 2t, Ossett 2g, 2t (awarded to Leeds St John's after protest)
Manningham 0, Leeds Parish Church 3t
Manningham Rangers 0, Hull Southcoates 1g, 1t
Mytholmroyd 0, Dewsbury 7g, 5t
Otley 2t, Bramley 0
Pudsey 0, Alverthorpe 1t
Rodley 2g, 1t, Adwalton Old 0
Salterhebble 1t, Saltaire 1g, 2t
Shepley 1t, Hebden Bridge 1g
Shipley 4g, Yeadon 1t
Skipton 4g, 5t, Middlesbrough 0
South Milford 1g, Harrogate 1g, 1t
Todmorden 1t, Normanton 0
Wakefield Trinity 4g, 6t, Dewsbury Clarence 0
York 2g, Low Moor St Mark's 1t
Byes: 31 teams drew a bye to next round

First Round Replay
Calverley 0, Horsforth 2g

Second Round
Alverthorpe 0, Ravensthorpe 0 (mp: 1-3, aet)
Batley 11g, 4t, Rodley 0
Birstall 1g, 6t, Eastmoor 0
Bradford Trinity 2g, Saltaire 1g
Buttershaw 4g, 2t, Woodlands United 1t
Cleckheaton 1g, 2t, Whitwood 2t
Crosland Moor 0, Selby 2t

Milestones & Stats 1869-1901

Second Round *continued*
Dewsbury 1t, Halifax 2t (replay ordered after protest)
Farnley Ironworks (Leeds) 0, Brighouse Rangers 4g, 2t
Goole 2g, Holbeck 1g
Greengates 0, Liversedge 4g, 1t
Hebden Bridge 0, North Leeds 1t
Heckmondwike 4g, 2t, Thornes 0
Horbury 3g, 1t, Ripon 0
Huddersfield 2g, 2t, Outwood Church (Wakefield) 0
Hull Southcoates 2t, Newtown (Leeds) 0
Keighley 1t, Pontefract 1g
Kirkstall 2t, Leeds Rifles 0
Knaresborough 0, Halifax Free Wanderers 2t
Leeds Parish Church 4g, Harrogate 0
Mirfield 1t, Castleford 1t (mp: 2-8)
Morley 2g, 1t, Dudley Hill 1g
Otley 0, Bingley 0 (mp: 8-0)
Paddock 0, Leeds St John's 4g, 1t
Skipton 1g, Greetland 0
Stanley 0, Hipperholme and Lightcliffe 2t
Todmorden 1g, 3t, Wibsey 1g
Wakefield Trinity 3g, 5t, Woodhouse 0
Windhill 0, Horsforth 0 (mp: 0-4)
Wortley 2t, Churwell 0
York 0, Shipley 0 (mp: 4-3, aet)
York St George's 0, Hull 1g, 6t

Second Round Replays
Halifax 3t, Dewsbury 1t
(at Bradford)
Ravensthorpe 0, Alverthorpe 0
(mp: 3-1, aet)
Shipley 0, York 0 (mp: 0-7)

Second Round Second Replay
Alverthorpe 0, Ravensthorpe 3g, 3t

Third Round
Batley 1t, Heckmondwike 2g
Bradford Trinity 0, Liversedge 2g, 3t
Brighouse Rangers 1t, Halifax Free Wanderers 0
Buttershaw 3g, 1t, Birstall 0
Goole 1t, York 0
Halifax 1g, 1t, Kirkstall 0
Hipperholme and Lightcliffe 1t, Leeds St John's 2g
Horsforth 1g, Hull 1g, 1t
Huddersfield 4g, 2t, Horbury 0
Leeds Parish Church 4g, North Leeds 0
Morley 3g, 1t, Todmorden 0
Pontefract 1t, Castleford 1g, 1t
Ravensthorpe 0, Otley 1t
Selby 1g, 2t, Cleckheaton 0
Wakefield Trinity 3g, 2t, Hull Southcoates 0
Wortley 2g, 1t, Skipton 1t

Fourth Round
Goole 0, Wakefield Trinity 2t
Halifax 1g, 2t, Otley 1t
Heckmondwike 1t, Wortley 1t (mp: 6-0)
Huddersfield 1g, 5t, Castleford 1t
Leeds Parish Church 1t, Hull 0
Leeds St John's 4t, Selby 0
Liversedge 1g, 2t, Buttershaw 0
Morley 0, Brighouse Rangers 0 (mp: 2-1, aet)

Fourth Round Replay
Brighouse Rangers 3t, Morley 1t

Fifth Round
Halifax 1t, Heckmondwike 0
Huddersfield 2g, 2t, Brighouse Rangers 0
Leeds St John's 1g, 1t, Liversedge 1t
Wakefield Trinity 1g, 2t, Leeds Parish Church 1g

Semi-finals
Halifax 2g, 1t, Huddersfield 0 (at Valley Parade, Bradford)
Wakefield Trinity 0, Leeds St John's 0 (mp: 12-0, at Crown Flatts, Dewsbury)

FINAL
Saturday 7 April 1888 at Cardigan Fields, Leeds
HALIFAX 2t *Back*: W Barratt. *Three-quarters*: JH Greenwood (t), J Dodd (capt), D Welsh. *Half-backs*: E Buckley, G Scholefield (t). *Forwards*: T Allbutt, W Baldwin, A Dennis, F Halliday, J Stansfield, A Watson, TW Watson, I Webster, HJ Wilkinson.
WAKEFIELD TRINITY 1 try *Back*: JH Fotherby. *Three-quarters*: A Ash (t), H Hayley, H Fallas. *Half-backs*: H Dawson, H Hutchinson (capt). *Forwards*: W Binks, P Booth, T Harrison, JH Jones, J Lathom, FW Lowrie, A Thompson, H Whitney, TH Wordsworth.
Attendance: 15,000   *Referee*: Rev F Marshall (Huddersfield)

COUNTY MATCHES

Saturday 29 October 1887 at Jesmond Ground, Newcastle
NORTHUMBERLAND 1 goal *Back*: MF Elsdon (Tynm). *Three-quarters*: AS Carr (NorFC), T Coulson (PerPk), RE Herbertson (PerPk, t). *Half-backs*: F Miller (Ben), H Welford (NEls). *Forwards*: H Angus (Nor), JW Coward (PerPk), A Gee (PerPk), T Gee (PerPk, c), JH Greenwell (Tynm), CW Harrison (Tynd), F Manford (Nor), GW Mole (NEls), RH Spence (PerPk).
CUMBERLAND 1 try *Back*: J Scott (CarlC). *Three-quarters*: W Selkirk (Egr), W Lewthwaite (Mary), R Little (Mary). *Half-backs*: WT Ridley (Asp), J Stamper (Egr). *Forwards*: J Geddes (Mary), J Grave (Cock), J Halliday (Mary), T Hodgson (Work), W Holmes (Cock), J Lewthwaite (Mary), B Nixon (Ellenborough, t), J Smith (Asp), J Thomson (capt, Pen).
Attendance: 1,000   *Referee*: CR Green (Durham)

Milestones & Stats 1869-1901   155

Wednesday 2 November 1887 at Irwell Lane, Runcorn
CHESHIRE 1 goal, 5 tries *Back*: C Hebden (BirkPk). *Three-quarters*: WH Cawley (Run, t), HC Speakman (Run), JF Taylor (Stock, t). *Half-backs*: H Hughes (Run, t), FW Spence (capt, BirkPk). *Forwards*: WH Broady (Run, t), W Faulkner (Run), J Fitchett (Stock), JG Gifford (NewB), W Hardy (Sale), W Haslam (Duk, c), W Hughes (Run, t), PH Lockwood (BirkPk), A Williams (NewB, t)..
NORTHAMPTONSHIRE 0 *Back*: RT Hughes (Marlborough Nomads). *Three-quarters*: W Disney (Richmond), C Dixon (Kettering), CA Kingston (Northampton). *Half-backs*: C Atkinson (Northampton), W Burgess (Rushden). *Forwards*: RS Abrams (Kettering), W Brudenhall (Rushden), W Godfrey (Northampton), J Greaves (Rushden), C Lewis (Kettering), JH Lowry (Northampton), T Phipps (Northampton), C Robinson (Kettering), HH Whitehead (Northampton).
Attendance: 4,000   *Referee*: AT Kemble (Lancashire)

Saturday 12 November 1887 at Aigburth, Liverpool
LANCASHIRE 3 goals, 2 tries *Back*: W Bull (ManFW). *Three-quarters*: J Valentine (Swi, t), J Robertson (BroR), FC Withers (Liv). *Half-backs*: AG Melly (Liv, 3c), J Mills (Swi, 2t). *Forwards*: C Anderton (ManFW), F Chambers (LivOB), H Eagles (Sal, 2t), AE Evans (Bro), AT Kemble (capt, Liv), JW Roberts (Sal), RL Seddon (Swi), TJ Smith (Sal), JH Tune (BroR).
CHESHIRE 1 try *Back*: TH Woods (Run). *Three-quarters*: JA Black (capt, BirkPk), HC Speakman (Run), WH Cawley (Run, t). *Half-backs*: H Hughes (Run), J Lingard (Duk). *Forwards*: J Cowan (BirkPk), W Faulkner (Run), JG Gifford (NewB), W Hardy (Sale), W Haslam (Duk), PH Lockwood (BirkPk), A Williams (NewB), AG Wood (BirkPk), W Wright (Run).
Attendance: 2,000   *Referee*: GR Hill (RFU Honorary Secretary)

Saturday 12 November 1887 at Jesmond Ground, Newcastle
NORTHUMBERLAND 0 *Back*: RH Robb (Tynd). *Three-quarters*: CS Gill (Nor), T Coulson (PerPk), AS Carr (NorFC). *Half-backs*: H Douglas (PerPk), WM Scott (NorFC). *Forwards*: H Angus (Nor), JW Coward (PerPk), T Elliott (Tynd), T Gee (PerPk), JH Greenwell (Tynm), CW Harrison (Tynd), F Manford (Nor), GW Mole (NEls), J Skelton (Newcastle Rangers).
YORKSHIRE 5 tries *Back*: JT Haslam (Bat). *Three-quarters*: AL Brooke (Hud, t), P Robertshaw (Brad, t), FT Ritchie (Brad, 2t). *Half-backs*: F Bonsor (capt, Brad, t), WJ Stadden (Dew). *Forwards*: H Bedford (Bat), C Brumfitt (Ship), J Garforth (Dew), JL Hickson (Brad), FW Lowrie (Wak), C Mathers (LeeStJ), C Sumner (LeeStJ), TW Watson (Hal), E Wilkinson (Brad).
Attendance: 2,000   *Referee*: Rev CH Newman (Durham)

Saturday 19 November 1887 at Whalley Range, Manchester
LANCASHIRE 2 goals, 6 tries *Back*: W Bull (ManFW). *Three-quarters*: J Valentine (Swi, 3t), EH Flower (Bro, t, c), L Hickson (LivOB, t). *Half-backs*: AG Melly (Liv, c), J Mills (Swi, 2t). *Forwards*: C Anderton (ManFW), TK Bell (Bar), HC Chapman (LivOB), H Eagles (Sal, t), AE Evans (Bro), J Groves (RochH), AT Kemble (capt, Liv), AH Stockley (Liv), JH Tune (BroR).
NORTHUMBERLAND 0 *Back*: MF Elsdon (Tynm). *Three-quarters*: RE Herbertson (PerPk), T Coulson (PerPk), AS Carr (NorFC). *Half-backs*: T Hoyle (Nor), WM Scott

(NorFC). *Forwards*: H Angus (Nor), JW Coward (PerPk), T Elliott (Tynd), A Gee (PerPk), T Gee (PerPk), CW Harrison (Tynd), F Manford (Nor), GW Mole (NEls), J Skelton (Newcastle Rangers).
Attendance: 5,000   *Referee*: WH Wallace (Cheshire)

Saturday 19 November 1887 at Cardigan Fields, Leeds
YORKSHIRE 4 goals, 1 try *Back*: JT Haslam (Bat). *Three-quarters*: P Robertshaw (Brad, t), FT Ritchie (Brad, 2t), AL Brooke (Hud, 4c). *Half-backs*: G Barrett (Norm), WJ Stadden (Dew). *Forwards*: H Bedford (Bat), J Garforth (Dew), G Harrison (capt, Hull, t), JL Hickson (Brad), FW Lowrie (Wak), C Mathers (LeeStJ, t), C Sumner (LeeStJ), TW Watson (Hal), E Wilkinson (Brad).
DURHAM 1 try *Back*: HO Hoy (HartR). *Three-quarters*: WH Wilson (Wes), H Burkett (Hum), JC Wilford (Sund). *Half-backs*: TM Jamieson (Con), AR Wilson (DurU). *Forwards*: B Cox (Sund), CH Elliot (Sund), J Hall (Gateshead Institute), A Hill (HartR), W Hodgson (Tud), FE Pease (HartR), JW Sowerby (NDur, t), H Wiley (Wes), W Yiend (HartR).
Attendance: 6,000   *Referee*: GR Hill (RFU Honorary Secretary)

Monday 21 November 1887 at Athletic Ground, Richmond
MIDDLESEX 1 goal, 1 try *Back*: W Williams (Harl). *Three-quarters*: WE Maclagan (LonS), SH Baker (Ken, t), JA Gould (Rich, t, c). *Half-backs*: JH Roberts (Rich), Alan Rotherham (Rich). *Forwards*: FC Cousins (Rich), EG Finch (MidW), WT Grenfell (LonHosp), J Hammond (Black), GL Jeffery (Black), ES McEwan (OChelt), JG Patterson (LonS), HP Surtees (Harl), N Vandergutch (LonHosp).
DURHAM 1 try *Back*: HO Hoy (HartR). *Three-quarters*: EP Thompson (Wes), H Burkett (Hum), GH Eyre (Wes). *Half-backs*: TM Jamieson (Con), WG Lohden (HartR, t). *Forwards*: R Barwick (Sund), B Cox (Sund), CH Elliot (Sund), J Hall (Gateshead Institute), W Hodgson (Tud), FE Pease (HartR), JW Sowerby (NDur), H Wiley (Wes), W Yiend (HartR).
Attendance: 500   *Referee*: GR Hill (RFU Honorary Secretary)

Saturday 26 November 1887 at Park Avenue, Bradford
YORKSHIRE 2 tries *Back*: JT Haslam (Bat). *Three-quarters*: AL Brooke (Hud), P Robertshaw (Brad), FT Ritchie (Brad). *Half-backs*: F Bonsor (Brad), WJ Stadden (Dew, t). *Forwards*: H Bedford (Bat, t), J Garforth (Dew), G Harrison (capt, Hull), JL Hickson (Brad), FW Lowrie (Wak), C Mathers (LeeStJ), C Sumner (LeeStJ), TW Watson (Hal), E Wilkinson (Brad).
LANCASHIRE 0 *Back*: W Bull (ManFW). *Three-quarters*: J Valentine (Swi), J Robertson (BroR), L Hickson (LivOB). *Half-backs*: AG Melly (Liv), J Mills (Swi). *Forwards*: HC Chapman (LivOB), H Eagles (Sal), AE Evans (Bro), J Groves (RochH), AT Kemble (capt, Liv), JE Orr (Man), RL Seddon (Swi), AH Stockley (Liv), JH Tune (BroR).
Attendance: 12,000/15,000   *Referee*: GR Hill (RFU Honorary Secretary)

Saturday 3 December 1887 at Upper Park, Birkenhead
CHESHIRE 2 goals, 1 try *Back*: AC Blain (BirkPk). *Three-quarters*: JA Black (capt, BirkPk), HC Speakman (Run, t), WH Cawley (Run). *Half-backs*: H Hughes (Run, dg), QJ Leitch (NewB, dg). *Forwards*: WH Broady (Run), J Cowan (BirkPk), W Faulkner (Run), JG Gifford (NewB), W Haslam (Duk), W Hughes (Run), PH Lockwood (BirkPk), A Williams (NewB), AG Wood (BirkPk).

DURHAM 1 try *Back*: HO Hoy (HartR). *Three-quarters*: H Brooks (DurC, t), AE Emmerson (HartR), EP Thompson (Wes). *Half-backs*: WG Lohden (HartR), J Turnbull (DurC). *Forwards*: B Cox (Sund), CH Elliot (capt, Sund), A Hill (HartR), W Hodgson (Tud), FE Pease (HartR), J Snowdon (HartR), JW Sowerby (NDur), H Wiley (Wes), W Yiend (HartR).
Attendance: 3,000   *Referee*: AN Hornby (Lancashire)

Monday 5 December 1887 at Belle Vue, Wakefield
YORKSHIRE 2 goals, 1 try *Back*: JH Fotherby (Wak). *Three-quarters*: FT Ritchie (Brad), P Robertshaw (Brad, t), JT Haslam (Bat, t, c, dg). *Half-backs*: F Bonsor (Brad), WJ Stadden (Dew). *Forwards*: H Bedford (Bat), P Booth (Wak), J Garforth (Dew), JE Gomersall (Wak), G Harrison (capt, Hull), FW Lowrie (Wak), J Robertshaw (Brad), C Sumner (LeeStJ), H Wilkinson (Hal).
ULSTER 1 goal *Back*: LJ Holmes (Lis). *Half-backs*: JP Ross (NIFC, c), WG Moffatt (BelA), TB Pedlow (QCB). *Quarter-backs*: JH McLaughlin (Bray), W Monypenny (QCB). *Forwards*: JB Bennett (QCB), R Dick (Lis), A Gibb (Rugby, t), HJ Johnston (NIFC), RH Mayne (BelA), James Moffatt (BelA), HJ Neill (capt, NIFC), E Stevenson (Lis), E Williams (QCB).
Attendance: 3,000   *Referee*: FT Parry (West Lancashire)

Monday 2 January 1888 at New Springs, Aspull
WEST LANCASHIRE 1 goal, 2 tries *Back*: J Pilkington (Asp). *Three-quarters*: J Slevin (Wig), F Shaw (Tyl, c), W Lund (StHR). *Half-backs*: D Hulme (Asp), J Pilkington (StHR). *Forwards*: J Atkinson (Wig, t), J Hampson (Tyl, t), J Holmes (Litherland), T Hughes (Wid), R Lawson (Lei, t), R Littlewood (War), J Lowe (Wigan Rovers), J Pyke (StHR), E Wardle (Wig).
WESTMORLAND 0 *Back*: J Bell (KenT). *Three-quarters*: J Armstrong (KenH), TG Baines (KenH), LE Wilson (KenT). *Half-backs*: J Berry (KenH), W Cross (KenH). *Forwards*: J Banks (Amb), RC Beard (KenH), J Carradus (KenT), DF Ellwood (KenH), I Hadwin (KenT), W Hodgson (Amb), RH Moore (Amb), R Nicholson (KenT), JW Wilkinson (KenH).
Attendance: 2,000/3,000   *Referee*: AN Hornby (Lancashire)

Saturday 14 January 1888 at The Recreation Ground, Weston-super-Mare
SOMERSETSHIRE 3 tries *Back*: H Merry (Well). *Three-quarters*: BWL Ashford (Well, t), R A Glass (capt, Wivel), SC Smith (Wes, 2t). *Half-backs*: R Escott (Wivel), FH Fox (Well). *Forwards*: PA Colmer (Yeo), HG Fuller (Bath), EL Hancock (Wivel), PF Hancock (Wivel/Black), AA Glass (Wivel), WH Manfield (Yeo), RMP Parsons (Crew), H Paterson (Weston), SMJ Woods (Bridg).
YORKSHIRE 0 *Back*: JT Haslam (Bat). *Three-quarters*: AL Brooke (Hud), P Robertshaw (Brad), RE Lockwood (Dew). *Half-backs*: C Lapping (LeeStJ), WJ Stadden (Dew). *Forwards*: H Bedford (Bat), JP Clowes (Hal), G Harrison (capt, Hull), JL Hickson (Brad), FW Lowrie (Wak), C Mathers (Bram), A Parker (Bat), H Wilkinson (Hal), EH Wynne (Brad).
Attendance: 4,000   *Referee*: H Vassall (RFU Honorary Treasurer)

Thursday 19 January 1888 at Mint's Feet, Kendal
WESTMORLAND 1 goal, 4 tries *Back*: J Allen (KenH). *Three-quarters*: WJ Walker (capt, KenH, t), J Armstrong (KenH, c), LE Wilson (KenT). *Half-backs*: J Berry (KenH, t), W Cross (KenH, t). *Forwards*: J Banks (Amb), RC Beard (KenH), J Carradus (KenT), DF Ellwood (KenH, t), W Hill (KenH, t), W Hodgson (Amb), R Nicholson (KenT), E Wilson (KenH).

NORTH LANCASHIRE 1 goal *Back*: E Elkin (More). *Three-quarters*: J Lambert (Lanc), Graham (Carn, dg), Markinson (Carn). *Half-backs*: WE Banks (KenT), C Miller (More). *Forwards*: R Chorley (KenT), W Cross (More), J Downie (Lanc), N Leigh (Lanc), OS Smith (Bar), AG Thornton (More), S Whineray (Carn), R Wilson (KenH).
Attendance: 2,000   *Referee*: FT Parry (West Lancashire)
Note: Agreed to play as a 'draw' due to the non-appearance of four North Lancashire players. After reorganising the teams, both had 14 players, North Lancashire including three Kendal-based players loaned by Westmorland.

Saturday 21 January 1888 at Wellington
SOMERSETSHIRE 1 try *Back*: H Merry (Well). *Three-quarters*: SC Smith (Wes), RA Glass (capt, Wivel), BWL Ashford (Well). *Half-backs*: FH Fox (Well), A Goodman (Bath, t). *Forwards*: PA Colmer (Yeo), HG Fuller (Bath), EL Hancock (Wivel), PF Hancock (Wivel/Black), AA Glass (Wivel), WH Manfield (Yeo), RMP Parsons (Crew), H Paterson (Wes), SMJ Woods (Bridg).
LANCASHIRE 1 goal *Back*: W Bull (ManFW). *Three-quarters*: EH Flower (Bro), J Standring (Man, t), J Valentine (Swi, c). *Half-backs*: W Bumby (Swi), J Mills (Swi). *Forwards*: C Anderton (ManFW), T Banks (Swi), H Eagles (Sal), AE Evans (Bro), AT Kemble (capt, Liv), T Kent (Sal), JE Orr (Man), RL Seddon (Swi), J Strang (Liv).
Attendance: 3,000   *Referee*: GR Hill (RFU Honorary Secretary)

Saturday 28 January 1888 at Friarage Field, Hartlepool
DURHAM 1 try *Back*: HO Hoy (HartR). *Three-quarters*: MH Horsley (HartR), VT Thompson (Sund), H Burkett (Hum). *Half-backs*: TM Jamieson (Con), J Turnbull (DurC). *Forwards*: R Barwick (Sund), B Cox (Sund), CH Elliot (Sund), A Hill (HartR), JB Johnson (DurC), FE Pease (HartR), JW Sowerby (NDur), JT Wetherell (DurC), W Yiend (HartR, t).
LANCASHIRE 1 try *Back*: J Pilkington (Asp). *Three-quarters*: A Durandu (Liv), RR Veale (BroR), J Standring (Man). *Half-backs*: W Bumby (Swi), J Nolan (RochH). *Forwards*: J Armstrong (Old), T Banks (Swi), J Barlow (BroR), H Eagles (Sal, t), AE Evans (Bro), Harry Hasleham (ManR), AT Kemble (capt, Liv), T Kent (Sal), J Strang (Liv).
Attendance: 3,000   *Referee*: Rev F Marshall (Yorkshire)

Saturday 28 January 1888 at Jesmond Ground, Newcastle
NORTHUMBERLAND 0 *Back*: H Haslam (NEls). *Three-quarters*: AS Carr (NorFC), T Coulson (PerPk), B Sutherland (Nor). *Half-backs*: H Douglas (PerPk), T Hoyle (Nor). *Forwards*: H Angus (Nor), A Gee (PerPk), T Gee (PerPk), JH Greenwell (Tynm), CW Harrison (Tynd), AS Haslam (NEls), F Manford (Nor), GW Mole (NEls), H Shotton (NEls).
CHESHIRE 0 *Back*: AC Blain (capt, BirkPk). *Three-quarters*: WH Cawley (Run), HC Speakman (Run), TH Davies (Run). *Half-backs*: H Hughes (Run), QJ Leitch (NewB). *Forwards*: J Clarke (Run), J Cowan (BirkPk), W Faulkner (Run), JG Gifford (NewB), W Hughes (Run), T Lings (Sale), PH Lockwood (BirkPk), GT Wainwright (Run), AG Wood (BirkPk).
Attendance: 'large'   *Referee*: CH Sample (Northumberland)

Monday 6 February 1888 at Queen's Club, London
MIDDLESEX 2 goals, 1 try *Back*: AS Johnstone (Black, c). *Three-quarters*: JA Gould (Rich, t, dg), D Gordon (LonS), GC Lindsay (LonS). *Half-backs*: JH Roberts (Rich), Alan Rotherham (Rich). *Forwards*: WG Clibborn (Rich), FC Cousins (Rich), ET Gurdon (Rich,

Milestones & Stats 1869-1901   159

t), WT Grenfell (Rich), J Hammond (Black), GL Jeffery (Black), TW Lambert (Rich), ES McEwan (OChelt), JG Patterson (LonS).
YORKSHIRE 1 try *Back*: JT Haslam (Bat). *Three-quarters*: H Simms (Bat), P Robertshaw (Brad), F Ash (Wak). *Half-backs*: F Bonsor (Brad), WJ Stadden (Dew, t). *Forwards*: H Bedford (Bat), HO Hamshaw (Wak), G Harrison (capt, Hull), T Harrison (Wak), W Jowett (Brad), FW Lowrie (Wak), C Mathers (Bram), H Simpson (Hull), A Stuart (Dew).
Attendance: 2,000   *Referee*: GR Hill (RFU Honorary Secretary)

Saturday 11 February 1888 at Upper Park, Birkenhead
CHESHIRE 1 goal *Back*: AC Blain (BirkPk, c). *Three-quarters*: JA Black (BirkPk), HC Speakman (Run), WH Cawley (Run). *Half-backs*: LM Holden (BirkPk), H Hughes (Run). *Forwards*: WH Broady (Run), J Cowan (BirkPk), W Faulkner (Run), JG Gifford (NewB), W Hughes (Run), T Lings (Sale), PH Lockwood (BirkPk), GT Wainwright (Run, t), AG Wood (BirkPk).
YORKSHIRE 1 try *Back*: HO Hamshaw (Wak). *Three-quarters*: F Ash (Wak), R Walton (LeeStJ), H Simms (Bat). *Half-backs*: E Buckley (capt, Hal), WJ Stadden (Dew). *Forwards*: T Harrison (Wak), T Hurworth (York), FW Lowrie (Wak, t), C Mathers (Bram), JW Moore (LeeStJ), H Simpson (Hull), A Stuart (Dew), J Watmough (LeeStJ), TH Wordsworth (Wak).
Attendance: 5,000   *Referee*: AN Hornby (Lancashire)

Saturday 11 February 1888 at Ashbrooke Ground, Sunderland
DURHAM 1 try *Back*: MH Horsley (HartR). *Three-quarters*: VT Thompson (Sund), H Brooks (DurC), AE Emmerson (HartR). *Half-backs*: TM Jamieson (Con), J Turnbull (DurC). *Forwards*: R Barwick (Sund), CH Elliot (Sund), JB Johnson (DurC), W Mathieson (NDur), FE Pease (HartR), JW Sowerby (NDur), JT Wetherell (DurC), H Wylie (Wes), W Yiend (HartR, t).
NORTHUMBERLAND 1 try *Back*: H Haslam (NEls). *Three-quarters*: CS Gill (Nor), HB Lockhart (Nor), AS Carr (NorFC, t). *Half-backs*: H Douglas (PerPk), MT Scott (Nor/CamU). *Forwards*: H Angus (Nor), T Carter (Ben), JW Coward (PerPk), A Gee (PerPk), T Gee (PerPk), R Harrison (Tynm), AS Haslam (NEls), F Manford (Nor), GW Mole (NEls).
Attendance: 2,000   *Referee*: CH Sample (Northumberland)

Monday 20 February 1888 at Fartown, Huddersfield
YORKSHIRE 3 tries *Back*: HO Hamshaw (Wak). *Three-quarters*: AL Brooke (Hud), J Dodd (Hal, t), H Simms (Bat). *Half-backs*: H Archer (Hud, 2t), WJ Stadden (Dew). *Forwards*: T Allbutt (Hal), E Birch (York), G Harrison (capt, Hull), W Jowett (Brad), FW Lowrie (Wak), C Mathers (Bram), JW Moore (LeeStJ), A Stuart (Dew), J Watmough (LeeStJ).
SURREY 0 *Back*: SS Wallis (GuyHosp). *Three-quarters*: KJ Key (Rich/OxfU), JJB Hannen (Harl), AB Whitehead (OLey). *Half-backs*: J Bryant (GuyHosp), J Sutherland (RIEC). *Forwards*: A Allport (GuyHosp), S Bowditch (OLey), WP Carpmael (Black/CamU), JW Cave (CamU), LF Elliott (Ken), JH Gould (OLey), HS Johnstone (Harl), CC Lambert (StTHosp), TM Lord (Harl).
Attendance: 3,000   *Referee*: JD Vans Agnew (Middlesex)

Monday 3 March 1888 at Raeburn Place, Edinburgh
EDINBURGH 4 goals, 3 tries *Back*: HF Chambers (EdinU). *Half-backs*: J Marsh (EdinIFP), HJ Stevenson (EdinA), GR Wilson (RHSFP). *Quarter-backs*: C Johnston (EdinU), A Ramsay (EdinW, gm). *Forwards*: CW Berry (EdinW, 3c), AT Clay (EdinA, t), A Duke (RHSFP), MC

McEwan (EdinA), C Reid (EdinA, t), A Robertson (EdinU, 3t), LG Stevenson (EdinU), T Walters (EdinA), TR White (EdinA, t).
LANCASHIRE 0 *Back*: A Royle (BroR). *Three-quarters*: J Valentine (Swi), J Robertson (BroR), J Standring (Man). *Half-backs*: W Bumby (Swi), J Nolan (RochH). *Forwards*: C Anderton (ManFW), T Banks (Swi), GNM Carmerson (Man), AE Evans (Bro), J Groves (RochH), Harry Hasleham (ManR), AT Kemble (Liv), J Kenyon (Swi), J Strang (Liv).
Attendance: 5,000   *Referee*: n/a

Saturday 3 March 1888 at Mint's Feet, Kendal
WESTMORLAND 0 *Back*: G Webster (KirkL). *Three-quarters*: JJ Armer (KenT), WJ Walker (capt, KenH), J Armstrong (KenH). *Half-backs*: J Berry (Tyl), W Cross (KenH). *Forwards*: J Banks (Amb), RC Beard (KenH), L Beetham (Amb), DF Ellwood (KenH), W Hill (KenH), RH Moore (Amb), WJ Parsons (KenH), JW Wilkinson (KenH), E Wilson (KenH).
CUMBERLAND 0 *Back*: J Scott (CarlC). *Three-quarters*: R Little (Mary), CW Dove (Mil), R Bollinger (CarlC). *Half-backs*: J Stamper (Egr), J Murchie (Work). *Forwards*: RN Burgess (CarlC), J Flynn (Mil), J Halliday (Mary), T Hodgson (Work), J Lewthwaite (Mary), J Pender (CarlC), E Shimmins (Egr), J Thomson (capt, Pen), J Wright (Whi).
Attendance: 2,000   Referee: R Westray (Cumberland)

Saturday 17 March 1888 at Whalley Range, Manchester
LANCASHIRE 2 tries *Back*: A Royle (BroR). *Three-quarters*: J Standring (Man), J Robertson (BroR, t), J Valentine (Swi). *Half-backs*: JH Payne (Bro), C Rome (Bro). *Forwards*: C Anderton (ManFW), JA Brodie (LivOB, t), T Coulthwaite (Swi), AE Evans (Bro), AT Kemble (capt, Liv), FS Moss (Bro), JE Orr (Man), WA Scholes (RochH), T Whittaker (Man).
MIDDLESEX 1 goal, 1 try *Back*: TJ Pryce-Jenkins (LonW). *Three-quarters*: JA Gould (Rich), WE Maclagan (capt, LonS), GC Lindsay (LonS, t, dg). *Half-backs*: WT Moffatt (MidW), JH Roberts (Rich). *Forwards*: EW Bishop (Old Millhillians), WG Clibborn (Rich), EG Finch (MidW), HH Fuster (Rich), JH Hodderwick (LonS), ES McEwan (OChelt), JG Patterson (LonS), F Pitts-Tucker (StTHosp), AA Surtees (Harl).
Attendance: 3,000   *Referee*: WH Wallace (Cheshire)

Thursday 26 April 1888 at Mint's Feet, Kendal
WESTMORLAND 0 *Back*: J Allen (KenH). *Three-quarters*: WJ Walker (capt, KenH), JJ Armer (KenT), E Johnson. *Half-backs*: J Berry (Tyl), W Cross (KenH). *Forwards*: J Banks (Amb), L Beetham (Amb), J Carradus (KenT), R Fisher (Amb), I Hadwin (KenT), W Hill (KenH), RH Moore (Amb), R Nicholson (KenT), JW Wilkinson (KenH).
WEST LANCASHIRE 0 *Back*: J Pilkington (Asp). *Three-quarters*: J Slevin (Wigan), F Shaw (capt, Tyl), F Plumpton (Wid). *Half-backs*: D Hulme (Asp), CH Le Peton (Wig). *Forwards*: J Atkinson (Wig), W Dillon (War), H Flynn (Widnes St Mary's), J Hampson (Tyl), W Kiddie (Wid), J Lindsay (Asp), D McLoughlin (StH), J Pyke (StHR), E Wardle (Wig).
Attendance: n/a   *Referee*: J Dodd (Halifax)
Note: Club not identified for E. Johnson (Westmorland).

ENGLAND TRIAL MATCH

Saturday 17 December 1887 at Whalley Range, Manchester
NORTH 1 try *Back*: HB Tristram (OxfU). *Three-quarters*: FT Ritchie (Brad), P Robertshaw (Brad), J Valentine (Swi, t). *Half-backs*: FHR Alderson (CamU), F Bonsor (Brad). *Forwards*: C Anderton (ManFW), H Bedford (Bat), J Cowan (BirkPk), B Cox (Sund), H Eagles (Sal), CH Elliot (Sund), JL Hickson (Brad), C Mathers (LStJ), RL Seddon (Swi).
SOUTH 1 try *Back*: AR St L Fagan (Rich). *Three-quarters*: J le Fleming (Black), RA Glass (Wivel), BWL Ashford (Exe, t). *Half-backs*: Alan Rotherham (Rich), MT Scott (CamU). *Forwards*: WG Clibborn (Rich), C Collier (Rich), JH Dewhurst (Rich), PF Hancock (Wivel/Black), GL Jeffery (Black), JH Oakley (Glo), A Robinson (Black/CamU), N Spurling (Black), L Stokes (Black).
Attendance: 8,000   *Referee*: GR Hill (RFU Honorary Secretary)

REPRESENTATIVE MATCH

Saturday 4 February 1888 at Rectory Field, Blackheath
SOUTH 1 goal, 1 try *Back*: AR St L Fagan (Rich, c). *Three-quarters*: BWL Ashford (Exe), RA Glass (Wivel), GC Hubbard (Black, t). *Half-backs*: H Fox (Well), Alan Rotherham (capt, Rich). *Forwards*: WG Clibborn (Rich) C Collier (Rich), JH Dewhurst (Rich), PF Hancock (Wivel/Black), GL Jeffery (Black), RM Parsons (Crew), A Robinson (Black/CamU), N Spurling (Black, t), SMJ Woods (Bridg).
NORTH 1 goal *Back*: JT Haslam (Bat). *Three-quarters*: P Robertshaw (Brad), J Valentine (Swi, c), J Standring (Man, t). *Half-backs*: F Bonsor (capt, Brad), J Mills (Swi). *Forwards*: C Anderton (ManFW), H Bedford (Bat), H Eagles (Sal), JL Hickson (Brad), T Kent (Sal), FW Lowrie (Wak), C Mathers (Bram), RL Seddon (Swi), W Yiend (HartR).
Attendance: 8,000   *Referee*: L Stokes (RFU President)

INTERNATIONAL CHAMPIONSHIP

Results
Wales 1t, Scotland 0
Ireland 2g, 1t, Wales 0
Scotland 1g, Ireland 0

Final table

	P	W	D	L	G-T	G-T
Ireland	2	1	0	1	2-1	1-0
Scotland	2	1	0	1	1-0	0-1
Wales	2	1	0	1	0-1	2-1

(Championship incomplete. Ireland, Scotland and Wales refused to play England due to the latter's refusal to join the International Board, founded by the aforementioned countries in 1886.)

ENGLAND TOUR OF AUSTRALIA AND NEW ZEALAND 1888

TOUR PARTY
RL 'Bob' Seddon (captain, Swinton)
Jack Anderton (Salford)
Tom Banks (Swinton)
Herbert Brooks (Durham City)*
Walter Bumby (Swinton)
Robbie 'Bob' Burnett (Hawick)
William 'Willie' Burnett (Hawick)
JP 'Jack' Clowes (Halifax)
Harry Eagles (Salford)
Tom Haslam (Batley)
Tom Kent (Salford)
Alex Laing (Hawick)
Charlie Mathers (Bramley)
Johnny Nolan (Rochdale Hornets)
Arthur Paul (Swinton)
Alf Penketh (Douglas, Isle of Man)
John Smith (unattached)*
Andrew Stoddart (Blackheath)
Angus Stuart (Dewsbury)
WH 'Willie' Thomas (London Welsh/Cambridge University)
Sam Williams (Salford)

Scottish-born Angus Stuart – an 1888 tourist – qualified for Yorkshire through playing with Dewsbury. *Athletic News, 1888*

*Most publications list Brooks and Smith – who were both doctors – as Edinburgh University players. In fact both were former Edinburgh University players having left that establishment several years earlier. Yorkshire-born Brooks played for Durham City during 1887-88, and Smith – having taken up Association football and represented Scotland ten times under that code – was no longer attached to a rugby club.

Lancashire's Sam Williams was one of four Salford players on the 1888 tour. *Black and White, 1887*

Milestones & Stats 1869-1901

TOUR RESULTS

Saturday 28 April – Otago (at Dunedin, NZ), won 8-3 (attendance: 10.000)
Wednesday 2 May – Otago (Dunedin, NZ), won 4-3 (8,000)
Saturday 5 May – Canterbury (Christchurch, NZ), won 14-6 (6,000)
Wednesday 9 May – Canterbury (Christchurch, NZ), won 4-0 (3,000)
Saturday 12 May – Wellington (Wellington, NZ), draw 3-3 (6,000)
Monday 14 May – Mr Roberts' XV (Wellington, NZ), won 4-1 (2,500)*
Wednesday 16 May – Taranaki (New Plymouth, NZ), lost 0-1 (3,000)
Saturday 19 May – Auckland (Auckland, NZ), won 6-3 (6,000)
Thursday 24 May – Auckland (Auckland, NZ), lost 0-4 (12,000)
Saturday 2 June – New South Wales (Sydney, NSW), won 18-2 (12,000)
Wednesday 6 June – Bathurst (Bathurst, NSW), won 13-6 (2,000)
Saturday 9 June – New South Wales (Sydney, NSW), won 18-6 (7,000)
Monday 11 June – Sydney Juniors (Sydney, NSW), won 11-0
Tuesday 12 June – King's School (Parramatta, NSW), draw 10-10 (1,200)
Monday 16 July – South Australia (Adelaide, SA), won 28-3 (2,500)
Wednesday 1 August – Melbourne (Melbourne, Qld), won 15-5 (5,000)
Saturday 4 August – New South Wales (Sydney, NSW), won 16-2 (5,000)
Monday 6 August – Sydney Grammar School (Sydney, NSW), draw 3-3 (2,000)
Wednesday 8 August – Bathurst (Bathurst, NSW), won 20-10 (1,600)
Saturday 11 August – Sydney University (Sydney, NSW), won 8-4 (2,000)
Saturday 18 August – Queensland (Brisbane, Qld), won 13-6 (12,000)
Tuesday 21 August – Queensland Juniors (Brisbane, Qld), won 11-3 (2,000)
Thursday 23 August – Ipswich (Ipswich, Qld), won 12-1 (3,000)
Saturday 25 August – Queensland (Brisbane, Qld), won 7-0
Wednesday 29 August – Northern Districts (Newcastle, NSW), won 14-7 (1,000)
Saturday 8 September – Auckland (Auckland, NZ), won 3-0 (7,000)
Wednesday 12 September – Mr O'Connor's XV (Auckland, NZ), draw 1-1 (2,000)**
Saturday 15 September – Hawke's Bay (Napier, NZ), won 3-2 (3,000)
Monday 17 September – Wairarapa (Masterton, NZ), won 5-1 (2,500)
Thursday 20 September – Canterbury (Christchurch, NZ), won 8-0 (1,000)
Saturday 22 September – Otago (Dunedin, NZ), draw 0-0 (3,000)
Wednesday 26 September – South Island (Dunedin, NZ), won 5-3 (4,000)
Saturday 29 September – South Island (Christchurch, NZ), won 6-0 (3,000)
Tuesday 2 October – Taranaki (Hawera, NZ), won 7-1 (2,000)
Wednesday 3 October – Wanganui (Wanganui, NZ), draw 1-1 (2,000)
*Replaced Wellington fixture (cancelled due to claims of 'rough play' on 12 May).
**Replaced North Island fixture (cancelled after dispute over share of gate money).

Note 1: Two different point systems were used during the tour as follows:
New Zealand (NZ) and Australian states Queensland (Qld), South Australia (SA) and Victoria (Vic): try – 1 point, conversion – 2, drop-goal – 3.
Australian state of New South Wales (NSW): try – 2 points, conversion – 3, drop-goal – 4.
Note 2: Above results do not include 19 matches played under Australian Football rules.
Note 3: Refer to appendix 5 for summary of players' records on 1888 tour.

These evocative images of the Maoris opening tour match against Surrey at Richmond made the front page. *Illustrated London News, 1888*

1888-1889

THE POPULAR GAME

In early August the *Yorkshire Post* heralded the new rugby season with a question or two for its readers: 'The reign of King Cricket is not yet over, nor will it be for another six weeks. The football season proper used to date from the first Saturday in October, not a week sooner; but since the game has become so popular its advent comes on now fully a month earlier. This encroaches upon the legitimate cricket season, much to the annoyance of those who participate in the summer game, who consider the act an act of trespass, and nothing short of poaching. Is it fair to cricketers? Is it reasonable that a game of the nature of Rugby football should be played in the month of August?'[91]

THE WEST LANCASHIRE UNION HITS SIXTY

The *Liverpool Mercury* wrote that the West Lancashire and Border Towns Rugby Union 'has again set on foot the enthusiasm which annually follows in its path. At the last meeting four new clubs enrolled, bringing the total strength to 60. Several others outside the prescribed radius expressed a wish at the close of last season to enlist, but the representatives [of the Union] deemed it inadvisable to further extend the boundary. The Union is now one of the strongest in the country [and] financially is in a very healthy state'.[92]

PENALTY GOAL INTRODUCED

In October 1888 the Rugby Football Union decided that if a team was awarded a 'free kick' they could attempt to score a goal (now referred to as a 'penalty goal') worth two points. The first such goal by a northern county was on 3rd November 1888, scored by Northumberland's John Dodd (Tynedale) against the touring New Zealand Native team, the ball hitting the cross-bar and rolling over. Penalty kicks had been introduced for offside in 1882 but with no goal attempt allowed. Penalties continued to be awarded solely for offside until 1892, after which they were given for all infringements.

THE MAORIS OPEN THEIR TOUR

The New Zealand Native Football Team, commonly and inaccurately referred to in the press at the time as 'The Maoris', was the first overseas rugby party to tour the British Isles. The *Manchester Guardian* noted: 'The invasion of the New Zealander has taken place at last, and their first game in this country came off yesterday [3rd October] at the Richmond Athletic Ground. A great deal of interest centred on the first appearance of the team and, among the three or four thousand spectators who watched Surrey being beaten, one noticed the faces of half the best-known footballers in and about London. The team received a very hearty greeting as they stepped into the field wearing their handsome mats trimmed with the feathers of the Kiwi. On divesting themselves of these adornments the men were found to be uniformly dressed in black jerseys and knickerbockers, the only touch of relief in their costume being a fern leaf embroidered in white on their breast. All the men played in boots, the hard-footed individuals who, report said, were in the habit of discarding all such luxuries as shoe leather, being either absent from the team or, what is perhaps more likely, having changed their minds after a short experience of English weather. The first peculiarity one noticed when the teams lined out was that the Maoris were playing only eight forwards, with three, instead of the customary two, half-backs.'[93]

THE NEW ZEALANDERS' TOUGH SCHEDULE

The New Zealanders' punishing tour schedule ran from October to March and covered an incredible 74 matches, 49 of which were won and five drawn. In addition to international fixtures with England, Ireland and Wales, they met county opposition 16 times, including Cumberland, Lancashire, Northumberland, Westmorland and Yorkshire (twice), whilst Cheshire and Durham did not have a fixture. Their ground breaking visit also included

45 games against club sides, 35 of which were in the north; Yorkshire had 16, Lancashire 13, Cheshire and Durham two each, Cumberland and Northumberland one each. They also opposed three northern area selections; East Cumberland, Liverpool District, and Barrow District.

INTOXICATING FACILITIES
A letter to the *Manchester Guardian* from 'An Old Footballer' bemoaned the lack of proper changing facilities: 'I have played in football matches for seven or eight years in various parts of England and Wales, with most of the leading clubs, and with but one exception no accommodation has been provided for players to dress and undress previous to and after the matches, except in public houses, which I consider a very great source of danger to the young men, causing them to indulge freely in intoxicating drinks. I would suggest as a remedy that the various clubs arrange for accommodation at a temperance hotel or some such place before the date of the match, so that the players may be sure of a suitable place to undress and dress, and also be provided with a good tea and wash, apart from the temptation to indulge in intoxicating drinks.'[94]

YORKSHIRE: SPLENDID EXPONENTS
Following Lancashire's 14-0 defeat to Yorkshire at Whalley Range on 24th November, the *Manchester Guardian* announced 'there can be no doubt that the Yorkshiremen are now splendid exponents of the game and that the County Palatine [Lancashire] will have to smarten up in future if the balance of victories is to be maintained on the right side'.[95]

THE NORTH SHORT-HANDED
When the North met the South at Rectory Field, Blackheath, on 15th December, they were short-handed for the opening 20 minutes, three-quarter Arthur Brooke (Huddersfield) being delayed on a foggy day due to a 'defective train service' and not reaching the ground until shortly before the match ended. Forward Fred Lowrie (Wakefield Trinity) started in the three-quarters and, when it was realised Brooke was unlikely to appear and with no reserve available, veteran forward Charles Fernandes, who had not played for several seasons, filled the vacancy in the forwards.[96]

NORTHUMBERLAND CUP RIVALRY
Tynemouth hosted Percy Park in round one of the Northumberland Cup on 9th March, in what was a keenly anticipated tie between two local rivals. One correspondent noted that it had 'excited much interest amongst

the patrons of the sport. For years the rivalry between the two has run very high, both having in turn won the Northumberland Cup. The Cricket Field has been properly staked off to prevent the players being hampered by spectators'.[97] Despite past successes, Tynemouth, who lost the match, ceased to exist after this season, having been founded in 1880.

CUMBERLAND CUP FINAL: AN ANIMATED SCENE

The Cumberland Cup final between Maryport and Millom, at Whitehaven on 16th March, stirred up plenty of enthusiasm, the *Cumberland Pacquet* commenting: 'The Cricket Field presented a most animated scene. The railway companies ran excursion trains from Millom, Maryport, Cockermouth, and intermediate stations, and issued tickets at reduced rates from Carlisle, Wigton, and Aspatria. The consequence was a large assemblage of football enthusiasts. The crush at the entrance to the ground was so great at times that two or three persons were injured, and not a small number managed to obtain admittance without payment. A better arrangement as to turnstiles ought to have been made. [William] Smith [Maryport] was suspended for about ten minutes [during the second half] for threatening to strike one of the Millom team, after which the referee allowed him to return.' The referee was Reverend Frank Marshall of Huddersfield, the Yorkshire County treasurer, who also presented the cup.[98]

WIGAN WIN THE WEST LANCASHIRE CUP

Wigan defeated their old adversaries Aspull in the final of the West Lancashire and Border Towns Cup, played at St Helens on 30th March. It was the fourth such final, Aspull having appeared in each of them. Unfortunately, the competitive nature that existed between them came to the surface, the *Athletic News* reporting: 'The same keenness and feeling of bitter rivalry comes to the front whenever they meet, and is always present in big bucketfuls. If the West Lancashire Cup competition is to have a future success, there will need to be a different style of play than that witnessed at St Helens on Saturday. If fighting for a cup means fighting and not football, then the sooner the competition comes to an end the better.'[99]

THE YORKSHIRE CUP: WAKEFIELD TRINITY EXPEL PLAYERS

Following their Yorkshire Cup semi-final defeat to Liversedge at Dewsbury on 30th March, the Wakefield Trinity committee held a meeting at their Holly Lodge rooms to discuss 'allegations made against certain members of the Trinity team', the outcome being that Fred Ross and Ralph

Dunn were both expelled. This brought about an interesting observation in the *Athletic News*: 'We question whether the Wakefield Trinity committee had any legal right to expel Ross and Dunn for going on the spree the night before the Cup tie with Liversedge. If every club adopted the Trinity method of procedure regarding their ale-drinking members, some organisations we know would have very few players left.'[100]

YORKSHIRE CUP FINAL: POST-MATCH MAYHEM

After Otley had overcome Liversedge in the Yorkshire Cup final at Cardigan Fields, Leeds, on 6th April, the *Yorkshire Post* noted: 'At the conclusion the members of both teams made for the committee's grandstand, where the Cup and medals were to be presented. The players were followed by some thousands of men and youths who had got through the enclosures and who in their headlong rush destroyed several of the barricades. The disorder caused by the pressing forward of the crowd continued for some minutes, but in the meantime the contents of two bottles containing a toothsome liquid were being poured into the Challenge Cup and the thirsty players were eagerly engaged upon their consumption.'[101]

YORKSHIRE DECLARED THE FIRST COUNTY CHAMPIONS

Although no county championship existed as such, the Rugby Football Union issued a circular on 6th February which stated they had 'decided to institute an annual match between the champion county of England and the rest of England'. The date of this encounter was given as 23rd February, and it was confirmed that the 'committee will decide which county shall be considered champion'. Middlesex believed they had a claim, but the choice of Yorkshire was ratified on Monday 18th February immediately after victory over Somersetshire at Wakefield, the sixth win from their six inter-county fixtures during the season. Yorkshire subsequently met the 'Rest of England' at Halifax on 23rd February, losing 9-0.[102]

1888-1889 STATISTICS

CUMBERLAND COUNTY CHALLENGE CUP (14 entries)
Try – 1 point; conversion, penalty goal – 2; drop-goal, field goal, goal from mark – 3.
If equal then majority of 3 minor points required to win.

First Round
Cockermouth 0, Aspatria 6
Flimby 17, Dearham 0
Millom 11, Whitehaven 1 (replay ordered after protest)
Moresby 0, Egremont 12
Seaton 9, Brampton 0
Workington 3, Maryport 4 (aet)
Byes: Broughton, Cleator

First Round Replay
Millom 7, Whitehaven 0

Second Round
Aspatria 0, Millom 4
Broughton 0, Maryport 7
Egremont 7, Flimby 3
Seaton 18, Cleator 0

Semi-finals
Maryport 6, Seaton 1
(at Egremont Athletic Club Grounds)
Millom 5, Egremont 0
(at Maryport Cricket Ground)

FINAL
Saturday 16 March 1889 at the Whitehaven Cricket Ground
MILLOM 3 *Back*: J Moore. *Three-quarters*: JH Buckett, I Moore, CW Dove (capt, dg).
Half-backs: J Denwood, J McGuire. *Forwards*: J Burns, A Flynn, J Flynn, T Harris, J Holme,
J Kidd, W Leck, T Whalen, H Wills.
MARYPORT 1 *Back*: J Robley. *Three-quarters*: R Little, E Banks, J Oliver. *Half-backs*:
W Coulthard (t), J Holliday, W Lewthwaite. *Forwards*: J Bewley, J Chambers, J Dobie,
J Foster, J Geddes, J Lewthwaite, WT Smith, J Thompson.
Attendance: 5,000   *Referee*: Rev F Marshall (Yorkshire RU)

DURHAM COUNTY CHALLENGE CUP (17 entries)
Most goals wins. If equal, most tries. If still equal, majority of 3 minor points.

First Round
Hartlepool YMCA 3t, Ryton 0
Byes: 15 teams drew a bye to next round

Second Round
Durham City 1g, 1t, Hartlepool YMCA 0
Hartlepool Rangers 3t, Consett 0
Hartlepool Rovers w/o Humbledon (disbanded)
Houghton-le-Spring 0, Westoe 1g, 3t
North Durham 1g, Boldon 1g (mp: 3-3, aet)
Stockton 0, Sunderland 5t
Tudhoe 1g, 3t, Gateshead Institute 0
West Hartlepool 5g, 3t, Henderson's Wanderers 0

Second Round Replay
Boldon 2t, North Durham 0

Third Round
Boldon 1t, Hartlepool Rangers 2t
Hartlepool Rovers 2g, West Hartlepool 1g
Tudhoe 0, Sunderland 1t
Weston 0, Durham City 3g, 3t

Semi-finals
Durham City 0, Sunderland 3g, 2t (replay ordered after protest)
Hartlepool Rovers 3g, 1t, Hartlepool Rangers 0

Semi-final Replay
Durham City 1g, 1t, Sunderland 0

FINAL
Saturday 6 April 1889 at Ashbrooke Ground, Sunderland
HARTLEPOOL ROVERS 1 goal, 3 tries *Back*: E Morison. *Three-quarters*: WE Kassell (2t, c), AE Emmerson, D McPherson. *Half-backs*: AC Scott, G Smith. *Forwards*: J Coates, T Danby, A Hill (capt, t), CM Huntley, FE Pease, A Robinson, J Snowdon (t), AC Stephens, W Yiend.
DURHAM CITY 0 *Back*: KA Ker. *Three-quarters*: JH Smeddle, FA Bulman, H Brooks. *Half-backs*: F Marston, J Turnbull (capt). *Forwards*: EH Bulman, J Davidson, S Davidson, JW Fogg-Elliot, FJ Hall, F Lumsden, T Raine, JT Wetherell, CTB Wilkinson.
Attendance: 8,000   *Referee*: A Cattell (Sheffield)

NORTHUMBERLAND COUNTY FOOTBALL CHALLENGE CUP (8 entries)
Most goals wins. If equal, most tries.

First Round
Northern 4g, 1t, North Elswick 0
Rockcliff 1g, 4t, Northumberland FC 1t
Tynedale 3g, 7t, Newcastle Rangers 0
Tynemouth 0, Percy Park 2g, 10t

Semi-finals
Percy Park 1g, Tynedale 1g
Rockcliff 1t, Northern 4g, 1t

Semi-final Replay
Tynedale 1g, 2t, Percy Park 3g

FINAL
Saturday 30 March 1889 at Jesmond Ground, Newcastle
NORTHERN 2 goals, 3 tries *Back*: E Emley. *Three-quarters*: CS Gill (capt), HB Lockhart, PH Morrison (2t). *Half-backs*: MT Scott, WM Scott (2t, c, dg). *Forwards*: H Angus, T Hoyle, J Livingstone, CA Ridley, C Scott, P Stanton, G Walters, W Watson, CE Winship.
PERCY PARK 0 *Back*: T Coulson. *Three-quarters*: J Arthur, RE Herbertson, F Finney. *Half-backs*: W Andus, T Stewart. *Forwards*: G Brewis, F Burn, J Craig, J Cuthbertson, A Gee, T Gee (capt), F Marshall, A Phillips, J Watkin.
Attendance: 5,000   *Referee*: G Swainston (Durham RU Honorary Secretary)

WEST LANCASHIRE AND BORDER TOWNS CHALLENGE CUP (13 entries)
Try – 4 points; conversion – 4; drop-goal, field goal – 6; minor – 1.
Majority of 3 points required to win.

First Round
Boothstown 0, Tyldesley 14
Eccles 7, Pemberton 28
Litherland w/o Blackrod (withdrew)
St Helens 1, Aspull 6
Southport Olympic 0, Wigan 29 (at Wigan; abandoned – bad light, replay ordered)
Tuebrook 11, Woodman Rovers (Wigan) 7
Bye: Walkden

First Round Replay
Wigan w/o Southport Olympic (withdrew)

Second Round
Aspull 11, Pemberton 1
Tuebrook 0, Walkden 15
Tyldesley 4, Wigan 6 (aet)
Bye: Litherland

Second Round Replay
Wigan 8, Tyldesley 4

Semi-finals
Aspull 14, Litherland 0 (at Lowerhouse Lane, Widnes)
Wigan 9, Walkden 0 (at Three Crowns, Leigh)

FINAL
Saturday 30 March 1889 at Dentons Green Lane, St Helens
WIGAN 17 *Back*: J Pilkington. *Three-quarters*: J Slevin (capt), R Seddon, J Mitchinson (t).
Half-backs: W Halliwell, J Hunter. *Forwards*: W Atkinson (t, c), T Brayshay, E Bullough,
E Dempsey (t), J Hatton, JE Lowe, F Swift, J Telford, EF Wardle.
ASPULL 4 *Back*: J Jackson. *Three-quarters*: J Baines, E Morris, J Roberts (t). *Half-backs*:
D Hulme, J Cartwright. *Forwards*: WH Birchall, G Croston, J Donnelly, W Haydock,
JW Holding, James Lindsay, John Lindsay, T Monks, J Mulroy,
Attendance: 7,000   *Referee*: E Beswick (Swinton)
Note: Wigan's score includes one minor point.

YORKSHIRE COUNTY FOOTBALL CHALLENGE CUP (100 entries)
Most goals wins (3 tries count as one 'goal'). If equal, most tries (excluding any already counted as equalling a 'goal'). If still equal, majority of 3 minor points.

Preliminary Round
Bowling Old Lane 2t, Kippax 1t
Bradford Trinity 1g, Kirkburton 1g, 1t
Ripon 1t, Mytholmroyd 0
Wakefield St Austin's 1g, 2t Greetland 0
Byes: 60 teams drew a bye to next round

Milestones & Stats 1869-1901

Qualifying Round
Barnsley 1g, Woodhouse 2g
Bowling 1g, Bankfoot 0
Bowling Old Lane 1g, 2t, Hull Southcoates 1g, 1t
Calverley 1g, 5t, Todmorden 1g
Dewsbury Clarence 1t, Laisterdyke 1t (mp: 7-4, aet)
Dodworth 1g, Birstall 1g (mp: 2-7)
Elland 0, Horbury 1t
Gomersal 2t, Dudley Hill 2g, 1t
Guiseley 1g, 3t, Hebden Bridge 2t
Halifax Free Wanderers 1g, 1t, Churwell 3t
Harrogate 2g, Wibsey 1g
Horsforth 3g, Yeadon 3t
Hull Athletic 0, Leeds Rifles 1g
Idle 1t, Otley 4g, 2t
Ingrow 1t, Manningham Rangers 2t
Knaresborough 2t, Eastmoor 3g, 1t
Lindley 1g, 1t, Lockwood 1g
Mirfield Rangers 1t, Windhill 3t
Newtown 2g, 1t, Paddock 1g
North Leeds 0, Kirkburton 1t
Outwood Church 1g, 3t, Bingley 1g, 2t
Primrose Hill 3t, Hipperholme and Lightcliffe 2t
Ravensthorpe 1g, 3t, Armley 1t
Saltaire 4g, 3t, Doncaster Town 0
Shepley 3t, Ripon 1t
Silsden w/o Dobcross (withdrew)
Skipton 1g, 2t, Heaton 1g
South Milford 0, Normanton 2g, 2t
Sowerby Bridge 2g, 4t, Keighley Shamrocks 1g
Warmfield 1g, Wakefield St Austin's 1g, 2t
Whitwood 3g, 2t, Low Moor St Mark's 1g, 2t (awarded to Low Moor after protest)
Wibsey Slack Side 1g, 2t, Alverthorpe 2g, 3t

First Round
(* *indicates 32 teams seeded to this round*)
Batley* 2t, Horsforth 0
Cleckheaton* 1g, 3t, Sowerby Bridge 1g
Dewsbury* 2t, Heckmondwike* 0
Dudley Hill 1t, Ravensthorpe 1g, 1t
Halifax Free Wanderers 0, Skipton 2g, 1t
Harrogate 0, Halifax* 2g, 1t
Horbury 1g, 1t, Alverthorpe 1g, 1t (mp: 6-2)
Huddersfield* 3g, 1t, Selby* 0
Hull* 1t, Brighouse Rangers* 1t (mp: 1-8)
Hunslet* 1g, Bramley* 1g (mp: 5-2, aet)
Kirkburton 1g, 1t, Keighley* 1g

First Round *continued*
Kirkstall* 0, Wakefield Trinity* 3g, 3t
Leeds Parish Church* 3t, Holbeck* 2g
Leeds Rifles 1g, Eastmoor 4t
Liversedge* 2g, Leeds St John's* 1g, 1t
Low Moor St Mark's 0, Shipley* 2t
Manningham* 2g, 1t, Windhill 0
Mirfield* 1t, Buttershaw* 0
Morley* 1g, Castleford* 1g, 1t
Newton 3g, Pudsey* 1t
Normanton 1g, 1t, Bowling Old Lane 1g, 2t
Ossett* 1g, 4t, Birstall 0
Outwood Church 1t, York* 1g
Pontefract* 2g, Goole* 0
Primrose Hill 3t, Bowling 2g, 1t
Saltaire 4g, 7t, Dewsbury Clarence 1g
Salterhebble* 2g, 1t, Silsden 0
Shepley 1g, 3t, Manningham Rangers 3g
Thornes* 1g, Lindley 1t
Wakefield St Austin's 2g, Otley 1g, 4t
Woodhouse 2g, 3t, Calverley 2t
Wortley* 1g, 4t, Guiseley 0

Second Round
Bowling Old Lane 1t, Kirkburton 0
Dewsbury 1g, 2t, Skipton 0
Eastmoor 2t, Cleckheaton 5t
Halifax 3t, Bowling 1g (mp: 5-1)
Horbury 1g, Huddersfield 3g, 1t
Manningham Rangers 2g, Manningham 1g, 1t
Mirfield 2g, Hunslet 2g (mp: 0-5)
Newtown 1t, Wakefield Trinity 1g, 5t
Ossett 1g, Salterhebble 1t
Otley 1g, Saltaire 1g (mp: 12-1)
Pontefract 3g, Brighouse Rangers 2g, 1t
Shipley 1g, 2t, Holbeck 1g, 3t
Thornes 2g, Castleford 1g, 3t (mp: 1-4)
Woodhouse 1t, Ravensthorpe 1g, 1t
Wortley 1g, Liversedge 2g
York 1t, Batley 1g, 1t

Third Round
Batley 1g, Dewsbury 1g (mp: 0-7)
Castleford 1g, 2t, Holbeck 3t (aet)
Cleckheaton 1g, 1t, Liversedge 2g, 2t
Halifax 2g, Hunslet 1t
Manningham Rangers 1t, Wakefield Trinity 6g, 1t
Ossett 0, Huddersfield 3g, 1t
Pontefract 3g, Bowling Old Lane 1g, 1t
Ravensthorpe 1g, 1t, Otley 5t

Fourth Round
Castleford 1g, 1t, Otley 2g
Huddersfield 1g, 2t, Halifax 1t
Pontefract 1g, 1t,
Liversedge 2g, 1t (aet)
Wakefield Trinity 4g, 3t,
Dewsbury 1t

Semi-finals
Liversedge 1g, Wakefield Trinity 1t (at Crown Flatts, Dewsbury)
Otley 1g, 3t, Huddersfield 2t (at Holderness Road, Hull)

FINAL
Saturday 6 April 1889 at Cardigan Fields, Leeds
OTLEY 1 goal,1 try *Back*: S Mawson. *Three-quarters*: S Hopkins (t), J Dawson, F Mudd (capt, pg). *Half-backs*: E Summerscales, M Wise. *Forwards*: A Briggs, J Chew, G Mitchell, DH Payne, R Ritchie, S Robinson, L Waddington, F Watkinson, A Whittaker.
LIVERSEDGE 1 goal *Back*: B Sharpe. *Three-quarters*: A Jones, W Fisher (capt, c), R Earnshaw. *Half-backs*: H Barker, H Varley. *Forwards*: A Ellis, W Jackman, W Medley, N Parkin (t), P Priestley, F Sharpe, G Smith, H Stott, A Wood.
Attendance: 10,000   *Referee*: M Newsome (Yorkshire RU President)

COUNTY MATCHES

Saturday 27 October 1888 at Lismore Place, Carlisle
CUMBERLAND 1 try *Back*: J Moore (Mil). *Three-quarters*: CW Dove (Mil), R Boyd (Mary), W Berwick (Asp). *Half-backs*: J McGuire (Mil), J Murchie (Work). *Forwards*: G Clark (Brou), JW Cowen (Asp), G Cuthell (Work), T Hodgson (Work), J Holliday (Mary), J Lewthwaite (Mary), J Mumberson (Asp), T Nettleton (Cock), J Thomson (Pen, t).
NORTHUMBERLAND 1 goal *Back*: H Haslam (NEls). *Three-quarters*: F Finney (PerPk), RE Herbertson (PerPk), E Emley (Nor). *Half-backs*: MT Scott (Nor), J Thompson (Nor). *Forwards*: A Benson (Rock), A Gee (PerPk), T Gee (PerPk), JH Greenwell (Rock), CW Harrison (Tynd), T Hoyle (Nor), T Hutchinson (NorFC), J Livingstone (Nor), GW Mole (NEls).
Attendance: 'large'   *Referee*: JM Mawson (Barrow)

Wednesday 31 October 1888 at Irwell Lane, Runcorn
CHESHIRE 3 tries *Back*: JW Brazendale (Run). *Three-quarters*: TH Davies (Run), WH Male (NewB), CJ Luya (NewB). *Half-backs*: H Hughes (Run), LR Paterson (BirkPk). *Forwards*: N Allardice (BirkPk), W Faulkner (Run), HA Howes (Sale), PH Lockwood (BirkPk), K Monteath (BirkPk), RF Muir (NewB, t), P Riley (Run), GT Wainwright (Run, 2t), AG Wood (BirkPk)
WESTMORLAND 0 *Back*: J Allen (StH). *Three-quarters*: G Webster (KirkL), E Hoggarth (KenT), WG Hoggarth (KenT). *Half-backs*: WE Banks (KenT), FE Exley (KenT). *Forwards*: RC Beard (KenH), L Beetham (Amb), J Carradus (KenT), I Hadwin (KenT), RH Moore (Amb), J Parkinson (KenT), WJ Parsons (KenH), E Richardson (KirkL), E Wilson (KenH).
Attendance: 1,500   *Referee*: AT Kemble (Lancashire)

Saturday 10 November 1888 at Upper Park, Birkenhead
CHESHIRE 0 *Back*: JW Brazendale (Run). *Three-quarters*: JA Black (capt, BirkPk), CJ Luya (NewB), WH Male (NewB). *Half-backs*: LM Holden (BirkPk), H Hughes (Run). *Forwards*: W Faulkner (Run), JG Gifford (NewB), HA Howes (Sale), W Hughes (Run), PH Lockwood (BirkPk), K Monteath (BirkPk), RF Muir (NewB), GT Wainwright (Run), AG Wood (BirkPk).
LANCASHIRE 8 tries *Back*: A Royle (BroR). *Three-quarters*: J Valentine (Swi, 3t), AH Molesworth (Man), J Standring (Man). *Half-backs*: J Mills (Swi, t), JH Payne (capt, Bro, t). *Forwards*: C Anderton (ManFW, 2t), W Atkinson (Wig), HC Chapman (LivOB, t), W Dillon (War), Harry Hasleham (ManR), JE Orr (Man), J Strang (Liv), T Whittaker (Man), G Woodward (Tyl).
Attendance: 5,000   *Referee*: GR Hill (RFU Honorary Secretary)

Saturday 10 November 1888 at Crown Point, Leeds
YORKSHIRE 4 goals, 3 tries *Back*: AE Bearpark (Hull). *Three-quarters*: AL Brooke (Hud, t), RE Lockwood (Dew, 2dg), JW Sutcliffe (Heck, 3t, 2c). *Half-backs*: F Bonsor (capt, Brad), WJ Stadden (Dew). *Forwards*: H Bedford (Mor), T Else (Bat), JL Hickson (Brad, t), G Jacketts (Hull), JH Jones (Wak), D Jowett (Heck), FW Lowrie (Wak), JT Toothill (Brad), H Wilkinson (Hal).
NORTHUMBERLAND 1 try *Back*: H Haslam (NEls). *Three-quarters*: F Finney (PerPk), RE Herbertson (PerPk), J Rishworth (NEls). *Half-backs*: JT Dodd (Tynd), J Winship (Ben). *Forwards*: A Benson (Rock), T Elliott (Tynd, t), A Gee (PerPk), T Gee (PerPk), CW Harrison (Tynd), T Hoyle (Nor), T Hutchinson (NorFC), GW Mole (NEls), E Taylor (Ben).
Attendance: 6,000   *Referee*: FW Burnand (Surrey)

Saturday 17 November 1888 at Friarage Field, Hartlepool
DURHAM 0 *Back*: WH Bell (Sund). *Three-quarters*: JH Smeddle (DurC), FA Bulman (DurU), AE Emmerson (HartR). *Half-backs*: CJ Sadler (Sto), AC Scott (HartR). *Forwards*: CW Burn (Sund), B Cox (Sund), A Hill (HartR), FE Pease (HartR), R Shields (DurC), JW Sowerby (NDur), T Tate (Hou), JT Wetherell (DurC), W Yiend (HartR).
YORKSHIRE 3 goals, 1 try *Back*: J Dodd (Hal). *Three-quarters*: H Simms (Bat), JW Sutcliffe (Heck, 2t, c, pg, dg), RE Lockwood (Dew). *Half-backs*: F Bonsor (capt, Brad), WJ Stadden (Dew). *Forwards*: H Bedford (Mor), W Binks (Wak), T Else (Bat), JL Hickson (Brad), G Jacketts (Hull), JH Jones (Wak), D Jowett (Heck), JT Toothill (Brad), H Wilkinson (Hal).
Attendance: 4,000   *Referee*: GR Hill (RFU Honorary Secretary)

Saturday 17 November 1888 at Jesmond Ground, Newcastle
NORTHUMBERLAND 2 goals *Back*: H Haslam (NEls). *Three-quarters*: F Finney (PerPk), RE Herbertson (PerPk), J Rishworth (NEls). *Half-backs*: MT Scott (Nor, dg, pg), J Winship (Ben). *Forwards*: A Benson (Rock), T Elliott (Tynd), A Gee (PerPk), T Gee (PerPk), JH Greenwell (Rock), CW Harrison (Tynd), T Hutchinson (NorFC), J Livingstone (Nor), GW Mole (NEls).
LANCASHIRE 5 goals, 4 tries *Back*: A Royle (BroR). *Three-quarters*: H Cook (Sal, t), AH Molesworth (Man, t), J Standring (Man, 3t). *Half-backs*: J Mills (Swi, t), JH Payne (Bro). *Forwards*: C Anderton (ManFW), HC Chapman (LivOB), W Dillon (War), EJ Green (Man), Harry Hasleham (ManR), JE Orr (Man), J Strang (Liv, 5c), T Whittaker (Man, 2t), G Woodward (Tyl, t).
Attendance: 'large'   *Referee*: Rev CH Newman (Durham)

Saturday 24 November 1888 at Whalley Range, Manchester
LANCASHIRE 0 *Back*: A Royle (BroR). *Three-quarters*: J Valentine (Swi), AH Molesworth (Man), J Standring (Man). *Half-backs*: J Mills (Swi), JH Payne (capt, Bro). *Forwards*: C Anderton (ManFW), HC Chapman (LivOB), W Dillon (War), H Eagles (Sal), EJ Green (Man), Harry Hasleham (ManR), JE Orr (Man), J Strang (Liv), G Woodward (Tyl).
YORKSHIRE 4 goals, 2 tries *Back*: J Dodd (Hal). *Three-quarters*: RE Lockwood (Dew), JW Sutcliffe (Heck, 2c, dg, gm), P Robertshaw (Brad). *Half-backs*: F Bonsor (capt, Brad, 2t), WJ Stadden (Dew). *Forwards*: H Bedford (Mor), T Else (Bat), JL Hickson (Brad, t), G Jacketts (Hull, t), JH Jones (Wak), D Jowett (Heck), FW Lowrie (Wak), JT Toothill (Brad), H Wilkinson (Hal).
Attendance: 10,000   *Referee*: GR Hill (RFU Honorary Secretary)

Saturday 1 December 1888 at Ashbrooke Ground, Sunderland
DURHAM 1 goal *Back*: WH Bell (Sund, c). *Three-quarters*: R Dixon (Tud), EP Thompson (Wes), FA Bulman (DurU). *Half-backs*: TM Jamieson (Con), GA Morgan (Sund). *Forwards*: R Barwick (Sund, t), B Cox (capt, Sund), A Hill (HartR), FE Pease (HartR), R Shields (DurC), JW Sowerby (NDur), JT Wetherell (DurC), CTB Wilkinson (DurU), W Yiend (HartR).
CHESHIRE 0 *Back*: C Holden (BirkPk). *Three-quarters*: JA Black (BirkPk), CJ Luya (NewB), WH Male (NewB). *Half-backs*: LM Holden (BirkPk), H Hughes (Run). *Forwards*: N Allardice (BirkPk), W Faulkner (Run), HA Howes (Sale), W Hughes (Run), PH Lockwood (BirkPk), K Monteath (BirkPk), RF Muir (NewB), GT Wainwright (Run), AG Wood (BirkPk).
Attendance: 1,500   *Referee*: W Cail (Northumberland)

Milestones & Stats 1869-1901

Monday 3 December 1888 at Fartown, Huddersfield
YORKSHIRE 2 goals, 5 tries *Back*: FW Richmond (Hud, 2c). *Three-quarters*: P Robertshaw (Brad, t), JW Sutcliffe (Heck, t), RE Lockwood (Dew). *Half-backs*: F Bonsor (capt, Brad), WJ Stadden (Dew, t). *Forwards*: H Bedford (Mor), T Else (Bat), E Holmes (Mann, 2t), G Jacketts (Hull), JH Jones (Wak), D Jowett (Heck, t), FW Lowrie (Wak), JT Toothill (Brad), H Wilkinson (Hal, t).
SURREY 1 goal *Back*: SS Wallis (GuyHosp). *Three-quarters*: TL Trethewy (RMC), CJ Prime (MidW, dg), HM Jordan (GuyHosp/LonW). *Half-backs*: J Bryant (GuyHosp), JHS McArthur (OLey). *Forwards*: A Allport (GuyHosp), GE Begbie (RMC), S Bowditch (OLey), HJ Cooper (StTHosp), TAM Forde (capt, StTHosp), DH Helps (Croy), CC Moxon (StTHosp), FPS Taylor (RMC), WJ Williams (StTHosp).
Attendance: 1,500/2,000   *Referee*: Rev F Marshall (Yorkshire)

Saturday 29 December 1888 at Jesmond Ground, Newcastle
NORTHUMBERLAND 2 tries *Back*: AS Carr (NorFC). *Three-quarters*: F Finney (PerPk), FHR Alderson (Tynd), CS Gill (Nor, 2t). *Half-backs*: WR Gray (NorFC), WM Scott (Nor). *Forwards*: T Anderson (Tynd), A Benson (Rock), A Gee (PerPk), T Gee (PerPk), JH Greenwell (Rock), CW Harrison (Tynd), G Leighton (PerPk), J Livingstone (Nor), W Watson (Nor).
WESTMORLAND 0 *Back*: J Allen (StH). *Three-quarters*: G Webster (KirkL), JK Robinson (KirkL), J Carradus (KenT). *Half-backs*: JJ Armer (KenT), FB Punchard (KirkL). *Forwards*: RC Beard (KenH), L Beetham (Amb), G Carradus (KenT), E Hine (KenH), RH Moore (Amb), R Nicholson (KenT), WJ Parsons (KenH), JW Wilkinson (KenH), R Wilson (KenH).
Attendance: 2,000   *Referee*: n/a

Saturday 26 January 1889 at Upper Park, Birkenhead
CHESHIRE 1 goal, 4 tries *Back*: C Holden (BirkPk). *Three-quarters*: AH Wolff (Alt), F Drinkwater (Sale), GT Wainwright (Run, 4t, dg). *Half-backs*: W Evans (Run), H Hughes (Run). *Forwards*: WH Broady (Run), W Faulkner (Run), HA Howes (Sale), W Hughes (Run), PH Lockwood (BirkPk), K Monteath (BirkPk), RP Moodie (BirkPk), A Williams (NewB), AG Wood (BirkPk).
NORTHUMBERLAND 0 *Back*: TS Graham (Nor). *Three-quarters*: AS Carr (NorFC), HB Lockhart (Nor), RE Herbertson (PerPk). *Half-backs*: T Stewart (PerPk), J Winship (Ben). *Forwards*: G Avery (NorFC), W Douglas (NEls), A Gee (PerPk), CH Hamilton (Rock), CW Harrison (Tynd), J Livingstone (Nor), J Nimmo (NorFC), H Shotton (NEls), W Watson (Nor).
Attendance: 2,000   *Referee*: FT Parry (West Lancashire)

Saturday 26 January 1889 at Whalley Range, Manchester
LANCASHIRE 3 tries *Back*: A Royle (BroR). *Three-quarters*: J Valentine (Swi, t), R Seddon (Wig, t), W Hastings (RochH/VicU). *Half-backs*: W Bumby (Swi), J Mills (Swi). *Forwards*: C Anderton (capt, ManFW), W Atkinson (Wig), W Dillon (War), JE Griffiths (RochH, t), Herbert Hasleham (ManR), N Hotchkiss (Swi), T Kent (Sal/Rad), T Whittaker (Man), G Woodward (Tyl).
DURHAM 1 try *Back*: WH Bell (Sund). *Three-quarters*: D McPherson (HartR), R Dixon (Tud), FA Bulman (DurU). *Half-backs*: TM Jamieson (Con), GA Morgan (Sund). *Forwards*: R Barwick (Sund), CW Burn (Sund), B Cox (capt, Sund), JW Fogg-Elliot (DurC), FE Pease (HartR), JW Sowerby (NDur), JT Wetherell (DurC), CTB Wilkinson (DurU, t), W Yiend (HartR).
Attendance: 3,000   *Referee*: F Cattell (Yorkshire)

Saturday 9 February 1889 at Jesmond Ground, Newcastle
NORTHUMBERLAND 2 tries *Back*: H Haslam (NEls). *Three-quarters*: CS Gill (Nor), HB Lockhart (Nor), F Finney (PerPk). *Half-backs*: MT Scott (Nor), T Stewart (PerPk). *Forwards*: T Anderson (Tynd), G Avery (NorFC), A Benson (Rock), A Gee (PerPk), T Gee (PerPk, 2t), CW Harrison (Tynd), J Livingstone (Nor), JJ McIntyre (Tynd), W Watson (Nor).
DURHAM 0 *Back*: TAF Crow (Sund). *Three-quarters*: WE Kassell (HartR), AE Emmerson (HartR), D McPherson (HartR). *Half-backs*: F Hutchinson (NDur), AC Scott (HartR). *Forwards*: R Barwick (Sund), CW Burn (Sund), B Cox (capt, Sund), JW Fogg-Elliot (DurC), CM Huntley (HartR), FE Pease (HartR), JW Sowerby (NDur), JT Wetherell (DurC), W Yiend (HartR).
Attendance: n/a   *Referee*: R Westray (Cumberland)

Saturday 9 February 1889 at Crown Flatts, Dewsbury
YORKSHIRE 3 goals, 3 tries *Back*: J Dodd (capt, Hal). *Three-quarters*: RE Lockwood (Dew), JW Sutcliffe (Heck, t, 3c), J Bradley (Goole). *Half-backs*: Jim Naylor (Bat), WJ Stadden (Dew). *Forwards*: H Bedford (Mor, t), T Else (Bat), E Holmes (Mann), G Jacketts (Hull), D Jowett (Heck, t), FW Lowrie (Wak, t), W Nichol (BrigR), S Ripley (Cleck), H Wilkinson (Hal, 2t).
CHESHIRE 1 try *Back*: F Drinkwater (Sale). *Three-quarters*: GT Wainwright (Run), J Riley (Run), AH Wolff (Alt). *Half-backs*: W Evans (Run), H Hughes (Run). *Forwards*: WH Broady (Run), HA Howes (Sale), W Hughes (Run, t), EW Hunt (Sale), PH Lockwood (BirkPk), RP Moodie (BirkPk), P Riley (Run), A Williams (NewB), AG Wood (BirkPk).
Attendance: 4,000   *Referee*: J MacLaren (Lancashire)

Saturday 16 February 1889 at Whalley Range, Manchester
LANCASHIRE 0 *Back*: WH Pennington (RochH). *Three-quarters*: EH Flower (Bro/Moss), J Winterbottom (Moss), W Hastings (RochH/VicU). *Half-backs*: W Bumby (Swi), J Nolan (RochH). *Forwards*: W Atkinson (Wig), W Dillon (War), N Hotchkiss (Swi), T Kent (Sal/Rad), JW Roberts (Sal), J Strang (capt, Liv), JH Tune (BroR), T Whittaker (Man), G Woodward (Tyl).
SOMERSETSHIRE 1 goal *Back*: E Bryant (Bridg). *Three-quarters*: CJB Moneypenny (Bath), FC Duckworth (Wes, t), SC Smith (Wes). *Half-backs*: FH Fox (capt, Well), R Sweet-Escott (Black). *Forwards*: JE Aldridge (Wes), HG Fuller (Bath), AA Glass (Well/OChelt, c), EL Hancock (Well), PF Hancock (Well/Black), WH Manfield (Yeo), F Soane (Bath), CJ Vernon (Well), GD White (Well).
Attendance: 2,000   *Referee*: F Cattell (Yorkshire)

Monday 18 February 1889 at Park Avenue, Bradford
YORKSHIRE 2 goals, 3 tries *Back*: WH Eagland (Hud). *Three-quarters*: RE Lockwood (Dew, t), JW Sutcliffe (Heck, pg, dg), AL Brooke (Hud). *Half-backs*: F Bonsor (capt, Brad), Jim Naylor (Bat). *Forwards*: E Holmes (Mann), G Jacketts (Hull), JH Jones (Wak), D Jowett (Heck), FW Lowrie (Wak), W Nichol (BrigR), JW Sykes (Bat, t), JT Toothill (Brad, t), E Wilkinson (Brad).
SOMERSETSHIRE 1 try *Back*: E Bryant (Bridg). *Three-quarters*: CJB Moneypenny (Bath), FC Duckworth (Wes, t), SC Smith (Wes). *Half-backs*: FH Fox (capt, Well), R Sweet-Escott (Black). *Forwards*: JE Aldridge (Wes), HG Fuller (Bath), AA Glass (Well/OChelt, c), EL Hancock (Well), PF Hancock (Well/Black), WH Manfield (Yeo), F Soane (Bath), CJ Vernon (Well), GD White (Well).
Attendance: 8,000/10,000   *Referee:* A Budd (Kent)

Thursday 28 February 1889 at Wilderspool, Warrington
LANCASHIRE 1 goal, 2 tries *Back*: WH Pennington (RochH, c). *Three-quarters*: J Anderton (Sal), S Roberts (Swi), W Hastings (RochH/VicU). *Half-backs*: W Bumby (Swi, t), JH Payne (capt, Bro, t). *Forwards*: C Anderton (ManFW), W Atkinson (Wig), W Dillon (War), G Hewitt (Wid), N Hotchkiss (Swi), T Kent (Sal/Rad), JW Roberts (Sal), T Whittaker (Man, t), G Woodward (Tyl).
CUMBERLAND 1 goal, 1 try *Back*: J Moore (Mil). *Three-quarters*: JJ Mitchell (Cock/EdinU), CW Dove (Mil), W Selkirk (Egr). *Half-backs*: J Murchie (Work), DN Pape (Work, pg). *Forwards*: JH Buckett (Mil), G Cuthell (Work), J Holme (Mil), G Jones (Whi), T Kirkpatrick (Brou), J Lewthwaite (Mary, t), J Mumberson (Asp), C Simpson (Cock/EdinU), WT Smith (Mary).
Attendance: 2,000   *Referee*: AN Hornby (Lancashire)

COUNTY CHAMPIONSHIP
Yorkshire declared as the first ever county champions by the Rugby Football Union based on their record during the season, having won all six inter-county fixtures.

COUNTY CHAMPIONS v THE REST

Saturday 23 February 1889 at Thrum Hall, Halifax
YORKSHIRE 0 *Back*: J Dodd (Hal). *Three-quarters*: RE Lockwood (Dew), JW Sutcliffe (Heck), AL Brooke (Hud). *Half-backs*: F Bonsor (capt, Brad), WJ Stadden (Dew). *Forwards*: H Bedford (Mor), E Holmes (Mann), G Jacketts (Hull), JH Jones (Wak), D Jowett (Heck), FW Lowrie (Wak), JW Sykes (Bat), JT Toothill (Brad), H Wilkinson (Hal).
REST OF ENGLAND 3 goals *Back*: A Royle (BroR). *Three-quarters*: AE Stoddart (capt, Black), FHR Alderson (CamU, t), J Valentine (Swi, t). *Half-backs*: MT Scott (Nor, 3c), WM Scott (CamU). *Forwards*: C Anderton (ManFW), JW Cave (CamU), H Eagles (Sal), F Evershed (Burt, t), T Gee (PerPk), PF Hancock (Well/Black), GL Jeffery (Black), A Robinson (Black), W Yiend (HartR).
Attendance: 12,000   *Referee*: GR Hill (RFU Honorary Secretary)

ENGLAND TRIAL MATCHES

Saturday 15 December 1888 at Rectory Field, Blackheath
SOUTH 1 try *Back*: WG Mitchell (GuyHosp/Rich). *Three-quarters*: GC Hubbard (Black), AE Stoddart (capt, Black), P Christopherson (Black/OxfU). *Half-backs*: AR Richards (OLey), WM Scott (CamU). *Forwards*: JW Cave (CamU), C Collier (Rich), JH Dewhurst (Rich), F Evershed (Burt, t), J Hammond (Black), PF Hancock (Well/Black), GL Jeffery (Black), A Robinson (Black), EH Wynne (Black).
NORTH 2 goals *Back*: A Royle (BroR). *Three-quarters*: JW Sutcliffe (Heck, c), RE Lockwood (Dew, dg), FW Lowrie (Wak). *Half-backs*: F Bonsor (capt, Brad), MT Scott (Nor). *Forwards*: C Anderton (ManFW, t), H Bedford (Mor), CWL Fernandes (unattached), JL Hickson (Brad), JH Jones (Wak), D Jowett (Heck), JT Toothill (Brad), H Wilkinson (Hal), W Yiend (HartR).
Attendance: 5,000   *Referee*: GR Hill (RFU Honorary Secretary)

Saturday 2 February 1889 at Park Avenue, Bradford
NORTH 3 goals *Back*: A Royle (BroR). *Three-quarters*: RE Lockwood (Dew), JW Sutcliffe (Heck, 2c, dg), J Valentine (Swi). *Half-backs*: F Bonsor (capt, Brad), J Wright (Brad, t). *Forwards*: C Anderton (ManFW), H Bedford (Mor), JL Hickson (Brad), JH Jones (Wak), D Jowett (Heck), FW Lowrie (Wak), JT Toothill (Brad, t), H Wilkinson (Hal), W Yiend (HartR).
SOUTH 0 *Back*: WG Mitchell (GuyHosp/Rich). *Three-quarters*: AE Stoddart (capt, Black), P Christopherson (Black/OxfU), FHR Alderson (CamU). *Half-backs*: AR Richards (OLey), WM Scott (CamU.). *Forwards*: JW Cave (CamU), JH Dewhurst (Rich), F Evershed (Burt), FW Goodhue (StTHosp/CamU), JH Gould (OLey), J Hammond (Black), PF Hancock (Well/Black), GL Jeffery (Black), A Robinson (Black).
Attendance: 10,000   *Referee*: GR Hill (RFU Honorary Secretary)

INTERNATIONAL CHAMPIONSHIP

Results
Scotland 2t, Wales 0
Ireland 0, Scotland 1g
Wales 0, Ireland 2t

Final table

	P	W	D	L	G-T	G-T
Scotland	2	2	0	0	1-2	0-0
Ireland	2	1	0	1	0-2	1-0
Wales	2	0	0	2	0-0	0-4

(Championship incomplete. Ireland, Scotland and Wales again refused to play England due to its refusal to join the International Board. England subsequently joined in 1890.)

MAORIS TOUR OF THE BRITISH ISLES 1888-89

TOUR PARTY
Joseph Warbrick (captain, Hawke's Bay)
W Anderson (Thames)
William Elliot (Grafton)
Thomas Ellison (Wellington)
David Gage (Wellington)
Charles Goldsmith (Te Aute College)
E Ihimaira (Hawke's Bay)
Wi Karauria (Hawke's Bay)
Patrick Keogh (Kaikorai)
Harry Lee (Riverton)
Charles Madigan (Grafton)
Richard Maynard (North Shore)
Edward McCausland (Gordon)
Wiri Nehua (Auckland)
Teo Rene (Nelson)
David Stewart (Thames)
Richard Taiaroa (Dunedin)
Alfred Warbrick (East Coast)
Arthur Warbrick (East Coast)
Frederick Warbrick (East Coast)
William Warbrick (East Coast)
Alexander Webster (Westport)
George Williams (Poneke)
George Wynyard (North Shore)
Henry Wynyard (North Shore)
William Wynyard (North Shore)

Milestones & Stats 1869-1901   181

MAORIS TOUR RESULTS
Wednesday 3 October – Surrey (at Richmond), won 4-1 (attendance: 6,000)
Saturday 6 October – Northamptonshire (Northampton), won 12-0 (3,000)
Wednesday 10 October – Kent (Blackheath), won 4-1 (7,000)
Saturday 13 October – Moseley, lost 4-6 (5,000)
Thursday 18 October – Burton-on-Trent, lost 3-4 (5,000)
Saturday 20 October – Midland Counties (Birmingham), won 10-0 (5,000)
Monday 22 October – Middlesex (Fletching, Sussex), lost 0-9*
Thursday 24 October – Hull, lost 0-1 (12,000)
Saturday 27 October – Dewsbury, won 6-0 (6,000)
Wednesday 31 October – Wakefield Trinity, lost 0-1 (6,000)
Saturday 3 November – **Northumberland** (Newcastle), draw 3-3 (3,000)
Monday 5 November – Stockton-on-Tees (Stockton), won 6-1 (3,000)
Wednesday 7 November – Tynemouth and District (North Shields), won 7-1 (1,500)
Saturday 10 November – Halifax, lost 4-13 (9,000)
Monday 12 November – Newcastle and District (Newcastle), won 14-0 (2,000)
Wednesday 14 November – Hartlepool Rovers, won 1-0 (8,000)
Saturday 17 November – **Cumberland** (Maryport), won 10-2 (2,000)
Tuesday 20 November – Carlisle, won 13-0 (2,000)
Thursday 22 November – Hawick, won 3-1 (5,000)
Friday 23 November – East Cumberland (Carlisle), won 12-9
Saturday 24 November – **Westmorland** (Kendal), won 3-1 (4,000)
Monday 26 November – Swinton, lost 0-2 (8,000)
Wednesday 28 November – Liverpool and District (Liverpool), won 9-0 (2,000)
Saturday 1 December – Ireland (Dublin), won 13-4 (3,000)
Monday 3 December – Dublin University, draw 4-4 (1,500)
Wednesday 5 December – North of Ireland FC (Belfast), won 2-0 (2,000)
Saturday 8 December – **Lancashire** (Manchester), lost 0-1 (10,000)
Monday 10 December – Batley, draw 5-5 (5,000)
Wednesday 12 December – **Yorkshire** (Bradford), won 10-6 (5,000)
Saturday 15 December – Broughton, won 8-0 (5,000)
Monday 17 December – Wigan, won 5-1 (8,000)
Wednesday 19 December – Llanelli, lost 0-3 (4,000)
Saturday 22 December – Wales (Swansea), lost 0-5 (7,000)
Monday 24 December – Swansea, won 5-0 (4,000)
Wednesday 26 December – Newport, won 3-0 (6,000)
Saturday 29 December – Cardiff, lost 1-4 (15,000)
Tuesday 1 January – Bradford, lost 1-4 (15,000)
Thursday 3 January – Leeds Parish Church, won 6-3 (1,500)
Saturday 5 January – Kirkstall, won 7-3 (4,000)
Monday 7 January – Brighouse Rangers, won 4-0 (4,000)
Wednesday 9 January – Huddersfield, won 7-6 (4,000)
Saturday 12 January – Stockport, draw 3-3 (4,000)
Monday 14 January – Castleford, lost 3-9 (4,000)
Thursday 17 January – Warrington, won 7-1 (6,000)
Saturday 19 January – **Yorkshire** (Wakefield), lost 4-16 (6,000)
Wednesday 23 January – Spen Valley District (Cleckheaton), won 8-7 (5,000)

MAORIS TOUR RESULTS *continued*
Saturday 26 January – Somersetshire (Wellington), won 17-4 (3,000)
Wednesday 30 January – Devonshire (Exeter), won 12-0 (3,000)
Thursday 31 January – Taunton and District (Taunton), won 8-0 (1,000)
Saturday 2 February – Gloucestershire (Gloucester), won 4-1 (8,000)
Monday 4 February – Midland Counties (Moseley, Birmingham), won 6-1 (2,000)
Wednesday 6 February – Blackheath, won 9-3 (5,000)
Saturday 9 February – United Services (Portsmouth), won 10-0 (2,000)
Saturday 16 February – **England** (Blackheath), lost 0-7 (9,000)
Monday 18 February – London Welsh (Richmond), won 2-1 (3,000)
Tuesday 19 February – Cambridge University, lost 3-7 (4,000)
Thursday 21 February – Oxford University, lost 0-6 (4,000)
Saturday 23 February – Manningham, won 4-0 (12,000)
Monday 25 February – Leeds St John's, won 9-0 (6,000)
Wednesday 27 February – Leigh, lost 1-4 (10,000)
Saturday 2 March – Runcorn, won 8-3 (8,000)
Monday 4 March – Oldham, lost 0-6 (4,000)
Tuesday 5 March – Halifax, won 6-0 (6,000)
Thursday 7 March – Barrow and District (Barrow), lost 0-3 (7,000)
Saturday 9 March – Widnes, won 8-1 (8,000)
Monday 11 March – Manchester, won 7-1 (4,000)
Wednesday 13 March – Walkden, won 6-1 (3,000)
Thursday 14 March – St Helens, won 9-0 (5,000)
Saturday 16 March – Salford, won 7-1 (10,000)
Monday 18 March – Rochdale Hornets, won 10-0 (7,000)
Wednesday 20 March – York, won 4-3 (5,000)
Saturday 23 March – Hull, draw 1-1 (12,000)
Monday 25 March – Widnes, won 6-1 (3,000)
Wednesday 27 March – Southern Counties (Leyton, London), won 3-1 (1,500)

*Played at Lord Sheffield's estate in Sheffield Park by private invitation only.
Note: Point system used during the tour: try – 1 point, conversion – 2, all other goals – 3.

Saturday 3 November 1888 at Jesmond, Newcastle
NORTHUMBERLAND 3 *Back*: P Horsley (PerPk). *Three-quarters*: F Finney (PerPk), RE Herbertson (PerPk), AS Carr (NorFC). *Half-backs*: JT Dodd (Tynd, pg), J Winship (Ben). *Forwards*: A Benson (Rock), T Elliot (Tynd), A Gee (PerPk), T Gee (PerPk), JH Greenwell (Rock), CW Harrison (Tynd), T Hutchinson (NorFC), J Livingstone (Nor), GW Mole (NEls).
MAORIS 3 *Back*: E McCausland (gm). *Three-quarters*: C Madigan, W Warbrick, D Gage. *Half-backs*: W Elliot, P Keogh, F Warbrick. *Forwards*: W Anderson, W Karauria, H Lee, R Maynard, R Taiaroa, Arthur Warbrick, A Webster, G Williams.
Attendance: 3,000   *Referee*: W Cail (Northumberland)

Saturday 17 November 1888 at Maryport Cricket Ground
CUMBERLAND 2 *Back*: A Lee (Brampton). *Three-quarters*: W Selkirk (Egr, t), CW Dove (Mil), RY Sutton (Whi). *Half-backs*: J Murchie (Work), I Stamper (Egr, t). *Forwards*:

JH Buckett (Mil), JW Cowen (Asp), G Jones (Whi), J Lewthwaite (Mary), W Leck (Mil). J Mumberson (Asp), E Shimmins (Egr), WT Smith (Mary), J Wright (Whi).
MAORIS 10 *Back*: W Warbrick. *Three-quarters*: W Wynyard (t), D Gage, C Madigan (t). *Half-backs*: P Keogh (t), F Warbrick, C Goldsmith. *Forwards*: W Anderson, T Ellison (t), W Karauria, R Maynard, R Taiaroa (t), Arthur Warbrick, A Webster, G Williams (2c).
Attendance: 2,000   *Referee*: JM Mawson (Barrow)
Note: Scorer for one Maoris try not reported.

Saturday 24 November 1888 at Mint's Feet, Kendal
WESTMORLAND 1 *Back*: G Webster (KirkL). *Three-quarters*: JJ Armstrong (KenH), E Hoggarth (KenT), WJ Walker (capt, KenH, t). *Half-backs*: J Berry (Tyl), W Cross (StH). *Forwards*: RC Beard (KenH), J Carradus (KenT), DF Ellwood (KenH), RH Moore (Amb), R Nicholson (KenT), WJ Parsons (KenH), E Richardson (KirkL), JW Wilkinson (KenH), E Wilson (KenH).
MAORIS 3 *Back*: W Warbrick. *Three-quarters*: EMcCausland (capt), W Wynyard (dg), F Warbrick. *Half-backs*: W Elliot, C Goldsmith, P Keogh. *Forwards*: W Anderson, T Ellison, WKarauria, T Rene, D Stewart, R Taiaroa, Alfred Warbrick, Arthur Warbrick.
Attendance: 4,000   *Referees*: M Greaves (Carnforth, 1st half), FS Prest (Barrow, 2nd half)

Saturday 8 December 1888 at Whalley Range, Manchester
LANCASHIRE 1 *Back*: A Royle (BroR). *Three-quarters*: F Prince (Bro), R Seddon (Wig), W Hastings (RochH/VicU). *Half-backs*: JH Payne (capt, Bro), HD Wood (LivOB). *Forwards*: C Anderton (ManFW), W Atkinson (Wig), W Dillon (War), H Eagles (Sal), Harry Hasleham (ManR), N Hotchkiss (Swi), T Kent (Sal/Rad, t), J Strang (Liv), JH Tune (BroR).
MAORIS 0 *Back*: D Gage. *Three-quarters*: W Wynyard, F Warbrick, H Wynyard. *Half-backs*: W Elliot, P Keogh, G Wynyard. *Forwards*: W Anderson, W Karauria, R Maynard, D Stewart, R Taiaroa, Arthur Warbrick, A Webster, G Williams.
Attendance: 10,000   *Referee*: WH Wallace (Cheshire)

Wednesday 12 December 1888 at Valley Parade, Bradford
YORKSHIRE 6 *Back*: HO Hamshaw (Wak). *Three-quarters*: J Dyson (Hud, 2t), J Bradley (Goole), FW Richmond (Hud). *Half-backs*: M Wise (Otley, t), H Wood (Heck). *Forwards*: W Binks (Wak), J Brooke (Bram), D Brown (York, c), P Dickinson (capt, Cas), J Fisher (Brad), E Holmes (Mann, t), P Jackson (Hud), H Noble (Heck), I Webster (Hal).
MAORIS 10 *Back*: E McCausland (2c). *Three-quarters*: W Elliot, W Wynyard, D Gage (t). *Half-backs*: Arthur Warbrick (t), P Keogh (t), H Wynyard (t). *Forwards*: W Anderson, T Ellison (2t), W Karauria, R Maynard, D Stewart, A Webster, G Williams, G Wynyard.
Attendance: 5,000   *Referee:* W Cail (Northumberland)

Saturday 19 January 1889 at Belle Vue, Wakefield
YORKSHIRE 16 *Back*: J Dodd (Hal). *Three-quarters*: RE Lockwood (Dew, t), JW Sutcliffe (Heck, 4c), J Bradley (Goole, dg). *Half-backs*: F Bonsor (capt, Brad), WJ Stadden (Dew, t). *Forwards*: H Bedford (Mor), W Binks (Wak), T Else (Bat), E Holmes (Mann, t), G Jacketts (Hull), JH Jones (Wak), D Jowett (Heck, 2t), FW Lowrie (Wak), H Wilkinson (Hal).
MAORIS 4 *Back*: W Warbrick. *Three-quarters*: C Madigan, W Wynyard, E McCausland (c). *Half-backs*: W Elliot (t), P Keogh, D Gage. *Forwards*: T Ellison (t), W Karauria, H Lee, T Rene, D Stewart, R Taiaroa, G Williams, G Wynyard.
Attendance: 6,000   *Referee*: GR Hill (RFU Honorary Secretary)

Saturday 16 February 1889 at Rectory Field, Blackheath
ENGLAND 7 *Back*: AV Royle (BroR). *Three-quarters*: JW Sutcliffe (Heck, t, c), AE Stoddart (Black, t), RE Lockwood (Dew). *Half-backs*: F Bonsor (capt, Brad), WM Scott (CamU). *Forwards*: C Anderton (ManFW), H Bedford (Mor, 2t), JW Cave (Rich), F Evershed (Burt, t), D Jowett (Heck), F Lowrie (Wak), A Robinson (Black), HJ Wilkinson (Hal), W Yiend (HartR).
MAORIS 0 *Back*: W Warbrick. *Three-quarters*: C Madigan, W Wynyard, E McCausland. *Half-backs*: P Keogh, D Gage, W Elliot. *Forwards*: W Anderson, T Ellison, H Lee, R Maynard, T Rene, R Taiaroa, G Williams, G Wynyard.
Attendance: 9,000   *Referee*: GR Hill (RFU Honorary Secretary)

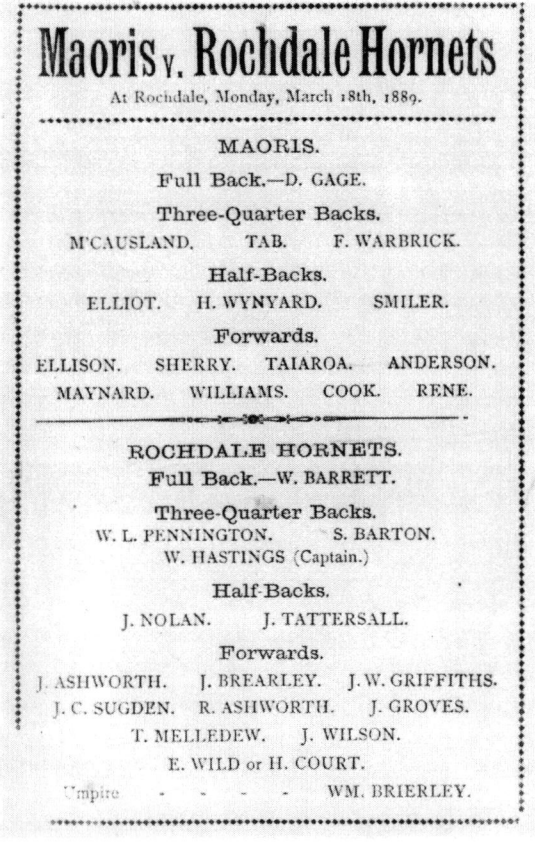

Team sheet for Rochdale Hornets versus Maoris, March 1889

1889-1890

WAKEFIELD TRINITY SUSPENDED

Wakefield Trinity were late commencing the 1889-90 season, having been suspended until 31st October for 'professionalism' due to an alleged payment of £50 towards a 'testimonial' for Teddy Bartram. In an era where an increasing number of clubs and individual players were being investigated for so-called professionalism Wakefield had appealed in vain.

THE WEST LANCASHIRE LEAGUE:
THE FIRST LEAGUE COMPETITION

The West Lancashire League was the first league competition organised for senior rugby clubs in the north. It effectively replaced the West Lancashire and Border Towns Challenge Cup, which had existed for four seasons as a knock-out contest. The first league encounter was St Helens versus Warrington on 7th September. The *Athletic News* reported: 'The West Lancashire League started on its wild career towards gilded greatness on Saturday last, when Warrington met St Helens, on the ground of the latter. Whether the League will furnish better expositions of football than those which were the outcome of the defunct West Lancashire Union remains to be shown, but there is the certainty that the results of these encounters will be more satisfactory and a better criterion of the superiority or otherwise of the teams engaged than the cup ties could prove. With good management and firm referees anything approaching the fiasco or exhibition which distinguished the final tie last season will be impossible.'[103]

THE YORKSHIRE COLTS
Yorkshire introduced a second tier county team named the Yorkshire Colts that met Cumberland at Manningham on Monday 21st October, winning 4-3. The 'Colts' sobriquet was reported as 'a term new to football, albeit familiar in the cricket world'. The exercise was repeated twelve months later when the Yorkshire Colts again opposed Cumberland at Manningham, claiming a second victory, 13-2.[104]

NORTHUMBERLAND: A MAN SHORT
When Northumberland met Cumberland at Jesmond, Newcastle, on 26th October, one of their forwards – Harry Greenwell (Rockcliff) – failed to arrive and the Northumbrians took to the field with fourteen players. At half-time George Brewis of the Northumberland club joined the game as his replacement for what was his only county appearance.

A REFEREE'S ROUGH TREATMENT
A meeting of the Yorkshire Committee was held at the Griffin Hotel, Leeds, on 4th November when it investigated complaints on the mistreatment of a referee at York. The *Manchester Guardian* reported: 'Mr. H. Sewell complained of rough treatment which he had received from spectators at a match played recently between the York and Otley teams [on 26th October]. During the game strong language was repeatedly used about him in his hearing, and a sod of earth was thrown at him, striking him in the back. As he left the ground stones and dirt were thrown after him, and if it had not been for the protection of two members of the York club, who were with him, he considered he would have been very severely handled. After consideration of the facts, the Committee decided that the York club should not be allowed to play a match on the York ground in the month of November.'[105]

THE WEST LANCASHIRE LEAGUE UNDER FLOODLIGHT
What is probably the first floodlit League fixture to take place in the north under Rugby rules took place at Aspull on Wednesday evening, 15th January, under Wells' patent lights. The West Lancashire League match, won 17-13 by visitors St Helens, commenced at 7.30 pm.[106]

LEEDS PARISH CHURCH SUSPENDED

The Leeds Parish Church club, which had been charged with professionalism, was the subject of a Yorkshire Committee meeting at the Griffin Hotel, Leeds, on 20th January. The *Yorkshire Herald* explained: 'It transpired that in April 1887 the sum of £68 was expended in touring South Lancashire and Cheshire. It was admitted money was spent in railway and other expenses for visiting theatres, concert halls, and having oyster suppers. In the same month the committee spent £37 on presents to members of the Cup teams, each player having either a suit of clothes or a watch given to him. It further transpired that R. Lumley, one of the regular playing members, had tendered for work in connection with the erection of new premises for the club and, having been accepted by the club committee, had the contract given to him for £160. It was decided to suspend the Leeds Parish Church Club until the end of February next.'[107]

A LEAGUE FOR CUMBERLAND

A meeting took place at the Commercial Hotel, Workington, on 6th February, with the object of creating a Cumberland League competition 'similar to that in West Lancashire'. It was claimed that letters of intent had been received from Workington, Maryport, Egremont, Broughton and Seaton, and it was decided to write to Penrith United, Whitehaven and Aspatria inviting them to join. It was agreed to name it the Cumberland Rugby Football League.[108] The proposed League did not, in fact, go ahead, the first Cumberland league competition not appearing until 1895-96.

WESTMORLAND PROVIDE A SHOCK

Westmorland produced a major shock in defeating Lancashire 5-2 at Prescott Street, Wigan, on Thursday 13th February. Although Lancashire 'turned out an indifferent team' it was reported that Westmorland 'deserved their success, and had all the best of the game until the last twenty minutes. Their passing was excellent and their tackling fearless, that of their opponents being just as feeble'.[109] It was the first meeting between the two counties, Westmorland failing to repeat the feat in seven further encounters during the 1890s.

THE YORKSHIRE CUP: UNUSUAL PROTESTS

Clubs protesting on the outcome of Yorkshire Cup ties had become a regular item for the Yorkshire Committee to deal with after each round. During the season there were three protests that stood out as being unusual by today's standard. All were upheld by the committee who ordered replays. Two of the reviewed ties were played in the first round on 1st March; York, who 'lost' at Sowerby Bridge, claimed the distance from the goal-line to the boundary was too short, whilst Pudsey protested that their 'loss' at Whitwood was due to their hosts wearing similar jerseys to themselves. After the third round on 15th March, Normanton complained that an official of their victorious hosts, Cleckheaton, had interfered by entering the playing area to speak to the players. In the replays York and Normanton overturned the original result, Whitwood repeating their earlier win.

LANCASHIRE TRAVEL TO IRELAND

Lancashire became the first northern county to play in Ireland when they met Ulster in Ormeau, Belfast, on 22nd March, losing 3-1. The *Manchester Guardian* provided several excuses for the defeat: 'First, the absence of such men as Flower, Mills and Whittaker weakened the team; secondly, the players had hardly recovered from the sea passage; and, thirdly, the miserable weather on Saturday made matters extremely uncomfortable. The Ulster team underwent many changes, half-a-dozen of those originally selected failing to answer to their names.'[110]

UP THE HILL TO HALIFAX

The Yorkshire Cup final between Huddersfield and Wakefield Trinity was staged at Thrum Hall, Halifax, on 5th April, which, the *Leeds Mercury*, with a hint of bias, claimed was not the best choice: 'The [Leeds] St John's ground in the Cardigan Fields, Leeds, was stated to be unsuitable for such a match, although most of the finals have been played there. There is nothing to complain of about the [Halifax] enclosure in Hanson Lane except its position. To paraphrase the lines of a popular ditty, "It's all right when you get there, but you have to get there first". This is accomplished by climbing one of the hills for which Halifax is justly famous. Had the majority of the County Committee known what denunciations and epithets were to be launched at them by mortals struggling up Pellon Lane, they would surely have hesitated before fixing on Halifax.'[111]

THE WEST LANCASHIRE LEAGUE:
CHAMPIONS VERSUS THE REST

The West Lancashire League set an end of season precedent which was replicated for many years to come by most League competitions. The *Athletic News* explained: 'The West Lancashire Union have decided to play a match on the same principle as England v Champion County, on the

The Lancashire team that met Middlesex at Kennington Oval, London, on 12th March 1887. Back: AH Stockley, AT Kemble, JW Roberts, R Walker (vice-president). Third row: V Slater (stood on bench), J Robertson, AN Hornby (president), S Roberts, FS Moss, C Anderton, H Eagles, RL Seddon (seated). Second row (seated, right): A Teggin. Front: HC Chapman, JH Payne, J Mills, J Valentine.

The Yorkshire team versus Lancashire at Bradford on 26th November 1887. Back: AE Hudson (president), TW Watson, C Sumner, E Wilkinson, FW Lowrie, P Robertshaw, JL Hickson, JA Miller (honorary secretary). Middle: WJ Stadden, JT Haslam, G Harrison, H Bedford, C Mathers. Front: F Bonsor, J Garforth, FT Ritchie, AL Brooke.

Tom Kent is the only Salford player to represent England at rugby union, making six appearances in the early 1890s. Described as a solid, hard working forward, he also played 35 times for Lancashire, three for the North, and was included in the 1888 tour of Australia and New Zealand. Initially signed from Radcliffe, he was a member of the Salford team that won the inaugural Lancashire Club Championship in 1892-93.

John Robinson of Kirkby Lonsdale made 23 appearances for Westmorland from 1888 to 1897, a record for the county he shared with Jack Carradus. He was described as a 'speedy' wing three-quarter and 'sure tackler'.

Jack Toothill played for Bradford, making the first of 50 appearances for Yorkshire in 1888, the highest total for the county during the Victorian era. He also played for England 12 times and the North on five occasions. Regarded as an excellent 'scrummager' and 'dribbler' he remained loyal to Bradford after they joined the Northern Union, continuing until 1898.

Jim Davidson was one of Cumberland's greatest forwards, making his county debut in 1889. He went on to accumulate 54 appearances for Cumberland and eight for the North, both record numbers for the Victorian era. He represented England five times and was a three-time winner of the Cumberland County Cup with Aspatria.

The 'Shaw and Shrewsbury' 1888 British touring team that visited Australia and New Zealand. Back: T Banks, AE Stoddart, JP Clowes, J Lawlor, Dr J Smith, AG Paul, F McShane. Middle: J Anderton, A Penketh, S Williams, R Burnett, WH Thomas, RL Seddon, H Eagles, T Kent, C Mathers. Front: HC Speakman, W Burnett, H Brooks, W Bumby, JT Haslam, J Nolan, A Stuart, A Laing. Note that Australian-based Jack Lawlor and Fred McShane joined the tour party to coach the players for their additional 19 matches played under Australian Rules.

The New Zealand Native team 1888-89 – referred to in the press as 'The Maoris' – that undertook a 74-match tour of the British Isles. Back: A Webster, G Wynyard, W Karauria. Third row (standing): P Keogh, T Eyton (treasurer), Arthur Warbrick, G Williams, T Ellison, JR Scott (manager), H Wynyard. Second row (seated): W Anderson, F Warbrick, J Warbrick, E McCausland, H Lee, D Stewart. Front: D Gage, W Elliot, W Wynyard, R Taiaroa.

Fred Alderson had a varied career, representing his native Northumberland county twice (1887-88) and Durham 17 times (1889-94). An outstanding three-quarter, he won the Northumberland County Cup with Tynedale and Durham County Cup with Hartlepool Rovers. He also captained England and had the distinction of representing both the North (5 times) and the South (once), the latter whilst at Cambridge University.

Ernest William Taylor, often referred to as 'EW' or 'Little Billy', was a brilliant half-back in a very successful Rockcliff team, contributing to eight Northumberland County Cup final victories. He represented Northumberland 34 times in the Victorian era (adding further appearances later), the North six and England 14. The latter was a record by a northern-based player during Victorian times, shared with Dicky Lockwood.

The Yorkshire team that took on the Rest of England at Halifax on 23rd February 1889, having been declared inaugural county champions. Back: JW Sykes, M Newsome (president), JT Toothill, FW Lowrie, G Jacketts, JA Miller (honorary secretary), H Wilkinson. Middle: WJ Stadden, RE Lockwood, F Bonsor, H Bedford, JH Jones, E Holmes. Front: J Dodd, JW Sutcliffe, AL Brooke, D Jowett.

Thirteen of Runcorn's players pictured during March 1888, all proudly wearing their Cheshire county caps and jerseys. Back: WH Broady, TH Woods, GT Wainwright, J Lewis, J Clarke, W Wright. Front: WH Cawley, H Hughes, TH Davies, HC Speakman, WA Riley, W Hughes, W Faulkner.

Oldham in 1889-90, the club's first season at Watersheddings. Back: J Darlington, S Pendlebury, J Giles, J Platt (treasurer), GF Holden, F Fitton, C Simpson. Middle: S Taylor (secretary), J Armstrong, J Bennett, W McCutcheon, Jack Hurst, WH Pennington, H Court (umpire). Front: E Blomley, James Hurst, J Thomas, J Nolan, D Gwynn, S Nuttall.

Sam Houghton was a dependable, calm full-back serving Runcorn from 1889 until 1909, excepting the opening months of the 1895-96 season when he briefly transferred allegiance to Birkenhead Wanderers after the former had joined the Northern Union. His list of representative honours were numerous; under the Rugby Union code he played for Cheshire (30 times), the North (4), and England (2), whilst, after rejoining Runcorn in the Northern Union, he added 15 Cheshire appearances.

Fred Lohden was a prominent forward, initially playing for local club Hartlepool Rovers, with whom he won the Durham County Cup in 1889-90 and 1890-91 and twice represented Durham county. From the 1892-93 season he began playing for Blackheath (London) which led to county selection for Surrey and two appearances for the South. In 1893 he was in the England team that opposed Wales at Cardiff Arms Park.

Tom Coop was a full-back who played for Leigh from 1888 to 1898, having begun his career with Tottington. Noted for his excellent tactical and goal-kicking, he achieved numerous representative honours in Rugby Union, playing for Lancashire (21 times including the 1890-91 county championship success), and once each for the North (1890) and England (1892). After Leigh joined the Northern Union in 1895 he made three further appearances for Lancashire.

William Bromet made the first of 17 Yorkshire appearances in 1890. A hard-working forward acclaimed for his dribbling skills, he later represented the North twice, England 12 times, and toured South Africa in 1891, participating in all three internationals against the hosts. After playing for his home-town Tadcaster club he later captained Richmond (London), in whose red, black and old gold jersey he is seen here, a move leading to three matches for the South and further county appearances with Middlesex.

Huddersfield 1889-90, winners of the Yorkshire County Cup. Back (standing): JW Dyson, G Harrop (joint-honorary secretary), WH Eagland, L Littlewood (umpire, in background), FW Richmond, JH Shaw, W Hirst (joint-honorary secretary, in background), JW Thewlis, TH Eagland, JP Crosland (president). Middle (seated): G Mitchell, P Jackson, H Archer, O France, J Schofield. Front: J Kaye, F Walker, W Lorriman, AL Brooke.

Wigan 1889-90, winners of the West Lancashire League and Wigan Union Charity Cup. Back: J Underwood (umpire), J Lowe, T Brayshay, J Hatten, J Slevin, J Halliwell, W Atkinson, E Bullough, J Bibby. Middle: J Telford, E Wardle, Richard 'Dick' Seddon, J Anderton, E Dempsey, Robert 'Bob' Seddon. Front: W Halliwell, J Mitchinson.

Liverpool's Sidney Wilson was regarded as an 'all-round' forward, reputedly skilled as a 'scrummager', line-out specialist, dribbler and place kicker. He appeared nine times for Lancashire from 1891 to 1894, having represented the South in 1890 whilst attached to Oxford University. He later took up refereeing.

Bill McCutcheon was a gifted Welsh three-quarter that joined Oldham from Swansea during December 1888, a move that led to 27 appearances for Lancashire. Unusually for the time, the first of his seven matches for Wales occurred after moving north. He remained with Oldham when they joined the Northern Union breakaway in 1895, continuing to play until 1897. He later refereed, having charge of the Northern Union Challenge Cup Final in 1906 and Championship deciders of 1913 and 1914.

The Northumberland team that played against Yorkshire in Newcastle on 21st November 1891. Back: JA Williamson (honorary secretary), HT Whiteling, W Young, A Styan, H Angus, E Emley, A Benson, W Cail (president). Middle: J Douthwaite, G Robson, S Brutton, JH Greenwell, PH Morrison. Front: R Harris, T Nicholson, EW Taylor, TP Alexander.

Wigan ground, on Wednesday evening next [16th April] when Wigan, as the champion club, will be opposed by a picked team of the Rest of the League. This will afford a capital test of the abilities of the Wigan team, who it will be remembered have defeated most of the best clubs in Lancashire. The Mayor of Wigan will present the Cup to Wigan at the close of the match.' Wigan subsequently won 16-10.[112]

1889-1890 STATISTICS

WEST LANCASHIRE RUGBY LEAGUE

Final table	P	W	D	L	For	Agst	Pts
Wigan	14	13	1	0	215	30	27
Leigh	14	6	3	5	87	72	15
Tyldesley	14	8	1	5	161	108	17
Warrington	14	7	0	7	146	131	14
Walkden	14	5	3	6	124	117	13
Aspull	14	5	3	6	125	175	13
Widnes	14	3	0	11	76	144	6
St Helens	14	3	1	10	71	228	7

CUMBERLAND COUNTY CHALLENGE CUP (12 entries)
Try – 1 point; conversion, penalty goal – 2; drop-goal, field goal, goal from mark – 3.
If equal then majority of 3 minor points required to win.

First Round
Aspatria 16, Cockermouth 0
Broughton 4, Maryport 1
Flimby w/o Bigrigg
Penrith United 2, Workington 6
Byes: Cleator, Crosby, Egremont, Seaton

Second Round
Broughton 2, Aspatria 5
Crosby 6, Workington 7
Egremont w/o Cleator (withdrew)
Flimby 3, Seaton 2

Semi-finals
Egremont 6, Aspatria 0 (at Maryport Cricket Ground)
Flimby 6, Workington 1 (at Egremont Athletic Club Grounds)

FINAL
Saturday 29 March 1890 at the Whitehaven Cricket Ground
EGREMONT 10 *Back*: T Adair (2c). *Three-quarters*: W Selkirk (capt), H Wallace, G Bowman (t). *Half-backs*: J Armstrong (2t), I Stamper. *Forwards*: L Cook (2t), W Cross (t), W Elliott, S Farrer, J Hyland, D Mulholland, W Parker, BT Rowe, H Simpson.
FLIMBY 0 *Back*: J Addison. *Three-quarters*: W Denwood, R Addison, T Whitehead. *Half-backs*: JW Holliday, W Stephenson. *Forwards*: G Addison, J Bethwaite, D Clark, G Crellin, JB Crellin, W Hodgson, G Southern, J Varty (capt), T Varty.
Attendance: 3,000   *Referee*: AM Crook (Manchester)

DURHAM COUNTY CHALLENGE CUP (16 entries)
Most goals wins. If equal, most tries. If still equal, majority of 3 minor points.

First Round
Consett 1g, Boldon 1g, 1t
Gateshead Institute 2t, Henderson's Wanderers 0
Hartlepool Rangers 3t, Sunderland 0 (replay ordered after protest)
Houghton-le-Spring w/o Hartlepool YMCA (disbanded)
North Durham 1g, 1t, Stockton 1t
Tudhoe 1t, Throston Wanderers (Hartlepool) 0
West Hartlepool 3g, 1t, Durham City 1t
Westoe 0, Hartlepool Rovers 2g, 4t

First Round Replay
Hartlepool Rangers 2t, Sunderland 0

Second Round
Gatehead Institute 0, Boldon 1g, 1t
Hartlepool Rangers 1g, 3t, Houghton-le-Spring 0
Hartlepool Rovers 1g, 3t, West Hartlepool 0
North Durham 0, Tudhoe 2t

Semi-finals
Boldon 1t, Hartlepool Rangers 1g
Tudhoe 1t, Hartlepool Rovers 6g, 2t

FINAL
Saturday 29 March 1890 at Friarage Field, Hartlepool
HARTLEPOOL ROVERS 6 goals, 2 tries *Back*: JW Horn. *Three-quarters*: D McPherson (t), WE Kassell (2t, 6c), FHR Alderson (t), AE Emmerson (t). *Half-backs*: JJ Rennie, AC Scott. *Forwards*: GE Boagey, J Coates, A Hill (capt, t), CM Huntley, FC Lohden, FE Pease (t), J Snowdon, W Yiend (t).
HARTLEPOOL RANGERS 1 goal *Back*: R Robinson. *Three-quarters*: R Dixon, W Davis, A Burdon. *Half-backs*: H Mulvey, J Nesbitt. *Forwards*: R Benvin, F Collins, T Emmerson, F Fleming (c), J Hastings, G Heppinstall (t), MH Horsley, R Mulvey, C Thompson (capt).
Attendance: 6,000   *Referee*: A Cattell (Sheffield)

NORTHUMBERLAND COUNTY FOOTBALL CHALLENGE CUP (8 entries)
Most goals wins. If equal, most tries.

First Round
Northern 0, North Elswick 1t
Northumberland FC 1g, 2t, Tynedale 1t
Percy Park w/o Benwell (withdrew)
Rockcliff 7g, 3t, Newcastle Rangers 0

Semi-finals
Percy Park 0, North Elswick 1t
Rockcliff 2g, 1t, Northumberland FC 1g

FINAL
Saturday 5 April 1890 at Jesmond Ground, Newcastle
ROCKCLIFF 3 goals, 4 tries *Back*: WB Shaw. *Three-quarters*: W Taylor (3t), S Brutton (t, dg), T Nicholson. *Half-backs*: EW Taylor (2c), J Winship. *Forwards*: Alf Benson, J Bolam (t), JH Greenwell, CH Hamilton (capt), C Lattimer, F Lattimer (t), Phillips, G Robson, HJ Vine.
NORTH ELSWICK 0 *Back*: B Oubridge. *Three-quarters*: W Bentham, H Haslam, H Wilkinson. *Half-backs*: W Curley, H Welford (capt). *Forwards*: J Carr, T Curtis, W Douglas, GA Highton, W Lattimer, GW Mole, TE Naish, A Sutton, E Taylor.
Attendance: 4,000   *Referee*: n/a

YORKSHIRE COUNTY FOOTBALL CHALLENGE CUP (107 entries)

Most goals wins (3 tries count as one 'goal'). If equal, most tries (excluding any already counted as equalling a 'goal'). If still equal, majority of 3 minor points.

Preliminary Round

Alverthorpe w/o Hull Southcoates (disbanded)
Buslingthorpe 4g, 2t, Keighley Shamrocks 0
Calverley w/o Leeds Rifles (disbanded)
Crosland Moor 1g, 1t, Saltaire 4g, 4t
Doncaster Town 1g, 1t, Lindley 0
Elland 1g, 2t, Armley 1t
Kippax 1t, Bankfoot 0
Knottingley Free Wanderers 1t,
Normanton St John's 2g, 3t
Mirfield Rangers 0, Newtown 2g, 2t
South Milford 3g, 2t, Laisterdyke 1t
Whitwood 3g, 1t, Bradford Britannia 0
Byes: 53 teams drew a bye to next round

Qualifying Round

Alverthorpe 4t, Birstall 0
Bingley 2g, 3t, Primrose Hill 1t
Bowling 1g, 4t, Knaresborough 0
Bradford Trinity 2g, 1t, Greetland 2g, 1t (mp: 0-6)
Buslingthorpe 2g, 1t, Methley 1g, 1t
Dobcross 0, Churwell 5g, 1t
Dudley Hill 2g, 3t, Lockwood 1t
Elland 3t, Kirkburton 0
Guiseley 1g, Horsforth 1g (mp: 8-2)
Heaton 0, Harrogate 1g, 1t
Hebden Bridge 1t, Sowerby Bridge 1g, 1t
Hipperholme and Lightcliffe 2g, 2t, Stanningley 1g, 1t
Horbury 2t, Doncaster Town 1t
Idle w/o Castleford Hornets
Ingrow 1g, 2t, Low Moor St Mark's 1g, 3t
Keighley Zingari 1g, Skipton 1g (mp: 0-9)
Kippax 2g, 4t, Yeadon 1t
Leeds East End 2t, Todmorden 1g
Newtown 2g, 1t, Dodworth 0
Normanton 1t, Wakefield St Austin's 0
Normanton St John's 1g, 1t, Barnsley 0
Outwood Church 1t, Silsden 0
Pateley Bridge 1g, Wibsey Slack Side 1g, 2t
Ravensthorpe 1g, 3t, Calverley 0
Ripon 2g, 6t, Yorkshire College (Leeds) 0
Saltaire 7g, 2t, Mytholmroyd 0
Salterbebble 1t, Windhill 1t (mp: 8-4, aet)
Shepley 1t, Paddock 1g, 2t
South Milford 1g, 1t, Manningham Rangers 1g, 2t
Tadcaster 1g, Buttershaw 1g, 4t
Whitwood 2g, 2t, Bowling Old Lane 1g, 1t
Woodhouse 4t, Wibsey 0

First Round

(* indicates 32 teams seeded to this round)
Alverthorpe 2g, Guiseley 1g
Batley* 1t, Manningham* 0
Bowling 2t, Mirfield* 0
Bradford* 1g, 1t, Dewsbury* 1t
Bramley* 1g, 4t, Leeds Parish Church* 1g
Brighouse Rangers* 1g, 2t, Pontefract* 1t
Buttershaw 2t, Holbeck* 1g, 1t (replay ordered after protest)
Castleford* 2g, 2t, Keighley* 0
Churwell 1g, Wibsey Slack Side 1t
Greetland 1g, Leeds St John's* 2g, 1t
Halifax* 3t, Thornes* 0
Harrogate 0, Salterhebble 1g
Huddersfield* 8g, 9t, Idle 0
Hull* 1g, 5t, Normanton St John's 0
Hunslet* 14g, 1t, Dudley Hill 0
Kirkstall* 2t, Elland 2g
Liversedge* 3g, 4t, Kippax 1t
Morley* 1g, 1t, Heckmondwike* 0
Normanton 1g, 2t, Bingley 1g, 1t
Ossett* 4t, Hipperholme and Lightcliffe 1t
Otley* 3g, 4t, Buslingthorpe 1t
Outwood Church 3g, 3t, Horbury 1g

First Round *continued*

Ripon 2t, Cleckheaton* 1g, 3t
Ravensthorpe 1t, Selby* 0
Saltaire 6g, 3t, Todmorden 0
Shipley* 1g, Paddock 2g, 1t
Skipton 1g, 1t, Newtown 1g, 1t (mp: 8-0)
South Milford 0, Goole* 1g
Sowerby Bridge 1g, 1t, York* 1g (replay ordered after protest)
Whitwood 1g, 1t, Pudsey* 2t (replay ordered after protest)
Woodhouse 3g, 3t, Low Moor St Mark's 0
Wortley* 0, Wakefield Trinity* 1t

First Round Replays

Buttershaw 1g, 3t, Holbeck 1g, 1t (at Manningham)
Sowerby Bridge 0, York 1t (at Leeds)
Whitwood 2g, Pudsey 1g, 1t

Second Round

Bradford 6g, 4t, Woodhouse 1g
Buttershaw 3t, Churwell 1t
Goole 3g, 4t, Whitwood 1g, 1t
Halifax 3t, Hull 1t
Hunslet 2g, 5t, Ossett 0
Leeds St John's 2g, 1t, Castleford 3g, 1t
Liversedge 0, Brighouse Rangers 0 (abandoned due to storm, replay ordered)
Morley 1t, Huddersfield 2g, 1t
Normanton 3g, 2t, Ravensthorpe 1t
Otley 2t, Bowling 1g
Paddock 1t, Bramley 1g
Saltaire 2t, Alverthorpe 2g, 1t
Salterhebble 1t, Batley 2g, 2t
Skipton 0, Cleckheaton 1t
Wakefield Trinity 4g, 3t, Elland 0
York 1t, Outwood Church 0

Second Round Replay

Liversedge 1t, Brighouse Rangers 1g, 2t (at Halifax)

Third Round

Alverthorpe 1g, 1t, Bowling 1g, 1t (mp: 8-3)
Brighouse Rangers 5g, 1t, Bramley 1g, 1t
Buttershaw 0, Bradford 2g, 5t
Castleford 1g, 1t, Hunslet 2g, 2t
Cleckheaton 1g, 1t, Normanton 1g, 1t (mp: 11-7, replay ordered after protest)
Goole 0, Halifax 1t
Huddersfield 3g, 1t, York 1g, 1t
Wakefield Trinity 1g, 1t, Batley 1t

Third Round Replay

Cleckheaton 1g, Normanton 2g, 1t (at Holbeck)

Fourth Round

Bradford 1g, 2t, Brighouse Rangers 1t
Huddersfield 3g, 7t, Alverthorpe 1g, 1t
Hunslet 2g, Halifax 2g (mp: 5-2)
Normanton 1t, Wakefield Trinity 2g

Semi-finals

Huddersfield 5g, 3t, Hunslet 1t (at Crown Flatts, Dewsbury)
Wakefield Trinity 1g, 1t, Bradford 0 (at Crown Point, Leeds)

FINAL

Saturday 5 April 1890 at Thrum Hall, Halifax
HUDDERSFIELD 1 goal *Back*: WH Eagland. *Three-quarters*: JW Dyson, FW Richmond (t), AL Brooke (c). *Half-backs*: H Archer (capt), J Kaye. *Forwards*: TH Eagland, O France, P Jackson, W Lorriman, G Mitchell, J Schofield, J Shaw, JW Thewlis, F Walker.
WAKEFIELD TRINITY 0 *Back*: H Stafford. *Three-quarters*: H Fallas (capt), JH Fotherby, M Varley. *Half-backs*: H Dawson, JH Thompson. *Forwards*: W Binks, P Booth, R Dawson, A Garforth, JE Gomersall, JH Jones, J Lathom, A Thompson, H Whiteley.
Attendance: 15,000   *Referee*: EB Holmes (Midland Counties RU President)

COUNTY MATCHES

Monday 21 October 1889 at Valley Parade, Bradford
YORKSHIRE COLTS 1 goal, 1 try *Back*: S Mawson (Otley). *Three-quarters*: JW Dyson (Hud), W Fisher (capt, Livs, c), I Newton (Mann). *Half-backs*: H Barker (Livs), G Scholefield (Hal). *Forwards*: W Harrison (Mann), P Jackson (Hud, t), J Leeming (Hull), W Lorryman (Dew), GB Naylor (LeeStJ), J Richards (Brad), JR Shaw (Pont), S Todd (Mor, t), RF Turner (LeePC).
CUMBERLAND 1 goal *Back*: J Moore (Mil, c). *Three-quarters*: JJ Mitchell (Cock/EdinU), CW Dove (Mil), W Selkirk (Egr). *Half-backs*: W Coulthard (Mary, t), J Murchie (Work). *Forwards*: JH Buckett (Mil), G Cuthell (Work), Jim Davidson (Asp), J Holme (Mil), J Hyland (Egr), J Lewthwaite (Mary), WH Mackereth (PenU), J Mumberson (Asp), J Thompson (Mary).
Attendance: 'moderate'   *Referee*: TR Sutton (Lancashire)

Saturday 26 October 1889 at Jesmond Ground, Newcastle
NORTHUMBERLAND 0 *Back*: H Haslam (NEls). *Three-quarters*: CS Gill (Nor), E Emley (Nor), F Finney (PerPk). *Half-backs*: T Stewart (PerPk), EW Taylor (Rock). *Forwards*: T Anderson (Nor), A Benson (Rock), G Brewis (NorFC), T Gee (capt, PerPk), J Livingstone (Nor), F Marshall (PerPk), GW Mole (NEls), C Scott (Nor), A Styan (Rock).
CUMBERLAND 1 goal *Back*: J Moore (Mil). *Three-quarters*: I Moore (Mil, dg), F Telford (Asp), TH Hodgkinson (CarlC). *Half-backs*: W Coulthard (Mary), J Murchie (Work). *Forwards*: JH Buckett (Mil), W Cross (Egr), J Holme (Mil), J Hyland (Egr), R Leck (Mil), J Lewthwaite (Mary), WH Mackereth (PenU), J Rumney (Asp), John Wilson (Work).
Attendance: 1,500   *Referee*: WH Humphreys (Durham)
Note: Northumberland began one player short due to non-arrival of J. H. Greenwell, G. Brewis taking his place during the second half.

Thursday 31 October 1889 at Maude's Meadow, Kendal
WESTMORLAND 1 goal, 1 try *Back*: T Hine (KenH). *Three-quarters*: JK Robinson (KirkL), J Allen (KenH), J Armstrong (KenH). *Half-backs*: R Chorley (KenT, t), RS Winskill (KenH). *Forwards*: J Atkinson (KenH), RC Beard (KenH, t), F Heap (KenH), G Machell (KenT), RH Moore (Amb), R Nicholson (KenT, c), J Parkinson (KenT), J Shepherd (KenT), JW Wilkinson (KenH).
CHESHIRE 2 goals *Back*: J Bancroft (Duk). *Three-quarters*: JT Haslam (Duk), JH Crompton (Run, 2t, 2c), WH Male (NewB). *Half-backs*: W Evans (Run), H Hughes (Run). *Forwards*: HA Howes (Sale), W Hughes (Run), RF Moodie (BirkPk), RP Moodie (BirkPk), R Morton (Alt), C Schofield (Alt), AG Wood (BirkPk).
Attendance: n/a   *Referee*: n/a.   *Note*: Names for two Cheshire forwards not reported.

Saturday 9 November 1889 at Whalley Range, Manchester
LANCASHIRE 3 goals, 3 tries *Back*: AG Paul (Swi, 2c, gm). *Three-quarters*: J Valentine (Swi, 2t), JH Marsh (Swi), EH Flower (Bro/Moss, t). *Half-backs*: J Mills (capt, Swi), J Nolan (Old). *Forwards*: C Anderton (ManFW), W Atkinson (Wig), Herbert Hasleham (ManR, t), CH Horley (Swi), N Hotchkiss (Swi), T Kent (Sal), T Melledew (RochH, t), T Whittaker (Man), G Woodward (Tyl).
CHESHIRE 2 tries *Back*: J Bancroft (Duk). *Three-quarters*: JH Crompton (Run, 2t), WH Male (NewB), JT Haslam (Duk). *Half-backs*: W Evans (Run), H Hughes (capt, Run). *Forwards*: R Dolan (Run), W Faulkner (Run), A Hampson (Run), WF Hancock (Run), HA Howes (Sale), W Hughes (Run), PH Lockwood (BirkPk), RP Moodie (BirkPk), AG Wood (BirkPk).
Attendance: 5,000   *Referee*: GR Hill (RFU Honorary Secretary)

Saturday 9 November 1889 at Crown Point, Leeds
YORKSHIRE 4 goals, 1 try *Back*: WH Eagland (Hud, 4c). *Three-quarters*: P Robertshaw (Brad), J Dyson (Hud, t), F Firth (BrigR). *Half-backs*: WJ Stadden (Dew), M Wise (Otley, t). *Forwards*: H Bedford (Mor), T Else (Paddock), JL Hickson (capt, Brad), E Holmes (Mann), FW Lowrie (Bat), J Richards (Brad, t), S Todd (Mor), JT Toothill (Brad, 2t), H Wilkinson (Hal).
DURHAM 1 try *Back*: WH Bell (Sund). *Three-quarters*: TAF Crow (Sund, t), FHR Alderson (HartR), WE Kassell (HartR). *Half-backs*: J Branfoot (Sund), AC Scott (HartR). *Forwards*: T Faulkner (Tud), A Hill (HartR), F Jones (NDur), FE Pease (HartR), FW Ranken (Sund), JT Wetherell (DurC), J Wheatley (Hou), CTB Wilkinson (DurC), W Yiend (HartR).
Attendance: 8,000   *Referee*: R Westray (Cumberland)

Saturday 16 November 1889 at Salthouse Road, Millom
CUMBERLAND 4 tries *Back*: J Moore (Mil). *Three-quarters*: I Moore (Mil, t), F Telford (Asp), TH Hodgkinson (CarlC). *Half-backs*: W Coulthard (Mary, t), J Murchie (Work). *Forwards*: Jim Davidson (Asp), T Hodgson (Work), J Holme (Mil, 2t), E Houston (Sea), J Lewthwaite (Mary), D Lowrey (Whi), J Mumberson (Asp), J Rumney (Asp), WT Smith (Mary).
WESTMORLAND 0 *Back*: WG Hoggarth (KenT). *Three-quarters*: J Armstrong (KenH), GH Bell (KenT), JK Robinson (capt, KirkL). *Half-backs*: W Berry (KenH), RS Winskill (KenH). *Forwards*: RC Beard (KenH), G Graham (KenT), F Heap (KenH), T Lupton (KirkL), R Moreton (KenT), A Park (KirkL), WJ Parsons (KenH), E Wilson (KenH), W Woodhouse (KirkL).
Attendance: 1,000   *Referee*: J Clegge (Lancashire)

Saturday 16 November 1889 at Jesmond Ground, Newcastle
NORTHUMBERLAND 1 try *Back*: H Haslam (NEls). *Three-quarters*: F Finney (PerPk), E Emley (Nor), CS Gill (Nor). *Half-backs*: MT Scott (Nor, t), T Stewart (PerPk). *Forwards*: T Anderson (Nor), A Gee (PerPk), T Gee (capt, PerPk), JH Greenwell (Rock), CW Harrison (Tynd), J Livingstone (Nor), F Marshall (PerPk), GW Mole (NEls), C Scott (Nor).
YORKSHIRE 1 goal, 4 tries *Back*: WH Eagland (Hud, c). *Three-quarters*: J Dyson (Hud, t), F Firth (BrigR), C Hammond (Cas). *Half-backs*: WJ Stadden (Dew), M Wise (Otley, t). *Forwards*: H Bedford (Mor), JL Hickson (capt, Brad, t), E Holmes (Mann), G Jacketts (Hull), JH Jones (Wak), FW Lowrie (Bat, t), J Richards (Brad), S Todd (Mor), JT Toothill (Brad, t).
Attendance: 3,000   *Referee*: T Swinburne (Durham)

Saturday 23 November 1889 at Park Avenue, Bradford
YORKSHIRE 1 goal *Back*: WH Eagland (Hud, c). *Three-quarters*: AL Brooke (Hud),
J Dyson (Hud), F Firth (BrigR). *Half-backs*: WJ Stadden (Dew), J Wright (Brad, t).
Forwards: H Bedford (Mor), JL Hickson (capt, Brad), E Holmes (Mann), G Jacketts (Hull),
JH Jones (Wak), FW Lowrie (Bat), J Richards (Brad), JT Toothill (Brad), H Wilkinson (Hal).
LANCASHIRE 0 *Back*: A Royle (BroR). *Three-quarters*: J Valentine (Swi), JH Marsh (Swi),
J Anderton (Wig). *Half-backs*: W Bumby (Swi), J Mills (capt, Swi). *Forwards*: C Anderton
(ManFW), W Atkinson (Wig), E Bullough (Wig), Herbert Hasleham (ManR), CH Horley
(Swi), T Kent (Sal), T Melledew (RochH), P Steel (Man), T Whittaker (Man).
Attendance: 15,000   *Referee*: GR Hill (RFU Honorary Secretary)

Saturday 30 November 1889 at Upper Park, Birkenhead
CHESHIRE 2 goals *Back*: JT Haslam (Duk). *Three-quarters*: WH Male (NewB),
JH Crompton (Run, 2c), W Stephens (Sale). *Half-backs*: W Evans (Run), H Hughes (Run).
Forwards: R Dolan (Run), W Faulkner (Run), A Hampson (Run), WF Hancock (Run, t),
HA Howes (Sale), W Hughes (Run), PH Lockwood (BirkPk), RP Moodie (BirkPk, t),
AG Wood (BirkPk).
DURHAM 4 goals, 1 try *Back*: WH Bell (Sund). *Three-quarters*: TAF Crow (Sund, t),
FHR Alderson (HartR), WE Kassell (HartR, t, 2c). *Half-backs*: FCL Hamilton (DurU, t),
G Smith (HartR). *Forwards*: CW Burn (Sund), T Faulkner (Tud), A Hill (HartR, t, c),
F Jones (NDur), F Lumsden (DurC), FE Pease (HartR), J Wheatley (Hou, dg),
CTB Wilkinson (DurC), W Yiend (HartR).
Attendance: 4,000   *Referee*: JH Payne (Lancashire)

Saturday 30 November 1889 at Whalley Range, Manchester
LANCASHIRE 2 goals, 4 tries *Back*: A Royle (BroR). *Three-quarters*: J Valentine (Swi, 3t,
2c), EH Flower (Bro/Moss, 2t), JR Harley (Bar, t). *Half-backs*: W Bumby (Swi), J Mills (capt,
Swi). *Forwards*: C Anderton (ManFW), W Atkinson (Wig), E Bullough (Wig), Herbert
Hasleham (ManR), CH Horley (Swi), T Kent (Sal), T Melledew (RochH), P Steel (Man),
GF Wormald (Bro).
NORTHUMBERLAND 1 goal *Back*: H Haslam (NEls). *Three-quarters*: F Finney (PerPk),
W Taylor (Rock), W Curley (NEls). *Half-backs*: MT Scott (Nor, t), T Stewart (PerPk).
Forwards: T Anderson (Nor), A Gee (PerPk), T Gee (capt, PerPk, c), JH Greenwell (Rock),
CW Harrison (Tynd), F Marshall (PerPk), GW Mole (NEls), CA Ridley (Nor), C Scott (Nor).
Attendance: 3,000   *Referee*: R Westray (Cumberland)

Monday 9 December 1889 at Thrum Hall, Halifax
YORKSHIRE 0 *Back*: WH Eagland (Hud). *Three-quarters*: AL Brooke (Hud), W Fisher
(Livs), J Dyson (Hud). *Half-backs*: M Wise (Otley), J Wright (Brad). *Forwards*: H Bedford
(Mor), EB Clarke (York), JL Hickson (capt, Brad), E Holmes (Mann), G Jacketts (Hull),
FW Lowrie (Bat), J Richards (Brad), JT Toothill (Brad), H Wilkinson (Hal).
MIDDLESEX 0 *Back*: C Moggridge (CamU/MidW). *Three-quarters*: AE Stoddart
(capt, Black), JA Gould (Rich), E Coulman (Rich). *Half-backs*: DG Anderson (LonS),
W Wotherspoon (CamU). *Forwards*: FC Cousins (Rich), FW Goodhue (LonS),
J Hammond (Black), GL Jeffery (Black), ROB Lane (OxfU), TW Lockwood (MidW),
A Robinson (Black), AA Surtees (Harl), RL Thomas (LonW).
Attendance: 5,000   *Referee*: AN Hornby (Lancashire)

Monday 16 December 1889 at Belle Vue, Wakefield
YORKSHIRE 2 goals, 4 tries *Back*: WH Eagland (Hud, c). *Three-quarters*: SN Eastwood (BrigR, 2t, c), HW Rhodes (York), J Dyson (Hud, 2t). *Half-backs*: Jim Naylor (Bat), J Wright (Brad). *Forwards*: H Bedford (Mor, 2t), P Booth (Wak), GO Brooke (Cas), FH Clay (Hal), JL Hickson (capt, Brad), G Jacketts (Hull), FW Lowrie (Bat), GB Naylor (LeeStJ), J Richards (Brad).
SURREY 1 goal, 1 try *Back*: AS Gedge (StTHosp). *Three-quarters*: AB Whitehead (OLey, t), ML McEwan (RMC, t), R Allport (ClapR), SE Hubbard (Croy). *Half-backs*: LH Gunnery (OMT), EW Senior (StTHosp). *Forwards*: WP Carpmael (capt, Black), W Daniel (LonW), TAM Forde (Harl), AH Gentle (StTHosp), DH Helps (Croy), WL Morgan (LonW), FC Nesbitt (RMC, c), WW Skilbeck (ClapR).
Attendance: 3,000   *Referee*: Rev F Marshall (Yorkshire)

Saturday 4 January 1890 at Wellington
SOMERSETSHIRE 0 *Back*: H Merry (Well). *Three-quarters*: FC Duckworth (Wes), CJB Moneypenny (Bath), SC Smith (Wes). *Half-backs*: FH Fox (Well), TN Parham (Bath). *Forwards*: J Aldridge (Wes), WH D'Ath (Yeo), EL Hancock (Wivel), PF Hancock (Wivel/Black), WH Manfield (Well), F Soane (Bath), H Smith (Wes), CJ Vernon (Well), SMJ Woods (Bridg/CamU).
YORKSHIRE 1 try *Back*: S Mawson (Otley). *Three-quarters*: AL Brooke (capt, Hud), I Newton (Mann), SN Eastwood (BrigR). *Half-backs*: Jim Naylor (Bat), J Wright (Brad). *Forwards*: H Bedford (Mor), FH Clay (Hal), E Holmes (Mann), G Jacketts (Hull), JH Jones (Wak), FW Lowrie (Bat, t), W Nichol (BrigR), J Richards (Brad), JT Toothill (Brad).
Attendance: 3,000   *Referee*: H Vassall (RFU Honorary Treasurer)

Monday 6 January 1890 at Clarence Street, York
YORKSHIRE 2 goals, 2 tries *Back*: S Mawson (Otley). *Three-quarters*: AL Brooke (capt, Hud), I Newton (Mann), SN Eastwood (BrigR, t). *Half-backs*: Jim Naylor (Bat), J Wright (Brad, t, 2c). *Forwards*: H Bedford (Mor), FH Clay (Hal), E Holmes (Mann), G Jacketts (Hull), JH Jones (Wak), FW Lowrie (Bat), W Nichol (BrigR), J Richards (Brad, t), JT Toothill (Brad, t).
KENT 0 *Back*: E Bromet (StTHosp). *Three-quarters*: P Christopherson (Black), GC Hubbard (Black), RL Aston (Black/CamU). *Half-backs*: AC Smith (Sydenham), EF Rowsall (Ken). *Forwards*: H Bone (RNC/WickPk), RD Budworth (Black/OxfU), VC le Fanu (Rich), S Kent (Harl), WJ McCanlis (London Caledonians), FJ Nisbet (GuyHosp), EHG North (Black/OxfU), HE Stanton (RA), AFV Wild (Ken).
Attendance: 4,000   *Referee*: JA Miller (Yorkshire)

Saturday 11 January 1890 at The Recreation Grounds, Weston-super-Mare
SOMERSETSHIRE 1 goal, 1 try *Back*: R Sweet-Escott (Car). *Three-quarters*: H Merry (Well), CJB Moneypenny (Bath), SC Smith (Wes). *Half-backs*: FC Duckworth (Wes), FH Fox (Well). *Forwards*: J Aldridge (Wes), WH D'Ath (Yeo), RA Clarke (Tau), EL Hancock (Wivel), L Hancock (Wivel, 2t), PF Hancock (Wivel/Black), WH Manfield (Well, c), F Soane (Bath), CJ Vernon (Well).
LANCASHIRE 2 goals, 2 tries *Back*: W Manwaring (Sal). *Three-quarters*: J Valentine (Swi, 3t, 2c), JH Marsh (Swi, t), EH Flower (Bro/Moss). *Half-backs*: W Bumby (Swi), J Mills (capt, Swi). *Forwards*: C Anderton (ManFW), W Atkinson (Wig), E Bullough (Wig),

H Eagles (Sal), Herbert Hasleham (ManR), CH Horley (Swi), T Melledew (RochH),
W Waugh (RochStC), T Whittaker (Man).
Attendance: 1,000   *Referee*: F Cattall (Yorkshire)

Saturday 25 January 1890 at Friarage Field, Hartlepool
DURHAM 0 *Back*: WH Bell (Sund). *Three-quarters*: TAF Crow (Sund), FHR Alderson (HartR), AE Emmerson (HartR). *Half-backs*: FCL Hamilton (DurU), G Smith (HartR). *Forwards*: B Cox (Sund), A Hill (HartR), F Lumsden (DurC), T Parker (Sund), FE Pease (HartR), JT Wetherell (DurC), J Wheatley (Hou), CTB Wilkinson (DurC), W Yiend (HartR).
LANCASHIRE 1 try *Back*: W Manwaring (Sal). *Three-quarters*: EH Flower (Bro/Moss), J Valentine (Swi), JH Marsh (Swi). *Half-backs*: W Bumby (Swi), J Mills (Swi). *Forwards*: C Anderton (ManFW), W Atkinson (Wig), E Bullough (Wig), H Eagles (Sal), Herbert Hasleham (ManR), CH Horley (Swi), T Kent (Sal, t), T Melledew (RochH), T Whittaker (Man).
Attendance: 7,000   *Referee:* GR Hill (RFU Honorary Secretary)

Saturday 25 January 1890 at Jesmond Ground, Newcastle
NORTHUMBERLAND 2 goals, 1 try *Back*: H Haslam (NEls). *Three-quarters*: W Taylor (Rock), E Emley (Nor), RE Herbertson (PerPk, t). *Half-backs*: MT Scott (Nor, dg), T Stewart (PerPk). *Forwards*: A Gee (PerPk), T Gee (capt, PerPk, gm), JH Greenwell (Rock), CW Harrison (Tynd), J Livingstone (Nor), JJ McIntyre (Tynd), F Marshall (PerPk), GW Mole (NEls), C Scott (Nor).
CHESHIRE 1 goal, 1 try *Back*: JW Brazendale (Run, c). *Three-quarters*: JT Haslam (Duk, t), WH Male (NewB), FP Jones (NewB). *Half-backs*: H Hughes (Run, t), FW Spence (BirkPk). *Forwards*: R Dolan (Run), RB Eskrigge (NewB), W Faulkner (Run), A Hampson (Run), WF Hancock (Run), PH Lockwood (BirkPk), P Riley (Run), C Schofield (Stock), WA Williams (NewB).
Attendance: 'large'   *Referee*: WH Humphreys (Durham)

Saturday 8 February 1890 at Upper Park, Birkenhead
CHESHIRE 1 goal, 1 try *Back*: JT Haslam (Duk). *Three-quarters*: FP Jones (NewB), JH Crompton (Run, t, c), WH Male (NewB). *Half-backs*: H Hughes (capt, Run), FW Spence (BirkPk, t). *Forwards*: R Dolan (Run), W Faulkner (Run), W Hughes (Run), PH Lockwood (BirkPk), RF Muir (NewB), P Riley (Run), C Schofield (Stock), WA Williams (NewB), AG Wood (BirkPk).
YORKSHIRE 4 tries *Back*: WH Eagland (Hud). *Three-quarters*: AL Brooke (Hud), RE Lockwood (Heck, t), J Dyson (Hud). *Half-backs*: Jim Naylor (Bat, 2t), WJ Stadden (Dew). *Forwards*: H Bedford (Mor), GO Brooke (Cas), JL Hickson (capt, Brad), E Holmes (Mann), JH Jones (Wak), D Jowett (Heck, t), W Lorryman (Dew), FW Lowrie (Bat), W Nichol (BrigR).
Attendance: 5,000   *Referee*: AN Hornby (Lancashire)
Note: Match drawn; 3 tries equal 1 goal.

Saturday 8 February 1890 at Ashbrooke Ground, Sunderland
DURHAM 3 tries *Back*: WH Bell (Sund). *Three-quarters*: TAF Crow (Sund, t), FHR Alderson (HartR, t), AE Emmerson (HartR). *Half-backs*: AC Scott (HartR, t), G Smith (HartR). *Forwards*: CW Burn (Sund), B Cox (Sund), A Hill (HartR), F Lumsden (DurC),

T Parker (Sund), FE Pease (HartR), J Wheatley (Hou), CTB Wilkinson (DurC), W Yiend (HartR).
NORTHUMBERLAND 1 try *Back*: H Haslam (NEls). *Three-quarters*: RE Herbertson (PerPk), E Emley (Nor), W Curley (NEls). *Half-backs*: MT Scott (Nor), T Stewart (PerPk). *Forwards*: H Angus (Nor), A Benson (Rock), A Gee (PerPk, t), T Gee (PerPk), JH Greenwell (Rock), J Livingstone (Nor), JJ McIntyre (Tynd), GW Mole (NEls), C Scott (Nor).
Attendance: 2,000   *Referee*: F Cattall (Yorkshire)

Thursday 13 February 1890 at Wigan Cricket Ground, Frog Lane
LANCASHIRE 2 tries *Back*: W Manwaring (Sal). *Three-quarters*: W Kendal (Ask), JH Marsh (Swi, t), W Hastings (RochH). *Half-backs*: W Bumby (Swi), J Mills (Swi). *Forwards*: W Atkinson (Wig), E Bullough (Wig), H Eagles (Sal), CH Horley (Swi), T Kent (Sal), T Melledew (RochH), W Waugh (RochStC, t), T Whittaker (Man), GF Wormald (Bro).
WESTMORLAND 1 goal, 2 tries *Back*: WG Hoggarth (KenT). *Three-quarters*: J Armstrong (capt, KenH, t), J Berry (Tyl), JK Robinson (KirkL). *Half-backs*: W Cross (StH, dg), W Ewan (KenT). *Forwards*: RC Beard (KenH), J Carradus (KenT), G Graham (KenT), P Ireland (KenT), G Machell (KenT), R Moreton (KenT, t), R Nicholson (KenT), E Wilson (KenH), RS Winskill (KenH).
Attendance: 2,500   *Referee*: n/a

Thursday 27 February 1890 at Whitehaven Cricket Ground
CUMBERLAND 0 *Back*: J Moore (Mil). *Three-quarters*: W Selkirk (Egr), DN Pape (Work), JJ Mitchell (Cock/EdinU). *Half-backs*: J Armstrong (Egr), J Murchie (Work). *Forwards*: JH Buckett (Mil), G Cuthell (Work), Jim Davidson (Asp), J Holme (Mil), M Humphrey (Mary), J Hyland (Egr), D Lowrey (Whi), J Pender (PenU), C Simpson (Cock/EdinU).
LANCASHIRE 2 goals, 1 try *Back*: W Manwaring (Sal). *Three-quarters*: F Miles (Sal), JH Marsh (Swi), J Hurst (Old). *Half-backs*: W Bumby (Swi), J Mills (Swi). *Forwards*: A Ashworth (Moss), W Atkinson (Wig), E Bullough (Wig, t), H Eagles (Sal), CH Horley (Swi), J Jackson (BroR), T Kent (Sal, t), T Melledew (RochH), AG Paul (Swi, c, pg).
Attendance: 5,000   *Referee*: AB Perkins (Yorkshire)

Saturday 22 March 1890 at Ormeau, Belfast
ULSTER 1 goal *Back*: DB Walkington (NIFC). *Half-backs*: S Lee (RBAI), LJ Holmes (Rugby), RW Dunlop (NIFC). *Quarter-backs*: John Moffatt (BelA), W Monypenny (QCB). *Forwards*: E Blow (NIFC), J Bristow (NIFC), S Ferguson (BelA), HJ Johnston (NIFC), JN Lytle (NIFC, c), HW Major (Rugby), RH Mayne (BelA), James Moffatt (BelA), RF Young (QCB, t).
LANCASHIRE 1 try *Back*: T Coop (Lei). *Three-quarters*: J Valentine (Swi), JH Marsh (Swi), F Miles (Sal). *Half-backs*: W Bumby (Swi), J Pilkington (StHR). *Forwards*: A Ashworth (Moss), W Atkinson (Wig), H Eagles (Sal), Herbert Hasleham (ManR), CH Horley (Swi), T Kent (Sal, t), T Melledew (RochH), AG Paul (Swi), P Steel (Man).
Attendance: 'small'   *Referee*: J Chambers (Ireland)

Milestones & Stats 1869-1901 199

COUNTY CHAMPIONSHIP
Yorkshire declared county champions for the second consecutive season based on their record of having won six and drawn two of its eight inter-county fixtures.

COUNTY CHAMPIONS v THE REST

Saturday 22 February 1890 at Park Avenue, Bradford
YORKSHIRE 1 goal, 3 tries *Back*: S Mawson (Otley). *Three-quarters*: J Dyson (Hud, 2t), SN Eastwood (BrigR), AL Brooke (Hud, c). *Half-backs*: Jim Naylor (Bat), WJ Stadden (Dew). *Forwards*: H Bedford (Mor), JL Hickson (capt, Brad, t), E Holmes (Mann), G Jacketts (Hull), JH Jones (Wak), D Jowett (Heck, t), W Nichol (BrigR), J Richards (Brad), JT Toothill (Brad).
REST OF ENGLAND 1 goal, 1 try *Back*: WG Mitchell (GuyHosp/Rich). *Three-quarters*: FHR Alderson (HartR), JH Crompton (Run, t, dg), PH Morrison (CamU). *Half-backs*: FH Fox (capt, Well/Black), MT Scott (Nor). *Forwards*: H Eagles (Sal), F Evershed (Black/Bur), PF Hancock (Wivel/Black), T Kent (Sal), JL Mayger (Burt), FE Pease (HartR), A Robinson (Black), JH Rogers (Mose), SMJ Woods (Bridg/CamU).
Attendance: 12,000   *Referee*: RS Whalley (London)

ENGLAND TRIAL MATCHES

Saturday 21 December 1889 at Whalley Range, Manchester
NORTH 1 goal *Back*: A Royle (BroR). *Three-quarters*: AL Brooke (Hud), FHR Alderson (HartR), J Valentine (Swi). *Half-backs*: MT Scott (Nor), J Wright (Brad, t). *Forwards*: C Anderton (capt, ManFW), H Bedford (Mor), T Gee (PerPk, c), E Holmes (Mann), CH Horley (Swi), FW Lowrie (Bat), JT Toothill (Brad), CTB Wilkinson (DurU), W Yiend (HartR).
SOUTH 4 tries *Back*: WG Mitchell (GuyHosp/Rich). *Three-quarters*: AE Stoddart (capt, Black, 2t), AB Whitehead (OLey), P Christopherson (Black). *Half-backs*: FH Fox (Well/Black), WRM Leake (Harl). *Forwards*: RD Budworth (Black/OxfU), JH Dewhurst (Rich), F Evershed (Black/Burt), PF Hancock (Wivel/Black, t), JL Mayger (Burt), A Robinson (Black), JH Rogers (Mose), AA Surtees (Harl, t), SMJ Woods (Bridg/CamU).
Attendance: 6,000   *Referee*: AN Hornby (Lancashire)

Saturday 1 February 1890 at Athletic Ground, Richmond
SOUTH 2 goals, 2 tries *Back*: WG Mitchell (GuyHosp/Rich). *Three-quarters*: SC Smith (Wes), AE Stoddart (capt, Black, t, c, dg), PH Morrison (CamU). *Half-backs*: FH Fox (Well/Black), PH Illingworth (Black/CamU). *Forwards*: RD Budworth (Black/OxfU), JH Dewhurst (Rich), F Evershed (Black/Burt, 2t), PF Hancock (Wivel/Black), JL Mayger (Burt), A Robinson (Black), JH Rogers (Mose), AA Surtees (Harl), SJM Woods (Bridg/CamU).
NORTH 1 goal *Back*: WH Bell (Sund). *Three-quarters*: FHR Alderson (HartR), J Dyson (Hud), J Valentine (Swi). *Half-backs*: W Bumby (Swi), MT Scott (Nor). *Forwards*: H Eagles (Sal), T Gee (PerPk, c), JL Hickson (capt, Brad), J Holme (Mil, t), E Holmes (Mann), D Jowett (Heck), T Kent (Sal), FW Lowrie (Bat), FE Pease (HartR).
Attendance: 7,000   *Referee*: AN Hornby (Lancashire)

INTERNATIONAL CHAMPIONSHIP

Saturday 15 February 1890 at Crown Flatts, Dewsbury
ENGLAND 0 *Back*: WG Mitchell (GuyHosp/Rich). *Three-quarters*: PH Morrison (CamU), AE Stoddart (capt, Black), J Valentine (Swi). *Half-backs*: FH Fox (Well/Black), JF Wright (Brad). *Forwards*: RD Budworth (Black/OxfU), JH Dewhurst (Rich), F Evershed (Black/Burt), PF Hancock (Wivel/Black), JL Hickson (Brad), FW Lowrie (Bat), A Robinson (Black), JH Rogers (Mose), SMJ Woods (Bridg/CamU).
WALES 1 *Back*: WJ Bancroft (Swa). *Three-quarters*: P Lloyd (Llan), JA Gould (capt, New), RM Garrett (Pen), D Gwynn (Swa). *Half-backs*: WJ Stadden (Dew, t), CJ Thomas (New). *Forwards*: AF Bland (Car), W Bowen (Swa), DW Evans (Car), J Hannan (New), J Meredith (Swa), S Thomas (Llan), WH Thomas (LonW), WEO Williams (Car).
Attendance: 4,000   *Referee*: RD Rainie (Scotland)

Saturday 1 March 1890 at Raeburn Place, Edinburgh
SCOTLAND 0 *Back*: G MacGregor (CamU). *Half-backs*: WE Maclagan (capt, LonS), HJ Stevenson (EdinA), GR Wilson (RHSFP). *Quarter-backs*: DG Anderson (LonS), CE Orr (WoS). *Forwards*: JD Boswell (WoS), A Dalgleish (Gala), FW Goodhue (LonS), HT Ker (GlasA), MC McEwan (EdinA), I MacIntyre (EdinW), RG Macmillan (WoS), DS Morton (WoS), JE Orr (WoS).
ENGLAND 6 *Back*: WG Mitchell (GuyHosp/Rich). *Three-quarters*: PH Morrison (CamU), RL Aston (Black/CamU), JW Dyson (Hud, t). *Half-backs*: FH Fox (Well/Black), MT Scott (Nor). *Forwards*: H Bedford (Mor), F Evershed (Black/Burt, t), JL Hickson (capt, Brad), E Holmes (Mann), D Jowett (Heck, c), A Robinson (Black), JH Rogers (Mose), JT Toothill (Brad), SMJ Woods (Bridg/CamU).
Attendance: 10,000   *Referee*: J Chambers (Ireland)
Note: Due to vagaries in the awarding of points, tries in this match were valued as two points (as preferred in Scotland) and valued as one in England's other games.

Saturday 15 March 1890 at Rectory Field, Blackheath
ENGLAND 3 *Back*: WG Mitchell (GuyHosp/Rich). *Three-quarters*: PH Morrison (CamU, t), RL Aston (Black/CamU), AE Stoddart (capt, Black, t). *Half-backs*: MT Scott (Nor), FW Spence (BirkPk). *Forwards*: H Bedford (Mor), F Evershed (Black/Burt), JL Hickson (Brad), E Holmes (Mann), D Jowett (Heck), A Robinson (Black), JH Rogers (Mose, t), JT Toothill (Brad), SMJ Woods (Bridg/CamU).
IRELAND 0 *Back*: DB Walkington (DubU). *Half-backs*: RW Dunlop (DubU), RW Johnston (DubU), T Edwards (Lans). *Quarter-backs*: BB Tuke (BecR), RG Warren (capt, Lans). *Forwards*: WJN Davis (Bess), EG Forrest (Wand), VC le Fanu (Lans), JN Lytle (NIFC), LC Nash (QCC), JH O'Conor (BecR), J Roche (Wand), R Stevenson (Dun), J Waites (BecR).
Attendance: 12,000   *Referee*: AR Don-Wauchope (Scotland)

Other results
Wales 1, Scotland 5
Scotland 4, Ireland 0
Ireland 3, Wales 3

Final table

	P	W	D	L	For	Agst
England	3	2	0	1	9	1
Scotland	3	2	0	1	9	7
Wales	3	1	1	1	5	8
Ireland	3	0	1	2	3	10

(England and Scotland share Championship)

1890-1891

LEEDS PLAY FIRST MATCH AT HEADINGLEY
The new Leeds club played its first match at Headingley on 20th September against visitors Manningham. The prospectus, published in March 1889, announced that the Clarendon Cricket Club and Leeds St John's Football Club would provide the cricket and football sections, respectively, of the Leeds Cricket, Football and Athletic Sports Company.[113] Leeds St John's had been founded in 1869, its former Cardigan Fields ground being earmarked for housing.

PROFESSIONALISM: LEEDS
The recently launched Leeds outfit soon found itself in trouble when the Yorkshire Committee met at the Green Dragon Hotel, Leeds, on 22nd October. One of its players, E. Southall, was accused of professionalism, having received £5 for secretarial work with the cricket section of the club. Southall, who failed to appear at the meeting, was declared a professional in his absence. The committee stated that had he appeared to provide an explanation they 'might have found reason to reconsider his case and reverse their decision'.[114]

PROFESSIONALISM: OLDHAM
Oldham officials were summoned to appear before the Lancashire Committee at the Grand Hotel, Manchester, on 23rd October. They were

instructed to bring with them the club books and all their first team players to answer charges of professionalism. The instigator of this action was the Reverend Frank Marshall, president of the Yorkshire Rugby Union. After speaking to several team members, particularly the Welsh trio of Bill McCutcheon, Dai Gwynn, and Dicky Thomas, it was decided to adjourn until Wednesday 29th October, the books being examined in the meantime. The subsequent meeting was again at the Grand Hotel when, having gone through the books and hearing additional evidence, it was decided to acquit Oldham of the charge.[115]

THE REVEREND FRANK MARSHALL

The part played by Reverend Frank Marshall in the case against Oldham did not go down too well in Lancashire. The *Manchester Guardian* scribe commented: 'What I regard as interference by the Rev. F. Marshall in Lancashire affairs is hardly appreciated. Surely the Lancashire Rugby Union are able to look after themselves, and if there is anything calling for inquiry they do not need to be prompted by Yorkshire officials. People are wondering why the Rev. F. Marshall has fixed his eye specifically upon Oldham, as they are no worse than other clubs in the county.'[116]

COUNTY CHAMPIONSHIP COMPETITION BEGINS

The north of England's first competitive county match took place on 8th November at Upper Park, Birkenhead, when Cheshire opposed Lancashire. A formal competition had been introduced this season to determine England's champion county, the northern counties being split into two groups; North Western (Cheshire, Cumberland, Lancashire, Westmorland) and North Eastern (Durham, Northumberland, Yorkshire). There was also two southern county groups, South Western and South Eastern, the four group winners meeting in a final group to decide the champions. In the preceding 1888-89 and 1889-90 seasons the Rugby Football Union had declared Yorkshire as county champions based on results during each campaign.

FOUR THREE-QUARTERS USED IN COUNTY FIXTURES

When Durham met Yorkshire, on 15th November in Sunderland, they became the first northern county to use four three-quarters in an inter-county match, the increase from three effectively reducing its forward strength from nine to eight players. One week later, on 22nd November, Northumberland became the second northern county to experiment with a four-man line, also against Yorkshire, at Headingley. In both matches

Yorkshire were the victors. Lancashire followed suit when meeting Devonshire at Exeter on 10th January. The four other northern counties waited a little longer; Yorkshire, Cheshire, Cumberland and Westmorland all taking the plunge during 1893.[117]

WHALLEY RANGE: STRUGGLING TO COPE

When Lancashire hosted Yorkshire on 29th November in front of 15,000 spectators, Manchester's Whalley Range enclosure struggled to cope with the crowd. The *Manchester Guardian* commented: 'Almost up to the very last there were grave doubts about the match being played owing to the severity of the weather at the end of the week. It was doubtless the uncertainty about the fixture being brought off that caused the discreditable scenes at the entrances to the enclosure. The bulk of the spectators seemed to rush up in a body almost at the last moment, and so many sought admission together that the means of entry was totally inadequate. At least half a dozen more pay-boxes were necessary. The patience of the tremendous crowd soon became exhausted, and many hundreds mounted the palings on different sides of the field, scores of pounds being thus lost, besides the damage to the fencing. Some of the players even were obliged to scale the boards, and altogether the scene was to be regretted in every way. The arrangements for such a big gathering were sadly at fault.'[118]

MIDDLESEX CRY OFF

Lancashire was due to receive Middlesex at Whalley Range on Monday 8th December. But, on the preceding Friday, it was announced that the match was cancelled as Middlesex could not raise a team. It was reported that 'something like 30 players were appealed to [but] it was the great difficulty of getting a reliable fifteen together that caused the authorities to cry off'.[119]

LET'S CALL IT A DRAW

When Northumberland met Durham at Jesmond, Newcastle, on 17th January, it was declared a draw even before kick-off! Heavy snowfalls had continued up to the morning of the match which, despite protecting the ground with straw, made conditions difficult. Therefore, it was decided to change the match to 'exhibition' status with two halves of just 20 minutes each, Durham providing the only score with a converted try.[120]

SENT OFF FOR FIVE MINUTES
Cumberland Cup holders Egremont hosted Aspatria in the first round of the 1890-91 competition on 14th February, three-quarter George Bowman rescuing them with an equalising try before being 'ordered off the field for five minutes for foul play'. Seven days later Aspatria won the replay 3-0 in a match notable for the joint-dismissals of Isaac Stamper (Egremont) and Joseph Mumberson (Aspatria) for having 'broken the rough play rule'. Stamper, who instigated the altercation by striking Mumberson, was suspended until the start of the following season.[121]

LANCASHIRE CLINCH COUNTY TITLE
Lancashire defeated Gloucestershire 14-0 at Whalley Range on 14th March to capture their first county championship title. The *London Daily News* commented: 'Lancashire secured beyond all dispute the right to the title of Champion County for 1890-91. They had previously defeated Yorkshire and Surrey, respectively, the strongest fifteens in the north-eastern and south-eastern districts of the country, so they had only to conquer Gloucestershire, the leading county of the south-western group, to obtain first honours. The present season is the first in which a systemised competition for the county championship has been decided, and though owing to the prolonged frost the early promise of the struggle was scarcely realised, the new departure has obtained a degree of success sufficient to warrant the expectation that in another year the contest will bear as important a relation to Rugby football as does the cup competition to the Association games.'[122]

THE 1891 ENGLAND TOUR
An invitation from the Western Province Union to tour South Africa was announced on 24th March at the Rugby Football Union's Annual General Meeting, held in the Westminster Palace Hotel, London. The offer was subsequently accepted, the Prime Minister of Cape Province, Cecil Rhodes, guaranteeing the expenses for the tour which would run from July until September 1891. The *London Daily News* observed that 'the side is composed almost exclusively of University and London club players,' adding – probably with thoughts of the professional stigma associated with the 1888 tour – that 'one of the most satisfactory features consists in the fact that it is under the auspices of the Rugby Union, and that consequently no question as to the purely amateur nature of the tour can possibly arise'.[123] Altogether 21 players from English and Scottish clubs were selected, seven with north of England connections: Edward Bromet

(born Tadcaster), William Bromet (born Tadcaster, younger brother of Edward, later played for Yorkshire), Paul Clauss (born Germany, later played for Birkenhead Park and Cheshire), John Hammond (born Skipton), Walter Jackson (born Gloucester, later played for Halifax), Bertwine Roscoe (born Liverpool, played for Manchester and Lancashire), Tom Whittaker (born Beckenham, played for Manchester and Lancashire). Tour captain Bill Maclagan, Robert Macmillan and William Wotherspoon were born in Scotland, Robert Thompson in Ireland. Clauss had also represented Scotland having been educated at Loretto School, near Edinburgh. Despite their presence, the tour party was referred to as England or the 'English team'. To reflect contemporary reports the tourists are called England in the statistics section.

WHALLEY RANGE: A WORTHY GROUND?

A letter from 'Lancastrian' appeared in the *Manchester Guardian* during April: 'Now that the football season has been brought to a close, many people are wishful to know if the Manchester club are taking any steps to provide a new ground worthy of the club and county and of the matches played by them, for really as a county football ground, or even a town's ground, the Whalley Range enclosure is altogether a shabby affair. The accommodation for large events is too limited, as was evident last Saturday, for quite five or six thousand people on the pavilion side were unable to see the progress of the match with anything like comfort, standing as they did six and seven deep, and only the front row having a really good view. Now, considering that the ground has for a number of years had all the principle fixtures in the county played on it, it is surprising the Manchester club has never wakened up and possessed itself of a ground such as those held by the leading Yorkshire clubs.'[124]

1890-1891 STATISTICS

WEST LANCASHIRE RUGBY LEAGUE

Final table	P	W	D	L	For	Agst	Pts
Walkden	12	11	1	0	207	48	23
Aspull	12	7	3	2	115	49	17
Wigan	12	7	1	4	153	86	15
St Helens	12	5	2	5	92	150	12
Leigh	12	3	1	8	69	103	7
Birkenhead Wanderers	12	2	2	8	75	155	6
Pemberton	12	2	0	10	34	154	4

CUMBERLAND COUNTY CHALLENGE CUP (12 entries)
Try – 1 point; conversion, penalty goal – 2; drop-goal, field goal, goal from mark – 3.
If equal then majority of 3 minor points required to win.

First Round
Cleator 1, Maryport 9
Cockermouth 0, Broughton 7
Egremont 1, Aspatria 1 (mp: 2-0, no extra time)
Workington 3, Seaton 5
Byes: Crosby, Flimby, Penrith United, Whitehaven

First Round Replay
Aspatria 3, Egremont 0

Second Round
Broughton 0, Seaton 0 (mp: 1-1, aet)
Crosby 0, Penrith United 0 (mp: 1-1, no extra time)
Flimby 0, Whitehaven 0 (mp: 4-2, aet)
Maryport 0, Aspatria 1

Second Round Replays
Penrith United 1, Crosby 0
Seaton 0, Broughton 0 (mp: 3-8)
Whitehaven 4, Flimby 1

Semi-finals
Aspatria 0, Penrith United 0 (mp: 5-0, at Cemetery Lane, Carlisle)
Broughton 1, Whitehaven 0 (at Egremont)

FINAL
Saturday 4 April 1891 at the Maryport Cricket Ground
ASPATRIA 3 *Back*: JH Blaylock. *Three-quarters*: Jerry Saul, L Beattie, W Berwick.
Half-backs: T Docker, Joe Nelson. *Forwards*: T Allison (t), JW Cowan, Jim Davidson,
T Grieve (capt, c), J Harker, R Mumberson, J Rumney, Joseph Saul, J Stanger.
BROUGHTON 0 *Back*: DG Lamonby. *Three-quarters*: R Kirkbride, W Harrison, W Lister.
Half-backs: T Lister, R Percival. *Forwards*: G Clark (capt), W Clark, W Graham,
T Kirkpatrick, J Moses, W Ray, J Renney, T Renney, J Studholme.
Attendance: 4,000   *Referee*: JH Walton (Barrow)

DURHAM COUNTY CHALLENGE CUP (15 entries)
Most goals wins. If equal, most tries. If still equal, majority of 3 minor points.

First Round
Consett 1t, Houghton-le-Spring 2g, 6t
Durham City 3g, 5t, Stockton 1t
Hartlepool Rangers 0,
Hartlepool Rovers 2g, 1t
North Durham 3g, Westoe 0
South Shields YMCA 8g, 2t,
Throston Wanderers 1g
Sunderland 1g, 2t, Tudhoe 2g, 2t
West Hartlepool 9g, 5t,
Gateshead Institute 0
Bye: Henderson's Wanderers

Second Round
Hartlepool Rovers 1g, 1t, Tudhoe 0
Houghton-le-Spring w/o
Henderson's Wanderers (disbanded)
South Shields YMCA 1t,
North Durham 3g, 2t
West Hartlepool 2t, Durham City 0

Semi-finals
Hartlepool Rovers 1g, 1t,
West Hartlepool 0
Houghton-le-Spring 3g, North Durham 0

FINAL
Saturday 4 April 1891 at Ashbrooke Ground, Sunderland
HARTLEPOOL ROVERS 2 goals, 1 try *Back*: JW Horn. *Three-quarters*: D McPherson (t), FHR Alderson (t, c), AE Emmerson, WE Kassell (c). *Half-backs*: AC Scott, G Smith. *Forwards*: J Coates, A Hill (t), FH Hunter, CM Huntley, FC Lohden, FE Pease, J Snowdon, W Yiend (capt).
HOUGHTON-LE-SPRING 2 tries *Back*: T Shields. *Three-quarters*: J Hugill, JT Dixon, R Clark. *Half-backs*: W Gregory, WA Johnson. *Forwards*: W Bassett, W Birtley, J Gibney, A Gowlands, J Johnson, R Robinson, N Smith (2t), J Wallace, J Wheatley.
Attendance: 3,000   *Referee*: n/a

NORTHUMBERLAND COUNTY FOOTBALL CHALLENGE CUP (8 entries)
Most goals wins. If equal, most tries.

First Round
Gosforth 1g, 1t, North Elswick 0
Northern 0, Rockcliff 5g, 3t
Northumberland FC 1t, Tynedale 3g, 1t
Wallsend 1t, Percy Park 0

Semi-finals
Rockcliff 3g, 1t, Wallsend 1t
Tynedale 0, Gosforth 1t

FINAL
Saturday 28 March 1891 at Jesmond Ground, Newcastle
ROCKCLIFF 8 goals, 2 tries *Back*: J Murray. *Three-quarters*: W Taylor (2t, c), S Brutton (t, dg), T Nicholson (3t). *Half-backs*: TP Alexander (t), EW Taylor (t, 6c). *Forwards*: Alf Benson, Ambrose Benson, J Bolam, JH Greenwell, CH Hamilton (capt), C Lattimer, F Lattimer (t), G Robson, A Styan.
GOSFORTH 0 *Back*: J Taylor. *Three-quarters*: H Farrer (capt), C Fairbairn, J Crone. *Half-backs*: P McAllum, S Punter. *Forwards*: W Armstrong, T Bell, TG Boss, R Brown, R Phillips, J Scott, A Swan, P Thompson, J Walker.
Attendance: 3,000   *Referee*: JA Williamson (Northumberland RU Honorary Secretary)

YORKSHIRE COUNTY FOOTBALL CHALLENGE CUP (129 entries)
Most goals wins (3 tries count as one 'goal').
If equal, most tries (excluding any already counted as equalling a 'goal').

Preliminary Round
Alverthorpe 2g, Paddock 0
Batley Mountaineers 0, Windhill 1g, 2t
Bankfoot 1t, Buslingthorpe 1g, 2t
Bowling 1g, 2t, Salterhebble 1g, 1t
Bradford Trinity 0, Bailiffe Bridge 2g, 5t
Churwell 2t, Greetland 2g, 1t
Doncaster Town 0, Normanton St John's 1t
Ferrybridge 1g, Barnsley Congregational 2g
Gildersome 4t, Bowling Old Lane 1g, 2t
Guiseley 2t, Bingley 2g
Haworth 1g, Pateley Bridge 0
Horbury w/o Thornes (withdrew)
Keighley Shamrocks 0,
Low Moor St Mark's 4t
Kippax 3g, 1t, Saltaire 1g
Kirkstall St Stephen's 2g, 1t,
Leeds East End 1g
Knaresborough 0, Bradford Britannia 1g
Knottingley Free Wanderers 1g, 2t,
West Ardsley Collieries 1t
Leeds Catholic Institute 0,
Woodhouse 1t

Preliminary Round *continued*

Luddendenfoot 2t, Hebden Bridge 0
Manningham Rangers 1g, 1t,
Hull Britannia 4g, 4t
Milnsbridge 1g, Mytholmroyd 4g, 1t
Morley Albion w/o
Hull White Star (withdrew)
Newtown 1g, 4t, Mirfield Rangers 1g, 2t
Nortonthorpe 2g, 1t, Hull St Paul's 1g
Outwood Church 1t, Mirfield 1g
Primrose Hill 2g, 2t, Keighley Hornets 1g, 2t

Ravensthorpe 1g, Sowerby Bridge 1g, 2t
Ripon 1g, 1t, Horsforth 3g
Selby 4t, Sedburgh 0
Silsden 1g, 2t, Stanningley 1t
Skipton 1g, 3t, Hull Three Crowns 0
Thornhill Lees Trinity 1g, 1t, Lockwood 0
Todmorden 1g, 2t, South Milford 2t
Byes: 31 teams drew a bye to next round

Qualifying Round

Armley 7g, 12t,
Knottingley Free Wanderers 0
Barnsley 3g, 4t, Leeds St John's 0
Barnsley Congregational 1t,
Crosland Moor 2t
Batley Gypsies 2g, 1t, Wibsey Slack Side 3t
Bingley 2g, 6t, Hull St Mary's 1t
Birstall 2g, 2t, Kirkburton 1g
Bowling 2g, 2t, Horbury 0
Bowling Old Lane 1g, 4t,
Hipperholme and Lightcliffe 1t
Cottingham w/o Calverley (withdrew)
Greetland 1g, Silsden 0
Haworth 3t, Beverley 1g, 1t
Honley 3g, 1t, Heaton 0
Hull Britannia 3g, 7t, Primrose Hill 0
Ingrow 2t, Keighley Zingari 0
Kippax 1t, Wakefield St Austin's 2g, 1t
Leeds Gaelic 0, Harrogate 2g, 6t
Low Moor St Mark's 3t, Alverthorpe 1g, 2t
Luddendenfoot w/o Stainland (withdrew)

Morley Providence 0, Mirfield 2g, 3t
Mytholmroyd 9t, Holmfirth 0
Newtown 2g, Buslingthorpe 3t
Normanton St John's w/o
Morley Albion (withdrew)
Nortonthorpe 1g, 1t, Whitwood 1g
Shepley w/o Otley Clarendon (withdrew)
Skipton 2g, 2t, Kirkstall St Stephen's 0
Sowerby Bridge 5g, 4t,
Thornhill Lees Trinity 0
Tadcaster 3g, 2t, Dudley Hill 1g
(replay ordered after protest)
Todmorden 1g, Horsforth 0
Wibsey 1g, 1t, Selby 1t
Windhill 0, Idle 2g, 1t
Woodhouse 7g, 5t, Bradford Britannia 1g
Yeadon 0, Bailiffe Bridge 2g, 1t

Qualifying Round Replay
Tadcaster 1g, 1t, Dudley Hill 1g

First Round
(* indicates 32 teams seeded to this round)
Alverthorpe 1t, Wakefield St Austin's 0
Barnsley 0, Bramley* 2g, 3t
Batley* 4g, 6t, Nortonthorpe 1t
Beverley 1g, 1t, Crosland Moor 2g, 1t
Bowling Old Lane 1g, 1t, Luddendenfoot 0
Brighouse Rangers* 2g, 9t, Wibsey 0
Buttershaw* 0, Holbeck* 1g, 2t
Castleford* 2g, 2t, Elland* 1t
Cleckheaton* 2g, 5t, Harrogate 0

Greetland 0, Goole* 1g
Halifax* 6g, 4t, Shepley 0
Heckmondwike* 4g, 13t, Cottingham 0
Honley 0, Bradford* 7g, 3t
Hull Britannia 0, Manningham* 1t
Hunslet* 5g, 5t, Normanton St John's 0
Idle 1t, Dewsbury* 4g, 2t
Ingrow 1t, Bailiffe Bridge 1t
Keighley* 2t, Bingley 0
Kirkstall* 0, Otley* 1t
Leeds* 0, Liversedge* 1g, 3t

First Round *continued*
Leeds Parish Church* 0, Pontefract* 1t
Mirfield 1g, 1t, Armley 1g
Newtown 3g, 1t, Mytholmroyd 2t
Ossett* 1g, 1t, Huddersfield* 1g, 3t
Pudsey* 0, Morley* 3t
Shipley* 5g, Todmorden 1t
Skipton 1g, 3t, Birstall 1g

Second Round
Alverthorpe 2g, Otley 1g, 1t
Batley 0, Wakefield Trinity 1t
Brighouse Rangers 1g, Bradford 4g
Castleford 2g, 2t, Bramley 1g, 1t
Cleckheaton 2t, Bowling Old Lane 0
Goole 1t, Shipley 0
Halifax 6g, 3t, Crosland Moor 0
Holbeck 3g, 3t, Ingrow 0
Hull 0, Dewsbury 1g
Hunslet 2g, 5t, Newtown 0
Keighley 0, Wortley 1g, 2t

Third Round
Alverthorpe 4g, 2t, Woodhouse 1g
Bradford 1g, Halifax 2g
Dewsbury 0, Huddersfield 1t
Hunslet 4g, 1t, Goole 1g
Morley 0, Castleford 2g
Pontefract 3g, Manningham 0
Wakefield Trinity 1g, 2t, Holbeck 1t
Wortley 1g, Cleckheaton 1t

Sowerby Bridge 0, Wakefield Trinity* 2g, 1t
Tadcaster 1t, Hull* 2g, 7t
Woodhouse 3g, 1t, Batley Gypsies 0
Wortley* 2g, Bowling 1t
York* 0, Normanton* 1g, 1t

First Round Replay
Bailiffe Bridge 1t, Ingrow 1g

Liversedge 1g, Huddersfield 2g, 4t
Manningham 1g, Heckmondwike 1t
(replay ordered after protest)
Mirfield 0, Woodhouse 0
Morley 3g, 1t, Normanton 1g, 1t
Pontefract 3t, Skipton 1t

Second Round Replays
Manningham 1t,
Heckmondwike 0 (at Halifax)
Woodhouse 3g, 1t, Mirfield 1t

Fourth Round
Halifax 0, Castleford 1g
Huddersfield 1g, Hunslet 0
Pontefract 1g, 1t, Alverthorpe 0
Wortley 1g, Wakefield Trinity 1g, 2t

Semi-finals
Pontefract 1g, 1t, Castleford 0
(at Crown Flatts, Dewsbury)
Wakefield Trinity 1t, Huddersfield 0
(at Park Avenue, Bradford)

FINAL
Saturday 11 April 1891 at Headingley, Leeds
PONTEFRACT 1 goal, 1 try *Back*: G Swift. *Three-quarters*: JW Goodhind (capt, t, c), T Booth, HJ Thackray. *Half-backs*: G Emmerson, E England. *Forwards*: H Adams, H Burton, E Crossland (t), C Heckingbottom, J Heckingbottom, T Holder, F Morley, H Thorpe, B Ward.
WAKEFIELD TRINITY 1 goal *Back*: T Collin. *Three-quarters*: JH Fotherby, C Overton, H Fallas. *Half-backs*: J Bedford (t), R Hudson. *Forwards*: W Binks, P Booth, J Dawson, R Dawson, J Harnell, JH Jones (capt), J Pickering, W Smith, H Whiteley (c).
Attendance: 17,720   *Referee*: WH Humphreys (Durham RU)

COUNTY CHAMPIONSHIP

NORTH WESTERN GROUP

Saturday 8 November 1890 at Upper Park, Birkenhead
CHESHIRE 0 *Back*: S Houghton (Run). *Three-quarters*: JT Haslam (Duk), WH Male (NewB), FP Jones (NewB). *Half-backs*: S Abram (Run), QJ Leitch (NewB). *Forwards*: WH Broady (Run), R Dolan (Run), W Faulkner (Run), PH Lockwood (BirkPk), R Morton (Alt), P Riley (Run), JH Smith (Stock), WA Williams (NewB), AG Wood (capt, BirkPk).
LANCASHIRE 7 *Back*: T Coop (Lei). *Three-quarters*: J Valentine (Swi, t, 2c), D Gwynn (Old), EH Flower (Bro, t). *Half-backs*: J Berry (Tyl), W Bumby (Swi). *Forwards*: W Atkinson (Wig, t), E Blomley (Old), E Bullough (Wig), P Fildes (StHR), Herbert Hasleham (ManR), J Jackson (BroR), T Kent (Sal), F Treweek (Bar), T Whittaker (Man).
Attendance: 8,000   *Referee*: GR Hill (RFU Honorary Secretary)

Saturday 22 November 1890 at Mint's Feet, Kendal
WESTMORLAND 0 *Back*: T Hine (KenH). *Three-quarters*: J Armstrong (KenH), JK Robinson (KirkL), J Whittam (KenT). *Half-backs*: W Ewan (KenT), W Whitehead (KenH). *Forwards*: J Carradus (KenT), T Fawcett (KenT), G Machell (KenT), RH Moore (Amb), R Nicholson (KenT), WJ Parsons (KenH), E Richardson (KirkL), JW Wilkinson (KenH), E Wilson (KenH).
LANCASHIRE 16 *Back*: T Coop (Lei, 4c). *Three-quarters*: J Valentine (Swi), D Gwynn (Old, t), EH Flower (Bro, 2t). *Half-backs*: J Berry (Tyl, t), W Bumby (Swi). *Forwards*: W Atkinson (Wig), T Brayshay (Wig), T Craven (Sal), T Kent (Sal, t), J Pyke (StHR, t), T Rothwell (Swi), J Strang (Liv, t), T Whittaker (Man), RP Wilson (LivOB, t).
Attendance: 3,000   *Referee*: HB Browning (Cheshire)

Saturday 7 February 1891 at Maude's Meadow, Kendal
WESTMORLAND 4 *Back*: T Hine (KenH). *Three-quarters*: J Allen (KenH, t), JK Robinson (KirkL, t), J Whittam (KenT). *Half-backs*: W Hall (KenH), J Lambert (Lanc). *Forwards*: J Carradus (KenT), T Fawcett (KenT), G Machell (KenT), RH Moore (Amb), R Nicholson (KenT, c), WJ Parsons (KenH), E Richardson (KirkL), E Wilson (KenH), RS Winskill (KenH).
CUMBERLAND 1 *Back*: J Sandwith (Sea). *Three-quarters*: J Johnston (CarlC, t), JH Buckett (Mil), G Bowman (Egr). *Half-backs*: L Cook (Egr), R Cuthbertson (Cock). *Forwards*: GB Atkinson (Whi), Jim Davidson (Asp), J Holme (Mil), M Humphrey (Mary), J Kidd (Mil), D Mulholland (Egr), J Mumberson (Asp), J Pender (PenU), C Simpson (Egr).
Attendance: n/a   *Referee*: AB Dewhurst (Lancashire)

Saturday 28 February 1891 at Whalley Range, Manchester
LANCASHIRE 12 *Back*: T Coop (Lei, c). *Three-quarters*: J Valentine (capt, Swi, 3t, 2c), D Gwynn (Old, t), W McCutcheon (Old). *Half-backs*: J Berry (Tyl), W Cross (StH). *Forwards*: W Atkinson (Wig), T Craven (Sal, t), T Kent (Sal), T Melledew (RochH), J Pyke (StHR), C Rome (Bro, t), T Rothwell (Swi), T Whittaker (Man), RP Wilson (LivOB).
CUMBERLAND 1 *Back*: JW Brown (South Vale Wanderers). *Three-quarters*: JP Graham (Whi, t), JH Buckett (capt, Mil), G Bowman (Egr). *Half-backs*: R Cuthbertson (Cock), J Murchie (Work). *Forwards*: GB Atkinson (Whi), JJ Bewsher (PenU), Jim Davidson (Asp), J Holme (Mil), E Houston (Sea), M Humphrey (Mary), J Kidd (Mil), J Leck (Mil), J Pender (PenU).
Attendance: 5,000   *Referee*: B Kilner (Yorkshire)

NORTH WESTERN GROUP *continued*

Final table	P	W	D	L	For	Agst	Pts
Lancashire	3	3	0	0	35	1	6
Westmorland	2	1	0	1	4	17	2
Cheshire	1	0	0	1	0	7	0
Cumberland	2	0	0	2	2	16	0

Note: Fixtures incomplete.

NORTH EASTERN GROUP

Saturday 15 November 1890 at Asbrooke Ground, Sunderland
DURHAM 1 *Back*: W Dooley (WHart). *Three-quarters*: TAF Crow (Sund), RCF Crow (Sund), WH Bell (Sund), FHR Alderson (HartR). *Half-backs*: AC Scott (HartR), G Smith (HartR). *Forwards*: HT Barmby (DurC), T Faulkner (Tud), FC Lohden (HartR), T Parker (Sund), P Turnbull (WHart), J Wheatley (Hou/Sund, t), CTB Wilkinson (DurC), W Yiend (HartR).
YORKSHIRE 5 *Back*: S Mawson (Otley). *Three-quarters*: J Dyson (Hud, t, dg), Joe Naylor (Dew), RE Lockwood (Heck, t). *Half-backs*: H Hartley (Hol), Jim Naylor (Bat). *Forwards*: H Bedford (Mor), WE Bromet (Tad), T Else (Hud), JL Hickson (capt, Brad), E Holmes (Mann), B Jackson (HebB), D Jowett (Heck), FW Lowrie (Bat), J Richards (Brad).
Attendance: 8,000   *Referee*: A McConnell (Northumberland)

Saturday 22 November 1890 at Headingley, Leeds
YORKSHIRE 9 *Back*: S Mawson (Otley). *Three-quarters*: SN Eastwood (BrigR), Joe Naylor (Dew), RE Lockwood (Heck, c). *Half-backs*: Jim Naylor (Bat, t), JH Potter (Lee, t). *Forwards*: H Bedford (Mor), WE Bromet (Tad, t), JL Hickson (capt, Brad), E Holmes (Mann), G Jacketts (Hull, t), D Jowett (Heck, t), FW Lowrie (Bat), W Nichol (BrigR), JT Toothill (Brad, t).
NORTHUMBERLAND 0 *Back*: E Emley (Nor). *Three-quarters*: T Nicholson (Rock), F Finney (PerPk), C Scott (capt, Nor), TS Graham (Nor). *Half-backs*: T Stewart (PerPk), EW Taylor (Rock). *Forwards*: H Angus (Nor), A Benson (Rock), TG Boss (Gos), G Davidson (PerPk), J Douthwaite (Tynd), F Marshall (PerPk), CA Ridley (Nor), G Robson (Rock).
Attendance: 8,000   *Referee*: E Beswick (Lancashire)

Tuesday 10 February 1891 at Holy Drift, Durham
DURHAM 2 *Back*: W Taylor (Tud). *Three-quarters*: RCF Crow (Sund), WH Bell (Sund), H Baty (SShYM, t), W Wainford (Tud, t). *Half-backs*: AC Scott (HartR), G Smith (HartR). *Forwards*: HT Barmby (DurC), WA Bell (Tud), T Faulkner (Tud), FE Pease (HartR), P Turnbull (WHart), J Wheatley (Hou/Sund), CTB Wilkinson (DurC), W Yiend (HartR).
NORTHUMBERLAND 1 *Back*: E Emley (Nor). *Three-quarters*: T Nicholson (Rock), F Finney (PerPk), S Brutton (Rock), W Taylor (Rock, t). *Half-backs*: T Stewart (PerPk), EW Taylor (Rock). *Forwards*: H Angus (Nor), TG Boss (Gos), G Davidson (PerPk), F Marshall (PerPk), CA Ridley (Nor), G Robson (Rock), C Scott (Nor), H Shotton (PerPk).
Attendance: 5,000   *Referee*: B Kilner (Yorkshire)
Note: This fixture was originally scheduled for 17 January at Newcastle but, due to a frozen ground, it was changed to 'exhibition' status and played over 2 halves of 20 minutes.

NORTH EASTERN GROUP continued

Final table	P	W	D	L	For	Agst	Pts
Yorkshire	2	2	0	0	14	1	4
Durham	2	1	0	1	3	6	2
Northumberland	2	0	0	2	1	11	0

SOUTH WESTERN GROUP

Results
Devonshire 3, Midland Counties 13
Somersetshire 7, Devonshire 0
Gloucestershire 5, Midland Counties 0
Gloucestershire 0, Somersetshire 0

Final table	P	W	D	L	For	Agst	Pts
Gloucestershire	2	1	1	0	5	0	3
Somersetshire	2	1	1	0	7	0	3
Midland Counties	2	1	0	1	13	8	2
Devonshire	2	0	0	2	3	20	0

Play-off to decide first place
Gloucestershire 3, Somersetshire 0

SOUTH EASTERN GROUP

Results
Middlesex 8, Kent 0
Surrey 5, Middlesex 3
Kent 1, Surrey 3

Final table	P	W	D	L	For	Agst	Pts
Surrey	2	2	0	0	8	4	4
Middlesex	2	1	0	1	11	5	2
Kent	2	0	0	2	1	11	0
Sussex	0	0	0	0	0	0	0

(Sussex withdrew without playing a match)

FINAL GROUP ('SECOND SERIES')

Saturday 29 November 1890 at Whalley Range, Manchester
LANCASHIRE 7 *Back*: T Coop (Lei, 2c). *Three-quarters*: J Valentine (capt, Swi, t), JH Marsh (Swi), EH Flower (Bro). *Half-backs*: J Berry (Tyl), W Bumby (Swi). *Forwards*: W Atkinson (Wig), T Brayshay (Wig), T Craven (Sal), T Kent (Sal), J Pyke (StHR), T Rothwell (Swi), J Strang (Liv, 2t), T Whittaker (Man), RP Wilson (LivOB).

YORKSHIRE 1 *Back*: S Mawson (Otley). *Three-quarters*: J Dyson (Hud), Joe Naylor (Dew), RE Lockwood (Heck). *Half-backs*: F Bonsor (Brad), Jim Naylor (Bat, t). *Forwards*: H Bedford (Mor), WE Bromet (Tad), JL Hickson (capt, Brad), E Holmes (Mann), G Jacketts (Hull), D Jowett (Heck), FW Lowrie (Bat), W Nichol (BrigR), JT Toothill (Brad).
Attendance: 15,000   *Referee*: RD Rainie (Scotland)

Monday 8 December 1890 at Belle Vue, Wakefield
YORKSHIRE 11 *Back*: F Blackburn (Heck, 2c). *Three-quarters*: J Dyson (Hud, 2t), Joe Naylor (Dew), RE Lockwood (Heck, 2t). *Half-backs*: J Bedford (Wak), Jim Naylor (Bat). *Forwards*: H Bedford (Mor, t), J Broadbent (Lee), WE Bromet (Tad), JL Hickson (capt, Brad), E Holmes (Mann), D Jowett (Heck), W Nichol (BrigR), J Richards (Brad, t), JT Toothill (Brad, t).
SURREY 0 *Back*: FB Hannen (Harl). *Three-quarters*: HL Turner (Croy), R Todd (RIEC), L Smith (LonS). *Half-backs*: R Chaldecott (RosPk), EW Senior (StTHosp). *Forwards*: R Allport (ClapR), JJE Biggs (GuyHosp), WP Carpmael (capt, Black), W Daniel (LonW), DH Helps (Croy), HT Hipwell (Croy), L Pitt-Brook (London and Westminster Bank), WW Skilbeck (ClapR), WH Smith (RIEC).
Attendance: 7,000   *Referee*: WH Humphreys (Durham)

Monday 16 February 1891 at Whalley Range, Manchester
LANCASHIRE 14 *Back*: T Coop (Lei, 2c). *Three-quarters*: J Valentine (capt, Swi, 2t, c), D Gwynn (Old, 2t), W McCutcheon (Old, t). *Half-backs*: J Berry (Tyl, t), W Cross (StH). *Forwards*: W Atkinson (Wig), T Brayshay (Wig), T Craven (Sal, t), T Kent (Sal), J Pyke (StHR, t), C Rome (Bro), T Rothwell (Swi), T Whittaker (Man), RP Wilson (LivOB).
SURREY 0 *Back*: EG Turner (Croy). *Three-quarters*: HL Turner (Croy), R Todd (RIEC), L Smith (Lennox). *Half-backs*: RF Easterbrook (LonS), LH Gunnery (OMT). *Forwards*: A Allport (capt, GuyHosp), HJ Barnett (RMC), WP Carpmael (Black), W Daniel (LonW), DH Helps (Croy), WW Skilbeck (ClapR), WH Smith (RIEC), FG Swayne (Rich), R Wallis (OxfU).
Attendance: 7,000   *Referee*: HB Browning (Cheshire)

Saturday 14 March 1891 at Whalley Range, Manchester
LANCASHIRE 14 *Back*: T Coop (Lei, c). *Three-quarters*: J Valentine (capt, Swi, 3t, 3c), D Gwynn (Old), W McCutcheon (Old). *Half-backs*: J Berry (Tyl, t), W Cross (StH). *Forwards*: W Atkinson (Wig, t), E Bullough (Wig), T Craven (Sal), T Kent (Sal), T Melledew (RochH), J Pyke (StHR), T Rothwell (Swi, t), T Whittaker (Man), RP Wilson (LivOB).
GLOUCESTERSHIRE 0 *Back*: AF Hughes (Glo). *Three-quarters*: CA Hooper (CamU), T Bagwell (Glo), WJ Jackson (Glo), WH Taylor (Glo). *Half-backs*: SA Ball (Glo), W George (Glo). *Forwards*: A Collins (Glo), T Collins (Glo), A Cromwell (Glo), RC Jenkins (Glo), SH Nicholls (Car), HV Page (capt, Glo), C Williams (Glo), GJ Witcomb (Glo).
Attendance: 6,000/7,000   *Referee*: HL Ashmore (Middlesex)

Final table	P	W	D	L	For	Agst	Pts
Lancashire	3	3	0	0	35	1	6
Yorkshire	2	1	0	1	12	7	2
Gloucestershire	1	0	0	1	0	14	0
Surrey	2	0	0	2	0	25	0

Note: Fixtures incomplete.

COUNTY CHAMPIONS v THE REST
Saturday 18 April 1891 at Whalley Range, Manchester
LANCASHIRE 3 *Back*: T Coop (Lei). *Three-quarters*: J Valentine (capt, Swi, t, c), D Gwynn (Old), W McCutcheon (Old). *Half-backs*: J Berry (Tyl), W Cross (StH). *Forwards*: W Atkinson (Wig), E Bullough (Wig), T Craven (Sal), T Kent (Sal), T Melledew (RochH), J Pyke (StHR), T Rothwell (Swi), T Whittaker (Man), RP Wilson (LivOB).
REST OF ENGLAND 4 *Back*: AS Johnston (Black). *Three-quarters*: RE Lockwood (Heck), FHR Alderson (capt, HartR, c), J Dyson (Hud). *Half-backs*: H Hughes (Run, t), EW Taylor (Rock). *Forwards*: WE Bromet (Tad), RD Budworth (Black), W Faulkner (Run), D Jowett (Heck), W Nichol (BrigR), EHG North (OxfU), JH Rogers (Mose), H Wilkinson (Hal), W Yiend (HartR).
Attendance: 18,000   *Referee*: ET Gurdon (RFU President)

NON-COUNTY CHAMPIONSHIP MATCHES
Wednesday 22 October 1890 at Irwell Lane, Runcorn
CHESHIRE 5 *Back*: S Houghton (Run). *Three-quarters*: FP Jones (NewB, 2t), JH Crompton (Run, t, c), J Cookson (Sale). *Half-backs*: S Abram (Run), RS Thorpe (Sale). *Forwards*: R Dolan (Run), RB Eskrigge (NewB), W Faulkner (capt, Run), PH Lockwood (BirkPk), TW Lockwood (BirkPk), R Morton (Alt), P Riley (Run), C Schofield (Stock), JH Smith (Stock).
MIDLAND COUNTIES 1 *Back*: JF Moore (OEdw). *Three-quarters*: AR Badger (OEdw, t), P Nichol (OEdw) W Auster (OEdw). *Half-backs*: CH Stone (Mose), A Slater (Cov). *Forwards*: A Bennett (Strat), T Cash (Cov), JR Deykin (Burt), F Evershed (Burt), JH Lory (Burt), K McAlpin (Leic), WA Maris (OEdw), WN Mayne (Mose), WH Sturges (Leic).
Attendance: 2,000   *Referee*: AN Hornby (Lancashire)

Monday 27 October 1890 at Valley Parade, Bradford
YORKSHIRE COLTS 13 *Back*: F Blackburn (Heck, 2c). *Three-quarters*: H Pickford (Hol), R Walton (Armley, 2t, dg), T Summersgill (Lee). *Half-backs*: H Hartley (Hol), B Pocock (capt, Mann, t, c). *Forwards*: W Binks (Wak), WE Bromet (Tad), T Else (Hud), H Halliday (Heck), HA Hardacre (Mann), H Hughes (BrigR), EG Load (Lee), H Lodge (Kirkburton, t), D McGreavy (Normanton St John's).
CUMBERLAND 2 *Back*: J Moore (capt, Mil). *Three-quarters*: JP Graham (Whi), H Wallace (Egr), I Moore (Mil). *Half-backs*: J Armstrong (Mil, t), R Cuthbertson (Cock, t). *Forwards*: GB Atkinson (Whi), JH Buckett (Mil), Jim Davidson (Asp), J Holme (Mil), M Humphrey (Mary), J Kidd (Mil), W Moore (Work), D Mulholland (Egr), J Mumberson (Asp).
Attendance: 3,000   *Referee*: WH Humphreys (Durham)

Saturday 1 November 1890 at Maryport Cricket Ground
CUMBERLAND 12 *Back*: J Moore (capt, Mil). *Three-quarters*: H Wallace (Egr), JP Graham (Whi, t, 3c), I Moore (Mil, t). *Half-backs*: J Armstrong (Mil), R Cuthbertson (Cock, t). *Forwards*: GB Atkinson (Whi, t), J Holme (Mil), E Houston (Sea), M Humphrey (Mary, t), J Kidd (Mil), D Mulholland (Egr), J Pender (PenU), J Sandwith (Sea), C Simpson (Egr, t).
NORTHUMBERLAND 0 *Back*: H Haslam (NEls). *Three-quarters*: F Finney (PerPk), E Emley (Nor), F Thompson (Tynd). *Half-backs*: MT Scott (capt, Nor), EW Taylor (Rock). *Forwards*: H Angus (Nor), JH Greenwell (Rock), F Lattimer (Rock), S Manford (Nor), F Marshall (PerPk), GW Mole (NEls), G Robson (Rock), C Scott (Nor), A Styan (Rock).
Attendance: 2,000   *Referee*: J MacLaren (Lancashire)

Milestones & Stats 1869-1901 215

Saturday 15 November 1890 at Jesmond Ground, Newcastle
NORTHUMBERLAND 1 *Back*: J Taylor (Gos). *Three-quarters*: F Finney (PerPk, t),
EW Taylor (Rock), T Nicholson (Rock). *Half-backs*: MT Scott (Nor), T Stewart (PerPk).
Forwards: H Angus (Nor), A Benson (Rock), TG Boss (Gos), , G Davidson (PerPk), JH
Greenwell (Rock), S Manford (Nor), G Robson (Rock), C Scott (Nor), H Shotton (PerPk).
LANCASHIRE 15 *Back*: T Coop (Lei, c). *Three-quarters*: J Valentine (capt, Swi, 4t, 2c),
D Gwynn (Old, t), EH Flower (Bro, t). *Half-backs*: J Berry (Tyl, t), W Bumby (Swi).
Forwards: W Atkinson (Wig), T Brayshay (Wig, t), T Craven (Sal), T Melledew (RochH),
G Pollard (ManR), T Rothwell (Swi), J Strang (Liv), T Whittaker (Man, t), RP Wilson
(LivOB).
Attendance: 5,000   *Referee*: WH Humphreys (Durham)

Saturday 6 December 1890 at Friarage Field, Hartlepool
DURHAM 1 *Back*: W Dooley (WHart). *Three-quarters*: TAF Crow (Sund), WH Bell (Sund),
FHR Alderson (HartR, t), W Wainford (Tud). *Half-backs*: AC Scott (HartR), G Smith
(HartR). *Forwards*: HT Barmby (DurC), A Burn (Sund), T Faulkner (Tud), A Hill (HartR),
P Turnbull (WHart), J Wheatley (Hou/Sund), CTB Wilkinson (DurC), W Yiend (HartR).
CHESHIRE 1 *Back*: S Houghton (Run). *Three-quarters*: JT Haslam (Duk), JH Crompton
(Run), FP Jones (NewB). *Half-backs*: S Abram (Run), F Drinkwater (Sale). *Forwards*:
R Dolan (Run), W Faulkner (Run), PH Lockwood (BirkPk, t), R Morton (Stock), P Riley
(Run), C Schofield (Stock), JH Smith (Stock), WA Williams (NewB), AG Wood (BirkPk).
Attendance: 5,000   *Referee*: Rev F Marshall (Yorkshire)

Saturday 10 January 1891 at Cemetery Lane, Carlisle
CUMBERLAND 4 *Back*: L Beattie (Asp). *Three-quarters*: JP Graham (Whi, t), JT Bell
(PenU), JH Buckett (Mil, c). *Half-backs*: J Armstrong (Mil), R Cuthbertson (Cock, t).
Forwards: Jim Davidson (Asp), J Holme (Mil), M Humphrey (Mary), J Kidd (Mil),
D Mulholland (Egr), J Mumberson (Asp), J Pender (PenU), J Ray (Whi), C Simpson (Egr).
SOUTH OF SCOTLAND 4 *Back*: G Cochrane (Gala). *Half-backs*: T Almers (Haw),
WS Oliver (Jed), AF McNee (Haw). *Quarter-backs*: W Wilson (capt, Jed), J Veitch (Lang).
Forwards: J Dalgleish (Gala, t), R Douglas (Jed, c), W Fairgrieve (Walkerburn), N Kemp
(Gala), W Mable (Hawick St Cuthbert's), M McAndrew (Haw, t), D Marchbanks (Jed),
TM Scott (Mel), W Stevenson (Lang).
Attendance: 1,000   *Referee*: M Newsome (Yorkshire)

Saturday 10 January 1891 at County Ground, St Thomas, Exeter
DEVONSHIRE 2 *Back*: GC Middleton (Barn). *Three-quarters*: CF Cash (DevA, t), FS Cox
(RNEC), AA Bearne (NewA). *Half-backs*: F Hall (DevA), F Penny (capt, Barn). *Forwards*:
GH Allington (DevA), R Biddell (Exe), Davenport (DevA), E Eastcott (DevA), JH Hills
(Exe), H Osmond (Exe), FJ Sellicks (NewA, t), S Thomas (Exe), BH Wallis (Exe).
LANCASHIRE 11 *Back*: T Coop (Lei, 2c). *Three-quarters*: F Miles (Sal, t), EH Flower (capt,
Bro, 2t), D Gwynn (Old), W McCutcheon (Old, 2t). *Half-backs*: J Berry (Tyl), W Cross
(StH). *Forwards*: W Atkinson (Wig), T Brayshay (Wig, t), E Bullough (Wig), T Kent (Sal),
J Pyke (StHR, t), C Rome (Bro), T Whittaker (Man), RP Wilson (LivOB).
Attendance: 3,000   *Referee*: SH Sparkes (Somersetshire)

Saturday 24 January 1891 at Whalley Range, Manchester
LANCASHIRE 6 *Back*: T Coop (Lei, p). *Three-quarters*: EH Flower (Bro, t), D Gwynn (Old), J Valentine (capt, Swi, 2t). *Half-backs*: J Berry (Tyl, t), W Cross (StH). *Forwards*: W Atkinson (Wig), T Brayshay (Wig), T Craven (Sal), T Kent (Sal), T Melledew (RochH), J Pyke (StHR), T Rothwell (Swi), T Whittaker (Man), RP Wilson (LivOB).
DURHAM 1 *Back*: W Dooley (WHart). *Three-quarters*: TAF Crow (Sund, t), FHR Alderson (capt, HartR), WH Bell (Sund), RCF Crow (Sund). *Half-backs*: AC Scott (HartR), WE Wilkinson (DurC). *Forwards*: HT Barmby (DurC), WA Bell (Tud), A Burn (Sund), T Faulkner (Tud), CM Huntley (HartR), P Turnbull (WHart), J Wheatley (Hou/Sund), W Yiend (HartR).
Attendance: 2,500   *Referee*: HB Browning (Cheshire)

Saturday 24 January 1891 at Park Avenue, Bradford
YORKSHIRE 7 *Back*: H Barnes (Hal, c). *Three-quarters*: I Newton (Mann), Joe Naylor (Dew), RE Lockwood (Heck, t, c). *Half-backs*: J Bedford (Wak, t), HJR Oxlade (Hull). *Forwards*: W Binks (Wak), WE Bromet (Tad), E Dewhirst (Brad), E Holmes (capt, Mann), D Jowett (Heck), W Nichol (BrigR), J Richards (Brad, t), JT Toothill (Brad), A Wilson (Hal).
SOMERSETSHIRE 0 *Back*: H Boucher (Wivel). *Three-quarters*: CF Mermagen (Well), H Merry (Well), NH Steed (Well). *Half-backs*: FC Duckworth (Wes), FH Fox (Well). *Forwards*: G Allen (Clif), H Fowler (Tau), PF Hancock (Wivel/Black), WH Manfield (Yeo), RMP Parsons (Crew), F Soane (Bath), CR Stack (Well), CJ Vernon (Well), SMJ Woods (Bridg/CamU).
Attendance: 4,000   *Referee*: T Hunter (Lancashire)

Saturday 14 February 1891 at Fartown, Huddersfield
YORKSHIRE 6 *Back*: H Barnes (Hal). *Three-quarters*: RE Lockwood (Heck, c), R Walton (Armley), I Newton (Mann). *Half-backs*: C Emmott (Brad, t), HJR Oxlade (Hull). *Forwards*: W Binks (Wak), A Briggs (Otley), J Broadbent (Lee), WE Bromet (Tad), E Holmes (capt, Mann, t), D Jowett (Heck, t), H Lodge (Hud), W Nichol (BrigR, t), A Wilson (Hal).
CHESHIRE 6 *Back*: S Houghton (Run, dg). *Three-quarters*: JT Haslam (Duk, dg), JH Crompton (Run), TH Davies (Run). *Half-backs*: S Abram (Run), H Hughes (Run). *Forwards*: W Faulkner (Run), J Gayter (Run), W Hughes (Run), PH Lockwood (BirkPk), TW Lockwood (BirkPk), P Riley (Run), JH Smith (Stock), WA Williams (NewB), AG Wood (BirkPk).
Attendance: 10,000   *Referee*: WH Humphreys (Durham)

Monday 9 March 1891 at Whalley Range, Manchester
LANCASHIRE 11 *Back*: T Coop (Lei). *Three-quarters*: J Valentine (Swi, 3c), D Gwynn (Old), F Miles (Sal). *Half-backs*: J Berry (Tyl), BG Roscoe (Man). *Forwards*: W Atkinson (Wig), E Bullough (Wig), T Kent (Sal), T Melledew (RochH), J Pyke (StHR, 2t), JW Roberts (Sal), C Rome (Bro, t), T Rothwell (Swi), T Whittaker (Man, 2t).
ULSTER 0 *Back*: DB Walkington (NIFC). *Half-backs*: RW Dunlop (NIFC), S Lee (NIFC), S Clarke (BelA). *Quarter-backs*: W Monypenny (QCB), R Pedlow (Bess). *Forwards*: W Bratton (QCB), WJN Davis (Bess), JS Dick (QCB), TJ Johnston (QCB), JN Lytle (NIFC), GH Moore (BelA), W Morell (QCB), R Stevenson (Dun), T Taggart (NIFC).
Attendance: 8,000   *Referee*: HB Browning (Cheshire)

ENGLAND TRIAL MATCH

Monday 29 December 1890 at Headingley, Leeds*
NORTH 1 goal, 3 tries *Back*: T Coop (Lei, c). *Three-quarters*: J Valentine (Swi), JH Marsh (capt, Swi), RE Lockwood (Heck, t). *Half-backs*: W Cross (StH), J Berry (Tyl). *Forwards*: W Atkinson (Wig), WE Bromet (Tad, 2t), D Jowett (Heck), T Kent (Sal), PH Lockwood (BirkPk), J Richards (Brad), JT Toothill (Brad, t), CTB Wilkinson (DurC), RP Wilson (LivOB).
SOUTH 1 goal *Back*: AS Johnstone (Black). *Three-quarters*: PH Morrison (CamU), WG Mitchell (GuyHosp/Rich), P Christopherson (capt, Black). *Half-backs*: WRM Leake (Harl), Arthur Rotherham (CamU, t). *Forwards*: A Allport (Black), E Bonham-Carter (OxfU), RD Budworth (Black), J Hammond (Black), EHG North (OxfU), LJ Percival (OxfU), JH Rogers (Mose), SE Wilson (OxfU), SMJ Woods (Bridg/CamU, c).
Attendance: 12,000   *Referee*: ET Gurdon (RFU President)
*Played in Leeds after two postponements at Blackheath due to frost.

INTERNATIONAL CHAMPIONSHIP

Saturday 3 January 1891 at Rodney Parade, Newport
WALES 3 *Back*: WJ Bancroft (Swa, c). *Three-quarters*: TW Pearson (Car, t), CS Arthur (Car), D Gwynn (Swa), P Lloyd (Llan). *Half-backs*: HM Ingledew (Car), CJ Thomas (New). *Forwards*: P Bennett (CarHarl), W Bowen (capt, Swa), DW Evans (Car), J Hannan (New), H Packer (New), EV Pegge (Nea), W Rice-Evans (Swa), RL Thomas (LonW).
ENGLAND 7 *Back*: WG Mitchell (GuyHosp/Rich). *Three-quarters*: RE Lockwood (Heck), FHR Alderson (capt, HartR, 2c), P Christopherson (Black, 2t). *Half-backs*: J Berry (Tyl), WRM Leake (Harl). *Forwards*: WE Bromet (Tad), RD Budworth (Black, t), D Jowett (Heck), T Kent (Sal), EHG North (OxfU), J Richards (Brad), JT Toothill (Brad), RP Wilson (LivOB), SMJ Woods (Bridg/CamU).
Attendance: 12,000   *Referee*: RD Rainie (Scotland)

Saturday 7 February 1891 at Lansdowne Road, Dublin
IRELAND 0 *Back*: DB Walkington (capt, NIFC). *Half-backs*: RW Dunlop (NIFC), S Lee (NIFC), R Montgomery (NIFC). *Quarter-backs*: AC McDonnell (DubU), BB Tuke (BecR). *Forwards*: WJN Davis (Bess), EG Forrest (Wand), VC le Fanu (Lans), JN Lytle (NIFC), LC Nash (QCC), JH O'Conor (BecR), J Roche (Wand), CV Rooke (DubU), J Waites (BecR).
ENGLAND 9 *Back*: WG Mitchell (GuyHosp/Rich). *Three-quarters*: PH Morrison (CamU), FHR Alderson (capt, HartR), RE Lockwood (Heck). *Half-backs*: J Berry (Tyl), WRM Leake (Harl). *Forwards*: WE Bromet (Tad), D Jowett (Heck), T Kent (Sal), EHG North (OxfU), LJ Percival (OxfU), J Richards (Brad), JT Toothill (Brad), RP Wilson (LivOB), SMJ Woods (Bridg/CamU).
Attendance: 10,000   *Referee*: WM Douglas (Wales)

Saturday 7 March 1891 at Athletic Ground, Richmond
ENGLAND 3 *Back*: WG Mitchell (GuyHosp/Rich). *Three-quarters*: P Christopherson (Black), FHR Alderson (capt, HartR, c), RE Lockwood (Heck, t). *Half-backs*: J Berry (Tyl), WRM Leake (Harl). *Forwards*: E Bonham-Carter (OxfU), RD Budworth (Black), D Jowett (Heck), T Kent (Sal), EHG North (OxfU) J Richards (Brad), JH Rogers (Mose), RP Wilson (LivOB), SMJ Woods (Bridg/CamU).

SCOTLAND 9 *Back*: HJ Stevenson (EdinA). *Half-backs*: PR Clauss (OxfU, dg), G MacGregor (CamU, 2c), W Neilson (MerCS, t). *Quarter-backs*: DG Anderson (LonS), CE Orr (WoS). *Forwards*: JD Boswell (WoS), WR Gibson (RHSFP), FW Goodhue (LonS), HTO Leggatt (Wat), MC McEwan (capt, EdinA), I McIntyre (EdinW), RG Macmillan (LonS), GT Neilson (WoS), JE Orr (WoS, t).
Attendance: 15,000   *Referee*: J Chambers (Ireland)

Other results	Final table						
Scotland 15, Wales 0		P	W	D	L	For	Agst
Ireland 0, Scotland 14	Scotland	3	3	0	0	38	3
Wales 6, Ireland 4	England	3	2	0	1	19	12
	Wales	3	1	0	2	9	26
	Ireland	3	0	0	3	4	29

ENGLAND TOUR OF SOUTH AFRICA 1891

TOUR PARTY
WE 'Bill' Maclagan (captain, London Scottish)
Randolph L Aston (Blackheath/Cambridge University)
Edward Bromet (St Thomas's Hosp.)
William E Bromet (Tadcaster)
Paul R Clauss (Oxford University)
John H Gould (Old Leysians)
John Hammond (Blackheath)
P Froude Hancock (Wiveliscombe/Blackheath)
Walter Jackson (Gloucester)
Robert G Macmillan (London Scottish)
Howard Marshall (Blackheath)
Edwin Mayfield (Cambridge University)
William G Mitchell (Guy's Hospital/Richmond)
Bertwine G Roscoe (Manchester)
Arthur Rotherham (Cambridge University)
Clement P Simpson (Cambridge University)
Aubone A Surtees (Harlequins)
Robert Thompson (Cambridge University)
William H Thorman (Cambridge University)
Tom Whittaker (Manchester)
William Wotherspoon (Cambridge University)

TOUR RESULTS
Thursday 9 July – Cape Town, won 15-1 (attendance: 6,000)
Saturday 11 July – Western Province (at Cape Town), won 6-0 (3,000)
Monday 13 July – Cape Colony (Cape Town), won 14-0 (2,000)
Saturday 18 July – Kimberley, won 7-0 (4,000)
Monday 20 July – Griqualand West (Kimberley), won 3-0 (3,000)
Saturday 25 July – Port Elizabeth, won 22-0 (4,000)
Tuesday 28 July – Eastern Province (Port Elizabeth), won 21-0 (4,000)

Milestones & Stats 1869-1901 219

TOUR RESULTS *continued*
Thursday 30 July – **South Africa** (Port Elizabeth), won 4-0 (5,000)
Saturday 1 August – Grahamstown, won 9-0 (3,500)
Tuesday 4 August – King William's Town, won 18-0 (3,000)
Thursday 6 August – King William's Town and East London (King William's Town), won 16-0 (3,000)
Tuesday 11 August – Pietermaritzburg, won 25-0 (2,000)
Saturday 15 August – Transvaal (Johannesburg), won 22-0 (5,000)
Wednesday 19 August – Johannesburg, won 15-0
Saturday 22 August – Transvaal (Johannesburg), won 9-0
Wednesday 26 August – Cape Colony (Kimberley), won 4-0
Saturday 29 August – **South Africa** (Kimberley), won 3-0 (3,000)
Thursday 3 September – Cape Colony (Cape Town), won 7-0 (3,000)
Saturday 5 September – **South Africa** (Cape Town), won 4-0 (3,000)
Monday 7 September – Stellenbosch College, won 2-0*
* Privately arranged unofficial match in college grounds, lasting one hour.

Thursday 30 July 1891 at the Port Elizabeth Cricket Ground
SOUTH AFRICA 0 *Back*: B Duff (WP). *Three-quarters*: HC Boyes (GW), JT Vigne (Tvl), MC van Buuren (Tvl). *Half-backs*: FH Guthrie (WP), AR Richards (WP). *Forwards*: E Alexander (GW), WM Bisset (WP), HH Castens (capt, WP), M Devenish (Tvl), F Hamilton (EP), EMM Little (GW), JS Louw (Tvl), J Merry (EP), M Versfeld (WP).
ENGLAND 4 *Back*: WG Mitchell. *Three-quarters*: PR Clauss, RL Aston (t), WE Maclagan (capt). *Half-backs*: A Rotherham (c), W Wotherspoon. *Forwards*: WE Bromet, JH Gould, J Hammond, PF Hancock, RG Macmillan, CP Simpson, AA Surtees, R Thompson, T Whittaker (t).
Attendance: 6,000   *Referee*: J Griffin (South Africa)

Saturday 29 August 1891 at Eclectics Ground, Kimberley
SOUTH AFRICA 0 *Back*: B Duff (WP). *Three-quarters*: HC Boyes (GW), JT Vigne (Tvl), A de Kock (GW). *Half-backs*: JM Powell (GW), AR Richards (WP). *Forwards*: E Alexander (GW), BH Heatlie (WP), JS Louw (Tvl), R Shand (GW), CW Smith (GW), D Smith (GW), RC Snedden (capt, GW), W Trenery (GW), M Versfeld (WP).
ENGLAND 3 *Back*: WG Mitchell (gm). *Three-quarters*: PR Clauss, RL Aston, WE Maclagan (capt). *Half-backs*: E Bromet, H Marshall. *Forwards*: WE Bromet, JH Gould, J Hammond, PF Hancock, RG Macmillan, E Mayfield, AA Surtees, R Thompson, T Whittaker.
Attendance: 3,000   *Referee*: P Ross-Frames (South Africa)

Saturday 5 September 1891 at Newlands, Cape Town
SOUTH AFRICA 0 *Back*: B Duff (WP). *Three-quarters*: AJ Hartley (WP), JT Vigne (Tvl), C Versfeld (WP). *Half-backs*: FH Guthrie (WP), AR Richards (capt, WP). *Forwards*: WM Bisset (WP), TW Chignell (WP), BH Heatlie (WP), EMM Little (GW), JS Louw (Tvl), JA McKendrick (WP), R Shand (GW), CG van Renen (WP), M Versfeld (WP).
ENGLAND 4 *Back*: WG Mitchell. *Three-quarters*: PR Clauss, RL Aston (t), WE Maclagan (capt, t). *Half-backs*: H Marshall, A Rotherham (c). *Forwards*: E Bromet, WE Bromet, J Hammond, PF Hancock, RG Macmillan, E Mayfield, AA Surtees, R Thompson, T Whittaker.
Attendance: 3,000   *Referee*: HH Castens (South Africa)

John 'Buff' Berry of Kendal Hornets, Tyldesley, Westmorland, Lancashire, the North, and England.
Lloyd's Weekly Newspaper, 1891

1891-1892

NEW SCORING MODE FOR YORKSHIRE
The Yorkshire Committee held a meeting at the Queen's Hotel, Leeds, on 11th August, when it was decided to adopt a point-scoring system for the Yorkshire Cup. It was based on the values agreed at the recent International Board meeting at the Grand Hotel, Manchester (8th August), and subsequently ratified at the Rugby Football Union's Annual General Meeting (Westminster Hotel, London, 16th September); converted try – 5 points, drop goal or goal kicked from a rolling ball (field goal) – 4 points, penalty goal – 3 points, unconverted try – 2 points.[125]

THE NORTH WESTERN LEAGUE
The North Western League was the second senior League competition launched in the north of England, embracing clubs from three counties; Cumberland (Millom), Lancashire (Askam, Barrow, Lancaster, Morecambe, Ulverston), and Westmorland (Kendal Hornets, Kendal Town). Millom, unbeaten during the season, were the inaugural champions.

DURHAM MEMBERSHIP IN DECLINE
The Durham County Union held its annual meeting at the Waltons Hotel, Sunderland, on 1st September. It was stated that the number of clubs at the start of the previous season had been 17 but Boldon, Consett, Henderson's Wanderers, and Throston Wanderers had since resigned. It

was agreed that West Hartlepool West End, by virtue of winning the Durham Junior Cup, were to be promoted to the senior rank and, therefore, admitted to the Union. This meant the number of clubs stood at 14, the committee expressing 'regret [at the] falling off in membership'.[126]

G. ROWLAND HILL MOBBED

When Cumberland met Lancashire at the Cricket Field, Whitehaven, on 21st November, the referee, Mr G. Rowland Hill, who was also Honorary Secretary of the Rugby Football Union, was subjected to abuse. The *Yorkshire Herald* reported: 'The Cumberland Rugby Union, consequent on the rough and unwarrantable behaviour of a section of the spectators towards the referee, decided that no match under their auspices should be played on the Whitehaven club ground during the present season, and no county match within a radius of fifteen miles until the end of next season.'[127]

WESTMORLAND FAIL TO KEEP THEIR APPOINTMENT

The Lancashire versus Westmorland match, scheduled for Whalley Range, Manchester, on 5th December, was cancelled by the visitors, a decision that led to controversy. The initial reaction in the Lancashire press was to criticise Kendal Hornets for having a League engagement on that date, and Kendal Town who, 'for some unexplained cause,' had resigned from the Westmorland Union. It was claimed that jealous rivalry existed between the two Kendal clubs, who provided the bulk of the county side, and that Town 'backed out [because] the Hornets received too much favour'. Kendal Hornets responded, a letter from their secretary appearing in the *Bradford Daily Telegraph*: 'The reason the fixture was abandoned was not owing to the action of Kendal Hornets, but to the unsportsmanlike secession of Kendal Town. Kendal Hornets have held the position of premier club of the county for the last 16 years, and have always supplied the majority of county players. In the match under notice the attendance of their players was excused, as they had an important fixture that day. Kendal Town took offence at only having three selected and, at the last moment, seceded from the [Westmorland] Union, making it impossible to get a team together.'[128]

DYSON SCORES FIVE TRIES

Jack Dyson's five tries for Yorkshire against Kent on 1st February was a County Championship record for a northern county player during the Victorian era. Previously John Lowthian Bell had scored five for Northumberland, but that had been in a friendly engagement against West

Cumberland on 16th March 1878. Yorkshire was on the receiving end when Glamorganshire's W. J. 'Billy' Trew registered five against them on 29th October 1900 in a non-championship fixture.

THE SENSELESS SCREECHING OF TIN TRUMPETS

Hartlepool Rovers hosted their neighbours West Hartlepool in the first round of the Durham Cup, a meeting that created tremendous interest. The *Yorkshire Herald* reported: 'Not even a Yorkshire County match, the presence of the Barbarians, nor even the Maoris, attracted such an immense gathering on the Friarage Field at Hartlepool, as last Saturday's [27th February] when, in spite of the north-east wind, the leaden sky, and drizzling rain, considerably over 10,000 spectators turned out to witness the antagonism of Hartlepool Rovers and West Hartlepool. So great was the interest that fully 5,000 arrived from the sister town [West Hartlepool]. As early as 1.30 pm upwards of 2,000 had paid for admission and the stream flowed steadily until, punctual to the minute, the teams appeared on the field, each being greeted with a perfect storm of applause, mingled with the senseless screeching of tin trumpets.'[129]

THE YORKSHIRE CUP: UNUSUAL REPLAYS

The Yorkshire Committee continued to arbitrate on Yorkshire Cup matters in circumstances that would be uncommon today. After Wibsey Slack Side had drawn 5-5 with Tadcaster in a qualifying round match on 12th March, Wibsey Slack Side protested that the Tadcaster players had received 'refreshments' during the game (one report suggested it was only one player, who received a 'wee drop' from a flask offered by 'a gentleman of the press'). It was decided Tadcaster should forfeit home advantage in the replay which took place at the Armley ground, Leeds, Tadcaster winning 14-5.[130] The Heckmondwike versus Harrogate first round tie on 19th March was postponed because Harrogate (on advice from the Harrogate Medical Officer) refused to go to Heckmondwike due to a smallpox outbreak in that town. Heckmondwike rejected Harrogate's suggestion of a different venue, but were eventually instructed to play at Cleckheaton on 23rd March. Heckmondwike won 30-7 despite the match being abandoned a few minutes from time after the ball burst, there being no replacement.[131]

SPIKED BOOTS IN THE CUMBERLAND CUP FINAL

After Aspatria defeated Whitehaven 4-0 in the Cumberland Cup final at Maryport on 10th April, the losers claimed victory on discovering Aspatria's Lewis Beattie had breached the rules by wearing spikes on his boots. The Cumberland Committee referred it to the Rugby Football Union, who decided Aspatria's win should stand. The referee, Reverend Frank Marshall, wrote about the incident in the *Yorkshire Evening Post*: 'It has been reserved for a Cumberland cup-tie to furnish one of the funniest and most complicated questions that I have had to deal with in my varied experience of cup-tie contests. The game had proceeded some 60 minutes when the appeal was made. Aspatria had scored a drop goal [and] at this period the Whitehaven captain claimed an Aspatria three-quarter had spikes in his boots. Examination showed the correctness of the claim, for the man had his boots studded with iron or steel pegs of cylindrical form. I immediately decided that these pegs were illegal. "Then I claim the match" said the Whitehaven captain. Here was a bonny kettle of fish for a bewildered referee. I ordered the player to go and change his boots, and commanded the Whitehaven men to continue the game as if nothing had happened, intimating that I would inform the committee that the appeal had been properly put before me. The whole occurrence was over in a twinkling, and none of the spectators knew more than that the player had been sent off to exchange his boots.'[132]

LEEDS IN A BOATING ACCIDENT

Leeds, who were due to meet Hunslet in the Yorkshire Cup final at Fartown, Huddersfield, on 23rd April, exercised in two boats near Knaresborough on the previous day. Unfortunately, the boats collided and half the team were immersed in the water, eight receiving injuries. Despite one pessimistic report stating 'it is doubtful whether they will be able to play today,' the final went ahead. Hunslet won 21-0, a *Pall Mall Gazette* journalist, referring to the accident, wrote 'whether this affected the result it is impossible to say'.[133]

NORTH EAST INTER-COUNTY CHALLENGE REVIVED

The inter-county challenge between the winners of the Durham Cup and Northumberland Cup was reintroduced following a seven-year gap, Tudhoe (Durham) opposing Rockcliff (Northumberland) at the Jesmond Ground in Newcastle on 23rd April. Its revival proved short-lived, lasting just two seasons.

1891-1892 STATISTICS

NORTH WESTERN LEAGUE

Final table	P	W	D	L	For	Agst	Pts
Millom	14	10	4	0	116	24	24
Lancaster	14	7	5	2	68	30	19
Barrow	14	8	2	4	89	48	18
Ulverston	14	7	3	4	90	31	17
Morecambe	14	6	1	7	71	64	13
Kendal Hornets	14	5	3	6	81	63	13
Kendal Town	14	3	0	11	49	123	6
Askam	14	1	0	13	34	215	2

WEST LANCASHIRE RUGBY LEAGUE

Final table	P	W	D	L	For	Agst	Pts
Aspull	8	6	0	2	38	14	12
Pemberton	8	5	0	3	101	42	10
Birkenhead Wanderers	7	3	0	4	40	33	6
Boothstown	8	3	0	5	39	36	6
Tottington	7	2	0	5	16	109	4

Note: Tottington v Birkenhead Wanderers postponed and not subsequently played.

CUMBERLAND COUNTY CHALLENGE CUP (12 entries)
Try – 2 points; conversion, penalty goal – 3; drop-goal, field goal, goal from mark – 4.
If equal then majority of 3 minor points required to win.

First Round
Flimby 0, Egremont 0 (mp: 1-1, no extra time)
Cockermouth 0, Whitehaven 21
Cummersdale Hornets 7, Workington 7 (mp: 3-1, aet)
Seaton 12, Penrith United 0
Byes: Aspatria, Broughton, Dearham, Maryport

Second Round
Egremont 18, Cummersdale Hornets 0
Maryport 0, Aspatria 0 (mp: 0-4)
Seaton 6, Dearham 0
Whitehaven 14, Broughton 2

Semi-finals
Aspatria 2, Seaton 0 (at Maryport Cricket Ground)
Whitehaven 10, Egremont 6 (at Cleator)

First Round Replays
Egremont 12, Flimby 0
Workington 0, Cummersdale Hornets 0 (mp: 4-3, aet)

First Round Second Replay
Cummersdale Hornets 9, Workington 4 (at Carlisle)

FINAL
Saturday 9 April 1892 at Maryport Cricket Ground
ASPATRIA 4 *Back*: JH Blaylock. *Three-quarters*: Jerry Saul, W Skelton (dg), L Beattie.
Half-backs: J Mumberson, Joe Nelson. *Forwards*: T Allison, JW Cowan, T Grieve (capt),
J Little, R Mumberson, T Robinson, Joseph Saul, J Stanger, J Todd.
WHITEHAVEN 0 *Back*: WH Younghusband. *Three-quarters*: T Johnstone, W Sharp (capt),
E Thornburrow. *Half-backs*: J Kitchin, Stewart. *Forwards*: GB Atkinson, R Burns,
J Campbell, D Cavender, W Lennox, D Lowrey, John Ray, Joseph Ray, J Wright
Attendance: 4,000   *Referee*: Rev F Marshall (Yorkshire RU)

DURHAM COUNTY CHALLENGE CUP (12 entries)
Try – 2 points; conversion, penalty goal – 3; drop-goal, field goal, goal from mark – 4.

First Round
Hartlepool Rovers 7, West Hartlepool 2
Houghton-le-Spring 2, Durham City 14
North Durham 0, Tudhoe 2
South Shields YMCA 46, Stockton 0
Sunderland w/o West Hartlepool West End (disbanded)
Westoe 4, Hartlepool Rangers 11

Second Round
Hartlepool Rangers 0, Durham City 4
Hartlepool Rovers 9, Sunderland 0
South Shields YMCA 0, Tudhoe 6

Semi-final
Durham City 2, Hartlepool Rovers 18
Bye: Tudhoe

FINAL
Saturday 2 April 1892 at Ashbrooke Ground, Sunderland
TUDHOE 2 *Back*: W Taylor. *Three-quarters*: W Wainford (t), J Robertshaw (capt), H Mills.
Half-backs: F Hindle, F Marston. *Forwards*: WA Bell, G Copley, J Duffey, T Faulkner,
J Gibbon, J Hamilton, JW Hodgson, J Lindsay, AJ Troupe.
HARTLEPOOL ROVERS 2 *Back*: W Smith. *Three-quarters*: T McDougal, FHR Alderson,
C Hodgson, JW Horn. *Half-backs*: W McSloy (t), AC Scott. *Forwards*: GE Boagey, J Burt,
J Coates, A Hill, CM Huntley, J Snowdon, W Snowdon, W Yiend (capt).
After extra time   *Attendance*: 8,000   *Referee*: H Knaggs (Yorkshire RU)

FINAL REPLAY
Saturday 9 April 1892 at Ashbrooke Ground, Sunderland
TUDHOE 2 *Back*: W Taylor. *Three-quarters*: W Wainford, J Robertshaw (capt), H Mills.
Half-backs: F Hindle, F Marston. *Forwards*: WA Bell, G Copley (t), J Duffey, T Faulkner,
J Gibbon, J Hamilton, JW Hodgson, J Lindsay, AJ Troupe.
HARTLEPOOL ROVERS 0 *Back*: JW Horn. *Three-quarters*: FHR Alderson, C Hodgson,
A Chivers, T McDougal. *Half-backs*: W McSloy, AC Scott. *Forwards*: GE Boagey, J Burt,
J Coates, A Hill, CM Huntley, J Snowdon, W Snowdon, W Yiend (capt).
Attendance: 10,000   *Referee*: H Knaggs (Yorkshire RU)

NORTHUMBERLAND COUNTY FOOTBALL CHALLENGE CUP (9 entries)
Try – 2 points; conversion, penalty goal – 3; drop-goal, field goal, goal from mark – 4.

First Round
Rockcliff 4, Tynedale 0
Byes: 7 teams drew a bye to next round

Semi-finals
Percy Park 19, Brighton 5
Rockcliff 51, North Elswick 0

Second Round
Northern 2, North Elswick 6
Northumberland FC 0, Brighton (Newcastle) 6
Percy Park 15, Gosforth 2
Rockcliff 7, Wallsend 0

FINAL
Saturday 2 April 1892 at Jesmond Ground, Newcastle
ROCKCLIFF 12 *Back*: J Murray. *Three-quarters:* T Nicholson, S Brutton (capt), W Taylor (t). *Half-backs*: TP Alexander (t), EW Taylor (2c). *Forwards*: Alf Benson, J Bolam, TG Boss, JH Greenwell, B Jobling, F Lattimer, G Robson, TC Stephenson (t), A Styan.
PERCY PARK 2 *Back*: J Taylor. *Three-quarters*: H Shotton (t), F Finney (capt), H Wilmot. *Half-backs*: HW Audus, T Stewart. *Forwards*: W Alexander, JW Coward, HF Craig, A Gee, H Newberry, H Smurthwaite, R Sopwith, RH Spence, J Wardle.
Attendance: 4,000/5,000   *Referee*: WH Humphreys (Durham RU)

DURHAM v NORTHUMBERLAND CHALLENGE MATCH
Saturday 27 April 1892 at Jesmond Ground, Newcastle
ROCKCLIFF (Northumberland Cup winners) **9** *Back:* J Murray. *Three-quarters*: W Taylor (t), S Brutton (capt), T Nicholson (2t). *Half-backs*: TP Alexander, EW Taylor (c). *Forwards*: Alf Benson, J Bolam, TG Boss, JH Greenwell, F Lattimer, GW Lee, G Robson, TC Stephenson, A Styan.
TUDHOE (Durham Cup winners) **4** *Back*: W Taylor. *Three-quarters*: H Mills, M Taylor, J Robertshaw (capt), G Copley. *Half-backs*: F Hindle, F Marston. *Forwards*: J Duffey, R Edwards, T Faulkner, J Gibbon (t), JW Hodgson, G Irwin, J Lindsay (t), AJ Troupe.
Attendance: 'large'   *Referee*: CS Gill (Northern)

YORKSHIRE COUNTY FOOTBALL CHALLENGE CUP (140 entries)
Try – 2 points; conversion, penalty goal – 3; drop-goal, field goal, goal from mark – 4.

Preliminary Round
Bankfoot 36, Chapel Allerton 2
Barnsley 4, Knottingley 0
Barnsley Parish Church 0, Armley 41
Batley Gypsies 0, Dobcross 16
Bingley 6, Horbury 0
Birstall 4, Stanningley 0
Bowling 10, Ripon 0
Bowling Old Lane 15, Keighley Shamrocks 0
Buttershaw 23, Whitwood 0
Cleckheaton White Star 25, Churwell 0
Crosland Moor 4, Keighley 2
Dewsbury St Mark's 0, Shipley 6
Farsley 4, Leeds Institute 0
Featherstone Trinity 25, Guiseley Parish Church 0
Greetland 0, Ingrow 3
Guiseley 16, Rothwell 2
Harrogate 19, Leeds Good Shepherd's 0
Harrogate Rangers 19, Rastrick Free Wanderers 0
Haworth 6, Knaresborough 0
Hebden Bridge w/o Hull St Paul's (withdrew)
Honley 4, Low Moor St Mark's 9

Preliminary Round *continued*
Horsforth 0, Newtown 4
Hull Kingston Rovers w/o Cottingham (withdrew)
Kippax 9, Buslingthorpe 0
Kirkburton 18, Hull Melbourne 0
Kirstall St Stephen's w/o Hipperholme and Lightcliffe (withdrew)
Liversedge Hornets 7, Doncaster Town 0
Lockwood 9, Shepley 0
Luddendenfoot 5, Saltaire 0
Methley 20, Holmfirth 0
Mirfield Rangers 4, Tadcaster 15
Normanton St John's w/o Bradford Trinity (withdrew)

Nortonthorpe 2, Hull White Star 10
Outwood Church 20, Pateley Bridge 0
Ravensthorpe 2, Pudsey 18
Salterhebble w/o Micklefield (withdrew)
Sedburgh w/o Netherton (withdrew)
Silsden 12 Todmorden 0
Skipton 21, Keighley Zingari 0
South Milford 5, Bailiffe Bridge 9
Wibsey 32, Hull Three Crowns 0
Wibsey Slack Side 14, East Leeds 5
Windhill 16, Yeadon White Star 6
Yorkshire College 0, Idle 18
Byes: 20 teams drew a bye to next round

Qualifying Round
Armley 34, Mytholmroyd 0
Bankfoot w/o Lockwood (withdrew)
Barnsley 15, Dewsbury St Paulinus 6
Batley Mountaineers 4, Harrogate 22
Bingley 11, Outwood Church 0
Birstall 8, Kirkburton 2
Bowling 34, Howarth 0
Buttershaw 21, Hull White Star 0
Cleckheaton White Star 2, Hebden Bridge 9
Dodworth 6, Barnsley Congregational 0
Farley w/o Sedburgh (withdrew)
Gildersome 6, Idle 2
Harrogate Rangers 0, Bailiffe Bridge 11
Hull Kingston Rovers 5, Selby 0
Ingrow w/o Yeadon (suspended)
Keighley Hornets 5, Windhill 12
Kippax 4, Bowling Old Lane 2
Kirkstall St Stephen's w/o Hull St Mary's (withdrew)

Methley 11, Luddendenfoot 4
Morley Providence 12, Beverley 2
Normaton St John's 41, Ferrybridge 0
Paddock 15, Featherstone Trinity 0
Primrose Hill 0, Low Moor St Mark's 14
Pudsey 21, Dudley Hill 0
Salterbebble 2, Guiseley 4
Shipley 19, Milnsbridge 0
Skipton 6, Liversedge Hornets 0
Thornhill Lees Trinity 0, Mirfield 4
Wakefield St Austin's 17, Crosland Moor 0
Wibsey 3, Silsden 0
Wibsey Slack Side 5, Tadcaster 5
York Leeman Wanderers 2, Newtown 7

Qualifying Round Replay
Tadcaster 14, Wibsey Slack Side 5

First Round
(* indicates 32 teams seeded to this round)
Alverthorpe* 7, Armley 5
Bailiffe Bridge 2, Pudsey 4
Batley* 17, Goole* 3
Bingley 9, Ingrow 12
Bowling 19, Woodhouse* 5
Bradford* 21, Pontefract* 0
Bramley* w/o Normanton* (suspended)
Buttershaw 2, Tadcaster 0

Cleckheaton* 11, Skipton 0
Dewsbury* 7, Hull Kingston Rovers 6
Dodworth 0, Sowerby Bridge* 9
Elland* 20, Paddock 0
Gildersome 18, Morley Providence 0
Heckmondwike* 30, Harrogate 7
Huddersfield* 44, Normanton St John's 0
Hull* 15, Morley* 2
Hull Britannia* 24, Windhill 2

First Round *continued*
Hunslet* 41, Birstall 0
Kippax 0, Brighouse Rangers* 19
Kirkstall* 11, Newtown 0
Leeds* 70, Wakefield St Austin's 2
Leeds Parish Church* 17, Guiseley 6
Liversedge* 7, Castleford* 0
Low Moor St Mark's 5, Hebden Bridge 0
Luddendenfoot 4, Barnsley 0
Manningham* 9, Shipley 0
Mirfield 10, Bankfoot 0
Ossett* 5, Holbeck* 3
Otley* 4, Halifax* 5
Wakefield Trinity* 23, Kirkstall St Stephen's 0
Wibsey 0, Wortley* 15
York* 9, Farsley 2

Second Round
Batley 11, Heckmondwike 10 (replay ordered after protest)
Bradford 12, York 2
Buttershaw 6, Hull 0
Cleckheaton 7, Leeds Parish Church 5
Dewsbury 17, Gildersome 5
Huddersfield 4, Halifax 12
Hull Britannia 2, Alverthorpe 4
Hunslet 24, Bramley 0
Ingrow 2, Liversedge 22
Kirkstall 5, Leeds 17
Low Moor St Mark's 0, Elland 6
Manningham 5, Brighouse Rangers 7 (aet)
Mirfield 6, Pudsey 0
Sowerby Bridge 6, Bowling 6 (aet)
Wakefield Trinity 3, Ossett 0
Wortley 11, Luddendenfoot 0

Second Round Replays
Bowling 9, Sowerby Bridge 7
Heckmondwike 11, Batley 0 (at Bramley)

Third Round
Alverthorpe 2, Hunslet 30
Bowling 15, Mirfield 3
Brighouse Rangers 2, Dewsbury 0
Buttershaw 5, Wakefield Trinity 8
Cleckheaton 4, Bradford 9 (aet)
Elland 0, Heckmondwike 2
Leeds 9, Halifax 6
Wortley 0, Liversedge 2

Fourth Round
Brighouse Rangers 4, Hunslet 13
Heckmondwike 0, Wakefield Trinity 2
Leeds 26, Bowling 2
Liversedge 5, Bradford 0

Semi-finals
Hunslet 12, Liversedge 3
(at Thrum Hall, Halifax)
Leeds 2, Wakefield Trinity 0
(at Park Avenue, Bradford)

FINAL
Saturday 23 April 1892 at Fartown, Huddersfield
HUNSLET 21 *Back*: W Goldthorpe (t). *Three-quarters*: J Goldthorpe (2t), AE Goldthorpe (t, 3c), C Wright. *Half-backs*: C Lapping (capt), W Townsend. *Forwards*: C Bennett, W Gilston, T Groves, E Kaye (t), E Liversedge, JW Moore, J Mossley, J Rathmel (t), J Skirrow.
LEEDS 0 *Back*: FT Wilkinson. *Three-quarters*: R Place, T Summersgill, B Walker. *Half-backs*: JH Potter (capt), T Watts. *Forwards*: T Cousins, W Donaldson, M Fletcher, J Lewthwaite, W Lorriman, JP Munroe, GB Naylor, J Pickles, W Watson.
Attendance: 15,484   *Referee*: WH Humphreys (Durham RU)

COUNTY CHAMPIONSHIP

NORTH WESTERN GROUP

Saturday 7 November 1891 at Whalley Range, Manchester
LANCASHIRE 10 *Back*: T Coop (Lei). *Three-quarters*: JB Stork (Liv, t), F Miles (Sal, 2t), W McCutcheon (Old). *Half-backs*: J Berry (Tyl), W Cross (StH). *Forwards*: E Bullough (Wig), Herbert Hasleham (ManR), J Holme (Wid), J Jolley (War), T Kent (Sal), R MacMasters (Lei), J Pyke (StHR, 2t), P Steel (Man), RP Wilson (capt, LivOB).
CHESHIRE 0 *Back*: S Houghton (Run). *Three-quarters*: FP Jones (NewB), JH Crompton (Run), TH Davies (Run). *Half-backs*: S Abram (Run), F Drinkwater (Sale). *Forwards*: AJ Chadwick (BirkPk), J Dobie (BirkW), JE Edmondson (Sale), O Hughes (Run), PH Lockwood (capt, BirkPk), TW Lockwood (BirkPk), HN Lowndes (NewB), P Riley (Run), WJ Tyack (Duk).
Attendance: 7,000   *Referee*: GR Hill (RFU Honorary Secretary)

Saturday 7 November 1891 at Maryport
CUMBERLAND 27 *Back*: DG Lamonby (Cock). *Three-quarters*: J Sandwith (Sea), T Johnston (Whi, t), TH Hodgkinson (CarlC, dg). *Half-backs*: R Cuthbertson (Cock), J Murchie (Work). *Forwards*: GB Atkinson (Whi), JH Buckett (capt, Mil, 3c), Jim Davidson (Asp), S Farrer (Egr, t), J Kidd (Mil, t), R Leck (Mil), W Moore (Work, 2t), J Mumberson (Asp, t), J Pender (PenU, t).
WESTMORLAND 0 *Back*: T Hine (KenH). *Three-quarters*: JK Robinson (KirkL), G Coleman (KenT), G Webster (KirkL). *Half-backs*: W Hall (KenH), FB Pollitt (KenT). *Forwards*: RC Beard (KenH), J Carradus (KenT), G Hargreaves (KenT), F Heap (KenH), G Machell (KenT), P Metcalfe (KirkL), T Nicholson (KenH), CB Punchard (KirkL), RS Winskill (KenH).
Attendance: 1,500   *Referee*: Rev F Marshall (Yorkshire)

Saturday 21 November 1891 at Whitehaven Cricket Ground
CUMBERLAND 5 *Back*: DG Lamonby (Cock). *Three-quarters*: T Johnston (Whi), J Sandwith (Sea), TH Hodgkinson (CarlC, t). *Half-backs*: R Cuthbertson (Cock), J Murchie (Work). *Forwards*: GB Atkinson (Whi), JH Buckett (capt, Mil, c), Jim Davidson (Asp), S Farrer (Egr), M Humphrey (Mary), W Leck (Mil), J Mumberson (Asp), J Pender (PenU), J Stephenson (Flimby).
LANCASHIRE 14 *Back*: T Coop (Lei). *Three-quarters*: J Valentine (Swi, 2c), JH Marsh (Swi, t), W McCutcheon (Old). *Half-backs*: J Berry (Tyl, t), W Cross (StH). *Forwards*: A Ashworth (Old), EW Bullen (LivOB), E Bullough (Wig), J Holme (Wid), J Pyke (StHR), T Rothwell (Swi), JA Squires (Bro), RP Wilson (LivOB, t), SE Wilson (Liv, t).
Attendance: 4,500   *Referee*: GR Hill (RFU Honorary Secretary)

Saturday 21 November 1891 at Mint's Feet, Kendal
WESTMORLAND 7 *Back*: T Hine (KenH). *Three-quarters*: WG Hoggarth (KenT), J Allen (KenH, t, c), JK Robinson (KirkL). *Half-backs*: W Hall (KenH), A Jowett (KirkL). *Forwards*: RC Beard (KenH), J Carradus (KenT), F Heap (KenH), G Machell (KenT, t), RH Moore (Amb), WJ Parsons (KenH), JH Thompson (KenH), E Wilson (KenH), RS Winskill (KenH).
CHESHIRE 0 *Back*: S Houghton (Run). *Three-quarters*: FP Jones (NewB), JD Watson

(BirkW), J Cookson (Sale). *Half-backs*: F Drinkwater (Sale), E Hurst (BirkW). *Forwards*: AJ Chadwick (BirkPk), J Dobie (BirkW), JE Edmondson (Sale), O Hughes (Run), PH Lockwood (BirkPk), HN Lowndes (NewB), R Morton (Stock), P Riley (Run), WA Williams (NewB).
Attendance: 2,000 *Referee*: HS Boyland (Cumberland)

Wednesday 30 December 1891 at Irwell Lane, Runcorn
CHESHIRE 11 *Back*: S Houghton (Run). *Three-quarters*: FP Jones (NewB), JH Crompton (Run, c, dg), TH Davies (Run, t). *Half-backs*: S Abram (Run), F Drinkwater (Sale). *Forwards*: AJ Chadwick (BirkPk), Dourides (NewB), SF Edmondson (Sale), F Little (NewB), D Massey (Run), P Riley (Run), W Shaw (Run), GD White (BirkPk, t), WA Williams (NewB).
CUMBERLAND 8 *Back*: DG Lamonby (Cock, dg). *Three-quarters*: T Johnston (Whi), TH Hodgkinson (CarlC), J Sandwith (Sea). *Half-backs*: R Cuthbertson (Cock), J Murchie (Work). *Forwards*: GB Atkinson (Whi), JJ Brewsher (PenU), JH Buckett (Mil, t), Jim Davidson (Asp, t), M Humphrey (Mary), J Kidd (Mil), R Leck (Mil), T McGerry (Mary), W Moore (Work).
Attendance: 3,000 *Referee*: JH Payne (Lancashire)

Final table

	P	W	D	L	For	Agst	Pts
Lancashire	2	2	0	0	24	5	4
Cumberland	3	1	0	2	40	25	2
Cheshire	3	1	0	2	11	25	2
Westmorland	2	1	0	1	7	27	2

Note: Fixtures incomplete.

NORTH EASTERN GROUP

Saturday 14 November 1891 at Holderness Road, Hull
YORKSHIRE 17 *Back*: W Goldthorpe (Hun, 3c). *Three-quarters*: J Dyson (Hud), AE Goldthorpe (Hun), RE Lockwood (Heck). *Half-backs*: J Bedford (Wak), WJ Stadden (Dew). *Forwards*: H Bradshaw (Bram), T Broadley (Bing, t), WE Bromet (capt, Tad), E Dewhirst (Brad, t), O Fletcher (Hal), D Jowett (Heck), W Nichol (BrigR, t), CJF Paisley (Hud), JT Toothill (Brad, t).
DURHAM 7 *Back*: W Taylor (Tud). *Three-quarters*: TAF Crow (Sund), RCF Crow (Sund), WH Bell (Sund), FHR Alderson (capt, HartR, t, c). *Half-backs*: F Marston (Tud), AC Scott (HartR). *Forwards*: WA Bell (Tud), GE Boagey (HartR), A Burn (Sund), T Faulkner (Tud), T Hurworth (WHart), J Lavell (WHart, t), TJ Lindsay (Tud), W Yiend (HartR).
Attendance: 10,000 *Referee*: R Henzell (Northumberland)

Saturday 21 November 1891 at Jesmond Ground, Newcastle
NORTHUMBERLAND 0 *Back*: E Emley (Nor). *Three-quarters*: T Nicholson (Rock), S Brutton (capt, Rock), PH Morrison (Nor). *Half-backs*: TP Alexander (Rock), EW Taylor (Rock). *Forwards*: H Angus (Nor), A Benson (Rock), J Douthwaite (Tynd), JH Greenwell (Rock), R Harris (NEls), G Robson (Rock), A Styan (Rock), HT Whiteling (Rock), W Young (Wall).

YORKSHIRE 32 *Back*: W Goldthorpe (Hun). *Three-quarters*: J Dyson (Hud, 3t), T Summersgill (Lee, 2t), RE Lockwood (Heck, 3c). *Half-backs*: J Bedford (Wak), A Briggs (Brad). *Forwards*: H Bradshaw (Bram), T Broadley (Bing, t), WE Bromet (capt, Tad, t, c), E Dewhirst (Brad), O Fletcher (Hal, t), D Jowett (Heck, t), W Nichol (BrigR), CJF Paisley (Hud, t), JT Toothill (Brad).
Attendance: 4,000   *Referee*: WL Oakes (Durham)

Saturday 23 January 1892 at Ashbrooke Ground, Sunderland
DURHAM 0 *Back*: W Taylor (Tud). *Three-quarters*: TAF Crow (Sund), FHR Alderson (capt, HartR), JH Wilkinson (DurC). *Half-backs*: AC Scott (HartR), WE Wilkinson (DurC). *Forwards*: WA Bell (Tud), A Burn (Sund), J Coates (HartR), G Copley (Tud), T Faulkner (Tud), J Hall (NDur), P Turnbull (WHart), J Wheatley (Hou), W Yiend (HartR).
NORTHUMBERLAND 4 *Back*: J Taylor (PerPk). *Three-quarters*: W Taylor (Rock), S Brutton (Rock), S Anderson (Wall), T Nicholson (Rock). *Half-backs*: TP Alexander (Rock, 2t), EW Taylor (Rock). *Forwards*: H Angus (Nor), A Benson (Rock), J Douthwaite (Tynd), H Finlay (Wall), JH Greenwell (Rock), O Heslop (NorFC), G Robson (Rock), W Young (Wall).
Attendance: 2,000   *Referee*: W Sewell (Yorkshire)

Final table

	P	W	D	L	For	Agst	Pts
Yorkshire	2	2	0	0	49	7	4
Northumberland	2	1	0	1	4	32	2
Durham	2	0	0	2	7	21	0

SOUTH WESTERN GROUP

Results
Devonshire 2, Midland Counties 7
Midland Counties 2, Somersetshire 0
Midland Counties 9, Gloucestershire 0
Devonshire 2, Somersetshire 14
Gloucestershire 9, Devonshire 0

Final table

	P	W	D	L	For	Agst	Pts
Midland Counties	3	3	0	0	18	2	6
Somersetshire	2	1	0	1	14	4	2
Gloucestershire	2	1	0	1	9	9	2
Devonshire	3	0	0	3	4	30	0

Note: Fixtures incomplete

SOUTH EASTERN GROUP

Results
Eastern Counties 2, Surrey 30
Kent 12, Middlesex 11
Eastern Counties 0, Middlesex 25
Surrey 7, Sussex 0
Kent 11, Eastern Counties 5
Surrey 0, Kent 7
Sussex 0, Middlesex 9
Middlesex 13, Surrey 5
Sussex 2, Kent 16
Eastern Counties 0, Sussex 5

Final table

	P	W	D	L	For	Agst	Pts
Kent	4	4	0	0	46	18	8
Middlesex	4	3	0	1	58	17	6
Surrey	4	2	0	2	42	22	4
Sussex	4	1	0	3	7	32	2
Eastern Counties	4	0	0	4	7	71	0

FINAL GROUP ('SECOND SERIES')

Saturday 28 November 1891 at Fartown, Huddersfield
YORKSHIRE 3 *Back*: W Goldthorpe (Hun). *Three-quarters*: J Dyson (Hud), RE Lockwood (Heck, pg), T Summersgill (Lee). *Half-backs*: J Bedford (Wak), A Briggs (Brad). *Forwards*: H Bradshaw (Bram), T Broadley (Bing), WE Bromet (capt, Tad), E Dewhirst (Brad), O Fletcher (Hal), D Jowett (Heck), W Nichol (BrigR), CJF Paisley (Hud), JT Toothill (Brad).
LANCASHIRE 0 *Back*: T Coop (Lei). *Three-quarters*: J Valentine (capt, Swi), JH Marsh (Swi), W McCutcheon (Old). *Half-backs*: J Berry (Tyl), W Cross (StH). *Forwards*: A Ashworth (Old), EW Bullen (LivOB), E Bullough (Wig), T Craven (Sal), T Kent (Sal), J Pyke (StHR), T Rothwell (Swi), RP Wilson (LivOB), SE Wilson (Liv).
Attendance: 23,000   *Referee*: JA Smith (Scotland)

Monday 1 February 1892 at Clarence Street, York
YORKSHIRE 27 *Back*: W Goldthorpe (Hun, t). *Three-quarters*: RE Lockwood (Heck, t, 2c), T Summersgill (Lee, t), J Dyson (Hud, 5t). *Half-backs*: A Briggs (Brad), C Emmott (Brad). *Forwards*: H Bradshaw (Bram), T Broadley (Bing), WE Bromet (capt, Tad, t), E Dewhirst (Brad), T Dickenson (Hud), E Hudson (Lee), W Nichol (BrigR), J Rathmel (Hun), E Redman (Mann, t).
KENT 5 *Back*: HJW Lovelace (Black). *Three-quarters*: GC Hubbard (Black), JHC Fegan (Black, t), EM Blair (RE). *Half-backs*: EF Bonsell (Black), P Northcote (StTHosp). *Forwards*: RD Budworth (Black), EG Chubb (OLey), WJH Holder (WickPk), P Maud (Black/RE, c), EHG North (Black), HB Palmer (Black), AC Scott (Black/RE), SH Shepherd (RE), T Whittaker (Harl/MidW).
Attendance: 5,000   *Referee*: W Cail (Northumberland)

Wednesday 10 February 1892 at The Reddings, Moseley, Birmingham
MIDLAND COUNTIES 0 *Back*: JP Ward (Burt). *Three-quarters*: A Sulley (Burt), A Rogers (Mose), AH Firth (Cov). *Half-backs*: WP Nichol (OEdw), A Rotherham (Cov). *Forwards*: F Evershed (Burt), A Gorton (Burt), ER Lycett (Mose), WA Marris (OEdw), HWT Patterson (Nott), LJ Percival (Rugby), W Rice (Cov), JH Rogers (Mose), H Staunton (Nott).

YORKSHIRE 8 *Back*: W Goldthorpe (Hun). *Three-quarters*: RE Lockwood (Heck, t, dg), T Summersgill (Lee), J Dyson (Hud). *Half-backs*: A Briggs (Brad), C Emmott (Brad). *Forwards*: H Bradshaw (Bram), T Broadley (Bing), WE Bromet (capt, Tad, t), E Dewhirst (Brad), D Jowett (Heck), W Nichol (BrigR), E Redman (Mann), JT Toothill (Brad), F Wood (BrigR).
Attendance: 3,000   *Referee*: A Budd (Kent)

Saturday 13 February 1892 at Whalley Range, Manchester
LANCASHIRE 4 *Back*: T Coop (Lei). *Three-quarters*: J Valentine (capt, Swi, t), JB Stork (Liv), W McCutcheon (Old). *Half-backs*: James Bate (War), W Cross (StH). *Forwards*: A Ashworth (Old), E Bullough (Wig), T Craven (Sal), T Kent (Sal), F Lomax (Swi), G Pollard (ManR), T Rothwell (Swi), RP Wilson (LivOB, t), SE Wilson (Liv).
MIDLAND COUNTIES 0 *Back*: JP Ward (Burt). *Three-quarters*: LA Marsden (Burt), A Rogers (Mose), WS Lowe (Burt). *Half-backs*: RH Cattell (Mose), WP Nichol (OEdw). *Forwards*: F Arblaster (OEdw), BH Cattell (Mose), SH Fisher (OEdw), AW Gorton (Burt), B Horton (Mose), ER Lycett (Mose), WAS Marris (OEdw), HWT Patterson (Nott), JH Rogers (Mose).
Attendance: 5,000   *Referee*: H Vassall (RFU Honorary Treasurer)

Final table

	P	W	D	L	For	Agst	Pts
Yorkshire	3	3	0	0	38	5	6
Lancashire	2	1	0	1	4	3	2
Midland Counties	2	0	0	2	0	12	0
Kent	1	0	0	1	5	27	0

Note: Fixtures incomplete

COUNTY CHAMPIONS v THE REST
Saturday 20 February 1892 at Headingley, Leeds
YORKSHIRE 4 *Back*: W Goldthorpe (Hun). *Three-quarters*: RE Lockwood (Heck), AE Goldthorpe (Hun), J Dyson (Hud). *Half-backs*: A Briggs (Brad), H Varley (Livs). *Forwards*: H Bradshaw (Bram), T Broadley (Bing), WE Bromet (capt, Tad), E Dewhirst (Brad), D Jowett (Heck, t), W Nichol (BrigR, t), E Redman (Mann), JT Toothill (Brad), F Wood (BrigR).
REST OF ENGLAND 0 *Back*: T Coop (Lei). *Three-quarters*: GC Hubbard (Black), J Valentine (Swi), A Rogers (Mose). *Half-backs*: RFC de Winton (Black), EW Taylor (Rock). *Forwards*: A Allport (Black), A Ashworth (Old), E Bullough (Wig), F Evershed (Black/Burt), T Kent (Sal), A Robinson (Black), JH Rogers (Mose), SMJ Woods (capt, Tau/Black), W Yiend (HartR).
Attendance: 20,000   *Referee*: ET Gurdon (RFU President)

NON-COUNTY CHAMPIONSHIP MATCHES

Wednesday 21 October 1891 at Belgrave Road Grounds, Leicester
MIDLAND COUNTIES 18 *Back*: FJ Byrne (Mose). *Three-quarters*: A Sulley (Burt, t, dg), A Rogers (Mose, 2c), CM Barham (Leic). *Half-backs*: RG Ley (Leic), RA Rotherham (Cov). *Forwards*: F Evershed (capt, Burt), A Gorton (Burt, t), ER Lycett (Mose), WAS Mavis

(OEdw), W Rice (Cov), JH Rogers (Mose, gm), H Rotherham (Cov), WH Sturges (Leic), LF Ward (Leic).
CHESHIRE 2 *Back*: S Houghton (Run). *Three-quarters*: FP Jones (NewB), JD Watson (BirkW), JT Haslam (Duk). *Half-backs*: S Abram (Run), WE Evans (Run). *Forwards*: AJ Chadwick (BirkPk), W Faulkner (Run), O Hughes (Run), PH Lockwood (BirkPk), TW Lockwood (BirkPk), HN Lowndes (NewB, t), J May (BirkW), P Riley (Run), WJ Tyack (Duk).
Attendance: 3,000   *Referee*: EB Holmes (Midland Counties)

Wednesday 4 November 1891 at Corpus College Ground, Cambridge
CAMBRIDGE UNIVERSITY 10 *Back*: W Neilson. *Three-quarters*: AB Fforde (t), WF Surtees, R Montgomery (c). *Half-backs*: H Marshall (t), JC Orr (c). *Forwards*: HJ Craig, RN Douglas, AE Elliott, CJ Hill, E Mayfield, CB Nicholl, BF Robinson, H Staunton, TWP Storey (capt).
LANCASHIRE 18 *Back*: T Coop (Lei). *Three-quarters*: JB Stork (Liv, t), JH Marsh (Swi, t), J Hurst (Old, 3t). *Half-backs*: James Bate (War, t), W Cross (StH). *Forwards:* E Bullough (Wig), GNM Carmerson (Man), Herbert Hasleham (ManR), T Kent (Sal), F Lomax (Swi), J Pyke (StHR, 2c), T Rothwell (Swi), T Whittaker (Liv), RP Wilson (LivOB).
Attendance: 'large'   *Referee*: HL Ashmore (Middlesex)

Saturday 5 December 1891 at Upper Park, Birkenhead
CHESHIRE 7 *Back*: S Houghton (Run). *Three-quarters*: FP Jones (NewB), JH Crompton (Run, t, c), TH Davies (Run). *Half-backs*: S Abram (Run), F Drinkwater (Sale). *Forwards*: AJ Chadwick (BirkPk, t), SF Edmondson (Sale), W Faulkner (Run), O Hughes (Run), PH Lockwood (BirkPk), P Riley (Run), GD White (BirkPk), WA Williams (NewB), AG Wood (BirkPk).
DURHAM 4 *Back*: W Taylor (Tud). *Three-quarters*: W Wainford (Tud), RCF Crow (Sund, t), WH Bell (Sund), FHR Alderson (capt, HartR). *Half-backs*: F Marston (Tud), AC Scott (HartR). *Forwards*: WA Bell (Tud), GE Boagey (HartR), J Coates (HartR), T Faulkner (Tud), T Hurworth (WHart), J Lavell (WHart, t), TJ Lindsay (Tud), W Yiend (HartR).
Attendance: 2,500   *Referee*: JH Payne (Lancashire)

Monday 21 December 1891 at Whalley Range, Manchester
LANCASHIRE 25 *Back*: T Coop (Lei, c, pg). *Three-quarters*: J Valentine (capt, Swi, 2t, c), JH Marsh (Swi, t), W McCutcheon (Old, 3t). *Half-backs*: James Bate (War), W Cross (StH). *Forwards*: A Ashworth (Old), J Brearley (RochH), EW Bullen (LivOB, t), T Craven (Sal, t), T Kent (Sal), F Lomax (Swi), G Pollard (ManR), J Pyke (StHR), RP Wilson (LivOB).
CAMBRIDGE UNIVERSITY 2 *Back*: CM Wells. *Three-quarters*: AB Fforde, W Neilson, R Montgomery (t). *Half-backs*: JC Orr, Arthur Rotherham. *Forwards*: HJ Craig, RN Douglas, AE Elliott, E Mayfield, CB Nicholl, JCA Rigby, BF Robinson, H Staunton, TWP Storey (capt).
Attendance: 1,000   *Referee*: LJ Percival (Oxford University)

Saturday 9 January 1892 at Wellington
SOMERSETSHIRE 7 *Back*: H Boucher (Tau). *Three-quarters*: CF Mermagen (Well), FH Fox (Well), GL Strachan (Bath, t, c). *Half-backs*: R Sweet-Escott (Car), H Merry (Well). *Forwards*: WH D'Ath (Tau). HT Gillimore (Wes), PF Hancock (Well/Black), WH Manfield

(Yeo), B Morris (Tau), F Soane (Bath), CJ Vernon (Well), BH Vincent (Bath), SMJ Woods (Tau/Black, t).
YORKSHIRE 19 *Back*: W Goldthorpe (Hun). *Three-quarters*: RE Lockwood (Heck, 2c), T Summersgill (Lee, 2t), J Dyson (Hud). *Half-backs*: A Briggs (Brad), C Emmott (Brad, t). *Forwards*: H Bradshaw (Bram), T Broadley (Bing), WE Bromet (capt, Tad), E Dewhirst (Brad, t), T Dickenson (Hud), D Jowett (Heck, c), W Nichol (BrigR, t), J Richards (Brad), JT Toothill (Brad).
Attendance: 2,000   *Referee*: HL Ashmore (Middlesex)

Monday 11 January 1892 at County Ground, St Thomas, Exeter
DEVONSHIRE 0 *Back*: W Hocken (DevA). *Three-quarters*: JM Wilcocks (Exe), GC Middleton (capt, Barn), W England (Exe). *Half-backs*: CHR Dalton (DevA), L Howell (RNEC). *Forwards*: GH Allington (DevA), R Biddell (Exe), SH Brooking (Torq), G Cox (Tiv), A May (DevA), FJ Sellicks (NewA), S Thomas (Exe), GA Trent (Exe), GH Valance (Sid).
YORKSHIRE 15 *Back*: W Goldthorpe (Hun). *Three-quarters*: R Place (Lee), RE Lockwood (Heck, t, c), J Dyson (Hud, 2t). *Half-backs*: J Bedford (Wak), C Emmott (Brad). *Forwards*: H Bradshaw (Bram), T Broadley (Bing, t), WE Bromet (capt, Tad), E Dewhirst (Brad), T Dickenson (Hud), E Hudson (Lee), W Nichol (BrigR, t), E Redman (Mann), JT Toothill (Brad, t).
Attendance: 3,000   *Referee*: Dr JA Macdonald (Somersetshire)

Saturday 6 February 1892 at Upper Park, Birkenhead
CHESHIRE 13 *Back*: JT Haslam (Duk). *Three-quarters*: FP Jones (NewB, 2t), JH Crompton (Run, t, c), TH Davies (Run). *Half-backs*: S Abram (Run), F Drinkwater (Sale). *Forwards*: AJ Chadwick (BirkPk), E Elliott (BirkW), W Faulkner (Run), O Hughes (Run), PH Lockwood (capt, BirkPk), EH Morley (Sale), P Riley (Run), WA Williams (NewB, 2t), G Wright (BirkPk).
YORKSHIRE 12 *Back*: F Blackburn (Cleck). *Three-quarters*: S Hopkins (Otley), AE Goldthorpe (capt, Hun, 2c), R Place (Lee). *Half-backs*: H Barker (Livs), H Varley (Livs). *Forwards*: F Clegg (Mann), L Donkin (Hull), B Jackson (Elland, t), R Munro (Brad), GB Naylor (Lee), J Pickles (Lee), J Rathmel (Hun, t), J White (Bowl, t), F Wood (BrigR).
Attendance: 3,000/4,000   *Referee*: EB Holmes (Midland Counties)

Saturday 6 February 1892 at Mansfield Park, Hawick
SOUTH OF SCOTLAND 4 *Back*: W Fairbairn (Mel). *Half-backs*: AF McNee (Haw, t), WS Oliver (Jed), R Murdison (Gala, t). *Quarter-backs*: JT Mabon (Jed), D Patterson (Haw). *Forwards*: R Douglas (capt, Jed), W Faston (Mel), D Gibson (Haw), R Hunter (Jed), A Jardine (Haw), J Linton (Sel), WL Oliver (Jed), AB Storrie (Haw), R Turnbull (Jed).
CUMBERLAND 6 *Back*: DG Lamonby (Cock). *Three-quarters*: TH Hodgkinson (CarlC), J Sandwith (Sea), JT Bell (PenU). *Half-backs*: W Coulthard (Mary), R Cuthbertson (Cock, dg). *Forwards*: J Addison (Flimby), GB Atkinson (Whi), JJ Brewsher (PenU), W Cross (Egr), Jim Davidson (capt, Asp), J Dodd (Asp), M Humphrey (Mary, t), W Leck (Mil), J Ray (Whi).
Attendance: n/a   *Referee*: C Reid (Scotland)

Wednesday 23 March 1892 at Whalley Range, Manchester
LANCASHIRE 16 *Back*: T Coop (Lei). *Three-quarters*: W McCutcheon (Old, t), JB Stork (Liv, t), WB Steel (Man). *Half-backs*: James Bate (War, t), W Cross (StH). *Forwards*:

A Ashworth (Old), EW Bullen (LivOB), E Bullough (Wig, t), R Case (Ulv), T Craven (Sal), S Hall (Swi), T Kent (capt, Sal), G Pollard (ManR, t), SE Wilson (Liv, 2c).
DEVONSHIRE 4 *Back*: T Causey (Aller Vale). *Three-quarters*: W Down (DevA), M Toller (Barn), W Bearne (NewA). *Half-backs*: J Davies (Torq), W Hannaford (Barn). *Forwards*: GH Allington (DevA, t), W Ashford (capt, Exe, t), W Biddell (DevA), SH Brooking (Torq), WT Bryant (DevA), J Collinge (DevA), G Cox (Tiv), F May (DevA), BH Wallis (Exe).
Attendance: 3,000   *Referee*: Rev F Marshall (Yorkshire)

ENGLAND TRIAL MATCH
Saturday 19 December 1891 at Jesmond Ground, Newcastle
NORTH 21 *Back*: S Houghton (Run). *Three-quarters*: RE Lockwood (Heck, 2t, 2c), FHR Alderson (capt, HartR, c, dg), J Dyson (Hud). *Half-backs*: A Briggs (Brad), EW Taylor (Rock). *Forwards*: A Ashworth (Old, t), WE Bromet (Tad), E Bullough (Wig, t), Jim Davidson (Asp), T Faulkner (Tud), D Jowett (Heck), W Nichol (BrigR), J Pyke (StHR), P Riley (Run).
SOUTH 12 *Back*: WB Thomson (Black). *Three-quarters*: A Rogers (Mose), GC Hubbard (capt, Black), AB Fforde (CamU, t). *Half-backs*: H Marshall (Black/CamU), Arthur Rotherham (CamU, c). *Forwards*: A Allport (Black), E Bonham-Carter (OxfU, t), F Evershed (Black/Burt), T Parker (Rich), LJ Percival (Rugby/OxfU, t), JH Rogers (Mose, c), F Soane (Bath), GJ Whitcombe (Glo), W Yiend (HartR).
Attendance: 6,000   *Referee*: ET Gurdon (RFU President)
Note 1: WE Bromet (North) was late arriving and after a few minutes play Arthur Hill (Hartlepool Rovers) took up his place. Following a further 20 minutes play Bromet arrived, replacing Hill following agreement by both captains and the referee.
Note 2: W Yiend (South) qualified for the South due to residing in his home town of Winchcombe (Gloucestershire) although contemporary match reports indicate he was playing for Hartlepool Rovers and Durham at the time.

INTERNATIONAL CHAMPIONSHIP

Saturday 2 January 1892 at Rectory Field, Blackheath
ENGLAND 17 *Back*: WB Thomson (Black). *Three-quarters*: RE Lockwood (Heck, 2c), FHR Alderson (capt, HartR, t, c), GC Hubbard (Black, t). *Half-backs*: A Briggs (Brad), C Emmott (Brad). *Forwards*: A Allport (Black), WE Bromet (Tad), E Bullough (Wig), F Evershed (Black/Burt, t), T Kent (Sal), W Nichol (BrigR, t), J Pyke (StHR), JT Toothill (Brad), W Yiend (HartR).
WALES 0 *Back*: WJ Bancroft (Swa). *Three-quarters*: RM Garrett (Pen), JA Gould (capt, New), W McCutcheon (Old), TW Pearson (Car). *Half-backs*: HP Phillips (New), GR Rowles (Pen). *Forwards*: AW Boucher (New), J Deacon (Swa), TC Graham (New), J Hannan (New), F Mills (Swa), CB Nicholl (Llan), RL Thomas (Llan), WH Watts (New).
Attendance: 15,000   *Referee*: MC McEwan (Scotland)

Saturday 6 February 1892 at Whalley Range, Manchester
ENGLAND 7 *Back*: S Houghton (Run). *Three-quarters*: RE Lockwood (Heck), J Marsh (Swi), GC Hubbard (Black). *Half-backs*: A Briggs (Brad), EW Taylor (Rock). *Forwards*: A Ashworth (Old), WE Bromet (Tad), E Bullough (Wig), F Evershed (Black/Burt, t), T Kent (Sal), LJ Percival (Rugby/OxfU, t), JT Toothill (Brad), SMJ Woods (capt, Tau/Black, c), W Yiend (HartR).

IRELAND 0 *Back*: T Peel (Lim). *Half-backs*: RW Dunlop (DubU), S Lee (NIFC), W Gardiner (NIFC). *Quarter-backs*: T Thornhill (Wand), BB Tuke (BecR). *Forwards*: WJN Davis (Bess), JS Jameson (Lans), TJ Johnston (QCB), VC le Fanu (capt, Lans), JH O'Conor (BecR), CV Rooke (DubU), RE Smith (Lans), AK Wallis (Wand), EJ Walsh (Lans).
Attendance: 15,000   *Referee*: JA Smith (Scotland)

Saturday 5 March 1892 at Raeburn Place, Edinburgh
SCOTLAND 0 *Back*: HJ Stevenson (EdinA). *Half-backs*: PR Clauss (OxfU), W Neilson (CamU), GT Campbell (LonS). *Quarter-backs*: DG Anderson (LonS), CE Orr (capt, WoS). *Forwards*: JD Boswell (WoS), WR Gibson (RHSFP), FW Goodhue (LonS), WA Macdonald (GlasU), MC McEwan (EdinA), RG Macmillan (LonS), JN Millar (WoS), GT Neilson (WoS), JE Orr (WoS).
ENGLAND 5 *Back*: T Coop (Lei). *Three-quarters*: RE Lockwood (Heck, c), FHR Alderson (capt, HartR). JW Dyson (Hud). *Half-backs*: A Briggs (Brad), H Varley (Livs). *Forwards*: H Bradshaw (Bram), WE Bromet (Tad, t), E Bullough (Wig), F Evershed (Black/Burt), T Kent (Sal), W Nichol (BrigR), JT Toothill (Brad), SMJ Woods (Tau/Black), W Yiend (HartR).
Attendance: 12,000   *Referee*: RG Warren (Ireland)

Other results
Wales 2, Scotland 7
Scotland 2, Ireland 0
Ireland 9, Wales 0

Final table

	P	W	D	L	For	Agst
England	3	3	0	0	29	0
Scotland	3	2	0	1	9	7
Ireland	3	1	0	2	9	9
Wales	3	0	0	3	2	33

1892-1893

THE LANCASHIRE CUP COMPETITION

A Lancashire league competition was launched at a meeting of the Lancashire Union held at the Grand Hotel, Manchester, on 5th August. The *Athletic News* reported: 'The vexed question of a League has at last been settled by the Lancashire County Committee. The action taken some time ago, and which resulted in the passing of a resolution by the Rugby Union giving that body the power to refuse or sanction the formation of a League, raised obstacles which have been surmounted.'[134] Officially named the Lancashire Cup Competition but more commonly referred to as the Lancashire Club Championship from 1893-94, it began in September 1892 with eight clubs; Broughton, Broughton Rangers, Oldham, St Helens Recreation, Salford, Swinton, Warrington and Wigan. The intention had been to operate a ten-team league but Liverpool and Manchester, historically the two most influential clubs in the county, opposed the idea, their proposed places being offered to Rochdale Hornets (who joined on 29th September) and Liverpool Old Boys (who declined). Tyldesley were later invited, restoring the contest to ten clubs from 19th October.

BIRTH OF THE YORKSHIRE SENIOR COMPETITION

The first League competition in Yorkshire was sanctioned during a meeting at the Queen's Hotel, Leeds, on 22nd August, when a dispute leading to the potential withdrawal of ten prominent clubs from the

Yorkshire Rugby Football Union was 'amicably settled'. It followed months of fractious negotiations between the Yorkshire Union and the Yorkshire Football Alliance, the latter having been created by the ten disaffected clubs; Batley, Bradford, Brighouse Rangers, Dewsbury, Halifax, Huddersfield, Hunslet, Leeds, Liversedge, and Wakefield Trinity. The Alliance had been founded three months earlier at the Saracen's Head Hotel, Leeds, on 17th May, placing them on a collision course with the Yorkshire Union who, at their annual meeting at the Queen's Hotel on 13th June, attempted to block the scheme through a resolution proposed by Reverend Frank Marshall. A series of meetings with the Yorkshire Union and an appeal to the Rugby Football Union failed to resolve the issue, the ten Alliance clubs then threatening to resign from the Yorkshire Union during their meeting at the Old George Hotel, Leeds, on 13th August. In fact, two Leagues were subsequently established, both commencing during September 1892; the Yorkshire Senior Competition and the Yorkshire Competition No. 2. Leeds, having withdrawn at an earlier stage, was replaced amongst the ten 'Senior' clubs by Manningham.[135]

THE DURHAM COUNTY CUP IN FIRE
When a fire broke out at a Spennymoor hotel on 18th September there were concerns about the safety of the Durham County Challenge Cup, the *Durham County Advertiser* reporting: 'Early on Sunday morning the North Eastern Hotel, Spennymoor, the largest hotel in the town, was destroyed by fire. The hotel, which was the headquarters of the Tudhoe Rugby Football Club [the cup holders], was three storeys high, and contained about 25 bedrooms, commercial room, smoke room, billiard room and a very commodious bar.' An update appeared in a separate section of the same issue, stating: 'Since going to press we have heard that this much-coveted trophy [the Durham Cup], which was in the fire, was found in the safe all right and sound, and is now in the possession of [hotel owner] Captain P. B. Junor, president of the Tudhoe Club.'[136]

SHOULD IT BE FIFTEEN OR THIRTEEN PLAYERS?
At a meeting of the Society of Referees, at the Green Dragon Hotel, Leeds, on 28th October, the Yorkshire Rugby Union President, Mr. J. A. Miller, argued for a reduction in players from 15 to 13. 'White Rose' of the *Yorkshire Evening Post* was unconvinced: 'It may be assumed that Mr. Miller's plea for a reduction in the number of players was the outcome of careful thought and calm deliberation on his part. We ought not to take Mr Miller's remarks so seriously were it not a matter of notoriety that the cry for diminution of

the number of players has already been raised by prominent authorities ranking very high in the football world. The views of the new school may eventually become law, but their arguments will be strongly opposed by the old school, who are at present in the majority on the Union Committee, and whose attachments to the old traditions of the game is too strong to be easily upset. To quote Mr Miller: "By lessening the number of the forwards [he was] convinced it would be a reform that would have precedence in the immediate future, and the adoption of which would bring the game nearer the perfected state [and] instead of admiring the physique and the pushing power of those giants who took part in the game, in the future they would be able to admire still more the skilful and scientific play of the game." In reply we may ask is the Rugby game to be played as a sport or to gain popular favour or, in other words, is it to be looked upon as a spectacular exhibition. The reformers must be prepared to show that the game, if with 13 men, will be a better game for the players for, after all, that is the real reason why the game ought to be played.'[137]

CUMBERLAND HOLDING THEIR OWN
After Cumberland surprisingly held Lancashire to a scoreless draw at Whalley Range, Manchester, on 19th November, one reporter claimed that 'the game has been fostered and developed in all directions, and counties that have hitherto ranked as second class can put into the field teams that can hold their own with the best'.[138]

ALLEGED PROFESSIONALISM OF BRADFORD
The continual drain of Westmorland players to Lancashire and Yorkshire came into focus when the combined committees of Westmorland and Yorkshire met at the Grosvenor Hotel, Manchester, on 21st December, to discuss the alleged professionalism of the Bradford club. The *Manchester Guardian* claimed 'the case has been regarded as one of the most sensational that the governing bodies have had to determine. It consisted in the allegations that [Enoch] Wilson, a forward, and [William] Hall, a half-back, had migrated from Kendal [Hornets] to Bradford on account of a monetary consideration with a direct view to assist the Bradford club'. Both players, on being interviewed by the Committee, denied any football-related inducement, claiming they went to Bradford after being offered employment. The Committee, after a lengthy debate, decided 'a professional element' could not be proved and granted the transfers and Bradford, reportedly, 'having scored a victory were jubilant over the result'.[139]

YORKSHIRE USE FOUR THREE-QUARTERS FOR THE FIRST TIME
Yorkshire defeated Middlesex 14-5 in Richmond on Monday 30th January, en route to claiming the County Championship, using four three-quarters for the first time, instead of its usual three. The *Yorkshire Post* commented: 'Congratulations have been expressed in Middlesex [towards Yorkshire's win] and a corresponding amount of fear felt in Yorkshire owing to the magnificent array of talent which the home county [Middlesex] had been able to select. Their backs were entirely composed of internationals – English, Scotch, and Welsh – but unfortunately for them the forwards did not come up to the same high standard of excellence. It was felt on all hands that, if Yorkshire were to win, it was to the forwards that they must look for victory. The four three-quarter backs were chiefly intended to play on defence, and the eight forwards relied upon to more than hold their opponents.'[140]

CUMBERLAND AND YORKSHIRE CANNOT AGREE
Yorkshire overcame Cumberland 17-2 at Lismore Place, Carlisle, on Thursday 16th February. As the two counties had each won their opening two matches in what was the final group stage of the county championship, it secured the title for Yorkshire. Despite the importance attached to the match, there had been difficulty in arranging a date; Cumberland had wanted to play on a Saturday, Yorkshire stating that that was impossible as it would interfere with club matches, preferring Monday, Tuesday, or Wednesday. The Cumbrian response was that those days were not acceptable, and, consequently, it was referred to the Rugby Football Union, who decided it should be played on a Thursday!

A RECORD GATE AT BRADFORD
The success of the new Yorkshire Senior Competition was demonstrated when Bradford met Halifax at Park Avenue on 4th March. The *Yorkshire Post* reported: 'The receipts proved a record for the club in ordinary club engagements at popular prices. The sum taken was £410, and the attendance was over 20,000 persons. The victory of Bradford proved immensely popular [and] the scene of enthusiasm which occurred in the field was such as has rarely been witnessed in the annals of club or Cup-tie football in Yorkshire. The victory of Bradford gives the club the honour of being the first winners of the new club championship. During the game there was an alarming escape from a serious disaster. The pressure at one end behind the goal posts was so great that the barriers gave way, and a number of persons fell forward in a heap into the field, but fortunately no

one was hurt. Before the match began a number of boys were sitting underneath the barriers, and the Bradford officials insisted on their leaving their places before the game commenced. But for this prompt action, in all probability, very serious results would have had to be recorded.'[141]

A RUPTURE BETWEEN BLACKHEATH AND BRADFORD

A North-South divide appeared evident, based on a report concerning Blackheath and Bradford that appeared in the *Manchester Guardian* during March: 'A rupture has occurred between these leading clubs. Blackheath recently wrote cancelling future fixtures with Bradford because of the style of play recently adopted by the latter. This unexpected step has greatly annoyed Bradford, who consider financial reasons to be the cause, Bradford having intimated that the subsidy given to Blackheath when playing away should cease, or Yorkshiremen be similarly treated in the south. They have cancelled their match with the Barbarians, of which team Mr. W. P. Carpmael [Blackheath] is also secretary, and are endeavouring to arrange instead a special match with Newport, at Park Avenue, Bradford.'[142]

WING-FORWARDISM

Two letters published in the *Yorkshire Post* during March condemned the disruptive influence of wing forward play. 'Bradfordian' argued that 'the greatest part of rough play is caused by wing forwards. It is very disheartening ... to go to a [rugby] football match with a view to seeing a genuine game, and there see nothing as regards football but two wing forwards pulling one another in a most shameful way, thereby hindering the men behind them from giving an exposition of football as it should and can be played'. His view was supported by 'Horsforth' who wrote: 'I quite agree as to the stamping out of wing-forwardism. I have been a half back player myself, and know what it is to play both with wing forwards and against them. If both teams are playing them, there is no half back play worth mentioning, and if only one team play them, well they hinder all four half backs from play. The sooner they get rid of such men the better.'[143]

EXCITEMENT AT THE NORTHUMBERLAND CUP FINAL

The meeting of keen rivals Rockcliff and Percy Park in the Northumberland Cup final, at Jesmond, Newcastle, on 25th March, attracted the largest crowd to date for the deciding match. The *Shields Daily News* noted: 'About 8,000 spectators paid for admission to the grounds, the majority of them were followers of the respective teams. The fisher folk from Whitley and Cullercoats were conspicuous by gorgeous rosettes and photographs of "Little Billy" [E. W. Taylor], the latter being fixed in the brim of their hats. They filed on to the field in hundreds, and greeted the arrival of their idol with vociferous cheers.'[144]

DURHAM COUNTY CUP FINAL CANCELLED

Hartlepool Rovers, having refused to play Tudhoe in the Durham Cup final at Mowbray Road, South Shields, on 8th April, were expelled from the competition, a decision taken by the Durham Committee at Walton's Hotel, Sunderland, on 11th April. It was also agreed to present the Cup to Tudhoe. Reports that the final was cancelled only surfaced in the press on 7th April, but it was later revealed that Tudhoe received a postcard from Hartlepool Rovers dated 29th March, stating the Rovers committee had 'decided they can only play in the final on the 15 April'. Hartlepool Rovers blamed the dilemma on the Durham Committee for advising its clubs to postpone their second round games on 4th March due to the England versus Scotland fixture at Headingley. This resulted in two ties being delayed, pushing subsequent rounds back by one week. The final was originally scheduled for 25th March and, for the Rovers, the new date came on the back of a four match Easter programme that included matches in South Wales and the South West the previous Monday and Tuesday. Possibly more significant was that it clashed with their attractive home fixture with Hull, which went ahead in front of a 3,000 crowd.[145]

A FOOTBALL RIOT AT WHITLEY

When Rockcliff hosted South Shields Young Men at their Whitley enclosure on 8th April, the *Northern Daily Mail* described the events that unfolded as 'a scene perhaps unprecedented in the history of football'. The report continued: 'About 5,000 were present, most were followers of the Young Men, and utmost partisanship was displayed. The contest was terribly rough, and the referee was frequently called upon to interpose. Hand-to-hand fights took place in the scrimmages, and these became so frequent the referee found it necessary to order two players off, one from each side. In the second stage, E. W. Taylor [Rockcliff] got over the line [for a try] and the point was being disputed when the same player landed [the] goal. A heated discussion took place, the referee deciding in favour of Rockcliff, the South Shields team [leaving] the field under protest. Immediately afterwards a scene of great disorder ensued. The referee sought protection in the grandstand, where Rockcliff supporters were assembled. A free fight ensued and many persons were seriously injured. The police succeeded in making several arrests, the pavilion being utilised as a prison house *pro tempore*. [South Shields] decided to again take the field, and this was communicated to Rockcliff. Considering the temper of the spectators, however, it was mutually agreed to abandon the match. The referee escaped by climbing railings at the rear of the grandstand, and sought refuge in a house hard by. The incident has created considerable excitement in the district.'[146]

SALFORD WIN LANCASHIRE CUP COMPETITION

The Lancashire Cup Competition, played on a league basis, did not run as smoothly as that of their Yorkshire counterparts with only two teams, Broughton and Broughton Rangers, completing the maximum 18 matches. In general, the clubs had been left to organise their own schedule and this led to an untidy finish with the two leading contenders, Salford and Swinton, arranging late fixtures. The *Manchester Guardian* commented: 'A match in this competition between Swinton and Rochdale Hornets was announced to be played at Swinton yesterday [26th April]. The Hornets, however, at a committee meeting on Monday [24th April] declined to carry out the arrangement and the match was cancelled. The result will be that the Swinton and Salford clubs will play an equal number of 15 matches and great interest will centre in the final match on Saturday [29th April] between Salford and Tyldesley, as the success of Salford will entitle that club to the Championship.'[147] Salford subsequently defeated visitors Tyldesley 19-2 at New Barnes to claim the trophy.

1892-1893 STATISTICS

LANCASHIRE CUP COMPETITION

Final table	P	W	D	L	For	Agst	Pts
Salford	15	10	4	1	77	29	24
Swinton	15	10	3	2	139	30	23
Tyldesley	12	7	2	3	48	35	16
Warrington	15	6	4	5	70	39	16
St Helens Recreation	15	6	3	6	81	67	15
Wigan	14	7	1	6	41	46	15
Oldham	16	6	3	7	73	69	15
Broughton Rangers	18	2	6	10	39	137	10
Rochdale Hornets	8	3	1	4	20	22	7
Broughton	18	1	3	14	27	141	5

Note: Fixtures incomplete; not all clubs arranged a full set of fixtures.

NORTH WESTERN LEAGUE

Final table	P	W	D	L	For	Agst	Pts
Lancaster	16	12	3	1	152	16	27
Millom	16	11	4	1	146	19	26
Morecambe	16	10	4	2	93	35	24
Barrow	16	7	1	8	101	94	15
Kendal Hornets	16	6	2	8	88	80	14
Ulverston*	16	7	5	4	103	35	13
Kendal Town	16	3	5	8	36	75	11
Askam	16	3	2	11	42	92	8
Dalton	16	0	0	16	10	325	0

*Six points deducted for using ineligible players

SOUTH EAST LANCASHIRE COMPETITION

Final table	P	W	D	L	For	Agst	Pts
Barton	18	9	7	2	86	29	25
Pendleton	18	7	9	2	61	19	23
Boothstown	18	7	9	2	60	23	23
Failsworth	18	6	7	5	59	31	19
Blackley Rangers	18	7	5	6	81	83	19
Radcliffe	18	3	10	5	41	32	16
Tottington	18	4	7	7	29	61	15
Manchester Athletic	18	2	10	6	15	68	14
Cheetham Hill	18	1	11	6	11	39	13
Milnrow	18	1	11	6	28	86	13

Note: 36 unplayed fixtures declared scoreless draws, affecting Cheetham Hill (11 matches), Milnrow (10), Manchester Athletic, Radcliffe (9 each), Boothstown (8), Pendleton (7), Barton (6), Failsworth (5), Tottington (4), Blackley Rangers (3).

YORKSHIRE SENIOR COMPETITION

Final table	P	W	D	L	For	Agst	Pts
Bradford	18	14	0	4	106	76	28
Hunslet	18	10	3	5	136	76	23
Halifax	18	10	2	6	92	56	22
Batley	18	9	3	6	98	77	21
Manningham	18	9	2	7	110	49	20
Brighouse Rangers	18	8	4	6	92	96	20
Huddersfield	18	8	1	9	111	106	17
Liversedge	18	7	2	9	130	108	16
Dewsbury	18	3	4	11	57	121	10
Wakefield Trinity	18	1	1	16	22	189	3

YORKSHIRE COMPETITION NO. 2

Final table	P	W	D	L	For	Agst	Pts
Holbeck	20	17	1	2	168	50	35
Elland	20	15	1	4	250	50	31
Morley	20	11	6	3	125	89	28
Leeds Parish Church	20	11	3	6	124	91	25
Cleckheaton	20	8	4	8	123	119	20
Wortley*	20	8	4	8	99	100	19
Otley	20	7	3	10	92	103	17
York	20	5	3	12	60	152	13
Pontefract*	20	5	2	13	56	184	13
Bramley**	20	4	4	12	71	105	10
Kirkstall	20	1	5	14	62	187	7

*Wortley versus Pontefract was played on hard ground, reduced to two periods of 20 minutes each. Wortley 'won' 3-0 but subsequently declared a draw on appeal, Wortley therefore deducted one point, Pontefract awarded one point
**Two points deducted for using ineligible player
Note: Seven unplayed fixtures declared scoreless draws, affecting Cleckheaton, Morley (3 matches each), Bramley, York (2 each), Leeds PC, Otley, Pontefract, Wortley (1 each).

CUMBERLAND COUNTY CHALLENGE CUP (14 entries)
Try – 2 points; conversion, penalty goal – 3; drop-goal, field goal, goal from mark – 4.
If equal then majority of 3 minor points required to win.

First Round
Brookland Rovers 0, Aspatria 11
Broughton 0, Whitehaven Recreation 5
Cockermouth 2, Penrith United 4
Cummersdale Hornets w/o Flimby (withdrew)
Egremont 2, Carlisle City 11
Whitehaven 2, Workington 4
Byes: Maryport, Seaton

Second Round
Penrith United 4, Carlisle City 7
Seaton 0, Aspatria 0 (mp: 1-7)
Whitehaven Recreation 0, Cummersdale Hornets 10
Workington 0, Maryport 7

Semi-finals
Cummersdale Hornets 3, Carlisle City 2 (at Lismore Place, Carlisle)
Maryport 2, Aspatria 0 (at Lonsdale Park, Workington)

FINAL
Saturday 1 April 1893 at Lonsdale Park, Workington
MARYPORT 4 *Back*: J Robley. *Three-quarters*: T McGerry (t), R Messenger, T Peters. *Half-backs*: G Davidson, W Stephenson. *Forwards*: R Barnes, JH Blacklock, G Crellin, J Holliday (capt), P Lowthian, WT Smith, J Thirlwell (t), J Thompson, J Turnbull.
CUMMERSDALE HORNETS 3 *Back*: E Smith. *Three-quarters*: G Boak, J Forsyth (capt), E Gardiner. *Half-backs*: J Ferguson, J Rogerson. *Forwards*: T Armstrong, J Blair (pg), J Foster, E Pringle, G Rogerson, J Talbot, G Tinkler, A Walsh, T Watson.
Attendance: 3,000   *Referee*: Rev F Marshall (Yorkshire RU)

DURHAM COUNTY CHALLENGE CUP (14 entries)
Try – 2 points; conversion, penalty goal – 3; drop-goal, field goal, goal from mark – 4.

First Round
Durham City 10, South Shields YMCA 0
Hartlepool Rovers 40, Jarrow 0
Sherburn House 18, Stockton 4
Sunderland 30, Hamsteels (Lanchester) 0
Tudhoe 36, North Durham 0
Westoe 4, Ryton 0
Byes: Houghton-le-Spring, West Hartlepool

Second Round
Hartlepool Rovers 30, Houghton-le-Spring 2
Sunderland 6, West Hartlepool 12
Tudhoe 8, Sherburn House 0
Westoe 0, Durham City 5

Semi-finals
Hartlepool Rovers 7, Durham City 2
West Hartlepool 7, Tudhoe 7 (aet)

Semi-final Replay
Tudhoe 4, West Hartlepool 0

FINAL
Saturday 8 April 1893 at Mowbray Road, South Shields
TUDHOE w/o HARTLEPOOL ROVERS
Cup awarded to Tudhoe.
Hartlepool Rovers refused to play on scheduled date and disqualified.

NORTHUMBERLAND COUNTY FOOTBALL CHALLENGE CUP (8 entries)
Try – 2 points; conversion, penalty goal – 3; drop-goal, field goal, goal from mark – 4.

First Round
Percy Park 27, Gosforth 0
Rockcliff 34, Brighton 0
Tynedale 3, North Elswick 6
Wallsend 6, Northern 0

Semi-finals
Rockcliff 13, North Elswick 0
Wallsend 0, Percy Park 12

FINAL
Saturday 25 March 1893 at Jesmond Ground, Newcastle
ROCKCLIFF 14 *Back*: J Murray. *Three-quarters*: W Taylor (t), T Nicholson (t), H Shotton. *Half-backs*: TP Alexander (dg), EW Taylor (capt, c, pg). *Forwards*: Alf Benson, J Bolam, JH Greenwell, GW Lee, AP Shiach, TC Stephenson, A Styan, B Taylor, John Taylor.
PERCY PARK 2 *Back*: Jack Taylor. *Three-quarters*: S Priest, H Knott, T Rycroft, CO Robinson (t). *Half-backs*: HW Audus, T Stewart (capt). *Forwards*: TG Boss, J Davidson, C Greaves, E Kerr, H Smurthwaite, FW Thompson. J Wardle, W Winter.
Attendance: 8,000   *Referee*: WH Humphreys (Durham RU)

DURHAM v NORTHUMBERLAND CHALLENGE MATCH
Saturday 29 April 1893 at Jesmond Ground, Newcastle
ROCKCLIFF (Northumberland Cup winners) **10** *Back*: R Baty. *Three-quarters*: T Rycroft, John Taylor, S Anderson, H Shotton. *Half-backs*: EW Taylor (capt, c, pg), W Turner. *Forwards*: Alf Benson, JH Greenwell, J Hall (t), GW Lee, AP Shiach (t), TC Stephenson, A Styan, B Taylor.

TUDHOE (Durham Cup winners) **7** *Back*: W Taylor. *Three-quarters*: M McGann, W Wainford (t, c), H Gibbon, J Robertshaw. *Half-backs*: F Marston (t), F Hindle. *Forwards*: WA Bell, J Duffey, R Edwards, T Faulkner (capt), R Gibbon, J Lindsay, A Stephenson, AJ Troupe.
Attendance: 2,000 / 3,000   *Referee*: H Hutchinson (Wakefield)

YORKSHIRE COUNTY FOOTBALL CHALLENGE CUP (146 entries)
Try – 2 points; conversion, penalty goal – 3; drop-goal, field goal, goal from mark – 4.

Preliminary Round
(112 teams in 15 districts; two from each, indicated by 'q', qualified for next stage)

Airedale: Guiseley (q), Guiseley Parish Church, Idle (q), Saltaire, Windhill, Yeadon
Batley: Batley Mountaineers, Birstall (q), Bruntcliffe (q), Gildersome, Morley Providence
Bradford: Bankfoot (q), Bowling Old Lane (q), Bradford Rangers, Brownroyd Recreation, Buttershaw, Thornton Rangers, Wibsey, Wibsey Slack Side
Castleford: Brotherton St John's, Featherstone Trinity (q), Ferrybridge, Garforth, Glasshoughton, Kippax, Knottingley (q), Methley, Normanton St John's, South Milford, Wheldale Rovers, Whitwood
Craven: Bingley, Bingley Grammar School Old Boys, Haworth, Ingrow, Keighley (q), Keighley Hornets, Keighley Zingari (q), Keighley Shamrocks, Silsden, Skipton
Dewsbury: Dewsbury St Mark's, Dewsbury St Paulinus (q), Horbury, Horbury Zingari, Mirfield (q), Mirfield Rangers, Thornhill Lees Trinity
East Leeds: Beeston, Leeds Good Shepherd's, Leeds Institute, Newtown (q), Rothwell and District (q)
Halifax: Bailiffe Bridge (q), Greetland (q), Halifax Gymnasium, Hebden Bridge, Luddendenfoot, Mytholmroyd, Salterhebble, Todmorden
Huddersfield: Crosland Moor (q), Holmfirth, Honley (q), Kirkburton, Lockwood, Milnsbridge, Netherton, Nortonthorpe, Old Almondburians, Paddock, Primrose Hill, Rastrick, Shepley

Hull and Ouse: Beverley (q), Hull Britannia (q), Hull Melbourne, Hull St Paul's, Hull Three Crowns, Hull White Star, Selby
Northern: Harrogate (q), Harrogate Rangers, Knaresborough, Pateley Bridge, Ripon, Tadcaster (q), York Leeman Wanderers
North Leeds: Burley, Chapel Allerton, Horsforth (q), Kirkstall St Stephen's, Leeds Northern, Woodhouse (q), Yorkshire College
Spen Valley: Cleckheaton White Star (q), Liversedge Hornets (q), Low Moor St Mark's
Wakefield: Barnsley, Barnsley Congregational, Barnsley Parish Church, Barnsley Volunteers, Darton Unity, Doncaster Town, Eastmoor, Kinsley, Outwood Church (q), Ryhill (q), Wakefield St Austin's
West Leeds: Farsley, Pudsey (q), Stanningley (q)

First Round
(* indicates 34 teams seeded to this round)
Bailiffe Bridge 2, Otley* 12
Batley* 38, Cleckheaton White Star 7
Beverley 0, Outwood Church 25
Bradford* 19, Hull Kingston Rovers* 5
Bramley* 12, Ryhill 0
Bruntcliffe 0, Morley* 19
Castleford* 43, Bankfoot 0
Crosland Moor 4, Mirfield 9
Dewsbury* 3, Alverthorpe* 8
Guiseley 5, Featherstone Trinity 0
Goole* 17, Stanningley 8
Halifax* 7, Elland* 0
Heckmondwike* 22, Liversedge Hornets 5
Holbeck* 12, Bowling Old Lane 5
Horsforth 2, Brighouse Rangers* 24
Hull* 0, Leeds* 15
Hull Britannia 10, York* 13
Hunslet* 2, Huddersfield* 0
Keighley 30, Woodhouse 0
Kirkstall* 5, Birstall 8
Leeds Parish Church* 7, Normanton* 2
Liversedge* 48, Dewsbury St Paulinus 4
Newtown 0, Manningham* 31
Ossett* 12, Greetland 0
Pontefract* 6, Bowling* 4
Pudsey 17, Honley 3
Rothwell and District 0, Cleckheaton* 2
Shipley* 4, Armley* 0
Sowerby Bridge* 27, Knottingley 2
Tadcaster 13, Idle 2
Wakefield Trinity* 10, Harrogate 0
Wortley* 24, Keighley Zingari 2

Second Round
Birstall 10, Mirfield 7
Bradford 25, Pontefract 3
Brighouse Rangers 5, Heckmondwike 6
Goole 15, Leeds 2
Guiseley 3, Alverthorpe 16
Holbeck 14, Bramley 2
Leeds Parish Church 0, Hunslet 4
Liversedge 6, Castleford 2
Manningham 24, Keighley 5
Ossett 9, Outwood Church 2
Otley 12, York 0
Pudsey 4, Batley 10
Shipley 2, Wortley 4 (replay ordered after protest)
Sowerby Bridge 6, Cleckheaton 0
Tadcaster 5, Morley 12
Wakefield Trinity 6, Halifax 29

Second Round Replay
Wortley 10, Shipley 7 (at Manningham)

Third Round
Alverthorpe 0, Bradford 7
Holbeck 5, Heckmondwike 8
Liversedge 49, Birstall 0
Manningham 10, Hunslet 2
Morley 5, Batley 19
Ossett 4, Halifax 5
Otley 7, Wortley 0
Sowerby Bridge 5, Goole 12

Fourth Round
Bradford 2, Halifax 11
Goole 5, Heckmondwike 10
Liversedge 4, Batley 7
Otley 0, Manningham 10

Semi-finals
Batley 9, Heckmondwike 4
(at Crown Flatts, Dewsbury)
Halifax 12, Manningham 4
(at Fartown, Huddersfield)

FINAL

Saturday 22 April 1893 at Headingley, Leeds
HALIFAX 8 *Back*: J Dodd. *Three-quarters*: AS Toothill, WH Keepings (c), F Firth. *Half-backs*: J Arnold, JA Rigg. *Forwards*: GF Dickenson, O Fletcher (capt), B Mellor, JW Mellor (t), T Watson, I Webster, H Wilkinson, A Wilson, RS Winskill (pg).
BATLEY 2 *Back*: Joe Naylor. *Three-quarters*: I Shaw, JB Goodall, H Simms. *Half-backs*: T Elliker, Jim Naylor (t). *Forwards*: W Farrar, JA Haigh, FW Lowrie (capt), J Oldfield, W Scott, M Shackleton, C Squires, C Stubley, A Thornton.
Attendance: 17,288   *Referee*: WH Humphreys (Durham RU)

COUNTY CHAMPIONSHIP

NORTH WESTERN GROUP

Saturday 29 October 1892 at Whalley Range, Manchester
LANCASHIRE 5 *Back*: L Rigg (RochStC). *Three-quarters*: W McCutcheon (Old), D Gwynn (Old), F Miles (Sal, t). *Half-backs*: W Bumby (Swi), W Cross (StH). *Forwards:* JB Andrew (Old), A Ashworth (Moss), W Atkinson (Wig), T King (Sal), J Newby (Moss), R Pierce (Liv), G Sharples (Swi), WB Stoddart (Liv), SE Wilson (capt, Liv, c).
WESTMORLAND 5 *Back*: T Hine (KenH). *Three-quarters*: JK Robinson (KirkL, t), J Allen (capt, KenH, c), CG Mason (Amb). *Half-backs*: W Hall (KenH), R Hill (KenH). *Forwards*: J Graham (KenH), RH Moore (Amb), J Newton (Amb), R Nicholson (KenH), WJ Parsons (KenH), JH Thompson (KenH), W Whiteley (KenH), W Wilson (KenH), RS Winskill (Hal).
Attendance: 4,000/5,000   *Referee*: CA Crane (Midland Counties)

Saturday 5 November 1892 at Upper Park, Birkenhead
CHESHIRE 7 *Back*: S Houghton (Run). *Three-quarters*: PR Clauss (BirkPk), JH Crompton (Run, c), FP Jones (NewB). *Half-backs*: S Abram (Run, t), F Drinkwater (Sale). *Forwards*: AJ Chadwick (BirkPk), E Elliott (BirkW), O Hughes (Run), EH Morley (Sale), P Riley (capt, Run, t), WB Smith (NewB), J Speet (Stock), H Williams (Run), WA Williams (NewB).
LANCASHIRE 6 *Back*: R Lewis (Ulv). *Three-quarters*: W McCutcheon (Old, t), D Gwynn (Old), DC Woods (Man). *Half-backs*: W Bumby (Swi), W Cross (StH). *Forwards*: JB Andrew (Old, t), A Ashworth (Moss), W Atkinson (Wig), H Case (Ulv, t), T King (Sal), J Newby (Moss), R Pierce (Liv), G Sharples (Swi), WB Stoddart (Liv).
Attendance: 8,000   *Referee*: GR Hill (RFU Honorary Secretary)

Monday 7 November 1892 at Salthouse Road, Millom
CUMBERLAND 2 *Back*: DG Lamonby (Brou). *Three-quarters*: T Forsyth (CumH), W Wilkinson (Mil), TH Hodgkinson (CarlC, t). *Half-backs*: J Armstrong (Mil), TL Jackson (Whi). *Forwards*: GB Atkinson (Whi), JJ Bewsher (PenU), JH Blacklock (Mary), C Callaghan (Work), JW Cowen (Asp), W Cross (Egr), J Fawcett (Mil), T Tervet (CarlC), T Whalen (Mil).
CHESHIRE 0 *Back*: S Houghton (Run). *Three-quarters*: PR Clauss (BirkPk), JH Crompton (Run), FP Jones (NewB). *Half-backs*: S Abram (Run), F Drinkwater (Sale). *Forwards*: AJ Chadwick (BirkPk), E Elliott (BirkW), W Faulkner (Run), O Hughes (Run), P Riley (Run), WB Smith (NewB), J Speet (Stock), H Williams (Run), WA Williams (NewB).
Attendance: 2,000   *Referee*: W Cail (RFU President)

Thursday 17 November 1892 at Upper Park, Birkenhead
CHESHIRE 5 *Back*: S Houghton (Run). *Three-quarters*: PR Clauss (BirkPk), JH Crompton (Run, c), FP Jones (NewB). *Half-backs*: S Abram (Run), G Robinson (Run). *Forwards*: AJ Chadwick (BirkPk), E Elliott (BirkW), W Faulkner (Run), EH Morley (Sale), JH Potts (Stock), P Riley (Run, t), J Speet (Stock), H Williams (Run), WA Williams (NewB).
WESTMORLAND 5 *Back*: T Hine (KenH). *Three-quarters*: J Allen (capt, KenH, t, c), JK Robinson (KirkL), GH Bell (Tyl). *Half-backs*: W Hall (KenH), R Hill (KenH). *Forwards*: RH Moore (Amb), J Newton (Amb), R Nicholson (KenH), T Nicholson (KenH), WJ Parsons (KenH), JH Thompson (KenH), W Whiteley (KenH), E Wilson (KenH), RS Winskill (Hal).
Attendance: 3,000   *Referee*: n/a

Saturday 19 November 1892 at Whalley Range, Manchester
LANCASHIRE 0 *Back*: J Boscow (War). *Three-quarters*: W McCutcheon (Old), A Barrett (Sal), J Valentine (Swi). *Half-backs*: W Bumby (Swi), W Parlane (ManR).
Forwards: A Ashworth (Moss), W Atkinson (Wig), H Case (Ulv), J Jolley (War), T Kent (Sal), T King (Sal), T Melledew (RochH), R Pierce (Liv), G Sharples (Swi).
CUMBERLAND 0 *Back*: DG Lamonby (Brou). *Three-quarters*: TH Hodgkinson (CarlC), T Forsyth (CumH), W Wilkinson (Mil). *Half-backs*: J Armstrong (Mil), J McGuire (Mil).
Forwards: GB Atkinson (Whi), JH Blacklock (Mary), JH Buckett (Mil), J Burns (Mil), Jim Davidson (Asp), J Fawcett (Mil), W Milligan (Work), J Rowe (Egr), T Whalen (Mil).
Attendance: 6,000   *Referee*: Rev F Marshall (Yorkshire)

Saturday 3 December 1892 at Mint's Feet, Kendal
WESTMORLAND 0 *Back*: T Hine (KenH). *Three-quarters*: GH Bell (Tyl), J Allen (capt, KenH), JK Robinson (KirkL). *Half-backs*: J Berry (Tyl), R Hill (KenH). *Forwards*: RH Moore (Amb), J Newton (Amb), R Nicholson (KenH), T Nicholson (KenH), WJ Parsons (KenH), JH Thompson (KenH), W Whiteley (KenH), W Wilson (KenH), RS Winskill (Hal).
CUMBERLAND 5 *Back*: DG Lamonby (Brou). *Three-quarters*: TH Hodgkinson (capt, CarlC), T Forsyth (CumH, t), W Wilkinson (Mil). *Half-backs*: J Armstrong (Mil), J McGuire (Mil). *Forwards*: GB Atkinson (Whi), JH Blacklock (Mary), JH Buckett (Mil, c), Jim Davidson (Asp), J Fawcett (Mil), W Milligan (Work), J Rowe (Egr), T Tervet (CarlC), T Whalen (Mil).
Attendance: n/a   *Referee*: Rev F Marshall (Yorkshire)

Final table

	P	W	D	L	For	Agst	Pts
Cumberland	3	2	1	0	7	0	5
Cheshire	3	1	1	1	12	13	3
Lancashire	3	0	2	1	11	12	2
Westmorland	3	0	2	1	10	15	2

NORTH EASTERN GROUP
Saturday 12 November 1892 at Friarage Field, Hartlepool
DURHAM 7 *Back*: N Devine (WHart). *Three-quarters*: S Morfitt (WHart), WH Bell (Sund), FHR Alderson (capt, HartR, t, c), W Wainford (Tud, t). *Half-backs*: F Hindle (Tud), F Marston (Tud). *Forwards*: J Duffey (Tud), T Faulkner (Tud), TJ Lindsay (SShYM), LG Nash (DurC), RF Oakes (HartR), P Turnbull (WHart), AE Thompson (SundN), W Yiend (HartR).
YORKSHIRE 13 *Back*: W Goldthorpe (Hun). *Three-quarters*: RE Lockwood (capt, Heck), AE Goldthorpe (Hun, t, 2c, pg), J Dyson (Hud). *Half-backs*: H Duckett (Brad), H Varley (Livs, t). *Forwards*: A Blakey (Wort), H Bradshaw (Bram), T Broadley (Brad), W Lorriman (Lee), B Mellor (Hal), E Redman (Mann), C Richardson (LeePC), H Speed (Cas), JT Toothill (Brad).
Attendance: 14,000   *Referee*: T Hunter (Lancashire)

Saturday 19 November 1892 at Headingley, Leeds
YORKSHIRE 17 *Back*: GE Lorimer (Mann). *Three-quarters*: TT Brook (Elland), AE Goldthorpe (Hun, t, c, 2dg), RE Lockwood (capt, Heck). *Half-backs*: H Barker (Livs), H Varley (Livs). *Forwards*: H Bradshaw (Bram, t), T Broadley (Brad), M Fletcher (Lee), W Lorriman (Lee, t), FW Lowrie (Bat), W Nichol (BrigR), E Redman (Mann), H Speed (Cas), JT Toothill (Brad).
NORTHUMBERLAND 12 *Back*: R Baty (Tynd). *Three-quarters*: H Knott (PerPk, t), S Anderson (Wall), F Finney (PerPk, t), T Nicholson (Rock, t). *Half-backs*: TP Alexander (Rock), EW Taylor (Rock, 2c). *Forwards*: W Armstrong (Gos), FC Garrett (Nor), JH Greenwell (Rock), R Harris (NEls), T Robson (Tynd), A Styan (Rock), AC Williams (Nor), R Wright (Brighton).
Attendance: 8,000   *Referee*: WH Humphreys (Durham)

Final table

	P	W	D	L	For	Agst	Pts
Yorkshire	2	2	0	0	30	19	4
Durham	1	0	0	1	12	17	0
Northumberland	1	0	0	1	7	13	0

(Northumberland v Durham on 21 January – too late for inclusion)

SOUTH WESTERN GROUP

Results

Gloucestershire 0, Somersetshire 0
Somersetshire 4, Devonshire 4
Gloucestershire 18, Cornwall 0

Devonshire 17, Gloucestershire 4
Devonshire 20, Cornwall 0
Note: Fixtures incomplete.

Final table

	P	W	D	L	For	Agst	Pts
Devonshire	3	2	1	0	41	8	5
Gloucestershire	3	1	1	1	22	17	3
Somersetshire	2	0	2	0	4	4	2
Cornwall	2	0	0	2	0	38	0

SOUTH EASTERN GROUP

Results

Surrey 9, Middlesex 25
Midland Counties 12, Surrey 7
Kent 0, Middlesex 17

Kent 5, Midland Counties 6
Middlesex 15, Midland Counties 5
Kent 5, Surrey 6

Final table

	P	W	D	L	For	Agst	Pts
Middlesex	3	3	0	0	57	14	6
Midland Counties	3	2	0	1	23	27	4
Surrey	3	1	0	2	22	42	2
Kent	3	0	0	3	10	29	0

FINAL GROUP ('SECOND SERIES')

Wednesday 18 January 1893 at Crown Flatts, Dewsbury
YORKSHIRE 11 *Back*: GE Lorimer (Mann). *Three-quarters*: F Firth (Hal, t), T Summersgill (Lee), AS Toothill (Hal). *Half-backs*: H Duckett (Brad, 2t), H Varley (Livs). *Forwards*: H Bradshaw (Bram), M Fletcher (Lee), D Jowett (Heck, c), H Lodge (Hud, t), W Lorriman (Lee), B Mellor (Hal), C Richardson (LeePC), H Speed (Cas), JT Toothill (capt, Brad).
DEVONSHIRE 0 *Back*: W Hockin (DevA). *Three-quarters*: P Webber (Paig), FS Cox (RNEC), WE Sowden (DevA), FE Greatwood (Tiv). *Half-backs*: J Davies (Torq), L Howell (RNEC). *Forwards*: GH Allington (DevA), RJ Harper (Barn), C Hawking (Torq), A May (DevA), B Parnell (Tot), FJ Sellicks (NewA), FH Toller (Barn), BH Wallis (Exe).
Attendance: 7,000/8,000   *Referee*: GR Hill (RFU Honorary Secretary)

Monday 30 January 1893 at Athletic Ground, Richmond
MIDDLESEX 5 *Back*: E Field (MidW). *Three-quarters*: GT Campbell (LonS), JA Gould (Rich, t), G MacGregor (LonS), AE Stoddart (Black, c). *Half-backs*: JC Orr (MidW), W Wotherspoon (LonS). *Forwards*: EW Bishop (RosPk), E Bonham-Carter (Black), FW Goodhue (LonS), J Hammond (Black), RG Macmillan (capt, LonS), E Prescott (OMT), HP Surtees (Harl), WP Wells (Ken).
YORKSHIRE 14 *Back*: WH Eagland (Hud). *Three-quarters*: J Dyson (Hud), RE Lockwood (capt, Heck, c), WH Keepings (Hal), F Firth (Hal). *Half-backs*: H Duckett (Brad), JA Rigg (Hal, 2t). *Forwards*: H Bradshaw (Bram, t), T Broadley (Brad), WE Bromet (Rich), M Fletcher (Lee), D Jowett (Heck, pg), C Richardson (LeePC), H Speed (Cas), JT Toothill (Brad, t).
Attendance: 8,000   *Referee*: WH Humphreys (Durham)

Thursday 9 February 1893 at Athletic Ground, Richmond
MIDDLESEX 0 *Back*: E Field (MidW). *Three-quarters*: CA Hooper (MidW), AL Brooke (OLey), ME Jardine (LonS). *Half-backs*: J Lamont (RosPk), JHS McArthur (OLey). *Forwards*: E Bonham-Carter (Black), N Davidson (RIEC), J Hammond (Black), WA Lindsay (OLey), E Prescott (OMT), CP Simpson (Rich), HP Surtees (Harl), AN Weir (OMT), WP Wells (Ken).
CUMBERLAND 2 *Back*: JT Bell (Mil). *Three-quarters*: W Wilkinson (Mil), T Forsyth (CumH), TH Hodgkinson (CarlC). *Half-backs*: J Armstrong (Mil), J McGuire (Mil).

Forwards: GB Atkinson (Whi, t), JH Blacklock (Mary), JH Buckett (Mil), J Burns (Mil), Jim Davidson (Asp), D Elliott (CarlC), W Milligan (Work), T Tervet (CarlC), T Whalen (Mil).
Attendance: 'small'   *Referee*: R Walker (Lancashire)

Saturday 11 February 1893 at County Ground, St Thomas, Exeter
DEVONSHIRE 0 *Back*: W Hockin (DevA). *Three-quarters*: FE Greatwood (Tiv), WE Sowden (DevA), P Webber (Paig). *Half-backs*: J Davies (Torq), JH Chipman (Torq). *Forwards*: GH Allington (DevA), RJ Harper (Barn), J Laverty (DevA), A May (DevA), B Parnell (Tot), FJ Sellicks (NewA), E Sloper (Tot), FH Toller (Barn), BH Wallis (Exe).
CUMBERLAND 8 *Back*: JT Bell (Mil). *Three-quarters*: T Forsyth (CumH, t), TH Hodgkinson (CarlC), JH Buckett (Mil). *Half-backs*: J McGuire (Mil), W Wilkinson (Mil, t). *Forwards*: GB Atkinson (Whi), JH Blacklock (Mary), J Burns (Mil), Jim Davidson (Asp, t), D Elliott (CarlC), W Milligan (Work, t), J Rowe (Egr), T Tervet (CarlC), T Whalen (Mil).
Attendance: 4,000   *Referee*: Rev F Marshall (Yorkshire)

Thursday 16 February 1893 at Lismore Place, Carlisle
CUMBERLAND 2 *Back*: JT Bell (Mil). *Three-quarters*: W Wilkinson (Mil), T Forsyth (CumH), TH Hodgkinson (CarlC). *Half-backs*: J Armstrong (Mil, t), J McGuire (Mil). *Forwards*: GB Atkinson (Whi), JH Blacklock (Mary), JH Buckett (Mil), Jim Davidson (Asp), D Elliott (CarlC), W Milligan (Work), J Rowe (Egr), T Tervet (CarlC), T Whalen (Mil).
YORKSHIRE 17 *Back*: WH Eagland (Hud). *Three-quarters*: F Firth (Hal), RE Lockwood (capt, Heck, c), J Dyson (Hud, 2t). *Half-backs*: H Duckett (Brad), JA Rigg (Hal, t). *Forwards*: H Bradshaw (Bram), T Broadley (Brad, t), M Fletcher (Lee, 2t), D Jowett (Heck, t), W Nichol (BrigR), E Redman (Mann), C Richardson (LeePC), H Speed (Cas), JT Toothill (Brad).
Attendance: 6,500   *Referee*: W Cail (RFU President)

Other result
Devonshire 13, Middlesex 0

Final table
	P	W	D	L	For	Agst	Pts
Yorkshire	3	3	0	0	42	7	6
Cumberland	3	2	0	1	12	17	4
Devonshire	3	1	0	2	13	19	2
Middlesex	3	0	0	3	5	29	0

COUNTY CHAMPIONS v THE REST
Saturday 25 February 1893 at Fartown, Huddersfield
YORKSHIRE 2 *Back*: WH Eagland (Hud). *Three-quarters*: J Dyson (Hud), RE Lockwood (capt, Heck), F Firth (Hal, t). *Half-backs*: H Duckett (Brad), JA Rigg (Hal). *Forwards*: H Bradshaw (Bram), T Broadley (Brad), WE Bromet (Rich), M Fletcher (Lee), D Jowett (Heck), H Lodge (Hud), E Redman (Mann), H Speed (Cas), JT Toothill (Brad).
REST OF ENGLAND 0 *Back*: WG Mitchell (Rich). *Three-quarters*: T Nicholson (Rock), JH Crompton (Run), FP Jones (NewB). *Half-backs*: F Marston (Tud), CM Wells (Harl/CamU). *Forwards*: Jim Davidson (Asp), F Evershed (capt, Black/Burt), JH Greenwell (Rock), T Kent (Sal), P Maud (Black), LJ Percival (Rugby), JJ Robinson (Burt/CamU), F Soane (Bath), W Yiend (HartR).
Attendance: 10,000   *Referee*: ET Gurdon (RFU Vice-President)

NON-COUNTY CHAMPIONSHIP MATCHES

Wednesday 19 October 1892 at Irwell Lane, Runcorn
CHESHIRE 9 *Back*: S Houghton (Run). *Three-quarters:* PR Clauss (BirkPk), JH Crompton (capt, Run, t, c, dg), C Kelly (BirkW). *Half-backs*: S Abram (Run), F Drinkwater (Sale). *Forwards*: AJ Chadwick (BirkPk), E Elliott (BirkW), O Hughes (Run), EH Morley (Sale), H Moss (Duk), P Riley (Run), WB Smith (NewB), J Speet (Stock), WA Williams (NewB).
MIDLAND COUNTIES 5 *Back*: JF Byrne (Mose). *Three-quarters*: RH Frith (Cov), A Rogers (Mose), W Frith (Cov). *Half-backs*: R Chaloner (Mose), WP Nichol (OEdw). *Forwards*: F Evershed (Burt), AW Gorton (Burt), G Carpenter (Cov), BH Cattell (Mose), CJ Hill (Cov), HD Hope (OEdw, t), ER Lycett (Mose), FS Pountney (Mose), RH Taylor (Handsworth).
Attendance: 2,000   *Referee*: n/a
Note: Scorer of Midland Counties conversion not reported.

Wednesday 19 October 1892 at Clarence Street, York
YORKSHIRE 31 *Back*: W Goldthorpe (Hun). *Three-quarters*: RE Lockwood (capt, Heck, t, c, dg), AE Goldthorpe (Hun, t, 2c, 2dg), T Summersgill (Lee). *Half-backs*: H Duckett (Brad), H Varley (Livs). *Forwards*: H Bradshaw (Bram), O Fletcher (Hal), E Hudson (Lee), D Jowett (Heck), W Nichol (BrigR, t), E Redman (Mann), W Smith (Wak), JT Toothill (Brad, 2t), F Wood (BrigR).
DEVONSHIRE 5 *Back*: T Causey (Aller Vale). *Three-quarters*: JM Wilcocks (Exe, c), GH Harding (Torq), FE Greatwood ((Tiv, t). *Half-backs:* JH Chipman (Torq), J Davies (Torq). *Forwards*: W Ashford (capt, Exe), SH Brooking (Torq), J Collinge (DevA), B Parnell (Tot), FJ Sellicks (NewA), E Sloper (Tot), WE Spreadbury (Crediton), F Tozer (Melville), BH Wallis (Exe).
Attendance: 4,000   *Referee*: W Cail (RFU President)

Monday 24 October 1892 at Whalley Range, Manchester
LANCASHIRE 2 *Back*: T Coop (Lei). *Three-quarters*: W McCutcheon (Old, t), D Gwynn (Old), GH Pierce (Bro). *Half-backs*: W Bumby (Swi), W Cross (StH). *Forwards*: A Ashworth (Moss), W Atkinson (Wig), EW Bullen (LivOB), T Craven (Sal), T Kent (Sal), G Pollard (ManR), J Pyke (StHR), T Rothwell (Swi), RP Wilson (LivOB).
GLAMORGANSHIRE 0 *Back*: WJ Bancroft (Swa). *Three-quarters*: CS Coke (Swa), AL Davies (CarHarl), RM Garrett (Pen), GW Shepherd (Pen). *Half-backs*: A Cross (Nea), W Thomas (Nea). *Forwards*: RG Edwards (Swa), I Griffiths (Aber), F Hutchinson (Nea), DH Lewis (Peny), D Mainwaring (Swa), F Mills (Swa), W Phillips (CarHarl), S Rice (Swa).
Attendance: 3,000   *Referee*: Rev F Marshall (Yorkshire)

Saturday 12 November 1892 at Jesmond Ground, Newcastle
NORTHUMBERLAND 13 *Back*: R Baty (Tynd). *Three-quarters*: H Knott (PerPk), F Finney (PerPk), T Nicholson (Rock, t), T Rycroft (PerPk). *Half-backs*: TP Alexander (Rock, t), EW Taylor (Rock, 2c, pg). *Forwards*: W Armstrong (Gos), FC Garrett (Nor), JH Greenwell (Rock), R Harris (NEls), T Robson (Tynd), A Styan (Rock), AC Williams (Nor), R Wright (Brighton).
SOUTH OF SCOTLAND 2 *Back*: G Cochrane (Gala). *Half-backs*: WS Oliver (Jed, t), T Almers (Haw), D Rutherford (Gala). *Quarter-backs*: T Brydon (Gala), JT Mabon (Jed).

Forwards: T Brown (Mel), J Ford (Gala), R Hunter (Jed), F Johnson (Gala), N Kemp (Gala), G Kyle (Gala), J Marchbanks (Haw), G Scott (Gala), A Stevenson (Haw).
Attendance: 4,000   *Referee*: WH Humphreys (Durham)

Monday 14 November 1892 at Corpus College Ground, Cambridge
CAMBRIDGE UNIVERSITY 5 *Back*: E Field. *Three-quarters*: DD Robertson, W Neilson, JJ Gowans (t). *Half-backs*: TL Jackson, FH Maturin. *Forwards*: DB Hill, WE Nelson, CB Nicholl (capt), HD Rendall, JCA Rigby, BF Robinson, JJ Robinson, TWP Storey (c), WE Tucker.
LANCASHIRE 0 *Back*: R Lewis (Ulv). *Three-quarters*: W McCutcheon (Old), D Gwynn (Old), W Pearson (Swi). *Half-backs*: GG Allen (Liv), W Parlane (ManR). *Forwards*: JB Andrew (Old), A Ashworth (Moss), W Atkinson (Wig), H Case (Ulv), T King (Sal), J Newby (Moss), R Pierce (Liv), G Sharples (Swi), WB Stoddart (Liv).
Attendance: 2,000/3,000   *Referee*: A Budd (Kent)

Wednesday 16 November 1892 at Fartown, Huddersfield
YORKSHIRE 5 *Back*: W Goldthorpe (Hun). *Three-quarters*: J Dyson (Hud, t), AE Goldthorpe (Hun, c), TT Brook (Elland). *Half-backs*: H Barker (Livs), H Varley (Livs). *Forwards*: H Bradshaw (Bram), T Broadley (Brad), WE Bromet (capt, Rich), O Fletcher (Hal), W Lorriman (Lee), E Redman (Mann), C Richardson (LeePC), H Speed (Cas), JT Toothill (Brad).
GLAMORGANSHIRE 5 *Back*: WJ Bancroft (Swa, c). *Three-quarters*: E Thorogood (Swa), GB Trick (Nea), JP Jago (CarHarl), J Davis (Pontardawe). *Half-backs*: I Grey (Morr, t), T Morgan (Peny). *Forwards*: RG Edwards (Swa), I Griffiths (Aber), J Harris (Aber), F Hutchinson (Nea), DH Lewis (Peny), D Mainwaring (Swa), S Rice (Swa), J Stead (Pon).
Attendance: 5,000   *Referee*: EB Holmes (Midland Counties)

Thursday 17 November 1892 at Corpus Ground, Cambridge
CAMBRIDGE UNIVERSITY 2 *Back*: E Field. *Three-quarters*: W Neilson, CM Wells, JJ Gowans (t). *Half-backs*: TL Jackson, FH Maturin. *Forwards*: DB Hill, WE Nelson, CB Nicholl (capt), HD Rendall, JCA Rigby, BF Robinson, JJ Robinson, TWP Storey, WE Tucker.
CUMBERLAND 4 *Back*: DG Lamonby (Brou). *Three-quarters*: T Forsyth (CumH), W Wilkinson (Mil), TH Hodgkinson (CarlC). *Half-backs*: J Armstrong (Mil), J McGuire (Mil). *Forwards*: GB Atkinson (Whi, 2t), JH Blacklock (Mary), JH Buckett (Mil), Jim Davidson (Asp), J Fawcett (Mil), W Milligan (Work), J Rowe (Egr), T Tervet (CarlC), T Whalen (Mil).
Attendance: 'large'   *Referee*: R Westray (Cumberland)

Saturday 26 November 1892 at Manchester Athletic Ground, Fallowfield
LANCASHIRE 2 *Back*: J Boscow (War). *Three-quarters*: W McCutcheon (Old, t), JH Marsh (Swi), DC Woods (Man). *Half-backs*: W Bumby (Swi), W Parlane (ManR). *Forwards*: W Atkinson (Wig), H Case (Ulv), J Jolley (War), T Kent (Sal), T King (Sal), T Melledew (RochH), R Pierce (Liv), T Rothwell (Swi), RP Wilson (LivOB).
YORKSHIRE 2 *Back*: GE Lorimer (Mann). *Three-quarters*: RE Lockwood (capt, Heck, t), AE Goldthorpe (Hun), J Dyson (Hud). *Half-backs*: A Briggs (Brad), H Duckett (Brad). *Forwards*: H Bradshaw (Bram), T Broadley (Brad), M Fletcher (Lee), D Jowett (Heck), W Lorriman (Lee), E Redman (Mann), C Richardson (LeePC), H Speed (Cas), JT Toothill (Brad).
Attendance: 15,000   *Referee*: AR Don-Wauchope (Scotland)

Saturday 3 December 1892 at Wood Terrace, Westoe, South Shields
DURHAM 11 *Back*: W Taylor (Tud). *Three-quarters*: W Wainford (Tud), FHR Alderson (HartR, t, c, gm), S Morfitt (WHart), WH Bell (Sund). *Half-backs*: F Hindle (Tud), F Marston (Tud, t). *Forwards*: J Duffey (Tud), T Faulkner (Tud), J Hall (NDur), TJ Lindsay (SShYM), LG Nash (DurC), RF Oakes (HartR), AE Thompson (SundN), W Yiend (HartR).
CHESHIRE 0 *Back*: S Houghton (Run). *Three-quarters*: FP Jones (NewB), JH Crompton (Run), PR Clauss (BirkPk). *Half-backs*: S Abram (Run), F Drinkwater (Sale). *Forwards*: AJ Chadwick (BirkPk), E Elliott (BirkW), W Faulkner (Run), EH Morley (Sale), JH Potts (Stock), P Riley (Run), WB Smith (NewB), H Williams (Run), WA Williams (NewB).
Attendance: 10,000   *Referee*: JA Miller (Yorkshire)

Saturday 14 January 1893 at Park Avenue, Bradford
YORKSHIRE 29 *Back*: GE Lorimer (Mann, t). *Three-quarters*: RE Lockwood (capt, Heck, 3c), T Summersgill (Lee, dg), J Dyson (Hud, t). *Half-backs*: A Briggs (Brad, t), JA Rigg (Hal, t). *Forwards*: H Bradshaw (Bram), T Broadley (Brad, 2t), M Fletcher (Lee), D Jowett (Heck), W Lorriman (Lee), E Redman (Mann), C Richardson (LeePC), H Speed (Cas), JT Toothill (Brad, 2t).
SOMERSETSHIRE 0 *Back*: H Boucher (Well). *Three-quarters*: CF Mermagen (Well), FH Fox (Well), SC Smith (Wes). *Half-backs*: H Merry (Well), TN Parham (Bath). *Forwards*: J Aldridge (Wes), PF Hancock (Tau/Black), WH Manfield (Yeo), H Smith (Wes), W Smith (Well), F Soane (Bath), J Taylor (Wes), BH Vincent (Bath), SMJ Woods (Tau/Black).
Attendance: 8,000   *Referee*: JH Payne (Lancashire)

Saturday 21 January 1893 at Jersmond Ground, Newcastle
NORTHUMBERLAND 4 *Back*: R Baty (Tynd). *Three-quarters*: T Nicholson (Rock), T Stewart (PerPk), S Anderson (Wall), H Knott (PerPk). *Half-backs*: TP Alexander (Rock), EW Taylor (capt, Rock, dg). *Forwards*: FC Garrett (Nor), JH Greenwell (Rock), R Harris (NEls), T Robson (Tynd), H Smurthwaite (PerPk), A Styan (Rock), AC Williams (Nor), R Wright (Brighton).
DURHAM 14 *Back*: W Taylor (Tud). *Three-quarters*: S Morfitt (WHart, dg), FHR Alderson (HartR, dg), WH Bell (Sund), W Wainford (Tud). *Half-backs*: F Hindle (Tud), F Marston (Tud). *Forwards*: WA Bell (Tud), CW Burn (Sund), T Faulkner (Tud, t), J Hall (NDur, t), TJ Lindsay (SShYM), LG Nash (DurC, t), RF Oakes (HartR), W Yiend (HartR).
Attendance: 4,000   *Referee*: JE Birkett (Cumberland)

Saturday 21 January 1893 at Thrum Hall, Halifax
YORKSHIRE 19 *Back*: WH Eagland (Hud). *Three-quarters*: J Dyson (Hud, t), T Summersgill (Lee), F Firth (Hal, 3c). *Half-backs*: H Duckett (Brad), JA Rigg (Hal, 2t). *Forwards*: H Bradshaw (Bram), T Broadley (Brad), M Fletcher (Lee, t), D Jowett (Heck, t), H Lodge (Hud), B Mellor (Hal), C Richardson (LeePC), H Speed (Cas), JT Toothill (capt, Brad).
CHESHIRE 5 *Back*: S Houghton (Run). *Three-quarters*: FP Jones (NewB), JH Crompton (Run, c), F Saville (Stock). *Half-backs*: S Abram (Run, t), G Robinson (Run). *Forwards*: E Elliott (BirkW), H Ellis (NewB), W Faulkner (Run), TW Lockwood (BirkPk), JH Potts (Stock), P Riley (Run), WB Smith (NewB), H Williams (Run), WA Williams (NewB).
Attendance: 10,000   *Referee*: ET Gurdon (RFU Vice-President)

Milestones & Stats 1869-1901 259

Saturday 4 February 1893 at Lismore Place, Carlisle
CUMBERLAND 5 *Back*: JW Brown (CarlC). *Three-quarters*: TH Hodgkinson (capt, CarlC), T Forsyth (CumH), T Johnston (Whi). *Half-backs*: R Cuthbertson (Cock, t), J Nelson (Asp). *Forwards*: GB Atkinson (Whi), JH Blacklock (Mary), Jim Davidson (Asp), D Elliott (CarlC), T Grieve (Asp, pg), W Milligan (Work), J Murray (PenU), J Rowe (Egr), T Tervet (CarlC).
SOUTH OF SCOTLAND 0 *Back*: J Edmondstone (Haw). *Half-backs*: T Almers (Haw), AF McNee (Haw), JW Dryden (Mel). *Quarter-backs*: M Elliot (Haw), JT Mabon (Jed). *Forwards*: A Douglas (Sel), J Dowson (Haw), R Hunter (Jed), J Johnstone (Jed), J Robson (Haw), TM Scott (capt, Mel), A Stevenson (Haw), AB Storrie (Haw), J Storrie (Haw).
Attendance: 3,000 *Referee*: Rev F Marshall (Yorkshire)

Wednesday 15 February 1893 at Ashbrooke Ground, Sunderland
DURHAM 6 *Back*: W Taylor (Tud). *Three-quarters*: W Wainford (Tud, t), FHR Alderson (capt, HartR), WH Bell (Sund), S Morfitt (WHart). *Half-backs*: F Hindle (Tud), F Marston (Tud, t). *Forwards*: CW Burn (Sund), J Hall (NDur, t), TJ Lindsay (Tud), T McKeon (SShYM), LG Nash (DurC), RF Oakes (HartR), AE Thompson (SundN), W Yiend (HartR).
LANCASHIRE 7 *Back*: J Boscow (War). *Three-quarters*: W Pearson (Swi, t)A Barrett (Sal), J Hurst (Old). *Half-backs*: H Brockbank (Swi), S Walch (Sal, t, c). *Forwards*: JB Andrew (Old), A Ashworth (Moss), W Atkinson (Wig), J Jolley (War), T Kent (Sal), T King (Sal), T Melledew (RochH), T Rothwell (Swi), T Whittaker (Walk).
Attendance: 5,000 *Referee*: W Cail (RFU President)

Saturday 18 March 1893 at St Helen's, Swansea
GLAMORGANSHIRE 0 *Back*: DT Lloyd (Peny). *Three-quarters*: WJ Bancroft (Swa), RM Garrett (Pen), C Wilding (CarHarl), H Kirkby (Pen). *Half-backs*: A Cross (Nea), W Thomas (Nea). *Forwards*: I Griffith (Aber), F Hutchinson (Nea), DH Lewis (Peny), F Mills (Swa), W Phillips (CarHarl), D Samuel (Swa), J Samuel (Swa), JH Stead (Pon).
LANCASHIRE 0 *Back*: J Boscow (War). *Three-quarters*: J Seddon (StHR), A Barrett (Sal), A Ashworth (Moss), R Holmes (More). *Half-backs*: H Brockbank (Swi), W Parlane (ManR). *Forwards*: JB Andrew (Old), H Case (Ulv), J Jolley (War), T Kent (Sal), T King (Sal), T Melledew (RochH), W Unsworth (Wig), T Whittaker (Walk).
Attendance: 8,000/10,000 *Referee*: WH Wilkins (Llanelli)

Monday 20 March 1893 at County Ground, St Thomas, Exeter
DEVONSHIRE 2 *Back*: P Webber (Paig). *Three-quarters*: JM Wilcocks (Exe), WE Sowden (DevA), WE Bildings (DevA), H Stoyle (Barn). *Half-backs*: J Davies (Torq), G Horwill (DevA). *Forwards*: GH Allington (DevA), W Ashford (Exe), RJ Harper (capt, Barn), A May (DevA), B Parnell (Tot, t), W Pitts-Tucker (Barn), FJ Sellicks (NewA), BH Wallis (Exe).
LANCASHIRE 14 *Back*: T Foulkes (StH). *Three-quarters*: A Ashworth (Moss, t), J Seddon (StHR), A Barrett (Sal), R Holmes (More). *Half-backs*: H Brockbank (Swi), W Halliwell (Wig). *Forwards*: JB Andrew (Old), H Case (Ulv), J Jolley (War, t), T Kent (Sal), T King (Sal), T Melledew (RochH, 2c, gm), W Unsworth (Wig), T Whittaker (Walk).
Attendance: 3,000 *Referee*: WM Douglas (Glamorganshire)

ENGLAND TRIAL MATCH
Saturday 17 December 1892 at Athletic Ground, Richmond
SOUTH 14 *Back*: E Field (MidW/CamU). *Three-quarters*: AE Stoddart (capt, Black, t), CA Hooper (MidW, t), A Rogers (Mose). *Half-backs*: RFC de Winton (Black/MarlN), H Marshall (Black, t). *Forwards*: A Allport (Black), WE Bromet (Rich), GHM Cookson (OxfU), F Evershed (Black/Burt, t), FC Lohden (Black), P Maud (Black), JJ Robinson (Burt/CamU), F Soane (Bath), SMJ Woods (Tau/Black, c, pg).
NORTH 0 *Back*: S Houghton (Run). *Three-quarters*: RE Lockwood (Heck), JH Marsh (Swi), FHR Alderson (capt, HartR), T Nicholson (Rock). *Half-backs*: W Parlane (ManR), EW Taylor (Rock). *Forwards*: T Broadley (Brad), H Case (Ulv), Jim Davidson (Asp), T Faulkner (Tud), W Faulkner (Run), JH Greenwell (Rock), E Redman (Mann), W Yiend (HartR).
Attendance: 10,000   *Referee*: W Cail (RFU President)

INTERNATIONAL CHAMPIONSHIP

Saturday 7 January 1893 at Cardiff Arms Park
WALES 12 *Back*: WJ Bancroft (Swa, c, pg). *Three-quarters*: W McCutcheon (Old), JA Gould (capt, New, 2t), J Conway-Rees (Llan), N Biggs (Car, t). *Half-backs*: FC Parfitt (New), HP Phillips (New). *Forwards*: AW Boucher (New), HT Day (New), TC Graham (New), J Hannan (New), AF Hill (Car), F Mills (Swa), CB Nicholl (Llan), HW Watts (New).
ENGLAND 11 *Back*: E Field (MidW/CamU). *Three-quarters*: RE Lockwood (Heck), FHR Alderson (HartR), AE Stoddart (capt, Black, c). *Half-backs*: RFC de Winton (Black/MarlN), H Marshall (Black, 3t). *Forwards*: H Bradshaw (Bram), T Broadley (Brad), WE Bromet (Rich), F Evershed (Black/Burt), JH Greenwell (Rock), FC Lohden (Black, t), P Maud (Black), JT Toothill (Brad), SMJ Woods (Tau/Black).
Attendance: 15,000   *Referee*: DS Morton (Scotland)

Saturday 4 February 1893 at Lansdowne Road, Dublin
IRELAND 0 *Back*: S Gardiner (BelA). *Half-backs*: T Edwards (Lans), W Gardiner (NIFC), S Lee (capt, NIFC). *Quarter-backs*: FE Davies (Lans), T Thornhill (Wand). *Forwards*: MS Egan (Garryowen), R Johnston (Wand), TJ Johnston (QCB), H Lindsay (DubU), JH O'Conor (BecR), CV Rooke (DubU), R Stevenson (Dun), AK Wallis (Wand), EJ Walsh (Lans).
ENGLAND 4 *Back*: E Field (MidW/CamU). *Three-quarters*: JW Dyson (Hud), RE Lockwood (Heck), T Nicholson (Rock). *Half-backs*: H Duckett (Brad), EW Taylor (Rock, t). *Forwards*: A Allport (Black), H Bradshaw (Bram, t), WE Bromet (Rich), F Evershed (Black/Burt), JH Greenwell (Rock), P Maud (Black), JT Toothill (Brad), SMJ Woods (capt,Tau/Black), W Yiend (HartR).
Attendance: 10,000   *Referee*: AR Don-Wauchope (Scotland)

Saturday 4 March 1893 at Headingley, Leeds
ENGLAND 0 *Back*: WG Mitchell (Rich). *Three-quarters*: JW Dyson (Hud), AE Stoddart (capt, Black), FP Jones (NewB). *Half-backs*: H Duckett (Brad), CM Wells (Harl/CamU). *Forwards*: H Bradshaw (Bram), T Broadley (Brad), WE Bromet (Rich), F Evershed (Black/Burt), LJ Percival (Rugby), JJ Robinson (Burt/CamU), F Soane (Bath), JT Toothill (Brad), W Yiend (HartR).

SCOTLAND 8 *Back*: HJ Stevenson (EdinA). *Half-backs*: GT Campbell (LonS, dg), G MacGregor (LonS), W Neilson (CamU). *Quarter-backs*: JW Simpson (RHSFP), W Wotherspoon (WoS). *Forwards*: JD Boswell (capt, WoS, dg), WB Cownie (Wat), RS Davidson (RHSFP), WR Gibson (RHSFP), TL Hendry (Clyd), HTO Leggatt (Wat), RG Macmillan (LonS), JE Orr (WoS), TM Scott (Mel).
Attendance: 25,000   *Referee*: WH Wilkins (Wales)

Other results
Scotland 0, Wales 9
Ireland 0, Scotland 0
Wales 2, Ireland 0

Final table

	P	W	D	L	For	Agst
Wales	3	3	0	0	23	11
Scotland	3	1	1	1	8	9
England	3	1	0	2	15	20
Ireland	3	0	1	2	0	6

The North versus South match at Fallowfield, Manchester, 16th December 1893.
Illustrated Sporting and Dramatic News, 1893

1893-1894

AN EXPANDED COMPETITION FOR YORKSHIRE
Such was the demand for places in Yorkshire's new league structure that an additional 36 clubs were to be included for 1893-94. The decision of the committee was that they be separated into three 'territorial groups' of 12 teams each. But it was an unpopular idea that caused the withdrawal of 14 of the applicants at the end of April 1893. The 22 clubs that remained created the new Competition No. 3 and were divided into two groups. During May the discontented clubs – which included Hull Kingston Rovers and Keighley – were granted permission to form their own competition. The resultant 14-team league was subsequently given the title of the Intermediate Competition and placed within the hierarchy below the existing Competition No. 2 but, controversially, above the new Competition No. 3.

NEW INTERNATIONAL SCORING VALUES
A revised set of scoring values for internationals, as recently agreed by the International Rugby Board, was put into operation this season, creating uniformity between the four home countries; converted try – 5 points, unconverted try – 3, drop goal or goal from a mark – 4, penalty goal – 3.

THE FOUR THREE-QUARTER SYSTEM SPREADS
With the Cardiff club credited as introducing four three-quarters, the *South Wales Echo* took a keen interest in developments elsewhere, noting that

'the success of the four three-quarter system adopted by Halifax is evidently influencing other teams to do likewise. Elland and Brighouse have selected four three-quarters for next Saturday [6th October], and it will be interesting to observe how the experiment acts'.[148]

YORKSHIRE SELECT A WESTMORLAND PLAYER

A controversy surrounding county selection was the increasing use of so-called 'foreigners' – players born outside the county. This often resulted in a player who, including his native county, represented two, or sometimes more counties. Such a situation arose after Bob Winskill, a former Kendal Hornets forward, joined Halifax in September 1892, bringing him within the domain of Yorkshire. The *Yorkshire Evening Post* defended its county, arguing: 'It became the duty of the Yorkshire authorities to select the best available fifteen [to meet Durham on 11th November], and this led to the nomination of Winskill. Some of the Committee were averse to the playing of a man not a born Tyke, but no such scruples are entertained by other counties, and there was a precedent in Yorkshire in the selection of several other players in past seasons. It is now officially stated that he has decided to play for Yorkshire although he has been selected to play for his native county Westmorland against Lancashire, at Kendal, next week.'[149] Winskill subsequently appeared for Westmorland (versus Lancashire on 9th November) before his Yorkshire debut two days later against Durham.

MINOR COUNTIES IMPROVING

The *Manchester Guardian* detected a wind of change in inter-county contests with Lancashire becoming less dominant against their northern rivals: 'Taking a line through the discouraging performances of Lancashire against Cheshire and Westmorland, and the ridiculously easy victory of Yorkshire over Durham on Saturday, this year's "war of the roses" should be a foregone conclusion. Two or three seasons ago, form, such as Lancashire have shown this year, would have been sufficient to discourage even their most enthusiastic supporters. Up to that time, the "minor" counties, as Cheshire, Cumberland and Westmorland were termed, really attracted very little attention. A mild deference was shown to Durham and Northumberland, but Lancashire and Yorkshire had so repeatedly shown their superiority that matches against the other counties aroused very little interest. Whether or not the improvement in play [by the other counties] is due to the introduction of the county championship, it would be difficult to say, but it is undoubtedly true that within the past two or three years a very considerable improvement has taken place, and that the days of placing second teams in the field, as Yorkshire did against Cheshire a year ago, have completely passed.'[150]

CLUB VERSUS COUNTY

When the Lancashire committee attempted to find a date for a play-off match with Cheshire (eventually played on Saturday 30th December) they came up against resistance, the introduction of the Lancashire club competition creating conflict with county requirements. The *Manchester Guardian* commented: 'The negotiations in regard to the match appear, unfortunately, to have created some little feeling. Lancashire find that, in assenting to the [club] championship competition they placed in the hands of the clubs a whip with which they may themselves be beaten. The ambitions of individual players are now subservient to the interests of the clubs. No matter what prospects a player may have, [it depends] entirely upon the attitude of his [club] committee. This is all right from the club point of view, but it is death to county football.'[151]

ENGLAND ADOPT FOUR THREE-QUARTER SYSTEM

England used four three-quarters for the first time on 6th January, beating Wales 24-3 at Birkenhead. The *Manchester Guardian* enthused: 'The advocates of the four three-quarter system may be excused if they regard the victory of England on Saturday as something of a triumph. It is difficult, of course, to say what would have happened under other circumstances, but it is certainly true that the game was much more open and interesting than is usually the case, and a great improvement on the old order of close scrimmaging. The system has by this time been pretty generally adopted, but a large number of the old school still refuse to be converted, and are likely to remain obdurate to the end. It was the very combination and mechanism of the Welsh team last season which took it to the top of the tree. From a spectator's point of view there is no comparison between the two systems. Properly played, as it was on Saturday, the four three-quarter game keeps the play alive and full of interest from beginning to end. The Welsh clubs have had something like ten years practice, and practically know no other game; but that it can be played to advantage by the skilled players of England was only too clearly demonstrated by the match of Saturday.'[152]

REFEREES EMPOWERED

Apart from revolutionising three-quarter play, it seems the Welsh also led the way in empowering the referee, one report claiming 'England is indebted to Wales for a useful extension of the powers of the referee, who is now empowered in the case of an infringement of rules to blow his whistle without an appeal. The system has been in vogue among the Welsh clubs for some time, and has proved of considerable value in the management of the game'.[153] Since referees were introduced in the 1870s they had lacked authority, acting as arbitrator between two umpires appointed by the clubs involved, with most disputes settled by committee. In 1893-94 the referee finally gained full control.

SWINTON: SOMEWHAT OUT OF THE WAY!
Lancashire hosted Devonshire at Chorley Road, Swinton, on 3rd February, a venue claimed by one journalist to be in 'a locality somewhat out of the way for a match of interest to the whole county'.[154] Nonetheless, some reports estimated an attendance numbering 6,000.

YORKSHIRE BORROW THE HUDDERSFIELD KIT
When Yorkshire entertained Midland Counties at Fartown, Huddersfield, on 7th February, the visitors took to the field wearing their usual white jerseys with a diagonal scarlet band. Consequently Yorkshire, who normally wore all white, had to borrow Huddersfield's blue and white reserve kit.

A NORTHERN RUGBY LEAGUE
With the cup-tie competitions almost completed for the season, the idea of forming a league for the North-East was raised by the *Shields Daily Gazette* which claimed: 'The advantages of a League competition are obvious. It secures at once a permanency of interest which is now limited to the cup ties, so far as Northumberland and Durham are concerned. The Association game rose to popularity after the institution of the Leagues in both England and Scotland. And with regard to the Rugby code, the same marked improvement has followed upon the League scheme wherever it has been put into operation. Yorkshire is the principle stronghold of the game and it is of significance that [it is] the very beau ideal of a League scheme. Lancashire, too, has its own League, and the immense popularity of football there is largely the outcome of it. We put before our readers a plan for a Northern League which will unite the whole of Northumberland and Durham. There is something like twenty-four eligible clubs in the two counties, sufficient for the formation of two divisions. Senior: Hartlepool Rovers, West Hartlepool, Tudhoe, Durham City, South Shields, Westoe, Sunderland Nomads, Rockcliff, Percy Park, Northern, North Elswick,

North Durham. Junior: Sunderland, Sherburn House, Wallsend, Tyne Dock, Houghton, Blaydon, Ryton, Brighton, Tynedale, Gosforth, Henderson's Creelers, Union British.'[155]

SUNDERLAND NOMADS SUSPENDED FOR PAYING FINE
When Sunderland Nomads defeated Houghton-le-Spring 11-0 in a Durham Cup match on 17th March, it proved costly. Houghton subsequently brought a charge of professionalism against George Wilson Trotter, who played for the Nomads under the name of George Wilson. At the Durham Committee meeting at Walton's Hotel, Sunderland, on 28th March, it was alleged he was professionalised due to the Nomads paying his 23 shillings (£1.15p) fine at Sunderland Magistrates court on 10th March for theft and assault. The Durham committee found him guilty and suspended the Nomads until 30th April 1894, awarding the tie to Houghton.[156]

NORTHUMBERLAND CUP FINAL: NO END OF EXCITEMENT
The Northumberland Cup final between Rockcliff and Percy Park, held at Jesmond, Newcastle, on 31st March, proved quite an occasion. The *Shields Daily News* correspondent 'Umpire' wrote: 'The followers of the two teams, to the number of some thousands, were early in the field, and whiled away the time with good-humoured banter. The colours of the opposing combination were freely worn, the gaudy yellow and red [of Rockcliff] being most conspicuous. The Cullercoats people turned out en masse to witness the conflict. I was told, by one of the natives, that there was not a man or woman left in the village. My informant could not have been far from the truth, for the neat costumes of the fishwives and the rough habiliments of fishermen were seen on every hand. Many of the fishermen made the most of the auspicious occasion, some of them driving to and from the grounds in open carriages, and creating no end of excitement among the Newcastle folk by their cries [for Rockcliff] of "gan on Wock, gud aad Wock!" When [the teams] entered the arena they were greeted with quite an ovation.'[157] The match ended scoreless, Rockcliff comfortably winning the replay the following week.

CUMBERLAND CUP FINAL: MARYPORT GO ON STRIKE
On the verge of their Cumberland Cup final date with Egremont Rangers on 7th April at Workington, the Maryport players threatened to go on strike for what would now be considered an unusual reason. The Maryport committee had notified the team that they would travel to Workington by train. The players response was that they would only go

by road in a four-horse char-a-banc, and be driven onto the field of play. Initially, the committee refused and said they would use the second team instead but eventually gave way, and the players travelled to Workington by road. One report stated: 'The affair caused considerable amusement in the town, but has left some bitterness behind in football circles. It will be noticed, however, that Maryport won the cup, and that may smooth matters over.'[158]

1893-1894 STATISTICS

LANCASHIRE CLUB CHAMPIONSHIP FIRST CLASS

Final table	P	W	D	L	For	Agst	Pts
Oldham	18	14	2	2	171	49	30
Swinton	18	11	6	1	124	23	28
Warrington	18	13	1	4	119	54	27
Wigan	18	9	5	4	85	25	23
Tyldesley	18	7	3	8	102	84	17
Salford	18	7	3	8	87	92	17
Broughton Rangers	18	5	5	8	75	84	15
Rochdale Hornets	18	5	3	10	32	77	13
Barrow	18	3	3	12	60	129	9
Broughton	18	0	1	17	40	278	1

LANCASHIRE CLUB CHAMPIONSHIP SECOND CLASS

Final table	P	W	D	L	For	Agst	Pts
St Helens	18	14	2	2	208	43	30
Leigh	18	13	3	2	189	47	29
Ulverston	18	13	1	4	225	59	27
Widnes	18	8	2	8	92	78	18
Rochdale St Clements	18	8	2	8	87	91	18
Lancaster	18	8	0	10	103	112	16
Walkden	18	7	1	10	85	106	15
Aspull	17	5	2	10	61	90	12
Mossley*	16	2	3	11	40	205	7
Blackley	17	2	0	15	17	276	4

*Mossley disbanded (April 1894), fixtures v Aspull and Blackley not fulfilled.

Promotion Test Matches
Leigh 6, Barrow 0 (at Well Street, Tyldesley)
St Helens 12, Broughton 5 (at Prescott Street, Wigan)
(Leigh, St Helens promoted to Lancashire First Class; Barrow, Broughton relegated)

LANCASHIRE CLUB CHAMPIONSHIP THIRD CLASS

Final table	P	W	D	L	For	Agst	Pts
Blackley Rangers	18	12	5	1	173	30	29
Pendleton	18	12	3	3	126	51	27
Werneth	18	8	7	3	116	46	23
Barton	18	7	7	4	74	40	21
Pemberton	18	9	2	7	97	73	20
Radcliffe	18	6	4	8	63	128	16
Boothstown*	18	5	3	10	63	114	11
Failsworth	17	4	3	10	60	120	11
Swinton Hornets	17	3	3	11	38	137	9
Bury*	18	2	5	11	47	118	7

*Two points deducted for using ineligible player
Note: Failsworth v Swinton Hornets not played.

Promotion Test Match
Blackley 6, Pendleton 0 (at Tetlow Fold, Barton)
(Blackley retain place in Lancashire Second Class)
Note: The test matches should have been Blackley v Blackley Rangers and Mossley v Pendleton but rearranged after Blackley Rangers successfully appealed that, as Third Class winners, they should automatically replace the disbanded Mossley in Second Class.

NORTH WESTERN LEAGUE

Final table	P	W	D	L	For	Agst	Pts
Millom	14	11	0	3	134	27	22
Ulverston	14	9	3	2	156	28	21
Morecambe	14	8	4	2	106	20	20
Lancaster	14	6	1	7	66	68	13
Barrow	14	6	0	8	56	96	12
Askam	14	5	1	8	74	91	11
Kendal Hornets	14	5	1	8	38	105	11
Kendal Town	14	0	2	12	4	199	2

WESTMORLAND JUNIOR LEAGUE (NORTH)

Final table	P	W	D	L	For	Agst	Pts
Staveley	8	8	0	0	89	6	16
Kendal Hornets 'A' *	8	5	0	3	42	32	8
Burneside	8	4	0	4	24	40	8
Ambleside	8	2	0	6	14	27	4
Windermere	8	1	0	7	16	80	2

*Two points deducted for using ineligible players

WESTMORLAND JUNIOR LEAGUE (SOUTH)

Final table	P	W	D	L	For	Agst	Pts
Kirkby Lonsdale	6	6	0	0	48	0	12
Burton & Holme Wanderers	6	1	3	2	6	19	5
Kendal Town 'A'	6	1	2	3	6	10	4
Milnthorpe	6	1	1	4	3	34	3

Westmorland Junior League Final
Staveley 3, Kirkby Lonsdale 0 (at Mint's Feet, Kendal)
(Bingley declared Westmorland Junior League winner)

YORKSHIRE SENIOR COMPETITION

Final table	P	W	D	L	For	Agst	Pts
Manningham	22	14	5	3	152	50	33
Brighouse Rangers	22	15	3	4	179	67	33
Halifax	22	12	1	9	236	74	25
Liversedge	22	11	3	8	166	106	25
Leeds	22	11	3	8	111	98	25
Huddersfield	22	10	2	10	89	84	22
Hunslet	22	9	3	10	113	116	21
Bradford	22	9	2	11	129	156	20
Wakefield Trinity	22	7	4	11	89	187	18
Hull	22	8	1	13	82	199	17
Batley	22	6	2	14	117	174	14
Dewsbury	22	4	3	15	46	198	11

Play-off to decide first place
Manningham 0, Brighouse Rangers 0 (at Thrum Hall, Halifax)

Replay
Manningham 9, Brighouse Rangers 3 (at Thrum Hall, Halifax)
(Manningham declared Yorkshire Senior Competition winner)

YORKSHIRE COMPETITION NO. 2

Final table	P	W	D	L	For	Agst	Pts
Leeds Parish Church	22	19	1	2	304	54	39
Holbeck	22	17	1	4	248	64	35
Bramley*	22	14	1	7	151	83	28
Morley	22	12	3	7	122	90	27
Bowling	22	10	2	10	134	93	22
Cleckheaton	22	8	5	9	134	153	21
Otley**	21	10	3	8	134	102	21
Elland	22	9	1	12	142	115	19
York	22	9	1	12	89	165	19
Kirkstall	22	5	0	17	63	248	10
Wortley	22	4	1	17	63	194	9
Pontefract***	21	4	1	16	57	280	5

*One point deducted for not fulfilling a fixture
**Two points deducted for using ineligible player
***Four points deducted for using ineligible players
Note: Otley v Pontefract postponed (frost) and not subsequently played.

YORKSHIRE INTERMEDIATE COMPETITION

Final table	P	W	D	L	For	Agst	Pts
Alverthorpe	26	20	1	5	183	53	41
Sowerby Bridge	26	17	4	5	156	63	38
Goole	26	14	6	6	200	70	34
West Riding	26	14	4	8	214	101	32
Ossett	26	13	4	9	126	86	30
Pudsey*	26	13	4	9	155	92	29
Normanton	26	13	3	10	175	154	29
Keighley	26	13	2	11	194	87	28
Hull Kingston Rovers	26	13	1	12	206	145	27
Bowling Old Lane	26	9	6	11	96	190	24
Shipley	26	8	6	12	106	148	22
Armley	26	4	5	17	59	294	13
Mirfield	26	5	2	19	66	263	12
Buttershaw**	26	2	0	24	36	226	4

*One point deducted for crowd assault on visiting players
**Suspended (Mar 1894) until 1st November for players leaving field during Yorkshire Cup tie, 6 remaining matches declared as win to opponents

YORKSHIRE COMPETITION NO. 3 (GROUP A)

Final table	P	W	D	L	For	Agst	Pts
Bingley	22	20	1	1	250	28	41
Stanningley	20	15	1	4	173	40	31
Skipton	22	14	3	5	175	57	31
Saltaire	22	12	3	7	106	107	27
Idle	22	11	4	7	166	86	26
Silsden	22	9	4	9	155	82	22
Guiseley	21	8	2	11	105	149	18
Windhill	22	6	2	14	73	133	14
Horsforth	21	5	2	14	79	181	12
Tadcaster	20	5	2	13	72	262	12
Newtown*	19	4	3	12	47	143	9
Ingrow	19	3	1	15	60	193	7

*Two points deducted for using ineligible player
Note 1: Seven unplayed fixtures declared scoreless draws, affecting Idle (3 matches), Newtown, Saltaire, Silsden (2 each), Guiseley, Skipton, Stanningley, Tadcaster, Windhill (1 each).
Note 2: Six matches not played for varying reasons and excluded from table, affecting Ingrow, Newtown (3 matches each), Stanningley, Tadcaster (2 each), Guisley, Horsforth (1 each).

YORKSHIRE COMPETITION NO. 3 (GROUP B)

Final table	P	W	D	L	For	Agst	Pts
Hebden Bridge	18	15	1	2	227	29	31
Paddock	18	10	3	5	113	60	23
Wibsey	18	11	0	7	149	146	22
Shepley	18	9	3	6	158	87	21
Kirkburton	18	9	2	7	156	139	20
Greetland	18	9	0	9	189	156	18
Luddendenfoot	17	8	2	7	88	108	18
Bailiffe Bridge	17	6	2	9	103	93	14
Low Moor St Mark's	18	4	0	14	63	271	8
Honley	18	1	1	16	65	222	3

Note 1: Three unplayed fixtures declared scoreless draws, affecting Bailiffe Bridge (2 matches), Honley, Kirkburton, Luddendenfoot, Paddock (1 each).
Note 2: Bailiffe Bridge v Luddendenfoot not played.

Yorkshire Competition No. 3 Final
Bingley 7, Hebden Bridge 3 (at Valley Parade, Bradford)
(Bingley declared Yorkshire Competition No. 3 winner)

Milestones & Stats 1869-1901

CUMBERLAND COUNTY CHALLENGE CUP (12 entries)
Try – 3 points; conversion – 2; penalty goal – 3; drop-goal, field goal, goal from mark – 4.

First Round
Cockermouth 29, Whitehaven 0
Cummersdale Hornets 3, Workington 8
Seaton 35, Penrith United 0
Maryport 11, Whitehaven Recreation 0
Byes: Aspatria, Broughton, Carlisle City, Egremont Hornets

Second Round
Carlisle City 0, Cockermouth 5
Egremont Hornets w/o Broughton (withdrew)
Seaton 3, Maryport 8
Workington 3, Aspatria 0

Semi-finals
Egremont Hornets 11, Cockermouth 3 (at Lonsdale Park, Workington)
Maryport 3, Workington 0 (at The Recreation Ground, Whitehaven)

FINAL
Saturday 7 April 1894 at Lonsdale Park, Workington
MARYPORT 8 *Back*: J Addison. *Three-quarters*: T Smith, M Humphreys (t), W Hodgson (c), T McGerry. *Half-backs*: G Davidson, Wells. *Forwards*: R Barnes, JH Blacklock (t), G Crellin, J Holliday (capt), W Orr, WT Smith, J Thompson, J Turnbull.
EGREMONT HORNETS 3 *Back*: J Deakin. *Three-quarters*: G Douglas (pg), J McGee, W Kelly, I Bruce. *Half-backs*: A Cook (capt), J Cook. *Forwards*: W Cross, S Farrer, W Grieves, W Head, J Hodgson, W Hodgson, J Rowe, G Todd.
Attendance: 5,000   *Referee*: Rev F Marshall (Yorkshire RU)

DURHAM COUNTY CHALLENGE CUP (18 entries)
Try – 3 points; conversion – 2; penalty goal – 3; drop-goal, field goal, goal from mark – 4.

First Round
Durham City 17, Hamsteels 0
Tudhoe 9, Blaydon 0
Byes: 14 teams drew a bye to next round

Third Round
Hartlepool Rovers 30, Tyne Dock 0
Sunderland 8, Tudhoe 28
Sunderland Nomads 11, Houghton-le-Spring 0
(awarded to Houghton after protest)
West Hartlepool 3, Durham City 5

Second Round
Houghton-le-Spring 17, Jarrow 0
Sherburn House 0, Durham City 6
South Shields 0, Hartlepool Rovers 5
Stockton 0, West Hartlepool 45
Sunderland Nomads 43, Ryton 0
Tudhoe 33, North Durham 0
Tyne Dock (South Shields) w/o Mount Pleasant (Spennymoor) (disbanded)
Westoe 0, Sunderland 3

Semi-finals
Hartlepool Rovers 8, Durham City 5
Houghton-le-Spring 0, Tudhoe 25

FINAL
Saturday 14 April 1894 at Mowbray Road, South Shields
HARTLEPOOL ROVERS 15 *Back*: GH Philbrick. *Three-quarters*: A Chivers, C Hodgson, FHR Alderson (2t, 3c), A Vallance (t). *Half-backs*: T McDougal, JT Thompson. *Forwards*: J Coates, W Dale, T Emmerson, J Finlay, J Hastings, WJ Le Cren, RF Oakes, W Yiend (capt).
TUDHOE 3 *Back*: W Taylor. *Three-quarters*: M McGann, JR Crone, R Edwards, H Mills. *Half-backs*: F Hindle, F Marston. *Forwards*: WA Bell, J Duffey (t), T Faulkner (capt), R Gibbon, J Lindsay, A Stephenson, AJ Troupe, G Urwin.
Attendance: 16,000   *Referee*: E Seddon (Lancashire RU)

NORTHUMBERLAND COUNTY FOOTBALL CHALLENGE CUP (8 entries)
Try – 3 points; conversion – 2; penalty goal – 3; drop-goal, field goal, goal from mark – 4.

First Round
Northern 3, Brighton 0
Percy Park 6, North Elswick 3
Tynedale 23, Gosforth 0
Wallsend 0, Rockcliff 27

Semi-finals
Percy Park 11, Northern 7
Rockcliff 32, Tynedale 3

FINAL
Saturday 31 March 1894 at Jesmond Ground, Newcastle
ROCKCLIFF 0 *Back*: W Jackson. *Three-quarters*: W Taylor, S Anderson, A Jackson, T Nicholson. *Half-backs*: J Scott, EW Taylor (capt). *Forwards*: J Bolam, JH Greenwell, GW Lee, J Nesbitt, TC Stephenson, A Styan, B Taylor, John Taylor.
PERCY PARK 0 *Back*: CO Robinson. *Three-quarters*: H Knott, F Finney (capt), J Miller, E Robinson. *Half-backs*: HW Audus, T Stewart. *Forwards*: H Angus, A Gee, O Heslop, T Leinster, FW Thompson, HA Town, J Wardle, W Winter.
After extra time   *Attendance*: 6,000   *Referee*: WH Humphreys (Durham RU)

FINAL REPLAY
Saturday 7 April 1894 at Jesmond Ground, Newcastle
ROCKCLIFF 29 *Back*: W Jackson. *Three-quarters*: W Taylor (t), S Anderson (t, dg), A Jackson (t), J Thompson (t). *Half-backs*: J Scott, EW Taylor (capt, t, 2c). *Forwards*: J Bolam, JH Greenwell (2t), WN Greenwell, GW Lee, J Nesbitt, A Styan, B Taylor, John Taylor.
PERCY PARK 0 *Back*: CO Robinson. *Three-quarters*: J Miller, H Knott, F Finney (capt), E Robinson. *Half-backs*: HW Audus, T Stewart. *Forwards*: H Angus, A Gee, O Heslop, T Leinster, FW Thompson, HA Town, J Wardle, W Winter.
Attendance: 7,000   *Referee*: WH Humphreys (Durham RU)

Milestones & Stats 1869-1901

YORKSHIRE COUNTY FOOTBALL CHALLENGE CUP (132 entries)
Try – 3 points; conversion – 2; penalty goal – 3; drop-goal, field goal, goal from mark – 4.

Preliminary Round
(98 teams in 15 districts; two from each, indicated by 'q', qualified for next stage)

Airedale: Guiseley, Guiseley Parish Church, Idle (q), Saltaire (q), Thackley, Windhill, Yeadon
Batley: Birstall (q), Bruntcliffe, Gildersome (q), Morley Providence
Bradford: Bowling Old Lane (q), Bradford Trinity, Brownroyd Recreation, Buttershaw, Thornton Rangers, Wibsey (q)
Castleford: Brotherton St John's (q) Featherstone Trinity (q), Ferrybridge, Garforth, Kippax, Knottingley, Methley, Normanton St John's, South Milford, Whitwood
Craven: Bingley (q), Bingley Grammar School Old Boys, Haworth, Ingrow, Keighley, Keighley Zingari, Silsden, Skipton (q)
Dewsbury: Dewsbury St Mark's, Dewsbury St Paulinus, Horbury (q), Mirfield (q), Thornhill Lees Trinity, Thornhill Parish Church
East Leeds: Beeston (q), Leeds Institute, Newtown, Rothwell and District (q)
Halifax: Bailiffe Bridge, Greetland, Halifax Gymnasium, Halifax West Mount, Hebden Bridge, Luddenden, Luddendenfoot (q), Mytholmroyd, Sowerby Bridge (q), Todmorden
Huddersfield: Crosland Moor, Holmfirth, Honley, Kirkburton, Lockwood, Milnsbridge, Netherton, Nortonthorpe (q), Paddock (q), Primrose Hill, Shepley
Hull and Ouse: Beverley, Hull Britannia (q), Hull Marlborough, Hull Melbourne, Hull Three Crowns, Selby (q)
Northern: Fulford Rovers, Harrogate, Harrogate Rangers, Harrogate St John's, Ripon (q), Tadcaster, York Leeman Wanderers (q)
North Leeds: Burley (q), Horsforth, West Riding (q)
Spen Valley: Liversedge Hornets (q), Low Moor St Mark's (q) (both had byes)
Wakefield: Barnsley, Barnsley Congregational, Darton, Dodworth, Doncaster Town (q), Eastmoor, Kinsley, Newmillerdam, Outwood Church (q), Ryhill, Streethouse, Wakefield St Austin's
West Leeds: Farsley (q), Stanningley (q) (both had byes)

First Round
(* indicates 34 teams seeded to this round)
Alverthorpe* 10, Birstall 3
Armley* 8, York Leeman Wanderers 0
Batley* 6, Otley* 3
Beeston 5, Paddock 14
Bingley 16, Brotherton St John's 0
Bradford* 48, Wibsey 0
Bramley* 13, Bowling Old Lane 8
Brighouse Rangers* 36, Hull Britannia 6
Castleford* 16, Sowerby Bridge 3
Cleckheaton* 31, Stanningley 0
Dewsbury* 23, Burley 3
Doncaster Town 0, Pudsey* 11
Elland* 16, Hull* 0
Farsley 0, York* 11
Featherstone Trinity 4, Bowling* 0
Heckmondwike* 0, Leeds* 3
Huddersfield* 24, Kirkstall* 3
Hull Kingston Rovers* 7, Shipley* 0
(replay ordered after protest)
Idle 0, Halifax* 13

First Round *continued*
Liversedge Hornets 3, Goole* 14
Luddendenfoot 0, West Riding (Leeds) 7
Mirfield 0, Holbeck* 16
Morley* 8, Wakefield Trinity* 16
Normanton* 3, Leeds Parish Church* 6
Nortonthorpe 7, Horbury 3
Ossett* 3, Liversedge* 6
Pontefract* 6, Low Moor St Mark's 5

Second Round
Alverthorpe 0, Wakefield Trinity 6
Batley 0, Halifax 0
Bingley 13, Nortonthorpe 0
Bradford 38, Wortley 0
Bramley 8, Dewsbury 5
Castleford 9, Elland 0
Cleckheaton 3, Liversedge 33
Hull Kingston Rovers 9, Hunslet 3
Leeds 5, Huddersfield 13
Manningham 5, Brighouse Rangers 5

Third Round
Bradford 18, Bingley 3
Bramley 4, Wakefield Trinity 0
Castleford 8, Leeds Parish Church 0
Featherstone Trinity 5, Manningham 26
Halifax 43, Liversedge 6
Pudsey 0, Huddersfield 9
Rothwell and District 0, York 4
West Riding 8, Hull Kingston Rovers 4

Semi-finals
Castleford 6, West Riding 0 (at Belle Vue, Wakefield)
Halifax 10, Bradford 0 (at Fartown, Huddersfield)

Ripon 11, Hunslet* 31
Rothwell and District 10, Gildersome 0
Selby 5, Manningham* 33
Skipton 6, Outwood Church 3
Wortley* 12, Saltaire 3

First Round Replay
Hull Kingston Rovers 14, Shipley 0
(at Castleford)

Pontefract 4, Leeds Parish Church 20
Pudsey 10, Holbeck 5
Rothwell and District 11, Paddock 0
Skipton 3, Featherstone Trinity 11
West Riding 5, Goole 4
York 18, Armley 0

Second Round Replays
Brighouse Rangers 0, Manningham 13
Halifax 35, Batley 0

Fourth Round
Bramley 3, West Riding 5
Huddersfield 3, Bradford 9
Manningham 3, Halifax 5
York 0, Castleford 5

FINAL
Saturday 21 April 1894 at Headingley, Leeds
HALIFAX 38 *Back*: JH Bromwich. *Three-quarters*: A Chorley, WH Keepings (t, 5c), WJ Jackson (t), F Firth (3t). *Half-backs*: J Arnold, JA Rigg (2t). *Forwards*: GF Dickenson, O Fletcher (capt), J Knowles, B Mellor, J Riley, S Ripley (t), A Robertshaw (2c), A Wilson.
CASTLEFORD 6 *Back*: E Rowlands. *Three-quarters*: DS Bonynge, T Jepson, T Bellerby, P Smith. *Half-backs*: B Burns, E Shaw (t). *Forwards*: T Hambleton (t), R Hanson, G Nowell, J Rhodes, H Speed (capt), A Starks, S Townend, W Walton.
Attendance: 16,093   *Referee*: H Hutchinson (Wakefield)

COUNTY CHAMPIONSHIP

NORTH WESTERN GROUP

Saturday 4 November 1893 at Whalley Range, Manchester
LANCASHIRE 3 *Back*: T Coop (Lei, pg). *Three-quarters*: W McCutcheon (Old), J Valentine (capt, Swi), A Barrett (Sal), J Hurst (Old). *Half-backs*: J Drummond (Wid), W Parlane (ManR). *Forwards*: JB Andrew (Old), H Case (Swi), JC Goold (LivOB), GH Murray (Swi), W Nevins (War), J Shepherd Tyl), J Simpson (RochH), W Unsworth (Wig).
CHESHIRE 14 *Back*: S Houghton (Run). *Three-quarters*: F Saville (Stock, t, c), AE Fenton (BirkPk), H Ashton (Stock, t), FP Jones (Swi, t). *Half-backs*: S Abram (Run), J Faulkner (Run). *Forwards*: J Davies (Run), E Elliott (BirkW), H Ellis (NewB, t), W Faulkner (capt, Run), J Langley (Run), F Little (NewB), T Morgan (BirkW), RT Reece (Run).
Attendance: 8,000   *Referee*: B Kilner (Yorkshire)

Thursday 9 November 1893 at Irwell Lane, Runcorn
CHESHIRE 3 *Back*: S Houghton (Run). *Three-quarters*: FP Jones (Swi), TH Warder (Run), AE Fenton (BirkPk), J Hutchinson (BirkPk). *Half-backs*: S Abram (Run), J Faulkner (Run, t). *Forwards*: J Davies (Run), E Elliott (BirkW), H Ellis (NewB), W Faulkner (Run), J Langley (Run), F Little (NewB), T Morgan (BirkW), RT Reece (Run).
CUMBERLAND 3 *Back*: DG Lamonby (Work). *Three-quarters*: JH Buckett (Mil), J Sandwith (Sea), T Fletcher (Sea, t), TH Hodgkinson (CarlC). *Half-backs*: J Armstrong (Mil), J Nelson (Asp). *Forwards*: GB Atkinson (Work), R Bell (Work), J Edwards (Sea), D Elliott (CarlC), J Fawcett (Mil), T Grieve (Asp), W Milligan (Work), T Tervet (CarlC).
Attendance: 3,000   *Referee*: T Ashton (Lancashire)

Thursday 9 November 1893 at Mint's Feet, Kendal
WESTMORLAND 3 *Back*: T Hine (KenH). *Three-quarters*: E Railton (KenH), J Berry (Tyl), J Goodman (Walk), JK Robinson (KirkL). *Half-backs*: W Cross (StH), W Hall (Ulv). *Forwards*: J Deason (KenH), T Jackson (BurHW), VS Jones (Burn), R Nicholson (KenH), WJ Parsons (KenH, t), T Rawlinson (Wind), R Simm (KenH), J Vity (Amb).
LANCASHIRE 5 *Back*: T Foulkes (StH). *Three-quarters*: W McCutcheon (Old, t), A Barrett (Sal), F Treweek (Roose), J Valentine (Swi, c). *Half-backs*: J Drummond (Wid), W Halliwell (Wig). *Forwards*: JB Andrew (Old), H Case (Swi), J Jolley (War), T King (Sal), GH Murray (Swi), J Simpson (RochH), W Unsworth (Wig), G Woodward (Tyl).
Attendance: 3,000   *Referee*: n/a

Thursday 16 November 1893 at Mint's Feet, Kendal
WESTMORLAND 0 *Back*: T Hine (KenH). *Three-quarters*: E Railton (KenH), J Goodman (Walk), J Berry (Tyl), W Whitehead (Wig). *Half-backs*: W Cross (capt, StH), W Hall (Ulv). *Forwards*: J Deason (KenH), T Jackson (BurHW), VS Jones (Burn), R Nicholson (KenH), WJ Parsons (KenH), R Simm (KenH), JH Thompson (KenH), J Vity (Amb).
CHESHIRE 0 *Back*: JT Haslam (Stock). *Three-quarters*: FP Jones (Swi), AE Fenton (BirkPk), F Saville (Stock), H Ashton (Stock). *Half-backs*: J Faulkner (Run), W Pickard (Stock). *Forwards*: Walter Bailey (Stock), E Elliott (BirkW), H Ellis (NewB), W Faulkner (Run), J Langley (Run), F Little (NewB), T Morgan (BirkW), RT Reece (Run).
Attendance: 2,000   *Referee*: n/a

Saturday 18 November 1893 at Lonsdale Park, Workington
CUMBERLAND 3 *Back*: DG Lamonby (Work). *Three-quarters*: JH Buckett (Mil),
J Sandwith (Sea), T Fletcher (Sea), TH Hodgkinson (CarlC). *Half-backs*: J Armstrong (Mil),
J Nelson (Asp). *Forwards*: R Bell (Work), JH Blacklock (Mary), D Elliott (CarlC), J Fawcett
(Mil), W Milligan (Work), J Pender (CumH), JG Phillips (Mil, t), T Tervet (CarlC).
LANCASHIRE 6 *Back*: T Foulkes (StH). *Three-quarters*: W McCutcheon (Old, t), A Barrett
(Sal), R Lewis (Ulv), R Holmes (More, t). *Half-backs*: James Bate (War), W Chapman (Bar).
Forwards: JB Andrew (Old), H Case (Swi), JC Goold (LivOB), J Jolley (War), T King (Sal),
J Simpson (RochH), W Unsworth (Wig), G Woodward (Tyl).
Attendance: 5,000   *Referee*: Rev F Marshall (Yorkshire)

Saturday 9 December 1893 at Lismore Place, Carlisle
CUMBERLAND 12 *Back*: JH Blaylock (Asp). *Three-quarters*: J Sandwith (Sea), JH Buckett
(Mil), TH Hodgkinson (CarlC, dg), T Fletcher (Sea, t). *Half-backs*: J Nelson (Asp, c),
S Northmore (Mil). *Forwards*: R Bell (Work), JH Blacklock (Mary), Jim Davidson (Asp),
D Elliott (CarlC), T McGerry (Mary), J Pender (CumH, t), JG Phillips (Mil), T Tervet
(CarlC).
WESTMORLAND 0 *Back*: T Hine (KenH). *Three-quarters*: CG Mason (Amb), E Railton
(KenH), J Allen (KenH), T Jackson (BurHW). *Half-backs*: F Dixon (KenH), J Garnett
(KenH). *Forwards*: J Deason (KenH), VS Jones (Burn), R Nicholson (KenH), WJ Parsons
(KenH), R Simm (KenH), JH Thompson (KenH), J Vity (Amb), T Wilson (KenH).
Attendance: 4,000   *Referee*: E Seddon (Lancashire)

Final table

	P	W	D	L	For	Agst	Pts
Lancashire	3	2	0	1	14	20	4
Cheshire	3	1	2	0	17	6	4
Cumberland	3	1	1	1	18	9	3
Westmorland	3	0	1	2	3	17	1

PLAY-OFF TO DECIDE FIRST PLACE
Saturday 30 December 1893 at Manchester Athletic Ground, Fallowfield
LANCASHIRE 11 *Back*: T Foulkes (StH). *Three-quarters*: J Valentine (capt, Swi, c),
A Barrett (Sal, t), R Holmes (More), W McCutcheon (Old, t). *Half-backs*: James Bate (War),
John Bate (War). *Forwards*: A Ashworth (RochH, t), H Case (Swi), JC Goold (LivOB),
J Jolley (War), T King (Sal), J Simpson (RochH), W Unsworth (Wig), G Woodward (Tyl).
CHESHIRE 3 *Back*: S Houghton (Run). *Three-quarters*: EH Drinkwater (NewB), TP Bate
(Sale), JT Haslam (Stock), TH Warder (Run). *Half-backs*: E Hurst (BirkW), H Parratt (Sale).
Forwards: Walter Bailey (Stock), W Beard (Stock), J Davies (Run), E Elliott (BirkW, t),
H Ellis (NewB), J Langley (Run), F Little (NewB), R Taylor (Sale).
Attendance: 4,000   *Referee*: WH Humpheys (Durham)

NORTH EASTERN GROUP

Saturday 11 November 1893 at Headingley, Leeds
YORKSHIRE 18 *Back*: H Ward (Brad). *Three-quarters*: A Davey (Norm, dg), B Sharpe (Livs), RE Lockwood (capt, Heck, t), F Firth (Hal). *Half-backs*: JA Rigg (Hal), R Wood (Livs, t, c). *Forwards*: H Bradshaw (Bram), T Broadley (Bing), F Clegg (Mann, t), G Nowell (Cas), H Speed (Cas), JT Toothill (Brad), O Walsh (Hun, t), RS Winskill (Hal).
DURHAM 0 *Back*: GH Philbrick (HartR). *Three-quarters*: W Wainford (Tud), FHR Alderson (HartR), S Morfitt (WHart), RCF Crow (SundN). *Half-backs*: F Hindle (Tud), F Marston (Tud). *Forwards*: T Burt (SherH), R Edwards (Tud), T Faulkner (Tud), J Geenty (WHart), J Hall (NDur), FC Lohden (HartR), RF Oakes (HartR), W Yiend (HartR).
Attendance: 10,000 *Referee*: H Williamson (Lancashire)

Saturday 18 November 1893 at Jesmond Ground, Newcastle
NORTHUMBERLAND 0 *Back*: R Baty (Tynd). *Three-quarters*: T Nicholson (Rock), WG Baty (Tynd/SSh), A Jackson (Rock), CO Robinson (PerPk). *Half-backs*: TP Alexander (Rock), EW Taylor (Rock). *Forwards*: A Buckley (Wall), AL Curry (PerPk), FE Dotchin (Nor), GW Lee (Rock), FC Garrett (Nor), JH Greenwell (Rock), WN Greenwell (Rock), A Styan (Rock).
YORKSHIRE 9 *Back*: H Ward (Brad). *Three-quarters*: A Davey (Norm), B Sharpe (Livs), RE Lockwood (capt, Heck), F Firth (Hal). *Half-backs*: JA Rigg (Hal, t), R Wood (Livs, t). *Forwards*: H Bradshaw (Bram), F Clegg (Mann), G Nowell (Cas), H Speed (Cas, t), JT Toothill (Brad), O Walsh (Hun), W Walton (Cas), RS Winskill (Hal).
Attendance: 1,000 *Referee*: WH Humphreys (Durham)

Final table

	P	W	D	L	For	Agst	Pts
Yorkshire	2	2	0	0	27	0	4
Northumberland	1	0	0	1	0	9	0
Durham	1	0	0	1	0	18	0

(Durham v Northumberland on 20 January too late for inclusion)

SOUTH WESTERN GROUP

Results
Somersetshire 6, Gloucestershire 5
Gloucestershire 0, Devonshire 16
Somersetshire 29, Cornwall 5
Devonshire 38, Cornwall 3
Devonshire 0, Somersetshire 0
Cornwall 0, Gloucestershire 16

Play-off to decide first place
Devonshire 3, Somersetshire 3

Replay
Somersetshire 8, Devonshire 0

Final table

	P	W	D	L	For	Agst	Pts
Somersetshire	3	2	1	0	35	10	5
Devonshire	3	2	1	0	54	3	5
Gloucestershire	3	1	0	2	21	22	2
Cornwall	3	0	0	3	8	83	0

SOUTH EASTERN GROUP

Results
Surrey 17, Kent 3
Midland Counties 6, Middlesex 3
Midland Counties 24, Kent 3
Middlesex 0, Surrey 5
Surrey 6, Midland Counties 8
Kent 11, Middlesex 10

Final table

	P	W	D	L	For	Agst	Pts
Midland Counties	3	3	0	0	40	12	6
Surrey	3	2	0	1	28	11	4
Kent	3	1	0	2	17	51	2
Middlesex	3	0	0	3	13	24	0

FINAL GROUP ('SECOND SERIES')

Saturday 25 November 1893 at Park Avenue, Bradford
YORKSHIRE 11 *Back*: H Ward (Brad). *Three-quarters*: A Davey (Norm, t), B Sharpe (Livs), RE Lockwood (capt, Heck, c), F Firth (Hal). *Half-backs*: JA Rigg (Hal), R Wood (Livs, 2t). *Forwards*: H Bradshaw (Bram), T Broadley (Bing), F Clegg (Mann), G Nowell (Cas), H Speed (Cas), JT Toothill (Brad), O Walsh (Hun), RS Winskill (Hal).
LANCASHIRE 3 *Back*: T Foulkes (StH). *Three-quarters*: W McCutcheon (Old, t), A Barrett (Sal), J Valentine (capt, Swi), S Lees (Old). *Half-backs*: James Bate (War), John Bate (War). *Forwards*: A Ashworth (RochH), H Case (Swi), JC Goold (LivOB), J Jolley (War), J Simpson (RochH), W Unsworth (Wig), RP Wilson (LivOB), G Woodward (Tyl).
Attendance: 10,000   *Referee*: T Potts (Durham)

Saturday 13 January 1894 at The Recreation Grounds, Weston-super-Mare
SOMERSETSHIRE 0 *Back*: AH Westcott (Bridg). *Three-quarters*: W Pattison (Bath), TC Rogerson (Bath), FE Duckworth (Wes), WH Culverwell (Bridg). *Half-backs*: T Gilmore (Bridg), G Vincent (Bath). *Forwards*: RH Barham (Bridg), RH Beiseigle (Crew), H Durie (Tau), P Ebdon (Well), B Morris (Tau), F Soane (capt, Bath), J Taylor (Well), CJ Vernon (Well).
YORKSHIRE 27 *Back*: H Ward (Brad). *Three-quarters*: A Davey (Norm), B Sharpe (Livs, 2c), RE Lockwood (capt, Heck, c), F Firth (Hal, 2t). *Half-backs*: JA Rigg (Hal, t), R Wood (Livs). *Forwards*: H Bradshaw (Bram, 2t), F Clegg (Mann), J Melvin (Lee), G Nowell (Cas), H Speed (Cas), JT Toothill (Brad), O Walsh (Hun, 2t), W Walton (Cas).
Attendance: 4,000   *Referee*: AJ Davies (Glamorganshire)

Wednesday 7 February 1894 at Fartown, Huddersfield
YORKSHIRE 9 *Back*: H Ward (Brad). *Three-quarters*: RE Lockwood (capt, Heck), B Sharpe (Livs), F Firth (Hal), A Davey (Norm, t). *Half-backs*: J Ingham (Otley), R Wood (Livs). *Forwards*: A Barraclough (Mann), H Bradshaw (Bram), T Broadley (Bing, t), G Nowell (Cas), H Speed (Cas), JT Toothill (Brad, t), O Walsh (Hun), W Walton (Cas).

MIDLAND COUNTIES 0 *Back*: JF Byrne (Mose). *Three-quarters*: A Fox (OEdw), HP Reynolds (Strat), AH Frith (Cov), FR Lovitt (Cov). *Half-backs*: A Slater (Cov), BB Tuke (Cov). *Forwards*: G Carpenter (Cov), BH Cattell (Mose), AE Cooke (Leic), AW Gorton (Burt), RW Hunt (Rugby), G Jones (Worc), ER Lycett (Mose), JJ Robinson (Burt).
Attendance: 3,000   *Referee*: J Higson (Lancashire)

Wednesday 14 March 1894 at Whalley Range, Manchester
LANCASHIRE 6 *Back*: T Foulkes (StH). *Three-quarters*: J Hurst (Old, t), T Anderton (Lei, t), S Lees (Old), J Valentine (Swi). *Half-backs*: H Varley (Old), S Walch (Sal). *Forwards*: S Bingham (Liv), T Butterworth (RochH), J Jolley (War), JJ Jones (Sal), R Pierce (Liv), B Ridehaugh (RochStC), J Simpson (RochH), G Woodward (Tyl).
SOMERSETSHIRE 5 *Back*: H Boucher (Black). *Three-quarters*: L Chard (Chedder), CF Mermagon (capt, Well, t), TC Rogerson (Bath), AH Westcott (Bridg, c). *Half-backs*: H Merry (Well), N Parham (OMT). *Forwards*: JBS D'Aguilar (Bath), P Ebdon (Well), RT Gilmore (Wes), ED Hancock (Wivel/GuyHosp), B Morris (Tau), J Roman (Bridg), J Taylor (Well), CJ Vernon (Well).
Attendance: 2,500   *Referee*: EB Holmes (Midland Counties)

Other result
Somersetshire 3, Midland Counties 0

Final table
	P	W	D	L	For	Agst	Pts
Yorkshire	3	3	0	0	47	3	6
Lancashire	2	1	0	1	9	16	2
Somersetshire	3	1	0	2	8	33	2
Midland Counties	2	0	0	2	0	12	0

COUNTY CHAMPIONS v THE REST

Saturday 3 March 1894 at Headingley, Leeds
YORKSHIRE 9 *Back*: H Ward (Brad). *Three-quarters*: F Firth (Hal), B Sharpe (Livs), RE Lockwood (capt, Heck), A Davey (Norm). *Half-backs*: JA Rigg (Hal, 2t), R Wood (Livs, t). *Forwards*: A Barraclough (Mann), H Bradshaw (Bram), T Broadley (Bing), G Nowell (Cas), H Speed (Cas), JT Toothill (Brad), O Walsh (Hun), W Walton (Cas).
REST OF ENGLAND 15 *Back*: JF Byrne (Mose). *Three-quarters*: CA Hooper (MidW), WJ Jackson* (Hal, t), S Morfitt (WHart, t), F Saville (Stock). *Half-backs*: W Hall (Ulv), EW Taylor (Rock, t, c, dg). *Forwards*: A Allport (Black), AE Elliott (StTHosp), W Faulkner (Run), J Hall (NDur), GE Lee (Rock), JJ Robinson (Burt/CamU), F Soane (Bath), WE Tucker (CamU).
Attendance: 15,000   *Referee*: W Cail (RFU President)
*Transferred from home town club Gloucester to Halifax during October 1893. He subsequently represented Yorkshire in 1894-95.

NON-COUNTY CHAMPIONSHIP MATCHES

Wednesday 25 October 1893 at Rugby Cricket Ground, Bilton Road, Rugby
MIDLAND COUNTIES 8 *Back*: JF Byrne (Mose, c). *Three-quarters*: A Rogers (Mose), HP Reynolds (Strat), GH Tuke (Cov). *Half-backs*: WP Nichol (OEdw), BB Tuke (Cov). *Forwards*: G Carpenter (Cov), BH Cattell (Mose), R Chaloner (Mose), AE Cooke (Leic), AW Gorton (Burt), HD Hope (OEdw), G Jones (Worc), C Norbury (Worc), W Rice (Cov, 2t).
CHESHIRE 4 *Back*: S Houghton (Run, dg). *Three-quarters*: F Saville (Stock), AE Fenton (BirkPk), PR Clauss (BirkPk). *Half-backs*: S Abram (Run), J Faulkner (Run). *Forwards*: J Baxter (BirkPk), H Ellis (NewB), W Faulkner (Run), J Langley (Run), F Little (NewB), T Morgan (BirkW), RT Reece (Run), WB Smith (NewB), WA Williams (NewB).
Attendance: 2,000   *Referee*: GR Hill (RFU Honorary Secretary)

Saturday 4 November 1893 at Mansfield Park, Hawick
SOUTH OF SCOTLAND 33 *Back*: J Edmondstone (Haw). *Half-backs*: AF McNee (Haw, 3t), T Almers ((Haw), G Grieve (Haw), WL Watson (Haw, 3t). *Quarter-backs*: M Elliot (Haw, t), D Patterson (Haw, t). *Forwards*: Frater (Mel), R Hunter (Jed), N Kemp (capt, Gala), T Murdison (Gala), J Scott (Haw, t), R Scott (Haw), TM Scott (Mel, 5c), AB Storrie (Haw).
NORTHUMBERLAND 0 *Back*: R Baty (Tynd). *Three-quarters*: T Nicholson (Rock), T Rycroft (PerPk), J Watt (NEls), JT Bell (PerPk). *Half-backs*: HW Audus (PerPk), EW Taylor (Rock). *Forwards*: A Buckley (Wall), FC Garrett (Nor), WN Greenwell (Rock), T Robson (Tynd), CS Shortt (Nor), H Smurthwaite (PerPk), TC Stephenson (Rock), A Styan (Rock).
Attendance: 3,000   *Referee*: n/a
Note: Scoring based on Scottish system: try – 2 points, conversion – 3 points.

Saturday 2 December 1893 at Edgeley Park, Stockport
CHESHIRE 3 *Back*: S Houghton (Run). *Three-quarters*: JH Crompton (Run), F Saville (Stock), J Hutchinson (BirkPk), FP Jones (Swi). *Half-backs*: S Abram (Run), J Faulkner (Run, t). *Forwards*: J Davies (Run), E Elliott (BirkW), H Ellis (NewB), W Faulkner (Run), J Langley (Run), F Little (NewB), T Morgan (BirkW), RT Reece (Run).
DURHAM 5 *Back*: GH Philbrick (HartR). *Three-quarters*: W Wainford (Tud, c), WE Kassell (SSh), S Morfitt (WHart), JW Tate (Wes). *Half-backs*: F Hindle (Tud), F Marston (Tud). *Forwards*: T Burt (SherH), R Edwards (Tud), J Hall (NDur, t), J Lavell (WHart), TJ Lindsay (Tud), RF Oakes (HartR), H Walker (DurC), W Yiend (HartR).
Attendance: 3,000   *Referee*: EB Holmes (Midland Counties)

Saturday 16 December 1893 at Lismore Place, Carlisle
CUMBERLAND 0 *Back*: JH Blaylock (Asp). *Three-quarters*: TH Hodgkinson (CarlC), M Nairn (Whi), J Sandwith (Sea), T Fletcher (Sea). *Half-backs*: J Armstrong (Mil), S Northmore (Mil). *Forwards*: R Bell (Work), JH Blacklock (Mary), D Elliott (CarlC), J Fawcett (Mil), T McGerry (Mary), J Pender (CumH), JG Phillips (Mil), T Tervet (CarlC).
CAMBRIDGE UNIVERSITY 13 *Back*: E Field. *Three-quarters*: LE Pilkington, CM Wells, JJ Gowans, W Neilson (dg, gm). *Half-backs*: AH Greg, RO Schwartz (t). *Forwards*: H Laing, F Mitchell, WE Nelson, HD Rendall, BF Robinson, TWP Storey, AF Todd, SE Whiteway (c).
Attendance: 2,000   *Referee*: JA Williamson (Northumberland)

Saturday 13 January 1894 at Jesmond Ground, Newcastle
NORTHUMBERLAND 8 *Back*: R Baty (Tynd). *Three-quarters*: CO Robinson (PerPk), WG Baty (Tynd/SSh, c), H Knott (PerPk),TP Galloway (Nor). *Half-backs*: TP Alexander (Rock, t), EW Taylor (Rock). *Forwards*: AL Curry (PerPk, t), FE Dotchin (Nor), JH Greenwell (Rock), WN Greenwell (Rock), R Harris (NEls), GW Lee (Rock), A Styan (Rock), R Wright (Brighton).
CUMBERLAND 0 *Back*: W Sharp (Whi). *Three-quarters*: TH Hodgkinson (capt, CarlC), J Sandwith (Sea), M Nairn (Whi), T Fletcher (Sea). *Half-backs*: A Cook (EgrH), J Nelson (Asp). *Forwards*: Jim Davidson (Asp), D Elliott (CarlC), W Moore (Work), G Rogerson (CarlC), G Steele (Asp), D Telford (Cock), T Tervet (CarlC), J Turnbull (Mary).
Attendance: 4,000   *Referee*: WH Humphreys (Durham)

Monday 15 January 1894 at St Helen's, Swansea
GLAMORGANSHIRE 0 *Back*: WJ Bancroft (Swa). *Three-quarters*: JE Elliott (Car), D Fitzgerald (Car), NW Biggs (Car), TW Pearson (Car). *Half-backs*: GW Shepherd (Pen), W Thomas (Nea). *Forwards*: RG Edwards (Morr), WB Gibbs (Pen), AF Hill (Car), W Howells (Aber), F Hutchinson (Nea), F Mills (Swa), W Phillips (CarHarl), SC Ramsay (Treorchy/Car).
YORKSHIRE 3 *Back*: WH Eagland (Hud). *Three-quarters*: T Summersgill (Lee), B Sharpe (Livs), RE Lockwood (capt, Heck), F Firth (Hal). *Half-backs*: JA Rigg (Hal), R Wood (Livs). *Forwards*: A Barraclough (Mann), H Bradshaw (Bram), D Jowett (Heck), G Nowell (Cas), H Speed (Cas), JT Toothill (Brad), O Walsh (Hun), W Walton (Cas, t).
Attendance: 12,000   *Referee*: JA Gould (Newport)

Saturday 20 January 1894 at Ashbrooke Ground, Sunderland
DURHAM 14 *Back*: GH Philbrick (HartR). *Three-quarters*: W Wainford (Tud), JJ Gowens (Wes, 2t), S Morfitt (WHart), JW Tate (Wes, t). *Half-backs*: F Hindle (Tud, c), F Marston (Tud). *Forwards*: T Burt (SherH), T Faulkner (Tud), J Geenty (WHart), J Hall (NDur), TJ Lindsay (Tud, t), RF Oakes (HartR), H Walker (DurC), W Yiend (HartR).
NORTHUMBERLAND 3 *Back*: R Baty (Tynd). *Three-quarters*: H Knott (PerPk), S Anderson (Rock), WG Baty (Tynd/SSh), CO Robinson (PerPk). *Half-backs*: TP Alexander (Rock), EW Taylor (Rock). *Forwards*: AL Curry (PerPk), FE Dotchin (Nor), GW Lee (Rock), FC Garrett (Nor), WN Greenwell (Rock), R Harris (NEls), T Robson (Tynd), A Styan (Rock, t).
Attendance: 5,000   *Referee*: A Hartley (Yorkshire)

Saturday 27 January 1894 at Upper Park, Birkenhead
CHESHIRE 6 *Back*: S Houghton (Run). *Three-quarters*: FP Jones (Swi, t), TP Bate (Sale), A E Fenton (BirkPk), PR Clauss (BirkPk, t). *Half-backs*: S Abram (Run), J Faulkner (Run). *Forwards*: J Davies (Run), E Elliott (BirkW), H Ellis (NewB), W Faulkner (Run), J Langley (Run), F Little (NewB), T Morgan (BirkW), RT Reece (Run).
YORKSHIRE 16 *Back*: H Ward (Brad). *Three-quarters*: RE Lockwood (capt, Heck, 3t, 2c), B Sharpe (Livs), A Davey (Norm), T Summersgill (Lee). *Half-backs*: J Ingham (Otley), JA Rigg (Hal, t). *Forwards*: H Bradshaw (Bram), T Broadley (Bing), F Clegg (Mann), G Nowell (Cas), H Speed (Cas), JT Toothill (Brad), O Walsh (Hun), W Walton (Cas).
Attendance: 4,000   *Referee*: T Hunter (Lancashire)

Saturday 3 February 1894 at Chorley Road, Swinton
LANCASHIRE 13 *Back*: T Foulkes (StH). *Three-quarters*: W McCutcheon (Old, t), S Lees (Old), A Barrett (Sal), J Valentine (Swi, 2c, pg). *Half-backs*: James Bate (War), H Varley (Old). *Forwards*: H Case (Swi), T Dixon (Ask), JC Goold (LivOB), J Jolley (War), G Rigby (Wig), J Simpson (RochH), T Whittaker (Walk), G Woodward (Tyl, t).
DEVONSHIRE 9 *Back*: H Gloynes (Tiv). *Three-quarters*: CF Donkin (NewA), JM Wilcocks (Exe), P Webber (DevA, pg), WE Bildings (DevA, t). *Half-backs*: W George (DevA), HC Nicolay (Barn). *Forwards*: GH Allington (DevA), J Bond (Torq), WC Chiswell (DevA), C Hawking (Torq), J Laverty (DevA), A May (DevA), B Parnell (Tot), C Thomas (Barn, t).
Attendance: 6,000   *Referee*: Rev F Marshall (Yorkshire)

Saturday 10 February 1894 at Mossilee, Galashiels
SOUTH OF SCOTLAND 0 *Back*: R Smith (Lang). *Half-backs*: R Renwick (Gala), WS Oliver (capt, Jed), T Crozier (Jed), G Grieve (Haw). *Quarter-backs*: JT Mabon (Jed), JH Oliver (Jed). *Forwards*: W Cairns (Lang), R Hunter (Jed), J McGregor (Gala Thistle), J Marchbanks (Haw), WL Oliver (Jed), W Purdie (Jed), Scott-Elliott (Haw), W Scott (Lang).
CUMBERLAND 0 *Back*: W Sharp (Whi). *Three-quarters*: TH Hodgkinson (capt, CarlC), JH Buckett (Mil), TH Hodgson (Mil), T Fletcher (Sea). *Half-backs*: J Armstrong (Mil), J McGuire (Mil). *Forwards*: R Bell (Work), M Boase (Mil), D Elliott (CarlC), J Fawcett (Mil), W Moore (Work), G Steele (Asp), T Tervet (CarlC), J Turnbull (Mary).
Attendance: n/a   *Referee*: RD Rainie (Scotland)
Note: Played only 20 minutes each half due to 'sodden pitch'.

ENGLAND TRIAL MATCH
Saturday 16 December 1893 at Fallowfield, Manchester
NORTH 16 *Back*: S Houghton (Run). *Three-quarters*: F Firth (Hal), S Morfitt (WHart, t), RE Lockwood (capt, Heck, 2c), F Saville (Stock). *Half-backs*: EW Taylor (Rock, t), R Wood (Livs). *Forwards*: T Broadley (Bing), H Case (Swi), Jim Davidson (Asp), J Hall (NDur, t), W Lee (Rock), H Speed (Cas), JT Toothill (Brad, t), G Woodward (Tyl).
SOUTH 9 *Back*: JF Byrne (Mose). *Three-quarters*: CA Hooper (MidW), A Latter (Black), JHC Fegan (Black), CF Donkin (NewA/RNEC). *Half-backs*: RH Castell (OxfU), CM Wells (capt, Harl, t). *Forwards*: AE Elliott (StTHosp), C Hawking (Torq), FC Lohden (Black), P Maud (Black), FO Poole (OxfU, t), W Rice (Cov), F Soane (Bath), WE Tucker (CamU, t).
Attendance: 6,000   *Referee*: W Cail (RFU President)

INTERNATIONAL CHAMPIONSHIP

Saturday 6 January 1894 at Upper Park, Birkenhead
ENGLAND 24 *Back*: JF Byrne (Mose). *Three-quarters*: F Firth (Hal), CA Hooper (MidW), S Morfitt (WHart, t), RE Lockwood (capt, Heck, t, 3c). *Half-backs*: EW Taylor (Rock, t, c, gm), CM Wells (Harl). *Forwards*: A Allport (Black), H Bradshaw (Bram, t), T Broadley (Bing), J Hall (NDur), F Soane (Bath), H Speed (Cas), JT Toothill (Brad), WE Tucker (CamU).
WALES 3 *Back*: WJ Bancroft (Swa). *Three-quarters*: W McCutcheon (Old), JA Gould (capt, New), J Conway-Rees (Llan), N Biggs (Car). *Half-backs*: FC Parfitt New, t), HP Phillips (New). *Forwards*: AW Boucher (New), DJ Daniel (Llan), TC Graham (New), J Hannan (New), AF Hill (Car), F Mills (Swa), CB Nicholl (Llan), WH Watts (New).
Attendance: 8,000   *Referee*: JA Smith (Scotland)

Saturday 3 February 1894 at Rectory Field, Blackheath
ENGLAND 5 *Back*: JF Byrne (Mose). *Three-quarters*: F Firth (Hal), CA Hooper (MidW), S Morfitt (WHart), RE Lockwood (capt, Heck, t). *Half-backs*: EW Taylor (Rock, c), R Wood (Livs). *Forwards*: A Allport (Black), H Bradshaw (Bram), T Broadley (Bing), J Hall (NDur), F Soane (Bath), H Speed (Cas), JT Toothill (Brad), WE Tucker (CamU).
IRELAND 7 *Back*: W Sparrow (DubU). *Half-backs*: HG Wells (BecR), S Lee (NIFC), W Gardiner (NIFC), LH Gwynn (DubU). *Quarter-backs*: WS Brown (DubU), BB Tuke (BecR). *Forwards*: TJ Crean (Wand), EG Forrest (capt, Wand, dg), H Lindsay (DubU), JH Lytle (NIFC), JN Lytle (NIFC, t), JH O'Conor (BecR), CV Rooke (DubU), G Walmsley (BecR).
Attendance: 15,000   *Referee*: WM Douglas (Wales)

Saturday 17 March 1894 at Raeburn Place, Edinburgh
SCOTLAND 6 *Back*: G MacGregor (LonS). *Half-backs*: GT Campbell (LonS), W Neilson (CamU), HTS Gedge (EdinW), JJ Gowans (CamU). *Quarter-backs*: JW Simpson (RHSFP), W Wotherspoon (WoS). *Forwards*: JD Boswell (capt, WoS, 2t), WB Cownie (Wat), WR Gibson (RHSFP), HTO Leggatt (Wat), WMC McEwan (EdinA), RG Macmillan (LonS), HF Menzies (WoS), WG Neilson (MerCS).
ENGLAND 0 *Back*: JF Byrne (Mose). *Three-quarters*: CA Hooper (MidW), WJ Jackson (Hal), S Morfitt (WHart), F Firth (Hal). *Half-backs*: EW Taylor (capt, Rock), CM Wells (Harl). *Forwards*: A Allport (Black), H Bradshaw (Bram), T Broadley (Bing), AE Elliott (StTHosp), J Hall (NDur), F Soane (Bath), H Speed (Cas), W Walton (Cas).
Attendance: 15,000   *Referee*: WH Wilkins (Wales)

Other results
Wales 7, Scotland 0
Ireland 5, Scotland 0
Ireland 3, Wales 0

Final table

	P	W	D	L	For	Agst
Ireland	3	3	0	0	15	5
England	3	1	0	2	29	16
Wales	3	1	0	2	10	27
Scotland	3	1	0	2	6	12

George Fisher of Holme Wanderers,
Lancaster and Westmorland.
Lancashire Daily Post, 1904

1894-1895

A NEW YORKSHIRE COMPETITION

The Yorkshire County Committee, who met at the Green Dragon Hotel, Leeds, on 30th July 1894, arrived at the decision to rename two of its leagues; the Intermediate Competition to become Competition No. 3, and the former Competition No. 3 to be called Competition No. 4. The *Yorkshire Evening Post* commented: 'The decision [to change] has been received with anything but satisfaction by the members of the old No. 3, and there are mutterings of revolt. Whether the revolt will go beyond protest to decline to adopt the designation of "No. 4" is doubtful, but it is pretty certain that the clubs will refuse to comply with a scheme which requires them to seek advancement by passing through the ranks of the new "No. 3," which is the old "Intermediate".'[159] Despite the misgivings, the proposed restructure went ahead.

CONTROLLING THE TRANSFER SYSTEM

The Lancashire Club Championship was causing its county authority problems in controlling abuse of the transfer system. Referring to the Lancashire Committee meeting at the Grand Hotel, Manchester, on 19th September, the *Manchester Courier* commented: 'Unless the committee insist upon some hard and fast conditions being observed, their position will become intolerable and their action the subject of ridicule. One suggestion to solve the difficulty is to abolish what we called "provisional" transfers and to adopt the rule in operation in other counties, viz., that every player transferring his membership from one club to another must obtain a transfer. That for a transfer to be sanctioned the player must make a personal written application, and must have the written sanction of the club he is leaving, and that until these are obtained he shall not be permitted to play for the club to which he proposes to transfer his services. The present system is to allow a man to play as soon as any club applies for his transfer.'[160]

PROFESSIONALISM: LEIGH SUSPENDED
The Leigh club was found guilty of professionalism at the Lancashire Committee meeting at the Grand Hotel, Manchester, on 19th September. The allegations had been made by Mr. G. Battersby, a former Leigh official who had been licensee of the Railway Hotel, the clubs headquarters. He claimed some players were paid and also received free dinners during the previous season. The allegations were sustained, the club and last year's players being suspended until the end of November.[161]

PROFESSIONALISM: LANCASHIRE RUMOURS
Rumours of professionalism in Lancashire were growing stronger as evidenced by the *Manchester Guardian* on 8th October: 'In local Rugby circles the outlook is growing more and more gloomy. Attempts to disguise professionalism seem to have been abandoned even among those who are in high places; with the result that the [Lancashire] County Committee will be engaged during the coming week in considering charges which are likely to involve four prominent clubs. Facts will be adduced that will show four at least of the [Lancashire] Competition Clubs have practiced professionalism for some time. One club in effect says "We are a professional club; but if we are going to be punished we will take care that we are not alone." And thus matters threaten to come to a crisis.'[162]

PROFESSIONALISM: RADCLIFFE AND SALFORD SUSPENDED
The Lancashire Committee suspended Radcliffe during their meeting at the Grand Hotel, Manchester, on 30th October. This followed an allegation by Salford that Radcliffe had paid three-quarter Joe Smith. In fact this was a counterclaim, Salford having themselves been suspended on 16th October until January for making inducements to Smith to join them. The charge against Radcliffe had been adjourned from the previous week because, on that occasion, Smith had refused to attend in the absence of a guarantee that he would be paid for presenting himself having already

been declared a professional at the time of Salford's suspension. The Committee decided Radcliffe had induced Smith to return to them by promising a job, and they were suspended until December.[163]

PROFESSIONALISM: THE RUGBY UNION MANIFESTO

The Rugby Football Union held a meeting at the Craven Hotel, London, on 1st November, when the following resolutions regarding professionalism were passed:

1. That a circular be at once issued by this Committee to the clubs of this Union, asking them whether they will undertake to comply with the letter and spirit of the bye-laws, rules and regulations of this Union as regards professionalism, and requesting a reply within 28 days from the date of this circular.
2. That offences committed by clubs after the issue of this circular, whether through themselves, their agents, officials, members, or ticket-holders, shall be punished by expulsion of such clubs and the permanent suspension of their members and officials.
3. That this Committee will consider applications for reinstatement on the part of any members.
4. That having regard to the notorious methods of concealment hitherto adopted by offending clubs, this Committee will, in dealing with future cases, consider that the burden of proof of innocence lies on the club or person charged.
5. That this Committee will not suspend or otherwise punish witnesses who voluntarily give evidence *bona fide* for the Union.
6. That when a player applies for his transfer, the burden of proof of the *bona fides* of his application lie on such player.[164]

WESTMORLAND: GATHERED FROM THE FOUR WINDS

Westmorland, whose best players were continually migrating to clubs based in Lancashire and Yorkshire, lost 19-0 to Lancashire at Watersheddings, Oldham, on 10th November. One scribe reflected on their increased difficulty in selecting a competitive team 'who appear to be gathered together from the four winds of heaven'.[165]

PROFESSIONALISM: WIGAN SUSPENDED

Salford was again the accuser when they exposed Wigan for poaching winger Frank Miles. The Lancashire Committee meeting at the Grand Hotel, Manchester, on 13th November, heard that Miles was allegedly paid

30 shillings (£1.50p) per week by the Wigan club during the close season with a view to securing him for their club. The Committee concluded that Miles had been paid by Wigan as an inducement to transfer to that club. Miles was found guilty of professionalism and Wigan suspended until February.[166]

PROFESSIONALISM:
LANCASHIRE AND YORKSHIRE JOIN FORCES

Representatives of Lancashire and Yorkshire's senior clubs met at the George Hotel, Huddersfield, on 21st November to consider the manifesto issued by the Rugby Football Union relating to professionalism. It was unanimously resolved: 'That in the opinion of this meeting, the resolutions passed by the Rugby Union Committee on November 1st 1894 regarding professionalism are not reasonable and just interpretations of the existing bye-laws of the Rugby Union, and cannot, as such, be accepted by us.' It was also agreed: 'That a requisition for a general special meeting of the Rugby Union be signed by the secretaries of the clubs here represented, and forwarded to the secretary of the Rugby Union, for the purpose of discussing the manifesto issued by the Union Committee regarding professionalism.'[167]

PROFESSIONALISM:
AN AUTOCRATIC ACTION BY THE RUGBY UNION?

The *Manchester Guardian* published a letter from 'Goalpost' that included the following observations: 'The recent autocratic action of the Rugby Union deserves, and is no doubt receiving, the most serious consideration of our clubs. I confess that I am personally in favour of a well-regulated professionalism. The word seems to be unpalatable to Rugby men; but we are not now living in 1870, but in 1894. Times and men have changed, but the Rugby Union apparently changeth not. The old-fashioned notions have gone forever, and Rugby football of today is the game of the masses; hence it is necessary that, unless the Union desires to become moribund and to let its place know it no more, they must accept a more sensible view of things. The ill-advised circular has met with more ridicule than could have been imagined. The present rules are quite strong enough, as is instanced by what is taking place, and if only the Union will have the wisdom and discretion that is common to most committees they will withdraw their circular. We should deeply regret to injure the Union, but we in Lancashire and Yorkshire ought to have our opinion respected.'[168]

PROFESSIONALISM:
YORKSHIRE REJECT RUGBY UNION CIRCULAR

The Yorkshire Rugby Union organised a special meeting of its clubs at the Queen's Hotel, Leeds, on 23rd November, to discuss the circular issued by the Rugby Union concerning professionalism. The Yorkshire Committee considered the circular and decided 'they could not ask the clubs of Yorkshire to submit to the monstrous conditions contained in its clauses'. Regarding the legality of the circular, they said 'the Rugby Union was a society for the mutual protection of the clubs in membership, and for the protection and furtherance of the Rugby game and its affairs had to be administered by a committee who had to act according to the bye-laws'. The following resolutions were subsequently carried:

1. That the clubs in the Yorkshire Union comply with the letter and spirit of the bye-laws, rules, and regulations of the Rugby Union as regards professionalism.
2. The Committee are of the opinion that the Rugby Union has exceeded its power by passing resolutions 2, 3, 4, and 5, which should be passed by a general (Rugby Football Union) meeting in accordance with bye-laws 11 and 13 before becoming law.[169]

BRAMLEY PLAYER IN LANCASHIRE TEAM

The Lancashire's team that faced Yorkshire on 24th November at Fallowfield included Bramley forward William Whiteley, the only Yorkshire-based player to appear for the Red Rose county during the Victorian era. Qualifying through being born in Bury, he had transferred from the Littleborough club in 1893 due to finding employment in the Leeds area. Having played three times for Lancashire he went on to represent Yorkshire in the 1895-96 season.

BROUGHTON WITHDRAW FROM LANCASHIRE CHAMPIONSHIP

The Broughton club withdrew from the Lancashire Second Class Competition on 13th December, due to financial reasons. Founded in 1869 it had stood alone in the Lancashire Competition as the only public school-related club competing in what was essentially a working class League. 'Lancashire Lad', whose letter was published in the *Manchester Courier*, supported their decision: 'The Broughton Football Club had the good sense and courage to withdraw from the Lancashire League. I am glad to see that one club has at last recognised the fact that these cups, leagues, and championships are mainly answerable for the very unsatisfactory state of rugby football in Lancashire and Yorkshire, and I am convinced that these unhealthy matches are neither good for the game itself nor pleasant for the players, but have, almost without exception, lowered the class of player and style of play.'[170]

A LANCASHIRE AND YORKSHIRE RUGBY UNION FORMED

The Lancashire and Yorkshire clubs held a meeting at the George Hotel, Huddersfield, on 30th January, passing the following resolutions:

1. That the premier clubs of Lancashire and Yorkshire, as here represented, do form themselves into a Union for the purpose of furthering the interests of Rugby football in the two counties.
2. That the Union be governed by one representative from each club.
3. That the champion club in the first division of the Lancashire Club Championship and the champion club of the Yorkshire Senior Competition play a match for the championship of the Union.

It was anticipated that the above rules would come into operation later in the year.[171]

LANCASHIRE WITHDRAW FROM COUNTY CHAMPIONSHIP

An anomaly of the county championship was accommodating traditional inter-county fixtures into the competition schedule. The Lancashire versus Yorkshire encounter was usually scheduled for November. As the pair dominated their respective North Western and North Eastern groups, they retrospectively included the result in the decisive 'Second Series' group table. This arrangement created an unusual circumstance after Lancashire had tied with Cumberland at the top of the 1894-95 North Western Group. Rather than travel to Cumberland for a play-off match to determine who progressed to the final group, Lancashire withdrew, making way for their rivals. The logic behind this generous gesture was that Yorkshire – who had already secured a place in the deciding group – had beaten Lancashire in their earlier meeting, a result that, when incorporated into the final 'Second Series' group table, gave Lancashire virtually no chance of securing the county title.[172] The annual Durham versus Northumberland fixture provided another conundrum. Steadfastly arranged for each January, its outcome was, for the third consecutive season, too late to incorporate into the North Eastern Group table.

A PROPOSED NORTHERN UNION

A further gathering of the leading Lancashire and Yorkshire clubs took place on 27th February, again at the George Hotel, Huddersfield, to discuss the formation of a Northern Union. The resolutions passed at the previous meeting were confirmed, and it was resolved that a sub-committee produce rules for the proposed Union to be submitted at a full meeting of the clubs before sending them to the Rugby Union. At a subsequent meeting at the George Hotel on 3rd April, it was stated that, 'having received an intimation from Mr. Rowland Hill [Rugby Football Union Honorary Secretary] that it is necessary to submit the rules direct to the Rugby Union, a copy of the rules now adopted be forwarded to the Rugby Union for approval'.[173] Rowland Hill's response was revealed at a further meeting at the same hotel on 24th May. It stated the RFU 'regret that they are unable to sanction the formation of such a body,' adding 'the proposed union is prejudicial to the best interests of the game'.

REFUSAL TO PLAY ON MANURE!

Silsden objected to playing on the Stanningley ground in a Yorkshire Competition No. 4 fixture on 23rd February, a matter referred to that Competition's 7th March committee meeting at the County Restaurant, Bradford. Stanningley claimed expenses against Silsden due to their refusal to play on a field covered with manure. The committee rejected the claim because they agreed that the ground was unfit for play, there being ice under the manure. It was decided the fixture should count as a draw.[174]

YORKSHIRE CUP: REPLAYED TIES

The Yorkshire Cup produced its usual quota of replayed ties, three of which are worthy of mention. Alverthorpe and Featherstone Trinity set a competition record during the first round, taking four meetings over eight days to arrive at a winner. The first two at Alverthorpe (16th March) and Trinity (20th March) finished scoreless, the third at Alverthorpe (21st March) ended 3-3, whilst the fourth, in Featherstone (23rd March) finished 17-0 in Trinity's favour. Also in the first round, Windhill hosted Elland on 16th March, losing 4-0 but subsequently protested that an Elland official had entered the field and supplied brandy to a player during a break in play. A replay was ordered at Fartown, Huddersfield, Elland again winning.[175] In a second round tie, Stanningley, having lost 3-0 at Horbury on 23rd March, successfully appealed that only 30 minutes (instead of the stipulated 40) was played in the first half, and that a few minutes before half-time the Horbury touch-judge 'handed a bottle to one of the home forwards who drank from it and returned it'. Stanningley won the replay which took place at Crown Point, Leeds.[176]

TUDHOE'S MEMORABLE LATE TRY

Durham Cup winners South Shields owed much of their success to Harry Swainston's memorable late try in a 3-0 semi-final victory over Tudhoe on 23rd March. With the match scoreless and time almost up, the *Shields Daily Gazette* reported: 'The ball was [kicked] past Race on the [Tudhoe] wing, and W. G. Baty coming smartly up dribbled past the [Tudhoe] full-back. Swainston was in close attendance and went off at top speed in pursuit of the oval which he picked up after crossing the half-way line. [Tudhoe's] Walter Taylor and others bounded off after him, but it was only a question of speed, and they were, as might be expected, left hopelessly in the rear, and Harry grounded the ball over the line. The demonstration which followed can be better imagined than described.'[177]

POSSIBLE WINDING UP OF THE MANCHESTER CLUB

The Manchester club, one of the oldest in existence and for so long the dominant organisation in Lancashire, came close to folding due to debts. The *Manchester Guardian* reported: 'A general meeting of the Manchester Football Club has been called for on Thursday [28th March] to confirm a resolution passed at a meeting on the 15th winding up the club. This step is considered necessary in consequence of the large liabilities [the club was £400 in debt], and in default of any prospect of covering future expenses. Everyone will regret that a club which has figured so prominently and for such a length of time in the history of Rugby football should come to such an untimely end.' The subsequent meeting, at the Albion Hotel (28th March) resolved 'that a strong endeavour be made to keep the old club in existence'. Members pledged donations and efforts were to be made to procure subscription arrears through the County Court.[178]

BOOTHSTOWN: TWO MATCHES IN ONE DAY

The *Leigh Chronicle* reported: 'Boothstown had a very arduous day on Saturday [20th April]. They went to Cheetham Hill in the afternoon and played their semi-final tie in the South East Lancashire Cup with the [Cheetham] Hill men. No sooner was the match over than Boothstown were driven in a wagonette to [Manchester] Exchange Station and left by the 6.20 pm train for Ellenbrook where another wagonette was in waiting, and in this they drove to their own ground at Boothstown where they met Failsworth in a Lancashire Third Competition match.'[179]

1894-1895 STATISTICS

LANCASHIRE CLUB CHAMPIONSHIP FIRST CLASS

Final table	P	W	D	L	For	Agst	Pts
Tyldesley	12	8	1	3	80	41	17
Oldham	12	7	2	3	118	47	16
St Helens	12	7	1	4	71	43	15
Broughton Rangers	12	4	2	6	63	84	10
Warrington	12	4	2	6	32	87	10
Swinton	12	2	5	5	26	44	9
Rochdale Hornets	12	3	1	8	39	83	7
Record expunged:							
Salford	4	1	1	2	18	23	3
Wigan	5	3	1	1	45	5	8

Note 1: Salford (Oct 1894), Wigan (Nov 1894) suspended for professionalism.
Note 2: Leigh suspended for professionalism (Sep 1894) without playing a match.

LANCASHIRE CLUB CHAMPIONSHIP SECOND CLASS

Final table	P	W	D	L	For	Agst	Pts
Barrow	16	15	0	1	260	13	30
Widnes	16	12	1	3	197	34	25
Lancaster	16	9	1	6	140	81	19
Ulverston	13	6	0	7	172	84	12
Rochdale St Clements	12	4	4	4	25	44	12
Walkden	14	5	1	8	48	109	11
Blackley Rangers	15	3	1	11	35	203	7
Aspull	10	3	0	7	23	134	6
Blackley	12	1	0	11	12	210	2
Record expunged:							
Broughton	8	2	1	5	17	66	5

Note 1: Broughton withdrew (Dec 1894). *Note 2*: Fixtures were incomplete.

LANCASHIRE CLUB CHAMPIONSHIP THIRD CLASS

Final table	P	W	D	L	For	Agst	Pts
Pemberton	15	11	3	1	148	30	25
Crompton	16	9	3	4	181	52	21
Morecambe	14	9	3	2	89	17	21
Barton	16	7	3	6	90	68	17
Boothstown	16	6	5	5	44	70	17
Werneth	16	6	3	7	64	94	15
Bury	15	5	2	8	61	73	12
Failsworth	14	2	1	11	39	125	5
Pendleton	14	1	1	12	15	202	3
Record expunged:							
Radcliffe	6	3	0	3	33	26	6

Note 1: Radcliffe suspended for professionalism (Oct 1894).
Note 2: Swinton Hornets withdrew (Sep 1894) without playing a match.
Note 3: Failsworth v Bury, Failsworth v Morecambe, Morecambe v Pendleton, Pemberton v Pendleton all postponed and not subsequently played.

NORTH WESTERN LEAGUE

Final table	P	W	D	L	For	Agst	Pts
Barrow	12	11	0	1	153	32	22
Millom	12	7	1	4	74	53	15
Ulverston	12	7	0	5	92	57	14
Kendal Hornets	12	5	1	6	44	106	11
Morecambe	12	3	4	5	58	36	10
Lancaster	12	4	2	6	56	67	10
Askam	12	1	0	11	11	137	2

WESTMORLAND JUNIOR LEAGUE

Final table	P	W	D	L	For	Agst	Pts
Staveley	12	8	2	2	69	19	18
Ambleside	11	6	1	4	55	34	13
Burneside	12	5	2	5	43	42	12
Kirkby Lonsdale	11	3	5	3	23	48	11
Kendal Hornets 'A' *	12	6	1	5	60	46	9
Windermere	12	2	3	7	6	60	7
Holme Wanderers**	10	2	2	6	27	34	6

*Four points deducted for using ineligible players
**Renamed from Burton and Holme Wanderers (Oct 1894)
Note: Holme Wanderers v Ambleside, Holme Wanderers v Kirkby Lonsdale not played

YORKSHIRE SENIOR COMPETITION

Final table	P	W	D	L	For	Agst	Pts
Liversedge	22	16	2	4	223	99	34
Manningham	22	14	4	4	170	74	32
Bradford	22	13	2	7	208	114	28
Leeds	22	10	5	7	147	80	25
Halifax	22	11	2	9	165	93	24
Hunslet	22	11	2	9	171	110	24
Brighouse Rangers	22	9	5	8	106	105	23
Huddersfield	22	10	1	11	101	142	21
Batley	22	8	4	10	83	172	20
Dewsbury and Savile	22	6	5	11	85	181	17
Hull	22	3	2	17	56	177	8
Wakefield Trinity	22	3	2	17	57	225	8

YORKSHIRE COMPETITION NO. 2

Final table	P	W	D	L	For	Agst	Pts
Morley	24	20	2	2	285	34	42
Castleford	24	20	1	3	456	63	41
Leeds Parish Church	24	18	1	5	209	77	37
Bramley	24	14	3	7	146	91	31
Bowling	24	11	2	11	143	152	24
Heckmondwike	24	9	5	10	113	113	23
York	24	10	2	12	105	173	22
Elland	24	8	5	11	76	165	21
Otley*	24	9	4	11	99	168	20
Holbeck	24	8	3	13	139	160	19
Wortley	24	7	1	16	97	162	15
Cleckheaton	24	3	3	18	38	252	9
Kirkstall*	24	2	2	20	54	350	4

*Two points deducted for using ineligible players

YORKSHIRE COMPETITION NO. 3

Final table	P	W	D	L	For	Agst	Pts
Pudsey	26	18	6	2	242	75	42
West Riding	26	19	2	5	321	69	40
Hull Kingston Rovers	26	17	2	7	192	112	36
Sowerby Bridge	26	12	6	8	163	70	30
Armley	26	13	4	9	129	112	30
Outwood Church	26	11	7	8	99	95	29
Ossett	26	12	3	11	130	159	27
Goole	26	10	5	11	119	165	25
Normanton	26	10	2	14	127	153	22
Keighley	26	8	5	13	96	152	21
Mirfield	26	10	0	16	92	207	20
Shipley	26	7	5	14	94	132	19
Alverthorpe	26	6	2	18	74	176	14
Bowling Old Lane	26	3	3	20	61	262	9

Promotion Test Match

Kirkstall v Pudsey (at Barley Mow, Bramley) – Kirkstall refused to play claiming they could not raise a team; Competition No. 2 committee therefore decided to promote Pudsey on proviso that the No. 3 Committee accept Kirkstall.

YORKSHIRE COMPETITION NO. 4 (GROUP A)

Final table	P	W	D	L	For	Agst	Pts
Stanningley	22	15	7	0	152	38	37
Saltaire	22	11	9	2	136	41	31
Skipton	22	8	12	2	100	39	28
Silsden	22	6	10	6	71	59	22
Farsley	22	6	9	7	69	73	21
Yeadon	22	6	9	7	51	67	21
Harrogate	22	5	9	8	67	105	19
Windhill	22	4	11	7	46	88	19
Idle	22	4	9	9	37	88	17
Bingley	22	5	7	10	92	94	17
Guiseley	22	3	10	9	51	113	16
Horsforth	22	4	8	10	54	121	16
Record expunged:							
Tadcaster*	22	6	4	12	71	200	14

*Two points deducted for using ineligible player
Note 1: Tadcaster expelled (Mar 1895) for not fulfilling a fixture.
Note 2: 33 unplayed fixtures (due to severe frost) declared scoreless draws, affecting Farsley (7 matches), Guiseley, Saltaire, Silsden, Skipton, Stanningley, Windhill, Yeadon (6 each), Bingley, Harrogate, Horsforth (5 each), Idle (2).

YORKSHIRE COMPETITION NO. 4 (GROUP B)

Final table	P	W	D	L	For	Agst	Pts
Hebden Bridge	20	10	10	0	137	23	30
Paddock	20	11	8	1	156	17	30
Mytholmroyd	20	10	6	4	97	58	26
Low Moor St Mark's	20	8	9	3	151	76	25
Luddendenfoot	20	6	8	6	63	56	20
Wibsey	20	7	6	7	104	106	20
Kirkburton*	20	6	8	6	114	66	18
Brownroyd Recreation	20	5	8	7	89	114	18
Horbury	20	4	6	10	101	110	14
Birstall	20	2	7	11	41	145	11
Primrose Hill	20	0	6	14	27	309	6
Record expunged:							
Shepley	8	2	0	6	20	104	4
Bailiffe Bridge*	14	4	6	8	67	83	12

*Two points deducted for ineligible player
Note 1: Shepley resigned November 1894.
Note 2: Bailiffe Bridge expelled March 1895 for not fulfilling a fixture.
Note 3: 30 unplayed fixtures declared scoreless draws, affecting Kirkburton (7 matches), Birstall, Hebden Bridge, Low Moor St Mark's, Luddendenfoot, Paddock, Primrose Hill (6 each), Boothroyd Recreation, Mytholmroyd (5 each), Wibsey (4), Horbury (3).

Play-off to decide first place
Hebden Bridge 5, Paddock 0 (at Park Avenue, Bradford)
(Hebden Bridge declared Yorkshire Competition No. 4 Group B winner)

Yorkshire Competition No. 4 Final
Stanningley 15, Hebden Bridge 3 (at Valley Parade, Bradford)
(Stanningley declared Yorkshire Competition No. 4 winner)

Promotion Test Match
Bowling Old Lane 7, Stanningley 5 (at Bowling FC ground, Usher Street, Bowling)
(Bowling Old Lane retain place in Yorkshire Competition No. 3)

CUMBERLAND COUNTY CHALLENGE CUP (12 entries)
Try – 3 points; conversion – 2; penalty goal – 3; drop-goal, field goal, goal from mark – 4.

First Round
Aspatria w/o Maryport (disqualified)
Carlisle w/o South Vale Hornets (Carlisle) withdrew)
Cockermouth 0, Workington 14
Whitehaven Recreation 8, Whitehaven 0
Byes: Brookland Rovers, Egremont Hornets, Penrith United, Seaton

Second Round
Aspatria 8, Whitehaven Recreation 0
Seaton 43, Egremont Hornets 0
Workington 5, Carlisle 0
Penrith United w/o Brookland Rovers (disqualified)

Semi-finals
Aspatria 9, Penrith United 0 (at Waterworks Lane, Carlisle)
Seaton 14, Workington 0 (at The Recreation Ground, Whitehaven)

FINAL
Saturday 20 April 1895 at Lonsdale Park, Workington
SEATON 13 *Back*: JG Sandwith. *Three-quarters*: E Sandwith, Joe Sandwith (capt, 2c),
T Fletcher (t), T Jackson (t). *Half-backs*: J Fisher, J Fletcher. *Forwards*: A Cary-Elwes,
W Denwood, J Edwards, E Houston, W Laybourne (t), T Little, T Owens, J Scott.
ASPATRIA 3 *Back*: JH Blaylock. *Three-quarters*: W Skelton, L Beattie, T Docker,
T Routledge. *Half-backs*: G Messenger, Joe Nelson. *Forwards*: JH Blacklock, T Blacklock,
T Grieve (capt), W Lazonby, J Mumberson, R Mumberson, T Robinson, G Steele (t).
Attendance: 3,000   *Referee*: Rev F Marshall (Yorkshire RU)

DURHAM COUNTY CHALLENGE CUP (17 entries)
Try – 3 points; conversion – 2; penalty goal – 3; drop-goal, field goal, goal from mark – 4.

First Round
Tyne Dock 0, Tudhoe 21 (replay ordered after protest)
Byes: 15 teams drew a bye to next round

First Round Replay
Tyne Dock 6, Tudhoe 14

Second Round
Durham City 19, Sunderland Nomads 8
Hamsteels 8, North Durham 0
Hartlepool Rovers 41, Jarrow 3
Houghton-le-Spring 0, Tudhoe 22
Ryton 0, South Shields 29
Sherburn House 4, Blaydon 0
Sunderland 9, Westoe 0
West Hartlepool 27, Stockton 0

Third Round
Hamsteels 0, Durham City 5
South Shields 7, Hartlepool Rovers 0
Tudhoe 8, Sherburn House 0
West Hartlepool 25, Sunderland 3

Semi-finals
South Shields 3, Tudhoe 0 (aet)
West Hartlepool 10, Durham City 5

FINAL
Saturday 30 March 1895 at Ashbrooke Ground, Sunderland
SOUTH SHIELDS 3 *Back*: J Frame (t). *Three-quarters*: HB Swainston, WG Baty, WE Kassell, A Ward. *Half-backs*: J Baty, A Smith (capt). *Forwards*: W Alden, R Langley, J Lyons, J Nichol, R Wake, RH Wood, T Woodman, S Young.
WEST HARTLEPOOL 0 *Back*: T Wood. *Three-quarters*: A Martin, S Morfitt, J Hughes, W Conning. *Half-backs*: J Liddle, J Morfitt. *Forwards*: J Carberry, J Conmy, W Dale, J Duffey, T Emmerson, J Geenty, T Gibbon, J Hopps.
Attendance: 10,000 *Referee*: A Hartley (Yorkshire RU)

NORTHUMBERLAND COUNTY FOOTBALL CHALLENGE CUP (8 entries)
Try – 3 points; conversion – 2; penalty goal – 3; drop-goal, field goal, goal from mark – 4.

First Round
Brighton 4, Wallsend 0
Northern w/o Gosforth (disbanded)
Percy Park 21, North Elswick 0
Rockcliff 8, Tynedale 0

Semi-finals
Brighton 6, Northern 4
Rockcliff 6, Percy Park 0

FINAL
Saturday 6 April 1895 at Jesmond Ground, Newcastle
ROCKCLIFF 28 *Back*: W Jackson. *Three-quarters*: W Taylor (3t, c), S Anderson, T Nicholson (t), J Thompson. *Half-backs*: TP Alexander (t, dg), EW Taylor (capt, t, 2c). *Forwards*: JH Greenwell, WN Greenwell, GW Lee, J Nesbitt, TC Stephenson, A Styan, B Taylor, John Taylor.
BRIGHTON 5 *Back*: H Pease. *Three-quarters*: T Peacock, C Ridley (capt), M Higgins, W Arrowsmith. *Half-backs*: J Gardner (c), G Mace. *Forwards*: J Aspery, C Hannah, J Scott, A Smith, G Taylor, G Tinn, W Williamson (t), R Wright.
Attendance: 2,000 *Referee*: n/a

YORKSHIRE COUNTY FOOTBALL CHALLENGE CUP (134 entries)
Try – 3 points; conversion – 2; penalty goal – 3; drop-goal, field goal, goal from mark – 4.

Preliminary Round
(100 teams in 15 districts; two from each, indicated by 'q', qualified for next stage)

Airedale: Eccleshill Parish Church, Guiseley (q), Guiseley Parish Church, Idle, Rawdon, Saltaire, Thackley, Windhill (q), Yeadon
Batley: Birstall, Bruntcliffe (q), Soothill (q)
Bradford: Allerton, Bowling Old Lane (q), Bradford Trinity, Brownroyd Recreation, Thornton Rangers, Wibsey (q), Woodville
Castleford: Allerton Bywater, Brotherton St John's, Featherstone Trinity (q), Ferrybridge, Garforth, Kippax, Knottingley (q), Methley, Normanton St John's, Pontefract, South Milford, Whitwood
Craven: Bingley, Haworth, Keighley (q), Keighley Shamrocks, Keighley Zingari, Silsden, Skipton (q), Sutton
Dewsbury: Dewsbury Moor Rangers, Dewsbury St Paulinus, Horbury (q), Horbury Athletic, Mirfield, Thornhill Lees Trinity (q), Thornhill Parish Church
East Leeds: Beeston (q), East Hunslet, Good Shepherd's Recreation, Leeds Institute, Rothwell (q)
Halifax: Bailiffe Bridge, Halifax Gymnasium, Hebden Bridge (q), Luddenden, Luddendenfoot, Mytholmroyd (q), Todmorden
Huddersfield: Crosland Moor, Honley, Kirkburton, Lockwood, Meltham and Meltham Mills, Milnsbridge (q), Netheroyd Hill, Netherton, Nortonthorpe, Paddock (q), Primrose Hill, Shepley, Turnbridge
Hull and Ouse: Beverley (q), Driffield, Holderness Falcons, Hull Marlborough, Selby (q)
Northern: Fulford Rovers, Harrogate, Ripon, Tadcaster (q), Thirsk (q), York Leeman Wanderers
North Leeds: Burley (q), Horsforth (q) (both had byes)
Spen Valley: Low Moor St Mark's (q), Wyke (q) (both had byes)
Wakefield: Barnsley, Cudworth, Dodworth, Doncaster Town, Eastmoor, Felkirk, Kinsley (q), Outwood Church, Royston, Ryhill, Streethouse (q)
West Leeds: Armley, Farsley (q), Stanningley (q)

First Round
(* indicates 34 teams seeded to this round)
Alverthorpe* 0, Featherstone Trinity 0
Batley* 20, Goole* 3
Beverley 5, Wibsey 3
Bowling* 13, Guiseley 3
Bowling Old Lane 24, Thirsk 0
Bradford* 54, Beeston 0
Bramley* 0, Castleford* 12
Brighouse Rangers* 11, Heckmondwike* 0
Burley 0, Thornhill Lees Trinity 17
Dewsbury* 6, Kirkstall* 0
Farsley 5, Paddock 8
Halifax* 26, Shipley* 0
Hebden Bridge 30, Soothill 0
Holbeck* 6, Wortley* 0
Horbury 13, Low Moor St Mark's 3
Huddersfield* 9, Hull* 5
Hull Kingston Rovers* 22, Horsforth 0
Hunslet* 26, Skipton 0
Keighley 6, Cleckheaton* 0
Liversedge* 3, Leeds* 0
Manningham* 20, Leeds Parish Church* 3
Milnsbridge 0, Sowerby Bridge* 13
Morley* 16, West Riding* 6
Mytholmroyd 14, York* 4
Ossett* 11, Tadcaster 5

First Round *continued*
Pudsey* 76, Bruntcliffe 0
Rothwell 7, Normanton* 0
Selby 3, Stanningley 23
Streethouse 0, Otley* 0
Wakefield Trinity* 32, Knottingley 0
Windhill 0, Elland* 4 (replay ordered after protest)
Wyke 5, Kinsley 9

Second Round
Batley 3, Halifax 0
Bowling 0, Keighley 6
Bradford 30, Bowling Old Lane 0
Castleford 32, Kinsley 4
Elland 5, Holbeck 0
Hebden Bridge 18, Beverley 0
Horbury 3, Stanningley 0
(replay ordered after protest)
Huddersfield 6, Morley 8
Hull Kingston Rovers 20, Mytholmroyd 0
Hunslet 7, Pudsey 0

Third Round
Bradford 0, Brighouse Rangers 3
Dewsbury 3, Wakefield Trinity 5
Hebden Bridge 0, Castleford 7
Hull Kingston Rovers 7, Hunslet 13
Morley 14, Keighley 0
Ossett 5, Batley 3
Rothwell 3, Elland 0
Stanningley 0, Manningham 16

First Round Replays
Elland 33, Windhill 0 (at Huddersfield)
Featherstone Trinity 0, Alverthorpe 0
Otley 27, Streethouse 0

First Round Second Replay
Alverthorpe 3, Featherstone Trinity 3

First Round Third Replay
Featherstone Trinity 17, Alverthorpe 0

Liversedge 0, Wakefield Trinity 20
Ossett 8, Featherstone Trinity 0
Otley 0, Dewsbury 5
Paddock 3, Manningham 18
Rothwell 19, Thornhill Lees Trinity 3
Sowerby Bridge 3, Brighouse Rangers 10

Second Round Replay
Stanningley 22, Horbury 9
(at Crown Point, Leeds)

Fourth Round
Castleford 3, Manningham 3
Hunslet 0, Brighouse Rangers 3
Rothwell 0, Ossett 0
Morley 15, Wakefield Trinity 0

Fourth Round Replays
Manningham 11, Castleford 3
Ossett 5, Rothwell 0

Semi-finals
Brighouse Rangers 5, Manningham 0 (at Fartown, Huddersfield)
Morley 16, Ossett 0 (at Crown Flatts, Dewsbury)

FINAL
Saturday 20 April 1895 at Headingley, Leeds
BRIGHOUSE RANGERS 16 *Back*: E Abbey (c). *Three-quarters*: I Rawnsley (t), L Brooke (2t), G Hartley (t), HG Waddington. *Half-backs*: E England, G Schofield. *Forwards*: E Croft, E Earnshaw, TH Hughes, W Jagger, W Nichol, RE Sugden, C Whiteley, F Wood (capt, c).
MORLEY 4 *Back*: F Blackburn. *Three-quarters*: J Gledhill (capt), JE Parker, W Thackray (dg), W Cosgrove. *Half-backs*: J Beaumont, T Stirk. *Forwards*: T Bedford, AW Crowther, J Holmes, F Scott, JH Shooter, S Stead, M Stone, G Wood.
Attendance: 14,038   *Referee*: W Emmott (Leeds)

COUNTY CHAMPIONSHIP

NORTH WESTERN GROUP

Saturday 3 November 1894 at Upper Park, Birkenhead
CHESHIRE 5 *Back*: J Smith (Stock). *Three-quarters*: William Bailey (Stock), F Saville (Stock, c), AE Fenton (BirkPk), FP Jones (NewB). *Half-backs*: PR Clauss (BirkPk, t), H Parratt (Sale). *Forwards*: Walter Bailey (Stock), J Davies (Run), E Elliott (BirkW), H Fletcher (Sale), J Langley (Run), J Mottershead (Stock), R Ould (BirkPk), A Taylor (Run).
LANCASHIRE 26 *Back*: J Valentine (capt, Swi). *Three-quarters*: W McCutcheon (Old, t), S Lees (Old, t), JP Taylor (Old, t), J Hurst (Old, t). *Half-backs*: W Hall (Ulv, t), H Varley (Old, t). *Forwards*: JC Goold (LivOB), J Johnson (Barton), J Jolley (War), GH Murray (Swi), G Rigby (Wig), J Simpson (RochH), SE Wilson (Liv, 4c), G Woodward (Tyl).
Attendance: 5,000   *Referee*: EB Holmes (Midland Counties)

Thursday 8 November 1894 at The Recreation Ground, Whitehaven
CUMBERLAND 11 *Back*: W Sharp (Whi/Bar). *Three-quarters*: JH Buckett (Mil, c), T Fletcher (Sea, t), W Skelton (Asp), WS Graham (Carl). *Half-backs*: J McGuire (Mil), S Northmore (Mil/Bar). *Forwards*: J Bell (Carl, t), R Bell (Work, t), Jim Davidson (capt, Asp), D Elliott (Carl), W Falcon (Mil/CamU), J Fawcett (Mil), W Moore (Work), G Steele (Asp).
CHESHIRE 0 *Back*: S Simpson (NewB). *Three-quarters*: F Saville (Stock), AE Fenton (BirkPk), TH Warder (Run), William Bailey (Stock). *Half-backs*: A McDonald (BirkPk), H Parratt (Sale). *Forwards*: J Davies (Run), E Elliott (BirkW), H Fletcher (Sale), F Gayter (Run), M King (Stock), R Ould (BirkPk), AH Spence (BirkPk), A Taylor (Run).
Attendance: 2,000   *Referee*: W Cail (RFU Honorary Treasurer)

Saturday 10 November 1894 at Watersheddings, Oldham
LANCASHIRE 19 *Back*: J Valentine (capt, Swi). *Three-quarters*: W McCutcheon (Old, t), S Lees (Old, t), JP Taylor (Old, t), J Hurst (Old, 2t). *Half-backs*: W Hall (Ulv), H Varley (Old). *Forwards*: JC Goold (LivOB), J Johnson (Barton), J Jolley (War), GH Murray (Swi), G Rigby (Wig), J Simpson (RochH), SE Wilson (Liv, 2c), G Woodward (Tyl).
WESTMORLAND 0 *Back*: A Chorley (Hal). *Three-quarters*: J Bell (Tyl), AS Dixon (Amb), CG Mason (Amb), J Allen (Dew). *Half-backs*: W Berry (Tyl), F Dixon (KenH). *Forwards*: WA Davis (BurHW), G Fisher (BurHW), W Jackson (BuHW), VS Jones (Burn), RH Moore (Old), RH Robinson (Burn), W Whiteley (StH), RS Winskill (Hal).
Attendance: 12,000   *Referee*: JH Potter (Yorkshire)

Saturday 17 November 1894 at Manchester Athletic Ground, Fallowfield
LANCASHIRE 3 *Back*: T Foulkes (StH). *Three-quarters*: W McCutcheon (Old, t), S Lees (Old), JP Taylor (Old), R Holmes (More). *Half-backs*: W Hall (Ulv), A Lees (Old). *Forwards*: JC Goold (LivOB), J Johnson (Barton), J Jolley (War), GH Murray (Swi), B Ridehaugh (RochStC), J Simpson (RochH), SE Wilson (Liv), G Woodward (Tyl).
CUMBERLAND 3 *Back*: W Skelton (Asp). *Three-quarters*: T Fletcher (Sea), W Nelson (Mil), T Ritson (Mil), W Cunningham (Mil). *Half-backs*: WS Graham (Carl), G Messenger (Asp). *Forwards*: J Bell (Carl), R Bell (Work), J Clague (Cock, t), Jim Davidson (capt, Asp), D Elliott (Carl), J Fawcett (Mil), W Moore (Work), G Steele (Asp).
Attendance: 7,000   *Referee*: Rev F Marshall (Yorkshire)

Thursday 22 November 1894 at Upper Park, Birkenhead
CHESHIRE 0 *Back*: S Houghton (Run). *Three-quarters*: Barker (Stockton Heath), F Saville (Stock), William Bailey (Stock), TH Warder (Run). *Half-backs*: S Abram (Run), H Parratt (Sale). *Forwards*: R Brown (Tranmere Wanderers), J Davies (Run), E Elliott (BirkW), W Faulkner (Run), M King (Stock), J Langley (Run), J Mottershead (Stock), A Taylor (Run).
WESTMORLAND 0 *Back*: A Chorley (Hal). *Three-quarters*: CG Mason (Amb), J Allen (Dew), AS Langley (KenH), R Doherty (StH). *Half-backs*: W Berry (Tyl), W Cross (StH). *Forwards*: J Deason (KenH), J Elliott (Burn), G Fisher (BurHW), T Garnett (Wind), T Gibson (Lanc), RH Moore (Old), W Whiteley (StH), RS Winskill (Hal).
Attendance: 2,000   *Referee*: n/a

Saturday 8 December 1894 at Mint's Feet, Kendal
WESTMORLAND 0 *Back*: A Chorley (Hal). *Three-quarters*: E Braithwaite (KenH), G Coleman (KenH), J Goodman (Rad), J Holmes (KenH). *Half-backs*: F Dixon (KenH), R Hill (KenH). *Forwards*: J Carradus (KenH), J Deason (KenH), T Fawcett (KenH), G Fisher (BurHW), T Garnett (Wind), WJ Parsons (KenH), W Whiteley (StH), W Wilson (KenH).
CUMBERLAND 3 *Back*: W Skelton (Asp). *Three-quarters*: W Nelson (Mil), T Fletcher (Sea, t), T Ritson (Mil), W Cunningham (Mil). *Half-backs*: WS Graham (Carl), G Messenger (Asp). *Forwards*: J Bell (Carl), R Bell (Work), J Clague (Cock), Jim Davidson (capt, Asp), E Doran (EgrH), E Houston (Sea), T Kitchin (Mil), W Moore (Work).
Attendance: 500   *Referee*: JH Potter (Yorkshire)

Final table

	P	W	D	L	For	Agst	Pts
Cumberland	3	2	1	0	17	3	5
Lancashire	3	2	1	0	48	8	5
Westmorland	3	0	1	2	0	22	1
Cheshire	3	0	1	2	5	37	1

(Cumberland declared winner after Lancashire withdrew from play-off)

NORTH EASTERN GROUP

Saturday 10 November 1894 at Victoria Ground, West Hartlepool
DURHAM 5 *Back*: W Taylor (Tud). *Three-quarters*: HB Swainston (SSh), S Morfitt (WHart), FHR Alderson (HartR, c), RCF Crow (SundN). *Half-backs*: F Marston (Tud), JT Thompson (HartR). *Forwards*: T Burt (SherH), J Geenty (WHart), T Gibbon (WHart), J Hall (NDur, t), TJ Lindsay (Tud), RF Oakes (HartR), AP Thompson (SundN), W Yiend (HartR).
YORKSHIRE 16 *Back*: H Ward (Brad). *Three-quarters:* A Davey (Cas), FW Cooper (Brad, t, 2c), WJ Jackson (Hal), F Firth (Hal, t). *Half-backs*: JA Rigg (Hal), R Wood (Livs). *Forwards*: A Barraclough (Mann), J Conley (LeePC), W Donaldson (Mann), J Knowles (Hal, t), Joe Riley (Lee, t), H Speed (Cas), JT Toothill (capt, Brad), W Walton (Cas).
Attendance: 12,000   *Referee*: J Ashton (Lancashire)

Saturday 17 November 1894 at Headingley, Leeds
YORKSHIRE 19 *Back*: H Ward (Brad). *Three-quarters*: TH Dobson (Brad, t, dg), FW Cooper (Brad, t, c, pg), WJ Jackson (Hal), F Firth (Hal). *Half-backs*: JA Rigg (Hal), R Wood (Livs). *Forwards*: A Barraclough (Mann), T Broadley (WRid), W Donaldson (Mann, dg), G Nowell (Lee), Jack Riley (Hal), Joe Riley (Lee), JT Toothill (capt, Brad), O Walsh (Hun).

NORTHUMBERLAND 5 *Back*: R Baty (Tynd). *Three-quarters*: J Thompson (Rock), H Knott (PerPk), S Anderson (Rock), GC Robinson (PerPk). *Half-backs*: H Mullin (Nor), EW Taylor (Rock, c). *Forwards*: A Buckley (Wall), FE Dotchin (Nor), JH Greenwell (Rock), WN Greenwell (Rock), GW Lee (Rock), J Nesbitt (Rock), T Robson (Tynd), A Styan (Rock, t). *Attendance*: 10,000   *Referee*: W Yiend (Durham)

Final table

	P	W	D	L	For	Agst	Pts
Yorkshire	2	2	0	0	35	10	4
Durham	1	0	0	1	5	19	0
Northumberland	1	0	0	1	5	16	0

(Northumberland v Durham on 27 February too late for inclusion)

SOUTH WESTERN GROUP

Results
Gloucestershire 0, Somersetshire 4
Cornwall 8, Somersetshire 16
Devonshire 16, Gloucestershire 9
Cornwall 6, Devonshire 23
Gloucestershire 8, Cornwall 3
Somersetshire 5, Devonshire 8

Final table

	P	W	D	L	For	Agst	Pts
Devonshire	3	3	0	0	47	14	6
Somersetshire	3	2	0	1	25	16	4
Gloucestershire	3	1	0	2	17	23	2
Cornwall	3	0	0	3	11	47	0

SOUTH EASTERN GROUP

Results
Middlesex 10, Kent 13
Surrey 11, Middlesex 5
Middlesex 11, Midland Counties 0
Kent 0, Midland Counties 10
Kent 6 Surrey 3
Midland Counties 16, Surrey 0

Play-off to decide first place
Midland Counties 6, Kent 3

Final table

	P	W	D	L	For	Agst	Pts
Midland Counties	3	2	0	1	26	11	4
Kent	3	2	0	1	19	23	4
Middlesex	3	1	0	2	26	24	2
Surrey	3	1	0	2	14	27	2

FINAL GROUP ('SECOND SERIES')

Monday 11 February 1895 at Welford Road, Leicester
MIDLAND COUNTIES 3 *Back*: JF Byrne (Mose). *Three-quarters*: AH Frith (Cov), EM Baker (Wolv, t), FR Lovitt (Cov), AR Badger (OEdw). *Half-backs*: RH Cattell (Mose), BB Tuke (Cov). *Forwards*: AAW Burton (Burt), BH Cattell (Mose), G Carpenter (Cov), AW Gorton (Burt), A Henshaw (Derby), G Jones (Leic), WA Marris (OEdw), E Redman (Leic).
YORKSHIRE 3 *Back*: H Ward (Brad). *Three-quarters*: FW Cooper (Brad), WJ Jackson (Hal), F Firth (Hal), A Davey (Cas). *Half-backs*: JA Rigg (Hal), R Wood (Livs, t). *Forwards*: A Barraclough (Mann), H Bradshaw (Bram), T Broadley (WRid), F Clegg (Mann), W Donaldson (Mann), Joe Riley (Lee), JT Toothill (capt, Brad), W Walton (Cas).
Attendance: 2,000   *Referee*: WM Douglas (Glamorganshire)

Wednesday 6 March 1895 at Home Park, Plymouth
DEVONSHIRE 5 *Back*: W Hocken (DevA, c). *Three-quarters*: W Down (DevA), WE Bildings (DevA), WE Sowden (DevA), EJ Salter (Exm). *Half-backs*: JH Chipman (Torq), W George (DevA). *Forwards*: GH Allington (DevA), G Dobell (Torq), J Laverty (DevA, t), F Long (DevA), A May (DevA), C Thomas (Barn), W Vanstone (Torq), C Vicary (Barn).
YORKSHIRE 12 *Back*: GE Lorimer (Mann). *Three-quarters*: FW Cooper (Brad), TH Dobson (Brad, t), JH Crompton (Brad), F Firth (Hal). *Half-backs*: JA Rigg (Hal, t), R Wood (Livs, t). *Forwards*: A Barraclough (Mann, t), T Broadley (capt, WRid), F Clegg (Mann), W Donaldson (Mann), G Nowell (Lee), M Sutcliffe (Hud), W Walton (Cas), JW Ward (Cas).
Attendance: 10,000   *Referee*: AJ Davies (Glamorganshire)

Thursday 14 March 1895 at Lonsdale Park, Workington
CUMBERLAND 14 *Back*: W Skelton (Asp). *Three-quarters*: T Ritson (Mil), W Nelson (Mil), T Fletcher (Sea, t), W Cunningham (Mil). *Half-backs*: WS Graham (Carl), G Messenger (Asp). *Forwards*: J Bell (Carl), R Bell (Work), Jim Davidson (capt, Asp, 2t), D Elliott (Carl, pg), W Falcon (Mil/CamU), J Fawcett (Mil), W Moore (Mil, c), G Steele (Asp).
MIDLAND COUNTIES 0 *Back*: AC Butlin (Rugby). *Three-quarters*: AH Frith (Cov), WP Nichol (OEdw), H Payne (Mose), E Patterson (Mose). *Half-backs*: AG George (OEdw), O Patterson (Mose). *Forwards*: E Aston (Derby), GC Buck (Rugby), R Chaloner (Mose), AW Gorton (Burt), WA Marris (OEdw), AV Payne (Cov), JJ Robinson (Burt), JG Wallis (OEdw).
Attendance: 2,000   *Referee*: Rev F Marshall (Yorkshire)

Thursday 21 March 1895 at Lismore Place, Carlisle
CUMBERLAND 11 *Back*: W Skelton (Asp). *Three-quarters*: T Ritson (Mil), W Nelson (Mil, 2t), T Fletcher (Sea),W Cunningham (Mil). *Half-backs*: WS Graham (Carl, t), G Messenger (Asp, c). *Forwards*: J Bell (Carl), R Bell (Work), JH Blacklock (Asp), Jim Davidson (capt, Asp), D Elliott (Carl), W Falcon (Mil/CamU), J Fawcett (Mil), W Moore (Mil).
DEVONSHIRE 5 *Back*: T Endacott (Torq). *Three-quarters*: H Stoyle (Barn), FS Cox (DevA, c), G Curtice (Barn), EJ Salter (Exm, t). *Half-backs*: GH Harding (Torq), T Porter (Barn). *Forwards*: G Dobell (Torq), T Fox (DevA), J Laverty (capt, DevA), W Little (DevA), T Phillips (Barn), C Thomas (Barn), W Thompson (Torq), W Vanstone (Torq).
Attendance: 2,000   *Referee*: EB Holmes (Midland Counties)

Wednesday 27 March 1895 at Valley Parade, Bradford
YORKSHIRE 5 *Back*: GE Lorimer (Mann, c). *Three-quarters*: A Davey (Cas), JH Crompton (Brad), OG Mackie (Wak), E Parkin (Livs, t). *Half-backs*: GE Mosley (LeePC), R Wood (Livs). *Forwards*: A Barraclough (Mann), T Broadley (WRid), F Clegg (Mann), G Nowell (Lee), M Sutcliffe (Hud), JT Toothill (capt, Brad), W Walton (Cas), JW Ward (Cas).
CUMBERLAND 3 *Back*: JH Moore (Mil). *Three-quarters*: T Ritson (Mil), W Nelson (Mil), T Fletcher (Sea), W Cunningham (Mil). *Half-backs*: WS Graham (Carl), G Messenger (Asp). *Forwards*: J Bell (Carl), R Bell (Work), JH Blacklock (Asp), Jim Davidson (capt, Asp), D Elliott (Carl), W Falcon (Mil/CamU), J Fawcett (Mil), W Moore (Mil, t).
Attendance: 4,000   *Referee*: J Ashton (Lancashire)

Other result
Midland Counties 8, Devonshire 8

Final table

	P	W	D	L	For	Agst	Pts
Yorkshire	3	2	1	0	20	11	5
Cumberland	3	2	0	1	28	10	4
Midland Counties	3	0	2	1	11	25	2
Devonshire	3	0	1	2	18	31	1

COUNTY CHAMPIONS v THE REST
Monday 8 April 1895 at Headingley, Leeds
YORKSHIRE 21 *Back*: GE Lorimer (Mann, c). *Three-quarters*: E Parkin (Livs), OG Mackie (Wak, t), FW Cooper (Brad, 2t, 2c), H Hainstock (Lee, t). *Half-backs*: JA Rigg (Hal, t), R Wood (Livs). *Forwards*: A Barraclough (Mann), T Broadley (WRid), F Clegg (Mann), G Nowell (Lee), M Sutcliffe (Hud), JT Toothill (capt, Brad), W Walton (Cas), JW Ward (Cas).
REST OF ENGLAND 3 *Back*: JF Byrne (Mose). *Three-quarters*: JHC Fegan (Black), EM Baker (OxfU), F Saville (Stock), S Morfitt (WHart). *Half-backs*: RH Cattell (Mose), EW Taylor (capt, Rock). *Forwards*: Jim Davidson (Asp), W Falcon (Mil/CamU), HW Finlinson (Black, t), AW Gorton (Burt), WN Greenwell (Rock), FO Poole (OxfU), G Steele (Asp), C Thomas (Barn).
Attendance: 8,000   *Referee*: CA Crane (Midland Counties)

NON-COUNTY CHAMPIONSHIP MATCHES

Wednesday 24 October 1894 at Irwell Lane, Runcorn
CHESHIRE 3 *Back*: S Houghton (Run). *Three-quarters*: William Bailey (Stock), F Saville (Stock), AE Fenton (BirkPk), FP Jones (NewB). *Half-backs*: J Faulkner (Run, t), G Robinson (Run). *Forwards*: Walter Bailey (Stock), J Davies (Run), W Faulkner (Run), M King (Stock), J Langley (Run), J Mottershead (Stock), R Ould (BirkPk), A Taylor (Run).
MIDLAND COUNTIES 8 *Back*: JF Byrne (Mose, c). *Three-quarters*: AH Frith (Cov, 2t), FR Lovitt (Cov), GH Tuke (Cov), FA Byrne (Mose). *Half-backs*: RH Cattell (Mose), WJ Foreman (Leic). *Forwards*: G Carpenter (Cov), AE Cooke (Leic), F Evershed (Burt), A Henshaw (Derby), G Jones (Leic), W Lamb (Cov), E Redman (Leic), WH Rowlands (Mose).
Attendance: 3,000   *Referee*: JH Smith (Lancashire)

Saturday 27 October 1894 at Lismore Place, Carlisle
CUMBERLAND 3 *Back*: A Smith (Carl). *Three-quarters*: JH Buckett (Mil), W Skelton (Asp), T Fletcher (Sea, t), WS Graham (Carl). *Half-backs*: G Messenger (Asp), J Nelson (Asp). *Forwards*: J Bell (Carl), R Bell (Work), J Clague (Cock), Jim Davidson (Asp), D Elliott (Carl), J Fawcett (Mil), W Moore (Work), G Steele (Asp).
DURHAM 12 *Back*: W Taylor (Tud). *Three-quarters*: J Morfitt (WHart), S Morfitt (WHart), C Hodgson (HartR), RCF Crow (SundN, c, dg). *Half-backs*: F Marston (Tud), JT Thompson (HartR). *Forwards*: T Burt (SherH, t), J Finlay (HartR), J Geenty (WHart), T Gibbon (WHart), J Hall (NDur), TJ Lindsay (Tud, t), FE Skinner-Jones (DurU), A Stephenson (Tud).
Attendance: 'large'   *Referee*: AM Crook (Lancashire)

Wednesday 31 October 1894 at Fartown, Huddersfield
YORKSHIRE 31 *Back*: H Ward (Brad). *Three-quarters*: A Davey (Cas), WJ Jackson (Hal, t, c), FW Cooper (Brad, t, 2c, dg), TH Dobson (Brad, 2t). *Half-backs*: GE Mosley (LeePC), JA Rigg (Hal). *Forwards*: A Barraclough (Mann, t), J Conley (LeePC), W Donaldson (Mann), S Priestley (LeePC), H Speed (Cas, 2t), M Sutcliffe (Hud), JT Toothill (capt, Brad), W Walton (Cas).
GLAMORGANSHIRE 0 *Back*: J Davies (Nea). *Three-quarters*: C Bowen (Llan), JP Jago (Wig), C Steer (Nea), HE Morgan (Pen). *Half-backs*: T Blackmore (Swa), I Grey (Morr). *Forwards*: C Bansey (Aber), T Deacon (Morr), E George (Pon), WB Gibbs (Pen), JA Harris (Aber), W Howells (Aber), AM Jenkins (Swa), J Reynolds (Nea).
Attendance: 4,000   *Referee*: J Mills (Lancashire)

Saturday 24 November 1894 at Manchester Athletic Ground, Fallowfield
LANCASHIRE 10 *Back*: T Foulkes (StH). *Three-quarters*: W McCutcheon (Old), S Lees (Old), JP Taylor (Old), J Valentine (capt, Swi). *Half-backs*: W Hall (Ulv, t), H Varley (Old). *Forwards*: J Dakin (War), E Furniss (Old), JC Goold (LivOB), J Johnson (Barton), J Jolley (War), W Whiteley (Bram), RP Wilson (LivOB, t), SE Wilson (Liv, 2c).
YORKSHIRE 26 *Back*: H Ward (Brad). *Three-quarters*: FW Cooper (Brad, c, pg), WJ Jackson (Hal), TH Dobson (Brad, t), F Firth (Hal). *Half-backs*: J Arnold (Hal), JA Rigg (Hal, t). *Forwards*: A Barraclough (Mann), T Broadley (WRid, t), W Donaldson (Mann, c, gm), G Nowell (Lee), Jack Riley (Hal), Joe Riley (Lee), JT Toothill (capt, Brad, t), W Walton (Cas, t).
Attendance: 15,000   *Referee*: RG Warren (Ireland)

Saturday 1 December 1894 at Brewery Field, Spennymoor
DURHAM 14 *Back*: RW Poole (HartR). *Three-quarters*: T Martin (Tud), S Morfitt (WHart, t), FHR Alderson (capt, HartR, 2c, dg), RCF Crow (SundN). *Half-backs*: F Marston (Tud), JT Thompson (HartR). *Forwards*: T Burt (SherH), J Geenty (WHart), T Gibbon (WHart), J Hall (NDur, t), TJ Lindsay (Tud), RF Oakes (HartR), AP Thompson (SundN), W Yiend (HartR).
CHESHIRE 3 *Back*: S Houghton (Run). *Three-quarters*: JAS Cannell (NewB, t), FP Jones (capt, NewB), J Butterworth (Run), William Bailey (Stock). *Half-backs*: H Parratt (Sale), G Robinson (Run). *Forwards*: Walter Bailey (Stock), R Brown (Tranmere Wanderers), J Davies (Run), M Fletcher (Sale), F Gayter (Run), F Ingham (BirkW), M King (Stock), J Stubbs (Run).
Attendance: 10,000   *Referee*: E Seddon (Lancashire)

Wednesday 27 February 1895 at Jesmond Ground, Newcastle
NORTHUMBERLAND 8 *Back*: W Jackson (Rock). *Three-quarters*: PW Oscroft (Nor), S Anderson (Rock), WG Baty (Tynd/SSh, 2t), GC Robinson (PerPk). *Half-backs*: TP Alexander (Rock), EW Taylor (Rock, c). *Forwards*: FE Dotchin (Nor), R Harris (NEls), CC Maughan (Nor), J Nesbitt (Rock), T Robson (Tynd), HJ Spencer (PerPk), A Styan (Rock), J Taylor (Rock).
DURHAM 9 *Back*: RV Hill (DurC). *Three-quarters*: T Martin (Tud), HH Lawrence (DurC), WE Kassell (SSh), JJ Gowans (Wes). *Half-backs*: CY Adamson (DurC, c, gm), F Marston (Tud, t). *Forwards*: W Alden (SSh), T Burt (SherH), J Hall (NDur), TJ Lindsay (Tud), A Stephenson (Tud), AP Thompson (SundN), H Walker (DurC), W Yiend (HartR).
Attendance: 1,500   *Referee*: n/a

Wednesday 27 February 1895 at Park Avenue, Bradford
YORKSHIRE 28 *Back*: GE Lorimer (Mann, c). *Three-quarters*: TH Dobson (Brad), JH Crompton (Brad, c), B Sharpe (Livs, t), E Parkin (Livs, 4t). *Half-backs*: GE Mosley (LeePC), R Wood (Livs). *Forwards*: A Barraclough (Mann, t), T Broadley (capt, WRid, 2t), F Clegg (Mann), W Donaldson (Mann), G Nowell (Lee), M Sutcliffe (Hud), W Walton (Cas), JW Ward (Cas).
CHESHIRE 0 *Back*: S Houghton (Run). *Three-quarters*: F Saville (Stock), William Bailey (Stock), J Butterworth (Run), AE Fenton (BirkPk). *Half-backs*: S Abram (Run), J Faulkner (Run). *Forwards*: J Baxter (BirkPk), R Brown (Tranmere Wanderers), W Faulkner (capt, Run), F Ingham (BirkW), M King (Stock), J Langley (Run), J Mottershead (Stock), R Ould (BirkPk).
Attendance: 4,000   *Referee*: J Higson (Lancashire)

Saturday 2 March 1895 at County Ground, St Thomas, Exeter
DEVONSHIRE 0 *Back*: T Endacott (Torquay Juniors). *Three-quarters*: FS Cox (DevA), GH Harding (Torq), EJ Salter (Exm), EJ Baker (Exe). *Half-backs*: F Pendleton (RNEC), T Porter (Barn). *Forwards*: G Cann (Torq), G Dobell (Torq), J Lake (Ply), T Oliphant (Tot), C Pearse (Barn), C Thomas (Barn), W Vanstone (Torq), C Vicary (Barn).
LANCASHIRE 20 *Back*: J Hacking (BroR). *Three-quarters*: J Valentine (Swi, t, c, pg), LE Pilkington (StHR/CamU, t), S Lees (Old), R Holmes (More). *Half-backs*: A Lees (Old), H Varley (Old, t). *Forwards*: E Bonser (Old), J Dakin (War), E Furniss (Old), C Gibson (Lanc), JC Goold (LivOB), JJ Jones (Sal), W Unsworth (Wig, t), W Whiteley (Bram, t).
Attendance: 4,000   *Referee*: CA Crane (Midland Counties)

Monday 4 March 1895 at Cardiff Arms Park
GLAMORGANSHIRE 3 *Back*: J Davies (Nea). *Three-quarters*: C Bowen (Llan), FJ Gordon (Swa), TD Davies (Morr), HE Morgan (Pen). *Half-backs*: A Cross (Nea), D Jones (Aber). *Forwards*: C Bansey (Aber), T Deacon (Morr), E George (Pon), T Hutchinson (Nea), TH Jackson (Swa, t), AM Jenkins (Swa), G Reynolds (Nea), R Thomas (Swa).
LANCASHIRE 0 *Back*: J Hacking (BroR). *Three-quarters*: J Valentine (Swi), LE Pilkington (StHR/CamU), S Lees (Old), R Holmes (More). *Half-backs*: A Lees (Old), H Varley (Old). *Forwards*: E Bonser (Old), J Dakin (War), C Gibson (Lanc), JC Goold (LivOB), J Jolley (War), JJ Jones (Sal), W Unsworth (Wig), W Whiteley (Bram).
Attendance: 2,000   *Referee*: WH Wilkins (Llanelli)

ENGLAND TRIAL MATCH
Saturday 15 December 1894 at Rectory Field, Blackheath
SOUTH 36 *Back*: JF Byrne (Mose, c, dg). *Three-quarters*: WB Thomson (Black, 3t), EM Baker (OxfU), FA Leslie-Jones (OxfU), JHC Fegan (Black, t). *Half-backs*: RH Cattell (Mose), CM Wells (Harl). *Forwards*: WE Bromet (Rich), GM Carey (OxfU), HW Finlinson (Black), F Mitchell (CamU, t, 3c), FO Poole (OxfU), C Thomas (Barn, t), WE Tucker (CamU), SMJ Woods (capt, Bridg/Black, 2t).
NORTH 0 *Back*: H Ward (Brad). *Three-quarters*: TH Dobson (Brad), FW Cooper (Brad), S Morfitt (WHart), F Firth (Hal). *Half-backs*: EW Taylor (Rock), R Wood (Livs). *Forwards*: A Barraclough (Mann), T Broadley (WRid), FE Dotchin (Nor), T Gibbon (WHart), WN Greenwell (Rock), J Hall (NDur), G Steele (Asp), RP Wilson (LivOB).
Attendance: 12,000   *Referee*: HL Ashmore (Middlesex)

INTERNATIONAL CHAMPIONSHIP

Saturday 5 January 1895 at St Helen's, Swansea
WALES 6 *Back*: WJ Bancroft (Swa). *Three-quarters*: TW Pearson (Car), O Badger (Llan), JA Gould (capt, New), WL Thomas (New). *Half-backs*: S Biggs (Car), B Davies (Llan). *Forwards*: AW Boucher (New), WK Elsey (Car, t), TC Graham (New, t), J Hannan (New), TH Jackson (Swa), F Mills (Car), CB Nicholl (Llan), WH Watts (New).
ENGLAND 14 *Back*: H Ward (Brad). *Three-quarters*: JHC Fegan (Black), WB Thomson (Black, t), FA Leslie-Jones (OxfU, t), EM Baker (OxfU). *Half-backs*: RH Cattell (Mose), EW Taylor (Rock). *Forwards*: WE Bromet (Rich), GM Carey (OxfU, t), HW Finlinson (Black), F Mitchell (CamU, c), FO Poole (OxfU.), C Thomas (Barn), WE Tucker (CamU), SMJ Woods (capt, Bridg/Black, t).
Attendance: 20,000   *Referee*: JA Smith (Scotland)

Saturday 2 February 1895 at Lansdowne Road, Dublin
IRELAND 3 *Back*: GR Symes (Monk). *Three-quarters*: W Gardiner (NIFC), S Lee (BecR), TH Stevenson (QCB), JT Magee (BecR). *Half-backs*: LM Magee (BecR, t), BB Tuke (BecR). *Forwards*: AA Brunker (Lans), AD Clinch (Wand), TJ Crean (Wand), TJ Johnston (QCB), H Lindsay (Arm), HC McCoull (BelA), JH O'Conor (capt, BecR), CV Rooke (Monk).
ENGLAND 6 *Back*: JF Byrne (Mose). *Three-quarters*: JHC Fegan (Black, t), WB Thomson (Black), FA Leslie-Jones (OxfU), EM Baker (OxfU). *Half-backs*: RH Cattell (Mose), EW Taylor (Rock). *Forwards*: WE Bromet (Rich), GM Carey (OxfU), HW Finlinson (Black), F Mitchell (CamU), FO Poole (OxfU), C Thomas (Barn, t), WE Tucker (CamU), SMJ Woods (capt, Bridg/Black).
Attendance: 8,000   *Referee*: DG Findlay (Scotland)

Saturday 9 March 1895 at Athletic Ground, Richmond
ENGLAND 3 *Back*: JF Byrne (Mose, pg). *Three-quarters*: JHC Fegan (Black), WB Thomson (Black), TH Dobson (Brad), EM Baker (OxfU). *Half-backs*: RH Cattell (Mose), EW Taylor (Rock) *Forwards*: WE Bromet (Rich), GM Carey (OxfU), HW Finlinson (Black), F Mitchell (CamU), FO Poole (OxfU), C Thomas (Barn), WE Tucker (CamU), SMJ Woods (capt, Bridg/Black).
SCOTLAND 6 *Back*: AR Smith (OxfU). *Half-backs*: R Welsh (Wat), W Neilson (LonS), JJ Gowans (LonS), GT Campbell (LonS). *Quarter-backs*: WP Donaldson (WoS), JW Simpson

(RHSFP). *Forwards*: WB Cownie (Wat), JH Dods (EdinA), WR Gibson (RHSFP), WMC McEwan (EdinA), RG Macmillan (capt, LonS), JN Millar (WoS), GT Neilson (WoS, t, pg), TM Scott (Haw).
Attendance: 20,000   *Referee*: WH Wilkins (Wales)

Other results
Scotland 5, Wales 4
Scotland 6, Ireland 0
Wales 5, Ireland 3

Final table

	P	W	D	L	For	Agst
Scotland	3	3	0	0	17	7
England	3	2	0	1	23	15
Wales	3	1	0	2	15	22
Ireland	3	0	0	3	6	17

England versus Wales at Blackheath, 4th January 1896.
Illustrated Sporting and Dramatic News, 1896

1895-1896

THE YORKSHIRE CUP: LATE WITHDRAWALS
The annual pre-season draw for the Yorkshire Cup ties was held at the Green Dragon Hotel, Leeds, on 2nd August. But, with the impending breakaway of clubs from the Rugby Union, there were significant absentees, the *Yorkshire Post* reporting: 'There was a very moderate attendance of club representatives, and none of the twelve clubs formerly comprising the [Yorkshire] Senior Competition were represented, nor was any communication received from them. As the County Committee decided on Monday [29th July 1895] to accept the resignations from the Union the officials had now no option but to proceed with the draw without including those clubs.'[180] The absent Senior Competition clubs referred to were Batley, Bradford, Brighouse Rangers, Dewsbury, Halifax, Huddersfield, Hull, Hunslet, Leeds, Liversedge, Manningham, and Wakefield Trinity. Despite their omission there were still 104 entries, although this was to reduce considerably during the forthcoming seasons.

ESTABLISHING THE NORTHERN UNION
The most momentous event to date in the Rugby code took place at the George Hotel, Huddersfield, on Thursday evening, 29th August, when 21 Lancashire and Yorkshire club representatives met to establish the Northern Rugby Football Union. The clubs involved were Batley, Bradford, Brighouse Rangers, Broughton Rangers, Dewsbury, Halifax,

Huddersfield, Hull, Hunslet, Leeds, Leigh, Liversedge, Manningham, Oldham, Rochdale Hornets, St Helens, Tyldesley, Wakefield Trinity, Warrington, Widnes, and Wigan. The *Huddersfield Chronicle* reported: 'After full discussion, which took place in private, it was decided to form a Northern Rugby Football Union, on the principle of payment for *bona fide* broken time only. Stockport were [also] admitted members of the union. The resignations to the English Rugby Union were handed in from 20 clubs, Dewsbury being the exception. It was resolved that each club represented at the meeting should sign a membership list, with the exception of Dewsbury, who were given till Tuesday to decide. A sub-committee of 10 were appointed to consider the bye-laws and rules of the Union. It was decided that meetings of the committee should be held alternatively in Huddersfield and Manchester. It was further resolved that there should be a Yorkshire Senior Competition, a Lancashire Senior Competition, and a Northern Rugby League consisting of 22 clubs, providing that Dewsbury agrees to join.'[181]

THE NORTHERN UNION: DEWSBURY WITHDRAW, RUNCORN JOIN

Dewsbury, although represented at the historic breakaway meeting at the George Hotel, decided to withdraw from the proposed Northern Union. The *Sporting Life* commented: 'Some little sensation was caused in Rugby Union circles in Yorkshire and Lancashire on Tuesday afternoon [3rd September] when it became known that the Dewsbury club had come to a decision not to throw in its lot with the revolted senior clubs in the Northern Rugby Union. It must be remembered that the president of the club, Mr. Mark Newsome, is also the president of the Yorkshire Rugby Union, and doubtless his influence would have considerable weight with the [Dewsbury] committee. The secession of Dewsbury has let in Runcorn, which has been elected by the [Northern Union] committee to membership of the new Union. The action of the Runcorn club has excited some surprise in the North, as it was not supposed that they would join the Union. They had always set their faces against professionalism, and the fact that they see no objection to joining the new Union should allay the fears of many other wavering clubs.'[182]

THE NORTHERN UNION: THOSE THAT REMAIN

Of the 22 clubs that founded the Northern Union, 14 still exist today: Batley, Halifax, Huddersfield, Hull, Hunslet, Leeds, Leigh, Oldham, Rochdale Hornets, St Helens, Wakefield Trinity, Warrington, Widnes and Wigan. Of the others, Bradford (who transferred to Association football in 1907) were replaced by Bradford Northern (now Bradford Bulls). The remaining seven, who no longer exist, are: Brighouse Rangers (founded 1878, defunct 1906), Broughton Rangers (founded 1877, renamed Belle Vue Rangers 1946, defunct 1955), Liversedge (founded 1877, renamed Cleckheaton 1902, defunct 1905), Manningham (founded 1876, transferred to Association football as Bradford City in 1903), Runcorn (founded 1876, defunct 1918), Stockport (founded 1881, defunct 1903), Tyldesley (founded 1879, defunct 1901).

THE CUMBERLAND SENIOR LEAGUE STARTS

The first match in the new Cumberland (Rugby Union) Senior League was on Saturday 21st September when Aspatria defeated visitors Maryport 13-0, three further fixtures taking place the following weekend. The creation of a league had been a talking point through the summer months before positive steps were taken during August. Eight clubs entered although the competition did not receive official backing at the start; County officials appeared cautious in the aftermath of the leading Lancashire and Yorkshire clubs breaking away to form the Northern Union and the Rugby Football Union had also not given approval.

CUMBERLAND CLUBS LOYAL TO THE RUGBY FOOTBALL UNION

The Cumberland Rugby Union Committee met at the Station Hotel, Workington, on 12th October, when the commitment of its clubs was discussed following further rumours of possible defections to the Northern Union should a league not be officially ratified. A circular had been sent to the clubs by Mr. R. Westray, the Cumberland President, to ascertain their desire, or otherwise, to form a league (despite the fact that the Cumberland Senior League had already begun in September) and to determine their loyalty should it not be sanctioned. The replies from the clubs was read out by Mr. Westray. The *West Cumberland Times* reported: 'From this correspondence [the committee] had the most conclusive proof that the clubs remained sound in their support of the executive. The sixteen leading clubs in the county had given all the assurance desired. This correspondence proved to him [Mr. Westray] that the allegation that strong feeling existed on the part of certain clubs in favour of severing their membership if a senior league was refused, was a myth, and never existed. This action of the clubs would give proof [that] instead of there being a crisis in this county, and a possibility of a split, nothing of the kind had ever existed, and that they stood stronger than ever.'[183] After its uncertain start, the league went ahead, Seaton winning the competition.

THE NORTHERN UNION: MOST PRAISEWORTHY

With the opening matches played, the *Manchester Guardian* offered an early verdict on the breakaway: 'So far as the Northern Union has gone, we have only to repeat what we have previously said, that its professions and performances have been most praiseworthy. The matches have been excellently managed, the play has been of good class, and the first symptom of revolt in the direction of open professionalism has been promptly suppressed. If the Union is only strong enough to live up to its ideal, it will establish a new era in the game.'[184]

THE RUGBY FOOTBALL UNION
MEET THE FOOTBALL ASSOCIATION

Representatives of the Rugby Football Union and the Football Association met at the offices of the latter in Chancery Lane, London, on 20th November. The *Manchester Guardian* reported: 'The conference had reference to the existing dispute between the Rugby Football Union and the recently formed Northern Union, and its primary object was to arrive at a definite understanding as to the course of action which would be pursued by the Football Association in their attitude towards players of the seceding clubs and members belonging to the Association sections of the same clubs, a question which on the face of it is an extremely difficult one to deal with. The proceedings were strictly private, and the representatives of the press were informed, on making inquiries, that no information whatever would be tendered to them.'[185]

THE RUGBY FOOTBALL UNION AND FOOTBALL ASSOCIATION: AN AGREEMENT

The Football Association appeared to have reached an understanding with the Rugby Football Union based on reports of a meeting by the former at their Chancery Lane offices in London on 16th December. The *Manchester Guardian* commented: 'The effect of the agreement is that in future each ruling body shall recognise each other's suspensions, whether referring to players, clubs, or grounds. In the event of a member or club being expelled from either body, the other shall not grant permission to play under its rules until a period of twelve months has expired. In cases where there are breaches of the laws after a club has resigned membership of either body, and such resignation has been accepted – and this is the point which affects the Northern Union – the embargo of the other body is not to apply.'[186]

The Lancashire team that took on the Rest of England in Manchester on 18th April 1891, having secured the county championship for the first time. Back: T Craven, T Rothwell, J Berry, W McCutcheon, J Pyke, T Kent, J Strang. Middle: EH Flower, T Whittaker, J Valentine, W Atkinson, W Melledew, T Coop. Front: E Bullough, D Gwynn, W Cross, RP Wilson. Note that Strang and Flower did not take part in this match.

Aspatria 1890-91 with the Cumberland County Cup, a competition they won six times during the Victorian era. Back; J Forester (treasurer), T Allison, JW Cowan, T Farrel (president), Jim Davidson, J Stanger, G Bell (secretary). Middle: J Rumney, J Mumberson, T Grieve, R Mumberson, J Harker, Joe Nelson. Front: W Berwick, T Docker, Joseph Saul, JH Tweddle, Jerry Saul, L Beattie.

Salford 1890-91. Back: H Clegg, T Kent, J Birch, J McVittie, JH Tune, F Knowles, J Shaw, S Whiteley (treasurer). Middle: J Horricks, (vice-president), A Barrett, JW Roberts, F Miles, D Wellwood (chairman), H Eagles, E Barrett, T King, J Higson (secretary). Front: G Tonge, S Walch. Salford subsequently won the inaugural Lancashire Club Championship in 1892-93.

Paul Clauss was a German-born three-quarter who represented Scotland six times, qualifying via his education at Loretto School in East Lothian. Known for his speed and strength, he later played for Oxford University during which time he was included in the 1891 tour of South Africa. After settling in Cheshire he joined Birkenhead Park, his residency earning a place in the Cheshire county team with 12 appearances from 1892 to 1895.

Edgar Redman, who began his career with the Yeadon and Guiseley clubs, gained the attention of Yorkshire's selectors after joining Manningham in 1891, making 12 appearances for the county and one for the North. In 1893 he transferred his allegiance to Leicester where he became captain and, rated one of the best forwards in the midlands area, represented Midland Counties.

Fred Clegg of Manningham, described as a forward who liked to 'open up the game', made 11 appearances for Yorkshire under Rugby Union rules from 1892 to 1895. A member of the Manningham team that won the first Northern Union championship in 1895-96, he gained five more Yorkshire caps under that code.

Harry Varley was a highly rated 'smart and strong' half-back who represented England against Scotland in 1892, claiming the rare distinction of appearing for Yorkshire (7 times) whilst with Liversedge and Lancashire (also 7) after transferring to Oldham during August 1893. When Oldham joined the Northern Union he continued to play for them until 1897, adding four more Lancashire appearances under that code. He subsequently turned out for Leeds during the 1900-01 season.

Cheshire's team versus Lancashire at Birkenhead on 5th November 1892. The players (in kit) are, standing: PR Clauss, AJ Chadwick, EH Morley, JH Crompton. Seated: S Houghton, F Drinkwater, O Hughes, P Riley, E Elliott, WA Williams, FP Jones. On ground: H Williams, J Speet, WB Smith, S Abram.

The Westmorland team that opposed Cumberland in Kendal on 3rd December 1892.
Back: G Webster (secretary), J Newton, GH Bell, R Nicholson, J Berry, T Nicholson, JK Robinson.
Middle: RH Moore, W Whiteley, W Wilson, WJ Parsons, J Allen, RS Winskill, T Hine.
Front: JH Thompson, R Hill.

Yorkshire's county championship-winning team that met the Rest of England at Headingley on 20th February 1892. Back: JT Toothill, E Dewhirst, W Nichol, D Jowett, F Wood, W Goldthorpe. Middle: H Bradshaw, H Varley, WE Bromet, T Broadley, E Redman, B Kilner (president, standing right). Front: A Briggs, J Dyson, RE Lockwood, AE Goldthorpe.

Millom 1891-92, first winners of the North Western League. Back: W Teasdale (committee), J Fawcett, J Burns, W Leck, J Dixon, T Whelan, M Boase, W Atkinson (treasurer). Middle: I Moore, J Davidson, J McGuire, JT Bell, S Warburton. Front: AG Fitzwilliam, TH Hodgson, W Wilkinson, S Northmore.

Swinton 1892-93, runner-up in the first Lancashire Club Championship. Back: A Sharples, H Murray, S Hall, T Hallam, CH Horley, T Rothwell, P Chapman. Middle: JT Lewis, H Brockbank, J Valentine, W Bumby, W Winterbottom, W Pearson. Front: N Hotchkiss, G Sharples.

Kendal Hornets 1891-92. Back: A George (umpire), E Railton, E Braithwaite, J Armstrong, J Allen, RS Winskill, T Nicholson, W O'Loughlin (umpire). Middle: W Wilson, W Hall, E Wilson, F Heap, R Simm, J Mitchell. Front: JH Thompson, W Whiteley, WJ Parsons. Only one player in this photograph (Mitchell) did not represent Westmorland, such was the Hornets dominance within the county.

The Durham team that opposed Yorkshire at Headingley on 11th November 1893.
Back: TM Swinburne (president), T Faulkner, FC Lohden, W Yiend, J Geenty, A Hill (honorary secretary). Middle: R Edwards, J Hall, RCF Crow, FHR Alderson, T Burt, W Wainford, RF Oakes. Front: S Morfitt, F Marston, GH Philbrick, F Hindle.

St Helens 1893-94, winners of the Lancashire Club Championship Second Class.
Back: TC Wilcock (chairman), J Appleton, E Ashcroft, W Whiteley, J Brownbill, W Wilson, J Gladwin, T Sudlow, J Edwards (committee). Middle (seated): T Foulkes, R Doherty, F Little, J Rennie. Front (kneeling): P Dale, W Cross, S Jones, J Graham.

Leigh 1893-94, runner-up in the Lancashire Championship Second Class and earning promotion via a play-off. Standing: E France, J Cheetham, J Eccleston, J Clark (honorary secretary, in background), P Taylor, J France, J Pemberton. Seated: F Green, C Wilding, A Wallwork, T Anderton, T Coop, G Boardman, R MacMasters. Front: J Shovelton, J Shaw, W Ewan.

Milford Sutcliffe made an early impression with Huddersfield following his first appearance as a 17-year-old in September 1894, his Yorkshire debut following one month later. Described as an industrious forward he played a further four times for Yorkshire at rugby union, adding another ten games under Northern Union rules. He later became the Huddersfield chairman.

Tom Dobson rose to prominence with Bradford having transferred from the Bowling club in February 1893. A speedy strong-running three-quarter and excellent passer of the ball, he had a breakthrough season in 1894-95, playing for Yorkshire five times and once each for the North and England. That was Bradford's last campaign before joining the Northern Union, Dobson continuing to play for them until 1900, appearing in their 1898 Challenge Cup Final line-up.

Halifax 1893-94, winners of the Yorkshire County Cup for a record fifth time. Back: J Riley, I Webster, A Wilson, B Mellor, J Knowles, EF Fookes, JH Bromwich. Middle: DG Wheelwright, A Robertshaw, WJ Jackson, O Fletcher, F Firth, H Bottomley. Front: A Rigg, J Arnold, GF Dickenson, A Chorley.

THE JAMES BROTHERS REINSTATED

The reinstatement of Welsh international half-back brothers David and Evan James was discussed at a Rugby Football Union meeting, held at the Queen's Hotel, Leeds, on 30th January. The pair had left the Swansea club in 1892 and played for Broughton Rangers until banned as professionals. After a lengthy discussion, it was announced: 'The Committee have decided that on the direct application of and in deference to the wishes of the Welsh Union, the brothers James are reinstated.'[187] The brothers again played for Swansea and Wales but returned to Broughton Rangers, then members of the Northern Union, in 1899.

THE YORKSHIRE CUP SUFFERS

The loss of the leading Yorkshire clubs had a severe impact on the Yorkshire (Rugby Union) Cup. The *Leeds Mercury* commented: 'It would be an exaggeration to state that the results of the matches in the first round of the Yorkshire Challenge Cup competition were awaited with the feverish anxiety manifested in previous years. The contest unquestionably suffers by reason of the absence of the clubs now to be found in the ranks of the Northern Union. It seems strange when looking over the list of organisations engaged in the fray to find so many familiar names wanting. Despite this great drawback, however, the struggle for the possession of the much-prized trophy will no doubt be fought to an issue with some approach to the enthusiasm we were accustomed to of old.'[188]

YORKSHIRE CUP SEMI-FINAL REPLAY ABANDONED

When Featherstone met West Riding (Leeds) in a replayed Yorkshire (Rugby Union) Cup semi-final at Barley Mow, Bramley, on Wednesday 15th April, the game ended in dramatic circumstances. In front of a 10,000 crowd the referee (Mr. E. Dunderdale of Keighley) ended the match 15 minutes into the second half with West Riding leading 3-0. Later that evening a special Yorkshire Committee meeting was held at the Green Dragon Hotel, Leeds, to consider what action to take. It was reported that the referee dismissed two Featherstone players, each for 'mistreating' an opponent. After the first incident an appeal by the referee to the Featherstone captain only resulted in 'abusive bad language being used to him'. During the interval the official addressed both teams 'but the Featherstone captain would not listen [and] more insulting language was used'. When the second sending off occurred he received 'more insulting language from the captain, and he accordingly declared the game at an end'. The committee awarded the match to West Riding. The *Huddersfield*

Chronicle gave a damming verdict: 'What an exhibition of sportsmanship we had in the semi-final, which we are told is played by clubs running under the strictly amateur banner. I don't remember such a disgraceful episode happening before, even when the clubs, now contemptuously dubbed "broken timers," were in the hunt for the "old tin pot".'[189]

SALFORD AND SWINTON JOIN THE NORTHERN UNION
Salford elected to resign from the Rugby Football Union at a meeting of its members held at the Hope Board School, Liverpool Street, Salford, on Thursday 16th April. Near-neighbours Swinton arrived at the same decision two weeks later during a meeting at St Peter's School on Thursday 30th April. Both clubs successfully applied for membership of the Northern Union.

FATAL SEQUEL TO COUNTY MATCH
Cumberland Rugby Union forward John Bell (Carlisle) died following injuries received in the match with Yorkshire at Workington on 8th February. Reportedly, he suffered a severe head injury following which he received treatment at Cumberland Infirmary. He eventually returned to his home, but passed away on 26th April as a result of the accident.[190]

BRAMLEY JOIN THE NORTHERN UNION
At their annual meeting on 29th May 1896, the members of the Bramley club, based in Leeds, elected to join the Northern Union for 1896-97.[191]

THE 1896 ENGLAND TOUR
During 1896 a second tour of South Africa was undertaken lasting from July to September, the Anglo-Irish party being managed by Rugby Football Union President and former Manchester player Roger Walker. The tour party, which was mostly student-based, had 21 players, including nine Irishmen and seven with north of England connections; Sydney Bell (born Newcastle-upon-Tyne), John Hammond (Skipton-born tour captain who had been in the 1891 squad in South Africa), George Lee (birthplace unknown, played for Hull, Rockcliff and Northumberland), Osbert Mackie (born Wakefield, previously played for Wakefield Trinity and Yorkshire), William Mortimer (born Warrington, played for Liverpool and Lancashire), Matthew Mullineux (born Barton, near Salford), Charlie Robinson (birthplace unknown, played for Percy Park and Northumberland). The nine Irish-born players were Cecil Boyd, Larry Bulger, Andrew Clinch, Thomas Crean, Robert Johnston, James Magee,

Louis Magee, Arthur Meares, and Jim Sealy. Another non-Englishman was Cuth Mullins who was born in South Africa. Despite the strong Irish presence the tourists were called England or 'the English' and are, therefore, referred to in the statistics section as England.

1895-1896 STATISTICS

NORTHERN UNION

NORTHERN RUGBY FOOTBALL LEAGUE

Final table	P	W	D	L	For	Agst	Pts
Manningham	42	33	0	9	367	158	66
Halifax	42	30	5	7	312	139	65
Runcorn	42	24	8	10	314	143	56
Oldham	42	27	2	13	374	194	56
Brighouse Rangers	42	22	9	11	247	129	53
Tyldesley	42	21	8	13	260	164	50
Hunslet	42	24	2	16	279	207	50
Hull	42	23	3	16	259	158	49
Leigh	42	21	4	17	214	269	46
Wigan	42	19	7	16	245	147	45
Bradford	42	18	9	15	254	175	45
Leeds	42	20	3	19	258	247	43
Warrington	42	17	5	20	198	240	39
St Helens*	42	15	8	19	195	230	36
Liversedge	42	15	4	23	261	355	34
Widnes	42	14	4	24	177	323	32
Stockport	42	12	8	22	171	315	32
Batley	42	12	7	23	137	298	31
Wakefield Trinity	42	13	4	25	156	318	30
Huddersfield	42	10	4	28	194	274	24
Broughton Rangers	42	8	8	26	165	244	24
Rochdale Hornets	42	4	8	30	78	388	16

*Two points deducted for using ineligible player

LANCASHIRE SENIOR COMPETITION

Final table	P	W	D	L	For	Agst	Pts
Runcorn	20	12	4	4	138	46	28
Oldham	20	13	2	5	176	70	28
Tyldesley	20	11	3	6	119	75	25
Wigan	20	10	4	6	117	55	24
Leigh	20	10	3	7	91	87	23
Warrington	20	9	4	7	87	84	22
St Helens*	20	7	5	8	94	97	17
Widnes	20	8	1	11	74	125	17
Stockport	20	5	5	10	75	127	15
Rochdale Hornets	20	3	5	12	45	162	11
Broughton Rangers	20	1	6	13	32	120	8

*Two points deducted for using ineligible player

Play-off to decide first place
Runcorn 6, Oldham 5 (at Wheater's Field, Broughton)
(Runcorn declared Lancashire Senior Competition winner)

YORKSHIRE SENIOR COMPETITION

Final table	P	W	D	L	For	Agst	Pts
Manningham	20	17	0	3	161	64	34
Halifax	20	13	2	5	133	76	28
Hunslet	20	12	2	6	119	76	26
Hull	20	10	1	9	124	67	21
Brighouse Rangers	20	9	3	8	95	60	21
Leeds	20	9	2	9	83	118	20
Bradford	20	6	5	9	74	86	17
Liversedge	20	7	2	11	112	138	16
Wakefield Trinity	20	6	1	13	77	168	13
Batley	20	5	3	12	54	129	13
Huddersfield	20	5	1	14	83	133	11

Milestones & Stats 1869-1901

COUNTY CHAMPIONSHIP

Monday 21 October 1895 at Edgeley Park, Stockport
CHESHIRE 0 *Back*: F Saville (Stock). *Three-quarters*: TH Warder (Run), G Robinson (Run), J Worsley (Stock), W Bailey (Stock). *Half-backs*: S Abrams (Run), J Faulkner (capt, Run). *Forwards*: H Farmer (Run), W Faulkner (Run), T Gibson (Stock), J Langley (Run), R Morton (Stock), J Mottershead (Stock), A Taylor (Run), C Wrigley (Stock).
LANCASHIRE 6 *Back*: J Winstanley (Wig). *Three-quarters*: F Barber (War, t), S Lees (Old), H Chapman (BroR, t), R Doherty (StH). *Half-backs*: A Lees (Old), H Varley (capt, Old). *Forwards*: E Bonser (Old), W Briers (StH), J Brown (Wig), W Nevins (War), W Roberts (Tyl), T Smith (Lei), W Unsworth (Wig), J Worthington (Tyl).
Attendance: 3,000   *Referee*: H Hutchinson (Wakefield)

Monday 25 November 1895 at Headingley, Leeds
YORKSHIRE 5 *Back*: GE Lorimer (Mann). *Three-quarters*: F Firth (Hal, t), WH Keepings (Hal), FW Cooper (Brad, c), A Boothroyd (Hud). *Half-backs*: JA Rigg (capt, Hal), R Wood (Livs). *Forwards*: A Barraclough (Mann), R Greig (Lee), Jack Riley (Hal), RE Sugden (BrigR), W Sugden (Brad), M Sutcliffe (Hud), O Walsh (Hun), W Walton (Wak).
CHESHIRE 9 *Back*: F Saville (Stock, 2pg). *Three-quarters*: TH Warder (Run), G Robinson (Run), J Worsley (Stock, t), H Myers (Run). *Half-backs*: J Faulkner (capt, Run), H Norris (Stock). *Forwards*: H Farmer (Run), W Faulkner (Run), T Gibson (Stock), J Langley (Run), R Morton (Stock), J Mottershead (Stock), A Taylor (Run), C Wrigley (Stock).
Attendance: 3,500   *Referee*: JH Smith (Widnes)

Saturday 7 December 1895 at Watersheddings, Oldham
LANCASHIRE 0 *Back*: J Winstanley (Wig). *Three-quarters*: F Barber (War), S Lees (Old), H Chapman (BroR), J Hurst (Old). *Half-backs*: A Lees (Old), H Varley (capt, Old). *Forwards*: E Bonser (Old), W Briers (StH), T Cleminson (BroR), A Hill (RochH), W Nevins (War), W Unsworth (Wig), J Worthington (Tyl), W Yates (Wig).
YORKSHIRE 8 *Back*: GE Lorimer (Mann). *Three-quarters*: B Sharpe (Livs, c), L Brooke (BrigR), A Boothroyd (Hud), F Firth (Hal). *Half-backs*: JA Rigg (capt, Hal, t), R Wood (Livs). *Forwards*: F Clegg (Mann), L Donkin (Hull), R Greig (Lee), TH Hughes (BrigR, t), Jack Riley (Hal), M Sutcliffe (Hud), O Walsh (Hun), W Walton (Wak).
Attendance: 9,059   *Referee*: J Bruckshaw (Stockport)

Wednesday 29 January 1896 at Wheater's Field, Broughton
LANCASHIRE 3 *Back*: T Coop (Lei). *Three-quarters*: F Barber (War), S Lees (Old), H Chapman (BroR, t), T Sudlow (StH). *Half-backs*: A Lees (Old), H Varley (capt, Old). *Forwards*: E Bonser (Old), W Briers (StH), T Cleminson (BroR), J Johnson (Wid), W Robinson (BroR), P Taylor (Lei), F Uttley (RochH), W Yates (Wig).
CHESHIRE 0 *Back*: S Houghton (Run). *Three-quarters*: J Butterworth (Run), H Myers (Run), P Sands (Stock), J Worsley (Stock). *Half-backs*: J Faulkner (capt, Run), G Robinson (Run). *Forwards*: H Farmer (Run), W Faulkner (Run), T Gibson (Stock), J Langley (Run), G Moores (Run), J Roberts (Stock), S Walker (Run), C Wrigley (Stock).
Attendance: 4,000   *Referee*: H Hutchinson (Wakefield)

Wednesday 12 February 1896 at Irwell Lane, Runcorn
CHESHIRE 6 *Back*: F Saville (Stock). *Three-quarters*: TH Warder (Run), H Myers (Run), P Sands (Stock), J Worsley (Stock, t). *Half-backs*: J Faulkner (Run), H Norris (Stock). *Forwards*: H Farmer (Run), W Faulkner (Run, t), A Garside (Stock), T Gibson (Stock), J Langley (Run), J Roberts (Stock), S Walker (Run), C Wrigley (Stock).
YORKSHIRE 16 *Back*: E Abbey (BrigR). *Three-quarters*: FW Cooper (Brad, t, 2c), L Brooke (BrigR), W Hannah (Hun), F Firth (Hal, 2t). *Half-backs*: R Sunderland (Mann), R Wood (capt, Livs, t). *Forwards*: F Clegg (Mann), L Donkin (Hull), R Greig (Lee), TH Hughes (BrigR), Jack Riley (Hal), M Sutcliffe (Hud), O Walsh (Hun), W Walton (Wak).
Attendance: 2,000   *Referee*: JH Smith (Widnes)

Saturday 29 February 1896 at Fartown, Huddersfield
YORKSHIRE 3 *Back*: GE Lorimer (Mann). *Three-quarters*: AE Goldthorpe (Hun), J Brown (Mann), F Firth (Hal), A Boothroyd (Hud, t). *Half-backs*: JA Rigg (capt, Hal), R Wood (Livs). *Forwards*: F Clegg (Mann), L Donkin (Hull), R Greig (Lee), TH Hughes (BrigR), Jack Riley (Hal), M Shackleton (Bat), O Walsh (Hun), W Walton (Wak).
LANCASHIRE 8 *Back*: T Coop (capt, Lei). *Three-quarters*: G Berry (BroR), S Lees (Old, t, c), T Anderton (Lei), T Sudlow (StH). *Half-backs*: J Berry (Tyl), W Berry (Tyl). *Forwards*: E Bonser (Old), W Briers (StH, t), T Cleminson (BroR), R Edwards (Old), W Robinson (BroR), P Taylor (Lei), F Uttley (RochH), J Wothington (Tyl).
Attendance: 5,300   *Referee*: W Jones (Runcorn)

Final table

	P	W	D	L	For	Agst	Pts
Lancashire	4	3	0	1	17	11	6
Yorkshire	4	2	0	2	32	23	4
Cheshire	4	1	0	3	15	30	2

RUGBY UNION

CUMBERLAND SENIOR LEAGUE

Final table	P	W	D	L	For	Agst	Pts
Seaton	14	12	0	2	181	24	24
Aspatria	13	11	0	2	134	18	22
Workington	14	8	1	5	73	52	17
Maryport	13	7	0	6	103	67	14
Brookland Rovers	13	4	2	7	33	76	10
Whitehaven	11	3	1	7	28	54	7
Whitehaven Recreation	14	2	2	10	30	130	6
Egremont Hornets	12	1	2	9	14	175	4

Note: Fixtures incomplete due to postponements.

LANCASHIRE CLUB CHAMPIONSHIP FIRST CLASS

Final table	P	W	D	L	For	Agst	Pts
Morecambe	20	18	1	1	223	40	37
Ulverston	20	16	0	4	164	56	32
Lancaster	20	12	3	5	153	83	27
Swinton	20	10	5	5	94	49	25
Barrow	18	8	3	7	112	51	19
Rochdale St Clements	19	8	3	8	85	73	19
Crompton	20	8	1	11	109	120	17
Walkden	19	5	3	11	67	152	13
Salford	20	5	1	14	42	111	11
Blackley Rangers	17	4	1	12	35	146	9
Blackley	19	1	1	17	29	232	3
Record expunged:							
Pemberton	15	4	2	9	65	134	10

Note 1: Fixtures incomplete due to postponements.
Note 2: Pemberton disbanded (Mar 1896).

LANCASHIRE CLUB CHAMPIONSHIP SECOND CLASS

Final table	P	W	D	L	For	Agst	Pts
Mossley	14	8	2	4	45	26	18
Barton	14	7	2	5	70	40	16
Radcliffe	14	5	6	3	35	23	16
Leigh Shamrocks	14	7	2	5	38	49	16
Littleborough	14	7	1	6	48	38	15
Werneth	14	5	2	7	49	56	12
Castleton Moor	14	3	4	7	28	60	10
Whitworth	14	3	3	8	29	50	9
Record expunged:							
Boothstown	15	0	2	13	12	139	2

Note 1: Boothstown expelled (April 1896) for not fulfilling final fixture.

NORTH WESTERN LEAGUE

Final table	P	W	D	L	For	Agst	Pts
Morecambe	12	11	1	0	84	20	23
Millom	12	9	2	1	136	21	20
Ulverston	12	5	3	4	102	35	13
Barrow	12	4	2	6	95	58	10
Lancaster	12	4	2	6	79	62	10
Kendal Hornets	12	2	2	8	35	135	6
Askam	12	1	0	11	21	221	2

WESTMORLAND JUNIOR LEAGUE

Final table	P	W	D	L	For	Agst	Pts
Staveley	8	5	2	1	52	6	12
Ambleside	8	5	1	2	46	17	11
Kirkby Lonsdale	8	4	2	2	49	25	10
Windermere*	7	2	1	4	11	34	3
Burneside	7	0	0	7	9	85	0
Record expunged:							
Holme Wanderers	2	0	0	2	8	24	0

*Two points deducted for using ineligible player.
Note 1: Holme withdrew (Oct 1895) having lost several players.
Note 2: Windermere v Burneside ordered to be replayed but not subsequently played.

YORKSHIRE COMPETITION NO. 1

Final table	P	W	D	L	For	Agst	Pts
Leeds Parish Church	26	22	2	2	271	53	46
Castleford	26	19	1	6	345	66	39
Morley	26	18	3	5	206	88	39
Bramley	26	16	2	8	171	99	34
Elland	26	13	5	8	174	87	31
Heckmondwike	26	11	3	12	98	120	25
Wortley	26	9	6	11	132	125	24
York	26	11	2	13	128	124	24
Holbeck	26	10	2	14	143	158	22
Pudsey*	26	10	6	10	172	156	20
Otley	26	9	1	16	68	182	19
Dewsbury	26	7	4	15	75	265	18
Bowling	26	5	0	21	100	287	10
Cleckheaton	26	2	3	21	34	307	7

*Six points deducted; two for inducing players, two for using ineligible players, two for providing incorrect list of players.

YORKSHIRE COMPETITION NO. 2

Final table	P	W	D	L	For	Agst	Pts
Shipley	26	19	4	3	207	43	42
Hull Kingston Rovers	26	19	1	6	273	81	39
West Riding	26	19	1	6	245	64	39
Sowerby Bridge	26	17	3	6	191	68	37
Keighley	26	14	5	7	177	77	33
Normanton	26	14	2	10	132	92	30
Stanningley	26	10	4	12	115	159	24
Goole	26	10	4	12	117	171	24
Bowling Old Lane	26	9	3	14	114	154	21
Ossett	26	9	3	14	136	138	21
Outwood Church	26	8	5	13	69	127	21
Mirfield	26	6	3	17	124	299	15
Alverthorpe	26	5	3	18	49	174	13
Armley	26	2	1	23	21	323	5

Promotion Test Match
Shipley 6, Cleckheaton 0 (at West Riding FC ground, Meanwood Road, Leeds)
(Shipley promoted to Yorkshire No. 1, Cleckheaton relegated)

YORKSHIRE COMPETITION NO. 3 (GROUP A)

Final table	P	W	D	L	For	Agst	Pts
Idle	24	19	2	3	177	58	40
Silsden	24	17	4	3	259	56	38
Skipton	24	18	2	4	221	43	38
Yeadon	23	15	3	5	193	64	33
Harrogate	24	11	3	10	83	156	25
Bingley	23	11	3	9	116	89	25
Keighley Shamrocks	24	10	2	12	90	118	22
Farsley	23	8	3	12	79	110	19
Horsforth	24	7	2	15	90	163	16
Guiseley	23	6	4	13	65	106	16
Windhill	24	5	4	15	68	199	14
Saltaire	23	2	4	17	44	196	8
Keighley Zingari*	23	5	2	16	46	173	6

*Six points deducted for using ineligible players on three occasions.
Note: Results not found for Bingley v Yeadon, Keighley Zingari v Guiseley, Saltaire v Farsley; probably not played.

YORKSHIRE COMPETITION NO. 3 (GROUP B)

Final table	P	W	D	L	For	Agst	Pts
Mytholmroyd	20	15	2	3	148	37	32
Luddendenfoot	20	15	1	4	206	40	31
Paddock	20	12	2	6	153	56	26
Hebden Bridge	20	11	4	5	124	78	26
Birstall	18	9	3	6	119	64	21
Milnsbridge	20	9	1	10	77	98	19
Todmorden	20	8	2	10	111	92	18
Wyke*	20	7	4	9	73	95	16
Horbury	18	4	1	13	53	131	9
Low Moor St Mark's*	18	3	4	11	58	230	8
Brownroyd Recreation	18	1	0	17	26	227	2
Record expunged:							
Kirkburton	13	0	1	12	6	186	1
Wibsey	15	2	3	10	35	130	7

*Two points deducted for using ineligible players
Note 1: Kirkburton (Dec 1895), Wibsey (Jan 1896) disbanded.
Note 2: Results not found for Birstall v Brownroyd Recreation, Brownroyd Recreation v Low Moor St Mark's, Horbury v Low Moor St Mark's, Birstall v Horbury; probably not played.

Yorkshire Competition No. 3 Final
Idle 5, Mytholmroyd 3 (at Albert Road, Saltaire)
(Idle declared Yorkshire Competition No. 3 winner)

Promotion Test Match
Idle v Armley
Armley withdrew ('practically defunct'); Idle promoted to Competition No. 2.

CUMBERLAND COUNTY CHALLENGE CUP (11 entries)
Try – 3 points; conversion – 2; penalty goal – 3; drop-goal, field goal, goal from mark – 4.

First Round
Carlisle 5, Whitehaven 0
Maryport 3, Brookland Rovers 3 (aet)
Whitehaven Recreation 7, Cockermouth 0
Byes: Aspatria, Egremont Hornets, Penrith United, Seaton, Workington

First Round Replay
Brookland Rovers 0, Maryport 3 (aet)

Second Round
Egremont Hornets 3, Penrith United 0
Maryport 9, Carlisle 0
Seaton 0, Aspatria 6
Whitehaven Recreation 3, Workington 4

Semi-finals
Aspatria 14, Workington 0
(at Sandy Lonning, Maryport)
Maryport 5, Egremont Hornets 0
(at Whitehaven Cricket Ground)

FINAL
Saturday 11 April 1896 at Lonsdale Park, Workington
ASPATRIA 13 *Back*: T Docker. *Three-quarters*: W Berwick, W Skelton (gm), JH Blaylock, T Routledge. *Half-backs*: Joe Nelson (t), John Nelson. *Forwards*: T Blacklock, T Blaylock, Jim Davidson (capt), T Grieve (t), J Mumberson, R Mumberson, G Steele (t), J Walker.
MARYPORT 4 *Back*: J Addison. *Three-quarters*: W Hodgson, JH Timney, M Humphrey (capt), D Semple (gm). *Half-backs*: J Bell, J Patterson. *Forwards*: R Barnes, J Bethwaite, R Kirkbride, S McCormick, W Orr, J Rogerson, WT Smith, J Thompson.
Attendance: 3,000   *Referee*: JM Mawson (Barrow)

DURHAM COUNTY CHALLENGE CUP (18 entries)
Try – 3 points; conversion – 2; penalty goal – 3; drop-goal, field goal, goal from mark – 4.

First Round
Ryton 0, Blackhill Rovers (Consett) 13
Sunderland Nomads 9, Stockton 4
Byes: 14 teams drew a bye to next round

Second Round
Blackhill Rovers 0, Sunderland 8
Blaydon 9, North Durham 8
Durham City 0, Hartlepool Rovers 8
Hetton Lyons (Sunderland) 6, Hamsteels 0
South Shields 27, Sunderland Nomads 0
Tudhoe 28, Houghton-le-Spring 0
Tyne Dock 6, West Hartlepool 0
Westoe 0, Sherburn House 3

Third Round
Hartlepool Rovers 11, Tyne Dock 5
South Shields 32, Blaydon 3
Sunderland 9, Hetton Lyons 3
Tudhoe 27, Sherburn House 0

Semi-finals
Sunderland 3, South Shields 13
Tudhoe 0, Hartlepool Rovers 3

FINAL
Saturday 28 March 1896 at Brewery Field, Spennymoor
HARTLEPOOL ROVERS 0 *Back*: RW Poole. *Three-quarters*: C Hodgson, W Fletcher, M Irvin, H Walker. *Half-backs*: W McSloy, JT Thompson. *Forwards*: J Athey, C Cox, S Dunning, J Finlay, D Gilchrist, M Hastings, J Huntley, RF Oakes (capt).
SOUTH SHIELDS 0 *Back*: J Frame. *Three-quarters*: HB Swainston, WG Baty, WE Kassell, MJ Wilkinson. *Half-backs*: WJ Baty, A Smith. *Forwards*: F Atkinson, T Bradford, A Peat, G Quest, R Wake, RH Wood, T Woodman, S Young.
After extra time   *Attendance*: 15,000   *Referee*: J Oakland (Yorkshire RU)

FINAL REPLAY
Saturday 4 April 1896 at Ashbrooke Ground, Sunderland
HARTLEPOOL ROVERS 7 *Back*: RW Poole. *Three-quarters*: W Fletcher, FHR Alderson (t, dg), M Irvin, H Walker. *Half-backs*: W McSloy, JT Thompson. *Forwards*: J Athey, GE Boagey, C Cox, S Dunning, J Finlay, M Hastings, J Huntley, RF Oakes (capt).
SOUTH SHIELDS 0 *Back*: J Frame. *Three-quarters*: HB Swainston, MJ Wilkinson, WE Kassell, H Purvis. *Half-backs*: WJ Baty, A Smith. *Forwards*: F Atkinson, T Bradford, A Peat, G Quest, R Wake, RH Wood, T Woodman, S Young.
Attendance: 8,000   *Referee*: J Oakland (Yorkshire RU)

NORTHUMBERLAND COUNTY FOOTBALL CHALLENGE CUP (6 entries)
Try – 3 points; conversion – 2; penalty goal – 3; drop-goal, field goal, goal from mark – 4.

First Round
Northern 7, Brighton 0
Tynedale 0, Wallsend 0 (aet)
Byes: Percy Park, Rockcliff

First Round Replay
Wallsend 0, Tynedale 5

Semi-finals
Percy Park 13, Tynedale 0
Rockcliff 10, Northern 5

FINAL
Saturday 28 March 1896 at Jesmond Ground, Newcastle
ROCKCLIFF 10 *Back*: G Taylor. *Three-quarters*: W Taylor (2t, dg), S Anderson, J Thompson, T Nicholson. *Half-backs*: TP Alexander, A Phillips. *Forwards*: JH Greenwell, GW Lee (capt), J McCarthy, J Nesbitt, TC Stephenson, A Styan, B Taylor, John Taylor.
PERCY PARK 0 *Back*: J Miller. *Three-quarters*: GC Robinson, W Bates, WA Mackay (capt), CO Robinson. *Half-backs*: SC Lockerby, CW Russell. *Forwards*: GT Bell, A Buckley, O Heslop, E Kerr, J McMenemy, A Nesbitt, H Robinson, G Thomson.
Attendance: 6,000/7,000   *Referee*: JH Reay (West Hartlepool)

YORKSHIRE COUNTY FOOTBALL CHALLENGE CUP (104 entries)
Try – 3 points; conversion – 2; penalty goal – 3; drop-goal, field goal, goal from mark – 4.

Preliminary Round
(70 teams in 15 districts; two from each, indicated by 'q', qualified for next stage)

Airedale: Eccleshill Parish Church, Guiseley, Idle (q), Thackley, Windhill (q)
Batley: Batley St Mary's. Birstall (q), East Ardsley, Soothill (q)
Bradford: Allerton (q), Brownroyd Recreation, Great Horton Church (q). Thornton Rangers, Wibsey
Castleford: Ackworth, Allerton Bywater, Brotherton St John's, Fairburn, Great Preston Old Hall, Kippax, Knottingley, Methley (q), Normanton St John's (q), Normanton United, Pontefract, South Milford, Whitwood
Craven: Keighley Shamrocks (q), Keighley Trinity, Silsden, Skipton (q)
Dewsbury: Dewsbury Moor Rangers, Dewsbury St Paulinus (q), Horbury, Horbury Athletic, Mirfield, Ravensthorpe Nelson (q), Thornhill Lees Trinity, Thornhill Parish Church

East Leeds: Beeston (q), Leeds Good Shepherd's (q) (both had byes)
Halifax: Luddendenfoot (q), Todmorden (q) (both had byes)
Huddersfield: Golcar, Kirkburton, Lockwood (q), Meltham and Meltham Mills, Milnsbridge (q), Nortonthorpe, Primrose Hill, Skelmanthorpe, Slaithwaite, Turnbridge
Hull and Ouse: Selby (q), Selby Mizpah (q) (both had byes)
Northern: Harrogate (q), Knaresborough, Tadcaster (q)
North Leeds: Horsforth (q), Yorkshire College (q) (both had byes)
Spen Valley: Low Moor St Mark's (q), Wyke (q) (both had byes)
Wakefield: Dodworth (q), Doncaster Town (q), Eastmoor, Kinsley, Ryhill, Streethouse
West Leeds: Farsley (q), Yeadon (q) (both had byes)

First Round
(* indicates 34 teams seeded to this round)
Birstall 19, Normanton St John's 3
Bowling* 27, Soothill 0
Bowling Old Lane* 5, Selby 16
Dewsbury St Paulinus 10, Skipton 4
Doncaster Town 0, Castleford* 14
Elland* 34, Armley* 10
Farsley 6, Low Moor St Mark's 0
Featherstone* 6, Bramley* 0
Great Horton Church 6, Idle 9
Harrogate 3, Shipley* 15
Heckmondwike* 16, Paddock* 5
Hebden Bridge* 27, Windhill 0
Holbeck* 10, Yeadon 0
Horsforth 7, Cleckheaton* 3
Hull Kingston Rovers* w/o
Yorkshire College (withdrew)
Keighley* 0, Alverthorpe* 0
Keighley Shamrocks 19, Ravensthorpe Nelson 0
Leeds Good Shepherd's 0, Goole* 22
Lockwood 0, York* 7
Luddendenfoot 11, Bingley* 4
Methley 13, Stanningley* 6
Milnsbridge 5, Leeds Parish Church* 23
Normanton* 26, Allerton 0
Ossett* 3, Rothwell* 0
Otley* w/o Kirkstall* (disbanded)
Outwood Church* 6, Wortley* 0
Selby Mizpah 3, Pudsey* 39
Sowerby Bridge* 20, Dodworth 3
Tadcaster 0, Morley* 17
Todmorden w/o Beeston (withdrew)
West Riding* 21, Saltaire* 0
Wyke 0, Mytholmroyd* 4

First Round Replay
Alverthorpe 5, Keighley 3

Second Round
Alverhorpe 3, Goole 9
Bowling 19, Methley 6
Castleford 40, Selby 0
Dewsbury St Paulinus 4, Sowerby Bridge 15
Featherstone 15, Heckmondwike 0
Hebden Bridge 0, Pudsey 26
Horsforth 0, Holbeck 32
Hull Kingston Rovers 12, Elland 0
Keighley Shamrocks 0, Morley 3
Mytholmroyd 0, Leeds Parish Church 36
Ossett 28, Todmorden 0
Otley 6, Farsley 0
Outwood Church 11, Luddendenfoot 6
Shipley 10, Normanton 0
West Riding 31, Birstall 0
York 17, Idle 3

Third Round
Featherstone 19, Shipley 0
Holbeck 3, Hull Kingston Rovers 3
Leeds Parish Church 26, Goole 0
Morley 6, Bowling 5
Otley 3, Ossett 0
Pudsey 8, Castleford 9
Sowerby Bridge 11, York 0
West Riding 19, Outwood Church 0

Third Round Replay
Hull Kingston Rovers 15, Holbeck 0

Fourth Round
Castleford 24, Otley 3
Hull Kingston Rovers 3, Featherstone 6
Sowerby Bridge 8, Morley 3
West Riding 15, Leeds Parish Church 5

Semi-finals
Castleford 20, Sowerby Bridge 0 (at Crown Point, Leeds)
West Riding 0, Featherstone 0 (at Crown Flatts, Dewsbury)

Semi-final Replay
West Riding 3, Featherstone 0 (at Barley Mow, Bramley – abandoned due to altercation and subsequently awarded to West Riding)

FINAL
Saturday 18 April 1896 at Scratcherd Lane, Morley
CASTLEFORD 3 *Back*: A Townend. *Three-quarters*: T Needham, A Kettlewell, Thomas, JT Taylor. *Half-backs*: J Beaumont (t), G Nowell. *Forwards*: Church, W Dooley, T Hambleton, W Holland, J Rhodes, H Speed, A Starks, JW Ward (capt).
WEST RIDING 0 *Back*: Horne. *Three-quarters*: J Whitley, G Newby, W Lister, C Halfyard. *Half-backs*: T Pickford, Scott. *Forwards*: C Brewster, T Broadley (capt), W Crosby, S Crowther, F Shaw, Stead, Vollans, Widdowson.
Attendance: 6,026   *Referee*: W Yiend (Peterborough)

COUNTY CHAMPIONSHIP

NORTHERN GROUP

Saturday 26 October 1895 at Prince Consort Road, Gateshead
DURHAM 11 *Back*: RW Poole (HartR). *Three-quarters*: HB Swainston (SSh), WE Kassell (SSh, c), J Taylor (Sund, t), T Martin (Tud, t). *Half-backs*: F Marston (Tud), JT Thompson (HartR). *Forwards*: T Burt (SherH), J Geenty (WHart, t), T Gibbon (WHart), J Hall (capt, NDur), TJ Lindsay (Tud), RF Oakes (HartR), A Stephenson (Tud), AJ Troupe (Tud).
CUMBERLAND 11 *Back*: JH Moore (Mil). *Three-quarters*: W Cunningham (Mil), T Fletcher (Sea), JH Timney (Mary, 2t), T Ritson (Cock c). *Half-backs*: WS Graham (Carl), G Messenger (Asp). *Forwards*: J Bell (Carl), R Bell (Work, t), JH Blacklock (Asp), Jim Davidson (capt, Asp), D Elliott (Carl), J Fawcett (Mil), R Mumberson (Asp), G Steele (Asp).
Attendance: 2,000   *Referee*: A Hartley (Yorkshire)

Saturday 2 November 1895 at Chorley Road, Swinton
LANCASHIRE 23 *Back*: W Manwaring (Sal). *Three-quarters*: JT Lewis (Swi), J Valentine (capt, Swi, 4c), LE Pilkington (StHR, t), R Holmes (More). *Half-backs*: GG Allen (Liv, 2t), W Parlane (Man, t). *Forwards*: GE Hughes (Bar), JJ Jones (Sal), R Moss (Sal), GH Murray (Swi), R Pierce (Liv), J Pinch (Lanc), WB Stoddart (Liv), S Walsh (Pem, t).
CHESHIRE 3 *Back*: S Houghton (BirkW). *Three-quarters*: FP Jones (capt, NewB), JAS Cannell (NewB, t), AE Fenton (BirkPk), F Hughes (BirkW). *Half-backs*: PR Clauss (BirkPk), H Parratt (Sale). *Forwards*: D Atkinson (BirkW), J Baxter (BirkPk), EH Bradshaw (Sale), AJ Chadwick (BirkPk), H Fletcher (Sale), S Hanson (Alt), F Ingham (BirkW), A Jones (BirkW).
Attendance: 4,000   *Referee*: A Hartley (Yorkshire)

Thursday 7 November 1895 at Upper Park, Birkenhead
CHESHIRE 5 *Back*: S Houghton (BirkW). *Three-quarters*: JAS Cannell (NewB), FP Jones (capt, NewB, t), J Anderson (BirkPk), F Hughes (BirkW). *Half-backs*: PR Clauss (BirkPk, c), ID Heyes (BirkW). *Forwards*: D Atkinson (BirkW), J Baxter (BirkPk), Benton (Sale), AJ Chadwick (BirkPk), H Fletcher (Sale), S Hanson (Alt), F Ingham (BirkW), A Jones (BirkW).
CUMBERLAND 8 *Back*: JH Moore (Mil, c). *Three-quarters*: W Cunningham (Mil), M Humphrey (Mary), T Fletcher (Sea), JH Timney (Mary, 2t). *Half-backs*: WS Graham

(Carl), G Messenger (Asp). *Forwards*: J Bell (Carl), R Bell (Work), JH Blacklock (Asp), Jim Davidson (capt, Asp), J Fawcett (Mil), R Mumberson (Asp), J Scott (Sea), G Steele (Asp).
Attendance: 500   *Referee*: J Ashton (Lancashire)

Saturday 9 November 1895 at Crown Point, Leeds
YORKSHIRE 19 *Back*: H Ward (Ship). *Three-quarters*: S Morfitt (HKR), JE Parker (Mor, t), EF Fookes (SowB, dg), A Hambrecht (Bram). *Half-backs*: GE Mosley (LeePC), H Myers (Bram, t). *Forwards*: JH Barron (Bing), T Broadley (capt, WRid, 2t), J Conley (LeePC, t), J Rhodes (Cas), A Starks (Cas), JW Ward (Cas), W Whiteley (Bram), H Woodhead (Goole).
DURHAM 0 *Back*: RW Poole (HartR). *Three-quarters*: RCF Crow (SundN), C Hodgson (HartR), WE Kassell (SSh), T Martin (Tud). *Half-backs*: F Marston (Tud), JT Thompson (HartR). *Forwards*: T Burt (SherH), J Geenty (WHart), T Gibbon (WHart), J Hall (NDur), GC Kerr (DurC), RF Oakes (HartR), FO Poole (Sund), AJ Troupe (Tud).
Attendance: 10,000   *Referee*: H Williamson (Lancashire)

Saturday 9 November 1895 at Mint's Feet, Kendal
WESTMORLAND 0 *Back*: WA Duff (KirkL). *Three-quarters*: CG Mason (KenH), J Goodman (Walk), AS Langley (KenH), JK Robinson (KirkL). *Half-backs*: R Hill (KenH), A Jowett (KirkL). *Forwards*: J Carradus (capt, KenH), WA Davis (Burn), C Heap (KenH), VS Jones (Burn), RH Robinson (Burn), R Simm (KenH), J Vity (Amb), W Woodhouse (KirkL).
LANCASHIRE 18 *Back*: W Manwaring (Sal). *Three-quarters*: R Holmes (More, t), LE Pilkington (StHR, t), J Valentine (Swi, t, 3c), JT Lewis (Swi). *Half-backs*: GG Allen (Liv, t), W Parlane (Man). *Forwards*: GE Hughes (Bar), JJ Jones (Sal), R Moss (Sal), GH Murray (Swi), R Pierce (Liv), J Pinch (Lanc), WB Stoddart (Liv), S Walsh (Pem).
Attendance: 'fair'   *Referee*: E Dunderdale (Yorkshire)

Saturday 16 November 1895 at Warwick Road, Carlisle
CUMBERLAND 5 *Back*: W Skelton (Asp). *Three-quarters*: TH Hodgkinson (Carl), T Fletcher (Sea), T Ritson (Cock), JH Timney (Mary, t). *Half-backs*: WS Graham (Carl), G Messenger (Asp, c). *Forwards*: J Bell (Carl), R Bell (Work), JH Blacklock (Asp), Jim Davidson (capt, Asp), D Elliott (Carl), R Mumberson (Asp), J Scott (Sea), G Steele (Asp).
LANCASHIRE 7 *Back*: W Manwaring (Sal). *Three-quarters*: R Holmes (More), R Lewis (More), J Valentine (Swi, dg, pg), JT Lewis (Swi). *Half-backs*: GG Allen (Liv), W Parlane (Man). *Forwards*: GE Hughes (Bar), JJ Jones (Sal), R Moss (Sal), GH Murray (Swi), R Pierce (Liv), J Pinch (Lanc), WB Stoddart (Liv), S Walsh (Pem).
Attendance: 2,000   *Referee*: Rev F Marshall (Yorkshire)

Saturday 16 November 1895 at Jesmond Ground, Newcastle
NORTHUMBERLAND 0 *Back*: W Jackson (Rock). *Three-quarters*: T Nicholson (Rock), S Anderson (Rock), WG Baty (Tynd/SSh), PW Oscroft (Nor). *Half-backs*: TP Alexander (Rock), EW Taylor (capt, Rock). *Forwards*: JH Greenwell (Rock), WN Greenwell (Rock), J Hobson (Tynd), GW Lee (Rock), J Nesbitt (Rock), T Robson (Tynd), HJ Spencer (PerPk), TC Stephenson (Rock).
YORKSHIRE 11 *Back*: CE Dixon (Alv). *Three-quarters*: EF Fookes (SowB), JE Parker (Mor), S Morfitt (HKR, t), A Hambrecht (Bram, t). *Half-backs:* GE Mosley (LeePC), H Myers (Bram, c). *Forwards*: JH Barron (Bing), T Broadley (capt, WRid, t), J Conley (LeePC), J Rhodes (Cas), A Starks (Cas), JW Ward (Cas), W Whiteley (Bram), H Woodhead (Goole).
Attendance: 5,000   *Referee*: WH Bell (Durham)

Thursday 21 November 1895 at Borrans Field, Ambleside
WESTMORLAND 3 *Back*: WA Duff (KirkL). *Three-quarters*: JK Robinson (KirkL), W Hall (Lanc), G Fawcett (Lanc, t), CG Mason (KenH). *Half-backs*: AS Dixon (Amb), A Jowett (KirkL). *Forwards*: J Carradus (KenH), G Fisher (Lanc), C Heap (KenH), VS Jones (Burn), CB Punchard (KirkL), RH Robinson (Burn), W Robinson (Amb), J Vity (Amb).
CHESHIRE 0 *Back*: S Houghton (BirkW). *Three-quarters*: JAS Cannell (NewB), W Fleet (Alt), JD Watson (BirkW), F Hughes (BirkW). *Half-backs*: ID Heyes (BirkW), HD Pagden (Sale). *Forwards*: D Atkinson (BirkW), J Baxter (BirkPk), AJ Chadwick (BirkPk), H Fletcher (Sale), J Gerrard (BirkW), S Hanson (Alt), F Ingham (BirkW), A Jones (BirkW).
Attendance: 500   *Referee*: J Mills (Lancashire)

Saturday 23 November 1895 at Upper Park, Birkenhead
CHESHIRE 0 *Back*: GR Ingham (BirkW). *Three-quarters*: JAS Cannell (NewB), W Fleet (Alt), J Anderson (BirkPk), EC Harvey (Sale). *Half-backs*: PR Clauss (BirkPk), H Parratt (Sale). *Forwards*: J Baxter (BirkPk), EH Bradshaw (Sale), AJ Chadwick (BirkPk), H Fletcher (Sale), S Hanson (Alt), RW Hooper (NewB), F Ingham (BirkW), W Palmer (Alt).
NORTHUMBERLAND 11 *Back*: W Jackson (Rock). *Three-quarters*: T Nicholson (Rock), S Anderson (Rock), WG Baty (Tynd/SSh, 2t), PW Oscroft (Nor). *Half-backs*: TP Alexander (Rock, t), EW Taylor (capt, Rock, c). *Forwards*: JH Greenwell (Rock), J Hobson (Tynd), GW Lee (Rock), J Nesbitt (Rock), T Robson (Tynd), J Smith (Wall), HJ Spencer (PerPk), TC Stephenson (Rock).
Attendance: 4,000   *Referee*: E Seddon (Lancashire)

Saturday 23 November 1895 at Meanwood Road, Leeds
YORKSHIRE 16 *Back*: CE Dixon (Alv). *Three-quarters*: EF Fookes (SowB), JE Parker (Mor, pg), S Morfitt (HKR), A Hambrecht (Bram, t). *Half-backs*: GE Mosley (LeePC), H Myers (Bram, 2c). *Forwards*: JH Barron (Bing, t), T Broadley (capt, WRid), J Conley (LeePC), J Rhodes (Cas), A Starks (Cas), JW Ward (Cas, t), W Whiteley (Bram), H Woodhead (Goole).
LANCASHIRE 5 *Back*: W Manwaring (Sal). *Three-quarters*: R Holmes (More), R Lewis (More), J Valentine (capt, Swi, t, c), JT Lewis (Swi). *Half-backs*: GG Allen (Liv), W Parlane (Man). *Forwards*: GE Hughes (Bar), JJ Jones (Sal), R Moss (Sal), GH Murray (Swi), R Pierce (Liv), J Pinch (Lanc), WB Stoddart (Liv), S Walsh (Pem).
Attendance: 10,000   *Referee*: DG Findlay (Scotland)

Saturday 7 December 1895 at Upper Park, Birkenhead
CHESHIRE 0 *Back*: S Houghton (BirkW). *Three-quarters*: JAS Cannell (NewB), W Fletcher (NewB), PR Clauss (BirkPk), EC Harvey (Sale). *Half-backs*: A Dillon (BirkW), ID Heyes (BirkW). *Forwards*: J Baxter (BirkPk), AJ Chadwick (BirkPk), H Fletcher (Sale), J Gerrard (BirkW), S Hanson (Alt), RW Hooper (NewB), F Ingham (BirkW), W Palmer (Alt).
DURHAM 9 *Back*: RW Poole (HartR). *Three-quarters*: RCF Crow (SundN), C Hodgson (HartR), WE Kassell (SSh, c, gm), T Martin (Tud). *Half-backs*: F Hindle (Tud), F Marston (Tud). *Forwards*: T Burt (SherH), T Gibbon (WHart), J Hall (NDur), RF Oakes (HartR), A Stephenson (Tud), AJ Troupe (Tud, t), G Urwin (Tud), H Walker (DurC).
Attendance: 'meagre'   *Referee*: T Hunter (Lancashire)

Saturday 7 December 1895 at Whitehaven Cricket Ground
CUMBERLAND 14 *Back*: JH Moore (Mil, c). *Three-quarters*: JH Timney (Mary), JC Broughton (Mary, t), T Fletcher (Sea), S Northmore (Mil). *Half-backs*: WS Graham (Carl, t), G Messenger (Asp). *Forwards*: J Bell (Carl), R Bell (Work), JH Blacklock (Asp), Jim Davidson (capt, Asp), F Gorman (Mil), E Knowles (Mil, t), R Mumberson (Asp), G Steele (Asp, t).
WESTMORLAND 10 *Back*: WA Duff (KirkL). *Three-quarters*: J Holmes (KenH), G Fawcett (Lanc, 2t, dg), JK Robinson (KirkL), AS Langley (KenH). *Half-backs*: AS Dixon (Amb), A Jowett (KirkL). *Forwards*: J Bigland (Wind), J Carradus (KenH), WA Davis (Burn), G Fisher (Lanc), C Heap (KenH), CB Punchard (KirkL), W Robinson (Amb), J Vity (Amb).
Attendance: 'good'   *Referee*: JM Mawson (Barrow)

Saturday 21 December 1895 at Jesmond Ground, Newcastle
NORTHUMBERLAND 11 *Back*: W Jackson (Rock). *Three-quarters*: CO Robinson (PerPk), S Anderson (Rock), WG Baty (Tynd/SSh, t), T Nicholson (Rock, t). *Half-backs*: TP Alexander (Rock, t), EW Taylor (capt, Rock, c). *Forwards*: FE Dotchin (Nor), WN Greenwell (Rock), GW Lee (Rock), A Nesbitt (PerPk), T Robson (Tynd), J Smith (Wall), HJ Spencer (PerPk), TC Stephenson (Rock).
WESTMORLAND 3 *Back*: WA Duff (KirkL). *Three-quarters*: G Fawcett (Lanc, t), HF Newton (Amb/OxfU), E Braithwaite (KenH), J Holmes (KenH). *Half-backs*: AS Dixon (Amb), A Jowett (KirkL). *Forwards*: J Carradus (capt, KenH), WA Davis (Burn), G Fisher (Lanc), C Heap (KenH), CB Punchard (KirkL), W Robinson (Amb), J Vity (Amb), W Woodhouse (KirkL).
Attendance: 500   *Referee*: n/a

Saturday 11 January 1896 at Manchester Athletic Ground, Fallowfield
LANCASHIRE 14 *Back*: W Manwaring (Sal). *Three-quarters*: R Robinson (Ulv), J Valentine (capt, Swi, t), J Seddon (StHR), R Holmes (More, 2t). *Half-backs*: W Hall (Ulv, t, c), W Parlane (Man). *Forwards*: GE Hughes (Bar), JJ Jones (Sal), W Mortimer (Liv/CamU), R Moss (Sal), J Pinch (Lanc), R Tickle (Swi), S Walsh (Pem), RD Wood (LivOB).
DURHAM 0 *Back*: RW Poole (HartR). *Three-quarters*: RCF Crow (SundN), W Wainford (Tud), J Taylor (Sund), P Moran (HartR). *Half-backs*: F Hindle (Tud), F Marston (Tud). *Forwards*: J Geenty (WHart), T Gibbon (WHart), GC Kerr (DurC), RF Oakes (HartR), A Stephenson (Tud), AJ Troupe (Tud), G Urwin (Tud), CS Wright (NDur).
Attendance: 4,000   *Referee*: W Oxley (Yorkshire)

Saturday 18 January 1896 at Blue House Ground, Hendon, Sunderland
DURHAM 9 *Back*: RW Poole (HartR). *Three-quarters*: RCF Crow (SundN, 2t), P Moran (HartR), WE Kassell (SSh), JW Tate (Wes, t). *Half-backs*: F Marston (Tud), JT Thompson (HartR). *Forwards*: J Geenty (WHart), T Gibbon (WHart), GC Kerr (DurC), P McDermid (TynD), RF Oakes (HartR), AJ Troupe (Tud), G Urwin (Tud), RH Wood (SSh).
NORTHUMBERLAND 3 *Back*: R Baty (Tynd). *Three-quarters*: GC Robinson (PerPk), WG Baty (Tynd/SSh), S Anderson (Rock), T Nicholson (Rock, t). *Half-backs*: TP Alexander (Rock), HS Bell (capt, Nor). *Forwards*: FE Dotchin (Nor), WN Greenwell (Rock), GW Lee (Rock), J Nesbitt (Rock), T Robson (Tynd), J Smith (Wall), HJ Spencer (PerPk), TC Stephenson (Rock).
Attendance: 2,500   *Referee*: A Wells (Yorkshire)

Saturday 18 January 1896 at Victoria Pleasure Grounds, Goole
YORKSHIRE 32 *Back*: H Ward (Ship). *Three-quarters*: EF Fookes (SowB, 2t, dg), S Morfitt (HKR, 2t), JE Parker (Mor, t), A Hambrecht (Bram, 2t). *Half-backs*: GE Mosley (LeePC), H Myers (Bram, c). *Forwards*: JH Barron (Bing, t), T Broadley (capt, WRid), J Conley (LeePC), W Duke (Hol, c), J Rhodes (Cas), H Speed (Cas), A Starks (Cas), JW Ward (Cas).
WESTMORLAND 0 *Back*: WA Duff (KirkL). *Three-quarters*: G Fawcett (Lanc), J Holmes (KenH), HF Newton (Amb/OxfU), JK Robinson (KirkL). *Half-backs*: E Braithwaite (KenH), A Jowett (KirkL). *Forwards*: J Carradus (capt, KenH), WA Davis (Burn), T Fawcett (KenH), G Fisher (Lanc), C Heap (KenH), W Robinson (Amb), E Vity (Amb), W Woodhouse (KirkL).
Attendance: 5,000   *Referee*: WH Clark (Durham)

Saturday 25 January 1896 at Upper Park, Birkenhead
CHESHIRE 0 *Back*: S Houghton (BirkW). *Three-quarters*: JAS Cannell (NewB), W Fletcher (NewB), W Hughes (BirkW), W Conning (BirkW). *Half-backs*: A Dillon (BirkW), ID Heyes (BirkW). *Forwards*: AJ Chadwick (BirkPk), H Fletcher (Sale), J Gerrard (BirkW), S Hanson (Alt), E Herschell (BirkPk), RW Hooper (NewB), F Ingham (BirkW), A Jones (BirkW).
YORKSHIRE 8 *Back*: CE Dixon (Alv). *Three-quarters*: EF Fookes (SowB), W Ward (LeePC), JE Parker (Mor, 2t), W Murgatroyd (Idle). *Half-backs*: GE Mosley (LeePC), H Myers (Bram). *Forwards*: JH Barron (Bing), T Broadley (capt, WRid), J Conley (LeePC), W Duke (Hol, c), J Rhodes (Cas), H Speed (Cas), A Starks (Cas), JW Ward (Cas).
Attendance: 3,000   *Referee*: E Seddon (Lancashire)

Saturday 8 February 1896 at Lonsdale Park, Workington
CUMBERLAND 0 *Back*: JH Moore (Mil). *Three-quarters*: W Rowe (Mil), T Fletcher (Sea), T Ritson (Cock), JH Timney (Mary). *Half-backs*: WS Graham (Carl), S Northmore (Mil). *Forwards*: J Bell (Carl), R Bell (Work), JH Blacklock (Asp), Jim Davidson (capt, Asp), D Elliott (Carl), E Knowles (Mil), J Mumberson (Asp), G Steele (Swi).
YORKSHIRE 12 *Back*: CE Dixon (Alv). *Three-quarters*: S Morfitt (HKR), JE Parker (Mor), A Hambrecht (Bram), W Murgatroyd (Idle). *Half-backs*: GE Mosley (LeePC), H Myers (Bram). *Forwards*: JH Barron (Bing), T Broadley (capt, WRid, t), J Conley (LeePC, t), H Lloyd (Bowl), J Rhodes (Cas), H Speed (Cas), A Starks (Cas, t), JW Ward (Cas, t).
Attendance: 6,000   *Referee*: J Higson (Lancashire)

Saturday 15 February 1896 at Jesmond Ground, Newcastle
NORTHUMBERLAND 5 *Back*: W Jackson (Rock). *Three-quarters*: GC Robinson (PerPk), WG Baty (Tynd/SSh), S Anderson (Rock), CO Robinson (PerPk, t). *Half-backs*: SC Lockerby (PerPk), EW Taylor (Rock, c). *Forwards*: FE Dotchin (Nor), JH Greenwell (Rock), W Hamilton (Tynd), GW Lee (Rock), J Nesbitt (Rock), T Robson (Tynd), HJ Spencer (PerPk), TC Stephenson (Rock).
CUMBERLAND 8 *Back*: W Skelton (Asp). *Three-quarters*: JH Timney (Mary, t, c), M Humphrey (Mary), T Fletcher (Sea), CW Barry (Asp). *Half-backs*: WS Graham (Carl, t), T James (Mil). *Forwards*: TD Bell (Carl), Jim Davidson (capt, Asp), F Gorman (Mil), E Knowles (Mil), W Moore (Sea), J Mumberson (Asp), G Rogerson (Carl), G Steele (Swi).
Attendance: 2,000   *Referee*: WH Bell (Durham)

Saturday 22 February 1896 at Hollow Drift, Durham
DURHAM 17 *Back*: J Frame (SSh). *Three-quarters*: WE Kassell (capt, SSh, c), J Gordon (Tud), J Morfitt (WHart), HB Swainston (SSh, t). *Half-backs*: F Hindle (Tud), F Marston (Tud, t). *Forwards*: T Burt (SherH, 2t), J Geenty (WHart), GC Kerr (DurC), P McDermid (TynD), AJ Troupe (Tud), G Urwin (Tud), J Wheatley (Hou, t), CS Wright (NDur).
WESTMORLAND 5 *Back*: J Holmes (KenH). *Three-quarters*: JK Robinson (KirkL), WC Skelton (Amb, t), G Fawcett (Lanc, c), R Vity (Amb). *Half-backs*: D Geddes (BurHW), A Jowett (KirkL). *Forwards*: J Carradus (KenH), J Elliott (Burn), T Fawcett (KenH), W Lancaster (Wind), CB Punchard (KirkL), W Robinson (Amb), JH Thompson (KenH), E Vity (Amb).
Attendance: 4,000/5,000   *Referee*: JA Miller (Yorkshire)

Saturday 29 February 1896 at Jesmond Ground, Newcastle
NORTHUMBERLAND 3 *Back*: W Jackson (Rock). *Three-quarters*: GC Robinson (PerPk), S Anderson (Rock), WG Baty (Tynd/SSh), CO Robinson (PerPk). *Half-backs*: SC Lockerby (PerPk, t), EW Taylor (Rock). *Forwards*: A Buckley (PerPk), FE Dotchin (Nor), JH Greenwell (Rock), WN Greenwell (Rock), W Hamilton (Tynd), GW Lee (Rock), HJ Spencer (PerPk), TC Stephenson (Rock).
LANCASHIRE 9 *Back*: J Crossley (StHR). *Three-quarters*: JT Lewis (Swi, 2t), J Valentine (Swi, t), R Lewis (More), R Holmes (More). *Half-backs*: W Chapman (Bar), G Cookson (Swi). *Forwards*: RW Forshaw (Ulv), GE Hughes (Bar), JJ Jones (Sal), W Lancaster (Swi), W Mortimer (Liv/CamU), R Pierce (Liv), J Pinch (Lanc), RD Wood (LivOB).
Attendance: 1,000   *Referee*: JB Hodgson (Middlesex)

Final table

	P	W	D	L	For	Agst	Pts
Yorkshire	6	6	0	0	98	5	12
Lancashire	6	5	0	1	76	27	10
Cumberland	6	3	1	2	46	50	7
Durham	6	3	1	2	46	52	7
Northumberland	6	2	0	4	33	40	4
Westmorland	6	1	0	5	21	92	2
Cheshire	6	0	0	6	8	62	0

SOUTH WESTERN GROUP

Results
Somersetshire 23, Gloucestershire 3   Somersetshire 5, Cornwall 0
Devonshire 22, Cornwall 3   Devonshire 3, Somersetshire 0
Gloucestershire 5, Devonshire 18   Cornwall 0, Gloucestershire 10

Final table

	P	W	D	L	For	Agst	Pts
Devonshire	3	3	0	0	43	8	6
Somersetshire	3	2	0	1	28	6	4
Gloucestershire	3	1	0	2	18	41	2
Cornwall	3	0	0	3	3	37	0

SOUTH EASTERN GROUP

Results
Middlesex 9, Surrey 14
Surrey 14, Kent 3
Midland Counties 18, Middlesex 4
Kent 0, Midland Counties 22
Surrey 0, Midland Counties 0
Kent 11, Middlesex 0

Play-off to decide first place
Midland Counties 0, Surrey 18

Final table	P	W	D	L	For	Agst	Pts
Surrey	3	2	1	0	28	12	5
Midland Counties	3	2	1	0	40	4	5
Kent	3	1	0	2	14	36	2
Middlesex	3	0	0	3	13	43	0

Southern Final
Surrey 16, Devonshire 0

COUNTY CHAMPIONSHIP FINAL
Thursday 20 February 1896 at Athletic Ground, Richmond
YORKSHIRE 16 *Back*: CE Dixon (Alv). *Three-quarters*: EF Fookes (SowB), S Morfitt (HKR), W Murgatroyd (Idle, t), A Hambrecht (Bram). *Half-backs*: GE Mosley (LeePC, t), H Myers (Bram). *Forwards*: JH Barron (Bing, t), T Broadley (capt, WRid), J Conley (LeePC, t), W Duke (Hol, 2c), J Rhodes (Cas), H Speed (Cas), A Starks (Cas), JW Ward (Cas).
SURREY 4 *Back*: KB Alexander (GuyHosp). *Three-quarters*: C Wells (Harl), HN Clarke (Harl/GuyHosp), WH Thorman (Rich), HT Wallis (Black/CamU). *Half-backs*: JH Curtis (RIEC), CM Wells (Harl). *Forwards*: W Ashford (Rich, gm), HW Dudgeon (Rich), DH Helps (Croy), RW Hunt (Harl), JH Kipling (Thornton Heath), FC Lohden (Black), SB Peech (Harl), FH Todd (RIEC).
Attendance: 10,000   *Referee*: AJ Davies (Glamorganshire)

NON-COUNTY CHAMPIONSHIP MATCHES

Wednesday 19 February 1896 at New Barnes, Salford
LANCASHIRE 11 *Back*: J Crossley (StHR). *Three-quarters*: GP Wincey (Man), J Valentine (Swi, t, c), J Seddon (StHR), D Traynor (StHR). *Half-backs*: W Parlane (Man, t), W Pearson (Swi). *Forwards*: GE Hughes (Bar, t), JJ Jones (Sal), W Lancaster (Swi), W Mortimer (Liv/CamU), R Pierce (Liv), J Pinch (Lanc), CEK Thompson (Lanc), S Walsh (Pem).
GLAMORGANSHIRE 3 *Back*: J Davies (Nea). *Three-quarters*: W Rees (Nea), F Gordon (Swa), T Davies (Tre), HE Morgan (Pen). *Half-backs*: D Jones (Aber), GW Shepherd (Pen, t). *Forwards*: H Davies (Morr), T Hayman (Bri), E Jones (Peny), J Jones (Aber), J Mackenzie (Pon), F Miller (Mou), T Phillips (Llwyn), JD Williams (Swa).
Attendance: 3,000   *Referee*: W Oxley (Yorkshire)

Milestones & Stats 1869-1901

Monday 2 March 1896 at St Helen's, Swansea
GLAMORGANSHIRE 0 *Back*: J Davies (Nea). *Three-quarters*: E Lloyd (Llan), HE Morgan (Pen), WJ Bancroft (Swa), F Gordon (Swa). *Half-backs*: D James (Swa), E James (Swa). *Forwards*: H Davies (Morr), D Evans (Peny), L Griffiths (Aber), F Hutchinson (Nea), J Jones (Aber), J Mackenzie (Pon), F Miller (Mou), JD Williams (Swa).
YORKSHIRE 6 *Back*: CE Dixon (Alv). *Three-quarters*: JE Parker (Mor, t), W Murgatroyd (Idle), A Hambrecht (Bram), EF Fookes (SowB, t). *Half-backs*: GE Mosley (LeePC), H Myers (Bram). *Forwards*: T Broadley (capt, WRid), J Conley (LeePC), W Duke (Hol), H Lloyd (Bowl), J Rhodes (Cas), H Speed (Cas), A Starks (Cas), JW Ward (Cas).
Attendance: 7,000/8,000   *Referee*: WH Wilkins (Llanelli)

Saturday 14 March 1896 at Whalley Range, Manchester
LANCASHIRE 6 *Back*: J Crossley (StHR). *Three-quarters*: J Sunderland (Swi), R Lewis (More, pg), J Seddon (StHR), CEL Beasley (Lit). *Half-backs*: W Chapman (Bar), G Cookson (Swi, t). *Forwards*: RW Forshaw (Ulv), J Johnson (Swi), JJ Jones (Sal), W Lancaster (Swi), R Moss (Sal), R Pierce (Liv), J Pinch (Lanc), RD Wood (LivOB).
DEVONSHIRE 3 *Back*: H Gloyne (DevA). *Three-quarters*: EJ Salter (Exm), WE Bildings (DevA), H Reed (Exe), EJ Baker (Exe, t). *Half-backs*: E Down (DevA), HC Nicolay (Barn). *Forwards*: GH Allington (capt, DevA), J Bond (Torq), V Howard (Torq), J Laverty (DevA), A May (DevA), C Pearse (Barn), J Powell (Exe), W Vanstone (Torq).
Attendance: 1,000   *Referee*: J Oakland (Yorkshire)

ENGLAND TRIAL MATCH

Saturday 14 December 1895 at Friarage Field, Hartlepool
NORTH 11 *Back*: S Houghton (BirkW). *Three-quarters*: EF Fookes (SowB), S Morfitt (HKR), J Valentine (Swi, t, c), R Holmes (More). *Half-backs*: W Parlane (Man), EW Taylor (capt, Rock, t). *Forwards*: T Broadley (WRid, t), Jim Davidson (Asp), WN Greenwell (Rock), J Pinch (Lanc), J Rhodes (Cas), A Starks (Cas), JW Ward (Cas), W Whiteley (Bram).
SOUTH 3 *Back*: JF Byrne (Mose). *Three-quarters*: EM Baker (OxfU), FA Leslie-Jones (OxfU), WB Thomson (Black), JHC Fegan (Black). *Half-backs*: RH Cattell (Black), FH Maturin (Black). *Forwards*: WE Bromet (capt, Rich), GM Carey (Black/OxfU, t), AE Elliott (StTHosp), W Falcon (CamU), LF Giblin (CamU), F Mitchell (CamU), JC Rigby (Black), C Thomas (Barn).
Attendance: 3,000   *Referee*: WH Bell (Durham)

INTERNATIONAL CHAMPIONSHIP

Saturday 4 January 1896 at Rectory Field, Blackheath
ENGLAND 25 *Back*: S Houghton (BirkW). *Three-quarters*: S Morfitt (WHart, 2t), J Valentine (Swi, c), EM Baker (OxfU), EF Fookes (SowB, 2t). *Half-backs*: RH Cattell (Black, 2t), EW Taylor (capt, Rock, c). *Forwards*: GM Carey (Black/OxfU), LF Giblin (CamU), F Mitchell (CamU, t), J Pinch (Lanc), J Rhodes (Cas), A Starks (Cas), JW Ward (Cas), W Whiteley (Bram).
WALES 0 *Back*: WJ Bancroft (Swa). *Three-quarters*: C Bowen (Llan), O Badger (Llan), JA Gould (capt, New), FH Dauncey (New). *Half-backs*: B Davies (Llan), D Morgan (Llan). *Forwards*: AW Boucher (New), E George (Pon), AM Jenkin (Swa), F Mills (Car), CB Nicholl (Llan), H Packer (New), SH Ramsey (Treorchy), WH Watts (New).
Attendance: 20,000   *Referee*: DG Findlay (Scotland)

Saturday 1 February 1896 at Meanwood Road, Leeds
ENGLAND 4 *Back*: JF Byrne (Mose, dg). *Three-quarters*: S Morfitt (WHart), J Valentine (Swi), EM Baker (OxfU), EF Fookes (SowB). *Half-backs*: RH Cattell (Black), EW Taylor (capt, Rock). *Forwards*: WE Bromet (Rich), GM Carey (Black/OxfU), LF Giblin (CamU), F Mitchell (CamU), J Pinch (Lanc), J Rhodes (Cas), A Starks (Cas), JW Ward (Cas).
IRELAND 10 *Back*: J Fulton (NIFC). *Three-quarters*: W Gardiner (NIFC), S Lee (capt, NIFC), TH Stevenson (EdinU, t), LQ Bulger (DubU, 2c). *Half-backs*: GG Allen (Der), LM Magee (BecR). *Forwards*: WG Byron (NIFC), AD Clinch (Wand), TJ Crean (Wand), H Lindsay (Wand), JH Lytle (NIFC), JH O'Conor (BecR), CV Rooke (Monk), J Sealy (DubU, t).
Attendance: 18,000   *Referee*: DG Findlay (Scotland)

Saturday 14 March 1896 at Hampden Park, Glasgow*
SCOTLAND 11 *Back*: G MacGregor (LonS). *Half-backs*: HTS Gedge (LonS, t), GT Campbell (LonS), CJN Fleming (EdinW, t), JJ Gowans (LonS, t). *Quarter-backs*: WP Donaldson (WoS), M Elliot (Haw). *Forwards*: A Balfour (Wat), JH Dods (LonS), WMC McEwan (EdinA), MC Morrison (RHSFP), GT Neilson (capt, WoS), TM Scott (Haw, c), HO Smith (Wat), GO Turnbull (WoS).
ENGLAND 0 *Back*: RW Poole (HartR). *Three-quarters*: S Morfitt (WHart), J Valentine (Swi), EM Baker (OxfU), EF Fookes (SowB). *Half-backs*: RH Cattell (Black), CM Wells (Harl). *Forwards*: JH Barron (Bing), T Broadley (WRid), GE Hughes (Bar), E Knowles (Mil), F Mitchell (capt, CamU), J Rhodes (Cas), H Speed (Cas), JW Ward (Cas).
Attendance: 20,000   *Referee*: WM Douglas (Wales)
*This venue was predecessor to the current Hampden Park.

Other results
Wales 6, Scotland 0
Ireland 0, Scotland 0
Ireland 8, Wales 4

Final table

	P	W	D	L	For	Agst
Ireland	3	2	1	0	18	8
Scotland	3	1	1	1	11	6
England	3	1	0	2	29	21
Wales	3	1	0	2	10	33

ENGLAND TOUR OF SOUTH AFRICA 1896

TOUR PARTY
John Hammond (captain, Richmond)
Sydney P Bell (Cambridge University)
Cecil Boyd (Dublin University)
Larry Bulger (Dublin University)
JF 'Fred' Byrne (Moseley)
Walter J Carey (Oxford University)
Andrew Clinch (Wanderers, Dublin)
Thomas Crean (Wanderers, Dublin)
P Froude Hancock (Wellington, Somersetshire)
Robert Johnston (Wanderers)
George W Lee (Rockcliff)
Osbert G Mackie (Cambridge University)
James T Magee (Bective Rangers)
AM 'Louis' Magee (Bective Rangers)
Arthur Meares (Dublin University)
William Mortimer (Cambridge University)
Matthew Mullineux (Blackheath)
RC 'Cuth' Mullins (Oxford University)
CO 'Charlie' Robinson (Percy Park)
Jim Sealy (Dublin University)
Alexander Todd (Cambridge University)

TOUR RESULTS
Saturday 11 July – Cape Town Clubs (at Cape Town), won 14-0 (5,000)
Monday 13 July – Suburban Clubs (Cape Town), won 8-0
Wednesday 15 July – Western Province (Cape Town), draw 0-0 (4,500)
Saturday 18 July – Griqualand West (Kimberley), won 11-9 (4,000)
Wednesday 22 July – Griqualand West (Kimberley), won 16-0 (4,000)
Saturday 25 July – Port Elizabeth, won 26-3 (3,500)
Tuesday 28 July – Eastern Province (Port Elizabeth), won 18-0 (2,000)
Thursday 30 July – **South Africa** (Port Elizabeth), won 8-0 (7,500)
Saturday 1 August – Grahamstown, won 20-0
Tuesday 4 August – King William's Town, won 25-0
Thursday 6 August – East London, won 27-0
Saturday 8 August – Queenstown, won 25-0
Wednesday 12 August – Johannesburg Country (Johannesburg), won 7-0
Saturday 15 August – Transvaal (Johannesburg), won 16-3
Monday 17 August – Johannesburg Clubs (Johannesburg), won 18-0
Wednesday 19 August – Transvaal (Johannesburg), won 16-5
Saturday 22 August – **South Africa** (Johannesburg), won 17-8 (5,000)
Wednesday 26 August – Cape Colony (Kimberley), won 7-0
Saturday 29 August – **South Africa** (Kimberley), won 9-3 (2,000)
Thursday 3 September – Western Province (Cape Town), won 32-0
Saturday 5 September – **South Africa** (Cape Town), lost 0-5 (3,500)

Thursday 30 July 1896 at Port Elizabeth Cricket Ground
SOUTH AFRICA 0 *Back*: D Lyons (EP). *Three-quarters*: PST Jones (WP), JH Anderson (WP), FTD Aston (Tvl), E Olver (EP). *Half-backs*: FH Guthrie (WP), FR Myburgh (capt, EP). *Forwards*: M Bredenkamp (GW), FW Douglass (EP), HC Gorton (Tvl), BH Heatlie (WP), PJ Meyer (GW), P Scott (Tvl), CG van Renen (WP), JJ Wessels (WP).
ENGLAND 8 *Back*: C Boyd. *Three-quarters*: L Bulger (t), JF Byrne (c), OG Mackie, R Johnston. *Half-backs*: AM Magee, M Mullineux. *Forwards*: WJ Carey (t), A Clinch, T Crean (capt), PF Hancock, W Mortimer, RC Mullins, J Sealy, A Todd.
Attendance: 7,500   *Referee*: HB Kemsley (South Africa)

Saturday 22 August 1896 at Wanderers Ground, Johannesburg
SOUTH AFRICA 8 *Back*: D Cope (Tvl, c). *Three-quarters*: TA Samuels (GW, 2t), HH Forbes (Tvl), WS Taberer (GW), FTD Aston (capt, Tvl). *Half-backs*: G St L Devenish (Tvl), A Larard (Tvl). *Forwards*: JB Andrew (Tvl), AM Beswick (Bdr), JH Crosby (Tvl), C Devenish (GW), T Mellett (GW), P Scott (Tvl), CW Smith (GW), JJ Wessels (WP).
ENGLAND 17 *Back*: JT Magee. *Three-quarters*: L Bulger, JF Byrne (2c), OG Mackie (dg), R Johnston. *Half-backs*: SP Bell, AM Magee. *Forwards*: WJ Carey, A Clinch, T Crean (t), J Hammond (capt), PF Hancock (t), W Mortimer, J Sealy, A Todd (t).
Attendance: 5,000   *Referee*: G Beves (South Africa)

Saturday 29 August 1896 at Athletic Club, Kimberley
SOUTH AFRICA 3 *Back*: TA Samuels (GW). *Three-quarters*: PST Jones (WP, t), JH Anderson (WP), AW Powell (GW), FTD Aston (capt, Tvl). *Half-backs*: W Cotty (GW), JM Powell (GW). *Forwards*: AM Beswick (Bdr), M Bredenkamp (GW), PJ Dormehl (WP), EW Kelly (GW), P Scott (Tvl), CW Smith (GW), DJ Theunissen (GW), JJ Wessels (WP).
ENGLAND 9 *Back*: A Meares. *Three-quarters*: L Bulger, JF Byrne (c, dg), OG Mackie (t), R Johnston. *Half-backs*: SP Bell, AM Magee. *Forwards*: WJ Carey, A Clinch, T Crean (capt), PF Hancock, W Mortimer, RC Mullins, J Sealy, A Todd.
Attendance: 2,000   *Referee*: WM Bissett (South Africa)

Saturday 5 September 1896 at Newlands, Cape Town
SOUTH AFRICA 5 *Back*: TA Samuels (GW). *Three-quarters*: PST Jones (WP), JH Anderson (WP), FTD Aston (Tvl), T Hepburn (WP, c). *Half-backs*: TE Etlinger (WP), A Larard (Tvl, t). *Forwards*: AM Beswick (Bdr), HA Cloete (WP), PJ Dormehl (WP), BH Heatlie (capt, WP), P de Waal (WP), P Scott (Tvl), HD van Broekhuizen (WP), CG van Renen (WP).
ENGLAND 0 *Back*: A Meares. *Three-quarters*: JT Magee, JF Byrne, OG Mackie, L Bulger. *Half-backs*: SP Bell, AM Magee. *Forwards*: WJ Carey, A Clinch, T Crean, J Hammond (capt), PF Hancock, WMortimer, J Sealy, A Todd.
Attendance: 3,500   *Referee*: AR Richards (South Africa)

1896-1897

TWO CASTLEFORD CLUBS

The defection of clubs from the Rugby Union to the Northern Union resulted in several towns having a team in both codes. Castleford was a case in point. The Rugby Union club, which began in 1877-78, still functioned but a splinter group had created the Castleford Northern Union club during May 1896. The *Yorkshire Evening Post* told its readers that 'interest in the coming football season at Castleford is already becoming intense, and the split which has occurred in the Rugby Union club has aroused, to use a mild term, a spirit of very keen rivalry. The [Northern Union] ground is within easy access of the town, being on the opposite side of Lock Lane, some 200 yards away from the Castleford Rugby Union enclosure'.[192] Both clubs later disbanded, the current Castleford rugby league team being founded as a junior club in 1912. There was also Morley and Featherstone clubs in both codes, from 1897-98 and 1898-99, respectively, the latter being unconnected to the current Featherstone Rovers club.

MAKING THE GAMES PAY

With commercialism growing in football, the *Manchester Guardian* gave its view on the financial implication of the Northern Union: 'Unfortunately it is not possible nowadays to play football for the sake of the game alone. Competition has rendered it necessary that the spectator should be taken into consideration, and the result is that it is necessary to take the best means possible to make the games pay. It is now a question not so much of interesting the player as the spectator, and it would be as well perhaps if this could be realised by those who are endeavouring to oppose the advance of professionalism. It is unfortunate, perhaps, but it is nevertheless true, that in the northern counties at least, amateurism is in a bad way at present, and that interest is concentrated in the Association League matches and the matches of the Northern Union. Amongst those who have followed Rugby football for years there is still a difference of opinion as to the ultimate outcome of the Northern Union, but it is impossible to disguise the fact that in Lancashire and Yorkshire the new organisation has made remarkable progress.'[193]

CASTLEFORD'S INTERNATIONAL FORWARDS CAUSE A SENSATION

The advent of Northern Unionism was creating unrest amongst several Rugby Union clubs whose leading players were rumoured to be transferring their allegiance to the new code. The Castleford Rugby Union Club was particularly hit with their three international and county forwards making the headlines. During October the *Leeds Mercury* reported: 'J. W. [Jack] Ward, John Rhodes, and Anthony Starks declined offers by Castleford Northern Union Club, and refused to play for Castleford Rugby Union Club. Many put their own construction on the *bona fides* of these players playing under amateur status when Ward transferred his services to Pudsey [Rugby Union], and Rhodes and Starks joined the ranks of the Hull Kingston Rovers [still Rugby Union at the time]. All three continued to be employed in Castleford [although] Ward has now been dismissed from his employment and Rhodes and Starks are given the option of playing under the banner of the Castleford clubs, or their notices are required. The case of the well-known players is exciting considerable interest in the town.'[194]

BATTLE OF THE ROSES

Lancashire met Yorkshire under both codes of rugby on 21st November, one scribe commenting 'it was a pity that two such important engagements clash, and it is to be hoped that some different arrangements will be made another season'.[195] Comparisons of the attendance provided a talking point as a barometer of how the two codes matched up in terms of crowd appeal. The Rugby Union fixture at the Manchester Athletic Ground, Fallowfield, had an attendance variously reported as 4,000 and

5,000, the Northern Union game at Watersheddings, Oldham, estimated between 15,000 and 20,000.

WESTMORLAND RECRUIT SPECTATORS

Westmorland Rugby Union continued its struggle to raise a competitive team, a dilemma highlighted when some players failed to turn up to oppose Cumberland at Millom on 5th December. The fixture had been switched from Westmorland to attract a better gate. It was reported that 'the visitors brought only a poor team, and were, besides, so short-handed that the side had to be made up by pressing into it a couple of spectators'.[196]

HULL KINGSTON ROVERS: ALLEGED PROFESSIONALISM

Accusations of professionalism still persisted in Rugby Union circles, a special meeting of the Yorkshire Rugby Union Committee taking place at the Green Dragon Hotel, Leeds, on 14th January to debate alleged payments by Hull Kingston Rovers. Amongst the players under scrutiny were forwards Anthony Starks and John Rhodes, and three-quarter Sam Morfitt, the latter having returned from the West Hartlepool club in September 1895. Rhodes and Starks defended themselves by stating that as Castleford had split into two clubs, they had joined Rovers 'rather than give local offence by playing for one club in preference to another'. They claimed they only received their railway fare. The committee, unable to find anything incriminating, decided the Rovers had not broken the professional laws.[197]

YORKSHIRE RUGBY UNION: MORE RUMOURS OF PROFESSIONALISM

Commenting on the shift from amateurism to professionalism in Yorkshire, the *Manchester Guardian* wrote: 'The Yorkshire Rugby Union is experiencing some of the difficulties that beset Lancashire last year. Rumours of professionalism among clubs professing amateurism are prevalent on every hand, and there are sinister accusations that next season will see some remarkable changes. Certainly there have been secessions from amateurism but there is no indication that the time has arrived for putting up the shutters of Rugby Unionism. There is no comparison, of course, between the amount of interest aroused between the matches under the two codes. The Northern Union have a considerable advantage. But the amateur clubs in Lancashire, at least, seem to be getting on pretty well. They are managing to provide very fair football. Yorkshire, on the other hand, is finding some difficulties in dealing with the so-called amateur clubs.'[198]

HULL KINGSTON ROVERS SUSPENDED

Hull Kingston Rovers again came under the microscope after the Rugby Football Union appointed a sub-committee to review their affairs, having been dissatisfied with the verdict of the Yorkshire Committee's enquiry on 14th January in Leeds. This time the meeting took place at the Station Hotel, York, on 2nd February, and the outcome was different. The *Pall Mall Gazette* reported: 'The sentence of suspension, pending a further report, passed on the Hull Kingston Rovers club caused little or no surprise in Yorkshire football circles. It was generally conceded that the inquiry which the committee of the Yorkshire Union held a week or two ago, at the instance of the professional sub-committee of the Rugby Union, was rather a lame affair. Naturally enough, the parent body were not satisfied and promptly deputed a special committee to silt the allegations against the amateur status of the Rovers to the very bottom. The decision is rather a "smack in the face" for the Yorkshire Rugby Union. It is no secret that many members of its committee were indignant when they learnt that the inquiry was to be reopened.'[199]

CHESHIRE LOSE EIGHT PLAYERS

The Cheshire Rugby Union team travelled to Newcastle on Friday evening, 5th February, ahead of their meeting with Northumberland at North Shields the next day, taking what was described as 'practically a scratch fifteen'. It was not unknown for Cheshire to suffer from late withdrawals and, on this occasion, they were short of three backs and five forwards from their selected team. Predictably, they lost the match 17-0.[200]

YORKSHIRE'S DILEMMA

The Rugby Union match between Yorkshire and Cheshire took place at Dewsbury on 13th February, but not without some problems in the preceding weeks. Originally it was to be at the Hull Kingston Rovers' ground on 23rd January but, when the two teams arrived, the surface was found to be hard with frost and it was postponed. Cheshire agreed to make the journey again to complete the group matches but, as the Rovers had been suspended in the meantime due to allegations of professionalism, a new venue was required, Dewsbury's Crown Flatts chosen at short notice. Yorkshire, meantime, had selection problems in the forwards; Hull Kingston Rovers' case meant Anthony Starks and John Rhodes were suspended, as was John Shooter (Morley), whilst Harry Barron (Bingley) was ill. The outcome was that four forwards made their Yorkshire debut.

HULL KINGSTON ROVERS: SUSPENSION CONFIRMED

The suspension of Hull Kingston Rovers was confirmed at a further meeting of the Rugby Football Union's professional sub-committee on 19th February, again held at the Station Hotel in York. The Committee decided Sam Morfitt and the club had committed breaches relating to professionalism and the Rovers were suspended until 2nd March. The verdict reopened wounds between the Yorkshire Rugby Union, having had its decision overturned, and the Rugby Football Union. It created an atmosphere leading to further defections to the Northern Union.[201]

A COLOUR CLASH DELAYS A YORKSHIRE CUP SEMI-FINAL

Featherstone and Shipley arrived at Oldfield Lane, Wortley, on 10th April for their Yorkshire (Rugby Union) Cup semi-final meeting where it was noticed there was a colour clash, both having turned up with white jerseys. Realising 'someone had blundered' a messenger was despatched to Leeds to purchase replacements. Apparently 'time passed very slowly to the impatient and anxious spectators' until, shortly before 4 pm, 'sarcastic cheers arose from one corner of the field [when] two brown paper parcels had been hurriedly taken into the dressing tent'. Amid great cheers, Featherstone emerged 'attired in the most vivid of blue jerseys'. Reportedly they 'retreated as rapidly, possibly to make sure that the colours were fast'. They reappeared shortly after and the match finally began.[202]

THE ONLY LANCASHIRE CUP FINAL

The first and only Lancashire (Rugby Union) Cup final to be played during the Victorian era took place at Quay Meadow, Lancaster, on 10th April, Ulverston defeating Castleton Moor 21-0. The referee was James Higson, secretary of the Lancashire County Club who, as a Salford official, had vehemently opposed its defection to the Northern Union earlier that season. After presenting the cup he took the opportunity to air his views on the Northern Union, the *Hull Daily Mail* reporting: 'He was surprised they had any teams left under the old regime [Rugby Union], when he considered the unsportsmanlike and contemptible wiles which the Northern Union had resorted to in order to tempt players and teams to go over. That while holding it illegal to tempt players with bribes, or pay more than six shillings per a match, they made offers of £10 and £50 down, and payments of 15 shillings [75 pence] to 50 shillings [2.50p] per week. No doubt his hearers would think he was speaking rather strongly, but there was nobody on that ground who knew so much as he did on the subject.' Whilst speaking, he was cheered (shouts of 'hear, hear') and heckled in equal measures.[203]

YORKSHIRE COMPETITION NO. 3 FINAL: A DISQUALIFICATION

Bingley and Hebden Bridge, leaders of Group A and Group B, respectively, of the Yorkshire (Rugby Union) Competition No. 3, met to decide the overall winners. After a 3-3 draw at Sowerby Bridge, Hebden Bridge won the replay 3-0 at Windhill on Tuesday 20th April. Bingley subsequently objected that Hebden Bridge had used four players who were not club members. Although the winners' shield and medals had been presented to Hebden Bridge after the match, the Competition Committee decided it should be replayed. However, as this extra match would encroach the 'close season' (after 30th April), the Rugby Football Union refused to sanction it. The Competition No. 3 Committee subsequently disqualified Hebden Bridge and awarded the shield and medals to Bingley.

BARROW JOIN THE NORTHERN UNION

At a special meeting of members of the Barrow club, held at the Central Hall on Tuesday 20th April, it was agreed to resign from the Rugby Union in favour of joining the Northern Union.

HULL KINGSTON ROVERS JOIN THE NORTHERN UNION

Hull Kingston Rovers decided at their meeting on 18th May 1897 to apply for membership of the Northern Union, the club being admitted at a meeting of the latter on 1st June at the George Hotel, Huddersfield.[204]

1896-1897 STATISTICS

NORTHERN UNION

LANCASHIRE SENIOR COMPETITION

Final table	P	W	D	L	For	Agst	Pts
Broughton Rangers	26	19	5	2	201	52	43
Oldham	26	20	2	4	243	59	42
Tyldesley	26	15	2	9	159	80	32
Runcorn	26	13	5	8	134	62	31
Stockport	26	14	2	10	157	137	30
Swinton	26	12	5	9	125	82	29
Warrington	26	11	5	10	100	124	27
Leigh	26	11	4	11	105	147	26
St Helens	26	10	4	12	122	160	24
Widnes	26	10	3	13	113	164	23
Wigan	26	8	7	11	73	118	23
Rochdale Hornets	26	8	1	17	121	167	17
Salford	26	3	5	18	76	191	11
Morecambe	26	3	0	23	52	238	6

YORKSHIRE SENIOR COMPETITION

Final table	P	W	D	L	For	Agst	Pts
Brighouse Rangers	30	22	4	4	213	68	48
Manningham	30	21	4	5	291	129	46
Halifax	30	18	4	8	219	112	40
Hunslet	30	16	4	10	211	138	36
Hull	30	15	6	9	152	125	36
Batley	30	15	5	10	164	126	35
Bradford	30	15	3	12	170	157	33
Wakefield Trinity	30	13	4	13	172	154	30
Castleford	30	11	6	13	178	161	28
Huddersfield	30	10	7	13	142	179	27
Liversedge	30	13	0	17	176	233	26
Leeds	30	10	4	16	115	123	24
Leeds Parish Church	30	9	4	17	129	162	22
Bramley	30	9	3	18	101	193	21
Holbeck	30	7	4	19	86	223	18
Heckmondwike	30	3	4	23	72	308	10

NORTHERN UNION CHALLENGE CUP (52 entries)

Try – 3 points; conversion – 2; penalty goal – 3; drop-goal, field goal, goal from mark – 4.

First Round
Bradford 7, Oldham 3
Broughton Rangers 0, Warrington 0
Castleford 43, Allerton 3
Eastmoor (Wakefield) 26, Oldham Juniors 8
Holbeck 38, Latchford Rangers 3
Hull 9, Walkden 0
Hunslet 75 Broughton Recreation (Salford) 5
Leeds 11, Rochdale St Clements 0
Leigh 0, Wakefield Trinity 0
Manningham 31, Dukinfield 3
Morecambe 8, Bramley 8 (at Bramley)
Rochdale Hornets 63, Waterhead Hornets (Oldham) 3
Runcorn 65, Warrington Locomotive 0
Runcorn Recreation 0, Leeds Parish Church 42 (at Leeds PC)
St Helens 58, Lees (Oldham) 0
Stockport Rangers 5, Halifax 55 (at Halifax)
Swinton 12, Huddersfield 4
Warrington St Mary's 0, Salford 28 (at Salford)
Widnes 55, Atherton Hornets 0
Wigan 3, Radcliffe 0
Byes: 12 teams drew a bye to next round

First Round Replays
Bramley 6, Morecambe 4
Wakefield Trinity 13, Leigh 4
Warrington 3, Broughton Rangers 0

Second Round
Bramley 0, Batley 11
Brighouse Rangers 11, Wakefield Trinity 4
Crompton 26, Bradford Church Hill 0
Eastmoor 3, Stockport 3
Leeds Parish Church 0, Halifax 11
Liversedge 9, Heckmondwike 4
St Helens 17, Castleford 3
St Helens Recreation 0, Rochdale Hornets 8 (at Rochdale Hornets)
Thornton Rangers 4, Runcorn 52 (at Runcorn)
Swinton 15, Hunslet 0
Swinton Church 3, Bradford 68 (at Bradford)

Second Round *continued*
Tyldesley 9, Leeds 3
Warrington 24, Holbeck 0
Werneth 0, Salford 30 (at Salford)
Widnes 11, Hull 0
Wigan 7, Manningham 0

Second Round Replay
Stockport 28, Eastmoor 8

Third Round
Batley 6, Brighouse Rangers 3
Bradford 4, Tyldesley 8
Crompton 0, Halifax 50 (at Halifax)
Rochdale Hornets 3, Swinton 3
St Helens 11, Wigan 0
Stockport 8, Salford 0
Warrington 6, Liversedge 0
Widnes 14, Runcorn 0

Third Round Replay
Swinton 10, Rochdale Hornets 0

Fourth Round
Batley 10, Widnes 0
St Helens 12, Tyldesley 0
Swinton 3, Stockport 0
Warrington 10, Halifax 8

Semi-finals
Batley 6, Warrington 0 (at Fartown, Huddersfield)
St Helens 7, Swinton 0 (at Wheater's Field, Broughton)

FINAL
Saturday 24 April 1897 at Headingley, Leeds
BATLEY 10 *Back*: A Garner. *Three-quarters*: WP Davies, D Fitzgerald, JB Goodall (capt, t),
I Shaw. *Half-backs*: H Goodall, J Oakland (dg). *Forwards*: F Fisher, J Gath, J Littlewood,
G Maine, JT Munns (t), M Shackleton, R Spurr, C Stubley.
ST HELENS 3 *Back*: T Foulkes (capt). *Three-quarters*: R Doherty, D Traynor (t), J Barnes,
W Jacques. *Half-backs*: F Little, R O'Hara. *Forwards*: W Briers, P Dale, T Reynolds,
S Rimmer, J Thompson, W Whiteley, T Winstanley, W Winstanley.
Attendance: 13,492   *Referee*: JH Smith (Widnes)

COUNTY CHAMPIONSHIP

Saturday 17 October 1896 at Edgeley Park, Stockport
CHESHIRE 0 *Back*: F Saville (Stock). *Three-quarters*: G Robinson (Stock), P Sands (Stock),
J Butterworth (Run), TH Warder (Run). *Half-backs*: A Allen (Stock), J Faulkner (Run).
Forwards: H Farmer (Run), W Faulkner (Run), A Garside (Stock), J Langley (Run),
E Longthorpe (Stock), H Moss (Duk), J Mottershead (Stock), S Walker (Run).
LANCASHIRE 8 *Back*: T Coop (Lei). *Three-quarters*: S Lees (Old), H Chapman (BroR),
J Valentine (Swi, t, c), R Holmes (More). *Half-backs*: J Berry (Tyl, t), G Messenger (BroR).
Forwards: E Bonser (Old), W Briers (StH), J Brown (Wig), T Cleminson (BroR), R Edwards
(Old), W Robinson (BroR), J Simpson (RochH), J Worthington (Tyl).
Attendance: 9,000   *Referee*: WH Bairstow (Wakefield)

Saturday 7 November 1896 at The Boulevard, Hull
YORKSHIRE 17 *Back*: GE Lorimer (Mann). *Three-quarters*: FW Cooper (Brad),
AE Goldthorpe (Hun, c, pg), F Firth (Hal), A Hambrecht (Bram, t). *Half-backs*: JA Rigg

(Capt, Hal), R Sunderland (Mann, t). *Forwards*: F Clegg (Mann, t), J Conley (LeePC), G Kitson (Hal, t), RJ Robertson (Brad), H Speed (Cas), RE Sugden (BrigR), O Walsh (Hun), W Walton (Wak).
CHESHIRE 10 *Back*: S Houghton (Run). *Three-quarters*: T Richardson (Run), J Butterworth (Run), F Saville (capt, Stock, dg), W Robinson (Stock). *Half-backs*: A Allen (Stock), B Booth (Stock, t). *Forwards*: A Garside (Stock), F Gayter (Run), T Gibson (Stock), O Hughes (Run), J Langley (Run), W Lightfoot (Run), H Moss (Duk), J Mottershead (Stock, t).
Attendance: 5,000   *Referee*: W Dillon (Warrington)

Saturday 21 November 1896 at Watersheddings, Oldham
LANCASHIRE 7 *Back*: H Eagland (Old). *Three-quarters*: S Lees (Old), H Chapman (BroR), J Valentine (capt, Swi, t), R Holmes (More). *Half-backs*: A Lees (Old), H Varley (Old, dg). *Forwards*: E Bonser (Old), W Briers (StH), J Brown (Wig), T Cleminson (BroR), R Edwards (Old), W Robinson (BroR), J Simpson (RochH), J Taylor (War).
YORKSHIRE 3 *Back*: GE Lorimer (Mann). *Three-quarters*: FW Cooper (Brad), J Brown (Mann), F Firth (Hal, t), A Hambrecht (Bram). *Half-backs*: JA Rigg (capt, Hal), R Wood (Livs). *Forwards*: T Broadley (Brad), F Clegg (Mann), J Conley (LeePC), G Kitson (Hal), H Speed (Cas), RE Sugden (BrigR), M Sutcliffe (Hud), W Walton (Wak).
Attendance: 15,000   *Referee*: J Bruckshaw (Stockport)

Final table

	P	W	D	L	For	Agst	Pts
Lancashire	2	2	0	0	15	3	4
Yorkshire	2	1	0	1	20	17	2
Cheshire	2	0	0	2	10	25	2

RUGBY UNION

LANCASHIRE CLUB CHAMPIONSHIP

Final table	P	W	D	L	For	Agst	Pts
Littleborough	13	10	3	0	129	21	23
Leigh Shamrocks	11	9	0	2	80	34	18
Cheetham Hill	10	5	1	4	51	44	11
Mossley	10	5	1	4	45	57	11
Castleton Moor	14	6	0	8	64	69	12
Whitworth	12	5	0	7	59	63	10
Rochdale Rangers	11	2	1	8	27	84	5
Boothstown	13	1	2	10	28	111	4
Record expunged:							
Barton	15	9	0	6	101	79	18
Blackley Rangers	14	7	2	5	83	33	16
Clifton	3	1	0	2	9	38	2

Note 1: Clifton withdrew (Jan 1897); last match played was Oct 1896.
Note 2: Barton, Blackley Rangers both withdrew Mar 1897 to join Northern Union.
Note 3: Further defections to the Northern Union caused the competition to be discontinued during March 1897 with several fixtures unfulfilled.

NORTH WESTERN LEAGUE

Final table	P	W	D	L	For	Agst	Pts
Millom	8	6	1	1	54	21	13
Lancaster*	7	5	1	1	58	10	9
Barrow	8	4	0	4	38	37	8
Ulverston	7	2	2	3	49	31	6
Askam	8	0	0	8	5	105	0

*Two points deducted for refusing to replay Ulverston (at Barrow) following crowd disturbance at Ulverston

YORKSHIRE COMPETITION NO. 1

Final table	P	W	D	L	For	Agst	Pts
Hull Kingston Rovers	25	22	0	3	293	64	44
Featherstone	26	20	2	4	319	93	42
Pudsey	25	14	2	9	140	160	30
Castleford	26	14	2	10	244	122	30
Cleckheaton	26	13	3	10	179	148	29
Morley	26	12	4	10	163	107	28
Sowerby Bridge	25	13	1	11	130	131	27
Shipley	26	12	2	12	130	140	26
York	26	11	3	12	165	158	25
Elland	26	10	4	12	152	147	24
Otley	26	9	2	15	121	220	20
Wortley	26	8	3	15	109	175	19
Dewsbury	25	6	4	15	88	218	16
Bowling	26	0	0	26	36	386	0

Note: Hull Kingston Rovers v Sowerby Bridge, Dewsbury v Pudsey not played.

YORKSHIRE COMPETITION NO. 2

Final table	P	W	D	L	For	Agst	Pts
Keighley	24	20	2	2	272	56	42
Alverthorpe	23	17	4	2	146	47	38
Normanton	24	13	5	6	165	86	31
Skipton	22	12	3	7	143	63	27
Ossett	23	8	6	9	145	142	22
Silsden	21	8	3	10	145	112	19
Mytholmroyd*	20	10	1	9	93	136	19
Stanningley	21	8	2	11	71	104	18
Goole	23	8	2	13	106	140	18
Outwood Church	22	7	4	11	67	153	18
Idle	22	8	1	13	143	156	17
Bowling Old Lane	24	4	2	18	62	201	10
Mirfield**	15	1	1	13	31	193	3

*Two points deducted for breach of professional rules
**Mirfield suspended (Jan 1897) for failing to fulfil two fixtures; results retained in table
Note: Fixtures incomplete due to postponements.

Yorkshire Competition No. 2 Promotion Test Match
Keighley 9, Bowling 8 (at Ring o' Bells Ground, Shipley)
(Keighley promoted to Yorkshire Competition No. 1, Bowling relegated)

YORKSHIRE COMPETITION NO. 3 (GROUP A)

Final table	P	W	D	L	For	Agst	Pts
Bingley	20	15	4	1	176	41	34
Farsley	20	15	2	3	229	53	32
Keighley Shamrocks	20	13	2	5	159	47	28
Harrogate	20	9	4	7	118	71	22
Saltaire	20	8	6	6	72	130	22
Yeadon	20	9	3	8	107	175	21
Brownroyd Recreation	20	7	5	8	90	64	19
Windhill	20	6	5	9	88	89	17
Sutton	20	4	3	13	41	148	11
Guiseley	20	3	2	15	37	176	8
Bradford Celtic	20	1	4	15	30	153	6

Note: Nine postponed fixtures declared scoreless draws, affecting Brownroyd Recreation, Saltaire (3 matches each), Bradford Celtic, Harrogate, Sutton, Windhill, Yeadon (2 each), Bingley, Guiseley (1 each).

YORKSHIRE COMPETITION NO. 3 (GROUP B)

Final table	P	W	D	L	For	Agst	Pts
Hebden Bridge	14	12	1	1	147	36	25
Birstall	14	11	2	1	145	14	24
Luddendenfoot	14	5	5	4	111	30	15
Wyke	14	5	3	6	37	62	13
Todmorden	14	4	3	7	47	81	11
Milnsbridge	14	3	3	8	33	91	9
Paddock	14	2	4	8	61	87	8
Low Moor St Mark's	14	3	1	10	30	210	7

Note 1: Six postponed fixtures declared scoreless draws, affecting Luddendenfoot, Wyke (3 matches each), Milnsbridge, Paddock (2 each), Hebden Bridge, Todmorden (1 each).
Note 2: Dewsbury St Paulinus, Lockwood (Huddersfield) and Turnbridge (Huddersfield) withdrew before the competition began.

Yorkshire Competition No. 3 Final
Hebden Bridge 3, Bingley 3 (at Beech Ground, Sowerby Bridge)

Yorkshire Competition No. 3 Final Replay
Hebden Bridge 3, Bingley 0 (at Windhill FC ground, Bradford)
Bingley protested that Hebden Bridge included 4 ineligible players and a second replay was ordered. Following the RFU's refusal to sanction the match (as it would have taken place after the season's deadline) the trophy was awarded to Bingley.

CUMBERLAND COUNTY CHALLENGE CUP (11 entries)
Try – 3 points; conversion – 2; penalty goal – 3; drop-goal, field goal, goal from mark – 4.

First Round
Brookland Rovers 10, Whitehaven 4
Maryport 3, Aspatria 22
Penrith United 6, Whitehaven Recreation 5
Byes: Carlisle, Cockermouth, Seaton, Wath Brow, Workington

Second Round
Aspatria 0, Seaton 3
Carlisle 5, Brookland Rovers 6
Wath Brow 0, Cockermouth 0
Workington 26, Penrith United 0

Second Round Replay
Cockermouth 12, Wath Brow 5

Semi-finals
Cockermouth 0, Workington 0 (at Sandy Lonning, Maryport)
Seaton 30, Brookland Rovers 0 (at Lonsdale Park, Workington)

Semi-final Replay
Cockermouth 10, Workington 3 (at Seaton)

FINAL
Saturday 17 April 1897 at the Whitehaven Cricket Ground
SEATON 14 *Back*: F Moran. *Three-quarters*: T Fletcher, E Sandwith, Joe Sandwith (capt, c), Joe Owens (t). *Half-backs*: R Fletcher, J Fisher (t). *Forwards*: J Edwards, R Falcon, JG Fletcher (t), M Linton, T Little, John Owens, W Studholme (t), J Wright.
COCKERMOUTH 0 *Back*: JC Turner. *Three-quarters*: H Welsh, J Jackson, W Jackson (capt), T Nicholson. *Half-backs*: L Bowe, R Cuthbertson. *Forwards*: H Banks, TG Banks, C Bulman, W Callister, R Harley, J Ritson, J Smallwood, J Thompson.
Attendance: 2,000/3,000   *Referee*: J Ashton (Lancashire RU)

DURHAM COUNTY CHALLENGE CUP (18 entries)
Try – 3 points; conversion – 2; penalty goal – 3; drop-goal, field goal, goal from mark – 4.

First Round
Durham City 9, West Hartlepool 13
Sherburn House w/o Blackhill Rovers (withdrew)
Byes: 14 teams drew a bye to next round

Second Round
Hamsteels 9, Sheburn House 0
Hartlepool Old Boys 0, Hartlepool Rovers 19
Hetton Lyons 6, Old Dunelmians (Durham) 13
Houghton-le-Spring 8, South Shields 11
Sunderland 9, North Durham 3
Tudhoe 0, West Hartlepool 5
Tyne Dock w/o Stockton (disbanded)
Westoe 41, Blaydon 0

Third Round
Hartlepool Rovers 12, Old Dunelmians 8
South Shields 0, Westoe 3
Sunderland 16, Tyne Dock 5
West Hartlepool 50, Hamsteels 0

Semi-finals
Hartlepool Rovers 6, West Hartlepool 0
Sunderland 6, Westoe 0

FINAL
Saturday 3 April at 1897 Hollow Drift, Durham
HARTLEPOOL ROVERS 12 *Back*: RW Poole. *Three-quarters*: H Yeoman (c), C Hodgson, M Irvin, AG Murrell. *Half-backs*: W McSloy, JT Thompson (2t, dg). *Forwards*: J Athey, C Cox, W Dale, D Gilchrist, RF Oakes (capt), R Snowdon, J Wheatley, CS Wright.
SUNDERLAND 0 *Back*: DB Burn. *Three-quarters*: EW Elliot, J Taylor, NS Cox, W Thompson. *Half-backs*: A Featherstonehaugh, E Featherstonehaugh. *Forwards*: A Burn, W Holland, E Hunter, H McGowan, G Player, FO Poole, HA Taylor, B Wilson.
Attendance: 5,000   *Referee*: A Turnbull (Scotland RU)

LANCASHIRE CHAMPIONSHIP CUP (14 entries)
Try – 3 points; conversion – 2; penalty goal – 3; drop-goal, field goal, goal from mark – 4.

North Division:
First Round
Dalton 58, Carnforth 0
Ulverston 40, Swarthmoor 0
Askam w/o Roose

Second Round
Askam 19, Dalton 0
Bye: Ulverston

Semi-final
Askam 3, Ulverston 6

South Division:
First Round
Boothstown w/o Barton (withdrew)
Mossley w/o Leigh Shamrocks (withdrew)
Rochdale Rangers 3, Littleborough 0
Whitworth 6, Castleton Moor 8

Second Round
Castleton Moor w/o Mossley (withdrew)
Rochdale Rangers 3, Boothstown 0

Semi-final
Castleton Moor 0, Rochdale Rangers 0

Semi-final Replay
Rochdale Rangers 0, Castleton Moor 5

FINAL
Saturday 10 April 1997 at Quay Meadow, Lancaster
ULVERSTON 21 *Back*: Murphy. *Three-quarters*: Newsham, R Lewis (t), W Hine (t, 3c), H Wilson (t). *Half-backs*: W Hall, McDonald. *Forwards*: T Backhouse, T Clements, R Forshaw (2t), I Ireland, J Jackson, J McNicholas, W Turner, J Whittle.
CASTLETON MOOR 0 *Back*: F Woodhead. *Three-quarters*: W Lord, H Lord, T Cosgrove, S Lee. *Half-backs*: H Howarth, J Rigg. *Forwards*: W Briggs, A Chatterton, W Emmerson, A Jones, F Mason, E Rangeley, J Thomas, J Walker.
Attendance: 'small'   *Referee*: J Higson (Lancashire RU)

NORTHUMBERLAND COUNTY FOOTBALL CHALLENGE CUP (7 entries)
Try – 3 points; conversion – 2; penalty goal – 3; drop-goal, field goal, goal from mark – 4.

First Round
Percy Park 40, Brighton 0
Rockcliff 8, Wallsend 5 (aet)

Tynedale 0, North Elswick 0 (aet)
Bye: Northern

First Round Replay
North Elswick 0, Tynedale 6

Semi-finals
Tynedale 3, Percy Park 14
Rockcliff 8, Northern 3

FINAL
Saturday 3 April at 1897 Jesmond Ground, Newcastle
PERCY PARK 6 *Back*: AK Tasker. *Three-quarters*: GC Robinson, W Bates (t), FW Stone, CO Robinson (t). *Half-backs*: J Johnson, CW Russell. *Forwards*: F Atkinson, GT Bell, TG Boss, T Leinster, J McMenemy, A Nesbitt, HJ Spencer (capt), W Winter.
ROCKCLIFF 3 *Back*: G Taylor. *Three-quarters*: W Taylor (capt), S Anderson, T Rycroft, T Nicholson. *Half-backs*: J Scott, EW Taylor. *Forwards*: G Brough, T Finlay, JH Greenwell, W Hill (t), E Housten, A Styan, B Taylor, John Taylor.
Attendance: 7,000   *Referee*: J Oakland (Yorkshire RU)

YORKSHIRE COUNTY FOOTBALL CHALLENGE CUP (86 entries)
Try – 3 points; conversion – 2; penalty goal – 3; drop-goal, field goal, goal from mark – 4.

Preliminary Round
(54 teams in 4 sections; eight from each, indicated by 'q', qualified for next stage)

Section A: (Airedale, Craven, Northern): Guiseley (q), Harrogate (q), Keighley Shamrocks (q), Keighley Trinity (q), Keighley Zingari, Knaresborough (q), Ripon, Sutton, Tadcaster (q), Windhill (q), Yeadon (q)
Section B: (Bradford, Halifax, Huddersfield): Bradford Celtic, Brownroyd Recreation (q), Lockwood (q), Low Moor St Mark's, Luddendenfoot (q), Meltham and Meltham Mills (q), Milnsbridge (q), Nortonthorpe (q), Primrose Hill, Roberttown, Skelmanthorpe, Slaithwaite, Todmorden (q), Turnbridge, Wyke (q)

Section C: (Castleford, Hull and Ouse, Wakefield): Ackworth, Allerton Bywater (q), Brotherton St John's (q), Carlton (q), Doncaster Town (q), Fairburn, Flockton (q), Horbury Athletic, Kinsley (q), Kippax, Knottingley, Methley (q), Normanton United, Pontefract, Purston (q), Ryhill
Section D: (Dewsbury, Leeds, Morley): Batley St Mary's (q), Birstall (q), Dewsbury Moor Rangers (q), Dewsbury St Paulinus (q), Farsley (q), Gawthorpe Old Boys (q), Leeds Good Shepherd's, Mirfield, Morley Wanderers (q), Ravensthorpe Nelson, Thornhill Lees Trinity (q), Thornhill Parish Church

First Round
(* indicates 32 teams seeded to this round)
Alverthorpe* 14, Brownroyd Recreation 0
Bingley* 0, Castleford* 0
Birstall 0, Cleckheaton* 0
Carlton 0, Windhill 9
Dewsbury St Paulinus w/o Batley St Mary's (disbanded)
Doncaster Town 15, Selby* 7
Elland* 30, Bowling* 3
Farsley 11, Sowerby Bridge* 8
Guiseley 15, Keighley Trinity 3
Harrogate 17, Wyke 0
Hull Kingston Rovers* 20, Idle* 6
Keighley* 8, Goole* 10
Keighley Shamrocks 16, Knaresborough 3
Lockwood 3, Bowling Old Lane* 0
Meltham and Meltham Mills 0, Rothwell* 9
Milnsbridge 13, Allerton Bywater 3
Morley Wanderers 9, Morley* 37
Mytholmroyd* 0, Ossett* 0

First Round *continued*
Normanton* 27, Flockton 0
Nortonthorpe 8, Kinsley 9
Paddock* 0, Luddendenfoot 3
Pudsey* 0, Dewsbury* 0
Saltaire* w/o Dewsbury Moor Rangers (disbanded)
Shipley* 9, York* 0
Silsden* 5, Outwood Church* 6
Skipton* 31, Gawthorpe Old Boys 0
Stanningley* 5, Hebden Bridge* 8
Tadcaster 0, Featherstone* 38

Thornhill Lees Trinity 49, Methley 0
Todmorden 8, Otley* 13
Wortley* 16, Brotherton St John's 0
Yeadon 3, Purston 3

First Round Replays
Castleford 26, Bingley 0
Cleckheaton 6, Birstall 0
Dewsbury 6, Pudsey 0
Ossett 3, Mytholmroyd 0
Purston 14, Yeadon 8

Second Round
Alverthorpe 6, Hebden Bridge 0
Cleckheaton 10, Otley 3
Doncaster Town 5, Farsley 0
Featherstone 22, Wortley 0
Harrogate 5, Thornhill Lees Trinity 6
Hull Kingston Rovers 17, Skipton 0
Keighley Shamrocks 4, Purston 0
Kinsley 13, Elland 0
Lockwood 8, Dewsbury 3
Milnsbridge 12, Guiseley 5
Morley 18, Dewsbury St Paulinus 0
Normanton 3, Castleford 10
Rothwell 3, Outwood Church 6
Saltaire 4, Goole 28
Shipley 32, Luddendenfoot 5
Windhill 9, Ossett 5

Third Round
Castleford 7, Alverthorpe 6
Cleckheaton 0, Kinsley 6
Featherstone 19, Thornhill Lees Trinity 3
Hull Kingston Rovers 27, Outwood Church 0
Keighley Shamrocks 9, Goole 0
Lockwood 11, Doncaster Town 3
Shipley 12, Morley 5
Windhill 6, Milnsbridge 5

Fourth Round
Featherstone 8, Castleford 4
Hull Kingston Rovers 30, Keighley Shamrocks 0
Shipley 8, Kinsley 3
Windhill 4, Lockwood 3

Semi-finals
Hull Kingston Rovers 30, Windhill 0 (at Clarence Street, York)
Shipley 4, Featherstone 0 (at Oldfield Lane, Wortley)

FINAL
Saturday 17 April 1897 at Meanwood Road, Leeds
HULL KINGSTON ROVERS 11 *Back*: J Spavieri (c). *Three-quarters*: D Morfitt, S Morfitt (t), T Ripton (capt), H Tullock. *Half-backs*: C Coyne, C Fletcher (t). *Forwards*: R Blades, J Geenty, M Gledhill, A Kemp, P McDermott, J Noble, J Rhodes (t), A Starks.
SHIPLEY 5 *Back*: H Ward (capt). *Three-quarters*: A Hargreaves, CE Jennings, H Hall, J Whiteley. *Half-backs*: C Emmott (c), J Lawrenson. *Forwards*: F Elstub, J Goldsborough, N Greenwood, H Moon, E Pearson, F Pratt, T Town (t), A Whittingham.
Attendance: 3,000   *Referee*: J Higson (Lancashire RU)

COUNTY CHAMPIONSHIP

NORTHERN GROUP

Saturday 24 October 1896 at Lonsdale Park, Workington
CUMBERLAND 6 *Back*: JH Moore (Mil). *Three-quarters*: J Young (Mil), FR Moore (Mil), JC Broughton (PenU), WS Graham (Carl). *Half-backs*: T James (Mil), S Northmore (Mil, 2t). *Forwards*: TD Bell (Carl), JH Blacklock (Asp), Jim Davidson (capt, Asp), R Falcon (BrookR), S Hoggarth (Mil), E Knowles (Mil), W Moore (Sea), W Young (Work).
DURHAM 0 *Back*: RW Poole (HartR). *Three-quarters*: JJ Gowans (Wes), WE Kassell (capt, SSh), CY Adamson (DurC), WJ Robertson (SSh). *Half-backs*: W Guy (Tud), F Marston (Tud). *Forwards*: T Burt (SherH), T Emmerson (WHart), GC Kerr (ODun), RF Oakes (HartR), G Spraggin (NDur), P Tunney (Tud), H Walker (ODun), CS Wright (HartR).
Attendance: 2,000   *Referee*: JM Mawson (Barrow)

Saturday 31 October 1896 at Jesmond Ground, Newcastle
NORTHUMBERLAND 34 *Back*: WW Gibson (Nor). *Three-quarters*: T Nicholson (Rock, t), W Bates (PerPk), S Anderson (Rock, t), GC Robinson (PerPk, 4t). *Half-backs*: W Douglas (Brighton), EW Taylor (Rock, 2t,5c). *Forwards*: AC Blackett (Nor), FE Dotchin (Nor), J Finlay (Wall), JH Greenwell (Rock), W Hamilton (Tynd), J Lindsay (Tud), J Smith (Wall), HJ Spencer (PerPk).
WESTMORLAND 0 *Back*: F Hoggath (Lanc). *Three-quarters*: JK Robinson (KirkL), J Holmes (Stav), W Hine (Ulv), HH Skelton (Amb). *Half-backs*: AS Dixon (Amb), G Dixon ('Kendal'). *Forwards*: L Bowe (Amb), GW Braithwaite ('Kendal'), J Carradus (Burn), J Harrison ('Kendal'), CB Punchard (KirkL), W Robinson (Amb), J Stavert (Burn), JH Thompson (Burn).
Attendance: 2,000   *Referee*: JH Reay (Durham)

Saturday 7 November 1896 at Upper Park, Birkenhead
CHESHIRE 0 *Back*: M Linton (BirkPk). *Three-quarters*: JAS Cannell (NewB), FP Jones (NewB), B Murphy (BirkW), AW Harris (NewB). *Half-backs*: A Dillon (BirkW), ID Heyes (BirkW). *Forwards*: J Baxter (BirkPk), EH Bradshaw (Sale), H Fletcher (Sale), J Gerrard (BirkW), E Herschell (BirkPk), F Ingham (BirkW), A Jones (BirkW), J Searle (Alt).
LANCASHIRE 17 *Back*: CE Crews (Man, t). *Three-quarters*: GP Wincey (Man, t), R Lewis (Ulv, c), T Bowker (Bar), R Bell (Bar, 2t). *Half-backs*: GG Allen (Liv), W Parlane (Man). *Forwards*: HP Bannerman (Man), RW Forshaw (Ulv), GE Hughes (Bar, t), R Pierce (Liv), WB Stoddart (Liv), CEK Thompson (Lanc), EB Thompson (Lanc), RD Wood (LivOB).
Attendance: 3,000   *Referee*: J Oakland (Yorkshire)

Saturday 7 November 1896 at Mowbray Road, South Shields
DURHAM 3 *Back*: RW Poole (HartR). *Three-quarters*: JJ Gowans (capt, Wes), WJ Robertson (SSh), JE Parker (WHart), GS Legard (ODun). *Half-backs*: CY Adamson (DurC), W Guy (Tud). *Forwards*: T Burt (SherH), GC Kerr (ODun), RF Oakes (HartR), A Stephenson (Tud), AJ Troupe (Tud, t), P Tunney (Tud), H Walker (ODun), CS Wright (HartR).
YORKSHIRE 15 *Back*: J Metcalfe (Fea). *Three-quarters*: EF Fookes (capt, SowB), W Murgatroyd (Idle, t), JT Taylor (Cas), I Rawnsley (Elland). *Half-backs*: H Myers (Kei),

T Stirk (Mor, t). *Forwards*: JH Barron (Bing), J Gath (Mor, t), T Lord (Fea), J Rhodes (HKR), JH Shooter (Mor, t), A Starks (HKR, t), WP Swabey (OutC), JW Ward (Pud).
Attendance: 5,000/6,000   *Referee*: JA Smith (Scotland)

Saturday 14 November 1896 at Warwick Road, Carlisle
CUMBERLAND 8 *Back*: R Petrie (BrookR). *Three-quarters*: J Young (Mil), FR Moore (Mil, 2t, c), JC Broughton (PenU), A Smith (Carl). *Half-backs*: T James (Mil), S Northmore (Mil). *Forwards*: R Bell (Work), TD Bell (Carl), JH Blacklock (Asp), Jim Davidson (capt, Asp), S Hoggarth (Mil), E Knowles (Mil), W Moore (Sea), W Young (Work).
CHESHIRE 0 *Back*: M Linton (BirkPk). *Three-quarters*: JAS Cannell (NewB), FP Jones (NewB), B Murphy (BirkW), JD Watson (BirkW). *Half-backs*: HD Pagden (Sale), H Parratt (Sale). *Forwards*: J Baxter (BirkPk), EH Bradshaw (Sale), H Fletcher (Sale), J Gerrard (BirkW), E Herschell (BirkPk), F Ingham (BirkW), A Jones (BirkW), J Searle (Alt).
Attendance: 'good'   *Referee*: J Ashton (Lancashire)

Saturday 14 November 1896 at Whalley Range, Manchester
LANCASHIRE 28 *Back*: CE Crews (Man). *Three-quarters*: GP Wincey (Man), R Lewis (Ulv, 2c), T Bowker (Bar), R Bell (Bar, 3t). *Half-backs*: GG Allen (capt, Liv, t), W Parlane (Man, t). *Forwards*: HP Bannerman (Man), RW Forshaw (Ulv, t), GE Hughes (Bar), R Pierce (Liv), WB Stoddart (Liv, 2t), CEK Thompson (Lanc), EB Thompson (Lanc), RD Wood (LivOB).
WESTMORLAND 0 *Back*: F Hoggath (Lanc). *Three-quarters*: JK Robinson (KirkL), J Holmes (Stav), JC Taylforth (KirkL), W Hall (Lanc). *Half-backs*: AS Dixon (Amb), F Workman (Amb). *Forwards*: L Bowe (Amb), J Elliott (Burn), T Gibson (Lanc), W Jackson ('Burton'), CB Punchard (KirkL), W Robinson (Amb), J Thompson (Stav), W Woodhouse (KirkL).
Attendance: 500   *Referee*: W Oxley (Yorkshire)

Saturday 14 November 1896 at Victoria Pleasure Grounds, Goole
YORKSHIRE 18 *Back*: J Metcalfe (Fea). *Three-quarters*: EF Fookes (capt, SowB, t), W Murgatroyd (Idle, dg), JT Taylor (Cas, dg, gm), F Murgatroyd (Idle). *Half-backs*: H Myers (Kei), T Taylor (Fea). *Forwards*: JH Barron (Bing), J Gath (Mor, t), EH Jacobson (Wort), J Rhodes (HKR), JH Shooter (Mor), A Starks (HKR), WP Swabey (OutC), JW Ward (Pud).
NORTHUMBERLAND 0 *Back*: WW Gibson (Nor). *Three-quarters*: GC Robinson (PerPk), S Anderson (Rock), WG Baty (SSh), T Nicholson (Rock). *Half-backs*: SC Lockerby (PerPk), EW Taylor (Rock). *Forwards*: AC Blackett (Nor), FE Dotchin (Nor), J Finlay (Wall), JH Greenwell (Rock), WN Greenwell (Rock), W Hamilton (Tynd), J Lindsay (Tud), HJ Spencer (PerPk).
Attendance: 3,000   *Referee*: JW Maclean (Lancashire)

Saturday 21 November 1896 at Upper Park, Birkenhead
CHESHIRE 37 *Back*: M Linton (BirkPk). *Three-quarters*: JAS Cannell (NewB, 2t, 2c), JD Watson (BirkW, t, 3c), B Murphy (BirkW, 2t), AW Harris (NewB). *Half-backs*: H Headen (NewB, t), NS Wood (BirkPk). *Forwards*: J Baxter (BirkPk), EH Bradshaw (Sale), H Fletcher (Sale, t), J Gerrard (BirkW, t), E Herschell (BirkPk), F Ingham (BirkW), A Jones (BirkW, t), J Searle (Alt).
WESTMORLAND 0 *Back*: F Sharpe ('Kendal'). *Three-quarters*: HT Wilson (Ulv), JK Robinson (KirkL), R Vity (Amb), E Vity (Amb). *Half-backs*: AS Dixon (Amb), D Geddes (Carn). *Forwards*: Adams ('Burton'), T Bell (KirkL), L Bowe (Amb), GW Braithwaite ('Kendal'), H Dean (KirkL), W Newton (Amb), W Robinson (Amb), J Whitwell (Bar).
Attendance: 3,000   *Referee*: WW Higgins (Lancashire)

Saturday 21 November 1896 at Manchester Athletic Ground, Fallowfield
LANCASHIRE 8 *Back*: CE Crews (Man). *Three-quarters*: GP Wincey (Man), R Lewis (Ulv), T Bowker (Bar, c), R Bell (Bar). *Half-backs*: GG Allen (capt, Liv, 2t), W Parlane (Man). *Forwards*: HP Bannerman (Man), RW Forshaw (Ulv), GE Hughes (Bar), R Pierce (Liv), J Pinch (Lanc), WB Stoddart (Liv), CEK Thompson (Lanc), RD Wood (LivOB).
YORKSHIRE 17 *Back*: J Metcalfe (Fea). *Three-quarters*: W Murgatroyd (Idle), JT Taylor (Cas), EF Fookes (capt, SowB, t, c), F Murgatroyd (Idle, t). *Half-backs*: H Myers (Kei), T Taylor (Fea). *Forwards*: JH Barron (Bing), J Gath (Mor), EH Jacobson (Wort, 2t), J Rhodes (HKR), JH Shooter (Mor), A Starks (HKR, t), WP Swabey (OutC), JW Ward (Pud).
Attendance: 4,000/5,000   *Referee*: W Yiend (Durham)

Saturday 28 November 1896 at Cavendish Park, Barrow
LANCASHIRE 0 *Back*: FJ Wildman (Bar). *Three-quarters*: GP Wincey (Man), T Bowker (Bar), R Bell (Bar), R Lewis (Ulv). *Half-backs*: G Cookson (Man), W Parlane (Man). *Forwards*: HP Bannerman (Man), RW Forshaw (Ulv), GE Hughes (Bar), R Pierce (Liv), J Pinch (Lanc), WB Stoddart (Liv), CEK Thompson (Lanc), RD Wood (LivOB).
CUMBERLAND 3 *Back*: JH Moore (Mil). *Three-quarters*: J Young (Mil), FR Moore (Mil), T Fletcher (Sea), W Cunningham (Bar, t). *Half-backs*: T James (Mil), S Northmore (Mil). *Forwards*: R Bell (Work), TD Bell (Carl), JH Blacklock (Asp), Jim Davidson (capt, Asp), S Hoggarth (Mil), E Knowles (Mil), H Nixon (BrookR), J Smitheram (Mil).
Attendance: 6,000   *Referee*: Rev F Marshall (Yorkshire)

Saturday 5 December 1896 at Ashbrooke Ground, Sunderland
DURHAM 21 *Back*: RW Poole (HartR). *Three-quarters*: WJ Robertson (SSh, t), JE Parker (WHart, dg), DR Thomas (WHart, t), CE Leslie-Jones (NDur, t). *Half-backs*: CY Adamson (DurC, t, c), JT Thompson (HartR). *Forwards*: T Burt (SherH), GC Kerr (ODun), RF Oakes (capt, HartR, t), G Quest (SSh), AJ Troupe (Tud), P Tunney (Tud), H Walker (ODun), CS Wright (HartR).
CHESHIRE 6 *Back*: M Linton (BirkPk). *Three-quarters*: T Lewis (BirkW, t), AW Harris (NewB), JD Watson (BirkW), B Murphy (BirkW, t). *Half-backs*: H Headen (NewB), NS Wood (BirkPk). *Forwards*: D Atkinson (BirkW), J Baxter (BirkPk), H Fletcher (Sale), J Gerrard (BirkW), E Herschell (BirkPk), F Ingham (BirkW), A Jones (BirkW), J Searle (Alt).
Attendance: 2,000   *Referee*: JA Miller (Yorkshire)

Saturday 5 December 1896 at Salthouse Road, Millom
CUMBERLAND 15 *Back*: JH Moore (Mil). *Three-quarters*: J Young (Mil, t), T Fletcher (Sea, t), A Smith (Carl),W Cunningham (Bar). *Half-backs*: T James (Mil, t), S Northmore (Mil, t). *Forwards*: JH Blacklock (Asp), Jim Davidson (capt, Asp), D Elliott (Carl, t), R Falcon (BrookR), S Hoggarth (Mil), E Knowles (Mil), J Walker (Asp), W Young (Work).
WESTMORLAND 0 *Back*: J Elliott (Burn). *Three-quarters*: HT Wilson (Ulv), JK Robinson (KirkL), J Stavert (Burn), E Vity (Amb). *Half-backs*: J Hugginson (Burn), H Reed (Burn). *Forwards*: L Bowe (Amb), J Hadwin (Ulv/'Kendal'), W Huck (Stav), F Lowery (Burn), J Major (Burn), W Robinson (Amb), J Whitwell (Bar), W Woodhouse (KirkL).
Attendance: 1,000   *Referee*: JM Mawson (Barrow)

Saturday 9 January 1897 at Victoria Ground, West Hartlepool
DURHAM 0 *Back*: RW Poole (HartR). *Three-quarters*: RA Moreland (DurU), JE Parker (WHart), DR Thomas (WHart), GS Legard (ODun). *Half-backs*: CY Adamson (capt,

DurC), W Guy (Tud). *Forwards*: T Burt (SherH), M Hastings (HartR), T Hope (Hou),
A Stephenson (Tud), AJ Troupe (Tud), P Tunney (Tud), H Walker (ODun), CS Wright (HartR).
LANCASHIRE 9 *Back*: FJ Wildman (Bar). *Three-quarters*: R Lewis (Ulv), T Bowker (Bar),
W Pierce (Liv), JDK Jones (Liv, t). *Half-backs*: C Danby (Lanc), W McDonald (Ulv).
Forwards: RW Forshaw (Ulv), A Long (Bla), W Mortimer (Liv), R Pierce (Liv), J Pinch
(Lanc), EB Thompson (Lanc, 2t), S Tillison (CasM), RD Wood (LivOB).
Attendance: 4,000   *Referee*: JD Boswell (Scotland)

Saturday 16 January 1897 at Scratcherd Lane, Morley
YORKSHIRE 19 *Back*: J Metcalfe (Fea). *Three-quarters*: EF Fookes (capt, SowB, t),
W Murgatroyd (Idle), JT Taylor (Cas, pg), F Murgatroyd (Idle). *Half-backs*: H Myers (Kei,
c), T Stirk (Mor, t). *Forwards*: J Gath (Mor, t), EH Jacobson (Wort), R Little (Skip), T Lord
(Fea), J Rhodes (HKR, t), JH Shooter (Mor), A Starks (HKR), WP Swabey (OutC, c).
WESTMORLAND 0 *Back*: C Pearson (Amb). *Three-quarters*: HF Newton (Amb/OxfU),
JK Robinson (KirkL), HR Palmer (KirkL/CamU), HT Wilson (Ulv). *Half-backs*:
J Hugginson (Burn), A Jowett (KirkL). *Forwards*: L Bowe (Amb), J Elliott (Burn),
T Fleming (Stav), J Jackson (Ulverston), J Major (Burn), W Robinson (Amb), J Whitwell
(Bar), W Woodhouse (KirkL).
Attendance: 2,000   *Referee*: JS Turnbull (Lancashire)

Saturday 6 February 1897 at Preston Avenue, North Shields
NORTHUMBERLAND 17 *Back*: WW Gibson (Nor). *Three-quarters*: F Wheler-Sime (Nor,
2t), S Anderson (Rock, t), W Bates (PerPk, c), JC Seymour (Wall, 2t). *Half-backs*: HS Bell
(Nor), SC Lockerby (PerPk). *Forwards*: AC Blackett (Nor), J Finlay (Wall), JH Greenwell
(Rock), WN Greenwell (Rock), J Lindsay (Tud), J Nesbitt (Wall), HJ Spencer (PerPk),
RC Stevenson (Nor).
CHESHIRE 0 *Back*: M Linton (BirkPk). *Three-quarters*: EC Harvey (Sale), W Hodgson
(Sale), JD Watson (BirkW), T Lewis (BirkW). *Half-backs*: HD Pagden (Sale), G Pendlebury
(Alt). *Forwards*: Barnett (Alt), J Hague (Sale), Hampson (Cheadle), HC Harvey (Sale),
E Herschell (BirkPk), A Jones (BirkW), J Murray (NewB), J Searle (Alt).
Attendance: 500   *Referee*: n/a

Saturday 13 February 1897 at Crown Flatts, Dewsbury
YORKSHIRE 14 *Back*: J Metcalfe (Fea). *Three-quarters*: EF Fookes (capt, SowB),
W Murgatroyd (Idle, t), JT Taylor (Cas, c), F Murgatroyd (Idle, 2t). *Half-backs*: H Myers
(Kei), CE Winpenny (Oss). *Forwards*: J Gath (Mor), T Hambleton (Cas), EH Jacobson (Wort,
t), R Little (Skip), R Rhodes (Cas), F Shaw (Cleck), WP Swabey (OutC), J Wilcock (Pud).
CHESHIRE 0 *Back*: M Linton (BirkPk). *Three-quarters*: JAS Cannell (NewB), JD Watson
(BirkW), B Murphy (BirkW), T Lewis (BirkW). *Half-backs*: G Pendlebury (Alt), NS Wood
(BirkPk). *Forwards*: J Baxter (BirkPk), EH Bradshaw (Sale), H Fletcher (Sale), J Gerrard
(BirkW), E Herschell (BirkPk), F Ingham (BirkW), A Jones (BirkW), J Searle (Alt).
Attendance: 3,000   *Referee*: H McBeath (Durham)

Saturday 13 February 1897 at Warwick Road, Carlisle
CUMBERLAND 0 *Back*: JH Moore (Mil). *Three-quarters*: J Young (Mil), T Fletcher (Sea),
FR Moore (Mil), A Smith (Carl). *Half-backs*: T James (Mil), S Northmore (Mil). *Forwards*:
JH Blacklock (Asp), Jim Davidson (capt, Asp), D Elliott (Carl), S Hoggarth (Mil),
E Knowles (Mil), W Moore (Work), J Walker (Asp), W Young (Work).

NORTHUMBERLAND 0 *Back*: WW Gibson (Nor). *Three-quarters*: JC Seymour (Wall), S Anderson (Rock), W Bates (PerPk), F Wheler-Sime (Nor). *Half-backs*: SC Lockerby (PerPk), EW Taylor (Rock). *Forwards*: AC Blackett (Nor), J Finlay (Wall), WN Greenwell (Rock), J Lindsay (Tud), J Nesbitt (Wall), T Robson (Tynd), HJ Spencer (PerPk), F Thew (Nor).
Attendance: 3,000   *Referee*: J Ashton (Lancashire)

Saturday 20 February 1897 at Wood Terrace, Westoe, South Shields
DURHAM 20 *Back*: RW Poole (HartR). *Three-quarters*: RA Moreland (DurU), JE Parker (WHart, t, gm), DR Thomas (WHart), GS Legard (ODun, 2t). *Half-backs*: J Moore (Wes), JT Thompson (HartR, 2c). *Forwards*: J Conley (Tud), GC Kerr (ODun), RF Oakes (capt, HartR), G Quest (SSh), A Stephenson (Tud), AJ Troupe (Tud), P Tunney (Tud), H Walker (ODun, t).
WESTMORLAND 0 *Back*: J Elliott (Burn). *Three-quarters*: JK Robinson (KirkL), HT Wilson (Ulv), HH Skelton (Amb), W Hall (Lanc). *Half-backs*: J Hugginson (Burn), A Jowett (KirkL). *Forwards*: L Bowe (Amb), E Brown, T Fleming (Stav), W Jackson ('Burton'), J Miller, G Murdock, J Whitwell (Bar), W Woodhouse (KirkL).
Attendance: 3,000   *Referee*: n/a
Note: Clubs not identified for E. Brown, J. Miller and G. Murdock (Westmorland).

Saturday 20 February 1897 at Lock Lane, Castleford
YORKSHIRE 3 *Back*: J Metcalfe (Fea). *Three-quarters*: RW Matterson (Selby), JT Taylor (Cas, pg), W Murgatroyd (capt, Idle), F Murgatroyd (Idle). *Half-backs*: H Myers (Kei), CE Winpenny (Oss). *Forwards*: J Gath (Mor), EH Jacobson (Wort), G Nowell (Kinsley), J Randall (Fea), R Rhodes (Cas), F Shaw (Cleck), JH Shooter (Mor), WP Swabey (OutC).
CUMBERLAND 9 *Back*: JH Buckett (Mil). *Three-quarters*: J Young (Mil, 2t), FR Moore (Mil), T Fletcher (Sea, t), W Cunningham (Bar). *Half-backs*: T James (Mil), S Northmore (Mil). *Forwards*: JH Blacklock (Asp), Jim Davidson (capt, Asp), D Elliott (Carl), S Hoggarth (Mil), E Knowles (Mil), W Moore (Work), J Walker (Asp), W Young (Work).
Attendance: 10,000   *Referee*: W Yiend (Durham)

Saturday 6 March 1897 at Quay Meadow, Lancaster
LANCASHIRE 8 *Back*: FJ Wildman (Bar). *Three-quarters*: R Bell (Bar), R Lewis (Ulv, c), T Bowker (Bar), PE Middleton (Man). *Half-backs*: G Cookson (Man), W Parlane (Man). *Forwards*: R Crabtree (Lit, t), WG Hogg (Man), GE Hughes (Bar), A Long (Bla), J Pinch (capt, Lanc, t), CEK Thompson (Lanc), T Tickle (Leigh Shamrocks), S Tillison (CasM).
NORTHUMBERLAND 19 *Back*: WW Gibson (Nor). *Three-quarters*: F Wheler-Sime (Nor), S Anderson (Rock, c), W Bates (PerPk), W Taylor (Rock, 3t). *Half-backs*: SC Lockerby (PerPk, 2t), EW Taylor (Rock, c). *Forwards*: AC Blackett (Nor), G Brough (Rock), J Finlay (Wall), JH Greenwell (Rock), J Munro (Wall), J Nesbitt (Wall), HJ Spencer (PerPk), F Thew (Nor).
Attendance: 5,000   *Referee*: JA Miller (Yorkshire)

Saturday 10 April 1897 at Jesmond Ground, Newcastle
NORTHUMBERLAND 28 *Back*: WW Gibson (Nor). *Three-quarters*: W Taylor (Rock, 3t), S Anderson (capt, Rock, 5c), W Bates (PerPk, t), GC Robinson (PerPk). *Half-backs*: HS Bell (Nor), C Samuel (PerPk). *Forwards*: AC Blackett (Nor), G Brough (Rock), J Finlay (Wall, 2t), COP Gibson (Nor), J Lindsay (Tud), J Nesbitt (Wall), HJ Spencer (PerPk), F Thew (Nor).
DURHAM 8 *Back*: W Taylor (Tud). *Three-quarters*: EW Elliot (Sund, t), JE Parker (WHart,

c), J Taylor (Sund), JD Taylor (Wes, t). *Half-backs*: A Featherstonhaugh (Sund), E Featherstonhaugh (Sund). *Forwards*: T Burt (SherH), J Conley (Tud), T Hope (Hou), GC Kerr (ODun), SV Lowrey (Wes), AJ Troupe (Tud), G Urwin (Tud), H Walker (ODun). *Attendance*: 3,000   *Referee*: n/a

Final table

	P	W	D	L	For	Agst	Pts
Cumberland	6	5	1	0	41	3	11
Yorkshire	6	5	0	1	86	20	10
Northumberland	6	4	1	1	98	34	9
Lancashire	6	3	0	3	70	39	6
Durham	6	2	0	4	52	64	4
Cheshire	6	1	0	5	43	77	2
Westmorland	6	0	0	6	0	153	0

SOUTH WESTERN GROUP

Results
Cornwall 5, Devonshire 10
Gloucestershire 6, Cornwall 0
Devonshire 13, Gloucestershire 6
Cornwall 0, Somersetshire 16
Gloucestershire 6, Somersetshire 11
Somersetshire 25, Devonshire 3

Final table

	P	W	D	L	For	Agst	Pts
Somersetshire	3	3	0	0	52	9	6
Devonshire	3	2	0	1	26	36	4
Gloucestershire	3	1	0	2	18	24	2
Cornwall	3	0	0	3	5	32	0

SOUTH EASTERN GROUP A

Results
Middlesex 5, Kent 8
Surrey 0, Midland Counties 16
Midland Counties 3, Kent 8
Middlesex 5, Midland Counties 10
Kent 18, Surrey 11
Surrey 6, Middlesex 0

Final table

	P	W	D	L	For	Agst	Pts
Kent	3	3	0	0	34	19	6
Midland Counties	3	2	0	1	29	13	4
Surrey	3	1	0	2	17	34	2
Middlesex	3	0	0	3	10	24	0

SOUTH EASTERN GROUP B

Results
Sussex 34, Eastern Counties 0
Sussex 6, Hampshire 15
Eastern Counties 3, Hampshire 15

Final table

	P	W	D	L	For	Agst	Pts
Hampshire	2	2	0	0	30	9	4
Sussex	2	1	0	1	40	15	2
Eastern Counties	2	0	0	2	3	49	0

South Eastern Group Final
Kent 25, Hampshire 0

Southern Final
Kent 7, Somersetshire 3

COUNTY CHAMPIONSHIP FINAL
Saturday 10 April 1897 at Warwick Road, Carlisle
KENT 9 *Back*: GW Gordon-Smith (Black). *Three-quarters*: A Latter (Black), WL Bunting (Rich, t), PMR Royds (RNC, t), W Walmsley (Southwark Home). *Half-backs*: R O'H Livesay (Black, dg), FC Wetherell (GuyHosp). *Forwards*: AG Gibson (LonS), F Jacob (CamU), AFC Luxmoore (CamU), NM Marples (Croy), P Maud (Black), F Mitchell (Black), AF Todd (Black), WE Tucker (Black).
CUMBERLAND 3 *Back*: JH Buckett (Mil). *Three-quarters*: J Young (Mil), T Fletcher (Sea), FR Moore (Mil), W Cunningham (Bar). *Half-backs*: T James (Mil), S Northmore (Mil). *Forwards*: JH Blacklock (Asp), Jim Davidson (capt, Asp), D Elliott (Carl), S Hoggarth (Mil), E Knowles (Mil), W Moore (Work, t), J Walker (Asp), W Young (Work).
Attendance: 5,000   *Referee*: DG Findlay (Scotland)

NON-COUNTY CHAMPIONSHIP MATCH
Saturday 26 October 1896 at Oldfield Lane, Wortley, Leeds
YORKSHIRE 11 *Back*: J Metcalfe (Fea, c). *Three-quarters*: EF Fookes (capt, SowB), W Murgatroyd (Idle), S Morfitt (HKR, t), I Rawnsley (Elland). *Half-backs*: H Myers (Kei), T Taylor (Fea). *Forwards*: JH Barron (Bing, t), T Broadley (Bing, t), EH Jacobson (Wort), T Lord (Fea), J Rhodes (HKR), JH Shooter (Mor), A Starks (HKR), JW Ward (Pud).
GLAMORGANSHIRE 5 *Back*: T Jones (Peny, c). *Three-quarters*: C Bowen (Llan), T Williams (Llwyn), TD Davies (Tre), R Messer (Swa). *Half-backs*: D Jones (Aber, t), W Phillips (Mou). *Forwards*: J Evans (Llwyn), I Griffiths (Aber), T Hayman (Bri), R Hellings (Llwyn), J Mackenzie (Pon), F Miller (Mou), J Rhapps (Peny), JT Williams (Swa).
Attendance: 4,000   *Referee*: E Seddon (Lancashire)

ENGLAND TRIAL MATCHES
Saturday 12 December 1896 at Athletic Ground, Richmond
SOUTH 3 *Back*: E Field (Rich). *Three-quarters*: FA Byrne (Mose), JF Byrne (Mose, t), FA Leslie-Jones (OxfU), WL Bunting (Rich). *Half-backs*: RO Schwarz (Rich), CM Wells (capt, Harl). *Forwards*: HW Dudgeon (Rich), PJ Ebdon (Well), LF Giblin (CamU), F Jacob (CamU), RH Mangles (Rich), W Mortimer (CamU), FM Stout (Glo), CE Wilson (Black).

Milestones & Stats 1869-1901

NORTH 0 *Back*: J Metcalfe (Fea). *Three-quarters*: EF Fookes (SowB), OG Mackie (CamU), T Fletcher (Sea), WJ Robertson (SSh). *Half-backs*: W Parlane (Man), EW Taylor (capt, Rock). *Forwards*: JH Barron (Bing), R Bell (Work), AC Blackett (Nor), RF Oakes (HartR), P Pierce (Liv), A Starks (HKR), WB Stoddart (Liv), JW Ward (Pud).
Attendance: 7,000/8,000   *Referee*: ET Gurdon (RU International Board)

Saturday 27 February 1897 at Crown Flatts, Dewsbury
NORTH 13 *Back*: J Metcalfe (Fea). *Three-quarters*: W Murgatroyd (Idle), JT Taylor (Cas), S Anderson (Rock, t, 2c), GC Robinson (PerPk). *Half-backs*: S Northmore (Mil), W Parlane (Man). *Forwards*: Jim Davidson (Asp), J Gath (Mor), S Hoggarth (Mil), E Knowles (Mil), RF Oakes (HartR), J Pinch (Lanc, 2t), WB Stoddart (capt, Liv), WP Swabey (OutC).
SOUTH 5 *Back*: AO Jones (Leic, c). *Three-quarters*: WN Pilkington (CamU, t), OG Mackie (CamU), FA Byrne (Mose), WL Bunting (Rich). *Half-backs*: R O'H Livesay (Black), CM Wells (capt, Harl). *Forwards*: HW Dudgeon (Rich), PJ Ebdon (Well), LF Giblin (CamU), F Jacob (CamU), RH Mangles (Rich), FM Stout (Glo), PC Tarbutt (Black), C Thomas (Barn).
Attendance: 6,000   *Referee*: W Cail (RFU Honorary Treasurer)

INTERNATIONAL CHAMPIONSHIP

Saturday 9 January 1897 at Rodney Parade, Newport
WALES 11 *Back*: WJ Bancroft (Swa, c). *Three-quarters*: C Bowen (Llan), EG Nicholls (Car), JA Gould (capt, New), TW Pearson (New, t). *Half-backs*: S Biggs (Car), D Jones (Aber, t). *Forwards*: AW Boucher (New, t), FH Cornish (Car), D Evans (Peny), J Evans (Llan), R Hellings (Llwyn), W Morris (Llan), H Packer (New), J Rhapps (Peny).
ENGLAND 0 *Back*: JF Byrne (Mose). *Three-quarters*: FA Byrne (Mose), T Fletcher (Sea), EM Baker (OxfU), EF Fookes (SowB). *Half-backs*: EW Taylor (capt, Rock), CM Wells (Harl). *Forwards*: W Ashford (Rich), JH Barron (Bing), PJ Ebdon (Well), F Jacob (CamU), RH Mangles (Rich), RF Oakes (HartR), WB Stoddart (Liv), FM Stout (Glo).
Attendance: 14,000   *Referee*: JT Magee (Ireland)

Saturday 6 February 1897 at Lansdowne Road, Dublin
IRELAND 13 *Back*: J Fulton (NIFC). *Three-quarters*: LQ Bulger (DubU, t, gm), TH Stevenson (EdinU), S Lee (NIFC), W Gardiner (NIFC, 2t). *Half-backs*: GG Allen (Liv), LM Magee (BecR). *Forwards*: WG Byron (NIFC), AD Clinch (Wand), EG Forrest (capt, Wand), JH Lytle (NIFC), JE McIlwaine (NIFC), CV Rooke (Monk), J Ryan (RockC), M Ryan (RockC).
ENGLAND 9 *Back*: JF Byrne (Mose, 2pg). *Three-quarters*: GC Robinson (PerPk, t), WL Bunting (Rich), JT Taylor (Cas), EF Fookes (SowB). *Half-backs*: S Northmore (Mil), EW Taylor (capt, Rock). *Forwards*: W Ashford (Rich), JH Barron (Bing), PJ Ebdon (Well), F Jacob (CamU), RH Mangles (Rich), RF Oakes (HartR), WB Stoddart (Liv), FM Stout (Glo).
Attendance: 12,000   *Referee*: DG Findlay (Scotland)

Saturday 13 March 1897 at Fallowfield, Manchester
ENGLAND 12 *Back*: JF Byrne (Mose, c, dg). *Three-quarters*: GC Robinson (PerPk, t), WL Bunting (Rich), OG Mackie (CamU), EF Fookes (SowB, t). *Half-backs*: EW Taylor (capt, Rock), CM Wells (Harl). *Forwards*: Jim Davidson (Asp), HW Dudgeon (Rich), LF Giblin (CamU), F Jacob (CamU), E Knowles (Mil), RF Oakes (HartR), J Pinch (Lanc), WB Stoddart (Liv).

SCOTLAND 3 *Back*: AR Smith (OxfU). *Half-backs*: AM Bucher (EdinA), W Neilson (LonS), T Scott (Haw), AW Robertson (EdinA). *Quarter-backs*: M Elliot (Haw), JW Simpson (RHSFP). *Forwards*: A Balfour (CamU), JH Dods (EdinA), WMC McEwan (EdinA), RG Macmillan (capt, LonS), MC Morrison (RHSFP), TM Scott (Haw), RC Stevenson (LonS), GO Turnbull (LonS).
Attendance: 10,000   *Referee*: JT Magee (Ireland)

Other result
Scotland 8, Ireland 3

Final table

	P	W	D	L	For	Agst
Wales	1	1	0	0	11	0
Ireland	2	1	0	1	16	17
Scotland	2	1	0	1	11	15
England	3	1	0	2	21	27

(Championship incomplete. Ireland and Scotland refused to play Wales following its presentation of the deeds of a house to Newport's J. Arthur Gould, which the aforementioned countries viewed as professionalism.)

1897-1898

ADVENT OF A FRESH SEASON

On the eve of the 1897-1898 season, the *Leeds Mercury* reflected on the progress of the Northern Union: 'Probably no close season since the formation of the Rugby Union has exercised a more potential influence upon the Rugby game than the one which has just come to an end. The great cleavage which resulted in the formation of the Northern Union was, of course, an event entirely without a parallel, but it was a revolution whose immediate effects were easily apparent, even if its future influence and far-reaching consequences were not instantly perceived. The Northern Union, having safely survived the two years prophesied as its utmost limit of existence, enters upon the coming season with an enormous accession of strength, as from the original 22 the number has now risen to upwards of 80, exclusive of those affiliated through such organisations as the Hull and Oldham District Unions, which would bring the membership up to considerably over 100 clubs. The [recent] extension, however, is mainly on the Lancashire side, where, in addition to high-class clubs like Barrow, Birkenhead Wanderers, Lancaster, Ulverston and Millom, a great number of good second grade clubs have thrown in their lot. In Yorkshire, on the other hand, only two clubs of note [Hull Kingston Rovers and Morley] have [recently] seceded to the newer body.'[205]

LANCASHIRE INCREASES NORTHERN UNION COMPETITIONS

With continuing defections from Rugby Union, the Lancashire Northern Union authorities created a Lancashire Second Competition for 1897-98. Consisting of 12 clubs, it was eventually won by Barrow, who defeated Millom in a play-off after they had tied for top place in the table. A Third Competition was also added with eight teams taking part.

CUMBERLAND DIAMOND JUBILEE LEAGUE LAUNCHED

The Cumberland (Rugby Union) Diamond Jubilee League began on 18th September when Whitehaven Recreation lost at home to Workington 8-0. The re-introduction of a Cumberland League – after it had been shelved for 1896-97 – was first reported in April 1897. The Cumberland authorities organised the competition in an attempt to deter clubs from joining the Northern Union. However, by the time the League commenced, Millom had already defected on 3rd July.[206]

A RUGBY INCIDENT GOES TO COURT

During the South Shields versus West Hartlepool Rugby Union match on 13th November, visiting forward Shadrock Dunning was dismissed after an incident in which William Baty, the Northumberland County three-quarter, fractured a rib. The matter was taken further with Dunning summoned to appear at South Shields Police Court on 10th December, charge with 'maliciously wounding' Baty. The defence argued that, since the summons was only served on 8th December, there was insufficient time to obtain evidence to refute the allegations and an adjournment was agreed. The case resumed on 17th December, when it was reported that 'since the summons was issued the complainant has had the fullest denial from Dunning that he committed the offence and, after explanation, [Mr. Baty] had generously accepted Mr. Dunning's assurance, and was wishful that the case be not proceeded with'.[207]

ANOTHER DOUBLE ROSES CLASH

For the second successive year Lancashire and Yorkshire opposed each other under both codes of rugby on the same day. On 20th November the Northern Union version drew a reported 11,000 to Park Avenue, Bradford, whilst at Crown Flatts, Dewsbury, an attendance of 'not more than 3,000' was stated for the Rugby Union meeting. One report advised that 'it was the first occasion in this long series of matches that the Crown Flatts enclosure was chosen as the scene of action. The choice of ground was made at a somewhat unfortunate time, for public interest in [Rugby] football in Dewsbury has fallen off considerably in recent years'.[208]

A NORTH-EAST RUGBY LEAGUE: THIRTEEN CLUBS IN FAVOUR
A circular, proposing a North-East Rugby Football League embracing the Durham and Northumberland Rugby Union teams was distributed during November by Mr. N. L. Dees of the Wallsend club. Thirteen were in favour, namely Blaydon, Hamsteels, Hartlepool Old Boys, Hetton Lyons, Houghton, Percy Park, Rockcliff, South Shields, Tudhoe, Tyne Dock, Tynedale, Wallsend, and West Hartlepool. Those opposing were Hartlepool Rovers, Old Dunelmians, and Sunderland, whilst Sherburn House was reportedly 'indifferent,' with no replies forthcoming from North Durham, North Elswick, Northern, and Westoe.[209]

DEWSBURY QUITS RUGBY
During a Yorkshire (Rugby Union) Competition No. 1 committee meeting at the Commercial Hotel, Leeds, on 1st December, Dewsbury announced its resignation from the contest, citing meagre support and difficulty in raising a team. They were bottom of the league table at the time. Having hosted the Yorkshire-Lancashire match a few weeks earlier, they abandoned playing rugby union to create the Dewsbury and Savile (Association) Football Club.

A NORTH-EAST RUGBY LEAGUE: IT IS DESIRABLE
Representatives of the leading Durham and Northumberland rugby union clubs met at the Sayer's Hotel, Newcastle, on 3rd December, to discuss the proposal for a North-East League. It was reported that 'in the opinion of this meeting it is desirable that a Rugby League be formed,' and the Durham and Northumberland Union officials should be approached 'to seek their sanction to the establishment of the league'.[210]

LANCASHIRE RUGBY UNION MORIBUND
Lancashire entertained Durham at Whalley Range, Manchester, on 8th December, the *London Evening Standard* commenting that 'as no more than 2,000 spectators saw Lancashire win, it would appear that Rugby Unionism is almost moribund in the Palatinate [Lancashire]. At Oldham, a few miles away, a big crowd [20,000] witnessed a meritorious win [under Northern Union] by Oldham over Widnes'.[211]

WESTMORLAND STRUGGLING
Westmorland Rugby Union was struggling to raise a county team, the drain of its leading players to Lancashire and Yorkshire clubs having taken its toll. Consequently, the county had not won a match since November 1895 and finances were poor. An unofficial game was arranged with North

Lancashire in Barrow on 8th January to help raise funds. The *Westmorland Gazette*, which described the attendance as 'very thin,' said 'the efforts to keep Rugby Unionism alive in North Lancashire and Westmorland seem doomed to failure, especially if Saturday's match at Barrow between teams representing the district named is a sample of what we may expect in the future. Mr. [John] Mawson was the organiser of the North Lancashire team, and he suffered numerous disappointments from well-known players. It is not necessary to state therefore, especially as Westmorland was moderately represented, that the standard of football was not such as the Barrow public had been used to since their club joined the Northern Union'.[212]

WESTMORLAND'S FINALE

Westmorland entertained Yorkshire at Maudes Meadow, Kendal, on 15th January in what would be its final match under Rugby Union rules. 'Half-Way' wrote in the *Westmorland Gazette*: 'It is clearly time Westmorland ceased to take part in the struggle for the County Championship if we are to have exhibitions of the character of the one on Maudes Meadow. Not a single club in the county is connected with the Rugby Union, and the [county] teams are made up of players who, from one match to another, never see a Rugby football, and a few connected with outside clubs. I estimated Saturday's gate at 700 or 800, but I must have been sadly out of it, as I understand the receipts amounted to the stupendous sum of £11. This is not calculated to pay the expenses of a county team.'[213]

A NORTH-EAST RUGBY LEAGUE: APATHY IN SUNDERLAND

A further meeting to discuss a (Rugby Union) league embracing Durham and Northumberland took place at Walton's Hotel, Sunderland, on 1st February. The chairman of the meeting (Mr. F. C. Davison) announced 'that this meeting of club representatives and others interested in the Rugby game in Northumberland and Durham have seen with regret the apathy and unfriendly attitude adopted by the Rugby Unions of the two counties to the proposals recently submitted to them, and it is the opinion of this meeting that in view of the encroachments of the Northern Union and of the enormous and growing popularity of the Association game, more up-to-date sentiments should be shown and a greater desire manifested by them to meet the wishes and assist clubs who are endeavouring to strengthen the game in this district'. One objection raised was that a league competition would lead to professionalism.[214]

A NORTH-EAST RUGBY LEAGUE: DURHAM DECIDES NO
The plan to create a Rugby Union league in the north-east came to an abrupt end on 15th February during a meeting of the Durham County committee at Walton's Hotel, Sunderland. Some of the Durham clubs still believed there was a way forward and the following resolution was discussed: 'That a league be formed in the county of Durham in connection with the Durham County Union.' The resolution, however, was not adopted.[215]

THE FIRST SUBSTITUTE?
In the North versus South (Rugby Union) match, played at the County Ground, Exeter, on 26th February, the South forward, C. E. Wilson of Blackheath, broke his leg in the opening minutes and, after some debate, was replaced by P. Baron of Sidmouth (Devon). The *Sporting Life* commented: 'We believe that it is the first time in this country that a substitute has been allowed to take the place of an injured man. It is, of course, the ordinary practice in America, but we must own that we do not like the theory of it, and hope this will not be regarded as a precedent to be followed.'[216]

THE CUMBERLAND CUP: PENRITH SUSPENDED
Penrith United were drawn away to Carlisle in the second round of the Cumberland (Rugby Union) Cup, the match being postponed from 5th March to 12th March due to Carlisle having to replay with Whitehaven Recreation in the previous round. Carlisle, however, had a lucrative fixture with Jed-Forest scheduled for 12th March and appealed to the Cumberland Committee for a further postponement of the cup tie. The Committee agreed, and the match was arranged for 19th March which upset Penrith who had a fixture with Langholm on that date. With their request for a mid-week date refused by the Committee, Penrith failed to keep their cup appointment, playing Langholm instead. The Cumberland Committee held an emergency meeting at the Red Lion Hotel, Carlisle, on the evening of 19th March and decided to suspend Penrith for the remainder of the season.[217]

THE DURHAM CUP:
WEST HARTLEPOOL INVOLVED IN TWO DISPUTES
The West Hartlepool club was involved in two separate disputes relating to the Durham (Rugby Union) Cup. The first came about after they had apparently beaten Hartlepool Old Boys 10-9 in a third round tie on 12th March. The Old Boys claimed they had a goal disallowed by the referee

because he said the ball was kicked before he blew his whistle. As the referee expressed some doubt to the Durham Committee, a replay was ordered, West Hartlepool again winning, 8-0. The second incident followed West Hartlepool's 12-3 semi-final defeat to Tudhoe on 26th March. West Hartlepool claimed that Tudhoe's Jimmy Gordon had been professionalised through accepting a fee to play for Hull Kingston Rovers. When the Durham Committee decided to take no action, an appeal was made to the Rugby Football Union. However, it was reported that 'the matter could not be decided before next Saturday [16th April when the final was to take place], so West's will simply have to grin and bear it'. West Hartlepool abandoned their protest, Tudhoe defeating Hartlepool Rovers 6-0 in the final.[218]

THE CUMBERLAND CUP:
MARYPORT JOIN THE NORTHERN UNION

Maryport decided at their meeting on 11th March to resign from the Rugby Union, upset at their treatment by the Cumberland authorities, in particular the suspension of John Hayton, who had been sent off in a recent match, a verdict they considered unjust. It created a problem for the Cumberland Committee because Maryport had won through to the semi-finals of the Cumberland Cup. The Committee held a meeting at the Station Hotel, Workington, on 14th March, representatives of the Maryport club being asked to attend regarding their secession to the Northern Union. Due to a remark made by county president Mr. Westray 'as to the manner in which the discussion would be conducted, they abruptly left the meeting'. It was subsequently decided that Maryport's semi-final opponents, Seaton, would receive a bye into the final.[219]

CUMBERLAND CUP: SEATON TO QUIT?

Rumours persisted that Seaton was about to join the evacuation of the Cumberland Union. The *Pall Mall Gazette* (17th March) commented: 'It appears that Seaton gave a promise to Workington to amalgamate with them [in the Northern Union]. After consideration, and influenced, no doubt, by the fact that the secession of Maryport left them in the final of the Cumberland Cup, Seaton withdrew their promise and decided to remain loyal to the Cumberland Rugby Union. The question now arises whether Seaton, having engaged to join a club which has already become professional by making arrangements with Northern Union clubs, is thereby disqualified from competing in the final for the Cumberland Challenge Cup.'[220]

THE RUGBY FOOTBALL UNION AND PROFESSIONALISM
Questioned during March on the subject of professionalism, Rugby Football Union secretary Mr. G. Rowland Hill told the *Pall Mall Gazette* that 'the secession of Yorkshire, Lancashire and Cheshire was a serious blow to the Rugby Union, but not a single club in the south had gone in for professionalism. But there was a danger of the extension of professionalism, because, where there was plenty of money, working men players wanted payment for their services'.[221]

WORKINGTON LEAVE THE RUGBY UNION
Problems continued to mount for Cumberland Rugby Union when Workington announced, after its meeting at Garfield School on 17th March, that it had unanimously decided to resign and apply for a place in the Northern Union.[222]

WESTMORLAND AND THE NORTHERN UNION
The Westmorland Union decided to adopt Northern Union towards the end of February, Lancashire hosting them in a county match under that code on Wednesday 2nd March at Broughton Rangers' Wheater's Field ground, situated in Salford. To assist the new organisation, the Lancashire authorities gave all proceeds, less costs, to their visitors. Unfortunately, a disappointing attendance meant the receipts were meagre.[223] As with the previous weekends North versus South match in Exeter, an injured player – two for Westmorland in fact – was replaced, much to the chagrin of the *Sporting Life* correspondent: 'If two substitutes are allowed, then why not three or four [and] we should in time arrive at a facsimile of the American [Football] system [which] is certain to encourage, as it does across the water, very rough play.'[224]

THE NORTHUMBERLAND CUP FINAL:
A FARCICAL CONCLUSION
The outcome of the Northumberland (Rugby Union) Cup final, played on 2nd April at Jesmond, Newcastle, between Rockcliff and Percy Park, turned into a farcical debate. Rockcliff were declared 5-0 winners after extra time, due to a converted try. Percy Park, however, protested that they scored a legitimate try during extra time which they claim the referee only disallowed after being spoken to by the Rockcliff captain. Despite the rules stating the referee was the sole judge of fact and all appeals should be made immediately to him at the time, the Northumberland Committee referred the matter to the Rugby Football Union. That body ruled Percy

Park's try should stand although, as a conversion had not been attempted, it hardly affected the result. The matter was still causing friction the following September (1898) when the Northumberland Committee asked the clubs to settle it between themselves. Rockcliff responded by stating the county committee should resolve it, whilst Percy Park wanted the competition declared void. Eventually the score was controversially adjusted to 5-3 for Rockcliff. The *Shields Daily News* commented: 'A more extraordinary decision could scarcely have been conceived. The Rugby Union, having allowed Percy Park the try, were entitled to give them an opportunity of converting it. It is rather too late to do that now, but considering that the try was scored between the posts and that the elements were favourable, the Union would have been justified in giving them a goal.'[225]

THE CUMBERLAND CUP FINAL: WILL IT TAKE PLACE?
With the Cumberland (Rugby Union) Cup final about to be decided on 9th April, questions were being asked. The *Sunderland Daily Echo* wrote 'some uneasiness is felt in Rugby circles in Cumberland as to whether the Cup final will take place. The clubs standing in the final are Carlisle and Seaton. The latter club, however, are going to the Northern Union, either after Easter or at the end of the season, and want the assurance of the [Cumberland] Rugby Union that if they succeed in winning the Cup they will be given the Cup and medals. Whether the Rugby Union will make this compact with Seaton is doubtful'.[226] The final did go ahead, Seaton defeating Carlisle 13-0 at the Cricket Field, Whitehaven, their anticipated defection not materialising until six months later.

THE YORKSHIRE CUP: WANING GLORIES
The Yorkshire (Rugby Union) Cup had lost much of its lustre following the desertion of the county's leading clubs, the *Leeds Mercury* lamenting: 'The waning glories of the old Yorkshire Challenge Cup were sufficiently marked on Saturday [9th April] by the attendances at the semi-finals, for although fairly good crowds assembled at Shipley [Keighley v Ossett] and Sowerby Bridge [Elland v Hebden Bridge], it could not be pretended they compared with the huge gatherings of some five or six or more years ago.'[227]

A NEW DEWSBURY CLUB JOINS THE NORTHERN UNION
On Thursday 21st April 1898 a meeting took place at the Black Bull Hotel, Dewsbury, to discuss the formation of a new Dewsbury club with the objective of joining the Northern Union. It was generally felt that rugby

had suffered in the town since the old Dewsbury team withdrew from the original list of clubs that created the Northern Union in 1895. A further meeting, at the Royal Hotel, Dewbury, on Tuesday 26th April, confirmed the decision, funds being pledged. On Tuesday 7th June 1898, during a Northern Union meeting at the Spread Eagle Hotel, Manchester, Dewsbury's admittance was confirmed.

YORK JOIN THE NORTHERN UNION
The York committee met at the club's headquarters, the Bar Hotel, on Monday 25th April, when it was decided to resign from the Rugby Union and seek membership of the Northern Union. The following evening at a meeting of the Northern Union, held at the George Hotel, Huddersfield, York's admittance was confirmed.

FEATHERSTONE DEFECT AFTER WINNING COMPETITION
Featherstone, having won the Yorkshire (Rugby Union) Competition No. 1, subsequently joined the Northern Union, playing an end of season match under that code against Castleford on Wednesday 27th April.

1897-1898 STATISTICS

NORTHERN UNION

LANCASHIRE SENIOR COMPETITION

Final table	P	W	D	L	For	Agst	Pts
Oldham	26	23	1	2	295	94	47
Swinton	26	20	3	3	321	83	43
Widnes	26	19	1	6	251	114	39
Salford*	26	16	3	7	275	182	33
Broughton Rangers	26	13	4	9	183	108	30
Wigan	26	11	1	14	124	173	23
Leigh*	26	11	2	13	176	170	22
St Helens	26	10	2	14	161	192	22
Warrington	26	10	2	14	131	178	22
Runcorn	26	9	2	15	142	184	20
Stockport	26	8	2	16	154	253	18
Tyldesley	26	8	1	17	111	281	17
Rochdale Hornets	26	7	0	19	146	247	14
Morecambe	26	4	2	20	74	285	10

*Two points deducted for using ineligible player

LANCASHIRE SECOND COMPETITION

Final table	P	W	D	L	For	Agst	Pts
Barrow	18	13	1	4	237	59	27
Millom	18	13	1	4	173	55	27
Ulverston	18	10	2	6	101	75	22
Radcliffe	18	9	2	7	107	117	20
Lancaster	18	9	1	8	94	96	19
Barton	18	8	2	8	107	114	18
Birkenhead Wanderers	18	7	2	9	118	94	16
Walkden	18	6	4	8	79	143	16
Altrincham	18	6	1	11	54	95	13
Fleetwood	18	1	0	17	41	263	2
Record expunged:							
St Helens Recreation	18	11	2	5	100	59	24
Crompton*	15	5	0	10	25	97	8

*Two points deducted for using ineligible player
Note: Crompton (Feb 1898), St Helens Recreation (Mar 1898) disbanded.

Play-off to decide first place
Barrow 0, Millom 0 (aet, at Askam)

Replay
Barrow 2, Millom 0 (at Quay Meadow, Lancaster)
(Barrow declared Lancashire Second Competition winner)

Promotion Test Match
Morecambe 10, Barrow 0 (at Quay Meadow, Lancaster)
(Morecambe retain place in Lancashire Senior Competition)

LANCASHIRE THIRD COMPETITION

Final table	P	W	D	L	For	Agst	Pts
Werneth	10	7	1	2	65	34	15
Whitworth*	10	6	1	3	68	28	11
Todmorden	10	5	1	4	32	41	11
Rochdale Rangers	10	4	0	6	39	59	8
Warrington St Mary's	10	3	1	6	34	53	7
Leigh Shamrocks	10	3	0	7	37	60	6
Record expunged:							
Boothstown	7	1	0	6	7	137	2
Mossley	8	1	2	5	27	57	4

*Two points deducted for using ineligible player
Note: Boothstown (Feb 1898), Mossley (Mar 1898) disbanded.

YORKSHIRE SENIOR COMPETITION

Final table	P	W	D	L	For	Agst	Pts
Hunslet	30	22	4	4	327	117	48
Bradford	30	23	2	5	319	139	48
Batley	30	17	3	10	234	111	37
Halifax	30	16	3	11	193	164	35
Manningham	30	15	4	11	276	181	34
Castleford	30	16	1	13	256	208	33
Wakefield Trinity	30	16	1	13	248	214	33
Leeds Parish Church	30	15	1	14	187	213	31
Leeds	30	13	4	13	186	171	30
Huddersfield	30	12	3	15	208	170	27
Hull	30	11	4	15	192	187	26
Bramley	30	11	4	15	156	199	26
Brighouse Rangers	30	9	5	16	143	172	23
Holbeck	30	11	0	19	171	310	22
Heckmondwike	30	9	2	19	148	315	20
Liversedge	30	3	1	26	76	449	7

Play-off to decide first place
Hunslet 5, Bradford 2 (at Headingley, Leeds)
(Hunslet declared Yorkshire Senior Competition winner)

NORTH WESTERN LEAGUE

Final table	P	W	D	L	For	Agst	Pts
Millom	8	5	1	2	49	21	11
Barrow	8	5	0	3	74	31	10
Lancaster	8	4	1	3	25	33	9
Morecambe	8	3	0	5	38	48	6
Ulverston	8	2	0	6	24	77	4

WESTMORLAND JUNIOR LEAGUE

Final table	P	W	D	L	For	Agst	Pts
Ambleside	4	3	1	0	37	8	7
Staveley	4	1	1	2	24	28	3
Holme	4	1	0	3	12	37	2

NORTHERN UNION CHALLENGE CUP (67 entries)
Try – 3 points; all goals – 2.

Qualifying Round
Abbey Hills (Oldham) w/o Radcliffe Hornets (withdrew)
Runcorn Recreation w/o Runcorn Victoria (withdrew)
Warrington St Mary's w/o Lowton St Mary's (withdrew)

First Round
Abbey Hills w/o Crompton (disbanded)
Altrincham 8, Salford St Bartholomew's 0
Barrow 13, Dalton 3
Barton 16, Rochdale Rangers 3
Batley 12, St Helens 7
Birkenhead Wanderers 17, Runcorn Recreation 0
Bradford 7, Swinton 2
Castleford 18, Wigan 2
Eastmoor 22, Smallbridge (Rochdale) 3
Fleetwood 6, Warrington St Mary's 3
Halifax 17, St Helens Recreation 0
Hull 8, Morecambe 0
Hull Kingston Rovers 46, Hull Marlborough 0
Hunslet 8, Lancaster 3
Leeds Parish Church 7, Bramley 10
Leigh 7, Heckmondwike 0
Lostock Gralam w/o Stockport Rangers (withdrew)
Manningham 5, Huddersfield 11
Millom 2, Salford 9 (at Salford)
Morley w/o Batley Purlwell (withdrew)
Mossley 0, Lees 9
Oldham 8, Leeds 3
Radcliffe w/o Waterhead Hornets (withdrew)
Rochdale Hornets 10, Holbeck 6
Stockport 5, Brighouse Rangers 6
Tyldesley 2, Broughton Rangers 3
Ulverston 2, Runcorn 19
Wakefield Trinity 5, Warrington 3
Walkden 22, Swinton Church 0
Werneth 14, Oldham Juniors 0
Whitworth 2, Rochdale Athletic 2
Widnes 26, Liversedge 0

First Round Replay
Rochdale Athletic 0, Whitworth 4

Second Round
Abbey Hills 0, Leigh 59 (at Leigh)
Altrincham 21, Eastmoor 2
Barton 16, Werneth 4
Birkenhead Wanderers 0, Bradford 5
Brighouse Rangers 3, Runcorn 3
Broughton Rangers 3, Wakefield Trinity 0
Castleford 14, Whitworth 7
Halifax 3, Oldham 8
Huddersfield 14, Barrow 6
Hull Kingston Rovers 11, Morley 0
Lees 2, Salford 65 (at Salford)
Lostock Gralam 0, Fleetwood 10
Radcliffe 0, Hull 18 (at Hull)
Rochdale Hornets 3, Bramley 4
Walkden 0, Batley 8 (at Batley)
Widnes 8, Hunslet 7

Second Round Replay
Runcorn 11, Brighouse Rangers 0

Third Round
Altrincham 0, Salford 16
Barton 3, Bramley 9
Castleford 4, Batley 10
Fleetwood 0, Hull Kingston Rovers 31
Huddersfield 0, Broughton Rangers 6
Hull 2, Bradford 6
Leigh 3, Widnes 3
Oldham 11, Runcorn 0

Third Round Replay
Widnes 22, Leigh 3

Fourth Round
Batley 3, Oldham 0
Bradford 7, Broughton Rangers 5
Hull Kingston Rovers 0, Widnes 0
Salford 12, Bramley 2

Fourth Round Replay
Widnes 6, Hull Kingston Rovers 5

Semi-finals
Batley 5, Salford 0
(at Watersheddings, Oldham)
Bradford 13, Widnes 0
(at Thrum Hall, Halifax)

FINAL

Saturday 23 April 1898 at Headingley, Leeds
BATLEY 7 *Back*: A Garner. *Three-quarters*: WP Davies (g), JB Goodall (capt, t, g), D Fitzgerald, E Fozzard. *Half-backs*: H Goodall, J Oakland. *Forwards*: F Fisher, J Gath, G Maine, JT Munns, J Rodgers, M Shackleton, R Spurr, S Stubley.
BRADFORD 0 *Back*: B Patrick. *Three-quarters*: TH Dobson, FW Cooper, W Murgatroyd, F Murgatroyd. *Half-backs*: H Prole, R Wood. *Forwards*: T Broadley (capt), J Fearnley, H Holden, B Holt, E Kelsey, J McLoughlin, RJ Robertson, JT Toothill.
Attendance: 27,941   *Referee*: JH Smith (Widnes)

COUNTY CHAMPIONSHIP

Saturday 16 October 1897 at Watersheddings, Oldham
LANCASHIRE 11 *Back*: T Foulkes (StH). *Three-quarters*: R Messer (Swi), S Lees (Old), J Valentine (capt, Swi, g), T Martin (Old, 3t). *Half-backs*: B Griffiths (Sal), A Lees (Old). *Forwards*: W Briers (StH), T Cleminson (BroR), R Edwards (Old), F Hampson ((Wid), J Johnson (Swi), G Whitehead (BroR), J Williams (Sal), J Worthington (Tyl).
CHESHIRE 10 *Back*: J Jolley (Run). *Three-quarters*: W Robinson (Stock, t), F Saville (Stock, t, g), J Butterworth (Run, g), J Worsley (Stock). *Half-backs*: A Allen (Stock), J Faulkner (Run). *Forwards*: H Barnett (Alt), S Hanson (Alt), C Holmes (BirkW), H Moss (Stock), J Mottershead (Stock), RT Reece (Run), A Taylor (Run), S Walker (Run).
Attendance: 7,000   *Referee*: F Renton (Hunslet)

Saturday 6 November 1897 at Edgeley Park, Stockport
CHESHIRE 3 *Back*: S Houghton (capt, Run). *Three-quarters*: W Robinson (Stock), F Saville (Stock, t), J Butterworth (Run), JD Watson (BirkW). *Half-backs*: J Faulkner (Run), J Jolley (Run). *Forwards*: H Barnett (Alt), F Ingham (BirkW), W Milligan (Stock), H Moss (Stock), W Palmer (Stock), RT Reece (Run), A Taylor (Run), S Walker (Run).
YORKSHIRE 22 *Back*: J Metcalfe (Wak). *Three-quarters*: FW Cooper (Brad, t, 4g), RE Lockwood (Wak, g), B Pollard (Brad), WP Davies (Bat). *Half-backs*: GE Mosley (LeePC, t), JA Rigg (capt, Hal, 2t). *Forwards*: T Broadley (Brad), J Gath (Bat), A Kemp (HKR), H Milnes (Hol), A Starks (HKR), M Sutcliffe (Hud), W Walton (Wak), JW Ward (Cas).
Attendance: 5,500   *Referee*: S Williams (Salford)

Saturday 20 November 1897 at Park Avenue, Bradford
YORKSHIRE 7 *Back*: S Walker (Lee). *Three-quarters*: FW Cooper (Brad, 2g), W Jacques (Hull), A Hambrecht (Bram, t), B Pollard (Brad). *Half-backs*: GE Mosley (LeePC), JA Rigg (capt, Hal). *Forwards*: T Broadley (Brad), J Gath (Bat), A Kemp (HKR), C Richardson (LeePC), A Starks (HKR), M Sutcliffe (Hud), W Walton (Wak), JW Ward (Cas).
LANCASHIRE 6 *Back*: RJ Baty (Wid). *Three-quarters*: T Martin (Old), S Lees (Old), J Valentine (capt, Swi), F Barber (War). *Half-backs*: A Lees (Old), J Nelson (BroR). *Forwards*: R Edwards (Old), F Hampson (Wid), J Johnson (Swi), G Steele (BroR), P Taylor (Lei), G Whitehead (BroR, t), H Woodhead (Sal, t), J Worthington (Tyl).
Attendance: 11,000   *Referee*: C Schofield (Stockport)

Final table

	P	W	D	L	For	Agst	Pts
Yorkshire	2	2	0	0	29	9	4
Lancashire	2	1	0	1	17	17	2
Cheshire	2	0	0	2	13	33	2

NON-COUNTY CHAMPIONSHIP MATCHES

Saturday 5 February 1898 at Parkside, Hunslet
YORKSHIRE 8 *Back*: J Metcalfe (Wak). *Three-quarters*: FW Cooper (Brad), RE Lockwood (Wak, g), A Hambrecht (Bram), H Bentley (Mann, 2t). *Half-backs*: GE Mosley (LeePC), JA Rigg (Hal). *Forwards*: H Eastwood (Hal), J Gath (Bat), A Kemp (HKR), R Rhodes (Hull), C Richardson (LeePC), W Walton (Wak), JW Ward (Cas), T Wilkinson (Mann).
CUMBERLAND 0 *Back*: JH Moore (Mil). *Three-quarters*: W Hannah (Hun), FR Moore (Mil), F Austin (Mil), J Young (Mil). *Half-backs*: S Northmore (Mil), J Whitehead (Mil). *Forwards*: JH Buckett (Mil), T Grenfell (Mil), S Hoggarth (Mil), T Kitchin (Mil), E Knowles (Mil), J McLaughlin (Brad), J Smitheram (Mil), W Young (Hun).
Attendance: 5,000   *Referee*: JH Smith (Widnes)

Wednesday 2 March 1898 at Wheater's Field, Broughton
LANCASHIRE 15 *Back*: RJ Baty (Wid). *Three-quarters*: H Chapman (BroR, t), T Williams (Sal), R Duck (BroR, 2t), J Hoskins (Sal, 2t). *Half-backs*: B Griffiths (Sal), J Lawton (Old). *Forwards*: G Boardman (Lei), W Briers (StH), J Johnson (Swi), J Moffatt (Old), G Steele (BroR), P Taylor (Lei), P Turner (Wig), J Worthington (Tyl).
WESTMORLAND 0 *Back*: F Hoggarth (Stock). *Three-quarters*: W Hall (Lanc), J Holmes (Stav), J Goodman (Swi), R Doherty (StH). *Half-backs*: W Cross (StH), J Threlfall (Stav). *Forwards*: J Elliott (Ulv), T Fawcett (Holme), G Fisher (Sal), J Hayton (Lee), G Jackson (Lanc), W Robinson (Amb), J Simpson (StH), J Thompson (StH).
Substitutes: W Whiteley (StH) replaced J Goodman (injured) during first half, G Whitwell ('Kendal') replaced W Robinson (injured) at half-time.
Attendance: 2,000   *Referee*: F Renton (Hunslet)

RUGBY UNION

CUMBERLAND DIAMOND JUBILEE LEAGUE

Final table	P	W	D	L	For	Agst	Pts
Aspatria	16	13	2	1	217	16	28
Seaton	16	13	1	2	153	24	27
Whitehaven Recreation	16	8	1	7	42	89	17
Workington*	16	6	2	8	42	36	14
Maryport*	16	5	3	8	17	19	13
Brookland Rovers	16	5	3	8	57	97	13
Whitehaven	16	6	0	10	39	167	12
Cockermouth	16	4	3	9	49	110	11
Penrith United**	16	4	1	11	47	105	9

*Withdrew Mar 1898 to join Northern Union; remaining matches declared as win to opponents
**Suspended Mar 1898 for non-fulfilment of Cumberland Cup match; remaining matches declared as win to opponents

YORKSHIRE COMPETITION NO. 1

Final table	P	W	D	L	For	Agst	Pts
Featherstone	28	20	3	5	278	63	43
Keighley	28	19	3	6	307	69	41
Castleford	28	15	4	9	199	124	34
Elland	27	15	4	8	199	127	34
Cleckheaton	27	16	2	9	155	141	34
Shipley	28	13	7	8	189	106	33
Otley	25	13	3	9	151	104	29
Morley	26	13	3	10	191	134	29
York	28	13	3	12	155	150	29
Ossett	27	12	5	10	121	127	29
Sowerby Bridge	28	12	5	11	131	163	29
Pudsey	27	8	7	12	113	216	23
Wortley	28	5	2	21	97	298	12
Bowling*	25	2	4	19	43	357	6
Dewsbury**	28	0	1	27	6	156	1

*Two points deducted for breach of rules
**Dewsbury disbanded (Dec 1897), 16 unplayed matches declared as win to opponents.
Note: Results not found for Bowling v Otley, Cleckheaton v Bowling, Elland v Otley, Morley v Pudsey, Ossett v Morley, Otley v Bowling; probably not played.

YORKSHIRE COMPETITION NO. 2

Final table

	P	W	D	L	For	Agst	Pts
Alverthorpe	24	19	3	2	253	54	41
Rothwell	24	17	3	4	304	93	37
Skipton	24	12	4	8	201	76	28
Hebden Bridge	24	11	5	8	134	106	27
Outwood Church	24	9	6	9	106	85	24
Mytholmroyd	24	10	4	10	190	126	24
Goole	24	10	4	10	150	159	24
Normanton	24	9	5	10	101	102	23
Stanningley	24	9	4	11	125	155	22
Bingley	24	9	3	12	105	162	21
Idle	24	9	3	12	161	188	21
Farsley	24	5	0	19	91	340	10
Silsden	24	3	4	17	29	304	10

Note: Four unplayed fixtures declared scoreless draws, affecting Hebden Bridge (3 matches), Rothwell, Silsden (2 each), Outwood Church (1).

YORKSHIRE COMPETITION NO. 3

Final table

	P	W	D	L	For	Agst	Pts
Luddendenfoot	20	16	1	3	202	51	33
Otley St Joseph's	20	16	0	4	179	37	32
Kirkstall St Stephen's	20	13	1	6	179	51	27
Birstall	19	12	1	6	152	64	25
Keighley Shamrocks	20	10	2	8	91	80	22
Windhill*	20	8	1	11	73	122	15
Holywell Brook	18	6	2	10	59	119	14
Saltaire*	20	7	0	13	71	187	12
Guiseley	20	5	1	14	62	164	11
Harrogate	20	4	3	13	73	171	11
Brownroyd Recreation	19	4	2	13	42	137	10

*Two points deducted for using ineligible player

Note: Holywell Brook v Birstall abandoned (due to late start) and Holywell Brook v Brownroyd Recreation postponed (former involved in a cup-tie) and not subsequently played.

Promotion Test Match
Luddendenfoot v Silsden (at Windhill FC ground, Bradford)
Not played as neither could raise a team.

CUMBERLAND COUNTY CHALLENGE CUP (12 entries)
Try – 3 points; conversion – 2; penalty goal – 3; drop-goal, field goal, goal from mark – 4.

First Round
Cockermouth 3, Aspatria 3
Maryport 11, Whitehaven 0
Egremont Hornets 0, Seaton 34
Whitehaven Recreation 3, Carlisle 3
Byes: Brookland Rovers, Penrith United,
Wath Brow, Workington

First Round Replays
Aspatria 12, Cockermouth 0
Carlisle 24, Whitehaven Recreation 3

Second Round
Brookland Rovers 5, Aspatria 3
Carlisle w/o Penrith United (suspended)
Maryport 9, Workington 3
Seaton 8, Wath Brow 0

Semi-finals
Carlisle 5, Brookland Rovers 3
(at Aspatria)
Seaton w/o Maryport (withdrew)

FINAL
Saturday 9 April 1898 at the Whitehaven Cricket Ground
SEATON 13 *Back*: R Petrie. *Three-quarters*: Joe Sandwith (capt, 2c), T Fletcher (2t),
W Meers (t), Joe Owens. *Half-backs*: J Fisher, R Fletcher. *Forwards*: J Edwards, R Falcon,
M Linton, H Murray, W Owens, E Richards, JG Sandwith, J Wright.
CARLISLE 0 *Back*: P Westray. *Three-quarters*: M Burrows, G Steel, A Smith, F Spottiswood.
Half-backs: J Fleming, WS Graham (capt). *Forwards*: G Brough, D Elliott, RH Graham,
G Scott, J Sewell, J Smith, J Stubbs, E Walsh.
Attendance: 'poor'   *Referee*: WH Humphreys (Durham RU)

DURHAM COUNTY CHALLENGE CUP (17 entries)
Try – 3 points; conversion – 2; penalty goal – 3; drop-goal, field goal, goal from mark – 4.

First Round
Hartlepool Old Boys 34, Darlington 5
Byes: 15 teams drew a bye to next round

Second Round
Blaydon 0, Durham City 5
Hamsteels 3, South Shields 13
Hartlepool Old Boys 8, Houghton-le-Spring 0
Hartlepool Rovers 13, Tyne Dock 4
Hetton Lyons 0, West Hartlepool 60
North Durham 9, Westoe 14
Old Dunelmians 0, Tudhoe 15
Sunderland 19, Sherburn House 0

Third Round
Hartlepool Old Boys 9,
West Hartlepool 10
(replay ordered after protest)
Hartlepool Rovers 8, South Shields 0
Sunderland 3, Tudhoe 12
Westoe 5, Durham City 0

Third Round Replay
West Hartlepool 8,
Hartlepool Old Boys 0

Semi-finals
Hartlepool Rovers 5, Westoe 3
West Hartlepool 3, Tudhoe 12

FINAL
Saturday 16 April 1898 at Ashbrooke Ground, Sunderland
TUDHOE 6 *Back*: JE Pickering. *Three-quarters*: W Taylor (2t), W Wainford, J Gordon, H Sinclair. *Half-backs*: J Levitt, F Marston. *Forwards*: J Carmedy, B Hamm, J Mason, G Richardson, R Shaw, A Stephenson (capt), J Stitt, G Urwin.
HARTLEPOOL ROVERS 0 *Back*: RW Poole. *Three-quarters*: H Yeoman, C Hodgson, AG Murrell, R Roberts. *Half-backs*: G Horsley, JT Thompson. *Forwards*: J Athey, C Cox, D Gilchrist, M Hastings, RF Oakes (capt), R Snowdon, J Wheatley, CS Wright.
Attendance: 5,000   *Referee*: WH Bell (Durham RU President)

NORTHUMBERLAND COUNTY FOOTBALL CHALLENGE CUP (7 entries)
Try – 3 points; conversion – 2; penalty goal – 3; drop-goal, field goal, goal from mark – 4.

First Round
North Elswick 0, Percy Park 29
Rockcliff 43, Tynedale 0
Wallsend w/o Brighton (disbanded)
Bye: Northern

Semi-finals
Percy Park 39, Northern 3
Rockcliff 19, Wallsend 6

FINAL
Saturday 2 April 1898 at Jesmond Grounds, Newcastle
ROCKCLIFF 5 *Back*: G Dick. *Three-quarters*: W Taylor (t), G Taylor, W Straughan, A Taylor. *Half-backs*: T Owen, EW Taylor (c). *Forwards*: FJ Bell, J Dobinson, T Finlay, JH Greenwell, E Houston, B Taylor, Joe Taylor, John Taylor.
PERCY PARK 3 *Back*: T Scotland. *Three-quarters*: FW Stone (t), W Bates, JS Miller, W Smith. *Half-backs*: SC Lockerby, CW Russell. *Forwards*: F Atkinson, G Buckham, PF Hardwick, J Lawson, T McKean, J McMenemy, HJ Spencer (capt), W Winter.
After extra time   *Attendance*: 7,000   *Referee*: J Oakland (Yorkshire RU)

YORKSHIRE COUNTY FOOTBALL CHALLENGE CUP (69 entries)
Try – 3 points; conversion – 2; penalty goal – 3; drop-goal, field goal, goal from mark – 4.

Preliminary Round
Brotherton St John's w/o Allerton Bywater (withdrew)
Doncaster Town 5, Kippax 0
Lockwood 18, Brownroyd Recreation 3
Purston 6, Knottingley 3
Skelmanthorpe 0, Slaithwaite 0
Byes: 27 teams drew a bye to next round

Preliminary Round Replay
Slaithwaite 28, Skelmanthorpe 0

First Round
(* indicates 32 teams seeded to this round)
Bingley* 4, Castleford* 0
Birstall 11, Normanton* 10
(replay ordered after protest)
Bowling* 0, Methley 0
Brotherton St John's w/o Horbury Athletic (withdrew)
Harrogate 10, Silsden* 13
Dewsbury* v Farsley*
(not played – both disbanded)
Dewsbury St Paulinus 0, Shipley* 31
Elland* 32, Bottomboat Trinity 6
Fairburn 0, Rothwell* 15

First Round *continued*
Goole* 3, Idle* 0
(replay ordered after protest)
Hebden Bridge* 8, Otley* 0
Kirkstall St Stephen's 11, Featherstone* 12
Knaresborough 8, Methley Mills 7
Lockwood 0, Keighley* 36
Luddendenfoot w/o Carlton (withdrew)
Milnesbridge w/o Todmorden (withdrew)
Morley* w/o Paddock   (disbanded)
Nortonthorpe 0, Outwood Church* 8
Ossett* 17, Keighley Trinity 0
Otley St Joseph's 9, Holywell Brook 3
Pontefract 18, Guiseley 8
Pudsey* 7, Doncaster Town 0
Purston 22, Bilton St John's 3
Ravensthorpe Nelson 0, Cleckheaton* 20
Saltaire* 0, Stanningley* 14
Sharlston 3, Alverthorpe* 11
Skipton* 10, Kinsley* 0
Slaithwaite 15, Thornhill Lees Trinity 5
Stainland 10, Keighley Shamrocks 5
Windhill* 6, Sowerby Bridge* 3
Wortley* 3, Mytholmroyd* 13
York* 38, Selby* 0

First Round Replays
Goole 17, Idle 6 (at Castleford)
Methley w/o Bowling (withdrew)
Normanton w/o Birstall (withdrew)

Second Round
Alverthorpe 13, Normanton 0
Bingley 25, Pontefract 0
Featherstone 16, Methley 0
Hebden Bridge 11, Goole 3
Keighley 6, Cleckheaton 0
Luddendenfoot 8, Brotherton St John's 0
Meltham and Meltham Mills 0, Elland 12
Mytholmroyd 8, Stanningley 0
Ossett 10, Otley St Joseph's 3
Outwood Church 11, Pudsey 7
Purston 16, Silsden 0
Rothwell 15, Morley 0
(replay ordered after protest)
Shipley 66, Milnsbridge 6
Skipton 10, York 3
Windhill 9, Slaithwaite 0
Bye: Stainland (due to disbanding of Dewsbury and Farsley)

Second Round Replay
Morley 0, Rothwell 9 (at Ossett)

Third Round
Alverthorpe 8, Rothwell 0
Bingley 3, Windhill 3
Elland 6, Skipton 0
Hebden Bridge 7, Purston 3
Keighley 0, Shipley 0
Ossett 6, Featherstone 0
Outwood Church 3, Mytholmroyd 0
Stainland 5, Luddendenfoot 3

Third Round Replays
Shipley 0, Keighley 3
Windhill 4, Bingley 8

Fourth Round
Alverthorpe 0 Keighley 11
Bingley 3, Hebden Bridge 8
Outwood Church 0, Ossett 4
Stainland 3, Elland 8

Semi-finals
Hebden Bridge 14, Elland 6
(at Beech Ground, Sowerby Bridge)
Ossett 3, Keighley 0
(at Ring o' Bells Ground, Shipley)

FINAL

Saturday 16 April 1898 at Oldfield Lane, Wortley, Leeds
OSSETT 13 *Back*: FA Ashton. *Three-quarters*: T Nutter, H Fisher (t), J Jackson (2c), L Land.
Half-backs: W Loughlin (t), CE Winpenny (capt, t). *Forwards*: E Biltcliffe, G Biltcliffe,
W Clarkson, H Clayton, J Dews, J Jones, J Walker, W Woodson.
HEBDEN BRIDGE 3 *Back*: WT North. *Three-quarters*: C Astin, W Astin, A Lee (t),
CE Sutcliffe. *Half-backs*: A Crabtree, E Sutcliffe. *Forwards*: H Blackburn, K Jagger (capt),
W McGregor, J Ogden, AS Priestley, H Sutcliffe, A Taylor, E Vity.
Attendance: 4,000   *Referee*: H Williamson (Lancashire RU)

COUNTY CHAMPIONSHIP

NORTHERN GROUP

Saturday 23 October 1897 at Prince Consort Road, Gateshead
DURHAM 16 *Back*: RW Poole (HartR). *Three-quarters*: EW Elliot (Sund, t), JE Parker
(WHart, 2c, 2pg), DR Thomas (WHart), GS Legard (ODun). *Half-backs*: W Guy (Tud, t),
JT Thompson (HartR). *Forwards*: T Burt (SherH), W Dale (HartR), JH Dods (DurC),
GC Kerr (ODun), J Knight (Hou), RK Oakes (capt, HartR), AJ Troupe (Tud), H Walker
(ODun).
CUMBERLAND 3 *Back*: R Petrie (Sea). *Three-quarters*: A Smith (Carl), T Fletcher (Sea),
Joe Owens (Sea), P Westray (Carl). *Half-backs*: J Fisher (Sea), WS Graham (Carl, t).
Forwards: JH Blacklock (Asp), G Brough (Carl), Jim Davidson (capt, Asp), Joe Davidson
(Asp), D Elliott (Carl), M Linton (Sea), J Walker (Asp), J Wright (Sea).
Attendance: 'fair'   *Referee*: A Turnbull (Scotland)

Saturday 30 October 1897 at Jesmond Ground, Newcastle
NORTHUMBERLAND 40 *Back*: P Moran (Wall). *Three-quarters*: JC Seymour (Wall),
S Anderson (Wall, 2t, 4c, 2pg), W Bates (PerPk), W Taylor (Rock, 2t, c). *Half-backs*:
SC Lockerby (PerPk), CW Russell (PerPk, t). *Forwards*: FJ Bell (Rock), J Finlay (WHart),
COP Gibson (Nor/OxfU), J McMenemy (PerPk), J Munro (Wall), T Scott (NEls, t),
HJ Spencer (PerPk), RC Stevenson (Nor, 2t).
WESTMORLAND 0 *Back*: N Shaw ('Staveley'). *Three-quarters*: W Whitehead ('Kendal'),
C Crossley ('Kendal'), F Stubbs ('Kendal'), A Bigland ('Windermere'). *Half-backs*: J Stavert
('Windermere'), G Whitwell ('Kendal'). *Forwards*: J Bigland ('Windermere'), C Causton
('Kendal'), W Cooper ('Kendal'), J Graham ('Kendal'), R Palmer ('Burneside'), F Sharpe
('Kendal'), J Tomlinson ('Kendal'), JW Wilkinson ('Kendal').
Attendance: 1,000   *Referee*: CH Thompson (Durham)

Saturday 6 November 1897 at Aigburth, Liverpool
LANCASHIRE 9 *Back*: F Woodhead (CasM). *Three-quarters*: AT Brettargh (LivOB, t),
FK Ashton (Bro), CEL Beasley (Lit, t), N Duckworth (Bro, t). *Half-backs*: GG Allen (capt,
Liv), G Cookson (Man). *Forwards*: AS Arkle (Liv), S Croggan (Bro), A Forman (Liv),
GW Hartham (OwC), A Long (Bla), JE Louden (Man), R Pierce (Liv), RD Wood (LivOB).
CHESHIRE 3 *Back*: S Simpson (BirkPk). *Three-quarters*: JAS Cannell (NewB), W Fletcher
(NewB), A Tipping (NewB), C Bradley (AshH). *Half-backs*: JC Marquis (BirkPk, t),
H Parratt (capt, Sale). *Forwards*: AL Auty (NewB), J Baxter (BirkPk), EH Bradshaw (Sale),
H Fletcher (Sale), J Hague (Sale), E Herschell (BirkPk), J Murray (NewB), H Spence (BirkPk).
Attendance: 2,000   *Referee*: GE Kinder (Yorkshire)

Saturday 6 November 1897 at Lock Lane, Castleford
YORKSHIRE 7 *Back*: CE Dixon (Alv). *Three-quarters*: EF Fookes (capt, SowB), JT Taylor (WHart, dg), S Neumann (Cleck), RW Collinson (Myth). *Half-backs*: H Myers (Kei), CE Winpenny (Oss, t). *Forwards*: J Glew (Fea), GE Hughes (Otley), EH Jacobson (Mor), H Moon (Ship), HE Ramsden (Bing), F Shaw (Cleck), JH Shooter (Mor), G Voyse (Cas).
DURHAM 9 *Back*: RW Poole (HartR). *Three-quarters*: EW Elliot (Sund, t), JE Parker (WHart), DR Thomas (WHart), GS Legard (ODun, dg). *Half-backs*: W McSloy (HartR), JT Thompson (HartR, c). *Forwards*: T Burt (SherH), W Dale (HartR), GC Kerr (ODun), RK Oakes (capt, HartR), A Stephenson (Tud), J Stitt (Tud), AJ Troupe (Tud), H Walker (ODun).
Attendance: 6,000   *Referee*: EB Holmes (Midland Counties)

Saturday 13 November 1897 at Upper Park, Birkenhead
CHESHIRE 8 *Back*: CR Hartley (Sale). *Three-quarters*: JAS Cannell (NewB, t, c), W Fletcher (NewB), A Tipping (NewB), H Greenham (BirkPk). *Half-backs*: JC Marquis (BirkPk), H Parratt (capt, Sale). *Forwards*: AL Auty (NewB), J Baxter (BirkPk, t), EH Bradshaw (Sale), J Hague (Sale), E Herschell (BirkPk), J Murray (NewB), H Spence (BirkPk), F Taylor (BirkPk).
CUMBERLAND 11 *Back*: J Tyson (Whi). *Three-quarters*: Joe Owens (Sea), T Fletcher (Sea), R Holywell (WickPk, c), P Westray (Carl, t). *Half-backs*: J Fisher (Sea, t), WS Graham (Carl, t). *Forwards*: R Barnes (Mary), JH Blacklock (Asp), G Brough (Carl), Jim Davidson (capt, Asp), D Elliott (Carl), M Linton (Sea), J Messenger (Asp), J Walker (Asp).
Attendance: 2,000   *Referee*: J Ashton (Lancashire)

Saturday 13 November 1897 at Jesmond Ground, Newcastle
NORTHUMBERLAND 3 *Back*: P Moran (Wall). *Three-quarters*: GC Robinson (PerPk), W Bates (PerPk, t), S Anderson (Wall), JG Bainbridge (Nor). *Half-backs*: SC Lockerby (PerPk), CW Russell (PerPk). *Forwards*: J Finlay (WHart), COP Gibson (Nor/OxfU), JH Greenwell (Rock), J Lindsay (Tud), J McMenemy (PerPk), J Nesbitt (Wall), T Scott (NEls), RC Stevenson (Nor).
YORKSHIRE 5 *Back*: CE Dixon (Alv). *Three-quarters*: EF Fookes (capt, SowB, t), JT Taylor (WHart, c), S Neumann (Cleck), F Goodfellow (Sha). *Half-backs*: H Myers (Kei), CE Winpenny (Oss). *Forwards*: H Blackburn (HebB), G Bryars (Goole), J Glew (Fea), EH Jacobson (Mor), H Moon (Ship), J Randall (Fea), JH Shooter (Mor), G Voyse (Cas).
Attendance: 5,000   *Referee*: JA Smith (Scotland)

Saturday 13 November 1897 at Maude's Meadow, Kendal
WESTMORLAND 0 *Back*: N Shaw ('Staveley'). *Three-quarters*: HT Wilson ('Kendal'), F Stubbs ('Kendal'), C Crossley ('Kendal'), R Fisher ('Staveley'). *Half-backs*: J Hall ('Kendal'), H Reed ('Burneside'). *Forwards*: J Bigland ('Windermere'), J Carradus ('Kendal'), J Major ('Kendal'), R Palmer ('Burneside'), F Sharpe ('Kendal'), JH Thompson ('Kendal'), J Tomlinson ('Kendal'), G Whitwell ('Kendal').
LANCASHIRE 11 *Back*: F Woodhead (CasM). *Three-quarters*: AT Brettargh (LivOB, c), CEL Beasley (Lit, t), FK Ashton (Bro, t), N Duckworth (Bro). *Half-backs*: G Cookson (Man), WK Roberts (Lancaster Royal Grammar School). *Forwards*: AS Arkle (Liv), S Croggan (Bro), A Forman (Liv), GW Hartham (OwC), A Long (Bla), JE Louden (Man, t), R Pierce (Liv), RD Wood (LivOB).
Attendance: 1,000   *Referee*: WW Belton (Yorkshire)

Saturday 20 November 1897 at Maude's Meadow, Kendal
WESTMORLAND 3 *Back*: N Shaw ('Staveley'). *Three-quarters*: HT Wilson ('Kendal'),
F Stubbs ('Kendal'), C Crossley ('Kendal'), H Fisher ('Staveley'). *Half-backs*: R Fisher
('Staveley'), PJ Maw ('Burneside'). *Forwards*: J Bigland ('Windermere'), J Carradus (capt,
'Kendal', t), FW Cragg ('Kendal'), J Hall ('Kendal'), J Major ('Kendal'), F Sharpe
('Kendal'), JH Thompson ('Kendal'), J Tomlinson ('Kendal').
CHESHIRE 8 *Back*: CR Hartley (Sale). *Three-quarters*: JAS Cannell (NewB, t, c), W Fletcher
(NewB), A Tipping (NewB, t), H Greenham (BirkPk). *Half-backs*: JC Marquis (BirkPk),
H Parratt (capt, Sale). *Forwards*: J Adams (AshH), AL Auty (NewB), J Baxter (BirkPk),
J Hague (Sale), E Herschell (BirkPk), J Murray (NewB), JB Royle (BirkPk), H Spence
(BirkPk).
Attendance: 500   *Referee*: JM Mawson (Barrow)

Saturday 20 November 1897 at Crown Flatts, Dewsbury
YORKSHIRE 25 *Back*: CE Dixon (Alv). *Three-quarters*: EF Fookes (capt, SowB, 2t, 2c),
JT Taylor (WHart, c, dg), AW Robinson (Bowl, t), F Goodfellow (Sha, t). *Half-backs*:
H Myers (Kei), CE Winpenny (Oss). *Forwards*: H Blackburn (HebB), R Blades (Kei),
J Glew (Fea), EH Jacobson (Mor), H Moon (Ship), HE Ramsden (Bing, t), F Shaw (Cleck),
JH Shooter (Mor).
LANCASHIRE 0 *Back*: F Woodhead (CasM). *Three-quarters*: GP Wincey (Man),
FK Ashton (Bro), AT Brettargh (LivOB), N Duckworth (Bro). *Half-backs*: GG Allen (Liv),
G Cookson (Man). *Forwards*: S Croggan (Bro), A Forman (Liv), JS Francomb (Man),
JW Hardicker (Lit), A Long (Bla), JE Louden (Man), R Pierce (Liv), RD Wood (LivOB).
Attendance: 3,000   *Referee*: W Yiend (Peterborough)

Saturday 27 November 1897 at The Recreation Ground, Whitehaven
CUMBERLAND 3 *Back*: J Tyson (Whi). *Three-quarters*: P Westray (Carl), R Holywell
(WickPk), T Fletcher (Sea, t), Joe Owens (Sea). *Half-backs*: J Fisher (Sea), WS Graham
(Carl). *Forwards*: R Barnes (Mary), JH Blacklock (Asp), G Brough (Carl), Jim Davidson
(capt, Asp), D Elliott (Carl), M Linton (Sea), J Messenger (Asp), J Walker (Asp).
LANCASHIRE 12 *Back*: F Woodhead (CasM, c). *Three-quarters*: GP Wincey (Man, t),
R Whitehead (Bla, dg), CEL Beasley (Lit), N Duckworth (Bro). *Half-backs*: G Cookson
(Man, t), WK Roberts (Royal Lancaster Grammar School). *Forwards*: S Croggan (Bro),
JS Francomb (Man), JW Hardicker (CasM), H Hodgkinson (Lit), A Long (Bla), JE Louden
(Man), R Pierce (capt, Liv), RD Wood (LivOB).
Attendance: 2,000   *Referee*: HB Browning (Cheshire)

Saturday 4 December 1897 at Upper Park, Birkenhead
CHESHIRE 0 *Back*: S Simpson (BirkPk). *Three-quarters*: JAS Cannell (NewB), A Tipping
(NewB), C Bradley (AshH), H Greenham (BirkPk). *Half-backs*: F Drinkwater (Sale),
NS Wood (BirkPk). *Forwards*: J Adams (AshH), AL Auty (NewB), J Baxter (BirkPk),
EH Bradshaw (Sale), H Fletcher (Sale), J Hague (Sale), J Murray (NewB), F Taylor (BirkPk).
DURHAM 8 *Back*: RW Poole (HartR). *Three-quarters*: EW Elliot (Sund), DR Thomas
(WHart), J Taylor (Sund, c), GS Legard (ODun, t). *Half-backs*: W McSloy (HartR),
JT Thompson (HartR, t). *Forwards*: T Burt (SherH), W Dale (HartR), JH Dods (DurC),
RK Oakes (capt, HartR), A Stephenson (Tud), J Stitt (Tud), AJ Troupe (Tud), H Walker (ODun).
Attendance: 'limited'   *Referee*: H Williamson (Lancashire)

Saturday 4 December 1897 at Lonsdale Park, Workington
CUMBERLAND 56 *Back*: J Tyson (Whi, c). *Three-quarters*: T Fletcher (Sea, 3t), R Holywell (WickPk, t), T Parkinson (Work, 4t), JC Broughton (PenU, t). *Half-backs*: J Fisher (Sea), WS Graham (Carl, 2t). *Forwards*: JH Blacklock (Asp, 2c), G Brough (Carl, c), D Elliott (Carl, t), M Linton (Sea, t), T McGerry (WhiR), J Messenger (Asp), J Ritson (Cock, 3t), J Walker (Asp).
WESTMORLAND 0 *Back*: F Sharpe ('Kendal'). *Three-quarters*: J Pickthall ('Burneside'), C Leather ('Kendal'), HT Wilson ('Kendal'), C Crossley ('Kendal'). *Half-backs*: R Fisher ('Staveley'), R Moore ('Burneside'). *Forwards*: J Bigland ('Windermere'), J Carradus (capt, 'Kendal'), W Chorley ('Kendal'), D McIntosh ('Kendal'), G Metcalf ('Kendal'), JH Thompson ('Kendal'), J Tomlinson ('Kendal'), G Whitwell ('Kendal').
Attendance: 1,200   *Referee*: HN Boyd (Scotland)

Saturday 4 December 1897 at Jesmond Ground, Newcastle
NORTHUMBERLAND 10 *Back*: P Moran (Wall). *Three-quarters*: R Thomas (Wall, t), S Anderson (Wall, 2c), W Bates (PerPk), JG Bainbridge (Nor). *Half-backs*: SC Lockerby (PerPk, t), CW Russell (PerPk). *Forwards*: FJ Bell (Rock), J Finlay (WHart), JH Greenwell (Rock), J Nesbitt (Wall), RM Robertson (NDur), T Robson (Tynd), J Smith (Wall), RC Stevenson (Nor).
LANCASHIRE 0 *Back*: F Woodhead (CasM). *Three-quarters*: GP Wincey (Man), CEL Beasley (Lit), R Whitehead (Bla), AT Brettargh (Liv). *Half-backs*: G Cookson (Man), WK Roberts (Royal Lancaster Grammar School). *Forwards*: S Croggan (Bro), JS Francomb (Man), JW Hardicker (CasM), H Hodgkinson (Lit), A Long (Bla), JE Louden (Man), R Pierce (capt, Liv), RD Wood (LivOB).
Attendance: 1,000   *Referee*: JA Smith (Scotland)

Saturday 8 January 1898 at Whalley Range, Manchester
LANCASHIRE 13 *Back*: F Woodhead (CasM). *Three-quarters*: GP Wincey (Man), R Whitehead (Bla, c), CEL Beasley (Lit), AT Brettargh (Liv). *Half-backs*: GG Allen (capt, Liv, c), G Cookson (Man). *Forwards*: R Crabtree (Lit), JW Hardicker (CasM), H Hodgkinson (Lit, t), A Long (Bla), JE Louden (Man, t), W McInnes (Bla, t), R Pierce (Liv), RD Wood (LivOB).
DURHAM 8 *Back*: RW Poole (HartR). *Three-quarters*: EW Elliot (Sund, t), DR Thomas (WHart), RF Cumberlege (ODun), GS Legard (ODun). *Half-backs*: F Marston (Tud, t), JT Thompson (HartR, c). *Forwards*: T Burt (SherH), W Dale (HartR), GC Kerr (ODun), RK Oakes (capt, HartR), A Stephenson (Tud), J Stitt (Tud), AJ Troupe (Tud), H Walker (ODun).
Attendance: 2,000   *Referee*: A Hartley (Yorkshire)

Saturday 15 January 1898 at Maude's Meadow, Kendal
WESTMORLAND 0 *Back*: N Shaw ('Staveley'). *Three-quarters*: JA Gott ('Heversham'/ CamU), C Crossley ('Kendal'), C Pearson (DonT), HF Newton (OxfU). *Half-backs*: J Gawith ('Kirkby Lonsdale'), G Whitwell ('Kendal'). *Forwards*: J Carradus (capt, 'Kendal'), F Causton ('Kendal'), FW Cragg ('Kendal'), J Hall ('Kendal'), F Sharpe ('Kendal'), JH Thompson ('Kendal'), J Tomlinson ('Kendal'), W Woodhouse ('Kirkby Lonsdale').
YORKSHIRE 40 *Back*: H Ward (Ship). *Three-quarters*: EF Fookes (capt, SowB, 2t, 2c), OG Mackie (CamU, t), AW Robinson (Bowl, 2t), F Goodfellow (Sha, t). *Half-backs*: C Emmott (Ship, t), H Myers (Kei, dg). *Forwards*: H Blackburn (HebB), J Glew (Fea), EH Jacobson (Mor), H Moon (Ship), A Priestley (Wort), HE Ramsden (Bing, 3t, c), F Shaw (Cleck), JH Shooter (Mor).
Attendance: 700   *Referee*: JM Mawson (Barrow)

Saturday 22 January 1898 at Upper Park, Birkenhead
CHESHIRE 5 *Back*: S Simpson (BirkPk). *Three-quarters*: JAS Cannell (NewB, c), W Fletcher (NewB, t), H Greenham (BirkPk), GM Bennett (BirkPk). *Half-backs*: JC Marquis (BirkPk), NS Wood (BirkPk). *Forwards*: H Alexander (BirkPk), J Baxter (BirkPk), EH Bradshaw (Sale), JS Darby (BirkPk), H Fletcher (Sale), J Hague (Sale), E Herschell (BirkPk), J Murray (NewB).
YORKSHIRE 5 *Back*: H Ward (Ship). *Three-quarters*: EF Fookes (capt, SowB, c), GH Marsden (Mor), H Wilkinson (Harr, t), F Goodfellow (Sha). *Half-backs*: C Emmott (Ship), H Myers (Kei). *Forwards*: R Blades (Kei), J Glew (Fea), EH Jacobson (Mor), H Moon (Ship), A Priestley (Wort), HE Ramsden (Bing), F Shaw (Cleck), JH Shooter (Mor).
Attendance: 2,000/3,000   *Referee*: H Williamson (Lancashire)

Saturday 29 January 1898 at Warwick Road, Carlisle
CUMBERLAND 8 *Back*: J Tyson (Whi). *Three-quarters*: A Smith (Carl, t), R Holywell (WickPk, c), T Parkinson (Work), JC Broughton (PenU). *Half-backs*: WS Graham (Carl, t), W Jackson (Cock). *Forwards*: JH Blacklock (Asp), G Brough (Carl), J Clague (Cock), Jim Davidson (capt, Asp), Joe Davidson (Asp), D Elliott (Carl), T McGerry (WhiR), J Walker (Asp).
YORKSHIRE 13 *Back*: H Ward (Ship). *Three-quarters*: JT Taylor (WHart), GH Marsden (Mor), EF Fookes (capt, SowB, t, gm), F Goodfellow (Sha, t). *Half-backs*: H Myers (Kei), CE Winpenny (Oss). *Forwards*: H Blackburn (HebB), J Glew (Fea, t), H Moon (Ship), A Priestley (Wort), HE Ramsden (Bing), F Shaw (Cleck), JH Shooter (Mor), LR Wood (Cleck).
Attendance: 3,000   *Referee*: J Ashton (Lancashire)

Saturday 29 January 1898 at Brewery Field, Spennymoor
DURHAM 0 *Back*: RW Poole (HartR). *Three-quarters*: EW Elliot (Sund), GS Legard (ODun), RW Adamson (ODun), WJ Robertson (SSh). *Half-backs*: F Marston (Tud), JT Thompson (HartR). *Forwards*: T Burt (SherH), J Knight (Hou), RK Oakes (capt, HartR), A Peat (SSh), A Stephenson (Tud), J Stitt (Tud), F Tully (SSh), H Walker (ODun).
NORTHUMBERLAND 3 *Back*: P Moran (Wall). *Three-quarters*: GC Robinson (PerPk, t), S Anderson (Wall), W Bates (PerPk), H Spencer (Nor/CamU). *Half-backs*: SC Lockerby (PerPk), CW Russell (PerPk). *Forwards*: FJ Bell (Rock), COP Gibson (Nor/OxfU), J Lindsay (Tud), JH Greenwell (Rock), J Nesbitt (Wall), T Robson (Tynd), J Smith (Wall), RC Stevenson (Nor).
Attendance: n/a   *Referee*: EB Holmes (Midland Counties)

Saturday 12 February 1898 at Jesmond Ground, Newcastle
NORTHUMBERLAND 6 *Back*: P Moran (Wall). *Three-quarters*: H Spencer (Nor/CamU), W Bates (PerPk), S Anderson (Wall, pg), EW Taylor (Rock, t). *Half-backs*: SC Lockerby (PerPk), CW Russell (PerPk). *Forwards*: FJ Bell (Rock), J Dobinson (Rock), JH Greenwell (Rock), J Nesbitt (Wall), T Robson (Tynd), T Scott (NEls), HJ Spencer (PerPk), RC Stevenson (Nor).
CUMBERLAND 0 *Back*: A Smith (Carl). *Three-quarters*: G Steel (Carl), R Holywell (Wick Pk), JC Broughton (PenU), T Parkinson (Work). *Half-backs*: WS Graham (Carl), J Nelson (Asp). *Forwards*: JH Blacklock (Asp), G Brough (Carl), J Clague (Cock), Jim Davidson (capt, Asp), Joe Davidson (Asp), D Elliott (Carl), John Owens (Sea), W Winskill (PenU).
Attendance: 3,000   *Referee*: A Turnbull (Scotland)

Wednesday 16 February 1898 at Upper Park, Birkenhead
CHESHIRE 0 *Back*: McIver (AshH). *Three-quarters*: H Greenham (BirkPk),
HP Hebblethwaite (BirkPk), W Fletcher (NewB), JAS Cannell (NewB). *Half-backs*:
F Drinkwater (Sale), NS Wood (BirkPk). *Forwards*: AL Auty (NewB), A Baker (Sale),
J Baxter (BirkPk), J Hague (Sale), E Herschell (BirkPk), J Murray (NewB), Nelson (AshH),
JB Royle (BirkPk).
NORTHUMBERLAND 11 *Back*: P Moran (Wall). *Three-quarters*: S Anderson (Wall, t, c),
W Bates (PerPk, t), EW Taylor (Rock), A Taylor (Rock). *Half-backs*: SC Lockerby (PerPk, t),
CW Russell (PerPk). *Forwards*: FJ Bell (Rock), J Dobinson (Rock), COP Gibson (Nor/Oxf),
GR Gibson (Nor), JH Greenwell (Rock), J Munro (Wall), J Nesbitt (Wall), T Robson (Tynd).
Attendance: 'satisfactory'   *Referee*: n/a

Final table

	P	W	D	L	For	Agst	Pts
Northumberland	6	5	0	1	73	5	10
Yorkshire	6	4	1	1	95	25	9
Durham	6	4	0	2	41	26	8
Lancashire	6	4	0	2	45	49	8
Cumberland	6	2	0	4	81	55	4
Cheshire	6	1	1	4	24	47	3
Westmorland	6	0	0	6	3	155	0

(Durham awarded win for unplayed match with Westmorland)

SOUTH WESTERN GROUP

Results
Devonshire 22, Cornwall 0
Gloucestershire 5, Devonshire 13
Somersetshire 11, Cornwall 5
Somersetshire 0, Gloucestershire 3
Cornwall 3, Gloucestershire 16
Devonshire 6, Somersetshire 0

Final table

	P	W	D	L	For	Agst	Pts
Devonshire	3	3	0	0	41	5	6
Gloucestershire	3	2	0	1	24	16	4
Somersetshire	3	1	0	2	11	14	2
Cornwall	3	0	0	3	8	49	0

SOUTH EASTERN GROUP A

Results
Kent 22, Middlesex 5
East Midlands 5, Kent 15
Midland Counties 0, Surrey 0
Midland Counties 28, Middlesex 11
Kent 3, Midland Counties 10
Surrey 9, East Midlands 9
East Midlands 3, Midland Counties 8
Middlesex 8, Surrey 13
Surrey 5, Kent 6
Middlesex 18, East Midlands 3

SOUTH EASTERN GROUP A *continued*

Final table

	P	W	D	L	For	Agst	Pts
Midland Counties	4	3	1	0	46	17	7
Kent	4	3	0	1	46	25	6
Surrey	4	1	2	1	27	23	4
Middlesex	4	1	0	3	42	66	2
East Midlands	4	0	1	3	20	50	1

SOUTH EASTERN GROUP B

Results
Sussex 13, Eastern Counties 3
Hampshire 0, Sussex 3
Eastern Counties 0, Hampshire 11

Final table

	P	W	D	L	For	Agst	Pts
Sussex	2	2	0	0	16	3	4
Hampshire	2	1	0	1	11	3	2
Eastern Counties	2	0	0	2	3	24	0

South Eastern Group Final
Midland Counties awarded win after Sussex withdrew

Southern Final
Devonshire 3, Midland Counties 5

COUNTY CHAMPIONSHIP FINAL

Saturday 26 March 1898 at The Butts, Coventry
NORTHUMBERLAND 24 *Back*: P Moran (Wall). *Three-quarters*: GC Robinson (PerPk), W Bates (PerPk, t), S Anderson (capt, Wall, c), FW Stone (PerPk, 3t). *Half-backs*: SC Lockerby (PerPk), EW Taylor (Rock, t, 2c). *Forwards*: FJ Bell (Rock), RW Bell (Nor/CamU), J Dobinson (Rock), COP Gibson (Nor/OxfU), GR Gibson (Nor), JH Greenwell (Rock), J Nesbitt (Wall), RC Stevenson (Nor, t).
MIDLAND COUNTIES 3 *Back*: JF Byrne (Mose). *Three-quarters*: G Birtles (Mose), WL Bunting (Bromsgrove), FA Byrne (Mose), JA Gould (Mose, t). *Half-backs*: RH Cattell (Mose), F Cattell (Mose). *Forwards*: BH Cattell (Mose), A St G Cummings (Wolv), AO Dowson (Mose), J Elsworth (Mose), CP Evers (Mose), J Hall (Rugby), DF Miller (Strat), JJ Robinson (Burt).
Attendance: 3,000   *Referee*: JD Boswell (Scotland)

NON-COUNTY CHAMPIONSHIP MATCHES

Saturday 19 February 1898 at County Ground, St Thomas, Exeter
DEVONSHIRE 8 *Back*: W Churchill (Ply). *Three-quarters*: EJ Salter (Exm), MH Toller (Barn), G Hutchings (Exe), T Fitzgerald (Sid, t). *Half-backs*: A Hannaford (Barn), S Labbett (Exe). *Forwards*: W Ashford (Exe, c), P Baron (Sid), D Hallings (Llwyn), P Rigby (Barn), JJ Sargent (RNEC), JF Shaw (RNEC), C Thomas (Barn, t), TH Thomas (Ply).
CUMBERLAND 5 *Back*: A Smith (Carl). *Three-quarters*: M Burrows (Carl), JC Broughton (PenU), JH Blaylock (Asp), JB Hewitson (Asp). *Half-backs*: J Nelson (Asp), J Steel (Asp, t). *Forwards*: G Brough (Carl), R Brown (Asp), Jim Davidson (capt, Asp, c), Joe Davidson (Asp), D Elliott (Carl), T McGerry (WhiR), W Winskill (PenU), J Walker (Asp).
Attendance: 6,000   *Referee*: EB Holmes (Midland Counties)

Monday 21 February 1898 at St Helen's, Swansea
GLAMORGANSHIRE 8 *Back*: WJ Bancroft (Swa, c). *Three-quarters*: EG Nicholls (Car), V Huzzey (Car, t), J Driscoll (Car), TD Davies (Tre, t). *Half-backs*: JE Elliott (Car), W Phillips (Mou). *Forwards*: WH Alexander (Llwyn), A Brice (Aber), FH Cornish (Car), H Davies (Swa), T Dobson (Car), D Evans (Peny), B Jones (Llwyn), R Thomas (Swa).
CUMBERLAND 3 *Back*: A Smith (Carl). *Three-quarters*: JH Blaylock (Asp), JB Hewitson (Asp), M Burrows (Carl), JC Broughton (PenU). *Half-backs*: J Nelson (Asp), J Steel (Asp). *Forwards*: G Brough (Carl), R Brown (Asp), Jim Davidson (capt, Asp), Joe Davidson (Asp, t), D Elliott (Carl), G Evans* (Llwyn), W Winskill (PenU), J Walker (Asp).
Attendance: 4,000   *Referee*: WH Wilkins (Llanelli)
*Guest from Glamorganshire to replace unavailable player.

Monday 7 March 1898 at Cardiff Arms Park
GLAMORGANSHIRE 6 *Back*: J Davies (Nea). *Three-quarters*: EG Nicholls (Car, t), TD Davies (Tre, t), V Huzzey (Car), J Driscoll (Car). *Half-backs*: S Biggs (Car), JE Elliott (Car). *Forwards*: WH Alexander (Llwyn), A Brice (Aber), FH Cornish (Car), H Davies (Swa), S Davies (Nea), T Dobson (Car), R Hellings (Llwyn), R Thomas (Swa).
YORKSHIRE 0 *Back*: H Ward (Ship). *Three-quarters*: F Goodfellow (Sha), JT Taylor (WHart), AW Robinson (Bowl), EF Fookes (capt, SowB). *Half-backs*: H Myers (Kei), T Stirk (Mor). *Forwards*: R Blades (Kei), J Cole (Fea), J Glew (Fea), EH Jacobson (Mor), H Moon (Ship), A Priestley (Wort), F Shaw (Cleck), LR Wood (Cleck).
Attendance: 10,000   *Referee*: DH Bowen (Llanelli)

ENGLAND TRIAL MATCHES

Saturday 18 December 1897 at Warwick Road, Carlisle
NORTH 7 *Back*: RW Poole (HartR). *Three-quarters*: JAS Cannell (NewB, t), S Anderson (Wall), JT Taylor (WHart, dg), EF Fookes (capt, SowB). *Half-backs*: WS Graham (Carl), JT Thompson (HartR). *Forwards*: JH Blacklock (Asp), W Dale (HartR), Jim Davidson (Asp), EH Jacobson (Mor), RF Oakes (HartR), R Pierce (Liv), HE Ramsden (Bing), F Shaw (Cleck).
SOUTH 9 *Back*: JF Byrne (capt, Mose). *Three-quarters*: PW Stout (Glo, t), WL Bunting (Rich), OG Mackie (CamU, t), WN Pilkington (CamU). *Half-backs*: Arthur Rotherham (Rich), GT Unwin (Black). *Forwards*: W Ashford (Exe), AJL Darby (CamU), HW Dudgeon (Rich), CP Evers (OxfU), AFC Luxmoore (CamU), FM Stout (Glo, t), W Mortimer (MarlN), CE Wilson (Black).
Attendance: 4,000/5,000   *Referee*: WH Bell (Durham)

Saturday 26 February 1898 at County Ground, St Thomas's, Exeter
SOUTH 34 *Back*: JF Byrne (capt, Mose, 5c). *Three-quarters*: R Forrest (Tau, t), WL Bunting (Rich), PMR Royds (Black, t), WN Pilkington (CamU, 3t). *Half-backs*: Arthur Rotherham (Rich), GT Unwin (Black, t). *Forwards*: W Ashford (Exe, t), AO Dowson (Mose), HW Dudgeon (Rich, t), F Jacob (Rich), FS Preston (MarlN), JF Shaw (RNEC). FM Stout (Glo), CE Wilson (Black). *Substitute*: P Baron (Sidmouth) replaced Wilson (broken leg) after 7 minutes.
NORTH 0 *Back*: H Ward (Ship). *Three-quarters*: GP Wincey (Man), JT Taylor (WHart), AT Brettargh (LivOB), GS Legard (ODun). *Half-backs*: JC Marquis (BirkPk), H Myers (Kei). *Forwards*: Jim Davidson (Asp), Joe Davidson (Asp), J Finlay (WHart), E Herschell (BirkPk), RF Oakes (capt, HartR), R Pierce (Liv), H Ramsden (Bing), F Shaw (Cleck).
Attendance: 8,000   *Referee*: GH Harnett (Kent)

INTERNATIONAL CHAMPIONSHIP

Saturday 5 February 1898 at Athletic Ground, Richmond
ENGLAND 6 *Back*: JF Byrne (capt, Mose, pg). *Three-quarters*: GC Robinson (PerPk, t), WL Bunting (Rich), OG Mackie (CamU), EF Fookes (SowB). *Half-backs*: PG Jacob (Black), H Myers (Kei). *Forwards*: JH Blacklock (Asp), HW Dudgeon (Rich), F Jacob (Rich), RF Oakes (HartR), R Pierce (Liv), F Shaw (Cleck), FM Stout (Glo), CE Wilson (Black).
IRELAND 9 *Back*: PE O'Brien-Butler (Monk). *Three-quarters*: FC Purser (DubU), S Lee (capt, NIFC), LH Gwynn (Monk), LQ Bulger (Lans, pg). *Half-backs*: GG Allen (Der), LM Magee (BecR, t). *Forwards*: WG Byron (NIFC), JL Davis (Monk), JG Franks (DubU), H Lindsay (Arm, t), JH Lytle (NIFC), JE McIlwaine (NIFC), M Ryan (RockC), J Ryan (RockC).
Attendance: 20,000   *Referee*: DG Findlay (Scotland)

Saturday 12 March 1898 at Powderhall, Edinburgh
SCOTLAND 3 *Back*: JM Reid (EdinA). *Half-backs*: AR Smith (capt, OxfU), TA Nelson (OxfU), RT Neilson (WoS), T Scott (Haw). *Quarter-backs*: M Elliot (Haw), JT Mabon (Jed). *Forwards*: JM Dykes (Clyd), GC Kerr (ODun), WMC McEwan (EdinA, t), A MacKinnon (LonS), MC Morrison (RHSFP), TM Scott (Haw), HO Smith (Wat), RC Stephenson (Nor).
ENGLAND 3 *Back*: JF Byrne (capt, Mose). *Three-quarters*: PW Stout (Glo), WL Bunting (Rich), PMR Royds (Black, t), WN Pilkington (CamU). *Half-backs*: Arthur Rotherham (Rich), GT Unwin (Black). *Forwards*: W Ashford (Exe), Jim Davidson (Asp), HW Dudgeon (Rich), F Jacob (Rich), RF Oakes (HartR), HE Ramsden (Bing), JF Shaw (RNEC), FM Stout (Glo).
Attendance: 15,000   *Referee*: J Dods (Ireland)

Saturday 2 April 1898 at Rectory Field, Blackheath
ENGLAND 14 *Back*: JF Byrne (capt, Mose, c). *Three-quarters*: PW Stout (Glo, t), WL Bunting (Rich), PMR Royds (Black), EF Fookes (SowB, 2t). *Half-backs*: R O'H Livesay (Black), Arthur Rotherham (Rich). *Forwards*: W Ashford (Exe), Jim Davidson (Asp), HW Dudgeon (Rich), F Jacob (Rich), RF Oakes (HartR), HE Ramsden (Bing), JF Shaw (RNEC), FM Stout (Glo, t).
WALES 7 *Back*: WJ Bancroft (capt, Swa). *Three-quarters*: V Huzzey (Car), W Jones (Car), EG Nicholls (Car), TW Pearson (New). *Half-backs*: S Biggs (Car), JE Elliott (Car). *Forwards*: WH Alexander (Llwyn), G Boots (New), FH Cornish (Car), DJ Daniel (Llan), H Davies (Swa), T Dobson (Car), D Evans (Peny), R Hellings (Llwyn).
Attendance: 20,000   *Referee*: JT Magee (Ireland)

Other results
Ireland 0, Scotland 8
Ireland 3, Wales 11

Final table

	P	W	D	L	For	Agst
Scotland	2	1	1	0	11	3
England	3	1	1	1	23	19
Wales	2	1	0	1	18	17
Ireland	3	1	0	2	12	25

(Championship incomplete. Scotland again refused to play Wales following the dispute over J. Arthur Gould's presentation.)

Ireland attack England's line at Richmond, 5th February 1898.
Illustrated London News, 1898

Albert Goldthorpe of Hunslet and Yorkshire.
Yorkshire Evening Post, 1903

1898-1899

NORTHERN UNION AND THE PROFESSIONAL PLAYER

The following appeared in the *Manchester Guardian* during October regarding the growth of professionalism: 'It is hard to work for a living when one can get that living by kicking a football, and it is unfortunately the fact that there are a great many of the footballers today whose aspirations do not exceed the kicking of a football. Certain [Northern Union] clubs, troubled with consciences, are going to the extreme of leaving out of their team's men who are unable to affidavit to prove that they are really working for a living. What is to become of the Union if this policy is pursued to the bitter end? For the [Lancashire] trial match at Warrington on Wednesday next [5th October], what is the Union going to pay? We have reason to believe that the players selected for that important match will receive considerably more than the statutory fee. There are "obvious reasons," it is said, why the fee should not be stated. This is written, apparently, on the assumption that there is still a small section of the football public which believes that the Northern Union is endeavouring, to some extent at least, to conform to the principles of amateurism. As far as can be gathered, the tendency among the Northern Union clubs is to become more and more professional every day.'[228]

SOUTH EAST LANCASHIRE REVIVAL
A new Northern Union competition called the South East Lancashire League was created with just seven teams, destined to last one season. A previous ten-team South East Lancashire competition existed under the Rugby Union code in 1892-1893 but also survived for one term.

KENDAL HORNETS RESURRECTED
Kendal Hornets, having disbanded in 1896, were resurrected, but as a Northern Union club, during a meeting held at the Golden Lion Hotel, Kendal, on 3rd October. It brought the strength of the Westmorland Northern Union up to three clubs, the others being Ambleside and Staveley. The Hornets first match took place on 8th October when they visited Staveley for a friendly fixture, winning 8-5.[229]

SEATON LEAVE THE RUGBY UNION
Cumberland Cup holders Seaton decided, at their meeting on 12th October, to resign from the Rugby Union and seek membership of the Northern Union. The reasons given were the poor finances of the club, and unlikely public support for fixtures arranged under Rugby Union rules.[230] They were subsequently asked to return the Cup but when the Cumberland Committee received it, it was found that the name of Seaton had been engraved on it in letters twice as large as any of the previous winners. The *Shields Daily Gazette* commented that 'no doubt the Seatonians thought that a good joke, but the Cumberland Committee were equal to it for they caused the offending engraving to be refilled with silver, and had the cup re-lettered in harmony with the rest, and finally deducted the cost of the work from money standing to the credit of the Seaton club'.[231]

CUMBERLAND RUGBY UNION STRUGGLING
With so many clubs migrating to the Northern Union, the Cumberland Rugby Union was struggling to select a county team for their opening match against Durham at Carlisle on 22nd October. The *Lancashire Daily Post* reported: 'Rugby Union football is dying in West Cumberland, Seaton have given it a blow from which it cannot recover. Whitehaven Recreation, who for some time past if rumour be not a lying jade, have stood hesitating on the brink. Aspatria, Whitehaven and Cockermouth will then be left deserted. Under these circumstances the loyalty of these three clubs will be severely tried.' Whitehaven, who 'were expected to hold the fort to the very last gasp,' subsequently resigned on 19th October, creating further selection problems ahead of the Durham fixture.[232]

RUGBY UNION STILL FLOURISHING

According to the *Manchester Guardian*, 'the county championship of the Rugby Union has perhaps lost some of its interest by reason of the advent of the Northern Union, but the North is not the whole of England, and it is well to recognise that the amateur game is still in existence. Outside Lancashire and Yorkshire "Rugby" appears to be flourishing as well as ever'.[233]

PROPOSAL FOR A DURHAM LEAGUE: NORTHUMBERLAND OBJECT

The Durham Rugby Union decided to form a League, the decision being taken at its meeting held at Walton's Hotel, Sunderland, on 8th November. The idea of a Durham-only competition resurrected the plan that had floundered earlier in the year. The clubs reported to have agreed to join were Durham City, Hamsteels, Hartlepool Old Boys, Houghton, Old Dunelmians, Sherburn House, South Shields, Sunderland, Tudhoe, Tyne Dock, West Hartlepool, and Westoe. The announcement put the Durham Union into conflict with neighbours Northumberland who were not consulted and, in a letter sent to the Durham officials, dated 22nd November, they asked to be included, but this request was turned down. A further letter was sent to the Durham hierarchy, dated 6th December, opposing the formation of a Durham-only league, stating 'it will do intolerable harm to the Rugby game in Northumberland,' explaining that 'Durham have about twelve senior clubs and Northumberland only five [and] if the Durham clubs, through their League engagements, are precluded from playing our clubs, our clubs must die a natural death from starvation of matches'.[234]

RUGBY UNION AND THE RE-INSTATEMENT OF PLAYERS

Professionalism was again the subject of a Rugby Union Sub-committee meeting, held at the Craven Hotel, London, on 17th November. The *Manchester Guardian* reported that they 'considered a number of applications for the reinstatement of players who had knowingly played with or against professional clubs after the 1st November, 1895. The Sub-committee, acting upon instructions by the General Committee, refused all such applications'.[235]

SEATON LOSE TOM FLETCHER

Although the Cumberland clubs were migrating almost *en masse* to the Northern Union, they still had issues when it came to retaining players. The case of Seaton's ex-England Rugby Union centre Tom Fletcher moving to Oldham was a typical one. A *Lancashire Daily Post* journalist commented: 'It is another case of the way Cumberland is sucked of its best men. The border county is nothing but a nursery for training players for Lancashire and Yorkshire clubs. It is drained of its best blood and muscle for the benefit of clubs with big cash bags. Well, I suppose one cannot grumble at a man for "bettering himself" as the saying goes, but this never ending migration of players has weakened the county and must have done the Rugby game great harm in Cumberland.'[236]

WHITEHAVEN RECREATION LEAVE THE RUGBY UNION
The Whitehaven Recreation club decided at its meeting on 9th January to secede from the Rugby Union. The decision had a major impact, being the last major Rugby Union team remaining in West Cumberland and a regular choice for hosting county fixtures. It reduced Cumberland to just four senior clubs in Aspatria, Carlisle, Cockermouth, and Penrith United. That quartet were the only participants in a much-reduced Cumberland Challenge Cup competition, the last to be held for several seasons until revived in 1907-08.[237]

NORTHUMBERLAND CLUBS TO BE BOYCOTTED
A meeting of the Durham Rugby Union Committee took place at Walton's Hotel, Sunderland, on 10th January, to consider for resolution: 'That it is the feeling of the clubs in Durham County that all fixtures with Northumberland clubs be cancelled at once for next season.' It brought to a head the dissatisfaction of some Durham organisations towards the alleged interference of Northumberland regarding the proposal to form a Durham County League, the Northumberland Committee having appealed to the Rugby Football Union on 13th December to intervene. The resolution was carried although it did not affect the current season's fixtures. However, feelings cooled and in early February it was reported that 'an important development is announced on the part of [Durham's] West Hartlepool, which has, like Sunderland and Hartlepool Rovers, repudiated the resolution of the Durham Union, and agreed to stand by the Northumberland clubs. Now it would appear that the exclusive Durham League is destined to utter failure'. The prediction was correct and, as with previous attempts, no league was subsequently formed.[238]

DURHAM: PUBLIC INTEREST DECLINING
The Durham City versus Hartlepool Rovers match on 14th January was poorly attended prompting the *Durham County Advertiser* to state it was

an 'indication of how fast the public interest in the Rugby game is declining. One has been accustomed on such occasions to see the stands packed, and spectators standing four and five deep round the ropes. On Saturday the whole of the spectators could have been accommodated in a fair sized room. The falling away of public interest and support [is] deplorable, especially from the point of view of those who prefer amateur sports, as well as most serious so far as the finances of the local club are concerned'.[239]

THE PRECARIOUS POSITION OF CUMBERLAND RUGBY UNION

Following the defection of three Cumberland clubs so far during the season – Seaton, Whitehaven and Whitehaven Recreation – and more rumoured to be joining them, the Rugby Union code in that county was looking precarious. The *Manchester Courier* reported during February: 'It may lead directly to the annihilation of the Cumberland Rugby Union. It is just possible that a single club may remain, that club being Carlisle. The whole trouble has been caused by the rapid development of Northern Unionism in the county. Aspatria, prominent as it is and has been for years in Rugby Union circles, are placed in a distressing position, being now, with one exception, entirely devoid of fixtures, and have not had a game at home since the beginning of December. The report was sprung a few days ago that Aspatria was going over to Northern Union, being involuntarily forced thither by mere force of circumstances. If Aspatria go over, the death knell of the Cumberland Union is sounded, for Penrith [United] and Cockermouth are bound to follow, and it is scarcely predictable that a County Union can exist with one club affiliated.'[240]

CARLISLE THREATEN TO LEAVE
THE CUMBERLAND RUGBY UNION

When the Yorkshire versus Cumberland rugby union match, scheduled for Keighley on 28th January, was postponed due to frost, it created problems for the Cumberland Union, whose team was mostly composed of players from Aspatria and Carlisle. Rearranged for 18th February, it clashed with Aspatria's match with West Hartlepool. A new date of 4th March was agreed with Yorkshire but Carlisle objected as it clashed with other fixtures and they threatened to resign from the Union unless it was changed. The *Yorkshire Post* was not impressed, claiming 'it is deplorable that the difficulties of the Cumberland Union should be aggravated by the unnecessary assertiveness of a club from who the Rugby Union had a right to expect the most loyal co-operation. The County Committee have been engaged in the extremely difficult task of upholding Rugby Union in Cumberland, and, outsiders at least, have not failed to observe how they have been hampered in quarters from which loyal assistance might have been expected'. Carlisle later rescinded their threat and the county match went ahead on 4th March.[241]

YORKSHIRE SECOND COMPETITION CHAMPIONSHIP FINAL

Todmorden, having won the West Division of the Northern Union's Yorkshire Second Competition, had to meet Hull Kingston Rovers, winners of the East Division, to determine the overall champions. The Second Competition committee decided they should play-off on Thursday 2nd March at the Boulevard ground of Rovers' near neighbour Hull. Todmorden felt the location was unfair and also objected to the date as it was two days before they were due to oppose Dewsbury in a Northern Union Challenge Cup qualifying tie. It was agreed to alter the date to 9th March and there was also a change of attitude by Todmorden on the venue, possibly influenced by financial considerations. The Boulevard was unavailable so Hull Kingston Rovers' Craven Street enclosure was chosen instead, with Todmorden's consent. Rovers won 36-0, earning a play-off Test Match against the Yorkshire Senior Competition's basement club, Heckmondwike, who they overcame 21-3 to gain promotion.[242]

THE NORTHUMBERLAND CUP: INTEREST FADING

Interest in the Northumberland (Rugby Union) Cup appeared to be fading, the *Athletic News* stating that 'with the falling away of Northumberland Rugby clubs, owing to failing interest, the Cup Competition becomes more restricted than ever. This season's contests began on Saturday [4th March]. There being only five clubs, the first round produced one match'.[243]

UNATTACHED PLAYERS

When Lancashire met Devonshire at Exeter on 4th March they were opposed by two 'unattached' Welsh players, namely J. Jones and W. Sims. They had qualified for Devonshire through joining Devonport Albion, the Welsh Union claiming they had done so for financial gain. The South Wales clubs, who had already seen many players defect for monetary reward to the Northern Union, saw the same situation happening with the West Country clubs, Devonport Albion and Torquay Athletic in particular. In a bid to halt the player-drain the Welsh Union had ruled that 'all Welsh clubs were prohibited from renewing fixtures with any English club playing men under suspension by any [other] Union'. As a consequence it was reported that Devonport 'have had to discard [the two Welsh players] in order to retain fixtures with Welsh clubs,' leaving both without a club. It was a curious situation because they were still considered to be amateurs in England and, therefore, the Devonshire county authorities selected both for the county fixture with Lancashire. Jones appeared as an 'unattached' player in further Devonshire fixtures over the next year including Durham (twice) and Northumberland.[244]

YORKSHIRE CUP ISSUES
Several incidents took place in the Yorkshire (Rugby Union) Cup during March. Nortonthorpe overcame visitors Mytholmroyd 5-4 in the first round but the latter protested that an 'attendant' entered the field for the hosts without permission. A replay was ordered at Ossett which finished scoreless, a second replay, at Shipley, being won by Mytholmroyd, 16-6. Also in the first round, Bingley won 6-0 at Stainland, the home team suffering further when it was suspended until 31st December 1899 'for not protecting the referee' who claimed that, after penalising Stainland several times, around 200 to 300 spectators surged round him and, when the final whistle blew, he was 'sodded, stoned and kicked' all the way to the passage leading from the field. He said that 'if it had not been for a Stainland official and the Bingley players, I believe I should have been killed'.[245] In the third round Harrogate, who lost 15-6 at home to Ossett, objected to an Ossett official acting as a touch judge after an appointed touch judge withdrew through illness, contravening the rule that in Cup-ties they should be neutral. Harrogate claim they were not consulted in the matter and a replay was ordered at Otley, Ossett again winning, 11-9.

THE YORKSHIRE CUP FINAL REPLAY
Alverthorpe and Sowerby Bridge fought out a scoreless draw in the Yorkshire (Rugby Union) Cup final at Keighley on Saturday 15th April, a result that caused a dilemma for the Yorkshire authorities. The Rugby Union season officially ended on 20th April, so a replay had to be on Wednesday 19th April at the latest, but Sowerby Bridge had several players involved in a charity match on that date. The Rugby Football Union was asked for permission to replay on Saturday 22nd April and, following a meeting on 17th April, consent was given, Sowerby Bridge winning 4-0 at Keighley.

THE 1899 ENGLAND TOUR
The first official Rugby Union tour to Australia lasted from June to August 1899, a plan to include New Zealand being shelved. Eight of the 21 players

had northern England connections: Charlie Adamson (born Durham, played for Durham City, Old Dunelmians and Durham county), Alan Ayre-Smith (born Richmond in Yorkshire), George Cookson (born Port Elizabeth, South Africa, played for Swinton, Manchester and Lancashire), John Francomb (born Blackburn, played for Manchester and Lancashire, later played for Bowdon, Sale and Cheshire), George Gibson (born Gateshead, played for Northern and Northumberland county), Matthew Mullineux (tour captain, born Barton, near Salford, toured in 1896), Elliot Nicholson (born Derby, played for Liverpool and Lancashire), Charlie Thompson (born Lancaster, played for Lancaster, Manchester and Lancashire). Of the others, Gerry Doran, Tom McGown, and Esmond Martelli were born in Ireland, Alf Bucher and Hugh Gray born in Scotland. Gwynne Nicholls (born England) played for Wales, Alec Timms (born Australia) played for Scotland, and Cookson, as previously mentioned, was born in South Africa. The badge worn by the players named the party as 'The Anglo-Australian Rugby Football Team' but despite that, and representation from all the home nations, they were known on tour as England or 'the English team' and are, therefore, referred to in this publication as England.

1898-1899 STATISTICS

NORTHERN UNION

LANCASHIRE SENIOR COMPETITION

Final table	P	W	D	L	For	Agst	Pts
Broughton Rangers	26	21	0	5	277	74	42
Oldham	26	20	0	6	385	58	40
Salford	26	18	2	6	206	113	38
Widnes	26	17	2	7	196	113	36
Leigh	26	17	0	9	168	125	34
Swinton*	26	16	2	8	228	79	32
Runcorn	26	15	2	9	193	113	32
St Helens	26	12	3	11	168	180	27
Warrington	26	11	1	14	134	217	23
Rochdale Hornets	26	9	3	14	112	216	21
Stockport	26	5	1	20	102	317	11
Tyldesley	26	3	5	18	82	240	11
Wigan	26	4	2	20	66	238	10
Morecambe	26	2	1	23	47	281	5

*Two points deducted for breach of professional rules

LANCASHIRE SECOND COMPETITION

Final table	P	W	D	L	For	Agst	Pts
Millom	16	15	1	0	301	15	31
Barrow	16	10	3	3	190	41	23
Lancaster	16	9	1	6	121	77	19
Ulverston	15	8	2	5	68	52	18
Altrincham	15	6	4	5	85	48	16
Radcliffe	16	7	1	8	119	69	15
Birkenhead Wanderers	16	7	1	8	101	126	15
Fleetwood	16	2	1	13	48	221	5
Blackpool	16	0	0	16	31	415	0
Record expunged:							
Barton	9	2	0	7	28	88	4
Walkden	12	1	0	11	22	424	2

Note 1: Barton (Dec 1898), Walkden (Feb 1899) disbanded.
Note 2: Altrincham v Ulverston not played.

Promotion Test Match
Millom 11, Morecambe 3 (at New Barnes, Salford)
(Millom promoted to Lancashire Senior Competition, Morecambe relegated)

YORKSHIRE SENIOR COMPETITION

Final table	P	W	D	L	For	Agst	Pts
Batley	30	23	2	5	279	75	48
Hull	30	23	1	6	429	101	47
Bradford	30	21	0	9	330	139	42
Leeds Parish Church	30	20	2	8	201	114	42
Hunslet	30	16	5	9	314	140	37
Huddersfield	30	15	3	12	169	147	33
Manningham*	30	15	2	13	222	212	30
Halifax	30	15	0	15	156	158	30
Wakefield Trinity	30	11	6	13	209	161	28
Brighouse Rangers	30	12	2	16	114	191	26
Leeds	30	11	3	16	127	186	25
Castleford	30	10	4	16	159	214	24
Holbeck	30	10	4	16	134	220	24
Bramley	30	7	3	20	62	266	17
Liversedge	30	5	3	22	131	439	13
Heckmondwike	30	4	4	22	70	343	12

*Two points deducted for breach of professional rules

YORKSHIRE SECOND COMPETITION (WEST)

Final table	P	W	D	L	For	Agst	Pts
Todmorden	16	12	1	3	121	36	25
Dewsbury	16	9	2	5	132	51	20
Eastmoor	16	8	2	6	47	83	18
Elland	16	8	1	7	89	64	17
Morley	16	8	0	8	138	79	16
Birstall	16	8	0	8	118	98	16
Bowling	16	7	1	8	66	96	15
Idle	16	4	2	10	69	131	10
Luddendenfoot	16	3	1	12	39	181	7

Note: Pudsey disbanded (Oct 1898) without playing a match

YORKSHIRE SECOND COMPETITION (EAST)

Final table	P	W	D	L	For	Agst	Pts
Hull Kingston Rovers	18	18	0	0	389	18	36
Featherstone	18	13	0	5	197	86	26
Outwood Church	18	11	2	5	65	71	24
York	18	11	0	7	170	96	22
Kinsley	18	10	2	6	111	77	22
Normanton	18	10	0	8	112	91	20
Goole	18	7	0	11	91	168	14
Rothwell	18	3	1	14	59	238	7
Pontefract	18	2	1	15	38	206	5
Ripon*	18	2	0	16	22	203	4

* Disbanded (Jan 1899), 8 remaining matches declared as win to opponents

Yorkshire Second Competition Final
Hull Kingston Rovers 36, Todmorden 0 (at Hull KR ground, Craven Street)
(Hull Kingston Rovers declared Yorkshire Second Competition winner)

Promotion Test Match
Hull Kingston Rovers 21, Heckmondwike 3 (at Crown Point, Leeds)
(Hull KR promoted to Yorkshire Senior Competition, Heckmondwike relegated)

NORTH WESTERN LEAGUE

Final table	P	W	D	L	For	Agst	Pts
Millom	14	14	0	0	183	13	28
Barrow	14	10	1	3	137	36	23
Workington	14	8	1	5	82	52	15
Dalton	14	6	1	7	45	118	13
Maryport	14	5	2	7	55	72	12
Lancaster	14	5	1	8	70	65	11
Ulverston	14	4	2	8	44	79	10
Askam	14	0	0	14	27	208	0

SOUTH EAST LANCASHIRE LEAGUE

Final table	P	W	D	L	For	Agst	Pts
Radcliffe	8	7	0	1	60	24	14
Whitworth	8	4	1	3	37	21	9
Werneth	8	4	0	4	67	40	8
Fleetwood	7	1	2	4	14	79	4
Altrincham	7	1	1	5	13	27	3
Record expunged:							
Barton	2	0	1	1	0	8	1
Blackpool	2	0	0	2	0	29	0

Note 1: Barton disbanded (Dec 1898), Blackpool withdrew (Jan 1899)
Note 2: Fleetwood v Altrincham not played

WESTMORLAND JUNIOR LEAGUE

Final table	P	W	D	L	For	Agst	Pts
Kendal Hornets	8	7	0	1	36	14	14
Ambleside	8	4	1	3	38	15	9
Staveley	8	0	1	7	10	55	1

NORTHERN UNION CHALLENGE CUP (91 entries)
Try – 3 points; all goals – 2.

Qualifying Round
Altrincham 8, Leigh Shamrocks 6
Askam 0, Millom 34 (at Millom)
Birkenhead Wanderers 8, Lostock Gralam 3
Birstall 2, Luddendenfoot 2
Blackpool 8, Fleetwood 13
Bowling 3, Morley 0
Elland w/o Pudsey (disbanded)
Hull Marlborough 0, Normanton 22 (at Normanton)
Hull Stoneferry 0, Outwood Church 8
Idle 2, Eastmoor 0
Latchford Rangers w/o Walkden (disqualified)
Maryport 2, Brookland Rovers 0
Pontefract 2, Goole 7
Rochdale Athletic w/o Pendleton (withdrew)
Rothwell w/o Ripon (disbanded)
Runcorn Hornets 0, Warrington St Mary's 14 (at Warrington)
Runcorn Recreation w/o Hazel Grove (disbanded)
Saddleworth Rangers 6, Lees 2
Salford St Bartholomew's w/o Oldham Juniors (withdrew)
Smallbridge 0, Radcliffe 42 (at Radcliffe)
Ulverston 11, Lancaster 6
Todmorden 0, Dewsbury 2
Wath Brow 3, Dalton 0
Werneth 13, Abbey Hills 5
Whitworth w/o Barton (disbanded)
Workington 31, Ambleside 0
York 13, Kinsley 4
Byes: Featherstone, Fletcher Russell and Company (Warrington), Groves United (Hull), Rochdale Rangers, Waterhead Hornets

First Round
Batley 38, Rochdale Athletic 0
Bowling 12, Warrington St Mary's 0
Bradford 8, Wakefield Trinity 0
Brighouse Rangers 10, Stockport 0
Broughton Rangers 59, Rothwell 0
Castleford 8, Halifax 0
Dewsbury 2, Tyldesley 0
Elland 13, Workington 5
Goole 0, Oldham 63 (at Oldham)
Groves United 3, Wigan 28 (at Wigan)
Heckmondwike w/o Waterhead Hornets (disbanded)
Holbeck 9, Birkenhead Wanderers 3
Hull 21, Featherstone 0
Hull Kingston Rovers 11, Manningham 2
Hunslet 11, Maryport 2
Leeds Parish Church 11, Idle 0
Leigh 14, Bramley 0
Liversedge 0, York 4
Millom 24 Ulverston 2
Morecambe 30, Latchford Rangers 0
Outwood Church 8, Altrincham 3
Radcliffe 0, Normanton 5
Rochdale Hornets 28, Dalton 0
Rochdale Rangers 0, Leeds 20 (at Leeds)
Runcorn Recreation 0, Runcorn 77 (at Runcorn)
Saddleworth Rangers 2, Huddersfield 43 (at Huddersfield)
St Helens 12, Whitworth 3
Salford 63, Luddendenfoot 3
Salford St Bartholomew's 2, Werneth 4 (at Werneth)
Swinton 40, Fletcher Russell and Company 5
Warrington 12, Barrow 2
Widnes 48, Fleetwood 3

Second Round
Batley 29, York 5
Bradford 19, Rochdale Hornets 5
Broughton Rangers 10, Hull Kingston Rovers 5
Castleford 10, Brighouse Rangers 2
Elland 10, Bowling 3
Huddersfield 17, Heckmondwike 0
Hull 21, Millom 0
Leeds 3, Wigan 0
Leigh 4, Runcorn 2
Normanton 7, Holbeck 2
Oldham 14, Warrington 0
Outwood Church 0, Leeds Parish Church 6
St Helens 0, Morecambe 0
Salford 31, Werneth 0
Swinton 0, Hunslet 2
Widnes 28, Dewsbury 0

Second Round Replay
Morecambe 5, St Helens 5

Second Round Second Replay
St Helens 17, Morecambe 5

Third Round
Bradford 3, Oldham 23
Broughton Rangers 6, Leeds Parish Church 7
Huddersfield 23, Normanton 2
Hull 86, Elland 0
Hunslet 16, Castleford 0
Leigh 16, Batley 6
Salford 16, St Helens 0
Widnes 11, Leeds 8

Fourth Round
Hunslet 9, Hull 0
Leeds Parish Church 5, Leigh 10
Oldham 20, Widnes 0
Salford 8, Huddersfield 0

Semi-finals
Hunslet 15, Salford 8
(at Park Avenue, Bradford)
Oldham 16, Leigh 2
(at Wheater's Field, Broughton)

FINAL

Saturday 29 April 1899 at Fallowfield, Manchester
OLDHAM 19 *Back*: RL Thomas (g). *Three-quarters*: S Williams (2t), S Lees (t, g), T Fletcher, TD Davies. *Half-backs*: J Lawton, A Lees (capt). *Forwards*: W Barnes, E Bonser, H Broome, H Ellis, G Frater, J Lees (t), J Moffatt (t), EW Telfer.
HUNSLET 9 *Back*: J Mitchell. *Three-quarters*: W Hannah, AE Goldthorpe (capt, 3g), W Goldthorpe (t), JW Wright. *Half-backs*: W Fletcher, H Robinson. *Forwards*: J Harrison, T Leach, J Ramage, R Rubrey, O Walsh, T Walsh, H Wilson, TC Young.
Attendance: 15,763   *Referee*: TH Marshall (Bradford)

COUNTY CHAMPIONSHIP

Saturday 15 October 1898 at Watersheddings, Oldham
CHESHIRE 5 *Back*: S Houghton (Run). *Three-quarters*: W Robinson (Stock), J Worsley (Stock), JD Watson (BirkW), F Saville (Stock, g). *Half-backs*: J Jolley (Run, t), G Robinson (Run). *Forwards*: J Davidson (Stock), F Gayter (Run), C Holmes (BirkW), W Lightfoot (Run), W Milligan (Stock), A Taylor (Run), S Walker (Run), F Ward (Lostock Gralam).
LANCASHIRE 4 *Back*: RJ Baty (Wid, 2g). *Three-quarters*: T Martin (Old), S Lees (Old), D Traynor (StH), J Valentine (capt, Swi). *Half-backs*: B Griffiths (Sal), W Pearson (Swi). *Forwards*: W Briers (StH), J Evans (Swi), J Johnson (Swi), J Moffatt (Old), G Steele (BroR), P Taylor (Lei), G Whitehead (BroR), J Williams (Sal).
Attendance: 4,000   *Referee*: WH Bairstow (Hunslet)

Saturday 29 October 1898 at Valley Parade, Bradford
YORKSHIRE 14 *Back*: J Metcalfe (Wak). *Three-quarters*: JE Parker (Mor), AE Goldthorpe (Hun, g), J Lumley (Lee, t), CC Lempriere (Hull). *Half-backs*: GE Mosley (LeePC), JA Rigg (Hal, 2t). *Forwards*: T Broadley (Brad), FH Chambers (Hud), J Gath (Bat), J Ramage (Hun), A Starks (HKR), M Sutcliffe (Hud, t), W Walton (Wak), T Wilkinson (Mann).
CHESHIRE 2 *Back*: S Houghton (Run). *Three-quarters*: W Robinson (Stock), J Worsley (Stock), F Saville (Stock, g), B Murphy (BirkW). *Half-backs*: J Jolley (Run), G Robinson (Run). *Forwards*: J Davidson (Stock), F Fields (Alt), F Gayter (Run), C Holmes (BirkW), W Lightfoot (Run), W Milligan (Stock), A Taylor (Run), S Walker (Run).
Attendance: 7,500   *Referee*: W McCutcheon (Oldham)

Saturday 5 November 1898 at New Barnes, Salford
LANCASHIRE 9 *Back*: RJ Baty (Wid). *Three-quarters*: J Hoskins (Sal, 2t), T Williams (Sal), O Badger (Swi), D Traynor (StH, t). *Half-backs*: G Messenger (capt, BroR), J Nelson (BroR). *Forwards*: W Briers (StH), J Evans (Swi), J Harrison (RochH), G Heslop (Wid), W McCarthy (Wig), P Taylor (Lei), G Whitehead (BroR), J Williams (Sal).
YORKSHIRE 20 *Back*: J Metcalfe (Wak). *Three-quarters*: JE Parker (Mor), AE Goldthorpe (Hun), J Lumley (Lee), FW Cooper (Brad, 4g). *Half-backs*: JA Rigg (capt, Hal, t), H Robinson (Hun, t). *Forwards*: T Broadley (Brad, t), FH Chambers (Hud), W Dale (Hull), J Gath (Bat), A Kemp (HKR, t), J Ramage (Hun), A Starks (HKR), T Wilkinson (Mann).
Attendance: 12,000   *Referee*: J Bruckshaw (Stockport)

Saturday 19 November 1898 at Irwell Lane, Runcorn
CHESHIRE 4 *Back*: F Hoggarth (Stock). *Three-quarters*: J Worsley (Stock), TH Warder (Run), W Robinson (Stock), F Saville (Stock, 2g). *Half-backs*: B Booth (Stock), R Findlow (Alt). *Forwards*: J Davidson (Stock), F Gayter (Run), C Holmes (BirkW), W Lightfoot (Run), W Simister (Stock), A Taylor (Run), S Walker (Run), F Ward (Lostock Gralam).
CUMBERLAND 3 *Back*: WJ Eagers (Mil). *Three-quarters*: J Young (Mil, t), T Fletcher (Sea), J Whitehead (Mil), W Mandle (Mary). *Half-backs*: S Northmore (capt, Mil), JD Wharton (Mil). *Forwards*: J Atkinson (Work), E Knowles (Mil), M Linton (Sea), J McLaughlin (Work), H Nixon (BrookR), WP Robinson (Mary), D Wilson (WathB), W Young (Mary).
Attendance: 1,000   *Referee*: JH Smith (Widnes)

Saturday 3 December 1898 at Lonsdale Park, Workington
CUMBERLAND 13 *Back*: WJ Eagers (Mil). *Three-quarters*: J Young (Mil), J Whitehead (Mil, t), T Fletcher (Sea), T Parkinson (Work). *Half-backs*: S Northmore (capt, Mil), JD Wharton (Mil). *Forwards*: JH Buckett (Mil, 2g), E Knowles (Mil), M Linton (Sea, t), J McLaughlin (Work), H Nixon (BrookR, t), WP Robinson (Mary), D Wilson (WathB), J Wright (Sea).
LANCASHIRE 5 *Back*: RJ Baty (Wid). *Three-quarters*: S Williams (Old), T Williams (Sal), H Chapman (capt, BroR, t, g), J Altham (More). *Half-backs*: J Lawton (Old), A Lees (Old). *Forwards*: W Briers (StH), J Evans (Swi), G Frater (Old), J Harrison (RochH), J Moffatt (Old), P Taylor (Lei), G Whitehead (BroR), J Williams (Sal).
Attendance: 4,000   *Referee*: PF Farrar (Halifax)

Saturday 28 January 1899 at Crown Point, Leeds
YORKSHIRE 8 *Back*: J Metcalfe (Wak). *Three-quarters*: JE Parker (Mor), AE Goldthorpe (Hun), A Hambrecht (Bram), FW Cooper (Brad, g). *Half-backs*: JA Rigg (capt, Hal, t), H Robinson (Hun). *Forwards*: T Broadley (Brad, t), W Dale (Hull), J Gath (Bat), A Kemp (HKR), J Ramage (Hun), A Starks (HKR), M Sutcliffe (Hud), T Wilkinson (Mann).
CUMBERLAND 5 *Back*: WJ Eagers (Mil). *Three-quarters*: J Young (Mil), J Whitehead (Mil), TH Hodgson (Mil, t), P Marshall (WathB). *Half-backs*: S Northmore (Mil), JD Wharton (Mil). *Forwards*: J Atkinson (Work), JH Buckett (capt, Mil, g), T Grenfell (Mil), S Hoggarth (Mil), E Knowles (Mil), M Linton (Sea), WP Robinson (Mary), D Wilson (WathB).
Attendance: 12,000   *Referee*: JH Smith (Widnes)

Final table

	P	W	D	L	For	Agst	Pts
Yorkshire	3	3	0	0	42	16	6
Cheshire	3	2	0	1	11	21	4
Cumberland	3	1	0	2	21	15	2
Lancashire	3	0	0	3	16	38	0

RUGBY UNION

YORKSHIRE COMPETITION NO. 1

Final table	P	W	D	L	For	Agst	Pts
Shipley	26	20	1	5	234	90	41
Keighley	26	16	4	6	236	109	36
Sowerby Bridge	25	16	3	6	210	83	35
Morley	26	16	2	8	208	127	34
Skipton	26	13	4	9	165	98	30
Alverthorpe	26	11	8	7	139	98	30
Ossett	26	11	5	10	141	128	27
Castleford	26	11	4	11	142	144	26
Featherstone	26	7	6	13	96	141	20
Cleckheaton	26	9	1	16	99	281	19
Otley*	25	7	5	13	72	159	18
Bingley	26	6	5	15	87	161	17
Mytholmroyd	26	5	4	17	70	158	14
Hebden Bridge	26	5	4	17	95	217	14

*One point deducted due to late start
Note: Sowerby Bridge v Otley not played.

YORKSHIRE COMPETITION NO. 2 (BRADFORD DIVISION)

Final table	P	W	D	L	For	Agst	Pts
Otley St Joseph's	16	13	2	1	244	19	28
Kirkstall St Stephen's	16	11	2	3	197	54	24
Harrogate*	14	9	0	5	103	80	16
Bilton St John's	15	6	4	5	45	60	16
Windhill	14	4	5	5	56	59	13
Knaresborough*	15	5	2	8	46	129	10
Farsley	14	3	3	8	26	187	9
Guiseley	16	3	2	11	62	157	8
Keighley Trinity**	16	1	6	9	32	66	8

*Two points deducted for using ineligible players
**Withdrew Jan 1899; six remaining fixtures declared scoreless draws
Note: Results not found for Farsley v Bilton St John's, Farsley v Harrogate, Windhill v Harrogate, Windhill v Knaresborough; probably not played.

YORKSHIRE COMPETITION NO. 2 (CASTLEFORD DIVISION)

Final table	P	W	D	L	For	Agst	Pts
Bottomboat Trinity	14	11	2	1	-	-	24
Knottingley	13	9	0	4	-	-	18
Kippax	13	8	1	4	-	-	17
Brotherton St John's	13	6	1	6	-	-	13
Doncaster Town	11	5	0	6	-	-	10
Fairburn	14	5	0	9	-	-	10
Record expunged:							
Hemsworth	6	0	0	6	-	-	0
Sharlston	9	7	0	2	-	-	14

Note 1: Hemsworth disbanded Nov 1898, remaining 8 fixtures declared wins for opponents.
Note 2: Sharlston suspended 3 Jan 1899 due to 'violent' play, remaining 5 fixtures declared wins for opponents.
Note 3: Results not found for three Doncaster Town matches (vs Brotherton St John's, Kippax, and Knottingley); probably not played.
Note 4: League tables published for this competition did not include points scored for and against. As the actual scores were also unpublished for approximately 50% of the matches it has proved impossible to calculate that information.

YORKSHIRE COMPETITION NO. 2 (HUDDERSFIELD DIVISION)

Final table	P	W	D	L	For	Agst	Pts
Stainland	12	10	1	1	148	19	21
Holywell Brook	13	10	1	2	142	20	21
Nortonthorpe	11	6	1	4	55	32	13
Slaithwaite	12	5	1	6	77	78	11
Dewsbury Commonside	9	4	2	3	87	31	10
Ravensthorpe Nelson	9	2	1	6	28	60	5
Skelmanthorpe	9	1	1	7	30	112	3
Meltham & Meltham Mills	3	0	1	2	0	8	1
Thornhill Lees Trinity	8	0	1	7	3	210	1

Note: Thornhill Lees Trinity (Nov 1898), Dewsbury Commonside (Feb 1899), Skelmanthorpe (Feb 1899) resigned. Meltham & Meltham Mills disbanded (Dec 1898). Results associated with all four clubs remained in table.

Yorkshire Competition No. 2 Final
Bottomboat Trinity 11, Otley St Joseph's 3 (at Ring o' Bells ground, Shipley)
Note: This should have been a three-team play-off but Stainland (Huddersfield Division winners) suspended until 31 December 1899 for crowd violence at home to Bingley in the Yorkshire Cup on 11 March 1899.

Promotion Test Match
Hebden Bridge v Bottomboat Trinity (at Hebden Bridge)
Note: Match cancelled after Hebden Bridge withdrew to join Northern Union.

Milestones & Stats 1869-1901

CUMBERLAND COUNTY CHALLENGE CUP (4 entries)
Try – 3 points; conversion – 2; penalty goal – 3; drop-goal, field goal, goal from mark – 4.

Semi-finals
Carlisle 0, Aspatria 3
Cockermouth 6, Penrith United 8

FINAL
Saturday 25 March 1899 at Warwick Road, Carlisle
ASPATRIA 8 *Back*: T Pattinson. *Three-quarters*: JB Hewitson, JH Blaylock (capt, c), J Varty, T Routledge. *Half-backs*: Joe Nelson, J Steel (t). *Forwards*: Jim Davidson, Joe Davidson (t), T Docker, D Graham, T Grieve, R Reed, J Walker, J Yeowart.
PENRITH UNITED 0 *Back*: J Broughton. *Three-quarters*: G Bell, J Murray, JC Broughton, L Taylor. *Half-backs*: E Dargue (capt), J Foley. *Forwards*: T Davidson, F Harryman, F Hodgson, A Pattinson, J Shawyer, T Stalker, T Wilson, W Winskill.
Attendance: 'moderate' *Referee*: G Cochrane (Galashiels)

DURHAM COUNTY CHALLENGE CUP (13 entries)
Try – 3 points; conversion – 2; penalty goal – 3; drop-goal, field goal, goal from mark – 4.

First Round
Durham City 0, West Hartlepool 13
Hartlepool Rovers 14, Tyne Dock 0
North Durham 3, Old Dunelmians 7
Tudhoe 53, Houghton-le-Spring 0
Westoe 5, South Shields 6 (replay ordered after protest)
Byes: Hamsteels, Hartlepool Old Boys, Sunderland

First Round Replay
South Shields 13, Westoe 0

Semi-finals
Tudhoe 17, Sunderland 0
West Hartlepool 13, South Shields 9

Second Round
Hartlepool Old Boys 0, Tudhoe 9
South Shields 12, Hamsteels 0
Sunderland 19, Old Dunelmians 0
West Hartlepool 11, Hartlepool Rovers 8

FINAL
Saturday 15 April 1899 at Ashbrooke Ground, Sunderland
TUDHOE 9 *Back*: JE Pickering. *Three-quarters*: W Taylor (2t), H Sinclair, G Holder, J Gordon (pg). *Half-backs*: J Levitt, R Levitt. *Forwards*: J Carmedy, J Foster, B Hamm, J Mason, G Richardson, R Shaw, A Stephenson (capt), J Stitt.
WEST HARTLEPOOL 0 *Back*: J Hogg. *Three-quarters*: C Boddy, A Edmunds, JT Taylor (capt), BS Wellock. *Half-backs*: C Coates, C Scott. *Forwards*: J Booth, S Dunning, J Finlay, G Freeman, GH Lewis, A McDonald, E Morton, JW Sutherst.
Attendance: 3,000 *Referee*: EB Holmes (Midland Counties RU)

NORTHUMBERLAND COUNTY FOOTBALL CHALLENGE CUP (6 entries)
Try – 3 points; conversion – 2; penalty goal – 3; drop-goal, field goal, goal from mark – 4.

First Round
Northern w/o North Elswick (disbanded)
Percy Park 3, Rockcliff 0
Byes: Tynedale, Wallsend

Semi-finals
Percy Park 12, Tynedale 0
Wallsend 5, Northern 0

FINAL
Saturday 1 April 1899 at Jesmond Ground, Newcastle
PERCY PARK 19 *Back*: AK Tasker. *Three-quarters*: GC Robinson (3t, 2c), W Bates (capt), JS Miller, FW Stone (t). *Half-backs*: CW Russell, EA Henderson. *Forwards*: G Buckham, PF Hardwick (t), C Hill, T McKean, J McMenemy, A Nesbitt, J Nesbitt, J Smith.
WALLSEND 0 *Back*: S Mason. *Three-quarters*: A Welburn, P Moran, J Richardson, J Knox. *Half-backs*: C Lawson, F Potts. *Forwards*: J McKenzie, J Martin, E Molyneaux, J Munro, Phillips, W Pullan, T Rodgers, T Tindle.
Attendance: 5,000   *Referee*: Captain Peveril (Hartlepool)

YORKSHIRE COUNTY FOOTBALL CHALLENGE CUP (40 entries)
Try – 3 points; conversion – 2; penalty goal – 3; drop-goal, field goal, goal from mark – 4

Preliminary Round
Goole Athletes 3, Fairburn 11
Holywell Brook 17, Brotherton St John's 0
Ilkley Olicana 30, Guiseley 0
Knaresborough 6, Leeds Good Shepherds 0
Knottingley 17, Milnsbridge 0
Nortonthorpe w/o Meltham and Meltham Mills (withdrew)
Thornhill Lees Trinity w/o Hemsworth (withdrew)
York Melbourne 6, Slaithwaite 0

First Round
(* indicates 24 teams seeded to this round)
Bottomboat Trinity* 22, Ilkley Olicana 9
Castleford* 8, Knottingley 3
Cleckheaton* 12, Doncaster Town* 3
Fairburn 5, Morley* 18
Harrogate* w/o Sharlston* (suspended)
Hebden Bridge* 11, Featherstone* 3
Holywell Brook 5, Otley* 6
Kippax* 3, Kirkstall St Stephen's* 7
Knaresborough 0, Alverthorpe* 10
Nortonthorpe 5, Mytholmroyd* 4 (replay ordered after protest)
Ossett* 25, Ravensthorpe Nelson* 5
Otley St Joseph's* w/o Thornhill Lees Trinity (disbanded)
Shipley* 32, York Melbourne 0
Sowerby Bridge* 22, Keighley* 3
Stainland* 0, Bingley* 6
Windhill* 0, Skipton* 3

First Round Replay
Normanton 0, Mytholmroyd 0 (at Ossett)

First Round Second Replay
Mytholmroyd 16, Nortonthorpe 6
(at Shipley)

Second Round
Alverthorpe 12, Morley 4
Bingley 13, Hebden Bridge 0
Bottomboat Trinity 27, Kirkstall St Stephen's 0
Harrogate 8, Mytholmroyd 3
Ossett 23, Cleckheaton 4
Otley St Joseph's 7, Skipton 0
Shipley 8, Otley 0
Sowerby Bridge 0, Castleford 0

Second Round Replay
Castleford 0, Sowerby Bridge 0

Second Round Second Replay
Sowerby Bridge 11, Castleford 0

Third Round
Alverthorpe 4, Shipley 0
Bingley 3, Sowerby Bridge 8
Harrogate 6, Ossett 15
(replay ordered after protest)
Otley St Joseph's 3, Bottomboat Trinity 0

Third Round Replay
Ossett 11, Harrogate 9 (at Otley)

Semi-finals
Alverthorpe 6, Otley St Joseph's 3
(at Queen's Park, Morley)
Sowerby Bridge 13, Ossett 0
(at Ring o' Bells Ground, Shipley)

FINAL
Saturday 15 April 1899 at Lawkholme Lane, Keighley
SOWERBY BRIDGE 0 *Back*: R Hatton. *Three-quarters*: J Thompson, A Habergham (capt), RW Mallinson, G Swaine. *Half-backs*: A Butterworth, J Morley. *Forwards*: J Birtwistle, JP Ellis, F Fox, H Hatton, J Hellawell, A Jagger, D Robinson, W Waddington.
ALVERTHORPE 0 *Back*: J Kaye. *Three-quarters*: E Sherwood, S Herberts, A Scratton, J Goodyear (capt). *Half-backs*: B Balmforth, J Clark. *Forwards*: JW Barstow, E Biltcliffe, G Biltcliffe, A Longley, S Mitchell, S Nunns, W Pidd, F Wild.
Attendance: 4,000   *Referee*: A Hartley (Yorkshire RU President)

FINAL REPLAY
Saturday 22 April 1899 at Lawkholme Lane, Keighley
SOWERBY BRIDGE 4 *Back*: R Hatton. *Three-quarters*: J Thompson, A Habergham (capt), RW Mallinson (gm), G Swaine. *Half-backs*: A Butterworth, J Morley. *Forwards*: J Eastwood, F Fox, Green, H Hatton, J Hellawell A Jagger, D Robinson, W Waddington.
ALVERTHORPE 0 *Back*: J Kaye. *Three-quarters*: E Sherwood, S Herberts, A Scratton, J Goodyear (capt). *Half-backs*: B Balmforth, J Clark. *Forwards*: JW Barstow, E Biltcliffe, G Biltcliffe, A Longley, S Mitchell, S Nunns, W Pidd, F Wild.
Attendance: 5,000   *Referee*: A Hartley (Yorkshire RU President)

COUNTY CHAMPIONSHIP

NORTHERN GROUP

Saturday 22 October 1898 at Warwick Road, Carlisle
CUMBERLAND 8 *Back*: A Smith (Carl). *Three-quarters*: F Spottiswood (Carl, t), JH Blaylock (Asp), JC Broughton (PenU), JB Hewitson (Asp, t). *Half-backs*: WS Graham (Carl), J Nelson (Asp). *Forwards*: JH Blacklock (Asp), T Cavaghan (Carl), Jim Davidson (capt, Asp, c), Joe Davidson (Asp), D Elliott (Carl), D Graham (Kes), T Grieve (Asp), E Walsh (Carl).
DURHAM 6 *Back*: HB Fawcus (ODun). *Three-quarters*: EW Elliot (Sund), W Smith (TynD), GS Legard (ODun), W Taylor (Tud). *Half-backs*: CY Adamson (ODun, 2 pg), F Marston

(Tud). *Forwards*: J Athey (HartR), GC Kerr (ODun), J Mason (Tud), RF Oakes (capt, HartR), R Shaw (Tud), A Stephenson (Tud), J Stitt (Tud), H Walker (ODun).
Attendance: n/a   *Referee*: G Cochrane (Scotland)

Saturday 5 November 1898 at Upper Park, Birkenhead
CHESHIRE 5 *Back*: S Simpson (BirkPk). *Three-quarters*: JDK Jones (BirkPk), H Greenham (BirkPk), W Fletcher (NewB), HP Hebblethwaite (BirkPk). *Half-backs*: HD Pagden (Sale), H Parratt (Sale, c). *Forwards*: AL Auty (NewB), J Baxter (BirkPk), EH Bradshaw (Sale), H Fletcher (Sale), J Hague (Sale), E Herschell (BirkPk, t), J Pickin (Sale), H Smith (BirkPk).
LANCASHIRE 8 *Back*: JD Martin (LivOB). *Three-quarters*: CEL Beasley (Lit, t, c), TH Kingscote (Man), AT Brettargh (LivOB), ET Nicholson (Liv). *Half-backs*: GG Allen (capt, Liv), G Cookson (Man, t). *Forwards*: H Beames (LivOB), RC Crabtree (Lit), H Hodgkinson (Lit), A Long (Bla), W McInnes (Bla), R Pierce (Liv), CVM Townsend (LivOB), RD Wood (LivOB).
Attendance: 2,000   *Referee*: T Shires (Yorkshire)

Saturday 5 November 1898 at Friarage Field, Hartlepool
DURHAM 10 *Back*: RW Poole (HartOB). *Three-quarters*: GS Legard (ODun), HB Fawcus (ODun, t), JD Taylor (Wes, t), W Smith (TynD). *Half-backs*: CY Adamson (ODun, 2c), J Levitt (Tud). *Forwards*: J Booth (WHart), DF Hardie (ODun), GC Kerr (ODun), J Mason (Tud), RF Oakes (capt, HartR), W Phillips (HartR), A Stephenson (Tud), R Watson (DurC).
YORKSHIRE 0 *Back*: H Ward (Ship). *Three-quarters*: EF Fookes (capt, Myth), JT Taylor (WHart), J Shepherd (DurC), W Jackson (York Melbourne). *Half-backs*: H Myers (Kei), EJ Walton (St Peter's School/Cas). *Forwards*: T Hanson (Otley), T Hollindrake (Kei), CE Holroyd (Holywell Brook), A Priestley (Ship), HE Ramsden (Bing), JH Shooter (Mor), H Wilson (Mor), LR Wood (Cleck).
Attendance: 5,000   *Referee*: A Turnbull (Scotland)

Saturday 12 November 1898 at Warwick Road, Carlisle
CUMBERLAND 3 *Back*: A Smith (Carl). *Three-quarters*: JH Blaylock (Asp), JB Hewitson (Asp), JC Broughton (PenU), F Spottiswood (Carl). *Half-backs*: WS Graham (Carl), J Nelson (Asp, t). *Forwards*: JH Blacklock (Asp), T Cavaghan (Carl), J Cox (Hensingham), Jim Davidson (capt, Asp), Joe Davidson (Asp), D Elliott (Carl), T Grieve (Asp), W Winskill (PenU).
CHESHIRE 0 *Back*: S Simpson (BirkPk). *Three-quarters*: JDK Jones (BirkPk), H Greenham (BirkPk), W Fletcher (NewB), HP Hebblethwaite (BirkPk). *Half-backs*: H Parratt (Sale), S Walker (NewB). *Forwards*: AL Auty (NewB), J Baxter (BirkPk), J Fernie (NewB), H Fletcher (Sale), J Hague (Sale), HC Harvey (Sale), G Hough (Wilmslow), F Taylor (BirkPk).
Attendance: n/a   Referee: WH Bell (Durham)

Saturday 12 November 1898 at Wharfeside, Otley
YORKSHIRE 3 *Back*: H Ward (capt, Ship). *Three-quarters*: G Middleton (Skip, t), GP Ackroyd (Skip), A Swaine (Mor), H Wilkinson (Harr). *Half-backs*: GH Marsden (Mor), J Shepherd (DurC). *Forwards*: H Clayton (Oss), J Glew (Kei), T Hambleton (Cas), GH Lewis (WHart), H Shaw (Cleck), JH Shooter (Mor), A Tillotson (Kei), F Wild (Alv).
NORTHUMBERLAND 18 *Back*: P Moran (Wall). *Three-quarters*: GC Robinson (PerPk, t), S Anderson (Rock, t, c), W Bates (PerPk), FW Stone (PerPk). *Half-backs*: SC Lockerby

(PerPk, t), EW Taylor (Rock, dg, pg). *Forwards*: FJ Bell (Rock), HW Dudgeon (Nor), J Dobinson (Rock), J Finlay (WHart), GR Gibson (Nor), JH Greenwell (Rock), J Nesbitt (Wall), RC Stevenson (Nor).
Attendance: 2,000/3,000   *Referee*: GH Harnett (Kent)

Saturday 19 November 1898 at Whalley Range, Manchester
LANCASHIRE 9 *Back*: JD Martin (LivOB). *Three-quarters*: CEL Beasley (Lit, t), TH Kingscote (Man), AT Brettargh (LivOB, t), ET Nicholson (Liv, t). *Half-backs*: GG Allen (Liv), G Cookson (Man). *Forwards*: H Beames (LivOB), RC Crabtree (Lit), AG Davidson (Bla), JS Francomb (Man), LB Hopper (Liv), A Long (Bla), R Pierce (Liv), RD Wood (LivOB).
YORKSHIRE 3 *Back*: H Ward (Ship). *Three-quarters*: S Carter (Cas), FF Glendinning (Mor), EF Fookes (capt, Myth), G Middleton (Skip). *Half-backs*: GH Marsden (Mor), H Myers (Kei). *Forwards*: T Hambleton (Cas), CE Holroyd (Holywell Brook), GE Hughes (Otley), A Priestley (Ship), HE Ramsden (Bing, t), H Shaw (Cleck), JH Shooter (Mor), LR Wood (Cleck).
Attendance: 2,000   *Referee*: EB Holmes (Midland Counties)

Saturday 3 December 1898 at Hollow Drift, Durham
DURHAM 16 *Back*: RW Poole (HartOB). *Three-quarters*: GS Legard (ODun), HB Fawcus (ODun), J Taylor (HartR), W Taylor (Tud). *Half-backs*: CY Adamson (ODun, t, 2c), J Levitt (Tud). *Forwards*: J Booth (WHart), J Conmy (WHart, t), GC Kerr (ODun, 2t), RF Oakes (HartR), W Phillips (HartR), A Stephenson (Tud), J Stitt (Tud), R Watson (DurC).
CHESHIRE 0 *Back*: S Simpson (BirkPk). *Three-quarters*: A Tipping (NewB), HP Hebblethwaite (BirkPk), J Hutchinson (BirkPk), CA Booth (NewB). *Half-backs*: H Parratt (Sale), S Walker (NewB). *Forwards*: A Baker (Sale), J Baxter (BirkPk), W Fearenside (NewB), J Hague (Sale), E Herschell (BirkPk), H Smith (BirkPk), F Taylor (BirkPk), E Walker (AshH).
Attendance: 1,800   *Referee*: EB Holmes (Midland Counties)

Saturday 3 December 1898 at Whalley Range, Manchester
LANCASHIRE 6 *Back*: JC Milnes (Man). *Three-quarters*: CEL Beasley (Lit), TH Kingscote (Man, t), AT Brettargh (LivOB, t), ET Nicholson (Liv). *Half-backs*: GG Allen (capt, Liv), G Cookson (Man). *Forwards*: H Beames (LivOB), AG Davidson (Bla), JS Francomb (Man), H Hodgkinson (Lit), LB Hopper (Liv), A Long (Bla), R Pierce (Liv), RD Wood (LivOB).
CUMBERLAND 6 *Back*: Joe Broughton (PenU). *Three-quarters*: F Spottiswood (Carl), JC Broughton (PenU), R Holywell (WickPk), JB Hewitson (Asp, 2t). *Half-backs*: WS Graham (Carl), J Nelson (Asp). *Forwards*: JH Blacklock (Asp), T Cavaghan (Carl), J Cox (Hensingham), Jim Davidson (capt, Asp), Joe Davidson (Asp), D Elliott (Carl), T Grieve (Asp), W Winskill (PenU).
Attendance: 4,000   *Referee*: GE Kinder (Yorkshire)

Saturday 10 December 1898 at Aigburth, Liverpool
LANCASHIRE 0 *Back*: JC Milnes (Man). *Three-quarters*: CEL Beasley (Lit), TH Kingscote (Man), AT Brettargh (LivOB), ET Nicholson (Liv). *Half-backs*: GG Allen (capt, Liv), G Cookson (Man). *Forwards*: H Beames (LivOB), AG Davidson (Bla), JS Francomb (Man), H Hodgkinson (Lit), LB Hopper (Liv), A Long (Bla), R Pierce (Liv), RD Wood (LivOB).
NORTHUMBERLAND 10 *Back*: P Moran (Wall). *Three-quarters*: W Bates (PerPk), GC Robinson (PerPk, t, dg), FW Stone (PerPk, t), S Anderson (Rock). *Half-backs*:

SC Lockerby (PerPk), EW Taylor (Rock). *Forwards*: FJ Bell (Rock), RW Bell (Nor), HW Dudgeon (Nor), J Finlay (WHart), GR Gibson (Nor), JH Greenwell (Rock), J Nesbitt (Wall), RC Stevenson (Nor).
Attendance: 1,500   *Referee*: A Rogers (Midland Counties)

Saturday 14 January 1899 at Jesmond Ground, Newcastle
NORTHUMBERLAND 26 *Back*: P Moran (Wall). *Three-quarters*: GC Robinson (PerPk, 2t), W Bates (PerPk), S Anderson (Rock, c), FW Stone (PerPk, t). *Half-backs*: SC Lockerby (PerPk, 3t), EW Taylor (Rock, 3c). *Forwards*: FJ Bell (Rock), HW Dudgeon (Nor), J Finlay (WHart), T Finlay (Rock), COP Gibson (Nor/OxfU), GR Gibson (Nor), JH Greenwell (Rock), RC Stevenson (Nor).
CHESHIRE 0 *Back*: CR Hartley (Sale). *Three-quarters*: EC Harvey (Sale), W Fletcher (NewB), HP Terry (Sale), J Hutchinson (BirkPk). *Half-backs*: H Parratt (Sale), S Walker (NewB). *Forwards*: J Adams (AshH), H Alexander (BirkPk), W Fearenside (NewB), J Hague (Sale), HC Harvey (Sale), McClay (AshH), EC Salvidge (NewB), E Walker (AshH).
Attendance: 3,000   *Referee*: Mr Saville (Durham)

Saturday 21 January 1899 at Queen's Park, Morley
YORKSHIRE 26 *Back*: H Ward (Ship). *Three-quarters*: J Goodyear (Alv, t), AW Robinson (Kei, 2t), C Pearson (DonT, t), EF Fookes (capt, Myth, 2t, c). *Half-backs*: GH Marsden (Mor), EJ Walton (St Peter's School/Cas). *Forwards*: F Alexander (Fea, t), J Glew (Kei), T Hambleton (Cas), CE Holroyd (Holywell Brook), GE Hughes (Otley), H Shaw (Cleck), JH Shooter (Mor, t), LR Wood (Cleck).
CHESHIRE 0 *Back*: S Simpson (BirkPk). *Three-quarters*: GM Bennett (BirkPk), HP Hebblethwaite (BirkPk), JDK Jones (BirkPk), CA Booth (NewB). *Half-backs*: H Parratt (Sale), S Walker (NewB). *Forwards*: J Adams (AshH), J Baxter (BirkPk), W Fearenside (NewB), J Hague (Sale), HC Harvey (Sale), EC Salvidge (NewB), H Smith (BirkPk), E Walker (AshH).
Attendance: 200*   Referee: E Seddon (Lancashire)
*Low attendance attributed to 'wretched weather' (*Yorkshire Post*, 23 January 1899).

Saturday 11 February 1899 at Warwick Road, Carlisle
CUMBERLAND 8 *Back*: A Smith (Carl). *Three-quarters*: JB Hewitson (Asp, t), R Holywell (WickPk, c), GH Muriel (Carl), JC Broughton (PenU). *Half-backs*: J Fleming (Carl), WS Graham (Carl, t). *Forwards*: JH Blacklock (Asp), G Brough (DevA), Jim Davidson (capt, Asp), Joe Davidson (Asp), D Elliott (Carl), T Grieve (Asp), J Walker (Asp), W Winskill (PenU).
NORTHUMBERLAND 22 *Back*: P Moran (Wall). *Three-quarters*: GC Robinson (PerPk, 4t), S Anderson (Rock, c), W Bates (PerPk), FW Stone (PerPk, t). *Half-backs*: SC Lockerby (PerPk, t), EW Taylor (capt, Rock, c). *Forwards*: FJ Bell (Rock), RW Bell (Nor), J Dobinson (Rock), HW Dudgeon (Nor), J Finlay (WHart), GR Gibson (Nor), J Nesbitt (Wall), RC Stevenson (Nor).
Attendance: 5,000   *Referee*: EB Holmes (Midland Counties)

Saturday 18 February 1899 at Wood Terrace, Westoe, South Shields
DURHAM 24 *Back*: RW Poole (HartOB). *Three-quarters*: BS Wellock (WHart), HB Fawcus (ODun, t), J Gordon (Tud, dg), W Taylor (Tud, t). *Half-backs*: CY Adamson (ODun, 2c, dg),

J Levitt (Tud). *Forwards*: J Booth (WHart), T Gowans (Wes, t), J Mason (Tud), RF Oakes (capt, HartR), W Phillips (HartR), R Shaw (Tud), A Stephenson (Tud), J Stitt (Tud, t).
LANCASHIRE 0 *Back*: JC Milnes (Man). *Three-quarters*: N Duckworth (Sale), R Kendal (Bla), BC Middleton (Man), ET Nicholson (Liv). *Half-backs*: G Cookson (Man), R Rothwell (Bla). *Forwards*: J Bamford (Lit), J Buckler (Bla), AG Davidson (Bla), JS Francomb (Man), H Hodgkinson (Lit), LB Hopper (Liv), A Long (Bla), RD Wood (LivOB).
Attendance: 3,000   *Referee*: EB Holmes (Midland Counties)

Tuesday 28 February 1899 at Jesmond Ground, Newcastle
NORTHUMBERLAND 20 *Back*: P Moran (Wall). *Three-quarters*: GC Robinson (PerPk, 3t), W Bates (PerPk), S Anderson (Rock), FW Stone (PerPk). *Half-backs*: CW Russell (PerPk, dg), EW Taylor (Rock, t, 2c). *Forwards*: FJ Bell (Rock), J Dobinson (Rock), HW Dudgeon (Nor), J Finlay (WHart), GR Gibson (Nor), JH Greenwell (Rock), J Nesbitt (Wall), RC Stevenson (Nor).
DURHAM 3 *Back*: JE Pickering (Tud). *Three-quarters*: W Taylor (Tud), J Gordon (Tud), HB Fawcus (ODun), GS Legard (ODun, t). *Half-backs*: J Levitt (Tud), BS Oughtred (HartR). *Forwards*: J Booth (WHart), GC Kerr (ODun), J Mason (Tud), J Nichol (SSh), RF Oakes (capt, HartR), R Shaw (Tud), A Stephenson (Tud), J Stitt (Tud).
Attendance: 5,000   *Referee*: JD Boswell (Scotland)

Saturday 4 March 1899 at Lawkholme Lane, Keighley
YORKSHIRE 5 *Back*: H Ward (Ship). *Three-quarters*: J Goodyear (Alv), AW Robinson (Kei), C Pearson (DonT, t), EF Fookes (capt, Myth). *Half-backs*: GH Marsden (Mor, c), EJ Walton (St Peter's School/Cas). *Forwards*: F Alexander (Fea), J Glew (Kei), T Hambleton (Cas), GE Hughes (Otley), HE Ramsden (Bing), H Shaw (Cleck), JH Shooter (Mor), LR Wood (Cleck).
CUMBERLAND 14 *Back*: A Smith (Carl). *Three-quarters*: JB Hewitson (Asp), F Spottiswood (Carl), GH Muriel (Carl, c), J Varty (Asp, t). *Half-backs*: J Nelson (Asp), J Steel (Asp). *Forwards*: Joe Davidson (Asp), T Docker (Asp, t), D Graham (Kes, t), T Grieve (Asp), J Ritson (Cock, t), J Sewell (Carl), J Walker (Asp), W Winskill (PenU).
Attendance: 3,000   *Referee*: W Yiend (Peterborough)

Final table

	P	W	D	L	For	Agst	Pts
Northumberland	5	5	0	0	96	14	10
Cumberland	5	3	1	1	39	39	7
Durham	5	3	0	2	59	28	6
Lancashire	5	2	1	2	23	48	5
Yorkshire	5	1	0	4	37	51	2
Cheshire	5	0	0	5	5	79	0

SOUTH WESTERN GROUP

Results
Cornwall 0, Devonshire 15
Gloucestershire 16, Cornwall 3
Cornwall 5, Somersetshire 8
Devonshire 0, Gloucestershire 0
Gloucestershire 7, Somersetshire 3
Somersetshire 0, Devonshire 7

Final table

	P	W	D	L	For	Agst	Pts
Devonshire	3	2	1	0	22	0	5
Gloucestershire	3	2	1	0	23	6	5
Somersetshire	3	1	0	2	11	19	2
Cornwall	3	0	0	3	8	39	0

Play-off to decide first place
Gloucestershire 0, Devonshire 3

SOUTH EASTERN GROUP A

Results
Middlesex 0, Kent 3
Surrey 6, Midland Counties 0
Middlesex 11 Midland Counties 0
Midland Counties 7, Kent 8
East Midlands 14, Surrey 3
Kent 11, East Midlands 0
Midland Counties 9, East Midlands 0
Surrey 16, Middlesex 10
East Midlands 8, Middlesex 8
Kent 19, Surrey 0

Final table

	P	W	D	L	For	Agst	Pts
Kent	4	4	0	0	41	7	8
Surrey	4	2	0	2	25	44	4
Middlesex	4	1	1	2	29	27	3
East Midlands	4	1	1	2	23	31	3
Midland Counties	4	1	0	3	16	25	2

SOUTH EASTERN GROUP B

Result
Eastern Counties 0, Hampshire 27

Final table

	P	W	D	L	For	Agst
Hampshire	1	1	0	0	27	0
Eastern Counties	1	0	0	1	0	27

South Eastern Group Final
Hampshire 0, Kent 8

Southern Final
Devonshire 6, Kent 0

COUNTY CHAMPIONSHIP FINAL
Saturday 8 April 1899 at Jesmond Ground, Newcastle
DEVONSHIRE 5 *Back*: FL Hitt (Exe). *Three-quarters*: C Bowen (DevA), WS Boyle (Barn), JC Matters (RNEC), SF Coopper (RNEC). *Half-backs*: T Dunn (Torq, t), J Jones (unattached). *Forwards*: A Brock (Exe), T Dobson (NewA), HN Gordon (RNEC), R Hellings (DevA), J Powell (Exe), FW Roberts (RNEC), W Spiers (DevA), C Thomas (Barn, c).
NORTHUMBERLAND 0 *Back*: P Moran (Wall). *Three-quarters*: GC Robinson (PerPk), W Bates (PerPk), WG Baty (SSh), FW Stone (PerPk). *Half-backs*: T Owen (Rock), CW Russell (PerPk). *Forwards*: FJ Bell (Rock), RW Bell (Nor), HW Dudgeon (Nor), J Finlay (WHart), COP Gibson (Nor/OxfU), GR Gibson (Nor), JH Greenwell (Rock), J Nesbitt (PerPk).
Attendance: 5,000   *Referee*: ET Gurdon (Middlesex)

NON-COUNTY CHAMPIONSHIP MATCHES

Saturday 4 March 1899 at County Ground, St Thomas, Exeter
DEVONSHIRE 6 *Back*: FL Hitt (Exe). *Three-quarters*: LJ Hammond (DevA), WS Boyle (Barn), EJ Vivyan (DevA), M Sturt (DevA, t). *Half-backs*: WE Bildings (DevA), J Jones (unattached). *Forwards*: P Baron (Sid), W Bulley (Ply), FWC Coles (DevA), H Parris (Barn), W Sims (unattached), G Sowden (DevA), W Spiers (DevA, t), C Thomas (Barn).
LANCASHIRE 3 *Back*: BT Walmsley (BroPk). *Three-quarters*: JC Milnes (Man), N Duckworth (Sale), BC Middleton (Man, t), PJ Caldicott (Lit). *Half-backs*: G Cookson (capt, Man), AE Sargent (Man). *Forwards*: C Anderson (LivOB), J Bamford (Lit), RC Crabtree (Lit), JS Francomb (Man), H Hodgkinson (Lit), CR Jackson (BroPk), A Long (Bla), W McInnes (Bla).
Attendance: 5,000   *Referee*: P Coles (Sussex)

Monday 6 March 1899 at Cardiff Arms Park
GLAMORGANSHIRE 18 *Back*: TJ Thomas (Car). *Three-quarters*: V Huzzey (Car), G Davies (Swa, 3t), D Rees (Swa), LJ Deere (Mou). *Half-backs*: S Biggs (Car, 3c), E Lewis (Tre). *Forwards*: WH Alexander (Llwyn), J Blake (Car), A Brice (Aber), FH Cornish (Car), G Dobson (Car, t), T Dobson (Car), W Parker (Swa), WE Rees (Pon).
LANCASHIRE 0 *Back*: BT Walmsley (BroPk). *Three-quarters*: N Duckworth (Sale), JC Milnes (Man), BC Middleton (Man), PJ Caldicott (Lit). *Half-backs*: G Cookson (Man), AE Sargent (Man). *Forwards*: C Anderson (LivOB), J Bamford (Lit), J Buckler (Bla), RC Crabtree (Lit), JS Francomb (Man), H Hodgkinson (Lit), CR Jackson (BroPk), A Long (Bla).
Attendance: 4,000   *Referee*: DH Bowen (Llanelli)

ENGLAND TRIAL MATCHES

Saturday 17 December 1898 at County Ground, Bristol
SOUTH 6 *Back*: HT Gamlin (Well). *Three-quarters*: R Forrest (Well), PMR Royds (Black), HBJ Taylor (Black, t), PW Stout (Glo, pg). *Half-backs*: Arthur Rotherham (capt, Rich), GT Unwin (Black). *Forwards*: J Daniell (CamU), AO Dowson (Mose), HW Dudgeon (Rich), CH Harper (OxfU), JW Jarman (Bris), W Mortimer (MarlN), FM Stout (Glo), WE Tucker (Black).
NORTH 3 *Back*: H Ward (Ship). *Three-quarters*: S Anderson (Rock), FW Stone (PerPk, t), JT Taylor (WHart), AT Brettargh (LivOB). *Half-backs*: CY Adamson (ODun), SC Lockerby

(PerPk). *Forwards*: J Baxter (BirkPk) JH Blacklock (Asp), Joe Davidson (Asp), COP Gibson (Nor/OxfU)), J Nesbitt (Wall), RK Oakes (capt, HartR), R Pierce (Liv), JH Shooter (Mor).
Attendance: 10,000   *Referee*: GH Harnett (Kent)

Saturday 25 February 1899 at Jesmond, Newcastle
NORTH 0 *Back*: RW Poole (HartOB). *Three-quarters*: EF Fookes (Myth), JT Taylor (WHart), AT Brettargh (LivOB), GC Robinson (PerPk). *Half-backs*: CY Adamson (ODun), G Cookson (Man). *Forwards*: RW Bell (Nor), Joe Davidson (Asp), GR Gibson (Nor), JH Greenwell (Rock), E Herschell (BirkPk), RF Oakes (capt, HartR), R Pierce (Liv), LR Wood (Cleck).
SOUTH 11 *Back*: HT Gamlin (Well). *Three-quarters*: PW Stout (Glo, c), WL Bunting (Rich, t), J Matters (RNEC, t), SF Coopper (RNEC, t). *Half-backs*: Arthur Rotherham (capt, Rich), RO Schwarz (Rich). *Forwards*: AO Dowson (Mose), HW Dudgeon (Rich), F Goulding (Glo), RFA Hobbs (Black), F Jacob (Rich), W Spiers (DevA), FM Stout (Glo), C Thomas (Barn).
Attendance: 6,000   *Referee*: WH Bell (Durham)

INTERNATIONAL CHAMPIONSHIP

Saturday 7 January 1899 at St Helen's, Swansea
WALES 26 *Back*: WJ Bancroft (capt, Swa, 4c). *Three-quarters*: V Huzzey (Car, 2t), RT Skrimshire (New), EG Nicholls (Car), W Llewellyn (Llwyn, 4t). *Half-backs*: D James (Swa), E James (Swa). *Forwards*: WH Alexander (Llwyn), J Blake (Car), A Brice (Aber), DJ Daniel (Llan), T Dobson (Car), JJ Hodges (New), W Parker (Swa), F Scrine (Swa).
ENGLAND 3 *Back*: HT Gamlin (Well). *Three-quarters*: GC Robinson (PerPk, t), PW Stout (Glo), PMR Royds (Black), R Forrest (Well). *Half-backs*: R O'H Livesay (Black), Arthur Rotherham (capt, Rich). *Forwards*: J Daniell (CamU), Joe Davidson (Asp), HW Dudgeon (Rich), GR Gibson (Nor), CH Harper (Barn/OxfU), F Jacob (Rich), W Mortimer (MarlN), RF Oakes (HartR).
Attendance: 20,000   *Referee*: A Turnbull (Scotland)

Saturday 4 February 1899 at Lansdowne Road, Dublin
IRELAND 6 *Back*: J Fulton (NIFC). *Three-quarters*: IG Davidson (NIFC), GRA Harman (DubU), JB Allison (Campbell College), WH Brown (DubU). *Half-backs*: GG Allen (Der, t), LM Magee (capt, BecR, pg). *Forwards*: T Ahearne (QCC), WG Byron (NIFC), HC McCoull (BelA), TMW McGown (NIFC), JE McIlwaine (NIFC), J Ryan (RockC), M Ryan (RockC), J Sealy (DubU).
ENGLAND 0 *Back*: JF Byrne (Mose). *Three-quarters*: S Anderson (Rock), PW Stout (Glo), JT Taylor (WHart), EF Fookes (Myth). *Half-backs*: Arthur Rotherham (capt, Rich), EW Taylor (Rock). *Forwards*: JH Blacklock (Asp), AJL Darby (CamU), Jim Davidson (Asp), HW Dudgeon (Rich), F Jacob (Rich), JH Shooter (Mor), FM Stout (Glo), C Thomas (Barn).
Attendance: 10,000   *Referee*: DG Findlay (Scotland)

Saturday 11 March 1899 at Rectory Field, Blackheath
ENGLAND 0 *Back*: HT Gamlin (Well). *Three-quarters*: JC Matters (RNEC), PW Stout (Glo), WL Bunting (Rich), EF Fookes (Myth). *Half-backs*: Arthur Rotherham (capt, Rich), RO Schwarz (Rich). *Forwards*: Jim Davidson (Asp), Joe Davidson (Asp), AO Dowson (Mose), HW Dudgeon (Rich), RFA Hobbs (Black), RF Oakes (HartR), JH Shooter (Mor), FM Stout (Glo).

SCOTLAND 5 *Back*: H Rottenburg (LonS). *Half-backs*: HTS Gedge (LonS), DB Monypenny (LonS), GAW Lamond (Kelvinside Academicals), T Scott (Lang). *Quarter-backs*: JJ Gillespie (EdinA, t), JW Simpson (RHSFP). *Forwards*: JM Dykes (LonS), GC Kerr (EdinW), WMC McEwan (EdinA), A Mackinnon (LonS), MC Morrison (capt, RHSFP), HO Smith (Wat), RC Stevenson (LonS), WJ Thomson (WoS, c).
Attendance: 20,000 *Referee*: JT Magee (Ireland)

Other results
Scotland 3, Ireland 9
Scotland 21, Wales 10
Wales 0, Ireland 3

Final table

	P	W	D	L	For	Agst
Ireland	3	3	0	0	18	3
Scotland	3	2	0	1	29	19
Wales	3	1	0	2	36	27
England	3	0	0	3	3	37

Artist's impression of England versus Scotland at Blackheath, 11th March 1899.
Illustrated Police News, 1899

ENGLAND TOUR OF AUSTRALIA 1899

TOUR PARTY
Matthew Mullineux (captain, Richmond)
CY 'Charlie' Adamson (Old Dunelmians)
Alan Ayre-Smith (Guy's Hospital)
Frederick Belson (Bath)
Alf Bucher (Edinburgh Academicals)
George Cookson (Manchester)
Gerry Doran (Lansdowne)
Guy Evers (Moseley)
John S Francomb (Manchester)
George R Gibson (Northern, Newcastle)
Hugh GS Gray (Melrose)
J Wallace Jarman (Bristol)
William Judkins (Coventry)
TMW 'Tom' McGown (Northern Ireland FC)
Esmond Martelli (Wanderers, Dublin)
Gwynne Nicholls (Cardiff)
Elliot T Nicholson (Liverpool)
Frank M Stout (Gloucester)
Blair Swannell (Northampton)
CEK 'Charlie' Thompson (Manchester)
Alec B Timms (Edinburgh Wanderers)

TOUR RESULTS
Wednesday 14 June – Goulburn, won 11-3 (attendance: 3,500)
Saturday 17 June – New South Wales (Sydney), won 4-3 (30,000)
Tuesday 20 June – Metropolitan Branch Union (Sydney), won 8-5 (14,000)
Saturday 24 June – **Australia** (Sydney), lost 3-13 (28,000)
Wednesday 28 June – Toowoomba, won 19-5 (3,000)
Saturday 1 July – Queensland (Brisbane), lost 3-11 (12,000)
Wednesday 5 July – Bundaberg, won 36-3 (2,000)
Saturday 8 July – Rockhampton, won 16-3 (4,000)
Tuesday 11 July – Mount Morgan, won 29-3 (3,000)
Saturday 15 July – Central Queensland (Rockhampton), won 22-3 (5,000)
Wednesday 19 July – Maryborough, won 27-8 (2,000)
Saturday 22 July – **Australia** (Brisbane), won 11-0 (15,000)
Tuesday 25 July – New England (Armidale), won 6-4 (2,000)
Thursday 27 July – Northern Districts (Newcastle), won 28-0 (4,000)
Saturday 29 July – New South Wales (Sydney), won 11-5 (14,000)
Tuesday 1 August – Metropolitan Branch Union (Sydney), lost 5-8 (5,000)
Saturday 5 August – **Australia** (Sydney), won 11-10 (20,000)
Wednesday 9 August – Western Districts (Bathurst), won 19-0 (5,000)
Saturday 12 August – **Australia** (Sydney), won 13-0 (10,000)
Tuesday 15 August – Great Public Schools (Sydney), won 21-3 (2,000)
Saturday 19 August – Victoria (Melbourne), won 30-0 (10,000)

Saturday 24 June 1899 at Sydney Cricket Ground
AUSTRALIA 13 *Back*: RH McCowan (Qld). *Three-quarters*: CJ White (NSW), FL Row (capt, NSW), SA Spragg (NSW, t, 2c). *Five-eighths*: WT Evans (Qld, t), PM Ward (NSW). *Half-back*: AS Gralton (Qld). *Forwards*: PJ Carew (Qld), J Carson (NSW), AJ Colton (Qld), W Davis (NSW), CS Ellis (NSW), AJ Kelly (NSW, t), H Marks (NSW), WH Tanner (Qld).
ENGLAND 3 *Back*: E Martelli. *Three-quarters*: A Bucher, G Nicholls (t), CY Adamson, G Doran. *Half-backs*: G Cookson, M Mullineux (capt). *Forwards*: A Ayre-Smith, F Belson, JS Francomb, GR Gibson, HGS Gray, JW Jarman, T McGown, FM Stout.
Attendance: 28,000   *Referee*: WG Gerrard (New Zealand)

Saturday 22 July 1899 at the Exhibition Ground, Brisbane
AUSTRALIA 0 *Back*: RH McCowan (capt, Qld). *Three-quarters*: T Ward (Qld), AR Henry (Qld), SA Spragg (NSW). *Five-eighths*: WT Evans (Qld), PM Ward (NSW). *Half-back*: EW Currie (Qld). *Forwards*: PJ Carew (Qld), RL Challoner (NSW), AC Corfe (Qld), CS Ellis (NSW), CS Graham (Qld), H Marks (NSW), NO Street (NSW), WH Tanner (Qld).
ENGLAND 11 *Back*: CEK Thompson. *Three-quarters*: HGS Gray, AB Timms, G Nicholls (t), G Doran. *Half-backs*: CY Adamson (t, c), G Cookson. *Forwards*: A Ayre-Smith (t), G Evers, GR Gibson, JW Jarman, W Judkins, T McGown, FM Stout (capt), B Swannell.
Attendance: 15,000   *Referee*: WH Beattie (Australia)

Saturday 5 August 1899 at Sydney Cricket Ground
AUSTRALIA 10 *Back*: WG Cobb (NSW). *Three-quarters*: SW Miller (NSW), FL Row (capt, NSW), SA Spragg (NSW, 2t, 2c). *Five-eighths*: IC O'Donnell (NSW), PM Ward (NSW). *Half-back*: A Boyd (NSW). *Forwards*: RFD Barton (NSW), SB Boland (Qld), RG Bouffler (NSW), PJ Carew (Qld), AJ Colton (Qld), W Davis (NSW), CS Ellis (NSW), W Webb (NSW).
ENGLAND 11 *Back*: CEK Thompson. *Three-quarters*: A Bucher (2t), AB Timms (t), G Nicholls, ET Nicholson. *Half-backs*: CY Adamson (c), G Cookson. *Forwards*: A Ayre-Smith, G Evers, GR Gibson, JW Jarman, W Judkins, T McGown, FM Stout (capt), B Swannell.
Attendance: 20,000   *Referee*: WS Corr (Australia)

Saturday 12 August 1899 at Sydney Cricket Ground
AUSTRALIA 0 *Back*: WG Cobb (NSW). *Three-quarters*: RH McCowan (Qld), FL Row (capt, NSW), SA Spragg (NSW). *Five-eighths*: IC O'Donnell (NSW), PM Ward (NSW). *Half-back*: AS Gralton (Qld). *Forwards*: SB Boland (Qld), PJ Carew (Qld), W Davis (NSW), CS Ellis (NSW), WR Hardcastle (NSW), JM O'Donnell (NSW), JH Sampson (NSW), W Webb (NSW).
ENGLAND 13 *Back*: CEK Thompson. *Three-quarters*: A Bucher (t), AB Timms, G Nicholls, ET Nicholson. *Half-backs*: CY Adamson (t, 2c, pg), G Cookson. *Forwards*: A Ayre-Smith, G Evers, GR Gibson, JW Jarman, W Judkins, T McGown, FM Stout (capt), B Swannell.
Attendance: 10,000   *Referee*: WS Corr (Australia)

William Bates of Percy Park made 21 appearances for Northumberland.
Newcastle Weekly Chronicle, 1896

1899-1900

THE LANCASHIRE AND YORKSHIRE BORDER TOWNS LEAGUE
A new competition, the Lancashire and Yorkshire Border Towns League, was launched under the Northern Union code. It was announced that the following clubs would be included: Hebden Bridge, Luddendenfoot, Radcliffe, Rochdale Rangers, Werneth and Whitworth. It was agreed that the fixtures between Radcliffe, Werneth and Whitworth will count in both the Lancashire Second Competition and the new league. Todmorden subsequently joined, making the numbers up to seven. In the previous season Radcliffe, Werneth and Whitworth had been members of the disbanded South East Lancashire League.[246]

THE NORTH WESTERN LEAGUE: A LATE FINISH!
Workington defeated Ulverston 16-0 on 2nd September to complete the North Western League table for the previous (1898-99) season. The match, under Northern Union rules, had been held over after complications following the originally fixture on 8th October 1898. Ulverston had beaten Workington 7-3 at home but were then found to have used two ineligible players. A replay was ordered at Workington but, after the two clubs failed to agree when that should be, the League Committee twice set dates – 31st March and 26th April 1899 – which Ulverston cancelled each time, citing financial issues. A further League meeting during May decreed Ulverston would not be allowed to participate in any matches during 1899-1900 until they played the outstanding fixture.

YORKSHIRE DEFECTIONS TO THE NORTHERN UNION
As the new season dawned, more defections from the Rugby Union were announced, including Shipley and Sowerby Bridge, winner and runner-up, respectively, of the 1898-99 (Rugby Union) Yorkshire Competition No. 1. In both cases the loss of key fixtures, due to other clubs joining the Northern Union, had created financial difficulties.[247]

CHANGES IN THE NORTH WESTERN LEAGUE
The Northern Union's North Western League underwent a few changes for 1899-1900. Whitehaven and Whitehaven Recreation were newcomers having left the Rugby Union, but north Lancashire clubs Askam, Lancaster and Ulverston withdrew because travelling to West Cumberland to fulfil fixtures was proving too costly.[248]

WESTMORLAND AND DISTRICT LEAGUE
Attempts were ongoing to revive the Rugby code in Westmorland. Having operated under Northern Union with a three-team Westmorland Junior League during 1897-98 and 1898-99, ambitious plans to create what would be the Westmorland and District League were reported in early September. The 'A' (second) teams of Lancaster and Morecambe had been invited to join along with the Lancaster-based Christ Church Hornets. The remaining six clubs in the nine-team League were announced as Ambleside, Carnforth, Holme, Kendal Hornets 'A', Kirkby Lonsdale, and Marsh Hornets (Lancaster). The League went ahead as reported except the Kendal Hornets first team replaced their 'A' team.[249]

THE NEW CUMBERLAND SENIOR COMPETITION
With the West Cumberland teams reunited under one code, the *Athletic News* opined that Northern Union in the area 'is found holding a much stronger and healthier position than was the case at this time last year. Then there were four clubs, now there are seven, and they have formed a [Cumberland] Senior Competition, which is confidently expected to do much to deepen and strengthen public interest. As all these clubs find a habitation and a home on the strip of coast between Whitehaven and Maryport, these competition matches will cost them little for travelling expenses, a consideration of weight with the West Cumberland clubs. Maryport, Workington and the two Whitehaven organisations, are also members of the North Western League. Seaton and Workington have been weakened by migration [of players to Lancashire and Yorkshire clubs], and Brookland Rovers have lost [Joe] Ferguson [to Oldham], yet several of the West Cumberland teams will be stronger this season than last'.[250]

LANCASHIRE CLUBS DISBAND

Not all news was positive for the Northern Union clubs, several defectors from the Rugby Union having run into difficulties. The *Yorkshire Evening Post*, previewing the 1899-1900 season, noted: 'The Barton club, one of the best of the second-class Lancashire teams last season, has been compelled to go to the wall [during December 1898] owing to increased expenditure and lack of support. Barton were rather unfortunately situated, their ground being too near Swinton and Salford to ensure them good "gates," and thus they could not pay their way. Barton are not alone among Lancashire clubs in failing to continue as a professional organisation, for such as St Helens Recreation, Dukinfield, and Walkden have also disbanded, to say nothing of Rochdale St Clement's, Failsworth, and Crompton. It is one of fate's little ironies that the Barton club's ground should have been taken by Eccles, an organisation playing under the auspices of the Rugby Union. And yet in certain parts of Lancashire, Northern Unionists expected that the old [Rugby Union] game would be smothered out of existence in their county.'[251]

PROBLEMS FOR LUDDENDENFOOT

Luddendenfoot, members of Northern Union's Yorkshire Second Competition (West) and the Lancashire and Yorkshire Border Towns League, ran into problems after hosting Dewsbury in the Yorkshire Second on 11th November. At the Yorkshire Committee meeting at the Green Dragon Hotel, Leeds, on 23rd November, one player was suspended for the season and the remaining 14 until mid-December for using bad language in continually disputing the referee's decisions. It had a disastrous effect on the finances of the club. Retired playing members helped fill the gaps but subsequent defeats affected attendances. The club held a meeting on 13th December and, having initially decided to break up, agreed to continue in the Yorkshire Second Competition but to withdraw from the Lancashire and Yorkshire Border Towns League.[252]

YORKSHIRE VERSUS LANCASHIRE: A FOGGY DAY

The start of Yorkshire's (Rugby Union) county championship match with Lancashire at Keighley on 18th November was delayed due to thick fog. Eventually it was agreed to play four 15-minute periods but, five minutes into the third quarter it was abandoned with no score. A Yorkshire Committee meeting was held that evening at the Wellington Hotel, Keighley, when it was decided to report back to the English Union for them to determine whether the match should count as a draw or be replayed. A replay was subsequently ordered and it was decided to play at Harrogate on 7th April, postponing the Yorkshire Cup final for one week to accommodate it. Yorkshire won the rematch 24-3.[253]

NORTHUMBERLAND VERSUS LANCASHIRE ABANDONED
The Northumberland versus Lancashire rugby union county championship game at Jesmond, Newcastle, on 9th December, was played on a hard ground due to frost. Several players were injured and critics argued that it should never have taken place. Ten minutes into the second half the two captains agreed to abandon the match at 3-3. Initially the result was declared void and a replay planned. However, with the counties occupying the bottom two places in the table the score stood.

LANCASHIRE SECOND COMPETITION TEAMS STRUGGLING
The Northern Union's Lancashire Second Competition was proving to be as much a battle of survival off the field as on it. The *Lancashire Daily Post* commented: 'The list of clubs in straitened circumstances is being added to [and] it is doubtful whether any, with the possible exception of Barrow, can make both ends meet. Outside the clubs north of the [River] Ribble, may be mentioned Altrincham, a team that has suffered heavily in the matter of travelling expenses. Werneth, too, are not near so well off as has been thought, whilst Whitworth are very poorly supported. Three clubs in the competition, namely Barton, Blackpool, and Walkden, all came to grief last season, and present appearances are far from bright for several of the remaining organisations maintaining their position. The area covered by the Competition is far too wide, hence the heavy travelling expenses.'[254]

WHITEHAVEN CLUB DISBANDED
The early season optimism for Northern Union in Cumberland suffered a blow with the demise of Whitehaven, a club which had been in existence since 1877. A meeting of its members at the Central Hotel, Whitehaven, on 1st March, arrived at the decision to fold, citing poor attendances and difficulties in raising a team. They competed in the North Western League and Cumberland Senior Competition.[255]

THE SOUTH-WEST LANCASHIRE AND BORDER TOWNS CUP
Eight prominent Lancashire and Cheshire Northern Union clubs met in the Minorca Hotel, Wigan, on 8th March to discuss a new cup competition. Those represented were Leigh, Runcorn, St Helens, Swinton, Tyldesley, Warrington, Widnes, and Wigan. A follow-up meeting took place at the

same hotel on 15th March when it was agreed to organise a knock-out competition for the new South-West Lancashire and Border Towns Challenge Cup. The contest commenced during April 1900.[256]

YORKSHIRE COMPETITION NO. 1 DISBANDED

The committee for the Yorkshire Competition No. 1 held a meeting at the Commercial Hotel, Leeds, on 14th March to vote on whether it should be discontinued. As Rugby Union's only remaining 'senior' league in the North of England, it contained just eight clubs. Morley had already decided they would not take part in any more competitive matches as they felt that, rather than promoting Rugby Union, the sport was deteriorating. The representatives of Cleckheaton, Castleford and Bingley all said they were in favour of discontinuing, whilst Keighley and Skipton felt it was no longer 'of a representative character'. It was unanimously decided not to continue after the current season.[257]

ROUGH PLAY IN THE YORKSHIRE CUP

The Cleckheaton versus Bottomboat Trinity second round Yorkshire (Rugby Union) Cup match on 24th March was abandoned 10 minutes from the end due to excessive 'roughness' by the forwards, the score standing at 0-0. The Yorkshire Committee, at their meeting at the Green Dragon Hotel, Leeds, on 26th March, felt that the referee should have talked to the captains before 'abruptly' ending the match, although the 'rough play' indulged in by both sets of forwards was censured. A replay was ordered at a neutral venue, Bottomboat Trinity winning 16-3 at Morley.[258]

THE WEST RIDING CHALLENGE CUP: A NEW COMPETITION

The Northern Union's Yorkshire clubs decided to organise a knock-out cup competition to replicate the one they had competed for under Rugby Union, calling it 'The Yorkshire Northern Rugby Union Challenge Competition'. After several meetings, they referred the matter to the Northern Union Committee for approval. Although it was forthcoming, there were two key conditions; the title was to be altered from 'Yorkshire' to 'The West Riding' and (with the competition due to take place during April) no match shall be played within a 12-mile radius of any Northern Union Challenge Cup tie taking place on the same date. Disappointingly for the organisers, only 12 clubs entered with Liversedge the only team from the Yorkshire Senior Competition, the remainder from the Yorkshire Second Competition.[259]

GLEN VIEW REPRESENT HEBDEN BRIDGE

Due to Hebden Bridge's involvement in the Northern Union's West Riding Challenge Cup, their local junior side Glen View were 'deputed' to take their place in two Lancashire and Yorkshire Border Towns League fixtures that clashed with the cup ties. On 7th April Glen View (as 'Hebden Bridge') lost 43-0 at Werneth and on Good Friday, 13th April, they were beaten 53-0 at Radcliffe.

KEIGHLEY JOIN THE NORTHERN UNION

Keighley, having just won the Rugby Union's Yorkshire Competition No. 1, decided to join the Northern Union during a special meeting of members at the Wellington Hotel, Keighley, on 12th April. It was reported that 'it was quite evident that interest has gone out of the Rugby Union so far as that district was concerned, and by going over to the other Union they hoped to get better gates, and to be relieved of the necessity of travelling such long distances to play matches'.[260]

THE WEST RIDING CUP: PROBLEMS WITH THE 12-MILE RADIUS

The new West Riding Challenge Cup competition was struggling to function, one report stating that 'the twelve-mile radius condition imposed by the Northern Union executive has reduced the West Riding Cup Competition to an affair of shreds and patches'. The West Riding Cup Committee claimed the ruling had meant four first round ties could not be played on the scheduled date of 7th April, one of which was delayed until Good Friday, 13th April, and two others were played on 14th April. The problem of rescheduling matches due to the 12-mile rule led to the withdrawal from the competition of Birstall, Dewsbury and Heckmondwike.[261]

SOUTH SHIELDS CONSIDER NORTHERN UNION

South Shields held a members meeting at St Thomas' Hall, South Shields, on 18th April, to consider joining the Northern Union. Approximately two-thirds of the members were in favour, the remaining third considering it 'premature and inopportune'. A final decision was deferred to ascertain the support of the other Durham and Northumberland clubs, a further meeting taking place at the same venue on 21st April. It was explained that, at the time of the previous meeting, they were under the impression Wallsend had already decided to join the Northern Union and others might follow. Wallsend now stated they 'would try and hold up [in Rugby Union] for another season' and, after further debate, it was agreed South Shields should not join the Northern Union.[262]

THE WEST RIDING CUP SEMI-FINAL:
A DISGRACEFUL SPECTACLE

The Northern Union's West Riding Challenge Cup semi-final between Liversedge and Ossett, played on the ground of Leeds Parish Church at Crown Point on 21st April, turned into mayhem. The *Leeds Mercury* wrote that during the second half 'the players commenced to be pugilistic, the spectators, who were apparently mostly neutrals, doing all in their power to encourage rough play in the field. For ten minutes the game was little more than a free fight, and four men in quick succession left the field by order of the referee; Jones, Clarkson and Glover of Ossett, and Wilshaw of Liversedge. This had a most beneficial effect, and for some time after the play was really interesting. Towards the finish, however, rough play again became the order, and before the [final] whistle blew, Spencer of Liversedge and Mellor and Ashton of Ossett were all severely injured. It was altogether a disgraceful spectacle'.[263]

LANCASHIRE AND YORKSHIRE BORDER TOWNS:
WERNETH AWARDED TITLE

The committee of the Lancashire and Yorkshire Border Towns League held a meeting in Rochdale on 26th April to determine the champions! Based on the published table, Werneth and Whitworth had equal points but Werneth raised an objection against a point credited to Whitworth. The problem related to a Christmas Day fixture between Whitworth and Rochdale Rangers. Due to the ground being hard with frost, it was agreed between the referee and both clubs that, whatever the result, it would be declared a draw with each club awarded one point each. Whitworth 'won' 3-2 and, despite the arrangement, credited with two points in the league table. Werneth argued that the original agreement should hold good. Their objection was upheld and they were awarded the championship.[264]

ASPATRIA FORMS A NORTHERN UNION CLUB

At a meeting held in the Reading Room, Aspatria, on 27th April, it was decided to form a new Aspatria club under Northern Union rules. It was anticipated that junior club Aspatria Hornets would join forces with former Aspatria rugby union players who had already moved to the Workington Northern Union club. It was a further blow to the Cumberland Rugby Union authorities with Aspatria and Carlisle considered its mainstays. The Aspatria rugby union club had struggled to arrange fixtures at home, the result being 'that the local interest in Rugby Union was almost dead'.[265]

THE WEST RIDING CUP FINAL: REPLAY HEADACHE

The West Riding Challenge Cup final, contested by Liversedge and Hebden Bridge at Thrum Hall, Halifax, on 28th April, led to more headaches for the organisers after it finished scoreless. A committee meeting was held in the club pavilion immediately afterwards when they asked the Halifax club if they would stage the replay the following Monday evening. The problem was that the Halifax ground was being prepared for its grandly titled 'World's Fair' to be held during July and August. The 'first sod' for its lake was to be cut on that day, having already been delayed to accommodate the original final. The replay eventually went ahead at Sowerby Bridge, Liversedge winning 10-3.[266]

LANCASHIRE SECOND COMPETITION: OUTSTANDING MATCHES

At a meeting of the Northern Union in Manchester on 1st May, officials of the Lancashire Second Competition inquired if they could play their outstanding matches during the close season. The application was refused.[267]

1899-1900 STATISTICS

NORTHERN UNION

LANCASHIRE SENIOR COMPETITION

Final table	P	W	D	L	For	Agst	Pts
Runcorn	26	22	2	2	232	33	46
Oldham	26	21	1	4	340	75	43
Swinton	26	19	1	6	210	108	39
St Helens	26	16	3	7	207	119	35
Widnes	26	12	4	10	174	146	28
Warrington	26	12	1	13	174	128	25
Broughton Rangers*	26	13	1	12	132	138	25
Salford	26	12	0	14	196	176	24
Stockport	26	10	2	14	126	136	22
Leigh	26	8	5	13	119	211	21
Rochdale Hornets*	26	9	1	16	90	181	17
Millom	26	7	1	18	112	234	15
Wigan	26	7	1	18	73	230	15
Tyldesley	26	2	1	23	66	336	5

*Two points deducted for breach of professional rules

LANCASHIRE SECOND COMPETITION

Final table	P	W	D	L	For	Agst	Pts
Barrow	20	17	2	1	254	34	36
Werneth	20	14	3	3	135	64	31
Morecambe	20	11	4	5	147	52	26
Birkenhead Wanderers	19	9	2	8	80	103	20
Whitworth	20	9	1	10	102	146	19
Altrincham	19	8	1	10	90	106	17
Lancaster	20	6	3	11	114	108	15
Fleetwood	19	6	3	10	48	110	15
Radcliffe	18	6	1	11	75	105	13
Ulverston	19	5	1	13	43	160	11
Dalton	16	3	1	12	38	138	7

Note: Fixtures incomplete due to postponements.

Promotion Test Match
Barrow 22, Tyldesley 8 (at Quay Meadow, Lancaster)
(Barrow promoted to Lancashire Senior Competition, Tyldesley relegated)

YORKSHIRE SENIOR COMPETITION

Final table	P	W	D	L	For	Agst	Pts
Bradford	30	24	2	4	324	98	50
Batley	30	21	6	3	219	72	48
Halifax	30	20	3	7	193	120	43
Wakefield Trinity	30	18	5	7	203	120	41
Huddersfield	30	17	4	9	181	110	38
Hull Kingston Rovers*	30	15	4	11	181	129	32
Hull	30	15	0	15	249	154	30
Hunslet	30	14	2	14	182	168	30
Manningham	30	13	3	14	207	203	29
Bramley	30	13	0	17	121	190	26
Castleford	30	11	3	16	155	199	25
Brighouse Rangers	30	9	3	18	80	231	21
Holbeck**	30	8	4	18	138	236	18
Leeds Parish Church	30	7	3	20	135	207	17
Leeds	30	7	3	20	103	225	17
Liversedge	30	5	1	24	94	303	11

*Two points deducted for breach of professional rules
**Two points deducted for using ineligible player

YORKSHIRE SECOND COMPETITION (WEST)

Final table	P	W	D	L	For	Agst	Pts
Heckmondwike	22	19	1	2	255	41	39
Dewsbury	22	14	4	4	162	42	32
Hebden Bridge	22	12	5	5	227	61	29
Todmorden	22	11	7	4	168	58	29
Shipley	22	12	3	7	126	120	27
Kirkstall	22	10	3	9	102	150	23
Elland	22	9	3	10	142	145	21
Birstall	22	7	4	11	97	168	18
Sowerby Bridge	22	7	3	12	75	104	17
Idle	22	3	7	12	57	135	13
Luddendenfoot	22	2	5	15	32	216	9
Windhill	22	2	3	17	53	256	7

Note: 12 unplayed fixtures declared scoreless draws, affecting Idle, Todmorden (5 matches each), Luddendenfoot (4), Dewsbury (3), Kirstall, Shipley (2 each), Birstall, Hebden Bridge, Windhill (1 each).

YORKSHIRE SECOND COMPETITION (EAST)

Final table	P	W	D	L	For	Agst	Pts
Normanton*	20	18	1	1	131	19	35
York	20	17	0	3	329	27	34
Featherstone	20	12	2	6	155	73	26
Ossett	20	10	3	7	61	76	23
Kinsley	17	9	1	7	115	75	19
Alverthorpe	18	9	1	8	66	91	19
Pontefract	19	5	3	11	59	173	13
Goole	20	6	1	13	58	158	13
Eastmoor	20	5	2	13	41	157	12
Outwood Church	20	4	4	12	28	105	12
Rothwell**	20	3	0	17	32	121	6

*Two points deducted for using ineligible player
**Disbanded (Jan 1900), 9 remaining matches declared as win to opponents
Note: Kinsley v Alverthorpe, Alverthorpe v Kinsley, Kinsley v Pontefract all postponed and not subsequently played.

Yorkshire Second Competition Final
Heckmondwike 2, Normanton 2 (at Crown Flatts, Dewsbury)

Yorkshire Second Competition Final Replay
Heckmondwike 9, Normanton 2 (at Crown Flatts, Dewsbury)
(Heckmondwike declared Yorkshire Second Competition winner)

Promotion Test Match
Liversedge 11, Heckmondwike 2 (at Park Avenue, Bradford)
(Liversedge retain place in Yorkshire Senior Competition)

CUMBERLAND SENIOR COMPETITION

Final table	P	W	D	L	For	Agst	Pts
Maryport	10	7	2	1	63	13	16
Workington	10	7	1	2	77	19	15
Seaton	10	5	2	3	45	35	8
Wath Brow	10	3	1	6	35	92	7
Whitehaven Recreation	10	2	2	6	23	54	6
Brookland Rovers	10	1	2	7	26	56	4
Record expunged:							
Whitehaven	9	0	0	9	0	148	0

Note: Whitehaven disbanded (Mar 1900).

LANCASHIRE AND YORKSHIRE BORDER TOWNS LEAGUE

Final table	P	W	D	L	For	Agst	Pts
Werneth	10	7	0	3	138	16	14
Whitworth	10	6	1	3	81	37	13
Radcliffe	10	6	1	3	97	45	13
Todmorden	10	5	2	3	50	47	12
Hebden Bridge	10	3	1	6	44	181	7
Rochdale Rangers	10	0	1	9	16	100	1
Record expunged:							
Luddendenfoot	4	0	0	4	0	36	0

Note: Luddendenfoot withdrew (Dec 1899).

NORTH WESTERN LEAGUE

Final table	P	W	D	L	For	Agst	Pts
Millom	8	5	1	2	60	25	11
Workington	8	4	3	1	44	23	11
Maryport	8	4	1	3	32	21	9
Barrow	8	3	1	4	46	39	7
Whitehaven Recreation	8	1	0	7	18	92	2
Record expunged:							
Whitehaven	5	0	0	5	2	58	0

Note: Whitehaven disbanded (Mar 1900).

WESTMORLAND AND DISTRICT LEAGUE

Final table	P	W	D	L	For	Agst	Pts
Kendal Hornets	16	13	0	3	229	55	26
Morecambe 'A'	15	11	2	2	117	37	24
Lancaster Marsh Hornets	16	11	2	3	132	51	24
Carnforth	16	9	3	4	100	59	21
Lancaster 'A'	16	6	4	6	72	89	16
Ambleside	16	5	2	9	46	95	12
Lancaster Christ Church H	15	3	3	9	51	100	9
Holme Wanderers	16	2	1	13	30	181	5
Kirkby Lonsdale	14	1	1	12	24	134	3

Note: Fixtures incomplete due to postponements.

NORTHERN UNION CHALLENGE CUP (64 entries)
Try – 3 points; all goals – 2.

First Round
Alverthorpe 2, Workington 8
Altrincham 24, Pontefract 0
Barrow 2, Bradford 3
Birkenhead Wanderers 4, Werneth 6
Bramley w/o Rothwell (disbanded)
Brighouse Rangers 16, Todmorden 5
Broughton Rangers 22, Lancaster 7
Castleford 0, Batley 0
Dewsbury 3, Wigan 0
Featherstone 2, Halifax 19 (at Halifax)
Goole 8, Heckmondwike 6
Hebden Bridge 0, Wakefield Trinity 15 (at Wakefield Trinity)
Holbeck w/o Whitehaven (disbanded)
Huddersfield 22, Idle 0
Hull 52, Wath Brow 0
Hull Kingston Rover 3, Millom 0
Kendal Hornets 0, Maryport 9
Leeds Parish Church 5, Seaton 0

Liversedge 8, Leigh 12
Manningham 3, Oldham 3
Morecambe 19, Whitehaven Recreation 0
Normanton 5, Leeds 0
Ossett 5, Elland 0
Outwood Church 5, Widnes 24
Radcliffe 13, Whitworth 0
Runcorn 42, Birstall 0
St Helens 0, Warrington 6
Salford 9, York 0
Stockport 2, Hunslet 0
Swinton 53, Eastmoor 0
Tyldesley 12, Brookland Rovers 0
Windhill 0, Rochdale Hornets 11

First Round Replays
Batley 5, Castleford 0
Oldham 18, Manningham 3

Second Round
Altrincham 3, Leeds Parish Church 15, (at Leeds PC)
Bramley 8, Hull 5
Bradford 12, Ossett 0
Brighouse Rangers 0, Wakefield Trinity 4
Dewsbury 0, Widnes 2
Halifax 5, Oldham 10
Holbeck 8, Swinton 17
Huddersfield 13, Workington 0
Leigh 2, Salford 9
Morecambe 0, Broughton Rangers 7 (at Broughton Rangers)
Normanton 0, Batley 3
Radcliffe 2, Werneth 0
Rochdale Hornets 13, Hull Kingston Rovers 5
Runcorn 12, Maryport 0
Stockport 5, Tyldesley 2
Warrington 44, Goole 0

Third Round
Bradford 0, Runcorn 0
Bramley 3, Widnes 3
Broughton Rangers 5, Wakefield Trinity 3
Leeds Parish Church 7, Batley 2
Rochdale Hornets 3, Warrington 0
Salford 6, Huddersfield 5
Stockport 24, Radcliffe 3
Swinton 14, Oldham 2

Third Round Replays
Runcorn 3, Bradford 3
Widnes 8, Bramley 0

Third Round Second Replay
Runcorn 6, Bradford 2
(at Wheater's Field, Broughton)

Fourth Round
Leeds Parish Church 5, Runcorn 5
Salford 11, Rochdale Hornets 3
Stockport 0, Widnes 3
Swinton 9, Broughton Rangers 0

Fourth Round Replay
Runcorn 6, Leeds Parish Church 8

Semi-finals
Salford 11, Widnes 0
(at Watersheddings, Oldham)
Swinton 8, Leeds Parish Church 0
(at Fartown, Huddersfield)

FINAL
Saturday 28 April 1900 at Fallowfield, Manchester
SWINTON 16 *Back*: A Chorley. *Three-quarters*: JT Lewis (t), R Messer (t), R Valentine (t), VR Hampson. *Half-backs*: D Davies (t), FJ Morgan. *Forwards*: J Evans, G Harris, GR Jones, B Murphy, C Pollitt, J Preston, J Valentine (capt, 2g), E Vigors.
SALFORD 8 *Back*: D Smith. *Three-quarters*: A Pearson (t), T Williams (capt, t), E Harter, H Hadwen. *Half-backs*: I Grey, B Griffiths (g). *Forwards*: W Brown, G Fisher, M Gledhill, J Rhapps, R Shaw, H Shore, P Tunney, J Williams.
Attendance: 17,864   *Referee*: F Renton (Hunslet)

SOUTH WEST LANCASHIRE AND BORDER TOWNS CHALLENGE CUP (8 entries)
Try – 3 points; all goals – 2.

First Round
St Helens 8, Leigh 0
Swinton v Warrington
(not played; both withdrew)
Widnes 23, Tyldesley 6
Wigan 0, Runcorn 0

First Round Replay
Runcorn 32, Wigan 0

Semi-final
Widnes 0, St Helens 3
Bye: Runcorn (due to withdrawal of Swinton and Warrington)

FINAL
Monday 30 April 1900 at Lowerhouse Lane, Widnes
ST HELENS 6 *Back*: T Foulkes (capt). *Three-quarters*: R Doherty, J Barnes (t), D Traynor, G Liversedge. *Half-backs*: J Appleton (t), P Boyle. *Forwards*: W Briers, P Dale, W Green, P Melvin, F Mooney, W Prescott, J Thompson, W Whiteley.
RUNCORN 0 *Back*: S Houghton. *Three-quarters*: D Jones, J Butterworth, TH Warder, C Butterworth. *Half-backs*: J Jolley, J Richardson. *Forwards*: F Darlington, H Farmer, F Gayter, O Hughes, J Langley, A Taylor, J Tomlinson, S Walker.
After extra time   *Attendance*: 3,000   *Referee*: W McCutcheon (Oldham)

WEST RIDING CHALLENGE CUP (12 entries)
Try – 3 points; all goals – 2.

First Round
Alverthorpe 0, Ossett 3
Elland 3, Sowerby Bridge 9
Heckmondwike w/o Birstall (withdrew)
Liversedge w/o Dewsbury (withdrew)
Todmorden 0, Hebden Bridge 2
Windhill 5, Idle 2

Second Round
Hebden Bridge 7, Sowerby Bridge 3
Liversedge w/o Heckmondwike (withdrew)
Byes: Ossett, Windhill

Semi-finals
Hebden Bridge 10, Windhill 2 (at Valley Parade, Bradford)
Liversedge 7, Ossett 2 (at Crown Point, Leeds)

FINAL
Saturday 28 April 1900 at Thrum Hall, Halifax
LIVERSEDGE 0 *Back*: R Walker. *Three-quarters*: C Walshaw, J Garnett, T Stead, F Swallow. *Half-backs*: G Smith, H Wear. *Forwards*: B Furniss, W Hall, F Howarth, T Midgley, N Parkin, W Osborne, GF Robinson, J Todkill (capt).
HEBDEN BRIDGE 0 *Back*: J Greenwood. *Three-quarters*: H Costello, H Bottomley, J Sutcliffe, W Astin. *Half-backs*: A Crabtree, F Hodgson. *Forwards*: H Blackburn (capt), W Clayton, W Crowther, N Greenwood, K Jagger, W Peel, Harry Sutcliffe, Horsfall Sutcliffe.
Attendance: 4,000   *Referee*: J Oakland (Batley)

FINAL REPLAY
Monday 30 April 1900 at Beech Ground, Sowerby Bridge
LIVERSEDGE 10 *Back*: R Walker. *Three-quarters*: C Walshaw, J Garnett (t), T Stead, F Swallow. *Half-backs*: G Smith (t), H Wear. *Forwards*: B Furniss, W Hall, F Howarth, T Midgley, N Parkin, W Osborne, GF Robinson, J Todkill (capt, 2g).
HEBDEN BRIDGE 3 *Back*: J Greenwood. *Three-quarters*: H Costello (t), H Bottomley, J Sutcliffe, W Astin. *Half-backs*: A Crabtree, F Hodgson. *Forwards*: H Blackburn (capt), W Clayton, W Crowther, H Eastwood, N Greenwood, K Jagger, W Peel, Harry Sutcliffe.
Attendance: 2,000   *Referee*: TH Marshall (Bradford)

COUNTY CHAMPIONSHIP

Saturday 30 September 1899 at The Recreation Ground, Whitehaven
CUMBERLAND 3 *Back*: WJ Eagers (Mil). *Three-quarters*: JH Timney (Mary), T Teasdale (WathB), J Leck (Mil), J Young (Mil). *Half-backs*: J Lomas (Mary, t), S Northmore (Mil). *Forwards*: J Atkinson (Work), JH Buckett (capt, Mil), S Hoggarth (Mil), M Linton (Mil), H Nixon (BrookR), WP Robinson (Mary), G Steele (Work), D Wilson (Mil).
CHESHIRE 0 *Back*: W Simister (Stock). *Three-quarters*: H Clayton (BirkW), J Worsley (Stock), J Butterworth (Run), T Wilkinson (Run). *Half-backs*: J Faulkner (Run), J Jolley (Run). *Forwards*: J Burrows (Stock), H Farmer (Run), F Gayter (Run), E Glover (BirkW), S Hanson (Alt), W Lightfoot (Run), A Taylor (capt, Run), S Walker (Run).
Attendance: 2,000   *Referee*: F Renton (Hunslet)

Saturday 21 October 1899 at Watersheddings, Oldham
LANCASHIRE 17 *Back*: RL Thomas (Old). *Three-quarters*: H Hadwen (Sal, t), T Fletcher (Old), TD Davies (Old, t), S Williams (Old, t). *Half-backs*: H Kruger (RochH), J Lawton (capt, Old, 2t). *Forwards*: G Aspey (Wid), W Briers (StH), G Frater (Old, g), J Harrison (RochH), D Morrison (War), P Taylor (Lei), P Tunney (Sal), E Vigors (Swi).
CUMBERLAND 7 *Back*: J Robley (Mary). *Three-quarters*: J Whitehead (Mil), J Leck (Mil, t, g), WJ Eagers (Mil), I Latham (Mil). *Half-backs*: J Lomas (Mary), R O'Hara (Work). *Forwards*: J Beetham (Mil), JH Buckett (capt, Mil, g), C Gowan (WathB), S Hoggarth (Mil), H Killen (Mary), W Milligan (Work), G Steele (Work), D Wilson (Mil).
Attendance: 8,500   *Referee*: F Renton (Hunslet)

Saturday 28 October 1899 at Park Station, Birkenhead
CHESHIRE 9 *Back*: S Houghton (capt, Run). *Three-quarters*: T Wilkinson (Run), J Butterworth (Run, t), F Bevan (Stock), J Worsley (Stock, t). *Half-backs*: B Booth (Stock, t), J Jolley (Run). *Forwards*: J Bramble (Stock), F Gayter (Run), E Glover (BirkW), W Lightfoot (Run), W Oram (Stock), W Simister (Stock), A Taylor (Run), S Walker (Run).
YORKSHIRE 8 *Back*: H Taylor (Hull). *Three-quarters*: H Tulloch (HKR), FW Cooper (Brad, g), R Lewis (LeePC), A Hambrecht (Bram). *Half-backs*: P Brady (Cas), JA Rigg (capt, Hal, t). *Forwards*: H Buckler (Hol), FH Chambers (Hud), J Gath (Bat), A Kemp (HKR), R Parkinson (Hull), A Starks (HKR), M Sutcliffe (Hud, t), H Walker (LeePC).
Attendance: 2,500   *Referee*: JH Smith (Widnes)

Saturday 4 November 1899 at Thrum Hall, Halifax
YORKSHIRE 13 *Back*: H Taylor (Hull). *Three-quarters*: J Driscoll (Hull), JE Parker (Bram, t, 2g), A Hambrecht (Bram), J Lumley (Lee). *Half-backs*: GE Mosley (LeePC), H Robinson (Hun, t). *Forwards*: T Broadley (capt, Brad), J Gath (Bat), A Kemp (HKR), A Proctor (Mann), J Ramage (Hun), A Starks (HKR), M Sutcliffe (Hud, t), W Walton (Wak).
LANCASHIRE 16 *Back*: RL Thomas (Old). *Three-quarters*: H Hadwen (Sal, g), T Fletcher (Old), TD Davies (Old, t), S Williams (Old, t). *Half-backs*: J Lawton (capt, Old, t), A Lees (Old). *Forwards*: G Aspey (Wid), W Briers (StH), G Frater (Old, g), J Harrison (RochH), C Pollitt (Swi), C Thompson (BroR), P Tunney (Sal, t), J Williams (Sal).
Attendance: 9,000   *Referee*: J Bruckshaw (Stockport)

Saturday 25 November 1899 at Salthouse Road, Millom
CUMBERLAND 5 *Back*: WJ Eagers (Mil). *Three-quarters*: P Marshall (Mil), J Leck (Mil), J Whitehead (Mil), J Young (Mil, t). *Half-backs*: J Lomas (Mary), S Northmore (Mil). *Forwards*: J Beetham (Mil), JH Buckett (capt, Mil, g), C Gowan (WathB), T Hall (Whi), H Killen (Mary), M Linton (Mil), E Mason (WhiR), D Wilson (Mil).
YORKSHIRE 7 *Back*: H Taylor (Hull). *Three-quarters*: A Hambrecht (Bram), J Driscoll (Hull), JE Parker (Bram, g), J Lumley (Lee). *Half-backs*: J Oakland (Bat, t, g), M Sullivan (Hud). *Forwards*: A Barker (Mann), J Gath (capt, Bat), G Hewlett (LeePC), A Kemp (HKR), TJ Phillips (Hud), A Proctor (Mann), W Walton (Wak), F Wright (Brad).
Attendance: 3,500   *Referee*: W McCutcheon (Oldham)

Saturday 2 December 1899 at Chorley Road, Swinton
LANCASHIRE 6 *Back*: RL Thomas (Old). *Three-quarters*: H Hadwen (Sal), T Fletcher (Old), TD Davies (Old), S Williams (Old, t). *Half-backs*: J Lawton (capt, Old, t), A Lees

(Old). *Forwards*: G Aspey (Wid), W Briers (StH), G Frater (Old), J Harrison (RochH), C Pollitt (Swi), C Thompson (BroR), P Tunney (Sal), J Williams (Sal).
CHESHIRE 0 *Back*: S Houghton (capt, Run). *Three-quarters*: F Saville (Stock), TH Warder (Run), F Bevan (Stock), J Worsley (Stock). *Half-backs*: J Faulkner (Run), J Jolley (Run). *Forwards*: J Bramble (Stock), H Farmer (Run), F Gayter (Run), S Hanson (Alt), W Lightfoot (Run), W Oram (Stock), W Simister (Stock), S Walker (Run).
Attendance: 10,000   *Referee*: W Robinson (Manningham)

Final table

	P	W	D	L	For	Agst	Pts
Lancashire	3	3	0	0	39	20	6
Yorkshire	3	1	0	2	28	30	2
Cumberland	3	1	0	2	15	24	2
Cheshire	3	1	0	2	9	17	2

RUGBY UNION

YORKSHIRE COMPETITION NO. 1

Final table	P	W	D	L	For	Agst	Pts
Keighley	14	9	3	2	203	34	21
Castleford	14	8	2	4	111	70	18
Skipton	14	7	4	3	161	42	18
Morley	14	6	3	5	103	92	16
Bottomboat Trinity	14	6	2	6	74	158	14
Otley St Joseph's	14	3	5	6	42	86	11
Cleckheaton	14	2	4	8	30	168	8
Bingley	14	2	3	9	22	96	7

Note: Ten unplayed fixtures declared scoreless draws, affecting Cleckheaton (4 matches), Bingley, Keighley, Otley St Joseph's. Skipton (3 each), Morley (2), Bottomboat Trinity, Castleford (1 each).

DURHAM COUNTY CHALLENGE CUP (12 entries)
Try – 3 points; conversion – 2; penalty goal – 3; drop-goal, field goal, goal from mark – 4.

First Round
Durham City w/o Houghton-le-Spring (disbanded)
Hartlepool Old Boys 29, North Durham 9
West Hartlepool 58, Tyne Dock 0
Westoe 0, Tudhoe 13
Byes: Hamsteels, Hartlepool Rovers, South Shields, Sunderland

Second Round
Durham City 3, South Shields 27
Hartlepool Rovers 3, West Hartlepool 11
Sunderland 0, Hartlepool Old Boys 3
Tudhoe 25, Hamsteels 0

Semi-finals
West Hartlepool 3, Hartlepool Old Boys 3 (aet)
Tudhoe 20, South Shields 0

Semi-final Replay
West Hartlepool 16, Hartlepool Old Boys 0

FINAL
Saturday 21 April 1900 at Wood Terrace, Westoe, South Shields
WEST HARTLEPOOL 6 *Back*: J Hogg. *Three-quarters*: BS Wellock, JT Taylor (capt, pg), W Phipps, T Hunter. *Half-backs*: T Gallagher (t), J Phillips. *Forwards*: C Boddy, J Booth, R Bradley, J Conmy, GH Lewis, E Morton, WJ Simms, J Waller.
TUDHOE 3 *Back*: JE Pickering. *Three-quarters*: J Lindsley, E Sleep, J Gordon, W Taylor. *Half-backs*: Jack Cockrayne (t), R Levitt. *Forwards*: J Carmedy, Joe Cockrayne, J Foster, J Frater, B Hamm, G Richardson, A Stephenson (capt), J Stitt.
Attendance: 10,000   *Referee*: EB Holmes (Midland Counties RU)

NORTHUMBERLAND COUNTY FOOTBALL CHALLENGE CUP (5 entries)
Try – 3 points; conversion – 2; penalty goal – 3; drop-goal, field goal, goal from mark – 4.

First Round
Percy Park 5, Wallsend 0
Byes: Northern, Rockcliff, Tynedale

Semi-finals
Tynedale 3, Rockcliff 26
Percy Park 7, Northern 0

FINAL
Saturday 7 April 1900 at Jesmond Ground, Newcastle
ROCKCLIFF 8 *Back*: C Pickering. *Three-quarters*: JC Seymour, S Anderson (capt), F Pickering (2t), T Scott. *Half-backs*: W Seymour, EW Taylor (c). *Forwards*: JW Bamborough, JH Dunn, T Finlay, JH Greenwell, T Hamblin, JLM Neilson, C Seys, TC Stephenson.
PERCY PARK 5 *Back*: T Scotland. *Three-quarters*: GC Robinson (c), W Bates, JS Miller (t), BS Robson. *Half-backs*: EA Henderson, CW Russell. *Forwards*: J Dobinson, A Gradon, PF Hardwick, E Holmes, T Leinster, RT Lockerby, J Nesbitt, HJ Spencer.
Attendance: 5,000   *Referee*: n/a

YORKSHIRE COUNTY FOOTBALL CHALLENGE CUP (18 entries)
Try – 3 points; conversion – 2; penalty goal – 3; drop-goal, field goal, goal from mark – 4.

Preliminary Round
Bradford Olicana 5, Bradford Wanderers 3
Headingley w/o Shipley Clarence (withdrew)
Note: 14 other teams seeded to First Round

First Round
Bottomboat Trinity 11, Otley 5
Bradford Olicana w/o Shipley (withdrew)
Cleckheaton 11, Headingley 3
Harrogate 8, Kippax 0
Knottingley 3, Castleford 10
Morley 0, Keighley 8
Mytholmroyd 3, Bingley 0
Skipton 16, Otley St Joseph's 0

Second Round
Bradford Olicana 0, Castleford 12
Cleckheaton 0, Bottomboat Trinity 0
(abandoned due to altercations, replay ordered)
Keighley 9, Skipton 0
Mytholmroyd 6, Harrogate 0

Second Round Replay
Bottomboat Trinity 16, Cleckheaton 13
(at Morley)

Semi-finals
Castleford 13, Keighley 9 (at Queen's Park, Morley)
Mytholmroyd 5, Bottomboat Trinity 3 (at Wharfedale Ground, Otley)

FINAL
Saturday 14 April 1900 at County Ground, Claro Road, Harrogate
MYTHOLMROYD 11 *Back*: JF Longbottom. *Three-quarters*: P Carter, EF Fookes (t),
RW Collinson, EW Collinson (t). *Half-backs*: DA Ashton (c), DG Wheelwright. *Forwards*:
JE Ashton, T Barker, H Clark, G Greenwood, T Heyhurst, C Milnes, W Newell,
W Stansfield (capt, t).
CASTLEFORD 0 *Back*: T Wood. *Three-quarters*: JW Milner, S Gover, J Pickering, G Yeld.
Half-backs: J Briggs, J Shepherd. *Forwards*: RG Bingham, W Cobby, H Doncaster, J Hague,
T Hambleton (capt), J Lawton, H Milner, W Pratt.
Attendance: 2,000/3,000   *Referee*: E Alderson (Yorkshire RU Secretary)

COUNTY CHAMPIONSHIP

NORTHERN GROUP

Saturday 21 October 1899 at Brewery Field, Spennymoor
DURHAM 3 *Back*: RW Poole (HartOB). *Three-quarters*: W Taylor (Tud), J Gordon (Tud, t),
NS Cox (Sund), BS Wellock (WHart). *Half-backs*: W Moffet (Sund), BS Oughtred (HartR).
Forwards: C Boddy (WHart), J Booth (WHart), DF Hardie (ODun), GC Kerr (ODun),
GH Lewis (WHart), J Nichol (SSh), DG Pearson (Durham School), A Stephenson (Tud).
CUMBERLAND 3 *Back*: T Pattinson (Asp). *Three-quarters*: A Smith (Carl), F Spottiswood
(SSh), G Bell (PenU), T Routledge (Asp). *Half-backs*: J Foley (PenU), J Hillary (Asp, t).
Forwards: Joe Davidson (Asp), T Docker (Asp), D Graham (Asp/NewB), T Grieve (Asp),
J Ritson (Wall), J Sewell (Carl), J Stubbs (Carl), J Walker (Asp).
Attendance: 4,000   *Referee*: H Welford (Northumberland)

Saturday 4 November 1899 at Aigburth, Liverpool
LANCASHIRE 17 *Back*: JC Milnes (Man). *Three-quarters*: BC Middleton (Man, t),
AT Brettargh (LivOB, t, c), RH Spooner (Liv, t), ET Nicholson (Liv, t). *Half-backs*: GG Allen
(capt, Liv), G Cookson (Man, t). *Forwards*: GWB Ainsworth (Liv), CE Allen (Liv),
H Beames (LivOB), CR Jackson (BroPk), WA Kingscote (Man), A Long (Bla),
CVM Townsend (LivOB), RD Wood (LivOB).
CHESHIRE 3 *Back*: CR Hartley (Sale). *Three-quarters*: HL Hampton (AshH),
EJ Hargreaves (BirkPk), T Hodgson (AshH), GM Bennett (BirkPk). *Half-backs*: JC Marquis
(BirkPk, t), H Parratt (Sale). *Forwards*: J Baxter (BirkPk), CS Edgar (BirkPk), W Fearenside
(NewB), RH Fry (Sale), J Hague (Sale), HC Harvey (Sale), E Herschell (BirkPk),
JH Stephens (Bow).
Attendance: 'meagre'   *Referee*: B Butterworth (Yorkshire)

Saturday 4 November 1899 at Whitcliffe, Cleckheaton
YORKSHIRE 21 *Back*: J Miller (Cas). *Three-quarters*: JT Taylor (capt, WHart),
AW Robinson (Kei, 2t), JE Hammond (BradO), S Neumann (BradO). *Half-backs*:
GH Marsden (Mor, t, 3c), H Myers (Kei, t). *Forwards*: W Cobby (Cas), A Cockerham

(BradO), CE Holroyd (Mor), HE Ramsden (Bing), Archie Ross (Skip, t), RF Russell (Cas), JH Shooter (Mor), AEN Yeadon (Head).
DURHAM 0 *Back*: J Hogg (WHart). *Three-quarters*: W Taylor (Tud), J Gordon (Tud), HB Fawcus (ODun), HM Imrie (DurC). *Half-backs*: W Moffet (Sund), BS Oughtred (HartR). *Forwards*: T Christian (Wes), J Frater (Tud), DF Hardie (ODun), GH Lewis (WHart), A Peat (SSh), A Stephenson (Tud), J Stitt (Tud), R Stoker (TynD).
Attendance: 1,000   *Referee*: EB Holmes (Midland Counties)

Saturday 11 November 1899 at Upper Park, Birkenhead
CHESHIRE 6 *Back*: CR Hartley (Sale). *Three-quarters*: T Hodgson (AshH), HL Hampton (AshH), EJ Hargreaves (BirkPk, t), JDK Jones (BirkPk). *Half-backs*: JC Marquis (BirkPk), H Parratt (Sale, t). *Forwards*: J Baxter (BirkPk), CS Edgar (BirkPk), W Fearenside (NewB), RH Fry (Sale), J Hague (Sale), HC Harvey (Sale), E Herschell (BirkPk), JH Stephens (Bow).
CUMBERLAND 8 *Back*: T Pattinson (Asp). *Three-quarters*: A Smith (Carl), F Spottiswood (SSh), G Bell (PenU, t), T Routledge (Asp). *Half-backs*: JW Bell (Asp), J Hillary (Asp, t). *Forwards*: Joe Davidson (Asp), T Docker (Asp), D Graham (Asp/NewB), T Grieve (Asp, c), J Murray (PenU), T Robinson (Cock), J Sewell (Carl), J Walker (Asp).
Attendance: 'small'   *Referee*: AT Kemble (Lancashire)

Saturday 11 November 1899 at Jesmond Ground, Newcastle
NORTHUMBERLAND 6 *Back*: P Moran (HartR). *Three-quarters*: GC Robinson (PerPk, 2t), S Anderson (Rock), W Seymour (Rock), FW Stone (PerPk). *Half-backs*: CW Russell (PerPk), EW Taylor (capt, Rock). *Forwards*: JW Bamborough (Rock), FJ Bell (Rock), J Dobinson (PerPk), JH Dunn (Rock), J Finlay (WHart), GR Gibson (Nor), JH Greenwell (Rock), PF Hardwick (PerPk).
YORKSHIRE 18 *Back*: J Miller (Cas). *Three-quarters*: JT Taylor (capt, WHart, dg), AW Robinson (BradO), JE Hammond (BradO, 2t), S Neumann (BradO). *Half-backs*: GH Marsden (Mor, 2t), H Myers (Kei). *Forwards*: D Adkins (Kei), RG Bingham (Cas), A Cockerham (BradO), CE Holroyd (Mor), HE Ramsden (Bing), Archie Ross (Skip), JH Shooter (Mor), G Yeld (Cas, c).
Attendance: 1,500   *Referee*: TH Peverill (Durham)

Saturday 18 November 1899 at Lawkholme Lane, Keighley
YORKSHIRE 0 *Back*: E Bottomley (BradO). *Three-quarters*: JT Taylor (capt, WHart), AW Robinson (BradO), JE Hammond (BradO), S Neumann (BradO). *Half-backs*: GH Marsden (Mor), H Myers (Kei). *Forwards*: D Adkins (Kei), RG Bingham (Cas), W Cobby (Cas), A Cockerham (BradO), CE Holroyd (Mor), HE Ramsden (Bing), Archie Ross (Skip), G Yeld (Cas).
LANCASHIRE 0 *Back*: JC Milnes (Man). *Three-quarters*: ET Nicholson (Liv), AT Brettargh (LivOB), RH Spooner (Liv), TH Kingscote (Man). *Half-backs*: G Cookson (capt, Man), W Parlane (Man). *Forwards*: CE Allen (Liv), H Beames (LivOB), AG Davidson (Bla), CR Jackson (BroPk), WA Kingscote (Man), A Long (Bla), CVM Townsend (LivOB), RD Wood (LivOB).
Attendance: 500   *Referee*: FK Ward (Midland Counties)
Note: Abandoned 5 minutes into 'third quarter' due to thick fog (replayed 7 April 1900).

Saturday 25 November 1899 at Kilgour's Field, Penrith
CUMBERLAND 8 *Back*: T Pattinson (Asp). *Three-quarters*: A Smith (Carl), JH Blaylock (Asp, c), G Bell (PenU, t), T Routledge (Asp). *Half-backs*: JW Bell (Asp), J Hillary (Asp). *Forwards*: Joe Davidson (Asp, t), T Docker (Asp), D Graham (Asp/NewB), T Grieve (Asp), J Murray (PenU), J Sewell (Carl), J Stubbs (Carl), J Walker (Asp).
LANCASHIRE 6 *Back*: JC Milnes (Man). *Three-quarters*: TH Kingscote (Man), BC Middleton (Man, t), RH Spooner (Liv), ET Nicholson (Liv). *Half-backs*: G Cookson (Man, t), W Parlane (Man). *Forwards*: CE Allen (Liv), H Beames (LivOB), AG Davidson (Bla), CR Jackson (BroPk), WA Kingscote (Man), A Long (Bla), CVM Townsend (LivOB), RD Wood (LivOB).
Attendance: 2,000   *Referee*: H Welford (Northumberland)

Saturday 2 December 1899 at Upper Park, Birkenhead
CHESHIRE 0 *Back*: CR Hartley (Sale). *Three-quarters*: GM Bennett (BirkPk), EJ Hargreaves (BirkPk), JDK Jones (BirkPk), D McLeod (BirkPk). *Half-backs*: JC Marquis (BirkPk), H Parratt (Sale). *Forwards*: J Baxter (BirkPk), CS Edgar (BirkPk), W Fearenside (NewB), H Fletcher (Sale), RH Fry (Sale), J Hague (Sale), HC Harvey (Sale), E Herschell (BirkPk).
DURHAM 14 *Back*: RW Poole (HartOB). *Three-quarters*: W Taylor (Tud, t), J Gordon (Tud, c), NS Cox (Sund, t), BS Wellock (WHart, t). *Half-backs*: H Gibbon (Ham), W Moffet (Sund). *Forwards*: C Boddy (WHart), J Carmedy (Tud), J Frater (Tud, t), DF Hardie (ODun), GH Lewis (WHart), A Peat (SSh), J Smith (HartOB), J Stitt (Tud).
Attendance: 'small'   *Referee*: AT Kemble (Lancashire)

Saturday 9 December 1899 at Jesmond Ground, Newcastle
NORTHUMBERLAND 3 *Back*: G Dick (Rock). *Three-quarters*: GC Robinson (PerPk), B Williams (PerPk), S Anderson (Rock), FW Stone (PerPk, t). *Half-backs*: C Lawson (Wall), CW Russell (PerPk). *Forwards*: FJ Bell (Rock), WH Dick (Nor), JH Dunn (Rock), J Finlay (WHart), T Finlay (Rock), JH Greenwell (Rock), PF Hardwick (PerPk), RT Lockerby (PerPk).
LANCASHIRE 3 *Back*: JC Milnes (Man). *Three-quarters*: ET Nicholson (Liv), RH Spooner (Liv), BC Middleton (Man), TH Kingscote (Man). *Half-backs*: GG Allen (capt, Liv), G Cookson (Man). *Forwards*: GWB Ainsworth (Liv), CE Allen (Liv), AG Davidson (Bla), WA Kingscote (Man), A Long (Bla), JE Louden (Man), CVM Townsend (LivOB), RD Wood (LivOB, t).
Attendance: 3,000   *Referee*: FK Ward (Midland Counties)
Note: Abandoned 10 minutes into second half due to hard ground, result stood.

Saturday 13 January 1900 at Upper Park, Birkenhead
CHESHIRE 10 *Back*: EJ Hargreaves (BirkPk). *Three-quarters*: HP Terry (Sale, t), J Hutchinson (BirkPk), JDK Jones (BirkPk), D McLeod (BirkPk). *Half-backs*: JC Marquis (BirkPk, t), H Parratt (Sale). *Forwards*: H Alexander (BirkPk, 2c), J Baxter (BirkPk), CS Edgar (BirkPk), W Fearenside (NewB), J Fernie (NewB), J Hague (Sale), J Pickin (Bow), H Smith (BirkPk).
NORTHUMBERLAND 9 *Back*: P Moran (HartR). *Three-quarters*: FW Stone (PerPk, t), W Bates (PerPk), JH Dunn (Rock, t), S Anderson (Rock, t). *Half-backs*: EA Henderson (PerPk), CW Russell (PerPk). Forwards: FJ Bell (Rock), RW Bell (Nor), J Bryant (Nor), WH Dick (Nor), COP Gibson (Nor/OxfU), PF Hardwick (PerPk), RT Lockerby (PerPk), J Nesbitt (PerPk).
Attendance: 1,000   *Referee*: WW Higgins (Lancashire)

 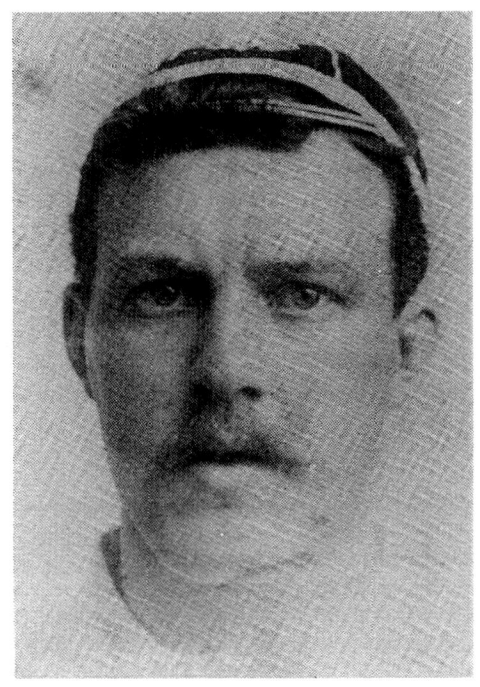

George 'Tot' Robinson was Northumberland's stand out winger during the Victorian era, registering a try in all but one of his eight England matches. A two-time winner of the Northumberland Cup with Percy Park, he represented the North four times and, following his county debut in 1894, played in 22 games for Northumberland during the Victorian era with further appearances thereafter.

Jack Pinch was Lancaster's only international player, the forward enjoying a purple patch from 1895 to 1897 whilst representing England (3 times), Lancashire (12) and the North (2). He continued to assist Lancaster after they joined the Northern Union in 1897, playing his final match in 1903.

The Yorkshire team that met Lancashire on 24th November 1894 in Manchester. Back: W Hirst (honorary secretary), W Donaldson, A Barraclough, G Nowell, Jack Riley, W Walton, JA Millar (president). Middle: T Broadley, J Arnold, JT Toothill, WJ Jackson, TH Dobson, F Firth. Front: Joe Riley, A Rigg, FW Cooper, H Ward.

The Lancashire team that played against Cheshire at Swinton on 2nd November 1895. Back: LE Pilkington, R Pierce, S Walsh, J Pinch, JJ Jones, W Parlane, SM Crook (honorary secretary). Middle: R Holmes, WB Stoddart, GE Hughes, GH Murray, J Valentine, JT Lewis, R Moss, FA Grover (vice-president). Front: GG Allen, W Manwaring.

The Cheshire side that took on Lancashire at Swinton on 2nd November 1895. Back: CC Harvey (honorary secretary), H Fletcher, EH Bradshaw, A Jones, F Ingham, AE Fenton, D Atkinson. Middle: J Baxter, JAS Cannell, H Parratt, FP Jones, S Houghton, F Hughes, AJ Chadwick. Front: S Hanson, PR Clauss.

The Durham side versus Cumberland in Gateshead on 26th October 1895. The players (in kit) are, back (standing): A Stephenson, F Marston. Third row (seated behind second row): AJ Troupe, JT Thompson. Second row (seated): RW Poole, T Martin, WE Kassell, HB Swainston, J Geenty. Front: RF Oakes, T Gibbon, J Hall (with ball), T Burt, J Taylor, TJ Lindsay.

The Cumberland team that opposed Durham on 26th October 1895 in Gateshead.
Back: T Fletcher, G Messenger, JH Blacklock, R Mumberson, G Steele, J Fawcett. Middle: IH Mawson (secretary, standing), JH Timney, J Bell, D Elliot W Cunningham, R Westray (president, standing). Front: JH Moore, R Bell, Jim Davidson, T Ritson, WS Graham.

The Westmorland team which met Northumberland in Newcastle on 21st December 1895. The players (in kit) are, back: G Fawcett, J Vity. Third row: WA Duff, W Woodhouse, E Braithwaite, W Robinson, HF Newton. Second row (seated): CB Punchard, WA Davis, J Carradus, C Heap, G Fisher. Front: AS Dixon, A Jowett, J Holmes.

Hartlepool Rovers, eight times Durham County Cup winners during the Victorian era, photographed in 1895. Back: A Quelch, M Irvin, W Burke, GE Boagey, R Snowdon, J Huntley, WH Allen (honorary secretary). Third row (standing behind seated players): E Carroll (honorary treasurer), T Richardson (president), FHR Alderson. Second row (seated): T Maynard, RW Poole, RF Oakes, D Gilchrist, C Hodgson. Front (on ground): W McSloy, P Moran, JT Thompson.

Barrow 1894-95, winners of the Lancashire Club Championship Second Class and North Western League. Back: GE Hughes, T McGerry, T Morgan, WC Sharpe, J Bowker, E Dickinson, F Hodgson (treasurer). Middle: JH Walton (secretary), G Woodhouse, C Kelly, T Dickinson, J Weatherall, C Jeffery, R Bell, R Parkinson. Front: E Dillon, R Messenger, S Northmore, W Sharp.

Rockcliff 1894-95 with the Northumberland Challenge Cup, won for seven consecutive seasons from 1889-90 to 1895-96. Back: G Steward, N Roxby (honorary secretary), WN Greenwell, A Styan, W Jackson, J Nesbitt, B Taylor, John Thompson (committee). Middle: J Taylor, S Anderson, JH Greenwell, GW Lee, EW Taylor, W Taylor, TP Alexander. Front: TC Stephenson, Joe Thompson, T Nicholson.

Tyldesley 1894-95, winners of the Lancashire Club Championship. Back: SL Warburton (president), W Roberts, R Berry, G Taylor (treasurer), G Woodward, J Berry, J Bell, GH Bell (honorary secretary). Middle: J Roberts, A Cooper, J Worthington, F Shaw, W Woodward, W Berry, J Shepherd. Front: J Harris, E Evans, J Lawton, J Miller, A Smith, H Fox.

Manningham 1895-96, first champions of the Northern Union. Back: H Jowett (honorary secretary), T Bamfort, T Wilkinson, H Tolson, F Clegg, J Thomas, H Whiteoak, A Proctor, W Robson. Middle: A Leach, W Atkinson, J Brown, A Barraclough, GE Lorimer, A Padgett, J Newton. Front: W Needham, J Williamson, R Sunderland, H Pickles.

Batley 1896-97, inaugural winners of the Northern Union Challenge Cup. Back: J Gath, JT Munns, FW Lowrie, T Wilby, JB Goodall, C Stubley, H Goodall, R Barraclough, F Fisher. Middle: M Shackleton, J Oakland, J Naylor, J Littlewood. Front: J Wilson (assistant trainer), I Shaw, AF Garner, R Spurr, G Maine, F Bennett (trainer).

Cumberland's team that lost to Kent in the County Championship final at Carlisle on 10th April 1897. The players (in kit) are, standing: W Moore, S Northmore, Jim Davidson (with ball), J Walker, S Hoggarth. Seated (left): J Young, E Knowles. Seated (right): D Elliott, JH Blacklock, T Fletcher. On ground: JH Buckett, W Young, T James, W Cunningham, R Moore.

Osbert Mackie was a strong-running three-quarter and captain of Wakefield Trinity who severed his connection with the club when it joined the breakaway Northern Union in 1895. He continued his rugby union career with Cambridge University adding a further Yorkshire appearance to two made whilst with Trinity. He went on to represent the North once, the South twice, England twice, and was a member of the 1896 touring side to South Africa.

Joe Davidson was a powerful presence in the Aspatria pack and capped 23 times for Cumberland during the Victorian period, adding further appearances beyond that. He also played four times for the North and twice for England, playing alongside older brother Jim in the match against Scotland at Blackheath in 1899.

Northumberland 1897-98, winners of the County Championship. Players (in kit) are, back: TP Galloway, P Moran, JH Greenwell, SC Lockerby, C Lawson, FW Stone, W Bates. Middle: A Taylor, RW Bell, RC Stevenson, J Dobinson, J Nesbitt, GR Gibson, T Robson, W Taylor. Front: COP Gibson, FJ Bell, S Anderson, EW Taylor, CW Russell.

Milestones & Stats 1869-1901

Saturday 20 January 1900 at Upper Park, Birkenhead
CHESHIRE 14 *Back*: CR Hartley (Sale). *Three-quarters*: JDK Jones (BirkPk, t), D McLeod (BirkPk), HP Terry (Sale, 2t), J Hutchinson (BirkPk, t). *Half-backs*: JC Marquis (BirkPk), H Parratt (Sale). *Forwards*: H Alexander (BirkPk, c), J Baxter (BirkPk), CS Edgar (BirkPk), W Fearenside (NewB), J Fernie (NewB), H Fletcher (Sale), J Hague (Sale), JH Stephens (Bow).
YORKSHIRE 9 *Back*: E Bottomley (BradO). *Three-quarters*: JT Taylor (capt, WHart, t, pg), S Neumann (BradO), G Smith (Bottomboat Trinity), JE Hammond (BradO). *Half-backs*: GH Marsden (Mor), HE Ramsden (Bing, t). *Forwards*: D Adkins (Kei), RG Bingham (Cas), A Cockerham (BradO), CE Holroyd (Mor), F Redman (Kei), Archie Ross (Skip), RF Russell (Cas), JH Shooter (Mor).
Attendance: 2,000   *Referee*: SE Wilson (Lancashire)

Saturday 27 January 1900 at Warwick Road, Carlisle
CUMBERLAND 6 *Back*: T Pattinson (Asp). *Three-quarters*: A Smith (Carl), F Spottiswood (SSh, t), G Bell (PenU), T Routledge (Asp). *Half-backs*: JW Bell (Asp, t), J Hillary (Asp). *Forwards*: Jim Davidson (Asp), Joe Davidson (Asp), T Docker (Asp), D Graham (Asp/NewB), T Grieve (Asp), T Robinson (Cock), J Sewell (Carl), J Stubbs (Carl).
YORKSHIRE 0 *Back*: W Phipps (WHart). *Three-quarters*: JT Taylor (capt, WHart), EE Walker (CamU), JE Hammond (BradO), S Neumann (BradO). *Half-backs*: GH Marsden (Mor), J Platts (Head). *Forwards*: D Adkins (Kei), W Cobby (Cas), A Cockerham (BradO), CE Holroyd (Mor), HE Ramsden (Bing), Archie Ross (Skip), RF Russell (Cas), JH Shooter (Mor).
Attendance: 1,500   *Referee*: H Welford (Northumberland)

Saturday 27 January 1900 at Horsley Hill, South Shields
DURHAM 16 *Back*: RW Poole (HartOB). *Three-quarters*: W Taylor (Tud, t), J Gordon (Tud, 2c), NS Cox (Sund), BS Wellock (WHart). *Half-backs*: H Gibbon (Ham), W Moffet (Sund, t). *Forwards*: C Boddy (WHart), J Carmedy (Tud), J Frater (Tud, t), GH Lewis (WHart, t), A Peat (SSh), J Smith (HartOB), A Stephenson (Tud), T Thornton (TynD).
NORTHUMBERLAND 0 *Back*: P Moran (HartR). *Three-quarters*: GC Robinson (PerPk), W Bates (PerPk), F Pickering (Rock), FW Stone (PerPk). *Half-backs*: HE Galloway (Nor), EA Henderson (PerPk). *Forwards*: JW Bamborough (Rock), WH Dick (Nor), JH Dunn (Rock), J Finlay (WHart), GR Gibson (Nor), PF Hardwick (PerPk), RT Lockerby (PerPk), RM Robertson (Rock).
Attendance: 4,000   *Referee*: EB Holmes (Midland Counties)

Saturday 3 March 1900 at Whalley Range, Manchester
LANCASHIRE 5 *Back*: TH Kingscote (Man). *Three-quarters*: ET Nicholson (Liv), T Brettargh (LivOB), RH Spooner (Liv), BC Middleton (Man). *Half-backs*: G Cookson (capt, Man, t), W Parlane (Man). *Forwards*: GWB Ainsworth (Liv), AG Davidson (Bla), LB Hopper (Liv), WA Kingscote (Man), A Long (Bla, c), A Mann (BroPk), CVM Townsend (LivOB), RD Wood (LivOB).
DURHAM 13 *Back*: J Hogg (WHart). *Three-quarters*: W Taylor (Tud), J Gordon (Tud, dg), NS Cox (Sund), EW Elliot (Sund, t). *Half-backs*: H Gibbon (Ham), W Moffet (Sund). *Forwards*: J Carmedy (Tud), J Frater (Tud, t), GH Lewis (WHart), J Nichol (SSh), A Peat (SSh), G Richardson (Tud), WJ Simms (WHart, t), GE Summerscales (DurC).
Attendance: 2,000   *Referee*: A Hartley (Yorkshire)

Saturday 3 March 1900 at Jesmond Ground, Newcastle
NORTHUMBERLAND 8 *Back*: T Scotland (PerPk). *Three-quarters*: GC Robinson (PerPk, c), W Bates (PerPk, t), FW Stone (PerPk), F Pickering (Rock, t). *Half-backs*: EA Henderson (PerPk), C Lawson (Wall). *Forwards*: RW Bell (Nor), WH Dick (Nor), JH Dunn (Rock), J Finlay (WHart), GR Gibson (Nor), PF Hardwick (PerPk), RT Lockerby (PerPk), S Woodburn (Wall).
CUMBERLAND 6 *Back*: T Pattinson (Asp). *Three-quarters*: F Spottiswood (SSh), A Smith (Carl, t), JB Hewitson (Asp), T Routledge (Asp). *Half-backs*: JW Bell (Asp, t), J Hillary (Asp). *Forwards*: Jim Davidson (Asp), Joe Davidson (Asp), T Docker (Asp), D Graham (Asp/NewB), T Grieve (Asp), T Robinson (Cock), J Stubbs (Carl), J Walker (Asp).
Attendance: 2,000   *Referee*: J Boyd (Scotland)

Saturday 7 April 1900 at County Ground, Claro Road, Harrogate
YORKSHIRE 24 *Back*: T Morgan (Skip). *Three-quarters*: EE Walker (CamU, t), JA Batley (Harr, dg), S Neumann (BradO, t), JE Hammond (BradO, t). *Half-backs*: GH Marsden (Mor, t), EJ Walton (Cas/OxfU). *Forwards*: RG Bingham (Cas), W Cobby (Cas, t, c), A Hodgson (Cleck), CE Holroyd (Mor), Alec Ross (Skip), Archie Ross (Skip), JH Shooter (Mor), W Stansfield (Myth, t).
LANCASHIRE 3 *Back*: JE Kidd (Eccles). *Three-quarters*: BC Middleton (Man), FWH Weaver (Liv), J Ricketts (BroPk), N Duckworth (Bla/Sale). *Half-backs*: G Cookson (Man), W Parlane (Man, t). *Forwards*: CR Jackson (BroPk), A Mann (BroPk), F Mason (Kersal), T Moore (Bla), RB Slacke (Man), JR Steele (Bla), JL Sylo-Jones (Waterloo), RD Wood (LivOB).
Attendance: 3,000   *Referee*: A Crosbie (Midland Counties)

Final table

	P	W	D	L	For	Agst	Pts
Durham	5	3	1	1	44	29	7
Cumberland	5	3	1	1	31	21	7
Yorkshire	5	3	0	2	72	29	6
Cheshire	5	2	0	3	33	57	4
Lancashire	5	1	1	3	34	51	3
Northumberland	5	1	1	3	26	53	3

PLAY-OFF TO DECIDE FIRST PLACE

Saturday 17 March 1900 at Noble Croft, Aspatria
CUMBERLAND 0 *Back*: T Pattinson (Asp). *Three-quarters*: F Spottiswood (SSh), GH Muriel (Rich), A Smith (Carl), JB Hewitson (Asp). *Half-backs*: JW Bell (Asp), J Hillary (Asp). *Forwards*: Jim Davidson (Asp), Joe Davidson (Asp), T Docker (Asp), D Graham (Asp/NewB), T Grieve (Asp), J Stubbs (Carl), J Walker (Asp), E Walsh (Carl).
DURHAM 5 *Back*: J Hogg (WHart). *Three-quarters*: W Taylor (Tud), J Gordon (Tud, c), NS Cox (Sund), EW Elliot (Sund, t). *Half-backs*: H Gibbon (Ham), W Moffet (Sund). *Forwards*: J Carmedy (Tud), J Frater (Tud), GH Lewis (WHart), A Peat (SSh), G Richardson (Tud), WJ Simms (WHart), A Stephenson (Tud), GE Summerscales (DurC).
Attendance: 'good'   *Referee*: EB Holmes (Midland Counties)

SOUTH WESTERN GROUP

Results
Devonshire 13, Cornwall 0
Cornwall 3, Gloucestershire 5
Somersetshire 6, Cornwall 3
Gloucestershire 3, Devonshire 16
Somersetshire 8, Gloucestershire 3
Devonshire 9, Somersetshire 0

Final table

	P	W	D	L	For	Agst	Pts
Devonshire	3	3	0	0	38	3	6
Somersetshire	3	2	0	1	14	15	4
Gloucestershire	3	1	0	2	11	27	2
Cornwall	3	0	0	3	6	24	0

SOUTH EASTERN GROUP A

Results
Kent 15, Middlesex 3
East Midlands 3, Midland Counties 6
Middlesex 6, East Midlands 8
Midland Counties 0, Surrey 7
Kent 9, Midland Counties 3
Surrey 3, East Midlands 3
East Midlands 14, Kent 8

Middlesex 13, Surrey 10
Midland Counties 0, Middlesex 6
Surrey 3, Kent 3

Play-off to decide first place
East Midlands 5, Kent 8

Final table

	P	W	D	L	For	Agst	Pts
Kent	4	2	1	1	35	23	5
East Midlands	4	2	1	1	28	23	5
Surrey	4	1	2	1	23	19	4
Middlesex	4	2	0	2	28	33	3
Midland Counties	4	1	0	3	9	25	2

SOUTH EASTERN GROUP B

Result
Hampshire 24, Eastern Counties 0

Final table

	P	W	D	L	For	Agst
Hampshire	1	1	0	0	24	0
Eastern Counties	1	0	0	1	0	24

South Eastern Group Final
Kent 29, Hampshire 0

Southern Final
Kent 3, Devonshire 12

COUNTY CHAMPIONSHIP FINAL

Saturday 7 April 1900 at County Ground, St Thomas, Exeter
DURHAM 11 *Back*: J Hogg (WHart). *Three-quarters*: W Taylor (Tud), J Gordon (Tud, c), NS Cox (Sund), EW Elliot (Sund). *Half-backs*: H Gibbon (Ham), W Moffet (Sund). *Forwards*: J Carmedy (Tud, t), J Frater (Tud), B Hamm (Tud), GH Lewis (WHart), G Richardson (Tud), WJ Simms (WHart), A Stephenson (Tud, t), GE Summerscales (DurC, t).
DEVONSHIRE 3 *Back*: A Richards (Barn). *Three-quarters*: HBJ Taylor (NewA/Black), EJ Vivyan (DevA), T Mills (RNEC), SF Coopper (RNEC). *Half-backs*: T Dunn (Torq), J Jones (unattached). *Forwards*: C Avery (Ply), P Baron (Sid), D Dobson (NewA), A Ferris (DevA), A O'Neill (Torq), C Thomas (capt, Barn), W Spiers (DevA), EW Roberts (RNEC, t).
Attendance: 12,000   *Referee*: EB Holmes (Midland Counties)

NON-COUNTY CHAMPIONSHIP MATCHES

Monday 30 October 1899 at Lock Lane, Castleford
YORKSHIRE 3 *Back*: AM Sullivan (Cas). *Three-quarters*: JT Taylor (capt, WHart), AW Robinson (Kei), JE Hammond (BradO, t), S Neumann (BradO). *Half-backs*: GH Marsden (Mor), J Shepherd (Cas). *Forwards*: D Adkins (Kei), W Cobby (Cas), A Cockerham (BradO), CE Holroyd (Mor), HE Ramsden (Bing), Archie Ross (Skip), RF Russell (Cas), AEN Yeadon (Head).
GLAMORGANSHIRE 5 *Back*: HB Winfield (Car, c). *Three-quarters*: V Huzzey (Car), G Davies (Swa, t), D Rees (Swa), W Llewellyn (Llwyn). *Half-backs*: G Hughes (Car), W Jones (Aber). *Forwards*: WH Alexander (Llwyn), J Blake (Car), H Davies (Swa), J Jenkins (Tre), V Jones (Aber), J Matthews (Bri), A Thomas (Nea), R Thomas (Swa).
Attendance: 3,000   *Referee*: JW Maclean (Lancashire)

Friday 1 December 1899 at Lansdowne Road, Dublin
COUNTY DUBLIN 39 *Back*: PE O'Brien-Butler (Monk). *Three-quarters*: GP Doran (Lans, 2t), BR Doran (Lans, t), J McKinlay (OWes, 2t), EF Campbell (Monk). *Half-backs*: LM Magee (BecR, 3c), G Meldon (Wand). *Forwards*: C Caffrey (Monk), JJ Coffey (Lans, t), GT Hamlet (OWes), HJ Knox (Lans, t), TJ Little (BecR, 2t), HJ Millar (Monk, t), CCH Moriarty (Monk, t), J Robinson (OWes).
CUMBERLAND 0 *Back*: T Pattinson (Asp). *Three-quarters*: AJ Richardson (PenU), G Bell (PenU), JH Blaylock (Asp), T Routledge (Asp). *Half-backs*: JW Bell (Asp), J Hillary (Asp). *Forwards*: Joe Davidson (Asp), T Docker (Asp), T Grieve (Asp), J Murray (PenU), J Sewell (Carl), J Stubbs (Carl), J Walker (Asp), J Yeowart (Asp).
Attendance: 1,500   *Referee*: RW Jeffares (Ireland)

Saturday 2 December 1899 at Agricultural Grounds, Balmoral, Belfast
ULSTER 39 *Back*: Watters (MethC). *Three-quarters*: IG Davidson (NIFC, 3t), C Reid (NIFC, t, dg), JB Allison (QCB, t), S McCausland (MethC, t). *Half-backs*: A Barr (capt, MethC), JH Ferris (QCB, t). *Forwards*: CWL Alexander (QCB, t), WG Byron (NIFC), F Gardiner (NIFC), AG Heron (QCB, t), ST Irwin (QCB, 4c), TMW McGown (NIFC), G Moffatt (BelA), James Moffatt (BelA).
CUMBERLAND 0 *Back*: T Pattinson (Asp). *Three-quarters*: G Bell (PenU), AJ Richardson (PenU), JH Blaylock (Asp), T Routledge (Asp). *Half-backs*: JW Bell (Asp), J Hillary (Asp). *Forwards*: Joe Davidson (Asp), T Docker (Asp), T Grieve (Asp), J Murray (PenU), J Sewell (Carl), J Stubbs (Carl), J Walker (Asp), J Yeowart (Asp).
Attendance: 1,000   *Referee*: C Lefevre (Ireland)

Milestones & Stats 1869-1901 449

Wednesday 10 January 1900 at Cardiff Arms Park
GLAMORGANSHIRE 21 *Back*: HB Winfield (Car, 3c). *Three-quarters*: W Jones (Car), PF Bush (Car, t), V Huzzey (Car, 2t), LJ Deere (Mou). *Half-backs*: R Jones (Swa), C Sweet-Escott (Car). *Forwards*: J Blake (Car), A Bolton (Peny), A Brice (Aber), G Dobson (Car), F Kirby (Pen, t), F Miller (Mou), F Scrines (Swa, t), J Wheeler (Car).
DURHAM 3 *Back*: W Hector (SSh). *Three-quarters*: W Taylor (Tud), J Gordon (Tud), NS Cox (Sund), EW Elliot (Sund). *Half-backs*: H Gibbon (Ham), W Moffet (Sund, t). *Forwards*: J Carmedy (Tud), J Frater (Tud), J Nichol (SSh), A Peat (SSh), J Smith (HartOB), J Stitt (Tud), HA Taylor (Sund), J Wilson (Ham).
Attendance: 2,000   *Referee*: ATW James (Newport)

Thursday 11 January 1900 at Kingsholm, Gloucester
GLOUCESTERSHIRE 18 *Back*: G Romans (Glo, t, 3c). *Three-quarters*: PL Nicholas (OxfU), FM Luce (OxfU), AS Dryborough (Bris), CC Smith (Glo). *Half-backs*: SH Foster (Bris), W Needs (Bris). *Forwards*: F Channon (Bris, 2t), M Courtney (Bris), T Downing (Lydney), C Hall (Glo, t), FW Harrison (Stroud), J Lewis (Glo), F Oswell (Glo), C Smith (Stroud).
DURHAM 6 *Back*: W Hector (SSh). *Three-quarters*: W Taylor (Tud, t), J Gordon (Tud), NS Cox (Sund), SH Irvin (HartOB). *Half-backs*: R Allison (TynD), BS Oughtred (HartR). *Forwards*: J Carmedy (Tud), J Frater (Tud), A Peat (SSh, t), J Smith (HartOB), J Stitt (Tud), GE Summerscales (DurC), T Thornton (TynD), G Wreford-Brown (Sund).
Attendance: 500   *Referee*: GH Harnett (Kent)

Saturday 13 January 1900 at County Ground, St Thomas, Exeter
DEVONSHIRE 14 *Back*: JE Knight (DevA). *Three-quarters*: SF Coopper (RNEC), WS Boyle (Barn), EJ Vivyan (DevA, c), T Fitzgerald (Sid). *Half-backs*: T Dunn (Torq, t), J Jones (unattached, t). *Forwards*: P Baron (Sid), A Brock (Exe), R Chichester (Barn), A Kelly (Tiv), J Masters (Ply), A O'Neil (Torq), T Ramsey (Ply), EW Roberts (RNEC, 2t).
DURHAM 8 *Back*: SH Irvin (HartOB). *Three-quarters*: W Taylor (Tud, t), J Gordon (Tud, c), NS Cox (Sund), EW Elliot (Sund). *Half-backs*: H Gibbon (Ham), W Moffet (Sund, t). *Forwards*: J Carmedy (Tud), J Frater (Tud), J Nichol (SSh), A Peat (SSh), J Smith (HartOB), J Stitt (Tud), GE Summerscales (DurC), J Wilson (Ham).
Attendance: 3,000   *Referee*: GH Harnett (Kent)

ENGLAND TRIAL MATCHES

Saturday 23 December 1899 at Upper Park, Birkenhead
NORTH 3 *Back*: CR Hartley (Sale). *Three-quarters*: ET Nicholson (Liv), AT Brettargh (LivOB), NS Cox (Sund), JE Hammond (BradO, t). *Half-backs*: JC Marquis (BirkPk), GH Marsden (Mor). *Forwards*: CE Allen (Liv), J Baxter (BirkPk), FJ Bell (Rock), RW Bell (Nor), W Cobby (Cas), A Cockerham (BradO), Joe Davidson (Asp), T Grieve (Asp).
SOUTH 0 *Back*: HT Gamlin (Well). *Three-quarters*: SF Coopper (RNEC/Black), WS Boyle (Barn), GW Gordon-Smith (Black), R Forrest (Black). *Half-backs*: RH Cattell (Black), RO Schwarz (Rich). *Forwards*: H Atterbury (Northn), CE Barry (OxfU), S Reynolds (Rich), EW Roberts (RNEC), AM Rouse (RIEC), MS Scott (Leic), AF Todd (Black), HT Weston (Northn).
Attendance: 3,000   *Referee*: A Hartley (Yorkshire)

Saturday 24 February 1900 at Welford Road, Leicester
SOUTH 22 *Back*: G Romans (Glo, 2c). *Three-quarters*: SF Coopper (RNEC/Black, 2t), WS Boyle (Barn), WL Bunting (Rich, t), R Forrest (Black, 2t). *Half-backs*: HE Kingston (Northn, t), GT Unwin (Black). *Forwards*: J Daniell (capt, CamU), NC Fletcher (OMT/CamU), C Hall (Glo), AFC Luxmoore (Rich), S Matthews (Leic), S Reynolds (Rich), CT Scott (CamU), AF Todd (Black).
NORTH 9 *Back*: RW Poole (HartOB). *Three-quarters*: ET Nicholson (Liv), AT Brettargh (LivOB, 2t), JT Taylor (capt, WHart), J Hutchinson (BirkPk). *Half-backs*: JC Marquis (BirkPk), GH Marsden (Mor). *Forwards*: H Alexander (BirkPk), RW Bell (Nor, t), A Cockerham (BradO), Jim Davidson (Asp), J Frater (Tud), J Hague (Sale), JH Shooter (Mor), RD Wood (LivOB).
Attendance: 4,000/5,000   *Referee*: GH Harnett (Kent)

INTERNATIONAL CHAMPIONSHIP

Saturday 6 January 1900 at Kingsholm, Gloucester
ENGLAND 3 *Back*: HT Gamlin (Well). *Three-quarters*: ET Nicholson (Liv, t), AT Brettargh (LivOB), GW Gordon-Smith (Black), SF Coopper (RNEC/Black). *Half-backs*: RH Cattell (capt, Black), GH Marsden (Mor). *Forwards*: J Baxter (BirkPk), FJ Bell (Rock), RW Bell (Nor/CamU), W Cobby (Cas), A Cockerham (BradO), JW Jarman (Bris), S Reynolds (Rich), CT Scott (CamU).
WALES 13 *Back*: WJ Bancroft (capt, Swa, 2c, pg). *Three-quarters*: W Llewellyn (Llwyn), D Rees (Swa), G Davies (Swa), WJ Trew (Swa, t). *Half-backs*: GH Lloyd (New), LA Phillips (New). *Forwards*: J Blake (Car), G Boots (New), A Brice (Aber), R Hellings (Llwyn, t), JJ Hodges (New), F Miller (Mou), R Thomas (Swa), WH Williams (Pontymister).
Attendance: 15,000   *Referee*: A Turnbull (Scotland)

Saturday 3 February 1900 at Athletic Ground, Richmond
ENGLAND 15 *Back*: HT Gamlin (DevA). *Three-quarters*: ET Nicholson (Liv), JT Taylor (WHart), GW Gordon-Smith (Black, t, dg), GC Robinson (PerPk, 2t). *Half-backs*: JC Marquis (BirkPk), GH Marsden (Mor). *Forwards*: H Alexander (BirkPk, c), J Baxter (BirkPk), RW Bell (Nor/CamU), J Daniell (capt, CamU), S Reynolds (Rich), CT Scott (CamU), JH Shooter (Mor), AF Todd (Black).
IRELAND 4 *Back*: PE O'Brien-Butler (Monk). *Three-quarters*: GP Doran (Lans), C Reid (NIFC), JB Allison (QCB, dg), EF Campbell (Monk). *Half-backs*: JH Ferris (QCB), LM Magee (capt, BecR). *Forwards*: CE Allen (Der), JJ Coffrey (Lans), F Gardiner (NIFC), ST Irwin (QCB), AWD Meares (Wand), PC Nicholson (DubU), M Ryan (RockC), J Sealy (DubU).
Attendance: 7,000   *Referee*: DG Findlay (Scotland)

Saturday 10 March 1900 at Inverleith, Edinburgh
SCOTLAND 0 *Back*: H Rottenburg (LonS). *Three-quarters*: T Scott (Lang), GT Campbell (LonS), AR Smith (LonS), WH Welsh (EdinU). *Half-backs*: JI Gillespie (EdinA), RT Neilson (WoS). *Forwards*: LHI Bell (EdinA), GG Kerr (EdinW), WMC McEwan (EdinA), A Mackinnon (LonS), MC Morrison (capt, RHSFP), R Scott (Haw), WP Scott (WoS), HO Smith (Wat).
ENGLAND 0 *Back*: HT Gamlin (DevA). *Three-quarters*: R Forrest (Black), WL Bunting

(Rich), GW Gordon-Smith (Black), GC Robinson (PerPk). *Half-backs*: JC Marquis (BirkPk), GH Marsden (Mor). *Forwards*: H Alexander (BirkPk), J Baxter (BirkPk), RW Bell (Nor/CamU), J Daniell (capt, CamU), AFC Luxmoore (Rich), S Reynolds (Rich), JH Shooter (Mor), AF Todd (Black).
Attendance: 20,000   *Referee*: MG Delaney (Ireland)

Other results
Wales 12, Scotland 3
Ireland 0, Scotland 0
Ireland 0, Wales 3

Final table

	P	W	D	L	For	Agst
Wales	3	3	0	0	28	6
England	3	1	1	1	18	17
Scotland	3	0	2	1	3	12
Ireland	3	0	1	2	4	18

Jim Buckett of Millom made a total 35 Cumberland appearances across both rugby codes.
Lancashire Daily Post, 1900

1900-1901

THE WESTMORLAND AND NORTH LANCASHIRE LEAGUE
The Westmorland and District League, played under the auspices of the Northern Union, was renamed the Westmorland and North Lancashire League for 1900-01, due to the fact that six of the nine competing clubs were based in the latter region.[268]

YORKSHIRE SECOND COMPETITION: KIRKSTALL CHANGE DIVISIONS
Kirkstall began 1900-01 in the West Division of Northern Union's Yorkshire Second Competition but, having played three matches, were transferred to the East Division during September by the County Committee in order to level up the two groups numerically. Otley were similarly ordered to transfer from West to East but refused, citing travel and financial issues. However, after Luddendenfoot and Elland, both of the West Division, disbanded, Otley were reinstated in the latter at the start of October.[269]

ASPATRIA RUGBY UNION: A NOMINAL EXISTENCE
When Cumberland's Rugby Union Committee selected the county team for its opening match against Durham at Carlisle on 20th October, they included four forwards whose 'club' was listed as 'Aspatria'. In fact, the Aspatria rugby union club did not play a match during the 1900-01 season, its members having helped create the new Aspatria Northern Union club.

The rugby union club was quoted as having a 'nominal existence,' the players selected for Cumberland being those still loyal to the older code.[270]

YORKSHIRE'S DECLINING REPUTATION

Following two heavy 'tour' defeats during October to Devonshire (24-0) and Glamorganshire (47-3), Yorkshire (Rugby Union) were beaten 21-0 by Durham in its opening county championship match at West Hartlepool on 3rd November. The *Leeds Mercury* bemoaned the demise of rugby union in the county: 'Rugby Unionism in Yorkshire cannot be said to be flourishing. There is for this probably more than one cause, but it may safely be asserted that the best interests of the game have not been promoted by Leagues [where] clubs financially weak were at a disadvantage. They could not offer the attractions to players held out by the financially strong organisations, and their performances in the field were in consequence not so attractive to followers of the game. Under these circumstances, it was inevitable that the weaker clubs should go to the wall. Everyone can see that such a system is inimical to genuine sport, and that only time was required to bring about the natural consequence – decay.'[271]

PENRITH UNITED JOIN THE NORTHERN UNION

A meeting of the Penrith United club took place at the Red Lion Hotel, Carlisle, on Wednesday 7th November, to discuss a proposal to join the Northern Union. It was seen as the only way to continue playing rugby in the town because it was difficult arranging fixtures as few clubs in the area still played under the Rugby Union code. The motion was carried and they were subsequently admitted to the Cumberland Senior League for 1900-01, playing their first match in the competition on 24th November 1900 at home to Wath Brow. Penrith were the fourth Cumbrian club to defect to the Northern Union since 1897. Only Carlisle and newcomer Aspatria Agricultural College remained as members of the Cumberland Rugby Union.[272]

LANCASHIRE VERSUS YORKSHIRE: A POOR ATTENDANCE

The traditional rugby union clash between Lancashire and Yorkshire took place on 17th November at Fallowfield, Manchester. The resultant 5-5 draw was considered a drab affair, not helped by cold and wet weather. The *Manchester Guardian* commented: 'The poor attendance on Saturday afternoon showed that the Lancashire Football Club has started none too soon to preserve the vital spark of Lancashire interest in the Rugby Union game from absolute extinction. The club is trying to rejuvenate itself, and at the same time to provide a permanent following for Rugby Unionism by creating what it has not hitherto possessed – an individual membership. It is a pity, of course, that Rugby Union football should no longer be able itself to command a large following in the county. For so exceptional a fixture as the Lancashire and Yorkshire match the gate did not number more than 600 or 700, and these, scattered around the large Fallowfield enclosure, appeared a mere handful of people.'[273]

LANCASHIRE VERSUS YORKSHIRE: THE CHOICE OF FALLOWFIELD

The choice of Fallowfield for the Lancashire versus Yorkshire rugby union match on 17th November drew some negative comment, with the *Yorkshire Post* particularly critical: 'It surprised many football men to find that the match was taken to a ground so removed from a centre of population as Fallowfield. The last match between the Unions took place at Whalley Range, the scene of many a big struggle in the palmy days of both county Unions. The reason why Fallowfield was chosen on this occasion is that the stands on the Whalley Range ground are so dilapidated that it is not safe to permit the public to use them. The ground is liable to be swallowed up any day by the vandals of the bricks and mortar trade, and any outlay on the stands is inadvisable, supposing the Manchester club had the wherewithal to attempt such an enterprise, which is doubtful. A large gate would not have been expected under any circumstances. The attractions of the Manchester City Association club, and of the Northern Union organisations, have left very lean pickings for the adherents of the Rugby Union in Cottonopolis.' Despite the downbeat appraisal, Whalley Range provided the venue for Lancashire's next match against Cumberland seven days later.[274]

THE VICTORIA UNIVERSITY

Victoria University were beaten 14-0 by Yorkshire under Rugby Union rules at Yorkshire College, Leeds, on 5th December. Victoria University was described as a 'Federal' University and created in 1880 as a joint enterprise by several northern colleges, an arrangement continuing until 1904. The University team included players from Owen's College (Manchester), University College (Liverpool), and Yorkshire College (Leeds).

BINGLEY'S POSTS REMOVED

Bingley was all set to entertain Shipley in the Northern Union's Yorkshire Second Competition (West Division) on 8th December but when the teams and spectators arrived it was discovered that the goal-posts had disappeared! The culprit was the landlord who claimed that Bingley was in arrears with the rent. The match was consequently cancelled.[275]

END OF AN ERA
The Victorian era ended with the death of Queen Victoria on Tuesday 22nd January. Several rugby union matches were postponed on the following Saturday out of respect, including Lancashire versus Victoria University, Northumberland versus Durham, and Yorkshire versus Cumberland, although many club matches still went ahead. On Saturday 2nd February, the day of Queen Victoria's funeral, every match across all codes of football was postponed.

THE NORTH WESTERN LEAGUE
Millom won the North Western League for the fifth consecutive year; the first under Rugby Union rules, the latter four with the Northern Union. Unlike previous seasons, when north Lancashire clubs had taken part, the five competing teams were all from Cumberland. Four of them also participated in the Cumberland Senior League, the exception being Millom who, based in south Cumberland, continued to ignore that competition. A report suggested that their performance in the North Western League demonstrated that Millom would be a strong contender if they entered the Cumberland Senior League. Maryport won the latter but finished last in the North Western League.[276]

SOUTH SHIELDS JOIN THE NORTHERN UNION
South Shields, the Durham Rugby Union County Cup holders, caused a sensation when its members unanimously elected to join the Northern Union, the first club from that county to defect. The decision was taken at a meeting held in St. Thomas's Hall on 21st June 1901 because 'promises made to them had come to naught, and the Durham [Rugby Union] League was as far off as ever'. They also believed that the Northern Union authorities 'were prepared to do a great deal to establish their game in the county [of Durham]'.[277] The Northern Union meeting at the Spread Eagle Hotel, Manchester, on 2nd July, confirmed their membership.

1900-1901 STATISTICS

NORTHERN UNION

LANCASHIRE SENIOR COMPETITION

Final table	P	W	D	L	For	Agst	Pts
Oldham	26	22	1	3	301	67	45
Swinton	26	21	2	3	283	66	44
Runcorn	26	20	0	6	240	100	40
Broughton Rangers	26	17	2	7	211	84	36
Salford	26	15	0	11	229	149	30
Warrington	26	12	3	11	149	126	27
Leigh	26	12	2	12	157	143	26
Barrow	26	10	2	14	140	169	22
Wigan	26	8	3	15	98	227	19
Rochdale Hornets	26	8	2	16	103	257	18
Millom	26	8	0	18	85	194	16
Stockport	26	6	3	17	102	184	15
St Helens*	26	6	2	18	82	228	12
Widnes	26	6	0	20	85	271	12

*Two points deducted for breach of professional rules

Play off to decide bottom place
St Helens 3, Widnes 0 (Wilderspool, Warrington)
(Widnes declared as finishing in bottom place)

LANCASHIRE SECOND COMPETITION

Final table	P	W	D	L	For	Agst	Pts
Morecambe	16	12	0	4	107	53	24
Birkenhead Wanderers	16	11	0	5	111	37	22
Lancaster	16	8	2	6	94	58	18
Altrincham	16	8	1	7	108	64	17
Radcliffe	16	8	1	7	72	95	17
Werneth	16	7	1	8	66	72	15
Whitworth	16	7	0	9	55	78	14
Tyldesley	16	6	1	9	59	89	13
Leigh Shamrocks	16	2	0	14	33	159	4
Record expunged:							
Fleetwood	5	0	1	4	10	40	1

Note: Fleetwood disbanded (Jan 1901).

Promotion Test Match
Widnes 7, Morecambe 0 (at Springfield Park, Wigan)
(Widnes retain place in Lancashire Senior Competition)

YORKSHIRE SENIOR COMPETITION

Final table	P	W	D	L	For	Agst	Pts
Bradford*	30	26	1	3	324	98	51
Halifax	30	22	3	5	219	72	47
Hunslet	30	20	0	10	193	120	40
Batley	30	17	5	8	203	120	39
Hull**	30	19	1	10	181	110	37
Huddersfield	30	17	1	12	181	129	35
Brighouse Rangers	30	16	0	14	249	154	32
Hull Kingston Rovers	30	15	2	13	182	168	32
Wakefield Trinity	30	14	3	13	207	203	31
Leeds Parish Church	30	12	6	12	121	190	30
Bramley	30	12	5	13	155	199	29
Manningham	30	9	1	20	80	231	19
Leeds	30	7	3	20	138	236	17
Holbeck*	30	7	3	20	135	207	15
Castleford	30	5	4	21	103	225	14
Liversedge	30	2	2	26	94	303	6

*Two points deducted for breach of professional rules
**Two points deducted for breach of work clause

YORKSHIRE SECOND COMPETITION (WEST)

Final table	P	W	D	L	For	Agst	Pts
Heckmondwike	20	17	0	3	263	40	34
Keighley	20	15	0	5	195	49	30
Sowerby Bridge	20	15	0	5	132	54	30
Shipley	20	14	1	5	144	60	29
Dewsbury	20	11	1	8	114	106	23
Hebden Bridge	20	8	2	10	91	119	18
Otley	20	7	3	10	114	106	17
Bingley	20	2	8	10	24	134	12
Todmorden	20	4	3	13	98	73	11
Idle	20	4	3	13	39	255	11
Windhill	20	2	1	17	33	251	5
Record expunged:							
Kirkstall	3	1	0	2	15	37	2
Luddendenfoot	3	0	0	3	0	36	0
Birstal	9	1	0	8	24	124	2

Note 1: Kirstall and Otley relocated from West Competition to East (Sep 1900). Otley objected and reinstated in West (Oct 1900).
Note 2: Luddendenfoot (Sep 1900), Birstal (Jan 1901) both suspended.
Note 3: Elland disbanded (Sep 1900) without playing a match.
Note 4: Nine unplayed fixtures declared scoreless draws, affecting Bingley (7 matches), Todmorden (3), Hebden Bridge, Idle, Otley (2 each), Shipley, Windhill (1 each).

YORKSHIRE SECOND COMPETITION (EAST)

Final table	P	W	D	L	For	Agst	Pts
York	22	21	0	1	438	34	42
Normanton	22	20	1	1	229	53	41
Outwood Church	22	11	4	7	81	126	26
Kinsley	22	11	3	8	124	104	25
Ossett*	22	11	3	8	104	128	23
Kirkstall	22	10	2	10	75	99	22
Goole	22	9	2	11	136	100	20
Featherstone	22	8	1	13	68	148	17
York Melbourne	22	7	2	13	65	134	16
Alverthorpe	22	6	2	14	55	140	14
Pontefract	22	4	1	17	54	197	9
Eastmoor	22	2	3	17	45	211	7

*Two points deducted for using ineligible player
Note: Three unplayed fixtures declared scoreless draws, affecting Kinsley (2 matches), Goole, Kirkstall, Pontefract, York Melbourne (1 each).

Yorkshire Second Competition Final
York 7, Heckmondwike 0 (at Clarence Street, Leeds)
(York declared Yorkshire Second Competition winner)

Promotion Test Match
York 0, Liversedge 0 (at Parkside, Hunslet)

Promotion Test Match Replay
York 0, Liversedge 0 (at Belle Vue, Wakefield)

Promotion Test Match Second Replay
York 10, Liversedge 6 (at Clarence Street, Leeds)
(York promoted to Yorkshire Senior Competition, Liversedge relegated)

CUMBERLAND SENIOR COMPETITION

Final table	P	W	D	L	For	Agst	Pts
Maryport	12	9	0	3	98	17	18
Workington	12	8	1	3	78	30	17
Whitehaven Recreation	12	7	1	4	69	27	15
Wath Brow	12	7	0	5	42	29	14
Seaton	12	5	2	5	61	30	12
Aspatria	12	4	0	8	38	48	8
Penrith United	12	0	0	12	5	210	0

NORTH WESTERN LEAGUE

Final table	P	W	D	L	For	Agst	Pts
Millom	8	6	0	2	72	12	12
Seaton	8	4	1	3	29	30	9
Whitehaven Recreation	8	4	1	3	24	34	9
Workington	8	2	3	3	21	26	7
Maryport	8	1	1	6	16	60	3

WESTMORLAND AND NORTH LANCASHIRE LEAGUE

Final table	P	W	D	L	For	Agst	Pts
Kendal Hornets	14	11	1	2	154	22	23
Lancaster Marsh Hornets*	13	9	2	2	89	33	18
Lancaster 'A'	10	7	1	2	94	20	15
Ulverston	11	7	1	3	87	22	15
Holme Wanderers	15	6	2	7	61	97	14
Carnforth	15	5	1	9	79	116	11
Morecambe 'A'*	9	4	0	5	35	45	6
Kirkby Lonsdale	13	1	0	12	16	179	2
Morecambe Parish Church	8	0	0	8	3	84	0

*Two points deducted for using ineligible players
Note 1: Morecambe Parish Church resigned 14 February; results remain in table.
Note 2: Fixtures incomplete due to postponements.

NORTHERN UNION CHALLENGE CUP (64 entries)
Try – 3 points; all goals – 2.

First Round
Aspatria 4, Altrincham 3
Barrow 11, Brighouse Rangers 0 (replay ordered after protest)
Batley w/o Elland (disbanded)
Birkenhead Wanderers 2, Millom 0
Bradford 7, Swinton 2
Dewsbury 9, Featherstone 5
Goole 2, St Helens 12
Hebden Bridge 6, Whitworth 0
Heckmondwike 8, Seaton 0
Huddersfield 6, Hull 3
Hull Kingston Rovers 4, Salford 0
Hunslet 8, Wath Brow 0
Keighley 13, Kinsley 0
Lancaster 3, Maryport 3
Leeds 0, Warrington 19
Leeds Parish Church 11, Radcliffe 0
Leigh 38, Alverthorpe 0
Liversedge 3, Normanton 2
Manningham 0, Castleford 0
Morecambe 11, Pontefract 0
Otley 0, Oldham 19 (at Oldham)
Outwood Church 2, Holbeck 5
Rochdale Hornets 3, Bramley 7
Runcorn 18, Wigan 0
Stockport 13, Shipley 2
Todmorden 2, Sowerby Bridge 11
Tyldesley 3, Broughton Rangers 24 (at Broughton Rangers)
Wakefield Trinity 28, Eastmoor 6
Whitehaven Recreation 0, Widnes 3
Windhill 3, Ossett 5
Workington w/o Werneth (withdrew)
York 10, Halifax 2

First Round Replays
Barrow 0, Brighouse Rangers 2
Castleford 21, Manningham 2
Maryport 3, Lancaster 0

Second Round
Aspatria 2, Wakefield Trinity 21 (at Wakefield Trinity)
Batley 6, Huddersfield 2
Bramley 7, Oldham 10
Castleford 3, Workington 2
Dewsbury 8, Morecambe 0
Hebden Bridge 3, Broughton Rangers 33
Holbeck 3, Bradford 6
Maryport 0, Hull Kingston Rovers 11 (at Hull KR)
Keighley 5, York 5
Liversedge 0, Leeds Parish Church 5
Ossett 5, Birkenhead Wanderers 5
Runcorn 16, Leigh 4
St Helens 0, Stockport 0
Sowerby Bridge 3, Brighouse Rangers 6
Warrington 19, Heckmondwike 2
Widnes 8, Hunslet 0

Second Round Replays
Birkenhead Wanderers 20, Ossett 2
Stockport 5, St Helens 11
York 12, Keighley 0

Third Round
Birkenhead Wanderers 2, Widnes 10
Brighouse Rangers 0, Hull Kingston Rovers 7
Broughton Rangers 4, Oldham 11
Dewsbury 3, Castleford 5
Runcorn 21, York 0
St Helens 5, Batley 7
Wakefield Trinity 4, Bradford 5
Warrington 11, Leeds Parish Church 0

Fourth Round
Batley 5, Runcorn 2
Hull Kingston Rovers 5, Castleford 5
Warrington 10, Bradford 8
Widnes 0, Oldham 8

Fourth Round Replay
Castleford 7, Hull Kingston Rovers 2

Semi-finals
Batley 9, Oldham 2 (at Fartown, Huddersfield)
Warrington 21, Castleford 5 (at Wheater's Field, Broughton)

FINAL
Saturday 27 April 1901 at Headingley, Leeds
BATLEY 6 *Back*: A Garner. *Three-quarters*: WP Davies (t), D Fitzgerald, JB Goodall, FWH Auty (t). *Half-backs*: J Midgley, J Oakland (capt). *Forwards*: F Fisher, E Fozzard, F Hollingworth, P Judge, G Maine, J Rodgers, R Spurr, C Stubley.
WARRINGTON 0 *Back*: J Hallam. *Three-quarters*: J Fish, D Isherwood (capt), G Dickenson, E Harris. *Half-backs*: R Bate, J Duckworth. *Forwards*: A Boardman, J Cunningham, J Eden, J Edmondson, T Fell, D Morrison, J Scholtz, J Swift.
Attendance: 29,563   *Referee*: J Kidd (Millom)

SOUTH WEST LANCASHIRE AND BORDER TOWNS CHALLENGE CUP (8 entries)
Try – 3 points; all goals – 2.

First Round
Leigh 15, Tyldesley 2
Swinton 6, Runcorn 5
Warrington 20, Widnes 7
Wigan 0, St Helens 7

Semi-finals
Swinton 0, Leigh 4
Warrington 6, St Helens 5

FINAL

Monday 29 April 1901 at Springfield Park, Wigan
LEIGH 0 *Back*: E Pearson (capt). *Three-quarters*: T Davies, S Johnson, T Kight, F Ganley.
Half-backs: JH Dunbavin, J Molyneux. *Forwards*: G Boardman, E Clare, J Eccleston,
H McMasters, J Ramsdale, J Roberts, W Roberts, W Webster.
WARRINGTON 0 *Back*: J Hallam. *Three-quarters*: J Fish, D Isherwood (capt),
G Dickenson, E Ratcliffe. *Half-backs*: J Allen, A Burgess. *Forwards*: A Boardman, J Eden,
J Edmondson, T Fell, DF Mereweather, D Morrison, J Swift, J Taylor.
Attendance: 6,000   *Referee*: J Kidd (Millom)

FINAL REPLAY

Tuesday 30 April 1901 at Lowerhouse Lane, Widnes
LEIGH w/o **WARRINGTON**
Cup awarded to Leigh, Warrington unable to raise a team.

COUNTY CHAMPIONSHIP

Saturday 20 October 1900 at Belle Vue, Wakefield
YORKSHIRE 40 *Back*: H Taylor (Hull). *Three-quarters*: A Hambrecht (Bram, 3t, g),
W Dewhirst (Hud), JE Parker (Bram, 2t, 2g), AW Robinson (HKR, t). *Half-backs*: D Frank
(Hull), GH Marsden (Brad). *Forwards*: A Barker (Mann), J Gath (capt, Heck, t), G Hewlett
(LeePC), J Hutt (Brad), A Laidlaw (Brad), A Lunn (Hun, g), A Starks (HKR, 4g),
H Topham (Bram, t).
CHESHIRE 0 *Back*: J Jolley (Run). *Three-quarters*: D Jones (Run), T Wilkinson (Run),
J Worsley (Stock), W Robinson (Stock). *Half-backs*: F Bevan (Stock), J Faulkner (capt, Run).
Forwards: F Darlington (Run), H Farmer (Run), W Oram (Stock), M Owen (Stock),
RT Reece (Run), W Simister (Stock), J Trotter (Stock), S Walker (Run).
Attendance: 6,000   *Referee*: W McCutcheon (Oldham)

Saturday 20 October 1900 at Lonsdale Park, Workington
CUMBERLAND 2 *Back*: W Little (Sea). *Three-quarters*: JH Timney (Mary), G Whitehead
(Mil), J Young (Mil), J Varty (Asp). *Half-backs*: J Leck (Mil), P Marshall (WathB). *Forwards*:
J Beetham (Mil), JH Buckett (Mil, g), T Hall (WhiR), GW Lamb (Mil), M Linton (Sea),
J McLaughlin (WhiR), G Steele (Work), D Wilson (WathB).
LANCASHIRE 21 *Back*: D Smith (Sal). *Three-quarters*: J Fish (War, 3g), A Field (RochH),
T Williams (Sal, t), S Williams (Old, 3t). *Half-backs*: D Davies (Swi), A Lees (Old).
Forwards: G Aspey (Wid), W Briers (StH, t), J Moffatt (Old), J Rhapps (Sal), C Thompson
(BroR), F Treweeke (Bar), P Tunney (Sal), E Vigors (Swi).
Attendance: 5,000   *Referee*: F Renton (Hunslet)

Saturday 3 November 1900 at Athletic Grounds, Rochdale
LANCASHIRE 24 *Back*: D Smith (Sal). *Three-quarters*: T Williams (Sal, 2t), R Valentine
(Swi, t, 2g), S Williams (Old, 2t), A Field (RochH, t). *Half-backs*: D Davies (Swi), A Lees
(capt, Old). *Forwards*: W Briers (StH), J Ferguson (Old, g), J Moffatt (Old), J Rhapps (Sal),
F Treweeke (Bar), P Tunney (Sal), E Vigors (Swi), G Whitehead (BroR).
YORKSHIRE 5 *Back*: H Taylor (Hull). *Three-quarters*: A Hambrecht (Bram), W Dewhirst
(Hud), JE Parker (Bram, g), AW Robinson (HKR). *Half-backs*: D Frank (Hull, t),

GH Marsden (Brad). *Forwards*: A Barker (Mann), J Gath (capt, Heck), G Hewlett (LeePC), J Hutt (Brad), A Laidlaw (Brad), A Lunn (Hun), A Starks (HKR), H Topham (Bram).
Attendance: 18,000   *Referee*: J Kidd (Millom)

Saturday 10 November 1900 at Park Station, Birkenhead
CHESHIRE 11 *Back*: S Houghton (capt, Run, t, g). *Three-quarters*: T Wilkinson (Run), TH Warder (Run), HA Harris (BirkW), H Clayton (BirkW, t). *Half-backs*: J Faulkner (Run), J Jolley (Run). *Forwards*: H Barnett (Alt), C Griffiths (BirkW), W Lightfoot (Run), W Oram (Stock), T Poole (BirkW), RT Reece (Run), J Trotter (Stock), S Walker (Run, t).
CUMBERLAND 3 *Back*: I Latham (Mil). *Three-quarters*: G Whitehead (Mil), J Young (Mil), J Hayton (Mary), J Varty (Asp). *Half-backs*: G Milburn (WhiR), JH Richardson (WhiR). *Forwards*: J Atkinson (Work), J Beetham (Mil), JH Buckett (capt, Mil, t), J Grimes (WathB), GW Lamb (Mil), M Linton (Sea), J McLaughlin (WhiR), S Warwick (WhiR).
Attendance: 2,500   *Referee*: JH Smith (Widnes)

Saturday 8 December 1900 at Edgeley Park, Stockport
CHESHIRE 0 *Back*: P Wilkinson (Alt). *Three-quarters*: T Wilkinson (Run), TH Warder (Run), J Richardson (Run), W Robinson (capt, Stock). *Half-backs*: B Booth (Stock), J Faulkner (Run), J Jolley (Run). *Forwards*: H Barnett (Alt), C Griffiths (BirkW), W Lightfoot (Run), W Oram (Stock), RT Reece (Run), W Simister (Stock), J Trotter (Stock), S Walker (Run).
LANCASHIRE 30 *Back*: D Smith (Sal). *Three-quarters*: A Field (RochH, 2t), R Valentine (Swi), T Williams (Sal), S Williams (Old, 2t). *Half-backs*: D Davies (Swi, t), A Lees (Old). *Forwards*: W Briers (StH), J Ferguson (Old, 6g), J Moffatt (capt, Old, t), J Rhapps (Sal), F Treweeke (Bar), P Tunney (Sal), E Vigors (Swi), G Whitehead (BroR).
Attendance: 6,000   *Referee*: W Robinson (Manningham)

Saturday 15 December 1900 at The Boulevard, Hull
YORKSHIRE 10 *Back*: H Taylor (Hull). *Three-quarters*: JE Jones (Hal, t), W Evans (LeePC), WP Davies (Bat, t, g), A Hambrecht (capt, Bram). *Half-backs*: D Frank (Hull), GH Marsden (Brad). *Forwards*: A Barker (Mann), G Hewlett (LeePC), J Hutt (Brad), A Laidlaw (Brad), A Lunn (Hun), A Starks (HKR, g), J Stephenson (HKR), H Topham (Bram).
CUMBERLAND 5 *Back*: W Little (Sea). *Three-quarters*: T Bell (Mary), J Coulthard (Work), J Young (Mil), I Latham (Mil, t). *Half-backs*: J Leck (Mil), J Whitehead (Mil). *Forwards*: J Atkinson (Work), J Beetham (Mil), J Bell (Mary), JH Buckett (capt, Mil, g), C Furness (Sea), J Hatchin (Work), W Irving (Sea), GW Lamb (Mil).
Attendance: 9,000   *Referee*: JH Smith (Widnes)

Final table

	P	W	D	L	For	Agst	Pts
Lancashire	3	3	0	0	75	7	6
Yorkshire	3	2	0	1	55	29	4
Cheshire	3	1	0	2	11	73	2
Cumberland	3	0	0	3	10	42	0

RUGBY UNION

DURHAM COUNTY CHALLENGE CUP (10 entries)
Try – 3 points; conversion – 2; penalty goal – 3; drop-goal, field goal, goal from mark – 4.

First Round
Hamsteels 4, North Durham 0
Hartlepool Rovers 0, West Hartlepool 6
Byes: Durham City, Hartlepool Old Boys, South Shields, Sunderland, Tudhoe, Westoe

Second Round
South Shields 11, Hartlepool Old Boys 4
Hamsteels 14, Sunderland 5
Tudhoe 3, Durham City 0
Westoe 8, West Hartlepool 14

Semi-finals
Hamsteels 0, West Hartlepool 13
Tudhoe 6, South Shields 11

FINAL
Saturday 13 April 1901 at Brewery Field, Spennymoor
SOUTH SHIELDS 6 *Back*: W Hector. *Three-quarters*: HB Swainston (capt), WJ Robertson, J Deakin (t), WJ Archer (t). *Half-backs*: J Crosbie, A Ward. *Forwards*: R Hindson, J Marshall, G Newman, J Nichol, A Peat, T Sowerby, F Tully, G Younger.
WEST HARTLEPOOL 0 *Back*: J Hogg. *Three-quarters*: BS Wellock, JT Taylor (capt), J Phillips, T Hunter. *Half-backs*: W Howe, A McDonald. *Forwards*: J Booth, R Bradley, J Conmy, J Duthie, G Freeman, E Morton, WJ Simms, J Waller.
Attendance: 8,000   *Referee*: J Ward (Leicester)

NORTHUMBERLAND COUNTY FOOTBALL CHALLENGE CUP (5 entries)
Try – 3 points; conversion – 2; penalty goal – 3; drop-goal, field goal, goal from mark – 4.

First Round
Tynedale 0, Northern 6
Byes: Percy Park, Rockcliff, Wallsend

Semi-finals
Percy Park 0, Rockcliff 18
Wallsend 0, Northern 9

FINAL
Saturday 23 March 1901 at Jesmond Ground, Newcastle
ROCKCLIFF 13 *Back*: S Anderson (2c, pg). *Three-quarters*: T Simpson, F Pickering, W Seymour, JC Seymour (t). *Half-backs*: O Chambers, EJ Joicey (t). *Forwards*: JW Bamborough, J Bolam, JH Dunn, T Finlay, JH Greenwell, T Hamblin, R Smith, J Trotter.
NORTHERN 0 *Back*: WW Gibson. *Three-quarters*: RA Morland, FH Jones, F Stanger-Leathis, WB Steel. *Half-backs*: TA Gibson, C Nelson. *Forwards*: WG Blackmarsh, T Carter, FR Cumberlege, WH Dick, COP Gibson, GR Gibson, A Nicholson, CWM Potts.
Attendance: 4,000   *Referee*: F Marsh (Westoe)

YORKSHIRE COUNTY FOOTBALL CHALLENGE CUP (10 entries)
Try – 3 points; conversion – 2; penalty goal – 3; drop-goal, field goal, goal from mark – 4.

First Round
Bradford Wanderers 0, Skipton 33
Castleford 26, Harrogate 0
Byes: Bottomboat Trinity, Headingley, Kippax, Knottingley, Morley, Mytholmroyd

Second Round
Bottomboat Trinity 7, Mytholmroyd 3
Castleford 31, Skipton 10
Kippax 3, Morley 4
Knottingley 3, Headingley 17

Semi-finals
Castleford 25, Headingley 3 (at Bowling Old Lane, Bradford)
Morley 8, Bottomboat Trinity 0 (at Lock Lane, Castleford)

FINAL
Saturday 20 April 1901 at County Ground, Claro, Harrogate
CASTLEFORD 20 *Back*: JW Milner. *Three-quarters*: E Avery-Jones (2t), T Sherwood, E Higgins, J Pickering. *Half-backs*: J Briggs, EJ Walton (t). *Forwards*: W Cobby, E Dickinson, H Doncaster (t), CW Hague (t), J Hague (t), T Hambleton (capt, c), W Pratt, RF Russell.
MORLEY 6 *Back*: JW Mason. *Three-quarters*: F Rhodes (capt), J Peel, HE Reynolds (t), J Richardson. *Half-backs*: JW Hodgson, M Naylor. *Forwards*: G Bullers, H Hepworth, R Heywood, S Hodgson, JW Kitchen, J Taylor, W Tolson (t), JW Wilson.
Attendance: 3,000   *Referee*: T Shires (Bottomboat)

COUNTY CHAMPIONSHIP

NORTHERN GROUP
Saturday 20 October 1900 at Warwick Road, Carlisle
CUMBERLAND 0 *Back*: J Wilson (Carl). *Three-quarters*: F Spottiswood (Carl), A Smith (Carl), D Jackson (Carl), M Burrows (Carl). *Half-backs*: J Fleming (Carl), C Warwick (PenU). *Forwards*: T Cavaghan (Carl), Joe Davidson ('Aspatria'), T Davidson ('Aspatria'), D Graham ('Keswick'), JT Scott (Carl), J Stubbs (Carl), E Walsh (Carl), J Yeowart ('Aspatria').
DURHAM 4 *Back*: J Hogg (WHart). *Three-quarters*: W Taylor (Tud), J Gordon (Tud), JT Taylor (WHart, dg), EW Elliot (Sund). *Half-backs*: H Gibbon (Ham), W Moffet (Sund). *Forwards*: J Carmedy (Tud), J Frater (Tud), GH Lewis (WHart), G Richardson (Tud), WJ Simms (WHart), A Stephenson (Tud), GE Summerscales (DurC), J Waller (WHart).
Attendance: n/a   *Referee*: J Boyd (Scotland)

Saturday 3 November 1900 at Upper Park, Birkenhead
CHESHIRE 0 *Back*: A Taylor (BirkPk). *Three-quarters*: D McLeod (BirkPk), J Hutchinson (BirkPk), A Hartley (Sale), H Parratt (Sale). *Half-backs*: PD Kendall (BirkPk), JC Marquis (BirkPk). *Forwards*: J Baxter (BirkPk), R Butterworth (AshH), JC Edgar (BirkPk), W Fearenside (NewB), JS Francomb (Bow), J Hague (Sale), H Smith (BirkPk), R Taylor (BirkPk).
LANCASHIRE 17 *Back*: CEK Thompson (Man). *Three-quarters*: ET Nicholson (Liv, c), AT Brettargh (LivOB), TS Harrison (LivOB), F Alcock (OwC, t). *Half-backs*: G Cookson (Man,

t), D Glass (Waterloo). *Forwards*: CE Allen (Liv), JG Graham (LivOB), TS Kelly (LivOB), A Long (Bow), FJ Milne (Man), HE Moore (OwC), RD Wood (LivOB, t), SG Wood (Liv, 2t).
Attendance: 2,000   *Referee*: SE Wilson (Lancashire)

Saturday 3 November 1900 at Victoria Ground, West Hartlepool
DURHAM 21 *Back*: J Hogg (WHart). *Three-quarters*: W Taylor (Tud, t), J Gordon (Tud), JT Taylor (WHart, 2t, c, dg), EW Elliot (Sund, 2t). *Half-backs*: H Gibbon (Ham), W Moffet (Sund). *Forwards*: J Carmedy (Tud), J Frater (Tud), GH Lewis (WHart), WJ Simms (WHart), J Smith (HartOB), A Stephenson (Tud), GE Summerscales (DurC), J Waller (WHart).
YORKSHIRE 0 *Back*: FF Glendinning (Mor). *Three-quarters*: GP Ackroyd (Skip), T Sherwood (Cas), S Neumann (capt, Leic), E Avery-Jones (Cas). *Half-backs*: J Knox (Skip), DG Wheelwright (Myth). *Forwards*: P Driver (Skip), GG Firth (Head), J Hague (Cas), W Pratt (Cas), RF Russell (Cas), JA Smith (Cas), W Stansfield (Myth), AEN Yeadon (Head).
Attendance: 6,000/7,000   *Referee*: EB Holmes (Midland Counties)

Saturday 10 November 1900 at Warwick Road, Carlisle
CUMBERLAND 0 *Back*: J Wilson (Carl). *Three-quarters*: F Spottiswood (Carl), M Burrows (Carl), D Jackson (Carl), AJ Richardson ('Penrith'). *Half-backs*: J Fleming (Carl), C Warwick ('Penrith'). *Forwards*: T Cavaghan (Carl), Joe Davidson ('Aspatria'), T Davidson ('Aspatria'), D Graham ('Keswick'), JT Scott (Carl), J Stubbs (Carl), E Walsh (Carl), J Yeowart ('Aspatria').
CHESHIRE 0 *Back*: A Taylor (BirkPk). *Three-quarters*: D McLeod (BirkPk), A Hartley (Sale), H Robinson (BirkPk), EG Thin (BirkPk). *Half-backs*: PD Kendall (BirkPk), JC Marquis (BirkPk). *Forwards*: WL Bird (BirkPk), JC Edgar (BirkPk), W Fearenside (NewB), JS Francomb (Bow), J Hague (Sale), H Smith (BirkPk), JH Stephens (Bow), T Welch (Bow).
Attendance: 'moderately good'   *Referee*: J Boyd (Scotland)

Saturday 10 November 1900 at Lock Lane, Castleford
YORKSHIRE 9 *Back*: FF Glendinning (Mor). *Three-quarters*: T Sherwood (Cas), GP Ackroyd (Skip), S Neumann (capt, Leic), E Avery-Jones (Cas). *Half-backs*: J Knox (Skip), DG Wheelwright (Myth). *Forwards*: P Driver (Skip), GG Firth (Head), J Hague (Cas), SB James (Head), W Pratt (Cas), RF Russell (Cas), W Stansfield (Myth, t), AEN Yeadon (Head, c, gm).
NORTHUMBERLAND 18 *Back*: AK Tasker (PerPk). *Three-quarters*: F Pickering (Rock), T Simpson (Rock, t), S Anderson (capt, Rock, t, 3c), JC Seymour (Rock, t). *Half-backs*: EA Henderson (PerPk), CW Russell (PerPk). *Forwards*: JW Bamborough (Rock), RW Bell (Nor), COP Gibson (Nor), GR Gibson (Nor), PF Hardwick (PerPk), RT Lockerby (PerPk), J Ritson (Wall, t), R Smith (Rock).
Attendance: 3,000   *Referee*: A Crosbie (Midland Counties)

Saturday 17 November 1900 at Manchester Athletic Ground, Fallowfield
LANCASHIRE 5 *Back*: CEK Thompson (Man). *Three-quarters*: F Alcock (OwC), AT Brettargh (LivOB), TS Harrison (LivOB), ET Nicholson (Liv, c). *Half-backs*: G Cookson (Man, t), W Parlane (Man). *Forwards*: WH Ainley (BroPk), JG Graham (LivOB), TS Kelly (LivOB), A Long (Bow), FJ Milne (Man), HE Moore (OwC), RD Wood (LivOB), SG Wood (Liv).
YORKSHIRE 5 *Back*: JF Longbottom (Myth). *Three-quarters*: S Neumann (capt, Leic), GP Ackroyd (Skip), E Avery-Jones (Cas), T Sherwood (Cas, t). *Half-backs*: J Knox (Skip), DG Wheelwright (Myth). *Forwards*: GG Firth (Head), J Hague (Cas), SB James (Head),

HO Mawson (Head), W Pratt (Cas), RF Russell (Cas), W Stansfield (Myth), AEN Yeadon (Head, c).
Attendance: 600/700   *Referee*: FW Nicholls (Midland Counties)

Saturday 24 November 1900 at Whalley Range, Manchester
LANCASHIRE 8 *Back*: JE Kidd (BroPk). *Three-quarters*: F Alcock (OwC, t), TH Kingscote (Man), TWS Pollock (Parkfield Old Boys), ET Nicholson (Liv, c). *Half-backs*: G Cookson (Man, t), W Parlane (Man). *Forwards*: CE Allen (Liv), JG Graham (LivOB), LB Hopper (Liv), TS Kelly (LivOB), A Long (Bow), FJ Milne (Man), RD Wood (LivOB), SG Wood (Liv).
CUMBERLAND 0 *Back*: J Wilson (Carl). *Three-quarters*: F Spottiswood (Carl), M Burrows (Carl), AJ Richardson ('Penrith'), RW Bell (LivOB). *Half-backs*: T Docker ('Aspatria'), EH Dodgson (AspAC). *Forwards*: T Cavaghan (Carl), Joe Davidson ('Aspatria'), T Davidson ('Aspatria'), D Graham ('Keswick'), JT Scott (Carl), J Stubbs (Carl), E Walsh (Carl), J Yeowart ('Aspatria').
Attendance: 1,000   *Referee*: B Butterworth (Yorkshire)

Saturday 1 December 1900 at Friarage Field, Hartlepool
DURHAM 14 *Back*: J Hogg (WHart). *Three-quarters*: W Taylor (Tud, 2t), J Gordon (Tud, c), JT Taylor (WHart, t, pg), EW Elliot (Sund). *Half-backs*: W Moffet (Sund), BS Oughtred (HartR). *Forwards*: J Carmedy (Tud), J Frater (Tud), GH Lewis (WHart), WJ Simms (WHart), J Smith (HartOB), A Stephenson (Tud), GE Summerscales (DurC), J Waller (WHart).
CHESHIRE 0 *Back*: CR Hartley (Sale). *Three-quarters*: J Hutchinson (BirkPk), H Robinson (BirkPk), A Hartley (Sale), EG Thin (BirkPk). *Half-backs*: PD Kendall (BirkPk), JC Marquis (BirkPk). *Forwards*: WL Bird (BirkPk), J Edmondson (Sale), W Fearenside (NewB), JS Francomb (Bow), J Hague (Sale), H Smith (BirkPk), JH Stephens (Bow), T Welch (Bow).
Attendance: 2,000   *Referee*: FK Ward (Midland Counties)

Saturday 8 December 1900 at Aigburth, Liverpool
LANCASHIRE 11 *Back*: JE Kidd (BroPk). *Three-quarters*: F Alcock (OwC), AT Brettargh (LivOB), TH Kingscote (Man, t), ET Nicholson (Liv). *Half-backs*: G Cookson (capt, Man, t, c), W Parlane (Man). *Forwards*: CE Allen (Liv), JG Graham (LivOB, t), LB Hopper (Liv), TS Kelly (LivOB), A Long (Bow), FJ Milne (Man), RD Wood (LivOB), SG Wood (Liv).
NORTHUMBERLAND 8 *Back*: WW Coull (PerPk). *Three-quarters*: T Simpson (Rock), S Anderson (capt, Rock, c), F Pickering (Rock), JC Seymour (Rock). *Half-backs*: EA Henderson (PerPk), BS Robson (PerPk). *Forwards*: JW Bamborough (Rock), RW Bell (Nor), JH Dunn (Rock), COP Gibson (Nor), GR Gibson (Nor), PF Hardwick (PerPk), J Ritson (Wall, 2t), J Smith (Wall).
Attendance: 'small'   *Referee*: E Alderson (Yorkshire)

Saturday 12 January 1901 at Jesmond Ground, Newcastle
NORTHUMBERLAND 24 *Back*: F Pickering (Rock). *Three-quarters*: JC Seymour (Rock), BS Robson (PerPk, c), S Anderson (capt, Rock, t, 2c, pg), GC Robinson (PerPk, 3t). *Half-backs*: EA Henderson (PerPk), CW Russell (PerPk). *Forwards*: JW Bamborough (Rock), JH Dunn (Rock), T Finlay (Rock), COP Gibson (Nor), GR Gibson (Nor), JH Greenwell (Rock, t), PF Hardwick (PerPk), J Ritson (Wall).
CHESHIRE 3 *Back*: CR Hartley (Sale). *Three-quarters*: E Smith (Sale), A Hartley (Sale, t), HP Terry (Sale), A Taylor (BirkPk). *Half-backs*: C Bradley (AshH), PD Kendall (BirkPk).

Forwards: JC Edgar (BirkPk), SF Edmondson (Sale), F Edwards (NewB), W Fearenside (NewB), J Hague (Sale), H Smith (BirkPk), R Taylor (BirkPk), T Welch (Bow).
Attendance: 3,000   *Referee*: Mr Butcher (Scotland)

Saturday 19 January 1901 at County Ground, Claro Road, Harrogate
YORKSHIRE 0 *Back*: JF Longbottom (Myth). *Three-quarters*: GP Ackroyd (Skip), JG McPhail (Head), E Avery-Jones (Cas), T Sherwood (Cas). *Half-backs*: J Knox (Skip), EJ Walton (capt, Cas/OxfU). *Forwards*: W Cobby (Cas), P Driver (Skip), N Haigh (Harr), SB James (Head), W Pratt (Cas), RF Russell (Cas), W Stansfield (Myth), AEN Yeadon (Head).
CHESHIRE 3 *Back*: CR Hartley (Sale). *Three-quarters*: EG Thin (BirkPk), A Hartley (Sale), D Davies (NewB, t), DN Hebblethwaite (BirkPk). *Half-backs*: PD Kendall (BirkPk), JC Marquis (BirkPk). *Forwards*: WL Bird (BirkPk), JC Edgar (BirkPk), SF Edmondson (Sale), W Fearenside (NewB), J Hague (Sale), H Smith (BirkPk), R Taylor (BirkPk), T Welch (Bow).
Attendance: 500   *Referee*: Rev HTS Gedge (Yorkshire)

Saturday 9 February 1901 at Warwick Road, Carlisle
CUMBERLAND 3 *Back*: J Wilson (Carl). *Three-quarters*: F Spottiswood (Carl), P Westray (Carl), A Smith (capt, Carl), RW Bell (LivOB). *Half-backs*: EH Dodgson (AspAC, t), J Fleming (Carl). *Forwards*: H Banks (Catford Bridge), T Cavaghan (Carl), Joe Davidson ('Aspatria'), T Davidson ('Aspatria'), T Docker ('Aspatria'), D Graham ('Keswick'), E Walsh (Carl), J Yeowart ('Aspatria').
NORTHUMBERLAND 3 *Back*: WW Gibson (Nor). *Three-quarters*: T Simpson (Rock, t), S Anderson (capt, Rock), FW Stone (PerPk), WW Coull (PerPk). *Half-backs*: EA Henderson (PerPk), BS Robson (PerPk). *Forwards*: JA Baty (Tynd), WH Dick (Nor), COP Gibson (Nor), GR Gibson (Nor), CWM Potts (Nor), J Ritson (Wall), D Sinclair (PerPk), J Smith (Wall).
Attendance: 'average'   *Referee*: J Boyd (Scotland)

Saturday 2 March 1901 at Hollow Drift, Durham
DURHAM 6 *Back*: J Hogg (WHart). *Three-quarters*: W Taylor (capt, Tud), JT Taylor (WHart, t), NS Cox (Sund), EW Elliot (Sund). *Half-backs*: H Gibbon (Ham), BS Oughtred (HartR). *Forwards*: J Carmedy (Tud), J Frater (Tud), GH Lewis (WHart, t), WJ Simms (WHart), J Smith (HartOB), A Stephenson (Tud), GE Summerscales (DurC), J Waller (WHart).
LANCASHIRE 3 *Back*: JE Kidd (BroPk). *Three-quarters*: N Duckworth (BroPk/Sale), AT Brettargh (LivOB), TWS Pollock (Parkfield Old Boys), ET Nicholson (Liv). *Half-backs*: G Cookson (Man), W Parlane (Man). *Forwards*: J Ainley (BroPk), JG Graham (LivOB, t), TS Kelly (LivOB), W McPhail (Man), FJ Milne (Man), HE Moore (OwC), RD Wood (LivOB), SG Wood (Liv).
Attendance: 5,000   *Referee*: EB Holmes (Midland Counties)

Saturday 30 March 1901 at Sandylands, Skipton
YORKSHIRE 6 *Back*: JF Longbottom (Myth). *Three-quarters*: GP Ackroyd (Skip, t), H Lalor (Harr), T Sherwood (Cas), G Middleton (Skip). *Half-backs*: DA Ashton (Myth), EJ Walton (capt, Cas/OxfU). *Forwards*: W Cobby (Cas, t), H Doncaster (Cas), N Haigh (Harr), SB James (Head), JJ Robinson (Harr), RF Russell (Cas), W Stansfield (Myth), AEN Yeadon (Head).

CUMBERLAND 6 *Back*: J Wilson (Carl). *Three-quarters*: P Westray (Carl), A Smith (Carl, t), F Spottiswood (Carl), RW Bell (LivOB). *Half-backs*: T Docker ('Aspatria'), EH Dodgson (AspAC). *Forwards*: H Banks (Catford Bridge, t), Joe Davidson ('Aspatria'), W Elliott (Catford Bridge), D Graham ('Keswick'), J Reay ('Aspatria'), JT Scott (Carl), JA Shawyer ('Penrith'), E Walsh (Carl).
Attendance: 2,000   *Referee*: Rev HTS Gedge (Yorkshire)

Final table

	P	W	D	L	For	Agst	Pts
Durham	4	4	0	0	45	3	8
Lancashire	5	3	1	1	44	19	7
Northumberland	4	2	1	1	53	26	5
Cheshire	5	1	1	3	6	55	3
Cumberland	5	0	3	2	9	21	3
Yorkshire	5	0	2	3	20	53	2

(Northumberland v Durham on 27 April too late for inclusion in table)

SOUTH WESTERN GROUP

Results
Gloucestershire 19, Cornwall 0
Cornwall 6, Somersetshire 0
Cornwall 0, Devonshire 6
Gloucestershire 29, Somersetshire 8
Devonshire 21, Gloucestershire 6
Somersetshire 0, Devonshire 19

Final table

	P	W	D	L	For	Agst	Pts
Devonshire	3	3	0	0	46	6	6
Gloucestershire	3	2	0	1	54	29	4
Cornwall	3	1	0	2	6	25	2
Somersetshire	3	0	0	3	8	54	0

SOUTH EASTERN GROUP A

Results
Surrey 0, Hampshire 8
Eastern Counties 3, Surrey 13
Eastern Counties 11, Hampshire 22
(Sussex withdrew without playing a match)

Final table

	P	W	D	L	For	Agst	Pts
Hampshire	2	2	0	0	30	11	4
Surrey	2	1	0	1	13	11	2
Eastern Counties	2	0	0	2	14	35	0
Sussex	0	0	0	0	0	0	0

SOUTH EASTERN GROUP B

Results
Midland Counties 0, East Midlands 22
East Midlands 6, Middlesex 0
Midland Counties 3, Kent 7
Kent 6, East Midlands 14
Middlesex 17, Midland Counties 15
Middlesex 6, Kent 0

Final table

	P	W	D	L	For	Agst	Pts
East Midlands	3	3	0	0	42	6	6
Middlesex	3	2	0	1	23	21	4
Kent	3	1	0	2	13	23	2
Midland Counties	3	0	0	3	18	46	0

South Eastern Group Final
Hampshire 5, East Midlands 19

Southern Final
Devonshire 17, East Midland 3

COUNTY CHAMPIONSHIP FINAL
Saturday 30 March 1901 at Victoria Ground, West Hartlepool
DEVONSHIRE 14 *Back*: G Fleet (Torq). *Three-quarters*: AJ Roberts (Barn, t), EJ Vivyan (DevA, 2t, c), T Mills (Ply), PL Nicholas (Honiton, t). *Half-backs*: W Duffin (DevA), S Hurrell (DevA). *Forwards*: W Bulley (DevA), D Dobson (NewA), W Dobson (NewA), R Hellings (Llwyn), A O'Neil (Torq), W Spiers (DevA), C Thomas (Barn), L Tosswill (Exe).
DURHAM 3 *Back*: J Hogg (WHart). *Three-quarters*: W Taylor (Tud), JT Taylor (WHart), NS Cox (Sund, t), EW Elliot (Sund). *Half-backs*: H Gibbon (Ham), BS Oughtred (HartR). *Forwards*: J Carmedy (Tud), J Frater (Tud), L Hopper (SSh), GH Lewis (WHart), WJ Simms (WHart), J Smith (HartOB), GE Summerscales (DurC), J Waller (WHart).
Attendance: 6,000   *Referee*: EB Holmes (Midland Counties)

NON-COUNTY CHAMPIONSHIP MATCHES

Saturday 27 October 1900 at Rectory Field, Devonport
DEVONSHIRE 24 *Back*: A Richard (Ply). *Three-quarters*: E Clarke (DevA, 2t), EJ Vivyan (DevA, t, 3c), T Mills (Ply, t), H Thomas (DevA, t). *Half-backs*: W Duffin (DevA), S Hurrell (DevA). *Forwards*: W Bulley (DevA, t), R Hellings (Llwyn), W Manning (DevA), A O'Neil (Torq), EJ Peard (DevA), EW Roberts (Exe), W Spiers (DevA), L Tosswill (Exe).
YORKSHIRE 0 *Back*: T Morgan (Skip). *Three-quarters*: JW Milner (Cas), JA Batley (Harr), GP Ackroyd (Skip), S Platts (YorksC). *Half-backs*: ST Crump (YorksC), J Downing (Knot). *Forwards*: J Butterfield (Bottomboat Trinity), P Driver (Skip), GG Firth (Head), KS Gregg (Knot), H Horner (Harr), Archie Ross (Skip), RF Russell (capt, Cas), AEN Yeadon (Head).
Attendance: 10,000   *Referee*: EB Holmes (Midland Counties)

Monday 29 October 1900 at Cardiff Arms Park
GLAMORGANSHIRE 47 *Back*: HB Winfield (Car, 5c). *Three-quarters*: EG Nicholls (Car, 2t), G Davies (Swa, t, dg), WJ Trew (Swa, 5t), WL Williams (Mou, 2t). *Half-backs*: J Jones (Aber), C Powell (Nea). *Forwards*: J Blake (Car), A Bolton (Peny), A Brice (Aber, t), DH Davies (Nea), H Jones (Tre), J Luke ((Maesteg), F Miller (Mou), R Thomas (Swa).
YORKSHIRE 3 *Back*: T Morgan (Skip). *Three-quarters*: GP Ackroyd (Skip, t), JA Batley (Harr), S Platts (YorkC), S Gover (Cas). *Half-backs*: ST Crump (YorksC), J Downing (Knot). *Forwards*: J Butterfield (Bottomboat Trinity), P Driver (Skip), GG Firth (Head), KS Gregg (Knot), H Horner (Harr), Archie Ross (Skip), RF Russell (capt, Cas), AEN Yeadon (Head).
Attendance: 4,000   *Referee*: T England (Newport)

Wednesday 5 December 1900 at Yorkshire College, Leeds
VICTORIA UNIVERSITY 0 *Back*: JD Davies (YC). *Three-quarters*: F Alcock (OC), TS Harrison (capt, OC), HP Lunn (OC), S Platts (YC). *Half-backs*: ST Crump (YC), DN Hebblethwaite (UC). *Forwards*: CJ Brierley (YC), WHA Elliot (YC), WO Meek (OC), WF Mitchell (UC), DP La Page (OC), HE Moore (OC), HL Scarborough (YC), AF Wood (YC).
YORKSHIRE 14 *Back*: JF Longbottom (Myth). *Three-quarters*: T Sherwood (Cas), GP Ackroyd (Skip), JG McPhail (Head), E Avery-Jones (Cas, t). *Half-backs*: DA Ashton (Myth), J Knox (Skip). *Forwards*: T Barker (Myth), P Driver (Skip), N Haigh (Harr), SB James (Head), HO Mawson (Head), W Pratt (Cas), RF Russell (Cas, t, c), AEN Yeadon (capt, Head, t, pg).
Attendance: 300/400   *Referee*: Rev HTS Gedge (Yorkshire)
Note: Abbreviations for Victoria University: OC – Owen's College (Manchester), UC – University College (Liverpool), YC – Yorkshire College (Leeds).

Saturday 27 April 1901 at Jesmond Ground, Newcastle
NORTHUMBERLAND 13 *Back*: S Anderson (capt, Rock). *Three-quarters*: T Simpson (Rock, 2t), FH Jones (Nor, 2c), F Pickering (Rock, t), BS Robson (PerPk). *Half-backs*: O Chambers (Rock), CW Russell (PerPk). *Forwards*: JW Bamborough (Rock), J Bolam (Rock), T Finlay (Rock), COP Gibson (Nor), JH Greenwell (Rock), PF Hardwick (PerPk), J Ritson (Wall), A Smith (Wall).
DURHAM 19 *Back*: RW Poole (HartOB, 2c). *Three-quarters*: HB Swainston (SSh, t), FJ Gowans (Wes, t), NS Cox (Sund), EW Elliot (Sund, 2t). *Half-backs*: J Knaggs (HartOB), BS Oughtred (HartR). *Forwards*: JD Blackburn (DurC), J Carmedy (Tud), L Hopper (SSh), GH Lewis (WHart), J Nichol (SSh, t), J Smith (HartOB), GE Summerscales (DurC), F Tully (SSh).
Attendance: 1,500   *Referee*: T Shires (Yorkshire)

ENGLAND TRIAL MATCHES

Saturday 15 December 1900 at County Ground, Bristol
SOUTH 18 *Back*: HT Gamlin (DevA, dg). *Three-quarters*: AH du Boulay (Black), EJ Vivyan (DevA, c), FH Jones (CamU, 2t), CC Smith (Glo, t). *Half-backs*: W Patrick (Northn), RO Schwarz (Rich). *Forwards*: AO Dowson (Mose), NC Fletcher (OMT/CamU), C Hall (Glo), AFC Luxmoore (Rich), A O'Neill (Torq, t), EW Roberts (RNEC), CT Scott (Black), FM Stout (capt, Glo).

NORTH 6 *Back*: J Hogg (WHart). *Three-quarters*: EW Elliot (Sund, 2t), AT Brettargh (LivOB), JT Taylor (WHart), ET Nicholson (Liv). *Half-backs*: B Oughtred (HartR), EJ Walton (Cas/OxfU). *Forwards*: H Alexander (BirkPk), COP Gibson (Nor), D Graham ('Keswick'), J Hague (Sale), J Ritson (Wall), RF Russell (Cas), A Stephenson (Tud), RD Wood (LivOB).
Attendance: 8,000   *Referee*: GH Harnett (Kent)

Saturday 23 February 1901 at Friarage Field, Hartlepool
NORTH 19 *Back*: CR Hartley (Sale). *Three-quarters*: EW Elliot (Sund, 2t, c), NS Cox (Sund), FH Jones* (Nor/CamU), GC Robinson (capt, PerPk, 2t, c). *Half-backs*: PD Kendall (BirkPk, t), B Oughtred (HartR). *Forwards*: H Banks** (Catford Bridge), CS Edgar (BirkPk), GR Gibson (Nor), D Graham ('Keswick'), JG Graham (LivOB), J Ritson (Wall), J Waller (WHart), RD Wood (LivOB).
SOUTH 6 *Back*: G Romans (Glo). *Three-quarters*: R Forrest (Black, t), T Crouch (Olney), AJR Roberts (Rich), PW Stout (capt, Rich). *Half-backs*: W Duffin (DevA), R Goddard (Glo). *Forwards*: NC Fletcher (OMT/CamU), C Hall (Glo, t), BC Hartley (Black/CamU.), S Matthews (Leic), A O'Neill (Torq), S Reynolds (Rich), F Rodda (Ply), HT Weston (Northn).
Attendance: 3,000   *Referee*: A Hill (Durham)
*Represented South in the earlier meeting with North this season.
**Qualified for North through being born in Cumberland.

INTERNATIONAL CHAMPIONSHIP

Saturday 5 January 1901 at Cardiff Arms Park
WALES 13 *Back*: WJ Bancroft (capt, Swa, 2c). *Three-quarters*: W Llewellyn (Llwyn), EG Nicholls (Car, t), G Davies (Swa), WJ Trew (Swa). *Half-backs*: J Jones (Aber), GL Lloyd (New). *Forwards*: J Blake (Car), G Boots (New), A Brice (Aber), R Hellings (Llwyn), JJ Hodges (New, t), F Miller (Mou), R Thomas (Swa), WH Williams (Pontymister, t).
ENGLAND 0 *Back*: JW Sagar (CamU.). *Three-quarters*: CC Smith (Glo), EJ Vivyan (DevA), JT Taylor (capt, WHart), EW Elliot (Sund). *Half-backs*: RO Schwarz (Rich), EJ Walton (Cas/OxfU). *Forwards*: H Alexander (Rich), NC Fletcher (OMT/CamU), COP Gibson (Nor), D Graham ('Keswick'), AFC Luxmoore (Rich), A O'Neill (Torq), EW Roberts (RNEC), CT Scott (Black).
Attendance: 40,000   *Referee*: A Turnbull (Scotland)

Saturday 9 February 1901 at Lansdowne Road, Dublin
IRELAND 10 *Back*: J Fulton (NIFC). *Three-quarters*: JG Davidson (NIFC, t), JB Allison (EdinU), BRW Doran (Lans), AE Freear (Lans). *Half-backs*: A Barr (MethC), LM Magee (capt, BecR). *Forwards*: CE Allen (Der), F Gardiner (NIFC, t), P Healey (Lim), AG Heron (QCB), ST Irwin (QCB, 2c), TJ Little (BecR), M Ryan (RockC), J Ryan (RockC).
ENGLAND 6 *Back*: JW Sagar (CamU). *Three-quarters*: GC Robinson (PerPk, t), WL Bunting (capt, Mose), JT Taylor (WHart), EW Elliot (Sund). *Half-backs*: RO Schwarz (Rich), EJ Walton (Cas/OxfU). *Forwards*: H Alexander (Rich, dg), NC Fletcher (OMT/CamU), C Hall (Glo), A O'Neill (Torq), S Reynolds (Rich), EW Roberts (RNEC), CT Scott (Black), RD Wood (LivOB).
Attendance: 12,000   *Referee*: DG Findlay (Scotland)

Saturday 9 March 1901 at Rectory Field, Blackheath
ENGLAND 3 *Back*: HT Gamlin (DevA). *Three-quarters*: GC Robinson (PerPk, t), WL Bunting (capt, Mose), NS Cox (Sund), EW Elliot (Sund). *Half-backs*: PD Kendall (BirkPk), B Oughtred (HartR). *Forwards*: H Alexander (Rich), CS Edgar (BirkPk), NC Fletcher (OMT/CamU), GR Gibson (Nor), C Hall (Glo), BC Hartley (Black/CamU), A O'Neill (Torq), HT Weston (Northn).
SCOTLAND 18 *Back*: AW Duncan (EdinU). *Three-quarters*: WH Welsh (EdinU, t), AB Timms (EdinU, t), P Turnbull (EdinA), AN Fell (EdinU, t). *Half-backs*: JI Gillespie (EdinA, t, 3c), RM Neill (EdinA). *Forwards*: DR Bedell-Sivright (FetLor), JA Bell (Clyd), JM Dykes (GHSFP), AB Flett (EdinU), A Frew (EdinU), MC Morrison (capt, RHSFP), J Ross (LonS), RS Stronach (GlasA).
Attendance: 20,000   *Referee*: RW Jeffares (Ireland)

Other results
Scotland 18, Wales 8
Scotland 9, Ireland 5
Wales 10, Ireland 9

Final table

	P	W	D	L	For	Agst
Scotland	3	3	0	0	45	16
Wales	3	2	0	1	31	27
Ireland	3	1	0	2	24	25
England	3	0	0	3	9	41

The fledgling Northern Union's growing
confidence is captured in this all-action image.
Salford Football Club Bazaar brochure, 1903

Notes

1. Adrian Harvey, 'The oldest rugby football club in the world?', *Sport in History*, vol.26 no.1, April 2006, pp. 150-152.
2. *London Daily News*, 23 March 1871.
3. *Huddersfield Chronicle*, 27 January 1872.
4. *Bradford Observer*, 11 January 1873 and 13 January 1873. *Yorkshire Rugby Football Union Commemoration Book 1914-19* and *Official Handbook 1919-20*, 1920, p.91.
5. *Rugby Advertiser*, 7 December 1874. *Manchester Courier*, 19 December 1887. The dividing line between North and South was subsequently moved further north to Staffordshire, the *Reynold's Newspaper*, 13 December 1896, referring to 'the keen rivalry of the divisions of England north and south of the Trent'.
6. *Yorkshire Post*, 13 April 1874.
7. *Leeds Mercury*, 19 January 1875.
8. *Athletic News*, 23 October 1875.
9. *Huddersfield Chronicle*, 17 January 1876.
10. *Athletic News*, 12 February 1876.
11. *Yorkshire Post*, 14 November 1876.
12. *Sunderland Daily Echo*, 29 January 1877.
13. *Manchester Guardian*, 26 February 1877.
14. *Carlisle Patriot*, 30 November 1877. A letter published on 28 December 1877 implied that the first ever Cumberland team (that met Northumberland on 26 February 1976 – the letter writer incorrectly gave the year as 1875) included one player from Kendal, three from Whitehaven, and the remainder from Carlisle.
15. *Yorkshire Post*, 4 December 1877.
16. *Yorkshire Post*, 31 December 1877.
17. *Athletic News*, 23 March 1878.
18. *Manchester Guardian*, 2 December 1878.
19. *Yorkshire Post*, 10 December 1878.
20. The Badsworth Hunt Rugby Football Club, based near Wakefield, was a team organised by Dr. George Wood of Ackworth to compete in the 1878-79 Yorkshire Cup. The nucleus of the side was made up by former players of the Ackworth club, disbanded a few years earlier. Badsworth did not possess a ground, using Smith's Field, in Ackworth.
21. *Yorkshire Post*, 14 April 1879.
22. *Huddersfield Chronicle*, 15 April 1879.
23. *Yorkshire Post*, 28 October 1879.
24. *Manchester Courier*, 1 December 1879. The reference to the Cheshire team as 'Cestrians' was common in the press at the time, indicating natives of the county town of Chester.
25. *Yorkshire Post*, 16 March 1880. At that time the Yorkshire Cup rules still gave goals precedence over tries.

26. *Durham County Advertiser*, 10 December 1880. C. Berkeley Cowell and E. Watts Moses, *Durham County Rugby Union 1876-1936*, 1936, p.139.
27. *Manchester Courier*, 13 December 1880.
28. *Yorkshire Post*, 15 February 1881.
29. *Leeds Mercury*, 28 March 1881.
30. Cheshire County minutes, 21 April 1881.
31. *Bolton Evening News*, 2 June 1881.
32. *Manchester Times*, 21 May 1881.
33. *Yorkshire Post*, 31 May 1881. A previous Leeds Football Club had existed from 1864 until the mid-1870s.
34. *Northern Echo*, 12 October 1881.
35. *Carlisle Journal*, 9 December 1881. The letter writers' arithmetic was slightly incorrect in that Whitehaven provided nine players, although the argument was still valid.
36. *Athletic News*, 14 December 1881.
37. Cantab is an abbreviation of Cantabrigian, a reference to a person associated with Cambridge University.
38. *Yorkshire Post*, 7 March 1882.
39. *Manchester Guardian*, 12 October 1882.
40. *Manchester Guardian*, 19 October 1882. *Leeds Mercury*, 19 January 1880. Since their introduction in 1875 referees for representative matches were mostly appointed by, and had ties to, the host country or county which inevitably led to accusations of bias. The first neutral referee for an international match was H. L. Robinson (Ireland) on 4 March 1882 when England met Scotland.
41. *Manchester Guardian*, 19 October 1882.
42. *Manchester Guardian*, 26 October 1882. The decision to count tries when goals are equal was taken in November 1875, not 1876 as stated.
43. *Manchester Guardian*, 2 November 1882.
44. *Manchester Guardian*, 27 November 1882.
45. *Maryport Advertiser*, 8 December 1882.
46. *Sporting Life*, 4 November 1882.
47. *Shields Daily News*, 19 March 1883.
48. *Dewsbury Reporter*, 7 April 1883.
49. *Athletic News*, 18 April 1883.
50. *Hull Packet*, 28 September 1883.
51. *Manchester Guardian*, 19 October 1883. Players were often selected based on the county of the club they played for rather than their county of birth.
52. *Manchester Guardian*, 26 October 1883.
53. *Liverpool Mercury*, 29 October 1883. *Manchester Guardian*, 25 February 1884.
54. *Manchester Guardian*, 9 November 1883.
55. *Athletic News*, 27 February 1884.
56. *Yorkshire Post*, 4 March 1884.
57. *Athletic News*, 7 May 1884.
58. *Leeds Mercury*, 15 July 1884. A team was credited with a minor point when the opposition was forced to touch the ball down in their own in-goal area or concede a dead ball behind their line.
59. *Liverpool Echo*, 15 November 1884.
60. *Yorkshire Post*, 2 March 1885.
61. *Yorkshire Post*, 2 March 1885.
62. *Athletic News*, 10 March 1885.
63. *Northern Daily Mail*, 13 March 1885.
64. *Northern Echo*, 24 March 1885.
65. *Leeds Mercury*, 6 April 1885.
66. *Bradford Daily Telegraph*, 1 March 1886.
67. *Yorkshire Post*, 1 March 1886.
68. *Athletic News*, 2 March 1886.
69. *Yorkshire Post*, 16 March 1886.
70. *Yorkshire Post*, 6 April 1886. *Leeds Mercury*, 8 April 1886.
71. *Liverpool Mercury*, 12 April 1886.
72. *Northern Daily Mail*, 24 September 1886.
73. *London Evening Standard*, 5 October 1886.
74. *Carlisle Patriot*, 22 October 1886 and 5 November 1886.
75. *Manchester Guardian*, 22 November 1886.
76. *Ambleside Herald*, 3 December 1886. Stephen Tate, *A History of the British Sporting Journalist*, 2020, p.131, pp.136-151.
77. *Manchester Guardian*, 16 and 17 March 1887. *Yorkshire Post*, 19 March 1887.
78. *Athletic News*, 29 March 1887.
79. *Leeds Mercury*, 1 October 1887.
80. *Bradford Daily Telegraph*, 6 December 1887.
81. *Manchester Guardian*, 17 January 1888.
82. *Lakes Chronicle*, 20 January 1888.
83. *Yorkshire Post*, 28 February 1888.
84. *Yorkshire Post*, 5 and 6 March 1888.
85. *Manchester Guardian*, 8 March 1888.
86. *Leigh Chronicle*, 9 March 1888. *Manchester Times*, 3 March 1888.
87. *Leeds Mercury*, 26 March 1888.
88. *Northern Daily Mail*, 26 March 1888.
89. *Lancashire Evening Post*, 14 April 1888.
90. *Athletic News*, 8 May 1888. The competition, competed for by clubs below the top tier, lasted for nine seasons,

Notes

winners being Blackley (1887-88), Radcliffe (1888-89, 1889-90), Tottington (1890-91), Barton (1891-92, 1892-93, 1893-94), and Clifton (1894-95, 1895-96). Regular entries included Blackley Rangers, Boothstown, Cheetham Hill, Failsworth, Levenshulme, Manchester Athletic, Oldham Borough, Whitworth, Swinton Hornets and Milnrow. It was at its peak in 1888-89 and 1889-90 with 36 entries on both occasions.

91. *Yorkshire Post*, 6 August 1888.
92. *Liverpool Mercury*, 17 September 1888.
93. *Manchester Guardian*, 4 October 1888. Although incorrect, the tourists are referred to in this publication as 'Maoris' to reflect newspaper coverage at that time.
94. *Manchester Guardian*, 7 November 1888.
95. *Manchester Guardian*, 26 November 1888.
96. *The Sportsman*, 17 December 1888.
97. *Shields Daily Gazette*, 8 March 1889.
98. *Cumberland Pacquet*, 21 March 1889.
99. *Athletic News*, 1 April 1889.
100. *North Eastern Daily Gazette*, 2 April 1889. *Athletic News*, 8 April 1889.
101. *Yorkshire Post*, 8 April 1889.
102. *Morning Post*, 7 February 1889.
103. *Athletic News*, 9 September 1889.
104. *York Herald*, 22 October 1889.
105. *Manchester Guardian*, 5 November 1889.
106. *Wigan Observer*, 18 January 1890. The first floodlit rugby match is believed to have taken place on Tuesday evening, 29 October 1978, when Broughton hosted Swinton in a friendly match played under two lamps powered by Gramme dynamo-electric machines.
107. *Yorkshire Herald*, 25 January 1890.
108. *Carlisle Patriot*, 7 February 1890.
109. *Manchester Guardian*, 14 February 1890.
110. *Manchester Guardian*, 24 March 1890.
111. *Leeds Mercury*, 7 April 1890. The Yorkshire Cup final returned to Leeds the following season when it was held at the new Headingley ground. The reference to Hanson Lane should not be confused with the former Halifax enclosure which was usually referred to under that name. Halifax had moved to the adjoining Thrum Hall in 1886-87 and both grounds connected to Hanson Lane.
112. *Athletic News*, 14 April 1890.
113. *Leeds Times*, 2 March 1889. There had been two previous Leeds Football Clubs in existence between 1864 and 1881.
114. *Yorkshire Evening Post*, 23 October 1890.
115. *Manchester Courier*, 24 October 1890. *Manchester Guardian*, 30 October 1890.
116. *Manchester Guardian*, 27 October 1890. Reverend Marshall had recently become Yorkshire Rugby Union President. A staunch advocate for amateurism, he gained a reputation for seeking out any hint of so-called professionalism. A school headmaster in Huddersfield, he was also a referee, and author of the acclaimed book, *Football: The Rugby Union Game*, published in 1892.
117. Cheshire had used four three-quarters on 2 January 1886 against Fettesian-Lorettonian, a team composed of Scottish 'Academicals'.
118. *Manchester Guardian*, 1 December 1890.
119. *Manchester Guardian*, 8 December 1890.
120. *Shields Daily News*, 19 January, 1891. The match was replayed on 10 February in Durham.
121. *Carlisle Patriot*, 20 and 27 February 1891.
122. *London Daily News*, 16 March 1891. The 1890-91 season appears to be the first in which a point scoring system was adopted for county matches, evidenced by the county tables published in the *Athletic News Football Annual* 1891, p.139. A later publication, *Durham County Rugby Union 1876-1936*, 1936, p.147, claims point scoring for county matches was introduced in 1888-89, although contemporary reports for 1888-89 and 1889-90 continued to report results in terms of goals and tries.
123. *London Daily News*, 16 June 1891.
124. *Manchester Guardian*, 21 April 1891. The writer is referring to the Lancashire versus Rest of England match at Whalley Range on 18 April 1891 which drew a reported 18,000.
125. *Manchester Courier*, 10 August 1891. *Yorkshire Post*, 12 August 1891. *London Evening Standard*, 17 September 1891.
126. *Sunderland Daily Echo*, 2 September 1891.
127. *Yorkshire Herald*, 18 December 1891.
128. *Manchester Courier*, 7 December 1891. *Lancashire Evening Post*, 7 December 1891.

Bradford Daily Telegraph, 9 December 1891. Kendal Town did not return to the Westmorland Union and disbanded after 1893-94.
129. *Yorkshire Herald*, 29 February 1892.
130. *Yorkshire Evening Post*, 14 March 1892. *Huddersfield Chronicle*, 19 March 1892. *The Umpire*, 20 March 1892.
131. *Yorkshire Evening Post*, 18 March 1892. *Huddersfield Chronicle*, 23 March 1892.
132. *Yorkshire Evening Post*, 13 April 1892.
133. *Manchester Guardian*, 23 April 1892. *Pall Mall Gazette*, 25 Apr 1892.
134. *Athletic News*, 8 August 1892.
135. *Yorkshire Evening Post*, 18 May 1892, 25 June 1892, 15 and 23 August 1892. *Sporting Life*, 15 June 1892.
136. *Durham County Advertiser*, 23 September 1892.
137. *Yorkshire Evening Post*, 2 November 1892.
138. *Manchester Guardian*, 21 November 1892.
139. *Manchester Guardian*, 22 December 1892.
140. *Yorkshire Post*, 31 January 1893.
141. *Yorkshire Post*, 6 March 1893.
142. *Manchester Guardian*, 11 March 1893.
143. *Yorkshire Post*, 11 and 15 March 1893.
144. *Shields Daily News*, 27 March 1893.
145. *Northern Daily Mail*, 12 April 1893. *Shields Daily Gazette*, 7 April 1893.
146. *Northern Daily Mail*, 10 April 1893.
147. *Manchester Guardian*, 27 April 1893.
148. *South Wales Echo*, 29 September 1893.
149. *Yorkshire Evening Post*, 3 November 1893.
150. *Manchester Guardian*, 13 November 1893.
151. *Manchester Guardian*, 11 December 1893.
152. *Manchester Guardian*, 8 January 1894. The Ireland and Scotland international teams also began using a four three-quarter system this season.
153. *Manchester Guardian*, 8 January 1894.
154. *Manchester Guardian*, 5 February 1894.
155. *Shields Daily Gazette*, 20 February 1894.
156. *Sunderland Daily Echo*, 29 March 1894.
157. *Shields Daily News*, 2 April 1894.
158. *Leeds Mercury*, 9 April 1894.
159. *Yorkshire Evening Post*, 31 July 1894.
160. *Manchester Courier*, 24 September 1894.
161. *Manchester Courier*, 24 September 1894.
162. *Manchester Guardian*, 8 October 1894. The 'professional club' referred to is almost certainly Salford who subsequently accused Radcliffe and Wigan of professionalism.
163. *Manchester Guardian*, 31 October 1894.
164. *Yorkshire Post*, 2 November 1894.
165. *Manchester Courier*, 12 November 1894.
166. *Manchester Guardian*, 14 November 1894.
167. *Leeds Mercury*, 22 November 1894.
168. *Manchester Guardian*, 23 November 1894.
169. *Yorkshire Post*, 24 November 1894.
170. *Manchester Courier*, 18 December 1894. Broughton subsequently disbanded in May 1898.
171. *Manchester Guardian*, 31 January 1895.
172. *Athletic News Football Annual* 1895, p.184.
173. *Manchester Guardian*, 28 February 1895 and 4 April 1895.
174. *Leeds Mercury*, 8 March 1895.
175. *Leeds Mercury*, 19 March 1895.
176. *Yorkshire Post*, 26 March 1895.
177. *Shields Daily Gazette*, 25 March 1895.
178. *Manchester Guardian*, 25 March 1895.
179. *Leigh Chronicle*, 26 April 1895. This was an unusual occurrence during an era when a club, in trying to fulfil two fixtures on the same day, would normally send its strongest side to what it considered their most important match and their 'A' (reserve) team to the other.
180. *Yorkshire Post*, 3 August 1895.
181. *Huddersfield Chronicle*, 30 August 1895.
182. *Sporting Life*, 5 September 1895.
183. *West Cumberland Times*, 16 and 23 October 1895 and 23 November 1895.
184. *Manchester Guardian*, 14 October 1895.
185. *Manchester Guardian*, 21 November 1895.
186. *Manchester Guardian*, 23 December 1895.
187. *Manchester Guardian*, 1 February 1896. The case of the James brothers was the only time 'professional' players were reinstated as amateurs prior to the end of the Second World War. Before Rugby Union became professional in 1995, only two other instances occurred, both due to involvement with Rugby League; in 1948, John Gregory (Blackheath) was reinstated after appearing for Huddersfield and, in 1949, Glyn John (St Luke's College, Exeter) was reinstated after signing with Leigh.
188. *Leeds Mercury*, 16 March 1896.
189. *Yorkshire Evening Post*, 16 April 1896. *Huddersfield Chronicle*, 17 April 1896.

190. *Manchester Guardian*, 28 April 1896. Fatalities in Rugby were not uncommon during the nineteenth century in what were less safety regulated times in football. Others reported included Ben Hudson (Idle) who died on 23 September 1894 following a severe back injury the previous day, William Conning (Birkenhead Wanderers and Cheshire) who died on 15 February 1896 following a kick to the head on 8 February, and William Kaye (Alverthorpe) who died on 20 March 1898 after he fractured his spine the previous day.
191. Bramley ceased to exist following the 1999 summer season. A new amateur club, Bramley Buffalos, was subsequently formed by supporters but failed to gain re-admission to the Rugby Football League, continuing along amateur lines.
192. *Yorkshire Evening Post*, 2 September 1896.
193. *Manchester Guardian*, 28 September 1896.
194. *Leeds Mercury*, 30 October 1896.
195. *Yorkshire Post*, 23 November 1896.
196. *Leeds Mercury*, 7 December 1896. Six of Westmorland's selected team were late withdrawals, although all their replacements, 'spectators' or otherwise, were experienced players.
197. *Yorkshire Evening Post*, 15 January 1897.
198. *Manchester Guardian*, 16 January 1897.
199. *Pall Mall Gazette*, 3 February 1897.
200. *Manchester Guardian*, 6 February 1897.
201. *Yorkshire Evening Post*, 20 February 1897.
202. *Yorkshire Evening Post*, 10 April 1897.
203. *Hull Daily Mail*, 12 April 1897. Lancaster and Ulverston both joined the Northern Union in 1897-98. The next Lancashire (Rugby Union) knock-out competition did not take place until 1971-72.
204. As there was no vacancy in the Yorkshire Senior Competition for 1897-98, Hull Kingston Rovers played only friendly matches that season although they did take part in the Northern Union Challenge Cup. They competed in the newly created Yorkshire Second Competition in 1898-99.
205. *Leeds Mercury*, 4 September 1897.
206. The Cumberland Diamond Jubilee League was so named to honour Queen Victoria's Diamond Jubilee in 1897 which celebrated sixty years on the throne.
207. *Northern Daily Mail*, 11 December 1897. *Shields Daily Gazette*, 17 December 1897.
208. *Yorkshire Post*, 22 November 1897.
209. *Shields Daily Gazette*, 30 November 1897.
210. *Shields Daily Gazette*, 4 December 1897.
211. *London Evening Standard*, 10 January 1898.
212. *Westmorland Gazette*, 15 January 1898.
213. *Yorkshire Evening Post*, 15 January 1898. *Westmorland Gazette*, 22 January 1898.
214. *Sunderland Daily Echo*, 2 February 1898.
215. *Sunderland Daily Echo*, 16 February 1898.
216. *Sporting Life*, 28 February 1898.
217. *Penrith Observer*, 22 March 1898.
218. *North-Eastern Daily Gazette*, 9 April 1898.
219. *Manchester Guardian*, 15 March 1898.
220. *Pall Mall Gazette*, 17 March 1898.
221. *Pall Mall Gazette*, 17 March 1898.
222. *Workington Star*, 18 March 1898.
223. *Westmorland Gazette*, 5 March 1898.
224. *Sporting Life*, 3 March 1898. This was the only county match that Westmorland played under the Northern Union code.
225. *Shields Daily News*, 28 September 1898. Seven of Rockcliff's winning team had the surname of Taylor.
226. *Sunderland Daily Echo*, 2 April 1898.
227. *Leeds Mercury*, 11 April 1898.
228. *Manchester Guardian*, 3 October 1898. At the Northern Union's annual meeting in June 1898 it was announced that professionalism, in contrast to the previous system of 'broken time' payment, would become legal, but players must also have *bona fide* employment.
229. *Lakes Herald*, 14 October 1898. The Kendal Hornets name had reappeared briefly on 19 March 1898 in a one-off Northern Union match at Lancaster, losing 17-0. The revival was short lived and the new club ceased to exist in 1904.
230. *Northern Daily Telegraph*, 13 October 1898.
231. *Shields Daily Gazette*, 15 May 1898.
232. *Lancashire Daily Post*, 14 October 1898.
233. *Manchester Guardian*, 24 October 1898.
234. *Sunderland Daily Echo*, 7 and 9 November 1898. *North-Eastern Daily Gazette*, 7 November 1898. The two letters referred to were subsequently published in the *Sunderland Daily Echo*, 11 January 1899.

235. *Manchester Guardian*, 18 November 1898.
236. *Lancashire Daily Post*, 19 November 1898.
237. *Leeds Mercury*, 11 January 1899.
238. *Sunderland Daily Echo*, 11 January 1899. *Athletic News*, 6 February 1899. In 1902-03 the Durham and Northumberland (Rugby Union) Inter-County Club Championship was inaugurated, embracing the leading clubs of both counties. It ran until 1910-11 after which a Durham Senior League briefly operated until 1913-14.
239. *Durham County Advertiser*, 20 January 1899.
240. *Manchester Courier*, 9 February 1899.
241. *Yorkshire Post*, 20 February 1899.
242. *Athletic News*, 20 and 27 February 1899.
243. *Athletic News*, 6 March 1899.
244. *South Wales Daily News*, 6 February 1899. *Athletic News*, 27 February 1899.
245. *Yorkshire Post*, 21 March 1899.
246. *Manchester Courier*, 9 August 1899.
247. *Yorkshire Evening Post*, 2 September 1899.
248. *Lancashire Daily Post*, 2 September 1899.
249. *Lancashire Daily Post*, 2 September 1899.
250. *Athletic News*, 4 September 1899.
251. *Yorkshire Evening Post*, 9 September 1899.
252. *Yorkshire Post*, 15 December 1899.
253. *Yorkshire Herald*, 20 November 1899 and 20 March 1900.
254. *Lancashire Daily Post*, 10 February 1900.
255. *Manchester Courier*, 3 March 1900.
256. *Manchester Guardian*, 8 March 1900. *Manchester Courier*, 16 March 1900. The competition was repeated as a knock-out contest in 1900-01 after which it was discontinued in favour of a League format.
257. *Yorkshire Post*, 15 March 1900.
258. *Yorkshire Post*, 27 March 1900.
259. *Hull Daily Mail*, 5 April 1900.
260. *Yorkshire Evening Post*, 13 April 1900.
261. *Leeds Mercury*, 14 April 1900.
262. *South Shields Gazette*, 19 and 23 April 1900.
263. *Leeds Mercury*, 23 April 1900.
264. *Manchester Courier*, 28 April 1900.
265. *Lancashire Daily Post*, 30 April 1900.
266. *Leeds Mercury*, 30 April 1900. Andrew Hardcastle, *The Thrum Hall Story*, 1986, p.43. The West Riding Cup was not competed for again, the Northern Union subsequently launching the Yorkshire Challenge Cup in 1905-06. The 'World's Fair' was organised by Halifax to help clear a debt of £600 but, partly due to poor weather, the event made a loss of £2,656.
267. *Manchester Courier*, 2 May 1900.
268. *Lancashire Daily Post*, 1 September 1900.
269. *Todmorden and District News*, 17 and 24 August 1900, 21 September 1900, 12 October 1900
270. *Lancashire Daily Post*, 20 October 1900.
271. *Leeds Mercury*, 5 November 1900.
272. *Yorkshire Post*, 9 November 1900. The leading Cumberland clubs that joined the Northern Union were Millom (defected 3 July 1897), Maryport (11 March 1898), Workington (19 March 1898), Wath Brow (29 March 1898), Brookland Rovers (14 April 1898), Seaton (12 October 1898), Whitehaven (19 October 1898), Whitehaven Recreation (9 January 1899), Aspatria (27 April 1900), and Penrith United (7 November 1900).
273. *Manchester Guardian*, 19 November 1900.
274. *Yorkshire Post*, 19 November 1900.
275. *Yorkshire Post*, 10 December 1900.
276. *Lancashire Daily Post*, 4 May 1901.
277. *Shields Daily Gazette*, 22 June 1901. South Shields played only friendly matches during 1901-02 although they did take part in the Northern Union Challenge Cup. They competed in the Northern Rugby League Second Division in 1902-03 and 1903-04 but failed to gain re-election at the 1904 Northern Rugby League annual meeting, ceasing to exist shortly after.

Appendix 1

RUGBY UNION COUNTY APPEARANCES (1869-70 TO 1900-01)

The following pages list every player known to have appeared for a northern county from the first match, in 1869-70, up to and including 1900-01. This is broken down by the seven northern counties of Cheshire, Cumberland, Durham, Lancashire, Northumberland, Westmorland, and Yorkshire.

The name of each player is shown in alphabetical sequence, with surname followed by first name or initial where known. A hyphen (-) is used where a first name or initial has not been identified. The name that the player was popularly referred to at the time (such as 'Billy'. 'Joe', etc.) is given where known.

This is followed by the name(s) of the team(s) each player was associated with at the time of his appearance(s). Where the name of the team appears in quotes it indicates that the player was unattached and reported at the time as being from the town where he was associated (this affected players selected for Cumberland in 1900-01 and Westmorland in 1896-97 and 1897-98). Where the word 'unidentified' appears it indicates that it was not possible to establish a player's team.

Next is the appearance total followed by the year of the first and final appearance. Only one year is given where a player made all his appearances in the same year or had just one appearance.

CHESHIRE

107 matches, 339 players

Abram, Sam (Runcorn) 22 (1890-1895)
Adams, J (Ashford House) 4 (1897-1899)
Alexander, Harry (Birkenhead Park) 4 (1898-1900)
Allardice, Norman (Birkenhead Park) 2 (1888)
Anderson, Jimmy (Birkenhead Park) 2 (1895)
Andrew, W (Marple) 3 (1881-1882)
Andrews, G (Alderley) 2 (1876-1877)
Ashton, Harry (Stockport) 2 (1893)
Atkinson, Benjamin S (New Brighton) 2 (1879-1881)
Atkinson, B (Birkenhead Park) 2 (1879)
Atkinson, Davy (Birkenhead Wanderers) 4 (1895-1896)
Auty, AL (New Brighton) 7 (1897-1898)

Bailey, Walter (Stockport) 5 (1893-1894)
Bailey, William (Stockport) 6 (1894-1895)
Baker, F (Sale) 1 (1876)
Baker, A (Sale) 2 (1898)
Bancroft, James (Dukinfield) 2 (1889)
Barber, J (New Brighton) 4 (1883-1885)
Barber, R (New Brighton) 4 (1884-1886)
Barker, - (Stockton Heath) 1 (1894)
Barlow, F (Marple) 1 (1881)
Barnett, Harry (Altrincham) 1 (1897)
Bate, Thomas P (Sale) 2 (1893-1894)
Baxter, James (Birkenhead Park) 28 (1893-1900)
Beard, W (Stockport) 1 (1893)
Beazley, Edwin A (Birkenhead Park) 1 (1881)
Beevor, Bertram D (Bowdon & Lymm) 1 (1879)
Bell, Henry (New Brighton) 5 (1882-1884)
Bennett, George M (Birkenhead Park) 4 (1898-1899)
Benton, - (Sale) 1 (1895)
Bingham, David A (Birkenhead Park) 11 (1881-1887)
Bird, Walter L (Birkenhead Park) 3 (1900-1901)
Black, John A (Birkenhead Park) 14 (1883-1888)
Blain, Arthur C (Birkenhead Park) 11 (1880-1888)
Bleakley, William H (Sale) 4 (1876-1878)
Blocksage, Henry (Dukinfield) 4 (1883-1884)
Blythe, Henry M (Birkenhead Park) 2 (1876)
Bolton, R (Sale) 1 (1884)

Booth, CA (New Brighton) 2 (1898-1899)
Boucher, William (Birkenhead Park) 2 (1878)
Bradley, C (Ashford House) 3 (1897-1901)
Bradshaw, EH 'Frank' (Sale) 11 (1895-1898)
Brandon, H (Birkenhead Park) 4 (1879-1880)
Brazendale, JW 'Jack' (Runcorn) 3 (1888-1890)
Broady, WH 'Bill' (Runcorn) 11 (1882-1890)
Brown R (Tranmere Wanderers) 3 (1894-1895)
Burton, - (Rock Ferry) 1 (1876)
Butterworth, Jimmy (Runcorn) 2 (1894-1895)
Butterworth, R (Ashford House) 1 (1900)

Cannell, John AS (New Brighton) 17 (1894-1898)
Carrington, Gus (Sale) 2 (1883)
Carroll, William (Sale) 2 (1882-1883)
Cawley, WH 'Harry' (Runcorn) 5 (1887-1888)
Chadwick, Arthur J (Birkenhead Park) 17 (1891-1896)
Clark, Charles WH (Birkenhead Park) 2 (1879)
Clarke, Jim (Runcorn) 1 (1888)
Clauss, Paul R (Birkenhead Park) 12 (1892-1895)
Clegg, Lionel JW (Bowdon) 2 (1885)
Cockerell, J (Cheadle) 1 (1884)
Conning, William (Birkenhead Wanderers) 1 (1896)
Cookson, H (Sale) 2 (1883)
Cookson, James (Sale) 2 (1890-1891)
Coubrough, Andrew S (New Brighton) 3 (1878-1880)
Coubrough, WE 'Willie' (New Brighton) 12 (1878-1882)
Court, Henry (Birkenhead Park) 1 (1882)
Cowan, J (Birkenhead Park) 6 (1886-1888)
Cowie, Gilbert (Birkenhead Park) 14 (1880-1886)
Crawford, - (Parkgate) 1 (1876)
Crawford, J (Birkenhead Park) 1 (1878)
Crawford, SD (New Brighton) 2 (1883-1884)
Crawley, E (Birkenhead Park) 2 (1879-1882)
Crompton, JH 'Jack' (Runcorn) 18 (1889-1893)
Crossland, George (Birkenhead Park) 2 (1882-1883)

Darby, JS (Birkenhead Park) 1 (1898)
Davies, D (New Brighton) 1 (1901)
Davies, EOW (Birkenhead Park) 1 (1886)

Davies, Frederick (Runcorn) 1 (1887)
Davies, Jack (Runcorn) 10 (1893-1894)
Davies, JE (New Brighton) 2 (1883-1884)
Davies, TH 'Tom' (Runcorn) 7 (1888-1892)
Dearden, CE (Alderley) 4 (1876-1879)
Dillon, Albert 'Alby' (Birkenhead Wanderers) 3 (1895-1896)
Dixon, HA (New Brighton) 2 (1879)
Dobie, John (Birkenhead Wanderers) 2 (1891)
Dolan, Richard (Runcorn) 7 (1889-1890)
Dourides, - (New Brighton) 1 (1891)
Drinkwater, Edgar H (New Brighton) 1 (1893)
Drinkwater, Fred (Sale) 14 (1889-1898)
Dun, F (Birkenhead Park) 4 (1885-1886)
Dunlop, John (Birkenhead Park) 1 (1883)

Edgar, Charles S (Birkenhead Park) 9 (1899-1901)
Edmondson, John E (Sale) 2 (1891)
Edmondson, James (Sale) 1 (1900)
Edmondson, Samuel F (Sale) 4 (1891-1901)
Edwards, Frank (New Brighton) 1 (1901)
Elliott, Edward (Birkenhead Wanderers) 16 (1892-1894)
Ellis, H (New Brighton) 8 (1893-1894)
Eskrigge, Robert B (New Brighton) 2 (1890)
Evans, WE 'Bill' (Runcorn) 6 (1889- 1891)
Ewer, W (New Brighton) 2 (1876-1877)

Faulkner, Jack (Runcorn) 8 (1893-1895)
Faulkner, Will (Runcorn) 34 (1887- 1895)
Fearenside, William (New Brighton) 13 (1898-1901)
Fenton, Albert E (Birkenhead Park) 10 (1893-1895)
Fernie, James (New Brighton) 3 (1898-1900)
Fitchett, John (Stockport) 1 (1887)
Fleet, William (Altrincham) 2 (1895)
Fletcher, Harold (Sale) 21 (1894-1900)
Fletcher, W (New Brighton) 10 (1895-1899)
Fletcher, WN (Marple, Manchester, Birkenhead Park) 8 (1881-1885)
Forrest, R (Sale) 1 (1879)
Francomb, John S (Bowdon) 3 (1900)
Fry, Robert H (Sale) 3 (1899)

Gayter, Fletcher (Runcorn) 2 (1894)
Gayter, Joseph (Runcorn) 1 (1891)
Gerrard, James (Birkenhead Wanderers) 8 (1895-1897)

Gifford, John G (New Brighton) 7 (1887-1888)
Goodwin, J (Birkenhead Park) 1 (1876)
Green, William H (West Derby) 1 (1876)
Greenham, Harold (Birkenhead Park) 7 (1897-1898)

Hague, Jack (Sale) 22 (1897-1901)
Hampson, - (Cheadle) 1 (1897)
Hampson, Abraham (Runcorn) 3 (1889-1890)
Hampson, J (Birkenhead Park) 1 (1886)
Hampton, HL (Ashford House) 2 (1899)
Hancock, WF 'Fred' (Runcorn) 3 (1889-1890)
Hanson, Sam (Altrincham) 6 (1895-1896)
Hardy, Claude (Bowdon) 1 (1884)
Hardy, Tom (Sale) 1 (1878)
Hardy, W (Sale) 2 (1887)
Hargreaves, EJ (Birkenhead Park) 4 (1899-1900)
Harris, Anthony W (New Brighton) 3 (1896)
Harrison, T Harnett (Rock Ferry) 2 (1876-1877)
Hart-Davies, SO (Birkenhead Park) 1 (1883)
Hartley, Alfred (Sale) 5 (1900-1901)
Hartley, Charles R (Sale) 10 (1897-1901)
Harvey, Ernest C (Sale) 4 (1895-1899)
Harvey, Harry C (Sale) 7 (1897-1899)
Haslam, JT 'Tom' (Dukinfield, Stockport) 12 (1889-1893)
Haslam, William (Dukinfield) 3 (1887)
Headen, Henry (New Brighton) 2 (1896)
Healing, J (Birkenhead Park) 1 (1876)
Healing, W (Birkenhead Park) 1 (1876)
Hebblethwaite, Harold P (Birkenhead Park) 5 (1898-1899)
Hebblethwaite, Douglas N (Birkenhead Park) 1 (1901)
Hebden, C (Birkenhead Park) 1 (1887)
Herron, James R (New Brighton) 2 (1885-1886)
Herschell, Ernest (Birkenhead Park) 17 (1896-1899)
Heyes, Ivie D (Birkenhead Wanderers) 5 (1895-1896)
Hodgson, T (Ashford House) 2 (1899)
Hodgson, W (Sale) 1 (1897)
Holden, Cecil (Birkenhead Park) 5 (1885-1889)
Holden, Louie M (New Brighton, Birkenhead Park) 5 (1884-1888)
Hooper, Ralph W (New Brighton) 3 (1895-1896)
Hough, G (Wilmslow) 1 (1898)
Houghton, Sam (Runcorn, Birkenhead Wanderers) 30 (1890-1896)

Houlder, - (Birkenhead Park) 1 (1876)
Howes, Herbert A (Sale) 8 (1888-1889)
Hughes, Edward (Runcorn) 1 (1891)
Hughes, Fred (Birkenhead Wanderers) 3 (1895)
Hughes, Hughie (Runcorn) 18 (1884-1890)
Hughes, Owen (Runcorn) 8 (1891-1892)
Hughes, W 'Bill' (Runcorn) 16 (1885- 1891)
Hughes, W 'Billy' (Birkenhead Wanderers) 1 (1896)
Hulme, HD (Bowdon, Marple, Birkenhead Park), 12 (1879-1884)
Hunt, E Wilson (Sale) 1 (1889)
Huntington, Frank W (New Brighton) 2 (1882-1883)
Hurst, Ellis (Birkenhead Wanderers) 2 (1891-1893)
Hutchinson, J (Birkenhead Park) 8 (1893-1900)

Ingham, Frank (Birkenhead Wanderers) 13 (1894-1897)
Ingham, George R (Birkenhead Wanderers) 1 (1895)

Jackson, Robert H (Birkenhead Park) 7 (1883-1886)
Jones, Arthur (Birkenhead Wanderers) 10 (1895-1897)
Jones, FP 'Freddie' (New Brighton, Swinton) 28 (1890-1896)
Jones, James DK (Birkenhead Park) 7 (1898-1900)
Jones, J Hampton (New Brighton) 4 (1884-1885)
Kelly, Charlie (Birkenhead Wanderers) 1 (1892)
Kendall, Edward C (Rock Ferry, Birkenhead Park) 6 (1876-1879)
Kendall, Percy D (Birkenhead Park) 5 (1900-1901)
Kerr, William J (New Brighton) 5 (1878-1880)
King, Michael (Stockport) 5 (1894-1895)

Langley, Jimmy (Runcorn) 11 (1893- 1895)
Lathom, CFS (Bowdon) 1 (1885)
Leatham, Octavius (New Brighton) 2 (1880-1881)
Leece, - (Birkenhead Park) 2 (1876)
Leitch, Quinton J (New Brighton) 3 (1887-1890)
Leitch, William S (New Brighton) 2 (1883)
Lewis, Jack (Runcorn) 4 (1885-1886)

Lewis, Tom (Birkenhead Wanderers) 3 (1896-1897)
Lingard, J (Dukinfield) 1 (1887)
Lings, Ernest (Sale) 8 (1883-1886)
Lings, Tom (Sale) 4 (1885-1888)
Linton, M (Birkenhead Park) 6 (1896-1897)
Little, Frank (New Brighton) 8 (1891-1894)
Lucas, W (Hyde) 1 (1880)
Luya, Charles J (New Brighton) 3 (1888)
Lockwood, Philip H (Birkenhead Park) 23 (1887-1892)
Lockwood, TW (Birkenhead Park) 5 (1890-1893)
Lowndes, Harold N (New Brighton) 3 (1891)

McClay, - (Ashford House) 1 (1899)
McDonald, A (Birkenhead Park) 1 (1894)
McDonald, D (New Brighton) 2 (1880-1881)
McFarlane, W (Sale) 1 (1884)
McIlwaine, AW (Birkenhead Park) 6 (1878-1880)
McIver, - (Ashford House) 1 (1898)
McLeod, Duncan (Birkenhead Park) 5 (1899-1900)
Male, William H (New Brighton) 9 (1888-1890)
Marquis, John C (Birkenhead Park) 13 (1897-1901)
Marsland, Frank (Northenden, Sale) 3 (1879-1883)
Marsland, Harry (Sale) 2 (1877-1885)
Marsland, S (Sale) 1 (1876)
Massey, Daniel (Runcorn) 1 (1891)
Maxwell, Hugh (New Brighton) 4 (1881-1883)
May, John (Birkenhead Wanderers) 1 (1891)
Middleton, Bernard B (Rock Ferry, Birkenhead Park) 9 (1876-1883)
Middleton, W (Birkenhead Park) 4 (1878-1880)
Monteath, K (Birkenhead Park) 4 (1888-1889)
Moodie, Robert Fitzpatrick (Birkenhead Park) 1 (1889)
Moodie, Robert Pomeroy (Birkenhead Park) 5 (1889)
Morgan, Tom (Birkenhead Wanderers) 6 (1893-1894)
Morley, Ernest H (Sale) 5 (1892)
Morton, R 'Bob' (Altrincham, Stockport) 5 (1889-1891)
Moss, Harry (Dukinfield) 1 (1892)
Mottershead, Jack (Stockport) 4 (1894-1895)
Moysey, - (Birkenhead Park) 1 (1876)
Muir, Robert F (New Brighton) 4 (1888-1890)

Murdoch, H (New Brighton) 2 (1884-1887)
Murphy, Bernard (Birkenhead Wanderers) 5 (1896-1897)
Murray, J (New Brighton) 7 (1897-1898)

Nelson, - (Ashford House) 1 (1898)
Nicholson, W (New Brighton) 1 (1878)

Ould, R (Birkenhead Park) 4 (1894-1895)

Pagden, GP (Sale) 4 (1876-1879)
Pagden, HD 'Harry' (Sale) 4 (1895-1898)
Palmer, Will (Altrincham) 2 (1895)
Parratt, Henry (Sale) 22 (1893-1900)
Parry, John B (Rock Ferry, Birkenhead Park) 8 (1876-1880)
Paterson, Leslie R (Birkenhead Park) 1 (1888)
Patterson, Henry S (New Brighton) 2 (1882)
Pendlebury, George (Altrincham) 2 (1897)
Percival, R (Northenden) 4 (1878-1880)
Phillips, Charles (Birkenhead Park) 3 (1880-1881)
Pickard, W (Stockport) 1 (1893)
Pickin, Joseph (Sale, Bowdon) 2 (1898-1900)
Pierce, John H (New Brighton) 1 (1883)
Potter, H (unidentified) 1 (1876)
Potts, James H (Stockport) 3 (1892-1893)
Potts, LF (New Brighton) 1 (1882)
Pullen, SE (New Brighton) 2 (1882)

Ransome, Herbert F (Bowdon) 5 (1885-1886)
Ravenscroft, John J (Birkenhead Park) 5 (1879-1881)
Reece, RT 'Dick' (Runcorn) 6 (1893-1894)
Reynolds, E (New Brighton) 1 (1884)
Rickman, Wilfred (Birkenhead Park) 1 (1876)
Riley, J (Runcorn) 1 (1889)
Riley, Peter (Runcorn) 20 (1888-1893)
Riley, WA 'Bill' (Runcorn) 1 (1886)
Robinson, George (Runcorn) 4 (1892-1894)
Robinson, H (Birkenhead Park) 2 (1900)
Rome, Walter (New Brighton) 8 (1882-1886)
Rowley, Hugh C (Bowdon) 2 (1876-1877)
Rowley, - (unidentified) 1 (1876)
Royds, - (unidentified) 1 (1880)
Royle, John B (Birkenhead Park) 2 (1897-1898)
Ryalls, HJ 'Harry' (New Brighton) 14 (1880-1886)
Rycroft, Walter (Bowdon & Lymm) 5 (1878-1880)

Salvidge, Edward C (New Brighton) 2 (1899)
Saville, Fred (Stockport) 10 (1893-1895)
Schofield, C (Stockport) 5 (1889-1890)
Scurfield, J (Birkenhead Park) 1 (1886)
Searle, John (Altrincham) 6 (1896-1897)
Shaw, Percy F (New Brighton) 17 (1878-1884)
Shaw, TW (New Brighton) 1 (1878)
Shaw, W 'Bill' (Runcorn) 1 (1891)
Simpson, Samuel (New Brighton, Birkenhead Park) 8 (1894-1899)
Sinclair, H (Marple) 1 (1882)
Sleigh, Robert (Birkenhead Park) 1 (1879)
Smith, E (Sale) 1 (1901)
Smith, Harold (Birkenhead Park) 9 (1898-1901)
Smith, J (Stockport) 1 (1894)
Smith, Dr John H (Stockport) 4 (1890-1891)
Smith, WB (New Brighton) 6 (1892-1893)
Smythe, George H (Birkenhead Park) 8 (1876-1881)
Smythe, William S (Birkenhead Park) 1 (1879)
Speakman, HC 'Harry' (Runcorn) 8 (1886-1888)
Speet, James (Stockport) 4 (1892)
Spence, Arthur H (Birkenhead Park) 4 (1894-1897)
Spence, Charles (Birkenhead School) 1 (1876)
Spence, Frederick W (Birkenhead Park) 8 (1885-1890)
Stephens, John H (Bowdon) 5 (1899-1900)
Stephens, W (Sale) 1 (1889)
Stewart, G (Birkenhead Park) 6 (1878-1881)
Stewart, Robert L (Birkenhead Park) 1 (1876)
Stubbs, JJ 'Jimmy' (Runcorn) 1 (1894)
Swainwick, FS (Alderley) 2 (1876-1877)

Taylor, Alf (Runcorn) 4 (1894)
Taylor, A (Birkenhead Park) 3 (1900-1901)
Taylor, F (Birkenhead Park) 4 (1897-1898)
Taylor, JF (Stockport) 1 (1887)
Taylor, R (Sale) 1 (1893)
Taylor, R (Birkenhead Park) 3 (1900-1901)
Terry, HP (Sale) 4 (1899-1901)
Thin, Edward G (Birkenhead Park) 3 (1900-1901)
Thorp, JW Hook (Macclesfield) 13 (1876-1882)
Thorpe, RS (Sale) 1 (1890)
Tipping, Arthur (New Brighton) 5 (1897-1898)
Trevor-Smith, Estrange T (Sale) 2 (1885)
Turner, W (Marple) 2 (1881-1882)
Twyford, Robert (Congleton) 2 (1881-1882)
Tyack, William J (Dukinfield) 2 (1891)

Wainwright, F (Bowdon, New Brighton) 3 (1884-1886)
Wainwright, George T (Runcorn) 7 (1888-1889)
Walker, E (Ashford House) 3 (1898-1899)
Walker, S (New Brighton) 4 (1898-1899)
Wallace, William H (Birkenhead Park) 5 (1876-1879)
Warburton, F (Sale) 1 (1884)
Warder, TH 'Tom' (Runcorn) 4 (1893-1894)
Watson, H (Birkenhead Park) 1 (1876)
Watson, JD 'Jack' (Birkenhead Wanderers) 8 (1891-1897)
Welch, Thomas (Bowdon) 4 (1900-1901)
White, George D (Birkenhead Park) 2 (1891)
Whitehead, E (Dukinfield) 2 (1883-1884)
Williams, A (New Brighton) 7 (1886-1889)
Williams, Harry (Runcorn) 5 (1892-1893)
Williams, William A (New Brighton) 16 (1890-1893)
Williamson, Archie (Birkenhead Park) 8 (1879-1885)
Williamson, Hugh (Salford, Sale) 1 (1882)
Wilson, Andrew B (Birkenhead Park) 2 (1879-1885)
Wilson, AW (Sale) 2 (1879
Wilson, JC (Sale) 2 (1876-1877)
Wilson, James N (Sale) 5 (1877-1879)
Wilson, John R (Birkenhead Park) 2 (1882)
Wolff, Arnold H (Altrincham) 2 (1889)
Wood, Alexander G (Birkenhead Park) 8 (1887-1891)
Wood, NS (Birkenhead Park) 6 (1896-1898)
Wood, Reggie (Birkenhead Park) 5 (1879-1881)
Woods, TH 'Tom' (Runcorn) 2 (1886-1887)
Wright, Rev G (Birkenhead Park) 1 (1892)
Wright, W 'Bill' (Runcorn) 6 (1883-1887)

20-plus appearances (1876-1901):
Will Faulkner 34
Sam Houghton 30
James Baxter 28
Freddie Jones 28
Philip H Lockwood 23
Sam Abram 22
Jack Hague 22*
Henry Parratt 22
Harold Fletcher 21
Peter Riley 20
*Further appearances after 1900-01

CUMBERLAND
97 matches, 344 players

Abbott, - (unidentified) 1 (1876)
Addison, Joseph (Flimby) 1 (1892)
Alderson, Rev William H (Whitehaven) 3 (1881-1883)
Anderson, John T (Whitehaven) 4 (1882-1883)
Armstrong, T (Penrith) 1 (1886)
Armstrong, Joe (Egremont, Millom) 14 (1890-1894)
Ashburner, George B (Barrow, Whitehaven) 2 (1880-1881)
Atkinson, John (Barrow, Egremont) 1 (1881)
Atkinson, D (Whitehaven) 6 (1882-1885)
Atkinson, George B (Whitehaven, Workington) 17 (1890-1893)

Bailey, Robert S (Carlisle City) 1 (1884)
Baker, - (Carlisle) 1 (1877)
Banks, H (Catford Bridge) 2 (1901)
Barnes, R (Maryport) 2 (1897)
Barry, CW (Aspatria) 1 (1896)
Bayman, J (Parton) 2 (1884)
Beagle, - (Carlisle) 1 (1877)
Beattie, J (Workington) 1 (1883)
Beattie, Lewis (Aspatria) 4 (1886-1891)
Bell, G (Carlisle City) 2 (1885)
Bell, George (Aspatria) 5 (1882-1885)
Bell, George (Penrith United) 6 (1899-1900)
Bell, John (Carlisle) 12 (1894-1896)
Bell, John T (Penrith United, Millom) 5 (1891-1893)
Bell, JW (Aspatria) 7 (1899-1900)
Bell, R 'Nobby' (Workington) 19 (1893-1896)
Bell, RW (Liverpool Old Boys) 3 (1900-1901)
Bell, Dr Thomas D (Carlisle) 4 (1896)
Bell, - (Carlisle) 1 (1877)
Berwick, William (Aspatria) 1 (1888)
Bewsher, Jefferson J (Penrith United) 4 (1891-1892)
Blacklock, Joseph H (Maryport, Aspatria) 35 (1892-1899)
Blair, C (Workington) 1 (1881)
Blair, James (Workington) 2 (1880)
Blair, Robert (Workington) 1 (1881)
Blake, GB (Eden Wanderers) 2 (1884-1885)
Blaylock, JH 'Joe' (Aspatria) 9 (1893-1899)
Bleasdale, W (Cockermouth) 2 (1885)
Boase, Matthew (Millom) 1 (1894)

Bollinger, R (Carlisle City) 1 (1888)
Bowman, George (Egremont) 2 (1891)
Boyd, Robert (Maryport) 1 (1888)
Braithwaite, R (Carlisle) 1 (1877)
Brockbank, James C (Whitehaven) 1 (1880)
Brockbank, - (Carlisle) 1 (1877)
Brough, Gil (Carlisle, Devonport Albion) 9 (1897-1899)
Broughton, Julius C (Maryport, Penrith United) 12 (1895-1899)
Broughton, Joe (Penrith United) 1 (1898)
Brown, J (Maryport) 7 (1883-1885)
Brown, Robert (Aspatria) 2 (1898)
Brown, JW (South Vale Wanderers, Carlisle City) 2 (1891-1893)
Buck, J (Carlisle) 2 (1877)
Buckett, JH 'Jim' (Millom) 26 (1888-1897)
Burgess, Robert N (Carlisle City) 1 (1888)
Burns, Johnny (Millom) 3 (1892-1893)
Burrows, Martin (Carlisle) 5 (1898-1900)
Busch, - (unidentified) 1 (1876)

Callaghan, Charlie (Workington) 1 (1892)
Capon, - (Carlisle) 1 (1877)
Carlton, Tom (Barrow, Whitehaven) 1 (1881)
Carruthers, - (Maryport) 1 (1881)
Cavaghan, T (Carlisle) 7 (1898-1901)
Challoner, AC (Northern) 1 (1881)
Chapman, Charles E (Eden Wanderers, Cambridge University) 2 (1884)
Clague, John (Cockermouth) 5 (1894-1898)
Clark, G (Broughton) 1 (1888)
Collins, - (Whitehaven) 1 (1881)
Cook, L (Egremont) 1 (1891)
Cook, A (Egremont Hornets) 1 (1894)
Corbitt, J (Carlisle) 1 (1877)
Coulthard, William (Maryport) 4 (1889-1892)
Cowen, JW 'Billy' (Aspatria) 3 (1888-1892)
Cox, J (Hensingham) 2 (1898)
Cross, W (Egremont) 3 (1889-1892)
Crow, - (Carlisle) 1 (1877)
Crump, Frank (Penrith) 1 (1886)
Cunningham, W 'Billy' (Millom, Barrow) 11 (1894-1897)
Cuthbertson, R (Cockermouth) 10 (1890-1893)
Cuthell, Guy (Workington) 4 (1888-1890)

Davidson, Jim (Aspatria) 54 (1889-1900)
Davidson, Joe (Aspatria) 23 (1897-1901)
Davidson, Tom (Aspatria) 4 (1900-1901)
Dawson, Edward H (Carlisle City) 1 (1884)

Dixon, J (Aspatria) 1 (1886)
Dobie, Tom (Aspatria) 7 (1880-1883)
Dobson, G (Cockermouth) 1 (1887)
Docker, Tom (Aspatria) 12 (1899-1901)
Dodd, J (Aspatria) 1 (1892)
Dodgshon, W (Carlisle City) 1 (1884)
Dodgson, Edward H (Aspatria Agricultural College) 3 (1900-1901)
Doran, J (Whitehaven) 1 (1881)
Doran, E (Egremont Hornets) 1 (1894)
Dove, CW 'Charlie' (Millom) 5 (1888-1889)

Eddis, Francis E (Whitehaven) 2 (1880-1881)
Edwards, J (Seaton) 1 (1893)
Elliott, Dave (Carlisle City, Carlisle) 35 (1893-1899)
Elliott, W (Catford Bridge) 1 (1901)
Essex, - (unidentified) 1 (1876)
Evans, George (Llwynypia) 1 (1898)

Falcon, Robert (Brookland Rovers) 2 (1896)
Falcon, William (Millom, Cambridge University) 4 (1894-1895)
Farrer, S (Egremont) 2 (1891)
Farrow, William H (Tynemouth) 1 (1886)
Fawcett, John (Millom) 16 (1892-1895)
Fidler, - (unidentified) 1 (1876)
Fielden, George (Workington) 1 (1883)
Fish, - (Carlisle) 1 (1877)
Fisher, Jack (Seaton) 4 (1897)
Fleming, Jack (Carlisle) 4 (1899-1901)
Fletcher, Tom (Seaton) 28 (1893-1897)
Flynn, J (Millom St James's, Millom) 2 (1885-1888)
Foley, J (Penrith United) 1 (1899)
Forsyth, Jack (Cummersdale Hornets) 8 (1892-1893)
Fotherby, JH 'Jack' (Carlisle City) 1 (1885)
Fothergill, Robert (Carlisle) 1 (1877)
Geddes, Joseph (Maryport) 1 (1888)
Gibson, George (Cockermouth) 7 (1883-1885)
Gorman, Alfred 'Fred' (Millom) 2 (1895-1896)
Graham, David (Keswick, Aspatria, New Brighton) 13 (1898-1901)
Graham, John (Aspatria) 1 (1883)
Graham, John P (Whitehaven) 4 (1890-1891)
Graham, WS 'Billy' (Carlisle) 24 (1894-1899)
Graham, - (unidentified) 1 (1876)
Grave, J (Cockermouth) 2 (1887)
Grieve, Tom (Aspatria) 15 (1893-1900)

Hadley, - (Carlisle) 1 (1877)
Halliday, John (Maryport) 2 (1887-1888)
Harker, J (Aspatria) 1 (1880)
Harris, Dr Charles (Whitehaven) 2 (1884-1885)
Harrison, Clayton (Whitehaven) 1 (1883)
Harrison, J (Cockermouth) 1 (1883)
Harrison, J (Millom) 1 (1886)
Hayton, - (Cockermouth) 1 (1881)
Hellon, Joseph C (Whitehaven) 3 (1880-1881)
Henderson, - (Carlisle) 1 (1877)
Hewitson, Joseph (Millom) 1 (1885)
Hewitson, Joseph B (Aspatria) 9 (1898-1900)
Highton, George (Keswick) 2 (1881-1882)
Higmore, J (Workington) 1 (1885)
Hillary, James (Aspatria) 8 (1899-1900)
Hilton, - (Whitehaven) 1 (1881)
Hodgkinson, Tom H (Carlisle City, Carlisle) 21 (1889-1895)
Hodgson, B (Whitehaven) 1 (1885)
Hodgson, T (Workington) 4 (1887-1889)
Hodgson, TH 'Tom' (Millom) 1 (1894)
Hoggarth, Sam (Millom) 7 (1896-1897)
Holder, - (unidentified) 1 (1876)
Holliday, John (Maryport) 1 (1888)
Holme, Joseph (Millom) 10 (1889-1891)
Holmes, W (Cockermouth) 7 (1883-1887)
Holmes, - (Carlisle) 1 (1877)
Holywell, Richard (Wickham Park) 7 (1897-1899)
Hough, Edwin L (Carlisle) 1 (1876)
Houston, Edward 'Ned' (Seaton) 4 (1889-1894)
Humphrey, Matthew (Maryport) 11 (1890-1896)
Hunter, J (Workington) 3 (1883-1885)
Hursthwaite, W (Whitehaven) 1 (1881)
Hutchinson, H (Workington) 1 (1882)
Huthart, Michael J (Eden Wanderers) 1 (18840
Hyland, Joseph (Egremont) 3 (1889-1890)

Jackson, Dan (Carlisle) 2 (1900)
Jackson, TL (Whitehaven) 1 (1892)
Jackson, William (Cockermouth) 1 (1898)
James, Tommy (Millom) 8 (1896-1897)
Johnston, J (Carlisle City) 1 (1891)
Johnston, Tommy (Whitehaven) 4 (1891-1893)
Johnstone, - (unidentified) 1 (1876)
Jones, G (Whitehaven) 2 (1888-1889)

Kidd, Jack (Millom) 7 (1890-1891)
Kirkpatrick, Thomas (Broughton) 1 (1889)
Kitchin, Tom (Millom) 1 (1894)
Knowles, Edward 'Ned' (Millom) 10 (1895- 1897)

Lamonby, Duncan G (Cockermouth, Broughton, Workington) 10 (1891-1893)
Leck, Robert (Millom) 3 (1889-1891)
Leck, James (Millom) 1 (1891)
Leck, William (Millom) 3 (1888-1892)
Lee, A (Brampton) 1 (1888)
Lees, - (Whitehaven) 3 (1880-1881)
Lewthwaite, Joe (Maryport) 10 (1886-1889)
Lewthwaite, W 'Bill' (Maryport) 6 (1884-1887)
Linton, Matthew (Seaton) 4 (1897)
Lishman, - (Carlisle) 1 (1877)
Lister, J (Cockermouth) 3 (1880-1881)
Lister, Tom 'Crackett' (Dearham) 2 (1886)
Little, R (Maryport) 2 (1887-1888)
Lowrey, David (Whitehaven) 2 (1889-1890)

McCallum, H (Carlisle) 1 (1877)
McGee, W (Aspatria) 1 (1882)
McGerry, Tom (Maryport, Whitehaven Recreation) 6 (1891-1898)
McGuire, John (Millom) 9 (1888-1894)
Mackereth, William H (Penrith United) 2   (1889)
McPhail, SR (Eden Wanderers, Edinburgh University) 2 (1884)
McQuhae, John W (Cockermouth) 2 (1883-1884)
Main, - (Carlisle) 1 (1877)
Maxwell, - (Carlisle) 2 (1876-1877)
Messenger, George (Aspatria) 10 (1894-1895)
Messenger, J (Aspatria) 3 (1897)
Milburn, - (Carlisle) 1 (1877)
Milligan, Charles (Whitehaven) 1 (1880)
Milligan, William (Workington) 9 (1892-1893)
Mitchell, JJ (Cockermouth, Edinburgh University) 3 (1889-1890)
Monkhouse, Henry (Aspatria) 1 (1883)
Moore, Ike (Millom) 4 (1889-1890)
Moore, Joe (Millom) 8 (1888-1890)
Moore, John H (Millom) 9 (1895-1897)
Moore, FR 'Bob' (Millom) 6 (1896-1897)
Moore, William (Workington, Millom, Seaton) 18 (1890-1897)
Mulholland, David (Egremont) 4 (1890-1891)
Mumberson, Joseph (Aspatria) 15 (1886-1896)
Mumberson, Robert (Aspatria) 4 (1895)
Murchie, John (Workington) 14 (1883-1891)
Muriel, Guy H (Carlisle, Richmond) 3 (1899-1900)
Murray, CW (unidentified) 1 (1876)
Murray, E (Maryport) 1 (1886)

Murray, J (Penrith United) 5 (1893-1899)
Murray, - (Carlisle) 1 (1877)
Musgrave, William H (Whitehaven) 1 (1885)

Nairn, M (Whitehaven) 2 (1893-1894)
Nelson, Joe (Aspatria) 13 (1893-1899)
Nelson, William (Millom) 5 1894-1895)
Nettleton, Thomas (Cockermouth) 2 (1887-1888)
Newton, - (Broughton) 1 (1887)
Nicholson, Fletcher (Cockermouth) 2 (1880)
Nicholson, Joseph C (Cockermouth) 3 (1880-1881)
Nicholson, - (Maryport) 1 (1881)
Nixon, B (Ellenborough) 1 (1887)
Nixon, Humphrey (Brookland Rovers) 1 (1896)
Norrie, - (unidentified) 1 (1876)
Northmore, Sammy (Millom, Barrow) 12 (1893-1897)

Ormeston, - (Carlisle) 1 (1877)
Owens, Joe (Seaton) 3 (1897)
Owens, John (Seaton) 1 (1898)

Paisley, H (Greysouthen) 2 (1886)
Paisley, J (Greysouthen) 2 (1886-1887)
Palmer, SR (Whitehaven) 4 (1881-1883)
Pape, David N (Workington) 2 (1889-1890)
Parkinson, Tom (Workington) 3 (1897-1898)
Pattinson, Thomas (Aspatria) 8 (1899-1900)
Pender, Jack (Carlisle City, Penrith United, Cummersdale Hornets) 12 (1885-1893)
Petrie, Richard (Brookland Rovers, Seaton) 2 (1896-1897)
Phillips, J George (Millom) 3 (1893)
Pike, - (unidentified) 1 (1876)
Pooley, H (Keswick) 1 (1882)

Ramsay, - (Carlisle) 1 (1877)
Ray, Joseph (Whitehaven) 2 (1891-1892)
Rayson, G (Aspatria) 2 (1886-1887)
Reay, Joseph (Aspatria) 1 (1901)
Richardson, Alfred J (Penrith United, 'Penrith') 4 (1899-1900)
Richardson, - (Carlisle) 1 (1877)
Ridgway, Samuel B (Whitehaven) 1 (1883)
Ridley, William T (Aspatria) 4 (1885-1887)
Ritson, Thomas (Cockermouth) 8 (1894-1896)
Ritson, James (Cockermouth, Wallsend) 3 (1897-1899)
Robinson, T (Cockermouth) 3 (1899-1900)

Robley, John (Maryport) 3 (1884-1887)
Rogerson, George (Carlisle City) 2 (1894-1896)
Routledge, Thomas (Aspatria) 7 (1899-1900)
Rowe, J (Egremont) 6 (1892-1893)
Rowe, W 'Billy' (Millom) 1 (1896)
Rumney, James (Aspatria) 2 (1889)

Sandwith, Henry (Aspatria) 3 (1886-1887)
Sandwith, John (Aspatria) 2 (1886)
Sandwith, Joe (Seaton) 11 (1890-1894)
Scott, Joe (Workington) 3 (1880-1881)
Scott, J (Carlisle City) 2 (1887-1888)
Scott, J (Seaton) 2 (1895)
Scott, John T (Carlisle) 4 (1900-1901)
Scott, - (Carlisle) 2 (1876-1877)
Selkirk, Willie (Egremont) 5 (1887-1890)
Senhouse, Humphrey P (Cockermouth) 3 (1883-1887)
Sewell, Johnny (Carlisle) 7 (1899-1900)
Sewell, W (Workington) 1 (1883)
Sharp, Walker (Whitehaven, Barrow) 3 (1894)
Sharpe, - (Maryport) 1 (1881)
Sharpe, R (Maryport) 1 (1882)
Shawyer, James ('Penrith') 1 (1901)
Shippen, John (Whitehaven) 5 (1883-1885)
Shippen, Thomas (Whitehaven) 1 (1885)
Shimmins, Edward (Egremont) 2 (1888)
Simpson, C (Cockermouth, Edinburgh University, Egremont) 5 (1889-1891)
Simpson, R (Whitehaven) 1 (1883)
Skelton, J (Cockermouth, Maryport) 4 1883-1886)
Skelton, William (Aspatria) 8 (1894-1896)
Smith, Albert (Carlisle) 22 (1894-1901)
Smith, Charles E (Workington) 1 (1882)
Smith, James L (Workington) 2 (1884)
Smith, J (Aspatria) 1 (1887)
Smith, William T (Maryport) 3 (1888-1889)
Smitheram, Jack (Millom) 1 (1896)
Spottiswood, Frank (Carlisle. South Shields) 14 (1898-1901)
Stamper, Isaac (Egremont) 3 (1887-1888)
Steel, Gordon (Carlisle) 1 (1898)
Steel, Jim (Eden Wanderers) 5 (1882-1885)
Steel, J (Aspatria) 3 (1898-1899)
Steele, George (Aspatria, Swinton) 12 (1894-1896)
Stephenson, J (Flimby) 1 (1891)
Stewart, - (unidentified) 1 (1876)
Strathern, R (Whitehaven) 2 (1880)
Stubbs, J (Carlisle) 10 (1899-1900)

Sutton, Richard Y (Whitehaven) 11 (1880-1888)

Tandy, G (Penrith) 1 (1886)
Telford, David (Cockermouth) 1 (1894)
Telford, Fred (Aspatria) 2 (1889)
Temperley, H (Aspatria) 1 (1886)
Tervet, Thomas (Carlisle City) 13 (1892-1894)
Thompson, J (Maryport) 2 (1885-1889)
Thompson, William (Aspatria) 4 (1880-1881)
Thompson, W (Dearham) 1 (1886)
Thompson, - (Carlisle) 2 (1876-1877)
Thomson, Dr J (Penrith) 6 (1885-1888)
Timney, John H (Maryport) 6 (1895-1896)
Tinkler, Robert H (Carlisle City) 2 (1885)
Todd, John (Aspatria) 2 (1885)
Tremble, John (Aspatria) 2 (1885)
Troughton, Stephen (Barrow) 1 (1880)
Turnbull, John (Workington) 1 (1882)
Turnbull, James (Maryport) 2 (1894)

Tyson, James (Whitehaven, Wickham Park) 4 (1897-1898)
Tyson, J (Whitehaven) 1 (1881)
Tyson, Rowell (Barrow) 1 (1880)

Varty, John (Aspatria) 1 (1899)

Walker, J (Carlisle) 1 (1877)
Walker, J (Aspatria) 20 (1896-1900)
Wallace, Hughie (Egremont) 2 (1890)
Walsh, E (Carlisle) 7 (1898-1901)
Warwick, Charles (Penrith United, 'Penrith') 2 (1900)

Webster, - (Carlisle) 1 (1877)
Westray, Percy (Carlisle) 5 (1897-1901)
Whalen, Tom (Millom) 7 (1892-1893)
White, Thomas J (Tynedale) 1 (1885)
Whitehead, - (Carlisle) 1 (1877)
Wilkinson, William (Millom) 7 (1892-1893)
Williams, Edward H (Whitehaven) 1 (1880)
Wilson, Joe (Workington) 1 (1884)
Wilson, John (Workington) 2 (1885-1889)
Wilson, Johnny (Carlisle) 5 (1900-1901)

Winskill, W 'Billy' (Penrith United) 7 (1898-1899)
Wood, W (Parton) 2 (1884-1885)
Wright, J (Whitehaven) 2 (1888)
Wright, John (Seaton) 1 (1897)
Wynne-Edwardes, HC (Eden Wanderers) 3 (1882-1885)

Yeowart, Joseph (Aspatria) 6 (1899-1901)
Young, Joe (Millom) 7 (1896-1897)
Young, William (Workington) 6 (1896-1897)

20-plus appearances (1876-1901):
Jim Davidson 54
Joseph H Blacklock 35
Dave Elliott 35
Tom Fletcher 28
Jim Buckett 26
Billy Graham 24
Joe Davidson 23*
Albert Smith 22
Tom H Hodgkinson 21
J Walker 20
*Further appearances after 1900-01

DURHAM

105 matches, 321 players

Adamson, CY 'Charlie' (Durham City, Old Dunelmians) 9 (1895-1899)
Adamson, RW 'Bob' (Old Dunelmians) 1 (1898)
Alden, William (South Shields) 1 (1895)
Alderson, FHR 'Fred' (Hartlepool Rovers) 17 (1889-1894)
Allison, R (Tyne Dock) 1 (1900)
Athey, Joseph (Hartlepool Rovers) 1 (1898)

Bagley, WR (Darlington) 4 (1877-1881)
Barmby, Henry T (Durham City) 4 (1890-1891)
Barnes, CE (Durham City) 3 (1873-1877)
Barwick, R (Sunderland Rovers, Sunderland) 18 (1885-1889)
Baty, Henry (South Shields YMCA) 1 (1891)
Bell, C Ernest (Darlington) 1 (1873)
Bell, CL (Durham) 1 (1875)
Bell, J Lowthian (Darlington) 4 (1873-1877)
Bell, William A (Tudhoe) 6 (1891-1893)
Bell, William H (Sunderland) 18 (1886-1893)
Best, WC (Darlington) 6 (1873-1877)
Bicknell, Robert H (Stockton) 2 (1875-1876)
Blackburn, JD (Durham City) 1 (1901)
Boagey, George E (Hartlepool Rovers) 2 (1891)
Boddy, C (West Hartlepool) 3 (1899-1900)
Booth, Joseph (West Hartlepool) 5 (1898-1899)
Boyd, RF 'Bob' (Sunderland) 2 (1876)
Branfoot, J (Sunderland) 1 (1889)
Brierley, R (Houghton-le-Spring) 2 (1876)
Briggs, L (Sunderland) 1 (1882)
Brooks, Fredrick W (Darlington) 1 (1874)
Brooks, Herbert (Darlington, Edinburgh University, Durham City) 10 (1876-1888)
Brooks, John H (Darlington) 9 (1874-1879)
Buckland, Henry B (Westoe) 3 (1881-1883)
Bulman, FA (Durham University) 3 (1888-1889)
Burkett, H (Humbledon) 3 (1887-1888)
Burn, Alleyn (Sunderland) 4 (1890-1892)
Burn, Charles W (Sunderland) 7 (1888-1893)
Burt, Tom (Sherburn House) 21 (1893-1898)

Carmedy, John (Tudhoe) 14 (1899-1901)
Carr, OC (Durham University) 3 (1876-1877)
Carrick, HH (North Durham) 8 (1884-1887)
Christian, Thomas (Westoe) 1 (1899)
Christison, RH (Gateshead) 1 (1875)

Coates, John (Hartlepool Rovers) 2 (1891-1892)
Coleby, Charles J (Darlington) 1 (1873)
Conley, J (Tudhoe) 2 (1897)
Conmy, Jimmy (West Hartlepool) 1 (1898)
Copley, George (Tudhoe) 1 (1892)
Cox, Burdon (Sunderland) 22 (1884-1890)
Cox, Norman S (Sunderland) 12 (1899-1901)
Coxon, W (Houghton-le-Spring) 4 (1883-1884)
Cross, William F (Sunderland Rovers) 6 (1883-1884)
Crosthwaite, Robert F (Westoe) 4 (1881-1882)
Crow, Ernest A (Sunderland Rovers, Houghton-le-Spring) 3 (1882-1883)
Crow, RCF 'Dick' (Sunderland, Sunderland Nomads) 13 (1890-1896)
Crow, TAF 'Tom' (Sunderland) 10 (1889-1892)
Crozier, J (Durham City) 3 (1883-1884)
Crozier, W (Durham City) 3 (1880-1881)
Cumberlege, Rutland F (Old Dunelmians) 1 (1898)

Dale, William (Hartlepool Rovers) 4 (1897-1898)
Davidson, T (North Durham) 3 (1883-1884)
Dearden, FC (Durham University) 1 (1880)
Dearden, JK (Durham University) 1 (1880)
Devine, N (West Hartlepool) 1 (1892)
Dickinson, G (unidentified) 1 (1882)
Dickinson, W (Sunderland) 2 (1881-1882)
Dixon, R (Tudhoe) 2 (1888-1889)
Dods, JH (Durham City) 2 (1897)
Dooley, William (West Hartlepool) 3 (1890-1891)
Douglas, EA (Crook, Cambridge University, Sunderland, Hendon Church Institute) 4 (1885-1887)
Duffey, John (Tudhoe) 2 (1892)
Dykes, EH (Gateshead, Durham City) 3 (1873-1877)

Eden, James (Darlington) 4 (1877-1880)
Eden, R (Darlington) 1 (1882)
Edlin, Herbert W (Darlington) 5 (1876-1880)
Edwards, R 'Bob' (Tudhoe) 2 (1893)
Elliot, Charles H (Sunderland) 19 (1882-1888)
Elliot, Edgar W (Sunderland) 18 (1897-1901)
Elliot, WS (Sunderland) 2 (1873-1874)

Elstob, SJ (Darlington, Durham University) 2 (1877-1878)
Elstob, T (Houghton-le-Spring) 2 (1876-1877)
Emmerson, AE 'Alf' (Hartlepool Rovers) 11 (1885-1890)
Emmerson, Thomas (West Hartlepool) 1 (1896)
Eyre, GH (Sunderland, Westoe) 7 (1885-1887)

Faulkner, Tom (Tudhoe) 14 (1889-1894)
Fawcus, CO (Stockton) 1 (1875)
Fawcus, Henry B (Old Dunelmians) 6 (1898-1899)
Fawcus, Henry William (South Shields) 2 (1874-1875)
Featherstonhaugh, Albany (Sunderland) 1 (1897)
Featherstonhaugh, Edward (Sunderland) 1 (1897)
Ferens, Henry E (Durham University) 1 (1883)
Ferguson, Ralph S (Durham University) 3 (1885-1886)
Finlay, James (Hartlepool Rovers) 1 (1894)
Fisher, GA (unidentified) 1 (1873)
Fletcher, JE (Durham City) 1 (1877)
Fogg-Elliot, John W (Durham City) 2 (1889)
Forrest, Frederick (Sunderland Rovers) 2 (1882-1883)
Forster, W (Houghton-le-Spring) 6 (1883-1885)
Fowler, J (Darlington) 1 (1879)
Fowles, J (Sunderland) 6 (1876-1882)
Frame, J (South Shields) 1 (1896)
Frater, John (Tudhoe) 14 (1899-1901)

Geenty, J (West Hartlepool) 10 (1893-1896)
Gibbon, Harry (Hamsteels) 11 (1899-1901)
Gibbon, Thomas (West Hartlepool) 8 (1894-1896)
Gibson, WJ (Darlington) 1 (1873)
Gordon, Jimmy (Tudhoe) 16 (1896-1900)
Gowans, Frank J (Westoe) 1 (1901)
Gowans, James J (Westoe) 4 (1894-1896)
Gowans, Thomas (Westoe) 1 (1899)
Green, GH (Houghton-le-Spring) 1 (1878)
Gray, GW (North Durham) 1 (1878)
Guy, W 'Billy' (Tudhoe) 4 (1896-1897)

Hall, FJ (Durham City) 1 (1884)
Hall, John (Gateshead Institute, North Durham) 16 (1887-1895)
Hall, RE (Darlington) 1 (1873)
Hallimond, William T (Bishop Auckland) 3 (1878-1880)

Hamilton, FCL (Durham University) 2 (1889-1890)
Hamm, Benjamin (Tudhoe) 1 (1900)
Hardie, DF (Old Dunelmians) 4 (1898-1899)
Hastings, Matthew (Hartlepool Rovers) 1 (1897)
Hector, W 'Billy' (South Shields) 2 (1900)
Hill, Arthur (Hartlepools, Hartlepool Rovers) 28 (1879-1890)
Hill, Robert V (Durham City) 1 (1895)
Hill, W (Stockton) 3 (1874-1877)
Hindle, Fred (Tudhoe) 10 (1892-1896)
Hodgson, Cud (Hartlepool Rovers) 3 (1894-1895)
Hodgson, H (Darlington) 1 (1885)
Hodgson, W (Tudhoe) 8 (1886-1887)
Hogg, Jimmy (West Hartlepool) 9 (1899-1901)
Hope, T (Houghton-le-Spring) 2 (1897)
Hopper, Luke (South Shields) 2 (1901)
Horsley, MH (Hartlepool Rovers) 7 (1885-1888)
Hoy, Henry O (Hartlepool Rovers) 13 (1884-1888)
Hudson, AGM (Sunderland) 3 (1876-1877)
Huntley, Cuthbert M (Hartlepool Rovers) 2 (1889-1891)
Hurworth, Thomas (West Hartlepool) 2 (1891)
Hutchinson, F (North Durham) 1 (1889)

Imrie, Henry M (Durham City) 1 (1899)
Irvin, Samuel H (Hartlepool Old Boys) 2 (1900)

James, Christian HS (Otterburn) 1 (1873)
Jamieson, TM (Houghton-le-Spring, Consett) 10 (1882-1889)
Johnson, JB (Durham City) 2 (1888)
Jones, F (North Durham) 2 (1889)
Junor, Patrick B 'Paddy' (Sunderland, Durham City) 5 (1874-1880)

Kassell, WE 'Billy' (Hartlepool Rovers, South Shields) 11 (1889-1896)
Kayll, Henry E (Sunderland) 8 (1875-1880)
Kayll, Hartley P (Sunderland) 8 (1874-1878)
Kayll, John J (Sunderland) 2 (1874-1879)
Ker, JJ (Westoe) 4 (1881-1883)
Kerr, Graham C (Durham City, Old Dunelmians) 17 (1895-1899)
Kerrich-Walker, George A (Durham City) 1 (1886)
Kidson, Charles (Sunderland) 4 (1874-1878)
Kidson, William A (Sunderland) 9 (1874-1882)

Kimpster, William (North Durham) 3 (1883-1886)
Knaggs, Jack (Hartlepool Old Boys) 1 (1901)
Knight, J (Houghton-le-Spring) 2 (1897-1898)

Laing, Arthur (Sunderland) 7 (1876-1881)
Laing, James (Sunderland) 6 (1876-1881)
Lavell, Jack (West Hartlepool) 3 (1891-1893)
Lawrence, Hugh H (Durham City 1 (1895)
Leary, R (Houghton-le-Spring) 1 (1880)
Leatham, OA (Darlington) 2 (1873-1874)
Legard, George S (Old Dunelmians) 12 (1896-1899)
Leslie-Jones, CE (North Durham) 1 (1896)
Levitt, J (Tudhoe) 4 (1898-1899)
Lewis, George H (West Hartlepool) 13 (1899-1901)
Lindsay, Jim (Tudhoe, South Shields YMCA) 13 (1891-1895)
Lohden, FC 'Fred' (Hartlepool Rovers) 2 (1890-1893)
Lohden, William G (Hartlepool Rovers) 2 (1887)
Lowrey, Samuel V (Westoe) 1 (1897)
Lumsden, F (Durham City) 9 (1885-1890)

McDermid, P (Tyne Dock) 2 (1896)
McKeon, Thomas (South Shields YMCA) 1 (1893)
McPherson, Danny (Hartlepool Rovers) 2 (1889)
McSloy, William (Hartlepool Rovers) 2 (1897)
Mallett, Richard H (Darlington) 3 (1878-1880)
Mann, AC (Sunderland) 1 (1877)
Marston, Fred (Tudhoe) 23 (1891-1898)
Martin, Tom (Tudhoe) 5 (1894-1895)
Mason, Dr Henry (Durham City) 1 (1881)
Mason, J (Tudhoe) 4 (1898-1899)
Mathieson, W (North Durham) 1 (1888)
Meiklejohn, N (Houghton-le-Spring) 3 (1882-1883)
Moffet, William (Sunderland) 12 (1899-1900)
Moore, Jack (Westoe) 1 (1897)
Moran, Percy (Hartlepool Rovers) 2 (1896)
Moreland, RA (Durham University) 2 (1897)
Morfitt, Jack (West Hartlepool) 2 (1894-1896)
Morfitt, Sammy (West Hartlepool) 10 (1892-1894)
Morgan, LG (Durham University) 1 (1879)
Morgan, George A (Sunderland) 2 (1888-1889)

Nash, Dr Llewellyn C (Durham City) 4 (1892-1893)
Newman, Rev Charles H (North Durham) 12 (1884-1887)
Nichol, Joe (South Shields) 6 (1899-1901)

Oakes, RF 'Bob' (Hartlepool Rovers) 28 (1892-1899)
Oakes, WL 'Will' (Hartlepool Rovers) 11 (1883-1887)
Ogden, W (Sunderland) 2 (1874-1875)
Oliver, F (Ryton) 1 (1881)
Oughtred, Bernard S (Hartlepool Rovers) 8 (1899-1901)

Paget, A (Sunderland) 1 (1880)
Parker, T (Sunderland) 3 (1890)
Parker, JE 'Jimmy' (West Hartlepool) 7 (1896-1897)
Parry, D (Durham University) 2 (1877-1879)
Pattinson, R (Hartlepool Rovers) 1 (1887)
Pearson, DG (Durham School) 1 (1899)
Pease, Frank E (Darlington, Hartlepool Rovers) 23 (1885-1891)
Pease-Watkin, Edward T (Darlington) 2 (1880-1881)
Peat, Alan (South Shields) 9 (1898-1900)
Penny, E (Gateshead) 1 (1874)
Peters, H (Sunderland) 1 (1874)
Philbrick, George H (Hartlepool Rovers) 3 (1893-1894)
Phillips, W (Hartlepool Rovers) 3 (1898-1899)
Pickering, John E (Tudhoe) 1 (1899)
Pimbury, G (Durham City) 1 (1887)
Pinchin, - (Sunderland) 2 (1877)
Poole, Rev Francis O (Sunderland) 1 (1895)
Poole, Robert W (Hartlepool Rovers, Hartlepool Old Boys) 23 (1894-1901)
Potts, T (Houghton-le-Spring) 1 (1878)
Powell, - (Stockton) 1 (1874)
Prest, SF (Bensham) 2 (1876-1877)
Prior, H (Darlington) 2 (1882-1883)
Purves, FW (Hartlepool Rovers) 4 (1884-1885)

Quest, George (South Shields) 2 (1896-1897)

Radford, J (Gateshead) 1 (1874)
Ranken, Frederick W (Sunderland) 1 (1889)
Read, TR (Darlington) 1 (1875)
Reed, FG (Sunderland) 6 (1882-1883)
Reed, RE (Sunderland) 11 (1881-1886)

Richardson, G (Tudhoe) 4 (1900)
Rickerby, TE (Durham City) 3 (1885)
Robertson, WJ (South Shields) 4 (1896-1898)
Robinson, HJ (Darlington) 2 (1882-1883)
Robson, F (Sunderland Rovers) 5 (1880-1882)
Rowntree, John R (Houghton-le-Spring) 1 (1880)
Russell, - (Darlington) 1 (1874)

Sadler, Cecil J (Durham School, Stockton) 2 (1887-1888)
Sample, Harold W (Westoe) 1 (1881)
Scott, AC 'Alex' (Hartlepool Rovers) 11 (1888-1892)
Scott, E (Sunderland) 1 (1877)
Shaw, Robert (Tudhoe) 3 (1898-1899)
Shewell, JC (Darlington) 2 (1873-1877)
Shewell, SC (Darlington) 5 (1874-1877)
Shields, R (Durham City) 2 (1888)
Simey, RJ (Sunderland) 3 (1885-1886)
Simms, WJ (West Hartlepool) 8 (1900-1901)
Simpson, FR (Sunderland) 6 (1883-1885)
Skinner-Jones, Frederick E (Durham University) 1 (1894)
Smeddle, John H (Durham City) 1 (1888)
Smith, George (Hartlepool Rovers) 7 (1887-1891)
Smith, J (Hartlepool Old Boys) 10 (1899-1901)
Smith, Walter (Tyne Dock) 2 (1898)
Snowdon, J (Hartlepool Rovers) 1 (1887)
Sowerby, George (Darlington) 2 (1874-1875)
Sowerby, JW 'Jack' (North Durham) 32 (1878-1889)
Spraggin, G (North Durham) 1 (1896)
Stephenson, Alec (Tudhoe) 26 (1894-1901)
Stephenson, O (Hartlepools) 3 (1880-1881)
Stitt, J (Tudhoe) 13 (1897-1900)
Stobart, J (Ryton) 1 (1885)
Stoker, R (Tyne Dock) 1 (1899)
Summerscales, George E (Durham City) 11 (1900-1901)
Swainston, Harry B (South Shields) 4 (1894-1901)
Swinburne, W (North Durham) 3 (1883-1884)

Tate, JW 'Jack' (Westoe) 3 (1893-1896)
Tate, T (Houghton-le-Spring) 1 (1888)
Taylor, HA (Sunderland) 1 (1900)
Taylor, J (Gateshead) 3 (1873-1875)
Taylor, J 'Ness' (Sunderland, Hartlepool Rovers) 5 (1895-1898)
Taylor, JD 'Joe' (Westoe) 2 (1897-1898)
Taylor, JT (Ryton) 4 (1883-1884)
Taylor, JT 'Jack' (West Hartlepool) 5 (1900-1901)
Taylor, W (Hartlepools) 1 (1881)
Taylor, Walter (Tudhoe) 29 (1891-1901)
Thomas, D Radley (West Hartlepool) 7 (1896-1898)
Thompson, AE (Sunderland Nomads) 6 (1892-1895)
Thompson, Edward P (Westoe) 3 (1887-1888)
Thompson, John T (Hartlepool Rovers) 13 (1894-1898)
Thompson, O (Sunderland) 3 (1881-1882)
Thompson, T (Darlington) 2 (1874-1875)
Thompson, Viginti T (Sunderland) 5 (1884-1888)
Thornton, T (Tyne Dock) 2 (1900)
Todd, JT (Houghton-le-Spring) 3 (1879-1882)
Todd, Thomas (Houghton-le-Spring) 2 (1877-1879)
Towers, William H (Hartlepool Rovers) 12 (1883-1886)
Tristram, Henry B (Durham City) 1 (1885)
Trotter, George MD (Stockton) 2 (1874-1877)
Troupe, AJ (Tudhoe) 15 (1895-1898)
Tully, F (South Shields) 2 (1898-1901)
Tunney, Pat (Tudhoe) 5 (1896-1897)
Turnbull, John (Durham City) 3 (1887-1888)
Turnbull, P (West Hartlepool) 6 (1890-1892)
Twining, John H (Durham University) 1 (1876)

Urwin, George (Tudhoe) 5 (1895-1897)

Wainford, Willie (Tudhoe) 11 (1890-1896)
Walker, H (Durham City, Old Dunelmians) 16 (1893-1898)
Walker, JH (Hartlepool Rovers) 6 (1886-1887)
Waller, J (West Hartlepool) 5 (1900-1901)
Watson, JL 'Leo' (Darlington) 4 (1879-1881)
Watson, R (Durham City) 2 (1898)
Watson, Thomas (Darlington) 2 (1873-1874)
Welford, R (Darlington) 1 (1875)
Wellock, BS 'Ben' (West Hartlepool) 4 (1899-1900)
Wetherell, John T (Durham City) 8 (1888-1890)
Wetherell, William C (Durham City) 2 (1882-1883)
Wheatley, Joseph (Houghton-le-Spring, Sunderland) 10 (1889-1896)
White, J (North Durham) 1 (1880)

Wilford, JC 'Jack' (Sunderland) 6 (1886-1887)
Wilkes, JG (Darlington) 3 (1874-1876)
Wilkin, William W (Westoe) 1 (1884)
Wilkinson, Charles TB (Durham University, Durham City) 9 (1888-1891)
Wilkinson, JH (Durham City) 1 (1892)
Wilkinson, William E (Durham City) 2 (1891-1892)
Willis, - (Boldon) 1 (1884)
Wilson, AR (Durham University) 9 (1884-1887)
Wilson, EC (Durham City) 1 (1877)
Wilson, J (Hamsteels) 2 (1900)
Wilson, Thomas F (Westoe) 6 (1880-1884)
Wilson, William H (Westoe) 1 (1887)
Wood, Ralph H (South Shields) 1 (1896)
Wreford-Brown, Rev G (Sunderland) 1 (1900)
Wright, CS (North Durham, Hartlepool Rovers) 6 (1896-1897)

Wylie, Herbert (Westoe) 4 (1887-1888)

Yiend, William (Hartlepool Rovers) 35 (1886-1895)

20-plus appearances (1873-1901):
William Yiend 35
Jack Sowerby 32
Walter Taylor 29*
Arthur Hill 28
Bob Oakes 28
Alec Stephenson 26
Fred Marston 23
Frank E Pearse 23
Robert W Poole 23*
Burdon Cox 22
Tom Burt 21
*Further appearances after 1900-01

LANCASHIRE
144 matches, 435 players

Ainley, J (Broughton Park) 1 (1901)
Ainley, William H (Broughton Park) 1 (1900)
Ainsworth, GWB (Liverpool) 3 (1899-1900)
Aitken, L (Manchester) 1 (1878)
Alcock, Frank (Owen's College) 4 (1900)
Allen, C Elliott (Liverpool) 7 (1899-1900)
Allen, G Glynn (Liverpool) 17 (1892-1899)
Anderson, Charlie (Liverpool Old Boys) 2 (1899)
Anderton, Charlie (Manchester Free Wanderers) 27 (1883-1889)
Anderton, Jack (Salford, Wigan) 2 (1889)
Anderton, Tom (Leigh) 1 (1894)
Andrew, FA (Manchester) 1 (1887)
Andrew, Harold H (Manchester Rangers) 6 (1879-1880)
Andrew, JB 'Ben' (Oldham) 9 (1892-1893)
Andrew, WG (Manchester Rangers) 1 (1878)
Arkle, AS (Liverpool) 2 (1897)
Armstrong, John (Oldham) 1 (1888)
Armytage, CE (Manchester) 1 (1871)
Arnott, A (Manchester) 1 (1870)
Ashton, FK (Broughton) 3 (1897)
Ashworth, Abe (Mossley, Oldham, Rochdale Hornets) 17 (1890-1893)
Atkinson, W 'Billy' (Wigan) 31 (1888-1893)

Bagshaw, F (Cheetham, Manchester Rangers) 2 (1879-1882)
Bagshaw, Joe (Swinton) 4 (1883-1884)
Bamford, James (Littleborough) 3 (1899)
Banks, Tom (Swinton) 6 (1884-1888)
Bannerman, HP (Manchester) 4 (1896)
Barlow, Charlie E (Oldham) 1 (1883)
Barlow, J (Broughton Rangers) 1 (1888)
Barrett, Alf (Salford) 10 (1892-1894)
Bate, James T (Warrington) 8 (1891-1894)
Bate, John T (Warrington) 2 (1893)
Bateson, Harold D (Liverpool) 2 (1878-1879)
Beames, H (Liverpool Old Boys) 7 (1898-1899)
Beard, Samuel B (Rochdale Hornets) 1 (1882)
Beasley, CEL (Littleborough) 10 (1896-1898)
Bell, Henry (Liverpool Old Boys) 2 (1884-1885)
Bell, Robert (Barrow) 5 (1896-1897)
Bell, Thomas K (Barrow) 1 1887
Berry, John 'Buff' (Tyldesley) 14 (1890-1891)
Beswick, E 'Ted' (Swinton) 5 (1879-1882)
Bingham, S (Liverpool) 1 (1894)
Blatherwick, Thomas (Manchester) 11 (1878-1881)
Blomley, E 'Ned' (Oldham) 1 (1890)

Blythe, J (Liverpool) 2 (1872-1873)
Bolton, JJ (Manchester) 1 (1870)
Bonser, Emanuel (Oldham) 2 (1895)
Boscow, Joseph (Warrington) 4 (1892-1893)
Bowker, Tom (Barrow) 6 (1896-1897)
Brandon, H (Liverpool) 1 (1882)
Brayshay, Tom (Wigan) 6 (1890-1891)
Brearley, John (Rochdale Hornets) 1 (1891)
Brettargh, Arthur T (Liverpool Old Boys) 16 (1897-1901)
Brickill, J (Cheetham) 1 (1878)
Brierley, Frank (Rochdale) 1 (1870)
Brierley, James C (Rochdale) 1 (1870)
Brockbank, Herbie (Swinton) 3 (1893)
Brodie, John A (Walton, Liverpool Old Boys) 3 (1881-1888)
Bromilow, G (Southport) 1 (1878)
Broughton, FD (Manchester) 1 (1870)
Buckler, J (Blackley) 2 (1899)
Bull, W (Manchester Free Wanderers) 4 (1887-1888)
Bullen, EW (Liverpool Old Boys) 5 (1891- 1892)
Bullough, E 'Ned' (Wigan) 17 (1889-1892)
Bulteel, Andrew J (Manchester) 2 (1874-1875)
Bumby, Walter (Swinton) 23 (1885-1892)
Burder, H (Manchester) 1 (1876)
Butterworth, Tom (Rochdale Hornets) 1 (1894)
Butterworth, Wilfred S (Rochdale Hornets) 11 (1877-1881)

Caldicott, P James (Littleborough) 2 (1899)
Carmerson, GNM (Manchester) 2 (1888-1891)
Carver, Charles W (Liverpool) 3 (1873-1875)
Case, Harry (Ulverston, Swinton) 12 (1892-1894)
Case, Robert (Ulverston) 1 (1892)
Chambers, F (Liverpool Old Boys) 1 (1887)

Chapman, HC (Liverpool Old Boys) 15 (1884-1888)
Chapman, William (Barrow) 3 (1893-1896)
Clarke, Charles WH (Liverpool) 1 (1876)
Clegg, RJ (Manchester) 2 (1880)
Cliff, E (Liverpool) 3 (1876-1877)
Colley, William F (Rochdale, Manchester) 3 (1870-1872)
Colquhoun, RW (Liverpool) 4 (1872-1875)
Cook, Herbert (Salford) 1 (1888)
Cooke, JB (Manchester Free Wanderers) 4 (1881-1882)
Cooke, W 'Billy' (Swinton) 1 (1882)

Cookson, George (Swinton, Manchester) 28 (1896-1901)
Coop, Tom (Leigh) 21 (1890-1893)
Coulthwaite, Tom (Swinton) 1 (1888)
Court, Harry (Oldham) 2 (1883)
Crabtree, R (Littleborough) 6 (1897-1899)
Craven, Tom (Salford) 13 (1890-1892)
Crews, Charles E (Manchester) 3 (1896)
Croggan, S (Broughton) 5 (1897)
Cross, W 'Billy' (St Helens) 16 (1891-1892)
Crossley, James (St Helens Recreation) 3 (1896)

D'Aguilar, Capt J (Manchester Free Wanderers) 1 (1878)
Dakin, John (Warrington) 3 (1894-1895)
Danby, Charlie (Lancaster) 1 (1897)
Darbishire, Godfrey (Manchester) 1 (1875)
Davidson, AG (Blackley) 8 (1898-1900)
Dean, RW (Liverpool) 1 (1875)
Deane, T (Broughton) 8 (1879-1885)
Dickenson, Walter (Swinton) 2 (1881-1882)
Dillon, Will (Warrington) 7 1888-1889)
Dixon, Tom (Askam) 1 (1894)
Drew, Daniel (Manchester) 2 (1877)
Drew, J (Manchester) 1 (1872)
Drummond, Joe (Widnes) 2 (1893)
Duckworth, N (Broughton, Sale, Blackley, Broughton Park) 9 (1897-1901)
Dunlop, G (Liverpool) 1 (1873)
Dunsmuir, George (Manchester) 1 (1875)
Durandu, Arthur (Liverpool) 6 (1883-1888)

Eagles, Harry (Salford) 18 (1886-1890)
Edwards, M (Liverpool) 1 (1873)
Emery, W (Birch) 1 (1878)
Evans, AE (Broughton) 7 (1887-1888)

Farr, Herbert (Swinton) 2 1878)
Farr, Tom (Swinton) 5 (1882-1883)
Fildes, Peter (St Helens Recreation) 1 (1890)
Fletcher, Abraham M (Oldham) 1 (1879)
Fletcher, JE (Manchester) 3 (1880)
Fletcher, JW (Manchester Rangers) 1 (1879)
Flower, EH 'Teddy' (Broughton, Mossley) 18 (1884, 1891)
Forman, A (Liverpool) 3 (1897)
Forshaw, RW 'Bob' (Ulverston) 7 (1896-1897)
Foulkes, Tom (St Helens) 9 (1893-1894)
Fowler, Frank D (Manchester) 2 (1878-1879)
Francomb, John S (Manchester) 9 (1897-1899)
Furniss, E 'Ted' (Oldham) 2 (1894-1895)

Genth, JS 'James' (Manchester) 6 (1870-1876)
Gibson, Arthur S (Manchester) 1 (1871)
Gibson, Charlie (Lancaster) 2 (1895)
Gibson, JG (Liverpool) 1 (1872)
Gibson, PM (Liverpool) 1 (1871)
Glass, D (Waterloo) 1 (1900)
Goold, JC (Liverpool Old Boys) 11 (1893- 1895)
Gordon, WA (Southport) 1 (1879)
Graham, John G (Liverpool Old Boys) 5 (1900-1901)
Grave, William 'Willie' (Manchester) 6 (1870-1878)
Gray, A (Liverpool) 2 (1875-1876)
Green, EJ (Manchester) 2 (1888)
Greg, Walter (Manchester) 7 (1872-1877)
Grey, C (Manchester) 1 (1872)
Griffiths, JE (Rochdale Hornets) 1 (1889)
Groves, Jack (Rochdale Hornets) 4 (1886-1888)
Gwynn, Dai (Oldham) 14 (1890-1892)

Hacking, Jack (Broughton Rangers) 2 (1895)
Hall, Sam (Swinton) 1 (1892)
Hall, W 'Billy' (Ulverston) 5 (1894-1896)
Halliwell, W 'Billy' (Wigan) 2 (1893)
Hardicker, John W (Littleborough, Castleton Moor) 4 (1897-1898)
Harley, John R (Barrow) 1 (1889)
Harrison, TS (Liverpool Old Boys) 2 (1900)
Hartham, GW (Owen's College) 2 (1897)
Hasleham, Harry (Manchester Rangers) 6 (1888)
Hasleham, Herbert (Manchester Rangers) 10 (1889-1891)
Hastings, Willie (Rochdale Hornets, Victoria University) 5 (1888-1890)
Hay-Gordon, James R (Liverpool) 6 (1871-1877)
Heggs, O (Birch) 1 (1878)
Henderson, W (Manchester Free Wanderers) 1 (1879)
Hermon, Sidney A (Preston Grasshoppers) 1 (1871)
Hewitt, George (Widnes) 1 (1889)
Hickson, L (Liverpool Old Boys) 2 (1887)
Higgins, TH (Liverpool) 1 (1880)
Higgins, WF (Liverpool) 2 (1875-1876)
Higgins, William W (Cheetham, Manchester) 12 (1882-1885)
Hodgkinson, H (Littleborough) 9 (1897-1899)
Hogg, WG (Manchester) 1 (1897)

Holme, Joseph (Widnes) 2 (1891)
Holmes, Robert 'Bratty' (Morecambe) 13 (1893-1896)
Holt, Thomas M (Rochdale Hornets) 1 (1883)
Hope, Albert (Swinton) 3 (1882)
Hopper, LB (Liverpool) 7 (1898-1900)
Hopper, W (Bolton) 1 (1879)
Horley, CH 'Charlie' (Swinton) 21 (1881-1890)
Hornby, Albert N (Blackburn, Preston Grasshoppers, Manchester) 12 (1876-1885)
Hotchkiss, Nat (Swinton) 8 (1886-1889)
Hughes, George E (Barrow) 12 (1895-1897)
Hulse, JW 'Joe' (Manchester Free Wanderers) 6 (1882-1884)
Hulse, William S (Manchester Free Wanderers, Manchester) 17 (1881-1886)
Hulton, Campbell G (Rochdale, Preston Grasshoppers) 4 (1870-1873)
Hulton, Jessop (Manchester) 1 (1870)
Hulton, JH (Preston Grasshoppers, Manchester) 4 (1874-1878)
Hunt, James T (Manchester, Preston Grasshoppers) 9 (1880-1884)
Hunt, Dr Robert (Preston Grasshoppers, Manchester) 9 (1878-1881)
Hunt, TH (Manchester, Preston Grasshoppers) 1 (1884)
Hunt, William H (Preston Grasshoppers) 5 (1876-1878)
Hunter, T (Birch) 1 (1879)
Hurst, Jack (Oldham) 7 (1890-1894)

Irving, Andrew (Rochdale Hornets) 2 (1874-1877)

Jackson, CR (Broughton Park) 6 (1899-1900)
Jackson, James (Salford) 1 (1886)
Jackson, Jerry (Broughton Rangers) 2 (1890)
Jellicorse, EH (Manchester) 1 (1875)
Johnson, Jack (Barton, Swinton) 5 (1894-1896)
Jolley, Jim (Warrington) 17 (1891-1895)
Jones, JDK (Liverpool) 1 (1897)
Jones, J Hampton (Walton) 4 (1883-1884)
Jones, JJ (Salford) 11 (1894-1896)
Jordan, EJ (Broughton) 2 (1883-1886)

Kelly, Thomas S (Liverpool Old Boys) 5 (1900-1901)
Kemble, Arthur T (Liverpool) 23 (1883-1888)
Kendal, R (Blackley) 1 (1899)
Kendal, W (Askam) 1 (1890)

Kent, Tom (Salford, Radcliffe) 35 (1888-1893)
Kenyon, James (Swinton) 1 (1888)
Kewley, Edward (Liverpool) 6 (1871-1877)
Kewley, JR (Liverpool) 1 (1871)
Kidd, JE (Eccles, Broughton Park) 4 (1900-1901)
King, Tom (Salford) 11 (1892-1893)
Kingscote, TH (Manchester) 10 (1898-1900)
Kingscote, WA (Manchester) 5 (1899-1900)
Kinnish, William (Barrow) 2 (1885-1886)
Kneen, John (Cheetham) 1 (1882)
Knowles, A (Manchester) 4 (1876-1880)
Knowles, Lees (Manchester) 2 (1876-1877)

Lancaster, William (Swinton) 3 (1896)
Leach, William E (Liverpool) 1 (1875)
Lees, Arthur (Oldham) 3 (1894-1895)
Lees, Sam (Oldham) 9 (1893-1895)
Lemonius, Francis (Liverpool) 1 (1871)
Lewis, R 'Bobby' (Ulverston, Morecambe, Ulverston) 13 (1892-1897)
Lewis, JT 'Jack' (Swinton) 5 (1895-1896)
Lindsay, GC (Manchester Rangers) 1 (1878)
Lings, E (Manchester Free Wanderers) 1 (1882)
Little, Alec (Barrow) 3 (1886-1887)
Lomax, Fred (Swinton) 3 (1891-1892)
Long, A (Blackley, Bowdon) 24 (1897-1900)
Longshaw, Walter (Swinton) 1 (1878)
Lonsdale, JB (Walton) 1 (1884)
Louden, JE (Manchester) 7 (1897-1899)
Lyon, Arthur (Liverpool) 4 (1872-1875)

McCutcheon, W 'Bill' (Oldham) 27 (1891-1894)
McDonald, William (Ulverston) 1 (1897)
McInnes, W (Blackley) 3 (1898-1899)
McIntosh, EA (Liverpool) 1 (1871)
MacLaren, David (Manchester) 4 (1871-1874)
MacLaren, James (Manchester) 4 (1870-1875)
MacLaren, William (Manchester) 2 (1870-1871)
MacMasters, R 'Bob' (Leigh) 1 (1891)
McNiven, Hugh J (Manchester) 2 (1885-1886)
McPhail, W (Manchester) 1 (1901)
Mann, Alex (Broughton Park) 2 (1900)
Mann, Edward (Manchester) 1 (1876)
Manwaring, W 'Billy' (Salford) 9 (1890-1896)
Markendale, Ellis T (Manchester Rangers) 6 (1876-1880)
Marriott, Ernest E (Manchester) 3 (1874-1876)
Marsh, J (Bolton) 1 (1878)

Marsh, James H (Swinton) 13 (1889-1892)
Martin, JD (Liverpool Old Boys) 2 (1898)
Mason, F (Kersal) 1 (1900)
Massey, W (Manchester Free Wanderers) 1 (1878)
Melledew, Tom (Rochdale Hornets) 19 (1889-1893)
Mellor, R (Manchester Free Wanderers) 1 (1876)
Melly, AG (Liverpool) 3 (1887)
Middleton, BC (Manchester) 8 (1899-1900)
Middleton, PE (Manchester) 1 (1897)
Miles, Frank (Salford) 6 (1890-1892)
Mills, Joe (Swinton) 28 (1882-1890)
Milne, FJ (Manchester) 5 1900-1901)
Milnes, James (Manchester) 9 (1898-1899)
Molesworth, AH (Manchester) 3 (1888)
Moore, C (Liverpool) 2 (1871-1872)
Moore, HE (Owen's College) 3 (1900-1901)
Moore, HFB (Manchester) 2 (1883-1885)
Moore, T (Blackley) 1 (1900)
Morgan, W (Broughton) 1 (1878)
Mortimer, William (Liverpool, Cambridge University) 4 (1896-1897)
Moss, Frederick S (Broughton) 15 (1882-1888)
Moss, R 'Bob' (Salford) 6 (1895-1896)
Murray, A (Walton) 1 (1882)
Murray, G Harold (Swinton) 9 (1893-1895)

Nevins, Will (Warrington) 1 (1893)
Newby, J (Mossley) 3 (1892)
Nicholson, Elliot T (Liverpool) 15 (1898-1901)
Nicholson, G (Southport) 2 (1878-1879)
Nolan, Johnny (Rochdale Hornets, Oldham) 4 (1888-1889)

Openshaw, William E (Manchester) 2 (1878)
Orr, John E (Manchester) 6 (1887-1888)
Osborne, Richard R (Rochdale, Manchester) 2 (1870-1871)

Parlane, Willie (Manchester Rangers, Manchester) 24 (1892-1901)
Patteson, F (Manchester) 2 (1873-1875)
Pattinson, JP (Manchester) 3 (1882)
Paul, Arthur G (Swinton) 3 (1889-1890)
Payne, John H (Broughton) 31 (1879-1889)
Pearson, W 'Billy' (Swinton) 3 (1892-1896)
Peel, R (Manchester) 1 (1873)
Pennington, William H (Rochdale Hornets) 2 (1889)

Penny, J (Liverpool) 1 (1871)
Pierce, George H (Broughton) 1 (1892)
Pierce, Richard (Liverpool) 28 (1892-1898)
Pierce, W (Liverpool) 1 (1897)
Pilkington, A (Manchester) 2 (1873-1874)
Pilkington, C (Manchester) 3 (1872-1875)
Pilkington, Jim (Aspull) 1 (1888)
Pilkington, Jimmy (St Helens Recreation) 1 (1890)
Pilkington, Lionel E (St Helens Recreation, Cambridge University) 4 (1895)
Pinch, Jack (Lancaster) 12 (1895-1897)
Pollard, G (Manchester Rangers) 5 (1890-1892)
Pollock, TWS (Parkfield Old Boys) 2 (1900-1901)
Prince, F (Broughton) 1 (1888)
Pyke, Jim (St Helens Recreation) 15 (1890-1892)

Radcliffe, Frank (Manchester) 1 (1873)
Radcliffe, Herbert (Rochdale) 1 (1870)
Reid, JM (Liverpool) 1 (1880)
Richardson, William R (Manchester) 4 (1880)
Ricketts, Jim (Broughton Park) 1 (1900)
Ridehaugh, Benjamin (Rochdale St Clements) 2 (1894)
Rigby, George (Wigan) 3 (1894)
Rigg, Louis (Rochdale St Clements) 1 (1892)
Roberts, AS (Cheetham) 1 (1882)
Roberts, AT (Birch) 1 (1880)
Roberts, JW 'Jack' (Salford) 5 (1887-1891)
Roberts, Sam (Swinton) 7 (1886-1889)
Roberts, W Kendrick (Lancaster Royal Grammar School) 3 (1897)
Robertson, John (Broughton Rangers) 15 (1882-1888)
Robinson, Roper (Ulverston) 1 (1896)
Rome, C (Broughton) 5 (1888-1891)
Roscoe, Bertwine G (Manchester) 1 (1891)
Rothwell, R (Blackley) 1 (1899)
Rothwell, Tom (Swinton) 16 (1890-1893)
Rowley, AB (Manchester) 5 (1880-1881)
Rowley, Hugh C (Manchester) 7 (1879-1881)
Royds, Ernest EM (Rochdale) 1 (1870)
Royle, Arthur V 'Artie' (Broughton Rangers) 9 (1888-1889)
Rye, John B (Oldham) 4 (1879-1885)

Sargent, AE (Manchester) 2 (1899)
Sawyer, Charles M (Broughton Wasps, Broughton) 9 (1877-1881)
Sawyer, James S (Broughton) 5 (1879-1880)
Sawyer, Walter S (Broughton Wasps, Broughton) 4 (1878-1884)
Schofield, George F (Southport) 3 (1877-1878)
Schofield, John W (Manchester) 9 (1880-1882)
Scholes, William A (Rochdale Hornets) 3 (1884-1888)
Seddon, James (St Helens Recreation) 5 (1893-1896)
Seddon, John T (Swinton) 4 (1882-1883)
Seddon, R 'Bob' (Swinton) 3 (1882-1883)
Seddon, R 'Dick' (Wigan) 2 (1888-1889)
Seddon, RL 'Bob' (Broughton, Broughton Rangers, Swinton) 18 (1881-1888)
Sharpe, W (Manchester) 1 (1870)
Sharples, George (Swinton) 4 (1892)
Shawe, G (Liverpool) 1 (1874)
Shepherd, Jim (Tyldesley) 1 (1893)
Sherriff, H (Cheetham) 1 (1880)
Shutt, R (Broughton Wasps) 1 (1878)
Sidebotham, Charles E (Manchester) 3 (1870-1873)
Simpson, Jack (Rochdale Hornets) 10 (1893-1894)
Simpson, Sam (Broughton Rangers) 1 (1886)
Slacke, RB (Manchester) 1 (1900)
Slater, Vic (Salford) 6 (1886-1887)
Smith, A (Broughton) 1 (1883)
Smith, CW (Manchester Rangers) 1 (1879)
Smith, ET (Manchester Rangers) 4 (1877-1879)
Smith, TJ 'Tommy' (Salford) 1 (1887)
Spooner, Reginald H (Liverpool) 5 (1899-1900)
Springmann, HH 'Harry' (Liverpool) 6 (1879-1887)
Squires, JA (Broughton) 1 (1891)
Standring, J (Manchester) 7 (1888)
Steel, Percy (Manchester) 4 (1889-1891)
Steel, WB (Manchester) 1 (1892)
Steele, JR (Blackley) 1 (1900)
Stockley, AH (Liverpool) 3 (1887)
Stoddart, LB (Liverpool) 3 (1886)
Stoddart, Wilfred B (Liverpool) 11 (1892-1896)
Storey, Edgar (Manchester) 5 (1882-1883)
Storey, Herbert L (Preston Grasshoppers) 1 (1878)
Stork, JB (Liverpool) 4 (1891-1892)
Strang, Alan (Liverpool) 3 (1885)
Strang, J (Liverpool) 11 (1888-1890)
Sunderland, Jack (Swinton) 1 (1896)
Sylo-Jones, J Llewellyn (Waterloo) 1 (1900)

Taylor, Charles M (Rochdale) 1 (1870)
Taylor, IP 'Ike' (Oldham) 4 (1894)
Taylor, R (Rochdale) 1 (1871)
Teggin, Alf (Broughton Rangers) 18 (1883-1887)
Thompson, Charlie EK (Lancaster, Manchester) 8 (1896-1900)
Thompson, Edward B (Lancaster) 3 (1896-1897)
Thorp, John WH (Manchester) 1 (1878)
Tickle, R 'Bob' (Swinton) 1 (1896)
Tickle, Tom (Leigh Shamrocks) 1 (1897)
Tillison, S (Castleton Moor) 2 (1897)
Todd, R (Manchester) 3 (1876-1877)
Touzel, Charles JC (Liverpool) 2 (1874-1877)
Townsend, CVM (Liverpool Old Boys) 6 (1898-1900)
Traynor, David (St Helens Recreation) 1 (1896)
Trevor-Smith, CW (Manchester Rangers) 1 (1879)
Trevor-Smith, ET (Manchester) 3 (1883-1884)
Treweek, Fred (Barrow, Roose) 2 (1890-1893)
Tune, JH 'Jack' (Broughton Rangers) 6 (1886-1889)
Turner, Fairfield 'Fair' (Warrington) 2 (1887)
Turner, H James C (Manchester) 3 (1870-1872)

Unsworth, W 'Bill' (Wigan) 9 (1893-1895)

Valentine, Jim (Swinton) 56 (1884-1896)
Varley, Harry (Oldham) 7 (1894-1895)
Veale, RR 'Bob' (Broughton Rangers) 1 (1888)
Verelst, Courtenay L (Liverpool) 2 (1876-1878)

Walkden, JT (Oldham) 1 (1886)
Walker, Roger (Manchester) 8 (1872-1880)
Warren, GJ (Liverpool) 1 (1872)
Walch, Sam (Salford) 2 (1893-1894)
Walmsley, BT (Broughton Park) 2 (1899)
Walsh, S (Pemberton) 6 (1895-1896)
Waugh, W 'Billy' (Rochdale St Clements) 2 (1890)
Weaver, FWH (Liverpool) 1 (1900)
Welsh, J (Liverpool) 3 (1883-1884)
Welsh, W (Manchester) 3 (1870-1874)
Whalley, A (Broughton Wasps) 1 (1877)
Whitehead, R (Blackley) 3 (1897-1898)
Whiteley, William (Bramley) 3 (1894-1895)
Whittaker, Tom (Manchester, Liverpool, Walkden) 27 (1888-1894)
Wilcock, R (Walton) 1 (1883)

Wildman, FJ 'Fred' (Barrow) 3 (1896-1897)
Williams, Sam (Salford) 4 (1886-1887)
Wilson, JH (Manchester) 1 (1881)
Wilson, Roger P (Liverpool Old Boys) 19 (1890-1894)
Wilson, Sidney E (Liverpool) 9 (1891-1894)
Wincey, Guy P (Manchester) 9 (1896-1898)
Winterbottom, Joe (Mossley) 1 (1889)
Withers, FC (Liverpool) 3 (1887)
Wood, E (Cheetham) 2 (1881)
Wood, Herbert D (Liverpool Old Boys) 1 (1888)
Wood, Robert D (Liverpool Old Boys) 30 (1896-1901)
Wood, Sydney G (Liverpool) 5 (1900-1901)
Woodcock, W (Broughton) 1 (1880)
Woodforder, EF (Manchester) 1 (1878)
Woodhead, Fred (Castleton Moor) 6 (1897-1898)
Woods, DC (Manchester) 2 (1892)
Woodward, George (Tyldesley) 16 (1888-1894)
Woolley, Henry (Manchester) 1 (1874)
Wormald, Joseph D (Bolton, Manchester) 5 (1879-1883)
Wormald, GF (Broughton) 2 (1889-1890)
Worthington, Dr D 'Doc' (Tottington) 1 (1887)
Wright, Frank T (Manchester) 6 (1882-1885)
Wrigley, AH (Liverpool) 4 (1882-1883)
Wyles, H (Broughton Wasps) 2 (1877-1878)

Yates, Harry (Swinton) 2 (1878-1879)

20-plus appearances (1870-1901):
Jim Valentine 56
Tom Kent 35
Billy Atkinson 31
John H Payne 31
Robert D Wood 30*
George Cookson 28*
Joe Mills 28
Richard Pierce 28
Charley Anderton 27
Bill McCutcheon 27
Tom Whittaker 27
A Long 24
Willie Parlane 24*
Walter Bumby 23
Arthur T Kemble 23
Tom Coop 21
Charlie Horley 21
*Further appearances after 1900-01

NORTHUMBERLAND

109 matches, 314 players

Adamson, C (unidentified) 1 (1876)
Adamson, J (unidentified) 1 (1876)
Alderson, FHR 'Fred' (Tynedale) 2 (1887-1888)
Alexander, Thomas P (Rockcliff) 13 (1891-1896)
Anderson, Stanley (Wallsend, Rockcliff) 38 (1892-1901)
Anderson, Tom (Tynedale, Northern) 5 (1888-1889)
Angus, Harry (Northern) 12 (1887-1892)
Armstrong, GH (Northumberland) 9 (1883-1885)
Armstrong, W (Gosforth) 2 (1892)
Atkinson, R (Northumberland) 1 (1876)
Atkinson, S (North Elswick) 1 (1886)
Audus, Henry W (Percy Park) 1 (1894)
Avery, G (Northumberland) 2 (1889)

Bagley, WR (Darlington) 1 (1877)
Bailey, J 'Gus' (Tynedale) 1 (1884)
Bainbridge, Arthur E (Northumberland) 2 (1885)
Bainbridge, John G (Northern) 2 (1897)
Bamborough, Joseph W (Rockcliff) 6 (1899-1901)
Barnes, CE (Durham City) 2 (1877)
Bates, Stuart F (Gosforth) 2 (1880-1881)
Bates, William (Percy Park) 21 (1896-1900)
Baty, Isaac (Tynedale) 1 (1885)
Baty, JA 'Jack' (Tynedale) 1 (1901)
Baty, R (Tynedale) 9 (1892-1896)
Baty, William G (Tynedale, South Shields) 12 (1893-1899)
Beadon, Dacres C (Northumberland) 2 (1877-1878)
Bell, FJ 'Fred' (Rockcliff) 15 (1897-1900)
Bell, GA (Northumberland) 18 (1880-1886)
Bell, GH (Tynedale) 1 (1884)
Bell, Henry S (Northern) 3 (1896)
Bell, J Lowthian (Northumberland) 4 (1876-1880)
Bell, JT (Percy Park) 1 (1893)
Bell, Robert W (Northern, Cambridge University) 8 (1898-1900)
Bennett, Joseph H (North Elswick) 1 (1881)
Benson, Alf (Rockcliff) 12 (1888-1892)
Blackett, Algernon C (Northern) 6 (1896-1897)
Bolam, John (Rockcliff) 1 (1901)

Boss, Thomas G (Gosforth) 3 (1890-1891)
Braithwaite, Robert (Northumberland, North Durham) 3 (1876-1878)
Bramwell, C (Tynemouth) 4 (1876-1883)
Brewis, George (Northumberland) 1 (1889)
Brough, Gil (Rockcliff) 2 (1897o
Brutton, Ernest B (Tynemouth) 5 (1882-1884)
Brutton, Septimus (Tynemouth, Rockcliff) 4 (1886-1892)
Bryant, James (Northern) 1 (1900)
Buckley, Arthur (Wallsend, Percy Park) 4 (1893-1896)
Burdon, John G (Northumberland) 2 (1880-1881)
Burridge, S (Northumberland) 3 (1877-1880)

Cadle, A (Northumberland) 6 (1876-1882)
Calder, HF (unidentified) 1 (1882)
Campbell, P (North Elswick) 1 (1880)
Carr, Rev AS (Northumberland) 8 (1887-1889)
Carr, W (Northumberland) 1 (1876)
Carter, T (Benwell) 1 (1888)
Challoner, AC (Northern) 4 (1885-1887)
Challoner, Frederick CT (Northumberland) 4 (1876-1878)
Chambers, O (Rockcliff) 1 (1901)
Charles, C (Northern) 1 (1885)
Coates, Rev Charles H (Northern) 4 (1884-1885)
Coull, William W (Percy Park) 2 (1900-1901)
Coulson, T (Percy Park) 4 (1887-1888)
Coward, J William (Percy Park) 24 (1881-1888)
Cowper, J (Tynedale) 1 (1880)
Crawford, S (Tynemouth) 3 (1880-1881)
Cubbold, - (unidentified) 1 (1876)
Cummins, W (Tynemouth) 1 (1880)
Curley, William (North Elswick) 2 (1889-1890)
Curry, Alexander L (Percy Park) 3 (1893-1894)

Dale, B (Northumberland) 3 (1876-1877)
Dale, CNM (Northumberland) 1 (1876)
Dale, R (Tynemouth) 11 (1881-1884)
Darling, A (Northumberland) 1 (1884)
Davidson, George (Percy Park) 3 (1890-1891)
De Jersey, JE (Northumberland) 1 (1876)
Dick, Geo (Rockcliff) 1 (1899)
Dick, William H (Northern) 5 (1899-1901)
Dickenson, WR (Northern) 3 (1880-1881)

Dixon, TR (Tynemouth) 2 (1885)
Dobinson, James (Rockcliff, Percy Park) 7 (1898-1899)
Dodd, John T (Tynedale) 11 (1882-1888)
Dotchin, Frederick E (Northern) 11 (1893-1896)
Douglas, H (Percy Park) 3 (1887-1888)
Douglas, W (North Elswick) 1 (1889)
Douglas, W (Brighton) 1 (1896)
Douthwaite, J (Tynedale) 3 (1890-1892)
Dudgeon, Herbert W (Northern) 6 (1898-1899)
Dunford, F (Northumberland) 1 (1876)
Dunn, - (unidentified) 1 (1882)
Dunn, JH (Rockcliff) 7 (1899-1901)

Edwards, J (Northumberland) 1 (1877)
Eichholtz, Albert (Northumberland) 9 (1877-1885)
Elliott, Jim (Tynedale) 1 (1883)
Elliott, Tom (Tynedale) 6 (1883-1888)
Elsdon, Matthew F (Tynemouth) 12 (1883-1887)
Emley, Edwin (Northern) 9 (1888-1891)

Farr, W (Gosforth) 4 (1880-1881)
Farrow, William H (Tynemouth) 1 (1882)
Fawcus, George D (Tynemouth) 8 (1877-1881)
Fawcus, William (Tynemouth) 3 (1876-1877)
Finlay, H (Wallsend) 1 (1892)
Finlay, James (Wallsend, West Hartlepool) 19 (1896-1900)
Finlay, T (Rockcliff) 4 (1899-1901)
Finney, F (Percy Park) 17 (1886-1892)
Fletcher, JE (Northumberland) 1 (1877)
Fowles, J (Sunderland) 1 (1878)

Gabbatt, WH (Northumberland) 1 (1877)
Galloway, Hubert E (Northern) 1 (1900)
Galloway, TP (Northern) 1 (1894)
Garrett, FC (Northern) 6 (1892-1894)
Gee, Arthur (Percy Park) 19 (1885-1890)
Gee, J (Percy Park) 2 (1883)
Gee, Tom (Percy Park) 22 (1885-1890)
Gibson, C (Northern) 1(1880)
Gibson, Charles OP (Northern, Oxford University) 14 (1897-1901)
Gibson, George R (Northern) 15 (1898-1901)
Gibson, WW (Northern) 7 (1896-1901)
Gill, Charles S (Northern) 12 (1885-1889)
Graham, TS 'Tom' (Northern) 2 (1889-1890)
Graves, R (Northumberland) 2 (1877)

Gray, WR (Percy Park, Northumberland) 6 (1884-1888)
Greenwell, JH 'Harry' (Tynemouth, Rockcliff) 49 (1885-1901)
Greenwell, William N (Rockcliff) 12 (1893-1897)

Hadley, T (Tynedale) 1 (1881)
Hamilton, CH (Rockcliff) 1 (1889)
Hamilton, W (Tynedale) 4 (1896)
Harding, JT (Northumberland) 4 (1876-1877)
Hardwick, Peter F (Percy Park) 9 (1899-1901)
Hargreaves, R (unidentified) 1 (1878)
Harris, Roger (North Elswick) 7 (1891-1895)
Harrison, CW 'Charlie' (Tynedale) 19 (1884-1890)
Harrison, R (Tynemouth) 1 (1888)
Haslam, AS (North Elswick) 6 (1886-1888)
Haslam, Hedley (North Elswick) 12 (1888-1890)
Hedley, T (Tynedale) 1 (1881)
Henderson, EA (Percy Park) 7 (1900-1901)
Hendlands, - (unidentified) 1 (1877)
Henzell, Robert (Northern) 1 (1881)
Herbertson, Robert E (Percy Park) 10 (1886-1890)
Heslop, O (Northumberland) 1 (1892)
Heywood, W (Rockcliff) 1 (1882)
Hobson, James (Tynedale) 2 (1895)
Hodge, B (Northumberland) 5 (1876-1877)
Hogg, Dr (Tynedale) 1 (1883)
Honeyman, John (North Elswick) 3 (1885)
Horsley, P (Percy Park) 1 (1888)
Hoyle, T (Northern) 4 (1887-1888)
Hughes, H (Northumberland) 1 (1876)
Hughes, HA (unidentified) 1 (1877)
Hutchinson, A (Northumberland) 1 (1876)
Hutchinson, T (Northumberland) 4 (1888)

Jackson, Arthur (Rockcliff) 1 (1893)
Jackson, Willy (Rockcliff) 6 (1895-1896)
Jones, FH (Northern, Cambridge University) 1 (1901)
Jones, HE (Northumberland) 1 (1882)

Kayll, Henry E (Sunderland) 1 (1878)
Knott, Harry (Percy Park) 6 (1892-1894)

Lattimer, Francis (Rockcliff) 1 (1890)
Lawson, Charlie (Wallsend) 2 (1899-1900)
Lee, George W (Rockcliff) 10 (1894-1896)
Leighton, George (Percy Park) 1 1888)
Liddell, E (Northern) 2 (1881-1882)

Lindsay, Jimmy (Tudhoe) 7 (1896-1898)
Livingstone, J (Northern) 16 (1885-1890)
Lockerby, SC 'Sammy' (Percy Park) 17 (1896-1899)
Lockerby, Robert T (Percy Park) 5 (1899-1900)
Lockhart, HB (Northern) 14 (1882-1889)
Logan, F (Northumberland) 5 (1876-1878)

McConnell, John (Percy Park) 8 (1880-1882)
McIntyre, JJ (Tynedale) 3 (1889-1890)
McMenemy, J (Percy Park) 2 (1897)
Maitland, G (Northern) 2 (1881-1882)
Maling, JT (Northern) 1 (1880)
Manford, Frank (Northern) 5 (1887-1888)
Manford, S (Northern) 2 (1890)
Mansell, D (Northumberland) 1 (1882)
Marshall, F (Northumberland) 5 (1880-1882)
Marshall, Frank (Percy Park) 7 (1889-1891)
Mason, George A (Northern) 2 (1882)
Maughan, CC (Northern) 1 (1895)
Miller, F (Benwell) 1 (1887)
Milvain, E (Northumberland) 2 (1877-1878)
Mole, George W (North Elswick) 21 (1885-1890)
Moran, Percy (Wallsend, Hartlepool Rovers) 16 (1897-1900)
Morgan, CE (Northern) 4 (1884-1885)
Morgan, O (Wallsend Wanderers) 1 (1882)
Morrell, William (North Elswick) 1 (1887)
Morrison, James (Northumberland) 1 (1880)
Morrison, Piercy H 'Dolly' (Northern) 1 (1891)
Morrison, TH 'Tom' (Percy Park) 3 (1880-1881)
Mullin, H (Northern) 1 (1894)
Munro, J (Wallsend) 3 (1897-1898)
Mursell, Arthur (Northern) 12 (1883-1885)

Nesbitt, A (Percy Park) 1 (1895)
Nesbitt, John (Rockcliff, Wallsend, Percy Park) 22 (1894-1900)
Nicholson, Tom (Rockcliff) 16 (1890-1896)
Nimmo, J (Northumberland) 1 (1889)

Ogilvie, Frank S (Tynemouth) 2 (1882-1883)
Oliver, S (Tynemouth) 16 (1880-1885)
Oscroft, Percy W (Northern) 3 (1895)
Owen, T (Rockcliff) 1 (1899)

Palmer, George R (Tynemouth) 11 (1880-1885)
Pattinson, Charles R (Northumberland) 3 (1880-1882)
Pattinson, Hugh L (Northumberland) 3 (1876-1877)
Pattinson, John S (Northumberland) 10 (1876-1882)
Pattinson, William (Tynedale) 5 (1883-1885)
Pattinson, William H (Northumberland) 1 (1880)
Pickering, Fred (Rockcliff) 6 (1900-1901)
Pigg, David J (Gosforth) 1 (1880)
Potts, Charles WM (Northern) 1 (1901)
Prest, Stanley F (Northumberland) 9 (1877-1882)

Ramsay, Francis W (Northumberland, Northern) 13 (1883-1886)
Redford, F (Northumberland) 2 (1876-1877)
Reed, B (Northumberland) 2 (1880-1881)
Richards, F (unidentified) 1 (1877)
Richards, JB (Northumberland) 1 (1877)
Ridley, Charles A (Northern) 3 (1889-1891)
Ridley, Edward T (Northern) 1 (1882)
Ridley, G Walter (Northern) 18 (1880-1885)
Ridley, William (Northern) 1 (1880)
Rishworth, J (North Elswick) 2 (1888)
Ritson, James (Wallsend) 5 (1900-1901)
Robb, RH 'Harry' (Tynedale) 22 (1880-1887)
Robertson, JA (Northern) 4 (1884-1885)
Robertson, RM (North Durham, Rockcliff) 2 (1897-1900)
Robinson, CO 'Charlie' (Percy Park) 6 (1893-1896)
Robinson, George C 'Tot' (Percy Park) 22 (1894-1901)
Robson, BS (Percy Park) 4 (1900-1901)
Robson, G (Tynedale) 1 (1882)
Robson, George (Rockcliff) 6 (1890-1892)
Robson, Tom (Tynedale) 29 (1881-1898)
Rogan, T (Northumberland, Tynedale) 3 (1885-1886)
Ross, D (Northern) 3 (1881-1882)
Rowell, Henry S (Northern) 3 (1883-1884)
Russell, CW 'Charlie' (Percy Park) 14 (1897-1901)
Rutherford, John VW (Northern) 12 (1880-1884)
Rutherford, Vickerman (Northern) 6 (1885-1886)
Rycroft, Thomas (Percy Park) 2 (1892-1893)

Sample, Charles H (Northumberland, Cambridge University) 12 (1883-1886)
Sample, Harold W (Northumberland, Cambridge University) 5 (1885-1886)
Sample, William C (Northumberland) 10 (1883-1884)

Samuel, C (Percy Park) 1 (1897)
Scotland, Thomas (Percy Park) 1 (1900)
Scott, Charlie (Northern) 9 (1889-1891)
Scott, E (Northumberland) 2 (1877-1878)
Scott, Fife J (Northern) 1 (1884)
Scott, H (Northern) 2 (1886)
Scott, Mason T (Northern, Cambridge University) 11 (1886-1890)
Scott, T (North Elswick) 3 (1897-1898)
Scott, WM 'Willie' (Northumberland, Northern) 9 (1884-1888)
Seymour, John C (Wallsend, Rockcliff) 6 (1897-1901)
Seymour, Willie (Rockcliff) 1 (1899)
Shortt, Charles S (Northern) 1 (1893)
Shotton, Henry (North Elswick, Percy Park) 7 (1882, 1891)
Simpson, Thomas (Rockcliff) 4 (1900-1901)
Sinclair, D (Percy Park) 1 (1901)
Skelton, Joseph (Newcastle Rangers) 2 (1887)
Smith, Albert (Wallsend) 1 (1901)
Smith, J (Gosforth) 2 (1881)
Smith, James (Wallsend) 8 (1895-1901)
Smith, Robert (Rockcliff) 1 (1900)
Smurthwaite, H (Percy Park) 2 (1893)
Sowerby, George (Bensham, North Durham) 3 (1876-1878)
Spence, Robert H (Percy Park) 3 (1886-1887)
Spencer, D (Northern) 1 (1886)
Spencer, Harry (Northern, Cambridge University) 2 (1898)
Spencer, Harry J (Percy Park) 15 (1895-1898)
Spencer, Henry WE (Northern) 4 (1886-1887)
Spencer, Richard EE (Northumberland) 3 (1883)
Stephenson, TC (Rockcliff) 7 (1893-1896)
Stevenson, RC (Northern) 12 (1897-1899)
Steward, G (unidentified) 1 (1882)
Stewart, Tom (Percy Park) 11 (1889-1893)
Stone, Frank W (Percy Park) 13 (1898-1901)
Strickland, Francis S (Northumberland) 2 (1881-1882)
Styan, A (Rockcliff) 12 (1889-1895)
Sutherland, B (Northern) 4 (1886-1888)
Swinburne, Joseph W (Northern) 17 (1881-1887)
Symington, H (Northern) 17 (1881-1885)

Tasker, Andrew K (Percy Park) 1 (1900)
Taylor, Andrew (Rockcliff) 1 (1898)
Taylor, E (Benwell) 1 (1888)
Taylor, EW 'Little Billy' (Rockcliff) 34 (1889-1899)
Taylor, Jack (Gosforth, Percy Park) 2 (1890-1892)
Taylor, John (Rockcliff) 1 (1895)
Taylor, W 'Long Billy' (Rockcliff) 7 (1889- 1897)
Thew, F (Northern) 3 (1897)
Thomas, R (Wallsend) 1 (1897)
Thomas, T (Percy Park) 2 (1886-1887)
Thompson, Frank (Tynedale) 1 (1890)
Thompson, John (Northern) 1 (1888)
Thompson, Joe (Rockcliff) 1 (1894)
Thompson, M (Northumberland) 4 (1884-1885)

Wallace, T (Northumberland) 1 (1885)
Walters, G (Northern) 2 (1885)
Walton, J (Tynemouth) 2 (1882-1884)
Warwick, J (Northern) 1 (1882)
Watkin, JT (Tynemouth) 1 (1883)
Watson, W (Northern) 3 (1888-1889)
Watt, James (North Elswick) 1 (1893)
Watts, AE (Northern) 1 (1885)
Welford, Henry (North Elswick) 3 (1886-1887)
Wheler-Sime, F (Northern) 3 (1897)
Whiteling, HT (Rockcliff) 1 (1891)
Williams, AC (Northern) 3 (1892-1893)
Williams, B (Percy Park) 1 (1899)
Williams, WS (Northumberland) 2 (1881)
Williamson, JA (Percy Park) 2 (1886)
Wilson, T (Tynemouth) 3 (1876-1877)
Winship, Charles E (Northern) 14 (1881-1886)
Winship, John (Benwell) 4 (1888-1889)
Winship, William A (Northern) 1 (1880)
Woodburn, Stephen (Wallsend) 1 (1900)
Wright, Robert (Brighton) 4 (1892-1894)

Young, W (Wallsend) 2 (1891-1892)

20-plus appearances (1876-1901):
Harry Greenwell 49
Stanley Anderson 38*
EW 'Little Billy' Taylor 34*
Tom Robson 29
J William Coward 24
Tom Gee 22
J Nesbitt 22*
Harry Robb 22
George C Robinson 22*
W Bates 21
George W Mole 21
*Further appearances after 1900-01

WESTMORLAND
44 matches, 169 players

Adams, - ('Burton') 1 (1896)
Alexander, John (Kendal Town) 2 (1886-1887)
Allen, Joe (Kendal Hornets, St Helens, Dewsbury) 13 (1888-1894)
Armer, John J (Kendal Town) 5 (1886-1888)
Armstrong, Jack (Kendal Hornets) 12 (1886-1890)
Atkinson, Joseph (Kendal Hornets) 1 (1889)

Baines, TG 'Tom' (Kendal Hornets) 3 (1887-1888)
Banks, Jim (Ambleside) 5 (1887-1888)
Banks, William E (Kendal Town) 3 (1887-1888)
Beard, RC 'Dick' (Kendal Town) 15 (1886-1891)
Beetham, Luke (Ambleside) 8 (1886-1888)
Bell, George H (Kendal Town, Tyldesley) 3 (1889-1892)
Bell, Jim (Kendal Town, Tyldesley) 2 (1888-1894)
Bell, T (Kirkby Lonsdale) 1 (1896)
Berry, John 'Buff' (Kendal Hornets, Tyldesley) 13 (1886-1893)
Berry, W 'Billy' (Kendal Hornets, Tyldesley) 3 (1889-1894)
Bigland, Alf ('Windermere') 1 (1897)
Bigland, Joseph (Windermere, 'Windermere') 5 (1895-1897)
Bowe, Leonard (Ambleside) 6 (1896-1897)
Braithwaite, Edwin (Kendal Hornets) 3 (1894-1896)
Braithwaite, George W ('Kendal') 2 (1896)
Brown, E (unidentified) 1 (1897)

Carradus, George (Kendal Town) 1 (1888)
Carradus, Jack (Kendal Town, Kendal Hornets, Burneside, ('Kendal') 23 (1888-1898)
Causton, C ('Kendal') 1 (1897)
Causton, F ('Kendal') 1 (1898)
Chorley, Alf (Halifax) 3 (1894)
Chorley, R 'Bob' (Kendal Town) 2 (1886-1889)
Chorley, Walter ('Kendal') 1 (1897)
Coleman, George (Kendal Town, Kendal Hornets) 2 (1891-1894)
Cooper, William ('Kendal') 1 (1897)
Cragg, FW 'Frank' ('Kendal') 2 (1897-1898)
Cross, W 'Billy' (Kendal Hornets, St Helens) 13 (1886-1894)
Crossley, Christopher ('Kendal') 5 (1897-1898)

Davis, William A (Holme Wanderers) 5 (1894-1896)
Dean, H (Kirkby Lonsdale) 1 (1896)
Deason, James (Kendal Hornets) 5 (1893-1894)
Dixon, Arthur S (Ambleside) 7 (1894-1896)
Dixon, Frank (Kendal Hornets) 3 (1893-1894)
Dixon, George ('Kendal') 1 (1896)
Doherty, R 'Bob' (St Helens) 1 (1894)
Duff, William A (Kirkby Lonsdale) 5 (1895-1896)

Elliott, John (Burneside) 6 (1894-1897)
Ellwood, DF 'Dan' (Kendal Hornets) 4 (1888)
Ewan, W 'Billy' (Kendal Town) 2 (1890)
Exley, FE 'Fred' (Kendal Town) 1 (1888)

Fawcett, George (Lancaster) 5 (1895-1896)
Fawcett, Tom (Kendal Town, Kendal Hornets) 5 (1890-1896)
Fisher, George (Holme Wanderers, Lancaster) 7 (1894-1896)
Fisher, H ('Staveley') 1 (1897)
Fisher, R (Ambleside) 4 (1886-1888)
Fisher, R 'Dick' ('Staveley') 3 (1897)
Fleming, Tom (Staveley) 2 (1897)

Garnett, J (Kendal Hornets) 1 1893)
Garnett, Tom (Windermere) 2 (1894)
Gawith, James ('Kirkby Lonsdale') 1 (1898)
Geddes, David (Holme Wanderers, Carnforth) 2 (1896)
Gibson, Tom (Lancaster) 2 (1894-1896)
Goodman, Johnny (Radcliffe, Walkden) 4 (1893-1895)
Gott, John A ('Heversham', Cambridge University) 1 (1898)
Graham. George (Kendal Town) 2 (1889-1890)
Graham, Jim (Kendal Hornets) 1 (1892)
Graham, J ('Kendal') 1 (1897)

Hadwin, Isaac (Kendal Town) 3 (1888)
Hadwin, J (Ulverston/'Kendal') 1 (1896)
Hall, J ('Kendal') 3 (1897-1898)
Hall, W (Lancaster) 3 (1895-1897)
Hall, W 'Billy' (Kendal Hornets, Ulverston) 7 (1891-1893)
Hargreaves, George (Kendal Town) 1 (1891)
Harrison, Jim ('Kendal') 1 (1896)

Heap, Charles (Kendal Hornets) 5 (1895-1896)
Heap, Frank (Kendal Hornets) 4 (1889-1891)
Henderson, Thomas (Kendal Hornets) 1 (1887)
Hill, R 'Dicky' (Kendal Hornets) 5 (1892-1895)
Hill, W (Kendal Hornets) 5 (1887-1888)
Hine, E 'Ned' (Kendal Hornets) 1 (1888)
Hine, Tom (Kendal Hornets) 11 (1889-1893)
Hine, William (Ulverston) 1 (1896)
Hodgson, William (Ambleside) 4 (1887-1888)
Hoggarth, Edwin (Kendal Town) 6 (1886-1888)
Hoggarth, Fred (Lancaster) 2 (1896)
Hoggarth, Walter G (Kendal Town) 6 (1887-1891)
Holmes, Jim (Kendal Hornets, Staveley) 7 (1894-1896)
Huck, W (Staveley) 1 (1896)
Hugginson, J (Burneside) 3 (1896-1897)

Ireland, Philip (Kendal Town) 1 (1890)

Jackson, James (Ulverston) 1 (1897)
Jackson, T (Burton & Holme Wanderers) 3 (1893)
Jackson, W (Holme Wanderers) 1 (1894)
Jackson, W ('Burton') 2 (1896-1897)
Johnson, E (unidentified) 1 (1888)
Jones, Vincent S (Burneside) 6 (1893-1895)
Jowett, A (Kirkby Lonsdale) 9 (1891-1897)

Knight, CH 'Charlie' (Kendal Hornets) 2 (1886-1887)

Lambert, Jack (Lancaster) 1 (1891)
Lancaster, W (Windermere) 1 (1896)
Langley, Arthur S (Kendal Hornets) 3 (1894-1895)
Leather, Charles ('Kendal') 1 (1897)
Lowery, F (Burneside) 1 (1896)
Lupton, T (Kirkby Lonsdale) 1 (1889)

Machell, George (Kendal Town) 6 (1889-1891)
McIntosh, Donald ('Kendal') 1 (1897)
Major, J (Burneside, 'Kendal') 4 (1896-1897)
Martin, William (Windermere) 3 (1886-1887)
Mason, CG 'Charlie' (Ambleside) 6 (1892-1895)
Maw, PJ ('Burneside') 1 (1897)
Metcalfe, G ('Kendal') 1 (1897)
Metcalfe, P (Kirkby Lonsdale) 1 (1891)
Miller, J (unidentified) 1 (1897)
Moore, Robert H (Ambleside, Oldham) 16 (1887-1894)

Moore, R ('Burneside') 1 (1897)
Moreton, R (Kendal Town) 2 (1889-1890)
Murdock, G (unidentified) 1 (1897)

Newton, Herbert F (Ambleside, Oxford University) 4 (1895-1898)
Newton, John (Ambleside) 3 (1892)
Newton, William (Ambleside) 1 (1896)
Nicholson, Rowland (Kendal Town, Kendal Hornets) 16 (1887-1893)
Nicholson, Thomas (Kendal Hornets) 3 (1891-1892)

Palmer, Herbert R (Kirkby Lonsdale, Cambridge University) 1 (1897)
Palmer, R ('Burneside') 2 (1897)
Park, A (Kirkby Lonsdale) 1 (1889)
Parkinson, Jim (Kendal Town) 3 (1888-1889)
Parsons, William J (Kendal Hornets) 15 (1887-1894)
Pearson, Cuthbert 'Cuth' (Ambleside, Doncaster Town) 2 (1897-1898)
Pickthall, J ('Burneside') 1 (1897)
Pollitt, Frank B (Kendal Town) 1 (1891)
Punchard, Charles B (Kirkby Lonsdale) 7 (1891-1896)
Punchard, Frederick B (Kirkby Lonsdale) 1 (1888)

Railton, Edward (Kendal Hornets) 3 (1893)
Rawlinson, Tom (Windermere) 1 (1893)
Reed, H (Burneside, 'Burneside') 2 (1896-1897)
Richardson, E (Kirkby Lonsdale) 4 (1888-1891)
Robinson, John K (Kirkby Lonsdale) 23 (1888-1897)
Robinson, Roland H (Burneside) 3 (1894-1895)
Robinson, W 'Bill' (Ambleside) 10 (1895-1897)

Saul, Robert (Ambleside) 1 (1886)
Sharpe, Frederick ('Kendal') 6 (1896-1898)
Shaw, Nat ('Staveley') 4 (1897-1898)
Shepherd, Jack (Kendal Town) 1 (1889)
Simm, Robert (Kendal Hornets) 4 (1893-1895)
Skelton, Herbert H (Ambleside) 2 (1896-1897)
Skelton, William C (Ambleside) 1 (1896)
Stavert, John (Burneside, 'Windermere') 3 (1896-1897)
Stubbs, Frederick ('Kendal') 3 (1897)

Taylforth, JC 'Charlie' (Kirkby Lonsdale) 1 (1896)

Thompson, Joe (Staveley) 1 (1896)
Thompson, John H (Kendal Hornets, Burneside, 'Kendal') 12 (1891-1898)
Tomlinson, J ('Kendal') 5 (1897-1898)
Tucker, Arthur (Windermere) 1 (1886)

Vity, Edward 'Ted' (Ambleside) 4 (1896)
Vity, John (Ambleside) 7 (1893-1895)
Vity, Robert (Ambleside) 2 (1896)

Walker, William J 'Will' (Kendal Hornets) 8 (1886-1888)
Webster, George (Kirkby Lonsdale) 5 (1888-1891)
Whitehead, William (Kendal Hornets, Wigan, 'Kendal') 3 (1891-1897)
Whiteley, W 'Bill' (Kendal Hornets, St Helens) 6 (1892-1894)
Whittam, Jack (Kendal Town) 2 (1890-1891)
Whitwell, George ('Kendal') 4 (1897-1898)
Whitwell, J (Barrow) 4 (1896-1897)
Wilkinson, John W (Kendal Hornets, 'Kendal') 10 (1887-1897)
Wilson, Enoch 'Knock' (Kendal Hornets) 10 (1888-1892)
Wilson, HT 'Harry' (Ulverston, 'Kendal') 7 (1896-1897)
Wilson, LE 'Leo' (Kendal Town) 2 (1888)
Wilson, R (Kendal Hornets) 1 (1888)
Wilson, Tom (Kendal Hornets) 1 (1893)
Wilson, William (Kendal Hornets) 3 (1892-1894)
Winskill, RS 'Bob' (Kendal Hornets, Halifax) 11 (1889-1894)
Woodhouse, William (Kirkby Lonsdale, 'Kirkby Lonsdale') 9 (1889-1898)
Workman, Frank (Ambleside) 1 (1896)

20-plus appearances (1886-1898):
Jack Carradus 23
John K Robinson 23

YORKSHIRE
178 matches, 513 players

Ackroyd, GP (Skipton) 9 (1898-1901)
Adkins, D (Keighley) 5 (1899-1900)
Alexander, F (Featherstone) 2 (1899)
Allbutt, Tom (Halifax) 4 (1882-1888)
Archer, Harry (Huddersfield) 4 (1887-1888)
Arnold, Joey (Halifax) 1 (1894)
Ash, Alfred 'Fred' (Wakefield Trinity) 2 (1888)
Ashby, LE (Bradford) 2 (1873)
Ashton, DA 'Dan' (Mytholmroyd) 2 (1900-1901)
Asquith, Sam (Bradford) 2 (1883)
Atkinson, AR (Leeds) 1 (1880)
Atkinson, J Cecil (Leeds) 9 (1877-1879)
Avery-Jones, E (Castleford) 5 (1900-1901)

Baldwin, J (Ilkley) 1 (1873)
Bardon, J (Heckmondwike) 1 (1880)
Barker, Harry (Liversedge) 3 (1892)
Barker, Tom (Mytholmroyd) 1 (1900)
Barnes, Herbert (Halifax) 2 (1891)
Barraclough, Alf (Manningham) 12 (1894-1895)
Barrett, G (Normanton) 1 (1887)
Barron, JH 'Harry' (Bingley) 11 (1895-1896)
Bartram, CE 'Teddy' (Wakefield Trinity) 16 (1880-1884)
Batley, JA (Harrogate) 3 (1900)
Beardsell, Charles W (Huddersfield) 1 (1871)
Beardsell, Harry (Huddersfield) 5 (1870-1873)
Bearpark, Albert E 'Lol' (Hull) 1 (1888)
Bedford, Harry (Batley, Morley) 32 (1886-1890)
Bedford, Fred (Halifax) 1 (1880)
Bedford, Jim (Wakefield Trinity) 6 (1890-1892)
Belt, George E (Hull) 1 (1884)
Bennett, - (unidentified) 1 (1873)
Bennett, T Oliver (Wakefield Trinity) 1 (1880)
Bethell, C (Hull) 1 (1874)
Beutler, JO (Bradford) 1 (1880)
Bingham, RG (Castleford) 4 (1899-1900)
Binks, W 'Billy' (Wakefield Trinity) 5 (1888-1891)
Birch, Edward (York) 3 (1887-1888)
Blackburn, Fred (Heckmondwike, Cleckheaton) 2 (1890-1892)
Blackburn, H (Hebden Bridge) 4 (1897-1898)
Blades, R 'Dick' (Keighley) 3 (1897-1898)
Blakey, Albert (Wortley) 1 (1892)

Bonsor, Fred (Bradford) 32 (1881-1890)
Bonsor, Morris (Bradford) 1 (1885)
Booth, Frank (Bradford Rangers) 1 (1880)
Booth, Paul (Wakefield Trinity) 2 (1887-1889)
Bottomley, E (Bradford Olicana) 2 (1899-1900)
Bottomley, George W (Huddersfield) 19 (1878-1884)
Bottomley, JW (Bradford) 1 (1883)
Bradley, Alfred (Huddersfield) 5 (1870-1873)
Bradley, Joe (Goole) 3 (1888-1889)
Bradshaw, Harry (Bramley) 28 (1891-1895)
Briggs, Arthur (Otley, Bradford) 9 (1891-1893)
Briggs, HE (Bradford) 3 (1878-1880)
Broadbent, Harry (Dewsbury) 2 (1880)
Broadbent, J (Leeds) 2 (1890-1891)
Broadhead, JC (Kirkstall) 2 (1879-1880)
Broadley, Tom (Bingley, Bradford, West Riding) 38 (1891-1896)
Bromet, William E (Tadcaster, Richmond) 17 (1890-1893)
Brook, GS (Huddersfield) 7 (1871-1876)
Brook, Herbert S (Huddersfield) 5 (1871-1876)
Brook, TT 'Tom' (Elland) 2 (1892)
Brooke, Arthur L (Huddersfield) 14 (1887-1890)
Brooke, George (Huddersfield) 2 (1873-1874)
Brooke, George O (Castleford) 2 (1889-1890)
Brooke, J (Bramley) 1 (1888)
Broughton, Horace (Bradford Junior, Bradford Rangers) 4 (1880-1881)
Brown, - (Bradford) 1 (1870)
Brown, D (York) 1 (1888)
Brown, JD (Leeds) 1 (1874)
Brumfitt, C (Shipley) 1 (1887)
Bryars, G (Goole) 1 (1897)
Buckley, Edmund (Halifax) 5 (1881-1888)
Burton, David F (Hull) 2 (1875-1876)
Butler, Roland (Leeds) 2 (1871-1872)
Butterfield, J (Bottomboat Trinity) 2 (1900)

Calvert, T Herbert (Huddersfield) 2 (1875-1877)
Calvert, WFB (Hull) 5 (1882-1885)
Cariss, Ben (Leeds) 5 (1870-1877)
Carter, S (Castleford) 1 (1898)
Carter, William P (Bradford) 2 (1885)
Chadwick, C (Dewsbury) 1 (1882)
Chambers, Tom (Halifax) 7 (1880-1883)
Chambers, HW 'Harry' (Sheffield) 1 (1870)
Champion, A (Bradford) 1 (1871)
Champney, C (Halifax) 1 (1875)
Christison, Alex 'Sandy' (York) 4 (1875-1877)
Christison, Robert H (York) 1 (1876)

Clarke, EB (York) 1 (1889)
Clay, F Howard (Halifax) 3 (1889-1890)
Clayton, H (Ossett) 1 (1898)
Clegg, Fred (Manningham) 11 (1892-1895)
Clowes, JP 'Jack' (Halifax) 1 (1888)
Coates, Rev Charles H (Leeds, Yorkshire Wanderers) 3 (1880-1881)
Cobby, William (Castleford) 7 (1899-1901)
Cockerham, Arthur (Bradford Olicana) 6 (1899-1900)
Cole, J (Featherstone) 1 (1898)
Collinson, Roy W (Mytholmroyd) 1 (1897)
Conacher, JH Sheard (Huddersfield) 5 (1875-1877)
Conley, Jim (Leeds Parish Church) 10 (1894-1896)
Cookson, Frank (Kirkstall) 1 (1882)
Cooper, FW 'Fred' (Bradford) 7 (1894-1895)
Coulman, Edward (Hull) 2 (1886)
Crompton, JH 'Jack' (Bradford) 3 (1895)
Crosland, TP (Huddersfield) 1 (1874)
Crossland, JH 'Johnny' (Halifax) 4 (1882-1884)
Crump, ST (Yorkshire College) 2 (1900)

Darbishire, Godfrey (Hull) 3 (1877-1879)
Davey, Albert (Normanton, Castleford) 11 (1893-1895)
Dawson, FR 'Fred' (Leeds St John's) 1 (1877)
Dawson, Harry (Wakefield Trinity) 1 (1884)
Dawson, M (Bradford) 1 (1873)
Dawson, MS (Leeds) 1 (1880)
Dawson, W Arthur (Bradford) 3 (1872-1873)
Denehey, DS (Leeds St John's) 2 (1878)
Dewhirst, Edgar (Bradford) 9 (1891-1892)
Dickenson, Peter (Castleford) 8 (1886-1888)
Dickenson, Tom (Huddersfield) 3 (1892)
Dixon, CE 'Charlie' (Alverthorpe) 9 (1895-1897)
Dobson, TH 'Tom' (Bradford) 5 (1894-1895)
Dodd, Jimmy (Halifax) 31 (1879-1889)
Donaldson, William 'Donny' (Manningham) 7 (1894-1895)
Doncaster, Harry (Castleford) 1 (1901)
Donkin, Laurie (Hull) 1 (1892)
Downing, J (Knottingley) 2 (1900)
Driver, P (Skipton) 6 (1900-1901)
Duckett, Horace (Bradford) 8 (1892-1893)
Duke, W (Holbeck) 4 (1896)
Dunsford, E (Bradford) 3 (1874-1875)
Dykes, Rev Ernest H (Leeds Parish Church) 4 (1878-1881)
Dyson, JW 'Jack' (Huddersfield) 27 (1888-1893)

Eagland, WH 'Will' (Huddersfield) 12 (1889-1894)
Eastwood, SN 'Sam' (Brighouse Rangers) 5 (1889-1890)
Ellershaw, N (Hull) 1 (1873)
Elliker, Tom (Batley) 2 (1887)
Ellis, W 'Bill' (Wakefield Trinity) 1 (1880)
Else, Tom (Batley, Paddock, Huddersfield) 8 (1888-1890)
Emmott, Charlie (Bradford, Shipley) 7 (1891-1898)
Eyre, JR (Sheffield) 1 (1870)

Fairburn, John E (Mirfield) 2 (1877-1878)
Fallas, Herbert (Wakefield Trinity) 14 (1882-1885)
Fawcett, Fred (Harrogate) 2 (1873-1874)
Fawcett, Tom (Harrogate) 1 1873)
Fawcett, WJ 'Billy' (Manningham) 3 (1887)
Fernandes, Charles WL (Wakefield, Leeds) 11 (1878-1881)
Firth, Alfred (Bradford) 3 (1870-1872)
Firth, Albert W (Halifax) 1 (1878)
Firth, Fred (Brighouse Rangers, Halifax) 20 (1889-1895)
Firth, GG (Headingley) 5 (1900)
Fisher, J (Bradford) 1 (1888)
Fisher, W 'Billy' (Liversedge) 1 (1889)
Fisher, WK (Dewsbury) 6 (1880-1882)
Fletcher, Mark (Leeds) 8 (1892-1893)
Fletcher, Otis (Halifax) 5 (1891-1892)
Fookes, Ernest F (Sowerby Bridge, Mytholmroyd) 24 (1895-1899)
Forrest, Arthur J (Yorkshire Wanderers, Leeds St John's) 4 (1882-1884)
Fotherby, JH 'Jack' (Wakefield Trinity) 1(1887)
Fowler, R Henry (Leeds) 3 (1876-1877)
Fox, CE 'Charlie' (Salterhebble) 9 (1885-1887)
Freeman, CE (Huddersfield) 5 (1870-1873)
Freeman, James (Bradford, Leeds) 4 (1873-1874)
French, JE 'Teddy' (Halifax) 2 (1880)

Garforth, Joe (Dewsbury) 22 (1882-1887)
Garnett, HWT 'Harry' (Bradford) 22 (1873-1880)
Gath, Jim (Morley) 6 (1896-1897)
Gibson, C (Leeds) 1 (1871)
Glaisby, E 'Ted' (York) 4 (1875-1877)
Glendinning, FF (Morley) 3 (1898-1900)

Glew, J (Featherstone, Keighley) 10 (1897-1899)
Goldthorpe, Albert E (Hunslet) 8 (1891-1892)
Goldthorpe, Walter (Hunslet) 11 (1891-1892)
Gomersall, JE 'Jack' (Wakefield Trinity) 1 (1887)
Goodfellow, F (Sharlston) 6 (1897-1898)
Goodyear, Jack (Alverthorpe) 2 (1899)
Gordon, FT 'Fred' (Leeds St John's) 1 (1878)
Gover, S (Castleford) 1 (1900)
Graham, JW 'Jack' (Dewsbury) 3 (1886-1887)
Greenhalgh, JH (Bradford) 1 (1878)
Greenwood, Arthur (Cleckheaton) 1 (1883)
Gregg, KS (Knottingley) 2 (1900)
Griesbach, AJ (Leeds) 2 (1871-1872)
Griffith, JF (York) 1 (1880)
Griffiths, WH (Bradford) 1 (1874)
Gwyther, RF (Bradford) 2 (1875)

Hague, J (Castleford) 3 (1900)
Haigh, Norman (Harrogate) 3 (1900-1901)
Haigh, S (Bradford) 1 (1884)
Hainstock, Harry (Leeds) 1 (1895)
Hambleton, Tom (Castleford) 5 (1897-1899)
Hambrecht, Albert (Bramley) 7 (1895-1896)
Hammond, C (Castleford) 1 (1889)
Hammond, James E (Bradford Olicana) 7 (1899-1900)
Hamshaw, Harper O (Wakefield Trinity) 8 (1884-1888)
Hanson, Tom (Otley) 1 (1898)
Hanson, WE 'Ted' (Dewsbury) 3 (1882-1883)
Harris, H (York) 5 (1874-1880)
Harrison, Gilbert (Hull, Leeds, Yorkshire Wanderers) 48 (1876-1888)
Harrison, E Walter (Hull) 2 (1872-1876)
Harrison, Tommy (Wakefield Trinity) 2 (1888)
Harrison, WR (Kirkstall) 2 (1878-1880)
Hartley, Herbert (Holbeck) 1 (1890)
Hartley, JH 'Joe' (Halifax) 1 (1878)
Haslam, JT 'Tom' (Batley) 14 (1884-1888)
Hastings, George (Bradford) 1 (1878)
Hawcridge, JJ 'Joe' (Manningham, Bradford) 5 (1884-1885)
Hayley, Arthur (Wakefield Trinity) 4 (1879-1880)
Hayley, Harry (Wakefield Trinity) 3 (1878-1879)
Henderson, HP (Leeds) 3 (1877-1878)
Heron, J (Selby) 1 (1885)
Heron, Tom (Huddersfield) 2 (1871-1872)
Hickson, J Laurie (Bradford) 28 (1883-1890)

Hirst, B (Leeds) 1 (1871)
Hirst, ET (Leeds) 2 (1878)
Hodgson, A (Cleckheaton) 1 (1900)
Hodgson, Richard (Hull) 12 (1873-1878)
Hodgson, William (Hull) 11 (1871-1878)
Hollingbury, EA (Hull) 2 (1873)
Hollindrake, T (Keighley) 1 (1898)
Holmes, A (Bradford) 2 (1870-1871)
Holmes, Edgar (Manningham) 25 (1886-1891)
Holmes, Percy F (Huddersfield) 5 (1881-1882)
Holroyd, CE (Holywell Brook, Morley) 10 (1898-1900)
Holwell, EB (Leeds) 4 (1880)
Hopkins, S (Otley) 1 (1892)
Horner, Howard (Harrogate) 2 (1900)
Hudson, E (Leeds) 3 (1892)
Hudson, William H (Leeds) 1 (1880)
Hughes, George E (Otley) 4 (1897-1899)
Hurworth, T (York) 1 (1888)
Hustwick, C (Hull) 3 (1873-1875)
Hutchinson, Herbert (Wakefield Trinity) 10 (1880-1887)
Hutchinson, William HH (Hull) 11 (1870-1876)
Huth, Frank (Huddersfield) 1 (1878)
Huth, Fred (Huddersfield) 9 (1877-1881)
Huth, Harry (Huddersfield) 15 (1874-1880)

Ibbotson, JW (Dewsbury) 2 (1880)
Ineson, Arthur (Batley) 1 (1886)
Ingham, J (Otley) 2 (1894)
Iveson, AP 'Tony' (Hull) 1 (1885)

Jacketts, George (Hull) 18 (1884-1890)
Jackson, Ben (Hebden Bridge, Elland) 2 (1890-1892)
Jackson, E (Batley) 9 (1885-1887)
Jackson, Paul (Huddersfield) 1 (1888)
Jackson, W 'Bill' (Wakefield Trinity) 1 (1882)
Jackson, Walter J (Halifax) 5 (1894-1895)
Jackson, W (York Melbourne) 1 (1898)
Jacobson, EH 'Eli' (Wortley, Morley) 12 (1896-1898)
James, SB (Headingley) 5 (1900-1901)
Johnson, - (Sheffield) 1 (1870)
Jolly, JH (York) 1 (1877)
Jones, EM (Leeds) 2 (1878)
Jones, J Hampton (Wakefield Trinity) 13 (1888-1890)
Jowett, Donald (Heckmondwike) 31 (1888-1894)
Jowett, Willie (Bradford) 5 (1886-1888)
Jubb, George (Wakefield Trinity) 4 (1881-1884)

Keepings, WH 'Bill' (Halifax) 1 (1893)
Kilner, Barron (Wakefield Trinity) 10 (1879-1881)
Kilner, JW 'Joe' (Wakefield Trinity) 2 (1880)
Knowles, Jimmy (Halifax) 1 (1894)
Knox, John (Skipton) 5 (1900-1901)

Lalor, Herbert (Harrogate) 1 (1901)
Lambert, Charles B (Hull) 6 (1870-1874)
Lapage, CC (Leeds) 3 (1874)
Lapping, Charlie (Leeds St John's) 1 (1888)
Lassen, Albert W (Bradford) 2 (1871-1872)
Lathom, Joe (Wakefield Trinity) 6 (1883-1884)
Leatham, Octavius 'Oct' (Leeds) 2 (1876-1877)
Lewis, George H (West Hartlepool) 1 (1898)
Lindley, WB (Leeds St John's) 1 (1880)
Little, R 'Bob' (Skipton) 2 (1897)
Lloyd, Harry (Bowling) 2 (1896)
Lockhead, JL 'Jimmy' (Halifax) 3 (1881-1882)
Lockwood, W (Sheffield) 1 (1870)
Lockwood, RE 'Dicky' (Dewsbury, Heckmondwike) 46 (1886-1894)
Lodge, Harry (Huddersfield) 4 (1891-1893)
Longbottom, Ben (Wakefield Trinity) 1 (1880)
Longbottom, JF 'Joe' (Mytholmroyd) 4 (1900-1901)
Lord, T (Featherstone) 3 (1896-1897)
Lorimer, George E (Manningham) 8 (1892-1895)
Lorriman, W 'Bill' (Leeds) 6 (1892-1893)
Lorryman, William (Dewsbury) 1 (1890)
Lowrie, FW 'Fred' (Wakefield Trinity, Batley) 27 (1887-1892)
Lupton, WC (Bradford) 1 (1870)

Macaulay, Auly (Leeds, Huddersfield, Mirfield) 8 (1870-1880
Mackenzie, WJ (York) 1 (1878)
Mackie, Osbert G (Wakefield Trinity, Cambridge University) 3 (1895-1898)
McLaurin, A (Bradford) 1 (1871)
McPhail, JG (Headingley) 2 (1900-1901)
Mann, Edward (Bradford) 1 (1878)
Manning, HJ (Leeds) 4 (1874-1876)
Margerison, R (Appleby Bridge, Bradford) 2 (1873-1874)
Marsden, George H (Morley) 13 (1898-1900)
Marshall, John W (Bradford) 9 (1881-1883)
Mathers, Charlie (Bramley, Leeds St John's) 14 (1885-1888)
Matterson, RW 'Bob' (Selby) 1 (1897)
Mawer, FL 'Fred' (Hull) 1 (1885)

Mawson, HO (Headingley) 2 (1900)
Mawson, Squire (Otley) 6 (1890)
Mellor, Ben (Halifax) 3 (1892-1893)
Melvin, J (Leeds) 1 (1894)
Metcalfe, Jimmy (Featherstone) 7 (1896-1897)
Middleton, G (Skipton) 3 (1898-1901)
Millar, George (Halifax) 1 (1884)
Miller, J (Castleford) 2 (1899)
Miller, James A (Leeds St John's) 5 (1880-1881)
Mills, Frederick W (Esholt) 1 (1875)
Mills, Reggie (Bradford) 11 (1874-1878)
Milner, Arthur (Harrogate) 2 (1874-1875)
Milner, JW (Castleford) 1 (1900)
Moon, Herbert (Shipley) 7 (1897-1898)
Moore, JW 'Jack' (Leeds St John's) 2 (1888)
Morfitt, Sammy (Hull Kingstone Rovers) 7 (1895-1896)
Morgan, T (Skipton) 3 (1900)
Mortimer, S (Dewsbury) 1 (1881)
Mosley, George E (Leeds Parish Church) 11 (1894-1896)
Moss, FB (Hull) 3 (1872-1873)
Munro, R (Bradford) 1 (1892)
Murgatroyd, Frank (Idle) 5 (1896-1897)
Murgatroyd, Willie (Idle) 11 (1896-1897)
Myers, Harry (Bramley, Keighley) 27 (1895-1899)

Naylor, George B (Leeds St John's, Leeds) 2 (1889-1892)
Naylor, Jim (Batley) 12 (1886-1890)
Naylor, JW 'Joe' (Dewsbury) 5 (1890-1891)
Naylor, T (Leeds) 1 (1871)
Neumann, Sydney (Cleckheaton, Bradford Olicana, Leicester) 12 (1897-1900)
Newsome, Alf (Dewsbury) 13 (1879-1883)
Newsome, Mark (Dewsbury) 6 (1879-1881)
Newton, Isaac 'Ike' (Manningham) 4 (1890-1891)
Nichol, W 'Billy' (Brighouse Rangers) 22 (1889-1893)
Noble, Harry (Heckmondwike) 1 (1888)
Nowell, George (Castleford, Leeds, Kinsley) 15 (1893-1897)

Oddy, Joe (Leeds Parish Church) 1 (1885)
Ogden, JB 'Joe' (Leeds St John's) 4 (1880- 1882)
Ogden, TJ 'Tom' (Leeds St John's) 1 (1875)
Ormerod, JR (Leeds St John's) 1 (1878)
Osborne, B (unidentified) 1 (1873)
Oxlade, HJR 'Harry' (Hull) 2 (1891)

Paisley, CJF 'Charlie' (Huddersfield) 3 (1891)
Parker, Albert (Batley) 3 (1884-1888)
Parker, Jack (Halifax) 3 (1885)
Parker, JE 'Jimmy' (Morley) 7 (1895-1896)
Parkin, Ernest (Liversedge) 3 (1895)
Peacock, TP 'Tom' (Leeds St John's) 13 (1880-1886)
Pearson, Cuth (Doncaster Town) 2 (1899)
Perkins, Arthur B (Dewsbury) 1 (1883)
Petty, R (York) 2 (1882)
Phipps, W 'Billy' (West Hartlepool) 1 (1900)
Pickles, Joe (Leeds) 1 (1892)
Pierce, WR (Badsworth Hunt) 3 (1878-1879)
Pitt, Joseph (Kirkstall) 4 (1879-1880)
Place, Roger (Leeds) 2 (1892)
Platts, Joe (Headingley) 1 (1900)
Platts, Sydney (Yorkshire College) 2 (1900)
Plint, T (Leeds) 1 (1870)
Potter, J Herbert (Leeds St John's, Leeds) 16 (1882-1890)
Pratt, W (Castleford) 5 (1900-1901)
Priestley, Arthur (Wortley, Shipley) 6 (1898)
Priestley, Sam (Liversedge) 1 (1894)

Ramsbotham, FS (Leeds) 1 (1872)
Ramsden, Harold E (Bingley) 14 (1897-1900)
Randall, J (Featherstone) 2 (1897)
Rathmel, J (Hunslet) 2 (1892)
Rawnsley, Israel (Elland) 2 (1896)
Redfern, P (Dewsbury) 3 (1882)
Redman, Edgar (Manningham) 12 (1892-1893)
Redman, Frank (Keighley) 1 (1900)
Rhodes, HW (York) 1 (1889)
Rhodes, Jack (Castleford, Hull Kingston Rovers) 13 (1895-1897)
Rhodes, R 'Dick' (Castleford) 2 (1897)
Richards, Joe (Bradford) 12 (1889-1892)
Richardson, J (Bradford) 1 (1875)
Richardson, Charlie (Leeds Parish Church) 8 (1892-1893)
Richmond, FW 'Fred' (Huddersfield) 2 (1888)
Rigg, JA 'Archie' (Halifax) 19 (1893-1895)
Riley, J (Luddendenfoot) 1 (1872)
Riley, Joe (Leeds) 4 (1894-1895)
Riley, Jack (Halifax) 2 (1894)
Ripley, Sam (Cleckheaton) 1 (1889)
Ritchie, Frank T (Bradford) 8 (1882-1887)
Robertshaw, A Rawson (Bradford) 9 (1885-1886)
Robertshaw, Herbert (Bradford) 7 (1884-1886)
Robertshaw, Jere (Bradford) 1 (1887)

Robertshaw, Percy (Bradford) 9 (1887-1889)
Robinson, Albert W (Bowling, Keighley, Bradford Olicana) 9 (1897-1899)
Robinson, John J (Headingley) 1 (1901)
Ross, AJ 'Archie' (Skipton) 9 (1899-1900)
Ross, Alexander 'Alec' (Skipton) 1 (1900)
Russell, Richard F (Castleford) 12 (1899-1901)

Scarborough, George D (Halifax) 2 (1885)
Scarborough, TL 'Tom' (Halifax) 9 (1880-1885)
Scharff, C (Bradford, Leeds) 8 (1878-1880)
Schofield, B (Huddersfield) 5 (1875-1881)
Schutt, Arthur (Bradford) 1 (1878)
Schutt, Fred (Bradford) 8 (1873-1877)
Seaton, E (Leeds) 3 (1877-1878)
Shann, HC (Leeds) 4 (1874-1875)
Sharpe, AC (Huddersfield) 4 (1881-1883)
Sharpe, Ben (Liversedge) 9 (1893-1895)
Sharpe, CM (Huddersfield) 1 (1876)
Sharpe, J (Hull) 1 (1873)
Shaw, Fred (Cleckheaton) 12 (1897-1899)
Shepherd, J (Durham City, Castleford) 3 (1898-1899)
Sherwood, Tom (Castleford) 6 (1900-1901)
Shooter, John H (Morley) 22 (1896-1900)
Sidgwick, A (Bradford) 3 (1873-1874)
Simms, Herbert (Batley) 6 (1885-1888)
Simpson, Harry (Hull) 2 (1888)
Smith, FJ (Bradford) 1 (1880)
Smith, G (Bottomboat Trinity) 1 (1900)
Smith, JA (Castleford) 1 (1900)
Smith, William (Wakefield Trinity) 1 (1892)
Smith, WH (Bradford) 3 (1880)
Speed, Harry (Castleford) 25 (1892-1896)
Speight, Sam (Kirkstall) 1 (1880)
Spink, EJ (Wakefield Trinity) 1 (1882)
Stadden, William J 'Buller' (Dewsbury) 21 (1887-1891)
Stansfield, William (Mytholmroyd) 6 (1900-1901)
Starks, Anthony (Castleford, Hull Kingston Rovers) 13 (1895-1897)
Steele, George (Wakefield Trinity) 13 (1878-1884)
Steinthal, Fred (Bradford) 1 (1877)
Stericker, Thomas (Bradford) 3 (1881-1882)
Stirk, Thomas (Morley) 3 (1896-1898)
Stuart, Angus (Dewsbury) 3 (1888)
Sullivan, AM (Castleford) 1 (1899)
Summersgill, Tommy (Leeds) 11 (1891-1894)
Sumner, Claude (Leeds St John's) 4 (1887)
Sutcliffe, John W (Heckmondwike) 8 (1888-1889)
Sutcliffe, Milford (Huddersfield) 5 (1894-1895)
Swabey, Dr W Percy (Outwood Church) 6 (1896-1897)
Swaine, Albert (Morley) 1 (1898)
Sykes, JW 'Jack' (Batley) 3 (1886-1889)
Sykes, WS (Leeds) 3 (1873)

Taylor, JT 'Jack' (Castleford, West Hartlepool) 18 (1896-1900)
Taylor, Tommy (Featherstone) 3 (1896)
Teal, W 'Billy' (Hull) 3 (1887)
Tennant, Cecil (Leeds) 2 (1876-1877)
Tennant, EJ (Leeds) 2 (1872-1873)
Tennant, J (Leeds) 1 (1872)
Tetley, TS 'Tom' (Bradford) 9 (1873-1877)
Thompson, - (unidentified) 1 (1873)
Thompson, George (Dewsbury) 2 (1886)
Thomson, - (Sheffield) 1 (1870)
Thomson, George T (Halifax) 29 (1877-1885)
Thursby, F (York) 2 (1876-1877)
Tillotson, A (Keighley) 1 (1898)
Todd, Sam (Morley) 2 (1889)
Toothill, AS 'Abe' (Halifax) 1 (1893
Toothill, JT 'Jack' (Bradford) 50 (1888-1895)
Tuckwell, AJ (Leeds) 1 (1873)

Ullathorne, Charles (Hull) 1 (1873)

Varley, Harry (Liversedge) 7 (1892-1893)
Vickerman, John B (Huddersfield) 2 (1873-1874)
Voyse, George (Castleford) 2 (1897)

Wade, H (Leeds St John's) 5 (1880-1882)
Wade, RJ (Hull) 5 (1870-1875)
Walker, Edward E (Cambridge University) 2 (1900)
Walker, JH (Mirfield) 1 (1878)
Walsh, Owen (Hunslet) 9 (1893-1894)
Waltham, R (Hull) 1 (1870)
Walton, Ernest J (St Peter's School, Castleford, Oxford University) 6 (1898-1901)
Walton, R 'Bob' (Leeds St John's, Armley) 2 (1888-1891)
Walton, W 'Bill' (Castleford) 14 (1893-1895)
Ward, Herbert (Wakefield Trinity) 11 (1884-1887)
Ward, Herbert 'Bert' (Bradford, Shipley) 23 (1893-1899)
Ward, JW 'Jack' (Castleford, Pudsey) 16 (1895-1896)

Rugby Union County Appearances (1869-70 to 1900-01)

Ward, Rufus A (Halifax) 1 (1878)
Ward, W (Leeds Parish Church) 1 (1896)
Watmough, J (Leeds St John's) 2 (1888)
Watson, Jack (Leeds St John's) 1 (1880)
Watson, TW 'Tom' (Salterbebble, Halifax) 9 (1885-1887)
Watson, W 'Billy' (Leeds St John's) 4 (1881-1883)
Webster, Isaac 'Ike' (Halifax) 1 (1888)
Welsh, Robert (Huddersfield) 3 (1875-1876)
Wheelwright, DG (Mytholmroyd) 3 (1900)
White, Jack (Bowling) 1 (1892)
Whiteley, Herbert (Thornes) 1 (1883)
Whiteley, William (Bramley) 3 (1895)
Wigglesworth, Henry (Thornes) 6 (1883-1884)
Wilcock, John (Pudsey) 1 (1897)
Wild, Frank (Alverthorpe) 1 (1898)
Wilkinson, Edgar (Bradford) 22 (1884-1889)
Wilkinson, Harry J (Halifax) 12 (1887-1889)
Wilkinson, H (Harrogate) 2 (1898)
Wilkinson, P (Leeds) 1 (1877)
Wilson, Arthur (Halifax) 2 (1891)
Wilson, H (Morley) 1 (1898)
Wilson, Harry B (Huddersfield) 5 (1881-1885)
Winpenny, Charles E (Ossett) 6 (1897-1898)
Winskill, RS 'Bob' (Halifax) 3 (1893)
Wise, Matt (Otley) 4 (1888-1889)
Wise, WL (Leeds) 2 (1880-1881)
Wolstenholme, Eli (Dewsbury) 6 (1884-1886)
Wolstenholme, W (Dewsbury) 5 (1883-1884)
Wood, Albert (Halifax) 10 (1882-1884)
Wood, Charlie (York) 6 (1878-1881)
Wood, Fred (Brighouse Rangers) 4 (1892)
Wood, Herbert (Heckmondwike) 1 (1888)
Wood, Jack (Halifax) 1 (1878)
Wood, JE (Halifax) 5 (1880)
Wood, JH (Halifax) 1 (1882)
Wood, Louis R (Cleckheaton) 6 (1898-1899)
Wood, R 'Bob' (Liversedge) 14 (1893-1895)
Woodhead, Ernest (Huddersfield) 5 (1879-880)
Woodhead, Herbert 'Harry' (Goole) 3 (1895)

Wordsworth, Tommy H (Wakefield Trinity) 1 (1888)
Wright, Howard (Leeds) 2 (1870-1871)
Wright, JF 'Jimmy' (Bradford) 6 (1887-1890)
Wrigley, PT (Huddersfield) 4 (1875-1878)
Wylde, JA (Leeds, Yorkshire Wanderers) 6 (1878-1882)
Wylie, JG (Doncaster) 1 (1874)
Wynne, EH (Bradford) 1 (1888)

Yeadon, Arthur EN (Headingley) 10 (1899- 1901)
Yeld, G (Castleford) 2 (1899)
Young, James (Harrogate) 1 (1873)

20-plus appearances (1870-1901):
Jack Toothill 50
Gilbert Harrison 48
Dicky Lockwood 46
Tom Broadley 38
Harry Bedford 32
Fred Bonsor 32
Jimmy Dodd 31
Donald Jowett 31
George T Thomson 29
Harry Bradshaw 28
J Laurie Hickson 28
Jack Dyson 27
Fred Lowrie 27
Harry Myers 27
Edgar Holmes 25
Harry Speed 25
Ernest F Fookes 24
Bert Ward 23
Joe Garforth 22
Harry Garnett 22
Billy Nichol 22
John H Shooter 22
Edgar Wilkinson 22
William J Stadden 21
Fred Firth 20

North versus South at Headingley, 29th December 1890.
Illustrated Sporting and Dramatic News, 1891

Appendix 2

NORTH APPEARANCES (1874 TO 1901)

The following is a complete list of the 285 players that appeared for the North (of England) from its first match in 1874 until 1901. The period covers a total of 37 matches; 36 versus the South (of England), one versus Wales in 1882. The breakdown of northern counties that the players were associated with are: Lancashire 93, Yorkshire 88, Cheshire 31, Durham 29, Northumberland 25, Cumberland 15. There is also one player from Staffordshire (Sydney H. Evershed) and three attached to the London-based Ravenscourt Park club (D. H. Brownfield, G. F. Congreve, G. F. Griffin), two of which – and probably all three – having northern connections. Note that Wakefield-born Osbert G. Mackie (Cambridge University) had played for Wakefield Trinity up to 1895.

The name of each player is shown in alphabetical sequence, with surname followed by first name or initial where known. The name that the player was popularly referred to at the time (such as 'Billy', 'Joe', etc.) is given where known. This is followed by the name(s) of the team(s) each player was associated with at the time of his appearance(s). Next is the appearance total followed by the year of the first and final appearance. Only one year is given where a player made all his appearances in the same year or had just one appearance.

Adamson, CY 'Charlie' (Old Dunelmians) 2 (1898-1899)
Alderson, FHR 'Fred' (Tynedale, Hartlepool Rovers) 5 (1887-1892)
Alexander, Harry (Birkenhead Park) 2 (1900)
Allen, C Elliott (Liverpool) 1 (1899)
Anderson, Stanley (Rockcliff, Wallsend 3 (1897-1898)
Anderton, Charley (Manchester Free Wanderers) 5 (1887-1889)
Andrew, Harold H (Manchester Rangers) 1 (1880)
Ashworth, Abe (Oldham) 1 (1891)
Atkinson, J Cecil (Leeds) 1 (1877)
Atkinson, W 'Billy' (Wigan) 1 (1890)

Banks, H (Cockermouth) 1 (1901)
Barraclough, Alf (Manningham) 1 (1894)
Barron, JH 'Harry' (Bingley) 1 (1896)
Bartram, CE 'Teddy' (Wakefield Trinity) 4 (1881-1883)
Bateson, Harold D (Liverpool) 1 (1879)
Baxter, James (Birkenhead Park) 2 (1898-1899)
Bedford, Harry (Batley, Morley) 5 (1887-1889)
Bell, FJ 'Fred' (Rockcliff) 1 (1899)
Bell, Henry (New Brighton) 1 (1883)
Bell, J Lowthian (Darlington) 2 (1876-1877)
Bell, R 'Nobby' (Workington) 1 (1896)
Bell, Robert W (Northern) 3 (1899-1900)
Bell, William H (Sunderland) 1 (1890)
Berry, John 'Buff' (Tyldesley) 1 (1890)
Beswick, E 'Ted' (Swinton) 2 (1881-1882)
Bingham, David A (Birkenhead Park) 1 (1884)
Black, John A (Birkenhead Park) 1 (1886)
Blackett, Algernon C (Northern) 1 (1896)
Blacklock, Joseph H (Aspatria) 2 (1897-1898)
Blatherwick, Thomas (Manchester) 2 (1879-1880)
Bonsor, Fred (Bradford) 7 (1883-1889)
Bottomley, George W (Huddersfield) 3 (1880-1882)
Brettargh, Arthur T (Liverpool Old Boys) 6 (1898-1900)
Briggs, Arthur (Bradford) 1 (1891)
Broadley, Tom (Bradford, Bingley, West Riding) 4 (1892-1895)
Brodie, John A (Walton) 1 (1881)
Bromet, William E (Tadcaster) 2 (1890-1891)
Brook, Herbert S (Huddersfield) 1 (1876)
Brooke, Arthur L (Huddersfield) 1 (1889)
Brooks, Herbert (Darlington) 1 (1884)

Brownfield, Douglas H (Ravenscourt Park) 2 (1876-1877)
Brutton, Ernest B (Tynemouth, Cambridge University) 1 (1885)
Bucknill, Frederick H (Crewe) 1 (1874)
Bullough, E 'Ned' (Wigan) 1 (1891)
Bulteel, Andrew J (Manchester) 2 (1874-1876)
Bumby, Walter (Swinton) 1 (1890)
Burton, David F (Hull) 1 (1876)
Butterworth, Wilfred S (Rochdale Hornets) 2 (1880)

Cannell, John AS (New Brighton) 1 (1897)
Carver, Charles W (Liverpool) 2 (1874)
Case, Harry (Ulverston, Swinton) 2 (1892-1893)
Clarke, Charles WH (Liverpool) 1 (1876)
Cliff, E (Liverpool) 3 (1874-1876)
Coates, Rev Charles H (Yorkshire Wanderers) 1 (1881)
Cobby, William (Castleford) 1 (1899)
Cockerham, Arthur (Bradford Olicana) 2 (1899-1900)
Colquhoun, Sutherland G (Liverpool) 1 (1874)
Congreve, Galfred F (Ravenscourt Park) 1 (1874)
Cookson, George (Manchester) 1 (1899)
Coop, Tom (Leigh) 1 (1890)
Cooper, FW 'Fred' (Bradford) 1 (1894)
Cowan, J (Birkenhead Park) 1 (1887)
Cowie, Gilbert (Birkenhead Park) 1 (1882)
Cox, Burdon (Sunderland) 1 (1887)
Cox, Norman S (Sunderland) 2 (1899-1901)
Cross, W 'Billy' (St Helens) 1 (1890)

Dale, William (Hartlepool Rovers) 1 (1897)
Davidson, Jim (Aspatria) 8 (1891-1900)
Davidson, Joe (Aspatria) 4 (1898-1899)
Dobson, TH 'Tom' (Bradford) 1 (1894)
Dodd, Jimmy (Halifax) 3 (1880-1882)
Dotchin, Frederick E (Northern) 1 (1894)
Durandu, Arthur (Liverpool) 1 (1886)
Dykes, Rev EH (Leeds Parish Church) 1 (1879)
Dyson, JW 'Jack' (Huddersfield) 2 (1890-1891)

Eagles, Harry (Salford) 3 (1887-1890)
Edgar, Charles S (Birkenhead Park) 1 (1901)
Elliot, Charles H (Sunderland) 2 (1885-1887)
Elliot, Edgar W (Sunderland) 2 (1900-1901)
Evershed, Sydney H (Burton-on-Trent) 2 (1882-1883)

Faulkner, Tom (Tudhoe) 2 (1891-1892)

North (of England) Appearances (1874 to 1901)

Faulkner, Will (Runcorn) 1 (1892)
Fenton, Aynsley (Rochdale Hornets) 1 (1876)
Fernandes, Charles WL (Leeds, unattached) 3 (1879-1888)
Finlay, James (West Hartlepool) 1 (1898)
Finney, Stephen (Crewe) 1 (1874)
Firth, Fred (Halifax) 2 (1893-1894)
Fletcher, Tom (Seaton) 1 (1896)
Fookes, Ernest F (Sowerby Bridge, Mytholmroyd) 4 (1895-1899)
Fowler, Frank D (Manchester) 1 (1879)
Frater, John (Tudhoe) 1 (1900)

Garforth, Joe (Dewsbury) 2 (1882-1883)
Garnett, HWT 'Harry' (Bradford) 4 (1874-1877)
Gath, Jim (Morley) 1 (1897)
Gee, Tom (Percy Park) 2 (1889-1890)
Genth, JS 'James' (Manchester) 3 (1874-1876)
Gibbon, Thomas (West Hartlepool) 1 (1894)
Gibson, Charles OP (Northern, Oxford University) 2 (1898-1900)
Gibson, George R (Northern) 2 (1899-1901)
Graham, David (Aspatria) 2 (1900-01)
Graham, John G (Liverpool Old Boys) 1 (1901)
Graham, WS 'Billy' (Carlisle) 1 (1897)
Grave, William 'Willie' (Manchester) 1 (1876)
Greenwell, JH 'Harry' (Rockcliff) 2 (1892-1899)
Greenwell, William N (Rockcliff) 2 (1894-1895)
Greg, Walter (Manchester) 5 (1874-1877)
Grey, C (Manchester) 1 (1876)
Grieve, Tom (Aspatria) 1 (1899)
Griffin, GF (Ravenscourt Park) 1 (1874)

Hague, Jack (Sale) 2 (1900)
Hall, John (North Durham) 2 (1893-1894)
Hammond, James E (Bradford Olicana) 1 (1899)
Harding, JT (Northumberland FC) 1 (1879)
Harrison, Gilbert (Hull, Leeds, Yorkshire Wanderers) 7 (1876-1886)
Hartley, Charles R (Sale) 2 (1899-1901)
Haslam, JT 'Tom' (Batley) 1 (1888)
Hawcridge, JJ 'Joe' (Bradford) 1 (1884)
Hay-Gordon, James R (Liverpool) 5 (1874-1877)
Herschell, Ernest (Birkenhead Park) 2 (1898-1899)
Hickson, J Laurie (Bradford) 7 (1883-1890)
Higgins, William W (Manchester) 1 (1884)
Hill, Arthur (Hartlepool Rovers) 1 (1891)
Hodgson, Richard (Hull) 1 (1874)
Hogg, Jimmy (West Hartlepool) 1 (1900)
Hoggarth, Sam (Millom) 1 (1897)

Holme, Joseph (Millom) 1 (1890)
Holmes, Edgar (Manningham) 2 (1889-1890)
Holmes, Robert 'Bratty' (Morecambe) 1 (1895)
Horley, CH 'Charlie' (Swinton) 3 (1884-1889)
Hornby, Albert N (Blackburn, Preston Grasshoppers, Manchester) 5 (1876-1880)
Houghton, Sam (Runcorn, Birkenhead Wanderers) 4 (1891-1895)
Hulse, William S (Manchester Free Wanderers, Manchester) 2 (1882)
Hunt, James, T (Manchester, Preston Grasshoppers) 4 (1980-1883)
Hunt, Dr Robert (Manchester) 3 (1879-1880)
Hunt, William H (Preston Grasshoppers) 3 (1876-1877)
Hutchinson, Herbert (Wakefield Trinity) 1 (1883)
Hutchinson, J (Birkenhead Park) 1 (1900)
Hutchinson, William HH (Hull) 2 (1874)
Huth, Harry (Huddersfield) 6 (1876-1882)

Jacobson, EH 'Eli' (Morley) 1 (1897)
Jones, FH (Northern, Cambridge University) 1 (1901)
Jones, J Hampton (Wakefield Trinity) 2 (1888-1889)
Jowett, Donald (Heckmondwike) 5 (1888-1891)

Kayll, Henry E (Sunderland) 2 (1877-1879)
Kemble, Arthur T (Liverpool) 2 (1884-1886)
Kendall, Percy D (Birkenhead Park) 1 (1901)
Kent, Tom (Salford) 3 (1888-1890)
Kewley, Edward (Liverpool) 5 (1874-1877)
Kilner, Barron (Wakefield Trinity) 1 (1880)
Knowles, Edward 'Ned' (Millom) 1 (1897)

Leach, William E (Liverpool) 1 (1874)
Leatham, Octavius 'Oct' (Leeds) 1 (1876)
Lee, George W (Rockcliff) 1 (1893)
Legard, George S (Old Dunelmians) 1 (1898)
Lemonius, Francis (Liverpool) 1 (1874)
Littledale Thomas AR (Liverpool) 1 (1874)
Lockerby, SC 'Sammy' (Percy Park) 1 (1898)
Lockwood, Philip H (Birkenhead Park) 1 (1890)
Lockwood, RE 'Dicky' (Dewsbury, Heckmondwike) 7 (1886-1893)
Lowrie, FW 'Fred' (Wakefield Trinity, Batley) 5 (1888-1890)
Lyon, Arthur (Liverpool) 2 (1874)

Mackie, Osbert G (Cambridge University) 1 (1896)

MacLaren, David (Manchester) 1 (1874)
MacLaren, James (Manchester) 2 (1874)
McNiven, Hugh J (Manchester) 1 (1885)
Markendale, Ellis T (Manchester Rangers) 3 (1876-1880)
Marquis, John C (Birkenhead Park) 3 (1898-1900)
Marriott, Ernest E (Manchester) 2 (1874-1876)
Marsden, George H (Morley) 2 (1899-1900)
Marsh, James H (Swinton) 2 (1890-1892)
Marshall, John W (Bradford) 2 (1881-1882)
Mathers, Charlie (Leeds St John's, Bramley) 2 (1887-1888)
Metcalfe, Jimmy (Featherstone) 2 (1896-1897)
Middleton, Bernard B (Birkenhead Park) 5 (1879-1882)
Mills, Joe (Swinton) 2 (1886-1888)
Morfitt, Sammy (West Hartlepool, Hull Kingston Rovers) 3 (1893-1895)
Moss, Charles W (Liverpool) 1 (1874)
Moss, Frederick S (Broughton) 3 (1883-1885)
Murgatroyd, Willie (Idle) 1 (1897)
Myers, Harry (Keighley) 1 (1898)

Nesbitt, John (Wallsend) 1 (1898)
Newsome, Alf (Dewsbury) 1 (1882)
Nichol, W 'Billy' (Brighouse Rangers) 1 (1891)
Nicholson, Elliot T (Liverpool) 3 (1899-1900)
Nicholson, Tom (Rockcliff) 1 (1892)
Northmore, Sammy (Millom) 1 (1897)

Oakes, RF 'Bob' (Hartlepool Rovers) 6 (1896-1899)
Oughtred, Bernard S (Hartlepool Rovers) 2 (1900-1901)

Parker, Sydney (Liverpool) 2 (1874)
Parlane, Willie (Manchester Rangers, Manchester) 4 (1892-1897)
Parry, John B (Birkenhead Park) 1 (1880)
Payne, John H (Broughton) 6 (1880-1885)
Peacock, TP 'Tom' (Leeds St John's) 1 (1885)
Pease, Frank E (Darlington, Hartlepool Rovers) 2 (1886-1890)
Phillips, Charles (Birkenhead Park) 1 (1880)
Pierce, Richard (Liverpool) 5 (1896-1899)
Pilkington, A (Manchester) 1 (1874)
Pilkington, C (Manchester) 2 (1874)
Pinch, Jack (Lancaster) 2 (1895-1897)
Poole, Robert W (Hartlepool Rovers, Hartlepool Old Boys) 3 (1897-1900)

Potter, J Herbert (Leeds St John's) 2 (1882-1884)
Pyke, Jim (St Helens Recreation) 1 (1891)

Ramsden, Harold E (Bingley) 2 (1897-1898)
Ransome, Herbert F (Bowdon, Cambridge University) 1 (1884)
Ravenscroft, John J (Birkenhead Park) 2 (1880-1881)
Redman, Edgar (Manningham) 1 (1892)
Rhodes, Jack (Castleford) 1 (1895)
Richards, Joe (Bradford) 1 (1890)
Richardson, William R (Manchester) 2 (1880-1882)
Riley, Peter (Runcorn) 1 (1891)
Ritchie, Frank T (Bradford) 1 (1887)
Ritson, James (Wallsend) 2 (1900-1901)
Roberts, Sam (Swinton) 1 (1886)
Robertshaw, A Rawson (Bradford) 1 (1885)
Robertshaw, Herbert (Bradford) 1 (1885)
Robertshaw, Percy (Bradford) 2 (1887-1888)
Robinson, George C 'Tot' (Percy Park) 4 (1896-1901)
Rowley, Hugh C (Manchester) 5 (1879-1882)
Royle, Arthur V 'Artie' (Broughton Rangers) 3 (1888-1889)
Russell, Richard F (Castleford) 1 (1900)
Ryalls, HJ 'Harry' (New Brighton) 2 (1882-1883)
Rycroft, Walter (Bowdon) 1 (1880)

Sample, Charles H (Northumberland FC, Cambridge University) 2 (1884-1885)
Saville, Fred (Stockport) 1 (1893)
Sawyer, Charles M (Broughton) 3 (1880-1881)
Sawyer, James S (Broughton) 2 (1880)
Schofield, George F (Southport) 1 (1877)
Scott, Mason T (Northern, Cambridge University) 3 (1888-1890)
Seddon, RL 'Bob' (Broughton Rangers, Swinton) 4 (1885-1888)
Shaw, Fred (Cleckheaton) 2 (1897-1898)
Shaw, Percy F (New Brighton) 1 (1882)
Shooter, John H (Morley) 2 (1898-1900)
Smith, ET (Manchester Rangers) 1 (1879)
Sowerby, JW 'Jack' (North Durham) 1 (1884)
Speed, Harry (Castleford) 1 (1893)
Springmann, HH 'Harry' 2 (1879-1886)
Standring, J (Manchester) 1 (1888)
Starks, Anthony (Castleford, Hull Kingston Rovers) 2 (1895-1896)
Steel, Jim (Eden Wanderers) 1 (1885)
Steele, George (Aspatria) 1 (1894)

North (of England) Appearances (1874 to 1901)

Stephenson, Alec (Tudhoe) 1 (1900)
Stericker, Thomas (Bradford) 1 (1881)
Stoddart, Wilfred B (Liverpool) 2 (1896-1897)
Stone, Frank W (Percy Park) 1 (1898)
Sutcliffe, John W (Heckmondwike) 2 (1888-1889)
Swabey, Dr W Percy (Outwood Church) 1 (1897)

Taylor, EW 'Little Billy' (Rockcliff) 6 (1891-1896)
Taylor, JT 'Jack' (Castleford, West Hartlepool) 7 (1897-1900)
Teggin, Alf (Broughton Rangers) 3 (1883-1886)
Tetley, TS 'Tom' (Bradford) 1 (1876)
Thompson, John T (Hartlepool Rovers) 1 (1897)
Thomson, George T (Halifax) 4 (1881-1884)
Thorp, John WH (Manchester) 1 (1882)
Todd, R (Manchester) 3 (1876-1877)
Toothill, JT 'Jack' (Bradford) 5 (1888-1893)
Tristram, Henry B (Oxford University, Durham City) 2 (1883-1887)

Valentine, Jim (Swinton) 7 (1887-1895)
Verelst, Courtenay L (Liverpool) 1 (1876)

Walker, Roger (Manchester) 5 (1874-1879)
Waller, J (West Hartlepool) 1 (1901)
Walton, Ernest J (Castleford) 1 (1900)
Ward, Herbert 'Bert' (Bradford) 3 (1894-1898)
Ward, JW 'Jack' (Castleford) 2 (1895-1896)
Whiteley, William (Bramley) 1 (1895)
Wigglesworth, Henry (Thornes) 1 (1883)
Wilkinson, Charles TB (Durham City) 1 (1889)
Wilkinson, Edgar (Bradford) 2 (1885-1886)
Wilkinson, Harry J (Halifax) 2 (1888-1889)
Wilkinson, JH (Durham City) 1 (1890)
Williams, Sam (Salford) 1 (1886)
Wilson, Roger P (Liverpool Old Boys) 2 (1890-1894)

Wincey, Guy P (Manchester) 1 (1898)
Wood, Albert (Halifax) 1 (1883)
Wood, E (Cheetham) 2 (1881-1882)
Wood, Louis R (Cleckheaton) 1 (1899)
Wood, Reggie (Birkenhead Park) 1 (1882)
Wood, R 'Bob' (Liversedge) 2 (1893-1894)
Wood, Robert D (Liverpool Old Boys) 3 (1900-1901)
Woodhead, Ernest (Huddersfield) 1 (1880)
Woodward, George (Tyldesley) 1 (1893)
Woolley, Henry (Manchester) 1 (1874)
Wormold, Joseph D (Manchester) 1 (1882)
Wright, JF 'Jimmy' (Bradford) 2 (1889)
Wynne, TR (Liverpool) 1 (1874)

Yiend, William (Hartlepool Rovers) 5 (1888-1892)

Note: Arthur Hill played for approximately 20 minutes in 1891 as a temporary replacement for William E. Bromet who arrived late.

Most appearances (1874-1901):
Jim Davidson 8
Fred Bonsor 7
Gilbert Harrison 7
J Laurie Hickson 7
RE 'Dicky' Lockwood 7
JT 'Jack' Taylor 7*
Jim Valentine 7
Arthur T Brettargh 6*
Harry Huth 6
RF 'Bob' Oakes 6
John H Payne 6
EW 'Little Billy' Taylor 6
*Further appearances after 1900-01

Scotland oppose England at Raeburn Place, Edinburgh, 1st March 1890.
Illustrated Sporting and Dramatic News, 1890

Appendix 3

ENGLAND APPEARANCES BY NORTHERN PLAYERS
(1871 TO 1901)

The following is a list of players associated with northern clubs that represented England from its first match in 1871 until 1901. Altogether there are 164 'northern' players (from an overall England total of 374 for the period) who contributed to an aggregate appearance total of 450 (from an overall England total 1,120). The period covers a total of 72 England matches; versus Scotland 28, Ireland 25, Wales 18, and the 'Maoris' 1.

Note that international matches played on the tours to South Africa (1891 and 1896) and Australia (1899) are not included. Although the tourists were inaccurately referred to as 'England' at the time – as reflected in this publication – they included Scottish and Irish-born players in their squads, modern records classifying them as 'British Isles' touring teams.

The name of each player is shown in alphabetical sequence, with surname followed by first name. Where known, the name that the player was popularly referred to at the time (such as 'Billy', 'Joe', etc.) is given. This is followed by the name(s) of the team(s) each player was associated with at the time of his appearance(s). Next is the appearance total followed by the year of the first and final appearance. Only one year is given where a player made all his appearances in the same year or had just one appearance.

Alderson, FHR 'Fred' (Hartlepool Rovers) 6 (1891-1893)
Alexander, Harry (Birkenhead Park, Richmond) 5 (1900-1901)
Anderson, Stanley (Rockcliff) 1 (1899)
Anderton, Charley (Manchester Free Wanderers) 1 (1889)
Ashworth, Abe (Oldham) 1 (1892)

Barron, JH 'Harry' (Bingley) 3 (1896-1897)
Bateson, Harold D (Liverpool) 1 (1879)
Baxter, James (Birkenhead Park) 3 (1900)
Bedford, Harry (Morley) 3 (1889-1890)
Bell, FJ 'Fred' (Rockcliff) 1 (1900)
Bell, Henry (New Brighton) 1 (1884)
Bell, J Lowthian (Darlington) 1 (1878)
Bell, Robert W (Northern) 3 (1900)
Berry, John 'Buff' (Tyldesley) 3 (1891)
Beswick, E 'Ted' (Swinton) 2 (1882)
Blacklock, Joseph H (Aspatria) 2 (1898-1899)
Blatherwick, Thomas (Manchester) 1 (1878)
Bonsor, Fred (Bradford) 6 (1886-1889)
Bradshaw, Harry (Bramley) 7 (1892-1894)
Brettargh, Arthur T (Liverpool Old Boys) 1 (1900)
Briggs, Arthur (Bradford) 3 (1892)
Broadley, Tom (Bingley, West Riding) 6 (1893-1896)
Bromet, William E (Tadcaster, Richmond) 12 (1891-1896)
Bullough, E 'Ned' (Wigan) 3 (1892)
Bulteel, Andrew J (Manchester) 1 (1875)

Clarke, Charles WH (Liverpool) 1 (1875)
Clayton, John H (Liverpool) 1 (1871)
Coates, Rev Charles H (Leeds, Yorkshire Wanderers) 2 (1881-1882)
Cobby, William (Castleford) 1 (1900)
Cockerham, Arthur (Bradford Olicana) 1 (1900)
Coop, Tom (Leigh) 1 (1892)
Cox, Norman S (Sunderland) 1 (1901)

Davidson, Jim (Aspatria) 5 (1897-1899)
Davidson, Joe (Aspatria) 2 (1899)
Dobson, TH 'Tom' (Bradford) 1 (1895)
Duckett, Horace (Bradford) 2 (1893)
Dyson, JW 'Jack' (Huddersfield) 4 (1890-1893)

Edgar, Charles S (Birkenhead Park) 1 (1901)
Elliot, Charles H (Sunderland) 1 (1886)
Elliot, Edgar W (Sunderland) 3 (1901)

Emmott, Charlie (Bradford) 1 (1892)

Fallas, Herbert (Wakefield Trinity) 1 (1884)
Fernandes, Charles WL (Leeds) 3 (1881)
Firth, Fred (Halifax) 3 (1894)
Fletcher, Tom (Seaton) 1 (1897)
Fookes, Ernest F (Sowerby Bridge, Mytholmroyd) 10 (1896-1899)
Fowler, Frank D (Manchester, Royal Indian Engineering College) 2 (1878-1879)
Fowler, R Henry (Leeds) 1 (1877)

Garnett, HWT 'Harry' (Bradford) 1 (1877)
Genth, JS 'James' (Manchester) 2 (1874-1875)
Gibson, Arthur S (Manchester) 1 (1871)
Gibson, Charles OP (Northern) 1 (1901)
Gibson, George R (Northern) 2 (1899-1901)
Graham, David (Aspatria) 1 (1901)
Greenwell, JH 'Harry' (Rockcliff) 2 (1893)
Greg, Walter (Manchester) 2 (1875-1876)

Hall, John (North Durham) 3 (1894)
Harrison, Gilbert (Hull) 7 (1877-1885)
Hawcridge, JJ 'Joe' (Bradford) 2 (1885)
Hickson, J Laurie (Bradford) 6 (1887-1890)
Holmes, Edgar (Manningham) 2 (1890)
Horley, CH 'Charlie' (Swinton) 1 (1885)
Hornby, Albert N (Manchester) 9 (1877-1882)
Houghton, Sam (Runcorn, Birkenhead Wanderers) 2 (1892-1896)
Hughes, George E (Barrow) 1 (1896)
Hunt, James T (Manchester) 3 (1882-1884)
Hunt, Dr Robert (Manchester) 4 (1880-1882)
Hunt, William H (Manchester) 4 (1876-1878)
Hutchinson, William HH (Hull) 2 (1875)
Huth, Harry (Huddersfield) 1 (1879)

Jackson, Walter J (Halifax) 1 (1894)
Jones, FP 'Freddie' (New Brighton) 1 (1893)
Jowett, Donald (Heckmondwike) 6 (1889-1891)

Kayll, Henry E (Sunderland) 1 (1878)
Kemble, Arthur T (Liverpool) 3 (1885-1887)
Kendall, Percy D (Birkenhead Park) 1 (1901)
Kent, Tom (Salford) 6 (1891-1892)
Kewley, Edward (Liverpool) 7 (1874-1878)
Kilner, Barron (Wakefield Trinity) 1 (1880)
Knowles, Edward 'Ned' (Millom) 2 (1896-1897)

Lockwood, RE 'Dicky' (Dewsbury, Heckmondwike) 14 (1887-1894)

Lowrie, FW 'Fred' (Wakefield Trinity) 2 (1889-1890)
Lyon, Arthur (Liverpool) 1 (1871)

Mackie, Osbert G (Cambridge University) 2 (1897-1898)
MacLaren, William (Manchester) 1 (1871)
Markendale, Ellis T (Manchester Rangers) 1 (1880)
Marquis, John C (Birkenhead Park) 2 (1890)
Marriott, Ernest E (Manchester) 1 (1875)
Marsden, George H (Morley) 3 (1900)
Marsh, James H (Swinton) 1 (1892)
Middleton, Bernard B (Birkenhead Park) 2 (1882-1883)
Morfitt, Sammy (West Hartlepool) 6 (1894-1896)
Moss, Frederick S (Broughton) 3 (1885-1886)
Myers, Harry (Keighley) 1 (1898)

Nichol, W 'Billy' (Brighouse Rangers) 2 (1892)
Nicholson, Elliot T (Liverpool) 2 (1900)
Nicholson, Tom (Rockcliff) 1 (1893)
Northmore, Sammy (Millom) 1 (1897)

Oakes, RF 'Bob' (Hartlepool Rovers) 8 (1897-1899)
Openshaw, William E (Manchester) 1 (1879)
Osborne, Richard R (Manchester) 1 (1871)
Oughtred, Bernard S (Hartlepool Rovers) 1 (1901)

Parker, Sydney (Liverpool) 2 (1874-1875)
Payne, John H (Broughton) 7 (1882-1885)
Pease, Frank E (Hartlepool Rovers) 1 (1887)
Phillips, Charles (Birkenhead Park, Oxford University) 2 (1881)
Pierce, Richard (Liverpool) 1 (1898)
Pinch, Jack (Lancaster) 3 (1896-1897)
Poole, Robert W (Hartlepool Rovers) 1 (1896)
Pyke, Jim (St Helens Recreation) 1 (1892)

Ramsden, Harold E (Bingley) 2 (1898)
Ravenscroft, John J (Birkenhead Park) 1 (1881)
Rhodes, Jack (Castleford) 3 (1896)
Richards, Joe (Bradford) 3 (1891)
Richardson, William R (Manchester) 1 (1881)
Roberts, Sam (Swinton) 2 (1887)
Robertshaw, A Rawson (Bradford) 5 (1886-1887)
Robinson, George C 'Tot' (Percy Park) 8 (1897-1901)
Rowley, Hugh C (Manchester) 9 (1879-1882)

Royle, Arthur V 'Artie' (Broughton Rangers) 1 (1889)
Ryalls, HJ 'Harry' (New Brighton) 2 (1885)

Sample, Charles H (Northumberland FC, Cambridge University) 3 (1884-1886)
Sawyer, Charles M (Broughton) 2 (1880-1881)
Schofield, John W (Manchester) 1 (1880)
Scott, Mason T (Cambridge University, Northern) 3 (1887-1890)
Seddon, RL 'Bob' (Broughton Rangers) 3 (1887)
Shaw, Fred (Cleckheaton) 1 (1898)
Shooter, John H (Morley) 4 (1899-1900)
Speed, Harry (Castleford) 4 (1894-1896)
Spence, Frederick, W (Birkenhead Park) 1 (1890)
Springmann, HH 'Harry' (Liverpool) 2 (1879-1887)
Starks, Anthony (Castleford) 2 (1896)
Stoddart, Wilfred B (Liverpool) 3 (1897)
Sutcliffe, John W (Heckmondwike) 1 (1889)

Taylor, EW 'Little Billy' (Rockcliff) 14 (1892-1899)
Taylor, JT 'Jack' (Castleford, West Hartlepool) 5 (1897-1901)
Teggin, Alf (Broughton Rangers) 6 (1884-1887)
Tetley, TS 'Tom' (Bradford) 1 (1876)
Thomson, George T (Halifax) 9 (1878-1885)
Tobin, Frank (Liverpool) 1 (1871)
Todd, Robert (Manchester) 1 (1877)
Toothill, JT 'Jack' (Bradford) 12 (1890-1894)
Touzel, Charles JC (Liverpool) 2 (1877)
Turner, Henry JC (Manchester) 1 (1871)

Valentine, Jim (Swinton) 4 (1890-1896)
Varley, Harry (Liversedge) 1 (1892)
Verselst, Courtenay L (Liverpool) 2 (1875-1878)

Walker, Roger (Manchester) 5 (1874-1880)
Walton, Ernest J (Castleford, Oxford University) 2 (1901)
Walton, W 'Bill' (Castleford) 1 (1894)
Ward, Herbert 'Bert' (Bradford) 1 (1895)
Ward, JW 'Jack' (Castleford) 3 (1896)
Whiteley, William (Bramley) 1 (1896)
Wigglesworth, Henry (Thornes) 1 (1884)
Wilkinson, Edgar (Bradford) 5 (1886-1887)
Wilkinson, Harry J (Halifax) 1 (1889)
Wilson, Roger P (Liverpool Old Boys) 3 (1891)
Wood, Albert (Halifax) 1 (1884)
Wood, R 'Bob' (Liversedge) 1 (1894)

Wood, Robert D (Liverpool Old Boys) 1 (1901)
Woodhead, Ernest (Huddersfield) 1 (1880)
Wright, Frank T (Manchester) 1 (1881)
Wright, JF 'Jimmy' (Bradford) 1 (1890)

Yiend, William (Hartlepool Rovers) 6 (1889-1893)

Note 1: Richmond (see Harry Alexander and William E. Bromet) refers to the London-based club, not the North Yorkshire town.
Note 2: The Royal Indian Engineering College (see Frank D. Fowler) was based in Egham, near London.
Note 3: Wakefield-born Osbert G. Mackie (Cambridge University) played for Wakefield Trinity until 1895.

Most appearances (1871-1901):
RE 'Dicky' Lockwood 14
EW 'Little Billy' Taylor 14
William E Bromet 12
JT 'Jack' Toothill 12
Ernest F Fookes 10
Albert N Hornby 9
Hugh C Rowley 9
George T Thomson 9
RF 'Bob' Oakes 8
George C 'Tot' Robinson 8
Harry Bradshaw 7
Gilbert Harrison 7
Edward Kewley 7
John H Payne 7

Appendix 4

NORTHERN UNION COUNTY APPEARANCES
(1895-96 TO 1900-01)

The early pioneers of representative rugby in the Northern Union were those selected for inter-county fixtures, all seven of the northern England counties embraced by this publication having an involvement.

The following pages list every player to appear in a Northern Union county match during the Victorian era from the first, in 1895-96, up to and including 1900-01. This is broken down by county, namely Cheshire, Cumberland, Lancashire, Westmorland, and Yorkshire. A combined Durham and Northumberland team subsequently operated from 1901-02 until 1903-04, the majority of its players provided by South Shields who were Northern Union members at that time.

Each player is listed in alphabetical sequence, with surname followed by first name or initial. The name that the player was popularly referred to at the time (such as 'Billy'. 'Joe', etc.) is given where known. This is followed by the name(s) of the team(s) each player was associated with at the time of his appearance(s).

Next is the appearance total for the period followed by the year of the first and final appearance. Only one year is given where a player made all his appearances in the same year or had just one appearance.

Note that an asterisk (*) indicates further county appearances were made after 1900-01.

CHESHIRE
17 matches, 65 players

Abram, Sam (Runcorn) 1 (1895)
Allen, Arthur (Stockport) 3 (1896-97)
Bailey, William (Stockport) 1 (1895)
Barnett, Harry (Altrincham) 4 (1897-1900)
Bevan, Frank (Stockport) 3 (1899-1900)
Booth, Ben (Stockport) 4 (1896-1900)*
Brimble, Joseph (Stockport) 2 (1899)
Burrows, Jim (Stockport) 1 (1899)
Butterworth, Jimmy (Runcorn) 7 (1896-1899)*
Clayton, H Val (Birkenhead Wanderers) 2 (1899-1900)
Darlington, Fred (Runcorn) 1 (1900)
Davidson, J (Stockport) 3 (1898)
Farmer, Harry (Runcorn) 8 (1895-1900)*
Faulkner, Jack (Runcorn) 11 (1895-1900)*
Faulkner, Will (Runcorn) 5 (1895-1896)
Fields, Fred (Altrincham) 1 (1898)
Findlow, R 'Bob' (Altrincham) 1 (1898)
Garside, Albert (Stockport) 3 (1896)
Gayter, Fletcher (Runcorn) 7 (1896-1899)*
Gibson, Tom (Stockport) 5 (1895-1896)
Glover, E 'Ted' (Birkenhead Wanderers) 2 (1899)
Griffiths, Charlie 'Chuck' (Birkenhead Wanderers) 2 (1900)
Hanson, Sam (Altrincham) 3 (1897-1899)
Harris, Harry (Birkenhead Wanderers) 1 (1900)*
Hoggarth, Fred (Stockport) 1 (1900)
Holmes, Charlie (Birkenhead Wanderers) 4 (1897-1898)
Houghton, Sam (Runcorn) 8 (1896-1900)*
Hughes, Owen (Runcorn) 1 (1896)
Ingham, Frank (Birkenhead Wanderers) 1 (1897)
Jolley, Jim (Runcorn) 10 (1897-1900)*
Jones, David (Runcorn) 1 (1900)*
Langley, Jimmy (Runcorn) 6 (1895-1896)*
Lightfoot, W 'Bill' (Runcorn) 9 (1896-1900)*
Longthorpe, Eddie (Stockport) 1 (1896)
Milligan, W 'Bill' (Stockport) 3 (1897-1898)
Moores, George (Runcorn) 1 (1896)
Morton, R 'Bob' (Stockport) 2 (1895)
Moss, Harry (Dukinfield, Stockport) 4 (1896-1897)
Mottershead, Jack (Stockport) 5 (1895-1897)
Murphy, Bernard (Birkenhead Wanderers) 1 (1898)
Myers, Herbert (Runcorn) 3 (1895-1896)
Norris, Harry (Stockport) 2 (1895-1896)
Oram, W 'Billy' (Stockport) 5 (1899-1900)*
Owen, Mansel (Stockport) 1 (1900)
Palmer, Will (Stockport) 1 (1897)
Poole, Tom (Birkenhead Wanderers) 1 (1900)
Reece, RT 'Dick' (Runcorn) 5 (1897-1900)
Richardson, Joe (Runcorn) 1 (1900)
Richardson, Tom (Runcorn) 1 (1896)*
Roberts, Jack (Stockport) 2 (1896)
Robinson, George (Runcorn) 6 (1895-1898)
Robinson, W 'Billy' (Stockport) 8 (1896-1900)*
Sands, Phil (Stockport) 3 (1896)
Saville, Fred (Stockport) 11 (1895-1899)
Simister, W 'Billy' (Stockport) 6 (1898-1900)*
Taylor, Alf (Runcorn) 9 (1895-1899)
Trotter, Jim (Stockport) 3 (1900)*
Walker, Sam (Runcorn) 14 (1896-1900)*
Ward, Albert E (Lostock Gralam) 2 (1898)
Warder, TH 'Tom' (Runcorn) 8 (1895-1900)*
Watson, JD 'Jack' (Birkenhead Wanderers) 2 (1897-1898)
Wilkinson, Phil (Altrincham) 1 (1900)
Wilkinson, Tom (Runcorn) 5 (1899-1900)*
Worsley, Jim (Stockport) 12 (1895-1900)
Wrigley, Charlie (Stockport) 4 (1895-1896)

CUMBERLAND
10 matches, 57 players

Atkinson, James (Workington) 5 (1898-1900)*
Austin, Fred (Millom) 1 (1898)*
Beetham, Jack (Millom) 5 (1899-1900)*
Bell, James (Maryport)1 (1900)
Bell TG 'Tom' (Maryport) 1 (1900)*
Buckett, JH 'Jim' (Millom) 9 (1898-1900)
Coulthard, Joe (Workington) 1 (1900)
Eagers, WJ 'Bill' (Millom) 6 (1898-1899)*
Fletcher, Tom (Seaton) 2 (1898)*
Furness, Crossthwaite (Seaton) 1 (1900)*
Gowan, Charles (Wath Brow) 2 (1899)
Grenfell, Tom (Millom) 2 (1898-1899)
Grimes, John (Wath Brow) 1 (1900)*
Hall, Thomas (Whitehaven, Whitehaven Recs) 2 (1899-1900)

Hannah, W 'Billy' (Hunslet) 1 (1898)
Hatchin, Jonathan (Workington) 1 (1900)
Hayton, John (Maryport) 1 (1900)
Hodgson, TH 'Tom' (Millom) 1 (1899)
Hoggarth, Sam (Millom) 4 (1898-1899)*
Irving, William (Seaton) 1 (1900)
Killen, James (Maryport) 2 (1899)
Kitchin, Tom (Millom) 1 (1898)
Knowles, Edward 'Ned' (Millom) 4 (1898-1899)
Lamb, George W (Millom) 3 (1900)
Latham, Ike (Millom) 3 (1899-1900)
Leck, Jack (Millom) 5 (1899-1900)*
Linton, Matthew (Seaton, Millom) 7 (1898-1900)
Little, W 'Billy' (Seaton) 2 (1900)*
Lomas, Jimmy (Maryport) 3 (1899)*
McLaughlin, Jack (Bradford, Workington, Whitehaven Recs) 5 (1898-1900)
Mandle, William (Maryport) 1 (1898)
Marshall, Parmley (Wath Brow, Millom) 3 (1899-1900)*
Mason, Edward (Whitehaven Recs) 1 (1900)
Milburn, George (Whitehaven Recs) 1 (1900)
Milligan, William (Workington) 1 (1899)
Moore, John H (Millom) 1 (1898)
Moore, RF 'Bob' (Millom) 1 (1898)
Nixon, Humphrey (Brookland Rovers) 3 (1898-1899)
Northmore, Sammy (Millom) 6 (1898-1899)
O'Hara, Richard (Workington) 1 (1899)
Parkinson, Tom (Workington) 1 (1898)
Richardson, John H (Whitehaven Recs) 1 (1900)*
Robinson, William P (Maryport) 4 (1898-1899)
Robley, Joe (Maryport) 1 (1899)*
Smitheram, Jack (Millom) 1 (1898)
Steele, George (Workington) 3 (1899-1900)*
Teasdale, Tom (Wath Brow) 1 (1899)
Timney, John H (Maryport) 2 (1899-1900)*
Varty, John (Aspatria) 2 (1900)*
Warwick, Silas (Whitehaven Recs) 1 (1900)*
Wharton, JD 'Jack' (Millom) 3 (1898-1899)
Whitehead, Jonathan 'Jont' (Millom) 7 (1898-1900)*
Whitehead, George (Millom) 2 (1900)*
Wilson, Dan (Wath Brow, Millom) 7 (1898-1900)
Wright, John (Seaton) 1 (1898)
Young, Joe (Millom) 9 (1898-1900)*
Young, William (Hunslet, Maryport) 2 (1898)*

LANCASHIRE
18 matches, 83 players

Altham, Jimmy (Morecambe) 1 (1898)
Anderton, Tom (Leigh) 1 (1896)
Aspey, George (Widnes) 4 (1899-1900)
Badger, Owen (Swinton) 1 (1895)
Barber, Fairfield (Warrington) 4 (1895-1897)
Baty, Robert J (Widnes) 5 (1897-1898)
Berry, George (Broughton Rangers) 1 (1896)
Berry, John 'Buff' (Tyldesley) 2 (1896)
Berry, W 'Billy' (Tyldesley) 1 (1896)
Boardman, George (Leigh) 1 (1898)*
Bonser, Emanuel (Oldham) 6 (1895-1896)
Briers, W 'Billy' (St Helens) 17 (1895-1900)*
Brown, Jack (Wigan) 3 (1895-1896)
Chapman, Harry (Broughton Rangers) 7 (1895-1898)
Cleminson, Tom (Broughton Rangers) 6 (1895-1897)
Coop, Tom (Leigh) 3 (1896)
Davies, Dai (Swinton) 3 (1900)
Davies, TD 'Tom' (Oldham) 3 (1899)
Doherty, R 'Bob' (St Helens) 1 (1895)
Duck R 'Dick' (Broughton Rangers) 1 (1898)
Eagland, Harry (Oldham) 1 (1896)
Edwards, R 'Bob' (Oldham) 5 (1896-1897)
Evans, Jack (Swinton) 3 (1898)*
Ferguson, Joe (Oldham) 2 (1900)*
Field, Archie (Rochdale Hornets) 3 (1900)
Fish, Jack (Warrington) 1 (1900)*
Fletcher, Tom (Oldham) 3 (1899)
Foulkes, Tom (St Helens) 1 (1897)
Frater, George (Oldham) 4 (1898-1899)*
Griffiths, Ben (Salford) 3 (1897-1898)
Hadwen, Herbert (Salford) 3 (1899)
Hampson, Fred (Widnes) 2 (1897)
Harrison, Jack (Rochdale H) 5 (1898-1899)
Heslop, Oliver (Widnes) 1 (1898)
Hill, Arthur (Rochdale Hornets) 1 (1895)
Holmes, Robert 'Bratty' (Morecambe) 2 (1896)
Hoskins, Joe (Salford) 2 (1898)
Hurst, Jack (Oldham) 1 (1895)
Johnson, Jack (Swinton) 4 (1897-1898)
Johnson, Jim (Widnes) 1 (1896)
Kruger, Harry (Rochdale Hornets) 1 (1899)
Lawton, Joe (Oldham) 5 (1898-1899)*
Lees, Arthur (Oldham) 12 (1895-1900)
Lees, Sam (Oldham) 9 (1895-1898)
McCarthy, W 'Billy' (Wigan) 1 (1898)

Martin, Tom (Oldham) 3 (1897-1898)
Messenger, George (Broughton Rangers) 2 (1896-1898)
Messer, R 'Bob' (Swinton) 1 (1897)
Moffatt, Jim (Oldham) 6 (1898-1900)
Morrison, David (Warrington) 1 (1899)
Nelson, Joe (Broughton Rangers) 2 (1897-1898)
Nevins, Will (Warrington) 2 (1895)
Pearson, W 'Billy' (Swinton) 1 (1898)
Pollitt, Charlie (Swinton) 2 (1899)
Rhapps, Jack (Salford) 3 (1900)*
Roberts, W 'Billy' (Tyldesley) 1 (1895)
Robinson, W 'Bill' (Broughton Rangers) 4 (1896)
Simpson, Jack (Rochdale Hornets) 2 (1896)
Smith, Dan (Salford) 3 (1900)*
Smith, Tom (Leigh) 1 (1895)
Steele, George (Broughton Rangers) 3 (1897-1898)
Sudlow, Tom (St Helens) 2 (1896)
Taylor, Jack (Warrington) 1 (1896)
Taylor, Peter (Leigh) 8 (1896-1899)
Thomas RL 'Dicky' (Oldham) 3 (1899)*
Thompson, Charlie (Broughton Rangers) 3 (1899-1900)
Traynor, David (St Helens) 2 (1898)
Treweeke, Fred (Barrow) 3 (1900)*
Tunney, Pat (Salford) 6 (1899-1900)*
Turner, Peter (Wigan) 1 (1898)
Unsworth, W 'Bill' (Wigan) 2 (1895)
Uttley, Frank (Rochdale Hornets) 2 (1896)
Valentine, Jim (Swinton) 7 (1896-1900)*
Varley, Harry (Oldham) 4 (1895-1896)
Vigors, Evan (Swinton) 4 (1899-1900)
Whitehead, George (Broughton Rangers) 7 (1897-1900)*
Williams, Jack (Salford) 6 (1897-1899)
Williams, Sam (Oldham) 7 (1898-1900)*
Williams, Tom (Salford) 6 (1898-1900)
Winstanley, John (Wigan) 2 (1895)
Woodhead, Herbert 'Harry' (Salford) 1 (1897)
Worthington, Joe (Tyldesley) 7 (1895-1898)
Yates, W 'Billy' (Wigan) 2 (1895-1896)

WESTMORLAND
1 match, 17 players

The following 17 players represented Westmorland in its only match under Northern Union rules (versus Lancashire, 2nd March 1898)

Cross, W 'Billy' (St Helens)
Doherty, R 'Bob' (St Helens)
Elliott, John (Ulverston)
Fawcett, Tom (St Helens)
Fisher, George (Salford)
Goodman, Johnny (Swinton)
Hall, W 'Billy'
Hayton, John (Leeds)
Hoggarth, Fred (Stockport)
Holmes, Jim (Staveley)
Jackson, George (Lancaster)
Robinson, W 'Bill' (Ambleside)
Simpson Jack (St Helens)
Thompson, Joe (St Helens)
Threlfall, Jim (Staveley)
Whiteley, W 'Bill' (St Helens)
Whitwell, George ('Kendal')

Note 1: Whiteley and Whitwell appeared as substitutes for Goodman and Robinson who were both injured during the match.
Note 2: Whitwell was unattached to a club at the time and reported as from 'Kendal' having previously played for Kendal Hornets.

Northern Union County Appearances (1895-96 to 1900-01)

YORKSHIRE
18 matches, 82 players

Abbey, Ernest (Brighouse Rangers) 1 (1896)
Barker, Arthur (Manningham) 4 (1899-1900)*
Barraclough, Alf (Manningham) 1 (1895)
Bentley, Harry (Manningham) 1 (1898)
Boothroyd, Alf (Huddersfield) 3 (1895-1896)
Brady, Phil (Castleford) 1 (1899)
Broadley, Tom (Bradford) 7 (1896-1899)*
Brooke, Lewis (Brighouse Rangers) 2 (1895-1896)
Brown, Jack (Manningham) 2 (1896)
Buckler, Herbert (Holbeck) 1 (1899)
Chambers, Frank H (Huddersfield) 3 (1898-1899)
Clegg, Fred (Manningham) 5 (1895-1896)
Conley, Jim (Leeds Parish Church) 2 (1896)
Cooper, FW 'Fred' (Bradford) 10 (1895-1899)
Dale, W 'Billy' (Hull) 2 (1898-1899)
Davies, WP 'Wattie' (Batley) 2 (1897-1900)*
Dewhirst, Walter (Huddersfield) 2 (1900)
Donkin, Laurie (Hull) 3 (1895-1896)
Driscoll, Jimmy (Hull) 2 (1899)
Eastwood, Harry (Halifax) 1 (1898)
Evans, William (Leeds Parish Church) 1 (1900)*
Firth, Fred (Halifax) 6 (1895-1896)
Franks, Demetrious 'Dimmy' (Hull) 3 (1900)
Gath, Jim (Batley, Heckmondwike) 11 (1897-1900)
Goldthorpe, Albert E (Hunslet) 5 (1896-1899)*
Greig, Robert (Leeds) 4 (1895-1896)
Hambrecht, Albert (Bramley) 11 (1896-1900)*
Hannah, W 'Billy' (Hunslet) 1 (1896)
Hewlett, George (Leeds Parish Church) 4 (1899-1900)
Hughes, Thomas H (Brighouse Rangers) 3 (1895-1896)
Hutt, John (Bradford) 3 (1900)*
Jacques, W 'Billy' (Hull) 1 (1897)
Jones, J Ernest (Halifax) 1 (1900)
Keepings, WH 'Bill' (Halifax) 1 (1895)
Kemp, Albert (Hull Kingston Rovers) 8 (1897-1899)*
Kitson, George (Halifax) 2 (1896)
Laidlaw, Alex (Bradford) 3 (1900)*
Lempriere, Charles C 'Lemp' (Hull) 1 (1898)
Lewis R 'Bobby' (Leeds Parish Church) 1 (1899)
Lockwood, RE 'Dicky' (Wakefield Trinity) 2 (1897-1898)
Lorimer, George E (Manningham) 5 (1895-1896)
Lumley, Jimmy (Leeds) 4 (1898-1899)
Lunn, Albert (Hunslet) 3 (1900)
Marsden, George H (Bradford) 3 (1900)*
Metcalfe, Jimmy (Wakefield Trinity) 5 (1897-1899)
Milnes, Herbert (Holbeck) 1 (1897)
Mosley, George E (Leeds Parish Church) 5 (1897-1899)
Oakland, Joe (Batley) 1 (1899)*
Parker, James E (Morley, Bramley) 7 (1898-1900)
Parkinson, Ralph (Hull) 1 (1899)
Phillips, Thomas J (Huddersfield) 1 (1899)
Pollard, Bairstow (Bradford) 2 (1897)
Proctor, Arthur (Manningham) 2 (1899)
Ramage, James (Hunslet) 4 (1898-1899)
Rhodes, R 'Dick' (Hull) 1 (1898)
Richardson, Charlie (Leeds Parish Church) 2 (1897-1898)
Rigg, JA 'Archie' (Halifax) 12 (1895-1899)*
Riley, Jack (Halifax) 4 (1895-1896)*
Robertson, RJ 'Bob' (Bradford) 1 (1896)
Robinson, Albert W (Hull Kingston Rovers) 2 (1900)
Robinson, Herb (Hunslet) 3 (1898-1899)
Shackleton, Mark (Batley) 1 (1896)
Sharpe, Ben (Liversedge) 1 (1895)
Speed, Harry (Castleford) 2 (1896)
Starks, Anthony (Hull Kingston Rovers) 10 (1897-1900)*
Stephenson, James (Hull Kingston Rovers) 1 (1900)
Sugden, R Edgar (Brighouse Rangers) 3 (1895-1896)
Sugden, William (Bradford) 1 (1895)
Sullivan, Michael (Huddersfield) 1 (1899)
Sunderland, Robert (Manningham) 2 (1896)
Sutcliffe, Milford (Huddersfield) 10 (1895-1899)
Taylor, Harry (Hull) 6 (1899-1900)*
Topham, Harry (Bramley) 3 (1900)*
Tulloch, Herbert (Hull Kingston Rovers) 1 (1899)
Walker, Harry (Leeds Parish Church) 1 (1899)
Walker, Sam (Leeds) 1 (1897)
Walsh, Owen (Hunslet) 5 (1895-1896)
Walton, W 'Bill' (Wakefield Trinity) 12 (1895-1899)
Ward, JW 'Jack' (Castleford) 3 (1897-1898)
Wilkinson, Tom (Manningham) 4 (1898-1899)
Wood, R 'Bob' (Liversedge) 5 (1895-1896)
Wright, Fred (Bradford) 1 (1899)

Jack Clowes of Halifax and Yorkshire travelled to Australia and New Zealand with the 1888 tour party but was unable to play having been declared a 'professional' by the RFU after the ship departed. *Athletic News, 1888*

Appendix 5

THE 1888 TOUR TO AUSTRALIA AND NEW ZEALAND

Of the four tours undertaken during the Victorian era – 1888, 1891, 1896 and 1899 – the former is the most significant for northern rugby as it featured 14 players attached to clubs that would later join the breakaway Northern Union. For that reason the individual playing records for 1888 are summarised here. They cover the 35 matches that took place under Rugby rules. A further 19 (not included overleaf) were played under Australian Football rules.

Player	Team	Apps	Tries	Conv	D-gls	Points
Anderton, Jack	Salford	29	13	10		40
Banks, Tom	Swinton	9	3			4
Brooks, Dr Herbert	Durham City	18	3			6
Bumby, Walter	Swinton	24	7			12
Burnett, R 'Bob'	Hawick	30	2		1	5
Burnett, William 'Willie'	Hawick	21				0
Clowes, JP 'Jack'*	Halifax	0				0
Eagles, Harry	Salford	35	15	1		25
Haslam, Tom	Batley	29	9		2	18
Kent, Tom	Salford	28	5	1		9
Laing, Alex	Hawick	24				0
Mathers, Charlie	Bramley	25	7			10
Nolan, Johnny	Rochdale Hornets	20	14			16
Paul, Arthur	Swinton	29		13	2	33
Penketh, Alf	Douglas	19	1			1
Seddon, RL 'Bob'	Swinton	20	4	1		9
Smith, John	unattached	9	1			1
Speakman, Harry	Runcorn	27	6		3	17
Stoddart, Andrew	Blackheath	27	23	12	2	67
Stuart, Angus	Dewsbury	23	1			1
Thomas, WH 'Willie'	London Welsh	24	1			1
Williams, Sam	Salford	33	8		1	15
Bryce, Tom	guest	1				0
McSwaine, David	guest	1				0
Wadsworth, Deacon	guest	1				0

*Did not play due to having been declared a professional by the Rugby Football Union.

Note 1: Appearances incomplete due to team line-ups not reported for three matches; 16 July v South Australia (4 names missing), 8 August v Bathurst (6), 29 August v Northern Districts (9).
Note 2: Two try scorers not reported for 16 July v South Australia.

Appendix 6

NORTHERN CLUB ROOTS IN THE VICTORIAN ERA

There are currently 21 professional and semi-professional clubs in membership of the Rugby Football League that can trace their history back to the Victorian era. However, there are several teams that existed during the nineteenth century that, whilst having similar names to present day clubs, are not directly connected. To avoid confusion a brief overview of the life of those particular teams is given here.

BRADFORD
The original Bradford club is believed to have been founded in 1866, although its roots can be traced back to 1863. A founder member of the breakaway Northern Union in 1895 it disbanded in 1907 in favour of Association football, becoming known as Bradford Park Avenue. Rugby enthusiasts subsequently reformed as Bradford Northern in 1907, renaming as Bradford Bulls in 1995.

CASTLEFORD
Castleford Rugby Union (RU) club was formed in 1877. In May 1896 a Castleford Northern Union (NU) club was created following a split within the original Castleford organisation and the two teams began 1896-97 with both grounds located on Lock Lane. Castleford NU disbanded in 1907, a new Castleford NU club being formed in 1912. The latter, which began as a 'junior' organisation, was the forerunner of today's Castleford club, gaining admission to the Rugby Football League in 1926. The original Castleford RU club disbanded in 1909, a new Castleford RU club being founded in 1927.

DEWSBURY

The original Dewsbury club was founded as Dewsbury Athletic in October 1875. It was renamed Dewsbury and Savile in 1886, although the team was commonly referred to as Dewsbury throughout the Victorian era. The club was represented at the Northern Union breakaway meetings in 1895 but decided to remain with the Rugby Union. After the team struggled in the 1897-98 Yorkshire Competition No. 1 it was decided, at the end of that season, to transfer to Savile Town as an Association club. A new Dewsbury rugby club was founded in September 1898, joining the Northern Union and playing at the same Crown Flatt ground as its predecessor.

FEATHERSTONE

Founded in 1889 as Featherstone Trinity, the club dropped the Trinity tag in 1894. It joined the Northern Union 1898 but disbanded in 1902. A new club was organised in 1902 as Featherstone Rovers but folded in 1906. Featherstone Rovers reformed during 1908 and, in 1911, another new club, called Featherstone, was also founded. The two clubs amalgamated in 1912 under the name of Featherstone Rovers, operating as a junior club until joining the Northern Rugby League in 1921.

LEEDS

The first Leeds (Rugby) Football Club was founded during March 1864, amalgamating with the Leeds Athletic Club in 1870 to create its football section, thereafter playing under the name of Leeds Athletic. In April 1876 a new Leeds (Rugby) Football Club was founded by former players of the Leeds Athletic Club, the latter subsequently ceasing football after 1878-79. The new Leeds Football Club was renamed Yorkshire Wanderers from 1881-82, retaining its Leeds base, but disbanding in 1883. Throughout the remainder of the 1880s the most prominent users of the 'Leeds' name were Leeds St John's (founded 1870) and Leeds Parish Church (founded 1874). The latter disbanded in 1901 whereas Leeds St John's amalgamated with the newly formed Leeds Cricket, Football and Athletic Company at Headingley in 1890, creating the (Rugby) Football section. That same club exists today having been an original member of the breakaway Northern Union in 1895.

WHITEHAVEN

The original Whitehaven club was founded in 1877. Having defected to the Northern Union in 1898, it disbanded during 1900. The other prominent team of that era was Whitehaven Colliery Recreation Football Club, otherwise known as Whitehaven Recreation, which added rugby to its portfolio around 1891. In 1899 they also transferred their allegiance to the Northern Union, continuing until around 1912, after which time Association football became its main focus. The current Whitehaven club was formed in 1948.

WORKINGTON

The first Workington club was founded in 1877 as the football section of the local cricket club. In 1898 it joined the Northern Union but folded in 1909. Today's Workington Town club was founded in 1945.

Appendix 7

RUGBY UNION REPRESENTATIVE HONOURS BY NORTHERN PLAYERS

This section lists the rugby union representative honours of players connected to clubs that later defected to the Northern Union (NU) from 1895 to 1901. The clubs featured are those that subsequently competed in the Northern Rugby League, Lancashire Senior Competition or Yorkshire Senior Competition. Note this list includes players attached to the original Dewsbury club which ceased playing rugby during December 1897, the current Dewsbury club being founded in April 1898.

ALTRINCHAM (NU from 1897-98, withdrew 1902)
Cheshire: Harry Barnett, William Fleet, Sam Hanson, Bob Morton, Will Palmer, George Pendlebury, John Searle, Arnold Wolff

BARROW (NU from 1897-98)
Cumberland: George Ashburner, John Atkinson, Tom Carlton, Billy Cunningham, Sammy Northmore, Walker Sharp, Stephen Troughton, Rowell Tyson
Lancashire: Robert Bell, Thomas Bell, Tom Bowker, William Chapman, John Harley, George Hughes, William Kinnish, Alec Little, Fred Treweek, Fred Wildman
Westmorland: J. Whitwell
England: George Hughes

BATLEY (NU from 1895-96)
Yorkshire: Harry Bedford, Tom Elliker, Tom Else, Tom Haslam, Arthur Ineson, E. Jackson, Fred Lowrie, Jim Naylor, Albert Parker, Herbert Simms, J. W. 'Jack' Sykes
North: Harry Bedford, Tom Haslam, Fred Lowrie
Tourist (1888): Tom Haslam

BIRKENHEAD WANDERERS (NU from 1897-98, withdrew 1904)
Cheshire: Davy Atkinson, William Conning, Alby Dillon, John Dobie, Edward Elliott, James Gerrard, Ivie Heyes, Sam Houghton, Billy Hughes, Fred Hughes, Ellis Hurst, Frank Ingham, George Ingham, Arthur Jones, Charlie Kelly, Tom Lewis, John May, Tom Morgan, Bernard Murphy, Jack Watson
North: Sam Houghton
England: Sam Houghton

BRADFORD (NU from 1895-96, withdrew 1907)
Yorkshire: L. E. Ashby, Sam Asquith, J. O. Beutler, Fred Bonsor, Morris Bonsor, J. W. Bottomley, Arthur Briggs, H, E. Briggs, Tom Broadley, -, Brown, William Carter, A. Champion, Fred Cooper, Jack Crompton, Arthur Dawson, M. Dawson, Edgar Dewhirst, Tom Dobson, Horace Duckett, E. Dunsford, Charlie Emmott, Alfred Firth, J. Fisher, James Freeman, Harry Garnett, J. H. Greenhalgh, W. H. Griffiths, R. F. Gwyther, S. Haigh, George Hastings, Joe Hawcridge, Laurie Hickson, A. Holmes, Willie Jowett, Albert Lassen, W. C. Lupton, A. McLaurin, E. Mann, John Marshall, Reggie Mills, R. Munro, Joe Richards, J. Richardson, Frank Ritchie, Herbert Robertshaw, Jere Robertshaw, Percy Robertshaw, Rawson Robertshaw, C. Scharff, Arthur Schutt, Fred Schutt, A. Sidgwick, F. J. Smith, W. H. Smith, Fred Steinthal, T. Stericker, Tom Tetley, Jack Toothill, Bert Ward, Edgar Wilkinson, Jimmy Wright, E. H. Wynn
North: Fred Bonsor, Arthur Briggs, Tom Broadley, Fred Cooper, Tom Dobson, Harry Garnett, Joe Hawcridge, Laurie Hickson, John Marshall, Joe Richards, Frank Ritchie, Herbert Robertshaw, Percy Robertshaw, Rawson Robertshaw, T. Stericker, Tom Tetley, Jack Toothill, Bert Ward, Edgar Wilkinson, Jimmy Wright
England: Fred Bonsor, Arthur Briggs, Tom Dobson, Horace Duckett, Charlie Emmott, Harry Garnett, Joe Hawcridge, Laurie Hickson, Joe Richards, Rawson Robertshaw, Tom Tetley, Jack Toothill, Bert Ward, Edgar Wilkinson, Jimmy Wright

BRAMLEY (NU from 1896-97, withdrew 1999)
Lancashire: William Whiteley
Yorkshire: Harry Bradshaw, J. Brooke, Albert Hambrecht, Charlie Mathers, Harry Myers, William Whiteley
North: Charlie Mathers, William Whiteley
England: Harry Bradshaw, William Whiteley
Tourist (1888): Charlie Mathers

BRIGHOUSE RANGERS (NU from 1895-96, withdrew 1906)
Yorkshire: Sam Eastwood, Fred Firth, Billy Nichol, Fred Wood
North: Billy Nichol
England: Billy Nichol

Rugby Union Representative Honours by Northern Players

BROUGHTON RANGERS (NU from 1895-96, renamed Belle Vue Rangers 1946, withdrew 1955)
Lancashire: J. Barlow, Jack Hacking, Jerry Jackson, John Robertson, Arthur Royle, R. L. 'Bob' Seddon, Sam Simpson, Alf Teggin, Jack Tune, R. R. 'Bob' Veale
North: Arthur Royle, R. L. 'Bob' Seddon, Alf Teggin
England: Arthur Royle, R. L. 'Bob' Seddon, Alf Teggin

DEWSBURY (NU from 1898-99)
Yorkshire: Harry Broadbent, C. Chadwick, W. K. Fisher, Joe Garforth, J. W. 'Jack' Graham, Ted Hanson, J. W. Ibbotson, Dicky Lockwood, William Lorryman, S. Mortimer, Joe Naylor, Alf Newsome, Mark Newsome, Arthur Perkins, P. Redfern, William Stadden, Angus Stuart, George Thompson, Eli Wolstenholme, W. Wolstenholme
Westmorland: Joe Allen
North: Joe Garforth, Dicky Lockwood, Alf Newsome
England: Dicky Lockwood
Wales: William Stadden
Tourist (1888): Angus Stuart

GOOLE (NU from 1898-99, withdrew 1902)
Yorkshire: Joe Bradley, G. Bryars, Herbert 'Harry' Woodhead

HALIFAX (NU from 1895-96)
Yorkshire: Tom Allbutt, Joey Arnold, Herbert Barnes, Fred Bedford, Edmund Buckley, Tom Chambers, C. Champney, Howard Clay, Jack Clowes, Johnny Crossland, Jimmy Dodd, Albert Firth, Fred Firth, Otis Fletcher, Teddy French, Joe Hartley, Walter Jackson, Bill Keepings, Jimmy Knowles, Jimmy Lockhead, Ben Mellor, George Miller, Jack Parker, Archie Rigg, Jack Riley, George Scarborough, Tom Scarborough, George Thomson, Abe Toothill, Rufus Ward, Tom Watson, Ike Webster, Harry Wilkinson, Arthur Wilson, Bob Winskill, Albert Wood, Jack Wood, J. E. Wood, J. H. Wood
Westmorland: Alf Chorley, Bob Winskill
North: Jimmy Dodd, Fred Firth, George Thomson, Harry Wilkinson, Albert Wood
England: Fred Firth, Walter Jackson, George Thomson, Harry Wilkinson, Albert Wood
Tourist (1888): Jack Clowes

HECKMONDWIKE (NU from 1896-97, withdrew 1903)
Yorkshire: J. Bardon, Fred Blackburn, Donald Jowett, Dicky Lockwood, Harry Noble, John Sutcliffe, Herbert Wood
North: Donald Jowett, Dicky Lockwood, John Sutcliffe
England: Donald Jowett, Dicky Lockwood, John Sutcliffe

HOLBECK (NU from 1896-97, withdrew 1904)
Yorkshire: W. Duke, Herbert Hartley

HUDDERSFIELD (NU from 1895-96)
Yorkshire: Harry Archer, Charles Beardsell, Harry Beardsell, George W. Bottomley, Alfred Bradley, G. S. Brook, H. S. Brook, Arthur Brooke, George Brooke, Herbert Calvert, Sheard Conacher, T. P. Crosland, Tom Dickenson, Jack Dyson, Tom Else, Will England, C. E. Freeman, Tom Heron, Percy Holmes, Frank Huth, Fred Huth, Harry Huth, Paul Jackson, Harry Lodge, Auly Macauley, C. J. F. 'Charlie' Paisley, Fred Richmond, B. Schofield, A. C. Sharpe, C. M. Sharpe, Milford Sutcliffe, John Vickerman, Robert Welsh, Harry Wilson, Ernest Woodhead, P. T. Wrigley
North: George W. Bottomley, H. S. Brook, Arthur Brooke, Jack Dyson, Harry Huth, Ernest Woodhead,
England: Jack Dyson, Harry Huth, Ernest Woodhead

HULL (NU from 1895-96)
Yorkshire: Albert E. 'Lol' Bearpark, G. E. Belt, C. Bethell, D. F. Burton, W. F. B. 'Bill' Calvert, Edward Coulman, Godfrey Darbishire, Laurie Donkin, N. Ellershaw, Gilbert Harrison, Walter Harrison, Richard Hodgson, William Hodgson, E. A. Hollingbury, C. Hustwick, William Hutchinson, Tony Iveson, George Jacketts, Charles B. Lambert, Fred Mawer, F. B. Moss, H. J. R. 'Harry' Oxlade, J. Sharpe, Harry Simpson, Billy Teal, Charles Ullathorne, R. J. Wade, R. Waltham
North: D. F. Burton, Gilbert Harrison, Richard Hodgson, William Hutchinson
England: Gilbert Harrison, William Hutchinson

HULL KINGSTON ROVERS (NU from 1897-98)
Yorkshire: Sammy Morfitt, Jack Rhodes, Anthony Starks
North: Sammy Morfitt, Anthony Starks

HUNSLET (NU from 1895-96)
Yorkshire: Albert Goldthorpe, Walter Goldthorpe, J. Rathmel, Owen Walsh,

KEIGHLEY (NU from 1900-01)
Yorkshire: D. Adkins, R. 'Dick' Blades, J. Glew, T. Hollindrake, Harry Myers, Frank Redman, Albert Robinson, A. Tillotson
North: Harry Myers
England: Harry Myers

LANCASTER (NU from 1897-98, withdrew 1903)
Lancashire: Charlie Danby, Charlie Gibson, Jack Pinch, Charlie Thompson, Edward Thompson
Westmorland: George Fawcett, George Fisher, Tom Gibson, W. Hall, Fred Hoggarth
North: Jack Pinch
England: Jack Pinch

LEEDS (NU from 1895-96)
Yorkshire: J. Broadbent, Mark Fletcher, Harry Hainstock, E. Hudson, W. 'Bill' Lorriman, J. Melvin, George Naylor, George Nowell, Joe Pickles, Roger Place, Herbert Potter, Joe Riley, Tommy Summersgill

LEEDS PARISH CHURCH (NU from 1896-97, withdrew 1901)
Yorkshire: Jim Conley, E. H. Dykes, George Mosley, Joe Oddy, Charlie Richardson, W. Ward
North: E. H. Dykes

LEIGH (NU from 1895-96)
Lancashire: Tom Anderton, Tom Coop, Bob MacMasters
North: Tom Coop
England: Tom Coop

LIVERSEDGE (NU from 1895-96, renamed Cleckheaton 1902, withdrew 1902)
Yorkshire: Harry Baker, Billy Fisher, Ernest Parkin, Sam Priestley, Ben Sharpe, Harry Varley, Bob Wood
North: Bob Wood
England: Harry Varley, Bob Wood

MANNINGHAM (NU from 1895-96, withdrew 1903)
Yorkshire: Alf Barraclough, Fred Clegg, William Donaldson, Billy Fawcett, J. J. 'Joe' Hawcridge, Edgar Holmes, George Lorimer, Ike Newton, Edgar Redman
North: Alf Barraclough, Edgar Holmes, Edgar Redman
England: Edgar Holmes

MILLOM (NU from 1897-98, withdrew 1906)
Cumberland: Joe Armstrong, John Bell, Matthew Boase, Jim Buckett, Johnny Burns, Billy Cunningham, Charlie Dove, William Falcon, John Fawcett, J. Flynn, Fred Gorman, J. Harrison, Joseph Hewitson, Tom Hodgson, Sam Hoggarth, Joseph Holme, Tommy James, Jack Kidd, Tom Kitchin, Ned Knowles, James Leck, Robert Leck, William Leck, John McGuire, Bob Moore, Ike Moore, Joe Moore, John Moore, William Moore, William Nelson, Sammy Northmore, George Phillips, Billy Rowe, Jack Smitheram, Tom Whalen, William Wilkinson, Joe Young
North: Sam Hoggarth, Joseph Holme, Ned Knowles, Sammy Northmore
England: Ned Knowles, Sammy Northmore

MORECAMBE (NU from 1896-97, withdrew 1906)
Lancashire: Robert Holmes, Bobby Lewis
North: Robert Holmes

NORMANTON (NU from 1898-99, withdrew 1906)
Yorkshire: G. Barrett, Albert Davey

OLDHAM (NU from 1895-96)
Lancashire: Ben Andrew, John Armstrong, Abe Ashworth, Charlie Barlow, Ned Blomley, Emanuel Bonser, Harry Court, Abraham Fletcher, Ted Furniss, Dai Gwynn, Jack Hurst, Arthur Lees, Sam Lees, Bill McCutcheon, Johnny Nolan, John Rye, Ike Taylor, Harry Varley, J. T. Walkden
Westmorland: Robert Moore
North: Abe Ashworth
England: Abe Ashworth
Wales: Dai Gwynn, Bill McCutcheon

RADCLIFFE (NU from 1896-97, withdrew 1902)
Lancashire: Tom Kent
Westmorland: Jonty Goodman

ROCHDALE HORNETS (NU from 1895-96)
Lancashire: Abe Ashworth, Samuel B. Beard, John Brearley, Tom Butterworth, Wilfred Butterworth, J. E. Griffiths, Jack Groves, Willie Hastings, Thomas M. Holt, Andrew Irving, Tom Melledew, Johnny Nolan, William H. Pennington, William A. Scholes, Jack Simpson
North: Wilfred Butterworth, Aynsley Fenton
Tourist (1888): Johnny Nolan

RUNCORN (NU from 1895-96, withdrew 1918)
Cheshire: Sam Abram, Bill Boady, Jack Brazendale, Jimmy Butterworth, Harry Cawley, Jim Clarke, Jack Crompton, Frederick Davies, Jack Davies, Tom Davies, Richard Dolan, Bill Evans, Jack Faulkner, Will Faulkner, Fletcher Gayter, Joseph Gayter, Abraham Hampson, Fred Hancock, Sam Houghton, Bill Hughes, Edward Hughes, Hughie Hughes, Owen Hughes, Jimmy Langley, Jack Lewis, Daniel Massey, Richard Dick, Bill Riley, J. Riley, Peter Riley, George Robinson, Bill Shaw, Harry Speakman, Jimmy Stubbs, Alf Taylor, George Wainwright, Tom Warder, Harry Williams, Tom Woods, Bill Wright
North: Will Faulkner, Sam Houghton, Peter Riley
England: Sam Houghton
Tourist (1888): Harry Speakman

ST. HELENS (NU from 1895-96)
Lancashire: Billy Cross, Tom Foulkes
Westmorland: Joe Allen, Billy Cross, Bob Doherty, Bill Whiteley
North: Billy Cross

SALFORD (NU from 1896-97)
Cheshire: Hugh Williamson
Lancashire: Jack Anderton, Alf Barrett, Herbert Cook, Tom Craven, Harry Eagles, James Jackson, J. J. Jones, Tom Kent, Tom King, Billy Manwaring, Frank Miles, Bob Moss, Jack Roberts, Vic Slater, Tommy Smith, Sam Walch, Sam Williams
North: Harry Eagles, Tom Kent, Sam Williams
England: Tom Kent
Tourist (1888): Jack Anderton, Harry Eagles, Tom Kent, Sam Williams

SOUTH SHIELDS (from 1901-02, withdrew 1904)
Durham: William Alden, Henry Fawcus, J. Frame, Billy Hector, Luke Hopper, Billy Kassell, Joe Nichol, Alan Peat, George Quest, W. J. Robertson, Harry Swainston, F. Tully, Ralph Wood
Northumberland: William Baty

SOWERBY BRIDGE (NU from 1899-1900, withdrew 1902)
Yorkshire: Ernest Fookes
North: Ernest Fookes
England: Ernest Fookes

STOCKPORT (NU from 1895-96, withdrew 1903)
Cheshire: Harry Ashton, Walter Bailey, William Bailey, W. Beard, John Fitchett, Tom Haslam, Michael King, Bob Morton, Jack Mottershead, W. Pickard, James Potts, Fred Saville, C. Schofield, John H. Smith, J. Smith, James Speet, J. F. Taylor
North: Fred Saville

SWINTON (NU from 1896-97)
Cheshire: Freddie Jones
Cumberland: George Steele
Lancashire: Joe Bagshaw, Tom Banks, Ted Beswick, Herbie Brockbank, Walter Bumby, Harry Case, Billy Cook, George Cookson, Tom Coulthwaite, Walter Dickenson, Herbert Farr, Tom Farr, Sam Hall, Albert Hope, Charlie Horley, Nat Hotchkiss, Jack Johnson, James Kenyon, William Lancaster, Jack Lewis, Fred Lomax, Walter Longshaw, James Marsh, Joe Mills, Harold Murray, Arthur Paul, Billy Pearson, Sam Roberts, Tom Rothwell, John Seddon, R. 'Bob' Seddon, R. L. 'Bob' Seddon, George Sharples, Jack Sunderland, Bob Tickle, Jim Valentine, Harry Yates
North: Ted Beswick, Walter Bumby, Harry Case, Charlie Horley, James Marsh, Joe Mills, Sam Roberts, R. L. 'Bob' Seddon, Jim Valentine
England: Ted Beswick, Charlie Horley, James Marsh, Sam Roberts, Jim Valentine
Tourist (1888): Tom Banks, Walter Bumby, Arthur Paul, R. L. 'Bob' Seddon

TYLDESLEY (NU from 1895-96, withdrew 1901)
Lancashire: John Berry, Jim Shepherd, George Woodward
Westmorland: George H. Bell, Jim Bell, Billy Berry, John Berry
North: John Berry, George Woodward
England: John Berry

WAKEFIELD TRINITY (NU from 1895-96)
Yorkshire: Fred Ash, Teddy Bartram, Jim Bedford, Oliver Bennett, Billy Binks, Paul Booth, Harry Dawson, Bill Ellis, Herbert Fallas, Jack Fotherby, Jack Gomersall, Harper Hamshaw, Tommy Harrison, Arthur Hayley, Harry Hayley, Herbert Hutchinson, Bill Jackson, Hampton Jones, George Jubb, Barron Kilner, J. W. 'Joe' Kilner, Joe Lathom, Ben Longbottom, Fred Lowrie, Osbert Mackie, William Smith, E. J. Spink, George Steele, Herbert Ward, Tommy Wordsworth
North: Teddy Bartram, Herbert Hutchinson, J. Hampton Jones, Barron Kilner, Fred Lowrie, Osbert Mackie
England: Herbert Fallas, Barron Kilner, Fred Lowrie

WARRINGTON (NU from 1895-96)
Lancashire: James Bate, John Bate, Joseph Boscow, John Dakin, Will Dillon, Jim Jolley, Will Nevins, Fairfield Turner

WIDNES (NU from 1895-96)
Lancashire: Joe Drummond, George Hewitt, Joseph Holme

WIGAN (NU from 1895-96)
Lancashire: Jack Anderton, Billy Atkinson, Tom Brayshay, Ned Bullough, Billy Halliwell, George Rigby, Dick Seddon, Bill Unsworth,
Westmorland: William Whitehead
Glamorganshire: J. Percy Jago
North: Billy Atkinson, Ned Bullough
England: Ned Bullough

YORK (NU from 1898-99)
Yorkshire: Edward Birch, D. Brown, Alex Christison, Robert Christison, E. B. Clarke, Ted Glaisby, J. F. Griffith, H. Harris, T. Hurworth, J. H. Jolly, W. J. Mackenzie, R. Petty, H. W. Rhodes, F. Thursby, Charlie Wood

Appendix 8

COMPETITION WINNERS (1877-78 TO 1900-01)

RUGBY UNION: LEAGUE COMPETITIONS

CUMBERLAND SENIOR LEAGUE
1895-96 Seaton

CUMBERLAND DIAMOND JUBILEE LEAGUE
1897-98 Aspatria

LANCASHIRE CLUB CHAMPIONSHIP FIRST CLASS
1892-93 Salford
1893-94 Oldham
1894-95 Tyldesley
1895-96 Morecambe
1896-97 Littleborough

LANCASHIRE CLUB CHAMPIONSHIP SECOND CLASS
1893-94 St Helens
1894-95 Barrow
1895-96 Mossley

LANCASHIRE CLUB CHAMPIONSHIP THIRD CLASS
1893-94 Blackley Rangers
1894-95 Pemberton

NORTH WESTERN LEAGUE
1891-92 Millom
1892-93 Lancaster
1893-94 Millom
1894-95 Barrow
1895-96 Morecambe
1896-97 Millom

SOUTH EAST LANCASHIRE COMPETITION
1892-93 Barton

WEST LANCASHIRE RUGBY LEAGUE
1889-90 Wigan
1890-91 Walkden
1891-92 Aspull

WESTMORLAND JUNIOR LEAGUE
1893-94 Staveley
1894-95 Staveley
1895-96 Staveley

YORKSHIRE SENIOR COMPETITION
1892-93 Bradford
1893-94 Manningham
1894-95 Liversedge
1895-96 Leeds Parish Church
1896-97 Hull Kingston Rovers
1897-98 Featherstone
1898-99 Shipley
1899-1900 Keighley

YORKSHIRE COMPETITION NO. 2
1892-93 Holbeck
1893-94 Leeds Parish Church
1894-95 Morley
1895-96 Shipley
1896-97 Keighley
1897-98 Alverthorpe
1898-99 Bottomboat Trinity

YORKSHIRE COMPETITION NO. 3
1893-94 Bingley
1894-95 Pudsey
1895-96 Idle
1896-97 Bingley
1897-98 Luddendenfoot

YORKSHIRE COMPETITION NO. 4
1894-95 Stanningley

YORKSHIRE INTERMEDIATE COMPETITION
1893-94 Alverthorpe

RUGBY UNION: CUP COMPETITIONS

CHESHIRE COUNTY CHALLENGE CUP
1877-78 Birkenhead Park
1878-79 Birkenhead Park
1879-80 New Brighton
1880-81 Birkenhead Park

CUMBERLAND COUNTY CHALLENGE CUP
1882-83 Aspatria
1883-84 Whitehaven
1884-85 Aspatria
1885-86 Carlisle City
1886-87 Millom
1887-88 Millom
1888-89 Millom
1889-90 Egremont
1890-91 Aspatria
1891-92 Aspatria
1892-93 Maryport
1893-94 Maryport
1894-95 Seaton
1895-96 Aspatria
1896-97 Seaton
1897-98 Seaton
1898-99 Aspatria

DURHAM COUNTY CHALLENGE CUP
1880-81 Sunderland
1881-82 Houghton-le-Spring
1882-83 North Durham
1883-84 Hartlepool Rovers
1884-85 Durham City
1885-86 no competition held
1886-87 Hartlepool Rovers
1887-88 Durham City
1888-89 Hartlepool Rovers
1889-90 Hartlepool Rovers

DURHAM COUNTY CHALLENGE CUP *continued*
1890-91 Hartlepool Rovers
1891-92 Tudhoe
1892-93 Tudhoe
1893-94 Hartlepool Rovers
1894-95 South Shields
1895-96 Hartlepool Rovers
1896-97 Hartlepool Rovers
1897-98 Tudhoe
1898-99 Tudhoe
1899-1900 West Hartlepool
1900-01 South Shields

LANCASHIRE CHAMPIONSHIP CUP
1896-97 Ulverston

NORTHUMBERLAND COUNTY FOOTBALL CHALLENGE CUP
1880-81 Northern
1881-82 Northern
1882-83 Tynemouth
1883-84 Northern
1884-85 Tynemouth
1885-86 Percy Park
1886-87 Tynedale
1887-88 Northern
1888-89 Northern
1889-90 Rockcliff
1890-91 Rockcliff
1891-92 Rockcliff
1892-93 Rockcliff
1893-94 Rockcliff
1894-95 Rockcliff
1895-96 Rockcliff
1896-97 Percy Park
1897-98 Rockcliff
1898-99 Percy Park
1899-1900 Rockcliff
1900-01 Rockcliff

WEST LANCASHIRE AND BORDER TOWNS CHALLENGE CUP
1885-86 Warrington
1886-87 Aspull
1887-88 Tyldesley
1888-89 Wigan

YORKSHIRE COUNTY FOOTBALL CHALLENGE CUP
1877-78 Halifax
1878-79 Wakefield Trinity
1879-80 Wakefield Trinity
1880-81 Dewsbury
1881-82 Thornes
1882-83 Wakefield Trinity
1883-84 Bradford
1884-85 Batley
1885-86 Halifax
1886-87 Wakefield Trinity
1887-88 Halifax
1888-89 Otley
1889-90 Huddersfield
1890-91 Pontefract
1891-92 Hunslet
1892-93 Halifax
1893-94 Halifax
1894-95 Brighouse Rangers
1895-96 Castleford
1896-97 Hull Kingston Rovers
1897-98 Ossett
1898-99 Sowerby Bridge
1899-1900 Mytholmroyd
1900-01 Castleford

RUGBY UNION: COUNTY CHAMPIONSHIP

1888-89 Yorkshire
1889-90 Yorkshire
1890-91 Lancashire
1891-92 Yorkshire
1892-93 Yorkshire
1893-94 Yorkshire
1894-95 Yorkshire

1895-96 Yorkshire
1896-97 Kent
1897-98 Northumberland
1898-99 Devonshire
1899-1900 Durham
1900-01 Devonshire

RUGBY UNION: INTERNATIONAL CHAMPIONSHIP

1882-83 England
1883-84 England
1884-85 competition incomplete
1885-86 England, Scotland (shared)
1886-87 Scotland
1887-88 competition incomplete
1888-89 competition incomplete
1889-90 England, Scotland (shared)
1890-91 Scotland
1891-92 England

1892-93 Wales
1893-94 Ireland
1894-95 Scotland
1895-96 Ireland
1896-97 competition incomplete
1897-98 competition incomplete
1898-99 Ireland
1899-1900 Wales
1900-01 Scotland

NORTHERN UNION: LEAGUE COMPETITIONS

NORTHERN RUGBY FOOTBALL LEAGUE
1895-96 Manningham

LANCASHIRE SENIOR COMPETITION
1895-96 Runcorn
1896-97 Broughton Rangers
1897-98 Oldham
1898-99 Broughton Rangers
1899-1900 Runcorn
1900-01 Oldham

LANCASHIRE SECOND COMPETITION
1897-98 Barrow
1898-99 Millom
1899-1900 Barrow
1900-01 Morecambe

LANCASHIRE THIRD COMPETITION
1897-98 Werneth

YORKSHIRE SENIOR COMPETITION
1895-96 Manningham
1896-97 Brighouse Rangers
1897-98 Hunslet
1898-99 Batley
1899-1900 Bradford
1900-01 Bradford

YORKSHIRE SECOND COMPETITION
1898-99 Hull Kingston Rovers
1899-1900 Heckmondwike
1900-01 York

CUMBERLAND SENIOR COMPETITION
1899-1900 Maryport
1900-01 Maryport

LANCASHIRE AND YORKSHIRE BORDER TOWNS LEAGUE
1899-1900 Werneth

NORTH WESTERN LEAGUE
1897-98 Millom
1898-99 Millom
1899-1900 Millom
1900-01 Millom

SOUTH EAST LANCASHIRE LEAGUE
1898-99 Radcliffe

WESTMORLAND JUNIOR LEAGUE
1897-98 Ambleside
1898-99 Kendal Hornets

WESTMORLAND AND DISTRICT LEAGUE
1899-1900 Kendal Hornets

WESTMORLAND AND NORTH LANCASHIRE LEAGUE
1900-01 Kendal Hornets

NORTHERN UNION: CUP COMPETITIONS

NORTHERN UNION CHALLENGE CUP
1896-97 Batley
1897-98 Batley
1898-99 Oldham
1899-1900 Swinton
1900-01 Batley

SOUTH WEST LANCASHIRE AND BORDER TOWNS CHALLENGE CUP
1899-1900 St Helens
1900-01 Leigh

WEST RIDING CHALLENGE CUP
1899-1900 Liversedge

NORTHERN UNION: COUNTY CHAMPIONSHIP

1895-96 Lancashire
1896-97 Lancashire
1897-98 Yorkshire
1898-99 Yorkshire
1899-1900 Lancashire
1900-01 Lancashire

Cup Competition.

Over thirty years ago a Cheshire Cup Tourney was started, and continued for four seasons only. The following were the winners :—

1877-8 Birkenhead Park beat Bowdon and Lymm at Manchester.
1878-9 Birkenhead Park beat New Brighton at Waterloo.
1879-0 New Brighton beat Birkenhead Park at Rock Ferry.
1880-1 Birkenhead Park beat New Brighton at Liverpool.

The old Cup is now in the custody of the " Park " and has been ever since its withdrawal from the competition.

The Cheshire County Challenge Cup results as shown in Birkenhead Park's 50th anniversary publication. *Jubilee Year Book, 1922*

Appendix 9

THE CHESHIRE CUP

The Cheshire County Challenge Cup, which survived four seasons during the Victorian era from 1877-78 to 1880-81, was notoriously difficult to research. Unlike other county league and cup competitions embraced by this publication, coverage of the Cheshire Cup, particularly by the Cheshire press, was minimal or non-existent. A prime example is Birkenhead Park who, despite involvement in every final, received virtually no mention of their achievements in Birkenhead's newspapers. However, every effort has been made to secure information from alternative sources, although it is still incomplete. An honest approach has been made by the author and anomalies are highlighted in the sections where the competitions results are provided. On the positive side, details for three of the four finals have been uncovered and included on the relevant pages.

The biggest mystery surrounds the 1878-79 final in which Birkenhead Park is credited with beating New Brighton. Published fixture lists had it scheduled for the 30th November but there is no report of it taking place on that date. In fact, details for this important match have proved elusive. Contemporary sources have been consulted including Charles W. Alcock's 1879 *Football Annual*, together with numerous newspaper and sporting publications. The Cheshire Rugby Football Union's minutes are absent for that season, whilst the Birkenhead Park and New Brighton club archives do not reach back that far. Curiously Birkenhead Park have two team photographs on display celebrating its Cheshire Cup successes of 1877-78 and 1880-81, but there is no such image for 1878-79.

The 1878-79 competition started, but did it finish? What evidence do we have that Birkenhead Park overcame New Brighton in the final? The first reference found was imbedded in reports for the following year's 1879-80 decider contested by the same two teams, the *Athletic News* and the *Sporting Chronicle* advising readers that Birkenhead Park 'have held the trophy for two years', the *Field* stating 'they are the holders of the cup having won it two years in succession'. The earliest historical recognition appears to be in Birkenhead Park's *Jubilee Year Book* (published in 1922) which commemorated the club's 50th anniversary. It contains a summary of the four finals but no scores, just the name of the winner, loser and venue. For 1878-79 it simply reads: 'Birkenhead Park beat New Brighton at Waterloo.' The 'Waterloo' in question would have been Waterloo Park near Liverpool, then home to the Northern Cricket Club. Waterloo rugby club was not founded until 1882.

This seemingly influences subsequent comments concerning that final, none of which provide a date or score. *Rugby Union in Lancashire and Cheshire* (1950) gives the outcome of the four finals, but is identical to, and probably copied from, the aforementioned *Jubilee Year Book*. There is no mention at all in *Birkenhead Park: The First Hundred Years* (1971) excepting a photograph of the 1880-81 winning team. *New Brighton Rugby Union Football Club 1875-1975* (1975) simply states 'the [Cheshire] Challenge Cup … was won for the first two years by Birkenhead Park'.

A clue leaning towards the 1878-79 final not having taken place is provided in *The History of Cheshire Rugby Football Union 1876-1976* (1976). Whilst reiterating that the trophy 'had been won three times by Birkenhead Park and once by New Brighton' it informs us that, after the competition was shelved, 'the Challenge Cup was subsequently lodged with Messrs. Elkingtons [silversmiths] … but was unfortunately lost in the Second World War'. This indicates Birkenhead Park still had access to the trophy when its *Jubilee Year Book* appeared in 1922 and it seems feasible that its author may have obtained the list of winners and losers from engravings on the trophy or plinth.

That, of course, is a theory. Whatever the truth, it is unusual for such a prestigious game not to be reported somewhere. Was Birkenhead Park awarded the trophy without the decisive match taking place? There was certainly a problem completing fixtures that season due to a disruptive severe frost from mid-December 1878 until late February 1879, leaving Cheshire with two weekend county fixtures to fulfil during March, the favoured month for the three other Cheshire Cup finals. Was there a dispute in agreeing a date? Maybe we will never know!

Laurie Hickson of Bradford made 32 Yorkshire appearances, also representing the North and England. *Athletic News, 1890*

Statistics Notes

COUNTY MATCHES

Official matches, as organised by each county committee following the creation of the various county unions, are included. The first county union (or County Club) was Yorkshire in 1874, followed chronologically by Cheshire and Durham (both 1876), Northumberland (1880), Lancashire (1881), Cumberland (1882), and Westmorland (1886). Also, matches played by a county prior to the forming of their county union are included in instances where they were organised by one or more of their senior clubs, a system that caused many disputes regarding selection policy. With the exception of Westmorland, all had played at least one county match prior to the creation of their county union. Matches arranged by individuals after the formation of the county union, for instance the 'Lancashire' versus 'Yorkshire' match at Stockport on 28th April 1888, are excluded as they were not organised by the county committee.

It will be seen that, apart from meetings with other counties, matches took place against the University teams of Cambridge, Oxford, Edinburgh and Victoria, whilst Irish opposition was provided by Ulster and County Dublin. The 1888-89 Maoris opposed five northern counties, and Yorkshire (on six occasions) and Lancashire (once) met a Rest of England selection in celebration of county championship success. Cumberland twice took on the Yorkshire Colts and Westmorland arranged fixtures with North Lancashire and West Lancashire. Other opposition to the counties included Edinburgh, Furness, North Country Cantabs and Fettesian-Lorettonian. Three club sides also provided fixtures; Barrow (versus Cumberland in 1880), Liverpool (Cheshire twice during 1876) and Dewsbury (Cumberland in 1883). All are featured in this publication and included in each players county appearances record.

Note that players are listed with the club they are attached to at the time of their county appearance.

PLAYING POSITIONS

Where representative or cup final line-ups are listed, the playing positions (backs, three-quarters, half-backs, forwards, etc.) are indicated. This is because, during the Victorian era, team formations varied and were often unfamiliar to what is seen today. There were always forwards (as many as 16 in the early 20-a-side games) and their numbers gradually reduced until the now accustomed eight (rugby union) or six (rugby league) was settled on as the optimum figure. Player's associated with the last line of defence were initially referred to as a 'back' which, by the start of the 1900s, evolved into the term 'full-back'. Although today we are used to having just one full-back, at the very beginning there could be two or even three.

The biggest variation though is on the remaining positions. A three-quarter line of four players only became the norm in the mid-1890s, whereas previously the number had been three and, going even further back, two or even one. Similarly the idea of two half-backs only became a settled number during the latter 1870s, teams having previously fielded one, three or even four half-backs.

Other positions that occurred in the earlier days were two-third backs and quarter-backs. In Australia and New Zealand the position of five-eighths (linking the half-back and three-quarter line) was created and utilised in the Australia versus England test matches in 1899.

One particular difference during the Victorian period was in the teams representing Ireland and Scotland. Although their formation was similar to that of England and Wales, there were differences in terminology. Whereas England and Wales had adopted the familiar three-quarters and half-backs, Ireland (from 1876-77 to 1893-94) and Scotland (up to 1898-99) preferred to call those positions half-backs and quarter-backs, respectively.

The roles within playing positions (notably half-backs and forward) were less defined during this period and players have, therefore, been listed alphabetically within each set of positions. A notable exception is in the three-quarter line. When the three man three-quarter line became established in the early 1880s, the idea of a centre and two wingmen became accepted, evolving into two centres and two wingmen by the early 1890s. To reflect this, the players in those three-quarter lines are listed in the sequence published at the time which in most cases (but unfortunately not all) give an indication as to which players occupied the centre and wing berths (wing-centre-centre-wing).

LEAGUE COMPETITIONS

League tables published in newspapers and football annuals during the period covered by this volume were notoriously inaccurate in their detail. Basic rules that a modern statistician might apply were clearly not adhered to. For instance the 'won' column total should equal that of the 'lost' column; the total matches played and total 'drawn' should both be equal in number; the points 'for' column total should equate to that of the 'against' column. In the vast majority of cases these figures did not all balance, although it has to be accepted that in Victorian times there were no computers or calculators readily available.

Usually it was the responsibility of the competition secretary to compile the tables but it was often the case that once an error occurred it remained in the table for the remainder of that season! Another sign of the times was that the frustrated secretary of rugby union's Yorkshire Competition No.2 (Bradford Division) resorted to adding the following comment for each update he supplied the press; 'The above table is as correct as I can make it owing to the results of some matches not having been sent'.

It has, therefore, been necessary, for two-thirds of the tables included in this publication, to research the result of every match in order to arrive at as accurate a final compilation as possible. A painstaking task but, hopefully, a worthwhile one. For that reason the more curious reader may find that tables included here differ to those published at the time.

The Westmorland Junior League tables are included, 'Junior' being a reference to the level of its competing clubs (as opposed to 'senior') rather than the age of its players as might be the case today. This league included the 'A' teams of senior clubs like Kendal Hornets and the north Lancashire teams Lancaster and Morecambe. The league tables are included to place on record the competitions competed in by clubs that, although considered of comparative lower status, provided many of the Westmorland county players.

ATTENDANCES

Where known, the attendance is given for representative matches and cup finals. Unlike today, attendances were not officially published and are, therefore, mostly taken from match reports with estimates provided by the journalist, hence those quoted usually end in '000', in other words rounded to the nearest thousand. Estimates for the same match can often vary from one newspaper to another and, wherever possible, the attendance given by the local paper has been the one used. If no attendance was quoted in the local press a consensus has been reached through referencing other publications. Although these figures are unofficial it is felt that their inclusion adds interest and provides an indication of attendances attracted at the time. There are instances where an attendance, whilst not quantified by numbers, is referred to by adjectives such as 'large' 'good', 'fair' and 'small'. Rather than give no attendance, it was decided to quote those descriptions, where given. As a rough guide, 'large' generally implies an attendance of around 7,000 to 10,000, whereas 'small' suggests 1,000 to 2,000. Note: 'n/a' indicates the attendance is not known.

REFEREES

Where known, the name of the referee is given for representative matches and cup finals. Prior to their introduction, umpires (usually one from each team) made the on-field decisions which often led to disagreement. Referees first began to appear in 1875 but were initially used as arbiters to settle disputes between the two umpires. It was not until 1893 that the referee gained full control of the match in that his decisions were final. Note: 'n/a' indicates that the name of the referee is not known.

CAPTAINS

Where known, the team captain is noted in the team line-up as 'capt'

SCORING BY INDIVIDUALS

Where teams are listed (for representative matches, cup finals) the individual scorers are recorded against the players name as follows: t – try (or tries), c – conversion(s), dg – drop goal(s), fg – field goal(s), gm – goal(s) from mark, pg – penalty goal(s), mp – minor point(s), g – goal(s). If a player has scored more than one try or goal, then the abbreviation is preceded by the appropriate number (e.g. 2t is 2 tries scored, 3t is 3 tries, and so on). Note that goals ('g') are shown for Northern Union matches from 1897-98 onward when all goals under that code counted as two points.

SCORING IN RESULTS

Prior to the creation of a points system, match results were decided by the number of goals and tries scored. In the round-by-round cup competition results under the latter system, all scores are abbreviated as 'g' for goal, or 't' for try. Where a team has scored more than one try or goal, then the abbreviation is preceded by the appropriate number (e.g. 2t is 2 tries scored, 3t is 3 tries, and so on). Note: 'aet' indicates extra-time played (usually two 10-minute halves), 'w/o' indicates a walk-over in favour of the first named team.

MINOR POINTS

Minor points ('mp'), also referred to as 'minors', were often reported in scorelines during the Victorian era along with goals and tries. Although not counting towards the result, it gave an indication of dominance. A team would be credited with a minor point when the opposition was forced to touch the ball down in their own in-goal area or concede a dead ball behind their line. However, minor points were taken into account in some knock-out cup competitions in order to determine the results of matches that would otherwise be drawn. In those instances minor points are included in the match result.

Joe Sandwith of Seaton and Cumberland.
Lancashire Daily Post, 1899

Representative Team Abbreviations

Australia (Rugby Union)
NSW – New South Wales, Qld – Queensland.

Cheshire (Rugby Union and Northern Union)
Ald – Alderley; Alt – Altrincham; AshH – Ashford House (Prenton); BirkPk – Birkenhead Park; BirkW – Birkenhead Wanderers; Bow – Bowdon (Bowdon & Lymm 1877-78, 1878-79); Con – Congleton; Duk – Dukinfield; Macc – Macclesfield; Man – Manchester; Mar – Marple; NewB – New Brighton (Wallasey); Nord – Northenden; RockF – Rock Ferry (Birkenhead); Run – Runcorn; Sal – Salford; Stock – Stockport; Swi – Swinton.
Not abbreviated: Birkenhead School, Cheadle, Hyde, Lostock Gralam, Parkgate (Wirral), Sale, Stockton Heath, Tranmere Wanderers, West Derby (Liverpool), Wilmslow.

County Dublin (Rugby Union)
See under 'Ireland'.

Cumberland (Rugby Union and Northern Union)
Asp – Aspatria; AspAC – Aspatria Agricultural College; Bar – Barrow; Brad – Bradford; BrookR – Brookland Rovers (Maryport); Brou – Broughton (Cumberland); CamU – Cambridge University; Carl – Carlisle; CarlC – Carlisle City; Cock – Cockermouth; CumH – Cummersdale Hornets; Dear – Dearham; DevA – Devonport Albion

(Plymouth); EdW – Eden Wanderers (Carlisle); EdinU – Edinburgh University; Egr – Egremont; EgrH – Egremont Hornets; Grey – Greysouthen; Hun – Hunslet; Kes – Keswick; LivOB – Liverpool Old Boys; Llwyn – Llwynypia (Glamorganshire), Mary – Maryport; Mil – Millom; NewB – New Brighton (Cheshire); Nor – Northern (Newcastle); Par – Parton; Pen – Penrith; PenU – Penrith United; Rich – Richmond (London); Sea – Seaton; SSh – South Shield (Durham); Swi – Swinton; Tynd – Tynedale (Northumberland); Tynm – Tynemouth (Northumberland); Wall – Wallsend (Northumberland); WathB – Wath Brow (Cleator Moor), Whi – Whitehaven; WhiR – Whitehaven Recreation; WickPk – Wickham Park (London); Work – Workington.
Not abbreviated: Brampton, Catford Bridge (London), Ellenborough, Flimby, Hensingham, Millom St James's, South Vale Wanderers (Carlisle).
Note: In 1900-01, many players were unattached due to the declining number of clubs in the Cumberland Union, contemporary reports listing their 'club' name as the town with which they had previously been connected. In those instances, the club name is shown in quotes in this publication.

Devonshire (Rugby Union)
Barn – Barnstaple; Black – Blackheath (London); DevA – Devonport Albion (Plymouth); Exe – Exeter; Exm – Exmouth; Llwyn – Llwynypia (Glamorganshire); NewA – Newton Abbot; Paig – Paignton; Ply – Plymouth; RNEC – Royal Naval Engineering College (Keyham); Sid – Sidmouth; Tiv – Tiverton; Torq – Torquay Athletic; Tot – Totnes.
Not abbreviated: Aller Vale (Kingskerswell), Crediton, Honiton, Melville (Plymouth), Torquay Juniors.

Durham (Rugby Union)
BishA – Bishop Auckland; CamU – Cambridge University; Con – Consett; Darl – Darlington; DurC – Durham City; DurU – Durham University; EdinU – Edinburgh University; Gate – Gateshead; Ham – Hamsteels; Hart – Hartlepools; HartOB – Hartlepool Old Boys; HartR – Hartlepool Rovers; Hou – Houghton-le-Spring; Hum – Humbleton (Sunderland); NDur – North Durham (Gateshead); ODun – Old Dunelmians; SherH – Sherburn House; SSh – South Shields; SShYM – South Shields Young Men's Christian Association; Sto – Stockton; Sund – Sunderland; SundN – Sunderland Nomads; SundR – Sunderland Rovers; Tud – Tudhoe; TynD – Tyne Dock; Wes – Westoe; WHart – West Hartlepool.
Not abbreviated: Bensham, Boldon, Crook, Durham, Durham School, Gateshead Institute, Hendon Church Institute, Otterburn (Northumberland), Ryton.

Edinburgh (Rugby Union)
See under 'Scotland'.

England (Rugby Union)
Asp – Aspatria; Barn – Barnstaple; Bar – Barrow; Bat – Batley; Bing – Bingley; BirkPk – Birkenhead Park; BirkW – Birkenhead Wanderers; Black – Blackheath; Brad – Bradford; BradO – Bradford Olicana; Bram – Bramley; Bridg – Bridgwater; BrigR – Brighouse Rangers; Bris – Bristol; Bro – Broughton; BroR – Broughton Rangers; Burt – Burton-on-Trent; CamU – Cambridge University; Cas – Castleford; ClapR – Clapham Rovers; Cleck – Cleckheaton; Clif – Clifton (Bristol); Darl – Darlington; DevA – Devonport Albion

Representative Team Abbreviations

(Plymouth); Dew – Dewsbury; Exe – Exeter; Gip – Gipsies (London); Glo – Gloucester; GuyHosp – Guy's Hospital (London); Hal – Halifax; Harl – Harlequins (London); HartR – Hartlepool Rovers; Heck – Heckmondwike; Hud – Huddersfield; KCHosp – King's College Hospital (London); Kei – Keighley; Lanc – Lancaster; Lee – Leeds; Lei – Leigh; Liv – Liverpool; LivOB – Liverpool Old Boys; Livs – Liversedge; LonHosp – London Hospital; Man – Manchester; ManFW – Manchester Free Wanderers; Mann – Manningham; ManR -Manchester Rangers; MarlN – Marlborough Nomads (London); MidW – Middlesex Wanderers (Richmond); Mil – Millom; Mor – Morley; Mose – Moseley (Birmingham); Myth – Mytholmroyd; NDur – North Durham; NewB – New Brighton; Nor – Northern (Newcastle); NorFC – Northumberland Football Club (Newcastle); Northn – Northampton; OChelt – Old Cheltonians; Old – Oldham; OMT – Old Merchant Taylors' (London); OxfU – Oxford University; PerPk – Percy Park (Tynemouth); QH – Queen's House (Greenwich); RavPk – Ravenscourt Park (London); RE – Royal Engineers (Chatham); Rich – Richmond; RIEC – Royal Indian Engineering College (near Egham); RMA – Royal Military Academy (Woolwich); RNC – Royal Naval College (Greenwich); RNEC – Royal Naval Engineering College (Keyham); Rock – Rockcliff; Run – Runcorn; Sal – Salford; Sea – Seaton; SowB – Sowerby Bridge; StGHosp – St George's Hospital (London); StHR – St Helens Recreation; Stock – Stockport; StTHosp – St Thomas's Hospital (London); Sund – Sunderland; Swi – Swinton; Tad – Tadcaster; Tau – Taunton; Tho – Thornes (Wakefield); Torq – Torquay Athletic; Tud – Tudhoe; Tyl – Tyldesley; UCHosp – University College Hospital (London); Ulv – Ulverston; Wak – Wakefield Trinity; Well – Wellington (Somersetshire); WHart – West Hartlepool; Wig – Wigan; Wim – Wimbledon (Wimbledon Hornets 1874-75); Wivel – Wiveliscombe; WKent – West Kent (London); WRid – West Riding (Leeds); YorksW – Yorkshire Wanderers (Leeds).
Not abbreviated: Bath, Hull, Law Club (London), Rugby.

Glamorganshire (Rugby Union)
See under 'Wales'.

Gloucestershire (Rugby Union)
Bris – Bristol; CamU – Cambridge University; Car – Cardiff; Glo – Gloucester; OxfU – Oxford University.
Not abbreviated: Lydney, Stroud.

Ireland (Rugby Union)
Arm – Armagh; BecR – Bective Rangers (Dublin); BelA – Belfast Albion; Bess – Bessbrook; CamU – Cambridge University; Der – Derry; DubU – Dublin University; Dun – Dungannon; King – Kingstown (Dublin), EdinU – Edinburgh University; Lans – Lansdowne (Dublin); Lim – Limerick; Lis – Lisburn; Liv – Liverpool; MethC – Methodist College (Belfast); Monk – Monkstown (Dublin); NIFC – North of Ireland Football Club (Belfast); QCB – Queen's College (Belfast); QCC – Queen's College (Cork); OWes – Old Wesley (Dublin); RBAI – Royal Belfast Academical Institute; RockC – Rockwell College (near Cashel); Tip – Tipperary; Wand – Wanderers (Dublin); Wind – Windsor (Belfast).
Not abbreviated: Belfast Academy, Bray, Campbell College (Belfast), Cork, Cork Bankers, Garryowen (Limerick), Kingstown School (Dublin), Rugby.

Kent (Rugby Union)
Black – Blackheath; CamU – Cambridge University; Cleve – Clevedon (London); GuyHosp – Guy's Hospital (London); Harl – Harlequins (London); Ken – Kensington (London); Laus – Lausanne (London); LonS – London Scottish; MidW – Middlesex Wanderers (Richmond); OChelt – Old Cheltonians; OLey – Old Leysians; OxfU – Oxford University; QH – Queen's House (Greenwich); RA – Royal Artillery (Woolwich); RE – Royal Engineers (Chatham); Rich – Richmond; RNC – Royal Naval College (Greenwich); StGHosp – St George's Hospital (London); StTHosp – St Thomas's Hospital (London); WickPk – Wickham Park (London).
Not abbreviated: Croydon, London Caledonians (Dulwich), Southwark Home (London). Sydenham,

Lancashire (Rugby Union and Northern Union)
Ask – Askam; Asp – Aspull; Bar – Barrow; Bla – Blackley; Bow – Bowdon (Cheshire); Bram – Bramley (Leeds), Bro – Broughton (Broughton Wasps 1876-77, 1877-78); BroPk – Broughton Park; BroR – Broughton Rangers; CamU – Cambridge University; Carn – Carnforth; CasM – Castleton Moor; Che – Cheetham; KenH – Kendal Hornets; KenT – Kendal Town; Lanc – Lancaster; Lei – Leigh; Lit – Littleborough; Liv – Liverpool; LivOB – Liverpool Old Boys; LivW – Liverpool Wanderers; Man – Manchester; ManFW – Manchester Free Wanderers; ManR – Manchester Rangers, More – Morecambe; Moss – Mossley; Old – Oldham; OwC – Owen's College (Manchester); Pem – Pemberton; PresG – Preston Grasshoppers; Rad – Radcliffe; Roch – Rochdale; RochH – Rochdale Hornets; RochStC – Rochdale St Clements; Run – Runcorn; Sal – Salford; Sou – Southport; StH – St Helens; StHR – St Helens Recreation; Swi – Swinton; Tyl – Tyldesley; Ulv – Ulverston; VicU – Victoria University; Walk – Walkden; War – Warrington; Wid – Widnes; Wig – Wigan.
Not abbreviated: Barton (Eccles), Birch, Blackburn, Bolton, Eccles, Kersal, Lancaster Royal Grammar School, Leigh Shamrocks, Litherland, Parkfield Old Boys (Liverpool), Roose, Sale, Tottington, Walton (Liverpool), Waterloo (Liverpool), Widnes St Mary's, Wigan Rovers.

Middlesex (Rugby Union)
Black – Blackheath; CamU – Cambridge University; ClapR – Clapham Rovers; Flam – Flamingoes (London); Gip – Gipsies (London); Harl – Harlequins (London); KCHosp – King's College Hospital (London); Ken – Kensington (London); Laus – Lausanne (London); LonHosp – London Hospital; LonS – London Scottish; LonW – London Welsh; MarlN – Marlborough Nomads (London); MidW – Middlesex Wanderers (Richmond); OChelt – Old Cheltonians; OLey – Old Leysians; OMT – Old Merchant Taylors' (London); OxfU – Oxford University; Rich – Richmond; RIEC – Royal Indian Engineering College (near Egham); RosPk – Rosslyn Park (London); StBHosp – St Bartholomew's Hospital (London); StGHosp – St George's Hospital (London); StTHosp – St Thomas's Hospital (London); UCHosp – University College Hospital (London); Walth – Walthamstow; Wim – Wimbledon.
Not abbreviated: Old Millhillians (Hendon).

Midland Counties (Rugby Union)
Burt – Burton-on-Trent; Cov – Coventry; Edg – Edgbaston Crusaders (Birmingham);

Leam – Leamington Rovers; Leic – Leicester; Mose – Moseley (Birmingham), Nott – Nottingham; OEdw – Old Edwardians (Birmingham); Rush – Rushden; Stour – Stourbridge; Strat – Stratford; Wolv – Wolverhampton; Worc – Worcester.
Not abbreviated: Bedford, Bromsgrove, Derby, Handsworth, North Stafford, Rugby, Stafford, Stoke.

North (Rugby Union)

Asp – Aspatria; Bat – Batley; Bing – Bingley; BirkPk – Birkenhead Park; BirkW – Birkenhead Wanderers; Bow – Bowdon; Brad – Bradford; BradO – Bradford Olicana; Bram – Bramley; BrigR – Brighouse Rangers; Bro – Broughton; BroR – Broughton Rangers; Burt – Burton-on-Trent; CamU – Cambridge University; Carl – Carlisle; Cas – Castleford; Che – Cheetham; Cleck – Cleckheaton; Darl – Darlington; Dew – Dewsbury; DurC – Durham City; DurU – Durham University; EdW – Eden Wanderers (Carlisle); EdinU – Edinburgh University; Fea – Featherstone, Hal – Halifax; HartOB – Hartlepool Old Boys; HartR – Hartlepool Rovers; Heck – Heckmondwike; Hud – Huddersfield; HKR – Hull Kingston Rovers; Kei – Keighley; Lanc – Lancaster; Lee – Leeds; LeeStJ – Leeds St John's; Lei – Leigh; Liv – Liverpool; LivOB – Liverpool Old Boys; Livs – Liversedge; Macc – Macclesfield; Man – Manchester; ManFW – Manchester Free Wanderers; Mann – Manningham; ManR – Manchester Rangers; Mil – Millom; More – Morecambe; Mor – Morley; Myth – Mytholmroyd; NDur – North Durham; NewB – New Brighton; Nor – Northern (Newcastle); NorFC – Northumberland Football Club (Newcastle); ODun – Old Dunelmians; Old – Oldham; OutC – Outwood Church; OxfU – Oxford University; PerPk – Percy Park (Tynemouth); PresG – Preston Grasshoppers; Pud – Pudsey; RavPk – Ravenscourt Park (London); RochH – Rochdale Hornets; Rock – Rockcliff; Run – Runcorn; Sal – Salford; Sea – Seaton; Ship – Shipley; Sou -Southport; SowB – Sowerby Bridge; SSh – South Shields; StH – St Helens; StHR – St Helens Recreation; Stock – Stockport; Sund – Sunderland; Swi – Swinton; Tad – Tadcaster; Tho – Thornes (Wakefield); Tud – Tudhoe; Tyl – Tyldesley; Ulv – Ulverston; Wak – Wakefield Trinity; Wall – Wallsend; WHart – West Hartlepool; Wig – Wigan; WRid – West Riding (Leeds); Work – Workington; YorksW – Yorkshire Wanderers (Leeds).
Not abbreviated: Catford Bridge (London), Crewe, Hull, Idle, Sale, Walton (Liverpool).

North Lancashire (Rugby Union)
See under 'Lancashire'.

Northumberland (Rugby Union)
Ben – Benwell; CamU – Cambridge University; Darl – Darlington; DurC – Durham City; Gos – Gosforth; HartR – Hartlepool Rovers; NDur – North Durham (Gateshead); NEls – North Elswick (Newcastle); Nor – Northern (Newcastle); NorFC – Northumberland Football Club (Newcastle); OxfU – Oxford University; PerPk – Percy Park (Tynemouth); Rock – Rockcliff; SSh – South Shields; Sund – Sunderland; Tud – Tudhoe; Tynd – Tynedale; Tynm – Tynemouth; Wall – Wallsend, WHart – West Hartlepool.
Not abbreviated: Bensham, Brighton (Newcastle), Newcastle Rangers, Wallsend Wanderers.

Northumberland & Durham (Rugby Union)
See under 'Northumberland'.

Rest of England (Rugby Union)
See under 'England'.

Scotland (Rugby Union)
CamU – Cambridge University; Clyd – Clydesdale; Craig – Craigmount; EdinA – Edinburgh Academicals; EdinAy – Edinburgh Academy; EdinIFP – Edinburgh Institution Former Pupils; EdinU – Edinburgh University; EdinW – Edinburgh Wanderers; FetLor – Fettesian-Lorretonian (Edinburgh); GHSFP – Glasgow High School Former Pupils; GlasA – Glasgow Academicals; GlasU – Glasgow University; Haw – Hawick; Jed – Jed-Forrest; Lang – Langholm; LonS – London Scottish; Lor – Loretto (Edinburgh); Mel – Melrose; Mer – Merchistonians (Edinburgh); MerCS – Merchiston Castle School (Edinburgh); Nor – Northern (Newcastle); ODun – Old Dunelmians (Durham); OxfU – Oxford University; RA – Royal Artillery (Woolwich); RE – Royal Engineers (Chatham); RHSFP – Royal High School Former Pupils (Edinburgh), RIEC – Royal Indian Engineering College (near Egham); Sel – Selkirk; StAndU – St Andrew's University; Wat – Watsonians (Edinburgh); WoS – West of Scotland.
Not abbreviated: Abertay (Dundee), Edinburgh Collegians, Gala (Galashiels), Gala Thistle (Galashiels), Hawick St Cuthbert's, Kelvinside Academicals (Glasgow), Paisley, Walkerburn.

Somersetshire (Rugby Union)
Black – Blackheath (London); Bridg – Bridgwater; CamU- Cambridge University; Car – Cardiff; Clif – Clifton (Bristol); Crew – Crewkerne; Exe – Exeter; GuyHosp – Guy's Hospital (London); MarlN – Marlborough Nomads (London); OChelt – Old Cheltonians; OMT – Old Merchant Taylors' (London); Tau – Taunton; Well – Wellington; Wes – Weston-super-Mare; Wivel – Wiveliscombe; Yeo – Yeovil.
Not abbreviated: Bath, Cheddar.

South (Rugby Union)
Barn – Barnstaple; BirkPk – Birkenhead Park; Black – Blackheath; Bridg – Bridgwater; Bris – Bristol; Burt – Burton-on-Trent; CamU – Cambridge University; ClapR – Clapham Rovers; Clif – Clifton (Bristol); Cov – Coventry; Crew – Crewkerne; DevA – Devonport Albion (Plymouth); Exe – Exeter; Gip – Gipsies (London); Glo – Gloucester; GuyHosp – Guy's Hospital (London); Harl – Harlequins (London); HartR – Hartlepool Rovers; KCHosp – King's College Hospital (London); Leic – Leicester; LonHosp – London Hospital; Man – Manchester; MarlN – Marlborough Nomads (London); MidW – Middlesex Wanderers (Richmond); Mose – Moseley (Birmingham); NewA – Newton Abbot; Northn – Northampton; OChelt – Old Cheltonians; OLey – Old Leysians; OMT – Old Merchant Taylors' (London); OxfU – Oxford University; Ply – Plymouth; QH – Queen's House (Greenwich); Rich – Richmond; RA – Royal Artillery (Woolwich); RavPk – Ravenscourt Park (London); RE – Royal Engineers (Chatham); RIEC – Royal Indian Engineering College (near Egham); RMA – Royal Military Academy (Woolwich); RNEC – Royal Naval Engineering College (Keyham); StGHosp – St George's Hospital; StTHosp – St Thomas's Hospital (London); Tau – Taunton; Tiv – Tiverton; Torq – Torquay Athletic; UCHosp – University College Hospital (London); Walth – Walthamstow; Well – Wellington (Somersetshire); Wes – Weston-super-Mare; Wim – Wimbledon; Wivel – Wiveliscombe; WKent – West Kent (London).
Not abbreviated: Bath, Olney, Rugby, Sidmouth.

Representative Team Abbreviations

South of Scotland (Rugby Union)
See under 'Scotland'.

South Africa (Rugby Union)
Bdr – Border, EP – Eastern Province, GW – Griqualand West, Tvl – Transvaal, WP – Western Province.

Surrey (Rugby Union)
Black – Blackheath; CamU – Cambridge University; ClapR – Clapham Rovers; Croy – Croydon; ESh – East Sheen (London); Flam – Flamingoes (London); Gip – Gipsies (London); GuyHosp – Guy's Hospital (London); Harl – Harlequins (London); Ken – Kensington (London); Laus – Lausanne (London); LonS – London Scottish; LonW – London Welsh; MarlN – Marlborough Nomads (London); MidW – Middlesex Wanderers (Richmond); OChelt – Old Cheltonians; OLey – Old Leysians; OMT – Old Merchant Taylors' (London); OxfU – Oxford University; Rich – Richmond; RosPk – Rosslyn Park (London); RIEC – Royal Indian Engineering College (near Egham); RMC – Royal Military College (Sandhurst); StTHosp – St Thomas's Hospital (London); Walth – Walthamstow; Wim – Wimbledon.
Not abbreviated: Lennox (Dulwich), London and Westminster Bank, Thornton Heath (London).

Ulster (Rugby Union)
See under 'Ireland'.

Wales (Rugby Union)
Aber – Aberavon; Black – Blackheath (London); Bri – Bridgend; CamU – Cambridge University; Car – Cardiff; CarHarl – Cardiff Harlequins; Dew – Dewsbury; Llan – Llanelli; LlanC – Llandovery College; Llwyn – Llwynypia; LonW – London Welsh; Morr – Morriston; Mou – Mountain Ash; Nan – Nantyglo; Nea – Neath; New – Newport; Old – Oldham; OxfU – Oxford University; Pen – Penarth; Peny – Penygraig; Pon – Pontypridd; Rua – Ruabon; Swa – Swansea; Tre – Treherbert; Wig – Wigan.
Not abbreviated: Bangor, Chepstow, Haverfordwest; Lampeter, Llandaff, Maesteg, Pontardawe, Pontymister, Rhymney, Treorchy.

West Cumberland (Rugby Union)
See under 'Cumberland'.

West Lancashire (Rugby Union)
See under 'Lancashire'.

Westmorland (Rugby Union and Northern Union)
Amb – Ambleside; Bar – Barrow; BurHW – Burton and Holme Wanderers; Burn – Burneside; CamU – Cambridge University; Carn – Carnforth; Dew – Dewsbury; DonT – Doncaster Town; Hal – Halifax; KenH – Kendal Hornets; KenT – Kendal Town; KirkL – Kirkby Lonsdale; Lanc – Lancaster; Lee – Leeds; Old – Oldham; OxfU – Oxford University; Rad – Radcliffe (Manchester); Sal – Salford; Stav – Staveley; Stock – Stockport; StH – St Helens; Swi – Swinton; Tyl – Tyldesley; Ulv – Ulverston; Walk – Walkden; Wig – Wigan; Wind – Windermere.
Not abbreviated: Holme.

Note: In 1896-97 and 1897-98, many players were unattached due to the declining number of clubs in Westmorland, contemporary reports listing their 'club' name as the town with which they had previously been connected. In those instances, the club name is shown in quotes in this publication.

Yorkshire (Rugby Union and Northern Union)
Alv – Alverthorpe; Bat – Batley; Bing – Bingley; Bowl – Bowling; Brad – Bradford; BradO – Bradford Olicana; BradR – Bradford Rangers; Bram – Bramley; BrigR – Brighouse Rangers; CamU – Cambridge University; Cas – Castleford; Cleck – Cleckheaton; Dew – Dewsbury; Don – Doncaster; DonT – Doncaster Town, DurC – Durham City; Fea – Featherstone; Hal – Halifax; Harr – Harrogate; Head – Headingley; HebB – Hebden Bridge; Heck – Heckmondwike; HKR – Hull Kingston Rovers; Hol – Holbeck; Hud – Huddersfield; Hun – Hunslet; Kei – Keighley; Kirk – Kirkstall; Knot – Knottingley; Lee – Leeds; LeePC – Leeds Parish Church; LeeStJ – Leeds St John's; Leic – Leicester; Livs – Liversedge; Lud – Luddendenfoot; Mann – Manningham; Mir – Mirfield; Mor – Morley; Myth – Mytholmroyd; Norm – Normanton; Oss – Ossett; OutC – Outwood Church; OxfU – Oxford University; Pont – Pontefract; Pud – Pudsey; Rich – Richmond (London); Salt – Salterhebble; Sha – Sharlston; Shef – Sheffield; Ship – Shipley; Skip – Skipton; SowB – Sowerby Bridge; Tad – Tadcaster; Tho – Thornes (Wakefield); Wak – Wakefield Trinity; WHart – West Hartlepool; WRid – West Riding (Leeds); Wort – Wortley; YorksC – Yorkshire College (Leeds); YorksW – Yorkshire Wanderers (Leeds).
Not abbreviated: Appleby Bridge, Armley, Badsworth Hunt (Ackworth), Bottomboat Trinity, Bradford Junior, Elland, Esholt (Bradford), Goole, Holywell Brook, Hull, Idle, Ilkley, Kinsley, Kirkburton (Huddersfield), Normanton St John's, Otley, Paddock, St Peter's School (York), Selby, Wakefield FC, York, York Melbourne.

Yorkshire Colts (Rugby Union)
See under 'Yorkshire'.

Bibliography

NEWSPAPERS

Altrincham and Bowdon Guardian
Ambleside Herald
Annandale Observer (Annan)
Athletic News (Manchester)
Barrow Herald
Belfast News-Letter
Bell's Life in London
Bicester Herald
Birkenhead and Cheshire Advertiser
Birkenhead News
Birmingham Daily Post
Black & White (London)
Blackburn Standard
Bolton Evening News
Bradford Daily Telegraph
Bradford Observer
Bury Times
Cheshire Observer (Chester)
Carlisle Express
Carlisle Journal
Carlisle Patriot
Coventry Herald
Cumberland Pacquet (Whitehaven)
Daily Express (Dublin)
Daily Nation (Dublin)
Daily Review (Edinburgh)
Daily Telegraph (London)
Devon and Exeter Gazette
Dewsbury Reporter
Durham County Advertiser (Durham)
Eastern Morning News (Hull)
English Lakes Visitor (Keswick)
Edinburgh Evening News
Evening Herald (Dublin)
Evening News and Star (Glasgow)
The Field (London)
Freeman's Journal (Dublin)
Glasgow Herald
The Graphic (London)
Hartlepool Mail
Huddersfield Chronicle
Hull Daily Mail
Hull Packet
Illustrated London News

NEWSPAPERS continued

Illustrated Police News (London)
Illustrated Sporting and Dramatic News (London)
Irish Daily Independent (Dublin)
Irish Times (Dublin)
Lakes Chronicle (Windermere)
Lakes Herald (Ambleside)
Lancashire Daily Post (Preston)
Lancashire Evening Post (Preston)
Lancaster Guardian
Leeds Mercury
Leeds Times
Leigh Chronicle
Leigh Journal
Lichfield Mercury
Liverpool Echo
Liverpool Mercury
Lloyd's Weekly Newspaper (London)
London Daily News
London Evening Standard
Manchester Courier
Manchester Guardian
Manchester Times
Maryport Advertiser
Millom Gazette
Morning Post (London)
Nantwich Guardian
Newcastle Daily Chronicle
Newcastle Daily Journal
Newcastle Daily Leader
Newcastle Weekly Chronicle
North British Daily Mail (Glasgow)
North Cumberland Reformer (Carlisle)
North-Eastern Daily Gazette (Middlesbrough)
Northern Daily Mail (Hartlepool)
Northern Daily Telegraph (Blackburn)
Northern Echo (Durham)
Northern Whig (Belfast)
Northwich Guardian
Oldham Chronicle
Pall Mall Gazette (London)
Penny Illustrated Paper (London)
Penrith Observer
Pontefract & Castleford Express
Preston Chronicle

Preston Herald
The Referee (London)
Reynold's Newspaper (London)
Rochdale Observer
Rugby Advertiser
St Helens Newspaper
St Helens Reporter
St James's Gazette (London)
Salford Reporter
The Scotsman (Edinburgh)
The Scottish Referee (Glasgow)
Sheffield Daily Telegraph
Sheffield Evening Telegraph
Sheffield Independent
Shields Daily Gazette
Shields Daily News
Shipley Times
The Sketch (London)
Soulby's Ulverston Advertiser
South Wales Daily News (Cardiff)
South Wales Echo (Cardiff)
Sport (Dublin)
Sporting Chronicle (Manchester)
Sporting Life (London)
The Sportsman (London)
Star of Gwent (Newport)
Sunderland Daily Echo
Toby, The Yorkshire Tyke (Leeds)
Todmorden and District News
The Umpire (London)
The Warder (Dublin)
Warrington Guardian
West Cumberland Times (Cockermouth)
Western Daily Press (Bristol)
Western Mail (Cardiff)
Westmorland Gazette (Kendal)
Wharfedale & Airedale Observer (Otley)
Wigan Observer
Workington Star
York Herald
Yorkshire Evening Post (Leeds)
Yorkshire Gazette (York)
Yorkshire Herald (York)
Yorkshire Post (Leeds)

BOOKS

Adams, David, *The Rise and Fall of Rugby League: Brighouse Rangers 1879-1906*, Halifax, 1995.
Allan, George A., *Birkenhead Park: Jubilee Year Book*, Birkenhead, 1922.
Balaam, Len, *125 MFC*, Manchester, 1985.
Barak, Monty, *A Century of Rugby at Sale*, 1962.
Beacall, Philip J., *Birkenhead Park: The First Hundred Years*, Birkenhead, 1971.
Carrick, Terry, *Aspatria: The History of a Rugby Union Football Club*, Worksop, 1991.
Cartwright, Brian F., *A Ton Full of Memories*, Batley, 1986.
Chester, Rod H. and McMillan, Neville A. C., *The Visitors*, Auckland (New Zealand), 1990.
Clarke, James, *History of Football in Kendal*, 1908.
Collins, Tony, *Rugby's Great Split*, London, 1998.
Collins, Tony, *A Social History of English Rugby Union*, Abingdon, 2009.
Collins, Tony, *How Football Began*, Abingdon, 2018.
Cowell, C. Berkeley and Moses, E. Watts, *Durham County Rugby Union 1876-1936*, Newcastle-upon-Tyne, 1936.
Croxford, Walter B. (ed.), *Rugby Union in Lancashire and Cheshire*, Liverpool, 1950.
Dagleish, J. Richard A., *Red, Black and Blue: The First 125 Years of Liverpool FC*, Swinton, 1983.
Dalby, Ken, *The Headingley Story 1890-1955*, Leeds, 1955.
Delaney, Trevor, *The Grounds of Rugby League*, Keighley, 1991.
Delaney, Trevor, *Rugby Disunion*, Keighley, 1993.
Dewhirst, John, *Room at the Top*, Shipley, 2016.
Dewhirst, John, *Life at the Top*, Shipley, 2016.
Edgar, Harry, *Chocolate, Blue and Gold*, Wetherby, 1998.
Eggleshaw, Maurice, *New Brighton Rugby Union Football Club 1875-1975*, New Brighton, 1975.
Evans, Craig, *A History of Millom Rugby League Football Club*, 2010.
Fagan, Sean, *The First Lions of Rugby*, Melbourne (Australia), 2013.
Gate, Robert, *Gone North (Volume One)*, Sowerby Bridge, 1986.
Gate, Robert, *Bradford Rugby League: Bradford, Northern and Bulls*, Stroud, 2000.
Godwin, Terry, *The International Rugby Championship 1883-1983*, London, 1984.
Godwin, Terry, *The Complete Who's Who of International Rugby*, Poole, 1987.
Griffiths, John, *The Phoenix Book of International Rugby Records*, London, 1987.
Hardcastle, Andrew, *The Thrum Hall Story*, Halifax, 1986.
Hardcastle, Andrew, *They Played for Halifax 1895-1987*, Halifax, 1987.
Hardcastle, Andrew, *Thrum Hall Greats*, Halifax, 1994.
Harvey, Adrian, *Football: The First Hundred Years*, Abingdon, 2005.
Henderson, Andrew, *The History of Cheshire Rugby Football Union 1876-1976*, Hale, 1976.
Huitson, Dave, *In The Beginning: Barrow Rugby, the Union Years 1875-1897*, Barrow, 2019.
Jones, J. R., *Encyclopaedia of Rugby Football*, London, 1958.
Latham, Michael, *They Played for Leigh*, Adlington (Lancs), 1991.
Latham, Michael, *Buff Berry and the Mighty Bongers*, Adlington (Lancs), 1995.
Latham, Michael, *The Home of Footballers*, Leeds, 2020.
Latham, Michael and Gate, Robert, *They Played for Wigan*, Adlington (Lancs), 1992.

BOOKS *continued*

Latham, Michael and Mather, Tom, *The Rugby League Myth*, Adlington (Lancs), 1993.
Little, Tom, *A Rugby League Goldmine*, Carlisle, 2023.
Macrory, Jennifer, *Running With the Ball*, London, 1991.
Marshall, Rev. Frank (ed.), *Football: The Rugby Union Game*, London, 1892.
Myers, Simon, *Sport Around Stockport*, Stockport, 2009.
Pierce, Duncan, Jenkins, John M. and Auty, Timothy, *Who's Who of Welsh International Rugby Players*, Bath, 2018.
Pugh, Roger, *The Robins: An Official History of Hull Kingston Rovers*, Leeds, 2016.
Robinson, B. Fletcher, *Rugby Football*, London, 1896.
Ryan, Greg, *Forerunners of the All Blacks*, Christchurch (New Zealand), 1993.
Rylance, Mike, *Trinity*, Brighouse, 2013.
Saxton, Irvin (ed.), *History of Rugby League* (Nos.1 to 6), Pontefract, 1980 and 1981.
Scargill, Tony, Fox, Bob and Crabtree, Ken, *The Official History of Dewsbury RLFC*, Ossett, 1989.
Service, Alex and Whittle, Denis, *All Local Lads*, London, 2008.
Smith Jed, *The Original Rules of Rugby*, Oxford, 2007.
Tate, Stephen, *A History of the British Sporting Journalist c.1850-1939*, Newcastle-upon-Tyne, 2020.
Thorburn, Sandy, *The History of Scottish Rugby*, London, 1980.
Titley, Uel A. and McWhirter, A. Ross, *Centenary History of the Rugby Football Union*, London, 1970.
Turner, Michael, *Oldham RLFC: The Complete History 1876-1997*, Oldham, 1997.
Walker, Brian, *Roughyeds ... The Story*, 2004.
Wild, Stephen M., *Swinton Lions: 150 Years*, 2017.
Williams, Graham, *The Code War*, Harefield (Middlesex), 1994.
Williams, Graham, *Glory Days*, Leeds, 1998.
Williamson, John, *Football's Forgotten Tour*, Applecross (Australia), 2003.
Yorkshire Rugby Football Union, *Commemoration Book 1914-19 and Official Handbook 1919-20*, York, 1920.

ANNUALS AND YEARBOOKS

The Athletic News Football Annual (1891 to 1901-02), London.
The Football Annual (1871 to 1894), London.
Rothmans Rugby Union Yearbook (1972 to 1999-2000), London.

WEBSITES

The British Newspaper Archive (britishnewspaperarchive.co.uk)
National Library of Australia newspaper archive (trove.nla.gov.au)
National Library of New Zealand newspaper archive (paperspast.natlib.govt.nz)
Oldham Rugby League Trust (orl-heritagetrust.org.uk)
Rugby League Record Keepers' Club (rugbyleaguerecords.com)
Saints Heritage Society (saints.org.uk)

Investigate our other titles and
stay up to date with all our latest releases at
www.scratchingshedpublishing.co.uk